EU ELECTRONIC COMMUNICATIONS LAW

Competition and Regulation in the European
Telecommunications Market

EU ELECTRONIC COMMUNICATIONS LAW

Competition and Regulation in the European Telecommunications Market

Paul Nihoul

Paul Nihoul is Professor of Law at the University of Louvain, Belgium, where he holds the Jean Monnet Chair on the European Information Society; he is also Professor of Law at the University of Groningen, The Netherlands.

Peter Rodford

Peter Rodford is a head of unit in the European Commission, Directorate General for the Information Society, with particular responsibility for the implementation of the European regulation on electronic communications.

OXFORD

UNIVERSITY PRESS

OXFORD
UNIVERSITY PRESS

Great Clarendon Street, Oxford OX2 6DP

Oxford University Press is a department of the University of Oxford.
It furthers the University's objective of excellence in research, scholarship,
and education by publishing worldwide in

Oxford New York

Auckland Bangkok Buenos Aires Cape Town Chennai
Dar es Salaam Delhi Hong Kong Istanbul Karachi Kolkata
Kuala Lumpur Madrid Melbourne Mexico City Mumbai Nairobi
São Paulo Shanghai Taipei Tokyo Toronto

Oxford is a registered trade mark of Oxford University Press
in the UK and in certain other countries

Published in the United States
by Oxford University Press Inc., New York

British Library Cataloguing in Publication Data

Data available

Library of Congress Cataloging in Publication Data

Data available

ISBN 0-19-926340-X

3 5 7 9 10 8 6 4 2

Typeset by Newgen Imaging Systems (P) Ltd., Chennai, India
Printed in Great Britain
on acid-free paper by
Antony Rowe Ltd., Chippenham

FOREWORD

The European Union is growing. Ten new Member States are joining now, and more will come aboard in the years ahead. However, the geographical dimension is only one aspect of the Union's expansion. There is also a legal dimension. The laws of the European Union are constantly being enriched and deepened. A major development in this regard is the drafting of a "Constitution for Europe", which is intended to reorganise the relations between all those who participate in the European project (Member States, European institutions and bodies, citizens, etc). In parallel, the Union is devising regulatory frameworks in a number of sectors that are important for European society, including electronic communications, for which new rules have been enacted recently.

As is well known, legislation on electronic communications has evolved significantly in recent decades. Originally, in most Member States, telecommunications services were offered by monopolies. Telecommunications markets were subsequently opened to competition. Competition, however, cannot develop or even subsist without some form of control or intervention by public authorities. Such control is necessary to ensure that competition is not impaired by market power. Markets are also required to fulfil public policy objectives that would not be achieved if they were granted complete freedom of action. Accompanying rules were accordingly adopted by the European institutions when telecommunications markets were opened to competition. These rules were revised in 2002, thereby putting in place a new regulatory framework, to which this book is devoted.

Electronic communications are an important sector for society. They provide a tool for interaction between people, undertakings and authorities. They create a platform of communication necessary for the development of social cohesion and economic activity. They are in this regard as important to society as energy production and distribution, the water industry, waste treatment or transport. It should be noted in this connection that the European rules on electronic communications are more elaborate than those adopted for other public service-related sectors. To many observers, given the degree of legal coverage and complexity achieved, the electronic communications framework could serve to a substantial extent as a model for further rules to be adopted in these other sectors.

The electronic communications regulatory framework can now be considered as being in essence complete. It has been designed and adopted through the interaction of the three European institutions which play a key role in the Union's legislative process—the Commission, the Council and the European Parliament. The time has now come for it to be applied in the Member States. This stage in implementation will show that a number of issues remains to be resolved. In a large number of cases these questions will be addressed by the European Court of Justice and/or the European Court of First Instance, which will thereby contribute to the development of the framework.

In this respect it may be useful to recall to what extent the European Court of Justice has already been influential in defining the rules applicable to electronic communications in the European Union. To give but a few examples, the Court confirmed in 1991 the power of the Commission to introduce competition on the telecommunications terminal markets.[1] That position was reiterated in 1993, with respect to telecommunications services markets.[2] In 1991 the Court also ruled that regulatory functions could not be granted to an undertaking where such functions would favour the undertaking concerned.[3]

The role of the European Court of Justice and the European Court of First Instance will not decrease in the years ahead. As the authors make clear, litigation is bound to increase in this area of the law. It is now for practitioners to probe deeply and bring proceedings where appropriate; it is for the European Courts to provide answers within the limits of their jurisdiction.

This book provides invaluable analytical insight in this complex area of the law.

Koen Lenaerts
Judge of the Court of Justice of the European Communities
Professor of European Law at the Katholieke
Universiteit Leuven (KULeuven), Belgium

---

[1] France *v* Commission Case 202/88 [1991] ECR I-1223.

[2] Spain, Belgium and Italy *v* Commission Joined Cases C 271, 281 & 289/90 [1992] ECR I-5833.

[3] Régie des télégraphes et des téléphones *v* GB-Inno-BM Case C-18/88 [1991] ECR I-5941.

PREFACE

Electronic communications services in the European Union are worth 250 billion euros annually. Rates of growth have in recent years consistently outstripped average European GDP growth, and are likely to reach even higher levels as revenues from broadband and mobile services begin to rise in virtually every Member State. This pattern is likely to be reproduced in the United States and Japan and in high-growth economies such as China and other Asian as well as South American countries.

The European e-communications services market is in a period of transition. Before 1998, fixed telephony services were provided in most Member States by monopoly organizations. These former incumbents still have large shares in their traditional markets, although new entrant providers are beginning to erode these market positions, in particular in Member States that liberalised early. New services markets, including for mobile voice and data, are in many instances more competitive, although legacy networks still provide the former incumbents with considerable competitive advantages in the provision of services such as high speed data.

The EU e-communications framework adopted in 2002 has been designed not only to regulate more competitive markets, but to continue to do so for the foreseeable future without major revision. In doing so the framework should enable ex ante rules to be relaxed in line with the growth of competition in individual market segments, with ex post competition rules gradually supplanting them. During this probably rather lengthy transitional period, several bodies of rules (sector specific regulation, general competition rules, national administrative rules) may be applicable simultaneously. At the same time, several authorities (national regulatory and competition authorities, national appeal bodies and courts, the European Commission, the Court of First Instance, possibly even the World Trade Organization) are likely to have jurisdiction to intervene or settle disputes, sometimes on their own initiative.

In order to manage this transition, the EU framework provides for regulatory obligations to be imposed on market actors on the basis of competition law principles, using the principle of market dominance to identify undertakings likely to require regulatory restraint. This logic should enable the framework to perform a number of feats: to take account of the appearance on the market of new and innovative services; to encompass the newly acceding countries of the Baltic, Central Europe and the Mediterranean; and to treat all existing and future technologies on an equal regulatory footing. This flexibility and rigour makes the new rules probably the most advanced in the world, and may provide a model for other countries and regions.

This book attempts to analyse the relationships between the bodies of law and the authorities called upon to implement them in the electronic communications field. It is written by an academic specialising in EU e-communications and competition law and a European Commission official with long experience in the implementation of EU e-communications directives. It is intended to address both the theoretical and practical problems likely to be encountered in this area of EU law by practitioners, civil servants, members of regulatory authorities, academics and students.

The opinions set out in this publication are those of the authors, and do not necessarily reflect the position of the European Commission.

Paul Nihoul, Peter Rodford
Brussels, 2 April 2004

CONTENTS—SUMMARY

CONTENTS

TABLES OF CASES

COURT OF FIRST INSTANCE

EUROPEAN COURT OF JUSTICE

COMMISSION DECISIONS

COUNCIL DECISIONS

TABLES OF EU/EC TREATIES AND LEGISLATION

DIRECTIVES

TABLE OF NON-EU/EC TREATIES

GLOSSARY OF DEFINED TERMS, EXPRESSIONS, AND ABBREVIATIONS

A. Terms and Expressions used in this Book

The following terms and expressions are used in this book to designate specific instruments or concepts.

1. General Terms

Basic regulatory principles.   The basic regulatory principles contain rules that must be complied with by national authorities in applying the NRF. Entities to which they apply must adopt behaviour based on objectivity, non-discrimination, proportionality and transparency. These rules typically apply to decision or other instruments taken by national regulatory authorities. In many cases they also apply to practices adopted by undertakings having significant market power.

Essential facilities doctrine.   Doctrine originally developed in American law. It is based on general competition law and implies that an undertaking must share access to a resource or facility placed under its control, where that resource or facility is essential for the performance of activities on a secondary market. The doctrine is at the heart of the access-related obligations imposed on undertakings with significant market power under the new regulatory framework. There is some discussion as to whether the doctrine is accepted or otherwise by the CFI and ECJ.

General competition law. This expression refers to the main competition rules, which at European level are Article 81 EC (anti-competitive agreements), Article 82 EC (abuse of dominant position), Article 86 EC (undertakings with links to national public authorities), Article 87 (State aids) and the Merger Regulation. In this book, a distinction is drawn between general competition law and the liberalisation directives. Admittedly, these latter directives have been adopted on the basis of Article 86(3) EC. However, they introduce general regulatory obligations where general competition law consists of the adoption of concrete decisions in specific cases. A distinction is also drawn with the harmonisation directives which, in principle, have no direct connection with competition.

New regulatory framework. The new regulatory framework (NRF) is made up of directives adopted by the European institutions with a view to reforming the rules applicable to the electronic communications sector, after the telecommunications review carried out in 1999. Most of the directives concerned were adopted in 2002. The new regulatory framework is not limited to directives adopted by the European Parliament and Council, but also contains the Consolidated Services Directive adopted by the Commission as well as supplementary instruments adopted in most cases by that latter institution to implement the above-mentioned directives.

Old regulatory framework. The old regulatory framework was made up of directives adopted by the Parliament and Council[1] prior to the telecommunications review in 1999. These directives mainly sought to ensure Open Network Provision (ONP) and were based on Treaty provisions allowing harmonisation of national measures having as their object the internal market. These directives have been replaced by those introduced in the new regulatory framework (NRF). Some provisions contained in these directives remain applicable during a transitional period.

Special regulatory procedure ('Article 7' procedure). This procedure is established in the Framework Directive and applies to certain decisions taken by national regulatory authorities. These decisions must be communicated in the form of a draft to the authorities of the other Member States as well as to the Commission. These authorities and the Commission may then submit comments which must be taken into account by the organ responsible for the decision. In some circumstances the Commission may veto a draft, with the result that the decision envisaged by the national regulatory authority cannot be adopted.

Specific obligations. This expression designates obligations imposed on undertakings with significant market power. They are distinguished from other, more

---

[1] In a first period these instruments were adopted by the Council with an intervention of the European Parliament (consultation). The situation changed when the co-decision procedure was introduced. This co-decision procedure now has to be used for the adoption of harmonisation directives.

general, obligations that are applied, or may be applied, on certain markets irrespective of the existence of (significant) market power. Most specific obligations concern access to networks and are introduced by the Access Directive. They are of a regulatory nature in that they have general scope[2] and are applied ex ante.

2. New Regulatory Framework

Framework Directive.   European Parliament and Council Directive (EC) 2002/21 on a common regulatory framework for electronic communications networks and services [2002] OJ L108/33

Access Directive.   European Parliament and Council Directive (EC) 2002/19 on access to, and interconnection of, electronic communications networks and associated facilities [2002] OJ L108/7

Universal Service Directive.   European Parliament and Council Directive (EC) 2002/22 on universal service and user's rights relating to electronic communications networks and services [2002] OJ L108/51

Authorisations Directive.   European Parliament and Council Directive (EC) 2002/20 on the authorisation of electronic communications networks and services [2002] OJ L108/21

e-Privacy Directive.   European Parliament and Council Directive (EC) 2002/58 concerning the processing of personal data and the protection of privacy in the electronic communications sector (Directive on privacy and electronic communications) [2002] OJ L201/37 and OJ L108/51

3. Supplementary Instruments

1998 Recommendation on interconnection.   Commission Recommendation (EC) 98/195 on interconnection in a liberalised telecommunications market (Part 1—Interconnection pricing) [1998] OJ L73/42[3]

1998 Accounting recommendation.   Commission Recommendation (EC) 98/322 on interconnection in a liberalised telecommunications market (Part 2—Accounting separation and cost accounting) [1998] OJ L141/6

1998 Tariff recommendation.   Commission Recommendation (EC) C(2002) 561 amending Recommendation 98/195/EC, as last amended by Recommendation 2000/263/EC, on Interconnection in a liberalised telecommunications market (Part 1—Interconnection Pricing) [2002] OJ L58/56

---

[2] Application to all undertakings placed in a given situation (possession of significant market power).

[3] This Recommendation has been modified several times—the last time through Commission Recommendation C(2002) 561 available on the internet site of the Commission—DG Information Society.

2002 Guidelines on market analysis and significant market power. Commission Guidelines 2002/C165/03 on market analysis and the assessment of significant market power under the Community regulatory framework for electronic communications networks and services [2002] OJ C165/3

Recommendation on relevant markets. Commission Recommendation C(2003)497 On Relevant Product and Service Markets within the electronic communications sector susceptible to ex ante regulation in accordance with Directive 2002/21/EC of the European Parliament and of the Council on a common regulatory framework for electronic communication networks and services [2003] OJ L114/45

4. European Commission

Consolidated Services Directive. Commission Directive (EC) 2002/77 on competition in the markets for electronic communications networks and services [2002] OJ L249/21

Notice on the relevant market. Commission Notice on the definition of relevant market for the purposes of Community competition law [1997] OJ C372/5

1991 Competition Guidelines. Commission Guidelines (EC) 91/C233/02 on the application of EEC competition rules in the telecommunications sector [1991] OJ C233/2

1998 Competition Guidelines. Commission Notice 98/C265/02 on the application of the competition rules to access agreements in the telecommunications sector [1998] OJ C265/2

Terminal Equipment Liberalisation Directive Commission Directive 88/301 of 16 May 1988 on competition in the markets in telecommunications terminal equipment [1988] OJ L131/73

5. Background Instruments

e-Commerce Directive. European Parliament and Council Directive (EC) 2000/31 on certain legal aspects of information society services, in particular electronic commerce, in the internal market [2000] OJ L178/1

6. Old Regulatory Framework—Parliament and Council

ONP Framework Directive. Council Directive (EEC) 90/387 on the establishment of the internal market for telecommunications services through the implementation of open network provision [1990] OJ L192/1, as amended several times

ONP Interconnection Directive. European Parliament and Council Directive (EC) 97/33 on interconnection in telecommunications with regard to ensuring universal service and interoperability through application of the principles of Open Network Provision (ONP) [1997] OJ L199/32[4]

ONP Voice Telephony Directive.   European Parliament and Council Directive (EC) 98/10 on the application of open network provision (ONP) to voice telephony and on universal service for telecommunications in a competitive environment [1998] OJ L101/24

ONP Leased Lines Directives.   Council Directive (EEC) 92/44 on the application of open network provision to leased lines [1992] OJ L165/27, amended several times

RTTE Directive 1999/5.   European Parliament and Council Directive (EC) 98/13 relating to telecommunications terminal equipment and satellite earth station equipment, including the mutual recognition of their conformity [1998] OJ L74/1

7. Liberalisation Directives

Services Directive.   Commission Directive (EEC) 90/388 on competition in the markets for telecommunications services [1988] OJ L192/10[5]

Satellites Directive.   Commission Directive (EEC) 94/46 amending Directive 88/301 and Directive 90/388 in particular with regard to satellite communications [1994] OJ L268/15

Cable TV 1 Directive.   Commission Directive (EC) 95/51 amending Directive 90/388 with regard to the abolition of the restrictions on the use of cable television networks for the provision of already liberalised telecommunications services [1995] OJ L256/49

Mobile Directive.   Commission Directive (EC) 96/2 amending Directive 90/388 with regard to personal and mobile communications [1996] OJ L20/59

Full Competition Directive.   Commission Directive (EC) 96/19 amending Directive 90/388/EEC with regard to the implementation of full competition in telecommunications markets [1996] OJ L74/24.

Cable TV 2 Directive.   Commission Directive (EC) 1999/64 amending Directive 90/388 in order to ensure that telecommunications networks and cable TV networks owned by a single operator are separate legal entities [1999] OJ L1175/39

---

[4] Amended by European Parliament and Council Directive (EC) 98/61 [1998] OJ L268/37.
[5] Amended by the directives following in the list.

B. Technical Terms and Abbreviations used in EU Legislation and Commission Documents

The definitions in this part of the glossary are taken from EU legislative acts and documents issued or adopted by the European Commission.

Access

The making available of facilities and/or services, to another undertaking, under defined conditions, on either an exclusive or non-exclusive basis, for the purpose of providing electronic communications services. It covers inter alia: access to network elements and associated facilities, which may involve the connection of equipment, by fixed or non-fixed means (in particular this includes access to the local loop and to facilities and services necessary to provide services over the local loop); access to physical infrastructure including buildings, ducts and masts; access to relevant software systems including operational support systems; access to number translation or systems offering equivalent functionality; access to fixed and mobile networks, in particular for roaming; access to conditional access systems for digital television services; and access to virtual network services.

ACTS

Advanced Communications Technologies and Services.

Adapter

PC translator that converts information to tidy packages that flow neatly down network wires. Every PC on a corporate network has one of these adapters, which come in the form of circuit boards.

ADSL

Asymmetric digital subscriber line.

ADTT

Advanced Digital Television Technologies.

Application program interface (API)

The software interfaces between applications made available by broadcasters or service providers and the resources in the enhanced digital television equipment for digital television and radio services.

Applications

Telematic services available in the professional and private spheres such as telework, telemedicine, tele-education and teletraining or telemanagement of traffic.

Asymmetrical Digital Subscriber Line (ADSL)

Existing telephone networks upgraded to allow VCR-quality video images (but not live or high-definition signals) to be transmitted.

ATM (Asynchronous transfer mode)

An international packet switching standard established by the CCITT. A system for organising a digital signal in such a way as to allow very high speed transmission of the signal while making optimum use of the network's transmission capacity. A standard agreed for B-ISDN networks.

Bandwidth

Definition of the transmission capacity of a cable. Highest for fibre optic, lowest for copper telephone wire.

Baud

Numerical data transmission speed unit. 1 baud corresponds to 1 bit/second. The minimum speed of a modem is currently 9,600 bauds.

B-ISDN (Broadband ISDN)

A single network capable of carrying several different types of service, based on voice, data, still or moving image, by means of digital transmission techniques. The ISDN (Integrated Services Digital Network) currently being deployed in Europe carries communications of up to 2 Megabits/second (Narrowband ISDN). Future networks will carry higher speed communications (Broadband ISDN).

Bits/Bytes

The smallest discrete elements in a binary system: eight bits comprise one byte.

Broadband

A popular way to move large amounts of voice, data and video. Broadband technology lets different networks coexist on a single piece of heavy-duty wiring. It isolates signals as a radio does, each one vibrating at a different frequency as it moves down the line. Its opposite is baseband, which separates signals by sending them at timed intervals.

Cable

A reception system available in areas that are cabled. Unlike satellite, the reception of a cable broadcast does not need an aerial on a roof or balcony.

CEN

Comité Européen de Normalisation; European Committee for Standardisation. CEN's mission is to promote voluntary technical harmonisation in Europe in conjunction with worldwide bodies and its partners in Europe.

CENELEC

Comité Européen de Normalisation Electrotechnique; European Committee for Electrotechnical Standardisation. Together with its members, affiliates and co-operating partners its aim is to develop a coherent set of voluntary electrotechnical standards as a basis for a Single European Market / European Economic Area without internal frontiers for goods and services inside Europe.

CEPT

Conference Européenne des Postes et des Télécommunications; European Conference of Postal and Telecommunications Administrations

CFI

Court of First Instance of the European Communities.

Coaxial cable

Better known as coax, this is the old fat wire used by cable TV companies and some data networks. It has more capacity than standard copper phone wire, but quite a bit less than fibre-optic lines.

COM

European Commission; Commission document: COM documents are issued by the Secretariat-General of the Commission and contain proposals or other communications from the Commission to the Council and/or other institutions (European Commission on the Interinstitutional Webserver EUROPA).

Community antenna television, cable television (CATV)

A public network for the delivery of television programmes to the home by cable. Existing systems use coaxial cable and are limited in Europe to approximately 30 channels of television. Future broadband systems will carry up to 500 channels.

Compact Disc Interactive (CD-I)

The interactive multimedia platform developed by Philips, based on a Motorola 68000 processor and compact disc drive, with universal technical specifications. CD-I supports three levels of audio in stereo and mono, four graphics formats at various levels, four image planes, in/out devices including a remote control unit and keyboard, and output to ordinary TV sets, under its own dedicated operating system (CD-RTOS).

Compact disc read only memory (CD-ROM)

The CD format principally devoted to text and data (and occasionally audio and graphics).

Compression

The technique of reducing the amount of data in a signal in order to reduce the amount of required transmission capacity, the signal being reconstructed in its original form at the receiving end. A device to do this is a 'codec' (coder-decoder).

Conditional access systems

Any technical measure and/or arrangement whereby access to a protected radio or television broadcasting service in intelligible form is made conditional upon subscription or other form of prior individual authorisation.

DECT

Digital European Cordless Telecommunications (European standard for digital cordless telecommunications).

DELTA

Developing European Learning through Technical Advance—Flexible and distance learning (1990–4). Specific EC programme of research and technological development in the field of telematic systems in areas of general interest.

DG

Directorate General of the European Commission.

Digital compression

A way of reducing the number of bits (ones and zeros) in a digital signal by using mathematical algorithms to eliminate redundant information thereby reducing the space it occupies when being transmitted or recorded.

Digital European Cordless Telecommunications (DECT)

DECT is the time division multiple access (TDMA)-based digital standard chosen by the European Telecommunications Standards Institute (ETSI) for future advanced wireless phones, wireless PBX, and radio-based public access telecom services.

Digital transmission

In a digital telecommunication service, the original source is transformed into and transmitted as a series of digits in binary code (ie ones or zeros). Voice, text, image or data are all equally capable of being coded as a digital signal, so that a single network can handle all four forms of transmission (multimedia). The string of binary digits can be abbreviated and then re-expanded on arrival, thus economising transmission capacity. Different strings of binary digits can be interleaved and transmitted together, thus permitting several separate conversations on a single line (multiplexing). The string of digits can be encrypted prior to transmission, to ensure a high level of information security and privacy. Through digitalisation, even a severely degraded transmission can be reconstructed to reproduce perfectly the original source.

Digital video interactive (DVI)

DVI is a mode of image compression conceived by Intel for use by PC microcomputers. Microsoft adopted it for their software Video for Windows, Apple for QuickTime, etc.

Direct broadcasting by satellite (DBS)

The use of satellites to transmit high-power TV signals in the BSS band for reception via small antennae direct to home (DTH). Such services can also be carried on cable.

Diskette

Storing device used to save information from computers and other instruments such as digital picture cameras.

DVB

Digital Video Broadcasting.

EBU

The European Broadcasting Union, the largest professional association of national broadcasters in the world. The EBU has its headquarters in Geneva and negotiates broadcasting rights for major sports events, operates the Eurovision and Euroradio networks, organises programme exchanges, co-ordinates co-productions, and provides a range of other operational, commercial, technical, legal and strategic services.

ec

Electronic commerce.

ECJ

Court of Justice of the European Communities.

EEA

European Economic Area. The Member States are the 15 European Union Member States (Austria, Belgium, Denmark, Finland, France, Germany, Greece, Ireland, Italy, Luxembourg, the Netherlands, Portugal, Spain, Sweden, United Kingdom (including Gibraltar)) and Iceland, Liechtenstein and Norway.

*e*Europe Initiative

On 8 December 1999 the European Commission launched an initiative entitled 'e-Europe: An Information Society for All', which proposed ambitious targets to bring the benefits of the Information Society within reach of all Europeans. The initiative focused on ten priority areas, from education to transport and from healthcare to the disabled.

EFTA

The European Free Trade Association was established in 1960 by the Stockholm Convention to eliminate tariffs and other restrictions on trade between EFTA members. The organisation is currently composed of just four Member States: Iceland, Liechtenstein, Norway and Switzerland.

Electronic data interchange (EDI)

A way unaffiliated companies can use networks to link their businesses. While electronic mail between companies is common, electronic data interchange passes bigger bundles that replace large paper documents such as bills and contracts. Besides saving paper, computers could save time by taking over transactions like regular purchase orders that now require human intervention.

Electronic-mail (e-mail)

The most common use of networks. A service which allows computer users to send electronic messages to other computer users. The use of sophisticated software ensures that the message sent will find its way along different networks until it reaches the correct address.

Enhanced digital television equipment

Set-top boxes intended for connection to television sets or integrated digital television sets, able to receive digital interactive television services.

Enhanced television

Designates a TV system which retains the scanning standards of the existing 625-line 50-field or 525-line 60-field systems, while providing various improvements in the quality of the picture and additional features such as the wide screen 16:9 aspect ratio, resulting from new signal processing, with or without modification of the transmission standards.

Ethernet

The most common sort of network used in corporations. Its top speed is 10 million bits/second. Because it works like a party line, if too many people try to send messages at once, the network slows dramatically.

ETNO

European Telecommunications Network Operators.

ETSI

European Telecommunications Standards Institute.

EUTELSAT

European Telecommunication Satellite Organisation.

Fibre

Fibre-optic cable, made of glass fibres instead of copper strands. Data, expressed as pulses of light rather than electrons, is transmitted by lasers or other devices. Optical fibre can carry billions of bits a second, many times more than coaxial or copper wire, and is less sensitive to electrical interference.

Fibre to the curb (FTTC), fibre to the home (FTTH)

Future optical fibre networks may extend optical fibre to the individual home (FTTH), or the fibre may terminate at a 'black box' located in the street, where the optical signal is converted into an electrical signal and carried the remaining distance to each home on the pre-existing copper wiring (FTTC).

Fire wall

One way to keep hackers out. Some networking devices can limit access to sensitive parts of a network. For example, a company might authorise access to its salary records only to a computer in a particular location that gives a secret password.

Flaming

Bombardment with messages by users of the internet of any other user or advertiser who breaks the 'etiquette' of the network. Can run to billions of bites of useless data intended to clog up the offender's computer.

Gateway

One of the most common usages for the term is an on-line service company that gives customers access to a server or a network such as the internet. Inside a company, the term usually refers to special hardware that connects two different types of systems, such as a main-frame to a local-area network.

GATS

General Agreement on Trade in Services.

GATT

General Agreement on Tariffs and Trade.

Generic service

A service such as electronic mail that can be used for a multitude of purposes and adapted to the needs of a particular application.

Gigabit network

A gigabit network is one that operates at a billion bits a second, ie 100 times Ethernet's speed.

Global System for Mobile Communications (GSM)

GSM is a pan-European standard for digital mobile telephony which provides a much higher capacity than traditional analogue telephones as well as diversified services (voice, data) and greater transmission security through information encoding for users across Europe.

GPS

Global Position System (US).

GSM

Global system for mobile communications.

Hard disc

High-capacity data storage device for computers.

HD-Mac

Europe's HDTV broadcast transmission standard supporting 1250-line resolution pictures, 50 Hz, in the 16 : 9 aspect ratio with digital stereo sound.

High definition television (HDTV)

System designed to allow viewing at about three times the picture height, such that the system is virtually, or nearly, transparent to the quality of portrayal that would have been perceived in the original scene or performance by a discerning viewer with normal visual acuity. Such factors include improved perception of depth.

Integrated broadband communications (IBC)

The global term for the future overall communications environment, embracing broadband-ISDN, narrowband-ISDN, mobile telephony and existing conventional telephone services together with data communications and cable TV.

INTELSAT

International Satellite Organisation.

Interactivity

Interactivity in a service implies a close control by the user of the service by means of an ongoing system of two-way communication between the user and the service provider.

Interconnection

The physical and logical linking of public communications networks used by the same or a different undertaking in order to allow the users of one undertaking to communicate with users of the same or another undertaking, or to access services provided by another undertaking. Services may be provided by the parties involved or other parties who have access to the network. Interconnection is a specific type of access implemented between public network operators.

Interconnectivity

Devices (computers, lines, application programmes, etc) are interconnected when they can communicate which each other, that is send and receive data. They use the same communication protocols, for example OSI (Open Systems Interconnection).

Interface

That which facilitates the communication between the computer and its user. It may be a graphic interface or a textual interface. An interface can also be that which facilitates communication between two appliances (for example, the PERITEL jack links a TV to a videotape recorder or a videodisc player).

Internet

The world's largest computer communication system, with an estimated 100 million users. Originated in the United States, though now operating world-wide, the internet is a loose confederation of principally academic and research computer networks. It is not a network but rather the interconnection of thousands of separate networks using a common language. Developed by the Pentagon, the internet first linked US government agencies and colleges. Now the net also connects thousands of companies and millions of individuals worldwide who subscribe to on-line services.

Interoperability

Devices, in particular application programmes, are interoperable when, in addition to communicating with each other, they can also execute together a common task. They co-operate. This requires additional standards, such as APIs (Application Programme Interfaces).

ISDN (integrated services digital network), N-ISDN, B-ISDN

A single network capable of carrying several different types of service, based on voice, data, still or moving image by means of digital transmission techniques. The ISDN currently being deployed in Europe carries communications of up to 2 Megabits/second (narrowband ISDN). Future networks will carry higher speed communications (broadband ISDN).

ISSS

Information Society Standardisation System. The mission of CEN/ISSS is to provide market players with a comprehensive and integrated range of standardisation-oriented services and products, in order to contribute to the success of the Information Society in Europe.

ITU

International Telecommunications Union is an international organisation with headquarters in Geneva within which governments and the private sector co-ordinate global telecom networks and services.

Latency

Time which elapses between ordering information and receiving it through an interactive system. PC users on a crowded Ethernet network get a demonstration of latency.

Laserdisc

Also known as CDV (Compact Disc Video) or Video Disc. Originally launched by Philips, it was renamed Laserdisc by Pioneer, Philips, Matsushita and Sony in 1990. It stores analogue images and digital sound. Laserdisc players can be connected to TVs and Hi-fi systems.

Letterbox

Format used to describe a TV image with black bands at the top and bottom of the screen to fit a movie format into a 4 : 3 TV screen format.

Local area network (LAN)

A network for communication between computers confined to a single building or in a closely located group of buildings, permitting users to exchange data, share a common printer or master a common computer, etc. Linked groups of LANs extended over a larger area are termed wide area networks (WANs). WANS may connect users in different buildings or countries. Networks which extend over city-wide areas are called metropolitan area networks (MANs).

Local loop

The section of the telephone transmission network between the local telephone exchange and the subscriber's premises, which currently consists of copper wiring. In the future, optical fibre or wireless will also be used.

Low earth orbit (LEO), LEOS (low earth orbit satellite)

System of personal telecommunications based on communication via a number of satellites in low orbit. The best known is the 'Iridium' project.

Metropolitan area network (MAN)

Network which extends over a city-wide area.

Minitel

The first global experience of telematics, started in France in 1984. The precursor of the electronic highway.

MM

Multimedia: the concept of closely combining voice, text, data, as well as still and moving image. A multimedia database, for example, would contain textual information, images, video clips and tables of data, all equally easy to access. A multimedia telecommunications service (such as B-ISDN) would permit the user to send or receive any of these forms of information, interchangeable at will.

Mobile telephone, cellular

A system of mobile telephony whereby a country is divided into thousands of small areas (cells), each of which is served by its own 'base station' for low-powered radio transmissions. This allows a user in one cell to transmit on the same frequency as another user in another cell without interfering with the other's conversation. Cellular networks may employ analogue or digital transmission.

Modem (modulator-demodulator)

Device which transforms analogue signals transmitted by telephone lines into digital signals which can be transmitted by computer and vice versa.

Multimedia

See MM.

Multiplexed analogue components (MAC)

TV transmission system, pioneered in the United Kingdom in the early 1980s, in which the colour signals are time division multiplexed, thus, interference between chrominance and luminance does not occur as in PAL. In the D2-MAC version, sound is carried as digital data sent in a duobinary form (hence the 'D' letter) at 10.125 Mbits/s.

Multiplexing

The carriage of multiple signals on a communications channel. In recent cable programming terminology, it refers to 'cloning' one cable channel, like MTV or HBO, into multiple, complementary channels to reach a broader audience. The device that makes this possible is called a 'multiplexer' or 'mux'.

Navigator's guide

In interactive TV, the system for selecting from among the programmes offered.

NCA

National competition authority.

Network

Communication networks correspond to a complete system of communications between user's terminals. Networks may be 'point to point' (the transmission goes from a fixed origin to a fixed destination), 'switched' (the transmission is switched so as to reach a single destination out of many) or 'broadcast' (the transmission goes simultaneously to multiple destinations). Networks may be 'public' (owned by an operator and open to any member of the public that subscribes) or 'private' (owned or leased by an individual or company or group of companies exclusively for its own use).

Network, data

A network specialising in the transmission of data rather than voice. Among such networks are circuit switched data networks (CSDN), packet switched data networks (PSDN), frame relay networks and switched multimegabit data service networks (SMDS).

Network, intelligent

An intelligent network includes sophisticated features superior to those of the ordinary telephone service, such as advanced software allowing the customisation of the services provided to individual customers. For example, it allows the called party to redirect calls intended for another terminal (for example, from a home phone to an office phone). It allows calls to be billed wholly or in part to somebody other than the caller ('free phone' services). It also provides virtual private network services.

Network operating system

Software that allows a PC or a larger server to manage files and handle other central networking functions.

N-ISDN (narrowband ISDN)

See ISDN.

Node

Point of connection and conversion between fibre optic and coaxial cable.

NRA

National regulatory authority.

NRF

New regulatory framework.

Open network provision (ONP)

Principle of non-discriminatory opening of telecommunication networks to all telecoms operators and service providers on the basis of the harmonisation of access and usage conditions of telecommunications infrastructures with a view to the development of a trans-European information market.

Optical fibre network

Telecommunication networks based on fine glass fibres down which signals may be sent by laser beam.

PABX (private automatic branch exchange), PBX (private branch exchange)

The private switchboard located on business premises by which a business subscriber controls the calls on its own internal telephones.

PAL (phase alternation line)

Colour TV system used in most of Europe, Africa, Australasia and South America. Like SECAM, PAL produces interlaced 625-line, 25 frame/second pictures.

Pay-per-view

Programming sold on a per-occasion or per-title basis. Access can be controlled electronically in response to subscriber orders using an addressable cable converter. Digital signals switching the service off or on are sent to that converter's unique 'address'.

PCM (pulse code modulation)

The most common way of converting an analogue source into digital form.

Personal communication network (PCN)

A form of cellular telephone network deployed in Europe and specifically adapted for personal portable use based on a technology known as DCS 1800. Similar services in the USA are referred to as PCS (Personal Communication Services).

Personal digital assistant (PDA)

A pocket-sized personal computer with advanced features and communications facilities, where text is introduced by handwriting on a screen; also referred to as a 'notepad' computer.

Portability

Used in reference to a computer program, portability means that the program can be executed on a number of different computers without or with only minimal changes.

Protocol

Standard rules that govern how computers communicate with each other.

PSTN (public switched telephone network)

The everyday telephone network used for the transmission of voice conversations, fax images and for low speed data transmission.

Sampling

The transformation of an analogue signal (sound, image) into a digital code. Sampling consists of the analysis of electronic signals at regular and brief intervals. A large number of synthesisers produce sounds created by sampling.

Security of information and systems

Has three basic components: confidentiality, integrity and availability. Confidentiality refers to the protection of sensitive information from unauthorised disclosure. Integrity means safeguarding the accuracy and completeness of information and computer software. Availability relates to ensuring that information and vital services are available to users when required.

Server

Anything from a PC to a supercomputer that shares files and other services with multiple users.

Smart card

A card that is able to store digital information and is used for many purposes (examples are credit cards, telephone cards).

Telematics

The application of information and communications technologies and services, usually in direct combination. A telematics application is a system or service meeting user needs.

Telematics infrastructure

The assemblage of telecommunications and information-processing systems and services that offers a base for telematics applications.

Teleservice

A service provided from a remote location using the telematics infrastructure.

Teleworking

Work carried out using the telematics infrastructure at a place other than that where the results of the work are needed. This definition covers work by home, mobile or 'telecottage'-based teleworkers employed by an organisation, by independent workers and by teleservice companies offering specific services to both companies and individuals.

Universal service

A set of basic services that must be made available at an affordable price to all users by public operators irrespective of the user's geographical location.

Value added service (VAS), value added network service (VANS)

Services other than those under monopoly may be offered by other service suppliers which use national networks as the basic transmission medium but 'add value' to the basic transmission facility. What is exactly included in the concept depends on the regulatory situation of each country.

Video-on-demand

Systems that enable viewers to order and see a given programme at the exact time the viewer specifies. Near-video-on-demand (NVOD) systems approximate this capacity by staggering the start of a programme every 15 or 30 minutes.

Virus

Small informatics programme able to disrupt the functioning of other programmes.

Wide area network (WAN)

A complement to LAN. A WAN consists of multiple local networks tied together, typically using telephone company services. WANs may connect users in different buildings or countries.

Wide-screen television service

A television service that consists wholly or partially of programmes produced and edited to be displayed in a full height wide-screen format. The 16 : 9 format is the reference format for wide-screen television services.

WIPO

World Intellectual Property Organisation—Organisation Mondiale de la Propriété Intellectuelle (OMPI).

WTO

World Trade Organization.

1

A NEW REGIME FOR ELECTRONIC COMMUNICATIONS MARKETS

A. General Observations

(1) Electronic communications and the law

Importance of electronic communications.   Electronic communications play **1.01** an essential role in society. They represent in their own right a substantial part of the European economy. Electronic communications are also important for the role they play in other activities, which they make possible or facilitate. They are

1

fundamental in relations between members of society, which are in turn central to business activities and a vehicle for social interaction between private individuals and groups. In short they are important as vectors of information and communication within society.

1.02 **Significant quantity of negotiation and dispute.** As electronic communications are pervasive, they require to be organised on a legal footing. There are no statistics showing the degree of legal or regulatory activity associated with electronic communications. It can, however, be submitted that the scope of such activity is not small. A handful of regulatory personnel is active on this front, producing instruments that influence fundamentally the behaviour of businesses of all kinds. Lawyers and legal counsel advise their clients; judges and arbitrators attempt to resolve disputes; and students struggle to master this area of the law, to serve later in those functions.

1.03 **Important to know and understand the rules.** The importance of electronic communications makes it necessary to know and understand the rules that are associated with them. Expertise must be developed in this field by undertakings engaged in any form of legal or regulatory activity, whether advising, litigating or lobbying. Undertakings active in electronic communications (for example as service or network providers) also need to develop a legal and/or regulatory knowledge-base in this area. How otherwise can they be made aware, in a timely fashion, of what is allowed and what is prohibited, in particular since they are engaged in markets where delays and mistakes are subject to heavy sanction?

(2) The approach proposed to practitioners

1.04 **Variety of applicable laws.** Developing an activity in electronic communications within the European Union is not an easy undertaking, as a result of the variety of rules that may apply. *(a)* As will be seen, these rules stem both from general competition law and from regulation which has been specifically adopted for these markets. *(b)* Lawyers are confronted on these markets with rules of national, European and international origin. *(c)* In some instances, the division of powers within Member States makes it even harder to identify the applicable rules. Electronic communications are also bound up with cultural questions, an area regulated in some Member States by regions or communities within the national organisation.

1.05 **An approach for practitioners.** Given the multiplicity of applicable rules, a method must be developed to address the issues. Generally, practitioners start with rules based in national law. This approach can be explained in several ways. *(a)* European rules frequently produce their effects in the national legal orders only as a result of implementation by national authorities. In most cases, European directives thus appear in the national legal orders through their national implementation measures. *(b)* The majority of practitioners in most European countries are still educated on the basis of national law and practice, despite the fact that a body of European law has existed for nearly 50 years.

The approach proposed in this book. Practitioners dealing with cases or **1.06** regulatory activities concerning electronic communications are invited to seek, in the first place, information and analysis concerning national law. That approach should not, however, be the last. Practitioners should systematically examine European law as a supplementary step. They should even consider a third approach, where national and European law are confronted with international rules.

(a) Start with national law. The advice is for anybody counselling on legal or **1.07** regulatory aspects related to electronic communications to turn, in the first place, to the national rules, since the purpose of the European directives is to indicate to the Member States the principles that require to be transposed into national law. National law is supposed in these circumstances to reflect the principles laid down at European level.

(b) Verify compliance with European law. After examining national rules, **1.08** practitioners should consult European law. The European legislator has been granted wide-ranging powers to fulfil the objectives assigned to the Communities. Substantial practice and case law have developed on the basis of these rules. They have established the 'primacy' of European law. Primacy implies that national rules must comply with European law in the States belonging to the Union. It means that professionals and students should always look at EU law if they want to ensure that their advice on electronic communications is complete. As is shown throughout this book, the European legislator has intervened extensively in this sector in the last 20 years. There is now very little activity that has not been fully regulated at European level in the electronic communications sector. To a substantial extent, the rules in force at national level are, or should be, identical to those agreed at a European level.

(c) Check compatibility with international law. A practitioner will also have **1.09** to go beyond national and European laws to examine international law. A substantial body of rules has been adopted in various international fora. These rules bind the countries and territories that have acceded to them. This is the case for European countries regarding several categories of rules, in particular some that have been agreed within the World Trade Organisation (WTO). These rules are to be complied with at national and European level, although enforcement mechanisms differ in these various contexts.

(3) An emphasis on European law

Relationship between these levels. As appears from the paragraphs above, the var- **1.10** ious levels at which rules may be adopted are linked one with another. The scenarios are not simple, as national law must comply with European law which, in turn, must comply with international law. The relationships between these various regulatory levels are examined in a systematic manner in Chapter 6 dealing with litigation.

1.11 **European law.** An emphasis is placed in this book on the rules established at European level. This choice is made for several reasons. *(a) No substantial difference.* In principle, there should be little difference between the rules applicable at the European and national levels. In most Member States the rules adopted by the European legislator have been taken over, unchanged, in national legislation. A good knowledge of European law thus enables the reader to master in substance the rules applicable at national level in all Member States. *(b) Future disputes.* Disputes are likely to emerge in the years ahead as to the interpretation to be given to the rules concerning electronic communications. These disputes are likely to involve some (substantial) European component. For instance, parties may argue that the rules in force at national level do not comply with European law. Parties may also seek in the European sphere the solutions which they do not find at a national level (complaints addressed to the Commission, preliminary rulings requested from the European Court of Justice (ECJ), etc). *(c) Global basis.* The rules relating to electronic communications are progressively being harmonised across the countries of the world. With increasing trade there is an expectation that these rules will gradually converge. One opinion is that these common rules will be based, to a significant extent, on those applicable in the European Union and in the United States.[1]

1.12 **National and international laws covered.** Despite the particular attention devoted to European rules in this book, national and international laws are also taken into account. As stated above, international rules bind the European Union and its Member States. It would not be useful to analyse European rules if the latter were to be disregarded as a result of their not being compatible with superior international requirements. Nor has national law been set aside. Wherever it appears appropriate, analysis is provided of the choices made at national level in the implementation of European rules.

(4) An era of intense litigation

1.13 **Intense litigation and negotiation ahead.** It can be safely predicted that intense litigation and negotiation will take place in the years ahead in matters relating to electronic communications networks and services. This prediction is made on the basis of the overall importance of electronic communications in society and the

---

[1] A global convergence towards the European and American models is likely to occur as a result of the political and economic influence they exert. In this context a good knowledge of the rules applicable across the European Union provides a good basis for understanding the content and scope of these new and emerging common rules.

wider economy. It can be further expanded in view of the difficulties likely to emerge in the application of the new rules. The rules applicable to electronic communications are complex. As a result, businesses and economic actors more generally are likely to engage in activities with some uncertainty as to the legal consequences attached to them. Disputes will emerge, implying the intervention of administrative and judicial authorities.

Frequent modifications during the last decade.   One reason explaining some of **1.14** the difficulty is that the rules dealing with electronic communications have been modified frequently in Europe over the last 20 years. As submitted in a later section (see paras 1.96–1.97), electronic communications have been governed for decades by national regulation. In the mid-1980s, the European legislator showed willingness to intervene in the sector. It used the next 15 years (1985–2000) to regulate the sector progressively. A systematic review was carried out in 1999. The 'new regulatory framework' (NRF) was then adopted. These various moves (assertion by the European legislator of its power to regulate the area, adoption and modification of rules, recent adoption of a new framework) have had an impact on the organisation of the sector. Electronic communications activities are now carried out in a more efficient manner. The succession of rules adopted has however led to the emergence of complex regulatory situations. It is sometimes accordingly difficult to predict with a reasonable degree of certainty what treatment undertakings and individuals may expect from a legal point of view.

Several bodies of rules.   One cannot say that there exists a single body of rules **1.15** governing electronic communications in Europe. It is more accurate to say that two major categories are applicable. On the one hand, the European legislator has adopted rules dealing specifically with electronic communications activities. On the other, it has applied to these activities other rules with more general scope, that is, general competition law.[2] The coexistence of these categories of rules does not always clarify the legal situation. The rules belonging to these categories should ideally form a coherent and consistent body. They are based, however, on sources and inspirations that are not always identical. Divergences cannot be excluded. As a result, legal predictability is sometimes variable, depending on the standard applied (general competition law, NRF).

Institutional aspects.   The coexistence of two categories of rules has institutional **1.16** consequences. Different authorities have been created to administer distinct bodies of rules. Contacts and relations are frequent among these authorities. It is however difficult to avoid all discrepancies between the decisions they take. Nor can institutional conflicts be excluded, as these authorities are likely to claim simultaneous competence to solve the same, or similar, cases.

---

[2] Competition rules have general application and apply to all activities in the absence of explicit derogation in the EC Treaty or in secondary legislation.

(5) Organisation of this book

1.17   In order to facilitate the task of the practitioner, this book is organised as follows:

1.18   **Chapter 1.**   Chapter 1 provides the background necessary to understand the reform carried out by the European legislator. As part of that background, the development of the current regulatory framework is examined. The scope of application given to the framework is also analysed, together with the institutional organisation of the sector.

1.19   **Chapter 2.**   The second chapter examines rules applicable throughout the regulatory framework. Among these rules, some concern the special and exclusive rights which have been abolished by the European legislator. Some embody regulatory principles applicable to all public interventions (particularly objectivity and proportionality). Rules also concern the acquisition, by foreigners or nationals, of shares in the capital of telecommunications undertakings. Finally, undertakings may be subject to authorisation prior to starting their activities on electronic communications markets. The rules applicable to these authorisations are examined in Chapter 2, as they provide conditions to be satisfied whatever the market concerned.

1.20   **Chapters 3 and 4.**   After examining these general rules, the main issues likely to confront undertakings are examined. These issues concern access to facilities operated by other undertakings, which are reviewed under the specific regulation that has been adopted in the electronic communications field (Chapter 3). They are also examined under general competition law. That body of law has a more general application but is also relevant for behaviour adopted on electronic communications markets (Chapter 4).

1.21   **Chapter 5.**   The fifth chapter addresses issues relating to universal service, public service and services of general interest. These issues dominated to a large extent some of the discussions that took place in the Member States and the European Union when the reform was introduced. It is important to remind readers that telecommunications, a sector which has now evolved towards electronic communications together with broadcasting and information technology, were organised, prior to the reform, in the form of a public service. In its generality, the reform may be interpreted as a slow movement with as its starting point the concept of public service.

1.22   **Chapter 6.**   Chapter 6 deals with litigation and dispute resolution. Here again the approach has been as concrete as possible. Various types of conflict likely to emerge are examined, the purpose being to supply practitioners with a clear typology of possible litigation. On this basis they will know what types of procedure are open to them. It should be emphasised that litigation is only just starting to develop in the sector concerned. Little experience has thus been accumulated on this point, with the result that it is often difficult to refer to individual cases.

Chapter 7. Various specific issues are addressed in Chapter 7. These relate to **1.23** problems not covered in other parts of the book but requiring some analysis. Among the subjects touched on is the progressive development of spectrum policy in the European Union. The rights granted to users under the new electronic communications regulation are also examined, and a special section is devoted to the rules applicable to broadcasting.

Equal weight, with two exceptions. Throughout the book, equal importance is **1.24** given to all of the relevant issues. The purpose is to provide a thorough overview from the practitioner's viewpoint. Exceptions are made, however, for matters likely to arise in connection with disputes. *(a)* This is the case with access and interconnection. Two chapters are devoted to these issues (one on sector-specific regulation and the other on general competition law). Access and interconnection are indeed keys in the reform, concerning as they do the possibility for new actors to access facilities owned by incumbent operators. Hence they condition the development of markets for electronic communications. *(b)* The second exception is universal service. A major reason is that intense litigation may also be expected in this area. A particular issue is to ensure that Member States do not favour their former national operators. Another reason is that the debate concerning universal service has dominated the agenda in some Member States. Devoting a substantial discussion to this topic reflects the concerns expressed in those countries.

(6) Relations between actors

Three types of relationship. As the organisation of chapters shows, the NRF **1.25** deals with various kinds of relations that undertakings may form on the markets. In each of these the law plays a specific role.

Business to competitor. One relation is between businesses and their competi- **1.26** tors. Relations between competitors are generally indirect. Rivals challenge one another through the offers they present to customers. In some instances, however, they come into direct contact with one another. An example is when an undertaking needs access to facilities controlled by another operator. The role of the law in this context is to verify that transactions are concluded in an equitable manner between the undertakings concerned. The fear is that the operator controlling facilities may use the possibly essential character of those resources to extract over-favourable conditions. Such conditions may not only be favourable to the powerful operator, but may also discourage the development of new activities by challengers. The interests of society would be affected, as competition would be harmed or would not develop as was intended.

Business to client. Another relationship organised by the NRF is that bet- **1.27** ween undertakings and their customers. This relationship again is governed by sector-specific regulation and by general competition law. The goal is on the one hand to ensure that users are treated correctly by undertakings, the concern again being that undertakings might treat the people or entities they come into contact with otherwise than correctly once they acquire a certain power on the market. On the other hand, the purpose is to ensure the provision of services considered essential in society to everyone, and under reasonable conditions.

1.28 **Business to authority.** The last category concerns relations between undertakings and authorities. These relations are pervasive. All rules introduced in the NRF concern the relationship with the authorities, as they translate the desire manifested by these authorities to structure, and organise, markets. Despite that pervasive character, some rules deal more specifically than others with that category of relation. These rules concern the conditions under which undertakings may enter the markets (authorisations). They also establish principles applicable to interventions by public authorities (regulatory principles).

(7) Who should consult this book?

1.29 **A book for practitioners.** This book provides practitioners with information and analysis concerning the rules applicable within the European Union to electronic communications services. The intention is to provide a clear and complete overview without entering into excessive detail. The approach is that practitioners should be provided with a description and analysis of the rules they are likely to encounter in practice. At the same time, they should remain aware of the structure of the framework and of the principles that have guided the European legislator.

1.30 **Attorneys, solicitors, barristers, legal counsel.** Among practitioners, special reference is made to the situation of professionals active in law firms and businesses (attorneys, solicitors, barristers). Consultants (including lobbyists, etc) are also concerned, to the extent that they are asked to provide their clients with their opinions based on the law and regulation applicable to electronic communications.

1.31 **Public bodies.** This book is not limited to use by private actors. Rules and discussions are presented in a neutral fashion. It thus provides useful analysis and information for public actors, particularly regulators, administrations, government departments and members of the judiciary.

1.32 **Education.** Its format and method make this book an ideal academic tool. The subject matter has been divided up to provide a useful basis for teaching.

1.33 **Help us continue.** Trends in the development of electronic communications mean that projects of common interest can be promoted on the basis of collective action. The development of Linux and other publicly licensed software provide useful examples. The authors of this book would like to initiate a project in the area of electronic communications, from a legal perspective. This book provides a basis for a work which could become a common enterprise. Please send your comments and suggestions. The names of contributors will be mentioned in subsequent editions.

B. Presentation of Applicable Instruments

(1) Market organisation

Main instruments. This section examines the main instruments adopted by the European legislator in the field of electronic communications. The NRF consists mainly of directives adopted by the Parliament and Council, each dealing with a specific subject. These directives are presented briefly in the following paragraphs.[3] **1.34**

Principles and institutional organisation. European Parliament and Council Directive (EC) 2002/21 on a common regulatory framework for electronic communications networks and services ('Framework Directive')[4] lays down the principles underlying the NRF. It also establishes the institutional organisation making it possible, for European and national authorities, to control markets and ensure the proper functioning of economic activity in this field. Beyond general provisions, the Framework Directive addresses certain specific issues, including the management of radio frequencies (Article 9); numbering, naming and addressing (Article 10); rights of way (Article 11); and co-location and facility sharing (Article 12). **1.35**

Market entry. European Parliament and Council Directive (EC) 2002/20 on the authorisation of electronic communications networks and services ('Authorisations Directive')[5] deals with conditions relating to market entry. Prior to starting their activities, undertakings may be required to carry out certain formalities, in some cases involving the imposition of conditions. In most cases these correspond to obligations imposed by other directives making up the NRF. **1.36**

Access to networks and facilities. European Parliament and Council Directive (EC) 2002/19 on access to, and interconnection of, electronic communications networks and associated facilities ('Access Directive')[6] deals with a major issue faced by undertakings on electronic communications markets. On these markets investments are often considerable in scope. Building and maintaining a network, for instance, requires quantities of capital which may not be available to all undertakings. As a result of these costs, facilities and other resources may need to be shared in the interests of competition and economic efficiency. Service providers, for instance, may need to negotiate access to existing networks, instead **1.37**

---

[3] These instruments have not been integrated in an Annex but are available from http://europa.eu.int
[4] [2002] OJ L108/33.
[5] [2002] OJ L108/21.
[6] [2002] OJ L108/7.

of systematically building their own installations. Another example is the situation of operators seeking interconnection to other facilities instead of trying to build out to all locations where end users are located.

1.38 **Public service, universal service.** Most issues concerning undertakings are covered by the provisions included in the above-mentioned instruments—the Framework, Authorisations and Access Directives. Policy objectives are, however, pursued beyond the correct and efficient functioning of the markets. These policy objectives have led the European legislator to introduce, and construct, the concept of 'universal service'. In the NRF this concept is organised in European Parliament and Council Directive (EC) 2002/22 on universal service and users' rights relating to electronic communications networks and services ('Universal Service Directive').[7]

1.39 **Users' rights.** In addition to issues relating to universal service, the Universal Service Directive addresses, and regulates, the relations between users and undertakings. Regulation of these relations was made necessary by the fundamental changes which have occurred in the sector. Electronic communications were in most of the Member States previously provided by an administration acting autonomously. In that context users had few individual rights, as services were provided in the interest of society. That system has been transformed into a model where users are now regarded as customers. In this new context, the relations between undertakings and their customers must be organised by the law.

(2) Execution of the main directives

1.40 **Execution of the main directives.** Several instruments have been adopted in execution of these four directives. As they are closely related to the directives, these instruments form part of the NRF, and are accordingly analysed in this book.

1.41 **Recommendation on relevant markets.** Among these instruments, some provide important explanatory material concerning essential concepts. The first such concept is that of 'market'. This concept is defined in general competition law. A special interpretation is, however, needed in the context of sector-specific regulation. To that effect, the Commission has adopted Recommendation COM(2003)497 on Relevant Product and Service Markets within the electronic communications sector susceptible to ex ante regulation in accordance with the European Parliament and Council Directive (EC) 2002/21 on a common regulatory framework for electronic communication networks and services.[8]

1.42 **Guidelines on market power.** A second concept is market power. As will be submitted, there is a need for clarification as to how this concept is to be interpreted in the context of electronic communications. To that effect, the European Commission has adopted the Guidelines 2002/C165/03 on market analysis and

---

[7] [2002] OJ L108/51.   [8] [2003] OJ L114/45.

the assessment of significant market power under the Community regulatory framework for electronic communications networks and services.[9]

List of standards and specifications. Among the instruments giving effect to the framework, mention must also be made of the List of standards and/or specifications for electronic communications networks, services and associated facilities and services in accordance with Article 17 of European Parliament and Council Directive (EC) 2002/21 on a common regulatory framework for electronic communication networks and services.[10]   **1.43**

Recommendations on interconnection. Finally, a word must be said about various recommendations adopted by the European Commission, giving clarification in relation to several provisions concerning interconnection. These recommendations were introduced under the old regulatory framework and are maintained under the new rules. The reason is that they concern issues which remain central to the new framework. *(a)* One relates to interconnection pricing. As stated elsewhere in this book (see paras 3.128–3.140), it is an objective of the reform to ensure that access to networks is provided under reasonable conditions. In this context, interconnection pricing is of fundamental importance. Commission Recommendation (EC) 98/195 on interconnection in a liberalised telecommunications market (Part 1—Interconnection pricing) was adopted to address price-related issues.[11] *(b)* Another issue is how undertakings facing specific obligations should calculate their costs. This issue is related to the subject covered by the first recommendation, as pricing based on costs may be imposed under the NRF. The technical aspects associated with these issues have been addressed in Commission Recommendation (EC) 98/322 on interconnection in a liberalised telecommunications market (Part 2—Accounting separation and cost accounting).[12]   **1.44**

(3) Other issues covered by sector-specific regulation

Radio spectrum. The use of radio spectrum is a significant issue in the context of electronic communications services. At the present time, radio spectrum in all its aspects cannot really be considered as being part of the NRF. In this field the European legislator has only just begun to develop a policy. Time and effort will be needed to achieve results. At the present time, the radio spectrum-related instruments adopted at European level have the function of providing a basis for co-ordination. The European legislator has attempted to organise co-ordination   **1.45**

---

[9] [2002] OJ C165/3.   [10] [2003] OJ C331/32.
[11] [1998] OJ L73/42. That instrument was amended several times. See Commission Recommendation (EC) C(2002)561 amending Recommendation 98/195/EC, as last amended by Recommendation (EC) 2000/263 on Interconnection in a liberalised telecommunications market (Part 1—Interconnection Pricing) [2002] OJ L58/56. For a last update of the figures mentioned in these Recommendations, see Recommendation C(2002)561 available on the internet site of the Commission—DG Information Society.   [12] [1998] OJ L141/6.

mechanisms between the Member States, so as to define common approaches to common problems. Action is also taken to increase awareness of the importance of action at European level in this field. These efforts have led to the adoption of European Parliament and Council Decision (EC) 676/2002 on a regulatory framework for radio spectrum policy in the European Community (Radio Spectrum Decision).[13] As follow-up to that instrument the Commission adopted Decision (EC) 2002/622 establishing a Radio Spectrum Policy Group.[14] It should be noted however that not all provisions concerning radio spectrum are included in these specific instruments, since the subject is also covered in the Authorisations and Framework Directives.

(4) General competition law

1.46 **A parallel body of law.** The instruments examined in the previous paragraphs compose the NRF—a body of law generally called 'sector-specific regulation'. It consists of rules and instruments which were adopted in view of the specific issues appearing on electronic communications markets. As a result, they apply only to electronic communication services, although they provide a model for the establishment of rules regarding other, but similar, sectors (network industries). Others are of course applicable to electronic communications, among them competition rules. The latter form a second, parallel, body of law, which applies to all sectors of the economy. Exceptions are allowed but they must comply with restrictive conditions.

1.47 **Liberalisation directives.** In the field of electronic communications services, the European Commission has adopted Directive (EC) 2002/77 on competition in the markets for electronic communications networks and services (Consolidated Services Directive).[15] This directive follows a series of instruments of the same nature, whereby the Commission had introduced competition on the markets for telecommunications networks and services. As is submitted in another section (see paras 1.96–1.107), the move started in 1988. Liberalisation directives were adopted from 1988 until 1996. These directives have been the source for most Member States of the opening of markets to competition and the possibility for new actors to enter the market.

1.48 **Application of Articles 81 and 82 EC.** In addition to the directives, the Commission has adopted notices to explain how general competition law must be applied to the electronic communications services sector. *(a)* A first interesting instrument is the Commission Guidelines (EC) on the application of EEC competition rules in the telecommunications sector.[16] These guidelines were adopted early in the liberalisation process. They concern all behaviour likely to be adopted on electronic communications markets and falling under Article 81 and/or Article 82 EC.

---

[13] [2002] OJ L108/1.   [14] [2002] OJ L198/49.
[15] [2002] OJ L249/21.   [16] [1991] OJ C233/2.

(b) A second instrument is Commission Notice 98/C265/02 on the application of competition rules to access agreements in the telecommunications sector.[17] That notice deals with specific issues relating to access. It has already been submitted in an earlier paragraph that access constitutes a key aspect for the development of activities on electronic communications markets. It is for that reason that a specific directive has now been devoted to the subject by the Parliament and Council (the Access Directive). The Commission in the meantime also sought to clarify some of the problems that undertakings may encounter when they seek access to facilities controlled by others, and the notice examined these problems from the perspective developed in general competition law.

Services of general interest. Several important instruments adopted by **1.49** the European Commission deal with services of general interest. Among these are Commission Communication (EC) 96/C281/03[18] and Commission Communication (EC) 2001/C17/04 on Services of general interest in Europe.[19] They are based on Article 86 EC, which provides that public undertakings or undertakings with special or exclusive rights are subject to competition rules. A derogation to that principle is provided in respect of undertakings carrying out a mission of general interest. The derogation is limited to circumstances where the mission entrusted to the undertaking in question is legitimate and the means used are compatible with the principle of proportionality.

Other instruments. Other instruments of a more general character concerning **1.50** all economic activities and not limited to the electronic communications sector or to other sectors presenting similar characteristics may apply. Among these is Council Regulation (EC) 1/2003 on the implementation of the rules on competition laid down in Articles 81 and 82 of the Treaty.[20] Another is the Commission Notice on the definition of relevant markets for the purposes of Community competition law.[21] Unlike the above-mentioned regulation, the notice is not binding; its object is rather to explain how the Commission, when applying competition rules, defines markets in such a way as to allow an assessment of the position acquired on those markets by the various parties in question.

(5) Implementation of European rules

Implementation reports. Each year the Commission issues a communication **1.51** providing information on the implementation, in the Member States, of the measures which have been taken at European level in the electronic communications (formerly telecommunications) sector. These reports contain important information about the situation of electronic communications markets within the European Union, together with an analysis of faults in the transposition or application of EU

---

[17] [1998] OJ C265/2. [18] [1996] OJ C281/3. [19] [2001] OJ C17/4.
[20] [2003] OJ L1/1. [21] [1997] OJ C372/5.

principles in national law. The reports published up to 2002 relate to the old regulatory framework. To that extent they contain analysis which, in some cases, may no longer be directly useful. These reports however remain important where the issues treated remain the same as those arising under the NRF, or as background documents to the extent that they show the evolution which has taken place at national level and point out issues which have been progressively solved at national or European level.

1.52 **Transposition of the NRF.** The report published in 2003 contains valuable information concerning the transposition of the NRF at national level. The data which it contains may have to be updated, as the process of transposition is currently under way and national legislation is for many Member States still in a state of flux. This document can be found on the Commission's website, and is essential for practitioners in that it points out issues which may not have been handled properly in some Member States.

(6) Issues not covered in this book

1.53 **Data protection.** The directives mentioned above (Framework, Authorisations, Access, Universal Service) provide a structure for relations between actors on markets. In that sense it can be said that they organise the markets. The NRF contains other instruments related to a lesser extent to market organisation which are accordingly not treated here. This is the case, for instance, for Parliament and Council Directive (EC) 2002/58 concerning the processing of personal data and the protection of privacy in the electronic communications sector ('e-Privacy Directive').[22] Instruments covering issues other than market organisation are also not addressed in this book.

1.54 **Equipment, including terminals.** The same principle applies to equipment, including terminal equipment.[23] A key objective pursued by the NRF is the development of the markets for services. The rules concerning terminals or, more generally, equipment, are therefore not examined here.[24]

1.55 **Public procurement.** Another issue not covered in this book is public procurement. Public procurement is related to market organisation to the extent that the rules relating to it ensure that candidates are treated equally by authorities and associated bodies tendering for the provision of equipment. Directive 93/38[25]

---

[22] [2002] OJ L201/37.

[23] Terminal equipment provides the interface between the user and the network and the services provided over it, and usually takes the form of handsets, mobile handsets, fax machines, computer terminals and so on.

[24] The rules applicable to equipment, particularly terminals, are included in European Parliament and Council Directive (EC) 1999/5 on radio equipment and telecommunications terminal equipment and the mutual recognition of their conformity [1999] OJ L91/10.

[25] Council Directive (EEC) 93/38 coordinating the procurement procedures of entities operating in the water, energy, transport and telecommunications sectors [1993] OJ L199/84.

provides that former telecommunications monopolies must in principle comply with certain administrative formalities. With the progress made in the reform it has however becomes clear that these rules will not be applied on electronic communications markets for very much longer. The reason is that activities are now carried out mainly, where not exclusively, by private undertakings in a liberalised environment. Public undertakings still exist,[26] but these too are subject to the pressure of competition, and must select suppliers offering the best quality for the lowest prices. Equality is thus respected, in principle, on the markets as a result of competition, without the need to maintain specific rules to that effect.

C. Definition of Electronic Communications

Electronic communications.   This book analyses the rules applicable to electronic communications networks and services in the European Union. A preliminary issue is to determine what electronic communications are. The concept of electronic communications is not explicitly defined in the NRF. A definition may however be extracted from definitions given to other concepts in the same framework. The concepts of electronic communications 'networks' and 'services' provide interesting indications in relation to three elements forming the core of the electronic communications as envisaged in the NRF (activity, electronic form, what is being transmitted). These are analysed in the following paragraphs.   **1.56**

> *Framework Directive, Article 2(a).* ' "[E]lectronic communications network" means transmission systems and, where applicable, switching or routing equipment and other resources which permit *the conveyance of signals by wire, by radio, by optical or by other electromagnetic means,*[27] including satellite networks, fixed (circuit- and packet-switched, including Internet) and mobile terrestrial networks, networks used for radio and television broadcasting, "powerline" systems and cable TV networks, irrespective of the type of information conveyed.'[28]

> *Framework Directive, Article 2(c).* ' "[E]lectronic communications service" means services provided for remuneration which consist wholly or mainly in *the transmission and routing of signals on electronic communications networks,*[29] including telecommunications services and transmission services in networks used for broadcasting, but excluding services providing, or exercising editorial control over, content transmitted using electronic communications networks and services.'

Activities concerned.   Using these two definitions, electronic communications may be regarded as being closely connected with activities consisting in conveying, transmitting or routing. A clear link exists between communication and transportation. 'Something' is taken from one place and transmitted to another place.   **1.57**

---

[26] Not all former national operators have been privatised.
[27] Authors' emphasis.   [28] See glossary.   [29] Authors' emphasis.

1.58 **A communication with an electronic form.** A second element is important, the electronic form of the activity. The communication takes the form of an electronic activity. It may be distinguished in this regard from other types of transmission having a more 'physical' nature. Where it comes to electronic communications, objects are not transmitted in their original form. They are translated, or transformed, into 'signals'. These signals are then conveyed through networks. When they reach their destination, they are transformed back into their original form.

1.59 **What is being transmitted.** The definitions above do not provide much information about what is transmitted in an electronic communication. They refer rather vaguely to 'signals'. Generally, three types of signal may be distinguished in this context. *(a) Sounds.* Historically, telecommunications were born with the transmission of Morse code through copper wires (telegraphy). The technique was thereafter refined to allow voice transmission. The use of this new possibility remained limited, however. Transmissions were limited in the first place to short distances. Amplifiers were installed to regenerate weakening sounds. They successively made it possible to convey voice messages over increasingly large distances. With these devices, communications were eventually made possible from one part of the globe to any other. *(b) Images.* Another traditional example is broadcasting. The transmission of images is considered a form of electronic communication under the NRF. No distinction is made, in this regard, between the communication of sounds and images. *(c) Data.* A third category is the transmission of data via electronic means. Data consists of pieces of information stored on a computer and sent electronically to others. Originally, data mainly encompassed texts and graphics. Progressively, however, sounds and images came to be expressed in computer language (digitalisation). As a result, they can also be stored on computers. In the light of these developments, the expression 'data' now usually includes any piece of information in digital form, whatever its nature (visual, audio, text, etc). In this sense, 'data' has now become a synonym for 'piece of information'.

D. Institutional Aspects

(1) Introduction

1.60 **Outline.** The NRF contains rules creating rights and obligations to be implemented by the Member States in their national legal orders. In addition to these material provisions, institutional rules organise how public intervention must take place. These institutional aspects of the rules concerning electronic communications are analysed in the following paragraphs, in the first instance at European, then at national, level. The intention is to present them briefly so as to inform practitioners about the institutional background against which the most important instruments were adopted.

(2) The European level

Parliament and Council.   The rules currently in force concerning the European   **1.61**
electronic communications market have been adopted, for the most part, by the
Parliament and Council. The instruments setting out these rules are harmonisation directives adopted on the basis of Article 95 EC (co-decision procedure). The
directives making up the old regulatory framework were adopted by the Council
acting alone. The Parliament intervened in the procedure only as a secondary
influence, as the directives involved were adopted prior to the introduction of the
co-decision procedure.

Other European bodies.   The procedures currently in force and leading to the   **1.62**
adoption of harmonisation directives involve public bodies other than the
Parliament and Council. The proposals are drafted by the Commission. Through
that mechanism, the Commission establishes the basis on which the Parliament and
Council are required to work. In its proposal the Commission sets the framework
within which, or from which, the institutional dialogue will take place. Among
other bodies likely to express an opinion are the Economic and Social Committee,
which consists of representatives of trade unions and economic actors. Also of
importance is the Committee of the Regions, which is made up of representatives of
the regions within the Member States.

The Communications Committee.   A series of bodies has been created in the   **1.63**
electronic communications sector to assist the Commission in several procedures or
decisions. One such body is the Communications Committee, which was established under the Framework Directive and consists of representatives of the Member
States meeting under the chairmanship of a representative of the Commission. In
general, the Communications Committee provides a forum where the national
authorities (generally, ministries and national regulatory authorities, but possibly
others such as radio communications agencies or broadcasting bodies) can meet.
(a) Among the tasks entrusted to the Communications Committee is the promotion
of discussion between the Member States and the Commission on all regulatory
issues concerning electronic communications. *(b)* An important aspect of these
discussions is the implementation of the NRF. The Member States have an opportunity to explain to the Commission how the European regulation is implemented
at national level. *(c)* The Communications Committee also provides a channel for
the Commission to transfer to the Member States information gathered through
enquiries, studies or negotiation at international level.

> *Framework Directive.* [a] 'The Communications Committee shall . . . foster the
> exchange of information between the Member States and between the Member
> States and the Commission on the situation and the development of regula-
> tory activities regarding electronic communications networks and services.'[30]

---

[30] Art 23(2).

[b] 'Member States shall ensure that up-to-date information pertaining to the application of this Directive and the Specific Directives is made publicly available.' 'They shall publish a notice in their national official gazette describing how and where the information is published.' 'Member States shall send to the Commission a copy of all such notices at the time of publication. The Commission shall distribute the information to the Communications Committee as appropriate.'[31] [c] 'The Commission shall provide all relevant information to the Communications Committee on the outcome of regular consultations with the representatives of network operators, service providers, users, consumers, manufacturers and trade unions, as well as third countries and international organisations.'

1.64   The Communications Committee (2).   The Framework Directive also entrusts a more specific responsibility to the Communications Committee, that is, to provide a forum for discussion in situations where a national regulatory authority (NRA) envisages a decision to adopt a regulatory measure with an impact on trade between Member States. In the draft of such a decision, the NRA may contemplate defining a relevant market differing from those identified by the Commission in the recommendation referred to above. Another possibility is a draft decision whereby the NRA plans to designate an undertaking as an entity having significant market power. These two types of decision are important, as they may influence activities outside the national territory.[32] For that reason, an opportunity must be provided to organise a discussion among the representatives of the Member States. Pursuant to the NRF, that discussion must take place within the Communications Committee. On the basis of the consultative opinion issued by that committee, a decision has to be taken by the Commission. That decision may go so far as to ask the NRA to withdraw the draft decision.

Framework Directive, Preamble, recital 15. 'The Commission should be able, after consulting the Communications Committee, to require a national regulatory authority to withdraw a draft measure where it concerns definition of relevant markets or the designation or not of undertakings with significant market power, and where such decisions would create a barrier to the single market or would be incompatible with

---

[31] Art 24(1) and (2). See also Framework Directive, Preamble, recital 37. 'National regulatory authorities should be required to cooperate with each other and with the Commission in a transparent manner to ensure consistent application, in all Member States, of the provisions of this Directive and the Specific Directives. This cooperation could take place, *inter alia*, in the Communications Committee or in a group comprising European regulators.'

[32] The first kind of decision is one whereby an NRA defines a relevant market. The definition of the relevant market is essential for the assessment of competition in a given sector or area. If the market is defined restrictively, a finding that one or several undertakings present on that market have significant market power is easier to reach. Such a finding has consequences on the obligations that may be imposed on this, or these, undertaking(s). Similarly, an NRA could designate an operator established in another Member State as having significant market power in the provision of services on the national territory. Such a decision would have an influence on the obligations likely to be imposed on that operator. As a result of a decision of that nature, the entry of such an operator on the national territory, as well as the exercise of activities on that territory, may be made more difficult.

Community law and in particular the policy objectives that national regulatory authorities should follow.'

Radio Spectrum Committee. A special committee has also been created in rela- **1.65** tion to spectrum,[33] in particular to carry out tasks in relation to the harmonisation of technical implementation measures. It is perhaps unclear why the tasks entrusted to this committee could not be carried out by the Communications Committee, and why a specific organ had to be created in this field. One reason could be that the Parliament and Council wished to establish a distinction between the competences which the European Union has in the field of spectrum and those which it has in other sectors of electronic communications. It should be recalled here that the competences of the European Union in general in the field of electronic communications are rather large, since the Parliament and Council have harmonised the entire sector on the basis of common rules regulating the sector. One exception was spectrum, where the European competence is more limited. By establishing a specific committee to cover this subject, the Parliament and Council have possibly wished to dissociate this more restricted competence from the others.

European Regulators' Group and Radio Spectrum Policy Group. An informal **1.66** body, the European Regulators' Group, which is not subject to the rules on committees, has been set up by the Commission to assist and advise it on electronic communications networks and services.[34] *(a)* The group is composed of representatives of the independent national regulatory authorities on electronic communications. Independent in this context can be taken to mean the independent agencies set up by the Member States to regulate the sector, excluding ministries in cases where Member States have designated them to fulfil some of the regulatory tasks assigned by the framework. *(b)* The Group is chaired by a representative of one of the members ie one of the independent regulatory authorities. *(c)* The group's function is to serve as a body for 'reflection, debate and advice', and in particular in the light of the regulators' interface with the industry (operators and service providers) at national level in the course of regulating national markets. A further body, the Radio Spectrum Policy Group ('Policy Group'),[34a] has been established to assist the Commission in defining spectrum policy. *(a)* The composition of the spectrum group and the committee does not on the face of it differ, as both of them consist of representatives of the Member States. *(b)* There are, however, major differences between the Radio Spectrum Policy Group set up by the Commission, and the Radio Spectrum Committee created by the

---

[33] See European Parliament and Council Decision (EC) 676/2002 on a regulatory framework for radio spectrum policy in the European Community (Radio Spectrum Decision) [2002] OJ L108/1, Arts 3 and 4.

[34] See Commission Decision 2002/627 establishing the European Regulators' Group for Electronic Communications Networks and Services [2002] OJ L200/38.

[34a] See Commission Decision (EC) 2002/622 establishing a Radio Spectrum Policy Group [2002] OJ L198/49.

Parliament and Council. *(c)* The fact that different institutions have created these bodies has an impact on their functions. The Policy Group is chaired by a national representative and assists the Commission in its longer-term strategic role, whereas the Committee is a classic consultative and regulatory committee set up in accordance with the 'Comitology Decision'[35] and chaired by a Commission representative. *(d)* Another difference appears in the functions allocated to the two groups. The Radio Spectrum Committee provides a forum where the Member States meet for regulatory discussions in relation to spectrum. It also provides a forum for interaction between the Commission and the Member States. By contrast, the 'Policy Group' appears more informal, and gathers representatives of the Member States to which experts may be added, with a view to helping the Commission in wider-ranging matters relating to spectrum.[36]

1.67 **Court of Justice and Court of First Instance.**   A word must be said about the interventions of the Court of Justice (ECJ) and the Court of First Instance (CFI) of the European Communities.[37] The interventions of these organs have a general character. They are not limited to electronic communications. However, they may play an important part in that sector. *(a)* First, the ECJ and the CFI may have an opportunity to assess the validity of acts adopted by the European legislator in the field of electronic communications. This review may be carried out in relation to decisions adopted by the Commission, but also on instruments of a general nature (directives) adopted by the Parliament and Council. In exercising this power of review, the ECJ and the CFI may check the compatibility between instruments regarding electronic communications and superior rules of law, such as Treaty provisions or general principles of law. *(b)* The ECJ can also interpret the provisions of European law in the course of various procedures. This enables the ECJ to influence the content of the law to an extent that has often been celebrated, or criticised, in academic treatises. *(c)* Finally, the ECJ has the competence to answer requests for opinions addressed to it by the Council and/or Parliament. Opinions of the ECJ are requested when the Parliament or Council are not certain about the state of the law regarding a given issue. They then turn to the ECJ for a reasoned opinion on that issue.[38]

---

[35] Council Decision 1999/468/EC laying down the procedures for the exercise of implementing powers conferred on the Commission [1999] OJ L184/23.

[36] See the Radio Spectrum Policy Group Decision, Preamble, recital 5. 'The Group should gather high-level governmental experts from the Member States and a high-level representative of the Commission. The Group could also include observers and invite other persons to attend meetings as appropriate, including regulators, competition authorities, market participants, user or consumer groups.'

[37] Interventions by the ECJ and the CFI are limited to situations where applications or requests are addressed to them. Details about these procedures may be found in the chapter dealing with litigation.

[38] As a general matter, the ECJ has the power to state what the law is, and to this extent can be said to hold supreme authority to interpret European law. See Art 220 EC: 'The Court of Justice and the Court of First Instance, each within its jurisdiction, shall ensure that in the interpretation and application of this Treaty the law is observed.'

Outline.   The following paragraphs analyse the rules concerning national regula-   **1.68**
tory authorities (NRAs). Emphasis is placed on rules of a general character,
ie those concerning the NRAs as such, irrespective of the actions undertaken by
those authorities. The particular actions that NRAs may undertake are not
analysed in this section, but rather in the following chapters (Chapter 2 for authorisations; Chapters 3 and 4 for access; Chapter 5 for universal service; Chapter 6 for
litigation; Chapter 7 for specific issues such as spectrum and users' rights).

(4) NRAs—Nature and composition

Sector-specific regulation

Designation by the Member States.   It is for the Member States to determine   **1.69**
what public organs are required to carry out, at national level, the tasks assigned to
NRAs under the NRF. The NRF, while entrusting NRAs with specific tasks and
missions, does not provide any indication concerning the identity of the bodies
which have to fulfil these tasks at national level. Only general constraints are formulated, the rest being left to the discretion of the Member States. This general
responsibility on the part of the Member States for designating public bodies
falling within the definition of 'national regulatory authority' is laid down in the
Framework Directive. Pursuant to the directive, the concept refers to the body, or
bodies, charged with any of the regulatory tasks attributed in the NRF. The general
competence thus recognised as belonging to the Member States appears in line
with the power on the part of the States to organise their administration as they
consider appropriate, as long as they respect European and international rules.

> *Framework Directive, Article 2g.* ' "[N]ational regulatory authority" means the body
> or bodies charged by a Member State with any of the regulatory tasks assigned in this
> Directive and the Specific Directives.'

Obligation to notify the identity of NRAs.   The corollary of the freedom left to   **1.70**
Member States is that they have to make clear how tasks are distributed at national
level. In other words, the Member States may entrust the tasks created in the NRF
to whichever body they wish. However, they are required publicly to indicate
what authority is responsible for what mission. This clear determination of competent bodies must make it possible for the Commission, other Member States,
undertakings and users to identify the relevant authority in each EU country. On
the basis of this information, the various actors are in a position to determine from
which entity they may expect action. They are also able to understand against
which entity an appeal, or a complaint, can be initiated.

> *Framework Directive, Article 3(6).* 'Member States shall notify to the Commission all
> national regulatory authorities assigned tasks under this Directive and the Specific
> Directives, and their respective responsibilities.'

1.71 **Limits derived from the EC Treaty.**   The power on the part of Member States to organise their administrations as they see fit is not without limit. It must indeed be combined with general obligations deriving from the EC Treaty. Pursuant to the EC Treaty (Article 10), Member States must refrain from taking actions which would undermine the goals of the Community and must take positive action to ensure these goals are met. These obligations imply that the NRF must be implemented to ensure that the goals pursued through the framework are attained. Any failing by a Member State in this regard would qualify as a violation of the directive(s), which the Member State in question would be regarded as not having implemented in a timely or appropriate way. It would also be analysed as a violation of the general obligations imposed on the Member States to ensure the objectives assigned to the Community are met.

> *Article 10 EC.* 'Member States shall take all appropriate measures, whether general or particular, to ensure fulfilment of the obligations arising out of this Treaty or resulting from action taken by the institutions of the Community. They shall facilitate the achievement of the Community's tasks. They shall abstain from any measure which could jeopardise the attainment of the objectives of this Treaty.'

1.72 **Competence.**   Two constraints regarding NRAs are imposed on the Member States by the Framework Directive. One is that the tasks assigned to the NRAs must be entrusted to a competent authority. There are arguments to interpret this obligation of 'competence' in a general manner. *(a)* It certainly means that these authorities must have qualified personnel, ie personnel able to analyse the situation existing on the markets and propose appropriate measures to remedy possible difficulties in line with the NRF. *(b)* The obligation also implies, more generally, that the authorities concerned must have the capacity to ensure that the tasks and missions entrusted to them are carried out. In addition to being equipped with the staff having the necessary training and experience, NRAs must also be given sufficient finance to carry out the tasks assigned to them.

> *Framework Directive, Article 3(1).* 'Member States shall ensure that each of the tasks assigned to national regulatory authorities in this Directive and the Specific Directives is undertaken by a competent body.' *Framework Directive, Preamble, recital 11.* 'National regulatory authorities should be in possession of all the necessary resources, in terms of staffing, expertise, and financial means, for the performance of their tasks.'

1.73 **Legal independence.**   A second constraint is that NRAs must be independent. Independence is to be understood, in this context, as a strict separation from any undertaking active in electronic communications markets (whatever the market concerned: equipment, networks or services). Pursuant to the Framework Directive, independence implies that the NRAs must be legally separate from these undertakings. It is not possible for Member States to designate one or several undertakings for the fulfilment of the tasks and missions entrusted to NRAs in the NRF. Economic activities and regulatory responsibilities must be separated completely.

Framework Directive, Article 3(2). 'Member States shall guarantee the independence of national regulatory authorities by ensuring that they are legally distinct from and functionally independent of all organisations providing electronic communications networks, equipment or services. Member States that retain ownership or control of undertakings providing electronic communications networks and/or services shall ensure effective structural separation of the regulatory function from activities associated with ownership or control.'

Functional independence. Another implication, which is clear from the extract **1.74** presented above, is that NRAs must be functionally independent from undertakings. Functional independence is more difficult to define than legal separation. *(a)* Legal separation merely implies that the two sorts of activities must be entrusted to bodies with different legal personalities. Such a requirement may be enforced, in principle, without excessive difficulty. *(b)* Functional independence has a wider meaning. It appears to imply that no connection may exist between the two functions (economic, regulatory), at whatever level. The requirement that NRAs must be functionally independent requires that policies must be drawn up, defined and implemented independently of any link with specific undertakings.

Structural separation. Another manner for the Parliament and Council to give **1.75** more force to the same requirement of independence is to demand structural separation between NRAs and undertakings. Such a requirement may raise issues in Member States where one or more undertakings are still public. The scenario is that of a Member State which has maintained the former national operator under public ownership. The State is then responsible, on the one hand, for the fulfilment of regulatory tasks, through the NRA, and, on the other hand, for the exercise of economic activities, as these activities are carried out by a public undertaking. In such a situation, the Member State concerned must take the measures necessary to ensure that the exercise of regulatory tasks is not affected, in any form whatsoever, by the stake held by that State in a public undertaking.

Framework Directive, Article 3(2). 'Member States that retain ownership or control of undertakings providing electronic communications networks and/or services shall ensure effective structural separation of the regulatory function from activities associated with ownership or control.'

Rights of way. In addition to this general requirement, structural separation **1.76** is required in a specific manner with respect to rights of way. These rights are prerogatives granted to undertakings to establish fixed or mobile networks on, under or above public or private properties. Intervention may be necessary on the part of a public authority in order to grant these rights. A difficulty may arise where the undertaking applying to receive these rights is controlled or owned by such an authority. In this kind of situation a public entity would be in charge of granting the rights to an entity which would also be a public body. To avoid conflicts of interest, the Framework Directive insists that the authority granting the rights must be separate from that which owns or controls the applicant.

> *Framework Directive, Article 11(2).* 'Member States shall ensure that where public or local authorities retain ownership or control of undertakings operating electronic communications networks and/or services, there is effective structural separation of the function responsible for granting the rights referred to in paragraph 1 from activities associated with ownership or control.'

1.77 **No power to require privatisation.** In the current state of opinion, there is little doubt that the situation most likely to give satisfaction regarding independence is that where regulatory tasks are assigned to public bodies and the performance of economic activities is left to private economic entities. In such a situation neither the government, the NRA nor the administration has a specific interest in favouring any undertaking. Such a situation may not be imposed, however, by the European legislator, since the Treaty (Article 295 EC) provides that Community law may not prejudice the system of property ownership in the Member States. This provision has generally been understood as implying that European law permits both private and public ownership. However, it has also been interpreted as implying that the European legislator should maintain a neutral attitude vis-à-vis forms of ownership. Member States, in other words, are free to nationalise, or privatise, undertakings, without any European law constraints weighing on these operations.

> *Article 295 EC.* 'This Treaty shall in no way prejudice the rules in Member States governing the system of property ownership.'

1.78 **No independence from other public bodies required.** The requirement of independence does not mean that no link may exist between NRAs and other public bodies, including the national governments or administrations. As stated, independence refers to the absence of connections with specific undertakings. There is no requirement in the NRF that NRAs must be given a special status in the administrative organisation of the Member States. There is similarly no provision requiring that NRAs adopt their decisions and, more generally, their attitudes, independently of all political considerations formulated by national public bodies. NRAs may be integrated into the administration of the Member States and function under the supervision of a political authority. Political considerations may thus influence the attitudes adopted by NRAs. There are however limitations on that influence. These have already been examined in the light of the obligation that Member States take all measures necessary to ensure the fulfilment of the objectives of the Treaty and must refrain from adopting measures which may undermine those goals (see Article 10 EC).

Liberalisation directives

1.79 **Independence in the liberalisation directives.** There is no requirement, in the Consolidated Services Directive, that NRAs must be independent of undertakings.

In fact there is in that directive no provision dealing with the institutional organisation of electronic communications within the European Union. The European Commission has thus refrained from intervening on this subject in the context of a directive. This was not the case earlier, as the Commission was the first European institution to introduce the requirement of independence regarding regulatory tasks. That requirement was introduced in regard to terminals and telecoms services respectively in the Telecommunications Terminal Equipment Directive (1988) and the Services Directive (1990).

> *Telecommunications Terminal Equipment Directive, Article 6.* 'Member States shall ensure that . . . responsibility for drawing up the specifications . . ., monitoring their application and granting type-approval is entrusted to a body independent of public or private undertakings offering goods and/or services in the telecommunications sector.' *Services Directive, Article 7.* 'Member States shall ensure that . . . the control of type approval and mandatory specifications, the allocation of frequencies and surveillance of usage conditions are carried out by a body independent of the telecommunications organisations.'

Conformity with general competition law. The validity of these measures intro- **1.80** duced by the Commission was assessed by the ECJ with respect to general competition law. In its judgments the ECJ gives a clear view concerning the compatibility of the requirement of independence with that body of the law. These issues were addressed in *French Republic v. Commission*,[39] in which the ECJ reviewed the validity of the Telecommunications Terminal Equipment Directive. In substance, the ECJ stated that undertakings must be equal on the markets as regards public intervention. Member States may not grant regulatory advantages to given undertakings. Undertakings would have an advantage if they could decide what rules applied to their activities and those carried out by competitors. Such a position could be used by these undertakings to impose rules favourable to their own situation, an unacceptable situation under general competition law.

> *French Republic v Commission.* '[A] system of undistorted competition, as laid down in the Treaty, can be guaranteed only if equality of opportunity is secured as between the various economic operators. To entrust an undertaking which markets terminal equipment with the task of drawing up the specifications for such equipment, monitoring their application and granting type-approval in respect thereof is tantamount to conferring upon it the power to determine at will which terminal equipment may be connected to the public network, and thereby placing that undertaking at an obvious advantage over its competitors.'[40] 'Consequently, the Commission was justified in seeking to entrust responsibility for drawing up technical specifications, monitoring their application and granting type-approval to a body independent of public or private undertakings offering competing goods and/or services in the telecommunications sector.'[41]

---

[39] Case C-202/88 *French Republic v Commission of the European Communities* [1991] ECR I-01223.
[40] Para 51.   [41] Para 52.

1.81 **Confirmation of the line taken.** This position was confirmed, although not explicitly, in *Spain v Commission*[42] concerning the validity of the Services Directive. The context was similar to the case examined above with respect to terminal equipment. As it had already ruled in *France v Commission* on the specific provisions contained in the Telecommunications Equipment Liberalisation Directive, the ECJ did not repeat its analysis regarding similar provisions contained in the directive under review. It addressed new arguments put forward by the parties regarding the powers of the Commission and rejected the thesis that the Commission had no competence to adopt liberalisation directives.

1.82 **Case unrelated to liberalisation directives.** The ECJ had an additional opportunity to examine the issue of independence in *Régie des télégraphes et des téléphones v GB-Inno-BM*.[43] That case had no link with liberalisation directives, although it also dealt with competition and telecommunications terminal equipment. In the case at issue, a supermarket was selling terminal equipment without indicating to potential clients that the equipment could not be connected to the network without prior authorisation by the *Régie des télégraphes et des téléphones* (RTT). The RTT was the former Belgian national operator. It performed economic activities, including the sale of terminal equipment. At the same time, the operator was in charge of the adoption and implementation of the regulation applicable to telecommunications on the Belgian market. That situation was found by the ECJ to be incompatible with competition rules.[44]

> *Régie des télégraphes et des téléphones v. GB-Inno-BM.* 'A system of undistorted competition, as laid down in the Treaty, can be guaranteed only if equality of opportunity is secured as between the various economic operators. To entrust an undertaking which markets terminal equipment with the task of drawing up the specifications for such equipment, monitoring their application and granting type-approval in respect thereof is tantamount to conferring upon it the power to determine at will which terminal equipment may be connected to the public network, and thereby placing that undertaking at an obvious advantage over its competitors.' [26] 'In those circumstances, the maintenance of effective competition and the guaranteeing of transparency require that the drawing up of technical specifications, the monitoring of their application, and the granting of type-approval must be carried out by a body which is independent of public or private undertakings offering competing goods or services in the telecommunications sector.'[45]

---

[42] Joined cases C-271/90, C-281/90 and C-289/90 *Kingdom of Spain, Kingdom of Belgium and Italian Republic v Commission of the European Communities* [1992] ECR I-05833.

[43] Case C-18/88 *Régie des télégraphes et des téléphones v GB-Inno-BM* [1991] ECR I-05941.

[44] On the issue of independence, see also the following cases, which concern terminal equipment: Case C-69/91 *Criminal proceedings against Francine Gillon, née Decoster* [1993] ECR I-5335; Case C-91/94 *Criminal proceedings against Thierry Tranchant and Telephone Store SARL* [1995] ECR I-3911; Case C-92/91 *Criminal proceedings against Annick Neny, née Taillandier* [1993] ECR I-5383.

[45] Para 25.

WTO provisions

Independence and impartiality. Independence and impartiality are also **1.83** required under WTO provisions, as regards services for which the Members of the Organisation have accepted commitments in the telecommunications sector. Pursuant to the Reference Paper, which is referred to at para 1.176, the regulatory body must be separate from market participants. Further, decisions and procedures must ensure non-discrimination.

> *Reference Paper, para 5.* 'The regulatory body is separate from, and not accountable to, any supplier of basic telecommunications services. The decisions of and the procedures used by regulators shall be impartial with respect to all market participants.'

Current situation in the Member States

Eighth implementation report. In its Eighth implementation report, the **1.84** Commission analyses the situation as regards NRAs in the Member States. The report mainly concerns the old framework, but the analysis is of interest for the application of the NRF, as the institutional provisions have not changed in substance with the adoption of the new framework.

Assignment of powers. A difficulty remains that powers assigned to NRAs **1.85** under European rules are divided among a variety of organs in the Member States. In most cases, ministries have kept some power. For the Commission, such a division of power does not literally contravene the rules of the Treaty, since Member States remain free to organise their administrations as they consider appropriate. In some instances, the division may however impair legal certainty and undermine the ability of the NRA to intervene efficiently on the markets. One may wonder whether, in these instances, the obligations imposed by the EC Treaty (Article 10) and examined above, are still being complied with.

> *Eighth implementation report, 18.* 'Two models for the assignment of regulatory powers have evolved. In some Member States an independent and autonomous body or agency exercises the full range of powers including those relating to licensing, interconnection, access, price controls, frequency assignment and numbering (Germany, Greece, Ireland, Austria, the Netherlands except for frequencies, Portugal), while in the others the regulatory body exercises regulatory powers to a greater or lesser extent with the relevant ministry. The dispersal of powers inevitably leads to a reduction of the regulatory certainty required by the market, in particular in cases where decisions by ministries relating to licensing or price controls may be seen by the market as being influenced by political considerations. Leaving aside such considerations, the overall performance of the independent body may quite simply be improved through the transfer of all regulatory powers from the ministry, . . .'

Lack of resources. A second concern mentioned by the Commission is the lack **1.86** of resources. In some countries, the NRA does not appear to have the means necessary to accomplish its functions in a satisfactory manner. Improvements may be sought, according to the Commission, in more resources being entrusted to the NRAs concerned or in organisational improvements.

> *Eight implementation report, 18.* 'Lack of resources on the part of NRAs is still identified by the market as a brake on effective regulation. In this context market players believe that regulators could maximise resources by making greater use of moral suasion and publicity in combating anti-competitive behaviour. In two Member States, although the number of staff employed by the NRA is relatively high, only a small proportion deal with regulatory tasks relating to telecommunications (Belgium, Luxembourg). In some cases, new entrants consider that there is room for organisational improvements to enable regulators to address issues in a timely and efficient manner (Belgium, the Netherlands, Finland).'

(5) NRAs—Procedural constraints

1.87 **Impartiality.** Under the Framework Directive, NRAs must carry out their duties impartially. *(a)* That requirement is not remote from the obligation that NRAs must be functionally independent from undertakings. Impartiality means that no undertaking may be favoured. No decision or attitude may be taken in favour of an undertaking or group of undertakings. Favours granted by public authorities are often explained by specific links existing between these authorities and the undertakings they favour. *(b)* Another relationship exists between the requirement of independence and the demand that decisions or positions adopted by authorities must be based on objective criteria. Objectivity implies that the line of action must be founded on criteria which are not related to the identity of the undertakings concerned. Pursuant to the Framework Directive and the NRF in general, objectivity must guide the line of action adopted by authorities. That line of action may not be changed, whatever the motive, to a situation where one or several undertakings are favoured.

> *Framework Directive, Article 3(3).* 'Member States shall ensure that national regulatory authorities exercise their powers impartially.'

1.88 **Tasks clearly defined.** Another procedural constraint imposed on NRAs is transparency. National authorities must adopt their opinions and decisions in a transparent manner. An implication of transparency is that Member States must identify publicly the authorities which they have entrusted with the various tasks and missions granted to NRAs in the NRF. This is particularly the case where general competition law, sector-specific regulation and the rules concerning consumer protection are applied by distinct bodies.

> *Framework Directive, Article 3(4).* 'Member States shall publish the tasks to be undertaken by national regulatory authorities in an easily accessible form, in particular where those tasks are assigned to more than one body.' 'Where more than one authority has competence to address such matters,[46] Member States shall ensure that the respective tasks of each authority are published in an easily accessible form.'

---

[46] Competition, regulation, consumer protection.

Transparency in the exercise of activities. An additional implication of trans-   **1.89**
parency is that all decisions and positions adopted by NRAs must result from
a process where transparency is practised. That requirement is stated as a principle
in the Framework Directive. It is further construed in various provisions which are
analysed in the following paragraphs.

> *Framework Directive, Article 3(3).* 'Member States shall ensure that national regula-
> tory authorities exercise their powers . . . transparently.'

Consultation of interested parties. Transparency requires that interested par-   **1.90**
ties must be heard and consulted whenever a decision with potentially adverse
consequences for the parties is envisaged by an NRA. The result of the consultation must be made public. Information must be readily available about the procedures used in the various Member States for such consultations. In each
Member State an information point must be set up through which users and
undertakings can at any time gather intelligence about all consultations in
progress.[47]

> *Framework Directive, Article 6.* 'Member States shall ensure that where national regu-
> latory authorities intend to take measures . . . which have a significant impact on the
> relevant market, they give interested parties the opportunity to comment on the
> draft measure within a reasonable period. National regulatory authorities shall pub-
> lish their national consultation procedures. Member States shall ensure the estab-
> lishment of a single information point through which all current consultations can
> be accessed. The results of the consultation procedure shall be made publicly avail-
> able by the national regulatory authority.'[48]

Transfer of information to the Commission. Transparency also means that   **1.91**
action by NRAs must be brought to the attention of the Commission. This
requirement has a link with the procedures that may be initiated by the
Commission against Member States infringing obligations deriving from
European law. The Commission needs information to assess the actions adopted
by NRAs. To that effect the communication of information by NRAs is essential.
It should however be noted that, despite the importance of this kind of transfer of
information, the NRF does not impose on NRAs an obligation systematically to
warn the Commission about national initiatives. Pursuant to the Framework
Directive, information must be provided only when the Commission so requests.
The request must also be reasoned. These limitations correspond, some may argue,
with the principle of subsidiarity.[49] The disadvantage, however, is that as a result

---

[47] This may be important for users and undertakings willing to participate in such consultation.
They must be able to find out quickly how they can provide their opinion.

[48] Exceptions are provided to the obligation to consult interested parties, where interim measures are needed. Specific arrangements are made, furthermore, to hear parties in procedures where
disputes are to be resolved. See Framework Directive, Art 6.

[49] Under the subsidiarity principle, actions must be taken at the most appropriate level. This
principle guides actions where competences are shared between the European legislator and the

the Commission is not in a position systematically to supervise action taken, or envisaged, by NRAs.

> *Framework Directive, Article 5(2).* 'Member States shall ensure that national regulatory authorities provide the Commission, after a reasoned request, with the information necessary for it to carry out its tasks under the Treaty. The information requested by the Commission shall be proportionate to the performance of those tasks.'

1.92 **Exchange of information among national authorities.** In the same vein, an exchange of information between NRAs is provided for. *(a)* Pursuant to the Framework Directive, the exchange is in general co-ordinated by the Commission. As submitted in the previous paragraph, the Commission receives information from NRAs. Once the information has been acquired by the Commission it is automatically transferred to the NRAs established in the other Member States. An NRA forwarding information to the Commission may however refuse to allow it to be passed on to the other Member States. To be valid, that refusal must be notified to the Commission. It must also be reasoned. *(b)* Another possibility is for the NRAs to exchange information directly among themselves. Here again the information is not provided spontaneously. A request must be made by the authority wishing to receive information, giving the reasons.

> *Framework Directive, Article 5.* [a] 'To the extent necessary, and unless the authority that provides the information has made an explicit and reasoned request to the contrary, the Commission shall make the information provided available to another such authority in another Member State.'[50] [b] 'Subject to the requirements of paragraph 3, Member States shall ensure that the information submitted to one national regulatory authority can be made available to another such authority in the same or different Member State, after a substantiated request, where necessary to allow either authority to fulfil its responsibilities under Community law.'[51]

Exchange of Information

(1) NRAs pass information to the Commission when the Commission so requests in a reasoned decision.
(2) Information passed by NRAs to the Commission is normally passed on to the NRAs in the other Member States; this can however be contested by the NRAs from which the information originates (reasoned request).
(3) An NRA in one Member State must comply with a request for information originating from an NRA from another EU country if, and where, a reasoned request has been made by the recipient NRA.

national authorities. Where competences are exclusive, they are reserved for the authority in charge of the actions concerned. There is then no margin to examine whether action should be taken at another level.

[50] Para 2.   [51] Para 2, second subparagraph.

(6) NRAs—Business confidentiality

Limitation on transparency. A constraint on transparency and the exchange of **1.93** information is that NRAs must observe confidentiality requirements. Transparency is limited by the right of undertakings to have business secrets safeguarded. An emphasis on confidentiality may for this reason be found in the NRF. Pursuant to the Framework Directive, information gathered by NRAs should be made public, particularly when the publication may have an impact on the development of an open and competitive market. This is clearly not the case, however, whenever business confidentiality is involved.

Framework Directive, Article 5 (4). 'Member States shall ensure that, acting in accordance with national rules on public access to information and subject to Community and national rules on business confidentiality, national regulatory authorities publish such information as would contribute to an open and competitive market.' *Framework Directive, Preamble, recital 13.* 'Information gathered by national regulatory authorities should be publicly available, except in so far as it is confidential in accordance with national rules on public access to information and subject to Community and national law on business confidentiality.'

Assessment by the originating authority. Pursuant to the Framework Directive, **1.94** the confidential character of a piece of information must be respected by the authorities to which it is passed. Where, for example, an NRA is requested to give information to the Commission or an NRA in another Member State, the first NRA may specify that the information be kept confidential. The authority receiving the information (Commission, NRA) is then under an obligation to ensure confidentiality. The assessment regarding the confidential nature of information is made by the authority from which the information originates. That assessment must be respected by those who receive it.

Framework Directive, Article 5(3). 'Where information is considered confidential by a national regulatory authority in accordance with Community and national rules on business confidentiality, the Commission and the national regulatory authorities concerned shall ensure such confidentiality.' *Framework Directive, Preamble, recital 35.* 'National regulatory authorities and national competition authorities should provide each other with the information necessary to apply the provisions of this Directive and the Specific Directives, in order to allow them to cooperate fully together. In respect of the information exchanged, the receiving authority should ensure the same level of confidentiality as the originating authority.'[52]

---

[52] See also Preamble, recital 14. 'Information that is considered confidential by a national regulatory authority, in accordance with Community and national rules on business confidentiality, may only be exchanged with the Commission and other national regulatory authorities where such exchange is strictly necessary for the application of the provisions of this Directive or the Specific Directives. The information exchanged should be limited to that which is relevant and proportionate to the purpose of such an exchange.'

1.95 **General and specific obligations.** The obligation to respect confidentiality is not limited to general provisions. It may also be found in specific provisions where the Parliament and Council address particular issues. *(a)* As an example, confidentiality must be respected where NRAs publish the results of consultations organised prior to adopting decisions with potentially significant consequences for undertakings. *(b)* Another example is where NRAs adopt decisions resolving disputes between undertakings. In that context the NRAs' decisions must be published, except where business confidentiality would be violated. *(c)* A third scenario is where NRAs publish accounting records in accordance with NRF obligations. Confidentiality then requires, as in the previous circumstances, that business secrets cannot be published. *(d)* NRAs must publish information about specific obligations imposed on undertakings with significant market power. In the course of the implementation of that obligation, they must avoid divulging business secrets.

> *Framework and Access Directives.* [a]'The results of the consultation procedure shall be made publicly available by the national regulatory authority, except in the case of confidential information in accordance with Community and national law on business confidentiality.'[53] [b] 'The decision of the national regulatory authority shall be made available to the public, having regard to the requirements of business confidentiality.'[54] [c] '[N]ational regulatory authorities shall have the power to require that accounting records . . . are provided on request. National regulatory authorities may publish such information as would contribute to an open and competitive market, while respecting national and Community rules on commercial confidentiality.'[55] [d] 'Member States shall ensure that the specific obligations imposed on undertakings . . . are published and that the specific product/service and geographical markets are identified. They shall ensure that up-to-date information, provided that the information is not confidential and, in particular, does not comprise business secrets, is made publicly available.'[56]

E. Historical Perspective

1.96 **Several steps.** The present section contains a brief overview of the developments which have taken place in the European Union in the last 20 years.[57] It is not possible, or advisable, to be exhaustive in such an overview. The purpose is not to provide a full account of the numerous episodes that have taken place, but rather to give a schematic review of how and why the current situation has been reached. In this book this evolutionary process is presented as encompassing four

---

53 Framework Directive, Art 6.   54 ibid, Art 20(4).
55 Access Directive, Art 11(2).   56 ibid, Art 15(1).
57 For a review of EU electronic communications law, see L Garzaniti, *Telecommunications, Broadcasting and the Internet* (2000); P Larouche, *Competition Law and Regulation in European Telecommunications* (2000); P Nihoul, *Droit européen des télécommunications—L'organisation des marchés* (2003); Simmons & Simmons, *Telecommunications: The EU Law* (1999); I Walden & J Angel, *Telecommunications Law* (2001).

steps. *(a)* The starting point was the situation that existed in the Member States before the reform was undertaken. *(b)* The process starts with initiatives taken by the Commission to open the sector to competition. *(c)* The Member States acting in the Council reacted with harmonisation measures, thereby giving rise to a second—in some respects concurrent—set of rules applicable to telecommunications. *(d)* The rules were then reviewed and a new—intentionally more consistent and coherent—regulatory framework was laid out.

(1) Monopoly in national telecommunications

National operators.   For decades, the telecommunications services (and terminals)   **1.97**
markets were characterised by national monopolies in Europe. Member States had entrusted one undertaking—often a department within their administrations— with the task of installing and operating a network on the national territory. That undertaking was also charged with providing services over the infrastructure. The services were in many instances limited to voice telephony. The monopoly undertaking had an exclusive right to sell terminal equipment. It was also vested with the right to establish the technical requirements to be satisfied for connection to the network and more generally to determine what rules applied in the sector.

(2) Liberalisation by the Commission

Initiative by the Commission.   The situation described above (national mono-   **1.98**
polies) was not deemed satisfactory by the European Commission.[58] It is often said that this line was motivated by a comparison with the state of affairs in the United States. American customers seemed to have access to better communications at lower prices. American companies appeared to have a technological advantage to which Europe would not be able to respond without immediate action.[59] Regulatory moves were being undertaken in America to encourage further development in the communications sector in that country. It was feared that Europe would be left behind if no similar moves were made on this side of the Atlantic.[60]

The 1987 Green Paper.   On this basis the Commission published a Green Paper[61]   **1.99**
in which it outlined measures to be taken in order to support and develop electronic

---

[58] European Commission, Towards a dynamic European economy—Green Paper on the development of the common market for telecommunications services and equipment, COM(87)290final (30 June 1987).

[59] Innovation in communications is essential for sustaining economic growth. First, communications are an important sector in the wider economy. Growth in that sector has a substantial impact on general economic activity. Second, innovation in communications has an impact on other activities depending on information and data exchange.

[60] Y Benkler, *Rules of the Road for the Information Superhighway: Electronic Communications and the Law* (1996); HJ Brands & ET Leo, *The Law and Regulation of Telecommunications Carriers* (1999); CH Kennedy, *An Introduction to US Telecommunications* (2001).

[61] Towards a dynamic European Economy—Green Paper on the development of the common market for telecommunications services and equipment, COM(87)290final (30 June 1987).

communications (then, telecommunications) in Europe. Among other measures, the Paper suggested the introduction of competition in telecommunications markets (liberalisation).

1.100 **Two liberalisation directives.** This proposal did not, to say the least, raise enthusiasm among most of the Member States. It was indeed perceived as a threat to the system that had governed electronic communications for decades on national territories. As stated above, these activities had been the exclusive preserve of one undertaking in virtually every Member State. The European Commission was proposing to set that system aside. Under its proposal, all interested undertakings would be allowed to enter the market. Member States voiced their opposition, but the Commission went ahead.[62] It adopted several directives in succession, which enshrined in law the liberalisation process envisaged in the Green Paper. Pursuant to these directives, competition was introduced successively on the markets for terminals,[63] services[64] and infrastructure.[65] As a result of these instruments, the Member States were compelled to remove all privileges (special and exclusive rights) previously granted to national operators.

1.101 **Article 86(1) EC.** As a legal basis for these instruments, the Commission used an EC Treaty provision that had hardly been examined earlier—Article 90 EC, now Article 86 EC.[66] The first paragraph of that Article states that Member States must respect Treaty provisions as regards undertakings with which they have close relationships. These may be in the form of a share in the capital of these entities. They may also derive from regulatory advantages granted to these undertakings in order to facilitate their activities (special or exclusive rights). Pursuant to Article 86(1) EC (formerly Article 90(1) EC), Member States may not take in respect of these undertakings any measure contrary to the Treaty. All rules contained in the Treaty are concerned, but those relating to competition are explicitly mentioned.

> *Article 86(1) EC.* 'In the case of public undertakings and undertakings to which Member States grant special or exclusive rights, Member States shall neither enact nor maintain in force any measure contrary to the rules contained in this Treaty, in particular to those rules provided for in Article 12[67] and Articles 81 to 89.'[68]

---

[62] For an excellent account, see P Larouche, *Competition Law and Regulation in European Telecommunications* (2000), 1–17.

[63] Commission Directive (EEC) 88/301 of 16 May 1988 on competition in the markets in telecommunications terminal equipment [1988] OJ L131/73.

[64] Commission Directive (EEC) 90/388 on competition in the markets for telecommunications services (1990) OJ L192/10.

[65] Commission Directive (EC) 96/19 amending Directive 90/388 with regard to the implementation of full competition in telecommunications markets [1996] OJ L74/13.

[66] See JL Buendia Sierra, *Exclusive Rights and State Monopolies under EC Law—Article 86 (former Article 90) of the EC Treaty* (2000).

[67] This provision contains a prohibition on discrimination based on nationality.

[68] These provisions set out the European rules on competition.

Article 86(2) EC.   The second paragraph of Article 86 EC (formerly Article 90   **1.102**
EC) concerns undertakings entrusted by the Member States with the operation of
services of general economic interest. According to that provision, these undertakings may be granted an exemption with respect to the rules of the EC Treaty,
including those on competition. In cases where an exemption is granted, the
undertakings concerned escape the application of the Treaty rules. An exemption
may be granted only where a legitimate objective is pursued. It applies only in so
far as it is useful and necessary to allow these undertakings to perform the particular tasks assigned to them, in connection with an objective of general interest.

> *Article 86(2) EC.* 'Undertakings entrusted with the operation of services of general
> economic interest or having the character of a revenue-producing monopoly shall be
> subject to the rules contained in this Treaty, in particular to the rules on competition,
> in so far as the application of such rules does not obstruct the performance, in law or
> in fact, of the particular tasks assigned to them. The development of trade must not
> be affected to such an extent as would be contrary to the interests of the Community.'

Link between paragraphs 1 and 2.   A link may be established between the first and   **1.103**
second paragraphs of Article 86 EC (formerly Article 90 EC). As was the case for
undertakings with an exclusive right, monopolies fall under the competition rules
(first paragraph). That situation does not appear, however, to conform entirely[69] to
the requirements of competition. Competition requires the presence of several
undertakings, all competing to obtain resources from potential partners. To justify
that apparent contradiction, Member States refer to the second paragraph of Article
86 EC (formerly Article 90 EC). They said that exclusive rights were necessary to
fulfil objectives of a public nature. According to them, the monopoly holder had to
be protected against rivals. In the absence of such a protection, it would not be in a
position to achieve the public objectives set for it. Objectives of that nature could
not be reached in a competitive environment.[70] An exemption is thus warranted,
along the lines laid down in Article 86(2) EC (formerly Article 90(2) EC).

---

[69]   The ECJ has repeatedly insisted that, as such, exclusive rights should not be considered contrary to competition rules. However, it has ruled that the exercise of these rights may be abusive in
violation of Art 82 EC (abuse of dominant position). See for instance Case 175/73 *Sacchi* [1974]
ECR 409. It subsequently considered that the exercise of exclusive rights necessarily leads to abuses.
According to the ECJ, the mere exercise of an exclusive right leads undertakings to abuse their dominant position. See for instance Case C-179/90 *Merci* [1991] ECR I-5889. The ECJ has accordingly
expressed its agreement with the general economic literature, pursuant to which an undertaking
tends to increase prices and decrease output where it is in a monopolistic situation.
[70]   The typical example is natural monopolies. Over a period of decades the Member States justified exclusive rights granted to their telecoms operators by stating that these rights merely
expressed in the law structure imposed by markets. In their view it was less costly for society to
finance one infrastructure and concentrate demand on it. The alternative—allowing competitors to
install their own network—would lead to redundancy, losses and bankruptcy. Granting exclusive
rights further granted national authorities an opportunity to impose public policy objectives on
undertakings holding monopolies. For instance, these undertakings were required in various
Member States to wire the whole national territory irrespective of the cost. Profit or even financial

1.104 **Article 86(3) EC.** In addition to regulating monopolies and the general interest, Article 86 EC (formerly Article 90 EC) contains an institutional measure (paragraph 3). Pursuant thereto, the Commission has the power to adopt directives or decisions as deemed necessary to implement the other provisions contained in the Article. The Commission is thereby granted the power to ensure the application of Treaty provisions to undertakings with special or exclusive rights (paragraph 1).[71] It is also assigned the power to verify that exemptions are conferred in accordance with the conditions laid down in the Treaty (paragraph 2).

> *Article 86(3) EC.* 'The Commission shall ensure the application of the provisions of this Article and shall, where necessary, address appropriate directives or decisions to Member States.'

1.105 **New organisation for the sector.** On the basis of Article 86 EC (formerly Article 90 EC), the Commission claimed a legal mandate to organise the European telecoms markets on a competitive basis. Article 86(1) EC (formerly Article 90(1) EC), it said, implies that competition should be introduced on telecoms markets. Competition rules apply, according to that provision, to all sectors of the economy, even those where States have special links with undertakings. How should competition be introduced? For the Commission, a competitive environment implies that markets should be opened to new entrants. Exclusive rights had to be eliminated as they impeded entry.

1.106 **Derogations.** After the elimination of these privileges, it appeared that derogations could be granted on the basis of Article 86(2) EC (formerly Article 90(2) EC). These derogations would result in the undertakings concerned being placed outside the reach of competition. Such a possibility would create risks for the project envisaged by the Commission. Competition would not be introduced if national operators could successfully claim the benefit of exemptions. To avoid such a result, the Commission construed strictly the conditions under which derogations can be granted. *(a)* As to scope, derogations must be limited to specific services. These services must qualify as a service of general economic interest. Qualification is granted by national legislation, but the criteria are laid down at European level (universal service obligations). *(b)* Derogations are to be made available to all undertakings without discrimination. No undertaking can be granted an automatic derogation in the name of the general interest. A procedure must be organised to determine who will provide the services covered by the derogation (universal service, where the result cannot be reached via market forces). It must be open to all interested undertakings. The selection must be based on merit.

---

balance were considered less important than establishing a national infrastructure. FM Scherer, *Industrial Market Structure and Economic Performance* (1980); W Sharkey, *The Theory of Natural Monopoly* (1982); R Schmalensee, *The Control of Natural Monopolies* (1979).

[71] As well as to public undertakings.

Intervention by the ECJ. The initiative taken by the Commission was not **1.107** accepted by all Member States. An application for annulment of the liberalisation directives was submitted to the ECJ. The Court issued two judgments, one for each directive. In both decisions it confirmed the Commission's power to act.[72] The position adopted by the ECJ substantially modified the *rapport de forces* between the Commission and the Member States. The ECJ in fact ruled that a legislative power was vested in the Commission to apply Treaty provisions to public monopolies. According to the ECJ, Article 86 EC (formerly Article 90 EC) entrusts the Commission with the power to specify by way of general instruments the consequences deriving from the Treaty for the organisation of economic activities carried out by those undertakings. The judgments thus confirmed the Commission in its willingness to act as a legislative authority to organise services of general economic interest and/or services provided under derogations (special or exclusive rights).[73]

(3) The debate between harmonisation and liberalisation

Legislative reaction by the Member States. As they did not win the judicial **1.108** debate against the Commission, the Member States decided to adopt measures of their own. Their intention was to regulate markets themselves. They accordingly adopted harmonisation directives by virtue of the power originally granted to the Council by the Treaty. It was thereafter extended to cover also the Parliament, and both institutions now co-decide on most harmonisation matters.

The harmonisation process. Harmonisation (officially called 'approximation of **1.109** laws') is organised by several Treaty provisions. Among them, Article 95 EC (formerly Article 100a EC) provides the standard basis. Pursuant to that provision, approximation may be carried out where national rules affect the establishment

---

[72] Cases C-202/88 *France v Commission* [1991] ECR I-1223 and C-271/90 *Spain v Commission* [1992] ECR I-5833. Through these judgments, the Commission was authorised to take action in relation to the telecoms sector. Other liberalisation directives were adopted in their wake, supplementing and, in some regards, going beyond the ideas submitted in the Green Paper. Competition was extended to infrastructure whereas that step had not earlier been envisaged.

[73] Before these judgments, some commentators considered that the legislative power was vested with the Council as regards the organisation of the sectors concerned. That attitude was in line with the general position that the Council was (then) the legislator in the European Community (that role is now shared with the European Parliament). Pursuant to the EC Treaty, the Council is made up of representatives of the Member States. It can thus be said that the Member States exercised legislative power on these matters through their representation in the Council, pursuant to the rules laid down in the Treaties. That competence had general scope, ie it was not limited to any given field. On the contrary, it applied to all activities directly or indirectly covered by the Treaty. For a discussion on these aspects, see P Nihoul, '*Authorities, competition and electronic communications—Towards institutional competition in the information society*' [2002] 1 Info 7-24. That situation was admittedly modified subsequently with the adoption and ratification of the new Treaties. The principal modifications brought about by these Treaties did not, however, affect the institutional balance between the Council and the Commission. They rather promoted the position of the Parliament vis-à-vis both institutions: the Parliament was progressively given a greater say in the legislative process. LWG Gormley, *Introduction to the Law of the European Communities* (1998), 209 et seq.

and/or the functioning of the internal market. In most cases, the difficulty to be solved through harmonisation originates from a discrepancy existing between national legislation. As a result of that discrepancy, undertakings must adapt their products to each national market. They are as a result prevented from taking full advantage of the internal market. Article 95 EC is meant to solve that difficulty. It provides the Parliament and the Council with a legal basis to establish a common field where undertakings carry out activities on a similar basis. In the process of approximating the rules, these institutions have the opportunity to decide the rules applicable to undertakings throughout the Union. Harmonisation is thus a process whereby the European legislator regulates entire sectors of the economy.

1.110 **Telecommunications harmonisation directives.** The Council and Parliament have adopted several telecommunications harmonisation directives.[74] These instruments are presented briefly in the following paragraphs, on the basis of the markets concerned by the directives (terminal equipment, provision of services, Open Network Provision, behaviour of operators, social measures).

1.111 **Terminal equipment.** Some directives regulate terminal equipment.[75] These rules establish the conditions under which terminal equipment may be marketed. They also set the conditions governing connection of terminals to infrastructure in the various Member States. The aim underlying these measures is to ensure that manufacturers do not have to adapt their products to specific technical requirements in force in each Member State. Technical standards are thus harmonised throughout the Union. The terminals manufactured in conformity with these standards must be accepted throughout the Union. The directives further harmonise the formalities that can be imposed at national level in order to assess conformity with these technical requirements.

1.112 **Authorisation.** Similar measures were taken with regard to services. Where an undertaking wanted to provide services in several European countries, it had to comply with the rules applicable in each territory involved. As a result of that constraint undertakings were not in a position to enjoy fully the benefits of the internal market. To avoid such a situation, a choice was made to determine at European

---

[74] See http://europa.eu.int/information_society/topics/telecoms/index_en.htm.

[75] Latest instrument, still in force: European Parliament and Council Directive (EC) 1999/5 on radio equipment and telecommunications terminal equipment and the mutual recognition of their conformity [1999] OJ L091/10. Prior instruments concerning terminal equipment were: Council Directive (EEC) 86/361 on the initial stage of the mutual recognition of type approval for telecommunications terminal equipment [1986] OJ L217/21; Council Directive (EEC) 91/263 on the approximation of the laws of the Member States concerning telecommunications terminal equipment, including the mutual recognition of their conformity [1991] OJ L128/1; Council Directive (EEC) 93/97 supplementing Directive (EEC) 91/263 in respect of satellite earth station equipment [1993] OJ L290/1; European Parliament and Council Directive (EC) 98/13 relating to telecommunications terminal equipment and satellite earth station equipment, including the mutual recognition of their conformity [1998] OJ L74/1.

level the obligations that could be imposed on undertakings providing electronic communications services. A rapprochement also took place with respect to the formalities that could be imposed on undertakings before they could start their activities in the different Member States.[76] Following these measures, the rules applicable in the Member States to the provision of services were brought into line. A common field was established where undertakings were subject to similar conditions and could thus compete on an equal basis.

Open Network Provision (ONP).   A third—and wider—set of measures was adopted with a view to opening networks throughout the Community. The goal was to ensure that networks could be interconnected easily across the Member States. Technical harmonisation was decided on for this purpose. The process facilitated transmissions involving several Member States, and measures were added to regulate the behaviour of former national operators vis-à-vis operators and service providers from other European countries.[77]   **1.113**

Behaviour of operators.   In the same context (Open Network Provision), the Council and the Parliament harmonised the conditions subject to which access was to be granted by network operators to service providers. The intervention was important to establish, throughout the European market, common conditions for access to existing facilities. It was not specifically related to network operators or service providers wishing to carry out cross-border activities. Through these measures, the Council and the Parliament simply regulated the behaviour of network operators. They determined for instance under what conditions interconnection should be granted. They imposed on operators an obligation to provide some kinds of services or infrastructure. They also established accountancy constraints, so that activities would be easier to control.   **1.114**

Social measures.   The Parliament and the Council adopted further measures aimed at protecting certain categories of the population. In the telecoms sector,   **1.115**

---

[76] European Parliament and Council Directive (EC) 97/13 on a common framework for general authorisations and individual licences in the field of telecommunications services [1997] OJ L117/15. Despite these measures, the situation remains that undertakings active on several territories are still subject to formalities in each Member State. The formalities carried out in one Member State accordingly do not provide a valid authorisation for the performance of activities on another national territory.

[77] Council Directive (EC) 90/387 on the establishment of the internal market for telecommunications services through the implementation of open network provision [1990] OJ L192/1; Council Directive (EC) 92/44 on the application of open network provision to leased lines [1992] OJ L165/27; European Parliament and Council Directive (EC) 97/33 on interconnection in telecommunications with regard to ensuring universal services and interoperability through application of the principles of Open Network Provision (ONP) [1997] OJ L199/32; European Parliament and Council (EC) Directive 97/51 amending Directives (EC) 90/387 and 92/44 for the purpose of adaptation to a competitive environment in telecommunications [1997] OJ L295/23; European Parliament and Council Directive (EC) 98/10 on the application of ONP to voice telephony and on universal service for telecommunications in a competitive environment [1998] OJ L101/24.

these social provisions pursued several goals. *(a)* Some provisions were adopted in consideration of handicapped persons or other groups deserving special protection.[78] Special services were to be made available to them. A possibility was provided for Member States to grant tariffs reductions for some categories of the population. *(b)* Beyond these measures directed at specific groups of the population, a more general system was set up to ensure the provision of fundamental services to the whole population under reasonable and non-discriminatory conditions (universal service). European provisions also determined how the system could be financed, that is, what costs could be taken into account and who could be asked to pay for them.

(4) The new regulatory framework

Convergence

1.116 **Convergence.** As stated, convergence gave rise—partially at least—to the amendment of the old regulatory framework. In the NRF, electronic transmissions are treated alike, whatever the sector they were previously related to. By contrast, content-related issues remain regulated according to the sector to which the activities in question belong. More developments are expected on the latter front, as well as regarding institutional aspects (co-operation between authorities, and possibly reorganisation of some of them).

Broadcasting

1.117 **Telecoms rules applied to broadcasting.** In many respects, convergence may be analysed, in substance, as the application to broadcasting of rules relating to telecommunications. So far, analysis has concentrated on the rules applicable to telecommunications. The regulatory environment concerning broadcasting has not been examined. The reason is that the reform hardly affected broadcasting in the past. It is at this point important, however, to provide information as to how broadcasting is regulated under the NRF.

1.118 **Public and national organisation.** In European countries, broadcasting was for a long time organised on a public and national basis. Broadcasting basically consisted in radio and television, and these services were operated by the State. The task was generally entrusted to an administrative department, or to a specific entity placed under public control. *(a)* That organisation was due to the influence radio and television can have on public opinion and behaviour. It was thought unacceptable that an influence of that magnitude could be left to private forces. *(b)* Furthermore, it was considered that pluralism ought to be ensured. All political and cultural currents would be expressed in radio and TV programmes. Democracy would be enhanced.

---

[78] In particular European Parliament and Council Directive (EC) 98/10 on the application of ONP to voice telephony and on universal service for telecommunications in a competitive environment [1998] OJ L101/24.

It was feared that pluralism would not be achieved if broadcasting were left to the private sector. In a competitive environment, broadcasters would give priority to lucrative programming. They would in short concentrate on profit and avoid programmes covering socially or culturally important subjects.

Competition and regulation. Part of the opinion presented in the paragraph **1.119** above remains current. It is still considered in most Member States that pluralism must be striven for. The judgment has however changed as to the method likely to produce that objective. Efficiency nowadays demands that activities be left to private undertakings. It has been established that public bodies tend to neglect economic constraints. To take this new development into account, competition has been introduced on the markets for broadcasting.[79] Competition concerns the number of actors allowed on the market. It implies that consumers are given a choice between providers. It also requires that providers be treated alike. No undertaking may be placed at an advantage, and competition must occur on the basis of merit.

Public goals. These aspects aside, competition does not influence the content of **1.120** regulation. Competition may thus be combined with other rules to achieve cultural or political objectives. This observation explains why the Member States have increasingly resorted to regulatory powers in parallel with the introduction of competition in the market. They thereby hoped to enhance efficiency while maintaining a grip on the markets in order to ensure public policy goals. Comparing sectors, one can say that, on the whole, developments in broadcasting and telecommunications have been similar. Competition has been introduced in both sectors, and efficiency played a leading role. New companies have entered broadcasting and telecommunications markets. New rules have been established in parallel with the introduction of competition. Constraints were thereby imposed on private undertakings to ensure that the profit motive did not set aside (entirely) the fulfilment of public goals.

Adapt legislation to the new environment

Convergence. One of the objectives sought in the NRF was to adapt existing **1.121** regulation to the changing environment. Technologies and industrial structures were changing quickly. The European legislator wanted to assess whether the existing rules were still appropriate. In this regard the European institutions paid special attention to convergence. As stated earlier, technologies and industries are growing towards each other in the broadcasting, telecommunications and information sectors. They wanted to draw regulatory consequences from this phenomenon.

---

[79] Public broadcasting companies still exist in some Member States. They are however increasingly subject to the constraints applicable to private undertakings. For instance, the Commission regularly carries out enquiries to ensure that public broadcasting companies do not receive subsidies for activities that could be performed by private undertakings. It is as a result becoming difficult for these public bodies to continue their activities.

Better co-ordination between sector-specific regulation and general competition law

1.122 **Need for better co-ordination.** The European legislator also wanted to improve the co-ordination between rules in the regulatory framework. As a result of harmonisation and the application of competition law, two categories of rules were applied. They were adopted by different authorities: the Council and Parliament for harmonisation; the Commission for competition law. They were based on diverging legal bases: Article 95 EC for harmonisation; Articles 81, 82 and 86 EC and the Merger Regulation for competition rules. They pursued different, although not necessarily contradictory, objectives: achieving the internal market in one case; enhancing efficiency in the other.

	Harmonisation	Competition
Authorities involved	Parliament and Council	Commission
Legal basis	Article 95 EC	Articles 81, 82 and 86 EC; Merger Regulation
Objectives	Internal market	Enhance competition

Two sets of rules in European electronic communications

1.123 **Similar issues.** Despite these differences, both categories were used to regulate similar issues. Liberalisation and competition were interpreted widely by the Commission. That institution thus considered it had to regulate anything that may affect competition directly or indirectly. All rules have an effect of this kind. As they force undertakings to act in given directions or constrain them in others, rules necessarily influence behaviour and positions on the market. Hence, the Commission undertook to regulate the electronic communications sector. In parallel, a similar perspective was adopted by the Council and Parliament through the harmonisation directives. These instruments sought to eliminate disparities affecting activities in the market. The purpose was to establish a common basis for activities across the European territory. Using these instruments, the Parliament and Council regulated behaviour in the electronic communications sector.

1.124 **Contradictions.** As both categories of rules governed similar issues, contradictions were inevitable. An exhaustive account of the relationship between the two sets of rules is not possible here. Other studies may be consulted in this connection.[80] One example only is given here, to explain what kind of situation may

---

[80] P Nihoul, 'European Telecommunications: A Real Departure from Regulation?' in G Haibach (ed), *Services of General Interest in the EU: Reconciling Competition and Social Responsibility* (1999), 127–166; P Nihoul, 'Convergence in European Telecommunications—A Case Study on the Relationship between Regulation and Competition (Law)' [1998] 2 Intl J of Communications L and Policy 1–39.

result from a divergence between the rules applicable to one sector and coming from different institutions.

Illustration—How should universal service be financed?   The illustration con- **1.125** cerns the undertakings on which an obligation to contribute to the cost of the universal service may be imposed.[81] As stated above, the Commission, Council and Parliament agreed that the Member States could organise the provision of fundamental services in accordance with particular conditions. These services would be performed at prices below cost. The loss would have to be compensated, either through public intervention or through contributions paid from a fund set up to that effect. In the latter case, the fund would collect payments from undertakings, and the question was to determine which undertakings could be required to pay.

Attitude of the Commission.   In this debate the attitude adopted by the Com- **1.126** mission was to avoid the imposition of excessive obligations on new entrants.[82] For that reason, it proposed that the fund should be financed by former national opera- tors. These operators would thus face an extra burden. In contrast, new entrants would bear no financial obligation. They would be at an advantage that would allow them to compete more effectively with former operators. The still enormous market share held by the latter would be harnessed in the interests of competition. In order to achieve that result, the Commission specified that universal service obligations could be financed only by operators of public networks—in fact former national monopolies—in the Member States where the cost would be financed by a fund.[83]

> *Services Directive, Article 4(c).* '[A]ny national scheme which is necessary to share the net cost of the provision of universal service obligations entrusted to the telecom- munications organisations, with other organisations whether it consists of a system of supplementary charges or a universal service fund, shall . . . apply only to under- takings providing public telecommunications networks.'

Council.   A different attitude was taken by the Member States, represented in the **1.127** Council. *(a)* The Member States thought that liberalisation would provide oppor- tunities for new entrants. It was legitimate, according to them, that part of the benefit acquired by these new undertakings should be transferred to the population in the form of universal service obligations. *(b)* The Member States also feared that placing an extra burden on former national operators might affect their financial situation adversely. Such an impact would further complicate the partial or total privatisation of these operators. It would also force operators to reduce their costs

---

[81] A full account may be found in P Larouche, *Competition Law and Regulation in European Telecommunications* (2000), 70 and in P Nihoul (n 80 above).

[82] Such obligations might indeed lead to a situation where these new undertakings would be deterred from entering the market. This would indicate the Commission had failed in its objective of introducing competition by allowing new participants on the market.

[83] See Commission Directive (EC) 96/19 amending Directive 90/388/EEC with regard to the implementation of full competition in telecommunications markets [1996] OJ L74/24.

drastically, principally at the expense of employees. For these reasons the Council sought to enlarge the circle of undertakings called on to contribute to the cost of universal service. The position adopted by that institution was that a contribution should be required from any undertaking active in the provision of public telecommunications network or in the provision of public voice telephony.[84]

> *ONP Directives.* 'Where a Member State determines . . . that universal service obligations represent an unfair burden on an organisation, it shall establish a mechanism for sharing the net cost of the universal service obligations with other organisations operating public telecommunications networks and/or publicly available voice telephony services.'[85]

1.128 **Contradiction.** As appears from the previous paragraphs, a contradiction emerged between the positions adopted by the Commission and the Council (with the Parliament). That contradiction was addressed by the Commission in a notice pursuant to which Member States could impose financial obligations in the context of the universal service on voice telephony providers (other than former national operators). The position of the Council (and the Parliament) was thus accepted, in principle, by the Commission. A limitation was imposed, however, as the financial obligations concerning the cost of the universal service had to be determined, for each undertaking, in proportion to its usage of public telecommunications networks.

> *Conciliation by the Commission.* 'The Commission will . . . interpret both Article[s] . . . as allowing contributions only to be imposed on voice telephony providers in proportion to their usage of public telecommunications networks.'[86] 'In line with the Full Competition Directive and the Interconnection Directive, only organisations providing public telecommunications networks and/or public voice telephony services may be required under National Schemes to contribute to a Universal Service Fund or to any system of supplementary charges . . . [C]ontributions may only be imposed on voice telephony providers in proportion to their usage of public telecommunications networks . . . [T]he Commission will, in the case of an application (extension) of obligations to new entrants and/or mobile operators, assess in particular if the burden is allocated according to objective and non-discriminatory criteria and in accordance with the principle of proportionality.'[87]

---

[84] See European Parliament and Council Directive (EC) 97/33 on interconnection in Telecommunications with regard to ensuring universal service and interoperability through application of the principles of Open Network Provision (ONP) [1997] OJ L199/32 and European Parliament and Council Directive (EC) 98/10 on the application of open network provision (ONP) to voice telephony and on universal service for telecommunications in a competitive environment [1998] OJ L101/24.

[85] Council and Parliament Directive (EC) 97/33 on interconnection in telecommunications with regard to ensuring universal services and interoperability through application of the principles of Open Network Provision (ONP) [1997] OJ L199/32, Art 5(1).

[86] Commission Communication on Assessment Criteria for National Schemes for the Costing and Financing of Universal Service in Telecommunications and Guidelines for the Member States on Operation of Such Schemes, COM (96)608, 27 November 1996, annex C: Commission Statement to the Minutes of the 1910th Meeting of Council (Telecommunications), on 27th March 1996 on Who Contributes to Universal Service.

[87] Commission Communication at note 36, Guidelines for National Regulatory Authority, point III.

F. Convergence[88]

(1) Convergence between fixed and mobile communications

Convergence. To many people, convergence means the relationship between   **1.129**
mobile and fixed communications. Telecommunications first developed over
fixed lines. Mobile technology was used to provide transmissions in situations
where resorting to wires would be impossible, difficult or costly. The development
of these technologies gave rise to a new industry.

Combining fixed and mobile technologies. Both (mobile and fixed) technolo-   **1.130**
gies are increasingly combined to provide services wherever the client is located.
A real convergence is unfolding between the two segments, which are growing
towards each other to a point where it will be difficult to distinguish them.
(a) Thus mobile communications are rarely conveyed from the transmitter to the
addressee using only mobile technology. Signals are transmitted by the mobile terminal. They are intercepted by a receiver (antenna) placed in the area. From that
point, they are sent to an antenna located in the area where the addressee is located.
The transmission between antennas takes place on fixed lines. From the second
antenna, the communication is sent to the addressee's terminal via mobile technology. *(b)* Mobile technology is also employed to facilitate the use of technologies traditionally associated with fixed communications. For instance, people sometimes
have at home a hands-free terminal. That device is connected to a fixed base which
is connected to a fixed network. *(c)* Services are now being provided by some undertakings using the model of a combination of fixed and mobile telephony. One number is assigned to the subscriber. The latter may use a fixed or mobile terminal to
make and receive communications. Through a simple operation the user indicates
to the network whether he wants to be reached via fixed or mobile technology.

---

[88] For preparatory documents on convergence, see Green Paper [COM(1997)623] on the
Convergence of the Telecommunications, Media and Information Technology Sectors, and the
Implications for Regulation. Towards an Information Society Approach (December 1997). See also
Communication COM(99)108: Results of the Public Consultation on the Green Paper on the
Convergence of the Telecommunications, Media and Information Technology Sectors (10 March
1999). Interested readers may also consult background studies: Squire Sanders & Dempsey/Analysys,
Adapting the EU Telecommunications regulatory framework to developing multimedia environ-
ment (January 1998), available at http://europa.eu.int/infosoc/telecompolicy/en/Study-en.
htm; KPMG report for the European Commission, Public Policy Issues Arising From
Telecommunications and Audio-visual Convergence (September 1996); Norcontel, Economic
implications of New Communication Technologies on the audio-visual Markets, available at http://
europa.eu.int/comm/avpolicy/legis/key_doc/new_comm/index.htm. In general, see Baldwin,
S McVoy & M Steinfeld (eds), *Convergence: Integrating Media, Information and Commun-
ication* (1996); C Blackman & P Nihoul, *The Convergence between Telecommunications and Other
Media: How Should Regulation Adapt?*, Telecommunications Policy, Special Issue, vol. 22, no 3;
International Telecommunication Union (ITU) (1996), *The Changing Role of Government in an
Era of Telecom Deregulation: Regulatory Implications of Telecommunications Convergence*
(11–13 December 1996, Geneva); P Nihoul, 'Convergence in European Telecommunications—A
Case Study on the Relationship Between Regulation and Competition (Law)' (n 80 above)

1.131 **Mobile technology further developed.** Convergence can also refer to another development which mobile communications are currently undergoing. Originally mobile technologies were used to provide voice telephony. Other functions were hardly possible, although they were well developed using fixed technology. For instance, e-mails could be sent via a fixed connection but not using mobile technology. Similarly, accessing the worldwide web did not seem possible with available mobile techniques although it was easily done through broadband fixed networks. That situation is likely to change. The development of third generation mobile terminals and networks will make it possible to perform all functions now provided through fixed connections, and the appropriate radio frequencies have been allocated in all Member States. It is, however, difficult to predict when the new generation of mobile services will develop fully, as technologies are complex and the financial situation of some operators was damaged by the stock market crisis.

1.132 **Regulatory convergence.** Apart from these technological developments, there is convergence between mobile and fixed communications from a regulatory point of view. Up to now, the rules applicable to these types of communication have not always been identical. Two differences are worth mentioning. The first concerns universal service and the second the obligations that are imposed on dominant network operators.

1.133 **(a) Universal service.** As stated above, the telecommunications industry was formerly organised on the basis of national monopolies. The undertakings enjoying monopoly power were subject to special obligations deriving from the importance of telecommunications in society. Governments wanted to make fundamental services available to the population under reasonable conditions ('public service'). That attitude has to a certain extent survived. Markets have been opened to competition. At the same time, provisions were introduced in the regulatory framework to maintain—partially at least—the same idea in the form of 'universal service'. Under the NRF, certain services still have to be performed under reasonable conditions.[89] Among these services are the provision of a fixed connection and access to fixed voice telephony. The system has not been extended to similar services in mobile communications. A difference thus exists between fixed and mobile networks and services with respect to universal service.[90]

---

[89] These conditions are different from those that prevail in a market organised on a competitive basis. On these markets, the price and the availability of service depend mainly on costs.

[90] It is believed in some quarters that mobile services should be included in the universal service. The European legislator does not, however, appear to be convinced of the necessity to do so. It has rather the impression that society is better served by a system based on competition, which drives prices down and increases quality and diversity, to the benefit of consumers and society as a whole. In a competition-based system, mobile services would be made available to society as a whole, including the less well-off, under better conditions than if they were provided in a 'public' or 'universal' system.

(b) Fixed networks.   Despite the reform, the former national operators have been **1.134** able to maintain, in most Member States, a level of dominance on fixed networks. Partial networks have been installed by competitors. These efforts have been limited, however, to dense areas (cities, etc) or links where telecommunications traffic[91] is high.[92] It remains too expensive for competitors to finance networks in other circumstances. In particular, competitors are not in a position to finance the construction of a new 'local loop'. That concept refers to the wire linking subscribers to a local area exchange. These wires are not used intensively but are limited to a few subscribers. As a result, the cost of installing these wires cannot be amortised on numerous customers or communications.

Regulation of the local loop.   This situation created a difficulty for the objective **1.135** sought by the European legislator. For these institutions, it was indeed essential to ensure the development of electronic communications services. Services would develop only if networks were available for the communications to be transmitted. Measures were taken, in this context, to facilitate access to existing infrastructure. It was also attempted to upgrade the broadcasting networks in order to be able to organise the transmission, through these networks, of traditional telecommunications services.

Mobile technology.   Not only did the former national operators dominate fixed **1.136** telecommunications for decades. They were in most EU countries also the first undertakings present on the market for mobile technology. This was due to their experience and their financial capacity. In most Member States, existing regulation also reserved mobile markets for the existing operator. The situation has however evolved. As was the case for fixed telecommunications, mobile markets were opened to competition. The result was the entry of new actors in all segments of the industry. Competition appeared on the market both for mobile services and networks, a development which had not occurred for fixed telecommunications.

Cost differences.   This difference mirrors the discrepancy in the costs to be **1.137** incurred installing and maintaining a fixed, or a mobile, infrastructure. The cost of carrying out activity in the mobile market is much lower than that relating to an activity in fixed communications. Since it is less expensive to establish a mobile network than to install a network for fixed communications, barriers to entry are lower. As a result, entrants were able to establish themselves rapidly on mobile markets. In most Member States, former national operators have been able to maintain a significant market share. That share is however generally lower than their presence on markets for fixed communications.

Specific regulations.   A difference thus remains between the network markets **1.138** for mobile and fixed technologies. Costs constitute a barrier to entry on the latter

---

[91] Traffic in terms of communications.   [92] eg between Europe and the US.

markets, less so on the former. As a result, competition has flourished on the former, and less so on the latter. That difference calls for an adaptation of the regulation to both kinds of market. Strict regulation must be maintained on the markets for fixed electronic communications, to ensure wide access to existing facilities. The same degree of regulation does not need to be established on the market for mobile services, where competition can more easily develop through the interaction of market forces.

(2) Convergence between broadcasting, telecommunications and the information technology industry

Introduction

1.139   **Digitalisation.**   A convergence is nowadays taking place between broadcasting, telecommunications and information or computer-related activities. These sectors were formerly considered as separate fields. They are now increasingly being brought together. The factor behind that process is mainly of a technological nature. Scientists have made it possible to express as computer data the signals that are transmitted in broadcasting and telecommunications. Broadcasting and telecommunications originally involved 'analogue signals'. In that technique, sounds and images are represented in the form of a wave. By contrast, data stored and processed on computers are represented in 'digital form'. They are divided into units that are represented by a particular sequence of electronic current.

1.140   **Technology, industry and the law.**   Scientific progress has made it possible to use digital techniques to express sounds and images. As a result, it is now possible to transmit these categories of data together. It is also possible to combine them and provide multimedia products/services. This technological development has been followed by moves within the industry. Businesses have realised they can offer new products and services to their customers. They have thus embraced convergence, in the hope of creating new markets. As technology and businesses have changed, regulators have realised they have to react.

1.141   **The 1999 Review.**   Convergence has given rise to regulatory debate within the European Union. The authorities were aware of the necessity of providing a framework within which activities would develop in conformity with values deemed essential at European level. The Commission therefore carried out in 1999 a thorough review of the existing European legislation.[93] An important challenge was to determine how convergence should be addressed in regulation. An approach was

---

[93] See Communication from the Commission to the European Parliament, the Council, the Economic and Social Committee and the Committee of the Regions, Towards a New Framework for Electronic Communications Infrastructure and Associated Services—The 1999 Communications Review, COM (1999) 539. Other documents are available on the site set up by the European Commission on the 1999 review. See http://europa.eu.int/infosoc/telecompolicy/review99/review99.htm.

adopted whereby two principles had to be combined. On the one hand, there was a desire that all transmissions should be treated alike. On the other hand, there remains a need for specific regulation adapted to particular issues arising in given segments of the electronic communications market.

Convergence for transmissions

All transmissions treated alike.   In the NRF, all transmissions are treated alike,   **1.142** whatever the segment they belong to. In this approach, the transmission of broadcast services is no longer distinguished from the transmission of telecommunications services. Distinct legal or regulatory regimes are no longer applied to them. The concepts of 'telecommunications' and 'broadcasting' may disappear, as far as the transmission of the related services is concerned. Both categories are designated using a single concept, 'electronic communications'.

> *Framework Directive, Preamble, recital 5.* 'The convergence of the telecommunications, media and information technology sectors means that all transmission networks and services should be covered by a single regulatory framework.'

Extension of regime applicable to telecommunications.   The regime applicable   **1.143** to the transmission of electronic signals is not completely new. To put that regime in place the European legislator has resorted to the rules that were applicable to telecommunications under the old framework. In the new approach, these rules are in substance extended to other forms of transmission (in particular broadcasting and data transmission).

Classic telecommunications activities.   This approach does not raise difficulties   **1.144** for classic telecommunications activities, that is, voice telephony. That service was subject to the regime applicable to telecommunications under the old framework. The rules then applicable to that service do not really change with the adoption of the NRF. A new regime applies but on this point does not differ in substance from the previous regime.

Broadcasting networks.   The situation is similar for broadcasting networks. As   **1.145** will be submitted, these networks have been progressively subjected to the rules applicable to telecoms networks. The authorities had realised that competition would not really develop as long as one network only could be used. To increase efficiency, they encouraged the use of broadcasting networks for the provision of telecommunications services.[94] Broadcasting networks were thus as regards this

---

[94] These networks can carry telecommunications, provided they are upgraded to allow interactive transmissions. Broadcasting normally implies unilateral transmissions. Services—typically TV programmes—are transmitted from the broadcaster to the recipients. By contrast, telecommunications imply interaction. Voice telephony, for example, consists of bilateral conversations being transmitted. As broadcasting and telecommunications converge, this difference will tend to disappear. TV programmes, for instance, make increasing use of interactivity. In parallel, telecommunications may also encompass unilateral aspects (eg data transmission).

aspect brought in the course of the reform within the scope of telecommunications rules. That development occurred prior to the adoption of the NRF. The entry into force of the NRF should thus change little as regards the regime applicable to these networks.

1.146 **Traditional broadcasting services.** A different analysis must be made for transmissions which were previously regarded as broadcasting. These transmissions were not subject to the old regulatory framework. The situation changes with the NRF, as these activities now fall under the application of the new rules. With the adoption of the NRF, broadcasting services are subject to a new, and different, regime.

Absence of convergence regarding content

1.147 **Content not subject to a single framework.** In the NRF, the Parliament and Council have separated transmission from content. For content, they have not used the approach adopted for transmission. Pursuant to the Framework Directive, content is not subject to the NRF. As a result, no rule dealing with the content of transmissions can be found, in principle, in the NRF.

> *Framework Directive, Preamble, recital 5.* 'It is necessary to separate the regulation of transmission from the regulation of content. This framework does not therefore cover the content of services delivered over electronic communications networks using electronic communications services.'[95]

1.148 **Influence of content on transmission.** A difficulty with this approach is that a distinction is not always easily made between content and transmission. Decisions on one aspect often have consequences for the other. Where, for example, an authority wants to ensure cultural pluralism in content production, it must allocate resources in a way impeding one production from taking precedence over others. In the absence of that policy, alternatives would be eliminated. Network capacity constitutes one of these resources. If that capacity is limited,[96] the authority must allocate it to allow producers of alternative programmes to reach customers. An objective relating to content (pluralism) thus has consequences on how capacity (transmission) is regulated.

1.149 **Influence of transmission on content.** Conversely, transmission may affect content. A distinction is generally made between various forms of transmission. *(a)* In some instances, one message is sent from a central point to a multitude of addressees. That mechanism is generally used in broadcasting, where films or programmes are transmitted to viewers from one channel or producer. *(b)* In other instances, data—

---

[95] For an example of content provided via electronic communications services, see Case C-384/93 *Alpine Investments BV v Minister van Financiën* [1995] ECR I-1141. In that case, undertakings offered financial services by telephone to potential recipients established in other Member States.
[96] If there is no limitation on capacity, there will be no difficulty; all producers will be able to reach their customers.

including video—are transmitted from one point to another. That system is used for individual communications. Users normally exchange information on a one-to-one basis. *(c)* With the development of the internet, the latter technique is increasingly used. It remains the standard for communication among individuals. At the same time, it becomes a useful technique for communications between broadcasters and users. Networks make it possible to adapt supply to individual demand. In that context, broadcasting tends to become a point-to-point communication as well. It sets in train a process whereby a producer provides a viewer with individualised or quasi-individualised[97] content.

One sort of content. These point-to-point, or point-to-multipoint techniques, **1.150** and their development, may be influenced by regulation. Suppose that authorities set standards for digital broadcasting via satellite. The establishment of standards allows manufacturers to use the same technology everywhere. Resorting to that technique becomes cheaper. The attention of content-producing undertakings is attracted, as they try to minimise their costs. Given the low price of the technology, these undertakings resort to satellite transmissions. Broadcasting satellites are however placed at high altitudes. They do not permit point-to-point communication. By contrast, they make it easy to broadcast data (images, etc) from one point to a multitude of viewers in a given region. These data must however be standard in nature. They cannot be transmitted via satellites with a substantial quantity of individual content.

Scenario influenced by regulation. In this scenario, one sort of data (standard **1.151** data) and thus of content is encouraged by the adoption of a specific regulation concerning transmission (standards). The imposition of a specific standard, regarding one form of transmission, has an influence on the type of content likely to be produced.

Rules applicable to content

No common rules for content. Another difficulty generated by the NRF is **1.152** that, despite convergence, content remains subject to different rules depending on the sector in which the service takes place. Thus, content is not treated in the same fashion in the broadcasting industry and in the telecoms field. On that point, convergence has not taken place.

What rules apply to content?. If content is not subject to the NRF, what rules **1.153** should then be applied to it? Indications are provided in the Framework Directive. According to the Preamble, the NRF does not bring any change to the rules governing content. Content issues must thus be solved outside the NRF in already

---

[97] For instance, transmission of video at the time requested by the viewer, change of sequences in a film according to the wishes expressed by the viewer, etc.

existing, or future, rules. Examples are provided in the Preamble. *(a)* Information Society services are covered by European Parliament and Council Directive (EC) 2000/31 on certain legal aspects of Information Society services, in particular electronic commerce, in the internal market ('e-Commerce Directive').[98] *(b)* The content of TV programmes is covered by Council Directive (EEC) 89/552 on the co-ordination of certain provisions laid down by law, regulation or administrative action in Member States concerning the pursuit of television broadcasting activities,[99] as amended by European Parliament and Council Directive (EC) 97/36.[100] *(c)* In the discussion on content, the Preamble to the Framework Directive finally refers to financial services. No specific instrument is, however, mentioned in connection with these services. The rules applicable to electronic communications with financial content may be found in other instruments.[101]

1.154 **European and national rules.** The examples presented in the previous paragraph refer to European instruments. The Framework Directive makes it clear, however, that national measures may also be applied. The rules applicable to content may thus have a European or a national origin.

> *Framework Directive, Preamble, recital 7.* The 'framework is . . . without prejudice to measures taken at Community or national level in respect of such services, in compliance with Community law'.

1.155 **Constraints on Member States.** In that respect, it should be recalled that limits are imposed on legislative activity by the Member States as a result of their membership of the European Union. *(a) Prohibition on hindering European goals.* Wherever they regulate, Member States must refrain from adopting measures which may adversely affect objectives pursued by the European Union (Article 10 EC). They are not allowed to take measures running counter to what is being sought in the NRF (for example the development of competition). *(b) Obligation to contribute to European goals.* Pursuant to the same provision (Article 10 EC), Member States must adopt measures that will facilitate the achievement of the Community's tasks. That obligation imposes a positive duty on the Member States. The latter must actively use, in the areas placed under their jurisdiction, the tools allowing them to contribute to the fulfilment of European objectives.[102] *(c) Harmonisation.* Wherever

---

[98] [2000] OJ L178/1.   [99] [1989] OJ L298/23.   [100] [1997] OJ L202/60.

[101] For a general analysis of the subject, see Report on E-commerce and Financial Services to the Financial Services Policy Group at http://europa.eu.int/comm/internal_market/en/finances/general/fspg-report.htm.

[102] An area where no power has been transferred to the European legislator remains, as far as powers are concerned, with the Member States. The European legislator does not intervene, even on the basis of implicit powers entrusted to it by the EC Treaty. In such an area, Member States will not, however, be able to regulate as they would like. They have to refrain from any behaviour that would jeopardise the attainment of European goals. They will also be obliged to adopt measures likely to contribute to the realisation of such goals.

the European legislator intervenes by way of harmonisation, the freedom of the Member States is limited. Such States may adopt regulation in the area only if, and to the extent, the harmonisation undertaken by the European legislator is not complete. When an area is harmonised, the Member States lose their power to adopt their own objectives and measures.[103]

Harmonisation.   These remarks concerning harmonisation merit some explana-   **1.156**
tion. Complete harmonisation implies that Member States are prevented from relying on justifications embodied in the Treaty. However, harmonisation is not always complete. An illustration can be taken from the Authorisations Directive. *(a)* That directive harmonises fully the formal and material conditions that may be attached to entry on the market. On these points, harmonisation can be deemed complete. From the Preamble to that directive, as well as from the provisions contained in that instrument, it appears that the European legislator sought to regulate completely the conditions imposed in connection with market entry. *(b)* One aspect is not covered, however. The European legislator has not decided that authorisations granted in one Member State are to be recognised in the other European countries. On that point, harmonisation cannot be deemed to be complete. Member States thus keep the power to apply their national legislation in this respect.

Limitations on national power.   The possibility of applying national legislation   **1.157**
does not imply that Member States are entirely free to act. For instance, they may not adopt any measure which contradicts the provisions contained in the directives or the objectives that are sought in those instruments (see Article 10 EC.) Furthermore, they are not allowed to adopt measures that may be regarded as barriers to the free provision of services within the Union. These measures may sometimes be justified on the basis of an exception or an essential requirement accepted under European law (these exceptions and requirements are embodied in Articles 45 and 46 EC via Article 55 EC, as regards the free provision of services within the Union). That justification is assessed by the Commission, and by the ECJ in cases where judicial proceedings are initiated. Once complete harmonisation takes place, Member States lose their right to invoke a requirement or an exception. They may not add any additional measure to those adopted at European level.

(3) Probable evolution

The institutional dimension of convergence

Rules and authorities.   Convergence has so far implied, from a regulatory point   **1.158**
of view, that rules concerning broadcasting, telecommunications and the information industry have been increasingly brought together as regards transmission.

---

[103] PJ Kapteyn & P Verloren van Themaat, *Introduction to the Law of the European Communities* (2000) et seq (ed L Gormley).

Few initiatives have, however, been taken to examine the institutional conse-quences of that development. Each sector was formerly governed by a specific set of rules, and by a particular authority. Through convergence, rules are being brought together. That development is likely to have an impact on how authori-ties carry out their activities.

1.159 **Co-operation, consultation, integration.** To take into account the institu-tional dimension of convergence, a first step was made by asking authorities to co-operate. Pursuant to the NRF, this co-operation may take the form of an exchange of information or mutual consultations before the adoption and/or the publication of decisions. That first step does not however solve all difficulties. Co-operation and mutual consultation probably help avoid contradictory deci-sions between the authorities concerned. They do not provide, however, any guar-antee against the adoption of conflicting positions. To avoid such an outcome, a second step should be taken. In that step, consideration should be given to the question whether it is necessary, or even useful, to maintain different authorities, if the fields concerned by convergence are in the process of merging. A reasonable prediction is that institutional approximations are bound to take place, with authorities being asked to integrate. A partial, or total, integration would facilitate the tasks of undertakings, as it would provide one-stop shopping for all issues relating to electronic communications.

A distinction between content and services

1.160 **Ambiguous concept.** 'Content' is by nature an ambiguous concept. When it uses that concept, the European legislator sometimes refers to the object of a transmission: voice, images, data. In other contexts, it designates, with that con-cept, the service performed via electronic communications. This is the case where the Parliament and Council refer to financial services in the discussion concern-ing content. In that context, the expression 'financial services' does not designate the content of the transmission as such. One does not say whether voice, images or data are being transmitted. The expression rather refers, as stated earlier, to the kind of service that is performed. In fact it designates the economic sector where the transmission is taking place. In this case, one would say that financial services are being performed. That performance may take place through a variety of elec-tronic channels. Thus, clients may be approached via the telephone (traditional telecommunications), through television programmes (classic broadcasting) or even by e-mails (data, information industry).

1.161 **Link between the two concepts.** Content in the first sense proposed above (what is being transmitted) has no connection with the services provided. As has been submitted, financial services may be provided through sound, images and data. As a corollary, one can say that one or several sorts of data may be used to provide various services. Images, for instance, may be used to provide financial services but also cultural programmes or a channel for customers to do their shopping.

Regulatory consequences.   The analysis has consequences for the enactment and implementation of regulation. Electronic communications are used for services or activities that belong to separate sectors of the economy. It does not make sense to subject them to the same rules for the sole reason that they are provided via electronic means. The channel used to provide services does not have an impact on the service provided. As a result, it should not have an effect on the regulation applied to it. For instance, cultural programme broadcasting cannot be treated like the provision of financial services. In both cases, special rules must be adopted in connection with the values attached to each sector (such as pluralism in cultural programmes and solvency in the banking sector). In that regard, one cannot regret that the European legislator has maintained separate rules for different activities. **1.162**

A regulation aimed at services.   By contrast, one should probably encourage authorities to treat similarly all transmissions relating to a single service. There is no reason, for instance, to distinguish services of a financial nature on the basis of the electronic channel used in order to contact clients. Financial services provided through telecoms or broadcasting ultimately raise identical issues. They are proposed at a distance. Hence, the consumer does not have the possibility of watching the provider.[104] Similarly, there is no reason to introduce different regulation for entertainment depending on the channel used to provide the service—television, computer, radio or telephone.[105] In such a context, the channel hardly matters. For instance, pornography ought to be prohibited in all entertainment services whatever the technology used to transmit communications. What really matters is the value to be protected—in this case children and public morality. **1.163**

An example taken from the e-Commerce Directive

e-Commerce Directive.   Progress can be expected in this direction. An example can be taken from the e-Commerce Directive. That instrument governs services provided to clients via electronic means throughout the internal market. It identifies, for instance, the rules applicable to the provision of services across borders in the European Union. Clearly, there would be room for applying identical rules to these services whatever the electronic communications channel used (voice, images, data). This orientation was followed in Article 2 of the directive. Pursuant to that provision, the e-Commerce Directive applies to 'information society **1.164**

---

[104] Where an undertaking wants to approach customers for financial services, it has a choice between various communications channels: broadcasting, telephony, e-mails. The contact with the prospective customer should probably be treated along the same lines, whatever the medium.

[105] Suppose an entertainment company wants to broadcast theatrical performances. Again, several possibilities are open to it: TV, radio, internet, mobile telephony. Why should these communications channels be treated differently, if the issues they raise are similar?

services'.[106] These services encompass all activities normally carried out in return for payment, at a distance, by electronic means, at the request of the recipient of the service. That definition contains no distinction based on the nature of the transmission. As specified further in the e-Commerce Directive, 'electronic' means that the services are provided with electronic equipment for the processing (including digital compression) and storage of data. It also means that the services are transmitted, conveyed and received by wire, by radio, by optical means or by other electromagnetic means.

1.165 **Exception.** An exception is made in the directive, however, for radio broadcasting as well as television broadcasting services.[107] As a result of that exception, radio broadcasting services do not fall under the ambit of the directive. Hence, information society services are not subject to the same rules where they are provided through different communicative channels (broadcasting, telecoms). Such a situation cannot really be accepted. As stated, the technology used to provide services should not constitute a prime concern for lawyers. There is no reason to submit services to different rules where they raise identical issues.

1.166 The regulatory treatment of convergence

Old regulatory framework	New regulatory framework (NRF)	Expected developments
Broadcasting, telecommunications and information-related activities were addressed in different regulations.	**Context.** Activities relating to these sectors progressively merge from an industrial and technological point of view. The European legislator indicates its intention of drawing the consequences of that development in terms of regulation.	**Context.** Convergence intensifies.
	Transmission. Transmission is treated alike in the NRF, irrespective of the sector it belongs to.[108] This new development is brought about through the extension of	**Transmission.** Unchanged.

(cont.)

---

[106] European Parliament and Council Directive (EC) 98/34 laying down a procedure for the provision of information in the field of technical standards and regulations, [1998] OJ L204/37, as amended by Directive (EC) 98/48 [1998] OJ L207/18.

[107] Within the meaning of Council Directive (EEC) 89/552 on the co-ordination of certain provisions laid down by Law, Regulation or Administrative Action in Member States concerning the pursuit of television broadcasting activities [1989] OJ L298/23.

[108] The term 'sectors' is still used to the extent that it is possible to distinguish sectors in communications and information-related activities. As stated, convergence brings sectors together, new products and services emerge and it is increasingly difficult to separate them.

Old regulatory framework	New regulatory framework (NRF)	Expected developments
	telecommunications regulation to all electronic communications, particularly broadcasting.	
	Content. The NRF does not apply to content. Content remains subject to other rules, which may be set out in European or national regulation. Limitations are imposed on the Member States, particularly in areas where the European legislator has already intervened.	**Content.** Convergence will probably occur in the regulation applicable to content. Services will probably be treated in the same fashion, independently of the nature of the services transmitted (voice, images, data).
		Institutional aspects. Convergence will also have institutional effects. Transmission is now subject to various authorities depending on the sector (broadcasting, telecoms, information). As sectors converge, the relevant authorities have to co-operate, and possibly integrate.

G. Main WTO Rules on Telecommunications

(1) The WTO architecture

Final Act. WTO law consists of several instruments, some of which are relevant **1.167** to determine the legal regime applicable to audiovisual and telecommunications services. *(a)* On top of the pyramid is the 'Final Act'.[109] This document was adopted at the end of the Uruguay Round. It is very short and basically refers to annexed documents that contain the bulk of the provisions adhered to by the Member States. The Final Act was meant to contain the signatures of the acceding States.

Agreement establishing the WTO. In its provisions, the Final Act refers, **1.168** among others, to the 'Agreement establishing the World Trade Organisation'.[110] This second document is probably the most important, as it not only creates the WTO but establishes the provisions under which that organisation will carry out its activities. The Agreement in fact lays down the new foundations for multilateral commercial relations and negotiations.

---

[109] http://www.wto.org/english/docs_e/legal_e/03-fa.pdf.
[110] http://www.wto.org/english/docs_e/legal_e/04-wto.pdf.

1.169 **Annexes.**   The Agreement itself has several annexes that organise the liberalisation process. Annex 1 contains the material provisions, ie provisions which state what rules apply on markets parties have agreed to open to world trade. These provisions are divided into three categories, depending on the issues that are dealt with. The liberalisation of goods is addressed in the 'General Agreement on Tariffs and Trade' (GATT);[111] that of services is dealt with in the 'General Agreement on Trade in Services' (GATS);[112] and intellectual property is addressed in the 'Agreement on Trade-Related Aspects of Intellectual Property Rights'.[113]

1.170 **Other annexes.**   Other Annexes[114] organise additional aspects of liberalisation. A mechanism is established to solve disputes (Annex 2). Another aims at reviewing trade policy (Annex 3). A final annex (Annex 4) deals with issues that are dealt with on a plurilateral, rather than multilateral basis (for example government procurement).

(2) Specific provisions on telecommunications

1.171 **No convergence.**   WTO rules continue to work on the basis of a distinction between the telecoms and broadcasting or audiovisual sectors. They have not taken into consideration, at this stage, the movement of convergence which is currently unfolding between these sectors and on which, as has been stated, the NRF is based. For this reason, a comparison between European and international rules remains difficult.

1.172 **Specific instruments.**   In addition to these general instruments, described in the previous section, specific documents are particularly important for telecommunications networks and services.[115] They are examined in the following paragraphs.

1.173 **Annex on telecommunications.**   A specific document on telecommunications has been annexed to the GATS. This document clarifies what measures may be adopted by States on their national territory on markets concerning telecommunications transport networks and services. It in fact mostly concerns liberalised non-telecoms activities (such as financial services) that require for their effective performance the use of telecoms networks and services. Suppose these firms were not allowed to use these telecoms-related facilities. This would in effect mean that they were prevented from making full use of existing means to enter the target market. Liberalisation would then be only nominal, but not effective.[116]

---

[111] http://www.wto.org/english/docs_e/legal_e/06-gatt.pdf.
[112] http://www.wto.org/english/docs_e/legal_e/26-gats.pdf.
[113] http://www.wto.org/english/docs_e/legal_e/27-trips.pdf.
[114] See generally http://www.wto.org/english/docs_e/legal_e/final_e.htm.
[115] See generally http://www.wto.org/english/tratop_e/serv_e/telecom_e/telecom_e.htm.
[116] http://www.wto.org/english/tratop_e/serv_e/12-tel_e.htm.

Ministerial decision. After adopting the Uruguay agreements, the representa- **1.174** tives of some Members decided to continue negotiating for further liberalisation in telecommunications. That decision was taken by Ministers, hence the name given to it: Ministerial Decision on Negotiations on Basic Telecommunications ('Ministerial Decision'). It was based on the benefits that, they thought, would flow from market opening in that sector. Telecommunications are indeed an important motor for economic growth—both per se and as tools necessary for firms to carry out their business.[117]

Fourth Protocol. Subsequent to the Ministerial Decisions, negotiations were **1.175** carried out on market opening for telecommunications transport networks and services. They resulted in the adoption of Commitments by a significant number of Members. Some demanded that various telecoms markets be exempted from the National Treatment Clause. The Schedules of Specific Commitments were gathered with the List of Exemptions in the 'Fourth Protocol to the General Agreement on Trade in Services' ('Fourth Protocol'), which was annexed to the GATS.[118]

Reference Paper. Finally, Members accepted the delineation of the kind of **1.176** regulations they thought would be appropriate in the new liberalised telecoms environment. An exercise of this kind had already been carried out in the Annex on Telecommunications. It was continued, and further developed, in the Reference Paper. This document is unique. It is the first to spell out what regulatory measures are considered appropriate. This book concentrates on these regulatory principles, where compatibility with WTO provisions is envisaged.

(3) Definition given to telecommunications networks and services

Generic definition. Telecommunications are generically defined in the Annex **1.177** on Telecommunications. Pursuant to that instrument, the term refers to the transmission of signals. The transmission must occur electronically. Additional information may be found in the same Annex in a discussion concerning the concept of 'public telecommunications transport service'. Telecommunications are then described in a similar fashion.

> *Annex on Telecommunications.* ' "Telecommunications" means the transmission and reception of signals by any electromagnetic means',[119] 'typically involving the real-time transmission of customer-supplied information between two or more points without any end-to-end change in the form or content of the customer's information.'[120]

Basic telecommunications. A distinction is made in WTO provisions, **1.178** including the Reference Paper, between Basic Telecommunications and Value Added Telecommunications. *(a)* Basic Telecommunications are defined as

---

[117] http://www.wto.org/english/tratop_e/serv_e/telecom_e/tel22_e.htm.
[118] http://www.wto.org/english/tratop_e/serv_e/4prote_e.htm.
[119] Annex on Telecommunications, para 3(a).   [120] Para 3 (b).

'telecommunications transport networks and services'.[121] In that expression, the concept of 'transport' plays an essential role. As defined in that expression, Basic Telecommunications consists of transmitting information. In principle, there is no contribution whatsoever in that process to the production or processing of such information. From that perspective, telecommunications is a purely mechanical device: information is being transported from one point to another, without intervention in content. *(b)* Value Added Telecommunications encompass all activities whereby an additional service is provided to the client. Suppliers do not limit their service to the transmission of information. They provide additional assistance, for example by enhancing the form or content or by providing storage and retrieval facilities.

1.179 **Regulatory regime.** Basic telecommunications were provided in most Members on a public monopoly basis at the time of the Uruguay Round. As a result, Members were reluctant to open their borders for these activities. By contrast, value added telecommunications were provided from the outset by private undertakings operating in a competitive environment. They encompass services based on new technologies requiring high levels of investment. As they lacked the necessary resources and expertise, public monopolies were not in a position to enter these markets. The regulatory principles that are examined in this book concern basic telecommunications networks and services, as effective competition is deemed to exist on the markets for value added telecommunications.

---

[121] Para 1.

2

PRINCIPLES AND GENERAL RULES APPLICABLE THROUGHOUT THE FRAMEWORK

A. The Prohibition of Exclusive Rights, Special Rights and Other Regulatory Restrictions

(1) A key feature of the reform

2.01 **Elimination of monopolies.** A key feature of the reform carried out in European electronic communications markets is the removal of exclusive rights. As stated above, European markets for electronic communications were reserved over many decades for one national operator per Member State (with the exception of Finland, which has a particular market structure). In the context of this book, exclusive rights are prerogatives granted by public authorities and allowing one undertaking to carry out activities on one or several given markets.[1] Exclusive rights thus appear as barriers to entry, granted to a single undertaking on each of the markets involved. These barriers to entry have a regulatory character and are established by a public authority.

2.02 **Legal and regulatory advantages.** The change was not limited to the abolition of exclusive rights. The reform took on a wider scope by initiating a move directed against any form of legal or regulatory advantage granted to undertakings in violation of basic regulatory principles. The purpose was to introduce competition on the market. That goal would only succeed if undertakings were assessed by the markets on the basis of their own merits. Following this logic, the measures taken regarding exclusive rights were extended with a prohibition directed against special rights. A similar prohibition was directed against all other forms of regulatory measure imposing undue restrictions on access by undertakings to electronic communications markets and/or the exercise of activities on those markets.

(2) Applicable instruments

2.03 **Original instruments.** The measures prohibiting exclusive rights, special rights and other regulatory restrictions have been introduced in various liberalisation directives adopted by the Commission over the last 15 years. There have in substance been two main liberalisation directives—one concerning terminal equipment and the other networks and services. These directives have been amended several times.

2.04 **Terminal equipment.** The first directive was Commission Directive (EEC) 88/301 on competition in the markets in telecommunications terminal equipment[2] ('Terminal Equipment Liberalisation Directive'). This is still in force

---

[1] In some instances, undertakings may also grant exclusive rights to their partners. This is the case, typically, for producers wishing to distribute their products in various zones organised on the basis of exclusive rights granted to their agents. On this subject, see Commission Regulation (EC) No 1400/2002 of 31 July 2002 on the application of Art 81(3) of the Treaty to categories of vertical agreements and concerted practices in the motor vehicle sector [2002] OJ L203/30.

[2] [1988] OJ L131/73. That directive was amended by Commission Directive (EC) 94/46 amending Directive 88/301/EEC and Directive 90/388/EEC in particular with regard to satellite communications [1994] OJ L268/15.

today. It deals with the marketing of terminal equipment across Member States in the internal market. This subject does not fall within the ambit of this book.

Networks and services.   The second instrument was Commission Directive **2.05** (EEC) 90/388 on competition in the markets for telecommunications services[3] ('Services Directive'). This is no longer in force, and has been replaced by another instrument, Commission Directive (EC) 2002/77 on competition in the markets for electronic communications networks and services[4] ('Consolidated Services Directive'). In the latter directive, as in the instruments that preceded it, the provision of access to networks is analysed as a service. For this reason it is considered that the new directive concerns networks and services.

In this book.   Two liberalisation directives are therefore applicable at the present **2.06** time: the Terminal Equipment Liberalisation Directive and the Consolidated Services Directive. This book focuses on the markets for services (including the provision of access to networks). As a result, emphasis is placed on the provisions contained in the Consolidated Services Directive. This does not imply that the directive on terminal equipment has lost all relevance, since it remains applicable to some markets in the European Union (marketing of terminal equipment across the Member States). Further, it contains principles that still have some relevance for the markets in networks and services. Under the case law, this directive determines obligations imposed on Member States by the rules of the EC Treaty, including the competition rules. It thus provides indications of the implications of that part of the law for the organisation of the electronic communications sector, even if these indications are not embodied in an instrument dealing specifically with networks and/or services.

(3) Historical perspective

Two main instruments.   As stated, the European Commission adopted at the **2.07** end of the 1980s and the beginning of the 1990s two instruments referred to here as the Terminal Equipment Liberalisation Directive and the Services Directive. These instruments were based on similar principles, which still serve as cornerstones for the organisation that was imposed on the markets.

---

[3] [1990] OJ L192/10. That directive has been amended by the following instruments: Commission Directive (EC) 94/46 amending Directive 88/301/EEC and Directive 90/388/EEC in particular with regard to satellite communications [1994] OJ L268/15; Commission Directive (EC) 95/51 amending Directive 90/388/EEC with regard to the abolition of the restrictions on the use of cable television networks for the provision of already liberalised telecommunications services [1995] OJ L256/49; Commission Directive (EC) 96/2 of 16 January 1996 amending Directive 90/388/EEC with regard to mobile and personal communications [1996] OJ L20/59; Commission Directive (EC) 96/19 amending Directive 90/388/EEC with regard to the implementation of full competition in telecommunications markets [1996] OJ L74/13; Commission Directive (EC) 1999/64 amending Directive 90/388/EEC in order to ensure that telecommunications networks and cable TV networks owned by a single operator are separate legal entities [1999] OJ L74/13.
[4] [2002] OJ L249/21.

2.08 **First modifications.** Following their adoption, these directives were amended several times. The first modifications were introduced as a result of a ruling issued by the ECJ. An application had been made by several Member States against the Terminal Equipment Liberalisation Directive. The ECJ issued a ruling confirming in substance the power of the Commission to intervene in the telecoms sector on the basis of Article 86(3) EC. At the same time, it sanctioned the Commission on two grounds. *(a)* The concept of special rights, which is examined later in this book, had not been sufficiently defined. *(b)* Some provisions contained in the directive imposed obligations on undertakings. This was considered a violation of the nature of the directives. Pursuant to the Treaty, directives create rights and/or obligations addressed to Member States.[5] After the judgment was given, the Commission amended the two directives to take these criticisms into account. The amendments were embodied in Commission Directive (EC) 94/46 amending Directive 88/301/EEC and Directive 90/388/EEC in particular with regard to satellite communications.[6]

2.09 **Subsequent changes.** Further amendments were made to these basic instruments as the reform unfolded. These modifications established new principles to be complied with by Member States in the organisation of their telecommunications markets. They affected mainly the instrument dealing with networks and services. The changes were made in substance by the following instruments: *(a)* Commission Directive (EC) 95/51 amending Directive 90/388/ECC with regard to the abolition of the restrictions on the use of cable television networks for the provision of already liberalised telecommunications services;[7] *(b)* Commission Directive (EC) 96/2 of 10 January 1990, amending Directive 90/38/EEC with regard to mobile and personal communications;[8] *(c)* Commission Directive (EC) 96/19 amending Directive 90/388/EEC with regard to the implementation of full competition in telecommunications markets;[9] *(d)* Commission Directive (EC) 1999/64 of 23 June 1999 amending Directive 90/388/EEC in order to ensure that telecommunications networks and cable TV networks owned by a single operator are separate legal entities.[10]

(4) The prohibition of exclusive rights

The prohibition

2.10 **Abolition of monopolies.** Pursuant to the Consolidated Services Directive, no exclusive right can be created or maintained on the markets for electronic communications networks and services on the European territory. The prohibition is formulated at Article 2 of the directive. It confirms that monopolistic

---

[5] More can be found on these aspects in the sections devoted to special rights and to provisions applying to undertakings (see paras 2.25–2.40).   [6] [1994] OJ L268/15.
[7] [1995] OJ L256/49.   [8] [1996] OJ L20/59.   [9] [1996] OJ L74/13.
[10] [1999] OJ L175/39.

organisations must be abandoned in the Member States as regards markets for electronic communications. As it is clear, precise and unconditional, this prohibition has direct effect. As a result of that direct effect, undertakings and individuals can bring cases to a national court in cases where the prohibition is not complied with. The State will then be ordered by the national court to put an end to the violation. It may also be compelled to repair any damage that may have been suffered.

> *Consolidated Services Directive, Article 2(1).* 'Member States shall not grant or maintain in force exclusive . . . rights for the establishment and/or the provision of electronic communications networks, or for the provision of publicly available electronic communications services.'

Broadcasting networks included.   The prohibition does not only concern for-   **2.11** mer telecommunications networks and/or services. It also applies to broadcasting networks, ie networks used to carry radio and/or television content. The prohibition means that the Member States may not impede undertakings from establishing new networks or providing new services. This marks a far-reaching development, as broadcasting networks and services have often been reserved to a few actors placed under public control or influence.

> *Consolidated Services Directive, Preamble, recital 8.* 'The definition of electronic communications networks should also mean that Member States are not permitted to restrict the right of an operator to establish, extend and/or provide a cable network on the ground that such network could also be used for the transmission of radio and television programming. In particular, special or exclusive rights which amount to restricting the use of electronic communications networks for the transmission and distribution of television signals are contrary to Article 86(1), read in conjunction with Article 43 (right of establishment) and/or Article 82(b) of the EC Treaty insofar as they have the effect of permitting a dominant undertaking to limit "production, markets or technical development to the prejudice of consumers".'

Difference with regard to old liberalisation directives.   The same prohibition   **2.12** existed in the Services Directive. The scope given to that prohibition has however changed. The prohibition was formerly limited to the telecommunications sector. As stated above, it now extends to broadcasting networks and/or services.[11]

> *Services Directive.* 'Members States shall withdraw all those measures which grant . . . exclusive rights for the provision of telecommunications services, including the establishment and the provision of telecommunication networks required for the provision of such services.'[12]

---

[11] A similar prohibition may be found in the Terminal Equipment Liberalisation Directive. See Art 2, as amended. 'Member States which have granted special or exclusive rights to undertakings shall ensure that all exclusive rights are withdrawn.' This prohibition is however limited, as regard appliances, to telecommunications equipment. This limitation does not stem from the desire on the part of the Member States to grant exclusive rights to radio and/or television broadcasting or receiving equipment, since the markets for these kinds of equipment are indeed open to competition.   [12] Services Directive, Art 2, as amended.

2.13 **Prohibitions on specific markets.** In addition to the general prohibition concerning exclusive rights, the Consolidated Services Directive contains more specific prohibitions directed against exclusive rights in given sectors or markets. Thus, the prohibition is explicitly stated with respect to directories. Similarly, exclusive rights are prohibited on the markets involving the use of radio frequencies.

> *Consolidated Services Directive, Article 5.* 'Member States shall ensure that all exclusive and/or special rights with regard to the establishment and provision of directory services on their territory, including both the publication of directories and directory enquiry services, are abolished.' *Consolidated Services Directive, Article 4.* 'Without prejudice to specific criteria and procedures adopted by Member States to grant rights of use of radio frequencies to providers of radio or television broadcast content services with a view to pursuing general interest objectives in conformity with Community law: *(1)* Member States shall not grant exclusive or special rights of use of radio frequencies for the provision of electronic communications services; *(2)* the assignment of radio frequencies for electronic communication services shall be based on objective, transparent, non-discriminatory and proportionate criteria.'

The nature of the concept

2.14 **Criteria for a definition.** Pursuant to the Consolidated Services Directive, an exclusive right is a privilege conferred on a single undertaking. That privilege consists of the right to carry out activities, alone, on a given market within a certain geographical area. Two criteria are important in this definition. *(a)* The first refers to the content of the right. Exclusive rights relate to market access. Through an exclusive right, a market is reserved for a business entity. *(b)* The second relates to the number of authorised undertakings. In a situation where exclusive rights are granted, only one undertaking receives an authorisation to enter a market.

> *Consolidated Services Directive, Article 1(6).* ' "[E]xclusive rights" shall mean the rights that are granted by a Member State to one undertaking through any legislative, regulatory or administrative instrument, reserving it the right to provide an electronic communications service or to undertake an electronic communications activity within a given geographical area.'

Why were monopolies abolished?

2.15 **Economic reason.** Telecommunications[13] were liberalised because the services provided by the operators which were then active on the markets were not deemed to be satisfactory. As a result of the exclusive rights granted over a long period of time by Member States to undertakings in their national markets, these undertakings were protected from competition from national businesses and foreign undertakings. Furthermore, monopolies often carried out their activities in close

---

[13] The term 'electronic communications' was not current when exclusive rights were abolished. The expression was introduced in the NRF as an attempt to forge a regime that would regulate the transmission of broadcast services together with telecommunications and other communications-related activities.

co-operation with the national political establishment. The result was that attempts to modernise these undertakings did not materialise. They had become instruments for the implementation of political objectives, which often had no connection with the efficient exercise of activities on the markets. The purpose of the reform was to shake up that organisation and bring the telecommunications industry into line with other economic sectors where decisions regarding entry into the market was left to undertakings and customers. The purpose was to allow the entry of new actors into the market. Customers would then be in a position to choose from whom they wished to obtain their services. In these circumstances, businesses would struggle to gain the confidence of customers, thereby decreasing prices, increasing quality and expanding the range of available products or services. Through this mechanism, the European telecommunications industry would be revitalised and, indirectly, the whole European economy.

> The improvement of telecommunications in the Community is an essential condition for the harmonious development of economic activities and a competitive market in the Community, from the point of view of both service providers and users.[14]

Political considerations.   The Commission was also motivated by political **2.16** considerations. Citizens are customers. As such, they have a right to choose the provider from which they wish to receive goods and services. Freedom of choice is intimately related to democracy. Could a system be called democratic where pluralism was promoted in the expression of ideas but did not exist in the economy because activities were reserved for national champions? A second political reason was related to the economic situation. The national monopoly system did not produce the hoped-for economic results. Consumers did not receive technologically advanced goods and services that were available in countries where a different economic organisation was in place. This situation was due to the inability of monopolies to innovate or even introduce on their territory innovations made by others. European public authorities considered it their duty to facilitate access by European citizens to advanced communications facilities. Third, the European Union was progressively suffering a disadvantage vis-à-vis competitors worldwide, in the absence of access to efficient communications systems. Urgent action was necessary.

Legal reasoning (1)—Internal market.   The elimination of exclusive rights was **2.17** legally justified on several grounds, as set out in the preamble to the various liberalisation directives. A first ground is that national monopolies hinder the realisation of the internal market. In a national monopoly system, activities are reserved for one undertaking on the national territory. Undertakings from other Member States are not allowed to enter that geographical market. This situation undermines the objectives sought in the internal market.

---

[14]   Services Directive, Preamble, recital 1.

Services Directive. 'The granting of . . . exclusive rights to one or more undertakings to operate the network derives from the discretionary power of the State. The granting by a Member State of such rights inevitably restricts the provision of such services by other undertakings to or from other Member States.'[15] *Terminal Equipment Liberalisation Directive.* 'Article 30 [now Article 28] of the Treaty prohibits quantitative restrictions on imports from other Member States and all measures having equivalent effect. The grant of . . . exclusive rights to import and market goods to one organization can, and often does, lead to restrictions on imports from other Member States.'[16] 'The . . . exclusive rights relating to terminal equipment enjoyed by national telecommunications monopolies are exercised in such a way as, in practice, to disadvantage equipment from other Member States, notably by preventing users from freely choosing the equipment that best suits their needs in terms of price and quality, regardless of its origin. The exercise of these rights is therefore not compatible with [the internal market].'[17]

2.18 **Legal reasoning (2)—Competition.** Furthermore, monopolies were found to breach the competition rules. Competition requires choice for customers. In a competitive environment, customers are allowed to choose their business partners freely. The competition rules aim to ensure that choice is maintained, and possibly enhanced. To that end, action is taken against undertakings acquiring market power through unilateral or multilateral behaviour. There is little sense in addressing circumstances where market power is acquired through commercial conduct, but leaving unchanged situations where market power is derived from other sources—particularly where it comes from exclusive rights granted by Member States. The necessity of giving market power the same treatment whatever its origin found an echo in Article 86 EC. Pursuant to that provision, undertakings with special or exclusive rights are subject to European law, including the competition rules. There is thus no safe harbour for market power as granted by Member States.

> *Terminal Equipment Liberalisation Directive.* 'The effect of the . . . exclusive rights granted to such bodies by the State to import and market terminal equipment is to: (a) restrict users to renting such equipment, when it would often be cheaper for them, at least in the long term, to purchase this equipment. This effectively makes contracts for the use of networks subject to acceptance by the user of additional services which have no connection with the subject of the contracts, (b) limit outlets and impede technical progress since the range of equipment offered by the telecommunications bodies is necessarily limited and will not be the best available to meet the requirements of a significant proportion of users. Such conduct is expressly prohibited by Article 86[18] (d) and (b), and is likely significantly to affect trade between Member States.'[19]
>
> *Services Directive.* 'Where a State grants special or exclusive rights to provide telecommunications services to organisations which already have a dominant position in creating and operating the network, the effect of such rights is to strengthen

---

[15] Services Directive, Preamble, recital 5.
[16] Terminal Equipment Liberalisation Directive, Preamble, recital 3.
[17] ibid, Preamble, recitals 3 and 5.   [18] Now Art 82 EC.
[19] Terminal Equipment Liberalisation Directive, Preamble, recital 13.

the dominant position by extending it to services.'[20] 'Moreover, the special or exclusive rights granted to telecommunications organisations . . . (a) prevent or restrict access to the markets . . . by their competitors, thus limiting consumer choice which is liable to restrict technological progress to the detriment of consumers; (b) compel network users to use the services subject to exclusive rights, and thus make the conclusion of network utilization contracts dependent on acceptance of supplementary services having no connection with the subject of such contracts. Each of these types of conduct represents a specific abuse of a dominant position.' [21]

Evolution in the legal reasoning.   A focus was originally placed on issues raised **2.19** by national monopolies with regard to the internal market. The reason is probably that the case law originally provided a comfortable basis to address the problem with the concepts developed in that area of the law. Later,[22] more emphasis was placed on the competition rules. Again, that development is apparently due to the changes appearing in the case law. The competition case law became more helpful as the ECJ issued several judgments on exclusive rights granted by Member States. In the meantime, the case law on the internal market had become less intrusive in the checks carried out on national legislation. In 1994, the ECJ restricted significantly the scope of those checks in the well-known case of *Keck and Mithouard.*[23]

Transitional arrangements

No transitional rule still valid today.   As of now, there is no transitional arrange- **2.20** ment in force with regard to the abolition of exclusive rights. Exclusive rights have thus all been abolished—or at least should have been. Situations where they have not, or not fully, are contrary to European law. Proceedings could be initiated against Member States in default. The abolition of exclusive rights did not mean however that the reform evolved in one step. There was no big bang in European electronic communications. The reform can be better described as a process,

---

[20] Services Directive, Preamble, recital 15.   [21] ibid, Preamble, recital 16.

[22] In the amendments to the liberalisation directives after 1994.

[23] Joined Cases (267 & 268/91 *Criminal proceedings against Keck and Mithouard* [1993] ECR I-6097). This judgment addresses the use of internal market provisions as a tool to deregulate the economy progressively. The ECJ observed that parties progressively challenged the compatibility of national measures, in an attempt to have these measures removed. The result of this move was that national measures were gradually set aside. There was a risk that a trend towards systematic deregulation—abolition of all national measures—might develop. The ECJ found that this development was not to be encouraged. In order to avoid further such developments, it decided that national measures concerning 'sales arrangements' would no longer be scrutinised (the only exception is where such arrangements are discriminatory). As a result of *Keck and Mithouard*, Member States are allowed to regulate relations between consumers and businesses. A difficulty is that monopolies may be regarded as 'sales arrangements', since they concern the commercial arrangements that are used to sell goods and services. On the basis of this case law, national measures granting monopolies on a territory thus seem to escape scrutiny under the rules concerning the internal market. For that reason, it currently appears more appropriate to address these monopolies under the competition rules.

where deadlines were set to ensure rapid implementation of measures adopted at European level.

Consistency with licences

2.21 **Monopolies created through licences.** A first possible difficulty regarding the prohibition of exclusive rights is to ensure consistency with measures allowing Member States to limit entry on the market. The old regulatory framework provided that the Member States were obliged to admit on the market all undertakings demonstrating that they complied with the obligations, or conditions, attached to entry. A possibility was provided for Member States to limit the number of undertakings present on specific markets. These undertakings were to obtain 'licences'. A risk was then created that, using that possibility, Member States would reintroduce a sort of exclusive right. That risk was set aside by the formulation of new obligations regarding regulation of entry by the Member States. As is examined at paras 2.125–2.138, the Member States must accept all undertakings on the markets, and the conditions they may attach to entry are limited. The possibility of limiting the number of entrants is restricted to activities involving the use of radio spectrum. As is submitted later in this book (see paras 2.185–2.215), the European legislator has remained prudent in the regulation of radio spectrum. In that aspect of the electronic communications market, the power to act seems to belong, currently and to a significant extent, to the Member States.

2.22 **Remote possibility.** The provisions contained in the NRF demonstrate the desire on the part of the European legislator to avoid all situations where monopolies, or quasi monopolies, could be reintroduced. Provisions have been laid down in the European regulation to avoid a repetition of these situations. *(a)* The number of licences may not be limited except in exceptional circumstances. The Consolidated Services Directive provides in this regard that a limitation may occur only for reasons relating to lack of availability of spectrum. Other reasons are not accepted. *(b)* Licences are to be granted pursuant to objective and non-discriminatory criteria. A sort of competition thus precedes the granting of licences. As a result, the system would in any event not be entirely monopolistic. *(c)* Licences are granted for limited periods. A possibility thus exists that a licence may not be renewed and that—in the case that the number of licences is limited— another holder may be chosen. If monopolies are created through the licence system, they are thus limited in time. That constraint places the licence-holder under pressure. Good results have to be produced in order to have the licence renewed.[24]

---

[24] The limitation of licences in time may be analysed in terms of potential competition. The beneficiary remains under pressure as the licence may be granted to a competitor if the results are not satisfactory.

Illustration.   These three considerations make it unlikely that monopolies may   **2.23**
be created and that—supposing that such a situation did occur—they would
reproduce the results against which the reform was directed. Suppose the number
of licences is limited to one (for the reasons explained above). That licence would
be granted after careful examination of all applications. The decision would have
to be justified. Recourse would have to be made possible to an independent body.
There would thus be a possibility that the decision would be reviewed. The licence
would be granted for a limited period. After its expiry, the work performed by the
licence-holder would be assessed, other applications considered, and the renewal
only granted if satisfactory results were achieved by the previous licence-holder.

Consistency with universal service

Universal service.   The provisions relating to universal service are discussed at   **2.24**
length in various sections of this book. In this particular section, the issue
addressed is the extent to which the elimination of exclusive rights may come into
conflict with rules concerning the organisation of universal service. As is submitted in Chapter 5, several options are open to ensure that policy objectives are fulfilled in addition to the establishment of a competitive environment. One of them
is to entrust the provision of universal service to one undertaking. The losses
incurred on that service by that undertaking may have to be compensated. They
may be financed by public funds or by contributions imposed on market participants, provided certain conditions are met.

Possible conflict.   If the latter option is chosen, activities are entrusted to one   **2.25**
undertaking. These activities are not necessarily lucrative. However, they may
become lucrative given the subsidies paid by authorities with public money or
through market contributions. A situation thus arises which is not very different
from the one encountered in the Member States prior to the reform. A monopoly
would indeed be created on given activities, with a transfer of funds to ensure
profitability.

A tool to circumvent the reform?   The mechanism could even provide a tool to   **2.26**
possibly reluctant national authorities to circumvent the reform and the elimination of exclusive rights prescribed by the European legislator. The Member States
have indeed retained a certain margin of manoeuvre in the determination of activities that can be organised on the universal service model. They could use that possibility to define universal service broadly. All activities covered by universal
service would then be withdrawn from market forces and entrusted to one undertaking, with obligations on market participants to finance losses incurred by that
undertaking on behalf of the public interest.

Limitations imposed by the European legislator.   Limitations are imposed by   **2.27**
the European legislator on the freedom recognised by Member States to determine

what activities should be considered as part of the universal service. Among these limitations, the provisions prescribing the elimination of exclusive rights play an important role. Pursuant to these provisions, monopolies are part of the past. They cannot be re-introduced. Behaviour whereby that principle was not complied with but was on the contrary circumvented could be analysed as an infringement of European law.

2.28 **Grounds.** Several grounds could be used to that end. *(a)* Article 86(1) EC could be invoked. Pursuant to that provision, Member States must comply with European law as regards undertakings to which they grant special or exclusive rights. That provision would be violated if a Member State broadened the scope of universal service to circumvent the elimination of exclusive rights. *(b)* Article 86(2) EC could also be used. Pursuant to that provision, exceptions may be granted to the competition rules—and other European rules—where necessary to ensure the provision of services of general economic interest specifically entrusted to one or several undertakings. In order to obtain the benefit of that derogation, conditions have to be fulfilled. One of them is compliance with the proportionality principle. That principle would not be complied with as other measures could be used to ensure the attainment of the objectives in question without hindering competition to such a significant extent.[25] *(c)* Article 10 EC could also be used. Pursuant to that provision, Member States must take all measures appropriate to ensure and facilitate the realisation of the goals entrusted to the European Community. On the basis of the case law, that rule would be breached where a Member State adopted legislation seeking to limit the scope of an important European prohibition. *(d)* Finally, the European concept of 'abuse of right' could also apply in the situation. Case law has developed progressively in this direction over the last decade. Pursuant to that case law, undertakings may not use a provision to realise an aim that is not the one underlying that provision. For instance, they may not export goods from the Union in order to obtain subsidies but afterwards reimport the goods to sell them on the internal market. The situation described with respect to universal service could probably be analysed along the same lines. A Member State would not be allowed to define universal service broadly in an attempt to

---

[25] These measures are those advocated by the Commission, in whose view it is possible to realise the goals enshrined in universal service while complying with competition rules. Activities can be organised on a competitive basis on all electronic communications markets. Tariffs are then based on costs and costs decrease under the pressure of business rivalry. The universal service can thus be limited to non-lucrative activities. These activities can be entrusted to an undertaking. Although one undertaking is in charge, the mechanism does not constitute a derogation from competition, since activities covered by universal service are not withdrawn from competition. An auction can take place to identify the undertaking to provide universal service. That auction should be open to all interested candidates. A subsidy can be paid to cover losses associated with the provision of universal service. The subsidy should however not exceed any losses. As it compensates costs rather than grants an advantage, it cannot be considered as an aid violating the Treaty.

attain another, national, objective, which would be to limit the scope of the prohibition directed against exclusive rights.

(5) The elimination of special rights

The prohibition

Same provision.   Special rights are prohibited, just as exclusive rights are. The **2.29** prohibition is contained in the same provision. As was the case for exclusive rights, there is no limitation on the prohibition applied to special rights.

> *Consolidated Services Directive, Article 2(1).* 'Member States shall not grant or maintain in force . . . special rights for the establishment and/or the provision of electronic communications networks, or for the provision of publicly available electronic communications services.'

The nature of the concept

Definition.   The concept of special rights is defined in the Consolidated Services **2.30** Directive. *(a)* Pursuant to that Directive, a special right is an advantage granted to a limited number of beneficiaries. The advantage can take various forms. In some cases, the advantage concerns access to the market. Pursuant to the directive, an undertaking has a special right when that undertaking receives the right to enter a market and when that right is limited to a few beneficiaries.[26] The other form does not relate to market entry, but is rather defined in more general terms, as a legal or regulatory prerogative affecting the ability of the beneficiary to carry out its activities on the market in competition with other players. *(b)* A second element appears important in the definition. Pursuant to the directive, legal and regulatory advantages only qualify as special rights when they are granted in a procedure based on unacceptable criteria. These criteria can be linked with the basic regulatory principles examined in this chapter. According to the directive, special rights are prerogatives granted in violation of the basic regulatory principles of objectivity, proportionality and non-discrimination.

> *Consolidated Services Directive, Article 1(5).* ' "[S]pecial rights" shall mean the rights that are granted by a Member State to a limited number of undertakings through any legislative, regulatory or administrative instrument which, within a given geographical area: (a) designates or limits to two or more the number of such undertakings authorised to provide an electronic communications service or undertake an electronic communications activity, otherwise than according to objective, proportional and non-discriminatory criteria, or (b) confers on undertakings, otherwise than according to such criteria, legal or regulatory advantages which substantially affect the ability of any other undertaking to provide the same electronic communications

---

[26] A mechanism of this kind has operated in the markets for third generation mobile communications (3G), where participants allowed to take part were designated by the national authorities on the basis of predetermined criteria.

service or to undertake the same electronic communications activity in the same geographical area under substantially equivalent conditions.'

Difference with regard to other liberalisation directives

2.31 **Absence of total correspondence.**   The definition, and the prohibition, concerning special rights, as included in the Consolidated Services Directive, are not altogether similar to the corresponding provisions included in the Terminal Equipment Liberalisation Directive. Nor is correspondence with the Services Directive total.

2.32 **First difference—Limitation or designation.**   A first difference seems rather ancillary. In the Terminal Equipment Liberalisation Directive and the Services Directive the definition refers to a third type of situation where the concept of 'special rights' can be used. Pursuant to these instruments, the concept also refers to cases where a limitation is imposed on the number of undertakings present on a market (see table at para 2.37). The reason why that situation does not appear in the Consolidated Services Directive is not entirely clear. One reason might be that there is no real difference between that situation (limitation of undertakings present on a market) and another situation already aimed at in the definition (designation of the undertakings allowed on a market). The main distinction is that one situation refers to the limited number of players admitted on a market (result) whereas the second emphasises the designation which has taken place to arrive at that limitation (process). The Commission probably considered that the distinction was not significant enough to maintain the two approaches.

2.33 **Second difference—Prohibition limited in scope.**   A second, more substantial, distinction concerns the prohibition affecting special rights. Under the Consolidated Services Directive, the prohibition concerns the two sorts of advantages that qualify as special rights. Pursuant to that prohibition, Member States may no longer designate a limited number of undertakings allowed on a market or grant any other form of legal or regulatory advantage to a limited number of beneficiaries (if in these two cases the rights are granted in violation of basic regulatory principles). This marks a difference with the old Liberalisation Directive, where only the first form of right was prohibited. Under the liberalisation Directive, the Member States could not limit access to a market to a few undertakings (in conditions contrary to the basic regulatory principles). The prohibition formulated in the directive did not extend, however, to the second form of special rights. It was thus not forbidden for Member States, under the Services Directive, to grant legal or regulatory advantages, as long as these advantages did not concern market entry (see table at para 2.37).

2.34 **Second difference not to be overestimated.**   This second difference should not be overestimated. The prohibition to grant legal or regulatory advantages did not appear in the Services Directive. This, however, did not imply that such rights were permitted. The Services Directive did not contain all rules applicable to the kind of behaviour likely to be adopted by Member States. General competition law also applied. Special rights are covered by Article 86 EC. The treatment granted to special rights under that provision is no different from that given to exclusive rights. As is the case with exclusive rights, special rights may not be granted unless they are justified by a legitimate objective. They must also comply with the principle of proportionality. Through these rules, special rights were, and are still, prohibited, when the Member States do not comply, while granting them, with basic regulatory principles.

Differences with regard to Terminal Equipment Liberalisation Directive. **2.35** These differences exist with respect to the Services Directive. It should be borne in mind, however, that the provisions contained in that directive are identical to those included in the Terminal Equipment Liberalisation Directive. This means that the differences still exist today between the two instruments in force.

The definition of special rights in the liberalisation directives **2.36**

Networks, services (Consolidated Services Directive)	Networks, services (Services Directive)	Terminals (Terminal Equipment Liberalisation Directive)
' "[S]pecial rights" shall mean the rights that are granted by a Member State to a limited number of undertakings through any legislative, regulatory or administrative instrument which, within a given geographical area:	'[The concept of] "special rights" means rights that are granted by a Member State to a limited number of undertakings, through any legislative, regulatory or administrative instrument, which, within a given geographical area,	'[The concept of] "special rights" means rights that are granted by a Member State to a limited number of undertakings, through any legislative, regulatory or administrative instrument, which, within a given geographical area,
	—limits to two or more the number of such undertakings authorised to provide a service or undertake an activity, otherwise than according to objective, proportional and non-discriminatory criteria, or	—limits to two or more the number of undertakings, otherwise than according to objective, proportional and non-discriminatory criteria, or
(a) designates or limits to two or more the number of such undertakings authorised to provide an electronic communications service or undertake an electronic communications activity, otherwise than according to objective, proportional and non-discriminatory criteria, or	—designates, otherwise than according to such criteria, several competing undertakings as being authorised to provide a service or undertake an activity, or	—designates, otherwise than according to such criteria, several competing undertakings, or

(cont.)

Networks, services (Consolidated Services Directive)	Networks, services (Services Directive)	Terminals (Terminal Equipment Liberalisation Directive)
(b) confers on undertakings, otherwise than according to such criteria, legal or regulatory advantages which substantially affect the ability of any other undertaking to provide the same electronic communications service or to undertake the same electronic communications activity in the same geographical area under substantially equivalent conditions.'[27]	—confers on any undertaking or undertakings, otherwise than according to such criteria, legal or regulatory advantages which substantially affect the ability of any other undertaking to provide the same telecommunications service or to undertake the same activity in the same geographical area under substantially equivalent conditions.'[28]	—confers on any undertaking or undertakings, otherwise than according to such criteria, any legal or regulatory advantages which substantially affect the ability of any other undertaking to import, market,connect, bring into service and/or maintain telecommunication terminal equipment in the same geographical area under substantially equivalent conditions.'[29]

2.37 The prohibition of special rights in the liberalisation directives

Networks, services (Consolidated Services Directive)	Networks, services (Services Directive)	Terminals (Terminal Equipment Liberalisation Directive)
'Member States shall not grant or maintain in force . . . special rights for the establishment and/or the provision of electronic communications networks, or for the provision of publicly available electronic communications services.'[30]	'Member States shall withdraw all those measures which grant: . . . (b) special rights which limit to two or more the number of undertakings authorised to supply such telecommunication services, otherwise than according to objective, proportional and non-discriminatory criteria, or (c) special rights which designate, otherwise than according to such criteria, several competing undertakings to provide such telecommunication services.'[31]	'Member States . . . shall ensure that all exclusive rights are withdrawn, as well as those special rights which (a) limit to two or more the number of undertakings within the meaning of Article 1, otherwise than according to objective, proportional and non-discriminatory criteria, or (b) designate, otherwise than according to such criteria, several competing undertakings.'[32]

---

[27] Consolidated Services Directive, Art 1(6).

[28] Services Directive, Art 1(1), third indent, as amended.

[29] Terminal Equipment Liberalisation Directive, Art 1(1), third indent, as amended.

[30] Consolidated Services Directive, Art 2(1). This prohibition must be combined with the provision containing the definition of the concept of 'special rights'. It then appears that the prohibition covers all of the types of special right distinguished in that provision.

[31] Services Directive, Art 2, as amended.

[32] Terminal Equipment Liberalisation Directive, Art 2, as amended.

Comparison with exclusive rights

Similarities and differences.   Special and exclusive rights have features in com- **2.38**
mon. They both appear in Article 86 EC, which places upon Member States an
obligation to comply with all rules of the Treaty—including the competition
rules—as concerns undertakings to which they grant special or exclusive rights.
The two concepts also appear together in the liberalisation directives adopted by
the Commission. Both concepts clearly refer to advantages conferred by Member
States on undertakings. But these advantages are not altogether identical. *(a)* In
one case (exclusive rights), the privilege is conferred on one undertaking whereas
it is granted to two or more in the other (special rights). *(b)* Exclusive rights only
concern market access, whereas other legal and regulatory advantages are considered in the concept of special rights. *(c)* No reference is made to procedural
requirements in the definition and the treatment of exclusive rights. By contrast,
such requirements play an important role in the definition as well as in the treatment of special rights.

	Exclusive rights	Special rights
Number of beneficiaries	• One undertaking	• Two or more undertakings
Nature of the advantage	• Access to market	• Access to market
		• Other legal and regulatory advantages
Procedure	• No procedural requirement	• Procedural requirements

Similarities and differences.   *(a)* An explanation may be found for the differ- **2.39**
ence regarding the number of undertakings concerned. Special rights do not
imply that advantages are conferred on a single undertaking. This is rather the
nature of exclusive rights. *(b)* The difference concerning the type of advantages
granted can also be easily understood. An exclusive right is exhausted once a limitation has been imposed on the number of undertakings authorised to enter
a market. By nature, exclusive rights concern access to a market, rather than the
conditions relating to the exercise of activities. The situation is different for special
rights, which encompass legal or regulatory advantages concerning the exercise of
activities. *(c)* By contrast, it is more difficult to ascertain why the Commission
refers to procedural requirements in the definition of special rights where no such
reference exists for exclusive rights.[33]

---

[33] The Commission's attitude is probably one of caution. As stated, the two liberalisation directives were annulled by the ECJ on the ground that special rights had not been defined and that their
incompatibility with the Treaty was not demonstrated. Presumably, the Commission did not want
to take any risks in proposing a new definition. In fact, the definition is already very ambitious as far
as its scope is concerned. As has been seen, the concept does not relate only to market access advantages but encompasses all legal and regulatory advantages. To balance this wide approach, references
to procedural requirements probably needed to be inserted. All types of advantage are covered, to the
extent that they are granted in violation of fundamental European principles.

2.40 **Explanation.** Through this reference to procedural requirements, the Commission emphasises a limitation on the actions undertaken against legal and regulatory advantages granted to undertakings by public authorities. These actions are not directed against all legal and regulatory advantages, a move that would amount to a warning addressed to Member States and prohibiting them from regulating activities in the future. They are rather limited to the advantages that are granted in violation of basic regulatory principles. In application of that measure, the Member States may still grant legal or regulatory advantages. However, these advantages should not be granted on subjective bases, in conditions implying that discrimination is exercised, or through measures which do not conform with the principle of proportionality.

(6) The elimination of other regulatory restrictions

2.41 **Abolition.** The reform was not limited to the abolition of special and exclusive rights. It extended to all other kinds of regulatory restriction imposed by the Member States on electronic communications activities. In the Services Directive, the Commission ordered the removal of all 'remaining restrictions' hindering the provision of networks and services. These restrictions were not deemed compatible with EC law and, in particular, with the concept of liberalisation inspiring the directives adopted by the European Commission.

> *Services Directive, Article 2(2)(3), as amended.* 'Member States shall . . . ensure that all remaining restrictions on the provision of telecommunications services . . . are lifted.'[34]

2.42 **Limitations.** The abolition ordered by the European Commission is however not unlimited. On the one hand, the action was taken only in the markets for networks and services. No similar provision ordering the abolition of all other regulatory restrictions can be found in the Terminal Equipment Liberalisation Directive. On the other hand, the measure has been reviewed in the Consolidated Services Directive. The reason for this change is probably that the concept of 'remaining restriction' was difficult to interpret. The expression appeared so wide as potentially to cover all measures possibly adopted by the Member States. Such an interpretation would have implied that Member States could no longer take any measure in the field of telecommunications. It is probably to avoid excessive generality that the prohibition was formulated in a more refined manner in the Consolidated Services Directive. Under that instrument, no restriction can be introduced or maintained by the Member States other than restrictions introduced by or under the NRF.

> *Consolidated Services Directive, Article 2(3).* 'Member States shall ensure that no restrictions are imposed or maintained on the provision of electronic communications services

---

[34] There is no such provision in the Terminal Equipment Liberalisation Directive.

over electronic communications networks established by the providers of electronic communications services, over infrastructures provided by third parties, or by means of sharing networks, other facilities or sites without prejudice to the provisions of Directives 2002/19/EC, 2002/20/EC, 2002/21/EC and 2002/22/EC.'

Barrier to entry. With the provision banning remaining restrictions, the **2.43** Commission appeared mainly concerned with national measures potentially affecting entry on the markets. Prior to the reform, markets had been reserved for decades for monopolists. With the reform, Member States were obliged to open their markets. As a result of that process, several participants were expected to take up liberalised activities. The opening of markets did not however imply that Member States gave up controlling and regulating entry. The fear was that Member States wanted to maintain their role in that regard. National authorities might have taken action that would have made it more difficult, or more costly, to enter the market.

Satellites. A provision is devoted in the Consolidated Services Directive to **2.44** space segment capacity. Pursuant to the directive, all restrictions of a legal or regulatory nature on offers on that market must be eliminated. Where these restrictions result from international commitments, the Member States must take all appropriate measures to undo these commitments.

> *Consolidated Services Directive, Article 7.* 'Member States shall ensure that any regulatory prohibition or restriction on the offer of space segment capacity to any authorised satellite earth station network operator are abolished, and shall authorise within their territory any space-segment supplier to verify that the satellite earth station network for use in connection with the space segment of the supplier in question is in conformity with the published conditions for access to such person's space segment capacity.' 'Member States which are party to international conventions setting up international satellite organisations shall, where such conventions are not compatible with the competition rules of the EC Treaty, take all appropriate steps to eliminate such incompatibilities.'

(7) Compatibility with general competition law and European law in general

Applications for annulment. In the 1990s, the ECJ had an opportunity to **2.45** assess the validity of the provisions prohibiting exclusive rights, special rights and other regulatory restrictions. The assessment was not limited to the provisions concerning these aspects. It extended to all rules introduced in the liberalisation directives then in force. The result was that, in general, the liberalisation directives were found valid. Only on minor provisions did the ECJ consider that the Commission had not complied with European law. The rulings were issued on the basis of applications submitted by several Member States against the liberalisation directives adopted by the Commission.[35]

---

[35] Case 202/88 *France v Commission* [1991] ECR I-1223. Joined Cases C 271, 281 & 289/90 *Spain, Belgium and Italy v Commission* [1992] ECR I-05833.

2.46 **Power of the Commission to liberalise.** An important point is that the ECJ confirmed the power of the Commission to intervene in the telecommunications sector (now the electronic communications sector) in order to apply, through provisions of a general nature, the rules contained in the EC Treaty. The ECJ found that the Commission had the right to adopt the directives in order to determine the implications of the provisions contained in the Treaty as regards sectors aimed at in Article 86(2) EC. As stated, that provision concerns sectors where special or exclusive rights are granted by Member States. It also concerns industries where undertakings are public or entrusted with tasks of general interest. The powers of the Commission recognised by the ECJ are substantial. Given their scope, and the clarity of the rulings issued by the ECJ, there is little doubt that the Commission can adopt directives, in the electronic communications sector or in other, like sectors, should it consider that the organisation existing on these markets does not comply with the EC Treaty.

> *France v Commission (1991).* [17] 'Article 90(3)[36] of the Treaty empowers the Commission to specify in general terms the obligations arising under Article 90(1)[37] by adopting directives. The Commission exercises that power where, without taking into consideration the particular situation existing in the various Member States, it defines in concrete terms the obligations imposed on them under the Treaty. In view of its very nature, such a power cannot be used to make a finding that a Member State has failed to fulfil a particular obligation under the Treaty.' [18] 'However, it appears from the content of the directive at issue in this case that the Commission merely determined in general terms obligations which are binding on the Member States under the Treaty. The directive therefore cannot be interpreted as making specific findings that particular Member States failed to fulfil their obligations under the Treaty, with the result that the plea in law relied upon by the French Government must be rejected as unfounded.'

2.47 **Prohibition of exclusive rights (1).** Beyond the confirmation that the Commission had the powers to liberalise the European telecommunications sector, the ECJ assessed the validity of all provisions contained in the Terminal Equipment Liberalisation Directive (terminals). In that context, it ruled that the Commission was right to order the prohibition of exclusive rights. The assessment was carried out on the basis of the rules concerning the internal market. At that time, the case law concerning that area of European law was more developed. For that reason, the Commission based its argumentation in favour of the abolition of exclusive rights mainly on internal market considerations. The ECJ found that these arguments were in conformity with the EC Treaty. Exclusive rights indeed restricted the free movement of goods (terminals). Though these are normally prohibited, restrictions can be justified. In that case, the Commission had determined in the Terminal Equipment Liberalisation Directive which requirements

---

[36] Now Art 86(3).   [37] Now Art 86(1).

could be taken into account in the assessment of the Member States' national legislation. That aspect was not contested by the French Republic. As a result, the position adopted by the Commission was held to be valid.

> *France v Commission (1991).* [33] 'With regard to exclusive importation and marketing rights, it should be borne in mind that, as the Court has consistently held . . . ,[38] the prohibition of measures having an effect equivalent to quantitative restrictions laid down in Article 30[39] of the Treaty applies to all trading rules enacted by Member States which are capable of hindering, directly or indirectly, actually or potentially, intra-Community trade.' [34] 'In that regard it should be noted first that the existence of exclusive importing and marketing rights deprives traders of the opportunity of having their products purchased by consumers.' [35] 'It should be pointed out, secondly, that the terminals sector is characterised by the diversity and technical nature of the products concerned and by the ensuing constraints. In those circumstances there is no certainty that the holder of the monopoly can offer the entire range of models available on the market, inform customers about the state and operation of all the terminals and guarantee their quality.' [36] 'Accordingly, exclusive importation and marketing rights in the telecommunications terminal sector are capable of restricting intra-Community trade.'[40]

Prohibition of exclusive rights (2).   Only in the second case did the ECJ exam-   **2.48** ine the compatibility of the measure prohibiting exclusive rights with general competition law. The outcome of the assessment did not differ. In the second case, the ECJ indeed decided that exclusive rights restrict competition and cannot be justified in the electronic communications sector.

> *Spain, Belgium and Italy v Commission (1992).* [35] 'The Court has held that the mere fact of creating a dominant position by granting exclusive rights within the meaning of Article 90(1) of the Treaty is not as such incompatible with Article 86.'[41] [36] 'However, the Court has also held that the extension of the monopoly on the establishment and operation of the telephone network to the market in telephone equipment, without any objective justification, was prohibited as such by Article 86, or by Article 90(1) in conjunction with Article 86, where that extension resulted from a State measure, thus leading to the elimination of competition.'[42] The same conclusion necessarily follows where the monopoly on establishment and operation extends to the market in telecommunications services.' [37] 'In that regard, it may be seen from the 16th recital in the Preamble to the contested directive, the terms of which have not been in any way challenged by the Italian Government, that the grant of exclusive rights to telecommunications organizations has been conducive to the latter's excluding competitors from the market for telecommunications services or,

---

[38] See, in particular, judgment in Case 8/74 *Procureur du Roi v Dassonville* [1974] ECR 837 at [5].

[39] Now Art 28.

[40] In its ruling the ECJ also examines the validity of the prohibition regarding exclusive rights with respect to the connection, bringing into service and maintenance of telecommunications terminal equipment. The same conclusion was reached. See *France v Commission* (n 35 above) 40–44.

[41] Joined Cases C 271, 281 & 289/90 *Spain, Belgium and Italy v Commission* [1992] ECR I-5833.

[42] See Case C-18/88 *Régie des télégraphes et des téléphones v GB-Inno-BM* [1991] ECR I-5941(2)4.

at least, restricting their access to that market. According to the same recital, all the services in question could in principle be supplied by providers established in other Member States.' [38] 'The Commission was therefore justified in requiring the withdrawal of such exclusive rights as regards the supply of certain telecommunications services. The plea in law relating to this matter must therefore be rejected.'

2.49 **Provisions annulled.** As stated earlier, the ECJ annulled two provisions in the directives, on minor grounds. The first concerned special rights. The ECJ found that no clear definition had been given of that concept. Hence, the directives had to be considered insufficiently reasoned as regards the provisions in which this concept appeared. The second was the inclusion, in the directives, of provisions containing obligations addressed to undertakings. These provisions were annulled, as the ECJ found that directives may only contain provisions directed to Member States.[43]

B. Issues Relating to Ownership and Public Control

(1) Public ownership

2.50 **Few public operators.** A significant number of players active on electronic communications markets are in private hands. Only a few undertakings remain under public control. This is the case, principally, for some former national operators which have not been privatised (or at least not fully). These operators now are an exception. The Member States increasingly seek to privatise them. Several reasons may be found to justify this attitude. *(a)* Governments need resources. An expedient manner to bolster national exchequers is to sell public assets. *(b)* For the same reason (lack of resources), governments are not in a position to provide the financial means necessary for the development of the undertakings present on the electronic communications markets. *(c)* In the current situation, the former national operators have to carry out their activities in a competitive environment. Measures are taken by management within these operators to ensure they can face up to competition. Generally, governments prefer not being associated with the imposition of unpopular working conditions. *(d)* There is no reason to maintain in public hands an undertaking which must carry out its activities as if it were private. These public undertakings may no longer be used to fulfil public policy objectives. Such an obligation would represent a threat for their financial equilibrium.

2.51 **Ongoing privatisation.** These reasons have led Member States to sell a part, or all, of the shares they held in their former national monopolies. The sale of public

---

[43] See *France v Commission* (n 35 above) at [5]–[47] (special rights) and [3]–[57] (provisions applicable to undertakings). See also *Spain v Commission* (n 41 above) at [8]–[32] (special rights) and [2]–[27] (provisions applicable to undertakings).

telecommunications assets started at the beginning of the 1980s, in Britain. The same process occurred, and continues, in most Member States. The reason some have not yet sold off all their public shares, however, seems to be contextual, in other words the financial climate, rather than political. It is probable that further sales will take place with the return of economic growth.

Neutrality in principle.   In principle, the trend towards privatisation is not sup-   **2.52** ported by the European institutions. These institutions must base their attitude on the EC Treaty, which provides that European rules do not prejudge the property rights regime in the Member States. The relevant provision (Article 295 EC) was understood as expressing the requirement that European law must remain neutral vis-à-vis the concept of public, or private, ownership. As an implication, European institutions do not have the power to order, or even encourage, governments to sell public assets (privatisation). Conversely, they do not have the power to discourage, or prohibit, the purchase of shares, or other assets (nationalisation).

> *Article 295 EC.* 'This Treaty shall in no way prejudice the rules in Member States governing the system of property ownership.'

Current economic opinion.   That neutrality in principle has not prevented the   **2.53** European institutions from developing a preference for privatisation. A call for privatisation is currently widespread in economic circles. It is thought that public management does not provide the best environment for developing efficiency in an organisation. It is also considered that public management is not able to alter the climate within an organisation, and introduce a spirit of customer-oriented practice. That opinion coincides with another, that modern States should progressively abandon the exercise of economic activity to concentrate on core competences (the exercise of regulatory powers).

Attitude in practice.   Authors have generally noted that the European institu-   **2.54** tions remain neutral or, at least attempt to do so, in regard to property rights in most economic sectors. They observe that no direct order or incentive has been given in favour of privatisation. Some, however, consider that the European institutions use legal mechanisms or processes in an attempt to reinforce, indirectly, the trend towards privatisation.[44]

(a) Liberalisation.   One of these mechanisms or processes is liberalisation.   **2.55** Liberalisation may be defined as the elimination of legal barriers impeding access to markets.[45] Liberalisation is not an equivalent to privatisation (the second concept

---

[44] See W Devroe, 'Privatisations and Community Law: Neutrality versus, Policy' [1997] CMLR 267; A Verhoeven, 'Privatisation and EC law: Is the European Commission "Neutral" with respect to Public versus Public Ownership of Companies' [1996] Intl and Comparative LQ 861.

[45] Access was made difficult or impossible on some markets, as a result of the presence of certain rules. Liberalisation is a process whereby these rules are set aside in an effort to allow new actors on the markets.

refers to the sale of some or all shares held by a public authority in an entity). However, the two processes are related. Liberalisation implies that private companies are allowed on a market which, often, was formerly reserved for a public monopoly. As a result of liberalisation, the former public monopoly is confronted by competition. To maintain a presence on the market, that latter operator must change its organisation, as well as its attitude to the markets. It must adopt the type of management that is typical of a private company. The incentive and, even, the possibility, of remaining in public hands, then disappears. The next step is the modification of the capital of the former monopoly to bring it in line with that of private competitors.[46]

2.56 **(b) State aids.** The application of the rules concerning State aids provides another illustration of a mechanism or process where an implicit desire to develop the trend towards privatisation appears. State aids are prohibited pursuant to the Treaty (Article 87 EC). Exemptions are allowed in limited circumstances. One issue is to determine when a State aid is granted. That question is particularly delicate when an economic entity is in public hands and the authority grants funds to that entity. The criterion used in the case law is that a transfer of funds qualifies as an aid when it would not have been made by an ordinary (that is, a private) investor. The operation is thus seen through the eyes of a private investor.[47] This calls into question the reason for public authorities to maintain control over undertakings. That reason is, precisely, to ask, or order, such undertakings to implement objectives which private undertakings would not fulfil of their own volition. There is no reason for governments to maintain control over undertakings if the objectives they seek to bring about through their ownership could be taken over by private undertakings.

2.57 **(c) The concept of undertakings.** The trend towards privatisation further appears in the case law developed regarding the concept of 'undertaking', which determines the application of the competition rules. European competition rules apply only to entities qualifying as undertakings. In various cases, the ECJ has identified criteria to define the concept.[48] The ECJ has taken the line that entities carrying out economic activities[49] are considered undertakings, and are hence

---

[46] This scenario is not uncommon, and indeed now it appears to be a natural trend. As markets open to private undertakings, former monopolies increasingly look like private companies. The resemblance first concerns the behaviour adopted by the former monopoly on the market. Then follows the structural resemblance, with part or all of the capital being sold to private investors.

[47] As a result of the application of that criterion, public entities are regarded, for the assessment of transfers of funds from shareholders, as private undertakings. Public authorities may not grant funds to undertakings placed under their control, in situations different from those where a private investor would have adopted the same behaviour.

[48] Case C-41/90 *Höfner & Else v Mactroton GmbH* [1991] ECR I-1979. Case C-475/99 *Ambulanz Glockner v Landkreis Sudwestpfalz* [2001] ECR I-8089.

[49] That is, providing goods and/or services.

subject to the competition rules. The content, or nature, of the activity is thus the determining factor. By contrast, the private or public status of the entity has no impact. An entity placed in public hands qualifies as an undertaking if, and to the extent, an economic activity is carried out. The irrelevance of its status implies that numerous entities in public hands are currently subject to competition law. They do not differ, in this regard, from private companies. As both kinds of entity are subject to the same rules, there is no reason to maintain public ownership. Such ownership has relevance only if public entities may be entrusted with tasks that are not, or would not be, carried out spontaneously by private undertakings.

(d) Independence of regulators.   Another area where private shareholding is **2.58** favoured is in relation to the rules concerning the independence that is required of regulators of electronic communications markets. As already stated, regulators may not be linked, in any manner, with undertakings. Only with that condition can equality of treatment be maintained among actors in the markets. This requirement of independence raises issues when an operator remains partly, or totally, in public hands. The government then has the power to regulate the markets and, at the same time, as a shareholder, the responsibility for the economic activities carried out by the undertaking. The only way in which to solve this difficulty on a lasting basis is to ensure that regulation remains a public prerogative whereas economic activities are carried out by private undertakings. The European institutions have not been willing so far to impose this opinion, as a result of the neutrality which they have to maintain regarding ownership regimes. Some commentators however argue that privatisation is an unavoidable implication of independence. For these observers, independence is only complete and thus totally legitimate in countries where the two activities have been separated through privatisation.

(2) Limitation on the shares held by foreign investors

In the aftermath of privatisation.   As operators are progressively privatised, an **2.59** issue that arises is the extent to which foreign investors may hold shares in the capital of former national operators. The issue is not limited to telecommunications or electronic communications, but concerns most industries where public undertakings are privatised, including the energy and transport sectors. In these industries, States generally want to retain a certain level of control over the investors holding the shares. They feel such control can be carried out more easily when those investors are nationals. In some instances, the necessity of residual control is explained by strategic reasons. For instance, it is essential for a State to ensure security and continuity in the supply of energy to the population and public bodies. In other cases, the wish to retain control is based on the provision of public services. States consider that public services will be provided in a more satisfactory manner if the shareholders are mainly national investors.

2.60 **Applicable instruments.** National rules concerning the acquisition, by investors, of shares in one or several undertakings fall under the provisions concerning the free movement of capital under the EC Treaty. Several provisions, and instruments, may apply in such a situation. *(a)* First, these national measures may be assessed as to their compatibility with EU law under Article 56 EC. *(b)* The concept of capital movement was further developed in the secondary legislation. An important instrument in this regard is Council Directive 88/361/EEC of 24 June 1988 for the implementation of Article 67 of the Treaty.[50] *(c)* In the case law the ECJ has on several occasions addressed the conditions under which Member States may or may not introduce restrictions on the purchase of shares by Community investors in national undertakings. *(d)* Finally, the Commission has issued a Communication on certain legal aspects concerning intra-EU investment.[51]

> *Article 56(1) EC.* ' Within the framework of the provisions set out in this chapter, all restrictions on the movement of capital between Member States and between Member States and third countries shall be prohibited.'

2.61 **Measures examined in the following paragraphs.** The following paragraphs examine various types of measure which can be adopted by Member States in order to maintain a level of control over the acquisition of shares in national undertakings or over several types of decisions adopted by the undertaking(s) concerned which may have an effect on the national interest. Measures prohibiting the acquisition of shares by foreigners beyond a certain threshold are examined first. The analysis then turns to measures imposing an (ex ante) authorisation, or allowing for a control (ex post) when investors, nationals and/or foreigners, purchase shares.

(3) Prohibition on foreigners acquiring more than a given threshold in the capital of a national undertaking

2.62 **The type of measure concerned.** Several limitations are generally imposed on the ability of Community investors to purchase holdings in the capital in undertakings located in another Member State. The most stringent measure is the straightforward imposition of a maximum of shares that can be held by non-nationals. As mentioned in the previous paragraph, such a measure is a restriction on the free movement of capital. It can be regarded as a discrimination. A limitation is imposed on foreigners which does not apply to nationals. Such measures are considered as being contrary to the internal market.[52]

---

[50] [1988] OJ L178/5. Art 67 EC is now Art 56 EC. It contains the general provision concerning free movement of capital.   [51] [1997] OJ C220/15.

[52] There is some controversy regarding the extent to which discriminatory measures can be justified. Restrictions are prohibited, but they can in principle be justified if the objective is legitimate and the means are proportional. Some authors argue that no justification may be invoked for discriminatory measures. Others claim that justifications are possible, but are not accepted in practice

Commission v Portugal (2002). A limitation on the number of shares that foreign,   **2.63**
Community, investors may hold was condemned by the ECJ in *Commission v
Portugal (2002).*[53] The case concerned Portuguese legislation organizing the privatisation of public entities engaged in economic activities. The legislation in question
provided, among other restrictions, that foreign investors could not acquire more
than 25 per cent of the shares in privatised undertakings. Another limitation was that,
on the basis of that legislation, the national authorities could impose other, possibly
lower, ceilings, in specific cases. These limitations were considered unacceptable
restrictions which could not be justified in any way.

> *Commission v Portugal (2002).* [40] 'As regards the prohibition precluding investors
> from other Member States from acquiring more than a given number of shares in cer-
> tain Portuguese undertakings, it is common ground—and, moreover, not disputed by
> the Portuguese Government—that this involves unequal treatment of nationals of
> other Member States and restricts the free movement of capital. The Portuguese
> Government does not plead any justification in that regard. . . . [42] Consequently, . . .
> non-compliance with . . . the Treaty is established.'

(4) *Obligation to obtain an authorisation from a public authority prior to purchasing shares*

The type of measure concerned. A second limitation which may be imposed by   **2.64**
a government is that whereby approval must be obtained from a public authority
when investors seek to purchase shares in the capital of a national undertaking. In
this scenario, approval must be obtained before the foreign investor is allowed to
purchase the shares. Such a regime of preliminary authorisation may be imposed
independently of the number of shares which investors seek to acquire. In most circumstances, however, that regime is limited to the acquisition of a given threshold.

Regime reserved to foreign investors. In some circumstances the prior authori-   **2.65**
sation regime may be limited to foreign investors. Under such a regime, foreign
investors must obtain an authorisation prior to acquiring shares, whereas the
requirement does not apply for purchases carried out by national investors. To
date, no case dealing with this specific situation seems to have been decided concerning the acquisition of shares in national undertakings. There is little doubt,
however, that such a system would be deemed contrary to the EC Treaty. It introduces a discrimination based on nationality. Such a result is strictly prohibited
under EU law, as appears from the case law of the ECJ (see the attitude adopted
by the ECJ in *Commission v Portugal (2002)*).

Regime applicable to all investors. Another possibility is to apply the regime of   **2.66**
prior authorisation to purchases made by all investors whatever their nationality.

---

as a discriminatory result must be considered excessive and hence contrary to the principle of
proportionality (third test).

[53] Case C-367/98 *Commission v Portugal* [2002] ECR I-4731.

Such a measure is said to be 'equally applicable', as it contains no distinction based on nationality or residence. A measure of this nature constitutes a restriction on the movement of capital, as investors cannot buy shares freely. As a result these measures are normally contrary to the EC Treaty. Exemptions may be obtained if the objective sought via the measure is legitimate and the means used to attain it are proportionate.[54]

> *Commission v Portugal (2002)*. [49] 'The free movement of capital, as a fundamental principle of the Treaty, may be restricted only by national rules which are justified by reasons referred to in Article 73d(1)[55] of the Treaty or by overriding requirements of the general interest and which are applicable to all persons and undertakings pursuing an activity in the territory of the host Member State. Furthermore, in order to be so justified, the national legislation must be suitable for securing the objective which it pursues and must not go beyond what is necessary in order to attain it, so as to accord with the principle of proportionality.' [50] 'As regards a scheme of prior administrative authorisation . . . , . . . such a scheme must be proportionate to the aim pursued, inasmuch as the same objective could not be attained by less restrictive measures, in particular a system of declarations *ex post facto*.' 'Such a scheme must be based on objective, non-discriminatory criteria which are known in advance to the undertakings concerned, and all persons affected by a restrictive measure of that type must have a legal remedy available to them.'

2.67　(a) **First condition—Legitimacy of the objective(s).**　The first issue is to determine whether the objectives pursued by the national governments can be considered legitimate. The ECJ on this subject has a fairly positive attitude. It concedes the right for Member States to maintain a level of control on undertakings, particularly where they are active on markets where services of general interest are provided or where national strategic interests can be affected.

> *ECJ case law.* '[I]t is undeniable that, depending on the circumstances, certain concerns may justify the retention by Member States of a degree of influence within undertakings that were initially public and subsequently privatised, where those undertakings are active in fields involving the provision of services in the public interest or strategic services.'[56]

---

[54] The attitude was confirmed in another judgment. In Case C-98/01 *Commission v UK* [2003] 2 CMLR 19, the ECJ was confronted with UK legislation preventing, without prior authorisation, the acquisition of shares giving right to more than 15% of the votes in the British Airports Authority. The measure was found to be a restriction on the movement of capital. The UK Government argued that the restriction contained no discrimination against foreign investors, as it applied to all investors irrespective of their nationality or residence. The ECJ replied that the EC Treaty also prohibits equally applicable measures, where such measures cannot be justified as being objective and proportionate. The UK Government did not present further arguments to justify the national regime.　　　　　　　　　　　　　　　　　　　　　　　　　　　　[55] Now Art 56 EC.

[56] This sentence is taken from *Commission v Portugal (2002)* (n 53 above) at [47]. The same sentence can be found in Case C-483/99 *Commission v France* [2002] ECR I-4789 at [43]; Case C-503/99 *Commission v Belgium* [2002] ECR I-4809 at [43]; and Case C-463/00 *Commission v Spain* [2003] ECR I-4581 at [66].

Non-legitimate objectives.   The ECJ thus accepts in general the legitimacy of a   **2.68**
government control, but more specific considerations must be put forward by governments to obtain an exemption. This was made clear in *Commission v Portugal
(2002)*. That case, as examined above, featured legislation prohibiting the acquisition of shares in national undertakings by foreign investors, beyond a given
threshold. Beyond that prohibition, the legislation imposed an obligation to
obtain an authorisation from the Minister of Finance prior to the acquisition of
the shares. The measure was not dependent upon investors being foreigners. It
applied to all investors, national and foreigners alike. *(a)* In its ruling, the ECJ
considered that the obligation to obtain an authorisation was a restriction on
the free movement of capital.[57] *(b)* An exemption could however be obtained if
the objective was legitimate and the means proportional. In this case, the objectives put forward by the Portuguese Government were rejected. The Portuguese
Government had argued that a regime of prior authorisation would serve the
financial interests of the State and provide the State with an opportunity to ensure
that, as a result of the acquisition, markets would function as desired. These objectives were found to be economic in nature—the kind of objectives that EC law
does not accept when it comes to restrictions on the internal market.

> *Commission v Portugal (2002)*. 'As regards the need to safeguard the financial interest
> of the Portuguese Republic, it must be recalled that, save in so far as they may fall
> within the ambit of the reasons set out in Article 73d(1)[58] of the Treaty, which relate
> in particular to tax law, the general financial interests of a Member State cannot con-
> stitute adequate justification. It is settled case law that economic grounds can never
> serve as justification for obstacles prohibited by the Treaty.' 'That reasoning is equally
> applicable to the economic policy objectives reflected in . . . [the Portuguese legisla-
> tion] and the objectives mentioned by the Portuguese Government in the present
> proceedings, namely choosing a strategic partner, strengthening the competitive
> structure of the market concerned or modernising and increasing the efficiency of
> means of production. Such interests cannot constitute a valid justification for restric-
> tions on the fundamental freedom concerned.'[59]

Non-legitimate objectives—A further example.   The same restrictive attitude   **2.69**
was adopted by the ECJ in *Commission v Spain (2003)*. The Spanish Government
claimed that it was legitimate to impose controls on the acquisition of shares in
a national tobacco undertaking as well as in several national commercial banks.
The objective was rejected because there was no indication that these undertakings provided a form of public service or that control would be justified by
strategic reasons.

---

[57] As far as the ECJ is concerned, EC provisions concerning the movement of capital are not limited to a prohibition of discrimination. They cover all measures which, although they apply equally
to all investors independent of their nationality, restrict the freedom of legal or natural persons to
invest wherever they wish.   [58] Now Art 56 EC.
   [59] At [52].

Commission v Spain (2003). 'Tabacalera SA, which produces tobacco, and Corporación Bancaria de España SA (Argentaria), a group of commercial banks which operate in the traditional banking sector and which are not claimed to carry out any of the functions of a central bank or similar body, are not undertakings whose objective is to provide public services. In merely referring to "certain lines of business" which in the past fell within the remit of public savings banks, the Spanish Government does not establish that there are particular circumstances as a result of which the banking group takes responsibility for a public-service function. It follows that the regimes relating to Tabacalera SA and Corporación Bancaria de España SA (Argentaria) cannot be justified.'[60]

2.70 **Legitimate objectives.** The decision adopted by the ECJ in *Commission v Portugal (2002)* appears to be an exception. In most cases featuring authorisation regimes, governments invoke non-economic considerations. In these cases, the ECJ admits that the objectives pursued by the governments concerned can be legitimate. In *Commission v Belgium (2002)*, for instance, the ECJ declared that reasoning relating to public security was acceptable. The case concerned acquisitions in undertakings active on energy markets. The purpose of the national measure, according to the governments concerned, was to secure energy supplies.[61]

> *Commission v Belgium (2002).* 'In the present case, the objective pursued by the legislation at issue, namely the safeguarding of energy supplies in the event of a crisis, falls undeniably within the ambit of a legitimate public interest. Indeed, the Court has previously recognised that the public-security considerations which may justify an obstacle to the free movement of goods include the objective of ensuring a minimum supply of petroleum products at all times . . . The same reasoning applies to obstacles to the free movement of capital, inasmuch as public security is also one of the grounds of justification referred to in Article 73d(1)(b)[62] of the Treaty.'

2.71 **Legitimate objectives—A further example.** Another example of legitimate objectives can be found in *Commission v Spain (2003)*. The Spanish legislation concerned several economic sectors—among which the tobacco industry and various commercial banks for which the objectives put forward by the Spanish Government were not accepted (see above). The Spanish legislation further concerned three other sectors—petroleum, telecommunications and the electricity industry. In these sectors the Commission accepted in principle the justification founded on public security.

> *Commission v Spain (2003).* 'As regards the three other undertakings concerned, which are active in the petroleum, telecommunications and electricity sectors, it is undeniable that the objective of safeguarding supplies of such products or the provision of such services within the Member State concerned in the event of a crisis may

---

[60] See *Commission v Spain (2003)* (n 56 above) at [70].
[61] The same attitude was adopted regarding objectives in *Commission v France (2003)* (n 56 above) at [47]. The ECJ however rejected the measure, which appeared contrary to the proportionality principle. [62] Now Art 56 EC.

constitute a public-security reason . . . and therefore may justify an obstacle to the free movement of capital.'[63]

(5) *Ability of a public authority to control* ex post facto *the acquisition of shares by foreigners and/or nationals*

The type of measure concerned. A third type of measure may be adopted by **2.72** Member States wishing to control the acquisition of shares in national undertakings. In this third regime, the control is not carried out prior to the operation taking place, but occurs afterwards. According to the case law, this difference in the timing of the control has an important consequence for the assessment of the measure. For the ECJ, the ex post character of the control shows that the decisions concerning the purchase of shares remains, in normal circumstances, in the hands of the market. In that context, public intervention remains an exception. The status of the intervention is an element in favour of a finding that the control is not excessive.

Ex post control applicable to all investors. *Commission v Belgium (2002)* is the **2.73** leading case regarding ex post control on acquisitions independently of the nationality of the investor(s). Under Belgian legislation, the Minister for energy had the power to appoint members of the board in two undertakings responsible for energy transmission.[64] These board members operated as a communication channel, reporting to the Minister decisions concerning acquisitions of shares. Special attention was paid to the acquisition, by a legal or a natural person, of 5 per cent or more of the shares in the undertakings concerned. Similar attention was paid to operations whereby a legal or natural person acquired more than 10 per cent of the capital of these undertakings. Pursuant to Belgian legislation, the Minister had the right to veto these operations where they could affect the national interest as regards energy.

Positive reaction. The ECJ found that the measure qualified as a restriction **2.74** on the free movement of capital. Thereafter, it enquired into the objectives and the instruments featured in the national legislation. For the ECJ, the objective sought by the national legislator through these measures appeared legitimate. It is acceptable, said the ECJ, for a country to secure continuity in energy supply. The ECJ also took a positive attitude regarding the instruments used by the national legislator to ensure the attainment of that objective. The ECJ noted the following in this regard: *(a)* The control was carried out after the operation had taken place. As a result, business operations were in principle left untouched, with an exception when intervention was mandated. The restriction was thus subsidiary.

---

[63] See *Commission v Spain (2003)* (n 56 above) at [71].

[64] The first undertaking was *Société nationale de transport par canalisation* (electricity supply) and the second *Distrigaz* (gas).

(b) An intervention by the Minister was possible only where policy objectives would otherwise be jeopardised. *(c)* An appeal before a national court was available against the decision taken by the Minister. There thus existed a possibility for any affected parties to obtain a review of the decision taken by the public authority.

> *Commission v Belgium (2002).* [48] 'It is necessary . . . to ascertain whether the legislation in issue enables the Member State concerned to ensure a minimum level of energy supplies in the event of a genuine and serious threat, and whether or not it goes beyond what is necessary for that purpose.' [49] 'First of all, it should be noted that the regime in issue is one of opposition. It is predicated on the principle of respect for the decision-making autonomy of the undertaking concerned, inasmuch as, in each individual case, the exercise of control by the minister responsible requires an initiative on the part of the Government authorities. No prior approval is required. Moreover, in order for that power of opposition to be exercised, the public authorities are obliged to adhere to strict time limits.' [51] 'Lastly, the Minister may intervene pursuant to . . . [the national legislation] only where there is a threat that the objectives of the energy policy may be compromised. Furthermore, . . . any such intervention must be supported by a formal statement of reasons and may be the subject of an effective review by the courts.' [52] 'The scheme therefore makes it possible to guarantee, on the basis of objective criteria which are subject to judicial review, the effective availability of the lines and conduits providing the main infrastructures for the domestic conveyance of energy products, as well as other infrastructures for the domestic conveyance and storage of gas, including unloading and cross-border facilities. Thus, it enables the Member State concerned to intervene with a view to ensuring, in a given situation, compliance with the public service obligations . . . whilst at the same time observing the requirements of legal certainty.'

2.75 **Ex post control reserved for foreign investors.** The legal regime examined by the ECJ in *Commission v Belgium (2002)* was not applied solely to foreigners. It applied to all investors, whatever their nationality or residence. One could thus speak of an 'equally applicable' regime (regime applicable to all investors without distinction based on residence or nationality). One may wonder how the case would have been decided if the regime had been limited to foreign investors. Could an exemption be granted to a regime exercising a discrimination as between investors based on residence or nationality when, that aspect aside, the regime presented the characteristics examined in the Belgian case (control ex post, limited period for public reaction, etc)? The answer is probably in the negative. In the internal market, discriminatory measures have no legitimacy. This was made clear in *Commission v Portugal (2002)*. Economic activities such as a public service can be carried out, even in strategic sectors, by undertakings and/or investors from other Member States. A discriminatory effect would be deemed excessive, under the principle of proportionality. Other measures could be found to bring about the same objective while hindering to a lesser extent the realisation of the internal market.

(6) Case concerning the electronic communications sector

Commission v Spain (2003).   Most of the situations examined so far do not   **2.76**
concern electronic communications specifically. One case, however, has featured
undertakings active in that sector. In *Commission v Spain (2003)*, the ECJ dealt
with various industries—tobacco, commercial banking, petroleum, electricity
and telecommunications. As regards that case, it is stated above that the ECJ
rejected as unacceptable the objectives put forward by the Spanish Government
to justify a regime of prior authorisation in two sectors (tobacco, commercial
banking). By contrast, the objectives were accepted in the other sectors, including
telecommunications.[65] The issue, then, was to determine to what extent the
Spanish measure could be found proportional. The ECJ concluded that the measure produced excessive effects because it gave the Spanish authorities a discretionary power to decide when an operation could be blocked.

> *Commission v Spain (2003)*. [74] 'Exercise of the State's right is not subject, under the
> relevant provisions, to any conditions. The investors concerned are given no indica-
> tion of the specific, objective circumstances in which prior approval will be granted
> or withheld.' [75] 'Such lack of precision does not enable individuals to be apprised
> of the extent of their rights and obligations deriving from Article 56 EC, with the
> result that such rules must be regarded as contrary to the principle of legal certainty.' [80]
> 'Given the lack of any objective, precise criteria deriving from the rules at issue, it
> must be held that the latter go beyond what is necessary to attain the objective relied
> on by the Spanish Government.'

(7) Criteria for practitioners

Check list.   It is now time to draw up a check list of the conditions under which   **2.77**
a regime of controls on share acquisitions may be accepted or rejected. This list is
important for practitioners, as it describes the situations where such a national
regime can be defended or must, on the contrary, be set aside.

Features to avoid.   Governments should avoid certain features in the regimes   **2.78**
they want to adopt or maintain to control the acquisition of shares in national

---

[65] The Spanish legislation provided that authorisation had to be obtained from a public authority prior to certain operations. The regime was rather complex. *(a)* First, certain general conditions
were applicable. These related to the context in which control would take place. The regime was
applicable only when these conditions were fulfilled. The conditions were the following: a decision
was taken to lower the public participation in the undertaking to less than 50% of the capital; the
operation would allow the investor to acquire 10% or more of the shares in the company; the operation, alone or with others, would have as a consequence that the public holding would indeed
decrease below 10% of the capital. *(b)* These conditions being satisfied, the Spanish legislation
determined the scenarios where the prior authorisation regime would apply. Two scenarios were
taken into account. In the first, the operation would lead to a diminution of the public participation
below a threshold of 10%. In the second, intervention would be mandated where the operation
would allow the investor to hold 10% or more of the undertaking's capital. For more details on these
conditions, see *Commission v Spain (2003)* (n 56 above) at [9].

undertakings. *(a)* A regime exclusively directed against investors would be considered contrary to the internal market. According to the case law, such a regime may not be redeemed by any reasoning. The application of such an illegal regime may lead foreign investors to suffer losses. On the basis of the case law, redress could be demanded before the national courts against the government concerned for causing damages. *(b)* Drawing 'equally applicable' measures does not necessarily save a regime of controls on share acquisition. The advantage of such measures is that they may not be found prima facie contrary to EU law. An investigation must be carried out into the objectives pursued through the national regime and the measures composing that regime. *(c)* Regarding objectives, economic justifications must be avoided. They are not accepted by the ECJ. Non-economic considerations, such as security or continuity of supply, are by contrast permitted. Other examples of acceptable justification may be found in the EC Treaty itself or in the case law. *(d)* Finally, measures must be proportional. This last requirement implies that obligations to obtain an authorisation prior to carrying out an operation are normally contrary to the EC Treaty. By contrast, ex post controls are acceptable, even when the control occurs on the basis of a notification which must be made before the operation is carried out. Restrictions must be limited to the minimum. For instance, the period within which the public control is carried out must be limited.

2.79 **Legal uncertainty.** An important obligation is to avoid legal uncertainty. This aspect was examined in *Commission v Spain (2003)*, the ruling in which was based on an earlier case where the ECJ had rejected French legislation organising a control without indicating the criteria that would be used by the public authority in accepting or rejecting the operation. The ECJ held that it was important that the national regime should be transparent and based on criteria which are set out clearly.

> *Commission v Spain (2003)*. [50] '[U]nder the system established by that provision, any direct or indirect shareholding which exceeds certain limits, regardless of its nature or legal form, must first be approved by the Minister for Economic Affairs in respect of each of the persons participating in that holding. According to the applicable provisions, the exercise of that right is not qualified by any condition, save for a reference, formulated in general terms . . ., to the protection of the national interest. The investors concerned are given no indication whatever as to the specific, objective circumstances in which prior authorisation will be granted or refused. Such lack of precision does not enable individuals to be apprised of the extent of their rights and obligations deriving from Article 73b of the Treaty. That being so, such a system must be regarded as contrary to the principle of legal certainty.' [51] 'Such a wide discretionary power constitutes a serious interference with the free movement of capital, and may have the effect of excluding it altogether. Consequently, the system in issue clearly goes beyond what is necessary in order to attain the objective pleaded by the French Government, namely the prevention of any disruption of a minimum supply of petroleum products in the event of a real threat.' [54] 'It must therefore be

held that, by maintaining in force the legislation in issue, the French Republic has failed to comply with its obligations under Article 73b[66] of the Treaty.'

Communication from the Commission. An interesting document for practi-   **2.80**
tioners regarding the limitations placed on ownership by foreign investors is the Communication from the Commission on certain legal aspects concerning intra-EU investment.[67] The Communication does not contain principles differing from the case law, but provides useful background and a general presentation of the issues and solutions in European law. In the Communication, the Commission distinguishes two sorts of measure that governments tend to adopt when they want to maintain control over the shareholdings in national undertakings in specific sectors (public utilities, including electronic communications). *(a)* The first kind of measure is the imposition of prohibitions, or obligations, on foreigners. Such measures, the Commission considers, are incompatible with the EC Treaty. As examples, the Commission mentions measures such as those discussed above, including the prohibition imposed on foreigners on acquiring more than a given number of shares or the obligation to obtain prior authorisation when the operation could lead to a holding of a given percentage by a foreigner. *(b)* The second type of measure contains no discrimination but is 'equally applicable' to all investors, national and foreigners alike. Such measures constitute restrictions contrary to the EC Treaty, but can be redeemed if the objective is legitimate and the means are proportional.

C. The Basic Regulatory Principles

(1) Introduction

Objectives and means. In the NRF, the Parliament and the Council have con-   **2.81**
sidered that the Member States, and the NRAs, should comply with various basic regulatory principles. These principles introduce constraints on the type of action that NRAs may undertake. These constraints concern, on the one hand, the objectives which they seek to fulfil through their actions. They also concern, on the other hand, the means or instruments to be used by the NRAs in order to attain these objectives.

Various constraints concerning means. The constraints relating to the object-   **2.82**
ives are enumerated explicitly in one specific provision within the Framework Directive. There are echoes of these same, or similar, objectives in other provisions throughout the NRF. The situation is less explicit for the constraints relating to the instruments which may be used by the NRAs. In one general provision, there

---

[66] Now Art 56 EC.   [67] [1997] OJ C220/15.

is an indication that the proportionality principle must be complied with. But no provision summarises the regulatory constraints imposed on NRAs regarding the instruments that they can use. This does not correspond with the general approach adopted by the Parliament and the Council. In the NRF, these institutions granted significant powers to the NRAs for the implementation of the framework. But these powers were not granted without limitation. The constraints imposed on NRAs are real. For this reason all constraints concerning instruments or modalities are concentrated in Chapter 2. As a result, the expression 'basic regulatory principles' is used in this book in a wider sense than the meaning explicitly granted to the concept of regulatory principles in the NRF. All obligations affecting in a general fashion the powers granted to NRAs are included under that heading.

2.83 **The status of the basic regulatory principles.** The basic regulatory principles are more than simple rules. They permeate the NRF. It is for this reason that they are called, in the NRF itself, 'principles'. A legitimate interpretation is that, as they are pervasive, these principles must be accorded the status of general principles of law. Such status implies that they apply in all situations. There is no need for a specific reference in a provision to ensure the application of the principle in the situation at stake. Given their general character, then, these principles apply in all circumstances (in the absence of an explicit derogation in line with superior rules of European law).

2.84 **Critical for practitioners.** The basic regulatory principles imposed on actions undertaken by NRAs are critical for practitioners. Any deviation from them may provide an argument for practitioners to seek the annulment of an action. *(a) Means.* The case is particularly clear where principles regarding the instruments to be used by NRAs are not complied with. Where for example a decision is taken without the requisite transparency (transparency being a regulatory principle imposed by the Parliament and Council in the NRF), any binding action taken by the NRA may be attacked on formal grounds. *(b) Objectives.* The same remark can be made with regard to objectives. Pursuant to the NRF, action by the NRAs must seek to achieve certain objectives. This implies that the powers entrusted to NRAs are granted only for the attainment of those objectives. Where an NRA decides to undertake an action: (i) in pursuance of the above-mentioned principle, the action can only be considered legitimate and, hence, valid, if and to the extent that action is taken to achieve an objective sanctioned, and imposed, by the NRF. A link with an objective thus appears as a condition for the legitimacy, and validity, of a given action undertaken by an NRA; (ii) the NRA must justify its action. As it is granted powers for the attainment of specific objectives, it has to demonstrate that these objectives are indeed likely to be brought about through the action undertaken. An obligation to justify is thus imposed on NRAs as a result of the principle that objectives are to be fulfilled.

Outline. In the following paragraphs, the objectives and instruments at European **2.85** level are examined successively. The analysis starts with the objectives that the NRAs must seek to attain through their actions. These objectives are, respectively, the promotion of competition, the development of the internal market and the promotion of the interests of the citizens of the Union. The analysis then turns to the principles guiding the choice of instruments that NRAs may use to bring about these objectives. These principles concern, as will be seen, non-discrimination, neutrality and proportionality. Finally, the principles relating to the environment in which NRA actions take place are examined. That environment also gives rise to principles: the NRAs' powers; independence of these bodies; transparency in the decision-making process and the publication of instruments; and the possibility of judicial review to ensure control of compliance with these various principles.

(2) Constraints relating to the objectives assigned to NRAs

Objectivity

First constraint. A first constraint is that decisions or attitudes adopted by NRAs **2.86** must be objective. That constraint is formulated in various of the directives making up the NRF. It was already introduced in the old regulatory framework. The excerpts below provide examples of provisions referring to the requirement of objectivity.

> *Framework Directive, Article 9(1).* 'Member States . . . shall ensure that the allocation and assignment of . . . radio frequencies by national regulatory authorities are based on objective . . . criteria.' *Framework Directive, Article 10(1).* 'National regulatory authorities shall establish objective, transparent and non-discriminatory assigning procedures for national numbering resources.' *Universal Service Directive Preamble, recital 48.* 'Co-regulation should be guided by the same principles as formal regulation, ie it should be objective, justified, proportional, non-discriminatory and transparent.'

The link with objectives imposed on NRAs. The difficulty with the constraint **2.87** relating to objectivity is that the content and implications of that constraint are not described in an explicit manner in any of the instruments composing the NRF. As a result of that silence, it is difficult to develop a clear idea as to the requirements deriving from objectivity. To interpret the concept, one method is to establish a link between the requirement of objectivity and the idea that, in all their actions, NRAs must ensure the attainment of objectives set out in the NRF. In that interpretation, objectivity means that decisions and attitudes may not aim at non-legitimate purposes. On the contrary, decisions and attitudes must be directed towards objectives that are considered acceptable at European level.

> *Framework Directive, Article 8(1).* 'Member States shall ensure that in carrying out the regulatory tasks specified in this Directive and the Specific Directives, the national regulatory authorities take all reasonable measures which are aimed at achieving the objectives set out in paragraphs 2, 3 and 4.'

The development of competition

2.88 **Competition-related constraints.** A fundamental goal is that competition must be developed. That goal guides the whole reform undertaken by the European legislator in the electronic communications sector. It thus comes as no surprise that NRAs are asked to pay particular attention in the course of their activities to competition. Attention to competition implies various requirements. *(a)* Behaviour or measures likely to distort competition must be eliminated (see (b) in the extract below).[68] *(b)* Decisions to be taken by NRAs must be guided by a desire to promote the interests of users ((a) below). The existence of choice must be ensured for customers. This implies that decisions must be taken with a view to obtaining a diminution in the prices charged to customers and/or an increase in the quality and the range of products which are offered to the public ((a) below). *(c)* In addition to these requirements, the Framework Directive introduces specific suggestions for given areas. In particular, the Parliament and Council require NRAs to devote special attention to investment in infrastructure, the promotion of innovation and efficiency in the use of scarce resources (frequencies, numbering) ((c) and (d) below).[69]

> *Framework Directive, Article 8(2).* 'The national regulatory authorities shall promote competition in the provision of electronic communications networks, electronic communications services and associated facilities and services by *inter alia*: (a) ensuring that users, including disabled users, derive maximum benefit in terms of choice, price, and quality; (b) ensuring that there is no distortion or restriction of competition in the electronic communications sector; (c) encouraging efficient investment in infrastructure, and promoting innovation; and (d) encouraging efficient use and ensuring the effective management of radio frequencies and numbering resources.'

2.89 **Similarity with general competition law.** An interesting observation is that the objective of competition assigned to NRAs in the NRF does not differ substantially from the requirements guiding the intervention of competition authorities in the application of the competition rules. Under EC provisions, competition authorities (national authorities and the European Commission) intervene against anti-competitive behaviour in the form of agreements (Article 81 EC) or unilateral practices (Article 82 EC). That intervention is aimed at ensuring a satisfactory degree of choice for customers, in the hope that pressure will be placed on undertakings to offer better products and services. Exemptions may be granted, allowing undertakings to escape the application of the competition rules. Conditions must however be fulfilled for exemptions to be granted. One condition is that the situation created by the undertakings concerned should not be unfavourable for

---

[68] Competition law in principle covers behaviour adopted by undertakings. It also addresses measures adopted by authorities where such measures may affect the objectives of European law.

[69] NRAs could for instance accept relatively high prices for access to infrastructure in given areas, because such prices would ensure that investment in infrastructure would continue to be made. Low access prices may on the other hand encourage undertakings to seek access rather than develop new or properly maintain existing infrastructure.

customers. Another is that the behaviour adopted by these undertakings must be compatible with legitimate values such as economic and/or technical progress.

A single authority?   A similarity may thus be observed in the goals assigned to **2.90** NRAs as regards competition and the requirement imposed on competition authorities. One may wonder, on the basis of this similarity, whether NRAs do not receive, thereby, an implicit mandate to apply the competition rules in the electronic communications sector. As a result of the obligations imposed on NRAs, two authorities are indeed granted a power to ensure that competition is safeguarded and develops, at national level, in the electronic communications sector. This similarity in objectives to be pursued by the two types of authority explains why some Member States have decided that all rules concerning the organisation and functioning of electronic communications markets should be handled by a single authority whatever the origin of these rules (NRF or competition law). As stated in Chapter 6, however, that scenario is not favoured in all European countries.

Comparison between sector-specific regulation and general competition law as regards **2.91** **objectives to be implemented**

	Competition-related guidance for NRAs in the implementation of sector-specific regulation[70]	Analysis to be made by competition authorities pursuant to general competition law[71]
Principle		
	Combat distortions or restrictions of competition in the electronic communications sector	Intervene against anti-competitive practices, whether collective (Article 81 EC) or unilateral (Article 82 EC)
Exceptions Legitimate objectives must be pursued	*(a)* Maximum benefits for users (choice, price, quality). *(b)* Efficient investment in infrastructure, promotion of innovation, efficient use and management of radio frequencies, efficient use and management of numbering	*(a)* Allow consumers a fair share of the resulting benefit. *(b)* Improvement in the production or distribution, promotion of technical or economic progress
The means must be proportionate	See the basic regulatory principles relating to the instruments chosen by the NRAs to implement the objectives	The means must be useful, necessary and may not be excessive

[70]   See Framework Directive, Art 9(2).
[71]   The constraints presented in this column are formulated explicitly in Art 81(3) EC (anti-competitive agreements). They may be found in the case law as regards the application of Art 82 EC (anti-competitive unilateral behaviour).

The development of the internal market

2.92 **Internal market.** Another goal that NRAs must seek to realise is the development of the internal market. As was the case for competition, several requirements are attached to that principle. *(a)* One aspect is that discrimination should be avoided. As a result, no undertaking may be treated less favourably when it is placed in situations which are not different from those of other businesses.[72] *(b)* The prohibition is not limited to discriminatory practices. Pursuant to the Framework Directive, non-discriminatory barriers should also be avoided. In general, NRAs must ensure that all remaining obstacles to the provision of networks or services across Europe are eliminated. *(c)* Positive measures must be taken, beyond a prohibition on action hindering inter-State commerce. Among these positive measures are the adoption of action likely to promote the trans-European character of networks and services. Trans-European networks must be favoured. Pan-European services must be made possible through improvements in interoperability. End-to-end connectivity must be enhanced.

> *Framework Directive, Article 8(3).* 'The national regulatory authorities shall contribute to the development of the internal market by *inter alia*: (a) removing remaining obstacles to the provision of electronic communications networks, associated facilities and services and electronic communications services at European level; (b) encouraging the establishment and development of trans-European networks and the interoperability of pan-European services, and end-to-end connectivity; (c) ensuring that, in similar circumstances, there is no discrimination in the treatment of undertakings providing electronic communications networks and services.'

2.93 **No real legal innovation.** A remark concerning convergence of objectives must be made here. There is no innovation in the obligations imposed on NRAs regarding objectives relating to the internal market. A similar prohibition of discrimination and other barriers to trade may be found in the Treaty provisions concerning goods and services. These provisions have direct effect. They apply, as a result, independently of any provision included in a source of secondary legislation—for instance a harmonisation instrument such as the Framework Directive. The duty to encourage pan-European services and trans-European networks may be

---

[72] The Framework Directive is not clear on the entities to which this prohibition on discrimination is addressed. *(a)* One possibility is that it applies to national authorities (including NRAs), meaning that they must avoid all discrimination. They further have a mandate to intervene against other national authorities exercising discrimination on electronic communications markets. Such an interpretation, however, does not really create a new rule, since discrimination is prohibited in internal market-related situations as a result of the Treaty itself (see inter alia Arts 12 and 30 EC). *(b)* Another possibility is that the prohibition is not limited to authorities but extends to undertakings. This interpretation would imply that undertakings cannot discriminate in their mutual relations. This would signal an interesting development, as anti-discrimination rules have been limited, so far, to authorities (with some exceptions, regarding for instance equality among workers and the prohibition on discrimination between customers imposed on dominant undertakings (Art 82 EC)).

interpreted along the same lines. It was stated that barriers to trade have to be dismantled. In the case law of the ECJ, barriers are defined in a rather wide manner, and any obstacle to the free movement of goods or the free provisions of services across frontiers should be removed. A consequence is that connections must be encouraged between networks and services in the various European countries. Another implication is that technical standards should be harmonised, wherever disparities impede interoperability.[73]

A coherent body of law.   In connection with the development of the internal   **2.94** market, a special effort is asked of NRAs to ensure the development of coherent, and consistent, regulatory practice throughout the Community in the field of electronic communications. That obligation in the Framework Directive shows that the Parliament and Council are aware of the risks that are inherent in a decentralised application of the NRF by NRAs. To understand the implications of the obligation, the model provided by Article 10 EC may be used. In that provision, an obligation is imposed on Member States to contribute to the attainment of the goals assigned to the Community.[74] Following that model, one can say that, through the obligation introduced in the Framework Directive, NRAs are indeed required to refrain from any action which may jeopardise coherence and consistency in the application of the NRF. They are also required to engage in whatever action is useful or necessary to ensure the development of such a body of law at European level.

> *Framework Directive, Article 8(3).* 'The national regulatory authorities shall contribute to the development of the internal market by *inter alia*: . . . (d) cooperating with each other and with the Commission in a transparent manner to ensure the development of consistent regulatory practice and the consistent application of this Directive and the Specific Directives.'

Serving the interests of citizens

Universal service, users' rights and social policy.   A third goal is that the inter-   **2.95** ests of citizens should be served. *(a)* That goal implies, first, that NRAs should favour the provision of universal service as mandated in the Universal Service. *(b)* Second, users and consumers should be duly protected in their transactions with undertakings. This requirement concerns the rights of consumers in their relations with undertakings. It also implies the protection of personal data and

---

[73] The only measure which may add to the case law is ultimately the recommendation that positive measures such as investment must be taken to promote trans-European networks.

[74] See Art 10 EC. 'Member States shall take all appropriate measures, whether general or particular, to ensure fulfilment of the obligations arising out of this Treaty or resulting from action taken by the institutions of the Community. They shall facilitate the achievement of the Community's tasks. They shall abstain from any measure which could jeopardise the attainment of the objectives of this Treaty.'

privacy. *(c)* Third, social action should be undertaken in line with the Universal Service Directive to address the needs of specific groups in society.[75]

> *Framework Directive, Article 8(4).* 'The national regulatory authorities shall promote the interests of the citizens of the European Union by *inter alia*: (a) ensuring all citizens have access to a universal service specified in Directive 2002/22/EC (Universal Service Directive); (b) ensuring a high level of protection for consumers in their dealings with suppliers, in particular by ensuring the availability of simple and inexpensive dispute resolution procedures carried out by a body that is independent of the parties involved; . . . (d) promoting the provision of clear information, in particular requiring transparency of tariffs and conditions for using publicly available electronic communications services; (e) addressing the needs of specific social groups, in particular disabled users.'

2.96 **Integrity and security of public networks.** In addition to the above-mentioned objectives, NRAs must ensure the integrity and security of public networks. The purpose, with these requirements, is to ensure the continuity of supply. As was observed at the outset of this book, electronic communications networks and services are essential in society. The European Union, and the Member States, cannot afford to be deprived of networks and/or services even for short periods. For that reason, measures must at all times ensure that integrity and security are maintained.

Comparison with the old framework

2.97 **Similarity concerning values.** The enumeration of objectives to be attained by NRAs may appear as an innovation in the NRF. There was no such enumeration in the old regulatory framework. However, the difference should not be exaggerated. There are in fact similarities between the two frameworks regarding the values promoted. These values do not appear to have changed, in substance, with the adoption of the NRF. From a comparison (see table at para 2.101 below) it may be concluded that there is no discrepancy between the two frameworks on this point.

2.98 **Difference regarding technique.** What was modified, by contrast, is the technique used by the European legislator to encourage, and compel NRAs to respect European values in electronic communications markets. *(a) New regulatory framework.* A list of objectives is included in the Framework Directive. These objectives are repeated in several provisions of that same Directive. They also appear in other instruments of the framework. In all these provisions, NRAs are compelled to take action in order to ensure the achievement of these goals. Their

---

[75] A last aspect relates to principles concerning privacy. As part of that obligation, personal data should only be transferred where the guarantees provided by the e-Privacy Directive are fulfilled (see Directive (EC) 2002/58 concerning the processing of personal data and the protection of privacy in the electronic communications sector (Directive on privacy and electronic communications) [2002] OJ L201/37).

opinions, and the instruments they adopt, must be reasoned. That reasoning must clearly demonstrate that one of the objectives included in the NRF has indeed been sought through the action. *(b) Old regulatory framework.* The method was slightly different in the old framework. In the latter, NRAs were to implement the regulation adopted at European level. Where no action was provided for in the framework, they remained free to take initiatives. These initiatives had to comply with general European law, in particular the rules concerning the internal market.[76] In the context of the internal market, these initiatives were accepted if they ensured the attainment of objectives, or values, deemed acceptable at European level. Among these objectives are some referred to in the Treaty. Others were developed in the case law. A third category was introduced through the harmonisation directives composing the old regulatory framework. These directives provided that national measures could be accepted, to the extent that they complied with values set out. Such values were called 'essential requirements'. National measures were deemed compatible with the internal market where they were justified by these essential requirements.[77]

Regulatory objectives and essential requirements   **2.99**

The new regulatory framework (NRF)	The old regulatory framework
Regulatory objectives	*Essential requirements*
Action taken by NRAs must be motivated by an objective enumerated in the NRF.	As a result of harmonisation, the Member States (including the NRAs) must implement the old regulatory framework. Their actions are considered contrary to the rules concerning the internal market, except when they aim at ensuring the realisation of an essential requirement. As a result, the essential requirements provide the only legitimate values justifying measures adopted by Member States

Explanation of the table.   A comparison is proposed in the table below between   **2.100** the values set out in the NRF and those accepted in the old regulatory framework.

---

[76] When a harmonisation directive is adopted, Member States give up powers. Two situations must be distinguished. *(a)* In the first, harmonisation carried out by the European institutions may be considered complete. Member States then lose any power to intervene with new initiatives. They may only implement European harmonisation measures. *(b)* Where harmonisation is not complete, Member States may then take new initiatives in addition to implementing the European harmonisation measures.

[77] In the old regulatory framework, these essential requirements were introduced not only in the harmonisation directives but also by the European Commission in the liberalisation directives. There was accordingly convergence between these two bodies of law (harmonisation, liberalisation), regarding the requirements considered essential and likely to justify national measures.

The values that explicitly appear in both frameworks are shown in **bold**. As the table shows, the list of objectives enunciated in the NRF is more complete. This is due, apparently, to a desire on the part of the European legislator to formulate in a didactic manner the values to which NRAs must pay particular attention. The presence of more objectives in the NRF should not give the impression, however, that there has been a substantial change regarding the type of values that is advocated by the European legislator. Most objectives appearing in the NRF are indeed an expression of values that were already applicable under the old regulatory framework, as a consequence of the rules concerning the internal market and those relating to competition.

2.101 Comparison of the values considered legitimate for action by NRAs

New regulatory framework	Old regulatory framework
(*a*) Promotion of competition Maximum benefits for users No distortion or restriction of competition Encourage efficient investment in infrastructure Promote innovation	
Encourage efficient use and management of radio frequencies and numbering resources	**Effective use of frequency spectrum, avoidance of harmful interference** [78]
(*b*) Development of the internal market Removing remaining obstacles Encourage trans-European networks, interoperability and end-to-end connectivity Non-discrimination Cooperation to develop consistent practice at European level	**Interoperability of services**
(*c*) Promotion of the interests of citizens Universal service Protection of consumers **Protection of personal data and privacy** Transparency Assistance to specific groups **Integrity and security of networks**	**Data protection**[79]
(*d*) Protection of the environment, town and country planning objectives	**Security of network operations, maintenance of network integrity**

[78] Between radio-based telecommunications systems and other, space-based or terrestrial, technical systems.

[79] Protection of personal data, confidentiality of information transmitted or stored, protection of privacy.

Final observations

European and national objectives.   One may reflect as to the reasons which have   **2.102**
led the Parliament and Council to specify objectives which NRAs are required to
fulfil. The objectives assigned to NRAs in the Framework Directive are not different, in fact, from those that underlie the whole NRF. One interpretation could be
that, through these provisions concerning objectives, the Parliament and Council
have explicitly formulated the objectives that they have sought to realise through
the adoption of the NRF. They have therefore required the NRAs to use all possible means to ensure the fulfilment of these goals.[80]

The importance of users.   In the three categories of objectives (competition,   **2.103**
internal market, interests of citizens), users' interests predominate. All of these
objectives are indeed focused on their needs. This is particularly clear for the third
category, which concerns the rights granted to users. But the same observation
may be made for the first and second. Competition is indeed established, and
developed, for users, the goal being to provide them with goods and services of
reasonable quality under affordable conditions. The same goes for the objectives
relating to the internal market. The internal market was originally intended to
ensure the interpenetration of national economies. Contacts and exchanges were
originally encouraged in order to foster peace on the continent. However, these
objectives have progressively evolved. The provisions relating to the internal market now provide interesting tools to develop competition among undertakings
from different Member States. Competition often depends on behaviour adopted
by undertakings, but also on the attitudes adopted by public authorities. The
internal market rules provide interesting tools to challenge national provisions
hindering inter-State competition, to the benefit of users.

(3) Constraints relating to the instruments that may be used by NRAs
Overview of the constraints

Other constraints.   The basic regulatory principles go further than imposing   **2.104**
an obligation to base national actions on objectives which can be deemed
acceptable. They also concern the instruments that the NRAs may use in order to
reach these objectives. These constraints are examined in the following paragraphs. Among them are the obligations for NRAs to avoid discrimination, comply with the principle of proportionality and remain neutral in technological
choices.

---

[80] This method or strategy does not differ from that used in the EC Treaty, where the Member
States have set out the missions entrusted to the European institutions and have explained what
actions they should undertake in order to ensure they are fulfilled.

Avoid discrimination

2.105 **A general principle of law.** The first requirement is to avoid discrimination. The prohibition of discrimination, in the context of electronic communications, comes as no surprise. Discrimination is prohibited as a general principle of law. That principle is expressed in various EC provisions, including Article 12 of the EC Treaty. The prohibition to discriminate also appears in specific provisions contained in the NRF. Some examples are provided below. They do not pretend to be exhaustive.

> *Article 12 EC.* 'Within the scope of application of this Treaty, and without prejudice to any special provisions contained therein, any discrimination on grounds of nationality shall be prohibited. The Council, acting in accordance with the procedure referred to in Article 251, may adopt rules designed to prohibit such discrimination.' *Framework Directive, Article 8(3).* 'The national regulatory authorities shall contribute to the development of the internal market by *inter alia*: . . . (c) ensuring that, in similar circumstances, there is no discrimination in the treatment of undertakings providing electronic communications networks and services.' *Framework Directive, Article 9(1).* 'Member States shall ensure the effective management of radio frequencies for electronic communication services in their territory in accordance with Article 8. They shall ensure that the allocation and assignment of such radio frequencies by national regulatory authorities are based on objective, transparent, non-discriminatory and proportionate criteria.'

2.106 **The possibility of justification.** One issue in the European case law is whether a discriminatory measure may be justified. Some argue that discriminatory measures (in this context, measures introducing differences of treatment based on nationality or residence) may never be justified because they prejudice the attainment of the internal market to an unacceptable extent. Others consider that justifications are admitted and that, as a result, discriminatory measures should be accepted when they are based on a legitimate objective and when the means are acceptable (these two conditions being cumulative). The pragmatic approach between these positions is to consider that a discrimination normally violates the third requirement attached to proportionality, ie the necessity of avoiding excessive effects or the prohibition on going beyond what is strictly necessary for the realisation of a legitimate objective. In that intermediate approach, justification is not a priori excluded. Hence no distinction is drawn from a theoretical point of view between measures depending on whether they are discriminatory. In practice, justification is not, however, acceptable given the excessive harm caused by discriminatory measures to the realisation of the internal market.

Actions must be proportionate

2.107 **Proportionality.** Another constraint imposed on NRAs is the obligation to comply with the proportionality principle in the action they take.

Framework Directive, Article 8(1). 'Member States shall ensure that in carrying out the regulatory tasks specified in this Directive and the Specific Directives, the national regulatory authorities take all reasonable measures which are aimed at achieving the [assigned] objectives . . . Such measures shall be proportionate to those objectives.'

General principle of law. The requirement that proportionality must be com- 2.108
plied with appears in the general provisions concerning basic regulatory principles. It also appears in numerous provisions dealing with specific actions. This
shows that, apart from the establishment of the rule in given contexts, proportionality must be considered a general principle of law that is applicable to all
actions undertaken by NRAs. This status of the proportionality principle was
already clear from the general case law of the ECJ. It has important consequences
for practitioners, since in all contexts it is possible to question the adequacy of
actions undertaken by NRAs by claiming that they lack proportionality.

Application in other contexts. The proportionality principle is not limited to 2.109
actions developed by NRAs. It is part of all major provisions of European law. A
significant illustration is the provisions concerning the internal market (free
movement of goods, services, capital; right of establishment). These provisions do
not contain an explicit reference to the principle that has been developed, to its
current extent, in the case law. In the case law concerning the internal market, it is
difficult to find a case where, when a measure has been found to be a restriction
on trade, the decision is not based on the proportionality, or the absence of proportionality, of the national measure under examination. Other examples concerning
the principle of proportionality may be found in the application of the competition rules. In this specific context, the application of the proportionality principle
has also been verified in a large number of cases. Under Article 81, for instance,
undertakings may enter into agreements which are normally prohibited if, and to
the extent that, an appropriate objective is pursued by the undertakings concerned and the means are found to be proportional. A similar approach can be
found in the case law concerning Article 82 EC, where dominant undertakings
may resort to behaviour which, in the absence of a legitimate objective and appropriate means, would qualify as a prohibited abuse.

Three tests. There is abundant case law on, and large quantities of academic 2.110
analysis of, the principle of proportionality. Courts and authors have attempted to
distinguish various tests in the application of the principle. An interpretation will
depend on three tests: the measure must be useful, it must be necessary and it may
not be excessive. These three tests are examined in the following paragraphs.

Useful measure. Under the first, the body carrying out the control must verify 2.111
that the measure is useful for the realisation of a legitimate objective. Under that

test, the idea is to verify whether the measure contributes to the realisation of the said objective. The purpose is to avoid non-relevant justifications.[81]

2.112 **Necessary measure.** Another test is to determine whether the measure is necessary. Under this test, the intention is to verify whether another measure could be used to attain the objective. The authority making the assessment then attempts to find possible alternative measures. The question is whether the objective can be realised otherwise than through the measure causing the hindrance. In the assessment, a preference is given to alternative measures if, and to the extent, the objective (or a similar goal) can be attained while hindering freedom of commerce and activity to a lesser degree. Under this second test, the measure adopted by the national authority will be deemed satisfactory in the absence of a plausible, satisfactory, alternative measure.

2.113 **Absence of excessive effect.** The last test concerns the effects produced by the measure at stake. Where, for example, a national measure leads to the realisation of a legitimate objective and cannot be replaced by another, the first and second tests are fulfilled. However, necessary as it may be, such a measure may be set aside if the negative consequences would be excessive in relation to freedom of commerce and activity. Here a balance is struck between values and effects. The reasoning goes as follows. One value is affected by the national restriction. At the same time, that restriction brings about the attainment of a legitimate value. What situation should be preferred in the light of the positive, and the negative, consequences produced by the measure in regard to the various values involved?

2.114 **Necessity and absence of excessive effect.** Of the three tests composing the proportionality assessment, the second and the third are generally used by the controlling entity to set aside the measures or behaviour examined. Parties are generally able to establish a link between the measure and a legitimate objective (usefulness test). By contrast, justification becomes more difficult when other possible measures are considered or an excessive effect must be avoided. Practitioners are thus advised to concentrate on the second and third tests, whether they are defending or challenging a measure adopted by a national authority.

Neutrality with respect to technology

2.115 **Neutrality.** Pursuant to the NRF, NRAs must remain technology neutral in the decisions or positions they adopt. This implies that no given technology may be favoured, in any manner.

---

[81] In some instances, Member States seek to explain legislation by arguing that these measures serve a goal that is acceptable at a European level. After examination, it however appears that there is no link between the objective and the measure which is supposed to lead to its realisation.

Framework Directive, Article 8(1). 'Member States shall ensure that in carrying out the regulatory tasks specified in this Directive and the Specific Directives, in particular those designed to ensure effective competition, national regulatory authorities take the utmost account of the desirability of making regulations technologically neutral.'

Link with other provisions. The requirement to respect technological neutral- **2.116** ity may be associated with other provisions. It appears similar to the requirement examined elsewhere in this chapter that European institutions must remain neutral regarding the system of ownership in force in the various Member States. It also appears close to the prohibition on exercising discrimination. Regarding this last prohibition, neutrality indeed requires the absence of the favourable, or unfavourable, treatment of one or several particular parties.[82]

Difficulty of ensuring neutrality. It is shown in this chapter how difficult it is to **2.117** remain neutral regarding ownership regimes. A similar observation must be made regarding technological neutrality. Virtually all decisions taken by NRAs indeed have an effect on technology. Regulations have an impact on costs, and the development of technology depends mainly on investments. It is not possible to ignore the consequences on technological choices of decisions affecting the costs incurred by an undertaking. Suppose that, pursuant to a decision taken by an NRA, an undertaking operating a telecommunications network must be subject to specific regulatory obligations. The consequence is that the costs incurred by that undertaking will rise (regulation often implies higher costs and lower profits). A corollary is that investment by new undertakings in alternative techniques (for instance, mobile technology) will, by comparison, appear more appealing. In such a situation, the alternative technology (in this case, mobile) ends up being favoured, indirectly, even in a context where the NRA would not consciously seek to produce that effect.

Legal force. Practitioners should be aware of the possibilities opened by the **2.118** obligation imposed on NRAs to remain neutral regarding different technologies. The obligation to respect neutrality appears to have binding force (in the absence of such force, the provision calling for neutrality would be meaningless). A significant number of decisions may be challenged on that basis before a national court. The only condition which, according to the NRF, should be satisfied for the action to be successful would be that the decision has indeed favoured a technology directly or indirectly, consciously or unconsciously.

---

[82] In this case, the discrimination would not be based on nationality or residence but would rather be founded on a preference, direct or indirect, conscious or unconscious, for one or several techniques. The prohibition on discrimination should not be limited, however, to differences of treatment based on nationality or residence. It has wider scope in European law. It may be associated with the principle of equality. Under both principles, legal or natural persons in a similar situation must be treated in a similar manner. A corollary is that legal or natural persons in different situations must be treated differently.

(4) Constraints relating to the entities and system concerned

2.119 **Supplementary constraints.** Some constraints relating to objectives, and others concerning instruments, have been examined. A third category of requirements concerns the system, or the context, in which NRAs are to develop their actions. The Member States have an obligation to create a regulatory environment where the actions adopted by the NRAs conform to the constraints dealing with objectives and instruments. The requirements forming part of that system are examined in other chapters of this book. For that reason they are not analysed at length in this section. It is however important to mention them in this context, as they are basic regulatory principles in the sense set out above.

2.120 **The entities concerned.** A first set of constraints concerns the entities in question and, in particular, their organisation. As stated, NRAs must be independent of all relations with undertakings. They must also have qualified personnel. Competence is an obligation if the NRAs are to be able to contribute to the attainment of the tasks allocated to the Community.

2.121 **The system.** Another set of constraints concerns the system in which NRAs develop their actions. These constraints must make it possible for a superior body to verify whether the actions undertaken by NRAs are compatible with European law. *(a)* A pre-condition for making a control possible is transparency. The decision-making process must be public. The procedures where decisions are taken must also be opened up to interested parties. *(b)* Another requirement is the possibility of judicial review. It would be pointless to introduce regulatory constraints and impose them on NRAs in the absence of a mechanism ensuring compliance. Judicial review, or the possibility of such review, is a necessity to ensure compliance, not only by undertakings but also public authorities.

(5) A regulatory model

2.122 **Summary of the basic regulatory principles.** With the introduction of these constraints regarding objectives, instruments and systems, the European institutions (Parliament, Council, Commission) have sketched a regulatory model. That model is represented in the table below, showing how intervention should develop at national level and the conditions that must be complied with for national action to be valid. The important aspect, for practitioners, is to realise that each of these constraints provides arguments for challenging the position or decision adopted by an NRA in a given situation. In this model, NRAs are required to bring about certain objectives. To attain these objectives, they are required to comply with the principles of proportionality, technology neutrality and non-discrimination. All this must take place in a context where information flows freely and there is transparency as to the intentions and actions of the NRAs. In this context there must also be room for judicial review. Authorities must also have the requisite power and be independent.

Examples of application. The regulatory model proposed by the European **2.123** institutions is apparent in various provisions of the NRF. It is not possible to give here an exhaustive account of these provisions. Examples are provided. The main idea is that all decisions and rules adopted by the NRAs must in principle comply with this model.

> *Framework Directive, Article 9(1).* 'Member States . . . shall ensure that the allocation and assignment of such radio frequencies by national regulatory authorities are based on objective, transparent, non-discriminatory and proportionate criteria.' *Framework Directive, Article 10.* 'National regulatory authorities shall establish objective, transparent and non-discriminatory assigning procedures for national numbering resources.' *Access Directive, Preamble, recital 4.* 'This Directive covers authorisation of all electronic communications networks and services whether they are provided to the public or not. This is important to ensure that both categories of providers may benefit from objective, transparent, non-discriminatory and proportionate rights, conditions and procedures.' *Access Directive, Preamble, recital 28.* 'Subjecting service providers to reporting and information obligations can be cumbersome, both for the undertaking and for the national regulatory authority concerned. Such obligations should therefore be proportionate, objectively justified and limited to what is strictly necessary.' *Universal Service Directive, Preamble, recital 21.* 'In the case of cost recovery by means of levies on undertakings, Member States should ensure that the method of allocation amongst them is based on objective and non-discriminatory criteria and is in accordance with the principle of proportionality.'

The regulatory model established in the NRF **2.124**

NRAs	→	Instruments	→	Objectives	System
NRAs		Absence of discrimination, Neutrality, Proportionality[83]		Objectivity[84]	Competence, Independence, Transparency, Judicial review

D. Authorisations and Formalities Prior to Starting Activities

(1) Introduction

Formalities. Undertakings may be asked to accomplish formalities before they **2.125** commence market activity. These formalities are, in substance, intended to inform the relevant public authorities as to the identity of the players present on the markets. A second aim is to impose obligations concerning the performance

---

[83] The measures adopted by the NRAs must be useful to realise the objectives; they must also be necessary; they may not produce excessive negative effects.

[84] The measures adopted by the NRAs must seek the realisation of an objective deemed acceptable at a European level.

of activities. Traditionally, obligations concerning the exercise of activities are imposed through regulation. In the NRF, a preference is expressed in favour of another method whereby a commitment to comply with certain rules is requested from the undertakings at the time they ask for an authorisation to commence market activity. Obligations are imposed, in this manner, by the authorities. These obligations, and the commitment that is given in return by the undertakings, form a type of contract agreed by the parties involved.

2.126 Applicable provisions. Most European rules concerning formalities are contained in Directive (EC) 2002/20 of the European Parliament and of the Council on the authorisation of electronic communications networks and services ('Authorisations Directive').[85] Some rules may also be found in Commission Directive (EC) 2002/77 on competition in the markets for electronic communications networks and services ('Consolidated Services Directive').[86] The rules coming from that second instrument are limited in scope, and number, regarding authorisations.[87]

2.127 Networks and services, not terminal equipment. As stated earlier, this book concerns the rules applicable to networks and services. The marketing of terminal equipment across the Member States also raises issues of formalities.[88] These issues are not, however, examined in this book.

2.128 Similar national legislations. The rules concerning formalities result from a desire, on the part of the European legislator, to harmonise the national laws concerning that subject matter. Without harmonisation, undertakings would have remained subject to different legislation in all national territories where they want to provide networks and services. In some instances, discrepancies may exist between these national laws. This may cause problems for undertakings, which would have to adapt to each national market. Such a situation is avoided through the harmonisation of the main elements on which the national laws are based. Harmonisation provides comfort to undertakings eager to develop activities in various countries. In each of these countries, these undertakings can expect similar formal and/or material obligations.

Authorisations Directive, Article 1(1). 'The aim of this Directive is to implement an internal market in electronic communications networks and services through the

---

[85] [2002] OJ L108/21.   [86] [2002] OJ L249/21.

[87] The approach has not been to address the rules introduced by these two instruments in separate sections, in view of the convergence between the rules concerning formalities in the two instruments. Furthermore, the number of rules introduced on this subject in the Consolidated Services Directive is limited. In that Directive, the Commission only introduce principles such as the need to allow all interested undertakings to commence activity under the best possible conditions.

[88] See Directive (EC) 1999/5 of the European Parliament and of the Council on radio equipment and telecommunications terminal equipment and the mutual recognition of their conformity [1999] OJ L91/10.

harmonisation and simplification of authorisation rules and conditions in order to facilitate their provision throughout the Community.'

No European passport.   A further step could be reached, where undertakings **2.129** would only have to ask for an authorisation in one Member State. On that further step, the authorisation obtained in one Member State would be valid for all European countries (one-stop shopping). That stage of integration has not been reached at the present time on electronic communications markets. Currently, undertakings still have to be authorised in each country where they want to perform an activity.

Conflicting principles.   In the Authorisations Directive, the European **2.130** Parliament and the Council have sought to attain a compromise between two conflicting principles. *(a)* Activities should be performed in a climate where the values deemed essential in European society are complied with. This first aspect has traditionally been important in Europe, where authorities regularly monitor and control economic activities in the light of policy objectives. *(b)* The second principle is that no excessive burden should be imposed on undertakings. That aspect is more recent in Europe, where it developed with liberalisation and the bringing into being of the internal market. To a large extent, the reform carried out in European electronic communications aimed at breaking the monopolies long held by national operators. The objective was to open markets. That object-ive could only be reached if new actors were not discouraged by excessive costs. To that effect, it was thought that formalities should be reduced to a strict minimum, thereby reducing entry expenses.

(2) Application to public and private operations
Scope of application of the directives

Both types of operation.   The rules introduced in the NRF and concerning **2.131** formalities are applicable to electronic communications networks and services intended for the public, as well as to those with a private character. Public and non-public networks and services are thus covered, in principle, by the NRF, as regards authorisations.

> *Authorisations Directive, Preamble, recital 4.* 'This [Authorisations] Directive covers authorisation of all electronic communications networks and services whether they are provided to the public or not. This is important to ensure that both categories of providers may benefit from objective, transparent, non-discriminatory and propor-tionate rights, conditions and procedures.'

A specificity compared to other rules.   The application of European rules to the **2.132** private provision of networks and services may come as a surprise. Other rules introduced in the NRF and regarding, for instance, network access, or universal service, are subject to a different regime. In those rules, a distinction is made between public and private activities. The former (public) activities are subject to the rules introduced at European level. By contrast, the latter (private activities) escape the application of these rules.

2.133 **Universal service.**   It is not easy to understand the difference made by the European legislator in the scope of the respective directives it has introduced (Access, Universal Service and Authorisations Directives). A reason emerges rapidly however for the application of the Universal Service Directive to public activities to the exclusion of private operations. Through universal service, the Parliament and the Council wanted to ensure the availability of basic services for the public throughout the territory under reasonable conditions. That objective by its nature concerns public networks and services. There is no need, for that reason, to extend obligations to private activities.

2.134 **Network access.**   Finding an explanation becomes more difficult when considering the Access Directive. In that Directive, the Parliament and Council sought to ensure the adequate provision of networks and services throughout the European Union. In order to bring about that situation, they promoted access by service providers to facilities operated by other undertakings. In the Access Directive, the Parliament and Council have limited these access-related obligations to facilities connected with the provision of a service to the public. Given their objective, networks and services would have developed, though, at a superior level, throughout the European Union, if these obligations had been applied to all types of infrastructure, public or private. There is little doubt that the Parliament and Council could have decided that all networks and, more generally, all facilities could be affected by access-related obligations. Such an option could have been taken in the name of the general interest (ensuring a development of all networks and services). The institutions have not however been willing to go so far. The measures have remained limited to facilities already having a public character. One reason could be the lack of political will. Another could be the competition law-based orientation of the reform.[89]

2.135 **Authorisations.**   By contrast with the other directives, such a limitation did not exist regarding authorisations. Making the European rules regarding authorisations applicable to all services, be they public or private, did not imply any supplementary sacrifice on the part of undertakings. The extension to private

---

[89] The obligation to grant access is based, to a significant extent, on the idea that dominant undertakings must share access to the essential facilities under their control. The context envisaged is a market where several undertakings compete for the provision of a service. On that market, one undertaking has an advantage as a result of the control it holds over a facility. By nature, that facility cannot be duplicated. There is thus only one such facility available on the market. In the absence of a measure taken by a public authority and ordering access to the unique existing facility, the market would remain monopolistic.

services only limits the sort of formalities and conditions that Member States may impose prior to the commencement of activity.

Private activities

Regime more favourable for private operations.   As stated above, the European   **2.136**
rules concerning authorisations apply to both the public and private provision of networks and services. This does not mean that the same conditions are applied to both categories. A distinction needs to be made, on the basis of the basic regulatory principles. In application of these principles, conditions such as those relating to network access have no relevance. As most conditions attached to authorisations refer to obligations introduced by other directives, the best method of determining whether a condition may be applied to the private provision of networks and services is to consider the scope of these directives. It then becomes clear that the number of conditions applicable to private activities is limited.

Applicable conditions.   It appears that only few conditions can be attached to a   **2.137**
general authorisation to provide private services: the payment of an administrative tax;[90] the obligation to respect the environment, or town and country planning rules;[91] the necessity to ensure the protection of privacy, including personal data;[92] and the obligation to ensure the safety, security and continuity of the network.[93] The situation is easier regarding rights of use. All conditions relating to numbers and frequencies would seem to apply, as they mainly provide indications about the legal regime applicable to those rights.

> *Authorisations Directive, Preamble, recital 16.* 'In the case of electronic communications networks and services not provided to the public it is appropriate to impose fewer and lighter conditions than are justified for electronic communications networks and services provided to the public.'

The presence of remuneration.   Private activities are thus subject to the rules   **2.138**
contained in the Authorisations Directive. In the NRF, 'private' means that the networks and/or services concerned are not meant for the public. They are kept for a limited, and closed, circle of individuals or undertakings. The NRF applies however only in situations where networks and services are provided against payment. The existence of remuneration is an essential criterion for the application of the NRF. The European Community is empowered to adopt harmonisation measures only where these measures concern the internal market. The internal market only concerns goods and services where remuneration is paid in consideration of their delivery or provision.

---

[90] See Authorisations Directive, Annex, Letter A, point 2.
[91] See ibid, Annex, Letter A, point 5.   [92] See ibid, Annex, Letter A, points 7 and 11.
[93] See ibid, Annex, Letter A, points 12, 13, 15 and 16.

> *Authorisations Directive, Preamble, recital 5.* 'This [Authorisations] Directive only
> applies to the granting of rights to use radio frequencies where such use involves
> the provision of an electronic communications network or service, normally for
> remuneration.'[94]

(3) Limitation of formalities and obligations

2.139 **Freedom to engage in activities.** The main principle concerning formalities
under the NRF is that undertakings should remain free to engage in the activities
they choose. Freedom is the principle regarding market entry in European electronic communications. This emphasis on freedom may be found in the
Authorisations Directive (Parliament and Council), as well as in the Consolidated
Services Directive (Commission). It is central for the interpretation of all provisions contained in these instruments.

> *Authorisations Directive, Article 3(1).* 'Member States shall ensure the freedom to
> provide electronic communications networks and services.' *Consolidated Services
> Directive, Article 2(2).* 'Member States shall take all measures necessary to ensure that
> any undertaking is entitled to provide electronic communications services or to
> establish, extend or provide electronic communications networks.'

2.140 **Self-restraint in regulation.** A corollary of freedom is that restrictions must be
limited to a minimum. Public authorities thus have a duty to limit their interventions, as they may otherwise discourage undertakings from entering and becoming active on the market. Authorities must refrain from adopting rules save in
exceptional circumstances. A consequence is that, under the NRF, regulatory
restrictions regarding market entry are only permitted if, and to the extent, they
are based on provisions of the NRF. In other words, the only restrictions permitted on electronic communications markets are those which have been established
in the NRF.

> *Authorisations Directive, Article 3(1).* 'Member States shall ensure the freedom to pro-
> vide electronic communications networks and services, *subject to the conditions set out
> in this Directive.*'[95] *Consolidated Services Directive, Article 2(3).* 'Member States shall
> ensure that no restrictions are imposed or maintained on the provision of electronic
> communications services over electronic communications networks established by the
> providers of electronic communications services, over infrastructures provided by third
> parties, or by means of sharing networks, other facilities or sites *without prejudice to the
> provisions of Directives 2002/19/EC, 2002/20/EC, 2002/21/EC and 2002/22/EC.*'[96]

2.141 **Institutional impact.** The limitation imposed on intervention by public
authorities mainly concerns the Member States. The European institutions are

---

[94] As a consequence, the self-use of radio terminal equipment, based on the non-exclusive use of
specific radio frequencies by a user and not related to an economic activity, such as use of citizens'
band by radio amateurs, does not constitute the provision of an electronic communications network
or service. It is therefore not covered by the NRF.   [95] Authors' emphasis.
[96] Authors' emphasis.

affected to a lesser degree. It is they that hold the power to introduce the measures that guide the activities carried out by the undertakings in the market. Member States do not in principle have the power to introduce restrictions supplementary to those established in the NRF.

Basic regulatory principles. An idea present throughout the Authorisations **2.142** Directive is that formalities must be compatible with the basic regulatory principles. These principles apply to the formal procedures that undertakings must accomplish to obtain authorisation. They also apply to the obligations that are imposed, through these formalities, to undertakings prior to the commencement of activities. In substance, these procedures and obligations must at all times be objective, non-discriminatory and proportionate. Among these requirements, emphasis is placed on the proportionality principle. According to that principle, Member States may not impose on undertakings formalities and/or obligations that are not necessary to ensure the attainment of legitimate objectives. The principle is breached where a similar result could be achieved through a less restrictive measure, or where the effect produced by the measure is excessive.

> *Consolidated Services Directive, Article 2(4).* 'Member States shall ensure that a general authorisation granted to an undertaking to provide electronic communications services or to establish and/or provide electronic communications networks, as well as the conditions attached thereto, shall be based on objective, non-discriminatory, proportionate and transparent criteria.' *Authorisations Directive, Article 6(1).* 'The general authorisation for the provision of electronic communications networks or services and the rights of use for radio frequencies and rights of use for numbers may be subject only to the conditions listed . . . in . . . the Annex. Such conditions shall be objectively justified in relation to the network or service concerned, non-discriminatory, proportionate and transparent.'

Judicial review available. It must be possible for undertakings which have **2.143** been refused authorisation to provide a network and/or a service to seek review of the NRA's decision. That review must be carried out by an organ that is independent of the parties. Ideally the review should take place before a judicial body. Where that is not possible, a further appeal before a judge must be made possible.

> *Consolidated Services Directive, Article 2(5).* 'Reasons shall be given for any decision . . . preventing an undertaking from providing electronic communications services or networks. Any aggrieved party should have the possibility to challenge such a decision before a body that is independent of the parties involved and ultimately before a court or a tribunal.' *Authorisations Directive, Article 10(7).* 'Undertakings shall have the right to appeal against measures [taken by NRAs and regarding formalities] . . . in accordance with the procedure referred to in Article 4[97] of Directive 2002/21/EC (Framework Directive).'

---

[97] That provision introduces a right of appeal against decisions adopted by NRAs.

2.144 **Obligation to reason decisions.** A corollary of judicial review is that negative decisions adopted by NRAs regarding authorisations must be reasoned. This obligation is provided for expressly in the Consolidated Services Directive. It may also be found in the Authorisations Directive, together with the Framework Directive (see para 2.143 above). NRAs must therefore explain precisely why they have reached a negative decision. The reasoning must also state how the procedure has unfolded (contact with undertakings, opinions expressed, etc.). The reasoning must allow the appellate body to verify whether the basic regulatory principles, and other constraints imposed on NRAs, have been complied with.

2.145 **Same constraints under WTO provisions.** These constraints are similar, in substance, to those formulated in the Reference Paper, which has been presented in the introductory chapter (see para 1.176) and introduces regulatory principles to be complied with by the Members of the Organisation which have taken commitments as regards basic telecommunications. Pursuant to that paper, transparency is of the essence. All terms and conditions relating to licences[98] have to be made public. Decisions whereby licences are denied must be reasoned.

> *Reference Paper, para. 4.* 'Where a licence is required, the following will be made publicly available: (a) all the licensing criteria and the period of time normally required to reach a decision concerning an application for a licence and (b) the terms and conditions of individual licences. The reasons for the denial of a licence will be made known to the applicant upon request.'

(4) What can the Member States do?

2.146 **Limited margin for manoeuvre.** As stated, Member States are limited in the restrictions they may introduce on electronic communications markets. Pursuant to the NRF, they may only introduce restrictions that have been decided at European level. In this context the margin of manoeuvre open to Member States is limited.

2.147 **Case law on harmonisation.** This limitation appears to be in line with the European case law on harmonisation, which states that Member States lose their power to regulate when a field of activity has been harmonised. The extent to which the power is lost depends on the harmonisation measure in question. *(a)* Complete harmonisation takes away all possibility for the Member States to intervene further in the area concerned. Action has been pre-empted by the European legislator through the adoption of harmonisation measures. As a result of that pre-emption, Member States lose their power to regulate further. According to the case law, all rules that Member States may adopt beyond the implementation of the harmonisation measures must be set aside as contrary to

---

[98] In WTO terminology, licences correspond to any form of (collective or individual) authorisation which undertakings must have prior to commencing activity.

European law. *(b)* A partial harmonisation has more limited implications for national powers. It leaves the power of the Member States unchanged as regards the non-harmonised part of the market. In these non-harmonised areas,[99] the Member States may introduce national regulation. This does not mean, however, that Member States are entirely free in those areas. They remain bound by other rules embodied in European law, among which, a prohibition on hindering the operation of the internal market. Any measure introduced by the Member States in a part of the market that is not completely harmonised must remain compatible with the rules concerning the internal market.[100]

Complete harmonisation.   The provisions contained in the Authorisations **2.148** Directive suggest that the European legislator has completely harmonised the laws of the Member States regarding formalities and authorisation. Pursuant to the directive itself, no restrictions may be introduced except those introduced at European level. This appears to imply that the European institutions have reserved for themselves the right to introduce restrictions regarding the freedom to enter markets and the conditions under which activities may be carried out.

Persistence of some ambiguity.   The impression created by the Authorisations **2.149** Directive is, however, ambiguous. In one provision, the Parliament and the Council announce that national restrictions are admissible when they are compatible with Treaty provisions. This provision does not explicitly grant Member States the right to intervene further in the field of authorisations and formalities. It does however create an ambiguous situation when the statement contained in the provision is compared with the case law on complete, or partial, harmonisation. As stated, complete harmonisation implies that national measures may only be adopted when they implement restrictions decided at European level. That standard seems to apply in the case of formalities and authorisations, as the Parliament and the Council indicate that no restrictions are allowed except those introduced in the NRF. In contradiction to this, the Parliament and Council make clear, in the provision discussed in this paragraph, that national restrictions are to be assessed, regarding their compatibility with European law, against the rules concerning the internal market. As was seen in the previous paragraphs, this last standard corresponds to an identification of the powers remaining to the Member States when harmonisation was only partial.

Authorisations Directive, Article 3(1). 'Member States shall ensure the freedom to provide electronic communications networks and services, subject to the conditions

---

[99] In the harmonised areas, the Member States lose all power to regulate markets further. See *(a)* in the same paragraph.

[100] They must conform, for instance, with the rules concerning the free movement of goods and/or the free provision of services. The only case where a national measure hindering the attainment of the internal market could be upheld is when a legitimate justification is available on the basis of the Treaty or the case law (acceptable means and objectives).

set out in this Directive. To this end, Member States shall not prevent an undertaking from providing electronic communications networks or services, except where this is necessary for the reasons set out in Article 46(1)[101] of the Treaty.'[102]

2.150 **Mixed harmonisation.** The reason for the ambiguity seems to be that the Parliament and Council have carried out 'mixed' harmonisation. *(a)* They have harmonised the content of the conditions to be fulfilled for entry on electronic communications market in the Member States. In this regard, harmonisation can be considered complete (see preceding paragraphs). *(b)* At the same time, they have maintained the principle of a procedure for each Member State. Under the NRF, authorisation remains necessary in each Member State prior to the commencement of activities in that State. No European passport has been created whereby authorisation granted in one Member State would be recognised in the others. The internal market in this regard remains incomplete.

2.151 **Combination of two approaches.** The 'mixed' character of the harmonisation that has taken place probably explains the persistence of the two approaches in the current version of the Authorisations Directive. *(a)* Regarding harmonisation of the conditions applicable to market entry, the NRF has carried out a complete harmonisation. In that context, the Member States are not allowed to introduce new conditions or formalities. This is compatible with the statement found in the Authorisations Directive whereby the Parliament and Council prohibit restrictions other than those introduced at European level. *(b)* On the need for a procedure in each Member State, the national authorities have retained their powers. The Member States have thus kept the right to apply their national legislation. The various national legislations must, however, comply with European law, including provisions relating to the internal market. In this context it is to be expected that the Authorisations Directive should contain an allusion to the obligation, for the Member States, to comply with Article 46(1) EC (free provision of services throughout the European Union).

2.152 **Oversight by the Commission.** The NRF announces that the Commission is bound to remain particularly vigilant concerning the procedures applied to market entry by the Member States. As stated, formalities must be complied with in each national market. The Commission intends to ensure that the application of separate national legislative provisions does not create unnecessary hindrances.

---

[101] Free provision of services.

[102] The ambiguity also appears in the Preamble. See Authorisations Directive, Preamble, recital 3. 'The objective . . . is to create a legal framework to ensure the freedom to provide electronic communications networks and services, subject only to the conditions laid down in this Directive and to any restrictions in conformity with Art 46(1) of the Treaty, in particular measures regarding public policy, public security and public health.' Art 46(1) EC concerns the free provision of services throughout the EU.

Authorisations Directive, Preamble, recital 35. 'The proper functioning of the single market on the basis of the national authorisation regimes . . . should be monitored by the Commission.'

(5) The concept of general authorisation

Normal situations

No authorisation. Pursuant to the Authorisations Directive, undertakings   **2.153** wishing to start activities on electronic communications markets may do so without having to comply with formalities or conditions. That principle corresponds to the general philosophy underlying the reform, whereby activities should be left to the markets where the circumstances so allow. That principle may be deduced from the formulation used in the Authorisations Directive. Pursuant to that instrument, activities may only be subject to general authorisation. The formulation indicates that general authorisation is a maximum that Member States may impose—and that lighter formalities and conditions are preferred by the European legislator.

> *Authorisations Directive, Article 3(2).* 'The provision of electronic communications networks or the provision of electronic communications services may . . . only be subject to a general authorisation.'

General authorisation. As indicated in the previous paragraph, the Author-   **2.154** isations Directive accepts that general authorisation may be imposed prior to activities being started. It remains to define what the European legislator means thereby. A legitimate interpretation is that an authorisation may only be called general where all candidate undertakings are admitted on the markets where they want to start activities. General authorisation thus appears as a mechanism whereby undertakings receive an automatic right to perform activities on a given market, dependent upon these undertakings committing themselves to comply with various obligations. Rights and obligations are thus intimately associated in the concept.

> *Authorisations Directive, Article 2(2).* ' "[G]eneral authorisation" means a legal framework established by the Member State ensuring rights for the provision of electronic communications networks or services and laying down sector specific obligations that may apply to all or to specific types of electronic communications networks and services.'

Features. Pursuant to that interpretation, the characteristics of general authori-   **2.155** sation are as follows. *(a)* The authorisation is general and activities must be opened to all candidate undertakings without restriction. *(b)* As indicated in the NRF, general authorisation is a procedure whereby a request does not need to be made by each undertaking, on the basis of the context in which that undertaking is situated. In other words, the undertakings do not need to explain why they want to enter a specific market and justify their plans. No specific action is requested, in principle, from the undertakings concerned. *(c)* Nor does general authorisation imply specific actions on the part of the NRAs. The procedure does not require NRAs to take a stance. Authorisation is granted automatically to all interested undertakings.

> *Authorisations Directive, Article 3(2).* 'The provision of electronic communications networks or the provision of electronic communications services may . . . only be subject to a general authorisation. The undertaking concerned . . . may not be required to obtain an explicit decision or any other administrative act by the national regulatory authority before exercising the rights stemming from the authorisation.'

First derogation

2.156 **Notification, declaration.**   A derogation has been admitted, in the Authorisations Directive, to the principle according to which all undertakings are necessarily, and automatically, admitted on the markets where they want to perform activities. That derogation is that a declaration or notification may be requested, if the Member State so desires, prior to the commencement of activities. The derogation confirms that, in normal circumstances, and, presumably, in most Member States, activities are not expected to be subject to any action on the part of the undertakings concerned. The possibility of requesting a notification, or a declaration, has been introduced, apparently, as a concession to parties which felt that a certain control still had to be exercised before activities could be started.

2.157 **Features.**   It is important to realise that, although it allows Member States to request a notification and/or declaration, the NRF remains restrictive as to the formalities and conditions that may be imposed. *(a)* Undertakings may not be asked to obtain a specific authorisation. Under the notification or declaration system, undertakings may thus be asked to accomplish a given action before activities can be started. However, Member States may not subject the commencement of activities to a specific action to be taken by an authority.[103] *(b)* Under normal circumstances, activities may commence as soon as the notification/declaration has been made. No other formality may thus be imposed. In countries where a notification or declaration is required, the undertakings may, at the same time, notify or declare—and start activities.

> *Authorisations Directive, Article 3.* [2] 'The provision of electronic communications networks or the provision of electronic communications services may . . . only be subject to a general authorisation. The undertaking concerned may be required to submit a notification . . . Upon notification, when required, an undertaking may begin activity.' [3] 'The notification . . . shall not entail more than a declaration by

---

[103] The NRF refers thereby to acts adopted by public authorities in reaction to an individual request made by a particular undertaking and allowing the latter undertaking to start an activity. See following paragraphs for more detail.

a legal or natural person to the national regulatory authority of the intention to commence the provision of electronic communication networks or services.'[104]

Second derogation

Request information.   As a second derogation to the principle, Member States   **2.158**
may subject general authorisation to the provision of information by the undertakings. Where that obligation is introduced, the provision of information appears as a second derogation: not only must the undertakings declare or notify their intention to start activities, but they have to submit specific information.

Strictly regulated possibility.   As this marks a second derogation to the prin-   **2.159**
ciple that activities should be started freely, the system whereby information is requested is strictly regulated in the NRF. Pursuant to the Authorisations Directive, Member States must limit their request for information to data necessary to identify the undertaking concerned and determine the market where it will carry out its activities. As identification, undertakings may be required to provide a company registration number and the name of a contact person as well as an address. As regards an undertaking's commercial intentions, information may be requested regarding the network or service that the undertaking plans to provide, together with an estimated date for starting the activity.

> *Authorisations Directive, Article 3(3).* Member States may require 'the submission of the minimal information which is required to allow the national regulatory authority to keep a register or list of providers of electronic communications networks and services'. 'This information must be limited to what is necessary for the identification of the provider, such as company registration numbers, and the provider's contact persons, the provider's address, a short description of the network or service, and an estimated date for starting the activity.'

Actions required from parties

Summary.   To avoid ambiguities, it is important to recapitulate the actions which   **2.160**
may be requested from the various parties, where an undertaking decides to start an activity. *(a)* Normally, undertakings should be allowed to start activities without any formality. This possibility stems from the general nature of the authorisation. *(b)* Member States may impose a system whereby a notification or declaration is requested. The concept of 'notification' is a synonym for declaration. In both cases,

---

[104] See also Authorisations Directive, Preamble, recital 8. 'Those aims [imposed by the NRF] can be best achieved by general authorisation . . . without requiring any explicit decision or administrative act by the national regulatory authority and by limiting any procedural requirements to notification only.' In some instances, Member States may require a proof that the notification has indeed been made. Under the NRF, they should accept, as evidence, any legally recognised postal or electronic acknowledgement of receipt. As clearly appears from the NRF, '[s]uch acknowledgement should in any case not consist of or require an administrative act by the national regulatory authority to which the notification must be made'.

the term refers to a communication made by an undertaking and whereby that undertaking expresses its intention to start an activity. *(c)* Going further, they may request that information be provided. That possibility is strictly regulated in the NRF. *(d)* Under no circumstance are they allowed by the NRF to subject the commencement of activities to a given action by the authorities in response to a declaration, notification or provision of information by an undertaking.

2.161 **No specific action by authorities.**   The NRF prohibits Member States from submitting activities to procedures whereby actions must be taken by undertakings and authorities. The prohibition is repeated several times in the Authorisation Directive—this is why an emphasis is placed on that aspect in the present section. Whatever the system chosen by a Member State (freedom to start activities, request for a declaration or notification, provision of information), the procedure leading to general authorisation being granted may not require any specific act or decision in answer to the request made by the undertaking. Authorisation must remain general. The formalities imposed on undertakings may not require any specific reaction from an authority. The procedure may not be individualised. It must be designed in general terms and apply to all undertakings planning to enter a given market.

2.162 **An official reaction.**   Despite the emphasis on the absence of a specific response by authorities, a form of public reaction has been deemed useful in certain circumstances. It may for instance reassure undertakings that their notification or declaration has indeed been received. A reaction may also be used to inform undertakings about the procedures and conditions to be respected if they wish to obtain rights of use. These possible advantages of an official reaction by an NRA have not been disregarded by the Parliament and Council. Here again, the objective has been to reach a compromise between potentially conflicting principles: on the one hand, the opportunity to react and, on the other hand, the need to avoid making general authorisation dependent upon a specific act by a national authority.

2.163 **Standard responses.**   In the event, it was decided that NRAs may send back a standard response, indicating that the declaration or notification has been received and providing information regarding applications to obtain rights of use. Ideally, such standard responses should be sent automatically by NRAs to the undertakings concerned, the objective being to avoid any delay and preventing authorisation from being made dependent upon an assessment by the authority.

> *Authorisations Directive, Article 9.* 'At the request of an undertaking, national regulatory authorities shall, within one week, issue standardised declarations, confirming, where applicable, that the undertaking has submitted a notification . . . and detailing under what circumstances any undertaking providing electronic communications networks or services under the general authorisation has the right to apply for rights to install facilities, negotiate interconnection, and/or obtain access or interconnection in order to facilitate the exercise of those rights for instance at other levels of government

or in relation to other undertakings. Where appropriate such declarations may also be issued as an automatic reply following the notification.'[105]

(6) Rights attaching to general authorisations

Right to start an activity. With the general authorisation, undertakings are   **2.164**
fully admitted on the electronic communications market in the Member State where the procedure has taken place. The effect of the formality possibly imposed by a Member State, once fulfilled, is that activity may start. No additional condition or formality may be imposed.

Other rights. The general authorisation further places the undertaking in a situ-   **2.165**
ation where it can claim rights created and organised under the NRF. Some of these rights are examined in the following paragraphs: the possibility of applying for rights of way; the right to ask for radio frequency or numbers, where these resources are necessary for the provision of the services for which authorisation is granted; the possibility of seeking protection under the regulation against powerful undertakings hindering access to resources; and the right to be taken into account for the provision of universal service.

Rights of way. A first possibility for an undertaking that has general authorisa-   **2.166**
tion is to apply for rights of way. The development of networks requires facilities to be established on, over or under public or private land. Under the laws of the Member States, these facilities may not be established without permission or 'rights of way' under the NRF. Under the Authorisations Directive, the possibility to apply for rights of way attaches to general authorisation. Undertakings may thus apply for these rights where they have a general authorisation. In at least one Member State the right to apply is automatic, as general authorisations are granted in collective fashion by legislation. In some cases, undertakings first have to declare or notify their intention to start an activity, and possibly provide certain information, before they can start activities, and thus, apply for rights of way.[106]

> *Authorisations Directive, Article 4(1), letter (b).* 'Undertakings authorised pursuant to Article 3,[107] shall have the right to: . . . have their application for the necessary rights to install facilities considered.'

---

[105] See also Authorisations Directive, Preamble, recital 25. 'Providers of electronic communications networks and services may need a confirmation of their rights under the general authorisation with respect to interconnection and rights of way, in particular to facilitate negotiations with other, regional or local, levels of government or with service providers in other Member States. For this purpose the national regulatory authorities should provide declarations to undertakings either upon request or alternatively as an automatic response to a notification under the general authorisation. Such declarations should not by themselves constitute entitlements to rights nor should any rights under the general authorisation or rights of use or the exercise of such rights depend upon a declaration.'

[106] Art 11 of the Framework Directive refers to the rights of way and obligations that must be complied with in the procedure leading to the allocation of these rights.

[107] This provision concerns the general authorisation to be obtained by undertakings prior to starting activities.

2.167 **Current situation concerning rights of way.**   Practitioners should be aware of the fact that there are significant problems throughout the European Union as regards rights of way. In many instances, the Commission notes, these rights are granted on a discriminatory basis, with a preference for incumbents. Another issue is that local, regional and national regulations are not clear, and sometimes contradict one another. In granting rights of way, authorities are further eager to impose a tax, or claim a payment, from the operators concerned. This brings about procedures between the various levels of the administrative organisation of the Member States.

> *Eighth implementation report, 40.* 'Previous reports have identified a variety of problems with regard to rights of way, such as the grant of specific rights to the incumbent, lack of transparency in regulations and procedures and the unclear division of competence between the different levels of authority with responsibilities in this field . . . This has led to disadvantages for new entrants and significant delays in the deployment of new infrastructure . . . An additional concern is the risk of proliferation of taxes or other charges levied by local or regional authorities on mobile network infrastructure located in the public domain.'

2.168 **Right to apply for numbers and/or frequencies.**   Another possibility attaching to general authorisation is that, once they have that authorisation, undertakings may apply for numbers and/or radio frequency. Frequency is necessary for the provision of some services, particularly mobile services. Numbers are necessary for the provision of networks and services where numbers are attached to users in order to ensure the direction of the communications. In both cases, access to these resources is not permitted where the undertaking does not have general authorisation to carry out activities on the market where numbers and/or resources are sought.

> *Authorisations Directive, Article 5(2).* 'Where it is necessary to grant individual rights of use for radio frequencies and numbers, Member States shall grant such rights, upon request, to any undertaking providing or using networks or services under the general authorisation, subject to the provisions of . . . this Directive and any other rules ensuring the efficient use of those resources.'

2.169 **Protection of undertakings seeking access.**   Undertakings with general authorisation may claim rights created by the Access Directive. As stated elsewhere, the Access Directive facilitates access for new entrant undertakings to services provided, and networks operated, by other undertakings. The purpose of these arrangements is to ensure the development of the market for networks and services, which is a condition for customers to have a real choice between suppliers. Only in these circumstances will markets produce the best possible results in a competitive environment. Suppose an undertaking seeks access to a network operated by a former national operator. If it has general authorisation to carry out activities it may request protection against an operator refusing access or subjecting access to unreasonable conditions. If, by contrast, no authorisation is held, the undertaking has no right to be present on the market and thus cannot avail itself of the protection granted by the regulation.

> *Authorisations Directive, Article 4(2)*. 'When such undertakings provide electronic communications networks or services to the public the general authorisation shall . . . give them the right to . . . negotiate interconnection with and where applicable obtain access to or interconnection from other providers of publicly available communications networks and services covered by a general authorisation anywhere in the Community under the conditions of and in accordance with . . . [the] Access Directive.'

Right to be taken into account for the provision of universal service.   A last   **2.170** prerogative is the right for an undertaking to apply to provide universal service, or part of it, on the market where that undertaking is authorised. The Universal Service Directive creates rights for users, and also provides guarantees for undertakings that they may be designated as the provider of the whole or part of the universal service, if it is capable of doing so. No discrimination is allowed among the candidates in the procedures for determining the undertaking or undertakings entitled to provide universal service. An undertaking authorised on a market has the right to apply for the provision of universal service on that market. In the absence of authorisation it has no right to be present on that market, and hence an application by such an undertaking to provide universal service would be inadmissible.

> *Authorisations Directive, Article 4(2)*. 'When such undertakings provide electronic communications networks or services to the public the general authorisation shall . . . give them the right to . . . be given an opportunity to be designated to provide different elements of a universal service and/or to cover different parts of the national territory in accordance with . . . [the] Universal Service Directive).'

(7) Limitation of rights of use concerning numbers and frequencies

Scarce resources

Scarce resources.   Among the rights attaching to general authorisation is the pos-   **2.171** sibility of applying for numbers and/or frequencies. As stated in this chapter, both can be considered potentially scarce resources. The numbers and frequencies available may be insufficient to satisfy demand, so that an allocation must be made, usually by a public authority that has the legitimate power to distribute such resources.

General authorisation

In principle.   Under the NRF, numbers and frequencies are normally part of the   **2.172** general authorisation. This means that any undertaking wishing to start an activity may need to declare, or notify, its intention to do so. It may also need to provide to the competent authority the information requested. After accomplishing these formalities, operations may be started without further condition.

> *Authorisations Directive, Article 5(2).* 'Where it is necessary to grant individual rights
> of use for radio frequencies and numbers, Member States shall grant such rights,
> upon request, to any undertaking providing or using networks or services under the
> general authorisation.'

2.173 Implicit for numbers. As appears from the extract in the previous paragraph, the principle of a general authorisation is stated implicitly with respect to numbers. In the extract, the Parliament and Council refer to a scenario where it would not be necessary to grant individual authorisations. They imply thereby that such a necessity does not exist in all circumstances. The consequence, for the Parliament and Council, is that a general authorisation should, in principle, be sufficient.

2.174 Explicit for frequencies. The statement quoted above does not only concern numbers. It also mentions frequencies. Pursuant to the analysis presented in the previous paragraph, one can also consider that, in the approach chosen by the Parliament and Council, a general authorisation should in principle be sufficient for an undertaking to receive frequencies on a given market. That analysis is confirmed, regarding frequencies, by an explicit provision included in the Authorisations Directive.

> *Authorisations Directive, Article 5(1).* 'Member States shall, where possible, . . . not
> make the use of radio frequencies subject to the grant of individual rights of use but
> shall include the conditions for usage of such radio frequencies in the general author-
> isation.'

Individual authorisation

2.175 In some cases. As thus appears from the NRF, numbers and frequencies are to be used, under normal circumstances, in the context of a general authorisation, ie without requesting any specific reaction on the part of an authority. The possibility that a general authorisation may not be sufficient in all circumstances only comes in a second step in the Authorisations Directive. Pursuant to the NRF, Member States may realise, after an enquiry, that the numbers and frequencies available are not sufficient to satisfy demand.

2.176 Harmful interference. In the NRF, the possibility to resort to individual authorisations is clearer for frequencies than for numbers. Under the NRF, a finding that frequencies are insufficient may be made when the State receives a notification announcing the intention of an undertaking to start an activity on a frequency that is already in use. Another circumstance where a limitation may be decided is where the provision of general authorisations creates a risk of harmful interference. Suppose that several undertakings decide to exercise an activity implying the use of radio frequencies. Imagine that they only need to declare or notify their intention to start that activity. That declaration or notification implies for them a right to start their operations. One cannot exclude the scenario where several undertakings will use the same frequency or frequencies close to one another. The consequence may be that, as a result of interference, the services may no longer be provided in a satisfactory manner on these frequencies. Under the NRF, the State concerned must in these circumstances adopt an act stating that general authorisations are not sufficient. This act implies that undertakings must obtain, prior to starting their activities, an individual authorisation or, in the NRF terminology, a right of use.[108]

> *Authorisations Directive, Article 5(1).* 'Member States shall, where possible, in particular where the risk of harmful interference is negligible, not make the use of radio frequencies subject to the grant of individual rights of use but shall include the conditions for usage of such radio frequencies in the general authorisation.' *Authorisations Directive, Article 2(2)(b).* ' "[H]armful interference" means interference which endangers the functioning of a radio navigation service or of other safety services or which otherwise seriously degrades, obstructs or repeatedly interrupts a radio communications service operating in accordance with the applicable Community or national regulations.'

Some services. The possibility of starting activities involving these resources **2.177** without a specific authorisation presupposes that these resources are available in sufficient quantity compared to demand. This does not necessarily correspond to the situation on all markets. For certain services, there is a clear discrepancy between demand and supply regarding numbers and the availability of spectrum. One reason for the Parliament and Council to insist on general authorisation may have been a desire on their part to limit the restrictions placed on the exercise of market activity. By encouraging the use of general authorisation, the institutions make clear their desire that individual authorisation must be restricted to narrowly defined circumstances.

Competitive and comparative selection procedures

Open procedures. An ambiguity arises from the provisions devoted in the NRF **2.178** to the procedures whereby individual rights of use concerning numbers and frequencies are to be allocated. As stated above, all interventions by NRAs are subject to the basic regulatory principles. These principles imply that the allocation of scarce resources must be guided by constraints relating to objectivity, non-discrimination and proportionality. They imply that all interested undertakings must be given a chance to participate in the procedures under which numbers and/or frequencies will be allocated.

---

[108] The concept of individual authorisation does not appear in the NRF, where individual authorisation is referred to as 'rights of use'. There is no explanation concerning the reasons why this terminology was adopted. Through the use of the expression 'rights of use', the European institutions have probably sought to avoid confusion between 'individual' and 'general' authorisation.

2.179 **Competitive and comparative procedures.** Despite this emphasis on the need for open procedures, the Parliament and Council appear to envisage, as a mere possibility, that competitive and comparative procedures may be organised to allocate these resources. That the allocation of these resources in an open procedure is presented as a possibility appears contrary to the constraints deriving from the application of the basic regulatory principles. It is difficult to envisage a procedure where these principles would apply outside a comparative and competitive context. For that reason it is difficult to interpret the statements included in the Authorisations Directive. A legitimate interpretation could be that there was a misunderstanding when the directive was drafted, and that competitive and comparative procedures are indeed an obligation rather than a mere possibility.[109]

> *Authorisations Directive, Article 7(4).* 'Where competitive or comparative selection procedures are to be used, Member States may extend the maximum period . . . for as long as necessary to ensure that such procedures are fair, reasonable, open and transparent to all interested parties.'

(8) The right to use numbers

2.180 **A scarce resource.** Numbers provide an example of what may be a scarce resource. Numbers for use on electronic communications markets may be available in limited quantities in comparison to the vast demand coming from undertakings and other interested entities. Numbers traditionally have three functions in the electronic communications sector. First, they provide an efficient tool to identify users. For instance, users are granted a number when they subscribe to a service. That number is used for identification purposes by the service provider, the network operator and potential correspondents. Second, numbers also allow an identification of the providers. Service providers are often granted complementary numbers by public authorities. This allows easy identification by the authority, the users and the other undertakings.[110] Third, numbers are used for technical purposes to identify the channels through which communications are transmitted.

2.181 **Same rules as for frequencies.** The limited quantity of numbers available makes it necessary for authorities to distribute numbers among interested undertakings and entities. To manage this sharing out, the same rules were chosen, in substance, as those applicable to radio frequencies (see paras 2.185–2.195). This comes as no surprise, given the similarities between them on the issues likely to arise.

---

[109] An open—thus competitive and comparative—procedure indeed appears as the only possibility of bringing about the objectives pursued in the NRF. On that subject, see the Authorisations Directive, Preamble, recital 23. 'National regulatory authorities should ensure, in establishing criteria for competitive or comparative selection procedures, that the objectives in Art 8 of Directive 2002/21/EC (Framework Directive) are met.'

[110] This function becomes less important with number portability. As a result of that mechanism, users are allowed to keep the same number when they switch service provider.

Basic regulatory principles.   The procedure for the distribution of numbers   **2.182**
must therefore comply with the basic regulatory principles: openness, transparency, non-discrimination. The obligation to comply with the proportionality
principle is not mentioned explicitly in connection with the allocation of numbers. This does not imply, however, that proportionality need not be respected. As
stated, proportionality constitutes a general principle of law. The characteristic of
that category of principles is that they apply independently of whether a specific
reference is made to them in a given context.

> *Authorisations Directive, Article 5(2).* 'Where it is necessary to grant individual rights
> of use for . . . numbers, . . . rights of use shall be granted through open, transparent
> and non-discriminatory procedures.'

Rapidity of the procedure.   As for frequencies, the procedure for sharing out   **2.183**
numbers must be carried out promptly. Pursuant to the NRF, decisions concerning the allocation of numbers must be taken, communicated and made public
within three weeks of receipt of the original application. That period may be
extended up to a total of six weeks. The basic period may be extended only where
a decision has been made to allocate numbers in a comparative and competitive
selection. Furthermore, the initial period may be extended only where the use of
a comparative and competitive procedure follows a national consultation where
all interested parties have had the possibility to intervene.

> *Authorisations Directive, Article 5.* [3] 'Decisions on rights of use shall be taken, com-
> municated and made public as soon as possible after receipt of the complete applica-
> tion by the national regulatory authority, within three weeks in the case of numbers
> that have been allocated for specific purposes within the national numbering plan.'
> [4] 'Where it has been decided, after consultation with interested parties . . . ,[111]
> that rights for use of numbers of exceptional economic value are to be granted
> through competitive or comparative selection procedures, Member States may
> extend the maximum period of three weeks by up to three weeks.'

Transfer of numbers.   The rules concerning number transfer are identical to   **2.184**
those applicable to frequencies (see para 2.200 below). Under the NRF, numbers
may be transferred. Regulation must however be adopted by the national authorities, making these transfers possible and laying down the legal regime applicable. The possibility of trading numbers may prove important. Suppose an
undertaking is allocated numbers but, as a result of financial difficulties, may not
use them. The right to use these numbers may be regarded as an asset with an
accounting value, any sums raised by their transfer being used to pay debts.

---

[111]   This consultation is regulated in the Framework Directive. See Framework Directive, Art 6.
Under that provision, NRAs must give interested parties an opportunity to comment on a measure
they have drafted when that measure would, if adopted, have a significant impact on the relevant
market. The Member States must publish the rules which they intend to follow in order to carry out
the consultation. They must also publish the results of the consultation.

Authorisations Directive, Article 5(2). 'When granting rights of use, Member States shall specify whether those rights can be transferred at the initiative of the right holder, and under which conditions.'

(9) The right to use frequencies

Another scarce resource

2.185 **The importance of radio frequencies.** Beyond general authorisation, the provision of some services requires the use of radio frequency over which communications will be transmitted. For the undertakings wishing to provide these services, obtaining radio frequency is of the essence. The difficulty, however, is that available frequency is often limited. Comparing the number of available frequencies to the number of entities wishing to use them, one must conclude that radio spectrum is in many cases a scarce resource. In a context where demand exceeds supply, an allocation must be made. This raises significant issues, which have been addressed in the NRF.

2.186 **Applicable provisions.** In this section issues relating to the sharing out of frequencies among interested undertakings are considered. These issues must be considered primarily under the Framework Directive (Article 9), which sets the principles concerning the right to use frequencies in order to provide electronic communications networks and services. These principles are further enunciated in the Authorisations Directive (in particular Articles 5, 6 and 7). Beyond the issues addressed in these provisions, radio frequencies give rise to other, policy-oriented, problems, which are analysed in Chapter 7. These problems are to be examined under Decision (EC) 676/2002 of the European Parliament and of the Council on a regulatory framework for radio spectrum policy in the European Community ('Radio Spectrum Decision').[112]

2.187 **Scenario 1—Enough radio frequencies.** Two scenarios can be distinguished in the Authorisations Directive regarding access to frequencies. In the first, the European institutions seem to consider, at least as a theoretical hypothesis, that there are enough radio frequencies to satisfy all interested entities. Under the Authorisations Directive, Member States may limit rights of use only for frequencies where no other solution is possible. In the same provision, the European legislator insists that Member States must comply with certain requirements when they decide to limit the number of radio frequencies made available to undertakings for the provision of services. A contrario, these statements imply that there indeed exist situations where Member States do not need to limit the number of frequencies that they accept to share among interested undertakings.

2.188 **Not a frequent scenario.** There are situations where enough radio frequencies are available to meet demand. These situations are not necessarily frequent. In most

---

[112] [2002] OJ L108/1.

cases, the issue in the Member States is to determine how existing frequencies may be shared among various uses[113] and, within each of these uses, among the interested entities. There is a hope that, with technological development, more frequencies and, within each frequency, more space, become available. The ideal situation where the supply of available frequencies outweighs demand is, however, remote.

Scenario 2—Not enough frequencies. The most plausible scenario is that more 2.189
undertakings ask for frequencies than there are frequencies available. Frequencies must thus be shared among candidates. The European legislator refers to that situation when it states that Member States may decide to limit the rights of use concerning frequencies. A decision to limit these rights of use results from an observation that frequencies are insufficient to satisfy the whole demand.

The decision to limit the number of rights of use

Decision to limit frequencies. An official act must then be adopted by the 2.190
Member States, stating that the available frequency is insufficient and that they will need to be allocated among users. This act is strictly regulated. Under the Authorisations Directive, the Member States must comply with several constraints that are similar in substance to the basic regulatory principles presented above. They are analysed in the following paragraphs (compatibility with European values, transparency and proportionality).

Compatibility with European values. The limitation must be compatible with 2.191
values deemed essential at European level. A decision to limit frequencies must also be compatible with the objectives set out in the NRF. Special emphasis is placed in this regard on the need to maximise benefits for users, together with the need to ensure the development of competition.

> *Authorisations Directive, Article 7(1).* 'Where a Member State is considering whether to limit the number of rights of use to be granted for radio frequencies, it shall *inter alia* . . . give due weight to the need to maximise benefits for users and to facilitate the development of competition.'

Transparency. An act whereby frequencies are declared as being limited in 2.192
quantity must be taken in accordance with the transparency principle. Consultation must take place prior to the decision being taken. That consultation must grant all interested parties an opportunity to express their views on the subject matter.[114] Any decision limiting rights of use must be made public, and the reasons why a limitation was decided stated with clarity.

> *Authorisations Directive, Article 7(1).* 'Where a Member State is considering whether to limit the number of rights of use to be granted for radio frequencies, it shall *inter*

---

[113] Defence, radio, television, mobile services, etc.
[114] The rules applicable to the organisation of the procedure must themselves be published by the Member State concerned. See Framework Directive, Art 6.

alia: . . . give all interested parties, including users and consumers, the opportunity to express their views on any limitation . . . ; publish any decision to limit the granting of rights of use, stating the reasons therefore.'

2.193 **Proportionality.** The limitation of the number of rights of use must further be compatible with the principle of proportionality. *(a)* A key test in this regard is whether another, less burdensome, measure might be introduced with a similar possibility of bringing about the same objective. Where a Member State wants to limit rights of use because it feels that some frequencies must be reserved for non-commercial uses, the question to be asked under the proportionality principle is whether that purpose may be achieved through measures which would entail a lesser restriction on the availability of frequencies for undertakings. *(b)* Another aspect of proportionality is that the negative effect on competition that can be expected from a decision to limit frequencies may not be excessive. Particular attention is paid in this connection by the European legislator to the length of the period during which rights of use may be limited. Decisions to limit rights of use must be reviewed at reasonable intervals. A review must also be made when interested undertakings ask for a reassessment and that request appears reasonable.

> *Authorisations Directive, Article 5(5).* 'Member States shall not limit the number of rights of use to be granted except where this is necessary to ensure the efficient use of radio frequencies.' *Authorisations Directive, Article 7(1).* 'Where a Member State is considering whether to limit the number of rights of use to be granted for radio frequencies, it shall *inter alia* . . . review the limitation at reasonable intervals or at the reasonable request of affected undertakings.'

2.194 **No special or exclusive right.** An echo may be found to the rules explained above, in the Consolidated Services Directive adopted by the Commission. For that institution, no special or exclusive right may be granted regarding the use of radio frequencies. Member States may not reserve for one undertaking the right to carry out activities on a market implying the use of frequencies. The number of undertakings enjoying rights to use frequencies may be limited. However, such a limitation may only intervene after a procedure has been followed ensuring that the decision complies with the basic regulatory principles.

> *Consolidated Services Directive, Article 4.* 'Without prejudice to specific criteria and procedures adopted by Member States to grant rights of use of radio frequencies to providers of radio or television broadcast content services with a view to pursuing general interest objectives in conformity with Community law: *(1)* Member States shall not grant exclusive or special rights of use of radio frequencies for the provision of electronic communications services; *(2)* the assignment of radio frequencies for electronic communication services shall be based on objective, transparent, non-discriminatory and proportionate criteria.'[115]

---

[115] Pursuant to the Preamble, the provision does not impede the granting of special or exclusive rights to undertakings providing radio or television content. The position taken in this book is that such a statement does not appear in line with general competition law. General competition law

Reassessment of the decision to limit the number of rights of use

Reassessment of the limitation and/or the number of frequencies. As stated, **2.195**
Member States are invited to reassess periodically any decision they might have
taken to limit the number of radio frequencies made available to undertakings
active on their national territories. A scenario where frequencies will be sufficient
to cover all possible uses is, however, likely to be rare. The most likely reassessment
will bear, as a result, on whether the number of frequencies to be made available
should be changed. If the Member State considers that that number must be
further reduced, the decision will have to be compatible with the constraints set
out above. Should the Member State find that the number should on the contrary
be increased, additional rights of use may then be granted. The increase must then
be announced officially and interested undertakings invited to submit offers. The
procedure for the allocation of supplementary rights must comply with the
constraints examined earlier.

> *Authorisations Directive, Article 7.* [1] 'Where a Member State is considering whether
> to limit the number of rights of use to be granted for radio frequencies, it shall *inter
> alia*: . . . review the limitation at reasonable intervals or at the reasonable request of
> affected undertakings.' [2] 'Where a Member State concludes that further rights of
> use for radio frequencies can be granted, it shall publish that conclusion and invite
> applications for such rights.'

Allocation of limited rights of use

Procedure for the allocation of frequencies. Where they decide that individual **2.196**
authorisations are necessary to provide frequency-based services, Member States
must organise procedures conforming with the basic regulatory principles.
Pursuant to the Authorisations Directive, procedures for the allocation of rights
of use must be *(a)* open, *(b)* transparent, *(c)* non-discriminatory and *(d)* proportionate. These constraints are introduced in the Framework Directive, the
Authorisations Directive and the Consolidated Services Directive.

> *Framework Directive, Article 9(1).* 'Member States . . . shall ensure that the alloca-
> tion and assignment of such radio frequencies by national regulatory authorities are
> based on objective, transparent, non-discriminatory and proportionate criteria.'
> *Authorisations Directive, Article 5(2).* [2] '[R]ights of use shall be granted through
> open, transparent and non-discriminatory procedures.' *Authorisations Directive,
> Article 7.* [1] 'Where a Member State is considering whether to limit the number of

---

prohibits exclusive rights, save in exceptional circumstances. As for special rights, they cannot be
considered compatible with general competition law as they imply legal or regulatory advantages
granted in violation of basic regulatory principles. See Consolidated Services Directive, Preamble,
recital 11. 'This [prohibition of special and/or exclusive rights] should be without prejudice to specific criteria and procedures adopted by Member States to grant such rights to providers of radio or
television broadcast content services with a view to pursuing general interest objectives in conformity with Community law.'

rights of use to be granted for radio frequencies, it shall *inter alia*: . . . (d) after having determined the procedure, invite applications for rights of use.' [3] 'Where the granting of rights of use for radio frequencies needs to be limited, Member States shall grant such rights on the basis of selection criteria which must be objective, transparent, non-discriminatory and proportionate. Any such selection criteria must give due weight to the achievement of the objectives of Article 8 of Directive 2002/21/EC (Framework Directive).'[116] *Consolidated Services Directive, Article 4.* 'Member States shall not grant exclusive or special rights of use of radio frequencies for the provision of electronic communications services.' 'The assignment of radio frequencies for electronic communication services shall be based on objective, transparent, non-discriminatory and proportionate criteria.'

2.197 Rapidity. Rapidity is of the essence in the granting of individual rights of use. Pursuant to the Authorisations Directive, decisions concerning the allocation of limited rights of use must be taken, communicated and made public within six weeks after receipt by the competent authority of the complete application by the undertakings concerned. The period may be extended where the correct progress of the procedure so requires.[117] In total, the period necessary to take a decision may not last more than eight months.

> *Authorisations Directive, Article 5(3).* 'Decisions on rights of use shall be taken, communicated and made public as soon as possible after receipt of the complete application by the national regulatory authority, . . . within six weeks in the case of radio frequencies that have been allocated for specific purposes within the national frequency plan.'[118] *Authorisations Directive, Article 7(4).* 'Member States may extend the maximum period of six weeks[119] . . . for as long as necessary to ensure that such procedures are fair, reasonable, open and transparent to all interested parties, but by no longer than eight months.'[120]

2.198 Harmonisation. A difficulty is that the procedures for the allocation of radio frequencies currently remain regulated by the Member States. No harmonisation has yet taken place in this regard. This does not mean that the Member States are free to organise the procedures as they wish. Their freedom is, as stated above, limited by the basic regulatory principles and by other constraints introduced in the NRF. There is a body of opinion that European spectrum policy should be

---

[116] Art 8 of the Framework Directive states the objectives that must guide the actions undertaken by the NRAs in their implementation of the national legislation transposing the NRF.

[117] It may be questioned whether it was necessary to impose such rapidity in the decision-making process. Would it not be more appropriate to give NRAs more time to consider applications with due care? The reason for a strict time limit to be imposed is probably to avoid excessive speculation. The right to use frequency has significant consequences on the financial standing of an undertaking.

[118] See Authorisations Directive, Art 5(3). 'The . . . time limit shall be without prejudice to any applicable international agreements relating to the use of radio frequencies or of orbital positions.'

[119] Under normal circumstances, radio frequencies must be assigned within a period of six weeks. See Authorisations Directive, Art 5(3).

[120] These time limits are without prejudice to any applicable international agreements relating to the use of radio frequencies and satellite co-ordination. See Authorisations Directive, Art 7(4).

allowed to develop beyond these principles and obligations. Such a policy would entail the definition of common procedures for the allocation of frequencies. Efforts are being made in this direction, and in the meantime the NRF merely provides that Member States will be obliged to comply with European rules for the allocation of frequencies when such rules exist as a result of harmonisation.

> *Authorisations Directive, Article 8.* 'Where the usage of radio frequencies has been harmonised, [and] access conditions and procedures have been agreed . . . , Member States shall grant the right of use for such radio frequencies in accordance therewith.'

Status of rights of use

Validity of rights in time. Pursuant to the NRF, the Member States can limit **2.199** the duration in time of rights of use of frequencies. In the Authorisations Directive there is an indication that the duration of rights of use must be appropriate. Apart from this indication, however, there is no restriction upon the freedom of the Member States to choose the duration they consider appropriate. Most Member States in fact limit the duration of rights of use of frequencies, since otherwise there would be no incentive for beneficiaries to use to the fullest the scarce resources allocated to them.

> *Authorisations Directive, Article 5(2).* 'Where Member States grant rights of use for a limited period of time, the duration shall be appropriate for the service concerned.'

Transfer of rights. Pursuant to the Framework and Authorisations Directives, **2.200** Member States may decide that rights of use that they allocate may be transferred to third parties. *(a)* The Authorisations Directive requires that the Member States take a clear stance on this issue. The holders of rights must know whether or not the rights are transferable. Further, undertakings that do not enjoy such rights must know whether they may have a chance of purchasing rights from another undertaking during the period for which the rights have been allocated. *(b)* Not only must the Member States decide whether the rights are transferable: they must also determine the conditions under which the transfer may occur. *(c)* The *procedure* for the transfer, at least, must be regulated. *(d)* In that procedure, the Member States must provide that an undertaking wishing to transfer some or all of the rights it holds must notify that intention to the NRA. *(e)* The transfer must also be made public, so that all participants on the markets are informed about the transaction. *(f)* The transfer must be compatible with general competition law.[121]

---

[121] This indication is provided in the Framework Directive. It was not necessary to specify that compatibility with general competition law was required, as that body of rules applies in any event. The transfer of rights may be seen as a merger where an undertaking acquires a company to obtain the rights of use allocated to that company. The provisions relating to merger control then apply. Art 81 EC may also apply as an agreement takes place which may restrict competition. Finally, an undertaking may be challenged under Art 82 EC if it is dominant and reinforces that position with the acquisition of rights.

Framework Directive, Article 9. 'Member States may make provision for undertakings to transfer rights to use radio frequencies with other undertakings.'[122] 'Member States shall ensure that an undertaking's intention to transfer rights to use radio frequencies is notified to the national regulatory authority responsible for spectrum assignment and that any transfer takes place in accordance with procedures laid down by the national regulatory authority and is made public. National regulatory authorities shall ensure that competition is not distorted as a result of any such transaction.'[123] *Authorisations Directive, Article 5(2).* 'When granting rights of use, Member States shall specify whether those rights can be transferred at the initiative of the right holder, and under which conditions, in the case of radio frequencies, in accordance with Article 9 of Directive 2002/21/EC (Framework Directive).'

2.201   **Possible discrepancies between the Member States.**   An issue arising is whether undertakings have a right to transfer frequencies assigned to them. As appears from the paragraph above, a decision must be taken in this regard by the Member States. The Member States thus have the power to determine whether or not rights may be transferred. A difficulty may arise for undertakings located in countries with a restrictive attitude in this regard. Where for example a Member State refuses to allow transfers of rights of use[124] and an operator that has sunk significant amounts to purchase rights of use faces financial difficulties, the sums paid for the acquisition of the frequencies may, as a result, be lost, whereas in another Member State it may have been able to sell the rights of use and so place itself in a more favourable financial position.

2.202   **Right to transfer.**   One question is whether the operator concerned may find in European law a right to transfer the frequencies, when the national legislation does not permit that kind of operation. In other words, do the provisions concerning the possibility to authorise transfers have direct effect allowing undertakings to claim their application against contrary national legislation? The answer must be in the negative. As appears from the provision quoted above, the NRF grants Member States a prerogative to determine whether they accept, or not, that rights of use may be transferred.[125]

Application to broadcasting

2.203   **All forms of transmission.**   As stated, the NRF applies to all electronic communications networks and services. This implies that the rules concerning radio

---

[122] Para 3.   [123] Para 4.

[124] Such an attitude may be explained in a variety of ways. One possibility for the State would be to compel undertakings not using their frequencies to return them to the State, instead of being allowed to sell them. In that event the State would be able to sell the same frequency twice.

[125] For political reasons it is probably difficult for Member States to resist pressure in favour of allowing transfers of rights. Undertakings holding rights of use are keen to have the possibility to transfer their rights. They gain thereby a guarantee that they will not lose their investment if their frequencies cannot be used. Challengers also gain from legislation allowing transfers of rights, in being able to purchase rights of use from other undertakings.

frequencies, including those relating to rights of use, normally apply to broadcasting. There should be no difference, in this regard, between broadcasting and telecommunications activities. As a result, broadcasting frequencies must be allocated in the European Union under the procedures and conditions laid down in the NRF.

Separation from content. As also stated, a distinction is made in the NRF **2.204** between the transmission of electronic communications and the content of those communications. The content aspects are outside the scope of application of the NRF, owing to the view by some Member States that the regulation of the content of audiovisual services on their territories should remain a national competence.

Influence on content. As was submitted in the examination of the scope of the **2.205** NRF, a difficulty is that transmission often influences content. This observation is particularly relevant for the allocation of frequency-related rights of use. Even though the allocation of frequencies for the transmission of audiovisual services should in principle be made in conformity with the rules under the NRF, in some instances Member States may wish to grant rights of use on another basis, and for several reasons: *(a)* One of them may be, for instance, the wish to ensure pluralism in audiovisual content, since open and competitive procedures may lead, to a certain extent, to the disappearance of non market-oriented content producers. *(b)* Another reason for Member States to retain oversight is that they may wish to influence content, in the case, for example, where a government of a particular political colour fears that broadcasters chosen on a competitive basis will favour market-based ideologies.

An exception for broadcasting. For these reasons the European legislator has **2.206** accepted that the procedures for the allocation of frequencies for the transmission of audiovisual content may be regulated by the Member States. An exception was thus introduced to the NRF for the selection of undertakings allowed to use frequencies for this kind of transmission. Pursuant to this exception, the Member States have the right to establish specific procedures for the allocation of broadcasting frequencies.

> *Authorisations Directive, Article 5(2).* The rules concerning rights of use for frequencies apply '[w]ithout prejudice to specific criteria and procedures adopted by Member States to grant rights of use of radio frequencies to providers of radio or television broadcast content services with a view to pursuing general interest objectives in conformity with Community law'.

Uncertainty regarding the scope of the exception. The scope of this exception **2.207** remains difficult to analyse. As appears from the extract in the paragraph above, the exception introduced for the allocation of frequency for broadcast services does not leave the Member States entirely free. First, the allocation procedures must be in line with objectives of general interest. Second, they must conform with European law. These conditions imply that the procedure has to be organised in line with the objectives stated in the NRF (these objectives are analysed in a previous section of this chapter). They also mean that a check must be carried out as to compliance by the Member States with the basic regulatory principles. As stated above, these principles are not limited in their application to the provisions where they are explicitly introduced. They also have a general and wider value. From these observations, one may conclude that Member States have a margin of manoeuvre in the organisation of the procedures leading to the designation of authorised broadcasters. Their organisation must, however, conform to the same constraints as those applicable to the allocation of other, non broadcasting-related, procedures (objectivity, technological neutrality, non-discrimination, proportionality, transparency, presence of a judicial review mechanism).

The need for a spectrum policy

2.208 **Disparity between national laws.** The allocation of frequencies for the development of third generation mobile technology across Europe has shown that serious divergences exist between the legislation in the various Member States. Among the Member States, some wish to maintain specific national legislation on the basis of the argument that frequencies must be allocated in harmony with policy objectives, which are specific to each country. Experience however seems to indicate that some approximation is desirable, and even necessary.

2.209 **Need for a certain degree of common policy.** All these aspects show that some degree of common policy is necessary, at this stage, in the European Union regarding the availability and use of spectrum. In Chapter 7, arguments pro and contra the existence of a common policy in this area are examined.

(10) Issues common to numbers and radio frequencies

2.210 **Prerequisite to have a right of use.** Pursuant to the Authorisations Directive, individual authorisations regarding numbers and frequencies may be granted only to undertakings which have a general authorisation. As was stated earlier, general authorisations may be granted automatically and collectively by national legislation to all undertakings that want to start activities. In some countries, however, a declaration or notification must be made, and information may even be requested. Where these formalities exist, they must be accomplished before rights of use may be claimed.

> *Authorisations Directive, Article 5(2).* 'Where it is necessary to grant individual rights of use for radio frequencies ..., Member States shall grant such rights, upon request, to any undertaking providing or using networks or services under the general authorisation.'

2.211 **Authorisation without regulation.** Pursuant to the NRF, numbers and frequencies are tradable if the Member States authorise these operations on their territories. Under the NRF, Member States, having made the decision to do so, must not only make transfers possible. They have to regulate the operations involved.

An issue could arise if a Member State authorised transfers, but did not regulate them. Could an argument be inferred, in such a situation, that the authorisation is not complete in the absence of real regulation? A negative answer must apparently be given. The NRF indicates a clear preference in favour of allowing transfers. That preference seems to imply that transfers may take place as soon as they are authorised in principle. In that interpretation, the obligation imposed on Member States to regulate transfers should not be regarded as a condition for the right of transfer to be activated. It rather places a responsibility on the shoulders of the Member States. In the light of the case law, Member States could be held liable if damages are suffered as a result of a lack of a clear regulatory framework.

Period to take a decision. There is a difference as to the period during which **2.212** a decision must be taken regarding the allocation of numbers as opposed to frequencies. *(a)* Under the NRF, numbers must be allocated within a period of three weeks. That initial period may be extended to up to six weeks. *(b)* The period is longer regarding frequencies. A maximum of eight months is allowed, after extension from an initial period of six months. *(c)* The difference may be explained by the technical difficulties relating to the allocation of frequencies. The allocation of frequencies implies more preparation on the part of the authority, and on the part of the undertakings involved.

Other (slight) differences. There exist other minor differences. *(a)* For instance, **2.213** there is no reference to the obligation for authorities to ensure that transfers of numbers comply with competition rules (Authorisations Directive). Such a reference may be found, by contrast, for the transfer of frequencies (Framework Directive). The difference should not be overestimated. Competition rules have a general scope of application. They apply in both cases, even if they are not mentioned explicitly in relation to numbers. (b) A similar analysis may be made with respect to the notification that undertakings must make of their intention to transfer a right of use. An obligation to notify is mentioned regarding frequencies (Framework Directive), but not with respect to numbers (Authorisations Directive). There is no difference, however, between the regimes applicable to the two resources. A notification must take place for the transfer of numbers despite the absence of an explicit obligation. It would make no sense for an undertaking to transfer numbers without informing the NRAs about the operation.[126]

Ambiguity regarding NRAs. There is also a certain ambiguity in the role **2.214** assigned to NRAs for the allocation of radio frequencies and numbers. As stated, NRAs have a general responsibility for the implementation of the NRF in the national legal orders. That responsibility is confirmed in the Framework Directive

---

[126] Authorities are responsible for the functioning of the market. To ensure proper functioning, they must be aware of the identity of undertakings operating services with various numbers.

regarding numbers and frequencies.[127] A different scenario emerges from the Authorisations Directive, where the authority to regulate seems to be conferred, in generic terms, on the Member States, rather than specifically to the NRAs.[128] No conclusion may, however, be drawn from that apparent absence of coherence. The Framework Directive is indeed very clear about the responsibilities conferred on the NRAs regarding numbers and frequencies. It would not be possible for Member States to argue, on the basis of the Authorisations Directive, that they are free to grant the regulatory powers to other entities as regards these issues.

2.215 **WTO provisions.** The Reference Paper, which has been presented in the introductory chapter and formulates regulatory principles applicable to basic telecommunications services, confirms the importance of the basic regulatory principles where authorisations are granted. The obligation to comply with these principles is all the more important where scarce resources are allocated.

> *Reference Paper, para 6.* 'Any procedures for the allocation and use of scarce resources, including frequencies, numbers and rights of way, will be carried out in an objective, timely, transparent and non-discriminatory manner. The current state of allocated frequency bands will be made publicly available, but detailed identification of frequencies allocated for specific government uses is not required.'

E. Conditions Attached to Formalities

(1) Introduction

2.216 **Imposition of obligations.** As submitted in the previous section, Member States may subject activities on electronic communications markets to formalities. These formalities may consist in particular of the requirement to make a notification or declaration. Undertakings may also be requested to provide information. In connection with these formalities, Member States may make market entry dependent upon compliance with given conditions. In this context, the imposition of conditions attached to formalities appears to be a regulatory tool for authorities to impose obligations on undertakings. The impact of these conditions/obligations should, however, not be overestimated. The conditions attached to formalities are no more than obligations deriving in any case from the NRF.

2.217 **Three categories of conditions.** Three types of condition are distinguished in the NRF. *(a)* The first category is made up of 'general conditions'. These are attached to the 'general' authorisation required of undertakings prior to the starting of any electronic communications service. *(b)* A second category is made up of the conditions that attach to rights of use. These conditions apply to undertakings

---

[127] See Framework Directive, Art 9.   [128] See Authorisations Directive, Arts 5 and 7.

seeking numbers and/or frequencies. They are not included in the general authorisation. *(c)* A third category consists of conditions referred to as 'specific' in the NRF. These conditions reflect the 'specific' obligations that may be imposed on undertakings as provided in the Access and Universal Service Directives. They are called 'specific' in view of their link with a particular group of undertakings, that is, operators with significant market power.

Additional national conditions.   As stated, Member States may not introduce   **2.218**
restrictions supplementary to those established at European level. This does not mean that no other national rule may be applied to undertakings during the performance of their activities. These national obligations should however not constitute a condition for market entry. As a result, they cannot be integrated in any sort of authorisation to be obtained prior to the starting of activities. They must comply with general European rules, including those relating to the internal market.[129]

> *Authorisations Directive, Article 6(3).* 'The general authorisation shall only contain conditions which are specific for that sector and are set out in . . . the Annex and shall not duplicate conditions which are applicable to undertakings by virtue of other national legislation.'

(2) Conditions that may be attached to general authorisations

General constraints.   The exercise of activities may be made dependent upon   **2.219**
undertakings committing themselves to complying with general conditions. These conditions are described in the Authorisations Directive (in particular Article 6 and the Annex). In accordance with a principle examined earlier, no other conditions than those established in the NRF can be imposed by the Member States.[130] These conditions must be compatible with the basic regulatory principles (particularly objectivity, non-discrimination and proportionality).[131]

> *Authorisations Directive, Article 6(1).* 'The general authorisation for the provision of electronic communications networks or services . . . may be subject only to the conditions listed . . . in part A . . . of the Annex. Such conditions shall be objectively justified in relation to the network or service concerned, non-discriminatory, proportionate and transparent.'

---

[129] Pursuant to the EC Treaty, no national rules may constitute a restriction on the internal market. This implies that national legislation may not hinder the movement of goods and the provision of services across national frontiers. Restrictions may be justified only if they are introduced in connection with legitimate objectives and encompass appropriate instruments.

[130] See Authorisations Directive, Art 3(1). 'Member States shall ensure the freedom to provide electronic communications networks and services, subject to the conditions set out in this Directive.'

[131] Pursuant to the NRF, the Member States have the power to introduce these conditions. They are not, however, compelled to do so. The Authorisations Directive thus contains an exhaustive list of conditions/obligations which may be imposed on undertakings. The Member States may, depending on national circumstances, impose only a limited number of these conditions, or indeed none at all.

2.220 **Method chosen in the following paragraphs.** The conditions that Member States may attach to general authorisations are presented in the following paragraphs. They are divided in accordance with the attitudes undertakings are expected to adopt on the markets. These attitudes are presented in chronological order, to the extent that they must in principle be adopted successively by the undertakings. Of the behaviour required, two aspects are explained in further detail in the next section, the obligation to provide information and the obligation to make payments.

2.221 **(1) Provide requested information.** Undertakings may be requested to provide information to NRAs before being allowed to start their activities. As was examined earlier, the power of the Member States is restricted regarding the type of information that may be required. The purpose of this restriction is to avoid imposing excessive obligations on undertakings (facilitation of entry).

> *Authorisations Directive, Annex, letter A.* [10] 'Information to be provided under a notification procedure in accordance with Article 3(3)[132] of this Directive and for other purposes as included in Article 11[133] of this Directive.'

2.222 **(2) Make payments.** Undertakings starting activities may have to make several payments. First, they may have to pay a contribution to the administrative costs relating to the necessity for the State to regulate and control markets (administrative charge). Second, undertakings present on electronic communications markets may be constrained to contribute to the cost of the provision of universal service.[134] The contribution depends upon the system chosen to finance these costs. Contributions are expected from market players where a choice is made to share the cost of the universal service between providers of electronic communications networks and services.[135]

> *Authorisations Directive, Annex, letter A.* [1] 'Financial contributions to the funding of universal service in conformity with Directive 2002/22/EC (Universal Service Directive).' [2] 'Administrative charges in accordance with Article 12 of this Directive.'[136]

---

[132] That provision concerns information to be provided in order to obtain an authorisation. Without the provision of information, the authorisation will not be provided.

[133] This provision defines, more generally, the information which may be requested from undertakings. The information may be requested as a condition attached to an authorisation. However, the commencement of activity may not be made dependent upon that information being provided. Other, specific, penalties may be imposed in case requested information is not provided.

[134] See Universal Service Directive, Art 11.

[135] A third payment must be made by undertakings seeking rights of use (usage fee). As it concerns rights of use (individual authorisation), that payment may not, however, be included in a general authorisation. The various payments which may be requested from undertakings are strictly regulated in the NRF. The relevant rules are examined in a later section (see paras 2.248–2.262).

[136] This provision concerns the administrative charge which may be levied on undertakings for their participation on an electronic communications market. The imposition of an administrative charge is part of an effort to divide the costs of market regulation and control among the undertakings concerned.

(3) Ensure safety, security and integrity.   A priority for undertakings starting   **2.223**
activities must be to ensure safety and security. An emphasis is placed on this
obligation in the conditions attached to general authorisations. *(a) European or
national catastrophe*. In the first place, the Parliament and Council wished to cover
the use of electronic communications networks in case of a major catastrophe
occurring on the European territory.

> *Authorisations Directive, Annex, letter A.* [12] 'Terms of use during major disasters to
> ensure communications between emergency services and authorities and broadcasts
> to the general public.'

(b) The state of the networks. A second source of concern is the state of networks.
Exposure of the public to electromagnetic radiation must be limited. Undertakings providing networks must also ensure that the networks are properly
maintained.

> *Authorisations Directive, Annex, letter A.* [13] 'Measures regarding the limitation of
> exposure of the general public to electromagnetic fields caused by electronic com-
> munications networks in accordance with Community law.' [15] 'Maintenance of
> the integrity of public communications networks in accordance with [the] . . .
> Access Directive and . . . [the] Universal Service Directive . . . including by condi-
> tions to prevent electromagnetic interference between electronic communications
> networks and/or services.'[137] [16] 'Security of public networks against unauthorised
> access.'[138]

(4) Respect users.   *(a) Privacy, personal data.* Some conditions attached to gen-   **2.224**
eral authorisations concern the protection granted to privacy and personal data.
That protection derives from the e-Privacy Directive. As stated, the rules introduced in that Directive are not examined here. The conditions may relate in general to the protection granted to individuals as regards these aspects. A particular
condition may be included regarding the co-operation that undertakings must
accept in order to assist authorities in their enquiries.

> *Authorisations Directive, Annex, letter A.* [7] 'Personal data and privacy protection
> specific to the electronic communications sector in conformity with Directive
> 97/66/EC of the European Parliament and of the Council of 15 December 1997
> concerning the processing of personal data and the protection of privacy in the
> telecommunications sector.' [11] 'Enabling of legal interception by competent
> national authorities.'[139]

---

[137] In that regard, see Council Directive (EEC) 89/336 on the approximation of the laws of the
Member States relating to electromagnetic compatibility [1989] OJ L139/19.

[138] In this regard see European Parliament and Council Directive (EC) 97/66 concerning the
processing of personal data and the protection of privacy in the telecommunications sector [1998]
OJ L24/1.

[139] See European Parliament and Council Directive (EC) 95/46 on the protection of individuals
with regard to the processing of personal data and on the free movement of such data [1995] OJ
L281/31 and European Parliament and Council Directive (EC) 97/66 concerning the processing of
personal data and the protection of privacy in the telecommunications sector [1998] OJ L24/1.

(b) Users' rights. Another set of conditions relates to rights granted to users. These rights are introduced in the Universal Service Directive. Some of them are associated with the protection which, for the Parliament and Council, must be granted to consumers. Other rights are more generally accessible to all categories of user (including the possibility of obtaining information on numbers used in the public network).

> *Authorisations Directive, Annex, letter A.* [8] 'Consumer protection rules specific to the electronic communications sector including conditions in conformity with [the] . . . Universal Service Directive.' [4] 'Accessibility of numbers from the national numbering plan to end-users including conditions in conformity with [the] . . . Universal Service Directive.'

(c) Regulation of content. Through the conditions attached to general authorisations, undertakings are informed about the existence of rules concerning content. An illustration is the prohibitions contained in the European directives concerning broadcasting. Another example is the regulation applicable to illegal content on the internet. In order to address this kind of content, rules were included by the Parliament and Council in the e-Commerce Directive.

> *Authorisations Directive, Annex, letter A.* [9] 'Restrictions in relation to the transmission of illegal content, in accordance with [the e-Commerce Directive][140] . . . and restrictions in relation to the transmission of harmful content in accordance with [the Directive on Television Broadcasting Activities].'[141]

2.225 **(5) Comply with applicable regulation.** Another set of conditions refers to the rules that are applicable to the markets. *(a)* Among these conditions, some have a technical nature. Electronic communications are characterised by constant technological innovation. One difficulty that arises in this context is interoperability between the standards used by the various undertakings active on the markets. To avoid problems, undertakings are reminded, through conditions attached to the general authorisations, of the obligation that may some times be imposed on them to comply with the technical standards and specifications adopted on the basis of the NRF.[142] *(b)* Another set of conditions concerns access to facilities. It has been argued throughout this book that significant issues arise on electronic communications markets in relation to existing resources. An important purpose pursued by

---

[140] See European Parliament and Council Directive (EC) 2000/31 on certain legal aspects of information society services, in particular electronic commerce, in the internal market [2000] OJ L178/1 ('Directive on electronic commerce').

[141] See Council Directive (EEC) 89/552 on the coordination of certain provisions laid down by Law, Regulation or Administrative Action in Member States concerning the pursuit of television broadcasting activities [1989] OJ L298/23, amended by European Parliament and Council Directive (EC) 97/36 amending Council Directive 89/552/EEC on the coordination of certain provisions laid down by law, regulation or administrative action in Member States concerning the pursuit of television broadcasting activities [1997] OJ L202/60 ('Directive on Television Broadcasting Activities'). [142] See paras 7.130–7.145 below.

the European legislator is to ensure that existing resources are used efficiently. To ensure proper use, access obligations are imposed. The application of these obligations is not made dependent upon the undertaking(s) concerned having significant market power. All undertakings are affected.

> *Authorisations Directive, Annex, letter A.* [3] 'Interoperability of services and interconnection of networks in conformity with [the] . . . Access Directive.' [18] 'Measures designed to ensure compliance with the standards and/or specifications referred to in [the] . . . Framework Directive.'[143] [14] 'Access obligations other than those provided for in Article 6(2)[144] of this Directive applying to undertakings providing electronic communications networks or services, in conformity with [the] . . . Access Directive.'

(6) Contribute to other policy objectives.   Finally, conditions attached to general authorisations remind undertakings that a contribution may be required of them by national authorities for public policy purposes, including the promotion of plurality and cultural diversity. To this end, 'must carry' obligations may be imposed on broadcasters. These obligations imply that broadcasters must allow the transmission, through their facilities, of content that they would not otherwise have transmitted. Another kind of objective relates to the environment or town and country planning. These aspects were mentioned in the old framework. As regards the NRF, their importance is evidenced through an allusion made to them in the Framework Directive, where co-location and common infrastructure may be ordered for reasons relating to these aspects.   **2.226**

> *Authorisations Directive, Annex, letter A.* [6] ' "Must carry" obligations in conformity with [the] . . . Universal Service Directive.' [5] 'Environmental and town and country planning requirements, as well as requirements and conditions linked to the granting of access to or use of public or private land and conditions linked to co-location and facility sharing in conformity with [the] . . . Framework Directive . . . and including, where applicable, any financial or technical guarantees necessary to ensure the proper execution of infrastructure works.'

(3) Conditions that may be attached to numbers and frequencies

Conditions common to numbers and frequencies

Rights of use.   The conditions examined in the previous paragraphs are attached to general authorisations. They correspond to obligations which, for the most part, are imposed under the NRF on all undertakings. Undertakings wishing to obtain the right to use numbers or radio frequencies may also have conditions imposed on them. These conditions are similar, in substance, for these two types of scarce resource. They are examined in the following paragraphs, together with   **2.227**

---

[143] See Framework Directive, Art 17.

[144] This provision refers to obligations relating to access and interconnection and regulatory controls an retail services and on leased lines.

the peculiarities reserved to one or other of them. Before starting the analysis, it should be emphasised that the conditions attached to rights of use introduce few new obligations.

2.228 **Regulatory principle.**   As is the case for general authorisations, the Member States must comply with the basic regulatory principles in the conditions they attach to rights of use concerning numbers and frequencies. The conditions imposed in connection with these resources must thus be objective, non-discriminatory, transparent and proportional.

> *Authorisations Directive, Article 6(2).* 'The . . . rights of use for radio frequencies and rights of use for numbers may be subject only to the conditions listed respectively in parts A, B and C of the Annex. Such conditions shall be objectively justified in relation to the network or service concerned, non-discriminatory, proportionate and transparent.'

2.229 **Typical scenario.**   Pursuant to the NRF, Member States may attach special conditions to the granting of rights of use. In those conditions they may not include the general conditions imposed in connection with general authorisations. In other words, the conditions relating to rights of use must remain specific.[145] The typical scenario unfolds as follows. *(a)* An undertaking wishing to obtain a right of use must have, in the first instance, general authorisation. That authorisation allows the undertaking in question to be present on the electronic communications market. To that general authorisation, conditions may be attached which must be complied with. *(b)* As it holds a general authorisation, the undertaking may apply for a right of use (numbers, frequency). Conditions may be attached to the rights of use granted by undertakings. These conditions are specific and relate to the nature of the scarce resource granted.

> *Authorisations Directive, Article 6(4).* 'Member States shall not duplicate the conditions of the general authorisation where they grant the right of use for radio frequencies or numbers.'

2.230 **What type of service?**   Authorities granting a right of use (numbers, frequencies) must specify the type of service concerned. In the case of numbers, undertakings must indicate what kind of service they plan to provide with these numbers. In the case of frequencies, they must inform the authority as to the service that will be provided through the frequency. This is particularly important for audiovisual services, as the Member States will wish to monitor the programmes transmitted.

---

[145] The purpose of the restriction is probably to avoid entry barriers on markets where numbers or radio frequencies are necessary. Candidate undertakings may be discouraged by the number of conditions imposed on them, if general and specific conditions are added. Member States may also be tempted to introduce new requirements under the 'general' conditions when they grant the rights of use.

Numbers. 'Designation of service for which the number shall be used, including any requirements linked to the provision of that service.'[146]	*Radio frequencies.* 'Designation of service or type of network or technology for which the rights of use for the frequency has been granted, including, where applicable, the exclusive use of a frequency for the transmission of specific content or specific audiovisual services.'[147]

Usage fees.   Usage fees may be charged to undertakings receiving rights of use   **2.231** concerning number and frequencies. These fees must be added to the administrative charge that is intended to provide a contribution from undertakings to the costs associated with regulation of the sector. As stated, a third type of payment may be requested on markets where, pursuant to a decision taken by the competent NRA, universal service should be financed by the undertakings active in the sector.

Numbers. 'Usage fees in accordance with Article 13[148] of this Directive.'[149]	*Radio frequencies.* 'Usage fees in accordance with Article 13 of this Directive.'[150]

Duration, transferability.   In the conditions attached to individual authorisations,   **2.232** the Member States must specify for what period rights of use are granted. This is essential to avoid any ambiguity, given the value of the rights of use for undertakings. Similarly, details must be provided in the conditions regarding the regime applicable to transfers. As stated above, rights of use may in principle be transferred. A decision, however, has to be made by the NRA in each national territory. Beyond deciding whether transfers are permitted, NRAs should also regulate these operations (determine the rights and obligations applicable to all parties in presence).

Numbers. 'Maximum duration in conformity with Article 5 of this Directive,[151] subject to any changes in the national frequency plan.'[152]	*Radio frequencies.* 'Maximum duration in conformity with Article 5 of this Directive, subject to any changes in the national numbering plan.'[154]
'Transfer of rights at the initiative of the right holder and conditions for such transfer in conformity with [the] . . . Framework Directive.'[153]	'Transfer of rights at the initiative of the right holder and conditions for such transfer in conformity with [the] . . . Framework Directive.'[155]

---

[146] Authorisations Directive, Annex, letter C, point 1.

[147] ibid, Annex, letter B, point 1.

[148] This provision regulates the sort of usage fee which may be claimed from undertakings in return for the use of numbers or frequencies. The rules established on this subject at European level are examined at paras 2.248–2.262 below.

[149] Authorisations Directive, Annex, letter B, point 6.   [150] ibid, Annex, letter C, point 7.

[151] ibid, Art 5 regulates in general terms the right to use numbers and frequencies. There is no specific reference in this provision to the duration that rights of use may, or should, have.

[152] ibid, Annex, letter C, point 5.   [153] ibid, Annex, letter C, point 6.

[154] ibid, Annex, letter B, point 4.   [155] ibid, Annex, letter B, point 5.

2.233 **Conditions relating to use.** Conditions may be imposed by NRAs to ensure effective and efficient use of scarce resources granted to undertakings. The possibility for Member States to impose usage-related conditions is mentioned only in the Authorisations Directive. No indication is provided about the actual conditions Member States could link to usage. This leaves the Member States with a margin of manoeuvre which may appear, in some respects, substantial. However, the scope of that margin should not be overestimated, since the conditions attached to authorisations must remain compatible with the basic regulatory principles. NRAs are therefore not entirely free to introduce the conditions of their choice.

Numbers. 'Effective and efficient use of numbers in conformity with [the] . . . Framework Directive.'[156]	*Radio frequencies.* 'Effective and efficient use of frequencies in conformity with [the] . . . Framework Directive . . ., including, where appropriate, coverage requirements.'[157]

2.234 **Other commitments.** Two other sources of commitment are finally mentioned in the Authorisations Directive. *(a)* Conditions may be attached to individual authorisations in order to specify the commitments that undertakings have made during the procedure in the course of which rights of use were granted. This kind of commitment is usual in procedures where candidates take part in a competitive procedure to provide a service. In these circumstances undertakings are ready to accept additional obligations in the hope of being selected in preference to the other candidates. The competitive character of the procedure thus places authorities in a situation where they can impose, indirectly, supplementary obligations on undertakings. *(b)* Another source of obligations is international agreements binding the Member States. As submitted at paras 7.30–7.94, no common policy has been developed at the present stage as regards spectrum. The consequence is that Member States have signed international agreements, some of them binding. The undertakings active on the territory of these Member States must comply with the obligations that have been implemented at national level in implementation of these agreements.

Numbers. 'Any commitments which the undertaking obtaining the usage right has made in the course of a competitive or comparative selection procedure.'[158]	*Radio frequencies.* 'Any commitments which the undertaking obtaining the usage right has made in the course of a competitive or comparative selection procedure.'[160]
'Obligations under relevant international agreements relating to the use of numbers.'[159]	'Obligations under relevant international agreements relating to the use of frequencies.'[161]

---

156 Authorisations Directive Annex, letter C, point 2.   157 ibid, Annex, letter B, point 2.
158 ibid, Annex, letter C, point 8.   159 ibid, Annex, letter C, point 9.
160 ibid, Annex, letter B, point 7.   161 ibid, Annex, letter B, point 8.

Conditions relating to numbers

Portability and information. In the previous section, conditions common to fre- **2.235** quencies and numbers were analysed regarding the rights of use that Member States may grant on electronic communications markets. In addition to these common obligations, Member States can impose conditions specific to the allocation by NRAs of numbers allowing the provision of services.[162] These conditions echo obligations introduced in the NRF. *(a)* A first condition is that numbers must be portable. Undertakings granted numbers may not reject a request made by users to take their number with them when changing service provider. *(b)* A second condition is the obligation for network and service providers to provide assistance in the provision of components of universal service (provision of information necessary to compile directories or to provide services such as operator assistance and directory enquiries).

> *Authorisations Directive, Annex, letter C.* [3] 'Number portability requirements in conformity with [the] . . . Universal Service Directive.' [4] 'Obligation to provide public directory subscriber information for the purposes of Articles 5[163] and 25[164] of [the] . . . Universal Service Directive.'

Conditions relating to frequencies

Exposure and interference. Specific conditions may also be attached to frequen- **2.236** cies. Again, these conditions are in line with the nature of the resource concerned. *(a)* One difficulty with regard to frequencies is that their use may damage public health. As a result, conditions may be imposed to decrease, to the extent possible, public exposure to electromagnetic fields. *(b)* Another issue is that services provided by undertakings using the same, or neighbouring, frequencies may interfere with one another. Conditions may be imposed to avoid harmful interference.

> *Authorisations Directive, Annex, Letter B, point 3.* 'Technical and operational conditions necessary for the avoidance of harmful interference and for the limitation of exposure of the general public to electromagnetic fields, where such conditions are different from those included in the general authorisation.'

Avoid additional hindrance. It was observed that, under the NRF, Member **2.237** States may not impose restrictions supplementary to those existing at European level. This prohibition is repeated in the provisions concerning frequencies. Pursuant to the Authorisations Directive, no condition, criterion or procedure may be added to those existing in the national legislation as a result of the transposition of the NRF. That restriction is introduced to ensure that activity may start as soon as conditions are fulfilled and frequencies have been granted.

---

[162] Undertakings wishing to provide services requiring numbers must comply with three types of condition: those relating to general authorisations (as a reminder, a general authorisation must be obtained before a requested may be presented to obtain a right of use); conditions common to numbers and frequencies; conditions specific to numbers.

[163] Relating to directory enquiry services and directories.

[164] Relating to operator assistance and directory enquiry services.

Authorisations Directive, Article 8. 'Provided that all national conditions attached to the right to use the radio frequencies concerned have been satisfied in the case of a common selection procedure, Member States shall not impose any further conditions, additional criteria or procedures which would restrict, alter or delay the correct implementation of the common assignment of such radio frequencies.'

The normative sources of the conditions attached to authorisations

2.238 **A variety of sources.** As appears from preceding paragraphs, the conditions attached to rights of use may come from a variety of sources. *(a)* The overwhelming majority of them result from the directives composing the NRF. The conditions set out in the Authorisations Directive correspond to obligations introduced in the other directives forming the NRF. *(b)* Another source is international agreements entered into by the Member States. These agreements still influence national legislation relating to spectrum,[165] given in particular that no common spectrum policy has been developed at the present stage. *(c)* A final category is made up of obligations that undertakings have proposed to comply with in the course of competitive procedures. In this kind of procedure, undertakings have little choice other than to offer additional commitments if they want to be selected.

2.239 **No national conditions.** In principle, no other source may be added to the categories mentioned in the preceding paragraph. In particular, national conditions are excluded. *(a)* As stated, Member States may not impose conditions to entry in addition to those introduced at European level. This is the result of the harmonisation that has taken place regarding authorisation in the electronic communications sector. The prohibition imposed on Member States results from the case law. It is also stated explicitly in the Authorisations Directive.[166] *(b)* This does not impede Member States from imposing obligations concerning the exercise of activities. That possibility is however subject to several restrictions. First, such obligations should not indirectly establish disguised restrictions affecting market entry. As a result, they may not be introduced in general or individual authorisations.[167] Second, obligations introduced by the Member States should not be aimed, specifically, at the electronic communications markets. Otherwise, the national rules would run contrary to the harmonisation process that has been carried out at European level.

2.240 **Margin of manoeuvre.** On the basis of the considerations in the preceding paragraph, it might be supposed that no margin was left to the Member States in the regulation of authorisations for entry on electronic communications markets. Such a conclusion would however neglect two mechanisms that may help Member States to lay down policy to a certain extent in this field. *(a)* First, Member States may impose conditions relating to usage. These conditions are not

---

[165] In the other fields complete harmonisation has been carried out. The consequence is that Member States have lost their competence to regulate further these other fields.

[166] See Authorisations Directive, Art 3(1). See also the Preamble, recital 3.

[167] See ibid, Art 6(3).

further defined in the NRF. The Member States are thereby left free to lay down their own obligations in this connection. *(b)* Second, Member States are encouraged to use competition-based procedures to allocate rights of use. In the course of such procedures they may favour candidates offering commitments that correspond to the policies they wish to carry out.

Warning. A warning is however addressed to the Member States that they **2.241** should not discriminate in the national rules they impose prior to market entry by undertakings. These conditions—including those relating to usage and the commitments they would wish to encourage from undertakings—can be assessed as to their compatibility with general European law. As stated on several occasions, the rules concerning the internal market play a special role in this regard, and provide a tool for the European Commission to verify that no restriction is imposed on the free provision of services across national boundaries.[168]

> *Authorisations Directive, Preamble, recital 35.* 'The proper functioning of the single market on the basis of the national authorisation regimes under this Directive should be monitored by the Commission.'

(4) Conditions concerning specific undertakings

Certain undertakings. The conditions that may be attached by the Member **2.242** States to general and individual[169] authorisations have been examined in the preceding paragraphs. These conditions are applicable to all undertakings interested in taking part in activities on electronic communications markets. In the remarks introducing the sections on authorisations, it was noted that extra conditions may be added in respect of certain undertakings. These undertakings are those designated as having significant power on a given market.

Access and universal service. Specific obligations may be imposed on under- **2.243** takings with significant market power regarding access to networks or, more generally, facilities under their control. Obligations may also be imposed on the same undertakings in connection with retail price control. The two sets of obligations are introduced, respectively, in the Access and Universal Service Directives and are analysed at paras 5.95–5.104.

Attached to conditions. The NRF establishes a link between these access and uni- **2.244** versal service obligations and the conditions that may be attached to authorisations. In the Authorisations Directive, the Parliament and Council accepted that these obligations may be referred to in general authorisations. This means that the specific obligations that may be imposed on undertakings with significant market power should in the interests of transparency be described in the documents associated, in the various Member States, with authorisation.

---

[168] Under the EC Treaty, restrictions may be allowed only where national measures are justified by legitimate means and objectives.   [169] Rights of use for numbers and frequencies.

Authorisations Directive, Article 6(2). 'Specific obligations which may be imposed on providers of electronic communications networks and services under Articles 5(1), 5(2), 6 and 8 of Directive 2002/19/EC (Access Directive) and Articles 16, 17, 18 and 19 of Directive 2002/22/EC (Universal Service Directive) or on those designated to provide universal service under the said Directive shall be legally separate from the rights and obligations under the general authorisation. In order to achieve transparency for undertakings, the criteria and procedures for imposing such specific obligations on individual undertakings shall be referred to in the general authorisation.'

2.245 **Transparency.** As appears from the extract set out in the previous paragraph, the possibility of referring to these specific obligations in authorisations was introduced in the Authorisations Directive out of a desire to enhance transparency. The Parliament and Council deemed it essential that all undertakings should be warned about the existence of the obligations imposed in connection with market power. As a result of that measure, undertakings on which these obligations may be imposed are informed of the legal regime which may be applied to them. In the same manner, the association of these obligations with authorisation makes it possible for other undertakings to be informed as to the constraints imposed on competitors with market power.

2.246 **Legally distinct conditions.** Despite the links established between conditions and specific obligations, the Parliament and Council have been willing to maintain a legal separation between these aspects. Pursuant to the Authorisations Directive, the obligations that may be imposed on undertakings with significant market power are legally distinct from the conditions attached to authorisation. This 'legal separation' clearly appears in the extract quoted above. It is not clear whether that separation has any particular implications. One interpretation is that there are no such implications. The presence of this distinction means, in this interpretation, that conditions and obligations have different statuses. *(a)* The conditions are attached to authorisations. They have to be fulfilled, in principle, before activities may be started. *(b)* Access and universal service obligations, by contrast, are not connected with the commencement of activities. They rather refer to the exercise of activities. Pursuant to the relevant directives, activities must be carried out in compliance with these obligations.

2.247 **General access-related conditions.** As already stated, the Access Directive introduces obligations which are not limited in scope to undertakings holding significant market power. Some access-related obligations apply to all undertakings present on electronic communications markets. These obligations may be attached, as conditions, to general authorisation.

(5) Payments

2.248 **Three types of payment.** Three types of payment may be required from undertakings. Undertakings may be asked to contribute to the cost of the provision of universal service. They may further be asked to pay usage fees in exchange for a right of use. Finally, they may be asked to pay administrative charges aimed at covering the administrative costs associated with the regulation of electronic communications markets. These various financial obligations are examined in the following paragraphs.

(1) Contribution to universal service costs.   Undertakings may be asked to pay **2.249** a contribution to cover the cost of the provision of universal service. A decision may be taken to this effect only after several conditions have been satisfied. *(a)* An assessment must take place, in each Member State, of the possibility that universal service may be provided through the interaction of market forces. The Member States may not intervene if, and to the extent that, market forces spontaneously produce a satisfactory situation. *(b)* If universal service objectives cannot be realised through markets, a decision may be taken to impose specific obligations on one or several undertakings. *(c)* The Member States concerned should then determine whether funds should be granted to these undertakings. Again, a decision of this nature is not automatic. An assessment must be made to determine whether, as a result of the obligations imposed on them, these undertakings bear an excessive burden. The assessment may only be started if a specific request to that effect is made by the undertakings concerned. *(d)* A final decision must be taken regarding the methods to be used to finance the provision of the service by these undertakings. One possibility is that the Member States concerned finance the service out of general taxation. Another possibility is that a fund may be created with contributions recovered from undertakings on the market.

The obligations which Member States may impose on undertakings to finance the universal service are not analysed in detail in the section, but in the chapter dealing with universal service (see paras 5.179–5.195).

(2) Usage fees.   Some undertakings receive specific rights allowing them to carry **2.250** out their activities. A payment may be required from these undertakings in return for the rights granted. Three types of right are considered in the NRF in connection with payment obligations: the right to use numbers and radio frequencies and the right to establish facilities on property belonging to an authority or to a private individual. In economic theory, the obligation to make payments in connection with numbers or frequencies is generally explained by the scarce character of the resources concerned. By imposing a price, authorities ensure that these resources will be put to the best possible use by the undertakings concerned.

> *Authorisations Directive, Article 13(1).* 'Member States may allow the relevant authority to impose fees for the rights of use for radio frequencies or numbers or rights to install facilities on, over or under public or private property.'

Public resources.   Experience shows that usage fees have been used by European **2.251** governments to raise public funds. In recent years, for example, governments have attempted to raise money for the national exchequers through frequency auctions.

2.252 **A national decision in principle.** The question arises as to who has the authority to determine how much should be paid in return for a right of use. As regards frequency, it is submitted in Chapter 7 that spectrum policy is only partially developed at European level. There is a hope and expectation that procedures for the allocation of frequencies, including financial contributions, will at some point be harmonised across Europe. However, that stage of integration has not yet been reached, and in the absence of a specific Community provision the Member States currently keep the competence to regulate these procedures, including their financial aspects.

2.253 **Limitations imposed by the EC Treaty.** This does not mean that Member States have entire freedom on this matter. A general limitation is imposed by Article 10 of the EC Treaty, pursuant to which the Member States must refrain from all actions that may hinder the attainment of objectives set out in the Treaty. Under the same provision the Member States are compelled to adopt measures necessary for the fulfilment of these goals. An issue arises as to whether that provision is infringed where a Member State uses rights of use as a channel to raise public money without taking into account the specific needs of the electronic communications sector.

2.254 **Basic regulatory principles.** Limitations are also imposed by the NRF in the secondary legislation. These limitations are more precise, and more concrete, than those coming from general provisions founded in the EC Treaty. The first limitation comes from the basic regulatory principles. Given their general nature, these principles apply to usage fees. This implies that the financial contributions imposed on undertakings in return for rights of use should be objective and proportional. They should contain no discrimination.

> *Authorisations Directive, Article 13.* 'Member States shall ensure that . . . [usage] fees shall be objectively justified, transparent, non-discriminatory and proportionate in relation to their intended purpose and shall take into account the objectives in Article 8 of [the] . . . Framework Directive.' *Authorisations Directive, Preamble, recital 32.* '[U]sage fees . . . should not hinder the development of innovative services and competition in the market.'

2.255 **Optimal use of resources.** A second, and analogous, limitation comes from the obligation imposed in the NRF that usage fees must be determined with a view to ensuring an optimal use of the resource concerned. This is particularly true where, under the NRF, available frequencies should be managed efficiently. Again, it is not clear that imposing a high fee qualifies as an efficient form of spectrum management. When fees are high, the undertakings which have obtained the rights of use may lack the financial strength, once they have made their payments, to develop the necessary technology at the required pace.

> *Authorisations Directive, Article 13(1).* 'Member States may allow the relevant authority to impose fees for the rights of use . . . which reflect the need to ensure the optimal use

of these resources. *Authorisations Directive, Preamble, recital 32.* '[P]ayment arrangements should ensure that . . . fees do not in practice lead to selection on the basis of criteria unrelated to the objective of ensuring optimal use of radio frequencies.'

Control on usage fees.   Pursuant to the Authorisations Directive (preamble), no   **2.256**
control may be carried out on the use made of the usage fees levied by Member
States. Member States may accordingly use these fees as they wish. This could be
interpreted as implying that Member States have a substantial margin of manoeuvre
in the determination of fees. If they are free to use the fees as they wish, why should
they be limited as to the amounts they may ask from undertakings? Such an interpretation may not, however, be compatible with the provisions examined earlier.
A clear distinction must be established between two realities. *(a)* On the one hand,
the objective which must be attained through the imposition of fees on undertakings wishing to obtain the right to use scarce resources: pursuant to the NRF, that
objective is, and must be, the efficient and optimal use of the resource concerned.
A control may be carried out to verify whether that objective has been served
adequately. *(b)* On the other hand, the objectives that may be realised by the
Member States with the money they have acquired as a result of the usage fees
being imposed on undertakings: in the current version of the NRF, no obligation
is imposed in this regard on the Member States. States are thus free, at the current
stage of integration, to use these funds as they wish.[170]

> *Authorisations Directive, Preamble, recital 32.* 'This [Authorisations] Directive is
> without prejudice to the purpose for which fees for rights of use are employed. Such
> fees may for instance be used to finance activities of national regulatory authorities
> that cannot be covered by administrative charges.'

Best practice.   An interesting development is that, under the Authorisations   **2.257**
Directive, the European Commission can carry out, and publish, benchmark
studies listing best practice among European countries as regards the allocation of
frequencies. In this context, usage fees determined by the Member States may be
assessed using these benchmarks. It will be difficult for public authorities to justify
a difference, if these best practices are based on scientific evidence and demonstrate how, in a given context, the Member States concerned could attempt to
manage scarce resources in an efficient manner.

> *Authorisations Directive, Preamble, recital 32.* 'The Commission may publish on a
> regular basis benchmark studies with regard to best practices for the assignment of
> radio frequencies'.

---

[170] Pursuant to the NRF, the Member States are thus under an obligation to impose the usage
fees which, according to their analysis, leads to the best possible use of rights of use. Once these fees
have been imposed, they must collect the funds. Under the current version of the NRF, these funds
may then be allocated as the Member States consider appropriate. No verification can be carried out
on the use of the funds. By contrast, verifications may be made about the usage fees to ensure
that, according to available information, they indeed permit the best possible use of the existing
resources.

2.258　**(3) Administrative fees.**　A third type of payment may be imposed on electronic communications markets. Administrative payments may be demanded from undertakings as a contribution to the costs associated with the drawing up and application of regulation on these markets. Traditionally, the cost of operating agencies such as NRAs is financed from the general budget of the State. New regulatory responsibilities have however emerged in recent decades, requiring the creation of new agencies. The States appear reluctant to finance the cost associated with these new entities with the general budget. A solution is that these must be financed by the undertakings carrying out their activities on the markets concerned.

2.259　**All undertakings.**　A difference with the two kinds of payment examined earlier is that the administrative charges concern all undertakings active on electronic communications markets. They thus have a general character, which is lacking in the other cases. As discussed above, usage fees are limited to undertakings obtaining rights to use a scarce resource (particularly numbers or frequencies). As for universal service contributions, they are only imposed when the necessary conditions are satisfied. They are as a result not imposed in all circumstances on electronic communications markets.

2.260　**What costs may be charged.**　The power to raise payment from undertakings is not without limit. A first constraint is a precise identification of the costs that may be imposed on undertakings via administrative charges. The purpose is to ensure that these charges remain reasonable, and as low as possible. Excessive administrative charges would in fact amount to an entry barrier, making market entry difficult for new actors. Pursuant to the NRF, NRAs are allowed to charge the cost relating to three regulatory schemes: the scheme relating to general authorisations, that concerning rights of use, and that linked to specific obligations imposed on undertakings (obligations relating to access and universal service obligations). Regarding these schemes, they may charge the costs associated with the preparation of the regulation, as well as the expenses incurred as a result of the need to monitor compliance.

> *Authorisations Directive, Article 12(1).* 'Any administrative charges imposed on undertakings providing a service or a network under the general authorisation or to whom a right of use has been granted shall: . . . in total, cover only the administrative costs which will be incurred in the management, control and enforcement of the general authorisation scheme and of rights of use and of specific obligations as referred to in Article 6(2),[171] which may include costs for international cooperation, harmonisation and standardisation, market analysis, monitoring compliance and other market control, as well as regulatory work involving preparation and enforcement of secondary legislation and administrative decisions, such as decisions on access and interconnection.'

---

[171] These obligations relate to access and universal service.

How may costs be charged?   A second constraint is the way in which costs may   **2.261**
be divided. No 'distribution key' is explicitly provided in the NRF. *(a)* The
distribution must however conform with the basic regulatory principles.
According to these principles, the costs must be shared using objective, non-
discriminatory and proportional criteria. *(b)* The mechanism used should be
simple. The purpose in this regard is to avoid excessive administrative costs.
(c) Indications are provided in the preamble to the Authorisations Directive
regarding specific methods that may be used. The Parliament and Council mention the possibility of resorting to a 'turnover related distribution key'. In countries where the administrative charge is limited, NRAs could use flat-rate charges,
or charges combining a flat rate basis with a turnover-related element.[172]

> *Authorisations Directive, Article 12(1).* 'Any administrative charges imposed on
> undertakings providing a service or a network under the general authorisation or to
> whom a right of use has been granted shall: . . . be imposed upon the individual
> undertakings in an objective, transparent and proportionate manner which mini-
> mises additional administrative costs and attendant charges.'

Controls on these costs.   The consequence of the administrative charge is that   **2.262**
NRAs are allowed to channel their costs to undertakings. In this situation there is
a risk that the costs associated with these agencies may grow and rapidly constitute
an obstacle for the development of the markets concerned. Measures were envisaged to avoid the occurrence of such a scenario. Again, the method is to place pressure, through the provision of information, on the entities concerned. Under the
NRF, NRAs must publish data relating to their costs and revenues. This provides
an opportunity for all interested parties to verify the financial aspects of NRA
activities.

> *Authorisations Directive, Article 12(2).* 'Where national regulatory authorities
> impose administrative charges, they shall publish a yearly overview of their adminis-
> trative costs and of the total sum of the charges collected. In the light of the difference
> between the total sum of the charges and the administrative costs, appropriate
> adjustments shall be made.'

(6) The provision of information

The role of information.   In many regards, the reform can be presented as an   **2.263**
attempt to create more transparency on the markets. In this context the provision of
information plays an essential role. Information must be provided by a number of
parties. We concentrate here on information to be provided by undertakings to
authorities in connection with authorisations, and four categories are distinguished.

---

[172] See Authorisations Directive, Preamble, recital 31. 'An example of a fair, simple and transparent . . . [method] for these charge attribution criteria could be a turnover related distribution
key. Where administrative charges are very low, flat rate charges, or charges combining a flat rate
basis with a turnover related element could also be appropriate.'

2.264 **(1) Identification purposes.** Pursuant to the NRF, general authorisation is normally granted automatically to undertakings to enable them to commence activity. Some Member States may however choose a system where a declaration or notification is requested or even a system where, in addition to a declaration or a notification, information has to be provided. In that latter case, it is for the NRAs to determine what information is requested. Limitations are imposed in the NRF to ensure that no excessive entry barrier is imposed. *(a)* Pursuant to the Authorisations Directive, NRAs may request only minimal information. *(b)* Information requested must be restricted to what is necessary to identify the parties. *(c)* In practice, NRAs may only ask for information for identification purposes. The objective must be to determine who is applying, for what service the application is made and when the service is expected to start.

> *Authorisations Directive, Article 3.* 'The notification . . . shall not entail more than a declaration . . . and the submission of the minimal information which is required to allow the national regulatory authority to keep a register or list of providers of electronic communications networks and services. This information must be limited to what is necessary for the identification of the provider, such as company registration numbers, and the provider's contact persons, the provider's address, a short description of the network or service, and an estimated date for starting the activity.'

2.265 **Penalties.** Penalties may be imposed on undertakings failing to provide the information necessary for identification purposes. These penalties are normally imposed by NRAs, or by any authority allowed by the Member States to deal with these matters. Issues related to penalties are discussed at paras 2.273–2.282. In this context it should be emphasised that while the Member States may determine what penalties should apply, they must comply with the basic regulatory principles. In particular, penalties must as a result be proportional.

2.266 **A condition for authorisation to be granted.** Beyond these general rules concerning penalties, the NRF provides that non-compliance with an obligation to provide information for identification purposes in connection with an authorisation may result in an undertaking being excluded from a market. The indications that may be found in the Authorisations Directive on this subject concern the information to be provided in order to obtain a right of use (numbers, frequency). No such indication may be found regarding general authorisation. There is thus an uncertainty about the scope of the measures that may be taken by the Member States. Sanctions such as exclusion from the market should, since they affect the rights of undertakings, be interpreted narrowly.[173]

---

[173] This should not be seen as a penalty, but rather as the result of the absence of information necessary to provide the services concerned. A declaration or notification are the only formalities required to obtain general authorisation. The authorisation is called general where it does not imply any specific intervention on the part of the authority. By contrast, rights of use are granted in an

Authorisations Directive, Article 11(1). NRAs 'may only require undertakings to provide information . . . for rights of use . . . that is proportionate and objectively justified for: . . . . (c) procedures for and assessment of requests for granting rights of use . . . '. 'The information referred to in points (a), (b), (d), (e) and (f)[174] of the first subparagraph may not be required prior to or as a condition for market access.' *Authorisations Directive, Preamble, recital 13.* 'As part of the application procedure for granting rights to use a radio frequency, Member States may verify whether the applicant will be able to comply with the conditions attached to such rights. For this purpose the applicant may be requested to submit the necessary information to prove his ability to comply with these conditions. Where such information is not provided, the application for the right to use a radio frequency may be rejected.'

(2) Control purposes.   The second category concerns information to be used **2.267** to verify that conditions attached to authorisations are complied with. Pursuant to the NRF, NRAs may ask undertakings to provide information for control purposes. Such request may be formulated as a result of a complaint leading to an investigation. It may also follow an investigation started by an NRA on its own initiative. Whatever the circumstance, the request must be compatible with the basic regulatory principles. The Directive also states expressly that information for control-related purposes may not be requested systematically, but only on a case-by-case basis. NRAs must have solid grounds before they can ask for information concerning compliance.

Authorisations Directive, Article 10(1). 'National regulatory authorities may require undertakings providing electronic communications networks or services covered by the general authorisation or enjoying rights of use for radio frequencies or numbers to provide information necessary to verify compliance with the conditions of the general authorisation or of rights of use or with the specific obligations referred to in Article 6(2).'[175] *Article 11(1).* NRAs 'may only require undertakings to provide information under the general authorisation . . . [or] for rights of use . . . that is proportionate and objectively justified for: . . . case-by-case verification of compliance with conditions as set out in the Annex where a complaint has been received or where the national regulatory authority has other reasons to believe that a condition is not complied with or in case of an investigation by the national regulatory authority on its own initiative'.

---

individual authorisation. This authorisation is termed individual because it requires a specific intervention on the part of the authority. The NRA must grant numbers or frequencies. A specific, individual, decision is necessary to that effect. These decisions may not be taken in the absence of certain information. For instance, the authorities would not be in a position to deliver numbers if they do not know for what service the numbers were to be used. A similar remark may be made for radio frequencies.

[174] These letters refer to other kinds of information, which are examined in the following paragraphs.

[175] This provision refers to specific obligations imposed on undertakings, in application of the Access and Universal Service Directives.

2.268 **Penalties.** The NRF specifically provides that financial penalties can be applied to undertakings failing to provide information requested for control purposes.

> *Authorisations Directive, Article 10(4).* 'Member States may empower the relevant authority to impose financial penalties where appropriate on undertakings for failure to provide information in accordance with obligations imposed under Article 11(1) . . . (b)[176] of this Directive.'

2.269 **(3) Payment-related information.** A third category of information that may be requested under the Authorisations Directive is that needed to verify that payments have been made in connection with activities in electronic communications activities (contribution to the universal service, usage fee, administrative charge).

> *Authorisations Directive, Article 11(1).* NRAs 'may only require undertakings to provide information . . . that is proportionate and objectively justified for: (a) systematic or case-by-case verification of compliance with conditions 1[177] and 2[178] of Part A, condition 6[179] of Part B and condition 7[180] of Part C of the Annex'.

2.270 **Penalties.** There is little indication concerning the penalties Member States may impose when undertakings fail to provide this third category information. The NRF limits situations where undertakings may be excluded from the market. The only case where exclusion is allowed is where identification-related information is withheld. A contrario, this may be interpreted as implying that no exclusion may be ordered when an undertaking fails to deliver information concerning payments due, and other penalties may be ordered (see paras 2.273–2.282 below). Financial penalties may certainly be imposed but, as in other cases, they must conform with the basic regulatory principles.

> *Authorisations Directive, Article 10(4).* 'States may empower the relevant authority to impose financial penalties where appropriate on undertakings for failure to provide information . . . under Article 11(1)(a)[181] . . . of this Directive . . . within a reasonable period stipulated by the national regulatory authority.'

2.271 **(d) Statistical purposes.** A fourth category concerns information which NRAs may request in order to analyse markets. Such information may be called 'general' to the extent that it does not concern specific undertakings. The data gathered may be used by the Commission in its reports on implementation of the regulatory framework and other analytical exercises, and by the NRAs for their own statistical purposes.

---

[176] This provision is quoted in the previous paragraph and states that information must be provided to ensure compliance with the conditions attached to authorisations.

[177] Contribution to universal service.   [178] Administrative charge.

[179] Fee for the use of radio frequencies.   [180] Fee for the use of numbers.

[181] This provision empowers the Member States to request information in order to verify that payments have been made.

Authorisations Directive, Article 11(1). NRAs 'may only require undertakings to provide information . . . that is proportionate and objectively justified for: . . . (d) publication of comparative overviews of quality and price of services for the benefit of consumers; (e) clearly defined statistical purposes; (f) market analysis for the purposes of [the] . . . Access Directive or [the] . . . Universal Service Directive'.

Penalties.   The NRF remains silent about possible penalties in the event that **2.272** general information is not provided. The imposition of penalties should not be excluded in principle. However, it should remain proportionate in accordance with the basic regulatory principles and, furthermore, should probably be moderate, since the obligation to provide general information does not appear essential in the system created by the NRF.

(7) Penalties in case of infringement

Enforcement.   The rules established by the Parliament and Council must be **2.273** complied with by all parties present on electronic communications markets. Member States have the power to determine how the rules are enforced. The NRF, however, creates several possible mechanisms, including the imposition of penalties. As regards authorisations in particular, penalties may be imposed on undertakings when they do not comply with the conditions attached to authorisations (general authorisations, rights of use). Undertakings may be requested to provide information showing that conditions attached to authorisations are being complied with. In the absence of compliance, penalties may be imposed. The rights of the undertakings are protected in the procedures leading to the imposition of penalties. In exceptional circumstances, Member States may take emergency measures against undertakings failing to comply with their obligations. These various aspects are analysed in the following paragraphs.

(1) Request information.   NRAs must ensure that the conditions attached to **2.274** authorisations are complied with. One way for them to monitor the markets is to carry out controls. Another is to request from undertakings information likely to establish whether the conditions are complied with. On the basis of the NRF, NRAs may request undertakings to provide information. A request may be made, for instance, to undertakings holding significant market power to determine to what extent they open the facilities under their control to other actors. All requests addressed to undertakings regarding information must conform to the basic regulatory principles. Requests must be limited to what is strictly necessary to ensure that the conditions are complied with.

Authorisations Directive, Article 10(1). 'National regulatory authorities may require undertakings providing electronic communications networks or services covered by the general authorisation or enjoying rights of use for radio frequencies or numbers to provide information necessary to verify compliance with the conditions of the general authorisation or of rights of use or with the specific obligations referred to in Article 6(2),[182] in accordance with Article 11.'[183]

2.275 **(2) Carry out an investigation.** After receiving information, NRAs must decide whether a condition has been infringed. The enquiry may be founded on information provided by the undertakings concerned. In most instances, NRAs gather further data through their own investigations. They may use all channels made available by national legislation. A restriction is that the interventions of the NRAs must remain compatible with the basic regulatory principles.

2.276 **(3) Impose penalties.** Where they consider that conditions have not been fulfilled, NRAs must impose penalties. Here again the basic regulatory principles apply. This implies that, among other constraints, penalties must be proportional (useful, necessary, non-excessive). As appears from the NRF, the Member States have a margin of manoeuvre in determining the penalties that may be imposed. The NRF allows Member States to impose financial penalties. There is, however, no obligation to resort to this form of penalty. Member States may use other measures if they consider them more appropriate.

> *Authorisations Directive, Article 10(3).* 'If the undertaking concerned does not remedy the breaches within the period as referred to in paragraph 2, the relevant authority shall take appropriate and proportionate measures aimed at ensuring compliance. In this regard, Member States may empower the relevant authorities to impose financial penalties where appropriate.'

2.277 **The possibility of exclusion.** The ultimate sanction may be the withdrawal of the right to perform market activities. That sanction may be imposed only in exceptional circumstances, and several preconditions must be complied with. *(a)* Under the NRF, an undertaking may only be excluded where it has breached a regulation several times. The Member States do not appear to have the power to exclude an undertaking from the market where one breach only is established.[184] *(b)* The breaches concerned must be serious. Exclusion is only possible under the NRF where an important obligation has been infringed.[185] *(c)* Other measures must be taken before an undertaking may be excluded. Exclusion thus appears as

---

[182] Obligations imposed on undertakings in relation to access and universal service.

[183] General provision concerning the information that may be requested from undertakings in connection with an authorisation (general authorisation or right of use).

[184] There is no indication about a threshold to be satisfied before breaches can be considered sufficient in number. As the NRF refers to 'several' breaches, one may consider that more than two breaches are necessary to qualify under this requirement.

[185] In principle, minor violations must be punished using other forms of penalty. An exception is when an undertaking repeatedly infringes the regulation. In such a circumstance, the minor nature of the infringement will not form an obstacle against exclusion.

an ultimate penalty that may be ordered only after other measures have been taken and have proved insufficient.[186]

> *Authorisations Directive, Article 10(5).* 'In cases of serious and repeated breaches of the conditions of the general authorisation, the rights of use or specific obligations referred to in Article 6(2),[187] where measures aimed at ensuring compliance as referred to in paragraph 3[188] of this Article have failed, national regulatory authorities may prevent an undertaking from continuing to provide electronic communications networks or services or suspend or withdraw rights of use.'[189]

(4) Respect the rights of the undertakings concerned. Throughout the proce- **2.278**
dures which may lead to the adoption of measures or penalties, the rights of the undertakings concerned must be respected. *(a)* Under normal circumstances, NRAs must inform the undertakings concerned of their findings that a rule has been infringed. *(b)* Similarly, the undertakings concerned must be granted an opportunity to express their views. There is therefore under the NRF a right to be heard for the undertakings concerned, before the imposition of penalties. *(c)* After an undertaking has been heard, a decision must be adopted. That decision must take into account the elements put forward by the undertaking, which are compared to the information the NRA holds concerning the breach. *(d)* Should the NRA decide that a breach has indeed been committed, the undertaking must be given a reasonable period to stop the infringement. The duration of the period should in principle be a month, starting on the day when the decision is notified. That duration may, however, be extended or shortened by the NRA, depending on the circumstances.[190]

> *Authorisations Directive, Article 10(2).* 'Where a national regulatory authority finds that an undertaking does not comply with one or more of the conditions of the general authorisation, or of rights of use or with the specific obligations referred to in Article 6(2), it shall notify the undertaking of those findings and give the undertaking a reasonable opportunity to state its views or remedy any breaches within one month after notification, or a shorter period agreed by the undertaking or stipulated by the national regulatory authority in case of repeated breaches, or a longer period decided by the national regulatory authority.'

(5) Adopt the necessary measures. At the end of the period, the NRA must **2.279**
determine whether the breach has been terminated. Where the breach continues,

---

[186] A certain period is necessary between the various beaches and the imposition of these measures, to see whether the undertaking abides by the penalty. To assess the duration of this period, time-periods mentioned in the NRF may be used (one month after notification of the breach).

[187] Obligations imposed on undertakings in relation to access and universal service.

[188] These measures are examined in the previous paragraph.

[189] See also Authorisations Directive, Preamble, recital 27. 'Save in exceptional circumstances, it would not be proportionate to suspend or withdraw the right to provide electronic communications services or the right to use radio frequencies or numbers where an undertaking did not comply with one or more of the conditions under the general authorisation.'

[190] The NRF provides, in particular, that a shorter deadline may be imposed when the undertaking has repeatedly failed to respect the law.

measures must be taken as provided in the paragraphs above. These measures must be communicated to the undertakings concerned in the week following their adoption. The obligation to communicate and provide reasoning for the measures concerned is not limited to one portion of the procedure. It continues to apply if new measures and, ultimately, exclusion, are ordered.

> *Authorisations Directive, Article 10(3)*. 'The measures and the reasons on which they are based shall be communicated to the undertaking concerned within one week of their adoption and shall stipulate a reasonable period for the undertaking to comply with the measure.'

2.280 **Right of appeal.** A right of appeal must be available against the measures adopted by NRAs against undertakings. Member States thus have an obligation to organise a procedure allowing a review, by a superior body, of the measures in question. The obligation is formulated in rather broad terms. This is important for the interpretation of the provision, since as far as the protection of undertakings is concerned, provisions relating to the right of defence should not be construed in a restrictive manner.

> *Authorisations Directive, Article 10(7)*. 'Undertakings shall have the right to appeal against measures taken under this Article in accordance with the procedure referred to in Article 4[191] of Directive 2002/21/EC (Framework Directive).'

2.281 **Appeal not restricted.** Under the NRF, an appeal must lie against all the measures which may be adopted by the NRAs. *(a)* A consequence of the wide terms used in the NRF is that the possibility of appealing should not be limited to the first range of measures which NRAs may adopt when they consider for the first time that a breach has been committed and that the undertaking has failed to terminate it within the period set by the NRA. *(b)* It should be possible to appeal against any penalties imposed thereafter, when it appears that the undertaking remains in breach. *(c)* An appeal should also be possible against decisions whereby NRAs exclude an undertaking from the market after a serious and repeated breach has been established. *(d)* Undertakings must also have the possibility to appeal against interim measures adopted by NRAs. As these measures are dictated by an emergency situation, they should not be suspended. Given the strict conditions applying to the adoption of emergency interim measures, a suspension could lead to significant damage for the public, users or providers.

2.282 **Ideally a court.** The provision introducing the right to an appeal refers to the Framework Directive, which organises rights of appeals against decisions adopted by NRAs (see extract above). This provision is examined in Chapter 6. At this stage, it is important, however, to note that the appeal must take place before an

---

[191] This provision imposes on the Member States an obligation to establish a right of appeal against decisions adopted by the NRAs. On this subject, see Chapter 6.

entity independent of the parties. If that body is not a court, a superior degree must be organised. At that stage the application must be reviewed by a court. Pending the outcome of the appeal, a decision by the NRA normally stands. A stay may where necessary be ordered by the appeal body. For the reasons set out above it is doubtful, however, that a stay may be ordered in appeals against interim measures.

(8) Interim measures

A temporary reaction. The NRF provides that interim measures may be adopted by Member States. These measures are independent of those which NRAs may take on the basis of the other provisions of the NRF and which have been analysed in the previous paragraphs. In a typical procedure, an undertaking would seek protection from an NRA against a competitor which it is claimed has not complied with the national legislation implementing the NRF. Interim measures would be requested to ensure that, during the procedure, the complainant does not suffer irreparable damage. These measures should only be temporary, until a final decision is adopted by the NRA. **2.283**

> *Authorisations Directive, Article 10(6).* '[W]here the relevant authority has evidence of a breach of the conditions of the general authorisation, rights of use or specific obligations referred to in Article 6(2)[192] that represents an immediate and serious threat to public safety, public security or public health or will create serious economic or operational problems for other providers or users of electronic communications networks or services, it may take urgent interim measures to remedy the situation in advance of reaching a final decision.'

Conditions. In accordance with the case law, interim measures may be adopted only if several conditions are satisfied, owing to the exceptional character of these measures. Such measures are indeed adopted by way of derogation from the normal development of a procedure. The conditions for the application of interim measures appear in the extract quoted above. Pursuant to the provision concerned, two scenarios are distinguished in the NRF. *(a)* In the first, interim measures are necessary to confront an immediate and serious threat to the public. The hypothesis is one where the safety, security or health of the public is at stake. *(b)* The second scenario is wider and may develop more frequently, and relates to a situation where there may be an economic or operational threat. It is immaterial whether these problems concern users or providers. **2.284**

Irreparable damage. Under European law, interim measures may be requested from a court or tribunal if it appears that in the absence of such measures irreparable damage would be suffered by the complainant. An allusion was made to this general condition in 2.283. **2.285**

---

[192] This provision refers to specific obligations imposed on undertakings in connection with access to facilities or the provision of universal service.

2.286 **Rights of the parties.** As they are required to counter an emergency, interim measures may be adopted without respecting all the rights granted to the undertakings under the NRF. Further, the steps normally taken by the NRAs before reaching a final decision may be bypassed. As provided in the NRF, the undertakings against which interim measures are adopted must be informed, although only after the interim measures have been taken. This is in derogation from the normal procedure where a penalty may be imposed only after information has been provided to the undertaking concerned, and the undertaking has been heard by the authority and given a certain period to comply with the regulation in question.

> *Authorisations Directive, Article 10(6).* 'The undertaking concerned shall thereafter[193] be given a reasonable opportunity to state its view and propose any remedies. Where appropriate, the relevant authority may confirm the interim measures.'

F. Changes Introduced by the New Regulatory Framework

2.287 **Previously applicable instruments.** Under the old regulatory framework, market entry-related authorisations were regulated by the following instruments: *(a)* Directive (EC) 97/13 of the European Parliament and of the Council on a common framework for general authorisations and individual licences in the field of telecommunications services;[194] *(b)* Commission Directive (EEC) 90/388 on competition in the markets for telecommunications services.[195]

2.288 **No significant discrepancy.** There exists no significant discrepancy between the old and the new regulatory frameworks as regards authorisations. Differences can of course be found. These differences, however, are not of such scope or magnitude that one could speak of a *substantial* change in the formalities and conditions imposed on undertakings in connection with market entry.

2.289 **Basic regulatory principles.** A similarity is that certain basic regulatory principles already applied under the old framework with which Member States had to comply. In application of these principles, public intervention had to be connected with an objective deemed essential at European level. The instruments used to reach that objective had to be proportional and free of discrimination. Obligations also applied to the regulatory system where such intervention was to take place (mainly transparency, independence and competence).

---

[193] After the interim measure has been ordered.   [194] [1997] OJ L117/15.
[195] As amended several times, [1990] OJ L192/10. The main provisions concerning authorisations were introduced by Commission Directive (EC) 96/19 amending Directive 90/388/EEC with regard to the implementation of full competition in telecommunications markets [1996] OJ L074/13.

Conditions attached to formalities.   The mechanism of attaching conditions to   **2.290**
formalities also existed in the old regulatory framework. As is the case in the NRF, the
conditions attached to authorisations in the old regulatory framework corresponded
with the obligations imposed by the various directives composing that framework.
The content of these conditions, or obligations, has not varied substantially. No
significant difference can be found between the frameworks regarding the condi-
tions/obligations attached to the various types of authorisations then distinguished.

Types of formality.   The main difference lies in the type of formality imposed on   **2.291**
undertakings. As stated in this section, authorisation may in principle only be
general under the NRF. Exceptions are provided for rights of use, in particular
those concerning frequencies and numbers.

Four situations.   The situation was different under the old framework, where a   **2.292**
distinction was made between four scenarios. *(a) Absence of formality.* In a first scenario, undertakings could start an activity without accomplishing any formality.
That scenario was preferred by the European Commission. The reason for that
preference is clear. In a situation where no formality needs to be accomplished,
there exists virtually no barrier to entry. *(b) Declaration.* In a second scenario, activities were subject to a declaration. In that declaration, interested undertakings were
to communicate to an authority their desire to start an activity on a given market.
In such a situation, barriers to entry are also limited. The undertakings only need
to send a declaration before starting activities. No reaction is required from any
authority. *(c) Authorisations.* In a third scenario, undertakings had to receive an
authorisation prior to starting an activity. That authorisation was designed in general terms. In that regard, it does not differ from the general authorisation imposed
under the NRF. In the old framework, undertakings had to manifest their intention to start an activity. They could then be requested to provide information
allowing the NRA to determine whether conditions were complied with. In the
absence of a specific intervention, the undertaking could start activities. For a few
weeks the authority had the opportunity to verify whether conditions were fulfilled. A procedure was organised to structure exchanges between undertakings and
the authority in case conditions were not complied with. *(d) Licence.* In the last scenario a licence was required. That formality was only used in connection with the
use of scarce resources, although an individual licence could also be required for the
provision of voice telephony and network services. The situations concerned were
not fundamentally different from those covered by individual authorisation under
the new Authorisations Directive (numbers, frequencies).

Main changes.   As appears from the discussion above, there is little difference   **2.293**
between the old and the new regulatory framework as regards authorisations.
Under the old framework, four situations could be distinguished (absence of formality, declaration, authorisation, licence). Under the NRF, the same possibilities

still exist. The absence of formality, the declaration (or notification) and the authorisation coexist in the general category called 'general authorisation', and are still possible. Licences have been replaced by the individual authorisations to be obtained in order to have the right to use a scarce resource (right of use).

G. Transitional Arrangements

2.294 **The transition.**   As was submitted in the previous section, the changes between the old and the new regulation are minor. It is possible, however, that Member States may use the transition to create new rights and/or obligations. Such a situation would create transitional issues. When do the new conditions and obligations apply to the undertakings? What rules apply in the meantime?

2.295 **24 July 2003.**   The date for the implementation of the NRF serves as the key indicator for the determination of the regime applicable during the transition. As stated, transposition was to be completed at the latest on 24 July 2003. As a result, authorisations granted to undertakings had to be adapted by that date. The new rules adopted by the Member States were to be applied to undertakings on the day following that deadline.

> *Authorisations Directive, Article 17(1).* 'Member States shall bring authorisations already in existence on the date of entry into force of this Directive into line with the provisions of this Directive by at the latest the date of application referred to in Article 18(1), second subparagraph.'[196]

2.296 **(1) Prolongation of the regime.**   Under the Authorisations Directive, the Member States can organise a transitional regime. That regime may be established in situations where the rights and obligations applicable to undertakings are modified as a result of the passage from the old to the new regulation. The transitional period may last, at a maximum, nine months. This implies that the new regime must, in all cases, be made applicable, at the latest, on 24 April 2004.

> *Authorisations Directive, Article 17(2).* 'Where application of paragraph 1[197] results in a reduction of the rights or an extension of the obligations under authorisations already in existence, Member States may extend the validity of those rights and obligations until at the latest nine months after the date of application referred to in Article 18(1),[198] second subparagraph, provided that the rights of other undertakings under Community law are not affected thereby. Member States shall notify such extensions to the Commission and state the reasons therefore.'

2.297 **Condition.**   The possibility for Member States to introduce a transitional regime is limited by the date at which that possible regime must end. It is also

---

[196] Under the last provision, the Authorisations Directive had to be transposed by the Member States on 24 July 2003 at the latest.   [197] The transition to the new authorisations regime.   [198] 24 July 2003.

limited by a condition introduced in the NRF and apparent in the extract quoted above. Pursuant to the Authorisations Directive, a transitional regime may be installed only if that regime does not alter the rights of other undertakings under Community law. That condition creates a source of contention for undertakings which may consider that their situation has not improved as a result of the application of the transitional regime.

(2) **Prolongation of isolated rights/obligations.** The Authorisations Directive **2.298** further allows the Member States to prolong isolated rights and obligations concerning access to facilities. It was submitted that, among the conditions attached to general authorisations, some related to the obligations imposed on undertakings with significant market power regarding access to facilities operated by these undertakings. It cannot be excluded that the change from the old to the new regulation, as implemented by the Member States, may create a situation whereby undertakings seeking access to these facilities are treated less favourably than formerly. In that situation, the Member States may exceptionally prolong the conditions relating to access.

> *Authorisations Directive, Article 17(3).* 'Where the Member State concerned can prove that the abolition of an authorisation condition regarding access to electronic communications networks, which was in force before the date of entry into force of this [Authorisations] Directive, creates excessive difficulties for undertakings that have benefited from mandated access to another network, and where it is not possible for these undertakings to negotiate new agreements on reasonable commercial terms before the date of application referred to in Article 18(1), second subparagraph,[199] Member States may request a temporary prolongation of the relevant condition(s).'

Conditions. The prolongation of isolated rights/obligations is possible only if **2.299** several conditions are fulfilled. These conditions appear in the extract quoted in the previous paragraph. *(a)* The prolongation concerns situations where an undertaking sought access to facilities but did not obtain them through commercial negotiation. A procedure was then initiated by the access seeker. As a result of the procedure, a decision ordering access subject to reasonable conditions was taken by the NRA. *(b)* The Member State should demonstrate that the change from the old to the new regime would affect that situation in a way detrimental to the undertaking previously enjoying access. Situations may be taken into account only where undertakings enjoying access would suffer excessive difficulties as a result of the change in the applicable regime. *(c)* A further condition applies to the extent that a prolongation could only be decided if the undertakings enjoying access were not in a position to negotiate a new agreement before the deadline for the implementation of the NRF. It is not required that any sort of agreement should be concluded. The undertaking is

---

[199] 25 July 2003.

in a position to ask for a prolongation, as long as it can establish that the agreement offered to it cannot be deemed commercially reasonable.

2.300 **Formalities.**   To these material conditions must be added certain formalities. *(a)* Pursuant to the Authorisations Directive, the application for a prolongation of an isolated condition had to be made at the latest on 25 July 2003. Only undertakings that have presented an application at that date may claim the benefit of a possible prolongation. It was not possible to submit, after that date, any sort of request to continue enjoying the benefit of previous conditions. *(b)* The final decision concerning the prolongation was not to be taken by the Member State but rather by the European Commission. The Member States were thus not competent to decide that a former condition may remain valid, in derogation from the application of the NRF after the deadline for implementation. The decisions taken by the European Commission in this kind of procedure had to indicate the scope and duration of the prolongation. They were to be published in the Official Journal.

> *Authorisations Directive, Article 17(3).* 'Such requests [to obtain a prolongation of an isolated condition] shall be submitted by the date of application referred to in Article 18(1), second subparagraph,[200] at the latest, and shall specify the condition(s) and period for which the temporary prolongation is requested. The Member State shall inform the Commission of the reasons for requesting a prolongation. The Commission shall consider such a request, taking into account the particular situation in that Member State and of the undertaking(s) concerned, and the need to ensure a coherent regulatory environment at a Community level. It shall take a decision on whether to grant or reject the request, and where it decides to grant the request, on the scope and duration of the prolongation to be granted. The Commission shall communicate its decision to the Member State concerned within six months after receipt of the application for a prolongation. Such decisions shall be published in the Official Journal of the European Communities.'

H. Future Changes and Transparency

2.301 (1) **Future changes.**   Member States could be tempted to introduce, in the future, changes in the rights and obligations applicable to undertakings. The extent to which the Member States can bring about these changes is regulated in the NRF. The objective, in this case, is to ensure legal certainty through the application of the basic regulatory principles. *(a)* As required under these principles, possible changes must be justified in connection with an objective accepted or promoted in the NRF. *(b)* Changes must be proportionate. Member States would not be allowed, for instance, to introduce major amendments in order to bring about an objective deemed accessory in the NRF. *(c)* Transparency is required.

---

[200] 25 July 2003.

In application of that principle, changes must be announced with clarity. The undertakings and users concerned must have an opportunity to express their views. *(d)* Finally, any changes introduced by the Member States must remain compatible with the provisions concerning authorisations in the NRF.

> *Authorisations Directive, Article 14(1).* 'Member States shall ensure that the rights, conditions and procedures concerning general authorisations and rights of use or rights to install facilities may only be amended in objectively justified cases and in a proportionate manner. Notice shall be given in an appropriate manner of the intention to make such amendments and interested parties, including users and consumers, shall be allowed a sufficient period of time to express their views on the proposed amendments, which shall be no less than four weeks except in exceptional circumstances.'

Limitation.   If they comply with the basic regulatory principles, the Member **2.302** States can thus modify the rights and obligations applicable to undertakings. Their freedom is affected by another limitation, which is expressed explicitly in the NRF. Under the Authorisations Directive, the Member States may not affect rights and obligations during the period for which they have been created. Member States must await the end of the period for which these rights and obligations have been introduced. Only then, at the end of the period, can they be modified.[201]

> *Authorisations Directive, Article 14(2).* 'Member States shall not restrict or withdraw rights to install facilities before expiry of the period for which they were granted except where justified and where applicable in conformity with relevant national provisions regarding compensation for withdrawal of rights.'

(2) Transparency.   There are a number of references in this book to obligations **2.303** imposed in the name of transparency. Practitioners should be aware that, in the NRF, transparency is not a vague word without concrete possibilities for action. Transparency is at the origin of numerous obligations imposed on authorities and undertakings in the various directives composing the NRF. These obligations are accompanied by remedies. Actions may be started, for instance, against powerful undertakings in situations where these undertakings fail to announce properly the conditions under which access may be sought to their facilities. Similarly, actions may be initiated against Member States failing to announce clearly the rights and obligations applicable to the markets. As is detailed in Chapter 6, these actions may seek payment in redress for damage caused by a lack of transparency.

> *Authorisations Directive, Article 15(1).* 'Member States shall ensure that all relevant information on rights, conditions, procedures, charges, fees and decisions concerning general authorisations and rights of use is published and kept up to date in an

---

[201] A decision can be taken before the end of the period, but this modification can become effective only at the expiry of this period.

appropriate manner so as to provide easy access to that information for all interested parties.'

2.304 **One-stop shop.** An innovation introduced in the NRF is that information regarding the rules introduced in a Member State and concerning electronic communications markets must be gathered at a single information point. It is the NRAs that are responsible for collecting information and preparing it for consultation by consumers and undertakings. Under that obligation, NRAs must make all efforts necessary to ensure a synthesis of the rules applicable on the territory where they are competent. Under the terms used in the Authorisations Directive the NRAs are not compelled to act without regard for the cost of such an operation. There is however room for judicial action if the provision of information occurs in a disorganised manner and no effort is made to resolve that situation.

> *Authorisations Directive, Article 15(2).* 'Where information . . . is held at different levels of government, in particular information regarding procedures and conditions on rights to install facilities, the national regulatory authority shall make all reasonable efforts, bearing in mind the costs involved, to create a user-friendly overview of all such information, including information on the relevant levels of government and the responsible authorities, in order to facilitate applications for rights to install facilities.'

3

ACCESS TO FACILITIES AND RESOURCES
CONTROLLED BY OTHER
UNDERTAKINGS—SECTOR-SPECIFIC
REGULATION

A. Principles

(1) The issue

3.01 **The difficulty to be resolved.**   One of the principal difficulties in electronic communications is that of ensuring access by undertakings to the facilities or resources needed to engage in market activity. This refers not to the financial resources obtainable through banks or stock markets, but to an even more basic need, that of gaining access to the infrastructure and services necessary to carry out market activities. Electronic communications is a complex area where players' activities cannot be carried out in isolation. To provide a service, they must be able to gain access to resources controlled by others, sometimes competitors.[1] In some cases, undertakings controlling facilities are willing to co-operate. For instance, they may allow service providers to use part of the capacity available on the network under their control. This is, however, not necessarily always the case. Refusal of access often arises where operator activities are not limited to network operation but extend to the provision of services. On some of these markets for services, operators may be in competition with providers requesting access. As a result they may be reluctant to share access to a resource they regard as having been built through their own efforts.

3.02 **Policy objectives.**   In such a situation, rules are needed to ensure that access is indeed provided under conditions that are satisfactory for the performance of market activity. In the absence of regulatory intervention such access would not be ensured, an outcome not in line with the policy expectations underlying the reform. Regulatory tools are therefore provided in the new regulatory framework (NRF) as well as under general competition law in order to ensure that access is granted under appropriate conditions. These measures are intended to achieve objectives that have been analysed in the first chapter. The most important of these are the following.

3.03 **Develop markets/or services.**   One goal pursued by the reform is the development of services within the European Union. The availability of a variety of services is essential to satisfy the needs of businesses and the public. Yet services markets will develop only to the extent that undertakings are able to enter them. Customers have an opportunity to choose between providers only if several of them are indeed allowed to provide services. This cannot be achieved if providers are forced to rely solely on their own resources. To ensure choice, access must be subject to regulation.

---

[1] Where, for instance, an undertaking wants to offer a telephony service, it must set up a network linking users and supplying them with a tool to exchange messages. Ideally, the network should cover many users, as the value of a network depends on the number of connected customers. In many instances, this goal will be attained only if the undertaking has access to networks operated by other undertakings.

Maximise the use of existing resources.   Economically, it would be disastrous if **3.04**
electronic communications resources were used only by their owner or operator.
This would imply that they could be amortised only on customers supplied by
these owners or operators. An underlying expectation of the reform is that existing resources should be used to the maximum by all interested parties. Again, this
result will be attained only if access is subject to regulation.

Services, networks and other facilities.   The premise stated above is not limited **3.05**
to services but extends to networks and other resources necessary or useful in providing electronic communications services. Suppose an undertaking wants to
build a network. This is only possible if that undertaking can make use of the
sections it installs as they are being prepared for use. In providing capacity, the
undertaking should not wait for the whole network to be established. Such an
attitude would be unrealistic: the undertaking concerned could not be expected
to continue investing year after year without a return. For such an undertaking
there would be no alternative to seeking interconnection between its developing
facilities and resource networks operated by other businesses.

(2) How to find the applicable law?

Access Directive.   The main instrument regarding access is European Parliament **3.06**
and Council Directive (EC) 2002/19 on access to, and interconnection of electronic
communications networks and associated facilities ('Access Directive').[2] This
Directive is based on Article 95 EC and accordingly belongs to the 'harmonisation
framework'.

Two implementing instruments.   The Access Directive is supplemented by two **3.07**
implementing instruments adopted by the Commission. These also contain
analysis based on general competition law, and for this reason can be regarded as
a synthesis of the interaction between these two categories of rules in the electronic communications sector. *(a)* Guidelines 2002/C165/03 on market analysis
and the assessment of significant market power under the Community regulatory
framework for electronic communications networks and services ('2002
Guidelines on market analysis and significant market power').[3] This document
was drafted to provide assistance to national regulatory authorities (NRAs) in
identifying the undertakings on which one or more regulatory obligations
must be imposed as a result of provisions contained in the Access Directive.
(b) Commission Recommendation C(2003)497 on relevant product and service
markets within the electronic communications sector susceptible to ex ante regulation in accordance with Directive 2002/21/EC of the European Parliament and
of the Council on a common regulatory framework for electronic communication
networks and services ('Recommendation on relevant markets').[4] This document

---

² [2002] OJ L108/7.   ³ [2002] OJ L108/7.   ⁴ [2003] OJ L114/45.

structures electronic communications activities into relevant markets in respect of which NRAs must assess whether competition is effective. Where competition is found not to be effective, undertakings with significant market power must be required to fulfil one or more regulatory obligations pursuant to the Access Directive.

3.08 **Liberalisation directives.** These rules are to be complemented by rules included in the liberalisation directives (Commission), in particular Commission Directive (EC) 2002/77 on competition in the markets for electronic communications networks and services ('Consolidated Services Directive'). A further category is general competition law, under which Article 82 EC has particular importance as it regulates abusive conduct adopted by undertakings in a dominant position in a given market (for instance abuse committed by undertakings controlling facilities or resources).[5]

3.09 **To what instrument should priority be given?** Faced with this variety of instruments, the question arises as to which priority should be given. The answer is not different from that given in other chapters: practitioners should look to the Access Directive as implemented through the two communications issued by the Commission. The liberalisation directives and general competition law should be consulted only in situations where the practitioner is not satisfied with the arguments found in the harmonisation framework.

3.10 **An additional source of complexity.** An additional source of complexity arises from the fact that the NRF does not necessarily apply in all circumstances, for the following reason. The implementation of the new rules in the Member States is expected to take some time. To ensure continuity, the European legislator has postulated a system whereby certain rules, put in place under the old regulation, remain in force as long as NRAs have not decided that the corresponding rules under the new framework should apply. The actual introduction of these new rules is thus dependent on a twofold intervention by the Member States: first, implementation of the NRF in the national legal order, and second, a decision by the NRAs that these rules should replace those from the old regulatory framework as maintained in the meantime. This mechanism leads to a situation where new rules may be adopted in some Member States whereas rules from the old regulatory framework may remain applicable in others.

3.11 Which rules apply?

(1) The rules under the old regulatory framework continue to apply.
(2) As an assessment takes place, the NRAs decide whether, and to what extent, these rules must be replaced with those established under the NRF.
(3) The situation may vary across the Union, as some Member States may introduce changes more rapidly than others.

---

[5] Explanations have been given concerning the application of this provision to electronic communications markets in two communications issued by the Commission: the Guidelines (EC) 91/C233/02 on the application of EC competition rules in the telecommunications sector [1991] OJ C233/2 ; and Commission Notice 98/C265/02 on the application of the competition rules to access agreements in the telecommunications sector [1999] OJ C265/2.

As soon as possible.   It should be observed that this second transitional arrange-   **3.12**
ment should not last for long. Pursuant to the regulation, a first evaluation by the
NRAs has to take place 'as soon as possible' after the entry into force of the Directive.
The object of this evaluation is to determine whether the old obligations must
remain or be changed. In the event that changes are decided, the parties affected by
the decision must be given sufficient notice. No indication is given in the Directive
as to the period necessary to ensure that notice is sufficient. This condition must
thus be interpreted by the NRAs in the light of internal rules applicable to similar
issues.

> *Access Directive, Article 6.* 'Member States shall ensure that, as soon as possible after the
> entry into force of this Directive, and periodically thereafter, national regulatory
> authorities undertake a market analysis . . . to determine whether to maintain,
> amend or withdraw these obligations'.[6] *Notice period.* 'An appropriate period of notice
> shall be given to parties affected by such amendment or withdrawal of obligations.'

The old or the new regulatory framework?   *(a)* The reflex, for a practitioner   **3.13**
confronted with an access-related issue, should be to look, in the first instance, at
the national laws, regulations or administrative provisions in force in the Member
State where the problem occurs. These rules are plainly applicable and are those to
which most interested parties, including the NRAs, will refer. *(b)* Only at a second
stage will European law arise as an issue, and in two circumstances. The first will
be when the practitioner wants to ensure that national provisions have implemented European law correctly.[7] If implementation is not correct or complete,
this will represent an argument that the national rules should be set aside on the
point being argued. A second situation is where the practitioner is unable to argue
his case in national law. An attempt may then be made to find arguments on the
basis of European law, in particular where the European provisions concerned
have direct effect.[8]

Identify the relevant rule.   In the latter case, the first issue will be to identify the   **3.14**
relevant EU rules, and in particular to determine whether the rules from the old

---

[6] Access Directive, Art 7(3).

[7] Suppose a practitioner represents a client requesting access to a resource owned by a competitor.
The practitioner should look at the national rules implementing the principles adopted at European
level, and in particular the correspondence between the two. Discrepancies may indeed be found in
some instances, although it is not entirely sure what the solution will be. If the solution is based on
a rule introduced by a Directive of the Parliament and Council, that rule can normally not be relied
on by the practitioner. The reason is that directive provisions do not, in normal circumstances,
have horizontal direct effect. The scenario may, however, be different if these rules are based on competition law. Competition law provisions do indeed have horizontal direct effects. They may thus be
used in conflicts involving legal and natural persons. These various concepts and mechanisms are
explained in further detail in Chapter 6.

[8] To illustrate this, the example examined in the previous note may be used. Where, for example,
he is not satisfied with the possibilities opened to him by national law, the practitioner may seek in
European law arguments that may help it in its case. This is particularly so where national law has not
entirely transposed European law or where specific interpretations have been made by the national
legislators of European law provisions, interpretations that may be questioned before a court.

regulatory framework still apply or whether the rules established under the NRF have been activated by the relevant NRA as a result of the market assessment under the new framework. For this one needs to look again at national law, since the decision whereby the NRA decides that the new rules should be introduced is clearly part of national law. The easiest way to find the appropriate document is probably to consult the internet site of the relevant NRA, where the latter's determination on the need or otherwise to modify the existing rules is likely to be published. If the existing rules have been maintained, an investigation should be made as to whether the national provisions implementing the old regulatory framework are indeed in conformity with it. If a decision has been taken to introduce the new rules, the investigation should focus on the compatibility between the NRF and the national provisions intended to implement it.

3.15   The rules or obligations concerned.   Not all rules relating to access and contained in the old regulatory framework may be maintained. This possibility exists only for certain obligations that are specifically mentioned in the Access Directive. These obligations mainly concern undertakings that have been designated as having significant market power, and are set out in the table below. For a comprehensive overview of the obligations in force, reference should be made to the relevant sections below, in which the obligations are analysed following the structure of the NRF. To see whether changes have been introduced in the new framework as regards that obligation, go to the section comparing the two frameworks.

3.16   Comparison between the old regulatory framework and the NRF

	Old regulatory framework	NRF
General obligation to provide access	Interconnection Directive, Article 4	
Non-discrimination	Interconnection Directive, Article 6	Access Directive, Article 10
Transparency	Interconnection Directive, Article 6	Access Directive, Article 9
Tariffs for interconnection	Interconnection Directive, Article 7	Access Directive, Article 13
Cost accounting	Interconnection Directive, Articles 7 & 8	Access Directive, Article 11; Framework Directive, Article 13
Co-location and facility sharing	Interconnection Directive, Article 11	Framework Directive, Article 12
Numbering	Interconnection Directive, Article 12	Framework Directive, Article 10
Publication	Interconnection Directive, Article 14	Access Directive, Article 15
Special network access	Voice Telephony Directive, Article 16	
Obligation to provide a minimum set of leased lines	Leased Lines Directive, Articles 7 & 8	

Conditional access systems.   The situation is further complicated through the   **3.17**
choice made by the European legislator in favour of another transitional mechanism for the rules concerning conditional access systems. As stated above, certain
obligations remain applicable as long as no decision has been taken by NRAs to
replace them by new ones. This is not the case as regards obligations relating to
conditional access systems. More precisely, all rules regarding these systems apply
as soon as transposition is completed in the Member State concerned. The entry
into force of the obligations concerning conditional access systems is thus made
dependent upon one single event, the implementation of the directives in the
national legal order.[9] Changes may however be introduced at a second stage, as
NRAs are invited to evaluate the necessity to change these rules. After that evaluation, the NRA may decide whether the rules may, or must, be maintained,
amended or repealed. There is thus no certainty that the rules contained in the
NRF will indeed be maintained as regards these systems, as a significant margin of
discretion is granted to the NRAs on this point.

Introduction of the new rules.   Three mechanisms have been put in place to   **3.18**
structure the introduction of new rules on electronic communications markets.
(a) The first, and overriding, principle is that the rules contained in the NRF apply
in the national legal orders when the implementation measures have been adopted
by the Member States. This principle is general in scope and applies in the absence
of any derogation. *(b)* An exception is provided for certain rules, particularly
obligations imposed on undertakings with significant market power. For these
obligations or rules, the former version, ie the version applicable under the old
regulatory framework, remains in force. The new rules are only made applicable
when a specific decision is taken to that effect by the NRAs, each acting in relation
to its own national territory. Decisions do not need to be all-encompassing: an
authority may decide to introduce certain new rules but not all of them.
(c) Further, an exception to the exception is introduced as regards conditional
access systems. In the absence of any derogation, the rules concerning these
systems would fall under *(b)* above. As they concern undertakings with significant
market power, the old rules should remain applicable pending a decision by the
NRAs. The principle is however reversed, and the new rules apply when the
implementation provisions have been adopted. NRAs can, however, review that
situation and decide to amend or remove these rules thereafter.

In this book.   The focus in this book is on the rules with which practitioners will   **3.19**
normally be confronted in most instances over the next few years. In principle,
these rules are those contained in the NRF. This does not mean that the old rules
should be neglected, and these are covered in a section where the main differences
between the old and the new obligations are considered. The purpose of that

---

[9] These rules must apply as of 25 July 2003.

section is to draw the attention of practitioners to the changes that have occurred, rather than analysing a complete second set of obligations. This will be done regarding the various instruments that have been adopted by the European legislator: the directives from the Parliament and Council, as well as those adopted by the Commission. Finally, it must be noted that general competition law should also be taken into account. That body of law contains rules with general application and that fact is often a source of inspiration for practitioners, as it opens wide possibilities for bringing forward new and innovative arguments. The rules of general competition law are examined in this chapter in the course of the discussion concerning the obligations imposed by regulation. Specific issues are also analysed independently, particularly the case law concerning abuse of a dominant position.[10]

3.20 **What should practitioners do if faced with an issue concerning access?**

(1) Look at national provisions.
(2) Then look at European law if not satisfied or to check conformity with European law.
(3) For each rule encountered in the national order, ask whether this rule is intended to transpose the old or the NRF.
(4) Go to the relevant framework and analyse the rule in question.

(3) The relation with the old regulatory framework

Some rules maintained

3.21 **The old regulatory framework.** Three instruments under the old regulatory framework concerning access and interconnection need to be taken into account. *(a)* The rules with the widest scope and the strongest binding force were[11] concentrated in European law in Parliament and Council Directive (EC) 97/33 on interconnection in telecommunications with regard to ensuring universal service and interoperability through application of the principles of Open Network Provision (ONP) ('Interconnection Directive').[12] *(b)* These rules were explained, commented on and supplemented in two instruments as regards the specific issue of local loop access. The first was the Commission Recommendation (EC) of

---

[10] In many respects, the liberalisation and harmonisation directives appear as a construct based on general competition law. They in fact apply, in the specific context of electronic communications, rules that derive from that body of law.

[11] In this book, the past tense is used to describe the rules applicable under the old regulatory framework. It should however not be forgotten that these rules are applicable in the Member States as long as the NRAs have not examined the situation and decided, on the basis of that examination, that changes must be brought by introducing the rules applicable under the NRF.

[12] [1997] OJ L199/32. As amended by European Parliament and Council Directive (EC) 98/61 [1998] OJ L268/37.

25 May 2000 on unbundled access to the local loop enabling the competitive provision of a full range of electronic communications services including broadband multimedia and high-speed internet ('Local Loop Recommendation').[13] *(c)* Since a Recommendation has no binding force, and because a number of issues relating to the local loop had to be resolved, a directly applicable regulation was adopted by the Parliament and the Council Regulation (EC) 2887/2000 on unbundled access to the local loop ('Local Loop Regulation').[14]

Application through the Access Directive.   The rules applicable under the **3.22** old regulatory framework regarding access and interconnection no longer have binding force, but have been abolished by a provision inserted to that effect in the Framework Directive.[15] However, pursuant to a clause in the Access Directive, some of the provisions contained in the Interconnection Directive are kept in force during a transitional period. This period is necessary to allow NRAs to assess whether the markets are competitive. Where competition is sufficient, the markets are supposed to produce satisfactory outcomes by themselves. In cases where competition is not deemed sufficient, intervention is warranted and authorities must determine what obligations to apply to undertakings with significant market power. These obligations may be those which were introduced in the old regulatory framework. These old obligations may also be replaced by rules established under the NRF, dependent upon a decision to be taken by the NRAs to that effect.[16]

> *Access Directive, Article 7(1)*. 'Member States shall maintain all obligations on undertakings providing public communications networks and/or services concerning access and interconnection that were in force prior to the date of entry into force of this Directive under . . . [ONP Interconnection] Directive 97/33/EC . . . such time as these obligations have been reviewed and a determination made in accordance with paragraph 3.'[17]

Following paragraphs.   The following paragraphs examine briefly the provisions of **3.23** the old regulatory framework which are temporarily maintained in force, the main differences vis-à-vis the rules introduced under the NRF, and the main changes brought in by the NRF.

Undertakings subject to obligations

Undertakings concerned.   The obligations introduced by the Interconnection **3.24** Directive were mainly applicable to undertakings with significant market power

---

[13] [2000] OJ L156/44.
[14] [2000] OJ L336/4.
[15] See Framework Directive, Art 26.
[16] Access Directive, Art 7(1). See also Framework Directive, Art 27, subpara 1.
[17] See also Framework Directive, Art 27.

providing public telecommunications networks and services.[18] A certain degree of flexibility was allowed in the determination of undertakings with significant market power. In principle, undertakings were presumed to have significant market power where they had more than 25 per cent of a particular telecommunications market in the geographical area in which it carried out its activities. However, NRAs could decide that undertakings with less than 25 per cent of the market in question should be designated. Conversely, they had the power to decide that undertakings with more than 25 per cent should not be designated. In each case, the determination had to be based on several criteria, including the ability of the undertaking to influence market conditions, turnover relative to the size of the market, control of access to end users, access to financial resources and experience in providing products and services in the market.

3.25 **Change.**   The change that has occurred is that, under the NRF, access-related obligations may be imposed only on undertakings in a dominant position, although the European regulation still refers to the concept of 'significant market power'. There is thus no discontinuity regarding terminology, but the definition has changed. This definition under the NRF and the criteria that may be used to identify undertakings with significant market power are examined below. In essence, a higher degree of market power is required under the NRF for access-related obligations to apply.

3.26 **Undertakings with SMP.**   Until the NRAs have carried out the assessment referred to above, the special obligations relating to access and contained in the Interconnection Directive continue to apply to the undertakings that have been notified as having significant market power under that directive. The undertakings currently subject to these obligations thus remain bound until the NRAs determine otherwise.

> *Framework Directive, Article 27(1).* 'Member States shall maintain all obligations under national law referred to in Article 7 of Directive 2002/19/EC (Access Directive) and Article 16 of Directive 2002/22/EC (Universal Service Directive) until such time as a determination is made in respect of those obligations by a national regulatory authority in accordance with Article 16 of this Directive.'[19]

---

[18]   Interconnection Directive, Art 4(2) and (3).
[19]   A reference is made in the extract quoted to the Local Loop Regulation. We have not included that reference in the quotation because in our view the principle established in the provision is also valid for other European rules. That principle is that undertakings designated as having significant market power under the old regulation remain such until another decision has been taken by the NRAs regarding their status. As a result of that principle, these undertakings remain submitted to old access-related obligations until such decision. This derives from Art 7(1) of the Access Directive and Art 27(1) of the Framework Directive. Pursuant to these provisions, specific provisions of the Interconnection Directive remain in force as long as NRAs have not taken a decision to the contrary. Among these provisions is the article providing that undertakings must be designated for the application of special obligations when they have significant market power.

Special obligations relating to access

Provisions maintained in force. As stated above, certain provisions from the **3.27**
Interconnection Directive have been maintained in force, and reappear mainly as
part of the menu of obligations that regulators may impose following their assessment of the level of competition in relevant markets.

Right and obligation to negotiate interconnection. Under the Interconnection **3.28**
Directive, undertakings have a right to negotiate interconnection.[20] An obligation to
negotiate is imposed on undertakings with significant market power. These rights
and obligations must allow the provision of networks and services throughout the
Community. No change has been introduced to this obligation under the NRF.
As will appear throughout this chapter, the same right and the same obligation are
provided for in the Access Directive.[21]

Non-discrimination. The Interconnection Directive imposes on undertakings **3.29**
with significant market power a prohibition on discrimination between undertakings requesting access to their networks and services.[22] The same provision has
been taken over in the NRF.[23] A difference is that the prohibition does not apply
automatically under the new rules. Its application is to be ordered by the NRA.[24]
Another nuance is that authorities are allowed to draw all possible consequences
from the prohibition on discrimination and to formulate these consequences in
the form of obligations/prohibitions. These two differences imply that the non-
discrimination principle will probably be applied in a more flexible manner under
the NRF.

Transparency. Pursuant to the Interconnection Directive, all information **3.30**
necessary to enable business decisions on access or interconnection to be taken[25]
must be made available.[26] A reference offer must also be published. These
obligations have been maintained under the NRF, although slight changes have
been introduced. Under the new rules, a reference offer is required to be published
where access is sought to the twisted metallic pair.[27] Publication may also be
ordered where a prohibition on discrimination is imposed, but this is dependent

---

[20] Interconnection Directive, Art 4(1).   [21] See Access Directive, Art 4(1).
[22] Interconnection Directive, Art 6, letter (a).   [23] Access Directive, Art 10.
[24] The prohibition to discriminate is normally in force as a result of the continued application of
the Interconnection Directive, as it is embodied in a provision that has been temporarily maintained. This provision remains in force as long as the NRAs decide that no change needs to be introduced. Should the authority consider that the prohibition is justified, this prohibition will continue
to apply. The only modification will then be the legal basis on which it is founded—the NRF and
not the old framework any longer. Where the authority feels that the prohibition does not need to
apply in a general form, it can decide not to impose it or to introduce nuances to it.
[25] Price, operational modalities, technical specifications, etc.
[26] Interconnection Directive, Art 6, letter (b); Art 7(3) and Art 14(1).
[27] Access Directive, Art 9(4).

upon a decision taken to that effect by the NRAs.[28] Apart from these two circumstances, transparency obligations may be imposed by the NRAs on undertakings with significant market power.[29] This obligation implies that specified information[30] must be made public.[31] It is for the NRAs to specify what sort of information must be made available, what level of detail is required in the publication and how publication must take place.[32]

3.31 **Access and interconnection charges.** Under the Interconnection Directive, access and interconnection charges had to be based on cost where access was sought to a facility controlled by an undertaking with significant market power. It was for the undertakings concerned to demonstrate that this obligation was complied with and these undertakings could be asked to justify their price behaviour. Offers were to be unbundled so as to provide the services needed by customers without forcing them to purchase unnecessary items.[33] These obligations have not been changed in the NRF, and have all been taken over in the Access Directive.[34] The presentation is, however, different to the extent that these obligations have not been made mandatory automatically. Here again, NRAs are granted substantial powers to determine what obligations apply. As an example, cost orientation is not made mandatory per se, but is presented as a tool that may be used by the NRAs where needed.

3.32 **Accounting separation.** The Interconnection Directive imposed on undertakings with significant market power an obligation to keep separate accounts for interconnection activities.[35] This obligation has been taken over in the NRF, with the nuance that the obligation only applies where the NRA so decides.[36] Here again, under the new framework, decisions relating to the application of access obligations must be taken by NRAs and are not made mandatory by the European regulation itself. Other obligations contained in the Interconnection Directive have been taken over and are now set out in the Framework and Access Directives. This applies in particular as regards the obligation imposed on undertakings providing public telecommunications networks and services to hold separate accounts when they have special or exclusive rights in other sectors.[37] Separate accounts had to be maintained for activities where such rights were held. A further requirement could be imposed in the form of an obligation to organise these activities in a separate legal entity, but this was to be done by the Member States where they considered the option to be necessary.[38] Certified financial reports had

---

[28] ibid, Art 9(2).   [29] ibid, Art 9(1).
[30] Such as prices, accounting information, technical specifications, network characteristics, terms and conditions for supply and use: see Access Directive, Art 9(1).   [31] ibid, Art 9(1).
[32] ibid, Art 9(3).   [33] For these obligations, see Interconnection Directive, Art 7.
[34] See Access Directive, Art 13.   [35] See Interconnection Directive, Art 8(2).
[36] See Access Directive, Art 11.   [37] See Interconnection Directive, Art 8(1).
[38] ibid, Art 8(2).

to be drafted and presented by undertakings with significant market power.[39] This latter obligation is maintained, but only applies to undertakings that are not subject to the requirements of company law and do not satisfy the small and medium-sized enterprise criteria of Community law accounting rules.[40]

Co-location, facility sharing and numbering.   The Interconnection Directive **3.33** contained provisions devoted to co-location,[41] facility sharing[42] and numbering.[43] Pursuant to the NRF, these provisions are maintained until a decision is taken on their subsistence by the NRAs.[44] It should be noted that the obligations relating to co-location and facility sharing have not been taken over in the Access Directive, but are transferred to the Framework Directive, where they are not submitted to any limitation or decision to be taken by the NRAs. The conclusion is that the obligations relating to co-location and facility sharing continue to apply pursuant to the Framework Directive.

Overview of changes

Resources concerned.   Several changes have been introduced in the NRF **3.34** with regard to access. Some concern the resources with respect to which access obligations apply. In the old framework, the main concern was to ensure access to the network. This concern was further developed in the Local Loop Regulation as well as in the Local Loop Recommendation. A more general perspective has been taken in the Access Directive, where access-related obligations are extended to all facilities or resources necessary to provide electronic communications services.

Powers granted to authorities.   A second change relates to the powers granted to **3.35** NRAs. As stated, obligations deriving from the European regulation were to be transposed by the Member States. Where the transposition into the national legal orders was completed, the obligations in question were applied to all the undertakings concerned. In the NRF, the application of the obligations is made dependent upon a specific decision to be taken by the NRA—each for its national territory. Pursuant to this power, the authorities can decide whether, and to what extent, the obligations must apply. In application of the powers granted to them, authorities can also decide that some obligations do not need to be applied.

Undertakings concerned.   A third change relates to the undertakings concerned **3.36** by access-related obligations. In the old as in the NRF, these obligations are imposed on undertakings with significant market power. As stated, the terminology has not changed but the content given to that concept has been modified, as a higher degree of market power is required for the application of the new rules.

---

[39] ibid, Art 8(3) and (4).   [40] See Framework Directive, Art 13(2).
[41] Interconnection Directive, Art 11.   [42] ibid, Art 11.   [43] ibid, Art 12.
[44] See Access Directive, Art 7(1).

3.37 **Type of access.** A fourth change relates to what is sought in the Access Directive. Under the old regulatory framework, the key objective was to ensure and facilitate interconnection. This implied the establishment of links between networks to allow the provision of end-to-end services across the Community. In the NRF, interconnection has become one among many issues relating to access. Access is understood as a more general concept implying all sorts of facilities or resources necessary to provide electronic communications services, with some emphasis placed on access to the local loop.

(4) The liberalisation directives

3.38 **Introduction.** Issues relating to access and interconnection cannot be examined only in the light of rules established by the Parliament and Council. The Commission has also played an important role, in that it was in fact the institution that in the first instance imposed specific regulatory obligations in this sector. In addition to the rules adopted in the harmonisation framework, account must be taken of the rules adopted by the Commission in the liberalisation framework, including in relation to access and interconnection. As stated above, these directives were adopted by the Commission on the basis of Article 86(3) EC. They mainly contain rules seeking to ensure that markets are accessible.[45] The Consolidated Services Directive brings together the liberalisation rules remaining in force in the field of electronic communications. However, as shown above, the old liberalisation directives remain important to the extent that they construe principles that derive directly from the Treaty.[46]

3.39 **No specific provision on access or interconnection.** There is no provision dealing specifically with access or interconnection in the Consolidated Directive. One may thus consider that the obligations that may be imposed on undertakings in the electronic communications sector by way of directives are contained in the instruments adopted by the Parliament and Council. From the absence of a provision on that subject in the Consolidated Directive, it can probably be deduced that the Commission is satisfied with the rules that have been introduced by the Parliament and Council.

3.40 **Vertically integrated undertakings.** The existence of one provision relating to access must, however, be emphasised, in relation to the behaviour of vertically

---

[45] Market entry indeed is, and remains, essential to ensure that competition is maintained and further developed.

[46] In our opinion, these principles could be used, as applied in the Services Directives, to challenge behaviour adopted by a Member State or NRA. It is more difficult to determine whether they could serve as a basis for a challenge directed against the validity of a provision included in a harmonisation directive. One could argue that these principles derive from the Treaty and must thus be respected by EC secondary law instruments such as Directives of that nature. At the same time, it would be difficult to give priority to a Directive adopted by the Commission where a provision has been enacted by the Parliament and the Council, which hold the legislative power within the Union.

integrated undertakings. Pursuant to the definition traditionally given of that economic configuration, these are undertakings carrying out activities at different stages of the economic chain where the activities in question are in some way related to each other. A typical example is the operator which is active on a market for network operations and, at the same time, develops activities in derived markets for services (data provision, telephony, etc). This example is at the core of the provision inserted in the Consolidated Services Directive as regards vertically integrated undertakings. Pursuant to that provision, such undertakings may not discriminate in favour of their own activities. The prohibition applies where three conditions are fulfilled: *(a)* the undertakings must be vertically integrated, in the sense referred to above; *(b)* they must provide electronic communications networks; *(c)* they must hold a dominant position on the network market.

> *Consolidated Services Directive, Article 3.* 'Member States shall ensure that vertically integrated public undertakings which provide electronic communications networks and are in a dominant position do not discriminate in favour of their own activities.'

Comparison with Access Directive.   The provision appears similar to another **3.41** which is examined later in this chapter (see paras 3.158–3.161) and which is formulated in the Access Directive adopted by the Parliament and Council. Pursuant to the latter provision, operators must apply equivalent conditions in equivalent circumstances to undertakings providing equivalent services. In particular, they must provide to other undertakings services and information under the same conditions and of the same quality as they provide for their own services, those of their subsidiaries or those of their partners.[47] In other words, all parties must be treated equally as regards access, irrespective of their identity and relation with the operator.

Comparison with Consolidated Services Directive.   The prohibition seems **3.42** identical in the Access Directive and the Consolidated Services Directive. Differences however appear when account is taken of specific, additional, requirements that appear to be attached to the prohibition laid down in the Consolidated Services Directive. First, the prohibition on discrimination is limited to public undertakings. This requirement is explicitly mentioned in the body of the directive (see citation above). Second, the prohibition is limited to operators which have established their networks under special and exclusive rights. This requirement is formulated in the Preamble to the directive:

> *Consolidated Services Directive, Preamble, para 10.* 'Public authorities may exercise a dominant influence on the behaviour of public undertakings, as a result either of the rules governing the undertaking or of the manner in which the shareholdings are distributed. Therefore, where Member States control vertically integrated network operators which operate networks which have been established under special or exclusive rights, those Member States should ensure that, in order to avoid potential breaches

---

[47] See Access Directive, Art 10(2).

of the Treaty competition rules, such operators, when they enjoy a dominant position in the relevant market, do not discriminate in favour of their own activities. It follows that Member States should take all measures necessary to prevent any discrimination between such vertically integrated operators and their competitors.'

3.43 **Non-discrimination in the Consolidated Services Directive**

Conditions	Obligation
(a) The undertaking operates a network *(b)* It is placed under public influence[48] *(c)* The network has been established under special and/or exclusive rights *(d)* The undertaking is active on derived markets for services	All undertakings seeking access to the network must be treated equally whatever their relation with the operator[49]

3.44 **Comparison with old liberalisation directives.** From the discussion above, it appears that the provision concerning discrimination and inserted in the liberalisation directives is formulated in rather narrow terms. Yet the scope of the intervention does not appear to have changed if one considers the liberalisation directives. In adopting the latter, the Commission was confronted with a market organisation where all operators were public and all networks had been established under special and exclusive rights. Imposing on these operators a prohibition on discrimination appeared, at that time, as a general measure, affecting all operators and all networks. The situation has however changed as markets have been opened and new (non-public) undertakings have started network activities. The result is that a measure which, previously, affected a whole sector may now be analysed, in its effects, as being limited to some market participants.

3.45 **Rules regarding access in the old liberalisation directives.** The liberalisation rules concerning access and interconnection were introduced in 1996.[50] These rules are briefly examined below. The reason why they are presented is that, as

---

[48] The term 'public' is not defined in the Consolidated Services Directive. More details are however given in the Preamble. Pursuant to that Preamble, undertakings may be considered public when they are placed under the influence of one or several public authorities. A public influence may result, among others, from the manner in which the shareholdings are distributed. On the basis of that criterion, an undertaking could be considered public where more than 50% of its shares are in public hands. Another criterion may be taken into account. Pursuant to the Preamble, an undertaking may also be said to be public when authorities are in a position to influence its decisions as a result of the rules governing the entity. That situation can be encountered, for instance, where certain decisions may only be taken by an undertaking after an approval has been received by a designated authority, even in situations where the majority of the shares are not held by a public authority.

[49] No preferential treatment may be granted by the network operator to its partners, its subsidiaries or even its own services.

[50] These rules were introduced by Commission Directive (EC) 96/19 of 13 March 1996 amending Directive 90/388/EEC with regard to the implementation of full competition in telecommunications markets [1996] OJ L74/24. They were inserted by that instrument in the Services Directive, Art 4a.

submitted above, they still have some force to the extent that they determine, or construe, principles that may be derived from the competition rules. As there is a direct link between those rules and the Treaty, even if they are not taken over explicitly in the Consolidated Services Directive, they can to a certain extent be said to remain valid, their substance having been taken over by the Parliament and the Council in the Access Directive.

(a) *Access.* Telecommunications incumbents must grant access to their public networks and services: 'Member States shall ensure that the telecommunications organisations provide interconnection to their voice telephony service and their public switched telecommunications network to other undertakings authorised to provide such services or networks.'[51]

(b) *Terms and conditions.* Conditions for access must comply with the basic regulatory principles (objectivity, necessity, proportionality, transparency). Access and interconnection must be granted 'on non-discriminatory, proportional and transparent terms, which are based on objective criteria'.[52]

(c) *Transparency.* Transparency specifically requires that the terms and conditions for access and interconnection must be published.[53] 'Member States shall ensure . . . that the telecommunications organisations publish . . . the terms and conditions for interconnection to the basic functional components of their voice telephony service and their public switched telecommunications networks, including the interconnection points and the interfaces according to market needs.'[54]

(d) *Negotiation, intervention.* Undertakings seeking special access may negotiate with the incumbents. In case no agreement is reached, the terms and conditions are fixed by the Member States. 'Member States shall not prevent that organisations providing telecommunications networks and/or services who so request can negotiate interconnection agreements with telecommunications networks regarding special network access and/or conditions meeting their specific needs. If commercial negotiations do not lead to an agreement within a reasonable time period, Member States shall upon request from either party and within a reasonable time period, adopt a reasoned decision which establishes the necessary operational and financial conditions and requirements for such interconnection without prejudice to other remedies available under the applicable national law or under Community law.'[55]

(e) *Accounting obligations.* The accounting method used by the incumbents must make it possible to identify the costs on which interconnection charges are based. 'Member States shall ensure that the cost accounting

---

[51] Services Directive, Art 4a(1).   [52] ibid, Art 4a(1).
[53] A deadline was set for publication: 1 July 1997.
[54] Services Directive, Art 4a(2).   [55] ibid, Art 4a(3).

system implemented by telecommunications organisations with regard to the provision of voice telephony and public telecommunications networks identifies the cost elements relevant for pricing interconnection offerings.'[56]

(5) Principles of the new regulatory framework

Negotiate first

3.46 **Undertakings must negotiate under normal conditions.** The principle underlying the NRF is that undertakings requesting access must seek contacts with undertakings controlling the relevant facilities or resources. Where for example an undertaking wants to provide voice telephony in a major European city but does not have the facilities necessary to provide that service, it is expected to contact operators controlling networks in the region and negotiate the conditions under which access may be obtained. On the basis of the offers received, the undertaking will presumably make a selection in favour of the facility operated by the operator offering the best conditions. In that system, commercial negotiation is the key procedure under normal market conditions.

3.47 **Little difficulty.** As the Commission notes, there should be little difficulty for undertakings to negotiate access and interconnection in a market where several participants are present and a selection may be made from among them. The hope is that this sort of market has been created thanks to the reform carried out in the telecommunications sector. In the context of efficiency-oriented markets, with effective competition one may expect undertakings receiving requests for access or interconnection to negotiate in good faith and conclude such agreements on a commercial basis. Intervention becomes relevant only where large differences in negotiating power between the parties remain. Another reason for intervention is when undertakings are active on several markets and may be tempted to use their position in one market to favour their position on another.[57]

A mixture of regulation

3.48 **Measures aimed at Member States and undertakings.** A consequence is that public authorities are allowed to intervene only when they feel that negotiation is impaired or rendered more difficult. Difficulties may in general come from two different sources: (*a*) In some cases the restrictions imposed on negotiations come from the Member States. As will be seen, an obligation is imposed on them to eliminate those restrictions. (*b*) In other—and more numerous—cases, restrictions

---

[56] Services Directive, Art 4a, para 4.

[57] As mentioned earlier, the typical example is where an undertaking controls a facility on a network market and uses that position to influence the position of other undertakings with which it is in competition on another market.

are imposed by undertakings. In that second category of circumstances, public intervention has to ensure that these restrictions are also eliminated. Generally, intervention concerning restrictions imposed by undertakings is limited to situations where choice disappears in the market. In these situations, the parties seeking access cannot by themselves find a satisfactory offer. The authorities are then asked to intervene with a view to restoring normal conditions.

Asymmetric and generally applicable rules. As mentioned above, and will be **3.49** analysed later in more detail (see paras 3.103–3.212), the NRF imposes regulatory obligations on undertakings which are in a position to prevent customers from making choices. This is the situation where dominance or significant market power has been acquired. Through regulatory obligations, undertakings with dominance or significant market power have specific responsibilities imposed on them. Their liberty to engage in whatever behaviour they like is curtailed. The constraints that are imposed on these undertakings can be said to be 'asymmetric' to the extent that they apply to certain market participants, and to those participants only. This does not mean that other undertakings are exempt from all obligations regarding access. As will be made apparent, general obligations are imposed on all undertakings present on certain markets independently of the dominance or market power they may have. For instance, a general duty to negotiate is imposed on all undertakings. In contrast to asymmetric regulation, these obligations can be said to be 'generally applicable'.

Case law. In *Commission v Belgium*,[58] the Belgian legislation provided a general **3.50** power for the NRAs to intervene in order to ensure that the general objectives underlying the old regulatory framework, and the national implementing legislation, would be fulfilled. The Commission, however, considered that that general power was inconsistent with the framework. For the Commission, it was essential to stipulate expressly in the national legislation that NRAs must be able to intervene at any moment in the negotiations leading up to an interconnection agreement. According to the Commission, the Community legislator clearly envisaged that the power to intervene must be distinct from the power to require changes to interconnection agreements already concluded. It was followed in its argumentation by the ECJ, which condemned Belgium.

> *Commission v Belgium.* 'The national legislation invoked by the Belgian Government . . . confers on the [NRA] either very general supervisory powers, which cannot be regarded as adequate implementation of a specific power to intervene in commercial negotiations, or specific powers to intervene in contexts which do not fully reflect those envisaged [in] . . . the Directive.'[59] 'The Commission's second complaint is therefore . . . well founded.'[60]

---

[58] Case C-221/01 *Commission v Belgium* [2002] ECR I-7835.   [59] Art [34].
[60] Art [34].

Protection of all parties

3.51 **In search of a balance.**   In general, it can be said that the NRF attempts to find a balance in order to impose obligations on all parties involved and to avoid placing an excessive burden on some of them. Several obligations are admittedly reserved to undertakings with dominance or significant market power. It would, however, be erroneous to consider that the regulation has been adopted at European level with the exclusive intention of monitoring the behaviour of these undertakings, which are often former national operators. Quite to the contrary, some provisions included in the regulatory framework attempt to limit the obligations that can be imposed on these undertakings. There is thus a concern that over-regulation should be avoided and that parties should be left free to develop their behaviour autonomously to the greatest extent possible.

3.52 **Illustration.**   A good illustration may be taken from provisions concerning tariffs, and more particularly those relating to accounting systems. These provisions can be said to have been drafted to protect operators as much as other parties. From these provisions it can be inferred that the European legislator has sought to introduce regulatory tools regarding two types of situation. On the one hand, it wanted tools to be made available in case authorities needed to intervene as a result of inappropriate prices charged by operators. On the other hand, intervention by the authorities had also to some extent to be constrained. The terms used in several provisions show that the European legislator wants to avoid a situation where authorities systematically intervene and impose heavy accounting obligations on operators.

One sign of this is that interventions are normally limited to where abnormal conditions are observed 'for the provision of specific types of interconnection and/or access'.[61] This shows that authorities may not impose general obligations that would apply independently of the type of access that is sought. Another sign is that the objectives to be promoted through accounting choices (efficiency, sustainable competition, consumer benefit) are mentioned in connection with decisions that are 'mandated' by the authorities—although it will become obvious that these objectives also apply to choices made freely by operators. Finally, the obligation to publish the bases on which the accounting system is founded is also formulated in connection with obligations 'mandated' by authorities. This obligation applies to dominant or powerful operators independently of the intervention of an authority.

---

[61] Access Directive, Art 13.

Scope of application

Services intended for the public.   The obligations concerning access apply to   **3.53**
networks used to provide services to the public.[62] Networks used for transmission
reserved for certain users are not subject to the rules contained in the Access
Directive. One important issue is how to distinguish between activities on the
basis of their private or public character. Undertakings may attempt to escape
obligations by giving to their activities some sort of private appearance. At present
there appears to be no European case law on this issue. There is, however, little
doubt that the Commission and the European courts will sooner or later deal with
the issue. When they are asked to take a position on this, they will have to rely on
the definitions given in the NRF. Pursuant to the Framework Directive, networks
can be said to be public when they are used, mainly or wholly, to provide services
intended for the public.[63] This definition seems to suggest that an assessment has
to be made about the proportion of services meant for the public when an authority must decide whether a network can be considered public or otherwise.

Relations among market participants

Relations among businesses (B2B).[64]   As has been submitted, the regulation   **3.54**
adopted by the European legislator intends to ensure the development of the
market for electronic communications services. This can only be achieved through
the maximum use of all resources making possible the provision of these services.
It is for this reason that regulatory obligations are introduced as regards access in
relations between businesses. Regulatory mechanisms are indeed introduced where
one undertaking seeks to gain access to resources placed under the control of
another—the purpose being to ensure the provision of a maximum of electronic
communications services of excellent quality. The European rules thus regulate the
relations between the various participants playing a role on the market in the hope
of ensuring an efficient use of resources. *(a) Relations between network operators.*
A first category of relations is between network operators. In that context, the purpose is to ensure that network elements can be interconnected wherever possible.
Interoperability is here of the essence, as a constraint is to ensure that information
can go from one network to another. All forms of network (fixed, mobile, virtual)

---

[62] Framework Directive, Art 2, letter (d). See also Preamble, recital 1. 'Non-public networks do
not have obligations under this Directive except where, in benefiting from access to public network,
they may be subject to conditions laid down by Member States.'

[63] These various resources (ducts, masts, buildings) are explicitly mentioned in the directive. One
should however remember that no limitation is placed in the directive on facilities to which access
may be sought under the protection of the NRF. All facilities and services are concerned, as soon as
access to them may be necessary to ensure the provision of electronic communications services.

[64] 'B2B' means 'Business to business'.

are concerned. *(b) Relations between service providers and network operators.* Another context where access is important is when a service provider seeks to use facilities operated by another undertaking in order to provide services. The relation is then between a service provider and an operator—or several entities belonging to these categories, as the case may be.

3.55 **Access for end users (B2C).**[65]   Another kind of relationship will be examined in the next chapter—that between businesses and consumers (or end users). The provisions relating to this kind of relationship do not endeavour to ensure an efficient use of existing resources. The purpose is rather to make sure that services considered as fundamental in society are made available under reasonable conditions to all persons belonging to that society. With relations between businesses and consumers, the field of economic law is abandoned. That field concerns mainly obligations imposed with a view to organising the market so that it functions efficiently. Relations with consumers concern to a substantial extent public, or even social, law, in so far as the provisions in question aim at organising society in an inclusive way.

B. Facilities and Resources Concerned

(1) All facilities and resources necessary for the provision of electronic communications services

3.56 **Variety of resources.**   The NRF imposes an obligation to provide access in certain circumstances. It is important to identify resources or facilities covered by this obligation. A division is proposed in the following paragraphs between facilities, depending on their nature. One should be aware of the subjective character of this division, which seeks only to clarify rules, and may be replaced by any other classification that would help the practitioner to understand the variety of situations that may arise in practice.

3.57 **Access to physical infrastructure.**   First, access must be granted to networks or network elements. This entails access to physical elements of infrastructure. As an example, providers or operators may ask for access to ducts in which lines and wires are placed. They may also obtain access to masts used for the transmission of communications over fixed or mobile networks. Another example is access to buildings where this is required to connect with the network. In the latter case, one can imagine a service provider asking for access to buildings where distribution frames are situated when this is needed to access installations relating to the local loop.[66] Regulatory obligations may also be imposed on undertakings controlling conditional access systems. These systems are generally used for the

---

[65] 'B2C' means 'Business to consumers'.   [66] Access Directive, Art 2(2), letter (a).

provision, and reception, of digital television services, and consist of equipment to which appropriate software is added.

> *Access Directive, Article 2(2), subpara 2, letter (a).* '"[A]ccess" . . . covers *inter alia:* access to network elements and associated facilities, which may involve the connection of equipment, by fixed or non-fixed means . . . , access to physical infrastructure including buildings, ducts and masts, . . . access to fixed and mobile networks, in particular for roaming, access to conditional access systems.'[67]

Interconnection.   A specific concept is used to refer to the linkage between two **3.58** networks. This linkage is called 'interconnection' in the NRF. Pursuant to the Access Directive, the concept is limited to situations where the installations involved are meant for public electronic communications. This stipulation should, however, have no practical impact, since the obligations contained in the Access Directive are in any case limited to public networks. A typical example of interconnection is where public network operators established in different Member States decide to link their facilities. Another example is where an undertaking establishes a new network for the provision of public electronic communications services and asks for access to the existing public telephone network in order to cover other parts of the territory.

> *Access Directive, Article 2(2), subpara 2, letter (b).* ' "Interconnection" is a specific type of access implemented between public network operators.' ' "[I]nterconnection" means the physical and logical linking of public communications networks used by the same or a different undertaking.'[68]

Access to software.   Access is not limited to physical items. Wires cannot be **3.59** reduced to conduits made of copper, as they are increasingly equipped with software resources. Regulatory obligations relating to access can also be applied to software where this is necessary to ensure the provision of electronic communications services and the other conditions mentioned in the regulation are fulfilled (in most instances the existence of significant market power). Examples of software facilities mentioned in the Access Directive are: operational support systems, access to number translation or systems offering equivalent functionality, and access to software ensuring the functioning of conditional access systems.

All resources necessary to provide electronic communications services.   Beyond **3.60** these specific resources, regulatory obligations may be imposed to facilitate access with respect to all facilities or resources necessary to ensure the provision of electronic communications services. No limit is thus placed on the facilities possibly concerned

---

[67] The purpose of interconnection is to allow the users of one undertaking to communicate with users of the same or another undertaking, or to access services provided by another undertaking. The services may be provided by the parties involved or by other parties who have access to the network.

[68] This means that more functions can be carried out through the networks as a result of the application of computer-based applications to the transmission of signals.

by regulatory obligations relating to access. Access is defined in general terms as regards the facilities concerned. In this approach, regulatory obligations are set in motion as soon as the conditions for their application are met—particularly the existence of significant market power, independently of the resource to which access is sought. This appears from the definition given to the concept of access in the regulatory framework:

> *Access Directive, Article 2(2), subpara 2, letter (a).* ' "[A]ccess" means the making available of facilities and/or services, to another undertaking, under defined conditions . . . for the purpose of providing electronic communications services.'

(2) Specific issues—the local loop

3.61 **Definition.**   One of the most important facilities to which access must be granted is the 'local loop'. This concept designates the part of the network that is located between a main distribution frame and the terminal installed in the premises of the user.

> *Access Directive, Article 2, subpara 2, letter (e).* ' "[L]ocal loop" means the physical circuit connecting the network termination point at the subscriber's premises to the main distribution frame or equivalent facility in the fixed public telephone network.'

3.62 **Issues raised.**   The local loop raises significant issues because it is potentially the most expensive part of the network to reproduce. Generally, each of the wires connecting users to the distribution frames is used by few people. The consequence is that the expenses incurred in installing and maintaining them must be amortised on limited usage. The amounts are so high that this can hardly be done by charging users the sums invested to connect them. For this reason, few undertakings are interested in investing the amounts necessary to link subscribers to the network. The lack of interest on the part of undertakings may also be explained by the existence of a comprehensive network already in place. As one network already exists, potential entrants hesitate to undertake the work necessary to establish a new one. The existence of this network is seen as a barrier to entry. Potential new entrants calculate that they could not compete on the network market if they had to install a totally new infrastructure, whereas the existing operator has only to maintain the existing one. The difficulty is reinforced by the conditions under which the first network has been amortised. Investments relating to that first network were made at a time when the operator was not subject to competition. This protection from competition allowed the operator to enjoy substantial revenues that could be used to amortise costs. Additionally, part of the costs was financed through a variety of techniques implying public intervention (public subsidies, cross-subsidisation etc).

3.63 **Mobile technology.**   A first hope has been nourished by the European legislator that competition would flourish on network markets as a result of the development of mobile technology. This hope was based on the apparently lower costs that are to be incurred in order to establish a mobile network. It was anticipated that, as lower investments were required, mobile networks would be installed throughout the Union. For competition to be possible between mobile and fixed networks, another condition had, however, to be fulfilled. Mobile networks can serve as an alternative to fixed installations only if the same applications can be run on both infrastructures. This is not the case at the present time. Businesses, and institutions, have been promising for some time the development of new technology which would bring about substitutability between the two kinds of technology. This stage is however some way from being attained if one is to believe current estimates.[69]

Cable TV networks.   For some time it was also thought that issues relating to   **3.64**
the local loop could be solved as a result of the presence of a second network which is already established in some regions within the European Union, the cable TV network. In those regions where such networks exist, a form of competition could be envisaged between the two infrastructures. The existence of an alternative was indeed supposed to make it possible for providers and users to choose the network through which they want to receive services. The hope was that a situation would be created where, as a result of the existence of competition, markets would function properly. Experience has however shown that issues relating to the local loop would not be solved spontaneously as a result of the presence of these public broadcasting networks.

No spontaneous solution.   The reasons for the absence of a spontaneous solution   **3.65**
are as follows. *(a)* First, not all regions have a public broadcasting network. The existence of such a network appears as an exception rather than a general phenomenon if one looks at the overall situation in Europe, including the accession countries. As a result, one cannot consider that public broadcasting networks provide a general solution to issues relating to the local loop across the European Union. *(b)* Second, existing public broadcasting networks are not always equipped and configured to allow the transmission of wider electronic communications services. Investments are necessary in order to make of these networks a real alternative to public telephone infrastructure. The existence of an alternative thus depends to a significant extent on decisions to be made by the operators of these networks. *(c)* Third, broadcasting networks are not always operated, where they exist, under satisfactory competitive conditions. In some instances, they are operated by the undertakings that also control the public telephone network. One cannot consider, in such a situation, that a real alternative is provided to customers. The operator is in a position to co-ordinate activities and strategies on the two markets, if these activities can be distinguished. Regulatory obligations are imposed, to a certain extent, in order to prevent this sort of scenario. Compliance with these obligations

---

[69] The reason for the delay seems to be in particular that technological progress still has to be made.

is, however, difficult to monitor. Another problem is that public broadcasting networks are operated, in various regions, by semi-public entities enjoying regulatory privileges. These privileges are to disappear as a result of the application of the NRF. The situation is, however, far from clear as, at the present time, the European legislator does not appear to be preparing a regulatory strategy to address these issues in the public broadcasting sector.[70] *(d)* Leaving aside the issues summarised above, there remains a last—difficult—problem to be addressed. The existence of parallel networks—the public telephone and the public broadcasting infrastructure—creates a situation where the market for networks is in the hands of two undertakings. As they are the only two on this market, the relevant undertakings quickly arrive at the conclusion that they have converging interests. This is typically a situation which, according to case law, is conducive to co-ordination. The undertakings in question are tempted to agree on a common course of action. In some instances, they do so by entering agreements. As anti-competitive agreements are however prohibited, they may limit co-ordination to alignment of their conduct.[71]

C. Obligations Imposed on Member States

3.66 **Eliminate restrictions imposed on negotiation.** The obligations introduced by the Access Directive are mainly addressed to undertakings, but some also impose on Member States specific behaviour with a view to facilitating access. In this context, it has been submitted above that access must in most circumstances be reached through negotiation among undertakings. A consequence is that the rules applicable in the Member States must provide an adequate framework for negotiation to unfold. To that effect, the Access Directive imposes on the Member States an obligation to eliminate all measures that may exist in their internal legal orders and that may have as their effect, or their object, to restrict the possibility for businesses to negotiate. As a result of that provision, no reason may be invoked by the Member States to justify a restriction that would exist in their legal order and would place an obstacle to negotiation—whatever the commercial or technical reasons to introduce such reasons. This obligation concerns negotiations that take place within single national territories. In the perspective of the internal market, it is extended to negotiations among undertakings established or providing services in different Member States:

> *Access Directive, Article 3(1).* 'Member States shall ensure that there are no restrictions which prevent undertakings in the same Member State or in different Member States

---

[70] The reason is probably that the sector is generally considered very sensitive for political and cultural reasons. European institutions seem reluctant to develop in that sector a strategy as comprehensive and far-reaching as that carried out in telecommunications, even if public broadcasting and telecommunications now belong to the same sector.

[71] As will be stated, conduct alignment may be apprehended under the rules of competition and under the regulatory framework. To that effect, the existence of significant market power must however be established. As we will see, the conditions to establish such market power are difficult to satisfy.

from negotiating between themselves agreements on technical and commercial arrangements for access and/or interconnection, in accordance with Community law.'

Publish and notify obligations imposed on undertakings. A second obligation **3.67** is that, pursuant to regulation, Member States must publish information about the regulatory obligations they impose on undertakings. This information must also be notified to the Commission. The requirement in general concerns all obligations Member States and their emanations impose on market participants, but a special emphasis is placed on publication and notification when it comes to undertakings on which specific duties are imposed as a result of the significant market power they have acquired.

> *Publication.* 'Member States shall ensure that the specific obligations imposed on undertakings . . . are published and that the specific product/service and geograph-ical markets are identified. They shall ensure that up-to-date information . . . is made publicly available in a manner that guarantees all interested parties easy access to that information.'[72] *Notification.* 'Member States shall send to the Commission a copy of all such information published. The Commission shall make this information avail-able in a readily accessible form.'[73] 'National regulatory authorities shall notify to the Commission the names of operators deemed to have significant market power for the purposes of this Directive, and the obligations imposed upon them under this Directive. Any change affecting the obligations imposed upon undertakings or of the undertakings affected under the provisions of this Directive shall be notified to the Commission without delay.'[74]

An essential obligation. This general obligation of publication and notification **3.68** is essential in the philosophy underlying the NRF. As will be made clear, similar obligations are imposed on undertakings. For instance, dominant undertakings may have to publish reference offers. These offers must make it possible for possible partners to be informed as to the conditions available on the markets. In a context where information is available, business decisions may be made, it is to be hoped, in an appropriate manner. The publication of reference offers also ensures that data are made available which will possibly be used in proceedings in case the undertaking is challenged for infringement of existing rules. The objectives are the same, when the NRF imposes on Member States and their emanations an obligation to notify and publish. Here again, the purpose is to ensure that all possible undertakings—those present on the markets and those which envisage entry—are made aware of the legal regime that applies to them, and to the other market participants. A second goal is also to ensure transparency so that possible infringements, by Member States or their emanations, of superior rules may be detected and challenged.

Ensure compliance. This last objective is particularly important for the **3.69** Commission. As has been made clear, that institution acts as the guardian of the

---

[72] Access Directive, Art 15(1).   [73] ibid, Art 15(2).   [74] ibid, Art 16(2).

Treaty. In that capacity it must ensure compliance with European law. Such action is, however, not possible without appropriate information. The provision of information concerning the behaviour of the Member States and their emanations is also important from the point of view of peer review. Member States can, on the basis of mutual information, monitor each other. This makes action possible wherever they consider that their own undertakings—those bearing their nationality—are not treated fairly in other European countries.[75]

3.70 **Practical aspects of publication.**   In many cases, publication has important consequences for undertakings. For this reason, it is important for practitioners to monitor regularly the information that is made available by the Member States and their emanations. A question arises as to where this information is published. There are nowadays so many publications that it becomes difficult to find the appropriate source. No indication is included in the Access Directive about a place where information concerning obligations imposed on markets should be made available by the Member States. The only requirement is that access must be easy. One suggestion would be to look at the internet site of the NRA of the Member State where practitioners are active. This site should normally contain this information or, at least, a link to other sites where this information could be found. Practitioners are also advised to refer regularly to the official journal of the Member States where they are active. Pursuant to the Framework Directive, information must be published in this publication about the application of the Directive. This information will not necessarily be comprehensive, but will at least contain an indication as to where complete information can be found. The best advice is to look for an electronic version of the official journal and use the 'search' functions.

> *Framework Directive, Article 24(1).* 'Member States shall ensure that up-to-date information pertaining to the application of this [Framework] Directive and the Specific Directives is made publicly available in a manner that guarantees all interested parties easy access to that information. They shall publish a notice in their national official gazette describing how and where the information is published.'[76]

3.71 **Confidential information.**   Another aspect of publication is that there is a risk that confidential information may be made available. This is the case, for instance, where obligations are imposed on undertakings which, it is alleged, have significant market power. The analysis carried out by the NRAs about that power may encompass confidential information. To avoid dissemination of that information,

---

[75] Where Member States feel treatment is not fair, they can intervene in the form of an Art 227 EC application before the ECJ. They can also make use of the possibilities opened to them in the Regulatory Procedure, where they are consulted about measures envisaged by NRAs across the EU.

[76] Pursuant to that provision, a first notice about where information can be found had to be published by the Member States before 25 July 2003. A notice must be published whenever there is any change in the information contained in the first notice.

and protect business interests, the Access Directive imposes on Member States and their emanations an obligation of confidentiality.[77]

D. Obligations Concerning One, Some or All Undertakings

(1) Various sets of obligations

Specific obligations reserved for undertakings with significant market power. **3.72** Pursuant to the regulation, NRAs may not extend to other undertakings the specific obligations which are imposed on undertakings with significant market power. This general prohibition appears in line with the philosophy underlying the reform. Pursuant to that philosophy, markets should be left free in situations where they can produce satisfactory outcomes. Such outcomes should normally be reached in situations where no market power has been acquired by any of the market participants.[78] The prohibition on extending obligations to other undertakings further conforms to the allocation of powers between national and European authorities as organised by the NRF. Pursuant to regulation, Member States, including NRAs, cannot introduce obligations in addition to those adopted at European level. In this context, certain obligations have been established in the regulation as regards undertakings with significant market power. Supplementary rules may not be introduced, for instance rules allowing an extension of European obligations to situations other than those envisaged in the European regulation.

> *Access Directive, Article 8(3), subpara 1, indent 3.* '[N]ational regulatory authorities shall not impose the obligations designated . . . on operators that have not been [identified as having significant market power].'

Two sets of obligations. As a result of the prohibition examined above, one can **3.73** say that two sets of obligations are introduced by the NRF as regards access. A first set contains provisions reserved for undertakings with significant market power. These obligations may not be imposed on undertakings not falling under this category, as seen above. A second set comprises obligations that are not reserved to those undertakings. These obligations are to be applied to the undertakings aimed at in the relevant provisions. Among these undertakings may be those with significant market power as well as entities with no such power.

---

[77] See Access Directive, Art 5(1), in fine. This obligation is not different in substance from that which is imposed on undertakings acquiring information on rivals as a result of commercial and technical negotiation: see ibid, Art 4(3).

[78] In the absence of market power, clients are supposed to choose their supplier. These choices place on undertakings a constraint which requires them to adapt to demand. Intervention is only mandated where this market-based mechanism ceases to function properly. According to mainstream economic theory, this takes place where power is acquired on the markets by one or several undertakings.

(2) Nuances

3.74 **Obligations are imposed on 'non-powerful' undertakings in the new regulatory framework.** Nuances must be brought to the prohibition to impose obligations on non-powerful undertakings. Other provisions included in the NRF make it indeed possible to take action vis-à-vis non-powerful undertakings. Three sources of obligations for non-powerful undertakings are specifically mentioned in the Access Directive.

3.75 **Access Directive itself.** First, the Access Directive itself provides that obligations may be imposed on all undertakings in connection with access. This possibility has already been examined (see paras 3.72–3.73) and there is no necessity, as a result, to come back to it in the present section. It is however important to note that the European regulation entrusts NRAs with far-reaching powers in this context.[79]

3.76 **Other directives.** Second, other directives from the NRF impose obligations independently of market power. Examples are specifically mentioned in the Access Directive.[80] For instance, undertakings controlling an essential facility must share this facility.[81] Undertakings with special or exclusive rights must hold separate accounts for these activities.[82] Commitments may be imposed on undertakings obtaining a usage right as a result of a competitive or comparative selection procedure.[83] All undertakings operating public telephone networks must handle all calls to the European telephony numbering space.[84] Non geographic numbers (for instance 0800, etc) must be accessible to end users from other Member States.[85] Undertakings must allow end users to retain their number(s) when changing supplier.[86]

3.77 **International commitments.** Third, one may not exclude the possibility that NRAs may be compelled by international commitments to impose obligations on undertakings which do not qualify as having significant market power under the Access Directive. Suppose one Member State has entered an international agreement pursuant to which obligations must be imposed on such undertakings. As it is an official emanation of that State, the NRA has little choice and must apply this commitment. In a context of that nature, it is important that the Commission has a chance to verify the reality of that commitment as well as its compatibility with European law. In order to make such verification possible, the European regulation provides that the NRA must notify its intention to impose obligations in situations not provided for in the regulation.

(3) Obligations that may be imposed on undertakings controlling access to end users

3.78 **Traditional telecommunications.** The Access Directive introduces for the NRAs the possibility of imposing obligations on undertakings controlling access

---

[79] See Framework Directive, Art 12.   [80] See ibid, Art 13.
[81] See Authorisations Directive, Annex, Part B, condition 7.
[82] Universal Service Directive, Art 27.   [83] ibid, Art 28.   [84] ibid, Art 30.
[85] See Access Directive, Art 8(5).   [86] ibid, Art 5(1), subpara 2, letter (a).

to end users. This possibility does not seem different from those concerning the local loop. It is however inserted in the directive in a section other than the provisions relating to the local loop. These measures are introduced 'without prejudice to measures that may be taken regarding undertakings with significant market power'. This implies that undertakings may have imposed on them obligations in connection with access to end users in situations where they have no significant market power. As a result of that possibility, there exists in the NRF a tool to extend obligations outside the circle of 'powerful undertakings'.[87] Pursuant to the regulation, NRAs may impose all sorts of obligations that are necessary to ensure end-to-end connectivity. In some cases, an obligation may be imposed on them to interconnect their network:

> *Access Directive, Article 5(1), subpara 2, letter (a).* '[W]ithout prejudice to measures that may be taken regarding undertakings with significant market power . . . , national regulatory authorities shall be able to impose: . . . to the extent that is necessary to ensure end-to-end connectivity, obligations on undertakings that control access to end users, including in justified cases the obligation to interconnect their networks where this is not already the case.'

Digital radio and television broadcasting services. A similar possibility is **3.79** envisaged in the Access Directive as regards access to end users for digital broadcasting services. The possibility is not limited to television but also concerns radio services. In the context of these services, obligations may be imposed on undertakings controlling access to end users. These undertakings need not have significant market power. Non-powerful undertakings may thus have obligations imposed on them. There is no indication as to the nature of the obligations that may be imposed. One can, however, suppose that the NRAs are given the power to select, from among the obligations meant for undertakings with significant market power, those which appear appropriate to ensure the realisation of the goals pursued. In all cases, the purpose must be to ensure access to radio and television broadcasting services. Not all services are concerned, only those specified by the Member State on the territory of which the measures are taken. Pursuant to the directive, the measures aimed at ensuring access may be extended to other facilities. Two are mentioned in particular, access to application programme interfaces (APIs) and access to electronic programme guides (EPGs).

> *Access Directive, Article 5(1), subpara 2, letter (b).* '[W]ithout prejudice to measures that may be taken regarding undertakings with significant market power . . . , national regulatory authorities shall be able to impose: . . . (b) to the extent that is necessary to ensure accessibility for end users to digital radio and television broadcasting services specified by the Member State, obligations on operators to provide access to the . . . facilities referred to in Annex I, Part II on fair, reasonable and non-discriminatory terms.'

---

[87] This confirms the nuance formulated above, about the prohibition for Member States to apply specific access-related obligations to undertakings with no significant market power.

3.80 **Universal service.** This provision in fact appears to introduce an embryo of universal service in the context of radio and digital broadcasting. The purpose is not merely to ensure that providers or operators have access to the facility where contacts may be sought with end users with a view to developing competition in the markets for services. It is also to ensure that end users themselves have access to some services that are deemed essential in modern society. The insertion of this provision in the Access Directive is probably the only means that the supporters of a radio or television universal service have been able to impose. This does not mean that the only purpose of the provision is to introduce a sort of universal service in digital radio and television broadcasting services. Providers must also be given a chance to access facilities in that sector in order to offer their services to end users. Electronic programme guides provide a good example of this. On the one hand, end users must be ensured access to these guides in order to make a selection among the programmes offered. On the other hand, providers must also have access to these guides in order to present their offering.

(4) Obligations that may be imposed on all undertakings

3.81 **Some obligations may be imposed on all undertakings.** A significant number of the obligations regarding access are imposed on undertakings with significant market power. This corresponds to the philosophy underlying the reform, pursuant to which public intervention is warranted only where market mechanisms do not lead to satisfactory outcomes. As will be evident with regard to universal service, this freedom, left to markets, is, however, controlled. A general duty is imposed on all market participants to negotiate. This is a way for the European legislator to indicate what it expects from market participants in this new liberalised era. Furthermore, some obligations are imposed on all undertakings concerning behaviour which is deemed unacceptable even where market power is not present.

3.82 **A right and an obligation to negotiate.** Pursuant to regulation, all undertakings seeking access have a right to negotiate with undertakings operating public networks. As the right granted to one party implies an obligation for the other party, public network operators have a duty to negotiate with undertakings seeking access. Admittedly, an obligation to negotiate does not necessarily imply that the party seeking access will obtain satisfactory conditions. In itself, the obligation imposed on operators means, however, that any refusal to negotiate may be regarded as a breach. It can be argued that the introduction of an obligation to negotiate fulfils an objective relating to the provision of information. As a result of the reform and the NRF, markets are no longer organised as they used to be. Changes have occurred in the tasks entrusted to the various actors. Stating an obligation to negotiate indicates to undertakings that they have a fundamental responsibility for fulfilling certain requirements.

> *Access Directive, Article 4(1).* 'Operators of public communications networks shall have a right and, when requested by other undertakings so authorised, an obligation

to negotiate interconnection with each other for the purpose of providing publicly available communications services, in order to ensure provision and interoperability of services throughout the Community.'

General obligation to provide access under reasonable conditions. The regu- **3.83** lation imposes a general obligation to grant access under reasonable conditions. This obligation applies to all undertakings irrespective of the existence of significant market power. More specifically, the regulation emphasises that access must be granted under conditions comparable to those imposed by NRAs. As has been shown, these authorities may intervene in situations where significant market power is held. Their purpose must then be to ensure that access is obtained under reasonable conditions. Pursuant to regulation, conditions of this nature must also be obtained on markets where no significant market is held. In this fashion, the regulation makes it clear that an overall homogeneity is expected as regards access conditions, independently of the existence of significant market power. The provision also creates a tool that may be invoked by practitioners where they represent a client which, in their view, is not granted reasonable conditions in a situation where no undertaking holds significant market power.

> *Access Directive, Article 3(2).* 'Operators shall offer access and interconnection to other undertakings on terms and conditions consistent with obligations imposed by the national regulatory authority.'

Confidentiality of information. In the negotiation process, parties obtain about **3.84** each other information that may be sensitive. One issue is what they will do with this information. Suppose a provider seeks access to the public telephone network for the provision of data-related services. Negotiations start with the relevant operator. In the course of the negotiation, information is given by the provider concerning the technical requirements needed for access, and vice versa. Information of that nature may have a commercial value. In a context where financial resources are important, the parties may be tempted to use this information. However, negotiation will never develop as the main tool for the resolution of access-related issues if the freedom of the parties is not limited regarding the use they can make of information gathered in the process regarding activities developed or envisaged by other undertakings. For this reason, obligations are imposed in order to ensure confidentiality of information. First, information acquired from other parties as a result of negotiation must be kept confidential. This information must remain within the service of the department involved in the negotiation. It cannot be communicated to other parties, even to other departments or services within the same undertaking. Second, information may be used only for the purpose at stake in the negotiation. If an operator acquires information following a request by another undertaking seeking access, this information cannot be used for other purposes:

> *Access Directive, Article 4(3).* 'Member States shall require that undertakings which acquire information from another undertaking before, during or after the process of

negotiating access or interconnection arrangements use that information solely for the purpose for which it was supplied and respect at all times the confidentiality of information transmitted or stored. The received information shall not be passed on to any other party, in particular other departments, subsidiaries or partners, for whom such information could provide a competitive advantage.'

3.85 **Non-discrimination—Unbundling of services.** In addition to a general duty to negotiate and keep information confidential, the regulation appears to impose specific obligations on all undertakings operating public networks. These obligations seem to apply irrespective of the position acquired by these entities on the markets, and are thus not limited to undertakings with significant market power. *(a)* The first obligation is that no discrimination may be exercised in the conditions under which access or interconnection is granted. Operators are not allowed to impose different conditions on various undertakings where access is requested for a similar application and where the circumstances are equivalent. *(b)* The second obligation is that operators may not make access dependent upon the candidate purchasing a service or an item not directly related to the access.

> *Access Directive, Article 3(2).* 'Member States shall not maintain legal or administrative measures which oblige operators, when granting access or interconnection, to offer different terms and conditions to different undertakings for equivalent services and/or imposing obligations that are not related to the actual access and interconnection provided.'

3.86 **Status of obligations.** For the sake of clarity, one must draw attention to an uncertainty concerning the status of these obligations that are imposed, it would appear, on all undertakings, irrespective of whether or not they hold significant market power. As is apparent from the extract reproduced above, the relevant provision is expressed in terms of obligations imposed on the Member States. Pursuant to this provision, Member States are to eliminate all measures imposing discrimination or service-bundling relating to access. The provision is thus not addressed to undertakings as such. A duty imposed on Member States to eliminate certain provisions does not imply, indeed, that the practices adopted by undertakings and aimed at in these provisions are to be abandoned. The main effect of the provision, as regards undertakings, is that, when the relevant provisions are eliminated, these undertakings are deprived of a legal basis to discriminate or bundle. This does not imply, however, that they may not resort to this behaviour. Under normal market conditions, businesses are indeed free to behave as they wish. The fact that different treatments are granted to various parties does not raise difficulties in such an environment, as the existence of several undertakings makes it possible for customers to choose the offer corresponding to their needs. The same applies to the other obligation. In a competitive environment, users will not suffer from service bundling as they will find unbundled offers elsewhere on the market. Under normal conditions, users can thus ensure they receive adequate offerings without the need for public intervention. Public intervention is necessary only where choice has disappeared as a result of the acquisition of a certain level of market power by one or several undertakings.

Independent of market power.   If the provisions of the regulation were to be **3.87** interpreted as implying a prohibition imposed on all operators from resorting to bundling and discriminatory behaviour, it would mean that the European legislator had decided to make general a prohibition normally limited only to undertakings with market power. This would not seem entirely consistent with the methodology underlying the NRF, where market forces are to operate freely and public intervention is limited to circumstances where undesirable outcomes are produced. In these circumstances, the imposition of these two obligations may only emphasise the importance of the concepts that they aim to protect. There is indeed a strong argument to impose the obligation independently of market power because non-discrimination favours equality and unbundling encourages an efficient use of existing resources.[88]

(5) Conditional access systems

Technical devices.   The rules examined so far mainly concern access to the net- **3.88** work segment located between the subscriber's premises and the main distribution frame. Their object is to ensure that service providers and network operators are physically in a position to present their offering to end users. The necessity to reach end users concerns all forms of electronic communications from classic voice telephony to digital services such as radio or television broadcasting. In some instances, access to end users does not depend merely on the physical conduit or frequencies. Conditional access systems may have been installed by operators. These systems are technical devices making access by end users to a given service dependent upon an authorisation being granted by the undertaking controlling that facility. Usually, authorisation is granted in exchange for payment.[89]

Issues raised by these systems.   Conditional access systems mainly raise issues **3.89** for service providers. These systems are very expensive to design and develop. As a result, it is unlikely that several undertakings will each seek to develop their own device. From a business point of view, the most likely scenario is that the first undertaking placing a conditional access system will be approached by other service providers seeking to offer similar services. In other words, the first undertaking placing a conditional access system will control a facility essential for the provision of like services by competitors. The issue is whether the undertaking controlling the device will accept to share access. Arguments in favour may be

---

[88] Access Directive, Art 3(2). As will be stated, a distinction is drawn between the prohibitions on discrimination, depending on whether they are applied to all undertakings or reserved to undertakings with significant market power. In the latter case, the obligation goes so far as to prohibit undertakings from granting to their own divisions or services treatment that would be more favourable than that given to third parties. See ibid, Art 10.   [89] ibid, Art 5(1), subpara 2, letter (b).

found, as the use of the device by several undertakings will allow the investment to be amortised more efficiently. It is however to be feared that undertakings controlling a conditional access system will, in most circumstances, use their control of that facility as a tool to reserve access to end users for their own services.

3.90 **Undertakings controlling conditional access systems.** For this reason, provisions are inserted in the European regulation with a view to ensuring access for all service providers through these technical devices. Pursuant to the Access Directive, obligations are to be imposed on undertakings controlling conditional access systems as soon as the Member States apply the new rules (25 July 2003). These obligations are imposed irrespective of the market power held by the undertakings concerned. The criterion for the application of the obligations is not the market power but the control by an undertaking over such a system.[90] A difference must be noticed on this point compared to obligations regarding other facilities, where only undertakings with significant market power are concerned:

> *Access Directive, Article 6(1).* 'Member States shall ensure that, in relation to conditional access to digital television and radio services broadcast to viewers and listeners in the Community, irrespective of the means of transmission, the conditions laid down in Annex I, Part I, apply.'

3.91 **Access may not be limited.** Obligations are imposed on all undertakings having control over the conditional access systems and the technologies on which these systems are based. These obligations are not different in their nature from those which are imposed on undertakings controlling the local loop or other facilities necessary to provide electronic communications services. Three rules may be distinguished and are examined in the following paragraphs.

3.92 **Obligation to grant access.** Undertakings controlling conditional access systems must allow undertakings seeking to provide services to end users to transit via their facility in situations where this is needed. Not only must access be granted. Obligations are also imposed regarding the conditions under which access must be granted. Pursuant to the regulation, conditions for access must be fair, reasonable and non-discriminatory.

> *Access Directive, Annex I, Part I, letter (b), first indent.* '[A]ll operators of conditional access services . . . are to . . . offer to all broadcasters, on a fair, reasonable, and non-discriminatory basis compatible with Community competition law, technical services enabling the broadcasters' digitally-transmitted services to be received by viewers or listeners authorised by means of decoders administered by the service operators, and comply with Community competition law.'

3.93 **Technology-related obligations.** Dangers concerning the development of digital radio and television services are not only created by the use—or abuse—that may be made of conditional access systems in some circumstances. Limitations may also

---

[90] Access Directive, Art 6.

come from undertakings holding intellectual property rights on a technology used in these systems. There is a danger that this technology may be reserved to one or a few undertakings. Such a limitation would not serve the purpose of developing the markets for digital radio and television broadcasting, and should as a result be void. For this reason, the regulation provides that undertakings holding intellectual property rights are under an obligation to make their technology available to all candidates. Here again, access must be fair, reasonable and non-discriminatory.

> *Access Directive, Annex I, Part I, letter (c).* '[W]hen granting licences to manufacturers of consumer equipment, holders of intellectual property rights to conditional access products and systems are to ensure that this is done on fair, reasonable and non-discriminatory terms.'

Combination of technologies. Dangers may further come from the limitation **3.94** which may be placed in some instances on the combination of technologies included in the conditional access systems. There is a temptation for undertakings developing these systems to introduce elements which make it impossible to use at the same time another—competing—technology. Again, a situation of that nature would impair the purpose pursued in this area by the NRF, ie the development of digital radio and TV broadcasting services. Accordingly, the regulation prohibits rights-holders from limiting the inclusion, in the conditional access systems, of devices allowing other technologies to be used (interface allowing connection between several access systems or inclusion, in one system, of elements specific to another).

> *Access Directive, Annex I, Part I, letter (c).* 'Taking into account technical and commercial factors, holders of rights are not to subject the granting of licences to conditions prohibiting, deterring or discouraging the inclusion in the same product of: [a] a common interface allowing connection with several other access systems, or [b] means specific to another access system, provided that the licensee complies with the relevant and reasonable conditions ensuring, as far as he is concerned, the security of transactions of conditional access system operators.'

Accounting dimension. A third aspect comes from the traditional fear that **3.95** vertically integrated undertakings may attempt to subsidise activities with profits obtained on markets where they have significant market power. In the context of conditional access systems, undertakings controlling these devices may be in a dominant position. This may make it possible for them to charge high prices for the use of these systems. The danger is that profits coming from this market where the undertaking is somehow protected from competition may be used to sponsor activities where the undertaking is in competition with service providers. This is a classic situation where a conflict of interest arises between the presence of an undertaking controlling an essential facility on one market and the activities carried out by that undertaking on a second market where it is in competition with other undertakings needing access to the facility to perform their tasks. This situation is normally resolved through two mechanisms. A first mechanism is that undertakings controlling access to essential facilities are not allowed to charge excessive prices. The possibility for them to obtain profits that will be used to sponsor other activities is thus in principle limited. A second mechanism is that undertakings may not transfer profits from one activity to another. Separate accounts are mandated for the respective activities, so as to monitor the prohibition.

> *Access Directive, Annex I, Part I, letter (b), second indent.* '[All] operators of conditional access services . . . are to . . . keep separate financial accounts regarding their activity as conditional access providers.'

3.96 **Necessity to allow technical control.** The regulation adds an obligation relating to technical control. Pursuant to the Access Directive, conditional access systems must be designed so as to allow technical control by the network operator. This is to ensure the proper functioning of the systems, which in effect condition the possibility for end users to access digital radio and broadcasting services.

> *Access Directive, Annex I, Part I, letter (a).* '[C]onditional access systems . . . are to have the necessary technical capability for cost-effective transcontrol allowing the possibility for full control by network operators at local or regional level of the services using such conditional access systems.'

3.97 **Possibility of amending obligations.** Changes may be made to the obligations imposed in application of the regulation. First, the Access Directive provides that these obligations may be changed in the light of market and technical developments. A procedure is established to organise the consultations and interactions that must take place for such a change to occur.[91] Second, Member States may allow NRAs to alter or even remove these obligations.[92] The power granted to the national authorities is, however, subject to several conditions that are examined below.

> *(a)* *First condition.* A first condition is that a decision to modify or eliminate obligations may only be taken after the authorities have reviewed market conditions. This indicates that such a decision has to be justified in a specific manner on the basis of the situation that may be observed on the market.
>
> > *Access Directive, Article 6(3).* 'Member States may permit their national regulatory authority . . . to review the conditions applied in accordance with this Article, by undertaking a market analysis . . . to determine whether to maintain, amend or withdraw the conditions applied.'
>
> *(b)* *Second condition.* A second condition is that obligations may be modified or suppressed only in respect of undertakings that are found by the NRAs to be without significant market power. This means that the obligations introduced in the Access Directive apply in all circumstances to undertakings controlling conditional access systems where these

---

[91] Access Directive, Art 6(2).   [92] ibid, Art 6(3).

undertakings have significant market power. There is thus no possibility of removing or modifying obligations where the latter are imposed on undertakings with significant market power.

Access Directive, Article 6(3), subpara 2. 'Where, as a result of this market analysis, a national regulatory authority finds that one or more operators do not have significant market power on the relevant market, it may amend or withdraw the conditions with respect to those operators.'

(c) *Third condition.* A third condition is that the modification or removal of obligations may not affect the access of end users to radio and television broadcasts, as well as to broadcasting channels and services, which have been specified by the Member States. Nor may the prospects for effective competition be affected in the markets for retail services, conditional access systems and other associated facilities.'

Access Directive, Article 6(3), subpara 2. '[A] national regulatory authority . . . may amend or withdraw the conditions . . . only to the extent that: (a) accessibility for end users to radio and television broadcasts and broadcasting channels and services specified . . . would not be adversely affected by such amendment or withdrawal, and (b) the prospects for effective competition in the markets for digital retail television and radio broadcasting services and conditional access systems and other associated facilities, would not be adversely affected by such amendment or withdrawal.'

(d) *Fourth condition.* The fourth condition—or group of conditions—is of a procedural nature. An appropriate period of notice must be given to the parties likely to be affected by the possible modification or removal of obligations. These changes may only be introduced after the special regulatory procedure has been complied with. This procedure has already been examined at length and only its essential features will be repeated. The procedure is set out in the Framework Directive; parties likely to be affected are to be consulted; the draft measure must be communicated for comment to the Commission as well as to NRAs in other Member States. The Commission has the power to decide that the measures may not be adopted by the NRA concerned.

A specific system.   The regime examined above in connection with conditional **3.98** access systems is different from that presented in connection with obligations that may be imposed generally on undertakings with significant market power. Presented in a summary manner, the differences are as follows: *(a)* The margin for manoeuvre which is granted to the NRAs seems more limited in the provisions concerning conditional access systems. NRAs do not automatically have the power to decide whether the obligations should be amended. This power depends upon a decision to be taken to that effect by each Member State as regards its NRA. Moreover, a decision to amend is submitted to stringent material and procedural conditions. *(b)* The obligations introduced in the directive have significant force compared to obligations imposed on other resources. They are entirely applicable, whereas the obligations introduced by the directive only apply in other cases where the NRA decides that the obligations deriving from the old regulatory regime must be amended.[93] *(c)* Obligations concerning conditional access systems apply to all undertakings controlling this type of facility, even where these undertakings do not have significant market power. By contrast, the other obligations apply only to undertakings with such market power, and the regulation specifically provides that they may not be extended to situations where no such power is held.

3.99 Pattern for the imposition of obligations relating to conditional access systems

(a) Obligations are imposed on the basis of the NRF
(b) NRAs may determine whether these obligations must be maintained, modified or removed. This is however made dependent upon a decision from the Member State to grant that power to its NRA. Furthermore, the decision to amend may only be taken where material and procedural conditions are fulfilled.

3.100 Possibility to impose access on other resources. The obligations that have been analysed concern conditional access systems. Apart from these obligations, there is a possibility, pursuant to the Access Directive, of imposing access obligations regarding resources that have similar characteristics to conditional access systems. These resources are application programme interfaces (APIs) and electronic programme guides (EPGs). Under the Access Directive, Member States must grant NRAs the power to impose on operators obligations to provide access to these facilities on fair, reasonable and non-discriminatory terms.

Access Directive, Article 5(1), subpara 2. '(W)ithout prejudice to measures that may be taken regarding undertakings with significant market power in accordance with Article 8, national regulatory authorities shall be able to impose: . . . (b) to the extent that is necessary to ensure accessibility for end users to digital radio and television broadcasting services specified by the Member State, obligations on operators to provide access to the other facilities referred to in Annex I, Part II on fair, reasonable and non-discriminatory terms.'

3.101 Uncertainty. There is an uncertainty as to the obligations that may be imposed on these resources. These resources are placed in Annex I to the Access Directive, where obligations concerning conditional access systems are formulated. This

---

[93] Pursuant to Art 6 of the Access Directive, the Member States must ensure that the conditions enumerated in the Annex to the directive, and concerning conditional access systems, are applied as of the implementation of the directive in the national legal order. By contrast, the implementation of obligations regarding other resources only implies that some provisions contained in the Interconnection Directive (old regulatory framework) are maintained, with a power for the NRAs to determine whether, and to what extent, the obligations introduced by these provisions must be changed. (See, on this latter point, Art 7 of the Access Directive.)

provides an argument that these obligations should be applied to these resources, should the NRAs make use of their power to impose access obligations in connection with them. On the other hand, this power is described in a context where obligations are imposed concerning access to other resources than conditional access systems. This seems to indicate that NRAs have the power, when the Member States so decide, to apply these old obligations to these resources. This difficulty is important because the answer given to the question has an impact on the legal regime applicable to the resources.

Former legislative history.   Most obligations inserted in the Access Directive   **3.102** and regarding conditional access systems are taken over from a specific directive that had been adopted by the Parliament and the Council as regards the transmission of television signals.[94] The obligations examined above were thus in force before the NRF was adopted. This means that the adoption of the framework has not affected the markets for the transmission of television signals, as far as regulation is concerned.[95]

E. Obligations Imposed on Undertakings with Significant Market Power

(1) Transitional period

Reminder.   As stated above, the rules presented in this section are those intro-   **3.103** duced by the NRF. They are in substance similar to those that were part of the old framework, with some changes. It has been stated that, in order to structure the introduction of the new rules, a transitional mechanism has been put in place according to which certain obligations under the old framework remain applicable. These obligations are only replaced, or changed, when, and to the extent, the NRAs take a decision to that effect. As a result, the entry into force of the said obligations is made dependent on two events—the implementation of the European regulation in the national legal order, and a decision to apply the new rules in preference to the old. The obligations concerned are identified above.

---

[94] European Parliament and Council Directive (EC) 95/47 on the use of standards for the transmission of television signals [1995] OJ L281/51. This Directive was repealed when the NRF was adopted. See Framework Directive, Art 16.

[95] The obligation to grant access (first obligation) was formulated in Art 4, letter (c) of the directive. The technology-related obligations were inserted at Art 4, letter (d). Accounting separation was mandated at Art 4, letter (c). Results obtained on the markets are not satisfactory where choice disappears as a result of the acquisition of market power by one or several undertakings. As choice disappears, users no longer have the possibility to select the provider or the operator presenting the best offer. They have to deal with the undertaking(s) having market power. As they are constrained in their relations, the dominant or powerful undertakings no longer feel the pressure of choice and competition.

In general terms, they are those that relate to access and are applied to undertakings with significant market power.

3.104 **Conditional access systems.** In the course of the discussion, it has been submitted that a specific system has been devised for conditional access systems. As regards these systems, the obligations introduced in the NRF apply with the implementation of the European provisions by the Member States. No specific decision needs to be taken by the NRAs, unlike under the mechanism described above. However, the NRAs can decide, after these measures have been introduced, whether, and to what extent, they should be amended or removed.[96]

(2) The decision to impose obligations

3.105 **Markets where choice is impaired.** Regulatory obligations are provided for in the new framework, but the question arises as to when, or in what circumstances, they may, or must, be applied to undertakings. To identify these circumstances, reference has to be made to the philosophy underlying the reform. In that philosophy, it is expected that market interaction will make it possible for undertakings to obtain access to the resources they need to provide electronic communications services. This outcome should be reached under 'normal' market conditions, ie where customers have a choice between suppliers. As choice exists, suppliers strive to ensure their goods and services correspond to the needs of customers, and where they do not, they may be set aside and another supplier preferred. The existence of choice thus ensures that the best possible economic outcome will be attained. The disappearance or impairment of choice has far-reaching consequences. Where customers no longer enjoy a choice, they have to accept the terms and conditions imposed by the supplier. Choice does not need to be totally removed for such a situation to occur. In some circumstances the possibility of choosing one's supplier is only impaired. However, due to market circumstances, this impairment is sufficient to make customers depend on the terms and conditions dictated by the supplier.

3.106 **Choice and power.** The concept of choice is intimately related to power. Where customers have a choice, they are not dependent in any fashion on the supplier. They may go to another supplier that may offer better terms and conditions. By contrast, customers become dependent on suppliers when choice disappears. They then have to accept the offer made by the supplier, or no longer purchase the good or service concerned.[97]

---

[96] Access Directive, Art 6(1) for the introduction of the obligations with the implementation by the Member States and Art 6(3) for the modifications that NRAs may bring to these obligations if they receive an authorisation to that effect by their Member State.

[97] The alternative on that occasion is not between various suppliers, but between access, or absence of access, to the good or service concerned—in our scenario to facilities and resources needed to provide electronic communications services. It was submitted that the European legislator is

Two scenarios. On the basis of this reasoning, two scenarios are envisaged in the **3.107** regulatory framework. On markets where choice is sufficient, and power has not been acquired, interaction among economic agents should lead to appropriate solutions. By contrast, intervention may be needed where choice has disappeared and power built up by one or several undertakings, to ensure customers' access to facilities and resources.

Intervention by NRAs. Under the regulation, NRAs may intervene at their **3.108** own initiative. They may also act at the request of another party—in most instances a competitor and/or customer. Requests of this nature will normally come to their attention where negotiations between two or more undertakings regarding access have failed. The party seeking access, and which has not obtained a satisfactory offer, will seek to obtain better terms and conditions through a complaint addressed to the NRA or through the courts.

> *Access Directive, Article 5(4).* 'With regard to access and interconnection, Member States shall ensure that the national regulatory authority is empowered to intervene at its own initiative where justified or, in the absence of agreement between undertakings, at the request of either of the parties involved, in order to secure the policy objectives of . . . [the] Framework Directive . . . in accordance with the provisions of this [Access] Directive and the procedures referred to in . . . [the] Framework Directive.'

Duty imposed on Member States and NRAs. Directives are addressed to **3.109** Member States and introduce obligations national authorities have to implement. As regards the subject matter covered in this section, the new framework imposes obligations on the Member States with respect to access. In substance, the obligation is to transform their internal legal order where necessary to ensure the NRAs have the necessary tools to impose constraints on undertakings where normal market conditions are impaired. Obligations are also imposed on NRAs that must be interpreted in the light of the general objectives set for them in the NRF. An obligation is imposed on them to ensure their action is motivated at all times by reference to these objectives. The objectives are relatively specific in the Access Directive, as regards the specific issue of access, namely to ensure adequate access and interconnection. NRAs must also take all necessary steps to ensure interoperability of networks and services. The decisions they take with a view to ensuring these objectives are met must at all times be governed by three criteria: the necessity to promote economic efficiency, secure sustainable competition and maximise benefits for end users.

> *Member States.* 'Member States shall ensure that national regulatory authorities are empowered to impose the obligations identified in [this Directive].'[98] *National regulatory authorities.* 'National regulatory authorities shall, acting in pursuit of the

---

endeavouring to facilitate access since, in the absence of such measures, electronic communications will not develop sufficiently. This explains why it has deliberately opted for intervention as soon as market power is acquired on a given market.

[98] Access Directive, Art 8(1).

objectives set out in . . . [the regulatory framework], encourage and where appropriate ensure . . . adequate access and interconnection, and interoperability of services, exercising their responsibility in a way that promotes efficiency, sustainable competition, and gives the maximum benefit to end users.'[99]

3.110 **Basic regulatory principles and special regulatory procedure.** Authorities must respect certain basic regulatory principles whenever they decide to impose constraints on undertakings designated as having significant market power. Objectivity, proportionality, transparency and non-discrimination are thus to be complied with systematically. To these material requirements are added certain formal conditions. Under the regulation, obligations may be imposed on undertakings with significant market power only after a specific procedure has been followed.[100] This procedure is described in the Framework Directive and comprises the following steps: *(a)* before the measure is adopted, interested parties must be given an opportunity to comment on the draft; *(b)* the result of the consultation must be made public except where confidentiality so mandates; *(c)* the draft measure must be communicated for comment to the Commission and the NRAs in other Member States.[101]

> *Access Directive, Article 8(4).* 'Obligations imposed . . . shall be based on the nature of the problem identified, proportionate and justified in the light of the objectives laid down in Directive 2002/21/EC (Framework Directive). Such obligations shall only be imposed following consultation in accordance with Articles 6 and 7 of that Directive.'[102]

3.111 **Power to veto.** A further step may have to be taken in certain circumstances, as the Commission is empowered to veto a draft decision presented by a national authority in some situations under the special regulatory procedure. This possibility does not, however, exist as regards decisions imposing obligations on undertakings with significant market power. It is limited to two sorts of decision: those defining a market or markets differing from those identified by the Commission; and those designating one or more undertakings as having significant market power.[103]

---

99 Access Directive, Art 5(1).

100 ibid, Art 8(4).

101 ibid, Art 8(4). Despite the impression created by the extract quoted above, only one part of the procedure described at Arts 6 and 7 of the Framework Directive is applicable where the NRA envisages to impose conditions on dominant or powerful undertakings. The latter parts of the procedure (possibility for the Commission to decide that the measure cannot be taken) are limited to situations where operators are designated as having significant market powers or where markets are defined otherwise than stipulated in the recommendation adopted by the Commission on that subject matter.

102 The Interconnection Directive was adopted by the Parliament and the Council pursuant to the concept of 'Open Network Provision (ONP)'. This idea in general implied that existing networks had to be made available for interconnection. The purpose was to make end-to-end services possible across the European territory.

103 For the procedure to be followed by the NRAs where they notify information or draft decisions in that procedure, see Commission Recommendation C(2003)2647 final of 23 July 2003

Proportionality.   An important issue in the assessments to be made by the   **3.112**
NRAs is proportionality. Proportionality has to be assessed in connection with
the objective which a measure is intended to bring about. The purpose of the
proportionality test is to verify whether other measures may be used to attain the
same objective while hindering competition or distorting market forces less.
Another aspect is to ensure that, even where no alternative exists, competition or
market interaction is not distorted to an excessive extent.

A complex exercise.   The assessment to be carried out by NRAs takes the form   **3.113**
of a complex exercise, and is subject to review by an appeal body. Decisions regarding access may therefore be annulled where the assessment has not been done correctly with respect to proportionality. The European legislator has attempted to
facilitate the NRAs' work by including general guidelines in the regulatory framework. These guidelines—which are very general and may be further construed in
subsequent documents from the Commission in implementation of the regulatory framework—are described below, in the form of 'do grant' or 'do not
grant' access in order to clarify and simplify the presentation.

Access to be granted.   Access should be granted where this will facilitate the pro-   **3.114**
vision of pan-European services. The availability of services of this kind is deemed
essential by the European legislator. The EC Treaty contains a provision to allow
action by the European legislator to bring about that objective. The development
of pan-European services is also the basis of the technical work that has been carried out to ensure, and improve, interoperability of networks and services.

Access not to be granted.   Access does not have to be granted where competing   **3.115**
facilities may be used or installed. In order to carry out this assessment, it is necessary to look at the technical and economic viability of resorting to potential competing facilities. It is appropriate here to look at the context in which the request
is formulated, particularly the type of access required and the rate at which the
market is developing. In some cases it may be appropriate not to intervene in the
light of the possible appearance of a competing network which is expected to be
operational within a reasonable period.

Nor should access be granted where this may result in the infringement of intellectual property rights. A situation of this kind may occur where the competing
provider would have access to resources protected by intellectual property and
would be in a position to infringe the rights in question without being subject to
control by the rights holder or an appropriate authority. This may be particularly
important where access is sought to software or other similar technologies.

---

on notifications, time limits and consultations provided for in Art 7 of Directive 2002/21/EC of the
European Parliament and of the Council of 7 March 2002 on a common regulatory framework for
electronic communications networks and services.

Access should not be granted where it is not feasible. Reasons why access may not be feasible are varied. In some cases the available capacity may be exhausted. However, the question arises whether an operator can reject a request on the grounds that granting access would require excessive investment. A situation of this kind may occur where the requesting party needs specific adaptations to the network to allow transmission of its service. Such a situation does not seem to provide an excuse for not granting access. Adapting the network will admittedly require investment. However, such investment can be charged to the requesting party, since nothing in the regulation forces operators to finance themselves the costs incurred in granting access. The obligation is to offer reasonable conditions. The fact that operators should not realise an excessive benefit in the transaction should not be interpreted as an obligation on operators not to recover costs.

Access should not be granted where the operator involved has made considerable investment in the facility to which access is sought. In some instances, the operator has made considerable efforts to develop a competitive advantage through the construction of a specific resource. Compelling such an undertaking to share the result of its efforts under conditions dictated by a regulatory authority may have the effect of frustrating future investment. A balance thus has to be struck between, on the one hand, the desire to make existing resources available to all in the interests of society and, on the other hand, the necessity of allowing industrious and talented people or undertakings to enjoy the results of their efforts.

3.116 **No obligation going beyond regulation.** In carrying out the tasks assigned to them, NRAs may find that the obligations provided for in the European regulation are not sufficient. Limitations are however placed on their capacity to impose additional obligations. Under the regulation, such obligations may be introduced only after a specific request has been made to the Commission. The request must be submitted by the authority which envisages imposing the additional obligations. The Commission has the power to authorise or prohibit the adoption of these obligations.

> *Access Directive, Article 8(3), subpara 2.* 'In exceptional circumstances, when a national regulatory authority intends to impose on operators with significant market power other obligations for access and interconnection than those set out . . . in this Directive, it shall submit this request to the Commission. The Commission . . . shall take a decision authorising or preventing the national regulatory authority from taking such measures.'

3.117 **Division of power.** This division of powers between the Commission and the NRAs indicates that in the eyes of the European legislator, complete harmonisation has taken place as regards the obligations that may be imposed on undertakings with significant market power. Pursuant to established case law, harmonisation deprives Member States of their right to regulate a matter where that harmonisation can be considered as being complete. In the context of obligations imposed on undertakings with significant market power, the rule that Member States may not introduce additional obligations may be interpreted as an indication that the harmonisation is considered as being complete by the European legislator. The possibility of asking the Commission for authorisation should not be interpreted as introducing an exception. It rather provides confirmation of the analysis set out above, to the extent that the decision to impose additional obligations is to be adopted, ultimately, at European level.

(3) Obligations that may be imposed—general presentation

A wide range of possibilities. The following sections examine in more detail **3.118** some of the circumstances in which choice may disappear from the market as a result of the acquisition of power by one or several undertakings. Intervention is warranted in these circumstances. The analysis presented in this book provides indications as to when obligations may, or must, be imposed. First, however, the obligations that may be imposed in markets where the conditions for intervention are fulfilled are set out. The new framework opens a range of possibilities as regards obligations that may be imposed. It is for NRAs to select those they consider appropriate in order to fulfil the objectives of the framework.

What obligations to select? Once NRAs have determined that one or more **3.119** undertakings may be considered dominant or powerful on a market, the question arises as to the obligations that can, and should, be applied to them. The purpose of these obligations is to remedy the distortion of competition arising from the presence of market dominance. In this context, it should be emphasised that not all of the obligations provided for in the regulation need to be applied. A choice has to be made by the NRA with a view to restoring in the market the mechanisms that may have been distorted or that may have disappeared altogether as a result of the acquisition of that power. As a result, the object is not to sanction or punish undertakings with significant market power, but rather to re-establish normal market conditions through specific—'surgical'—regulatory intervention.

> *Access Directive, Article 8(2).* 'Where an operator is designated as having significant market power on a specific market . . . , national regulatory authorities shall impose the obligations set out in Articles 9 to 13 of this Directive as appropriate.'

Basic regulatory principles. It should be borne in mind in this context that the **3.120** basic regulatory principles apply to the decisions adopted by the NRAs. These requirements provide tools for assessing whether the obligations imposed on undertakings are appropriate. As a result of these requirements, obligations must be proportionate to the objectives sought and must also be objective, non-discriminatory and transparent.

Case law. An interesting ruling has been issued by the ECJ regarding the **3.121** margin of discretion which NRAs have in deciding what obligations should be applied to undertakings with significant market power. That ruling was issued under the old regulatory framework and concerns, as a result, the undertakings which were, then, subject to specific obligations. It, however, provides interesting indications about the margin of discretion which, according to the ECJ, must be granted by national legislation to the NRAs. The case—*Telefónica de España*[104]—concerns the transposition of the Interconnection Directive (old regulatory framework) in the Spanish legal order. The issue was whether NRAs could impose ex ante obligations for interconnection prior to negotiation between the parties concerned. The ECJ ruled that obligations of that nature could indeed be imposed, as NRAs have the general power to ensure an efficient allocation of interconnection resources.

> *Telefónica de España.* '[T]he fact that such operators are required under . . . the directive to satisfy only reasonable requests for interconnection does not mean that Member States are precluded under that provision from permitting their national regulatory authorities to impose *ex ante* on those operators conditions or obligations with regard to access.' '[T]he directive cannot therefore be construed as precluding a Member State from adopting provisions authorising a national regulatory authority to require an operator having significant power on the market to provide access to the local subscriber loop and to offer interconnection at local and higher-level switching centres.'[105]

(4) Obligation to grant access

3.122 **Negotiate in good faith.** The first obligation with which undertakings must comply under the new framework is that of negotiating access in good faith. This obligation has already been presented above and is so important that it is explicitly repeated in the list of measures that may be adopted by the NRAs with respect to access. It applies to all undertakings without being limited to those with significant market power. This obligation comes as no surprise as, in the philosophy underlying the framework, access-related issues must normally be solved through market interaction. This is not sufficient in all circumstances, however. Furthermore, establishing good or bad faith is not easy for the party on which the burden of proof is imposed. The consequence is that the NRA is often compelled to intervene.

> *Access Directive, Article 12(1), subpara 2, letter (b).* 'Operators may be required *inter alia*: . . . (b) to negotiate in good faith with undertakings requesting access.'

3.123 **An obligation to provide access.** Intervention may take the form of an obligation imposed on undertakings with significant market power to provide access to

---

[104] Case C-79/00 *Telefónica de España SA v Administración General del Estado* [2001] ECR I-10075.
[105] Paras [32] and [33].

facilities and resources under their control. This obligation may come into play when negotiations regarding access have not given the expected results. In such a context, intervention restores equality among partners by imposing on the operator an obligation to grant access.

> *Access Directive, Article 12(1).* 'A national regulatory authority may . . . impose obligations on operators to meet reasonable requests for access to, and use of, specific network elements and associated facilities.'

Duty to co-operate.   The far-reaching character of the provision quoted above **3.124** should not be underestimated. It must be remembered that freedom is key for the organisation of markets. It is often considered that markets perform satisfactorily only if, and when, undertakings exercise their activities as they wish. Undertakings understand that obligations may be imposed on them for social reasons.[106] The obligation discussed here goes further, however, in that it imposes on some undertakings a duty to co-operate with others irrespective of the relations that may exist between the parties. Suppose the parties are competitors: this will not take away the possibility that one may be obliged to provide assistance to the other even in circumstances where this could be detrimental to its own operations.

Nuances.   As the obligation to provide access may be perceived as being exten- **3.125** sive by some undertakings, the European legislator has sought to bring nuances to the debate. As one can see from the extract set out above, the obligation is limited to providing a positive answer when *(a)* a request is formulated that *(b)* is reasonable and *(c)* specific. Concerning this third nuance, it should be emphasised that the request may concern any element of a network or associated facilities. The scope of the obligation is thus rather wide as regards the facilities or resources concerned by the obligation. However, the request will have to be accepted only if it is specific, ie in circumstances where it concerns specific facilities and is formulated in specific terms.

Illustrations provided in the regulation.   It is stated in the previous paragraph **3.126** that the possibility of ordering access under reasonable conditions is established in the regulation. In some respects this 'obligation in principle' may appear vague. It indeed provides NRAs with far-reaching powers they can use as they see fit in all sorts of circumstances. Such an approach entails significant risks for undertakings against which access may be ordered. These undertakings may have duties and obligations imposed on them, with significant consequences as to their ability to perform their business activities. On the other hand, it does not appear appropriate to include in regulation a catalogue of measures available for NRAs with obligations on those authorities regarding the choice of tools they should use in particular circumstances. Such an approach would be over-rigid. Situations are

---

[106] On this subject, see Chapter 5.

likely to be created where access is impeded but authorities may not intervene because the tool they would like to use is not included in the catalogue. As a compromise, the regulation goes further than establishing a principle, and provides examples of measures that may be taken. These examples give clearer indications regarding the scope of the measures that may be envisaged, without limiting excessively the margin for manoeuvre granted to authorities.

> *Access Directive, Article 12(1), subpara 2.* 'Operators may be required *inter alia*: (a) to give third parties access to specified network elements and/or facilities, including unbundled access to the local loop; . . . (c) not to withdraw access to facilities already granted; (d) to provide specified services on a wholesale basis for resale by third parties; (e) to grant open access to technical interfaces, protocols or other key technologies that are indispensable for the interoperability of services or virtual network services; (f) to provide co-location or other forms of facility sharing, including duct, building or mast sharing; (g) to provide specified services needed to ensure interoperability of end-to-end services to users, including facilities for intelligent network services or roaming on mobile networks; (h) to provide access to operational support systems or similar software systems necessary to ensure fair competition in the provision of services; (i) to interconnect networks or network facilities.'[107]

3.127 **Various situations.** In the examples provided above, various situations are examined. The first is where access is sought to infrastructure. In this connection the regulation provides that third parties may be granted access to specified network elements and/or facilities (letter a). An obligation may be imposed not to withdraw access to facilities where this access has already been granted (letter c). Similarly, operators may be constrained to provide co-location or other forms of facility sharing—including duct, building or mast sharing (letter f). The second situation relates to technologies that are necessary to ensure effective access. Here the regulation provides that access may be imposed regarding technical interfaces, protocols or other key technologies that are indispensable for the interoperability of services (letter e). A similar obligation may be imposed with respect to operational support systems or similar software systems that are necessary to ensure the proper performance of services (letter h). The third situation concerns interoperability (letters g and i). Interoperability is particularly important where services must be provided from end users to end users. The classic example is telephony. This kind of service must be provided from the calling to the called party. No interruption can be admitted, because this would in effect imply that the service

---

[107] The approach adopted by the European legislator is not exempt from criticism. The main critique relates to the difficulty that authorities face when they attempt to envisage in advance all of the situations that may occur and the kinds of remedies that could be applied to address these situations. This difficulty has obviously been encountered by the European legislator, when drafting the Access Directive. The result is that the institutions have limited their approach to providing a few illustrations which can be related to various sorts of resource. In doing so, they have in effect done little more than give a reminder of the various sorts of facilities concerned and that an obligation to grant access may be imposed in relation to these various kinds of resource.

is not provided. In this context, an obligation to provide access implies that, in some circumstances, the service provider must be given access to equipment, technology and services that are necessary to ensure that no interruption to service is suffered.

(5) Conditions relating to access

Fair, reasonable and timely service.   Not only do the NRAs have a power to   **3.128**
order access. They may also impose measures relating to the terms and conditions under which access must be granted. The reason is that access would be meaningless if terms and conditions were not reasonable. Suppose, as an example, that access is provided but constantly delayed. The request for access will have been accepted in principle, but the conditions under which access have been granted make it in effect impossible for the provider to carry out its activities in a satisfactory manner. Intervention is warranted in such a situation. The purpose sought by the European legislator is to ensure that access may be obtained by providers under the best possible conditions, without which the market for the provision of electronic communications services would be unable to develop. To make sure that this result may be obtained, tools are made available to the NRAs. Under the Access Directive, the NRAs may impose all measures necessary to ensure that the conditions for access are fair, reasonable and appropriate regarding the time constraints faced by the undertaking seeking access.

> *Access Directive, Article 12, subpara 3.* 'National regulatory authorities may attach to those obligations conditions covering fairness, reasonableness and timeliness.'

Flexible system.   It is clear from this that the European legislator has again opted   **3.129**
in favour of a flexible system where tools are presented in general terms. The purpose is probably, once more, to avoid a situation where authorities could, as a result of excessively detailed provisions, lack the tools necessary to intervene. This approach creates difficulties, however, as the accuracy of the obligations likely to be imposed on operators ultimately depends on decisions taken by NRAs. It is to be hoped that, on this point, the NRAs will be able to build a common approach within the European Union. In the absence of such an approach, diverging traditions will undoubtedly be created across the Member States which will make it difficult for operators to build European-wide strategies.

Technical and operational conditions.   The regulation further provides that   **3.130**
NRAs may impose technical and/or operational conditions where they consider this to be appropriate to maximise access. In application of this power, NRAs may determine how access must be granted in practical terms—what the beneficiaries have to do to connect their equipment, etc. Another implication is that NRAs may issue technical specifications to be met by the access provider. In all cases, the decisions or other instruments issued by the NRAs must comply with the basic regulatory principles (objectivity, non-discrimination, proportionality, and transparency).

Access Directive, Article 5(2). 'When imposing obligations on an operator to provide access . . . , national regulatory authorities may lay down technical or operational conditions to be met by the provider/and or beneficiaries of such access, in accordance with Community law, where necessary to ensure normal operation of the network.'[108]

3.131 **Control on access charges.** An essential element to take into account in an access maximisation perspective is the tariff charged by operators for access. Suppose a provider needs access to the telephone network to provide internet access. Access is originally denied but ultimately granted as a result of an intervention made by the NRA. The tariff imposed by the operator, however, remains high. With a tariff of this nature, the provider would not be in a position to carry out its activities on a competitive basis with other providers. This would be the case, in particular, if the provider is in competition in a market for services with the network operator (most operators do not remain confined to network markets, but develop activities in services).

3.132 **Tariffs based on costs.** Given the special importance of tariffs, a specific provision has been included in the Access Directive. Member States may thus rely on a specific legal basis when they envisage action regarding tariffs. They do not need to base their action on the general obligation mentioned above concerning fairness/reasonableness in conditions regarding access. Under the regulation, NRAs may impose a requirement that tariffs be calculated on costs. Such an obligation implies that, when they fix tariffs for access and/or interconnection, operators must take as a basis for their decision the cost that is incurred in providing access.

Access Directive, Article 13(1). 'A national regulatory authority may . . . impose obligations relating to price controls, including obligations for cost orientation of prices.'

3.133 **No excessive profit.** The obligation to base tariffs on costs does not entail a prohibition for operators to realise a profit—profits are essential to finance projects and further develop activities. However, there must exist a reasonable relation between tariffs and costs. The difference between both, ie the profit, may not be unreasonable. A classic scenario for an authority to intervene is thus where tariffs are charged at a level which can be deemed excessive with respect to the costs.

Access Directive. 'A national regulatory authority may . . . impose obligations relating to . . . price controls . . . in situations where a market analysis indicates that a lack of effective competition means that the operator concerned might sustain prices at an

---

[108] Where technical specifications are imposed, this has to take place in accordance with the rules established in the Framework Directive on standardisation. See Framework Directive, Art 5(3). See Access Directive, Art 5(3) for the obligation to respect the basic regulatory principles. The provision quoted in the body of the text concerns conditions to be met by the providers, ie the undertakings seeking access. On that basis, one may consider that the provision imposes obligations on providers. In fact, the intention pursued by the European legislator is probably the opposite. In our view, that provision allows authorities to determine themselves what conditions may be obtained rather than let the operator fix on his own initiative conditions that would probably be less favourable.

excessively high level . . . to the detriment of end-users.'[109] 'National regulatory authorities . . . may, where appropriate, require prices to be adjusted.'[110]

No price squeeze.   Another situation where authorities may intervene is when   **3.134**
an operator granting access squeezes customers (providers) through a carefully designed tariff policy. Price squeezing is a typical form of conduct that dominant undertakings may use to reinforce their market position. Suppose a territory is covered by a comprehensive network. In addition to its network activities, the operator is active on certain markets for services. One undertaking present on one of these markets for services requests access to the network. Access is granted under reasonable conditions. The result of this conduct is that it cannot be claimed that the operator has charged excessive tariffs. However, the situation is complicated where a decision is taken by the operator to decrease prices on the market for services. As a result of that decision, the provider is placed in a situation where it has to charge lower prices on the retail market, whereas tariffs do not vary on the market where capacity is purchased. The costs thus increase but the provider is not in a position to carry that increase over to its customers. The result is that the provider is progressively squeezed and ultimately has to leave the market. At the end of the operation, a competitor has disappeared from a market for services where the operator has reinforced its position.

> Access Directive. 'A national regulatory authority may . . . impose obligations relating to . . . price controls . . . in situations where a market analysis indicates that a lack of effective competition means that the operator concerned might . . . apply a price squeeze, to the detriment of end users.'[111] 'National regulatory authorities . . . may, where appropriate, require prices to be adjusted.'[112]

Evaluation of costs.   An important issue in assessing the relation between tariffs   **3.135**
and costs is the methodology for determining costs. Significant differences may arise, depending on the methodology used. Historical costs are those that have been incurred by the operator to build, upgrade and maintain the network. They are considerable, and any decision to base access pricing on them will imply that tariffs will normally be high. By contrast, operators (and regulatory authorities) may decide to calculate prices on the basis of current value. That value is the value that may be attributed to the network as an asset allowing the undertaking to generate income under current conditions. Any methodology based on this approach will lead to tariffs being set at a lower level.

No particular methodology.   The NRF does not opt for a particular method-   **3.136**
ology. Pursuant to the Access Directive, costs are to be established in conformity with three criteria: *(a)* the assessment must be based on the investment made by

---

[109] Access Directive, Art 13(3).   [110] ibid, Art 13(1).   [111] ibid, Art 13(1).
[112] ibid, Art 13(3).

the operator;[113] *(b)* operators must be allowed to obtain a reasonable return on capital; and *(c)* decisions regarding cost assessment made by operators or authorities must seek the development of competition to the benefit of consumers. To these criteria, the Access Directive adds one suggestion, to set tariffs on the basis of a comparison with the practice on comparable markets.

> *Investment.* 'National regulatory authorities shall take into account the investment made by the operator.'[114] *Reasonable return.* 'National regulatory authorities shall . . . allow him a reasonable rate of return on adequate capital employed, taking into account the risks involved.'[115] *Enhance competition.* 'National regulatory authorities shall ensure that any cost recovery mechanism or pricing methodology that is mandated serves to promote efficiency and sustainable competition and maximise consumer benefits.'[116] *Suggestion.* '[N]ational regulatory authorities may . . . take account of prices available in comparable competitive markets.'[117]

3.137 **Costs.** These indications are not very extensive, and even give NRAs contradictory instructions. Costs may be assessed using historical or current values. An obligation to use historical costs seems to flow from two requirements in the regulation, that the investment must be taken into account and that a reasonable rate of return must be ensured. The need to enhance competition by contrast seems to suggest that costs are to be evaluated on the basis of current costs.[118] The requirement relating to competition is echoed in the suggestion in the new framework that comparable markets be used to determine appropriate interconnection tariffs.[119]

3.138 **Instruments adopted by the Commission on interconnection pricing.** As can be seen, the provisions concerning tariffs and costs do not introduce clear-cut rules. This may raise significant issues, because these aspects are important for the

---

[113] In that perspective, the costs originally incurred by the operator are introduced into the system. This is by contrast to the replacement costs, ie the costs that would have to be incurred today if the network had to be replaced. Replacement costs are traditionally lower, because new technologies have made it less expensive to install and develop networks.

[114] Access Directive, Art 13(1), second sentence.

[115] ibid, Art 13(1), second sentence. See also ibid, Art 13(3), first sentence.

[116] ibid, Art 13(2), first sentence.   [117] ibid, Art 13(2), second sentence.

[118] Competition indeed does not make it possible for undertakings to base their cost assessment on past values. If they do not want to lose customers, they have to fix prices taking into account the tariffs proposed by competitors. This always implies that the assets are only valued at their current value. These aspects are discussed at paras 3.189–3.212, where the criteria set forth by the Commission for cost assessment in one communication and two recommendations are examined.

[119] This suggestion corresponds to the method used under the old regulatory framework. At that time, the Commission considered that tariffs should be based on long-run average incremental costs. It however observed that research concerning the economic models to calculate these costs was not sufficiently advanced. Its proposal was then to calculate tariffs taking into account the 'best practices' encountered within the Union. On these aspects, see later the discussion on the communication and the two recommendations issued by the Commission on interconnection pricing, at paras 3.189–3.212.

development of a competitive market. Given the margin for manoeuvre left to them in the implementation of these provisions, the NRAs might be expected to turn to the Commission for guidance. At the present time, the Commission has issued no instruction as to how pricing obligations should be implemented. There is however little doubt that, should it be asked for guidance on these issues by market participants or NRAs, it would restate the position it has taken in various instruments adopted under the old framework. These instruments—one communication and two recommendations—are examined in a later section, where the relation between the NRF and other provisions on pricing are analysed.

Power to impose changes to the reference offer.   A power is granted to NRAs to **3.139** impose obligations aiming at fairness and reasonableness in access. This power entitles NRAs to modify the conditions offered by undertakings with significant market power in order to make them more compatible with the objectives sought in the regulatory framework. A similar possibility is set out with respect to reference offers. Pursuant to the regulation, authorities may impose changes to reference offers where they consider it appropriate. Again, these powers may not be exercised in arbitrary fashion, but are subject to basic regulatory principles which are of general application as regards public action in the regulatory framework.

> *Access Directive, Article 9(2).* 'The national regulatory authority shall, *inter alia*, be able to impose changes to the reference offers to give effect to obligations imposed under this [Access] Directive.'[120]

Modification of a reference offer.   A scenario where a reference offer is modified **3.140** may unfold as follows. Suppose an undertaking is obliged to publish. Where, following publication of a reference offer, market participants and possibly even the NRA notice that an obligation imposed pursuant to the European regulation has not been respected, the reputation of the undertaking concerned may be affected and continued market activity, as well as relations with other market players, made more difficult. In addition to this general market-based mechanism, a regulatory power is granted to the NRA to take action whenever, on the basis of a published reference offer, it realises that an obligation has been infringed. Pursuant to the regulation, the authority may impose changes to the reference offer so as to ensure the elimination of the infringement.

(6) Offer must be transparent

Obligation to publish information.   Obligations may be imposed on under- **3.141** takings with significant market power in order to ensure access under appropriate

---

[120] The situations where these obligations are not complied with by an undertaking may give an indication of a pattern as regards this undertaking. As they observe that rules are not respected by this undertaking, other undertakings may fear that they will not be treated properly either if they deal with it. They may thus be reluctant to engage in relations with that undertaking.

conditions. To these obligations, the regulation adds measures that are aimed at verifying whether these obligations are indeed complied with.[121] These measures mainly take the form of a duty to make information available. Here again, it is a principle of the reform that markets will function better if appropriate information is provided and that authorities will be able to perform their tasks better when they also receive an appropriate level of information.

3.142 **Information to be provided.**   Pursuant to the regulation, undertakings with significant market power may be compelled to publish information regarding access. This obligation is introduced in a general provision.[122] Where an NRA decides to make use of this general provision, it must specify the information to be published. In this context, financial information may be requested from undertakings with significant market power. Publication may also be ordered as regards technical information. Finally, the undertakings concerned may be required to provide data as to the terms and conditions under which they grant access.

> *Access Directive, Article 9(1).* 'National regulatory authorities may . . . impose obligations for transparency in relation to interconnection and/or access, requiring operators to make public specified information, such as accounting information, technical specifications, network characteristics, terms and conditions for supply and use, and prices.'[123]

3.143 **General reference offer.**   In some instances NRAs may go so far as to request the publication of reference offers by undertakings with significant market power. Reference offers are offers where operators specify in detail the terms and conditions under which access may be obtained to the facilities under their control. Players seeking access may refer to these offers in order to know what conditions would apply to them if they were to deal with the suppliers in question. They can compare offers and choose the most attractive. Another purpose is to obtain data from which it is possible to determine whether candidates are treated alike or otherwise. In this regard, the publication of reference offers appears a useful complement to a prohibition on discrimination between undertakings seeking access. For this reason the two measures are presented in combination in the regulation. In this context, an obligation to publish a reference offer may thus be regarded as a tool to compel network operators to apply the same terms and conditions to all access-seekers. Should the principle of non-discrimination not be applied, the disadvantaged access-seeker will have data to produce in court. The same

---

[121] Through that mechanism, two sorts of regulatory layer are created. On the first layer are material obligations concerning the behaviour of undertakings. On the second are obligations aiming at ensuring that the first, main obligations, are complied with.

[122] More specific provisions are examined in the following paragraphs and concern special forms of information to be provided.

[123] It is important to note the wide scope that is given to that obligation to publish information. The data mentioned earlier are only examples. The terms used in the provision ('such as') imply that no limit is imposed on what the national authorities may require to be published.

applies to NRAs, which will then have all the necessary information to decide whether sanctions should be applied.

> *Access Directive, Article 9(2).* '[W]here an operator has obligations of non-discrimination, national regulatory authorities may require that operator to publish a reference offer . . . giving a description of the relevant offerings broken down into components according to market needs, and the associated terms and conditions including prices.'[124]

Reference offer for access to the local loop.   Undertakings controlling access **3.144** to the local loop must publish a reference offer ensuring that access-seekers know what conditions will apply to them. The publication of a reference offer also makes it possible to compare the conditions offered by the operator to its partners, subsidiaries or services, as well as to undertakings that have no relation with it or are even competitors. Obligations concerning the publication of a reference offer for access to the local loop are examined at paras 3.147–3.157.

Reference offer linked to an obligation of non-discrimination.   Pursuant to **3.145** the European regulation, a requirement to publish a reference offer must be imposed on undertakings subject to an obligation not to discriminate. The information published as a result of this obligation may serve in comparisons carried out to detect possible differentiation made between undertakings despite similar circumstances.

> *Access Directive, Article 9(2).* '[W]here an operator has obligations of non-discrimination, national regulatory authorities may require that operator to publish a reference offer, . . . giving a description of the relevant offerings broken down into components according to market needs, and the associated terms and conditions including prices.'

Power to determine what information must be published, and how.   It is for **3.146** NRAs to determine what information must be published and how publication must take place. In general, the authorities have a general mandate to organise further the obligation to publish. The same power appears to be granted as regards obligations deriving from transparency. Where they make use of these powers, NRAs must comply with the general obligations imposed on them, particularly the basic regulatory principles.

> *Access Directive, Article 9(3).* 'National regulatory authorities may specify the precise information to be made available, the level of detail required and the manner of publication.'

---

[124] The formulation used in that provision may create the impression that an obligation to impose the publication of a reference offer is limited to cases where a prohibition of non-discrimination is implied. In our view, such an interpretation would not be correct. On the basis of the general provision concerning publication, NRAs are indeed allowed to impose duties of the same nature. Through the combination which is made of the two measures, the regulation indeed appears to encourage national authorities to impose a reference offer as soon as discrimination is prohibited.

(7) Access must be provided to the local loop

3.147 **Specific regulation for the local loop.** Access to the local loop raises significant issues, as network competition is limited on the last segment of the network between the main distribution frame and the subscriber's premises. The limitation of network competition on that segment makes it all the more necessary to ensure access to that facility. As stated above, terms and conditions must be reasonable so that effective use can be made of the right of access; in addition, the non-discrimination principle applies in order to ensure that competition is not distorted. Any such distortion would lead in the final instance to the elimination of undertakings from the market and thus to the weakening of competition. Another danger flowing from discrimination is that undertakings are not treated according to their merits, which must be avoided in an environment where efficiency is sought. The importance of the local loop has led the European legislator to adopt specific rules aimed at organising this segment of the network. General provisions have been included in the Access Directive, while more specific rules have been set out in a Regulation on the subject. Various recommendations have also been adopted. They introduce important principles although they naturally do not have the same binding force as a regulation or decision.

3.148 **Obligation to provide a detailed reference offer.** The Access Directive grants to the NRAs the power to impose the publication of a reference offer on undertakings controlling the local loop. In other areas where a reference offer may be imposed, the conditions to be set out in the offer are left to the discretion of the NRAs. The subject matter is, however, so important that the European legislator has deemed it necessary to regulate it in detail. The rules are included in Annex II to the Access Directive. Reference is made to this Annex in Article 9(4) of that directive.

> *Access Directive, Article 9(4).* '[W]here an operator has obligations . . . concerning unbundled access to the twisted metallic pair local loop, national regulatory authorities shall ensure the publication of a reference offer containing at least the elements set out in Annex II.'[125]

3.149 **Various kinds of access.** Annex II explains various concepts relating to access to the local loop. These concepts correspond to the different kinds of access that may be granted. In some instances, access is provided to the full frequency spectrum of the twisted metallic pair. Access is then said to be 'fully unbundled'. In terms of service provision, this means that players obtaining access have the technical possibility of offering any sort of service they want via the local loop. In other circumstances, access-seekers have access only to part of the frequency spectrum.

---

[125] The insertion, in an Annex, of the conditions to be mentioned in the reference offer provides more room for manoeuvre if these conditions must be modified. Annex II may be modified in the light of market and technological developments. See Access Directive, Art 9, para 5.

This situation is encountered where the network operator continues to use the local loop for the provision, itself, of telephony services to the public. This use does not imply that other undertakings have no access to the local loop. Their access is, however, limited, and they may only provide services using other frequencies on the metallic pair. In these circumstances, access is said to be 'shared'. These two hypotheses—full unbundling and shared access—are referred to as 'unbundling of the local loop'. This last expression must thus be interpreted as a general concept referring to local loop access without specifying what sort of access is granted.

> *Full unbundled access.* ' "[F]ull unbundled access to the local loop" means the provision to a beneficiary of access to the local loop . . . of the notified operator authorising the use of the full frequency spectrum of the twisted metallic pair.' *Shared access.* ' "[S]hared access to the local loop" means the provision to a beneficiary of access to the local loop . . . of the notified operator, authorising the use of the non-voice band frequency spectrum of the twisted metallic pair; the local loop continues to be used by the notified operator to provide the telephone service to the public.' *Unbundled access.* ' "[U]nbundled access to the local loop" means full unbundled access to the local loop and shared access to the local loop.'[126]

Information on how to obtain access.   Annex II provides that information must   **3.150** be given in the reference offer as to how access may be obtained. *(a)* First, information must be given as to the elements to which access is granted, ie full or shared access. *(b)* Second, information must be provided as to how the access-seeker may physically enter sites where access is granted.[127] *(c)* Third, technical information must be provided as to how access may occur.[128] Various technologies are used in networks, and access-seekers are not necessarily aware of the specific technology used on the local loop. In order to avoid technical difficulties, information must be provided on the technical conditions applicable to access and use of the local loops including the technical characteristics of the twisted metallic pair. *(d)* Finally, general information must be provided on how the relation between the operator and access-seeker will be structured, in particular the arrangements for ordering and for the actual supply of loops. In this context, special emphasis is placed on usage restrictions, which must be spelled out with clarity to avoid misunderstandings after the agreement has been signed.

> *Conditions for access.* The reference offer must contain information on the following items: '1. Network elements to which access is offered covering in particular the following elements:(a) access to local loops; (b) access to non-voice band frequency spectrum of a local loop, in the case of shared access to the local loop; 2. Information concerning the locations of physical access sites, availability of local loops in specific

---

[126] ibid, Annex II, letters (a) to (d).
[127] ibid, Annex II, letter A(2). For instance, personnel of the parties seeking access must be able to enter sites where network segments can be interconnected or where equipment for the provision of services may be installed.   [128] ibid, Annex II, letter A(3).

parts of the access network; 3. Technical conditions related to access and use of local loops, including the technical characteristics of the twisted metallic pair in the local loop; 4. Ordering and provisioning procedures, usage restrictions.'[129]

3.151 **Conditions for co-location services.**   Obligations regarding access may imply that, in some circumstances, operators are compelled to share premises or physical locations. The regulation uses the term 'co-location' to refer to a situation where a fixed facility is shared by two or several undertakings. This sharing of locations may occur in a variety of situations—for instance where single antennas are used by two or more mobile operators. In the context of the local loop, co-location is particularly important, since access to the local loop implies that undertakings share given locations, for instance the main distribution frame. To cope with this special situation, information must be made available in the reference offer as to how the operator proposes that facilities should be shared.

> *Co-location services.* The reference offer must contain information on the following items: '1. Information on the notified operator's relevant site. 2. Co-location options at the sites indicated under point 1 (including physical co-location and, as appropriate, distant co-location and virtual co-location). 3. Equipment characteristics: restrictions, if any, on equipment that can be co-located. 4. Security issues: measures put in place by notified operators to ensure the security of their locations. 5. Access conditions for staff of competitive operators. 6. Safety standards. 7. Rules for the allocation of space where co-location space is limited. 8. Conditions for beneficiaries to inspect the locations at which physical co-location is available, or sites where co-location has been refused on grounds of lack of capacity.'[130]

3.152 **Current situation in the Member States.**   In the Eighth Implementation Report, the Commission notes that there are currently difficulties concerning co-location in the Member States. An issue is that, in some circumstances, separate co-location space is too expensive. A solution could be that the various undertakings concerned could share the same space, or even equipment. That possibility raises security concerns, however. There is also a risk that business confidentiality may be breached. Where a new entrant is approached by potential clients, that entrant has to enquire with the incumbent about the technical feasibility of serving these clients. The incumbent may then address a better offer to the potential clients.

> *Eighth Implementation Report, 28.* 'New entrants in a number of Member States are still experiencing problems in the practical implementation of co-location, particularly the conditions for effective co-location in the site of the incumbent (Germany, Ireland, Portugal).' 'One issue . . . is whether application of th[e] principle [non-discrimination] should lead to "co-mingling" instead of separate collocation, particularly where a new entrant only requires a relatively small surface area and where separate co-location space is proportionately much more expensive.' '[T]here are some clear security concerns related to the siting of exchanges and the release of access codes.' 'The pricing of the rental of co-location space in the incumbent's

---

[129] Access Directive, Annex II, Letter A.   [130] ibid, Annex II, Letter B.

premises raises difficulties.' 'The Commission intends to examine this question further with the NRAs.' 'Another problem is the risk of discrimination where the marketing division of an incumbent may have access to information about customers who are thinking of changing provider when a new entrants seeks information about the addressing and technical feasibility of those potential clients.'

Conditions for access to information systems.   Access does not only mean that **3.153**
equipment or network segments are to be connected to the facilities controlled by the network operator. These facilities are increasingly equipped with software. As stated above, access may be ordered to information resources and computer-based functions where they are controlled by undertakings with significant market power. Information must be provided by these undertakings as to how access may be obtained to these supplementary resources.

Information systems. The reference offer must contain information on: 'Conditions for access to notified operator's operational support systems, information systems or databases for pre-ordering, provisioning, ordering, maintenance and repair requests and billing.'[131]

General contractual conditions.   Finally, Annex II specifies the contractual con- **3.154**
ditions regarding access on which information must be provided in the reference offer. *(a)* First, information must be given about the tariffs charged by the network operator. Tariffs are to be mentioned for each feature or function to which access may be sought. *(b)* Second, information must be provided on the terms and conditions that are generally associated with this sort of contract. The regulation refers, in this regard, to 'standard contract terms'. These terms may include information about the compensation that would have to be paid in case obligations are not complied with. *(c)* Third, access-seekers must be informed about the quality of service they can expect from the operator giving access. This includes indications as to the lead time for the operator to respond to requests. It also implies information about the quality access-seekers may expect for the transmission of their service. Information must in addition be given as to how faults would be resolved and the kind of procedures to be used to return to a normal level of service.

Supply conditions. The reference offer must contain information on the following items: '1. Lead time for responding to requests for supply of services and facilities; service level agreements, fault resolution, procedures to return to a normal level of service and quality of service parameters. 2. Standard contract terms, including, where appropriate, compensation provided for failure to meet lead times. 3. Prices or pricing formulae for each feature, function and facility listed above.'[132]

Local Loop Regulation.   Prior to adopting the NRF, and after bringing forward **3.155**
the Interconnection Directive, the Council and Parliament Regulation adopted

---

[131] ibid, Annex II, Letter C.   [132] ibid, Annex II, Letter D.

a regulation dealing specifically with access to the local loop. It is important to determine whether the obligations contained in that regulation remain applicable and to what extent they compare with those in the new framework. The specific instruments previously adopted with respect to the local loop are, in chronological order: *(a)* Commission Recommendation (EC) 2000/417 on unbundled access to the local loop: enabling the competitive provision of a full range of electronic communications services including broadband multimedia and high-speed internet, and *(b)* European Parliament and Council Regulation (EC) 2887/2000 on unbundled access to the local loop.

3.156   **The relation between the various instruments.**   Of the two measures, attention should clearly be focused on the regulation as a binding instrument; a recommendation has no such force. The regulation and the recommendation are however inspired by a similar philosophy and contain provisions that are in substance similar. The recommendation was adopted in the first instance by the European Commission to respond to the need for an instrument officially stating that access to the local loop should be unbundled. The Commission was later able to convince the Parliament and Council of the need for more forceful action, and the principles formulated in the recommendation were carried over into the regulation. The recommendation now has only historical value.[133]

The link between the regulation and the Access Directive is similar; the provisions of the regulation have been taken over in the Access Directive. However, the obligations contained in the regulation remain applicable during a transitional period consisting of the time necessary to assess competition and decide on the basis of that assessment whether the obligations in question should be maintained, withdrawn or replaced by the obligations introduced by the NRF.[134]

As shown in the table below, there is full consistency in the obligations that have been introduced in the recommendation, the regulation and the Access Directive

---

[133] It may still be used, however, as a background document to obtain information about some of the rules which have been later taken over in the regulation—and as a matter of fact in the Access Directive. The recommendation is particularly useful for the detail it provides about the information that must be granted by designated operators in the reference offer. See the Annex attached to the recommendation. That Annex corresponds in substance to the Annex included in the regulation with the same purpose, as well as to Annex II to the Access Directive. It, however, contains more details and explanation about the information to be provided by the operators.

[134] The application of the transitional mechanism is not provided in the body of the directive, but in the Preamble. This does not seem, however, to have any application on the binding force that may be recognised in the obligations contained in the regulation during the transitional period. See the Access Directive, Preamble, recital 12. 'In order to ensure continuity of existing agreements and to avoid a legal vacuum, it is necessary to ensure that obligations for access and interconnection imposed under [the old regulatory framework] . . . are initially carried over into the NRF, but are subject to immediate review in the light of prevailing market conditions. Such a review should also extend to those organisations covered by European Parliament and Council Regulation (EC) 2887/2000 on unbundled access to the local loop.'

as regards unbundled access to the local loop.[135] The changes have been limited, ultimately, to the legal basis on which these obligations are founded. As concerns the present situation, the obligations are based on a directive, which must be implemented by the Member States for the obligations to be given effect within the national legal order. As stated above, these obligations were previously directly applicable through their enactment in the regulation.

Correlation access to the local loop   **3.157**

	Interconnection Directive	Rules from the Interconnection Directive which are maintained in the NRF for as long as no determination has been made	NRF rules
General			
Definitions	Article 2	—	Article 2
Member States must eliminate restrictions on access and interconnection	Article 3(1)	—	Article 3(1) Article 3(2) (unbundling)
Member States must ensure access, interconnection and interoperability	Article 3(2)	—	Article 5(1) (duties of NRAs)
Powers and responsibilities of NRAs	Article 9	—	Article 5
Essential requirements	Article 10	—	Partly taken over in Article 5 and in the Framework Directive, Article 8
General obligations on undertakings			
Confidentiality of information	Article 3(3); Article 6 (d)	Article 6(d) maintained	Article 4(3)
Rights and duties of undertakings to obtain and grant interconnection	Article 4(1)	Maintained	Article 4(1)
Determination of undertakings on which special obligations may be imposed	Article 4(2) and (3)	Maintained	Article 8
Obligations			
Non-discrimination	Article 6(a)	Maintained	Article 10
Transparency	Article 6(b) and (c)	Maintained	Article 9
Price control	Article 7(1)	Maintained	Article 13
	Article 7(2) (reference offer)	Maintained	Article 9(2) and (4)
	Article 7(3) (unbundling)	Maintained	Article 3(2) and Article 9(2)

(cont.)

---

[135] At the time the provisions were formulated in the recommendation, they did not have any binding force. The purpose was, however, clearly to indicate to the Member States what they ought to do in order to avoid more affirmative action. One can thus say that a material constraint was exercised through the adoption of the recommendation.

	Interconnection Directive	Rules from the Interconnection Directive which are maintained in the NRF for as long as no determination has been made	NRF rules
Accounting separation	Article 8	Maintained	Article 11
Co-location and facility sharing	Article 11	Maintained	Article 12(1), subparagraph (2)(f); Framework Directive, Article 12
Numbering	Article 12	Maintained	Number portability: Universal Service Directive, Article 30; Distribution of numbers among undertakings: Framework Directive, Article 10
Technical standards	Article 13	—	Framework Directive, Article 17; for interoperability, Access Directive, Preamble, para 9 and Article 5(2)
Publication and access to information	Article 14	Maintained	Article 15
—	—	—	Provisions have been added on conditional access systems and digital radio/television services. See Article 4(2); Article 5(1), subpara 2(b); Article 6; and Annex I. These provisions have mainly been taken over from Directive (EC) 95/47.

(8) Non-discrimination in access conditions

3.158 **Two separate prohibitions.** Another obligation that may be imposed on dominant operators as regards access is non-discrimination. An obligation of non-discrimination is imposed in the regulation on all undertakings, independently of any significant market power they may have acquired in the market. This may be due to the importance that egalitarian principles have in society. Pursuant to the non-discrimination principle, business actors must be treated equally whenever they and the circumstances in which they are operating are similar. This principle is also stated in connection with obligations that may be imposed on undertakings with significant market power. A specific provision is devoted to non-discrimination in that context.

3.159 **The difference between these prohibitions.** The question is to determine to what extent the obligation of non-discrimination imposed on dominant undertakings differs from that imposed on all undertakings. The coexistence of the same obligation in two contexts indeed raises issues of interpretation. The reason for introducing two separate prohibitions is probably that more stringent obligations may be imposed on undertakings where competition is impaired. This can be deduced from the terms used in the Access Directive, under which *obligations* (plural) may be imposed by NRAs on undertakings with significant market power on the basis of the principle of non-discrimination. The use of the plural in a provision regarding powerful undertakings must probably be interpreted as implying that NRAs may derive all sorts of consequences from the principle of non-discrimination and may give to these consequences the status of obligations.

> *Access Directive, Article 10(1).* 'A national regulatory authority may . . . impose obligations of non-discrimination, in relation to interconnection and/or access.'

All access-seekers to be treated as third parties.   More liberty thus seems to   **3.160** be given to NRAs in contexts where competition is impaired. An example of a situation where that liberty could be used is presented in the Access Directive. Pursuant to Article 10, the principle of non-discrimination does not merely require that equivalent conditions must be applied in equivalent circumstances to undertakings providing equivalent services. Where it is applied to undertakings with significant market power, the principle also implies an obligation for these undertakings to treat as third parties all those seeking access. More specifically, these undertakings are, pursuant to regulation, under an obligation to extend to other parties the conditions they grant to their partners, subsidiaries or even their own departments entrusted with the activities for which access is sought.

> *Access Directive, Article 10(2).* 'Obligations of non-discrimination shall ensure . . . that the operator applies equivalent conditions in equivalent circumstances to other undertakings providing equivalent services, and provides services and information to others under the same conditions and of the same quality as it provides for its own services, or those of its subsidiaries or partners.'

Reference offer.   In order to ensure compliance with obligations relating to non-   **3.161** discrimination, NRAs are authorised to impose on dominant undertakings an obligation to publish a reference offer. This reference offer will make it possible to verify that conditions offered to those seeking access are similar to those provided to partners or even to the department which is entrusted with a task similar to that envisaged by the provider within the organisation itself. The reference offer must be detailed, so as to allow comparison on specific elements. A consequence of the comparison is that amendments may be imposed by NRAs, in order to eliminate all discrimination.

> *Access Directive, Article 9(2).* '[W]here an operator has obligations of non-discrimination, national regulatory authorities may require that operator to publish a reference offer . . . giving a description of the relevant offerings broken down into components

according to market needs, and the associated terms and conditions including prices. The national regulatory authority shall, *inter alia*, be able to impose changes to reference offers to give effect to obligations imposed under this Directive.'[136]

3.162 **Consolidated Services Directive.** A similar emphasis is placed in the Consolidated Services Directive on the obligation for dominant undertakings to avoid any discrimination. The situation envisaged in that instrument is the dominance exercised by an undertaking that is vertically integrated. As the competence of the Commission is limited to these undertakings, only public undertakings are taken into account.[137]

> *Consolidated Services Directive, Article 3.* 'Member States, shall ensure that vertically integrated public undertakings which provide electronic communications networks and which are in a dominant position do not discriminate in favour of their own activities.'

(9) Accounting obligations

3.163 **Liberty of undertakings and limitations placed on that liberty.** In principle, undertakings are free to choose the accounting system they consider appropriate to their activities in the context in which they operate. This is in line with the basic precept that, in normal circumstances, market players must have the freedom necessary to develop their operations subject only to market forces. Limitations are however imposed to ensure that activities are carried out in a manner compatible with the objectives laid down in the Regulatory Framework. These limitations are varied in their nature, and normally concern exclusively undertakings with significant market power; they are examined in the following paragraphs.

3.164 **Obligation to adopt a cost-based system.** NRAs may impose on undertakings having significant market power an obligation to install accounting systems capable of determining input costs. An accounting system of that kind is intended to provide the undertakings involved with the management tools necessary to set tariffs at an appropriate level in a liberalised environment. In this regard, it should not be forgotten that most telephone network operators, to which obligations regarding access often apply, were until recently administrations or public undertakings enjoying monopoly conditions. In such a situation, there was no need for them to resort to a cost accounting system. The reason was that the main purpose of these undertakings was not to realise a profit—ie obtain a return through tariffs fixed at a higher level than costs. Their purpose

---

[136] Access Directive, Art 9(2).

[137] The Consolidated Services Directive has been adopted by the Commission on the basis of Art 86 EC. That provision concerns special or exclusive rights granted by Member States, as well as public undertakings or undertakings to which special missions of general interest have been granted.

was rather to provide services in conformity with policy objectives. As they are now placed in a new context as a result of the reform and the adoption of the Regulatory Framework, these undertakings need to change the tools on which their decisions were based in the past.

Tool for verification.   In addition to providing an adequate management tool **3.165** for undertakings, the adoption of a cost accounting system is also important for regulatory authorities. Through such a system, regulators are provided with an instrument allowing them to verify that certain obligations are complied with. Several provisions have been examined in the previous paragraphs, pursuant to which NRAs are allowed to impose obligations where costs play a central role. Among them is the prohibition on charging tariffs that would be excessive or engaging in price squeeze activity.[138] Another obligation is to avoid discrimination in access conditions,[139] or cross-subsidising one market from another.[140] All these obligations or prohibitions imply that, in order to monitor compliance, regulators and undertakings must be able to identify costs.

> *Excessive prices or price squeeze.* 'A national regulatory authority may . . . impose obligations . . . concerning cost accounting systems relating to . . . price controls . . . in situations where a market analysis indicates that . . . the operator concerned might sustain prices at an excessively high level, or apply a price squeeze, to the detriment of end users.'[141] *Discrimination and unfair cross subsidies.* '[A] national regulatory authority may require a vertically integrated company to make transparent its wholesale prices and its internal transfer prices *inter alia* to ensure compliance where there is a requirement for non-discrimination . . . . or, where necessary, to prevent unfair cross-subsidy.'[142]

Obligation to keep separate accounts.   A constraint may also be imposed on **3.166** undertakings with significant market power to hold separate accounts for certain activities. The provision is formulated in rather broad terms, with the consequence that NRAs are authorised to impose accounting separation in an array of circumstances. Emphasis is, however, placed in the NRF on one situation where separation is particularly warranted, that is, when an undertaking with significant

---

[138] That prohibition has a clear link with costs. Excessive prices are indeed defined as tariffs without a reasonable relation to costs. As for price squeezing, it is a strategy whereby an undertaking forces a competitor into a situation where prices are lower than costs.

[139] In that context, undertakings seeking access must be treated in the same fashion. Differences may only be explained by underlying differences in the costs incurred in the provision of access. Suppose the connection of one network to another implies additional expenses, due for instance to a difference in the technologies used on the two installations. That technological difference will imply a cost difference, which may be used in order to establish different access charges.

[140] That latter prohibition has a link with costs. In order to identify possible transfers, costs must be allocated among activities. One is only capable of showing that funds have been transferred between markets if one can demonstrate that the sums should normally be allocated to certain activities and that that allocation has not been respected where the transfer has been made.

[141] Access Directive, Art 13(1).   [142] ibid, Art 11(1).

market power is vertically integrated. Vertical integration is a characteristic of an undertaking which is present on various markets, where these markets are related to each other to the extent that a presence on one market may help the undertaking to develop activities on another. In a situation of vertical integration, material obligations may be imposed, and the undertakings concerned may be compelled to extend to third parties the terms and conditions they make available to associated undertakings or even to their own services carrying out the activity in question. A prohibition may also be imposed on the transfer of funds from one market to another. In both instances, monitoring by the undertaking and the regulator requires that costs relating to all activities concerned must be identified with accuracy. As a result, accounting separation is necessary for all of the activities concerned.

> *Access Directive, Article 11(1).* 'A national regulatory authority may . . . impose obligations for accounting separation in relation to specified activities related to interconnection and/or access. In particular, a national regulatory authority may require a vertically integrated company to make transparent its wholesale prices and its internal transfer prices *inter alia* to ensure compliance where there is a requirement for non-discrimination.'[143]

3.167 **Criteria which the accounting systems must satisfy.** The accounting choices made by undertakings with significant market power must promote efficiency, sustainable competition and consumer benefits. These objectives are formulated in general terms in the framework, terms so general that undertakings and regulators may have difficulty in taking concrete instructions from them. A general principle is at least formulated that a check may be carried out by NRAs on the choices made by undertakings as regards their accounting systems. Undertakings are also required to justify their choices—and this justification must be in line with the objectives mentioned above. In other words, undertakings must be in a position to demonstrate that their accounting choices do indeed promote the objectives of the NRF.

> *Access Directive, Article 13(2).* 'National regulatory authorities shall ensure that any cost recovery mechanism or pricing methodology . . . serves to promote efficiency and sustainable competition and maximise consumer benefits.'[144]

3.168 **Publication of information concerning the accounting system.** Undertakings with significant market power may also be required to publish information

---

[143] Vertically integrated undertakings are also aimed at in the Consolidated Services Directive adopted by the Commission. Pursuant to that instrument, vertically integrated undertakings must refrain from exercising discrimination. The provision is limited to public undertakings, as the competence of the Commission is limited to special or exclusive rights, as well as to public undertakings or undertakings with a special mission relating to a service of general interest. See Consolidated Services Directive, Art 3. 'Member States, shall ensure that vertically integrated public undertakings which provide electronic communications networks and which are in a dominant position do not discriminate in favour of their own activities.'

[144] Access Directive, Art 13(2). There appears to be a certain ambiguity in the provision. According to the terms used by the European legislator, the obligation is mainly imposed on

regarding the accounting system they have chosen. The objective here is to compel them to explain clearly to all interested parties the choices they have made. The obligation concerning publication does not apply to the day-to-day decisions made by undertakings, but to the fundamental principles on which these decisions are based. Pursuant to the framework, the accounting system chosen by the undertaking must also be described: the main categories where costs are to be allocated must be presented, together with the rules that will be followed in the allocation of costs among these categories.

> *Access Directive.* 'National regulatory authorities shall ensure that . . . a description of the cost accounting system is made publicly available, showing at least the main categories under which costs are grouped and the rules used for the allocation of costs.'[145] 'National regulatory authorities may . . . impose obligations for transparency in relation to interconnection and/or access, requiring operators to make public specified information, such as accounting information.'[146]

This measure is intended to expose the operators concerned to scrutiny by market participants. Where an operator installs a system that differs widely from the standard in the market, this will be rapidly picked up by other market participants. Reactions will come from parties seeking access to the network operated by that undertaking and a claim is likely to be made that the tariffs are not appropriate because they are not founded on an adequate basis. Publication also provides NRAs with information allowing them to monitor the principles guiding the accounting system chosen by an undertaking. Finally, one should not underestimate the influence publication may have on the behaviour of investors. Where an operator chooses an accounting system that differs from those selected by other market participants, investors may begin to ask questions, leading to a loss of confidence.

Availability of accounting records—Confidentiality. An additional limitation **3.169** takes the form of an obligation to submit accounting records, an obligation that may be imposed on undertakings with significant market power. Pursuant to the framework, NRAs may request access to accounting records kept by undertakings with significant market power. When they receive these records, NRAs are in a position to verify whether obligations have been respected or otherwise. No exception seems to be provided. This appears to mean that no undertaking with significant market power may refuse access to these documents, under any circumstance. The framework furthermore grants NRAs the right to publish accounting records wherever they feel this could help bring about the objectives pursued in the reform. That possibility is however constrained by several limitations.

---

authorities. Pursuant to the provision, the cost recovery mechanism or pricing methodology 'that is mandated' must conform with the said objectives. In our view, the obligation however concerns accounting choices made by all parties.

[145] ibid, Art 13(4).　　　　　　　　　　　　　　　　　　　[146] ibid, Art 9(1).

Publication may occur only where it contributes to the attainment of an open and competitive market. Furthermore, national and European rules regarding confidentiality must be complied with.

> *Access Directive, Article 11(2).* '[T]o facilitate the verification of compliance with obligations of transparency and non-discrimination, national regulatory authorities shall have the power to require that accounting records, including data on revenues received from third parties, are provided on request. National regulatory authorities may publish such information as would contribute to an open and competitive market, while respecting national and Community rules on commercial confidentiality.'

3.170 **Possibility for third parties to use other data.**   Another restriction imposed is that an accounting system installed by an undertaking with significant market power may be set aside as a result of the use by other parties of other data to contest the decisions made by that undertaking.

Suppose an undertaking makes a choice in favour of a given accounting system. That undertaking is bound by the data contained in this system. This implies, for instance, that the costs identified in the system can be used against the undertaking by an adversary in litigation. These costs can also be used by an NRA as a basis to demonstrate that tariffs are excessive or not appropriate compared to normal business behaviour.

The question arises whether other parties are bound to the same extent by the accounting data provided by the undertaking. Where an NRA considers that tariffs charged by that undertaking are excessive, should it be bound by the decisions made by that undertaking as regards costs identified in the accounting system? Or can the NRA establish costs using another method? Compelling NRAs—and other parties—to use the accounting choices made by an operator would in fact make them dependent upon the choices made by that undertaking. This would place the SMP operator in a position where it could influence in advance the assessments made regarding its tariffs. The only obligation that would then remain on it would be to have a consistent accounting system—even if that system did not correspond to normal business practice. To avoid this, the framework provides that NRAs are not bound by accounting choices made by market players, but can resort to other data in order to monitor the pricing strategy used by the undertakings in question. One possibility is to compare tariffs with those sustained by other undertakings in similar circumstances.

> *Access Directive.* 'For the purpose of calculating the cost of efficient provision of services, national regulatory authorities may use cost accounting methods independent of those used by the undertaking.'[147] '[N]ational regulatory

---

[147] Access Directive, Art 13(3). A question is whether this possibility may be used by other parties as well. Suppose a provider feels that access-related tariffs are excessive. Is such a provider bound by the decisions made by the operators as regards costs? Our feeling is that the reasoning developed

authorities may . . . take account of prices available in comparable competitive markets.'[148]

Burden of proof. A further limitation takes the form of an obligation on SMP **3.171** operators to justify accounting choices. This obligation to provide justification is organised in the framework around the allocation of the burden of proof among parties. An important issue in regard to tariffs is: who must demonstrate that tariffs are reasonable, ie neither excessive nor insufficient. Suppose an operator charges excessive tariffs for access to its network. Imagine that the proof of the excessive character of the tariffs is to be provided by an access-seeker.[149] The latter would have to establish the costs incurred by the operator and demonstrate that the return obtained by that undertaking was higher than that obtained in comparable business circumstances. In providing these elements, it would face severe difficulties, as it would not have access to all relevant information about the tariffs charged by the undertaking. In view of this difficulty, the European legislator decided that the burden of proof as regards tariffs should be placed on the undertaking providing access. Operators thus have to demonstrate that their tariffs are not unreasonable, where a claim is made to the contrary. To that effect, they have to establish their costs and show that the return they obtain in providing access is not unreasonable, taking into account the costs they face.

> *Access Directive.* 'Where an operator has an obligation regarding the cost orientation of its prices, the burden of proof that charges are derived from costs including a reasonable rate of return on investment shall lie with the operator concerned.'[150] 'National regulatory authorities may require an operator to provide full justification for its prices.'[151]

Control by an independent and qualified body. A final limitation is that an **3.172** independent party must be appointed to verify that the accounting system is respected by undertakings on which accounting obligations have been imposed as a result of their significant market power. A statement must be issued every year by that body, to certify that the rules chosen by the undertakings concerned have been complied with.

> *Access Directive, Article 13(4).* 'Compliance with the cost accounting system shall be verified by a qualified independent body. A statement concerning compliance shall be published annually.'[152]

---

above concerning NRAs may be used for other parties—be they private or public—to have their decisions regarding costs and, as result, tariffs accepted.　　　　　[148] ibid, Art 13(2).

[149] A similar difficulty would be encountered by an NRA if that authority were to intervene in respect of excessive tariffs in a context where the burden of proof fell on it. Admittedly, the authority would have better access to information than another private party as a result, for instance, of the obligation to provide accounting records that may be imposed on undertakings with significant market power. It remains however easier for an authority, or a third party, to criticise proof provided by the network operator.　　　　　[150] Access Directive, Art 13(3).
　　[151] ibid, Art 13(3).　　　　[152] ibid, Art 13(4).

3.173 **Case law.** That provision does not differ from that which was included, with the same object, in the old regulatory framework. In connection with that old provision, a ruling of the ECJ should be mentioned. In *Commission v Belgium*,[153] the Commission argued that, under the regulatory framework, compliance with the cost accounting system must be verified and that a statement concerning compliance must be published annually. These requirements did not appear in the Belgian legislation. Belgium was, as a result, found against by the ECJ.

(10) Obligation to lease lines

3.174 **Obligation to lease lines.** An important factor for the development of markets for services is the possibility, for service providers, to rent, or lease, lines from network operators. With these leased lines, undertakings can provide their services to their customers. To ensure the availability of leased lines, the new regulatory framework provides that obligations to lease lines to service providers may be imposed on undertakings having significant market power. The steps preliminary to the imposition of these obligations are similar to those concerning other obligations imposed on such undertakings. First, an analysis must be made of the market. The question to be addressed in that analysis is whether, and to what extent, the market can be considered to be effectively competitive. The second step, after a lack of effective competition has been observed, is to identify the undertakings with significant market power on the markets concerned.

> *Universal Service Directive, Article 18(1).* 'Where, as a result of the market analysis . . . , a national regulatory authority determines that the market for the provision of part or all of the minimum set of leased lines is not effectively competitive, it shall identify undertakings with significant market power in the provision of those specific elements of the minimum set of leased lines services in all or part of its territory.'

3.175 **Technical specifications.** As stated above, one purpose of the obligation regarding leased lines is that a defined set of lines must be made available to undertakings needing them in order to provide their services. A constraint is that these lines must be compatible throughout the Community. Only if the lines are compatible is the provision of services throughout the Community possible. To ensure effective compatibility, the new regulatory framework empowers the Commission to determine technical specifications for the provision of these lines. These specifications may be modified, if necessary, by the Commission, in line with technical progress.

> *Universal Service Directive, Article 18(1).* 'The national regulatory authority shall impose obligations regarding the provision of the minimum set of leased lines, as identified in the list of standards published in the Official Journal of the European Communities in

---

[153] Case C-221/01 *Commission v Belgium* [2002] ECR I-7835.

accordance with . . . Directive 2002/21/EC (Framework Directive) . . . on such undertakings in relation to those specific leased line markets.' *Universal Service Directive, Article 18(3)*. 'The minimum set of leased lines with harmonised characteristics, and associated standards, shall be published in the Official Journal of the European Communities as part of the list of standards referred to in . . . Directive 2002/21/EC (Framework Directive). The Commission may adopt amendments necessary to adapt the minimum set of leased lines to new technical developments and to changes in market demand, including the possible deletion of certain types of leased line from the minimum set.'

Non-discrimination, costs and transparency. Under the new regulatory frame- **3.176** work, the leased lines referred to in the paragraph above must be provided in conformity with the principles of equality (non-discrimination), cost-oriented tariffs and transparency. Among these principles, two (equality, transparency) refer explicitly to the basic regulatory principles already analysed in this book. The third (cost-oriented tariffs) is related to another of these principles (objectivity).[154]

> *Universal Service Directive, Annex VII*. 'National regulatory authorities are to ensure that provision of the minimum set of leased lines . . . follows the basic principles of non-discrimination, cost orientation and transparency.'

Absence of discrimination. Under the principle of discrimination, undertak- **3.177** ings with significant market power must treat equally all requests for leased lines where these requests are similar. No distinction may be made between requests, depending on the identity of the undertakings ordering them. No preference may be given to partners, subsidiaries or even departments or divisions within the organisation of undertakings having significant market power.

> *Universal Service Directive, Annex VII, point (1)*. 'National regulatory authorities are to ensure that the organisations identified as having significant market power . . . adhere to the principle of non-discrimination when providing leased lines.' 'Those organisations are to apply similar conditions in similar circumstances to organisa- tions providing similar services, and are to provide leased lines to others under the same conditions and of the same quality as they provide for their own services, or those of their subsidiaries or partners, where applicable.'

Approval by NRAs. A corollary of the obligation to respect equality is that **3.178** undertakings with significant market power must ask for an authorisation, or approval, when they intend to make distinctions in the treatment granted to applicants. As is stated below, tariffs and financial conditions for access to the leased lines must be published. This ensures that all applicants have access to the

---

[154] Objectivity requires that the rules must be justified by an objective which is deemed legit- imate at European level. In this case, the obligation to base tariffs on costs can be associated with the goal of developing competition. In a competitive environment, tariffs are spontaneously based on costs as undertakings tend to fix their prices as close as possible to costs. Only where they follow that strategy may undertakings avoid being undercut by competitors and losing market share to the benefit of the latter.

same conditions. Under the new regulatory framework, any undertaking required to provide leased lines must obtain an authorisation, or approval, where it feels that the leased lines may not be provided under the conditions set forth in the list of tariffs published by that undertaking.

> *Universal Service Directive, Annex VII, point (3.2).* 'Where, in response to a particular request, an organisation identified as having significant market power . . . considers it unreasonable to provide a leased line in the minimum set under its published tariffs and supply conditions, it must seek the agreement of the national regulatory authority to vary those conditions in that case.'

3.179 **Cost orientation.** In addition to the obligations examined above, the leased lines identified under the new regulatory framework must be provided at tariffs based on costs. This does not imply that the tariffs must be equal to the costs. Surveillance is however carried out to ensure that the undertakings providing these lines do not obtain an excess profit. In case of excessive profit, public intervention will be carried out on the basis of sector-specific regulation and/or general competition law (Article 82 EC). That surveillance implies that the undertakings concerned must have an adequate accounting system. Information may be requested by the Commission from NRAs concerning the accounting system of undertakings having to provide a harmonised minimum set of leased lines in accordance with the principles laid down in the regulatory framework.

> *Universal Service Directive, Annex VII, point (2).* 'National regulatory authorities are, where appropriate, to ensure that tariffs for leased lines . . . follow the basic principles of cost orientation. To this end, national regulatory authorities are to ensure that undertakings identified as having significant market power . . . formulate and put in practice a suitable cost accounting system. National regulatory authorities are to keep available, with an adequate level of detail, information on the cost accounting systems applied by such undertakings. They are to submit this information to the Commission on request.'

3.180 **Transparency.** Information regarding access to leased lines must be published. As indicated above, this is a condition for access to occur properly. The plans envisaged by the applicant undertakings for the development of their activities would be undermined if they did not have a clear idea about the conditions under which access may be obtained. Furthermore, transparency is a condition for law enforcement. Only if they are aware of the access conditions imposed by undertakings with significant market power can the authorities monitor compliance with the applicable requirements.

3.181 **Technical information.** In order to ensure transparency, undertakings with significant market power may be required to publish information regarding the technical aspects of access.

> *Universal Service Directive, Annex VII, point (3.1).* 'National regulatory authorities are to ensure that the following information in respect of the minimum set

of leased lines . . . is published in an easily accessible form.' [1] 'Technical characteristics, including the physical and electrical characteristics as well as the detailed technical and performance specifications which apply at the network termination point.'

Tariffs.   Another obligation is to publish the tariffs at which lines may be leased.   **3.182**
Indications concerning tariffs must include information regarding the initial connection charge, the periodic rental charge and other elements which are taken into account by the undertaking with significant market power in order to establish the total price due.

> *Universal Service Directive, Annex VII, point (3.2)*. 'Tariffs, including the initial connection charges, the periodic rental charges and other charges. Where tariffs are differentiated, this must be indicated.'

Supply conditions.   All conditions other than technical or financial must   **3.183**
also be indicated. Among these conditions are the following: the procedure to be followed in order to obtain leased lines, the time necessary to obtain the lines, the period for which the use of the lines may be obtained, the time necessary to carry out repairs, and the procedures to be used in order to obtain refunds where appropriate.

> *Universal Service Directive, Annex VII, point (3.3)*. 'Supply conditions, including at least the following elements: information concerning the ordering procedure, the typical delivery period,[155] the contractual period,[156] the typical repair time,[157] the existing refund procedures.'

Additional national objectives.   Under the new regulatory framework, the NRAs   **3.184**
may add to the objectives described above other objectives to be reached by undertakings with significant market power. This ensures a balance between the needs which may be observed on a given territory and the obligations which are imposed

---

[155] Under that expression, the NRF refers to the period necessary between the date when the user has made a firm request for a leased line and the date when that user has effectively received access. That period must be the same for all similar requests. The delivery period may be said to be 'typical' when it is in force for 95% of the requests addressed to the undertakings with significant market power. The period referred to in the published conditions must be established on the basis of the actual delivery periods of leased lines during a recent time interval of reasonable duration. The calculation must not include cases where late delivery periods were requested by users. See the Universal Service Directive, Annex VII, point (3.3).

[156] The contractual period includes the period which is in general laid down in the contract and the minimum contractual period which the user is obliged to accept. See the Universal Service Directive, Annex VII, point (3.3).

[157] The repair time is the period necessary for the undertaking with significant market power to address the defect, counted from the time when a failure message has been given to the responsible unit within the undertaking and the time when the line has been re-established and in appropriate cases notified back in operation to the users. The typical repair time is the repair time taken to repair 80% of the error messages received by the undertaking. Where different classes of quality of repair are offered for the same type of leased lines, the different typical repair times must be published, See the Universal Service Directive, Annex VII, point (3.3).

on that territory. To maintain consistency, additional objectives must remain consistent with those established at European level.

> *Universal Service Directive, Annex VII, point (3.3).* '[W]here a Member State considers that the achieved performance for the provision of the minimum set of leased lines does not meet users' needs, it may define appropriate targets for the supply conditions listed above.'

3.185 **Immediate application.** The obligation to provide a harmonised minimum set of leased lines is imposed in the new regulatory framework, but was already introduced under the old. As is the case for the other specific obligations, the obligation imposed under the old framework remains applicable until NRAs analyse markets to determine whether competition is or is not effective. Only if the degree of effective competition is sufficient may the obligation be set aside.[158]

3.186 **Removal of obligations.** As was stated above, obligations regarding leased lines may only be imposed if a market is found not to be effectively competitive. The consequence of this principle is that, once a market is found to be competitive, the obligations have to disappear. This mechanism, under which public intervention is warranted only in cases where markets fail to reach the objectives which have been set, is an essential part of the new regulatory framework.

> *Universal Service Directive, Article 18(2).* 'Where as a result of . . . [a] market analysis . . . , a national regulatory authority determines that a relevant market for the provision of leased lines in the minimum set is effectively competitive, it shall withdraw the obligations referred to . . . in relation to this specific leased line market.'

3.187 **Universal Service Directive.** The provision concerning leased lines has been inserted by the European legislator in the Universal Service Directive. This may appear surprising, to the extent that the presence of leased lines concerns the ability on the part of undertakings to access resources or facilities under the control of another undertaking. That impression is reinforced by the fact that the obligations regarding leased lines were not part of the universal service provisions in the old regulatory framework. A change has thus occurred, apparently, in the approach adopted by the European legislator, even if the content of the provisions do not necessarily diverge between the old and the new regulatory framework.

---

[158] See the Universal Service Directive, Annex VII. '[P]rovision of the minimum set of leased lines under the conditions established by Directive 92/44/EC should continue until such time as the national regulatory authority determines that there is effective competition in the relevant leased lines market.' Directive 92/44, which is mentioned in this extract, is the instrument in which the obligation was introduced under the old regulatory framework. See Council Directive (EEC) 92/44 on the application of open network provision to leased lines [1992] OJ L165/27 ('ONP Leased Lines Directive'), several times amended.

A change in the interpretation of the universal service.   The reason explaining   **3.188**
this change may be due to a change in the European legislator's attitude to
universal service. In the old regulatory framework the emphasis was placed on
the social dimension of universal service. The purpose of universal service was to
ensure the adequate provision of basic services to the population, in particular to
the underprivileged. In the new framework the universal service is designed in
terms of objectives to be fulfilled in order have adequate electronic communications services in a modern society. One of these objectives is the presence of a
given quantity of leased lines available for the performance of adequate services.
The supply of these lines is thus interpreted, in the new regulatory framework,
as an objective to be fulfilled, as for other items which are part of the universal
service, by the markets or, in the event markets fail to achieve this objective, by
public intervention.

(11) Link with other provisions or instruments

Other instruments containing useful analysis.   The various obligations exam-   **3.189**
ined in the sections above have been introduced in the NRF. They are formulated
in rather general terms and it will be for the NRAs to determine what these
obligations entail in practice. Here again, it is to be hoped that a common
approach will evolve and that the Commission will take an active role in developing it. At this stage, guidance as to what these obligations may imply as regards
tariffs and accounting may be gleaned from the communication and two recommendations already published by the Commission. Another possibility is to
seek inspiration in general competition law, which imposes rules similar to
those introduced in the framework. The following paragraphs examine more
closely the content of the communication and the recommendations referred to
above. The obligations derived from general competition law are analysed in
Chapter 4.[159]

Instruments adopted by the Commission under the old regulatory framework.   **3.190**
The Commission issued under the old regulatory framework several instruments
intended to assist the implementation of certain obligations introduced by the
Interconnection Directive. The first recommendation concerns interconnection
tariffs in the light, mainly, of the obligation imposed on designated operators, to
base tariffs on costs. The second recommendation deals with accounting constraints resulting from that obligation, as well as those flowing from the necessity

---

[159] The reason why general competition law is addressed in Chapter 4 is that one cannot
exclude, at the present stage, that the case law may evolve in the future in the two contexts in diverging directions. It thus remains preferable to present the two contexts separately, while indicating
the relations and the differences. Practitioners are strongly encouraged to use these differences and
similarities in order to build their argumentation, on the basis of the facts with which they are
confronted.

to prevent designated operators from transferring revenues among markets. The Communication provides useful background for the two previous documents. Among others, it explains the content of the provisions included in the recommendation as well as the reasons why these provisions were introduced.

(*a*) Commission Recommendation (EC) 98/195 on interconnection in a liberalised telecommunications market (Part 1—Interconnection pricing) ('1998 Tariff Recommendation');[160]

(*b*) Commission Recommendation (EC) 98/322 on interconnection in a liberalised telecommunications market (Part 2—Accounting separation and cost accounting) ('1998 Accounting Recommendation');[161] and

(*c*) Commission Communication on interconnection pricing in a liberalised telecommunications market ('1998 Communication on Interconnection').[162]

3.191 **Do these instruments still apply?** These instruments have played a major role in organising access and interconnection under the old regulatory framework. They have indeed provided concrete indications as to the implications of the more abstract provisions in the Interconnection Directive. A question arises as to whether these instruments continue to apply after the introduction of the NRF. This would appear to be the case for two main reasons. (*a*) In an earlier discussion (see paras 3.21–3.23), it has been shown that certain obligations imposed by the Interconnection Directive remain applicable during a transitional period.[163] Application of these obligations continues to be facilitated by the two recommendations as well as the communication. There is no reason why the obligations should remain valid but deprived of the accompanying instruments adopted to explain their content, scope and the reasons for their introduction. (*b*) The obligations that the two recommendations and the communication seek to implement have been taken over into the NRF: undertakings with significant market power may still be required to calculate access tariffs on the basis of costs, to adopt a cost-based accounting system and to keep separate accounts for certain activities.[164] There is no reason why these obligations should be interpreted differently from those under the old framework.

---

[160] [1998] OJ L73/42.   [161] [1998] OJ L141/6.   [162] [1998] OJ C84/3.

[163] This period will last the time necessary for NRAs to assess the markets and determine whether regulatory obligations must be imposed in the light of the existing degree of competition.

[164] There are differences between the two frameworks, but they do not appear to be substantial as regards the obligations concerned. A significant difference concerns the conditions under which the obligations may be imposed. In the old regulatory framework, the obligations concerned were imposed on all designated operators. Under the new framework, a decision must be taken by the NRAs to impose such obligations in view of the circumstances and the necessity of the measure to reach the objectives assigned to these authorities. That difference does not concern, however, the content of the obligation, but rather the institutions which are empowered to impose them.

Minor adaptations.   For these reasons, the obligations to calculate tariffs on the   **3.192**
basis of costs and comply with certain accounting principles must still be interpreted, in principle, in the light of the recommendations and communication.
This does not imply that the provisions contained in those instruments must not
be adapted on minor points. This observation is particularly important for the
1998 Tariff Recommendation, which focuses on interconnection charges, ie on
tariffs charged by operators providing other operators with access to the infrastructure placed under their control.[165] This perspective is rather specific and can be
explained by the context in which the recommendation was adopted. At that time,
the main concern was to ensure interoperability among networks so as to make
possible the provision of end-to-end services throughout the Community. Since
then, the centre of interest has moved towards access envisaged in a more general
fashion. The European legislator now seeks to promote all forms of access, independently of the activity carried out by the access-seeker (operator or provider) as
long as it could increase the provision of electronic communications services. This
new orientation does not imply that the 1998 Tariff Recommendation no longer
has relevance, indeed quite the contrary. The change in perspective must however
be taken into account and attention focused on the provisions of the recommendation that are relevant to the priorities of the new framework. That being said, it
is clear that interoperability remains one of the Commission's key objectives.

Cost orientation of tariffs.   It has been submitted that, under the NRF, an   **3.193**
obligation may be imposed on undertakings with significant market power to base
access tariffs on costs. In examining that obligation it has already been remarked that
the indications provided in the Access Directive are not altogether clear, and even
seem contradictory on some points. NRAs may find guidance on these points in the
1998 Communication on Interconnection, the 1998 Tariff Recommendation and
the 1998 Accounting Recommendation. As explained in these various instruments,
the cost orientation principle implies that prices charged for the provision of a service should reflect the underlying costs incurred in providing that service. Thus in
arriving at principles for interconnection pricing, it is necessary to analyse the way
in which the act of interconnection imposes costs on a network. *(a)* Most of the costs
involved in an electronic communications network are one-off costs. Such costs
may be incurred, for example, when trenches are dug, ducts and cable installed and
switches purchased and programmed. *(b)* Other costs, for instance, maintenance,
switch reprogramming and administration expenses are on-going. *(c)* To be complete, one must also include, in the costs taken into account for the calculation of
interconnection charges, the investment made by operators in capacity. If a network

---

[165] As a reminder, interconnection is a specific form of access. The term 'access' generally designates the possibility for operators or providers to use facilities or resources under the control of
another undertaking. 'Interconnection' refers to the establishment of a link between two networks,
or network elements. See the Access Directive, Art 2, subpara 2, letters (a) and (b).

has to handle peak-hour traffic from other interconnected networks, additional capacity is necessary to maintain the desired quality. An analysis of the capacity costs required to provide that quality should enable costs to be apportioned among interconnecting parties.[166]

3.194 **Costing methodology.** When an obligation is imposed to base tariffs on costs, an issue that arises is the nature of the methodology used to assess the costs. Several may be used for that purpose.[167] Selecting one is by no means an easy task, given the consequences attached. In substance, one method implies an evaluation based on the costs the undertakings have faced in order to build and maintain infrastructure. The purpose of this method is to allow the undertakings concerned to amortise the initial investment. Another method is based on the value which assets have at the time the evaluation is made.

3.195 **Amortisation.** Incumbents generally favour the first method, because it allows them to obtain a reimbursement for all sums that have been spent in connection with the establishment, upgrade and maintenance of the network. However, it is not regarded by the Commission as necessarily being the most appropriate. According to that institution, the method used to evaluate assets must be in line with the context in which the market operates. In this case, it must be compatible with the competitive character of the environment where activities are carried out. However, in such an environment the price paid for an asset does not govern its value. From the moment an investment is made,[168] the value of that investment depends on what the undertaking does with it. One possibility is to sell the asset. The value is then the sum that the undertaking may get on the market at the time the asset is sold. Another possibility is to use the asset in order to generate income. In that activity, the undertaking competes with other undertakings. Where these are more efficient, the undertaking then has to lower prices rather than continue pricing on the basis of historic costs. In that strategy, the value must be scaled down to match the ability of the assets concerned to produce income in the circumstances in which the undertaking is placed.[169]

---

[166] See the 1998 Communication on Interconnection, para 3.2.

[167] For a description of these methods, see the 1998 Communication on Interconnection, para 3.4, and the 1998 Accounting Recommendation (in particular the Appendix to that recommendation).

[168] At that time, the investment cannot be reversed without significant cost.

[169] According to the Commission, a competitive environment implies that assets must be assessed, as to their value, on the basis of current circumstances, and not on the basis of the historic cost. Undertakings may only use historic cost as a basis for evaluation when they dominate a market. Only when an undertaking has substantial market power is it possible for it to demand from customers a price calculated to provide a required rate return on past investments. The situation is quite different on a competitive market, where assets are valued on the basis of their ability to generate income in a situation where the undertaking has to compete with other undertakings. The presence of such an environment, and the necessity to adapt the value of the assets in view of the evolution of market conditions, is a major source of risk in market economies. It is a reason why an undertaking's value, as measured by the value of its shares, can change significantly in a short period. See the 1998 Communication on Interconnection, para 3.3 and note 9.

Methods used to calculate interconnection charges.   Considerable research has   **3.196**
been carried out to identify the costs which should be used by operators in order
to set interconnection charges. The purpose has been to determine what price
would be appropriate to take account of the value of the assets and, at the same
time, the need to favour competition. This research has shown that the long-run
average incremental cost (LRAIC) provides an appropriate basis. This involves a
'bottom-up' approach, in which interconnection costs are calculated by aggregat-
ing the costs of individual network elements. This approach is generally opposed
to the 'top-down' method, which takes as a starting point the current cost
accounts of an operator and seeks to arrive at an interconnection cost by a process
of allocation and elimination of cost elements. It is generally suggested that the
two methods should be combined, with a comparison between the results arrived
at when using the two approaches.[170]

Intense debate.   Under the old regulatory framework, the economic models   **3.197**
constructed in order to calculate interconnection charges on the basis of these
approaches gave rise to intense debate. The results of the research carried out have
in most cases not yet been incorporated into regulated interconnection prices. In
addition, very few regulators have the technical expertise to calculate interconnection charges based on actual estimates of long-run average incremental costs
(LRAIC: current costs, as opposed to historic costs). Nonetheless, equitable interconnection charges must be determined to ensure access under reasonable conditions. In order to solve this difficulty, the Commission proposed the use, as an
interim measure, of the 'best current practice' approach. This approach entailed
a comparison of interconnection charges set in various countries. The prices
obtained were based on the interconnection charges observed in the three lowest
priced Member States. They were provided in the 1998 Tariffs Recommendation
(Annex II) and frequently updated.[171]

Current situation in the Member States.   The current situation concerning the   **3.198**
type of costs taken into account is not entirely consistent. The LRAIC methodology has been used in some Member States, but not all. This brings about disparities in the internal market, a circumstance which gives a legal basis for the
European institutions to intervene.

> *Eighth Implementation Report, 36.* '[I]n most Member States current costs are used as
> the cost base for pricing interconnection and unbundled local loops.' '[T]heir use for
> leased lines and voice telephony is [however] more limited.' 'For interconnection
> charges, historic costs are still used in the systems applied by the notified operators in
> Denmark, Luxembourg, Portugal, Finland and Sweden, although most of them have

---

[170] Where the results converge, the determination of the interconnection charge raises no
difficulty. Where a lack of convergence is observed, an additional assessment must be made.

[171] Our suggestion to practitioners wishing to obtain the latest estimates is to look at the internet
site of the Commission—DG Information Society.

started the process of migrating towards a system reflecting current costs.' 'Regarding the cost standard implemented for modelling interconnection costs, the LRAIC methodology is already applied in a first group of incumbents in six Member States (Germany, Greece, France, Ireland, the Netherlands for termination charges, and the United Kingdom).' 'Several other Member States are currently developing LRAIC models under the supervision of the NRA (Belgium, Denmark, Spain, Italy, Luxembourg).'

3.199 **Tariff comparisons.** In the light of market developments, the best practice approach has finally been abandoned.[172] It had become apparent that the interconnection fees charged in the Community were progressively being reduced to the levels recommended by the Commission. Therefore, the Commission found that it was no longer necessary to use that approach and update the price suggestions originally included in the Recommendation. Despite that decision, it should be emphasised that, although it is no longer imposed as a general measure, the best practice method remains important in that it provides an interesting methodology to assess possible excessive prices. Excessive prices may be prohibited under the NRF and general competition law, where they are set by undertakings with significant market power. One method of ascertaining the excessive character of prices may be to compare tariffs across several Member States. Practitioners wishing to use that method will no longer find prices suggested in the recommendation. They may however carry out a comparison using their own means, if they believe that the interconnection fees charged to their clients are excessive.

3.200 **Cost accounting systems.** Designated operators were compelled under the old regulatory framework to calculate interconnection charges on the basis of the cost incurred to provide interconnection. A corollary of that obligation was the constraint imposed on them to install accounting systems. The Interconnection Directive does not specify the particular cost accounting system that must be adopted by these undertakings. It merely requires transparency of the system used. At the time the obligation was imposed, most incumbent operators had accounting systems based on historic costs. That methodology had developed in the monopoly situation in which they operated. In that environment, the incumbents were able to charge customers the full costs incurred to provide the networks, as they were not subject to competitive pressure. This system could no longer be used after markets had been opened to competition. As explained above, values cannot be based on an assessment of historic costs in a competitive environment. As the Commission has made clear, the use of historic costs for calculating interconnection charges is not consistent with a competitive market.[173]

---

[172] See Commission Recommendation (EC) C(2002)561 amending Recommendation 98/195/EC, as last amended by Recommendation 2000/263/EC, on Interconnection in a liberalised telecommunications market (Part 1—Interconnection Pricing) [2002] OJL58/56.

[173] See the 1998 Communication on Interconnection, para 3.4.

Accounting Recommendation. The obligation to keep cost-based accounting **3.201** systems and, in some instances, separate accounts for diverse activities, is fully articulated in the 1998 Accounting Recommendation. That Recommendation has not lost its value with the adoption of the NRF. A reference is even made to it in the Framework Directive, pursuant to which that Recommendation clearly remains in force despite the changes in regulation.[174]

Other issues dealt with. The 1998 Tariff Recommendation and the 1998 **3.202** Communication on Interconnection also deal with other, less central, issues which deserve to be mentioned because of the importance of the rules on which they comment. They concern: the charges to be set by mobile operators when granting access or interconnection to their networks; the differences that may appear in interconnection charges when the call originates on a fixed or a mobile network; the difficulties relating to the inclusion of a universal service contribution in the interconnection charge; and the issues raised by the inclusion of an access deficit contribution as part of the interconnection charge.

(a) Interconnection provided by a mobile operator. Under the old framework **3.203** the obligation to use costs as a basis to calculate interconnection charges applies independently of the nature of the network concerned. It thus applies to mobile networks as much as to fixed infrastructure, provided the mobile operators have significant market power in the national market for interconnection. However, not all mobile operators can be deemed to have accumulated such power. There is thus a difference compared to fixed network markets, which are still dominated by incumbents as a result of the control held by these undertakings over the local loop. The consequence is that the obligation to base tariffs on costs does not apply, in many circumstances, to mobile operators. These undertakings thus remain free to set the tariffs for interconnection to their network. As they have no significant market power, they do not have to resort to the best practice method in order to calculate these tariffs.[175]

(b) Interconnection demanded by a mobile operator. There is generally a **3.204** considerable difference in the interconnection fees charged when the undertaking seeking access is a mobile, rather than a fixed, operator or provider. As the Commission notes, interconnection charges for the termination of traffic from fixed to mobile networks are often considerably higher than the charges between

---

[174] That reference is made in the context of accounting separation. There is no reason, however, not to use the recommendation as regards the obligation to have cost-based systems as well as the methods to be used to assess costs. See Access Directive, Preamble, recital 18. 'Accounting separation allows internal price transfers to be rendered visible, and allows NRAs to check compliance with obligations for non-discrimination where applicable. In this regard the Commission published Recommendation 98/322/EC of 8 April 1998 on interconnection in a liberalised telecommunications market (Part 2—accounting separation and cost accounting).'

[175] See the 1998 Communication on Interconnection, para 5.1.1.

fixed networks. However, the cost of conveying a particular call from a point of interconnection to its destination on the terminating mobile network is roughly the same whether the call originates on a mobile network or another fixed network. As a result, there is no objective justification to charge different rates depending on the network on which the call originates. The difficulty should be solved, as recommended by the Commission, through the application of the 'best practice' method. According to the Commission, the prices contained in the 1998 Tariff Recommendation must be applied on a non-discriminatory basis in all circumstances where interconnection or access is requested, irrespective of the networks (mobile or fixed) concerned.[176]

3.205 **(c) Interconnection charge and universal service.**   In the old regulatory framework, it was accepted that the contribution due to finance the universal service could be paid as a portion of the interconnection fee. This mechanism was made possible by the fact that the undertaking entrusted with the universal service was, in most circumstances, the operator controlling the fixed infrastructure. As the sums relating to the universal service had anyway to be paid to that undertaking, it was deemed more appropriate to make the payment straight to the undertaking which was to receive it. The solution was found more appropriate than organising transit through an administrative entity, a system which would have little added value and would have increased costs. In that context, an issue was raised about the undertakings from which a contribution could be asked for the provision of universal service. Suppose an operator or a provider located in one Member State seeks interconnection to infrastructure located in another European country. In that case, the purpose of interconnection is to ensure end-to-end transmission of electronic communications services across national borders. An issue is whether such an operator or provider established in another Member State could be asked to pay a contribution to the universal service to be organised on the national territory.

3.206 **Strict position.**   The Commission adopted a strict position on this point. According to that institution, the purpose of a universal service charge is to ensure that the social cost of universal service in a Member State is shared by the players on that market. The consequence, for the Commission, was that the social costs incurred in one Member State should not be subsidised by telephone users in other Member States. Thus, contributions to universal service should not be imposed, either directly or indirectly, on undertakings which merely interconnect

---

[176] See the 1998 Communication on Interconnection, para 5.1.1. This does not mean that no difference at all will appear in the interconnection charges, depending on the nature of the network where the calls originates. These differences will however be accepted in limited circumstances— only where they correspond to a difference in the cost incurred to provide interconnection. Interconnection charges paid by mobile operators may differ as a result, for instance, of variations in the distribution of points of interconnection, call destinations, call durations, and differences in the 'time of day' calling pattern.

to deliver traffic to another Member State and do not actually offer telecommunications services in the latter Member State. The corollary is that contributions to be made by undertakings in a Member State to universal service costs should not be calculated taking into account the traffic of these undertakings which is incoming from other Member States.[177]

Universal service. The statements made by the Commission in the 1998 Communication and Recommendations on this point are not entirely relevant, because the contributions to the universal service may no longer be paid as part of the interconnection charge. When the NRAs decide that the cost of providing the universal service must be shared, this may be done only through the establishment of a cost-sharing mechanism that is administered by such authorities or by an independent body.[178] The two instruments referred to are however still important, in that they exclude the participation of undertakings from other Member States in the mechanism established for the financing of the universal service.[179] **3.207**

(d) Access deficit charges. A similar attitude has been adopted by the Commission with respect to access deficit charges. Prior to the reform, local communications were subsidised, to a significant extent, by international communications. High profits were made on the latter market and were used to compensate losses incurred on the local market ('local access deficit'). This compensation mechanism implied that international communications users were in effect subsidising local communications users. For the Commission, such a system could be accepted within a single Member State. This was due to the fact that a Member State is supposed to form a community, where financial movements may be organised within several parts of the population out of policy concerns. The system could not have as a consequence, however, that users from other Member States could be called upon to contribute to the cross-subsidisation policy implemented in a given European country. **3.208**

> *1998 Communication on Interconnection, para 5.2.* '[A]n "access deficit" implies that profits from national and international services provide a cross-subsidy to the "local access" business. Presently, under the international accounting rate system, incumbent operators are earning significant revenues when terminating calls from other countries. The "excess profits" earned from terminating incoming calls from other Member States represent a cross-subsidy to consumers in one Member State from callers in all the other Member States. Thus when operators in other Member States interconnect to deliver traffic to a Member State, it is inappropriate that they should contribute either directly or indirectly to any access deficit type scheme in that Member State.'[180]

---

[177] See the 1998 Communication on Interconnection, para 5.2.
[178] See the Universal Service Directive, Art 13(1) and (2).
[179] This has been confirmed by ibid, Art 13(4), second sentence.
[180] 1998 Communication on Interconnection, para 5.2. That last aspect addressed by the 1998 Tariff Recommendation is still relevant, to the extent that NRAs are still allowed to establish, for instance, in the context of the universal service, schemes whereby prices are averaged on a geographic basis.

3.209 **Apportionment of costs to activities.** In the 1998 Accounting Recommendation, the Commission recommends the Member States to adopt a system where costs, capital and revenues are apportioned among activities. A minimal disaggregation into broad business lines is proposed regarding these items. The business lines considered by the Commission are as follows.[181]

> *(a)* Core network: activities covering the provision of interconnection services, transit services and carrier's carrier services.
> *(b)* Local access network: provision of connections to the telephony network
> *(c)* Retail: mainly, the commercial provision of fixed telephony services and leased lines to end users.
> *(d)* Other activities: activities provided by the notified operator which may include unregulated activities as well as other types of regulated activities.

3.210 **Cost causation.** In the Recommendation, the Commission further specifies an allocation of costs, capital and revenue in accordance with the principle of cost causation. The system used by undertakings on which accounting obligations are imposed should permit, as far as possible, an allocation of costs to unbundled network components, in particular to determine the cost of unbundled interconnection services. It is thought that a well-defined cost-allocation system should enable at least 90 per cent of the costs to be allocated on the basis of direct or indirect cost-causation. Unattributable costs, ie costs which can be attributed only on an arbitrary basis, should be clearly identified in a specific account. They should further be distributed according to the rules determined by each Member State, in accordance with the Community's competition rules and in compliance with the principles of transparency and proportionality.

3.211 **Transfer charges.** The 1998 Accounting Recommendation further contains interesting indications on accounting obligations to be respected by undertakings with significant market power, where transfers occur within their organisation. Suppose a network operator is also active on certain markets for services. These services will be provided on the basis of infrastructure owned by the undertaking. The contribution of one department, or division, within an undertaking, to another, in order to allow an activity to be carried out, must be expressed in the accounts of that undertaking. This is important to ensure that costs are correctly allocated to activities.[182] It is also essential to determine whether revenues are transferred from one department to another—in fact from one market to another. It will be recalled that cross subsidies are not allowed when undertakings have

---

[181] The scope of these business lines is further explained in the Annex (section 1) to the recommendation.

[182] Let us remember that tariffs must be based on costs, as far as access is concerned when access is granted by an undertaking with significant market power. In order to establish costs with accuracy, it is important to identify all activities carried out with assets the costs of which are to be established.

significant market power.[183] In order to ensure that transfers are reflected in an appropriate fashion in the accounts, the Commission recommends that a system of transfer charges should apply to services and products provided, within an undertaking, from one line of business to another. There should be a clear rationale for the transfer charges used. Each charge should be justifiable, charges should be non-discriminatory, and there should be transparency of transfer charges in the separate accounts. The transfer charges for internal usage should be determined as the product of usage and unit charges. The charge for internal usage should be equivalent to the charge that would be levied if the product or service were sold externally rather than internally. For accounting separation purposes, it should be assumed that an operator's retail business pays the same interconnection charge for the same service.

Principles of cost allocation.   The 1998 Accounting Recommendation further   **3.212**
sets out principles to be followed in order to allocate costs, capital and revenues for the purposes of preparing separate accounts. Accounting separation should be based on the principle of causation. As a result, costs and revenues should be allocated to those services or products that cause those costs or revenues to arise. This requires the implementation of appropriate and detailed cost allocation methodologies. In practice, this requires that operators review each item of cost, capital employed and revenue; establish the driver that caused each item to arise, and use the driver to allocate each item to individual businesses. All allocations may be subject to review by NRAs. Each item of cost and revenue must be allocated to the products and services provided by operators. In the case of revenue, it is anticipated that most, if not all, revenues can be allocated directly to those products or services to which they are related. This is not the case for costs, however, because a relatively high proportion of operators' costs is shared between different products and services.

F. Markets Where Specific Obligations May be Imposed (Market Definition and Selection)

(1) How to deal with the issue?

When must specific obligations be imposed?   In previous sections, an analysis has   **3.213**
been provided of the specific obligations[184] that may be imposed on undertakings in

---

[183] That prohibition is established in the NRF as well as in general competition law. See Access Directive, Art 11(1). '[A] national regulatory authority may require a vertically integrated company to make transparent its wholesale prices and its internal transfer prices *inter alia* to ensure compliance where there is a requirement for non-discrimination . . . or, where necessary, to prevent unfair cross-subsidy.' Rules prohibiting cross subsidies in general competition law are examined in Chapter 4.

[184] As stated above, obligations may be divided into two groups. Some are reserved to undertakings with significant market power. These obligations apply on markets where competition is not deemed effective. They can be said to be 'specific', as they can only be imposed on specific undertakings.

connection with access to electronic communications facilities and/or resources. As mentioned in the Framework Directive, the application of these obligations depends upon an assessment of the degree of competition existing on the various markets concerned. That assessment must be carried out by NRAs. It must allow these authorities to determine whether competition is effective. Pursuant to case law, an assessment of the existing degree of competition implies that the authority in charge of the exercise must analyse to what extent consumers have a choice, within a given territory, among various products or services serving a similar function. If the possibility to choose is considered sufficient, the markets will be said to be effectively competitive. In these circumstances, no specific obligation normally needs to be imposed. The common understanding is that markets will themselves produce, through commercial interaction, the best possible economic outcome. In the absence of sufficient choice, intervention will be warranted because competition does not exist to a satisfactory degree. Specific obligations may, or must, then in principle be imposed. The question is which should be selected and in what circumstances should they apply.

3.214 **Applicable instruments.** The application of specific obligations thus depends upon an assessment of competition, which in turn implies that markets must be defined. The reason for this is that competition may be assessed only in respect of given goods/services and given territories. An authority cannot reach a conclusion as to the existence, or absence, of competition if it has not determined the framework within which competition will be examined. Market definition is a frequent exercise in the application of competition law. It is a step that must be taken prior to examining whether undertakings have acquired a position that prevents competition from being effective and calls for intervention. The definition of markets must be made in accordance with several instruments, which are reviewed briefly in the following paragraphs and examined throughout this section. Among these instruments, a distinction must be made between those that are particularly important for the assessment exercise and others that can provide useful background information. Apart from the Framework Directive, all useful instruments come from the Commission. This should not come as a surprise, to the extent that market definition is an exercise that is typically associated with competition law and this institution with others is entrusted with the application of this body of rules within the European Union.

3.215 **(a) Instruments of particular interest.** There are three main instruments to be taken into account as regards market definition for the application of regulatory

---

The second category comprises obligations that may be applied to other undertakings. In some instances, these obligations also concern specified groups of undertakings (for instance, undertakings controlling access to end users or undertakings with control of conditional access systems). These obligations are however considered in the regulation as being more general because they apply irrespective of an assessment of competition existing on the markets where they are active.

obligations in European electronic communications: the Framework Directive, the Recommendation on relevant markets and the 2002 Guidelines on market analysis and significant market power.

Framework Directive.   The most fundamental is Parliament and Council   **3.216**
Directive (EC) 2002/21 on a common regulatory framework for electronic communications networks and services (Framework Directive).[185] Several provisions of that directive have already been examined above. The rules dealing specifically with market definition and the assessment of competition are located in Articles 14 and 15 of that instrument. A list of markets considered as relevant by the Parliament and Council is included in Annex I to the directive.

Recommendation on relevant markets.   On the basis of that directive, the Com-   **3.217**
mission has adopted a recommendation on relevant product and service markets ('Recommendation on relevant markets').[186] Despite its general title, the recommendation has limited scope. Its object is to identify markets where competition must be assessed for the application of regulatory obligations in electronic communications. A second list of markets is thus provided in that recommendation.

2002 Guidelines.   Finally, the assessment of market power must be carried out   **3.218**
in conformity with Commission Guidelines 2002/C165/03 on market analysis and the assessment of significant market power under the Community regulatory framework for electronic communications networks and services.[187] To avoid confusion with another instrument issued by the Commission in the same sector, the 2002 Guidelines are referred to here as the '2002 Guidelines on market analysis and significant market power'. As with the recommendation, the guidelines were adopted on the basis of the Framework Directive. They contain an important analysis of how markets may, or must, be defined in electronic communications. In this regard, they provide a useful complement to the recommendation, which itself only identifies the relevant market without presenting the methodology or explaining how the Commission has reached its conclusions.

(b) Useful background information.   In addition to the documents mentioned   **3.219**
above, practitioners may find it useful to resort to background information provided by more general instruments. These instruments are the Notice on relevant markets, the 1991 Competition Guidelines and the 1998 Competition Guidelines.

Notice on relevant markets.   An interesting analysis of the methodology to be   **3.220**
used in order to define markets is provided in the Commission Notice on the

---

[185] [2002] OJ L108/33.

[186] The NRF is limited to services and does not relate to equipment. Access to equipment is considered but this is analysed as a service in the regulation. 'Products' appear to have been mentioned without any specific intent in the official denomination of the recommendation.

[187] [2002] OJ C165/3.

definition of relevant markets for the purposes of Community competition law ('Notice on relevant markets').[188] It should however be noted that that instrument is rather general and does not contain any indication as to how this methodology must be used in the specific context of electronic communications.

3.221 **1991 Competition Guidelines.** Practitioners will also find general background about the application of general competition law to the telecommunications sector in the Commission Guidelines (EC) on the application of EEC competition rules in the telecommunications sector ('1991 Competition Guidelines').[189] These were issued at a time when reform was gathering pace, but the analysis remains limited as it was then rather early (1991) to have a clear view on the subject matter. For the sake of clarity, the instrument is referred to here as the '1991 Guidelines'.

3.222 **1998 Competition Guidelines.** Access-related issues are at the centre of Commission Notice 98/C265/02 on the application of competition rules to access agreements in the telecommunications sector ('1998 Competition Guidelines').[190] That notice analyses how the competition rules may, and should, be used in order to ensure that access is provided under reasonable conditions, and is interesting in shedding light on the measures adopted by the Parliament and Council on access and interconnection. However, it provides little insight into market definition.

(2) Methodology for the definition of relevant markets

3.223 **Importance of methodology.** As mentioned above, the European legislator has established two lists of markets considered important for the imposition of specific obligations on undertakings with significant market power. Pursuant to the regulation, these markets are to be examined by the NRAs when the latter carry out their assessment of the existing degree of competition. In general terms, markets are defined in order for authorities to assess the degree of competition existing between various goods or services within a given territory. The extent to which the supply of a service in a given geographical area constitutes a relevant market depends on the existence of competitive constraints weighing on the behaviour of the undertakings concerned. Two competitive constraints are generally considered. On the one hand, authorities analyse substitutability on the demand side. This concept is intended to measure the extent to which consumers are prepared to substitute other services for the service in question. On the other hand, authorities also examine supply-side substitution. The latter concept indicates whether other suppliers are in a position to switch their line of production rapidly in order to offer the relevant service without incurring significant costs and/or risks.

---

[188] [1997] OJ C372/5.   [189] [1991] OJ C233/2.   [190] [1999] OJ C265/2.

Hypothetical monopolist test. The classic method to assess substitution— **3.224** both on the demand and supply sides—is the so-called 'hypothetical monopolist test'. Under this test, authorities examine the consequence of a small but significant and lasting increase in the price at which a given service is made available. Admittedly, the concrete impact of price increases depends on consumers' individual preferences.[191] However, the underlying idea behind economic analysis is that these individual differences do not hinder the formulation of a general trend. Using that idea, economists generally consider that two services may be considered substitutable in a given community where a significant[192] number of consumers in that community shift from one service to another as a reaction to a price increase of 10 per cent.[193]

(a) Demand-side substitution. Pursuant to the case law, the relevant service **3.225** market comprises all items that are sufficiently interchangeable or substitutable in the eyes of consumers. Demand-side substitution is the main tool for the definition of markets in a competition law system that is oriented towards ensuring that consumers have a choice between services and suppliers. In technical terms, demand-side substitution enables authorities to determine the substitutable range of services to which consumers could easily switch in case of a relative price increase.[194] The assessment of substitutability is primarily based on objective characteristics, ie what makes the service capable of satisfying a particular need for consumers. Normally,[195] barely interchangeable services do not constitute a market together. For this reason, a good and practical method for defining markets is

---

[191] For instance, *x* may find internet telephony not to be substitutable for classical telephony whereas *y* will consider that the two services are entirely similar.

[192] The number is significant where the production of the service is not viable any longer as a result of the shifting movement observed among consumers towards the other service. Thus, service *A* can be considered as substitutable for service *B* if consumers shift to *B* where the price for *A* increases by 10% to an extent that the production of *A* is no longer viable as a result of consumer desertion.

[193] What matters is the reaction adopted by consumers as a result of a variation in prices. As a result, products may be viewed as substitutes even where they are offered at different prices. A low quality service sold at a low price could appear as an effective substitute for a higher quality service sold at higher prices. The assessment must be based on likely responses by consumers to a relative price increase.

[194] In determining the existence of demand substitutability, the NRAs are invited to use evidence of consumers' behaviour. For instance, these authorities could examine historical price fluctuations between potentially competing products, records of price movements and other relevant tariff information wherever available. An ideal situation is when authorities have evidence showing that consumers have shifted to other services in response to price changes, and this should be given appropriate consideration. In the absence of such information, the NRAs are invited to use all available means to assess the likely response of consumers and suppliers to a relative price increase for the service in question.

[195] Services which are not interchangeable on the demand side may be considered as forming part of the same market if they can be deemed substitutable on the supply side, ie if it is observed that suppliers can rapidly shift to the production of a service without incurring significant costs and/or risks.

to commence the analysis by grouping services that are used by consumers for the same purposes (end use).[196]

3.226 **Three aspects.** In the definition of markets, authorities should devote attention to three aspects. *(a)* As market definition depends on the function attributed by consumers to specific services, differences may appear among consumer groups. These differences may lead to a definition of different markets for the same products or service, depending on the consumers that are concerned. For instance, the Commission and the NRAs may consider defining separate markets for business and residential customers for a service that would appear the same if the focus were placed exclusively on its function.[197] *(b)* Substitutability among electronic communications services increases with the convergence that is developing among information and communication technologies. The increasing use of digital systems makes it possible to provide services traditionally offered with the assistance of other technologies. The result is that a similar function may be ensured by different technologies.[198] As a consequence, the technology used in a given context may not provide an adequate criterion to distinguish services. *(c)* Substitutability may be hindered by considerable switching costs. Consumers who have invested in a specific technology may be unwilling to incur additional costs where such costs must be made in order to switch to another service which would otherwise be considered as substitutable. Similarly, customers of existing providers may be 'locked in' by long-term contracts or by the prohibitively high cost of switching terminals. In a situation where users face significant switching costs, services do not form part of the same market because they are not perceived by consumers as being interchangeable in practice, despite their similarity as regards function.

3.227 **(b) Supply-side substitution.** In assessing the scope for supply-side substitution, the Commission and the NRAs must take into account the probability that undertakings not currently providing a given service may decide to start that activity within a reasonable timeframe. Such a decision is generally taken after a

---

[196] In some instances, different kinds of services may be affected to the same end. For instance, consumers may use dissimilar services such as cable and satellite connections for the same purpose, namely to access the internet. In such a case, the services concerned (cable and satellite access) may be included in the same market. That observation is however not always valid. Take paging services and mobile telephony services. The two types of service appear to be capable of offering the same functionality—dispatching two-way short messages. Yet they may be found to belong to distinct markets if they are perceived differently by consumers as regards their functionality.

[197] Take the provision of international electronic communications services. With the assistance of available technology, operators are able to apply different tariffs whether these services are meant for residential or, on the contrary, business customers. This possibility of treating differently two groups of consumers may lead to a decision that these two groups form separate markets as far as the said services are concerned.

[198] A packet-switched network may be used, for instance, to transmit digitised voice signals in competition with traditional voice telephony.

price increase has been observed on the market for the relevant service. As a result of that increase, the undertaking calculates that a profit could be made by entering the market. In such a situation, the service originally offered by the undertaking may be included in the market. To that effect, several conditions must be fulfilled. These conditions are an attempt to express in what circumstances the undertaking could start this new activity. There is a high probability that such a start would take place where: *(a)* the cost of switching production, or increasing production, is limited; *(b)* the risks relating to the new activity are reduced; *(c)* and the new activity can be started rapidly.

Investment.   From these conditions it can be seen that the shift or increase in **3.228** production depends mainly on the investments to be made in order to start the new activity. The move may be facilitated by the existence of assets already owned by the undertaking and which make it possible to provide the service in question. However, the presence of such assets is not decisive. In some instances, they do not spare undertakings from the necessity of making significant additional investments. The investments to be made appear, in this context, as barriers that may hinder, and thus make less likely, the provision of the service. As a result, one can consider that these investments form an obstacle to the two services being considered part of the same market. Apart from this economic barrier, one also has to consider legal, statutory or other regulatory requirements which may hinder a time-efficient entry into the relevant market. For instance, the provision of new services and the deployment of new networks may be impeded by delays and obstacles in concluding interconnection or co-location agreements, by negotiating any other form of network access or by obtaining rights of way for network expansion.

Hypothetical substitution.   The possibility for an undertaking to shift or **3.229** increase production is not the only factor to be taken into consideration. Supposing an undertaking is able to start the new activity, the relevant authorities need to ascertain whether it would actually make use of that possibility and in reality switch its productive assets to offering the relevant service. Hypothetical supply-side substitution is not sufficient for the purposes of market definition. A decision to shift production facilities may, however, be affected by a variety of factors that can have a determining influence.[199]

(c) The existence of a third constraint.   Apart from demand and supply-side **3.230** substitution, a third constraint—potential competition—is used in the assessment of the level of competition existing on a given market. This constraint is

---

[199] Suppose, as an example, that an undertaking is committed under long-term supply agreements. That undertaking will not be able to change the destination of its assets in a relatively short time with the consequence that the service currently provided by that undertaking cannot be considered as substitutable for the service in question for the purpose of market definition.

referred to at this stage in order to avoid confusion with supply-side substitution. The criterion relating to potential competition allows a determination to be made of the extent to which undertakings present on *other* markets could start an activity on the relevant market. By contrast, supply-side substitution examines to what extent a service may be considered substitutable for another in the eyes of a provider. The condition will be satisfied, as was stated, in the latter case (supply-side substitution) when the supplier providing the first service can switch rapidly to the second without incurring substantial costs or risks and would probably make use of that possibility, should prices increase on the market for the second service. If these circumstances are present, the two services would be considered as part of *the same market*.

3.231 **Link with supply-side substitution.** As immediately appears, there is a link between potential competition and supply-side substitution. In both cases, one looks at the behaviour of undertakings which are not currently providing the service under consideration. The status as given to the criteria are, however, different. Potential competition is analysed where the purpose is to measure the degree of competition existing on a given market. By contrast, supply-side substitution is examined in the course of market definition.[200] A distinction is made between the two situations to take account of the various degrees in the rapidity and ease with which undertakings can start providing the service in question. In supply-side substitution, one looks at undertakings which may respond promptly to a price variation without incurring substantial risk or cost. As undertakings in this situation can so easily decide to provide the service in question, one considers that the service originally offered by these undertakings can be considered substitutable.[201] Entry is so probable, in such a situation, that one may consider the services currently proposed by these undertakings as already present on the market.[202]

---

[200] Markets must be defined before the degree of competition existing on a market can be assessed. Supply-side substitution is thus examined before potential competition. The examination of potential competition only comes into play when the markets have been defined and the authority (possibly the Commission) wonders whether the position acquired by one or several undertakings is rendered questionable by the possibility that other undertakings may enter the market. The existence of potential competition is an argument to conclude there is an absence of a significant market power on the part of the undertaking(s) concerned.

[201] It should yet be rememberd that substitutability is to be understood, in that case, as the result of a perception by the supplier. This is by contrast with demand-side substitution, where substitutability is analysed in the eyes of consumers.

[202] As mentioned earlier, potential competition is examined at a later stage of the competition based analysis, ie where authorities attempt to determine whether one or several undertakings hold significant market power. The answer will be that no market power has been acquired where other undertakings have the possibility to come from other markets and this possibility impedes the undertaking in question controlling prices and other commercial conditions on the market. The possibility of entry is seen as a threat which obliges the undertaking to behave in a competitive environment. This implies that the undertaking is not in a position to behave independently. The main condition for the presence of dominance is thus not fulfilled.

(d) Geographic market.   Once the service market is identified, the next step is to   **3.232**
define the geographical dimension of the market. Pursuant to the case law, the relevant geographic market comprises an area in which undertakings and consumers
are involved in the supply and demand of the service in question. Normally, this
area is characterised by conditions of competition which are similar or sufficiently
homogeneous. These conditions must be appreciably different from those in force
in neighbouring areas.[203]

Same method.   To define the geographic market, one has to proceed along the   **3.233**
lines presented above in connection with substitutability. Demand and supply-side
substitution must thus be examined again—this time, however, from a different
perspective. The purpose here is to identify the territory concerned by examining
the geographic behaviour of consumers and suppliers in case prices vary. It would
no longer be a method to analyse consumers' and suppliers' patterns in terms of
services provided as a response to a particular need. *(a)* Regarding consumers, the
question would be whether consumers are likely to shop elsewhere if a price
increase is decided in a given area. *(b)* As far as supply-side substitution is concerned, authorities should consider whether operators or providers not currently
engaged in a given area could rapidly enter without incurring risks or costs in the
event of a relative price increase in the services provided in the area in question. If
one considers the electronic communications sector, a careful examination of the
case law shows that, where the two aspects of substitution are taken into account
(demand and supply-side), the geographical scope of the market has traditionally
been determined by the network through which services may be provided as well
as by the regulatory conditions applicable to suppliers. On these issues, the reader
may consult, for practical examples, the analysis provided in Chapter 4.

(3) Not all markets are relevant

Regulated markets.   The lists annexed to the Framework Directive and con-   **3.234**
tained in the Recommendation on Relevant Markets do not enumerate all existing
electronic communications markets. Nor do these documents contain any systematic analysis of all activities, actual or potential, carried out in the sector, in an
attempt to divide them into categories that may be considered as markets, depending on their nature and/or characteristics. The definition exercise has been limited
in the Framework Directive and Recommendation on Relevant Markets to the
identification of markets where specific obligations might have to be applied.

Framework Directive, Article 15(1). 'The recommendation shall identify . . . those
product and service markets within the electronic communications sector, *the*

---

[203] The definition of the geographic market does not require the conditions of competition to be
perfectly homogeneous. For various areas to form the same geographic market, it is sufficient that
the conditions are similar in these various areas. By contrast, different areas cannot be deemed to
form the same market where they are characterised by 'heterogeneous' conditions of competition.

characteristics of which may be such as to justify the imposition of regulatory obligations set out in the Specific Directives.'

3.235 **Conditions to be satisfied.** This limitation has been construed by the Commission in the 2002 Guidelines on market analysis and significant market power and in the Recommendation on relevant markets adopted on the basis of the Framework Directive. Pursuant to these instruments, several conditions must be satisfied before a market must be taken into consideration as being likely to justify the imposition of regulatory conditions. The interpretation given by the Commission is formulated in the extract below, and is further explained in the following paragraphs.

> *Recommendation on Relevant Markets, para 16.* '[W]hether an electronic communications market . . . [can] be identified . . . as justifying possible ex ante regulation would depend on the persistence of high entry barriers, on the second criterion measuring the dynamic state of competitiveness and thirdly on the sufficiency of competition law (absent ex ante regulation) to address persistent market failures.'

3.236 **(a) No potential competition.** As appears from the extract in the previous paragraph, a first condition is that there must exist high and persistent barriers impeding entry on the market. Markets with no, low or temporary entry barriers are not taken into consideration for the competition assessment exercise. The reason is that such markets do not require, in principle, any intervention from a public authority. In the absence of barriers with these characteristics, one can indeed expect newcomers to enter the market in a move which will allow competition to produce satisfactory outcomes. Pursuant to economic theory, barriers may have an economic or a regulatory nature.

3.237 **Economic barriers.** Economic barriers may stem from a variety of circumstances. An example is when markets allow participants to benefit from large economies of scale or scope. Where such economies are available, incumbents have an advantage that newcomers are not able to compensate because they cannot quickly build up activities on a large scale. Another example is when entry implies high sunk costs. The presence of these costs may deter entry, as newcomers may fear that they would lose investments if they cannot develop their activities in a satisfactory manner.[204]

3.238 **Legal and regulatory barriers.** Legal and regulatory barriers must also be considered. These barriers are not based on economic conditions. They rather result

---

[204] See Recommendation on Relevant Markets, para 10. In the recommendation, the Commission states that entry barrier may also come from the control by incumbents of a resource that cannot be technically duplicated or can only be duplicated at a cost that makes it uneconomic for competitors. This situation cannot really be distinguished from the concept of high sunk cost. To enter the markets where that resource is necessary, the newcomers should invest heavily and that may deter them given the risk attached to such an operation.

from legislative, administrative or other state measures that have an effect on the conditions under which entry is possible as well as on the relative position of the participants on the markets. A typical example is the limitation that is imposed in some circumstances on the number of undertakings allowed to take part in an activity. Such a limitation was inherent in the monopolistic system that lasted for decades on European telecommunications markets. Meanwhile, other forms of restriction have been introduced, such as a limitation on the number of undertakings allowed to access spectrum in order to provide mobile services.[205]

(b) No market-based solutions. A second condition for a market to be considered   **3.239** is that it must have characteristics that do not make it possible to solve competition-related issues spontaneously.[206] Suppose issues relating to competition arise on a given market as a result of the acquisition of significant market power by one or several undertakings. For instance, there is a danger that prices may be increased for interconnection as a result of significant market power acquired by the network operator established in that region. The existence of market power and the possibility that issues may arise from that situation do not imply per se that regulatory obligations must be imposed. Pursuant to the regulation, intervention through regulatory mechanisms is necessary only where markets cannot solve issues by themselves.

Highly innovative markets. Several examples are provided in the Recom-   **3.240** mendation of markets on which, as a result of structural characteristics, competition-related issues may be solved spontaneously. A typical illustration is markets with high innovation potential. On markets with high technological content, incumbents apparently remain under threat. However important the market share they have been able to build, they remain subject to the threat that new technologies may be developed by competitors to which customers would then switch rapidly. This constant threat would force incumbents to remain vigilant, as a result of which they would continue to behave as if the market were fully competitive despite the market power they may already have at a given time.

Other examples. Other examples are more classic in nature. For instance,   **3.241** a market may be found to be sufficiently competitive despite the existence of significant market power where there is excess capacity on that market. The existence of overcapacity makes it possible for competitors to expand output rapidly in case the incumbent behaves as if it were protected from competitive pressure. Another circumstance is the presence of high price elasticity on the demand side. This characteristic is present where demand reacts rapidly to changes in prices. Any decision taken by incumbents to increase prices may induce customers to change supplier. As a corollary, any decision by competitors to decrease prices may have

---

[205] Other examples of legal or regulatory barriers are price controls imposed on undertakings. Such measures may impede new entrants from setting the prices at a low level in the hope of developing market share.   [206] See Recommendation on Relevant Markets, paras 12–14.

the consequence that competitors' market shares may increase rapidly to the detriment of incumbents.[207]

3.242 New or emerging markets. The situation of new or emerging markets is discussed in the Framework Directive, the Recommendation on relevant markets and the 2002 Guidelines on market analysis and significant market power. On this subject, the policy adopted by the European legislator is not altogether clear. On the one hand, the desire is expressed that obligations should not be imposed too quickly on markets having these characteristics. The suggestion is thus that regulatory obligations should not be imposed even if significant market power has been acquired by one or several undertakings. The reason for this attitude is that, according to the European legislator, excessive regulation should be avoided, since excessive regulation is traditionally considered a hindrance to the development of technologies or applications. On the other hand, a wish is expressed in the regulation not to see incumbents dominate new markets. Such domination may emerge as a result of the power incumbents hold on classic, adjacent, activities. The fear is that incumbents may deter entry by taking an aggressive stance on these new or emerging markets, to the detriment of the development of competition in these activities.

3.243 Conclusion. In conclusion, one can say that two apparently conflicting sets of instructions are provided by the European legislator as regards the attitude to be adopted by NRAs with respect to the imposition of regulatory obligations on new or emerging markets. The practical consequence is that these authorities should be particularly cautious in assessing whether obligations must be imposed. The best attitude is probably to refrain from imposing regulatory obligations, since it is always possible for NRAs to review the situation regularly and assess competition again. Obligations should, however, be imposed where competition is deterred to an excessive level.

> *Avoid foreclosure.* '[F]oreclosure of such emerging markets by the leading undertaking should be prevented.' *Do not impose excessive regulation.* 'New and emerging markets in which market power may be found to exist because of "first-mover" advantages should not in principle be subject to ex-ante regulation.'[208] '[E]merging markets, where de facto the market leader is likely to have a substantial market share, should not be subject to inappropriate ex-ante regulation. This is because premature imposition of ex-ante regulation may unduly influence the competitive conditions taking shape within a new and emerging market.'[209] *Be overall cautious.* 'Without prejudice to the appropriateness of

---

[207] The influence of high price elasticity on the behaviour of undertakings and the state of competition on a market is reinforced where undertakings have diverging cost structures. The absence of similarity in costs makes it difficult for undertakings to base decisions on anticipation of price policies supposed to be carried out by other market participants. The divergence in cost structure also makes it possible for one undertaking to economise and use this opportunity to decrease prices whereas others remain subject to constant cost pressure.

[208] Recommendation on Relevant Markets, para 15.

[209] 2002 Guidelines on market anlysis and significant market power, para 32. See also Framework Directive, recital 27.

intervention by the competition authorities in individual cases, NRAs should ensure that they can fully justify any form of early, ex-ante intervention in an emerging market, in particular since they retain the ability to intervene at a later stage, in the context of the periodic re-assessment of the relevant markets.'

(c) No general competition law-based solution. Finally, markets are not taken **3.244** into consideration where the issues could be solved through the application of general competition law. This last condition is explicitly mentioned in the Recommendation on relevant markets, pursuant to which markets should not be considered from the perspective of regulatory obligations when competition law is to be preferred. No further analysis is however provided on this subject in any of the instruments concerned (Framework Directive, Recommendation, 2002 Guidelines on market analysis and significant market power). How can this silence be explained? It is not possible to determine whether preference must be given to general competition law at the moment when authorities are considering in abstracto what markets are to be defined for an assessment of competition. It could be argued that a general preference may be expressed in favour of general competition law, since it appears to imply light intervention compared to the imposition of ex ante obligations. However, a real decision as to what body of the law to apply in a given context may be taken only when an issue arises and authorities can analyse the concrete circumstances of the case. As a result, no balance between general competition law and sector specific regulation can be made at the stage where markets are defined in their functional component. Such a balance may only be made in concrete circumstances, at the time when NRAs determine the geographical component of the market.

(4) *The markets identified in the regulation*

An important issue.   An important issue is to determine who has the power to **3.245** identify markets. The power to define markets has a strategic value because market definition has an impact on findings relating to the existing degree of competition. Suppose a market is defined widely. The chances are then rather high that several competitors are present on the market. One will thus conclude in principle that no undertaking has significant market power. By contrast, if a market is defined in a rather narrow fashion, the probability is substantial that a limited number of undertakings will be considered to be present on that market, with the concomitantly high chance that one of these undertakings may be deemed to have significant market power. Given the stakes attached to market definition, one can expect the parties concerned to strive in order to have their own definition retained, in case litigation arises.[210]

---

[210] A typical example of argument presented by parties on that subject matter can be found in *United Brands*. The Commission sought to reduce the amplitude of the market by proposing that

3.246 **Identification by the European legislator.** Given the importance of the issue, it comes as no surprise that the European legislator has wished itself to define the markets on which competition has to be assessed. Pursuant to the Framework Directive, the responsibility for the task is primarily entrusted to the European legislator. Two instruments contain essential elements in this respect. *(a)* First, a list of markets was drafted by the Parliament and Council. This list is set out in Annex I to the Framework Directive, and enumerates the markets which, according to these institutions, must at least be considered separately for the assessment of competition. As will be seen, these markets were already defined, in substance, in their present form, under the old regulatory framework. *(b)* Another list was drafted by the Commission in implementation of the Access Directive. This list is included in the Recommendation on relevant markets, and identifies the markets where regulatory obligations might have to be applied. The Recommendation contains hardly any other information than this listing of relevant markets.

> *Recommendation on relevant markets, para 17.* 'When reviewing existing obligations imposed under the previous regulatory framework, in order to determine whether to maintain, amend or withdraw them, NRAs should undertake the analysis on the basis of the markets identified in this Recommendation.'[211]

3.247 **Comparison and regular review.** A comparison of the markets set out in the two lists shows that a correspondence exists between them. The Commission does not appear to have added markets in the Recommendation as compared to the list drafted by the Parliament and Council, but seems rather to have taken over those identified in Annex I to the Framework Directive.[212] Pursuant to the Framework Directive, the Recommendation must be reviewed 'regularly';[213] this is confirmed in the Recommendation. For the Commission, a review is required on the basis of the constant changes that occur in the characteristics of products and services. It may also be rendered necessary by changes in demand and supply substitution. Pursuant to the Recommendation, the first review must be carried out before 31 December 1994.[214]

---

the market should be defined as encompassing bananas—and these fruit only. On that market, United Brands could be found to have a dominant position in application of Art 82 EC. United Brands counteracted with a proposal that the market should be defined as including all fresh fruit (oranges, etc). On that market defined in such a wide manner, the undertakings could not be found to have such a position. The position defended by the Commission was ultimately upheld by the Court and this led to the condemnation of the undertaking. See Case 27/76 *United Brands v Commission* [1978] ECR 207.

[211] See also Access Directive, Art 7(2).

[212] This correspondence is explained by the Commission on the basis of the consistency which must exist between the two frameworks (the old and the new) during the transitional period: 'this first Recommendation has to be consistent with the transition from the 1998 regulatory framework to the new regulatory framework' (Recommendation, para 3). The correspondence also provides a clue about the difficulty faced by the Commission in prospectively identifying markets in a general manner. In the framework of competition law, the Commission has indeed been accustomed to defining markets on the basis of facts which have already occurred.

[213] Framework Directive, Art 15(1), subpara 2.

[214] Recommendation on Relevant Markets, para 18.

Relevant markets identified by the European legislator and the Commission   **3.248**

Framework Directive	Recommendation on relevant markets
'Segments' identified in the Framework Directive	*Markets enumerated in the Recommendation on relevant markets*
Universal service	**Retail level (B2C)**
Access to the public telephone network at a fixed location	Same analysis, but division of the segment into two markets: *(a)* residential customers *(b)* non-residential customers
Publicly available telephone services provided at a fixed location	Same analysis, but division into four segments depending on type of communication and type of public: *(a)* local and/or national telephone services for residential customers *(b)* idem for non-residential customers *(c)* international telephone services for residential customers *(d)* international telephone services for non-residential customers
Minimum set of leased lines	Idem
Access and interconnection	**Wholesale level (B2B)** **3.249**
Call origination on the public telephone network provided at a fixed location	Idem
Call termination on individual public telephone networks provided at a fixed location	Idem
Transit services in the fixed public telephone network	Idem
Access to the fixed public telephone network, including unbundled access to the local loop	Same analysis, but division into two markets *(a)* Wholesale unbundled access (including shared access) to metallic loops and sub loops for the purpose of providing broadband and voice services *(b)* wholesale broadband access
Leased lines interconnection; wholesale provision of leased lines capacity to other suppliers of electronic communications networks or services	Same analysis, but division into two markets *(a)* wholesale terminating segments of leased lines *(b)* wholesale trunk segments of leased lines
'Segments' identified in the Framework Directive	*Markets enumerated in the Recommendation on services*
Mobile networks and services	
Call origination on public mobile telephone networks; access to public mobile telephone networks, including carrier selection	Access and call origination on public mobile telephone networks
Call termination on public mobile telephone networks	Voice call termination on (public) individual mobile networks *(correspondence)*
The national market for international roaming services on public mobile telephone networks	The wholesale national market for international roaming on public mobile networks
Broadcasting networks and services	
—	Broadcasting transmission services and distribution networks to deliver broadcast content to end users

3.250 Powers granted to NRAs.   The Commission is not the only body authorised to play a role in the identification of markets for the assessment of competition before a decision can be taken for the application of regulatory obligations. NRAs may also intervene, although their role is more limited. Pursuant to the regulation, NRAs are to identify, on the basis of national circumstances, the markets they consider relevant for the assessment to be made of competition on their respective national territories. In application of that mandate, these authorities are expected to adopt a list similar to that in the Recommendation, identifying the markets where, in their opinion, competition must be assessed.

3.251 Consistency.   To safeguard the internal market, a certain level of consistency must exist between these national lists and the Recommendation. The Framework Directive therefore provides that NRAs are under an obligation to base their assessment on the market definition provided by the Commission. There is little doubt that the Commission would take action should it have the impression that the Recommendation or the 2002 Guidelines on market analysis and significant market power were not followed. Admittedly, the obligation is not expressed in formal terms. The necessity for NRAs to comply is however indicated with clarity. In the three instruments under examination, national authorities are asked to take the 'utmost account' of the Recommendation and guidelines.[215] In the 2002 Guidelines on market analysis and significant market power the Commission adds that it will review with care the decisions taken on this point by the NRAs with a view to assessing their legality and proportionality.

> *2002 Guidelines on market analysis and significant market power, para 7.* 'Under Article 15(3) of the Framework Directive, NRAs should take the utmost account of these guidelines. This will be an important factor in any assessment by the Commission of the proportionality and legality of proposed decisions by NRAs, taking into account the policy objectives laid down in Article 8 of the Framework Directive.'

3.252 Corollary.   A corollary of this obligation is that NRAs may not assess competition on the basis of their own definition of the relevant markets where this definition is different from that established at European level. In case of divergence, national authorities must submit their analysis to the Commission. *(a)* In some instances, the Commission may be convinced that markets must be defined differently from what is being provided in the Recommendation on relevant markets. In that scenario, the Commission may take the idea over and insert it in the Recommendation. Consistency will thus be maintained, as the European analysis will be made to conform to the national. *(b)* Another possibility is that a national authority may not succeed in convincing the Commission that one or several

---

[215] See Framework Directive, Art 15(3); Recommendation on Relevant Markets, recital 7 and Art 1; and 2002 Guidelines on market analysis and significant market power, para 7.

markets should be defined differently than proposed by the latter. In that case, no modification will be accepted by the Commission, the Recommendation will have precedence and the national instrument will have to be made consistent with it.

> *Framework Directive, Article 15(3).* 'National regulatory authorities shall, taking the utmost account of the recommendation and the guidelines, define relevant markets appropriate to national circumstances, in particular relevant geographic markets within their territory, in accordance with the principles of competition law. National regulatory authorities shall follow the procedures referred to in Articles 6 and 7 before defining the markets that differ from those defined in the recommendation.'[216]

Geographic definition of the market. We have seen that market definition encompasses a functional and a geographical component. In the functional component, one attempts to determine whether a choice exists between various goods or services. These goods/services are items which serve the same function and must thus make it possible to satisfy a given need for the consumer. In the geographical component, one measures the possibility for consumers of obtaining within a given territory the goods and services which are considered as functionally equivalent.   **3.253**

Division of powers (1). These two components are treated differently in the NRF as regards the distribution of powers. In the presentation made above, it has been stated that the main competence is attributed to the European legislator as regards the functional determination. Another solution has been adopted for the geographical component. Pursuant to the regulation, the task of carrying out the analysis in connection with this latter component is entrusted to the NRAs. Pragmatism is at the origin of this difference in treatment. In general, services may be analysed in an abstract manner. The analysis can thus be made by the Commission, without the constraint for that institution to collect factual data implying complex and burdensome procedures. Another attitude has been taken with respect to the geographical component of market definition. The analysis to be carried out in connection with that component implies a factual examination which the European legislator has considered should be entrusted to NRAs.   **3.254**

Division of powers (2). As a consequence of this division of powers, one should not expect the Commission to engage in an exercise where, for instance, it would have to consider whether a market for a given service is limited to a given municipality or province. The definitions given to markets at European level do not cover, as a result, the whole range of issues relating to market definition. There remains some margin of manoeuvre for NRAs, even if that margin appears somewhat limited.   **3.255**

---

[216] Arts 6 and 7 of the Framework Directive, to which a reference is made in that provision, organise the special regulatory procedure. Pursuant to that procedure, decisions envisaged by NRAs must be communicated in the form of a draft to the like authorities in the Member States as well as to the Commission. These authorities and the Commission then have the possibility to submit observations that must be taken into account by the author of the document. When it comes to decisions concerning market definitions, the Commission also has the power to veto the adoption of the draft.

The power left to NRAs to determine the geographic extension of the markets is acknowledged in the Framework Directive. It is also discussed in the 2002 Guidelines on market analysis and significant market power, which indicate that the Commission has responsibility for the functional component of market definition whereas NRAs must mainly turn their attention to the geographical dimension of the market.

> *2002 Guidelines on market analysis and significant market power.* 'National regulatory authorities shall . . . define relevant markets appropriate to national circumstances, in particular relevant geographic markets within their territory.'[217] '[I]n practice the task of NRAs will normally be to define the geographical scope of the relevant market.'[218]

3.256 **Transnational markets.** In some instances, markets may cover several Member States or portions of national territories. An issue is then who is responsible for the definition of the relevant market. It should be borne in mind that the definition exercise is important because it has an impact on the assessment of competition. That exercise may be used by an NRA to impose more, or fewer, regulatory obligations.[219] A certain level of co-ordination is desirable if contradictory decisions are to be avoided. Discrepancies between evaluations made by national authorities may indeed lead to legal uncertainty and hinder the attainment of the internal market.[220] This kind of problem may be avoided or resolved only if a form of co-operation is introduced in situations where markets may cover several Member States or portions of national territories. This concern is covered by the Framework Directive, which entrusts the Commission with the power of adopting a decision identifying transnational markets. In transnational situations, the definition of the markets is thus taken over by the Commission. Beyond market definition, a European mechanism also comes into play for the assessment of market power. Pursuant to the regulation, co-ordination must take place between the NRAs concerned in the conduct of the assessment.[221]

> *Framework Directive, Article 15(4).* 'After consultation with national regulatory authorities the Commission may . . . adopt a Decision identifying transnational markets.'

---

[217] Framework Directive, Art 15(3).

[218] 2002 Guidelines on market analysis and significant market power, para 36.

[219] Suppose an NRA wants to carry out a rather liberal policy. That policy implies that undertakings are to be left free to develop their activities and that regulatory obligations must be kept, as a result, to a minimum. One manner to orchestrate that policy is to define markets in rather broad terms. This may only be done at national level for the geographic component because an exclusive power has been granted to the Commission for the determination of the functional component. In application of this, the NRA may define in broad terms the geographical market where an undertaking is present. With such a definition, it will be difficult to demonstrate that this undertaking has significant market power.

[220] Suppose that an authority from a Member State considers that a market is limited to its own territory and, on the basis of this assessment, decides that competition is not effective. A decision of that nature may be questioned by an authority from an adjacent Member State, on the ground that the market covers part of its territory as well and that, with that element taken into consideration, competition can be deemed sufficient.

[221] These mechanisms—European Decision identifying transnational markets and co-ordination among national authorities concerned—still have to be worked out. As of now, no Decision has been published by the Commission on transnational markets. The co-ordination has not been organised either.

(5) Market definition under the NRF and general competition law

The context of market definition.　An important debate in the context of mar- **3.257**
ket definition is the relationship between the harmonisation directives and general competition law, since markets are defined under the two bodies of rules. The
question arises whether the definition is the same in the two contexts or whether
differences appear. This is important because the two bodies of rules would appear
to be capable of being applied to the same issues. Before choosing in favour of one
or the other, the similarities and differences as regards the subject matter at issue
(market definition) must be analysed.

General competition law used in sector-specific regulation.　The issue of market **3.258**
definition may not be considered independently of the general rapprochement
that has taken place between the two bodies of rules with the adoption of the NRF.
In this regard, one should note the growing emphasis placed by the European
legislator on the increasing force of general competition law principles in the electronic communications sector. This appears with clarity in several instruments,
in particular the Framework Directive, where the Parliament and Council insist
that the NRF is based on concepts used in general competition law. A further indication may be found in the choice made by the European legislator to consider
that regulatory obligations must be applied to undertakings with significant market power. In this context the concept of market power acquires a central role. This
role is essential in the NRF, as the existence of 'significant market power' determines the application of regulatory obligations. It is also at the core of general
competition law, under which obligations are applied, in principle, where undertakings acquire 'dominance' unilaterally or jointly through their own conduct or
by means of anti-competitive agreements. However, the two concepts are
regarded in the NRF as being equivalent. Pursuant to the regulation, the concept
of significant market power used in the harmonisation directives corresponds to
the concept of dominance which appears in general competition law. Regulatory
obligations are thus imposed under the NRF in situations where obligations are
traditionally imposed under general competition law.

Rapprochement.　From this fact it can be concluded that the NRF has evolved **3.259**
so that the conditions for the application of regulatory obligations have been
assimilated in the harmonisation directives to those under general competition
law. This evolution is emphasized in the three instruments under examination in
this section, ie the Framework Directive, the Recommendation and the 2002
Guidelines on market analysis and significant market power.

Framework Directive. 'The Commission shall define markets in accordance with the
principles of competition law.'[222] 'The Commission shall publish . . . guidelines for

---

[222] Framework Directive, Art 15(1).

market analysis and the assessment of significant market power . . . which shall be in accordance with the principles of competition law.'[223] 'National regulatory authorities shall . . . define relevant markets appropriate to national circumstances . . . in accordance with the principles of competition law.'[224] *Recommendation on Relevant Markets.* 'Under the new regulatory framework, relevant markets are defined in accordance with the principles of competition law.'[225] 'This approach differs from the practice under the 1998 regulatory framework, where ex-ante regulation was applied to market areas defined in a more general manner and not always in accordance with competition law principles.'[226] *2002 Guidelines on market analysis and significant market power.* '[U]nder the new regulatory framework, in contrast with the 1998 framework, the Commission and the NRAs will rely on competition law principles and methodologies to define the markets to be regulated ex-ante and to assess whether undertakings have significant market power . . . on those markets.'[227]

3.260 **Advantages and difficulty.** The rapprochement between the two bodies of law has several advantages. One of them is that it increases legal certainty. As rules are now based on similar concepts, the risk of discrepancies diminishes. Another advantage is that a definition along the same lines of the circumstances in which authorities must intervene should normally lead to a decrease in intervention. The two bodies of law indeed merge, as far as concepts are concerned. The consequence is that a second set of rules (for instance regulatory obligations) does not need to be applied where the other (for example general competition law) is already in use. This leads to a situation which appears to conform with the principle that markets must be distorted the least—a principle that has a central role in the NRF.

3.261 **Ambiguity.** The rapprochement between the harmonisation directives and general competition law thus appears to be a positive development. However, the European legislator has adopted a rather ambiguous position vis-à-vis that rapprochement. On the one hand, it has claimed that legal certainty would be increased as a result of the decision to found regulatory obligations on concepts used in general competition law. On the other hand, it has emphasised that differences may subsist in the application of certain concepts. This position, which acknowledges a rapprochement and maintains differences, is expressed in several instruments. In the Framework Directive, for instance, the Parliament and Council state that markets must be defined for the imposition of regulatory obligations in conformity with the principles applicable in general competition law. However, they also state that this should not preclude the Commission or national authorities from arriving at divergent conclusions where they define markets 'in specific cases under competition law'. This observation makes clear that, in the eyes of the European legislator, a difference may exist between the markets

---

[223] Framework Directive, Art 15(2). [224] ibid, Art 15(3).
[225] Recommendation on Relevant Markets, para 5. [226] ibid, para 5.
[227] 2002 Guidelines on market analysis and significant market power, para 5. See also para 24.

defined in the Recommendation on relevant markets for the application of regulatory obligations and the markets defined in connection with a procedure relating to general competition law.

> *Framework Directive, Article 15(1).* 'The recommendation shall identify . . . those product service markets . . . the characteristics of which may be such as to justify the imposition of regulatory obligations . . . without prejudice to markets that may be defined in specific cases under competition law.'[228]

Reasons for this ambiguity. The reasons for the differences that may appear in the ways markets are defined in the two contexts are explained in the 2002 Guidelines on market analysis and significant market power. The first reason given by the Commission—and a reason that is traditionally put forward to explain the differences between the two bodies of law—relates to the nature of public intervention in regulation and general competition law. In the traditional analysis,[229] competition law is said to be made up of rules which apply ex post facto—after facts harmful to competition have been observed and in an attempt to make these facts disappear so that competition may be restored. By contrast, ex ante regulation is said to imply the application of obligations before distortive situations arise. Another aspect is that, in general competition law, rules are applied with a view to putting an end to a situation where specific conduct in violation of competition rules has been detected. By contrast, the attitude is more general and abstract in regulation where competition must be assessed in overall terms.[230]   **3.262**

> *2002 Guidelines on market analysis and significant market power, para 27.* 'Although NRAs and competition authorities, when examining the same issues in the same circumstances and with the same objectives, should in principle reach the same conclusions, it cannot be excluded that, given the differences outlined above, and in particular the broader focus of the NRAs' assessment, markets defined for the purposes of competition law and markets defined for the purpose of sector-specific regulation may not always be identical.'

Danger of discrepancy. The result of these differences is that there may be divergences as regards market definition depending on the context in which the exercise takes place. Markets may thus be defined in different, and diverging, fashions, even though the harmonisation directives and general competition law are   **3.263**

---

[228] This reservation made by the European legislator in the Framework Directive is heavily relied upon by the Commission in order to justify the possibility that differences may appear between sector specific regulation and general competition law.

[229] See 2002 Guidelines on market analysis and significant market power, para 26.

[230] The Commission accepts that merger control does not imply an evaluation of past conduct but rather an assessment about how competition would further develop in a specific market as a result of the operation under investigation. However, it writes, the markets are assessed at the time when the decision is taken. That decision is normally not subject to review thereafter. The perspective is different when an assessment is made before deciding that regulatory obligations must apply as this assessment will be repeated regularly. See the 2002 Guidelines on market analysis and significant market power, paras 26 and 28.

based on the same principles and a similar methodology used. These differences may create uncertainty. Difficulties may thus outweigh the advantages that have been presented as deriving from the establishment of a conceptual equivalence between the two areas of the law. It should be recalled that no provision in the NRF prevents authorities from applying concurrently obligations deriving from the harmonisation directives and from general competition law. One can expect authorities to act consistently where these two bodies of law are applied by the same entities.[231] It is however legitimate to reflect on the outcome where different bodies are entrusted with the application of the rules pertaining to the two bodies of law.

3.264 **Solutions available in the new regulatory framework.** The difficulty may in the Commission's view be resolved through several mechanisms. First, an obligation is imposed on all parties to strive for consistency. It is accepted that divergences may appear in concrete circumstances where the concepts are applied. The methodology is however the same under the two bodies of law, and the authorities are urged to maintain that methodological coherence. The same principles should thus be used in the two areas in order to define the relevant markets. Furthermore, procedures are organised to ensure co-ordination between the various authorities likely to intervene in the application of the two bodies of rules.

> *Methodological coherence.* 'NRAs should . . . seek to preserve, where possible, consistency in the methodology adopted between, on the one hand, market definitions developed for the purposes of ex-ante regulation, and on the other hand, market definitions developed for the purposes of the application of the competition rules.'[232]
> *Co-ordination procedures.* 'In order to prevent any adverse effects on the functioning of the internal market, NRAs must ensure that they implement the provisions to which these guidelines apply in a consistent manner. Such consistency can only be achieved by close coordination and cooperation with other NRAs, with NCAs and with the Commission.'[233]

3.265 **Discrepancies to be avoided.** The possibility that market definitions may differ depending on the context in which they are formulated should not, however, be overemphasised. According to the Commission, variations can be explained, where they occur, by the differences existing between the two bodies of the law concerned. These differences are possibly exaggerated. In particular, a general opposition between ex ante general regulatory obligations and ex post facto competition law interventions does not appear convincing.[234] To bring a nuance to

---

[231] In some Member States, the NRAs are the same entities as those designated as NCAs.

[232] 2002 Guidelines on market analysis and significant market power, para 37.

[233] ibid, para 23.

[234] In other publications, it has been shown that, if any, the differences between the two bodies of law are minimal. See P Nihoul, 'European Telecommunications: A Real Departure from Regulation?' in G Haibach (ed), *Services of General Interest in the EU—Reconciling Competition and Social Responsibility* (1999), 127–166; P Nihoul, 'Convergence in European Telecommunications—A Case Study on the Relationship between Regulation and Competition (Law)' [1998] 2 Intl J of Communications L and Policy 1–39.

this opposition, it should be borne in mind at least that competition law is used to restore market conditions in situations where competition has been impaired. The role played by competition law is thus not different, in this regard, from the function attributed to regulatory obligations. Furthermore, it should be observed that general instruments are increasingly used under competition law to regulate ex ante situations that may harm competition. An example is the various regulations that are adopted by the Commission or the Council in application of Article 81(3) EC where an exemption is granted from a prohibition affecting anti-competitive agreements. This technique does not appear very distant from that used with the imposition of regulatory obligations.

Where differences appear. These reasons lead to the submission that there **3.266** should normally be no differences between market definitions, whether the exercise takes place in application of the NRF or of general competition law. Should differences appear, practitioners could introduce a proceeding before a national court in cases where the issue is handled by a national authority. In the course of that national proceeding, a preliminary question could be submitted to the ECJ. This procedure should allow the ECJ to state how the relevant market(s) must be defined. It will then emerge whether the differences in market definitions are due to aspects of the law that are intended to be applied, or to an error made by the national authority responsible for the case.[235]

G. Undertakings with Significant Market Power

(1) When may specific obligations be imposed?

National authorities must assess competition. After markets have been **3.267** defined, authorities must analyse the degree of competition existing on them. Pursuant to the regulation, this analysis must take place as soon as possible after the adoption of the Recommendation on relevant markets by the Commission. Another analysis must be made after each revision of the Recommendation. As the Recommendation must be reviewed at the latest in 2004, one can expect assessments by NRAs to be made again soon after that date. As the analysis implies

---

[235] The reason behind the possibility of diverging applications may ultimately have an institutional nature. Within the Commission, one Directorate General is in charge of general competition law and another is in charge of issues relating to the information society. This means that different teams intervene in the application and the determination of the two bodies of rules. This organisation implies that different teams are entrusted with the task of applying similar rules. This creates the conditions for contradictions. It should be noted that this institutional difficulty is not limited to the European level but has been reproduced within the Member States. In the Member States, one authority is in charge of competition law. Another has been created to ensure the correct application of the harmonisation directives. To the extent that the two bodies of rules are based on the same principles, two authorities are thus competent to apply similar rules.

the use of competition law concepts, Member States are advised to organise co-operation between their national authorities entrusted with the implementation of the NRF and the application of general competition law.

> *Framework Directive, Article 16(1).* 'As soon as possible after the adoption of the recommendation or any updating thereof, national regulatory authorities shall carry out an analysis of the relevant markets, taking the utmost account of the guidelines. Member States shall ensure that this analysis is carried out, where appropriate, in collaboration with the national competition authorities.'

3.268 **The purpose is to decide whether obligations must be imposed.** The purpose of the assessment exercise is to determine whether competition is effective on a given market. The existence of an effective or, in other words, of a sufficient degree of competition is important in determining whether specific obligations must be applied on these markets. Where competition is sufficient, it is thought that markets will produce by themselves the best economic outcome possible. Where competition is defective, intervention may be warranted in order to compensate for the defect which is observed on these markets. A decision then has to be taken by NRAs whether to impose specific obligations, and which.

> *Framework Directive, Article 16(2).* 'Where a national regulatory authority is required . . . to determine whether to impose, maintain, amend or withdraw obligations on undertakings, it shall determine on the basis of its market analysis . . . whether a relevant market is effectively competitive.'

3.269 **The decision depends on the degree of competition.** As seen from the last paragraph, the decision to impose specific obligations depends on the degree of competition existing on a given market. Where competition is effective, there is no need to apply these obligations, since markets are expected to solve issues spontaneously. On these markets, some obligations may have been introduced under the old regulatory framework. On the basis of the assessment carried out by the NRAs, these obligations may be lifted. In some circumstances they must absolutely be withdrawn as specific obligations may in principle be imposed only in situations where significant market power is established.[236] A different attitude has to be adopted on markets where competition is not effective. On these markets issues cannot be expected to be solved spontaneously, and intervention is thus warranted. On these markets, some obligations introduced under the old regulatory framework may still exist. The NRAs will have to determine whether these obligations will compensate for the deficit observed in the existing degree of competition. If the response to that question is in the negative, changes will have to be made to these obligations and the obligations introduced under the NRF applied.

> *Competition is effective.* 'Where a national regulatory authority concludes that the market is effectively competitive, it shall not impose or maintain any of the specific

---

[236] See Access Directive, Art 8(3).

regulatory obligations.' 'In cases where sector specific regulatory obligations already exist, it shall withdraw such obligations placed on undertakings in that relevant market.'[237] *Competition is not effective.* 'Where a national regulatory authority determines that a relevant market is not effectively competitive, it shall identify undertakings with significant market power on that market . . . and the national regulatory authority shall on such undertakings impose appropriate specific regulatory obligations . . . or maintain or amend such obligations where they already exist.'[238]

The existence of significant market power. Pursuant to the regulation, the **3.270** assessment to be made by NRAs concerning the possible existence of significant market power is equivalent, in principle, to the analysis which is carried out by competition authorities concerning the possible existence of a dominant position. Given that equivalence, the assessment must be made in conformity with the principles and the method guiding competition authorities. Competition is considered not to be effective in the presence of one or several undertakings holding 'significant market power'. Pursuant to the definition provided in the regulation, undertakings are said to hold such market power where they have a position of economic strength which allows them to behave independently of other market participants (competitors, customers, consumers). That definition corresponds to the one which is given under the concept of 'dominant position' in general competition law—a reason why the assessment by NRAs must be made in accordance with the competition rules and, wherever possible, in co-operation with national competition authorities (NCAs).

> *Framework Directive.* 'It is essential that ex ante regulatory obligations should only be imposed where there is not effective competition, ie in markets where there are one or more undertakings with significant market power.'[239] 'An undertaking shall be deemed to have significant market power if, either individually or jointly with others, it enjoys a position equivalent to dominance, that is to say a position of economic strength affording it the power to behave to an appreciable extent independently of competitors, customers and ultimately consumers.'[240]

Additional conditions to be fulfilled before intervention. Pursuant to the regula- **3.271** tion, conditions additional to the absence of effective competition must be fulfilled before specific obligations can be applied. These conditions have been examined under the analysis of the markets listed by the Commission in the Recommendation, as well as those designated by the Parliament and Council in Annex I to the Framework Directive.[241] According to these instruments, there are three conditions to be fulfilled for markets to be taken into consideration for the imposition of specific

---

[237] Framework Directive, Art 16(3).   [238] ibid, 16(4).   [239] ibid, recital 27.
[240] ibid, Art 14(2), subpara 1.
[241] As a reminder, these documents must be used by NRAs as a basis to carry out the assessment. It is worth recalling these conditions at the present stage, while referring to the previous section for more details.

regulatory obligations:[242] first, the existence of high and persistent barriers to entry (of an economic or a regulatory nature); second, the absence of structural characteristics allowing issues to be resolved spontaneously; third, the impossibility of resolving these issues through the application of general competition law.

3.272 **A check list of conditions to be fulfilled before applying specific obligations.** These three conditions have been examined in connection with market definition, and play an important role in the decision as to whether or not to impose specific regulatory obligations. It may be useful to integrate them in a check list of conditions to be satisfied before obligations of this nature can be imposed. Summarising these conditions, it can be said that specific obligations[243] may be imposed on undertakings with significant market power in the following circumstances: *(a)* the market is dominated by one or several undertakings; *(b)* entry is unlikely as a result of the existence of high and persistent (economic and/or regulatory) entry barriers; *(c)* there are no structural characteristics allowing competition to be restored through 'natural' means; *(d)* the issues likely to emerge as a result of the absence of effective competition cannot be resolved through the application of general competition law.

(2) The relationship between dominance and significant market power

3.273 **Significant market power defined.** As stated above, the existence of significant market power has far-reaching consequences, as it implies that specific obligations may be applied to the undertakings concerned. According to the Framework Directive, significant market power is deemed to exist where, individually or jointly with others, an undertaking enjoys a position equivalent to dominance. Dominance is defined in that directive as a position of economic strength giving the undertaking the possibility of behaving to an appreciable extent independently of competitors, customers and ultimately consumers.[244] It is a concept central to general competition law, where Article 82 EC prohibits abusive practices adopted by dominant undertakings, and the Merger Regulation empowers the Commission to block mergers where they could lead to the creation or the reinforcement of a dominant position.

> *Framework Directive, Article 14(2).* 'An undertaking shall be deemed to have significant market power if, either individually or jointly with others, it enjoys a position equivalent to dominance, that is to say a position of economic strength affording it the power to behave to an appreciable extent independently of competitors, customers and ultimately consumers.' *Article 82 EC.* 'Any abuse by one or more

---

[242] These conditions must be combined, thus a market will only be considered to the extent that the three conditions are fulfilled.

[243] These conditions are, on the one hand, those which have been introduced by the NRF and, on the other hand, those which were established under the old regulatory framework and remain applicable during a transitional period as a result of the mechanism instituted by the European legislator to prepare the implementation of the NRF.

[244] See Framework Directive, Art 14(2), subpara 1.

undertakings of a dominant position within the common market or in a substantial part of it shall be prohibited as incompatible with the common market in so far as it may affect trade between Member States.' *Merger Regulation, Article 2(3).* 'A concentration which creates or strengthens a dominant position as a result of which effective competition would be significantly impeded in the common market or in a substantial part of it shall be declared incompatible with the common market.'

Evolution in the interpretation. It is worth noting that the European legislator **3.274** has decided to maintain the concept of significant market power. The introduction of the concept under the old regulatory framework was then regarded as a regulatory innovation, as no similar concept was used in traditional telecommunications or competition law. The NRF still refers to significant market power as the central criterion for deciding whether regulatory obligations should be applied. The persistence of the concept does not mean, however, that it is to be interpreted in the same fashion under the new framework.

Old regulatory framework. Under the old regulatory framework, the notion of **3.275** significant market power was not defined conceptually. There was a general statement that regulatory obligations should be imposed on undertakings holding significant market power. These undertakings were identified with the assistance of a threshold formulated in terms of market share (25 per cent). Undertakings with a market share above that threshold were deemed to have significant market power. Regulatory obligations then had in principle to be imposed on them. Undertakings with a lower market share were not supposed to have significant market power, and obligations were accordingly not in principle applied to them.[245] Under that approach, the finding that an undertaking had a significant market share was mainly based on an evaluation to be made by NRAs about the necessity of applying special obligations to particular undertakings.

NRF. The approach is different under the NRF. In the new framework the **3.276** point of departure is not a desire to impose special obligations. It is rather an observation that competition is impaired on a given market. The finding that an undertaking has significant market power is thus based on a careful analysis, the purpose of which is to determine whether competition still functions effectively. A second difference over the old regulatory framework is the threshold, which is placed at a higher level.[246] Under the NRF, undertakings with a market share higher than 50 per cent are deemed to be dominant. In the event that the market

---

[245] Some flexibility was introduced in the system, to the extent that undertakings with less than 25% could be added to the group. As a corollary, undertakings with more than 25% could be withdrawn from the group of undertakings to be submitted to regulatory obligations. In each case, several criteria had to be taken into account, among which was the ability to influence market conditions.

[246] As stated above, the concept of significant market power is made equivalent to that of dominance in the NRF. The consequence is that significant market power must be determined with the criteria used to evaluate dominance in general competition law. The threshold for dominance is however placed at a higher level.

share is smaller, a more complex assessment must take place. A similar evaluation must be carried out when the market share is higher but where, for various reasons, competition does not appear to be impaired.

3.277   **Assessment to be made by NRAs**

Under the old regulatory framework	Under the NRF
(a) NRAs consider a market. *(b)* Their conclusion is that regulatory obligations must be imposed on one or several undertakings present on that market. *(c)* These obligations may be imposed where undertakings hold a market share higher than 25%.	*(a)* Similarly, NRAs consider a market. *(b)* and *(c)* They decide that competition is impaired on that market as a consequence of the power acquired by one or several undertakings. That power allows the undertakings concerned to behave independently of competitors, customers and consumers. This assessment may be based on several criteria, including market share.

3.278   **Differences between the two approaches**

Under the old regulatory framework	Under the NRF
(d) The finding that an undertaking has significant market power is based on a wish on the part of the authority that obligations be applied to one or several undertakings. From this point of view, the finding flows from the desire, by the authorities, that obligations be imposed. The finding appears to be based on the possibilities that it opens, in terms of obligations that can be imposed. *(e)* The possibilities for applying these obligations are wider. This flows from the fact that the conditions to be fulfilled are relatively light (low threshold).	*(d)* The finding that an undertaking has significant market power is based on an analysis of the market and a finding that competition is impaired on that market. The finding is made independently of the wish or otherwise to impose obligations. The obligations appear as a consequence of the finding. *(e)* The possibilities for applying the conditions are more restricted. This results from the stringent nature of the conditions to be fulfilled (high threshold).

3.279   **Why was equivalence established between dominance and significant market power?**   The question arises why the European legislator has made the concept of significant market power equivalent to that of dominance. Some explanation is provided in the Preamble to the Framework Directive. As explained there, the concept of significant market power was introduced under the old regulatory framework in order to ensure the development of competitive markets. That perspective is maintained in the NRF, but the Parliament and Council have announced that the concept should be interpreted differently in the light of market developments. The extract quoted here clearly states the existence of an equivalence between the two concepts, but provides little information about the evolution allegedly undergone by the markets or about the changes that were to follow in the interpretation given to the concept.

> *Framework Directive, Preamble, recital 25.* 'The definition of significant market power in the [Interconnection] Directive . . . has proved effective in the initial stages of

market opening as the threshold for ex ante obligations, but now needs to be adapted to suit more complex and dynamic markets. For this reason, the definition used in this Directive is equivalent to the concept of dominance as defined in the case law of the Court of Justice and the Court of First Instance of the European Communities.'

Several reasons.   In the absence of an official explanation, one can think of **3.280** several reasons why significant market power may have been made equivalent to dominance. A first reason might have been that, with the establishment of such equivalence, the same concepts would ultimately be used in the two bodies of the law. That rapprochement would increase legal certainty, as identical solutions would be applied to given situations on the basis of these two bodies of law. Another reason might have been that NRAs would be entitled to use the substantial case law developed in competition law. This, again, would increase legal certainty and facilitate public intervention, as such intervention could be modelled on action already undertaken under competition law. The situation would have been more difficult had the NRAs faced the necessity of building up an entirely new body of case law based on purely regulatory concepts. An additional reason might have been that an alignment between the concepts decreases regulatory activity. As stated above, the NRF is based upon an idea that intervention should be limited. There is little doubt that the parallel application of two identical bodies of law would not satisfy that criterion.[247]

Similar situations.   All these reasons may have played a role, but the main reason **3.281** is probably that the two concepts ultimately refer to situations that are not really different. As observed above, the purpose claimed by the European legislator as a reason to apply regulatory obligations is to ensure that markets function properly.[248] That is also the purpose pursued on the basis of competition law. The ideas underlying each body of law do not appear to diverge one from the other. In the two contexts, markets are supposed to work in an adequate fashion where undertakings strive to improve supply under the pressure of competition. That mechanism falters where competition is altered as a result of power or dominance being acquired by one or several undertakings. Where power or dominance is acquired, the market participants are no longer free to choose their suppliers. The result is that the latter are no longer under pressure constantly to improve the services they offer. In such a situation, public intervention must take place in order to compensate for the negative effects of power/dominance and to restore normal conditions on the markets.

Is there complete congruence?   Although dominance and significant market **3.282** power are thus formally regarded as being equivalent, a certain degree of ambiguity

---

[247] It would indeed be of no use to apply the same rules twice to the same situation.

[248] Cf Framework Directive, Preamble, recital 25. 'There is a need for ex ante obligations in certain circumstances in order to ensure the development of a competitive market.'

remains about the exact scope of that equivalence. Take the name given to market power in the NRF. The European legislator officially states that specific obligations may be imposed when undertakings can behave independently of customers, competitors and consumers. Although that definition, as stated above, corresponds to the concept of dominance in competition law, the European legislator does not impose that concept and persists in its willingness to maintain a specific concept.[249] A second source of ambiguity is that the statements made concerning equivalence are not very specific. No indication is provided about the status of equivalence or about the consequences that may derive from it. A good illustration is the emphasis placed by the Parliament and Council on the necessity for NRAs to comply with 'Community law' and the 2002 Guidelines on market analysis and significant market power when assessing the existence of significant market power. However, these institutions apparently refrain from referring specifically to competition law, even though the concept of dominance, which is central in that body of the law, provides the main criteria for that analysis.

> *Framework Directive.* '[N]ational regulatory authorities shall, when assessing whether two or more undertakings are in a joint dominant position in a market, act in accordance with Community law and take into the utmost account the guidelines on market analysis and the assessment of significant market power published by the Commission.'[250] 'In determining whether an undertaking has significant market power in a specific market, national regulatory authorities should act in accordance with Community law and take into the utmost account the Commission guidelines.'[251]

3.283 **The relationship between the concepts is construed in the 2002 Guidelines.** The Commission explains in the 2002 Guidelines on market analysis and significant market power how the NRAs must assess significant market power. In that document, the Commission construes to an extent the relations existing between dominance and significant market power. In that analysis, one finds an echo of the ambiguity already pointed out as existing in the Framework Directive. According to the 2002 Guidelines on market analysis and significant market power, the two concepts are in principle equivalent. That equivalence is mainly located at the methodological level, ie in the methods to be used by the respective authorities. At the same time, the Commission stresses the divergences that may appear in the way the concepts are applied. These differences, the Commission explains, are due

---

[249] In other words, although they have decided to establish a relation of equivalence between the two notions, it is not clear why, in these circumstances, the European legislator has not accepted, or decided, to abandon the notion of significant market power and turn resolutely to that of dominance. When two notions have the same content, there is no reason to maintain a difference between them. The difference may only be a source of divergence for future interpretation. Admittedly, undertakings, customers and authorities were used to the expression 'significant market power'. In our view, this does not provide a sufficient reason to maintain different concepts. The realities referred to are presented as 'equivalent' — why is that equivalence not reflected in the terms used to designate these realities?   [250] Framework Directive, Art 14(2), subpara 2.
[251] ibid, Preamble, recital 28.

to differences in the perspective adopted by the authorities in the respective situations. *(a)* A prospective view should be adopted by NRAs when applying the NRF. In that context, authorities have to determine whether obligations must be applied in the future. *(b)* A different attitude has to be taken in the application of competition law. In that context, authorities have to focus on specific conduct in the past.

> *Possible differences in the applications.* 'The designation of an undertaking as having SMP[252] . . . for the purpose of ex-ante regulation does not automatically imply that this undertaking is . . . dominant for the purpose of Article 82 EC Treaty.'[253] '[T]he application of the new definition of SMP, ex-ante, calls for certain methodological adjustments to be made regarding the way market power is assessed. In particular, when assessing ex-ante whether one or more undertakings are in a dominant position in the relevant market, NRAs are, in principle, relying on different sets of assumptions and expectations than those relied upon by a competition authority applying Article 82, ex post, within a context of an alleged committed abuse.'[254]
>
> *Equivalence in principle.* 'NRAs will . . . impose obligations on undertakings only where the markets are considered not to be effectively competitive as a result of such undertakings being in a position equivalent to dominance within the meaning of Article 82 of the EC Treaty.'[255] '[U]nder the new regulatory framework, in contrast with the 1998 framework, the Commission and the NRAs will rely on competition law principles and methodologies to define the markets to be regulated ex-ante and to assess whether undertakings have significant market power . . . on those markets.'[256] 'Under the regulatory framework, markets will be defined and SMP will be assessed using the same methodologies as under competition law.'[257] '[T]he assessment of effective competition by NRAs should be consistent with competition case-law and practice.'[258] 'The new framework has aligned the definition of SMP with the Court's definition of dominance within the meaning of Article 82 of the Treaty. Consequently, in applying the new definition of SMP, NRAs will have to ensure that their decisions are in accordance with the Commission's practice and the relevant jurisprudence of the Court of Justice and the Court of First Instance on dominance.'[259]

Equivalence at an abstract level with possible differences in application. On the basis of these extracts, it can be concluded that equivalence is acknowledged in principle but remains rather abstract, as the concepts may be applied differently in practice. This is no different from the conclusion drawn from the analysis made of market definition in competition law and the NRF. We observed there that emphasis was placed by the European legislator on the necessity of using the same method when markets were to be defined, irrespective of whether such definition takes place under competition law or the regulatory framework. Nonetheless, the reservation was made concerning the possibility that markets may be defined differently in 'specific' competition law cases. This shows that the European legislator has been

3.284

---

[252] Significant market power (authors' note).
[253] 2002 Guidelines on market analysis and significant market power, para 30.
[254] ibid, para 70.   [255] ibid, para 5.   [256] ibid, para 5.   [257] ibid, para 24.
[258] ibid, para 24.   [259] ibid, para 70.

willing to establish a link between the concepts used in the NRF and general competition law. This willingness has been translated into rather ambitious statements according to which concepts and mechanisms have been said to be equivalent. The way has however been opened for divergences to appear in concrete cases.

3.285 **Consequences for practitioners.** These remarks open interesting possibilities for practitioners. The statement that 'equivalence' exists between dominance and significant market power may be used as an argument by those who, in specific cases, would like to use the case law on dominance (competition law). At the same time, the reservations made by the European legislator about possible divergent applications make it possible for practitioners to claim that the concepts must be applied differently where they do not want to rely on that case law. In view of these possibilities, one may expect conflicting claims to be made. The result will probably be a rich, but complex, body of case law concerning differences and similarities between the concepts. The discussion will be made further complex by the institutional organisation between the two areas of the law. As will be seen in Chapter 6, conflicts concerning the application of the NRF must in principle be resolved by the NRAs. By contrast, issues concerning general competition law must be brought before NCAs or national courts. It can be expected that the existence of distinct bodies responsible for applying these concepts will reinforce the trend for diverging, and probably contradictory, decisions—a trend acknowledged in advance by the European legislator when it accepted that concepts and mechanisms may lead to different applications despite the equivalence which has been established between them.

(3) Assessing significant market power

3.286 **Elements of the definition.** Central to the definition of significant market power is the possibility for the undertaking(s) concerned of behaving independently of other market participants. This definition refers to behaviour an undertaking is supposed to adopt in the course of its activities on a competitive market. *(a) Customers.* On such a market, a normal attitude for an undertaking would be to care about the reaction of customers before taking a decision. If for example an undertaking envisages increasing prices it would, on a competitive market, normally consider whether this may affect the behaviour of customers. *(b) Competitors.* Another attitude that can be expected from undertakings on competitive markets is that they will pay attention to the reaction of competitors before engaging in a particular course of action. Before actually increasing prices, an undertaking will analyse what the consequences could be on the behaviour of competitors. Where the price is actually increased, will competitors adopt the same strategy, in which case customers would have little incentive for turning to another supplier? Or will competitors take advantage of the situation to maintain, or even reduce, prices in the hope of attracting dissatisfied customers?

Considerable strength. An undertaking can be considered to acquire domin- **3.287**
ance or significant market power where this mechanism—attention to the likely
influence of an action on customers and competitors—no longer works properly
on a given market. In some situations, undertakings have built a position of considerable strength which makes it possible for them to disregard the likely impact
of a given decision. Dominance in the sense set out above is typical of the position
acquired by telecommunications incumbents on the market for access to subscribers (local loop). As stated above, most Member States have only one infrastructure providing access to a variety of electronic communications services, and
that infrastructure is in the hands of one undertaking. *(a)* As a result of that situation, customers have little choice if they want to access electronic communications services—they have to use that infrastructure. A decision by the network
operator to increase prices is not likely to have a significant impact on the number
of customers.[260] *(b)* A similar remark may be made with respect to competitors.
As there is only one infrastructure, there are no competitors able to take advantage
of a price increase in order to attempt an increase in their own market share to the
detriment of the operator. The result is that the network operator is unlikely to
hesitate in increasing prices.[261]

Domination does not need to be complete. Under general competition law, **3.288**
authorities look at the degree of competition existing on the markets. Where they
consider that choice does not exist to a sufficient degree, they conclude that competition is not effective.[262] The assessment depends on the degree of competition
deemed necessary to achieve the objectives assigned to the markets. Where that
degree is not sufficient, the authorities conclude that competition is not effective.
The possibility then arises, under competition law, of sanctioning undertakings
when they adopt behaviour infringing such law. In the NRF, authorities must consider whether regulatory obligations should be imposed. In both cases, authorities
may conclude dominance or significant market power exist where no undertaking
is in a position to determine entirely the conditions under which activities are carried on. In other words, a finding that an undertaking has a dominant position does

---

[260] The only incidence would be that some customers would decide not to use a variety of electronic communications services. Such a result does not have negative consequences for the undertaking in all circumstances. The undertaking will be able to obtain superior profits if the revenues
generated by the price increase outweigh the decrease in output.
[261] The decision to increase prices may have as an effect that the provider will decide not to offer
the service. Such an outcome may have an influence on the turnover realised by the undertaking.
However, the diminution of the turnover may be compensated by a higher benefit as a result of the
price increase.
[262] If choice indeed is no longer sufficient, the undertakings concerned no longer base their
actions on a careful evaluation of possible reactions by customers and/or competitors. The pressure
that competition places on market participants no longer exists to a sufficient degree. In these situations, the mechanisms on which markets are based are somehow impaired and markets can no
longer produce the best economic outcome by themselves.

not imply that competition has disappeared from the relevant market. Conversely, the presence of a certain degree of competition does not preclude the existence of a dominant position.[263]

3.289   **(a) Principal criterion—market share.**   When they assess competition, authorities have to determine whether one or several undertakings have acquired the power to behave independently of the reactions of other participants—ie to ignore the mechanisms allowing the markets to achieve in principle the best allocation of resources. Criteria have been developed in the case law to determine when such power is acquired. The first criterion is the market share held by the undertaking. Market share normally gives an idea about the relative importance, and strength, of an undertaking vis-à-vis competitors on a given market. Authorities often refer to it, because it provides a rather objective basis for a decision.[264] Data may be taken from the statistics provided by various bodies or the accounting information published by undertakings present on the market concerned.[265] In practice, market share is mainly useful in setting boundaries within which a decision can be taken, with little probability of error, that an undertaking has significant market power or otherwise. A distinction is generally made between three situations, depending on the size of the market share in question.

3.290   **No significant market power under 25 per cent.**   Authorities generally consider that undertakings with market shares lower than 25 per cent do not enjoy a dominant position. Under that threshold, they normally decide that no further investigation is necessary. The reason is that other undertakings are present on the market in a proportion that makes it necessary, for the undertaking in question, under normal conditions to analyse possible reactions by competitors, and customers, before undertaking any course of action.

3.291   **Significant market power above 50 per cent.**   Market shares also provide a hint about the probable existence of dominance above a threshold of 50 per cent. According to established case law, market shares of that size normally indicate that the undertaking indeed has a dominant position or significant market power.[266]

---

[263] A certain margin of appreciation is thus involved in the finding that one or several undertakings are dominant or have significant market power. See 2002 Guidelines on market analysis and significant market power, para 22. 'In the exercise of their regulatory tasks . . . , NRAs enjoy discretionary powers which reflect the complexity of all the relevant factors that must be assessed (economic, factual and legal) when identifying the relevant market and determining the existence of undertakings with SMP.'

[264] The reality is that, in an economy-oriented legal discipline, quantitative analysis is preferred to qualitative assessment.

[265] This method is particularly appreciated because, it must be remembered, the laws of competition and the tools for their application have mainly been developed by economists.

[266] See Case C-62/86 *AKZO CHEMIE BV v Commission* [1991] ECR I-3359 at [60]; Case T-228/97 *Irish Sugar v Commission* [1999] ECR II-2969 at [70]; Case 85/76 *Hoffmann-La Roche & Co AG v Commission* [1979] ECR 461 at [41].

Under normal circumstances, market share on this scale demonstrates that the undertaking provides services under conditions that please customers to such an extent that the majority of them have decided to turn to it rather than choose another supplier. This relationship with customers cannot be explained without considering the competitive advantages that have been built by the undertaking. In most cases these advantages relate to unique resources that have been collected by the undertaking in the course of its activities.

Necessity of a more complex assessment between the two thresholds. The real **3.292** difficulty lies in situations where undertakings have more than 25 per cent but less than 50 per cent of a given market. In these situations, market shares do not provide sufficient indications, and further investigation is then warranted on the basis of other criteria, some of which are presented below.

How to calculate market share? The method used to calculate market share **3.293** may have a considerable impact. Generally, the share is calculated on the basis of the value generated by the operations performed by the undertakings in the market. Suppose market share has to be established on the market for mobile electronic communications services. The normal method is to see how much value each undertaking has obtained by selling its services. After establishing the total value obtained on the market, a division may be made to obtain the proportion of each undertaking. Another possibility is to look at the quantity of products sold, or the number of customers served, by an undertaking. These latter figures may however seem less relevant because they do not provide an indication as to the relative importance of the undertakings. Where an undertaking has 100,000 customers each spending 10 euros while another has 10,000 customers with expenditure of 1,000 euros per person, the second will probably have more power than the first, because it generates more value and probably has lower costs. In the example considered, the answer will depend on the definition of the relevant market. If customers are so distinct that they constitute different markets, no comparison will have to be carried out between the two undertakings. If the customers are identical in nature, and the difference merely lies in the quantity of the services they require, the undertaking with the lower number of customers but the higher turnover has more power than the other.

Link with relevant market. The criteria to be used ultimately depend on the **3.294** characteristics of the relevant market. It is for the NRAs to decide which to use for their evaluation. Examples are provided below, on the basis of the 2002 Guidelines on market analysis and significant market power and the case law adopted by the Commission.[267] *(a)* On the markets for leased lines, the relative strength of undertakings may be measured by leased lines revenues, leased capacity or numbers of

---

[267] See 2002 Guidelines on market analysis and significant market power, para 77.

leased line termination points.[268] *(b)* On the markets for retail services, authorities can refer to retail revenues, call minutes, number of fixed telephone lines or number of subscribers. *(c)* On the market for interconnection, power may be measured on the basis of revenues accrued for terminating calls to customers on fixed or mobile networks.[269]

3.295 **(b) Other elements to be taken into account.** It is important to stress that dominance cannot be established on the basis solely of an analysis of market shares. As stated above, strong indications can be inferred in situations where an undertaking has less than 25 per cent or more than 50 per cent. This analysis however needs to be confirmed by an examination of other criteria. These criteria are even more important where the undertaking holds a market share between these two thresholds. There is no definitive list of criteria to taken into account. Similarly, none of these criteria is decisive in itself. A conclusion that an undertaking has acquired dominance or significant market power may come only from a combination of these criteria. A thorough overall analysis of the economic characteristics of the relevant market must therefore be undertaken before coming to a conclusion. Experience shows that some criteria repeatedly appear as factors explaining why an undertaking acquires a strong position on a market. As mentioned above, most of these criteria relate to competitive advantages that have been acquired by undertakings in the course of their activities, and explain why customers turn to them rather than to competitors to obtain the service required.

> — *Control of resources, facilities or technologies that are not available to competitors.* The best advantage is to have under one's control a resource, facility or technology which is necessary to provide a service and to which competitors do not have access. The typical example is a comprehensive electronic communications infrastructure which, even now, is only in the possession of incumbents. An advantage of that nature ensures the undertaking superiority which inevitably brings dominance.
>
> — *Product/service diversification.* This protects undertakings against fluctuations in demand on a given market, allows them to build up economies of scope and provides an opportunity to satisfy a range of customer needs.
>
> — *Economies of scale or economies of scope.* These characteristics make it possible for undertakings to produce at lower costs and thus charge lower prices than competitors. They may be associated with the *overall size of*

---

[268] As the Commission pointed out, however, the number of termination points does not take into account the various types of leased line available on the market: analogue voice quality or high-speed digital leased lines, short-distance or long-distance international leased lines. One should thus prefer the revenues extracted by the various undertakings as a basis to measure their strength.

[269] Revenue indeed integrates the different values that call minutes may have (ie local, long distance and international). It thus measures market presence taking into account the number of customers as well as the network coverage.

the undertaking, which may allow it to shift resources easily from one market to another one depending on needs.

— *Vertical integration*. This organisation allows an undertaking to control production, improve delivery, co-ordinate operations and use advantages possibly acquired on one or several markets of the economic chain.

(c) Potential competition.   The market power acquired by an undertaking does   **3.296** not depend exclusively on the strengths and weaknesses it has built, or suffered, throughout the years. That power is also dependent upon the position and dynamism of competitors. Among these competitors, special consideration must be given to those outside the market when power is analysed but which may come into it, at that point posing a threat to the undertaking. In other words, the market power acquired by an undertaking can be constrained by the existence of potential competitors. Here again, authorities must measure the probability of entry through an analysis of the behaviour likely to be adopted by potential competitors in answer to a durable and significant price increase. This analysis implies an assessment of difficulties possibly faced by undertakings in entering the market. In principle, the absence of barriers to entry will lead undertakings with significant market power to behave cautiously. For instance, such undertakings generally avoid charging excessive prices out of fear that such prices would attract potential competitors that would not hesitate in entering the market given the absence of barriers.

Entry barriers.   Various types of entry barrier likely to be encountered on elec-   **3.297** tronic communications markets have been examined above. This examination has taken place in conjunction with market definition. *(a)* In some cases, barriers are of an economic nature. Examples may be found on markets where entry requires large investments, for instance to establish a network. It should however be emphasised that economic barriers should not be overestimated in electronic communications. The reason is that this is an area where innovation and technology play an important role. In electronic communications, competitive constraints may come from innovative threats posed by potential competitors that are not currently on the market. *(b)* In other circumstances, barriers are regulatory in nature. This sort of barrier still appears in electronic communications, where special and exclusive rights have been eliminated but other situations have been created where the presence on a given market depends upon an authorisation or a decision to be taken by an authority (such as GSM/DCS or 3G mobile services).

(4)   Who has the power to assess competition and impose specific obligations?

Assessment by NRAs and control through various mechanisms.   Pursuant to   **3.298** the regulation, competition must be assessed by NRAs. That power is granted by the Framework Directive (Article 16) and the Access Directive (Article 8). Limitations are imposed, however. In particular, the assessment must be based on the 2002 Guidelines on market analysis and significant market power and the Recommendation on relevant markets issued by the Commission. It must further be carried out in accordance with concepts used in general competition law. The requirements set forth in the NRF as regards action undertaken by authorities—in particular the basic regulatory principles—also need to be respected. Several mechanisms are established to ensure that these rules are complied with in the course of the assessment. They are examined in the following paragraphs.

3.299 **The special regulatory procedure.**   The main mechanism is the special regulatory procedure established in the Framework Directive. It may be used in respect of the decisions envisaged by the NRAs in several circumstances, including the decisions concerning market definition and assessment of competition. Under that procedure, NRAs must communicate to the Commission and the authorities of the other Member States the draft decisions they intend to take. As regards the subject matter under consideration, the obligation to communicate thus applies to authorities for the decisions they envisage concerning their competition assessment. The communication cannot be limited to the operative part of the envisaged decisions, but must set out the reasoning on which the latter is based. Once the communication has been made, two possibilities may be envisaged.

3.300 **Procedure under normal conditions.**   The normal procedure is that, on the basis of the communication, the Commission may provide comments. A period of one month is granted to that effect. That period may not be extended. The same possibility is open to NRAs established in other Member States. Pursuant to the regulation, the comments must be taken into account by the author of the draft. This formulation implies that the comments made by the Commission or the other authorities do not necessarily have to be accepted. An explanation should then be provided, by the drafting authority, as to the reasons why it has chosen not to accept these comments.[270]

3.301 **Additional powers granted to the Commission.**   In some circumstances, the Commission is granted powers additional to the possibility of submitting comments. These powers are set out in the Framework Directive as part of the special regulatory procedure. They apply when the decision that is envisaged by an NRA concerns the designation of one or several undertakings as having significant market power. Such designation takes place where the authority considers that

---

[270] In our opinion, an authority which does not accept some or all comments made by the Commission or other NRAs may be requested to explain its position. In that scenario, two constraints would weigh on that authority. On the one hand, it would have to reason the content of the decision it has adopted. This obligation to provide reasoning derives from the protection that is provided to legal and natural persons. The right to obtain an explanation is acknowledged as a fundamental right in the EU. On the other hand, the authority should also explain the reasons which have led it not to accept the comments it has received. A control would be open on both counts, using the mechanisms described in the next paragraph.

competition is not effective on a given market. The designation of this or these undertakings thus follows the observation that competition is impaired to an unacceptable degree on that market.

Compromise.   These powers are organised with care in the regulation, and in **3.302** fact gave rise to difficult discussions during the preparation of the NRF. The final mechanism reflects the compromise reached by the parties to the legislative process. *Conditions.* These powers are only available where the draft measure would create a barrier to the single market or does not appear to conform with European law. *Prerequisites.* Comments as to these two grounds must have been made by the Commission during the period described above (see para 3.300). *Timing.* A new period is opened during which no decision may be adopted by the NRA. This provides a 'cooling-off' period during which the reasons underlying the draft decision may be examined again. *Outcome.* The Commission can ask the national authority to withdraw the measure. This request must be made during the period referred to above, and must be accompanied by an analysis explaining the reasons why the draft should not be adopted. The Commission must at the same time make concrete proposals as to how the draft could be improved.

Other mechanisms allowing oversight of the competition assessment.   Other **3.303** mechanisms may be used to check the assessment made by NRAs as regards effective competition. The regulation provides that parties likely to be affected must be kept aware of decisions envisaged by NRAs. Pursuant to the regulation, these parties must be given an opportunity to submit observations prior to the adoption of the decision. This procedure has general application, and may thus be used for decisions whereby markets are defined and/or decisions regarding the assessment of competition.[271] Information must be published about the existence of the procedure so that interested parties may make effective use of it.[272] The results of the consultation must be made public, with the exception of confidential information.[273]

> *Framework Directive, Article 6.* '[W]here national regulatory authorities intend to take measures . . . which have a significant impact on the relevant market, they should give interested parties the opportunity to comment on the draft measure within a reasonable period.'

Review.   Another mechanism is that the analysis carried out by the NRAs may **3.304** also be reviewed by a national body or bodies. As provided in the NRF, the Member States must organise in their national legal orders a procedure whereby decisions

---

[271] It should be noted that the said procedure is limited to decisions likely to have a significant impact on the relevant markets. Where the regulation is transposed using the same terms in the national legal orders, parties thus have to establish that two conditions are fulfilled before being granted a right to submit information. *(a)* They have to demonstrate that the decision would have a significant impact on markets. *(b)* They must establish that they would be particularly affected by the decision—and hence have a specific interest in letting their views be known.

[272] Framework Directive, Art 6.   [273] ibid, Art 6.

taken by the NRAs can be reviewed by an independent body. This mechanism provides a guarantee that claims made by consumers, customers and/or competitors will be heard and addressed on their merits.

> *Framework Directive, Article 4(1).* 'Member States shall ensure that effective mechanisms exist at national level under which any user or undertaking . . . who is affected by a decision of a national regulatory authority has the right of appeal against the decision to an appeal body that is independent of the parties involved. This body . . . shall have the appropriate expertise . . . to carry out its functions. Member States shall ensure that the merits of the case are duly taken into account and that there is an effective appeal mechanism.'[274]

3.305 **General European law.** Finally, the traditional procedures laid down in general European law may be used. By nature, their intervention is limited to situations where European rules are breached. They may thus be used in situations where NRAs breach Treaty provisions or secondary law—for example, a rule contained in the NRF. Among the available procedures, particular mention must be made of the possibility of requesting a preliminary ruling from the ECJ.[275]

3.306 **Check list for the special regulatory procedure**

(1) The NRA envisages the adoption of a measure.
(2) In normal circumstances, it is free to adopt its decision but must ensure that it complies with national and European law. Where European and/or national laws are not complied with, procedures can be initiated against the national authority before national tribunals. This procedure is appropriate for undertakings and individuals affected by the decision. Another possibility is to bring a case before the ECJ against the Member State of the authority in question. This procedure is reserved for the Commission and the Member States.

(cont.)

---

[274] There is no obligation for this independent body to have a judicial nature. In some instances, the review could thus be carried out by an administrative entity. Serious guarantees are, however, provided in the regulation, for the review to be thorough and effective: *(a)* the body in charge of the appeal must have the technical expertise needed to carry out that task properly; *(b)* the merits of the case must be taken into account; *(c)* the appeal mechanism must be effective. Additional obligations are provided for the situations where the appeal is not heard by a court: *(d)* the decisions taken by the entity entrusted with the appeal must be issued in writing; *(e)* an appeal must be possible against that decision—and that appeal must be brought to a court. See Framework Directive, Art 4(2).

[275] Pursuant to the traditional presentation, this procedure allows natural and/or legal persons to ask questions about the interpretation to be given to a European rule in a context where litigation has arisen. (The preliminary procedure may also be used to ask questions about the validity of European acts. This possibility is, however, not relevant in the present situation, as the focus is placed on decisions taken by NRAs.) In practice, the preliminary procedure is used to confront a national decision with European law. Where the national decision is found to violate European law, it has to be set aside by the national court that has initiated the procedure. Another useful mechanism is provided in Arts 226 and 227 EC. Under these provisions, an application may be brought to the ECJ by the Commission (first provision) or another Union Member (second one) when a Member State has failed to fulfil obligations imposed by European law. As NRAs are organs of Member States, the States may be held accountable for actions taken by their authorities and decisions taken by them. An Art 226 or 226 EC procedure can thus be initiated against a Member State, when the NRA of that State has breached European law in the fulfilment of its tasks.

(3) The special regulatory procedure must be followed only in particular circumstances, that is, where the decision envisaged by the authority concerns specific regulatory obligations to be imposed on undertakings with significant market power in circumstances where inter-State commerce would be affected.

    (3.1) The use of the special regulatory procedure implies the communication of a reasoned draft to the Commission and the other NRAs. These entities have one month to respond and the NRA must justify its position where it decides to go ahead without accepting the comments made.

    (3.2) Where the decision defines markets in a manner that differs from that proposed by the Commission or designates an undertaking with significant market power, the Commission may oppose the adoption of the draft. Opposition must occur within two months starting after the expiry of the first period (total = three months). It may occur only where the decision envisaged would create a barrier to the internal market or does not comply with the goals assigned to the NRAs.

(4) In all cases, NRAs may take urgent decisions without complying with the procedure described above. These decisions may, however, not be extended or made permanent without going through the special regulatory procedure, where the conditions for the application of that procedure are fulfilled. Decisions must conform to the basic regulatory requirements (objectivity, proportionality, transparency). They may be challenged before national courts or the ECJ along the lines set out above.

(5) Leverage effect

Significant market power on adjacent markets.   The NRF specifically examines **3.307** situations where an undertaking is dominant or has significant power on one market and uses that power in order to reinforce its position on a second, related, market. Pursuant to the framework, the existence of significant power on the first market may be a cause for NRAs to consider that that undertaking is also powerful on the second market. The undertaking may then be said to hold significant market power if several conditions are fulfilled: *(a)* significant power is held on another market, *(b)* the two markets are related, and *(c)* the position acquired on the first market may be used by the undertaking to improve its position on the second market.

> *Framework Directive, Article 14(3).* 'Where an undertaking has significant market power on a specific market, it may also be deemed to have significant market power on a closely related market, where the links between the two markets are such as to allow the market power held in one market to be leveraged into the other market, thereby strengthening the market power of the undertaking.'

Not an exceptional situation.   The circumstances described in the Framework **3.308** Directive are not exceptional. They often arise in the context of Article 82 EC, which prohibits abusive practices adopted by dominant undertakings. In general, the situations falling under that prohibition are divided into two categories, and are described below, together with leverage on the basis of that classification.

Exploitative practices.   The first category concerns undertakings which have **3.309** built significant market power on a given market. These undertakings make use of that position in order to extract excessive prices from customers. More generally, they offer terms and conditions which are not favourable to customers, that is, are less favourable than those which could be obtained in a competitive environment. These practices are generally called 'exploitative'.

Illustration. A typical example is the situation of former telecommunications operators before markets were opened to competition. These undertakings controlled infrastructure and were the only ones able to provide services through that infrastructure.[276] For that reason, they could charge excessive prices to customers, and naturally enough, customers were in general not satisfied with the terms and conditions under which the goods and services were supplied by these undertakings.[277]

3.310 **Exclusionary practices.** The second category covers undertakings that have acquired control of the resources necessary to carry out certain activities. These resources are located on one market and the activities which can be carried out with them on a second. As these resources are a prerequisite, undertakings present on the second market have to obtain access to them. These undertakings are thus in the position of customers vis-à-vis the undertaking on the first market. As it controls resources, the undertaking present on the first market also develops an activity on the second market. It is, however, faced with competition on that second market. This complex environment creates intricate relationships between market participants. On the first market, the undertaking acts as supplier and the other undertakings as customers. On the second market, the undertaking and the other undertakings are competitors. These intermingled relationships provide the undertaking with an opportunity to acquire advantages. In particular, it may be tempted to use the first relationship (where undertakings depend on it) to improve its position in the second relation (where all undertakings are competitors). This may be done, for instance, through charging excessive prices or imposing unsatisfactory terms and conditions on the first market in the hope that the position of the competitors will be altered on the second.

Illustration. A classic example is the position acquired by the former incumbent telecommunications operators after the markets for services were opened to competition. The introduction of competition in services made it possible to distinguish the formerly undivided telecom activities into two series of markets (infrastructure, services). The current situation is that activities relating to network operation can be located on a first market whereas the provision of services through infrastructure belongs to a second market—or rather, on secondary markets several activities may also be distinguished among the services. On the first

---

[276] A good indicator of that peculiar situation is that no distinction was made in terms of markets between the activities involved. This provides a sign that all these activities were considered part of a single market, which was reserved to the telecom operator.

[277] For an undertaking to be found in violation of Art 82 EC, there is no need for the unsatisfactory terms and conditions proposed to customers to be the result of a so-called perverse desire to obtain profits to the detriment of these customers. It is sufficient that these terms and conditions are not equivalent to what could be found on a competitive market. In many instances, the dominant undertaking does not wilfully seek to exploit its dominance. As a result of the lack of competition, it does not strive constantly to improve supply. Pursuant to case law, that is a sufficient reason to consider that the position is being exploited.

market, the incumbent has dominance or significant market power. It controls infrastructure necessary for carrying out activities on the secondary markets. As a result of that position, the incumbent may be tempted to use the dependence of competitors vis-à-vis infrastructure as a tool to improve its position on the secondary markets.

Complementarity between these situations. The situations described above **3.311** are often presented as being opposed to each other. In that sense, exploitative practices are opposed to exclusionary conduct. Observation however shows that these 'labels' do not really conflict with each other and, for that reason, should rather be presented as complementary. Exclusionary practices could indeed be interpreted as exploitative practices which are presented in a peculiar fashion as a result of the presence of the undertaking on several markets and the use it makes of its position on a first market to improve its situation on the others. According to our presentation, exclusionary conduct indeed refers to practices that may be called exploitative in the first place. They primarily consist of terms and conditions that are offered to customers and are unsatisfactory compared to what could be obtained in a competitive environment. These exploitative practices acquire a particular coloration as a result of the context in which they take place. The unsatisfactory terms and conditions are indeed imposed by the dominant undertaking as a tool to improve its position on a second market. Through that behaviour, competitors are excluded on that second market.

Various abusive practices **3.312**

First situation Exploitative practices	Second situation Exclusionary practices
(a) An undertaking holds a dominant position or significant market power on one market.	Idem
(b) That position allows the undertaking to offer terms and conditions which are inferior to those that could be obtained on competitive markets.	
(c) These terms and conditions are considered 'exploitative'.	
	(d) The undertaking is also present on a second market.
	(e) Its customers on the first market are its competitors on the second.
	(f) The unsatisfactory terms and conditions offered on the first market are a tool for the undertaking to improve its situation on the second market.
	(g) As these terms and conditions do not allow competitors to perform correctly on the second market, they may be called 'exclusionary'.

3.313 **The specific status of leverage.** Leverage corresponds to the situation described in the second category presented above. In that situation, an undertaking uses a dominant position or significant market power acquired on a first market as a lever to improve its situation on a second. One issue is to measure the influence provided by leverage on the second market. Where for example an undertaking is present on a first market where it holds a dominant position and that position allows it to influence the terms and conditions applied on a second market, it may, as a result of the power acquired on the first market, determine for instance who has access to the second market. It would be classic conduct for that undertaking to limit access to the second market. As a result of that limitation, competition will be impaired on that second market and the terms and conditions applied will not be satisfactory. In such a situation, one can say that the undertaking holds a dominant position on the first market and, probably, on the second as well. The dominance acquired on the first market and the leverage between the activities appear to provide it with tools to behave independently on the second market.

3.314 **Use power on first market to develop on second.** A difficulty arises where an undertaking dominates a market and, through leveraging, attempts to influence activities on a second market, yet without dominating it. In that set of circumstances, it may be appropriate for authorities to intervene at an early stage, before dominance is acquired on the second market as a result of leveraging. Such intervention is possible on the basis of Article 82 EC. The case law accepts that that provision can be applied in circumstances where dominance was held on one market and the effects of that dominance are felt on another.[278] The problem is more complex under the NRF. In that context, a finding that an undertaking holds significant market power implies that an NRA may impose regulatory obligations on the undertaking concerned. In normal circumstances, these obligations must however relate to the activities where significant market power is established.[279] In normal circumstances, such obligations may not be imposed with respect to activities where no significant market power exists. That limitation is however set aside through a provision included in the NRF and concerning leverage specifically (see extract in para 3.307 above). As a result of that provision, regulatory obligations may be imposed on a market where no finding of significant market power can be made using the traditional indicators of dominance, but links exist with a first market where significant market power is held and may be used as leverage to influence activities on that second market.

---

[278] A typical illustration is the joint offers sometimes made by dominant undertakings. In that mechanism, the undertaking has a dominant position on the market for one good or service. That position has the consequence that customers wishing to acquire that good or service have to accept the terms and conditions imposed by that undertaking. The said undertaking makes use of that dependence and forces customers to purchase additional goods and services.

[279] A link is indeed established in the NRF between the assessment which must be carried out of the state of competition on a given market and the possibility, for authorities, to impose obligations where competition is not deemed effective on that market. See Access Directive, Art 8.

Evaluation. The European legislator is probably right in allowing regulatory **3.315** obligations to be imposed on markets where leverage can be exerted. However, the legal technique that has been used to introduce that mechanism in the regulation is not satisfactory, since a distinction should be maintained between the two kinds of circumstances that are involved in leveraging. *(a)* In the first, an undertaking holds significant market power on one market and has already extended that position to a second. On that second market it is capable of behaving independently of customers, competitors and ultimately consumers. Regulatory obligations may thus be imposed, on the basis of the general principle ('obligations on markets where significant market power is held'). *(b)* In another set of circumstances, an undertaking dominates a market and attempts to acquire and/or increase its influence through leveraging on a second market without yet having achieved dominance on that second market. In those circumstances the undertaking does not hold substantial market power on the second market, nor do the traditional indicators associated with dominance show that significant influence has been acquired on the second market. Pursuant to the principle mentioned above, regulatory obligations cannot be imposed, in normal circumstances, in relation to activities belonging to such a second market. An extension is however allowed by the provision concerning leveraging in the NRF. This provision makes it possible to apply regulatory obligations in regard to activities on that second market, despite the absence of significant market power on the second market, in an attempt to impede the acquisition of dominance on the second market.

Distinction between circumstances. A distinction should probably be main- **3.316** tained between the two sets of circumstances, since obligations imposed by NRAs must comply with the proportionality principle. In certain circumstances, proportionality may require less stringent obligations to be imposed on markets where no significant market power is held.[280]

H. Joint Market Power

(1) Principles

Abnormal functioning of the market. The regulation mentions situations **3.317** where one or several undertakings together acquire significant market power. The scenario which is referred to is the following. Pursuant to the regulation, an NRA carries out an assessment to ascertain whether competition is effective on the

---

[280] There is also an ethical objection against the European legislator treating alike the two sets of circumstances. In the NRF, it is emphasised that an undertaking may be said to have significant market power in situations where influence can be increased through leveraging from a first market. In our view, it is not appropriate to state that significant market power may be deemed to exist in a situation where no such power may indeed be observed using the indicators relating to dominance. It is more appropriate to provide that obligations may be imposed in the absence of significant market power where this is felt necessary as a result of the dangers posed by leverage.

markets under its control. As stated above, competition can be deemed effective where no significant market power is acquired on a given market. On competitive markets, undertakings are supposed to consider the possible reactions of competitors and customers before engaging in action. In the philosophy underlying the reform, competition places on undertakings a constant pressure forcing them to pay ever-increasing attention to customers so as not to be set aside in favour of another supplier.[281] In the course of their assessment, the NRA comes to the conclusion that no single undertaking has acquired significant market power acting on its own. However, market-based mechanisms do not appear to function properly. On closer examination, the authority realises that, on a given market, some undertakings, and in some cases all of them, have ceased acting under the pressure of competition. To use the formula attached to the definition of significant market power, these undertakings are in effect behaving independently of competitors and customers. They may be said to be in a position similar to that held by undertakings unilaterally holding dominant positions. As the diagnosis is identical (dominance), with the difference that the undertakings concerned are several in number, the situation is described as one of 'collective' or 'joint' dominance.[282]

3.318 **Behaviour independent of competitors and customers.** This goes back to the concept of market power, which plays a central role in competition law. As submitted above, the idea underlying competition rules is that undertakings must be placed under certain constraints in order to deliver good economic results. Such a result is attained when customers have a choice among suppliers. The existence of choice places undertakings at the risk that they may be set aside in favour of other suppliers if, and to the extent, they do not offer satisfactory goods/services. This competition-based mechanism is impaired where customers have no choice among suppliers. As they have no choice, customers must accept the offer which is made to them. Their only alternative is not to purchase the relevant good/service. Relations with competitors can be analysed along the same lines. Undertakings normally watch the behaviour adopted, or likely to be adopted, by their rivals. In the absence of such an attitude, they risk being set aside by these competitors in the race to win customers' approval. In some situations undertakings may, however, stop worrying about competitors because the latter are not in a position to react. When customers and competitors lose the opportunity to react, it can be said that the supplier can behave independently of them. Whatever its behaviour, its offer will be accepted by customers without reaction from competitors. In these situations, the supplier is said to dominate the market: it can impose the conditions under which transactions are made on the market without possible reaction by customers and competitors.

---

[281] As a result of that pressure, undertakings are supposed to strive in order to decrease prices, increase output, improve quality, broaden variety, etc.

[282] Various expressions are used to designate these situations: joint market power, collective dominance, joint dominance, collective market power.

Independence resulting from co-ordination.   The disappearance of choice may   **3.319**
be encountered in situations where one undertaking has acquired a dominant
position. Criteria have been examined above to address these situations (see paras
3.286–3.297). These situations are normally considered under Article 82 EC and
the Merger Regulation.[283] Other situations may also be considered. In various
circumstances, dominance or market power[284] may be acquired by several entities. These entities do not act unilaterally and the position they acquire on the
market is the result of a kind of co-ordination which can take various forms.

Agreements/decisions of associations.   The first form is when two or more   **3.320**
undertakings enter into an agreement whereby they determine one or several elements of their future conduct. Another possibility is that they belong to an association which takes decisions binding the members. The elements on which an
agreement is concluded or a decision is taken will have been an object of competition among the parties in the absence of the agreement or decision.[285] The presence
of the agreement or decision puts an end, however, to competition between the
parties. The difficulty is the same under competition rules as that examined in relation to unilateral dominant positions. As a result of the co-ordination that has
taken place, customers indeed lose their freedom of choice in the absence of possible reactions by competitors.[286]

Concerted practices.   A variation is when undertakings co-ordinate their behavi-   **3.321**
our but the authority is unable to demonstrate the existence of an agreement or a
collective decision. Pursuant to case law, it is then accepted that an agreement or
a decision may be inferred on the basis of the interdependent conduct adopted by
the alleged parties. This is known as 'concerted practice theory', under which the
inference is accepted to the extent that no other explanation can be put forward to
explain the interdependence in behaviour.

Collective dominance.   A third situation is where two or more undertakings   **3.322**
co-ordinate conduct without concluding an agreement or adopting a collective
decision. Through co-ordination, the undertakings present themselves on the markets as a collective entity. It is this situation that is called 'collective dominance'.

---

[283] In the case of the Merger Regulation, the analysis is prospective. The purpose is to avoid the
acquisition or the reinforcement of a dominant position on a relevant market.

[284] These concepts are used as synonyms in this book.

[285] For instance, undertakings would have competed to provide the good or service at the better
price.

[286] Suppose two undertakings decide to fix the prices at which they will market a given service in
a determined geographical area. As a result of that agreement, the parties will no longer propose to
their clients different prices. They will in effect make the same offers. The result is that the client has
lost part of the freedom of choice he had beforehand. As was submitted above, the situation cannot
be accepted under the rules of competition, because the purpose of these rules is to ensure that customers have a choice between suppliers, thereby forcing suppliers to improve economic output.

The difficulty created by this situation is not different from that resulting from agreements, collective decisions or concerted practices. In that context also, undertakings behave independently of preferences expressed by customers and reactions by competitors, a situation that cannot be accepted for the reasons seen above.

3.323   Various forms of collusion or co-ordination of behaviour

Various forms of co-ordination of behaviour	Agreement/decision by associations	Concerted practices	Collective dominance
Agreements	Parties agree on future conduct (Article 81 EC)		
		An agreement has been concluded. There is however no need to establish it directly. Its existence can be inferred from interdependent conduct in the absence of other possible explanations. (Article 81 EC)	
			No agreement has been concluded and co-ordination has occurred as a result of market characteristics. (Article 82 EC)
No agreement			

3.324   **Origin and development of the concept.**   The case law concerning undertakings holding dominance on the same market has emerged in the application of Article 82 EC, which prohibits abuse of a dominant market position. It was then extended to the assessment made by the Commission under the Merger Regulation. This extension raises some difficulties. Under Article 82 EC, the collective dominance theory is indeed used to assess the behaviour of undertakings that have allegedly engaged in abusive conduct. In this context attention is focused on an undertaking which may have behaved illegally. The attitude is however different when the theory is considered in relation to the Merger Regulation. In that context, a notified operation is assessed in the light of the possibility that collective dominance may be created as a result of the position held by third undertakings and more generally of market conditions. As a result of that perspective, an operation could be prohibited for reasons independent of the parties themselves. The objection was set aside on the ground that restricting the focus to the operation would reduce the effect sought by the control carried out on mergers. Suppose an operation could go ahead in a situation where collective dominance might be created. The purpose of merger control would not be attained, since it is put in place precisely to avoid the creation of situations where competition ceases to function.[287]

Terminology.   Various terms and expressions are used in the legislation, the case   **3.325**
law and the literature to designate the situations discussed in the following sections and paragraphs. It is important to state how these terms and expressions are to be understood here. For instance, no distinction is made between the terms 'market power', 'significant market power' and 'dominance',[288] since they refer to the same reality—the position of one or several undertakings which may behave independently of customers or competitors as a result of factors that have already been examined (unilateral dominance) or are discussed below (joint dominance).

Concepts such as 'parallel behaviour', 'correspondence in behaviour', 'common course of action' are used to refer to situations where co-ordination has taken place among economic agents. In these situations, undertakings do not implement a strategy that they have chosen on their own. They rather follow a course of action that is the result of the co-ordination that has taken place—whatever the form of that co-ordination (agreement, collective decision, concerted practice or undertakings forming associations). Such a situation may be encountered for instance where market participants increase prices at the same time. As a result of that common move, clients are deprived of the possibility of choosing a supplier offering a lower price. In other cases the behaviour will not be identical but complementary. Suppose one undertaking increases prices and a second restricts output. The two behaviours are different but they may be explained by a common underlying purpose, to create a situation where customers pay more for less. As is apparent from these two examples, there may exist differences in behaviour where undertakings have co-ordinated their actions. These differences do not take away the co-ordinated character of these actions and the possibility that the latter are encompassed under competition rules as a result of the restriction that is then imposed on customers in situations where competitors (if any) are unable to react.

Two kinds of situation.   The situations where the theory of collective dominance   **3.326**
is used in European case law are discussed in the following sections. These situations may be divided into two categories. In the first, authorities are confronted with a situation where undertakings hold dominant positions on contiguous territories. They decide to consider these positions as a whole covering a substantial

---

[287] See Joined Cases C-68/94 & C-30/95 *France and Société commerciale des potasses et de l'azote (SCPA) and Entreprise minière et chimique (EMC) v Commission* [1998] ECR I-1375 at [152]–[177]; Case T-102/96 *Gencor v Commission* [1999] ECR II-753, at [123]–[140].

[288] In our terminology, market power means the same as dominance. The European legislator refers to *significant* market power in the NRF because it wishes to continue using this expression which already appeared in the old framework. No difference is made between market power and significant market power.

part of the common market. In a second type of situation, several undertakings adopt a common course of action on the same geographical market. As a result of their common approach, and for other reasons also, these undertakings form a collective entity able to behave independently of customers and competitors.

(2) Juxtaposition of unilateral dominant positions

3.327 **Distinct territories.** In the first category, a series of undertakings dominate distinct geographical territories. Although they are held on distinct territories, these positions are not analysed individually. They are considered as forming a whole, as a result of which the authority can conclude that a dominant position is held on a substantial part of the common market. The consequence is that European competition law can be applied.[289]

3.328 **Leading case.** The leading case in this category is *Almelo*, which involved the production and distribution of electricity in the Netherlands.[290] A joint company had been formed by the four producers of electricity active on the territory of the Netherlands at the time the case arose. The object of the agreement was to organise the marketing of the electricity supplied by the producers in question. Within that joint company, it was agreed that distribution would occur on a geographical basis. The national territory was divided into geographical areas and exclusivity was granted to each distributor in a given area. The case arrived at the ECJ as a result of a tariff increase decided by a distributor and contested by a customer. In its ruling, the ECJ remarked that each distributor dominated a specific geographical area as a result of the exclusive right that had been granted to it. For the ECJ, the possibility existed of considering these positions together: links existed between the undertakings concerned and these links were strong enough to consider the latter as forming a collective entity.

> *Almelo.* 'Although the conclusion cannot automatically be drawn that a dominant position is held in a substantial part of the common market by an undertaking which . . . has a . . . concession covering only part of the territory of a Member State, a different assessment must apply where that undertaking belongs to a group of undertakings which collectively occupy a dominant position.'[291] '[I]n order for such a collective dominant position to exist, the undertakings in the group must be linked in such a way that they adopt the same conduct on the market.'[292]

---

[289] European competition rules only apply where interstate commerce is affected. The condition is explicitly formulated in the various provisions or legal instruments applying these rules (Art 81 EC, Art 82 EC and the Merger Regulation).

[290] Case C-393/92 *Municipality of Almelo v NV Energiebedrijf Ijsselmij* [1994] ECR I-1477.

[291] At [41].

[292] At [42]. In that judgment, the Court considers that several undertakings may form a group holding a dominant position. The Court uses a terminology that is similar to that used in the theory pursuant to which several companies belonging to the same group form a single undertaking for the application of competition law. By referring to the existence of a 'group', the Court extends that theory to the situation where various undertakings form a unit or an entity characterised by a common course of action.

La Crespelle.   Another illustration may be found in *La Crespelle*,[293] a case con-   **3.329**
cerning artificial insemination of bovine animals in France. Pursuant to the rules
in force in that country, insemination could be performed only in, and by, centres
authorised for the purpose. These centres were granted a monopoly in a defined
geographical area. None of them had a dominant position on a substantial part of
the internal market. It was, however, possible to aggregate these positions to consider that a form of collective dominance was created by the French legislator on
a substantial part of the internal market.

> *La Crespelle.* '[B]y making the operation of the insemination centres subject to
> authorization and providing that each centre should have the exclusive right to serve
> a defined area, the national legislation granted those centres exclusive rights. By thus
> establishing, in favour of those undertakings, a contiguous series of monopolies ter-
> ritorially limited but together covering the entire territory of a Member State, those
> national provisions create a dominant position . . . in a substantial part of the com-
> mon market.'[294]

Bodson.   Another—yet less clear—example appears in *Bodson*,[295] which con-   **3.330**
cerned the market for 'external services' of funerals.[296] In that case, 5,000 French
communes, out of a total of 36,000 (approximately 45 per cent of the population
of France) had granted to private undertakings a concession to provide these
'external services'. An issue was raised about allegedly high tariffs charged by a
group composed of several of these companies active in various municipalities.
The issue was brought to the ECJ in a request for a preliminary ruling. The ECJ
found that Article 81 EC could not be applied because the various companies
were controlled by the same shareholders and could not be considered, as a result,
as separate undertakings. These companies could on the contrary be considered as
forming one undertaking in their aggregate. A question raised in the case was
whether one could consider in their aggregate the dominant positions held by the
members of this group, and those held by other undertakings in other municipalities where exclusive rights had also been granted for the provision of the external
services.

---

[293] Case C-323/93 *Société Civile Agricole du Centre d'Insémination de la Crespelle v Coopérative
d'Elevage et d'Insémination Artificielle du Département de la Mayenne* [1994] ECR I-5077.
[294] At [17]. It should be noted that the Court refrains in that case from using the expression 'collective dominance'. It rather refers to a situation where dominant positions are juxtaposed. It is difficult to infer from the choice of these words any conclusion as to the position of the Court regarding
the application of the collective dominance theory in these circumstances. Our feeling is that the
theory applies, but that the circumstances dealt with in *La Crespelle* are specific to the first category
of situation aimed at by the theory.
[295] Case 30/87 *Bodson v Pompes funèbres des regions libérées* [1988] ECR 2479.
[296] These services cover the carriage of the body after it has been placed in the coffin, the provision of hearses, coffins and external hangings of the house of the deceased, conveyances for mourn-
ers, the equipment and staff needed for burial and exhumation and cremation. They are
distinguished from the 'internal services', which relate to the religious services, or the 'unregulated
services' which cover non-essential funeral services such as the supply of flowers and marble work.

3.331 **Characteristics of the first category.** The cases pertaining to the first category have characteristics in common. First, the expression 'collective dominance' is hardly used explicitly in the judgments issued in these cases. It appears, in fact, in only one case, *Almelo*. No explicit mention is made of the concept in the two other cases. This is however probably because the cases at issue are rather old, and were issued at a time when the theory of collective dominance had not really emerged, let alone been developed.

A second remark concerns the definition of markets. Dominance must normally be interpreted with reference to a given market. The ECJ appears however to consider that a dominant position has been created on various markets and to conclude that these markets may ultimately be joined to constitute a substantial part of the common market. This analysis does not appear appropriate, from a technical point of view. One cannot define the relevant market, in the first instance, as covering a limited geographical area, and then consider, in a second stage, that it covers various segments where an exclusive right has been granted.

Third, one may wonder whether the ECJ has indeed accepted to give a ruling in the cases at issue. The cases concern exclusive rights granted to undertakings on separate territories. On these territories, the presence of exclusive rights made it impossible for competitors to enter the markets and for customers to have a choice between suppliers. A situation was thus created which is typical of economic dominance. This does not automatically imply, however, that European rules must be applied. Pursuant to the Treaty, Article 82 EC—the provision that was at stake in the cases under review—can apply only where dominance is observed on a substantial part of the common market. The impossibility of applying European law, if each territory was considered individually, does not imply, however, that no solution could be found to the case at issue. National competition rules could indeed be applied, in particular as regards the French[297] or the Netherlands[298] territories, where rules have been adopted and authorities have been created for that purpose. It is not sure, however, that the application of these national rules would have led to the censuring of the exclusive rights granted by the undertakings concerned. The liberalisation and opening of markets characterised by exclusive rights is a process which has originated in European law. The probability is thus that the ECJ has been justified in applying European law to the cases at issue. In fact, the position adopted by the ECJ—considering the various dominant positions as forming a whole—can somehow be interpreted as a mechanism implemented to ensure the application of European law in situations where national laws could just as well have been applied.

---

[297] For *La Crespelle* (n 294 above) and *Bodson* (n 296 above).
[298] For *Almelo* (n 291 above).

In the electronic communications sector. A juxtaposition of dominant posi- **3.332**
tions may be encountered on some electronic communications markets. An example is the situation of broadcasting networks in some European countries. In
these countries, the networks in question have been installed by entities with limited
geographical competence. In Belgium, for instance, the networks have been established and are maintained by private entities with the participation of municipalities
which may not act beyond their geographical territory. These entities have a dominant position on each of these markets. However, this dominance is not sufficient to
imply the application of European rules as the markets are too limited. European
law may however apply, if one considers these juxtaposed positions to form a whole
with the size necessary to imply the application of European rules.[299]

(3) Collective dominance on the same market

Introduction of the concept

Same geographical market. In the second category, undertakings are present on **3.333**
the same geographical (and product) market, where they hold together a dominant position. The main issue in this context has been to define the factors that may
lead undertakings to dominate such a market collectively. The case law on this
point has developed in several stages. The first step has been rather elusive, with
the European legislator introducing the concept without really defining it or
attempting to spell out the conditions to be fulfilled in order to consider that collective dominance is held. The concept was introduced in 1992 in *Società Italiana
Vetro (SIV)*.[300] This case concerned flat glass production, which the Commission
considered as being in infringement of Article 81 EC and Article 82 EC. As
regards the latter provision, the contention was that the undertakings which were
fined held a position of collective dominance and had made abusive use of that
position. The case came to the CFI, which upheld the position adopted by the
Commission regarding the existence and abuse of collective dominance.[301]
In that judgment, the CFI stated that several undertakings may hold together
a collective dominant position. For the CFI, a dominant position may exist where
undertakings are united by economic links.

---

[299] Before they can conclude the existence of collective dominance, NRAs must however enquire
whether there are substitutes for the distribution of TV programmes. The market must be extended
to the public telephone network if it appears that the latter network provides an alternative for the
distribution of these programmes. This is however far from being so in most countries as technology
and investment have not yet made it possible to provide TV services through the telephone in most
countries.

[300] Joined Cases T 68, 77 & 78/89 *Società Italiana Vetro (SIV) v Commission* [1992] ECR II-
1403. This judgment was rendered on an application against a decision of the Commission:
Commission Decision (EEC) 89/93 relating to a proceeding under Articles 85 and 86 of the EEC
Treaty (IV/31.906, flat glass) [1989] OJ L33/44.

[301] Other parts of the decision were annulled but these are not relevant to our discussion.

> *SIV v Commission.* 'There is nothing, in principle, to prevent two or more independent economic entities from being, on a specific market, united by such economic links that, by virtue of that fact, together they hold a dominant position *vis-à-vis* the other operators on the same market.'[302]

3.334 **Electricity.** A similar observation was made two years later (1994) by the ECJ in *Almelo*,[303] examined above, a case concerning the production/distribution of electricity in the Netherlands. In that case, the ECJ stated that a finding of collective dominance can be made where links exist among undertakings on a given market and those links are strong enough to allow the undertakings to adopt a common course of action.

> *Almelo.* '[I]n order for . . . a collective dominant position to exist, the undertakings . . . must be linked in such a way that they adopt the same conduct on the market.'[304]

3.335 **Subsequent cases.** The position adopted in *Almelo* was referred to in a series of subsequent cases with one feature in common—they involved decisions made by a public authority after consultation of a committee where economic agents were represented.[305] These cases do not bring any real contribution to the theory of collective dominance. They concentrate on the question whether dominance was held rather than attempting to determine under what conditions a collective entity may emerge on a market with several autonomous undertakings. In each of the cases at issue, a question arose whether the economic agents concerned were in a position to influence conditions on the markets. Arguments were raised that their participation in the committee conferred power on these economic agents. The plea was however dismissed by the ECJ, as the administrative decisions at stake were ultimately fixed, in all cases under review, by a public authority. Admittedly economic agents participated in the procedure, but their role was limited to an advisory function. That function was not deemed sufficient for the ECJ to consider that real influence was exerted by them on the markets. These economic agents could thus not be found to hold dominance.

> *Centro Servizi Spediporto.* 'Article 86 of the Treaty prohibits abusive practices resulting from the exploitation by one or more undertakings of a dominant position on the common market or in a substantial part of it in so far as those practices may affect

---

[302] *SIV* (n 301 above) at [358].

[303] This case was examined earlier in connection with the first category of situations where the concept of collective dominance is used. The facts of the case correspond to those envisaged in the first category (juxtaposition of exclusive rights granted by public authorities). See paras 3.327–3.332 above for more details. The case must also be examined in the second category, because it contains the legal formula which was used as a basis for the development of the jurisprudence in subsequent cases pertaining to the second category.   [304] N 291 above, at [42].

[305] See Case C-96/94 *Centro Servizi Spediporto v Spedizioni Marittima del Golfo* [1995] ECR I-2883 (tariffs for road-haulage). An identical ruling was given on similar cases in Joined Cases C 140, 141 & 142/94 *DIP v Comune di Bassano del Grappa* [1995] ECR I-3257 (administrative decision to open new shops) as well as Case C-70/95 *Sodemare v Regione Lombardia* [1997] ECR I-3395 (regulation reserving to non-profit organisation participation in certain social activities).

trade between Member States.' 'However, in order for it to be held that . . . a collective dominant position exists, the undertakings in the group must be linked in such a way that they adopt the same conduct on the market.' 'National legislation which provides for . . . [decisions to be taken] by the public authorities cannot be regarded as placing economic agents in a collective dominant position characterized by the absence of competition between them.'[306]

Precision as to the nature of links between undertakings

3.336

Shipping companies. A second step was necessary to construe further the conditions under which dominance may be acquired collectively.[307] In that second step, the ECJ attempted to distinguish better two conditions that must be fulfilled for the application of the collective dominance theory. This was made in *Compagnie maritime belge*,[308] a case concerning shipping companies participating in a shipping conference.[309] The first condition is that undertakings must form a collective entity of some sort. This condition is satisfied when undertakings are engaged in a common course of action, ie they act or present themselves as an entity on the market. The second condition is that this collective entity must be found to dominate the market.

Compagnie maritime belge. '[F]or the purposes of analysis under Article 86 of the Treaty, it is necessary to consider whether the undertakings concerned together

---

[306] At [32] to [34]. In these various cases, the theory of collective dominance was not ultimately applied. This does not mean, however, that it could not apply had the circumstances been different. Suppose that decisions concerning tariffs were effectively taken by a committee and that this committee was made up of representatives of economic agents. Using the criteria presented by the ECJ, one would have to conclude that links exist among undertakings and that a common course of action was followed. The conditions would thus be fulfilled for the application of the collective dominance theory (Art 82 EC). It is however probable that the ECJ would then have merely considered that the co-ordination taking place in the committee could be analysed as an anti-competitive agreement falling under the prohibition contained in Art 81(1) EC.

[307] The case law was not very developed in that first step. The Court only emphasised the necessity of strong links among undertakings before the latter can be said to form a collective entity. In the other cases, the Court did not elaborate on conditions to be fulfilled for the notion of collective entity to apply but rather concentrated on dominance: the undertakings were not found to be in a position to influence market conditions.

[308] Joined Cases C395 & 396/96 P *Compagnie maritime belge v Commission* [2000] ECR I-1365. Appeal against decision of 8 October 1996 in Joined Cases T 24–26 & 28/93 *Compagnie Maritime Belge Transports v Commission* [1996] ECR II-1201. Commission Decision (EEC) 93/82 relating to a proceeding pursuant to Articles 85 (IV/32.448 and IV/32.450: Cewal, Cowac and Ukwal) and 86 (IV/32.448 and IV/32.450: Cewal) of the EEC Treaty [1993] OJ L34/20.

[309] A shipping conference is an organisation made up of members active on the same or similar markets and which has as its object the organisation of relations among its members and the defence of their interests. At European level, shipping conferences are regulated by Council Regulation (EEC) No 4056/86 of 22 December 1986 laying down detailed rules for the application of Articles 85 and 86 of the Treaty to maritime transport [1986] OJ L378/4. In this case, the conference was made up of shipping companies operating a regular liner service between the ports of Angola/Zaire (now Congo) and those of the North Sea (with the exception of the UK). The Commission had received complaints that the members of the conference were engaged in abusive conduct. No member however held a dominant position on its own. Art 82 EC could thus not be applied, unless it could be demonstrated that dominance was held collectively by the members.

constitute a collective entity . . . It is only where that question is answered in the affirmative that it is appropriate to consider whether that collective entity actually holds a dominant position.'[310]

3.337 **The nature of links.** No emphasis was placed in the judgment on the second condition (dominance), which appeared to be interpreted in terms similar to those concerning dominance as applied to single undertakings. For this reason, a focus is placed on the first condition, ie the factors explaining that undertakings may form a collective entity in certain circumstances. For the ECJ, various factors may be taken into account. *(a) Legal links.* A collective character may come from legal links existing among undertakings. Such links existed in the case at issue, as undertakings participated in a shipping conference through legal arrangements. Mutual agreements were concluded and collective decisions were taken by the organisation. The existence of these links made it possible for the undertakings to act as one single entity on the market. *(b) Economic links.* Although it could find sufficient evidence about the existence of legal links among the undertakings concerned, the ECJ added that a collective entity may also be created as a result of economic links among the entities concerned. This statement brought new light to the concept, although there are no indications in the judgment to provide clarification as to what forms of link are referred to.[311] The ECJ only mentioned that a finding of collective dominance could be based on an economic assessment of, among other things, the structure of the market in question.

> *Compagnie maritime belge.* '[A] dominant position may be held by two or more economic entities legally independent of each other, provided that from an economic point of view they present themselves or act together on a particular market as a collective entity.'[312] 'In order to establish the existence of a collective entity . . . , it is necessary to examine the economic links or factors which give rise to a connection between the undertakings concerned.'[313] 'A finding that two or more undertakings hold a collective dominant position must, in principle, proceed upon an economic assessment of the position on the relevant market of the undertakings concerned.'[314]

3.338 **Collective dominance resulting from market characteristics**

Third step. In a third step, the ECJ maintained the distinction between two conditions to be fulfilled for a finding of collective dominance to be made. Characteristic of that period is the judgment issued by the ECJ in *France, SCPA and EMC v Commission*[315] concerning a decision taken by the Commission allowing a merger between two German chemical undertakings (Kali und Salz and

---

[310] At [39].
[311] The reason was that the Court did not need to elaborate on these other connecting factors, as the undertakings were linked by legal relations in the case at issue and these links provided a sufficient basis for them to be considered as a collective entity. [312] At [36].
[313] At [41].   [314] At [38].   [315] See n 288 above.

Mitteldeutsche Kali). The first condition is that the undertakings concerned must be in a position to behave independently of competitors, customers and consumers. As seen earlier, this standard is no different from the one applied in situations where unilateral dominance is considered. The second condition concerns factors explaining why a collective entity emerges on certain markets.

> *France, SCPA and EMC v Commission* [221] 'In the case of an alleged collective dominant position, the Commission is . . . obliged to assess . . . whether the concentration . . . leads to a situation in which effective competition in the relevant market is significantly impeded by the undertakings involved in the concentration and one or more other undertakings *which together, in particular because of correlative factors which exist between them, are able to adopt a common policy on the market and act to a considerable extent independently of their competitors, their customers, and also of consumers.*'[316]

Factors explaining dominance. In the judgment, the ECJ devotes considerable **3.339** energy to analysing the various factors which may explain the emergence of such a collective entity. Among these factors are: the degree of concentration on the market, the relative position of competitors, the possible countervailing economic power held by purchasers, the characteristics of the goods sold on the relevant market, the existence of parallel behaviour and the existence of structural links between the undertakings concerned. These factors have been taken over by the European legislator in the regulation as factors to be taken into account in order to assess the effectiveness of competition on electronic communications markets, and are analysed in the section dealing with that subject (see paras 3.343–3.378).

Current state of the case law

Airtours. The latest case law as regards the conditions to be fulfilled for a finding of **3.340** collective dominance has recently been issued by the CFI in *Airtours*.[317] No judgment of the ECJ is available at the present time, although an appeal has been lodged against the ruling issued at first instance. The case concerned a planned merger between tour operators in the United Kingdom. The operation was notified to the Commission, which refused to grant authorisation on the ground that the operation would create a collectively dominant position between the entity resulting from the operation and the other undertakings present on the market. The decision was annulled by the CFI, on the ground that all conditions for the establishment of collective dominance

---

[316] Authors' emphasis. Decision of the Commission: Commission Decision (EEC) 94/449 relating to a proceeding pursuant to Council Regulation (EEC) No 4064/89 (Case No IV/M.308—Kali + Salz/MdK/Treuhand) [1994] OJ L186/38. In that case, no judgment was issued by the CFI because the application for annulment was introduced by a Member State. (The EC Treaty provides that the Court is competent in that situation.)

[317] Case T-342/99 *Airtours v Commission* [2002] ECR II-2585. The judgment was issued against decision (EC) 2000/276 of the Commission (Case IV/M.1524—Airtours/First Choice) [2000] OJ L93/1.

had not been fulfilled. In its judgment, the CFI specified these conditions as follows:

> *Airtours v Commission.* '[T]hree conditions are necessary for a finding of collective dominance as defined:
>
> — first, each member of the dominant oligopoly must have the ability to know how the other members are behaving in order to monitor whether or not they are adopting the common policy. As the Commission specifically acknowledges, it is not enough for each member of the dominant oligopoly to be aware that interdependent market conduct is profitable for all of them but each member must also have a means of knowing whether the other operators are adopting the same strategy and whether they are maintaining it. There must, therefore, be sufficient market transparency for all members of the dominant oligopoly to be aware, sufficiently precisely and quickly, of the way in which the other members' market conduct is evolving;
>
> — second, the situation of tacit coordination must be sustainable over time, that is to say, there must be an incentive not to depart from the common policy on the market. As the Commission observes, it is only if all the members of the dominant oligopoly maintain the parallel conduct that all can benefit. The notion of retaliation in respect of conduct deviating from the common policy is thus inherent in this condition. In this instance, the parties concur that, for a situation of collective dominance to be viable, there must be adequate deterrents to ensure that there is a long-term incentive in not departing from the common policy, which means that each member of the dominant oligopoly must be aware that highly competitive action on its part designed to increase its market share would provoke identical action by the others, so that it would derive no benefit from its initiative;
>
> — third, to prove the existence of a collective dominant position to the requisite legal standard, the Commission must also establish that the foreseeable reaction of current and future competitors, as well as of consumers, would not jeopardise the results expected from the common policy.'[318]

3.341 **Dominance.** From this extract it appears that several conditions must be fulfilled for a finding of collective dominance to be made. The following analysis disregards the presentation given in the judgment. The third indent in the extract above may be related to the requirement that, for dominance to be established, undertakings must be able to behave independently of competitors, customers and consumers. That indent refers to the possibility for competitors and customers to react against the dominance exercised by the collective entity. This possibility is inherent in a competitive market and disappears where dominance is acquired, whether by one or several undertakings. This requirement does not therefore really concern factors leading to the existence of a collective entity but rather the existence of dominance on the market.

3.342 **Collective entity.** The other indents concern conditions which must be satisfied, according to the CFI, for several undertakings to be considered as forming a collective entity. Pursuant to the judgment, a collective entity may emerge on

---

[318] At [62]. See also (n 288 above) at [276]–[277].

a market with several undertakings when these undertakings *(a)* have at their disposal various means allowing them to establish a common strategy, *(b)* are in a position to monitor compliance with the common strategy by the members, *(c)* have the necessary tools to retaliate as soon as the strategy is not respected and *(d)* are aware of the advantages resulting from interdependence rather than competition. This last point is particularly important: there should exist awareness, among the participants, that the benefits likely to be obtained through individual conduct are outweighed by the losses that would inevitably flow from retaliation.

(4) Collective dominance in the regulation

The concept as taken over in the regulation.   The concept of joint dominance   **3.343** is taken over in the ex ante regulation. By contrast to the approach it has taken in other provisions, the European legislator has not adopted the terminology of joint significant market power. It simply refers to joint dominance—a concept that is also used in general competition law, although as observed above, the case law has so far favoured the expression 'collective dominance'. There is no reason to believe the concept should evolve in different, let alone diverging, directions in the regulation and general competition law.[319] In the regulation, the Parliament and Council make it clear that regulatory action is mandated where significant market power is acquired by two or more undertakings. Joint market power is addressed at Article 14 of the Framework Directive and the concept is further construed in Annex II to the Directive.[320] Article 14 gives little information as to how the concept should be applied in practice. More insight is provided in Annex II, where criteria are given for assessing the concept:

> *Framework Directive.* 'An undertaking shall be deemed to have [a collective] significant market power if . . . jointly with others, it enjoys a position equivalent to dominance, that is to say a position of economic strength affording it the power to behave

---

[319] The regulation does not specify that both concepts must be construed in the same manner. The only reference made in the regulation is to the Guidelines issued by the Commission and, more generally, to Community law. No specific allusion is thus made to general competition law. This lack of allusion should however not be overestimated. Apparently, the European legislator is not convinced that regulatory provisions and general competition law will necessarily evolve, in all circumstances, in the same direction. In this provision, as in others, they may have been willing to introduce a caveat by not linking the two bodies of the law in a manner that may be deemed excessive. There is no reason, however, why such a difference should appear, as the notion of 'collective dominance' has been carefully construed in the jurisprudence in order to remedy difficulties of the same kind as those occurring in electronic communications.

[320] The reason for rules to be inserted in an Annex is that it is easier to modify them without touching the body of the directive. This is particularly indicated for rules or items that are likely to evolve quickly. For instance, the case concerning joint dominance has not yet completely stabilised. There is thus a significant likelihood that an evolution may take place in the years ahead. By placing in an Annex the description of the notion as it is understood today, the European legislator makes it easier to change it in order to conform with future developments.

to an appreciable extent independently of competitors, customers and ultimately consumers.'[321] 'In particular, national regulatory authorities shall, when assessing whether two or more undertakings are in a joint dominant position in a market, act in accordance with Community law and take into the utmost account the guidelines on market analysis and the assessment of significant market power published by the Commission pursuant to Article 15. Criteria to be used in making such an assessment are set out in Annex II.'[322]

3.344 **To which of the categories does the regulation refer?** It has been submitted that two categories of situation may be distinguished as regards the application of the collective dominance theory. In the first category, undertakings hold individual dominant positions on contiguous territories and these positions may be considered as covering a substantial part of the common market when considered collectively. In the second category, two or more undertakings are present on the same geographical (and product) market where, as a result of links between them or of market characteristics, they are in a position to behave as a collective entity independently of competitors, customers and consumers. No reference is made in the regulation to one or both of these categories. The inclusion of collective dominance in the regulation therefore implies that the two categories are to be considered.

3.345 **No specific link necessary between undertakings.** Details are given in Annex II to the directive concerning the criteria to be taken into account for an authority to conclude that a collective dominant position exists.[323] As appears from these criteria, the European legislator has opted for a definition in line with the latest development in the case law. This holds, as was stated above, that there is no necessity to establish the existence of links between the undertakings concerned, but rather to examine the characteristics of the markets—characteristics producing a situation where undertakings have a common interest, carry out a common strategy and are able to monitor and enforce that common policy.

> *Joined Cases C-68/94 and C-30/95.* 'Two or more undertakings can be found to be in a joint dominant position . . . even in the absence of structural or other links between them . . . [if] they operate in a market the structure of which is considered to be conducive to coordinate effects.'

3.346 **Criteria to be examined.** As was stated in connection with individual dominance, authorities are attempting to identify criteria to be examined in order to assess whether competition is sufficient. A list was inserted in Annex II to the Framework Directive, enumerating criteria which correspond to those singled out

---

[321] Art 14(2).   [322] Art 14(3).

[323] These criteria have probably been inserted in an Annex because this facilitates future amendments. The European legislator can easily amend the list of criteria to be taken into account for a situation of collective dominance to be established. If these criteria had been included in the body of the directive, the provisions would have to have been changed in the event that an amendment had to be made.

by the CFI and the ECJ in the latest stage of the case law.[324] The list is not exhaustive. Other criteria may thus be taken into account in the course of the assessment, as long as they are useful in showing that the undertakings concerned form a collective entity able to behave independently of other market participants.[325] Nor should the criteria be deemed to be cumulative. They do not have to be satisfied in all cases before a finding can be made that collective dominance exists. Authorities can come to such a conclusion where certain that these criteria are fulfilled.[326]

> *Framework Directive, Annex II.* 'Two or more undertakings can be found to be in a joint dominant position . . . where the market satisfies a number of appropriate characteristics . . . mentioned below: [i] mature market, [ii] stagnant or moderate growth on the demand side, [iii] low elasticity of demand, [iv] homogeneous product, [v] similar cost structures, [vi] similar market shares, [vii] lack of technical innovation, mature technology, [viii] absence of excess capacity, [ix] high barriers to entry, [x] lack of countervailing buying power, [xi] lack of potential competition, [xii] various kinds of informal or other links between the undertakings concerned, [xiii] retaliatory mechanisms, [xiv] lack or reduced scope for price competition.'

Dominance by undertakings forming a collective entity

Dominance.   These criteria may be divided into several categories, along the lines   **3.347** developed in the analysis set out above. Some of these criteria relate to dominance. As stated above, the European legislator has a tendency to aggregate these criteria with those concerning the existence of a collective entity on the market. The two situations may however be distinguished. Pursuant to the case law, dominance is defined as the ability to behave independently of competitors and customers. In criterion [viii] (absence of excess capacity), the focus is placed on competitors already present on the market. As they have no capacity in reserve, these competitors do not have the capability to increase output in case the undertakings belonging to the collective entity set conditions that are not those found on a competitive market. Criterion [ix] (high barriers to entry) and criterion [xi] (lack of potential competition) are related to the situation of undertakings located outside the market which may enter the latter in case, for instance, prices are increased by a certain margin. The room for manoeuvre of these competitors is, however, limited if entry is beset by barriers. A possibility is also that, independently of existing barriers, no undertaking is present on adjacent markets and ready to start a new activity.[327] Finally, criterion [x] (lack of countervailing power) concerns customers rather than competitors. Customers are sometimes in a position to influence the supply of

---

[324] In particular, see *France, SCPA and EMC v Commission* (n 288 above) at [179]–[250] *Airtours* (n 318 above) at [79]–[293].

[325] See Framework Directive, Annex II, subpara 2.   [326] See ibid, Annex II, subpara 2.

[327] This may be due to a variety of reasons. For instance, there may be undertakings on adjacent markets but these undertakings do not have the financial and/or the technical resources necessary to enter the relevant market. Another possibility is that undertakings able to enter the market exist but are put off by the collective dominance detained by the market participants.

a service. Often, their bargaining power depends on the quantity they order and/or on their readiness to engage in negotiations with the various undertakings present on the market in order to obtain a better deal. Where no bargaining power exists, or buyers are not ready to use the power they have, there is an increased likelihood that collective dominance may be acquired by suppliers.

3.348

Criteria relating to dominance

. . .
[viii] absence of excess capacity,
[ix] high barriers to entry,
[x] lack of countervailing buying power,
[xi] lack of potential competition,
. . .

Common interest for members of the entity

3.349 **Somnolence.** A second group of criteria relates to the existence of a common interest among the undertakings forming the collective entity. As seen earlier in the case law, economically autonomous entities only form a wider entity if, and to the extent, they consider that they all have the same interest. The collective character of the entity is bound to collapse if any of the members believes that it may gain from individual action. The existence of a common interest may be explained in many circumstances by the absence of future perspectives for the undertakings. Where undertakings present on a market do not see how they can develop further, they become caught in a sort of somnolence. Such a situation may be observed for several reasons.

3.350 **No incentive to engage in competition.** The first is where undertakings have no incentive to engage in competitive behaviour. A situation of this nature is encountered on markets where demand is not elastic (criterion). Low elasticity implies that customers do not easily move to another supplier in case prices vary. This characteristic makes it unattractive for an undertaking to decrease prices, as such an initiative would not allow it to increase market share. A similar criterion is when there is a lack or reduced scope for competition on a given market (criterion). This criterion also concerns situations where engaging in price competition would not bring any benefit to the undertaking.[328] A final reason is when undertakings present on

---

[328] Suppose that, for instance, prices are set at the level of costs without any perspective to decrease costs further. In that situation, a decision to lower prices would serve no purpose as the undertaking would lose money. In such a scenario, the perspective for price competition can be said to be non-existent. The only possibility would be for the undertaking to sell at a loss for a certain period in the hope that another market participant would be driven out of the market. Such behaviour is allowed under competition law as long as the undertaking does not have market power. A practice of that kind will however bring little benefit in situations where market participants are fairly strong.

the market have no excess capacity. The absence of overcapacity implies that investments are to be made in case output is to be increased. Undertakings cannot limit themselves to expanding output in the hope of amortising investments more effectively (criterion).[329]

Stagnant markets.   A second reason for markets to be caught in somnolence is **3.351** when demand is stagnant or grows only moderately. Undertakings have no possibility of growing on markets where no development is expected on the demand side. The only possibility for them to expand would be to engage in fierce competition—but that perspective does not appear attractive on a market conducive to co-ordination as a result of the presence of other criteria mentioned in the list (criterion [ii]). Another reason for lack of dynamism is when the relevant market can be considered mature (criterion [i]). Maturity sometimes comes from characteristics of demand. Suppose the only customers asking for the good or service are already served on the market and no other customer is expected: this will not lead to dynamism for the undertakings concerned. Maturity may also be related to a lack of technological innovation. This is observed where, for various reasons, undertakings are not able to innovate. Another reason is where one does not see, for technical reasons, how that technology could be replaced or how another technology could be developed to fulfil the same function (criterion [vii]).

Criteria relating to a common interest among the members of the entity   **3.352**

---

    [i] mature market,
    [ii] stagnant or moderate growth on the demand side,
    [iii] low elasticity of demand,

. . .

  [vii] lack of technical innovation, mature technology,
  [viii] absence of excess capacity,

. . .

  [xiv] lack or reduced scope for price competition

. . .

Possible existence of links between undertakings

Links.   The criteria examined above are related to the conditions under which a **3.353** collective entity may emerge. Although it is possible to identify factors conducive

---

[329] In our opinion, the absence of excess capacity can be taken in two contexts. On the one hand, as an element explaining that undertakings present on a given market have little incentive to engage in competitive behaviour—whereby the perspective for this undertaking of forming a collective entity with other undertakings is increased. On the other hand, as an element explaining that the collective entity acquires dominance when (actual or potential) competitors have no excess capacity that they could use in order to react should the collective entity set conditions not favourable for customers. In one case, the situation of an undertaking participating in the collective entity is considered; in the other, that of an actual or potential competitor.

to co-ordination, it is difficult to predict where, and why, a common course of action will actually appear and be followed up by the members. The emergence of such a common course of action will depend on the attitude of the undertakings concerned. These undertakings must be willing to discover whether equilibrium of a kind may be reached between the members of the collective entity. They must also actively seek to discover, and establish, such equilibrium. This at least supposes research and enquiry on the part of the undertakings involved, which must attempt to anticipate the behaviour likely to be adopted by other undertakings. In this process, contacts and links among market participants may provide substantial assistance. For this reason the existence of links, whatever their nature, is mentioned as a possible criterion in the list drafted by the European legislator. It has however been made clear that this criterion could by no means be considered indispensable. The Commission has insisted that a collective entity may emerge in situations where no such links exist or where, although they exist, they cannot be proved.

3.354 **Criteria relating to the possible existence of links between undertakings**

. . .

[xii] various kinds of informal or other links between the undertakings concerned,

. . .

Surveillance and retaliatory mechanisms

3.355 **Compliance with collective strategy.** It is submitted above that a collective entity can emerge, and be maintained, only if the participants have at their disposal various means allowing them to ensure that the strategy followed in common is effectively being respected by the members. This implies the surveillance mechanisms referred to in various of the criteria in the list above. Surveillance is easier where markets are transparent. Transparency can be created through a variety of mechanisms. For instance, it is relatively easy for undertakings to understand the position of the other market participants where products are homogenous on the markets. Given homogeneity, they can use information on their own undertaking in order to understand the situation, and anticipate the reaction, of the other members of the collective entity. Another factor of transparency is the presence of a similar cost structure within the undertakings concerned. Again, this similarity between them allows each of these undertakings to use information on its own operations to understand and anticipate the position adopted by other participants.

3.356 **Retaliation.** According to the case law, retaliation is an important factor explaining why undertakings form a collective entity. They will not maintain collective behaviour in situations where they feel that individual action may bring them more benefit than maintenance of the common course of action, except where the fear that retaliation would inflict severe damage forces them to conform. This aspect, which has been emphasised in the case law,[330] appears in the list drafted by the European legislator and should be given particular emphasis in the assessment of competition.

Similar market shares. A final circumstance may be that actors have similar shares **3.357** on the market. It appears easier for undertakings to define and carry out a common strategy in circumstances where they have equal force. The reason is that there is always a risk, should market participants be of diverging strengths, that one of them will consider itself to have the capability of driving one or several competitors out of the market. The presence of equilibrium in terms of power on the market makes it difficult for any member to pursue an individual strategy because it would then fear that others will react with a strength that is comparable to its own strength.

Criteria relating to surveillance and retaliation   **3.358**

. . .

  [iv] homogeneous product,
  [v] similar cost structures,
  [vi] similar market shares,
  . . .

[xiii] retaliatory mechanisms,
. . .

---

(5) Division of powers for findings concerning the existence of collective dominance

Who decides whether collective dominance is held? Collective dominance may be **3.359** found to exist under the NRF and/or general competition law. These two possibilities are examined successively. Under the NRF, the power to decide that a group of undertakings collectively holds a dominant position belongs, in principle, to the NRAs, each acting on its national territory. In application of the Framework Directive, a decision determining the existence of collective dominance is however submitted to the special regulatory procedure. Under that procedure, draft decisions must be notified to the other NRAs as well as to the Commission. These various bodies then have the opportunity to submit comments, which must be taken into account by the NRA concerned. In some circumstances, the Commission has the power to veto the adoption of the draft. This option is available as regards decisions that a group of undertakings holds a dominant position. The veto may only be expressed where the Commission considers that the decision, if adopted, would create a barrier to the single market or is incompatible with Community law, and in particular the objectives to be fulfilled in the NRF. Where the Commission decides to use its veto, it may justify that decision and make proposals for amending the draft measures.

Framework Directive, Article 7(4). 'Where an intended measure aims at: . . .
(b) deciding whether or not to designate an undertaking as having . . . jointly with

---

[330] See in the last instance, *Airtours* (n 318 above) at [183]–[216].

others, significant market power, . . . and would affect trade between Member States and the Commission has indicated to the national regulatory authority that it considers that the draft measure would create a barrier to the single market or if it has serious doubts as to its compatibility with Community law . . . , then the draft measure shall not be adopted for a further two months. This period may not be extended. Within this period the Commission may . . . take a decision requiring the national regulatory authority . . . to withdraw the draft measure.'[331]

3.360 **General competition law.** Findings as to collective dominance may also be made on the basis of general competition law. In order to determine what authority has power to adopt these rules, one must consider the various possibilities that may arise. *(a)* Collective dominance may be found in application of the Merger Regulation. The power to make such a finding belongs to the Commission, which has exclusive competence for the application of that regulation. In this context the Commission will attempt to determine whether collective dominance may be created by the entity formed as a result of the operation and third undertakings present on the same market. *(b)* Collective dominance may also be investigated under Article 82 EC. In that context, the relevant authorities will attempt to determine whether collective dominance is currently held by undertakings on a given market. The Commission has competence for the application of that provision. As it has direct effect, Article 82 EC may also be applied by national authorities, the latter in fact being under an obligation to ensure the application of European law, including the competition rules.[332] National courts are thus required to apply Article 82 EC in proceedings brought before them where this provision is relevant for the resolution of a case. A similar duty exists for NCAs.[333]

3.361 **May various provisions be combined?** A question must be raised as to the possibility of applying these various rules simultaneously. Different possible combinations are examined below, although they should normally occur only in rare circumstances. This is due to the perspective adopted in the various contexts and to the timeframe within which the assessment must take place.

3.362 **Article 82 EC and Merger Regulation.** Article 82 EC and the Merger Regulation may not be applied together, as a result of the exclusive character of

---

[331] This procedure has been analysed in detail in another section (see paras 3.299–3.306). The relations between the Commission and the NRAs are analysed, as regards that procedure, in Commission Recommendation C(2003)2647 final of 23 July 2003 on notifications, time limits and consultations provided for in Article 7 of Directive 2002/21/EC of the European Parliament and of the Council of 7 March 2002 on a common regulatory framework for electronic communications networks and services.

[332] Pursuant to Art 10 EC Member States must take all appropriate measures to ensure the fulfilment of the obligations arising from European law. They must facilitate the achievement of the Community's tasks. They must abstain from any measure which could jeopardise the attainment of the objectives of the Treaty.

[333] In most cases, NCAs apply the national rules of competition. These rules are not different, in most cases, from those adopted at European level. There will thus not be a specific need to apply Art 82 EC where the corresponding national provision may be applied.

that regulation. Pursuant to this principle, issues submitted to the Merger Regulation may not be resolved through the application of other provisions.[334]

Merger Regulation and NRF. The Merger Regulation and the NRF will in principle not be applied simultaneously as regards issues relating to collective dominance. This is due to the difference in the perspectives adopted in the two contexts. The NRF concerns the present. As regards collective dominance, the question is whether two or more undertakings are able to behave independently at the time the assessment is made. By contrast, under the Merger Regulation the perspective is oriented towards the future, the purpose being to evaluate the probability that collective dominance may be held in the future by the new entity and third undertakings. **3.363**

Article 82 EC and NRF. The only possibility of simultaneous application concerns Article 82 EC and the NRF. The NRF supposes an examination of the current situation with a view to determining whether collective dominance exists and regulatory obligations must apply. Article 82 EC implies an assessment of a situation that has existed and may still exist at the time the evaluation is made. The purpose is to verify whether collective dominance was held and whether abusive use has been made of it. If these conditions are fulfilled, a sanction is imposed as well as a prohibition on continuing or renewing the infringement. Given the perspectives in the two contexts, simultaneous application may be envisaged in several scenarios. A typical scenario would be that a collective dominant position has existed at a given moment and that abusive use has been made of it, thereby implying the possibility of applying Article 82 EC. The situation has however persisted and the NRAs decide, in view of this persistence, that regulatory obligations should be applied. **3.364**

Discretionary powers of authorities, marginal control by courts. The finding that two or more undertakings together hold a dominant position implies complex assessments of economic facts. In the cases examined above, these assessments were made, in most instances, by the Commission. In the cases concerning the application of the Merger Regulation, the European courts have emphasised the discretionary power that the Commission holds in order to carry out these assessments.[335] Pursuant to these rulings, judicial oversight is possible but limited, as in all cases where such powers are granted, to internal coherence and compliance with procedure. This recognition of a discretionary power is not given in cases where collective dominance is assessed on the basis of Article 82 EC. However, the principle remains the same. In order to conclude that collective dominance exists, the Commission must investigate market characteristics, and **3.365**

---

[334] Art 21 of the Merger Regulation. This does not preclude the application of the Merger Regulation and Art 81 EC to distinct issues relating to the same operation.
[335] *France, SCPA and EMC v Commission* (n 288 above) at [221]–[224].

this task inevitably escapes judicial control to a certain extent. One should not expect the division of powers to be different in the NRF. The only difference is that the assessment will in that context normally[336] be made by NRAs rather than by the Commission.[337]

3.366 **Administrative authorities.** The practical consequence is that practitioners should not expect stringent judicial review of analysis regarding the existence of collective dominance on a given market. The situation will not be different whether the analysis is carried out pursuant to the NRF and/or on the basis of general competition law. The same attitude will be adopted by the courts whether the control is to be carried out on a finding made by the Commission (European courts), by an NRA (national courts) or by a NCA (national courts). In all these cases, the power to decide whether collective dominance exists belongs to an administrative authority with little chance of redress at judicial level. Practitioners should thus concentrate their efforts to convince these authorities rather than hoping that a remedy will be obtained at judicial level.[338]

(6) Evaluation of the regulation and case law

3.367 **The situations considered under the theory.** The state of the regulation and the case law as regards collective dominance have been examined in the paragraphs above. It is now time to formulate a judgment on the development of the case law in that area and the subsequent integration of the concept in the regulation. Some inconsistency must also be recognised as regards the two categories of situation covered by the theory of collective dominance. The first category, as stated above, contains cases where various undertakings hold a dominant position in contiguous geographical areas. Circumstances are different in the second category, where undertakings are present on the same geographical (and product) market and build together, on that market, a position of collective dominance. The application of the

---

[336] Draft decisions concluding the existence of collective dominance have to be communicated to other NRAs and to the Commission, with a possibility for that latter institution to express a veto in certain circumstances. See Framework Directive, Art 7.

[337] In most instances, the cases concerning collective dominance were brought to a European court in a direct application seeking the annulment of a decision taken by the Commission. In a limited number of procedures, they were brought to Luxembourg in preliminary procedures. In these procedures, national courts asked the ECJ for an explanation of European rules to be applied in a given case. In these procedures, the Court stated that the economic appreciation as to the existence of collective dominance belonged to the national courts. See *Almelo* (n 291 above) at [43]. 'It is for the national court to consider whether there exist between the regional electricity distributors in the Netherlands links which are sufficiently strong for there to be a collective dominant position in a substantial part of the common market.'

[338] This analysis must somehow be nuanced. The European courts have consistently maintained the idea that their control should remain marginal as the assessment is made at the authorities' discretion. However, they have attempted to define in detail the conditions that have to be fulfilled in order for the authorities to conclude that collective dominance is indeed being held. This attempt has culminated in the enumeration of the conditions made by the CFI in *Airtours* (n 318 above).

theory can be understood in the second category, as the cases belonging to that group concern the possibility for customers of choosing between suppliers within a given market.[339] The reasoning of the European legislator is apparently different in the cases pertaining to the first category. The real difficulty, with these cases, is that the positions built by each undertaking on its individual market cannot be considered sufficient to cover, by itself, a substantial part of the common market. The connection with the common market—a condition to apply competition law—is obtained through the consideration that these various positions form a whole. The purposes pursued by the European courts with collective dominance are thus different in the two contexts (to ensure the existence of choice for customers in one case and to ensure the application of European law in the other).

Collective dominance 3.368

First category	Second category
—The first category concerns several undertakings	—Idem
—These undertakings are present on distinct geographical areas	—These undertakings are present on the same geographical (and material) market
—On each of these areas, a member has a dominant position	—They collectively hold a dominant position
—That position does not cover a substantial part of the common market	
—That condition is however fulfilled when these areas are considered as a whole	—This position covers a substantial part of the common market

Autonomy of undertakings belonging to a collective entity. It should be noted 3.369 that the concept of collective domination does not appear to be consistent in itself. As is apparent from Treaty provisions, competition rules apply to undertakings. The concept of 'undertaking' is defined, in competition law, as designating autonomous economic entities. This requirement of autonomy does not seem to be compatible with the idea that several undertakings may form a single entity when considered collectively. There are serious doubts that the Commission, the CFI and the ECJ have ever noticed the difficulty created by the juxtaposition of these two—possibly contradictory—ideas, that competition law applies to autonomous economic entities and that several of these entities may form an overall economic entity. The ECJ has in various judgments formulated the difficulty without providing an answer.

Compagnie maritime belge v Commission. 'In terms of Article 86 of the Treaty, a dominant position may be held by several undertakings. The Court of Justice has held, on

---

[339] As they are present on the same market, the undertakings involved should normally behave as competitors. At some point, the authority however notices that competition ceases to function and is replaced by co-ordination. In that context, the customers lose the possibility of choosing from among suppliers the one which corresponds to their needs.

many occasions, that the concept of undertaking . . . presupposes the economic independence of the entity concerned.' 'It follows that the expression one or more undertakings in [Article 82 EC] implies that a dominant position may be held by two or more economic entities . . . provided that from an economic point of view they present themselves or act together on a particular market as a collective entity.'[340]

3.370 **Two scenarios.**   How can the problem be resolved? Two scenarios should be distinguished and there should be no confusion between them. *(a)* A first possibility is for entities active on a certain market to be considered as autonomous. This supposes, and implies, that these entities decide their course of action in full independence.[341] Competition law can then be applied to them, as to distinct undertakings. *(b)* A second possibility is for various entities to constitute jointly a larger entity. This scenario has been accepted for companies belonging to the same group of companies. It has been acknowledged that, in normal circumstances, these companies follow a common course of action, which is decided at the level of the group. On the basis of this finding, a decision has been made that these companies should not be considered as distinct undertakings.

3.371 **Same group.**   In cases concerning companies belonging to the same group, it has been decided that agreements concluded between these companies are not subject to Article 81 EC. This followed the fact that these companies cannot be regarded as separate undertakings. Pursuant to case law, their situation must be examined under Article 82 EC. In this context one must consider whether they as a group hold a dominant position, which they possibly abuse. The same analysis should apply with respect to undertakings found to hold collective dominance under the current case law. As these undertakings hold a common course of action, they should be considered as one undertaking. Their behaviour could thus be covered under Article 82 EC.

3.372 **The relationship between Articles 81 and 82 EC.**   A third difficulty concerns the distinction between Articles 81 and 82 EC, which constitute the main provisions for the application of European competition law. It has long been considered that the former applies to situations involving several undertakings whereas the second is reserved for situations where single undertakings behave unilaterally. In *Continental Can*, the ECJ emphasised the relations existing between the two provisions. Pursuant to that judgment, these provisions aim at the same result, ie ensure that competition is not distorted or eliminated in the common market.

> *Continental Can.* '[A]rticle [81] is part of the chapter devoted to the common rules on the community's policy in the field of competition'; 'this policy is based on article

---

[340] N 309 above, at [35]–[36].

[341] In the course of their activities, they take into account the possible reactions of competitors and customers. This cannot, however, be considered as a lack of independence as it is a normal attitude on a competitive market. This attitude implies, in principle, that undertakings always attempt to meet better to the needs of the customers.

3 (f) of the treaty according to which the community's activity shall include the institution of a system ensuring that competition in the common market is not distorted';
'Article [81] concerns agreements between undertakings, decisions of associations of
undertakings and concerted practices, while Article 86 concerns unilateral activity of
one or more undertakings'; 'Articles [81] and [82] seek to achieve the same aim on different levels, ie the maintenance of effective competition within the common market';
'Articles [81] and [82] cannot be interpreted in such a way that they contradict each
other, because they serve to achieve the same aim'.[342]

Compagnie maritime belge.   The relationship between Articles 81 and 82 EC   **3.373**
was addressed in *Compagnie maritime belge*, in the context of the discussion on
collective dominance. In that case, the ECJ ruled that a difference existed between
these provisions regarding their focus. According to the ECJ, the focus is placed in
Article 81 EC on the presence of an agreement, whereas Article 82 EC focuses on
the power acquired or held by one or several undertakings.

> *Compagnie maritime belge v Commission.* 'Article [81 EC] . . . applies to agreements,
> decisions and concerted practices which may appreciably affect trade between
> Member States, *regardless of the position on the market of the undertakings concerned.*
> Article [82 EC] . . . , on the other hand, deals with the conduct of one or more eco-
> nomic operators consisting in the abuse of a position of economic strength which
> enables the operator concerned to hinder the maintenance of effective competition
> on the relevant market by allowing it to behave to an appreciable extent indepen-
> dently of its competitors, its customers and, ultimately, consumers.'[343]

Difficulties.   This approach adopted by the ECJ raises several difficulties. First, the   **3.374**
two provisions appear to contain criteria that may be considered not to be homo-
genous. Article 81 EC applies to agreements independent of the power possibly
acquired, or not, by the parties. Similarly, Article 82 EC applies to situations where
power is acquired, whether this power results from an agreement or not. The consequence is that the two provisions may be applied to the same situations. Suppose two
undertakings conclude an agreement whereby they acquire power on a market. On
the basis of the distinction proposed by the ECJ, the situation could be addressed
under Article 81 EC and Article 82 EC. This does not, however, create a harmonious
situation, as the provisions are not exactly the same as regards the legal regime they
contain.[344] It would possibly be more appropriate to construe these provisions as
aiming at different situations which they address in pursuit of the same goal.

Agreements.   Second, there is no reason to cover agreements under competition   **3.375**
law irrespective of the existence of market power on the markets. Agreements do

---

[342] Case 6/72 *Europemballage and Continental Can v. Commission* [1973] ECR 215 at [23]–[25].
[343] N 309 above, at [34].
[344] Art 81(3) EC provides that exemptions may be granted whereas such a possibility does not
appear in the text of Art 82 EC. As, pursuant to the distinction proposed by the Court, the two provisions can be applied to the same situations, one could have a situation where an agreement would
be exempted under Art 81 EC but sanctioned under Art 82 EC.

not per se constitute a threat to competition—quite the contrary, as undertakings have to share resources in order to use them more efficiently. Agreements raise difficulties under the competition rules where they create situations leading to the acquisition or maintenance of market power. The purpose of competition law is to ensure that choice continues to exist on the markets so that customers may choose their supplier freely, and suppliers are forced to continue to adapt to the needs of customers. As stated in *Continental Can*, Articles 81 and 82 EC strive towards the same goal, to ensure the existence of competition. Yet this identity between the goals pursued by these provisions would appear to be endangered if an economic perspective is adopted in one case (Article 82 EC, control over market power) and an administrative vision in the other (Article 81 EC, control over agreements).

3.376 **Economic theory.** Finally, the position adopted by the ECJ in *Compagnie maritime belge* makes a rapprochement more difficult with US antitrust law. In the United States, competition law is interpreted in a more systematic manner on the basis of economic theory. Pursuant to that theory, intervention is mandated, and only permitted, where market power is acquired. In the absence of market power there is no necessity to intervene, as competition-based mechanisms normally lead to the best possible outcome from an economic point of view. This view is fundamentally different from that advocated in *Compagnie maritime belge*, where control must occur on all agreements independently of their effect on the markets. Placing an emphasis on a control of such an administrative nature thus creates difficulties for a rapprochement between the two most important bodies of rules concerning competition.

3.377 **The reasons for the introduction of the theory.** One may ultimately wonder about the reasons why the theory of collective dominance has been introduced in European competition law. One interpretation is that, although based on Article 82 EC, the theory originally developed as a variation on the concept of agreements. As is well known, anti-competitive agreements are not permitted under Article 81 EC.[345] A difficulty with this provision is that the relevant authorities are not always in a position to establish the existence of an agreement. Market participants have become aware of the prohibition and seek to hide anti-competitive agreements whenever concluded, with the result that such agreements have become increasingly invisible. Yet the problem created by these agreements remains. At a certain moment, competition disappears from the market and action must be taken to restore choice for customers and the normal functioning of market mechanisms. As an answer to

---

[345] Suppose a market counts three undertakings and these undertakings agree to increase tariffs. If the cartel is strong enough, each of these market participants may charge a higher tariff without fearing that customers will turn to competitors. Agreements of that nature are normally prohibited under Art 81 EC and may only be exempted from the prohibition if severe conditions are fulfilled.

that evolution, the European institutions have developed the theory of 'concerted practices'. This theory is based on the same provision as that applied to anti-competitive agreements, ie Article 81 EC. Pursuant to this theory, undertakings may be presumed to have entered into an anti-competitive agreement where they adopt interdependent practices that can be explained only through inferring that the undertakings have agreed on conduct.

This theory relating to 'concerted practices' has been applied in some cases, but it has rapidly become evident that economists are able to present arguments showing that the correspondence between practices may be explained by other reasons.[346] The European institutions have thus been led to develop another theory, aimed at catching interdependent behaviour without having to infer, for the prohibition to apply, that an agreement has indeed taken place. That theory has centred around the idea of collective dominance. Under this interpretation, the creation of the collective dominance theory may thus be explained as a remedy brought by the European institutions to the difficulties of establishing the existence of an agreement and even inferring the existence of such. This interpretation seems in line with the emphasis placed in early case law on the existence of links between the undertakings having collective dominance.[347]

It is only as a second step that links have not been deemed essential for a finding of collective dominance to be made. The emphasis was then placed on characteristics present on the markets and explaining why, in certain circumstances, a common course of action develops. This development can also be analysed in relation to the case law concerning companies belonging to the same group. As stated above, competition law applies to undertakings and the concept of 'undertaking' is interpreted widely as encompassing all entities forming an 'economic unit'. Case law has been developed on this basis, pursuant to which companies belonging to the same group must be considered as forming one economic unit for the application of competition law. A single economic unit is supposed to be formed when parties do not enjoy enough freedom to pursue their own course of action. In other words, different entities are analysed as forming an economic unit when a common course of action is pursued.[348] These entities are considered as forming

---

[346] See in particular Joined Cases C 89, 104, 114, 116, 117 and 125–129/85, *A. Ahlström Osakeyhtiö v Commission* [1993] ECR I-1307.

[347] In *Compagnie maritime belge* (n 309 above), for instance, the undertakings formed a conference and adopted interdependent behaviour. The Commission, the Court and the CFI successively argued that these undertakings were united by links allowing them to hold collective dominance.

[348] The consequence is that agreements possibly concluded by these companies cannot be examined under Art 81 EC. An agreement indeed presupposes the presence of different undertakings. The companies are not however considered as separate entities but as forming a single undertaking for the application of competition rules. As a result, possible agreements among these entities have to be assessed in the light of Art 82 EC and competition authorities must enquire in that context whether the group—the economic unit—holds market power. See Case 15/74, *Centrafarm v Sterling Drug*

one single undertaking for the application of competition law and the behaviour collectively[349] adopted by them is analysed under Article 82 EC.

This line of reasoning appears to have been continued by the case law on collective dominance, under which the idea that various entities may form a single economic unit is extended to a situation where these entities are not part of the same group but generally appear to follow a common course of action. The substance of the approach made by competition authorities is thus identical in both cases, although differences appear in the vocabulary. Thus the various entities are not analysed as forming a single undertaking in the collective dominance theory. The case law accepts that these entities are different undertakings, the key factor for the application of the theory being the common course of action.

3.378 Collective dominant position and the concept of undertaking

Companies within the same group	Collective dominant position
The situation concerns companies within the same group. These companies do not have any autonomous course of action. For this reason they can be considered as forming one 'economic unit'. Under competition law, they are said to be one 'undertaking' under competition law. Conduct adopted by that undertaking is subject to Article 82 EC	The concept is applied to undertakings which, although they do not belong to the same group, are also characterised by a common course of action. The common character of this course of action implies that they must be considered as a single 'economic entity'. The jurisprudence does not go so far as to consider them as forming a single 'undertaking'. The conduct adopted by these undertakings is also subject to Article 82 EC

I. Potential Difficulties Associated with Transnational Markets

3.379 **Issue raised by transnational markets.**   Electronic communications are becoming increasingly internationalised. Nonetheless, the mechanisms which are established for maintaining controls on undertakings remain, in most instances, national, in particular since the authorities in charge of monitoring markets and restoring normal conditions are national bodies. One may wonder whether there is not a contradiction in entrusting national bodies with regulatory tasks on markets transcending national boundaries. Suppose that, in the European Union, one NRA is empowered to regulate a market overlapping national markets[350] (these markets are called

---

[1974] ECR 1147. See also *Bodson* (n 296 above) at [19]: 'Article 85 . . . is not concerned with agreements or concerted practices between undertakings belonging to the same concern and having the status of parent company and subsidiary, if the undertakings form an economic unit within which the subsidiary has no real freedom to determine its course of action on the market.'

[349] As stated above, these entities do not have enough freedom to follow their own course of action.

[350] This sort of market can be encountered where inhabitants of regions located on both sides of a national frontier have similar habits. Take a country like Belgium, which has a German-speaking

'transnational' in the European terminology). Pursuant to the NRF, that authority would have to carry out several tasks—identify the relevant markets, assess competition on them, decide whether obligations should be imposed and make a selection among the regulatory tools available. In fulfilling these tasks, that authority would probably be equipped in an adequate fashion to regulate the portion of the market that is located on its national territory. It would, however, lack information about the portions situated elsewhere. Furthermore, the tasks entrusted to that authority would require decisions to be taken. If it was empowered to regulate a transnational market, the authority would adopt instruments binding customers, undertakings and possibly other public bodies in areas beyond what is generally considered the normal scope of action for public entities, ie the national territory.

Solutions are meagre in the new regulatory framework.   To prevent, and rem-   **3.380** edy, such difficulties, the European legislator has adopted several measures. These however fall short of covering all issues potentially created by transnational markets. They do not establish a procedure which could be used as a general mechanism to address these transnational situations.

Co-operation among authorities.   Pursuant to the NRF, there is a need for NRAs   **3.381** to co-operate where markets are transnational. This observation is made by the European legislator in the preamble to the Framework Directive. No principle is however established, pursuant to which authorities have a duty to co-operate. No obligation is formulated in the NRF for the NRAs to examine common cases where they are confronted with markets exceeding the scope of their respective territories.

> *Framework Directive, Preamble, recital 27.* 'National regulatory authorities will need to cooperate with each other where the relevant market is found to be transnational.'

Obligation of joint or concerted action in some circumstances.   That introduc-   **3.382** tory observation made by the European legislator about the 'need' for co-operation is supplemented by a mechanism which is established, and organised, in the regulation. That mechanism unfolds in several phases. *(a)* The regulation provides that the Commission may adopt a decision identifying transnational markets. That provision does not imply that an obligation is imposed on the Commission—it rather creates a right or grants a power to that institution.[351] When the Commission

---

community with habits similar to those of the German citizens located on the other side of the frontier. As patterns are not different, one may contemplate defining a geographic market as encompassing both sides of the frontier. Such a finding would be made if customers are shown to go from one side of the border to the other in reaction to a price increase. This sort of behaviour is frequently adopted where customers can find standard products on either side of a frontier. A typical example is petrol. Customers may buy petrol of the same trade mark in all European countries. They can easily cross frontiers to buy cheaper petrol, in particular since movement is no longer restricted at the border and a comparison may easily be made among tariffs in countries using the euro.

[351] This implies, inter alia, that the Commission cannot be found to have failed to fulfil its mission if no decision is adopted. In procedural terms, no application for failure to act (Art 232 EC) may be brought against the Commission before the ECJ or the CFI. Similarly, the Commission

decides to identify transnational markets, it must consult the NRAs prior to adopting the decision. Through that procedure, the authorities may comment on the decision envisaged by the Commission. Their comments are not binding, and the Commission may decide to pursue its objectives despite the reluctance or disagreement of one, several or even all the national authorities.[352]

> *Framework Directive, Article 15(4).* 'After consultation with national regulatory authorities the Commission may, acting in accordance with the procedure referred to in Article 22(3), adopt a Decision identifying transnational markets.'[353]

(b) After the decision is adopted, the NRAs have to fulfil their mission on the basis of the identification made by the Commission. This mission encompasses, as stated above, several tasks—assessment of competition, decision as to whether specific obligations should be imposed, choice among the available regulatory tools, including possibly a decision to leave unchanged some obligations imposed under the old regulatory framework.[354] The regulation provides that these tasks may not be carried out separately by the NRAs involved. The first task mentioned above—competition assessment—must be carried out 'jointly'. The second and the third tasks—decision as to the application of specific obligations—must be implemented 'in a concerted fashion'.

> *Framework Directive, Article 16(5).* 'In the case of transnational markets identified in the Decision referred to . . . , the national regulatory authorities concerned shall jointly conduct the market analysis taking the utmost account of the guidelines and decide on any imposition, maintenance, amendment or withdrawal of regulatory obligations . . . in a concerted fashion.'

(c) It should be emphasised that the co-ordination requested from the NRAs does not go so far as to require that decisions must be adopted by them in common. The decisions to be taken on the basis of the joint assessment and the identification provided by the Commission apparently remain, pursuant to the NRF, a national prerogative. It is thus for each NRA to decide, for the territory placed under its competence, what kind of obligations have to be fulfilled. To avoid excessive divergence, the special regulatory procedure is made applicable to these decisions.[355] This implies that the decisions envisaged by the national authorities

---

could not be deemed liable for damages possibly incurred by authorities, undertakings or customers as a result of the absence of a decision identifying transnational markets. (Arts 235 and 288 EC.)

[352] The decision must of course be compatible with superior European rules, otherwise it may be challenged in its validity. See Arts 230 and 231 EC.

[353] The procedure referred to in that provision is analysed in Chapter 6.

[354] In normal circumstances, the first task to be fulfilled by the NRA is to define markets. As stated above, markets are defined in their functional component, in all circumstances, by the Commission. National authorities may make suggestions, but the Commission holds the ultimate decision-making power. By contrast, NRAs have the competence to define markets geographically. But that competence is set aside in the case of transnational markets when a decision is adopted by the Commission to identify these markets.   [355] See Framework Directive, Art 16(6).

concerned have to be communicated to the Commission and to the authorities in the other Member States. Comments may then be made within a period of one month. They must be taken into account by the authority planning the decision. Pursuant to the regulation,[356] the Commission ultimately has the power to oppose the adoption of the decision where the latter would create a barrier to the single market or serious doubts can be raised about the compatibility of that decision with the objectives pursued in the NRF.

Check list of the scenarios that may occur.   On the basis of the analysis presented **3.383** above, several scenarios may occur in practice, and practitioners should be prepared to take an appropriate stance in each of them. In the first, the Commission decides to make use of the power that is granted to it by the regulation. It thus adopts a decision identifying transnational markets. On the basis of that decision, the NRAs concerned examine in common the degree of competition existing on these markets. They also consider in a concerted fashion whether specific obligations should be imposed, and which. On the basis of this common analysis, they prepare draft decisions. These decisions must circulate and the other NRAs may submit comments. The decision may be vetoed by the Commission.[357]

Second scenario.   In a second scenario, the Commission does not adopt a decision **3.384** identifying transnational markets. The measures examined above, which are included in the NRF, do not, as a result, apply.[358] The consequence is that there is no obligation for the NRAs involved to carry out a common assessment of competition nor to decide in a concerted fashion whether obligations should be imposed. There remains only the 'need' for co-operation as referred to in the preamble to the Framework Directive, but this 'need' by no means implies any obligation for the NRAs. To this 'need' must be added the special regulatory procedure; it must however be emphasised that that procedure only applies in part in the second scenario. This limited application is due to a restriction of the circumstances in which the special powers granted to the Commission apply. Pursuant to the regulation, the decisions envisaged by the NRAs in respect of transnational markets must be circulated.[359] The other authorities, as well as the Commission, may then submit

---

[356] The special powers allocated to the Commission in the special regulatory procedure do not have a general application. They are limited to specific circumstances which are set forth in the regulation. Among them is the adoption of a decision by an NRA after a common analysis by the various authorities concerned, on the basis of the act taken by the Commission and identifying the transnational markets. See the Framework Directive, Art 16(4), letter (b).

[357] That scenario is based on the measures examined in para 3.382 above.

[358] These measures are indeed designed in the regulation, as related one to another. The obligation of a joint or concerted action only applies when the Commission makes use of the power to identify the transnational markets and the special power whereby the Commission may block draft decisions proposed by national authorities is limited to situations where a joint or concerted action has taken place.

[359] This mechanism applies for all decisions likely to be taken by these authorities in relation to transnational markets: decisions whereby markets are defined by the authorities as to their geographic

comments. These comments must be taken into account by the drafting authority. However, the regulation does not provide the Commission with a power to oppose the adoption of the decision, even when that institution considers that the objectives pursued in the NRF would be infringed or a barrier to entry would be created.[360]

3.385 **Third scenario.** A third scenario remains to be analysed, where a decision identifying transnational markets is adopted by the Commission but that decision does not mention a specific market which some authorities, undertakings and/or customers consider to be transnational. The situation is uncertain, in that it cannot really be addressed in the categories organised by the regulation. For that reason, the possibility would remain open of challenging the decision adopted by the Commission. Pursuant to the regulation, the Commission may adopt a decision identifying transnational markets. This implies, as mentioned, that a power, not an obligation, is granted to the Commission. The corollary is that, once the Commission has chosen to make use of that power, the decision must identify *all* existing transnational markets.[361] If it fails to do so, the decision does not comply with that obligation and could probably be annulled.[362]

3.386 **Are there many transnational markets?** The question arises whether many markets with a transnational character can be expected to be encountered in European electronic communications. In answer it should be borne in mind that the NRF is limited in its scope to services intended for the public as well as to networks used for the provision of such services.[363] These markets in most cases

---

extension; decisions assessing competition existing on these markets; and decisions about obligations possibly to be maintained, or imposed, on the said markets.

[360] The only possible action, in that second scenario, would be for the Commission to use the ordinary Art 226 procedure against the Member State of which the NRA is an organ. That procedure may be initiated after the decision has been taken. Pursuant to case law, the procedure may also be launched to get interim or provisional relief. It would thus be possible for the Commission to obtain a legal review of the decision by the ECJ prior to the adoption of that act. The same possibility is open to the Member States, on the basis of Art 227 EC. Undertakings and customers may react—but they have to use the proceedings available at national level.

[361] This interpretation is warranted by the French version of the Framework Directive. 'Après consultation des autorités réglementaires nationales, la Commission peut . . . adopter une décision *recensant* les marches transnationaux.' Pursuant to that version, the Commission may not limit its intervention to an identification of some transnational markets. A list must be established, with all markets having those characteristics.

[362] It should be emphasised that, although the instrument is called a decision, it has a general nature because it identifies all transnational markets. Such an instrument may be challenged by various European institutions and the Member States before the ECJ. The difficulty is, however, that a strict deadline (two months) has to be respected to that effect. The incomplete character of the decision will however probably appear after that deadline has expired. The above-mentioned applicants will then have lost their right of action. Action, however, remains possible for legal or natural persons. To that effect, they must initiate a procedure before a national court against an act, or failure to act, by the NRA. In their challenge, the applicants must request the national court to ask the ECJ preliminary questions about the validity of the decision adopted by the Commission.

[363] This is particularly true for the specific obligations to be imposed on undertakings with significant market power. These obligations only apply to markets concerning services meant for the public.

correspond with national territories, given the division of the European territory into networks that correspond, in most instances, with national territories. The division into national spheres may also be explained by the regulation that is applied. This regulation still has a national character to the extent that it is applied, and administered, by national authorities, even if divergence between the national laws is avoided as a result of harmonisation. As rules still have a national character (although they have a European origin), providers must analyse the rules in force in a given territory before they can engage in an activity on that territory. The conditions of competition are influenced by these rules. It thus comes as no surprise that customers do not turn to suppliers from other countries when they need a service—unless that supplier is also active on the territory where the customer is located, in which case it may not really be regarded as a foreign supplier.[364]

Not many markets. In conclusion, one should not expect many markets to have **3.387** a transnational character. This implies that practitioners should not worry, at this stage in the development of electronic communications markets, about the rather uncertain procedures established under the NRF as regards these markets. This conclusion is limited to the activities that must be examined under the regulation. The position is different as regards markets to be analysed under the competition rules. In general competition law there already exist, as of now, several examples of markets overlapping national borders and raising difficulties as a result of the acquisition of significant market power by one or several undertakings.[365]

J. Compatibility with WTO Provisions

In line with European law. As has been stated in the introductory chapter, the **3.388** Reference Paper contains principles applicable to basic telecommunications networks and services in the Members of the Organisation, where these Members

---

[364] Suppose a British customer wants to use internet services. One should not expect that customer to turn to a French provider if the prices for the service increase in the British territory. The reason is that the French provider may only offer a service to a British customer if it has access to a British network. That network corresponds to the British territory as regards its geographic scope. A similar analysis can be made with respect to providers. To return to our example, a French provider will not turn easily to the British market if tariffs increase on that latter territory. A geographical move may be envisaged if the provider feels that it could increase profits by entering the British market. This move will however require time, investment and risks. However, different locations are only considered as parts of the same market in circumstances where a supplier can move from one to another rapidly and without risk or substantial investment.

[365] In several cases, the Commission and the European courts have defined electronic communications markets on a transnational basis. In *BT/MCI I*, for instance, the market was considered to be worldwide. A more limited market was retained for *BT/MCI II* where, for one of the issues raised, the Commission deemed that competition would be impaired on the market for transatlantic communications. These cases, however, have not been dealt with under the NRF, but on the basis of general competition law.

have made commitments in those areas (this is the case for the European Union and its Member States). These principles are in line with those introduced at European level. There is thus consistency between the rules existing at European and international level, as regards access.

3.389 **Interconnection.** No distinction is drawn in the WTO terminology between access and interconnection. As stated above, a difference has been introduced in the European terminology between these concepts, with access keeping its general meaning and interconnection being reserved to the linking of networks. These concepts are gathered under the term 'interconnection' in the Reference Paper.

> *Reference Paper, para 2.1.* Interconnection is the 'linking with suppliers providing public telecommunications transport networks or services in order to allow the users of one supplier to communicate with users of another supplier and to access services provided by another supplier, where specific commitments are undertaken.'

3.390 **Non-discrimination.** The main obligation imposed on major suppliers under the Reference Paper is to provide interconnection under non-discriminatory conditions. As in the NRF, non-discrimination means that major suppliers may not treat some undertakings better—or worse—than others. It also implies that major suppliers may not impose on other undertakings less favourable conditions than those used for their own services.

> *Reference Paper, para 2.2., letter (a).* 'Interconnection with a major supplier . . . at any technically feasible point in the network . . . is provided . . . under non-discriminatory terms, conditions (including technical standards and specifications) and rates and of a quality no less favourable than that provided for its own like services or for like services of non-affiliated service suppliers or for its subsidiaries or other affiliates.'

3.391 **Transparency, reasonable conditions, unbundling.** Other obligations are imposed on major suppliers, in particular to *(a)* to ensure transparency in the conditions under which interconnection may be obtained; *(b)* to propose fair and reasonable conditions; *(c)* to avoid bundling, so that service providers only need to purchase the service that they require.

> *Reference Paper, para 2.2., letter (b).* 'Interconnection with a major supplier . . . at any technically feasible point in the network . . . is provided . . . in a timely fashion, on terms, conditions (including technical standards and specifications) and cost-oriented rates that are transparent, reasonable, having regard to economic feasibility, and sufficiently unbundled so that the supplier need not pay for network components or facilities that it does not require for the service to be provided.'

3.392 **Negotiations.** As in the NRF, the key principle for services providers, pursuant to the Reference Paper, is to negotiate with major suppliers. Only where interconnection may not be obtained under satisfactory conditions will public intervention be warranted. To facilitate negotiation, the Reference Paper provides that major suppliers must make publicly available the procedure to be used to negotiate with them. A reference interconnection offer must be made available. Service providers must have access to an independent body, within the national legal order of each Member of the Organisation, where the conditions proposed by the major suppliers are not satisfactory, in view of the obligations imposed on these latter undertakings.

> *Reference Paper, para 2.3, 2.4 and 2.5.* 'The procedures applicable for interconnection to a major supplier will be made publicly available.' 'It is ensured that a major supplier will make publicly available either its interconnection agreements or a reference interconnection offer.' 'A service supplier requesting interconnection with a major supplier will have recourse . . . to an independent domestic body . . . to resolve disputes regarding appropriate terms, conditions and rates for interconnection within a reasonable period of time, to the extent that these have not been established previously.'

Major supplier.   One issue is to determine to which undertakings these obligations apply. Pursuant to the Reference Paper, the obligations presented in the paragraphs above apply to major suppliers. Under that paper, major suppliers are undertakings which may influence the conditions on a market as a result of control over essential facilities. Facilities are considered essential where no alternative exists from an economic or technical point of view.   **3.393**

> *Reference Paper, point 1.* 'A major supplier is a supplier which has the ability to materially affect the terms of participation (having regard to price and supply) in the relevant market for basic telecommunications services as a result of: *(a)* control over essential facilities; or *(b)* use of its position in the market.' 'Essential facilities mean facilities of a public telecommunications transport network or service that *(a)* are exclusively or predominantly provided by a single or limited number of suppliers; and *(b)* cannot feasibly be economically or technically substituted in order to provide a service.'

Triple consistency.   That definition shows that there is a triple consistency between European and international rules relating to interconnection. *(a)* The obligations imposed on the markets and relating to access, and/or interconnection, are similar in the two bodies of the law. *(b)* These obligations may, or must, be imposed, depending on the case, on the same undertakings. Under the NRF and the Reference Paper, the undertakings concerned are those which, as a result of market power, may influence market conditions. *(c)* The definition which is given to 'major suppliers' in the Reference Paper is identical for the regulatory principles introduced in that paper, as well as for the competition rules which are also formulated in that instrument.   **3.394**

4

ACCESS TO FACILITIES AND RESOURCES CONTROLLED BY OTHER UNDERTAKINGS—GENERAL COMPETITION LAW

A. Access to Resources

(1) What should practitioners do?

The relationship between the two bodies of law. The rules governing access in **4.01** the new regulatory framework (NRF) are examined in the previous chapter. In the course of the discussion, it is made clear that a relationship exists between the rules contained in the framework and general competition law. This chapter analyses the rules concerning access to resources under general competition law.

4.02 Priority to the framework. When dealing with access-related issues, practitioners should, wherever possible, first examine whether the rules contained in the NRF may be applied. The reasons for adopting this line are twofold: first, the specialised character of these sector-specific rules, which have been tailored to the needs of the electronic communications market, and second, the presence of dedicated authorities specifically equipped to apply the sector-specific regulation to the particular circumstances that arise in this market.

4.03 General competition law as a second step. General competition law may be used as a second resort. It provides useful tools in three sets of circumstances. *(a)* General competition law may be used where there is a lacuna in the NRF. It has general scope and may thus apply in all circumstances where no other rule is applicable. *(b)* General competition law may also be useful in interpreting the NRF where rules belonging to that framework are not clear. This is particularly true since the European legislator has aligned the basic concepts and methods of the framework with general competition law.[1] *(c)* Finally, general competition law may prove useful where the NRF does not support the attitude which practitioners want to take in order to argue their case. Where, for instance, a practitioner considers that a strong case cannot be constructed on the basis of the NRF, other arguments may be sought in general competition law.

4.04 Applicable instruments. Most of the basic provisions of general competition law are located in the EC Treaty. They are, however, implemented and further construed in a number of complex cases and regulations. *(a)* Special consideration is given in this chapter to Article 82 EC, which prohibits abuses committed by undertakings in a dominant position and which is the main provision of general competition law governing issues relating to access to facilities and resources. *(b)* Article 81 EC concerns agreements concluded between two or more undertakings and, more generally, all forms of co-ordination among undertakings. The Merger Regulation applies to operations whereby undertakings acquire each other, merge with each other or create joint ventures changing their structure in a substantial manner. The case law relating to Article 81 EC and the Merger Regulation is not examined in this book. *(c)* Article 86 EC addresses situations where undertakings have special ties with public authorities.[2] The case law relating to that provision, together with the concept of universal service, is analysed in Chapter 5. Article 87 EC, which concerns State aids, is also examined there. In this manner, all specific links between undertakings and public authorities are examined in Chapter 5 dealing with universal service.

---

[1] In particular the concept of significant market power (dominance) and the methods used to define markets.

[2] Public undertakings, undertakings with special or exclusive rights, undertakings entrusted with the task of providing a service of general economic interest.

No need for secondary instruments.   Article 82 EC produces effects directly,   **4.05**
without the need for one or several instruments to be adopted in order to implement it.[3] The same now also applies for Article 81 EC, although the situation
used to be different regarding that provision.[4] This new situation whereby both
provisions have full direct effect has been created by Council Regulation (EC)
1/2003 on the implementation of the rules on competition laid down in Articles
81 and 82 of the Treaty.[5]

Guidelines published by the Commission.   The prohibition laid down in Article   **4.06**
82 EC has been interpreted in the case law of the Commission and the European
courts, with further detail concerning the electronic communications sector in two
notices. These notices do not contain binding rules. As mentioned above, Article 82
EC produces effects without the need for implementing instruments. The goal of
the Commission, through these notices, was to announce the position it is likely to
adopt where cases involving the application of that provision are brought to its
attention. *(a)* The first instrument is the Commission Guidelines (EC) on the application of EEC competition rules in the telecommunications sector.[6] *(b)* The second
is Commission Notice 98/C265/02 on the application of the competition rules to
access agreements in the telecommunications sector.[7]

How to get information.   Practitioners wishing to obtain official information   **4.07**
about the application of Article 82 EC in the electronic communications sector
should consult the website of the Commission, DG Competition. *(a)* All cases
dealt with by the Commission on the basis of that provision are presented there.
(b) Practitioners may also find there the Competition Report published annually
by the Commission. This report analyses all cases addressed during the previous
year on a provision per provision basis, including cases concerning electronic
communications. *(c)* The website further contains a newsletter (the Competition
Newsletter), which is published regularly by the Commission on issues currently
being addressed. *(d)* Press information about pending or possible cases is also
available on the site. This source of information is important, given the increasingly informal character of law enforcement in competition matters. *(e)* Finally,
the site provides electronic addresses where information can be found on cases

---

[3] This means that Art 82 EC can be applied directly, without a need for implementation instruments in order further to construe the prohibition that it contains. It also implies that the provision
can be applied directly by national entities—whether these entities are national courts or specialised
competition authorities.

[4] A distinction was made earlier, concerning Art 81 EC, between two parts of the provision.
(a) First, Art 81 EC prohibits anti-competitive agreements (para 1). The prohibition contained in
that article produces direct effects, without the need for implementation instruments. The situation
was not different from Art 82 EC, as regards that part of the provision. *(b)* Second, Art 81 EC contains an exemption clause, which allows agreements to be saved, despite their effect on competition,
when certain conditions are fulfilled (para 3). Until recently, that part of the provision did not have
direct effect. Instruments were to be adopted in order to implement it.

[5] [2003] OJ L1/1.   [6] [1991] OJ C233/2.   [7] [1999] OJ C265/2.

treated by the CFI and ECJ. The website of the two latter institutions provides a rather sophisticated case law search function.

(2) General presentation of Article 82 EC

4.08   **The content of the provision.**   As mentioned above, Article 82 EC prohibits abusive practices adopted by dominant undertakings. Several conditions must be fulfilled for that provision to apply. *(a)* At the time when the alleged practice took place, the undertaking in question must have had a dominant position. *(b)* An abusive usage must have been made of that position. *(c)* The internal market must have been affected by that conduct.[8] *(d)* To these conditions, which are explicitly formulated in the provision, another is sometimes added in the case law as well as the literature. This last condition is that no objective justification must be available to take away the abusive character of the practice.

> *Article 82 EC.* 'Any abuse by one or more undertakings of a dominant position within the common market or in a substantial part of it shall be prohibited as incompatible with the common market insofar as it may affect trade between the Member States. Such abuse may, in particular, consist in: *(a)* directly or indirectly imposing unfair purchase or selling prices or other unfair trading conditions; *(b)* limiting production, markets or technical development to the prejudice of consumers; *(c)* applying dissimilar conditions to equivalent transactions with other trading parties, thereby placing them at a competitive disadvantage; *(d)* making the conclusion of contracts subject to acceptance by the other parties of supplementary obligations which, by their nature or according to commercial usage, have no connection with the subject of such contracts.'

4.09   **Dominance and significant market power.**   Among these concepts, dominance plays a prominent role. It is not relevant that a practice may be deemed abusive, if the undertaking adopting that practice is not dominant. A rapprochement has taken place between this concept and that of significant market power used in the NRF.[9] Under the framework, the two concepts are made equivalent.[10] In the classic definition, dominance refers to the position of economic strength acquired by an undertaking and which permits that undertaking to behave, to an appreciable extent, independently of competitors, customers and ultimately consumers.[11]

---

[8] That latter condition is expressed in two places within the provision. First, dominance must be held within the common market or in a substantial part of it. That condition has generally been interpreted as implying that purely national dominant positions should not be addressed under European general competition law. Second, the abuse may only be addressed under Art 82 EC when trade between Member States is affected. Both conditions are expressed in the first paragraph of the provision.   [9] See the Framework Directive, Art 14.

[10] This general equivalence does not take away the possibility that differences may appear in specific cases. These variations are mainly due to the context in which the authorities operate. Authorities applying competition rules normally look at past situations, and attempt to determine whether the undertaking had a dominant position at the time the allegedly abusive practices were adopted. By contrast, the NRAs applying the NRF must take a prospective view and assess whether competition is impaired on a given market in a context in which that difficulty will not be solved by the markets operating on their own. See the 2002 Guidelines on market analysis and significant market power, para 70.   [11] See the Framework Directive, Art 14(2).

The concept of significant market power, and that of dominance, are analysed in Chapter 3 dealing with access under sector-specific regulation. The analysis provided there covers the concept as interpreted in the NRF as well as in general competition law. There is no need to repeat the analysis here.

Joint dominance.   The concept of joint dominance is also examined in Chapter 3   **4.10** dealing with access under sector-specific regulation. As submitted there, this concept has also been made equivalent by the European legislator to the concept of joint significant market power, an expression that the European legislator does not explicitly use.[12] As is the case with dominance, more analysis is provided in Chapter 3 dealing with access under the NRF.

Focus on abuse.   As the concepts of dominance and joint dominance are exam-   **4.11** ined elsewhere, this chapter concentrates on the concept of abuse. In the discussion on that concept, a general approach is adopted in the first instance. This approach is essential as, in the absence of developed specific case law on electronic communications, practitioners often have to refer to the general case law. It is thus important for them to have an overall understanding of the content, and the scope, of this case law. After this general approach, various types of behaviour or circumstance are analysed. These can be associated with situations where an undertaking dominates a given market.

Little case law on electronic communications.   As mentioned in the previous   **4.12** paragraph, there is little specific case law on the application of Article 82 EC to the electronic communications sector by the Commission or European courts. This may be due to the strategy increasingly adopted by the Commission in the application of general competition law. The main source for practitioners and academics of information concerning Commission practice is normally the decisions formally adopted by that institution and published in the Official Journal. This mechanism has numerous advantages in terms of transparency.[13] Despite these advantages, the Commission appears to handle an increasing proportion of cases on an informal basis. Where a negotiation is successful, a frequent occurrence given the Commission's negotiating power, no decision needs to be taken, and no publication is therefore necessary.[14] The practical consequence of the relative

---

[12] There is thus a discrepancy of a kind in the terms used in the NRF. The European legislator systematically uses the specific expression 'significant market power' although that expression is made equivalent to that, more common, of dominance. But it prefers the notion of 'dominance' when describing a situation where power is acquired by two or more undertakings. The reason for that choice is probably purely accidental—'joint significant market power' is not a felicitous expression.

[13] Among these advantages: the publication of formal decisions provides hindsight about how the rules are applied in practice; it also forces the Commission to explain the reasons why a decision was adopted.

[14] The absence of a formal decision, and the lack of an official publication, appears to create a danger for transparent and accurate legal information. As a remedy to that situation, the Commission attempts to publish notices or communications—instruments of a general character which explain

absence of specific case law on electronic communications is that practitioners have to rely on ordinary case law in order to determine how Article 82 EC can be applied in that sector.

(3) *The concept of abuse*

4.13 **Practices enumerated in Article 82 EC.** Article 82 EC does not provide a definition of the concept of abuse. It merely provides a list of practices which are deemed abusive. That list does not permit a general definition to be extracted. *(a)* First, it contains only examples, without being exhaustive. *(b)* Second, diverging criteria appear in the list.[15] *(c)* Third, these criteria are not homogeneous as regards their level of abstraction.[16] The result of these various difficulties is that the case law is not always consistent in the division of situations into categories. Where, for example, a dominant operator formally grants access to its electronic communications networks but makes it dependent on the payment of a high tariff, this behaviour could be analysed as unfair, since it is a practice which is explicitly mentioned in Article 82 EC. Further, through this behaviour the dominant operator in effect refuses access to its network. Admittedly, access is granted in formal terms, but the conditions are so demanding that they in effect amount to a refusal.

4.14 **A general approach favoured.** The difficulties raised by the list appearing in Article 82 EC are of such magnitude that the Commission and European courts hardly refer to the examples mentioned in the provision. They merely label a practice as abusive, once they consider that that practice corresponds to the general understanding of what abuses are under general competition law. This attitude has solid practical implications. Practitioners do not need to qualify the facts with reference to an example mentioned in Article 82 EC. They should rather seek to demonstrate how the practice does or does not correspond to what can be deemed abusive in general. Such a general approach is taken in the present section. In the next sections, various practices, or types of practice, are examined. These practices are generally associated with the existence of dominant undertakings on a given market.

4.15 **Business-to-customer and business-to-competitor.** It is often considered that the practices falling under this provision may be divided in two general categories.

---

the policy carried out in given sectors. These notices or communications are useful for practitioners to understand the general attitude envisaged by the Commission for different types of situation. They do not, however, remedy the situation altogether as they have, by nature, a general character, and do not bring as a result any assistance in understanding how rules are applied in practice.

[15] Three practices mentioned in the list are specific (discrimination, unfair trading, tying up), whereas the fourth refers to an effect observed on a market and which could be the result of numerous practices, including those mentioned in the first instance.

[16] Unfair terms and conditions, for instance, is a very general category which may encompass discrimination and tying up. The result is an overlap between the practices mentioned in the list. Where, for instance, a dominant undertaking imposes discriminatory treatment on a customer, that practice could be apprehended under two of the items in the list (discrimination and unfair treatment).

(a) The first contains practices called 'exploitative'. This term refers to conduct adopted by an undertaking which takes advantage of its power to impose on customers conditions that are not satisfactory, that is, are inferior to the conditions that could be found on a competitive market (excessive prices, reduced output, limited innovation, etc). *(b)* The second category comprises 'exclusionary practices', that is, practices adopted to eliminate competitors or make it more difficult for them to carry out their activities. This categorisation is analysed in Chapter 3 dealing with access under the NRF, in connection with leverage. It is submitted there that the distinction between exploitative and exclusionary practices should not be overemphasised. It is generally assumed that exploitative practices become exclusionary when they are adopted on a first market vis-à-vis a customer which is a competitor on a second market.

Illustration.   As an example, suppose that a dominant undertaking imposes unfair   **4.16**
conditions for network access on a service provider. These unfair conditions qualify as exclusionary when the effect of the practice is considered on the derived market for services, where the provider is not in a position to carry out activities under reasonable conditions as a result of the high costs it has to face for access to the infrastructure. In cases like this, the scenario is as follows. *(a)* Unsatisfactory conditions are offered on a first market. *(b)* As a result of the unsatisfactory character of these conditions, the practice can on that market be deemed to be exploitative, on the basis of the definition given above. *(c)* These conditions acquire an exclusionary effect when one considers the consequences that they have on a second, derived, market. *(d)* On that market, these conditions in fact impede competitors' performance.

Customers and competitors.   Despite its limitation, the division of the case law   **4.17**
concerning Article 82 EC into two categories provides a useful basis for analysis. In particular it shows that the abuses aimed at in that provision are principally directed, in some instances against customers[17] and in others against competitors. Where practices are deemed 'exploitative', this label is the result of a focus which is placed on the relations between the undertaking and its customer(s) (business-to-customer relations). When the practices are considered 'exclusionary', that conclusion derives from an emphasis placed on the relations between the undertaking and its competitors (business-to-competitor relations).

In this chapter.   In this chapter, emphasis is placed on business-to-competitor   **4.18**
practices, which are generally considered under the concept 'exclusionary'. The rights granted to users are examined in Chapter 7 dealing with specific issues, and it is accordingly in that context that business-to-customer practices generally deemed 'exploitative' are addressed.[18]

---

[17] Whether these customers are end users or businesses which will make use of the goods or services on another market, where they are not in competition with the undertaking.
[18] Despite that division, it should be clear that there does not exist any real difference between the core of the practices whether they are exploitative or exclusionary. Excessive prices may for instance

(4) Evolution of the concept

4.19 An evolution. As mentioned in the previous paragraphs, the concept of abuse has evolved over time in the direction of a wider interpretation. As a result the concept of abuse is defined in wider terms, in that undertakings are deemed to engage in abusive practices in wider circumstances than in the past. In other words, it is easier today for a practitioner to demonstrate that an undertaking abuses a dominant position, and correspondingly more difficult to defend an undertaking to which abusive practices are attributed. The developments that have taken place do not take away the possibility that cases may be decided on the basis of a standard set at an earlier stage. In other words, practitioners may face situations that were dealt with at an early phase in the case law. In such instances they may refer to earlier case law by way of precedent. For that reason, it is probably more accurate to consider that markers, rather than steps, exist in the case law. This means that an evolution has indeed taken place, but that the standards set at earlier stages have not lost all relevance and may still be invoked in litigation.

Deviation from standard economic behaviour

4.20 Marker/step 1. The case law originally placed emphasis on infringements allegedly committed by dominant undertakings. According to this interpretation, undertakings were deemed to abuse their dominant position where they adopted behaviour which could be considered as constituting an infringement. As in other sectors of the law, an infringement can be defined, in broad terms, as behaviour breaching a specific rule or, more generally, a moral or social standard. This interpretation of the concept of abuse may be labelled 'subjective', because it contains a reproach made against a person or entity for unacceptable behaviour.

4.21 Following paragraphs. This subjective interpretation was applied in numerous cases from which it is not easy to extract principles, due to the prominent role that facts often play in the decisions taken by competition authorities. Three typical situations are examined below where this interpretation has been applied. They are described in an abstract manner and illustrated afterwards by a leading case. Although it cannot be claimed that this analysis is exhaustive, it is hoped that the specific situations practitioners may encounter may be analysed using these categories. The infringement by the dominant undertaking is presented in these various examples as a deviation from the economic behaviour that undertakings are expected to adopt in a competitive environment. In such an environment, undertakings are supposed to concentrate their resources on the production of goods or services for the benefit of their customers. They are expected to strive in order to improve the service offered and thereby benefit if their merits outweigh those displayed by competitors.

---

be deemed abusive, whether they concern prices charged to customers or to competitors. The core of the provision does not depend on the identity of the parties involved—customers or competitors.

(a) Elimination of a competitor.   One kind of practice is the willingness on   **4.22**
the part of a dominant undertaking to eliminate a competitor. In the example examined below, a dominant undertaking engages in behaviour with no economic justification, but merely oriented towards the objective of eliminating a competitor. In
situations of this kind, the dominant undertaking shows a specific intent to eliminate
a competitor where other, more acceptable, behaviour was possible, and even recommended, had the undertaking concentrated on business development. In this part of
the case law, the authority makes the observation that the dominant undertaking did
not engage in the standard economic behaviour that is expected from an undertaking,
that is, offer goods and services in an environment where success is based on merit.

Leading case.   The leading case in this category is *National Carbonising*,[19] where an   **4.23**
undertaking held a dominant position (97 per cent) on the market for the produc-
tion of coal. That undertaking was also present on a secondary market, where the coal
was refined for industrial or domestic use. The dominant undertaking was subject to
competition on that second market. The competitor (there was only one) depended
on the dominant undertaking for supply. It had to purchase raw coal from the dominant undertaking on the first market in order to refine it and sell it to domestic or
industrial customers on the second. Taking advantage of that situation, the dominant undertaking increased the price for raw coal, although the price increase was not
passed on to final customers. In other words, the increase in the price paid to obtain
raw coal on the first market did not result in an increase of the price charged on the
second market to end users, whether individuals or businesses. As a result of that
practice, the competitor faced higher costs without being able to increase the revenues in due proportion.[20] The result was that, in the absence of intervention by an
authority, the competitor would have been squeezed out of the market.

Commission and ECJ.   The behaviour adopted by the dominant undertaking   **4.24**
was found unacceptable by the Commission and the ECJ. The reasoning underlying the decisions taken by these institutions may be presented as follows. In
a market-based environment, undertakings are expected to behave according to
economic standards. One standard is that if costs increase, that increase must be
reflected in the prices charged to end users. The only situation where that consequence can be avoided is where undertakings succeed in making their operations
more efficient to an extent matching the cost increase. However, a scenario of that
nature did not materialise in the case under review. Normal economic behaviour
would have implied an increase in the prices charged on the second market. Such

---

[19] See Commission Decision of 15 October 1975 (not published). See also the Order adopted
by the President of the ECJ, *National Carbonising Company v Commission*, 22 October 1975, 1193
and Commission Decision (CECA) 76/185 adopting interim measures concerning the National
Coal Board, the National Smokeless Fuels Ltd and the National Carbonising Company Ltd [1976]
OJ L35/6.
[20] Sale prices could not be increased by that competitor on the second market because customers
would have turned to the main undertaking for supply.

an increase would have followed, logically, the rising costs of supply. Such an increase did not however take place. The reason is that the decision to raise prices on the first market, and leave them stable on the second, was inspired not by an economic justification, which would have been related to an improvement of product supplied to customers, but rather the intention of eliminating a competitor. According to the analysis made by the Commission and the ECJ, there was a deliberate strategy to eliminate a competitor, a practice deemed abusive under Article 82 EC.

4.25 (b) **System of practices hindering competition.** Another typical situation is where an undertaking resorts to a combination of practices meant to impede the normal economic process. Considered individually, each of these practices already forms, in itself, an obstacle to competition. What is however striking in this second kind of situation is the combination of these practices, a combination that demonstrates that a deliberate strategy has been orchestrated by the dominant undertaking to hinder the economic process. These practices leave no doubt concerning the purpose sought by the dominant undertaking, that is, the maintenance of a position that is not founded on economic merit but rather on a capacity to constrain the economic freedom of partners and competitors.

4.26 **Leading case.** The leading case is *Hilti*,[21] in which an undertaking sold related products—nail guns, cartridges and nails. Each of these products constituted a separate market, as they could not be considered interchangeable. The undertaking enjoyed a dominant position on the market for nail guns. Its position was more precarious on the market for nails.[22] In order to improve its position on that latter market, the undertaking established a link between the various markets. Several practices were used to that effect; they were in fact so numerous that only some examples can be provided. One of them was to make the purchase of nail guns dependent on the purchase of nails. As a result of that link between the two markets, any customer wishing to acquire nail guns from the dominant undertaking—there was little alternative on the market—was also forced to buy nails from that same undertaking. The dominant undertaking prohibited the sale of nail guns to resellers which did not apply that policy. It also refused to provide a warranty where nail guns manufactured in its factories were used with

---

[21] Commission Decision (EEC) 88/138 relating to a proceeding under Article 86 of the EEC Treaty (IV/30.787 and 31.488—Eurofix-Bauco v Hilti) [1988] OJ L65/19; Case T-30/89 *Hilti AG v Commission* [1990] ECR II-163; Case T-30/89 *Hilti AG v Commission* [1991] ECR II-1439; Case C-53/92 P *Hilti AG v Commission* [1994] ECR I-667; Case C-53/92 P *Hilti AG v Commission* [1994] ECR I-667.

[22] The difference in the strength acquired by the undertaking on the two markets was for the following reasons. On the nail gun market, the undertaking was protected by entry barriers such as: the amount of investment required to produce nail guns, the technology needed to that effect and the intellectual rights obtained on that market. Entry was easier on the nail market, as no significant investment is necessary to start producing nails, nor any specific technology, and the production of nails is not protected by intellectual property.

nails produced by competitors. This made the production of nails on the basis of its technology impossible, or at least very difficult.[23] Confronted with these various practices, the Commission found that the undertaking had abused its dominant position. The decision adopted by that institution was later confirmed by the ECJ.

(c) **Causing disproportionate harm to a competitor.** A last type of situation is where a dominant undertaking causes disproportionate harm to a competitor. In that kind of circumstance, the European institution involved examines the situation of the various undertakings concerned. It weighs the benefits, and the costs, that result for each party from the behaviour adopted by the dominant undertaking. It also analyses the costs, and the benefits, that the adoption of other behaviour would have implied, for all parties. The purpose of this exercise is to assess whether the competitor was treated fairly. In that evaluation, the possibly disproportionate character of the behaviour adopted by the dominant undertaking, and that of the harm caused to the competitor, is measured in connection with, among other factors, the past relations between the parties. Have these relations been lengthy? Have they been useful for the dominant undertaking, as much as for the competitor? **4.27**

Leading case. The leading case is *Hugin*, which again involved two markets.[24] The first was for the manufacture and sale of cash registers. On that market, the undertaking concerned (Hugin) had a dominant position.[25] A second market was deemed to encompass derived, or secondary, activities, such as maintenance, repair and hiring out. On that market, Hugin and associated companies were also present. There, they were in competition with an independent undertaking (Lipton). The latter undertaking had previously served as a distributor for Hugin over a certain period. At a certain juncture Hugin had decided that distribution would take place in the future only with associated companies. Given the dominance held by Hugin, that business decision implied that Lipton was no longer allowed to carry out a distribution activity on the market in question. One may wonder whether that decision could not be analysed, in itself, as an abusive practice, in the context of the domination exercised by Hugin. No complaint was however **4.28**

---

[23] The production of the nail guns was protected by intellectual property rights. In the UK, however, holders of such rights may be compelled to grant licences. Due procedure must be used to that effect. That procedure had been used by several undertakings, which had obtained such a licence in that manner. The undertaking however accumulated legal obstacles in order to make it more difficult or, as mentioned in the text, practically impossible to use these licences and start producing the nail guns.

[24] Commission Decision (EEC) 78/68 relating to a proceeding under Article 86 of the EEC Treaty (IV/29.132—Hugin/Liptons) [1978] OJ L22/23; Case 22/78 *Hugin Kassaregister AB and Hugin Cash Registers Ltd v Commission* [1979] ECR 1869.

[25] In the case, the Commission, followed by the ECJ, defined the functional market in a rather narrow fashion. It considered that the market could be limited to the cash registers produced by a given company—the undertaking which was engaged in abusive practices.

lodged by Lipton. On the contrary, the latter company sought to develop the secondary activities mentioned above, that is, maintenance, repairs and hire. That intention was however made impossible as a result of a document sent by Hugin to all associated companies, pursuant to which they were prohibited from selling spare parts to Lipton in the future. The result of that order was that Lipton was in effect deprived of the possibility of carrying out any of the activities which it had exercised in the past. The business decision taken by Hugin thus had the consequence that Lipton was sentenced to economic death.

4.29 **Commission and ECJ.**   The case was brought to the Commission, which issued a decision later confirmed by the ECJ. According to these two institutions, the dominant undertaking had engaged in abusive behaviour. Before they reached that decision, the Commission and the ECJ assessed the relative positions of the parties. In the course of that discussion, Lipton is presented as an undertaking which had acted as a faithful distributor for Hugin when it was included in the network distribution. Lipton is also presented as being bound to disappear as a result of the decision taken by the dominant undertaking to prohibit the supply of spare parts. According to the Commission and the ECJ, there was no economic justification to explain that decision in an acceptable manner. Ultimately, the damage suffered by Lipton outweighed significantly the benefits that the dominant undertaking was supposed to extract from it. This was deemed unacceptable in the light of the exemplary behaviour of Lipton at the time when the two undertakings were in business relations.

Focus on effects

4.30 **Marker/step 2.**   In a second step the Commission and European courts considered that an infringement no longer needed to be demonstrated. By abandoning this fault-related requirement, the institutions accepted that a subjective interpretation was no longer required. In such an interpretation, the focus is placed on the behaviour adopted by a person or entity. That behaviour is declared unacceptable when, as in the first category presented above, a legal or moral standard is infringed. From the moment that requirement was set aside, the Commission and European courts moved towards a more objective interpretation of the provision. In that approach, the authorities look at the market and at the effect produced by the behaviour in question.

4.31 **Shift in the evolution.**   The shift took place in *Continental Can*.[26] That case is generally considered important because it made the fact obvious that concentrations

---

[26] Décision (EEC) 72/21 de la Commission, du 9 décembre 1971, relative à une procédure d'application de l'article 86 du traité CEE (IV/26 811—Continental Can Company) [1972] OJ L7/14 and 25 (no English version available); Case 6-72 *Europemballage Corporation and Continental Can Company Inc v Commission* [1973] ECR 215.

could not be addressed in a satisfactory manner under Articles 81 or 82 EC, and that specific regulation was needed to deal with these operations. The case is also important as regards the interpretation which the Commission and ECJ give in it to the concept of abuse under Article 82 EC. In that case, an American undertaking sought to acquire a European competitor. In the absence of specific merger regulation, the operation was addressed under Article 82 EC. In its decision, the Commission sought to establish that the acquisition of a competitor had to be deemed abusive in the context in which the operation took place. That position was later confirmed by the ECJ.

Commission and ECJ.   In their rulings, the two institutions accepted that the   **4.32** behaviour adopted by the American undertaking, ie the mere acquisition of an undertaking by another, cannot be deemed, in itself, as abusive. Nothing indeed prevented an undertaking, at that time, in law, from buying another. Such an operation could not even be deemed contrary to normal economic behaviour, as acquisitions are often justified by the economies of scale that can be created as a result of the combination of the operations carried out by previously independent entities. According to the decisions reached, the focus on behaviour must however be set aside in circumstances such as those present in this case. For the Commission and Court, the abusive character does not depend on the behaviour as such but rather on the effect that that behaviour may produce on the market. In the case at issue, the acquisition of a competitor had as a consequence that the already limited degree of competition existing on the market would have been further reduced, a consequence deemed unacceptable.

> *Argument presented by Continental Can.* 'Article [82] . . . reveals that the use of economic power linked with a dominant position can be regarded as an abuse of this position only if it constitutes the means through which the abuse is effected.' 'But structural measures of undertakings—such as strengthening a dominant position by way of merger—do not amount to abuse of this position within the meaning of Article [82] . . . of the Treaty. The decision contested is, therefore, said to be void as lacking the required legal basis.'[27] *Position of the ECJ.* 'The distinction between measures which concern the structure of the undertaking and practices which affect the market cannot be decisive, for any structural measure may influence market conditions, if it increases the size and the economic power of the undertaking.'[28]

Increased focus on effect

Marker/step 3.   In a third step, the case law continued to insist on the effect   **4.33** produced by behaviour adopted by a dominant undertaking. On that point, there is continuity with the second step. There is however a difference between the two stages, in the intensity of the emphasis placed on the market. At the third stage, positive obligations are imposed on dominant undertakings whereas the

---

[27] Judgment of the ECJ, at [19].   [28] Judgment of the ECJ, at [21].

constraint imposed on them was previously limited to prohibitions (negative obligations).

4.34 **Leading case.** The landmark example is *Stena Sealink*.[29] In that case, one undertaking dominated the market for port facilities on the main maritime route between Ireland and the United Kingdom. That route could be accessed only from these facilities, which were owned by a particular undertaking. That undertaking was also present on derived or secondary markets, the markets for maritime services (links) between the countries involved. On one of these secondary markets, the undertaking was confronted with potential competition.[30] In order to impede the entry of a competitor on that market, the dominant undertaking used the dominant position it had acquired on the market for facilities. The behaviour was deemed abusive by the Commission. An interim decision was issued, ordering the dominant undertaking to give access to the competitor under certain conditions. The Commission considered that a dominant undertaking must share facilities placed under its control when access is needed by competitors to carry out activities on a derived market. Not only must access be granted, but the terms and conditions must also be similar, if not equivalent, to those granted to business partners or even, internally, to the departments or divisions responsible, within the dominant undertaking, for the services provided on the derived market.

A special responsibility for dominant undertakings

4.35 **Avoid any effect on competition.** The discussion above describes the evolution that took place in the case law concerning the concept of abuse. Among the cases examined, some are analysed in more detail in the following sections. What is important is that, as a result of that evolution, a special constraint is imposed on undertakings enjoying a dominant position. That constraint was already formulated in the second step examined above. At that stage, the constraint implied, and still implies today, a prohibition on engaging in behaviour, whatever the nature of the action, where that behaviour is likely to bring about a further reduction in the degree of competition existing on the relevant market. Accordingly, undertakings active on electronic communications markets have to refrain from any behaviour whatsoever which may have such an effect, where these undertakings have a dominant position. In the third step, that constraint was made even heavier since an obligation was placed on dominant undertakings to assist competitors in the exercise of their activities, and thus in the development of competition, by giving access to facilities or resources under their control.

---

[29] Commission Decision EC (94/19) relating to a proceeding pursuant to Article 86 of the EC Treaty (IV/34.689—Sea Containers v. Stena Sealink—Interim measures) [1994] OJ L15/8.

[30] The reason for competition to exist on the second market, but not on the first, is not different from those mentioned earlier in connection with other cases. The undertaking is protected on the first market, as a result of the investment to be made in order to enter that market.

Any behaviour. The practical consequence is that undertakings in a dominant **4.36** position may not behave like any other undertaking. Practitioners representing such undertakings should draw the attention of the latter to the necessity for such undertakings to be mindful that any behaviour, whatever its nature, may qualify as an abuse, depending on the effect produced on the market. As a corollary, practitioners engaged in litigation against this type of undertaking may find arguments against any behaviour producing a comparable effect on the market.

> *Case law.* 'Article [82] . . . of the Treaty imposes on an undertaking in a dominant position, irrespective of the reasons for which it has such a dominant position, a special responsibility not to allow its conduct to impair genuine undistorted competition on the common market.'[31] *Literature.* 'Article [82] . . . prohibits practices which may be permissible in a normal competitive situation but are not permissible for dominant undertakings which have a "special responsibility" because of the prejudice their activities may cause to competition in general and to the interests of competitors, suppliers, customers and consumers in particular.'[32]

Following sections. In the following sections, practices and situations that may **4.37** be considered typical for practitioners confronted with dominant undertakings are examined. The following behaviour or situations are analysed successively: refusal to grant access, the imposition of discriminatory conditions, various practices involving prices, and situations where objective justifications may be raised by dominant undertakings to explain their behaviour. The final section of this chapter is devoted to the *essential facilities doctrine*, which is sometimes described as the theory underlying the major part of the case law relating to Article 82 EC.

B. Refusal to Deal or Grant Access

(1) Principles

Not an unexpected business decision. The most simple—and also the most **4.38** audacious—practice that a dominant undertaking may adopt to promote its position

---

[31] Joined Cases T 24-26 & 28/93 *Compagnie Maritime Belge Transports v Commission* [1976] ECR II-1201 at [106]. 'Article [82] . . . covers all conduct of an undertaking in a dominant position which is such as to hinder the maintenance or the growth of the degree of competition still existing in a market where, as a result of the very presence of that undertaking, competition is weakened.' See in the same direction Case T-83/91 *Tetra Pak International SA v Commission (Tetra Pak II)* [1994] ECR II-755 at [106]. See in an older case, 322/81 *Nederlandsche Banden Industrie Michelin v Commission* [1983] ECR 3461 at [10]: 'A finding that an undertaking has a dominant position is not in itself a recrimination but simply means that, irrespective of the reasons for which it has such a position, the undertaking concerned has a special responsibility not to allow its conduct to impair genuine undistorted competition on the common market.'

[32] C Bellamy & G Child, *Common Market Law of Competition* (London: Sweet & Maxwell, 1993, ed V Rose), 9-049. See also R Subiotto, 'The Special Responsibility of Dominant Undertakings Not to Impair Genuine Undistorted Competition' [1995] World Competition 11; M Waelbroeck & A Frignani, 'Concurrence', in *Commentaire Mégret: le droit de la CE* (Editions de l'université de Bruxelles) vol 4, 274; R Whish & B Sufrin, *Competition Law* (London–Edinburgh: Butterworths, 1993), 270.

is probably to refuse access to facilities and resources placed under its control. This kind of attitude may be expected, particularly, when the undertaking feels that granting access would harm its interests or, even, more generally, when it considers that granting access would not serve its interests. The undertaking in question may have devoted considerable resources to building a competitive advantage. Another undertaking, sometimes a competitor, is seeking access to that advantage. An advantage clearly loses its edge if it is shared with others, in particular where the entities to which access is allowed cannot be considered as allies or partners. It may readily be understood that, in these circumstances, the dominant undertaking may be reluctant to grant the access requested. Any doubts they may have appear all the more sensible if one takes into account the case law and the regulation applicable to the electronic communications sector. According to this case law and regulation, access must be granted to third parties under conditions equivalent to those charged to partners, or even to those applied to divisions or departments which are responsible, within the undertaking, for the activity concerned. That obligation takes away all the benefits that undertakings seek to obtain through vertical integration, that is, to enjoy better conditions than if the resources had to be obtained from a third supplier.

4.39 **Market-based mechanism.** These arguments help to understand why undertakings are often reluctant to accept the idea of granting access to the competitive advantages they have built over the years. This kind of reaction is inherent in the purpose generally assigned to undertakings, that is, to increase revenues and profits. It does not depend on the size of the undertaking or on the position acquired by the undertaking on a given market. All things considered, refusing access is thus not a decision that can be criticised on the basis of business founded arguments, indeed quite the contrary.

4.40 **Public intervention.** Despite the 'normal', negative, reaction by undertakings where requests for access are made, the European institutions responsible for implementing European general competition law (Commission, European courts) have decided to prohibit refusal of access in cases where an undertaking dominates a market. The reason is that access refusal is not deemed compatible with the policy objectives that authorities wish to implement.[33] In the market for electronic communications, an objective pursued by public authorities—a major one—is to ensure the development of the market for services. That objective cannot be attained if the facilities and resources available in that sector are used only by the undertakings controlling them. The development of services on the contrary requires that infrastructure must be made available to all undertakings interested in these activities, whatever their relation with the undertaking

---

[33] As electronic communications are considered in this book, this observation mainly concerns that sector. It should however be clear that these observations can be extended to (most) other sectors with comparable characteristics.

controlling access (partnership, competition, etc). It also requires that access must be granted under the best possible conditions to service providers. Only then are the costs for these activities low enough to attract newcomers onto the relevant markets.

Policy objectives. These policy objectives explain why authorities have imposed on dominant undertakings an obligation to share access. That obligation is formulated in the NRF. It is, however, not a new rule. The obligation to grant access had already been introduced under the old regulatory framework. It was also present in the decisions of the European institutions on general competition law. Pursuant to that case law, an undertaking must grant access to facilities or resources under its control when that undertaking holds a dominant position on a market for access. Formulated in a negative form, the rule implies that undertakings in that situation cannot refuse access where a reasonable request is made to that effect.[34] **4.41**

Essential facilities doctrine. In general competition law, decisions on refusal to grant access are sometimes associated with a theory known as the 'essential facilities doctrine'. Under that doctrine, undertakings must grant access when they control a facility or resource deemed essential for the exercise of derived activities and where no other option is available to competitors at a reasonable cost. When these circumstances are present, access must be granted under reasonable conditions. Conditions are considered to be reasonable where they are identical, or equivalent, to those under which access is granted to partners or divisions within the same undertaking. These aspects are discussed in another section of this chapter (see paras 4.325–4.365). **4.42**

(2) Facilities or resources concerned

Several types of facilities or resources. There exists substantial case law on access refusal. That case law in fact goes beyond access-related issues. It generally covers all situations where dominant undertakings refuse to deal with others. For that reason, this part of the case law is often referred to as covering 'refusal to deal'.[35] The case law on refusal to deal may be presented on the basis of the facilities or resources concerned.[36] Four kinds of resources may be considered: *(a)* networks or **4.43**

---

[34] The obligation is expressed in a negative form ('cannot refuse access') in the case law regarding general competition law. The reason is that authorities intervene, in that context, ex post. Their intervention is meant to sanction behaviour where access has been refused. By contrast, the obligation has a positive formulation ('must grant access') when it comes to regulatory intervention. In that kind of intervention, authorities impose obligations before problems arise (ex ante intervention).

[35] Access appears as one form of relation that may exist among undertakings. For that reason, the variety of situations where a refusal may be expressed is better termed 'refusal to deal'. The importance of access has only appeared at a recent stage, with the development of the case law and regulation concerning electronic communications and other forms of networks.

[36] Again, this division is the result of an interpretation. Others may be proposed.

systems, *(b)* other forms of installation, *(c)* items necessary to manufacture goods or provide services, and *(d)* products/substances embodied in the provision of other goods or services.

4.44 **All cases relevant.** All cases examined in connection with these various resources are important for practitioners engaged in electronic communications-related counselling or litigation. The type of case which may be useful depends on the resources involved. Cases concerning networks (first category) have a special relevance for access to electronic communications infrastructure. They are not the only ones, however, that practitioners can use. Where, for instance, an undertaking refuses to provide access to buildings or antennae despite the fact that these are essential for a competitor to place its own installations (collocation), the situation could be handled on the basis of the case belonging to the second category (other installations). Another example is where an undertaking needs information to prepare telephone books. That situation could be analysed using the cases pertaining to the third category (items necessary to manufacture goods or develop services). A final illustration is where technology is needed to provide a certain service. A refusal to provide that technology could be addressed under cases examined in the fourth category (product/substance embodied in the provision of goods and/or services).

Networks and systems

4.45 **First category.** The first category refers to cases where access is sought to computer data networks, public broadcasting networks and other forms of network. As mentioned above, these cases are close to those concerning access to electronic communications networks. For that reason, the solution given to them is important for practitioners seeking backing to argue their cases.

4.46 **Computer networks.** In *London European v Sabena*,[37] a competitor was seeking access to a computer network used for flight reservations. The network was owned and managed by Sabena, the former Belgian national airline company. It was the only network allowing reservations for flights originating from the national airport (Zaventem). The network was used by national travel agencies to consult information made available by airline companies admitted to the network.[38] The case arose when a competitor sought to be admitted to the network. The request was not refused but was made dependent on several conditions. To be granted access, the competitor had to align tariffs to those charged by Sabena.

---

[37] See Commission Decision (EEC) 88/589 relating to a proceeding under Article 86 of the EEC Treaty (IV/32.318, London European—Sabena) [1988] OJ L317/47.

[38] Apart from the undertaking seeking access, only two airline companies did not participate in the system. The absence of participation on their part was not the result of a refusal by the national company to provide access. It was justified as a marketing choice made by the two companies involved, which had opted for another method of distribution for their tickets.

It also had to entrust to the latter undertaking certain ground services such as plane maintenance. These conditions were not deemed acceptable by the competitor, nor indeed by the Commission, and the latter found that Sabena had abused its dominant position.

Public broadcasting networks.   In another case (*Telemarketing*),[39] an operator   **4.47** dominated the market for television broadcasting in a Member State (Luxembourg). An independent service provider was seeking access to that broadcasting network in order to provide publicity-related services. A contract was signed between the companies involved for the provision of a service called 'telemarketing'. That service required a call centre to be made available. The call centre could be contacted by viewers when they wished to receive information about products or services publicised in the programmes broadcast by the operator. At the end of the contract, the operator notified the service provider that no renewal would take place. The operator had understood that it would increase profits by taking over that service. The refusal to renew the contract was challenged before a national court, which sought to obtain from the ECJ an explanation as to how the case could be analysed in the light of European competition rules. In its preliminary ruling, the ECJ decided that the behaviour adopted by the operator was abusive. In its ruling the ECJ set forth the idea that an undertaking controlling a market may not refuse access to that market in the hope of reserving the activities concerned for itself. In the specific context of the case, the ruling implied that an undertaking controlling the market for broadcasting of advertisements could not refuse access to another party seeking to perform publicity-related services.

> *Telemarketing.* '[T]hat refusal is not justified by technical or commercial requirements relating to the nature of the television, but is intended to reserve to the agent any telemarketing operation broadcast by the said station, with the possibility of eliminating all competition from another undertaking, such conduct amounts to an abuse prohibited by Article [82] . . .'[40]

Other forms of electronic networks.   A third form of electronic communica-   **4.48** tions network was involved in *Decca*.[41] In that case, an undertaking dominated the market for network transmission of signals used to locate ships in the North Sea. That network was made up of stations located in several countries. Signals were transmitted from these stations and received by terminals on the ships, thereby allowing their geographical position to be fixed. The undertaking involved had acquired dominance on the network market, as a result of heavy barriers to entry making it difficult for potential competitors to start a similar

---

[39] Case 311/84 *Centre belge d'études de marché—Télémarketing (CBEM) v SA Compagnie luxembourgeoise de télédiffusion (CLT) and Information publicité Benelux (IPB)* [1985] ECR 3261.
[40] At [26].
[41] Commission Decision (EEC) 89/113 relating to a proceeding under Articles 85 and 86 of the EEC Treaty (IV/30.979 and 31.394, Decca Navigator System) [1988] OJ L43/27.

activity.[42] Its position was more fragile, however, on the market for terminals, where several competitors had developed the technology. In order to improve its position on the latter market, the undertaking resorted to several practices. One was to modify unilaterally and without warning the frequency used for the signals transmitted. The purpose was to ensure that the signals could be received only by the terminals produced by it. This behaviour was found unacceptable. It could not be admitted that an undertaking may risk accidents and the disturbance of maritime traffic through behaviour designed to improve its own business situation.

> *Decca.* 'By the above conduct, Racal Decca aimed at protecting the monopoly position it enjoyed for commercial receivers.'[43] 'Racal Decca intended to exclude . . . competitors . . . from the market for commercial receivers.'[44] '[I]t obstructed and coerced those competitors.' 'By so doing, Racal Decca abused its dominant position, not because it defended this position, but because the actions it took for this purpose went beyond normal competitive behaviour. Normal competitive behaviour would have been to compete with the newcomers in the market for commercial receivers in terms of price, quality and after-sales service. Moreover, Racal Decca's behaviour prejudiced users because it limited their freedom of choice in that market.'[45]

Physical infrastructure

4.49 **Second category.** The second category of cases concerns access to physical, or material, infrastructure. These cases are also relevant for the analysis of electronic communications situations. It will be recalled that the Access Directive specifically refers to several types of physical resource to which access is needed to perform services.[46] The leading case, in that category, is *Stena Sealink*.[47] That case was already mentioned above, in connection with the analysis carried out regarding the concept of abuse (evolution). As mentioned above, the Commission decided in that case that an undertaking must grant access to facilities under its control when these facilities are needed to carry out activities on a derived market. In the case, the facilities were located in Ireland. There existed no alternative to the use of these facilities, if the potential competitor wanted to provide a maritime link between Ireland and Great Britain.[48]

---

[42] Significant investment would have been needed, as well as authorisation by the countries involved in order to build the stations on their territory.   [43] At [98] (excerpts).

[44] At [99] (excerpts).   [45] At [99].

[46] cf the Access Directive, Art 2(2), letter (a), where the concept of access is defined. Reference is made, in that definition, to physical infrastructure including buildings, ducts and masts. See also the Access Directive, Art 12(1), (2), letter (f), where co-location is envisaged as well as other forms of facility sharing, including duct, building or mast sharing.

[47] Commission Decision (EC) 94/19 relating to a proceeding pursuant to Article 86 of the EC Treaty (IV/34.689—Sea Containers v Stena Sealink—Interim measures) [1994] OJ L15/8.

[48] A similar attitude was adopted by the same institution in other, rather similar, cases, all concerning port facilities. *(a)* One of these cases is *Rodby*. In that case, an undertaking sought access to port facilities allowing the provision of a maritime link between Denmark and Germany. Access was refused. The behaviour was deemed abusive by the Commission for the reason explained in

Reference to essential facilities doctrine. As shown in the extract presented **4.50**
below, the ruling issued by the Commission in that case contains a specific reference to the *essential facilities doctrine*. These facilities are described as resources
necessary to serve customers on derived markets. Pursuant to the ruling, discrimination is prohibited. The terms and conditions under which access is granted
must be similar to those granted to partners or even the divisions entrusted with
the relevant activity within the dominant undertaking.

> *Stena Sealink.* 'An undertaking which occupies a dominant position in the provision
> of an essential facility and itself uses that facility (ie a facility or infrastructure, with-
> out access to which competitors cannot provide services to their customers), and
> which refuses other companies access to that facility without objective justification
> or grants access to competitors only on terms less favourable than those which it gives
> its own services, infringes Article [82] . . . if the other conditions of that Article are
> met.' 'An undertaking in a dominant position may not discriminate in favour of its
> own activities in a related market.' 'The owner of an essential facility which uses its
> power in one market in order to protect or strengthen its position in another related
> market, in particular, by refusing to grant access to a competitor, or by granting
> access on less favourable terms than those of its own services, and thus imposing
> a competitive disadvantage on its competitor, infringes Article [82] . . .'[49]

Data, information, knowledge

Third category. Another form of resource to which access must be granted, or **4.51**
in relation to which a dominant undertaking may not refuse to deal, is information or, more generally, data. This kind of resource may also be important for the
exercise of electronic communications activities. This category may encompass
knowledge, for instance in the form of technology. One could thus use cases
belonging to that category in order to compel an undertaking to deal with another
undertaking, possibly a competitor, in situations where access to knowledge is
necessary for the provision of services.

Leading case. The leading case in this category is *RTE v Commission*. In that **4.52**
case, three broadcasting companies refused to communicate to another company
information concerning their TV programmes. The information was needed by
the other company to publish a television guide. An analysis of the market showed
that there was a demand, on the part of the public, for a publication providing

---

Stena Sealink. *(b)* Another case in the same vein is *Roscoff*. In that case, an undertaking asked for
access to port facilities to provide a service between France and Ireland. Access was first granted—
but then suspended. It had to be resumed at the request of the Commission. *(c)* It should be observed
that these two latter cases (*Rodby* and *Roscoff*) concern decisions taken by certain authorities. The
issue was thus not related to access refused by a private undertaking but rather by an entity having a
public character (a ministry in the first case and a local chamber of commerce, with apparently public status, in the second one). That feature does not take away the relevance of the two cases for the
point under discussion. In both cases, a decision was taken by the Commission to order access
against the will of the entity controlling the facility. The identity of that entity does not appear relevant in regard to the decision ordering access.   [49] At [66].

information on all TV programmes available in the area in question. The broad-casting companies were reluctant to divulge information and allow publication because they wanted to continue publishing their own information concerning their own programmes. The publication of a guide would have formed an obs-tacle on that path, to the extent that the public would have had access to infor-mation concerning all programmes at once. The refusal to grant access to this information and allow publication was deemed abusive by the Commission, the CFI and ultimately the ECJ itself.

Products/substances embodied in other goods/services

4.53 **Last category.**   The last category concerns material products, or substances, which, without being an infrastructure, are necessary to manufacture a(nother) good or provide a(nother) service. The cases contained in that category are classic to the extent that they concern traditional sectors of the economy. This does not deprive them of relevance as regards electronic communications. These cases provide important background permitting the formulation of a general principle pursuant to which dominant undertakings may not refuse to deal with other undertakings, even if they are competitors. In the various cases at stake, an under-taking controls a market where a basic item is sold and uses that position to hinder competition on a second market on which the derived items are marketed.

4.54 **Leading case.**   The leading case, *Commercial Solvents*,[50] is one of the oldest in which an obligation to deal or, in more modern terms, to grant access, was expressed with clarity. In that case, the market for a given substance (ethambutol) was dominated by an American undertaking. That substance was necessary for the manufacture of medicines against tuberculosis (second market). There was no alternative but to deal with that dominant undertaking on the first market. At least one other undertaking was present on the second market, and the case concerns the unfair treatment afforded to that undertaking, which was a customer on the first market and a competitor on the second. At a given point in time, the dominant undertaking decided to increase prices on the first market on which the substance was acquired. As a result of that practice, the competitor turned to other possible suppliers but could find no alternatives. Shortly thereafter, a decision was taken by the dominant undertaking to stop selling the substance altogether. That decision was motivated by the desire on the part of the undertaking concerned not to refrain from selling the substance, but rather to keep the whole production of the available substance in order itself to manufacture the derived medicines and market them directly to end users. In other words, the strategy amounted to interrupting

---

[50] See décision 72/457/CEE de la Commission relative à une procédure d'application de l'article 86 du traité instituant la Communauté économique européenne (IV/26.911—ZOJA/CSC-ICI), [1972] OJ L299, 51 (text not available in English). See also Joined Cases 6 & 7–73 *Istituto Chemioterapico Italiano S.p.A. and Commercial Solvents Corporation v Commission* [1974] ECR 223.

the sale of the raw material for the purpose of becoming the only undertaking selling the end product.

Commission and ECJ.   The behaviour was found abusive by the Commission   **4.55** and ECJ. For the Commission, the decision to increase prices and successively withdraw the substance from the market hindered competition on the secondary market. These practices also limited production, to the extent that access to the secondary market was limited to one undertaking—the dominant one. The case was later examined by the ECJ, which ruled that undertakings may not use a dominant position acquired on a first market to improve their position on a second, related, one.

> *ECJ.* '[A]n undertaking being in a dominant position as regards the production of raw material and therefore able to control the supply to manufacturers of derivatives, cannot, just because it decides to start manufacturing these derivatives (in competition with its former customers) act in such a way as to eliminate their competition which in the case in question, would amount to eliminating one of the principal manufacturers of ethambutol in the common market.'. '[A]n undertaking which has a dominant position in the market in raw materials and which, with the object of reserving such raw material for manufacturing its own derivatives, refuses to supply a customer, which is itself a manufacturer of these derivatives, and therefore risks eliminating all competition on the part of this customer, is abusing its dominant position within the meaning of Article [82] . . .'[51]

Other illustrations

Goods and services necessary.   All cases where the Commission has concluded   **4.56** that a dominant undertaking cannot refuse to deal with another company can be classified in one of these categories. Of these categories the last is probably the more general. Many cases concern situations where goods or services are needed to perform other activities. As they attempt to build competitive advantage, undertakings often seek to control these strategically important items. Where they succeed, they acquire a dominant position, which in turn implies that they have to share access as a result of the application of competition rules.

All economic stages.   A pattern of this nature may be encountered at all stages of   **4.57** the economic chain. In the example examined above (*Commercial Solvents*), an undertaking controls access to raw materials needed to manufacture end products. In other situations, an undertaking dominates the market where the product is sold at an intermediary level. *British Sugar* is examined below in this connection. In a last type of situation, an undertaking dominates access to customers. A reference has already been made, in this respect, to the difficulties encountered by service providers seeking access to customers on electronic communications markets but hindered by the control exercised by dominant operators over the

---

[51] At [25].

final loop. This sort of control may be analysed as a power over the service or network necessary to reach customers. It is no different, in principle, from the control exercised in some regions by distributors which sometimes dominate a market and are thus in a position to impose unsatisfactory terms and conditions on producers or wholesalers which need their intervention to access final customers.

4.58 **Intermediate level.** The domination of an intermediate level in the economic chain is illustrated by *British Sugar v Commission*.[52] In that case an undertaking dominated the market for the production of sugar (sugar beet) in the United Kingdom. The product was sold to several distributors and packaged by them in several sizes depending on their destination (industrial or individual use). The undertaking was aware of the profits relating to sales made directly to end users. In that context it did not accept the intention announced by one of the distributors of starting a retail business, ie selling the sugar to end users. The dominant undertaking sought to prohibit this development interrupting deliveries to that intermediary. This action was deemed contrary to Article 82 EC.

> *British Sugar.* 'BS has abused its dominant position by refusing to supply industrial sugar to NB without objective necessity, the intention or foreseeable result of which would have been to precipitate the removal of NB from the United Kingdom retail sugar market, thereby reducing competition on that market.'[53]

4.59 **Parallel markets.** In some instances, the pattern does not really concern the behaviour adopted by an undertaking vis-à-vis a partner or competitor located at another (higher or lower) level of the economic chain. It may relate rather to markets which are in some way parallel to each other. Although it may appear rather technical, this observation is important because it shows that the case law concerning the refusal to deal, or to grant access, should not be limited to a classical pattern. Contexts where it can be applied are diverse. They should not be reduced in their variety. A good example of that variety is provided by *Hugin*, a case discussed above in connection with the concept of abuse.[54] In that case, an undertaking dominated the market for cash registers. It refused to provide spare parts to an undertaking which had recently left the official distribution network in order to start up as an independent undertaking on adjacent markets (repairs, maintenance, hire, second-hand sales). The behaviour adopted by the dominant undertaking was found to violate Article 82 EC. For the Commission, the behaviour

---

[52] Commission Decision (EEC) 88/518 relating to a proceeding under Article 86 of the EEC Treaty (Case No IV/30.178 Napier Brown—British Sugar) [1988] OJ L284/41.

[53] At [64].

[54] Commission Decision (EEC) 78/68 relating to a proceeding under Article 86 of the EEC Treaty (IV/29.132—Hugin/Liptons) [1978] OJ L22/23; Case 22/78 *Hugin Kassaregister AB and Hugin Cash Registers Ltd v Commission* [1979] ECR 1869 (Opinion of AG Reischl); Case 22/78 *Hugin Kassaregister AB and Hugin Cash Registers Ltd v Commission* [1979] ECR 1869.

was a barrier to the development of competition on various markets derived from the main market relating to the manufacture and sale of cash registers.[55]

> *Hugin*. 'Hugin . . . abused its dominant position by prohibiting its subsidiaries . . . and its independent distributors . . . from supplying spare parts outside the Hugin distribution network. [S]uch conduct shelters Hugin from all effective competition in the matter of service, maintenance and repair of Hugin cash registers and from competition from reconditioning and rented Hugin cash registers throughout the common market.'[56]

(3) Additional analysis

Type of resource irrelevant

All resources concerned.   The examples examined with respect to networks or **4.60** systems are particularly relevant to address situations relating to access to electronic communications infrastructure. Situations of this nature are likely to emerge as undertakings seek access to networks to deliver their services. It should not be concluded from this observation that the nature of the resource is decisive for the application of the case law. On the contrary, the nature of the resource does not appear to be a determining factor in the decisions taken by the Commission or European courts to impose specific obligations on undertakings refusing to deal or to grant access. The terms used by these institutions show that the case law can be used in all circumstances where resources, whatever their nature, are needed. In the case law, the obligation to grant access relates to the position held by the undertaking (dominance), not to the type of resource over which that undertaking has control.

Conditions under Article 82 EC.   The general character of the prohibition **4.61** concerning facilities and resources appears to result from the conditions that must be fulfilled for Article 82 EC to apply. As stated above, this provision addresses situations where an undertaking dominates a market. In these situations, dominance may come about for a variety of reasons. In most circumstances it appears as a consequence of a competitive advantage which the undertaking has been able to acquire and maintain. By its nature, this advantage cannot be duplicated easily. Should duplication be easy, potential competition would be rather considerable.

---

[55]   In that case, the behaviour adopted by the dominant undertaking may also be analysed as an exclusionary practice vis-à-vis a competitor located on a market at another stage of the economic chain. The market for spare parts may indeed be analysed as an upstream market compared to the adjacent markets concerned (repairs, maintenance, hire, secondhand sales). These adjacent markets, however, cannot really be placed in the same chain as the traditional sale of normal cash registers. They rather concern activities that may be labelled as being parallel to the main sales activity. In the case at issue, the dominant undertaking sought to hinder activities on these adjacent markets because it feared that a parallel circuit of repairs, maintenance, hire and secondhand sales might not serve its development on the principal market for the sale of new cash registers.

[56]   Decision of the Commission, 32.

The consequence would be that the undertaking would probably not be dominant. As submitted above, dominance indeed does not exist where entry is easy on the relevant market.[57]

4.62 **Relationship with the NRF.**   On the basis of the observations made above, the case law concerning refusal to deal or to grant access may be formulated as encompassing an obligation to share access where a resource is deemed necessary for the exercise of an activity. That reformulation is rather close to the obligations which are introduced in the NRF as regards access. It should be recalled that the framework allows national regulatory authorities (NRAs) to impose access-related obligations in respect of all resources necessary for the provision of electronic communications services.[58] Examples of the facilities and resources concerned are provided in the Access Directive. These are only examples, however, as the obligation to grant access under reasonable conditions appears as a general clause applicable to all facilities and resources necessary to provide electronic communications services. The regulatory framework thus sets out an obligation with scope similar in its extent to that in general competition law.

4.63 **Access under the NRF**

NRF General clause	NRF Specific examples
All facilities and/or services for the purpose of providing electronic communications services.[59]	(a) Access to network elements and associated facilities, which may involve the connection of equipment, by fixed or non-fixed means; (b) access to physical infrastructure including buildings, ducts and masts; (c) access to relevant software systems including operational support systems, access to number translation or systems offering equivalent functionality; (d) access to fixed and mobile networks, in particular for roaming; (e) access to conditional access systems for digital television services; (f) access to virtual network services.[60]

---

[57] The fact that competitors may easily enter the market implies that, whatever its market share, the undertaking may not behave independently of competition. The decisions taken by that undertaking—for instance a price increase—always create a risk that competitors may enter the market if they feel that they could make a profit.

[58] See the Access Directive, Art 2(2), letter (a), where access is defined as 'the making available of facilities and/or services, to another undertaking, under defined conditions, on either an exclusive or non-exclusive basis, for the purpose of providing electronic communications services'. The main limitation, as regards their scope, of the obligations introduced by the NRF, is related to the public character which is required for the application of these obligations.

[59] See Access Directive, Art 2(2), letter (a), first sentence.

[60] See ibid, Art 2(2) letter (a), second sentence.

Expression of the refusal

Methods of expression.   As was stated in the above paragraphs, the nature of   **4.64**
the resource concerned is not essential to bring about the application of the case
law concerning refusal to deal or grant access. The same remark may be made as
regards the methods used by undertakings to express refusal. The Commission
and European courts do not distinguish, depending on these methods. *(a)* In
some instances, the refusal is stated explicitly. An example is *Rodby*, where access
was requested to port facilities in order to perform a maritime link between two
European countries. The request was explicitly turned down by the entity which
had authority to grant approval. *(b)* Blunt refusals are however rare, as entities
expressing a refusal generally disguise their attitude. All sorts of practices may
be found in the case law, whereby access is granted but later denied as a result of
practices adopted by the dominant undertaking. In some cases, the undertaking
promises access but does not adopt the behaviour requested to make access available in practice.[61] In other contexts, the undertaking arranges a situation where
access is impossible for technical reasons.[62] In a third set of circumstances, access
is made dependent on conditions which make it impossible for the competitor
without incurring a loss.[63]

Same line in the NRF.   General competition law and the NRF are inspired by   **4.65**
the same attitude. In both areas of the law, the methods used to express refusal do
not appear to be decisive. In the Access Directive, for instance, the European
legislator refers to measures that NRAs can take with respect to access. These
measures are designed as remedies to counter behaviour that may be adopted by
undertakings with significant market power. The types of behaviour concerned
are no different from those which may be found in the case law concerning refusal
to deal or to grant access. There thus exists a similarity between the practices

---

[61] See *Stena Sealink* (n 47 above) where the undertaking constantly delayed the provision of
the facilities necessary to ensure the maritime link between the countries concerned. In that case,
the dominant undertaking raised numerous technical difficulties which allegedly made it impossible for it to deliver access. It argued that, as a result of difficulties of that nature, access could not
be granted to the western part of the port. Nothing had however been done in order to solve these
difficulties. The undertaking had accepted the construction of new facilities by the access-seeker
in the eastern part of the port. It appeared, after examination, that these facilities could not have
been used, as a result of works planned in that zone by the dominant undertaking itself. The
plans for these works were repeatedly modified without consultation of the access-seeker, in spite
of the consequences resulting from these modifications for the planning of activities. Ultimately,
the dominant undertaking started itself to provide the link which was envisaged by the access-
seeker before the latter was allowed to use or build the infrastructure necessary for it to start the
service.
[62] See *Decca* (n 41 above) where frequencies were changed to avoid reception by terminals made
by competitors.
[63] See *Commercial Solvents* (n 50 above) where an excessive price was charged to obtain the
substance and *Sabena* (n 37 above) where the competitor could only obtain access if tariffs were
aligned to those set by the dominant undertaking.

against which intervention is sought, as between the NRF and general competition law.[64]

Do circumstances matter?

4.66 **No relevance.** On the basis of this analysis, it may be concluded that the nature of the resources, and the ways in which refusal is expressed, are not relevant for the application of the case law concerning refusal to deal or grant access. It must now be determined whether, irrespective of the method used to express it, refusal is sufficient to give rise to the application of the case law or whether additional circumstances or conditions are to be fulfilled.

4.67 **Ambiguity.** There exists a certain level of ambiguity on this point in the case law. *(a)* In general, the Commission and European courts seem to accept that refusal to deal or grant access is sufficient for general competition law to apply. That position was for instance adopted in *Stena Sealink*. In that case, the undertaking apparently accepted the request presented by the potential competitor but made access impossible in practice. The behaviour thus amounted to a refusal. No other condition was necessary. The Commission merely ruled that an undertaking must share access to a resource under its control, where that resource is necessary to carry out certain activities.[65] *(b)* In other cases, the Commission and European courts take great care in assessing the circumstances in which refusal takes place. This attention to circumstances, and the careful assessment of the relations between the parties concerned, seem to indicate that, in the eyes of the institution which adopted the decision, a mere refusal may not be sufficient.

4.68 **Cases where circumstances matter (1).** Several cases pertaining to this second category are examined in this book. One case, *Hugin*, concerns behaviour adopted by an undertaking manufacturing cash registers. That undertaking forbade the supply of cash registers to a former distributor in order to hinder the development of activity by the latter distributor on secondary markets (particularly hire, repairs, second-hand sales). The refusal to deal came in spite of the significant contribution that the distributor had made to the marketing of the manufacturer's products over a relatively long period.[66]

---

[64] See for instance the Access Directive, Art 12(1) (2). In that provision, the European legislator envisages various sorts of behaviour: refusal to grant access (letter a), bad faith negotiation (letter b); withdrawal of access after access has first been granted (letter c); proposing unreasonable or inequitable conditions (subpara 3).

[65] That case is not isolated. It can be encountered in all situations concerning access to port facilities. The same position is also adopted in other types of case—for instance *Commercial Solvents* (n 50 above) where the dominant undertaking interrupted supplies and *Telemarketing* (n 39 above) where a dominant undertaking refused to renew a contract at the expiry of an existing agreement.

[66] That case has been analysed in connection with the evolution undergone by the concept of abuse. It will not be re-examined at length in the present section.

Cases where circumstances matter (2).   Another case is *British Midland*, in   **4.69**
which a UK airline company decided to fly the route between London and
Dublin. That business decision caused it to enter into competition with the Irish
national airline, Aer Lingus. The latter company dominated the market. It refused
to grant its potential competitor a facility called 'interline'. That facility is traditionally provided between airline companies, even where they are competitors,
and allows them to issue tickets for journeys flown by other companies. In that
case, the Commission considered that the refusal to provide the interline service
had to be regarded as a refusal. The reason is that the refusal was not in line
with usages within the airline industry. There was also a discrepancy between the
damage suffered by the potential competitor and that which would have been
undergone by Aer Lingus, had the interline service been granted.[67]

Cases where circumstances matter (3).   A third case where authorities have   **4.70**
apparently requested more than a refusal to apply the case law is *BBI/Boosey and
Hawkes*.[68] That case concerned the production of certain musical instruments in
the United Kingdom. The market relating to that activity was dominated by one
undertaking. The instruments produced by that undertaking were sold by several
intermediaries. The market for distribution could be regarded as a second market.
Among the intermediaries present on that second market, one decided to expand
its activities and start producing musical instruments, using thereby the knowledge it had acquired as a distributor and taking advantage of the contacts it had
built with customers. Strategically, the intention was to develop a presence on the
first market (production) while maintaining and possibly further developing
activities on the second (distribution). The announcement of that intention was
greeted with shock by the dominant manufacturer, which decided to interrupt all
supplies to the intermediary concerned. This behaviour was found to be in breach
of general competition law. In its decision, the Commission analyses the relations
between the parties concerned. Pursuant to the decision, the musical instrument
producer had overwhelming dominance on the market. The survival of the
intermediary depended upon its receiving a regular supply of these instruments
for distribution. In these circumstances, the behaviour could only lead to a fatal
result for the intermediary, which was forced to put an end to its activities.

> *BBI/Boosey and Hawkes*. '[A] refusal of supplies by a dominant producer to an estab-
> lished customer without objective justification may constitute an abuse under Article
> [82] . . . ' 'On the facts of the present case, the dependence of . . . [the distributor]

---

[67] Commission Decision 92/213 relating to a procedure pursuant to Articles 85 and 86 of the
EEC Treaty (IV/33.544, British Midland v Aer Lingus) [1992] OJ L96/34. That case is not
addressed at length in the present section. For a full analysis of the case, see paras 4.319–4.324 dealing with objective justifications.
[68] That case has been dealt with by the Commission. See Commission Decision (EEC) 87/500
relating to a proceeding under Article 86 of the EEC Treaty (IV/32.279—BBI/Boosey & Hawkes:
Interim measures) [1987] OJ L286/36.

on B&H products is such that there was a substantial likelihood of . . . [its] going out of business as a result of the withholding of supplies.'[69]

4.71 **What conclusion can be drawn from these cases.** It is difficult to draw a definitive conclusion from these cases relating to refusal to deal or grant access. However, decisions apparently requiring other conditions than refusal are associated with relatively old case law. Using the terms introduced above, one may say that these cases belong to the first level or step singled out in the development of the concept of abuse. In that step, the abuse is still interpreted by reference to an infringement. The reference to an infringed standard is clear in *British Midland*, where the undertaking refused to provide a service which was customarily provided among airline companies. In *BBI* and *Hugin*, the willingness to eliminate a potential competitor clearly comes out. There is also a feeling, in these latter cases, that the victim is granted unfair treatment in consideration of the long and satisfactory relationship that had existed between the parties; the abrupt modification of that situation as a result of the decision taken by the dominant undertaking; and the economic risks that that modification implied for the subsistence of the victim.

4.72 **More objective interpretation.** The later steps analysed in the development of the concept seem to be focused on a more objective interpretation. In that interpretation, emphasis is placed on the market rather than on the behaviour or situation of the parties. The main concern is whether the practice at stake impedes, or hinders, the development of competition, even where competition is only potential. In the light of these observations, it can be concluded that, in principle, a mere refusal to deal or grant access is to be sanctioned. Additional circumstances or conditions do not need to be established. The existence of such conditions or circumstances may however of course be useful in facilitating the adoption of a decision against the dominant undertaking and setting aside all attempts by that undertaking to provide justification.

The structure of the markets involved

4.73 **Similar structure.** All of the cases examined above have a similar structure, as regards the markets concerned by the behaviour deemed abusive. These cases concern activities which develop on several markets. On one market, an undertaking develops a dominant position. Illegal use is made of that position on a second market.[70] These markets are present at different level of the economic chain.

---

[69] At [19] (extracts).

[70] In the first category of cases examined above, dominance was exercised on a market concerning a resource essential for the development of another activity on a second market: publicity broadcasting (*Telemarketing* (n 39 above)), seat reservation (*Sabena* (n 39 above)) and positioning of ships (*Decca* (n 41 above)). In the second category (ports), an undertaking dominated the market for facilities intended to grant access to a maritime link. In these cases, infrastructure was essential for the provision of the maritime service under consideration. In the third and fourth categories of

This type of structure is typical of vertical integration, where undertakings are located at different levels in the economic chain in an attempt to access upstream and downstream markets under conditions which are better than those they could obtain from normal commercial transactions. Such a structure is rather frequent in electronic communications cases. A classic example is the operators controlling public infrastructure and using that facility to provide services. Other examples may be found in this sector where infrastructure plays an important role and technology increasingly appears as an asset necessary for the development of market activity. In all these examples, it is feared that dominance acquired over a resource (first market) may be used to obtain an advantage on the market for services (second market) which require, for their provision, access to that resource.

Avoid entry or eliminate a competitor. In most cases examined above, the refusal takes place in order to avoid entry by a potential competitor. In these various contexts, entry sometimes has a geographical implication. An undertaking is active on a geographical market. The case may arise when it attempts to extend the geographical scope of its activities, a move not accepted by an undertaking already active on that geographical market (see *British Midland*). In other cases, entry has a material connotation. An undertaking carries out a given activity and attempts to develop a new one. This latter scenario may be observed, to take a few examples, in *Hugin*, where the idea is to impede the development of activities on secondary markets (hire, etc); in *BBI*, where the undertaking wants to avoid entry in the market for the manufacture of musical instruments; in *British Midland*, where the undertaking seeks to make it impossible for the new competitor to enter the market in a lasting manner; and in *Stena Sealink*, where the purpose is to avoid the development of a rapid maritime link. In some instances the competitor is already present. The undertaking concerned then adopts an abusive practice in order to drive that competitor out of business. In *Commercial Solvents*, for instance, the undertaking increases prices for the substance, and then withdraws the substance from the market in order to remain the sole producer on the market. **4.74**

Starting a new activity. Where entry has a material connotation (starting a new activity instead of expanding the geographical scope of current activities), the behaviour adopted by the dominant undertaking develops upstream or downstream. In most examples, the undertaking holds dominance on a primary market and uses that situation in order to obtain an advantage on a secondary market located downstream. That scenario is typical where control is held over a resource which is necessary to carry out an activity. The resource, and the market on which dominance is held, can be located upstream. The activity which is carried out with **4.75**

cases data, products or information were found necessary for the exercise of another activity which consisted in the production of another good or the provision of another service.

the assistance of that resource must be located, as far as it is concerned, downstream. The situation may be encountered on markets for electronic communications, where a network is used by a dominant undertaking in order to promote its position on markets for services. In some instances, one may find undertakings active on a downstream market and attempting to use domination they have acquired on that market in order to establish themselves and/or develop their operations on an upstream market. Where, for instance, an undertaking comes to control markets relating to conditional access systems for the provision of broadcasting services, that undertaking would be in a strong position to develop upstream, and start for instance a network activity or even engage in an activity relating to the production of content.

C. Discrimination

(1) The behaviour concerned

4.76 **Prohibition of discriminatory practices.** Discriminatory behaviour is explicitly prohibited by Article 82 EC, when such behaviour is adopted by undertakings holding a dominant position. Pursuant to that provision, prohibited abusive practices may consist in 'applying dissimilar conditions to equivalent transactions with other trading parties, thereby placing them at a competitive disadvantage'. The prohibition directed against discrimination was interpreted as implying an obligation to take into account, when determining the conditions for a transaction, the context in which the parties are placed. According to case law, several implications may be taken over from that obligation. *(a)* A first implication is that customers must be treated equally by dominant undertakings when they are in similar situations. *(b)* A second implication is that differences existing in the situations where customers are placed must be taken into consideration. As a result, customers may not have imposed on them similar treatment by dominant undertakings where some of them are placed in different situations.

4.77 **Correspondence between situations.** In both instances (first and second implications), an analysis must be made of the situation in which customers are placed and the treatment which is granted to them. This analysis must compare the situations, determine whether differences exist, decide whether these differences are relevant and, if so, conclude whether a correspondence exists between the differences existing in the situations and the treatment granted to the customers. That correspondence may be examined using the tools provided by the principle of proportionality. In the context of discrimination, that principle implies that: *(a)* the disadvantage imposed on customers must effectively contribute to the realisation of the purpose claimed by the dominant undertaking; *(b)* no other option is available to realise the same goal while implying a lesser disadvantage for customers; and *(c)* the disadvantage is not excessive.

How to assess behaviour in the light of the prohibition on discrimination?	**4.78**

(1) Customers in similar situations must be treated in the same fashion.
(2) Customers in different situations must be treated in a different manner.
(3) There must exist a correspondence between the situation in which the customers are placed and the treatment which is granted to them.

Discrimination against competitors and/or consumers. As appears from **4.79** Article 82 EC, the prohibition on discrimination refers explicitly to customers which, as a result of discriminatory practices, are placed at a competitive disadvantage. The prohibition is thus analysed, in that provision, in connection with the consequences that discriminatory practices have on businesses. That specific reference to businesses does not imply, however, that dominant undertakings may discriminate against consumers. Two situations may in fact be distinguished— business-to-business, as well as business-to-consumer, relations. These are discussed in the following paragraphs.

Business-to-business relations. In the first situation, the dominant undertak- **4.80** ing imposes a disadvantage on a customer which carries out an economic activity. That situation is explicitly covered in Article 82 EC, pursuant to which the behaviour adopted by the dominant undertaking is unacceptable because, as a result of the treatment accorded to it, the customer is placed at a disadvantage in the economic activity it carries out. This kind of practice is central to this section of the book, which concerns business-to-business (or rather, business-to-competitor) transactions.

Business-to-consumer relations. In another type of situation, customers **4.81** affected by discriminatory behaviour do not carry out an economic activity, but are end users (consumers). The situation where consumers are affected by discriminatory practices is not explicitly considered in Article 82 EC. This does not mean that such practices are acceptable. They also fall also under a prohibition, but based on a general clause prohibiting unfair treatment imposed by dominant undertakings. To refer to these situations, the term 'business-to-consumer' relations is used. These relations, and the practices that are adopted in that context by dominant undertakings, are not considered here, but are analysed in the chapters dealing with universal service and the protection of rights granted to users.

(2) Link with other behaviour

Link with refusal to deal or grant access. Discriminatory behaviour must be **4.82** analysed in connection with the behaviour examined in the previous section, refusal to deal or grant access. Undertakings controlling a facility or resource are not likely to refuse access to a competitor openly. In most circumstances, their personnel or at least certain members of the organisation are aware of the obligations and prohibitions deriving from competition rules, as well as those resulting from regulation. They know that a blatant refusal would conjure up a strong reaction on the part of the competitor(s) seeking access, thereby drawing the attention of competition and/or regulatory authorities. For that reason one can expect dominant undertakings to adopt a more prudent or cautious approach. This might take the form of discriminatory treatment inflicted on undertakings representing a threat for the dominant undertaking. The discrimination can be introduced in any of the elements involved in transactions between dominant undertakings and competitors. Discriminations in tariffs are a classic example, but there are many more examples when it comes to practices hindering the activities of competitors.

4.83 **Difficulty in distinguishing the two types of behaviour.** From the outset it must be emphasised that discriminatory practices can rarely be distinguished from refusal to deal or grant access. Often, discriminatory practices are adopted by a dominant undertaking because, as mentioned above, they provide an adequate tool to bring about two objectives: not to refuse access blatantly for fear of the consequences that such an attitude could have and, at the same time, avoid giving access to facilities or resources under conditions allowing rivals to compete on a successful basis with the dominant undertaking.

4.84 **Two markets involved.** The practices at stake (refusal to deal, discriminatory practices) concern situations where two markets are involved.[71] In that kind of situation, a competitor needs access to a facility or resource under the control of another undertaking. These resources are located on a first market and are necessary to carry out an activity on a second. Confronted with a request made by a competitor, the dominant undertaking has a choice between two possibilities. The first is to refuse access—the competitor then has no chance of entering the market. A second possibility is to grant access, but apply discriminatory conditions. In the second scenario, the competitor has the tools necessary to enter the market. However, the conditions under which access is given implies that it will not be in a favourable position to compete successfully. The result is that, in the absence of special circumstances, the competitor will sooner or later disappear—a result which is not different in substance from that obtained with a refusal to deal or grant access.

4.85 **Important yet underdeveloped case law.** The conclusion of these observations is that refusal to deal or grant access, and discriminatory practices, normally lead to similar results. Given this conclusion, it should come as no surprise that the two types of behaviour are analysed by the Commission and the European courts as practices posing significant threats to the development of competition. It is

---

[71] That is the case, at least, for situations where discrimination occurs vis-à-vis one or several competitors. Discriminatory practices that may be adopted vis-à-vis consumers are addressed in the last chapter of this book.

surprising in this regard that the case law appears to be less developed on discrimination. The reason is probably historical. The case law on refusal to deal is rather old. Competition authorities, particularly the Commission, have long concentrated their attention on cases where abuses were blatant. In that context they addressed situations where undertakings stopped supplying competitors despite a long, and satisfactory, business relationship. At a later stage they broadened their approach and expressed a general obligation to grant access independently of the relations existing between the undertakings. The case law on discriminatory practices developed only afterwards. When the focus was placed on market opening, the first goal was to ensure that access would be granted. That goal being reached, competition authorities observed that a second wave of practices had been adopted by dominant undertakings, which obeyed literally the obligation to grant access but made that obligation ineffective through imposing discriminatory conditions on competitors.

(3) Establishing discrimination

Burden of proof. An important issue when dealing with discriminatory prac- **4.86** tices is to identify the party which has to prove the existence of discrimination. The answer to that question depends on the procedure in which the existence of discrimination is alleged. A distinction must be made in this regard between two possible procedures.[72] *(a)* Generally, parties claiming that general competition law has been infringed may address a claim to the national competition authority (NCA) and/or, where the European market is affected, the Commission. On the basis of that claim, these authorities enquire whether discriminatory practices have indeed taken place.[73] In the context of such an enquiry, the parties are not, on one side, the author of the claim and, on the other, the dominant undertaking. The competition authority is investigating practices adopted by an undertaking. In such a context, it is for the competition authority to establish the existence of discrimination. *(b)* A second type of procedure is where an undertaking initiates an action before a court because it considers that competition rules have been infringed. In that kind of situation, the burden of proof then lies on the party initiating the procedure. That party has to establish that the treatment granted to it is not appropriate in regard of the one granted to other undertakings.

---

[72] These procedures are analysed in further detail in Chapter 6. They are, however, presented briefly here, to examine the consequences for the proof to be brought concerning the existence of a discrimination.

[73] According to case law, the said authorities are not compelled to launch an enquiry in all circumstances. On the contrary, they have a margin for manoeuvre which allows them to determine the cases to which they consider their limited resources will be adequately allocated. As a result of that possibility for authorities to choose their cases, practitioners representing a claimant are advised to carry out themselves, as much as possible, the work relating to the enquiry. It is tempting for the Commission or a competition authority to take up a case when they have the sense that the case is already prepared.

4.87 **Response to the claim.**   In both instances (procedure before a competition authority or a national court), the dominant undertaking may provide two sorts of answer to the claim that discrimination took place. *(a)* The first possible response is to question the facts put forward by the other party. In that kind of defence, the dominant undertaking may attempt to establish, for instance, that there was no difference in treatment, or that the situations were dissimilar. *(b)* A second answer, if the undertaking accepts that different treatment has indeed been granted, is to justify that attitude by stating that the difference may be explained by objective reasons. The possibility of showing justification is analysed in a later section of this chapter (See paras 4.317–4.324).

4.88 **Illustration on evidence (CFI).**   The division of tasks between parties as regards evidence can be illustrated by several rulings adopted by the Commission and/or the European courts. An interesting case in this regard is *Tetra Pak II*.[74] In that case, a dominant undertaking was selling identical machines to various customers but was charging different prices for an identical transaction. The behaviour was deemed abusive by the Commission. The same conclusion was reached by the CFI. The reasoning presented by the latter is illustrative of the approach taken by competition authorities vis-à-vis claims that discrimination is present. Following this reasoning, the CFI observes, first, that different prices have indeed been charged for identical transactions. This finding is based on evidence provided by the Commission and not questioned by the dominant undertaking. Second, the CFI observes that the difference in treatment is not explained or justified with objective arguments by the dominant undertaking. The result, the CFI concludes, is that the practice must be found discriminatory.

> *Tetra Pak II.* '[A] detailed analysis of the majority of contracts for the sale or lease of machines in Italy from 1976 to 1986 reveals short-term differences from the prevailing price of 20 to 40%, even in certain cases of 50% to more than 60%, for both aseptic and non-aseptic machines. In the absence of any argument by the applicant which might provide objective justification for its pricing policy, such disparities were unquestionably discriminatory.'[75]

4.89 **Further illustration (Commission).**   Another interesting case, emphasising this time action by the Commission, is *Régie des voies aériennes*.[76] That case concerns the fees claimed by a national undertaking from airline companies using the Belgian national airport (Zaventem). Companies were asked to pay these fees in return for the use of certain facilities. According to the presentation made by the

---

[74] Commission Decision (EEC) 91/535 declaring the compatibility with the common market of a concentration (Case No IV/M068—Tetra Pak/Alfa-Laval) Council Regulation (EEC) No 4064/89 [1991] OJ L290/35; Case T-83/91 *Tetra Pak International SA v Commission* [1994] ECR II-755. Case C-333/94 P *Tetra Pak International SA v Commission* [1996] ECR I-5951.

[75] Judgement of the CFI, at [207].

[76] Commission Decision (EEC) 95/364 relating to a proceeding pursuant to Article 90(3) of the Treaty [1995] OJ L216/8.

Commission, the fees were fixed by the Government but collected by the national undertaking in question. In its fee policy, the Government decided that a rebate could be granted to certain undertakings, calculated on the basis of the number of take-offs and landings on behalf of the undertakings concerned. These criteria used by the authority were however found to be discriminatory by the Commission. *(a)* The first reason was that the threshold for the application of the lower rebates was fixed at a high level. The consequence was that three airline companies only could benefit from the rebate. The rebate policy thus benefited a few actors without being opened to all participants. *(b)* The second reason related to the thresholds fixed for the allocation of the highest possible rebates. These rebates were introduced as a special measure to support undertakings making intensive use of the airport. The result was that, according to the Commission, an even greater discrimination was introduced, these thresholds being apparently designed to favour the national airline company (Sabena).

> *Régie des voies aériennes.* 'Sabena received final-step discounts (30%) equivalent to an overall reduction of 18% on its fees, whereas the other qualifying airlines (Sobelair and BA) were eligible for only a first-step discount (7,5%). No other airline operating at Brussels Airport qualifies for a reduction in its landing fees.'[77]

Tentative explanation. A tentative explanation was put forward by the under- **4.90** taking, which considered that the benefit obtained from the fee policy by the national airline company was objectively justified as it was based on a criterion that did not depend on the nationality or the residence of the company. The thresholds were indeed calculated on the basis of the number of take-offs and landings. In that context, the rebates could be compared to a special price granted to customers as a result of the quantity purchased by the latter. The argument was not accepted by the Commission. The position adopted by that institution was based on the case law concerning rebates, considered under competition rules. Pursuant to that case law, rebates are authorised only where they reflect an economy realised by the supplier in the transaction made with that customer. A typical case is where large quantities are purchased. The quantity ordered then allows the supplier to realise economies. Under competition rules, the supplier is allowed, in that context, to pass on to the customer part of the economy realised as a result of the size of the order placed by that customer.

Commission's position. That justification could not be used, in the opinion of **4.91** the Commission, in the case at issue. As appears from the extract set out below, the costs incurred by the airport operator did not depend, according to the Commission, on the number of take-offs and landings. The only costs possibly relating to the number of operations were those incurred in calculating the total sum to be paid by the companies. For those which make intensive use of the facilities, that cost

---

[77] Decision of the Commission, [13] at 11, col b.

could be lower as a result of the possibility of covering many operations in one bill, but these economies of scale were limited.

> *Régie des voies aériennes.* The airways authority has not demonstrated to the Commission that handling the take-off or landing of an aircraft belonging to one airline rather than to another gives rise to economies of scale. The handling of the landing or take-off of an aircraft requires the same service, irrespective of its owner or the number of aircraft belonging to a given airline. The airways authority might, at most, argue that economies of scale occur at the level of invoicing since a single invoice covering a large number of movements can be issued to a carrier with a high level of traffic whilst many invoices covering only a few movements are needed for other carriers. Such economies of scale are, however, negligible.'[78]

(4) Resources concerned

4.92 **Nature of resource again irrelevant.** As was mentioned in connection with refusal to deal, the practices adopted by the dominant undertaking and addressed under Article 82 EC do not really depend on the nature of the facility or resource concerned. In many instances, practitioners are confronted with issues relating to infrastructure. A typical case is an operator owning infrastructure but imposing discriminatory prices and conditions. Abusive practices are not limited, however, to networks. Other types of facility or resource may be involved. In fact, all types of resource may provide an opportunity for dominant undertakings to adopt discriminatory practices. For this reason it can be said that the nature of the facility or resource involved is not relevant for the application of the prohibition. The relevant criteria are elsewhere—*(a)* in the dominance held by an undertaking on one of the markets involved, *(b)* in the practice adopted by that undertaking and *(c)* in the effect of that practice on the degree of competition existing on one of the markets involved.

4.93 **Example of non network-related resource.** An example of a resource which is not related to a network is provided by a case dealt with by the Commission regarding access to data necessary to make telephone guides.[79] Such data are generally collected by operators when they open an account for subscribers. Operators then register the name, address and other data necessary to provide the service. As appears from their nature, electronic communications only have relevance for society if people can contact other subscribers easily. Telephone directories are essential for that purpose, whatever their form (electronic, paper, etc). The case concerned the market for the preparation of telephone directories in Belgium. Such directories cannot be prepared if the relevant data are not communicated by the operator. At the time the case arose, there were two undertakings on the market for the preparation of directories—ITT Promedia (an independent undertaking, hereinafter 'ITT') and a subsidiary of the former national operator

---

[78] Decision of the Commission, at [16].

[79] *Belgacom Directory Services v ITT Promedia* [1997] Competition Policy Newsletter 13.

(Belgacom Directory Services, hereinafter 'Belgacom'). As appears from the description given by the Commission, Belgacom charged high tariffs to ITT for the supply of information.

Analysis by the Commission.   The practice was analysed under the prohibition   **4.94**
laid down in Article 82 EC. Two arguments were raised by the Commission in concluding that the practice was abusive. *(a)* The first basis was to say that the tariffs were discriminatory. The tariffs were higher for the communication of data to ITT than for Belgacom. *(b)* In addition, the tariffs charged to ITT were excessive. That finding was based on an enquiry into the method used by Belgacom to calculate these tariffs. As transpired from that enquiry, the tariffs charged by Belgacom were not based on costs incurred in collecting data and treating and transmitting them. They were rather founded on the revenues that, according to Belgacom, ITT could be expected to obtain on the market for telephone guides.[80]

Commission's proposal.   To resolve the conflict between the two undertakings,   **4.95**
the Commission proposed that the tariffs charged for the communication of data should be based henceforth on the costs incurred by the operator in connection with the collection and processing of the data. To these costs the Commission accepted that a reasonable profit could be added. According to the Commission, the tariffs resulted from the sum of these two elements. They had to be identical whatever the undertaking seeking access to the data. In application of that principle, the tariff could not be higher for ITT than for Belgacom.[81]

Method used by Belgacom	Method imposed by the Commission
(a) The operator calculates the anticipated revenues of ITT. *(b)* It charges ITT a tariff that confiscates these revenues.	*(a)* The operator must calculate the costs incurred by it in collecting, processing and transmitting information. *(b)* These costs serve as a basis for the establishment of the tariffs. *(c)* The tariffs must be identical for all customers.

(5) Types of discrimination

Many possibilities.   Discriminatory practices may affect all aspects of the trans-   **4.96**
actions between a dominant undertaking and its customers. In most instances,

---

[80] Belgacom had calculated the revenues that it thought would be obtained by ITT on the relevant market. It was charging ITT so as to absorb the entirety of these revenues—or close to that amount. In effect, Belgacom was confiscating a part—as large as possible—of the anticipated revenues of the competitor. Using that method, Belgacom had estimated that the total to be paid by ITT amounted to 34% of the turnover realised by the latter undertaking on the relevant market. The method had been dissimulated through charging that client an amount based on the number of lines of communicated data (about 200 Belgian francs per line)—creating in this manner an impression that the tariff had been obtained using another method.

[81] Ultimately, the tariffs that were agreed by the undertakings amounted, in total, to about 16% of the turnover realised by ITT on the market. A price of 65 Belgian francs per line was agreed.

the discrimination is visible in the tariffs applied to those customers. Several examples are examined above where, in the case law relating to general competition principles, undertakings use their dominance to impose on certain customers different prices despite the fact that these customers are in identical situations. This does not mean, however, that discriminatory practices may not affect other aspects of the transaction. A typical situation is where a party controls information that can be crucial for another. Suppose that access to the public telephone infrastructure is necessary to deliver services. Access is sought, and obtained, from the operator. Prices are reasonable. The operator fails, however, to deliver the technical information necessary to adapt the equipment used by the provider, whereas that information is made available to other undertakings, including the division which, within the organisation of the operator, is entrusted with the provision of competing services. Such behaviour must be deemed abusive, even though it does not affect prices but other aspects of the transaction.

Link with rebates

4.97 **Rebates in exchange for an advantage.** An important part of the case law concerning discrimination relates to rebates granted by dominant undertakings to certain customers. These rebates are often given in exchange for an advantage granted to the dominant undertaking. In some cases, the customer commits itself to placing all of its orders with the undertaking (exclusivity). In others, the customer must order given quantities from the dominant undertaking regularly (fidelity). In a third type of circumstance, the customer must promise to enter into a partnership in exchange for which rebates are given. These practices are often encountered in the markets and have given rise to substantial case law.

Discrimination based on residence or nationality

4.98 **Non-competitors.** In many instances, practitioners are confronted with discrimination practised against competitors. They should be aware that the case law on discrimination originally developed in situations where a distinction was imposed on the basis of the nationality of the undertaking suffering the discrimination. In that kind of situation, the dominant undertaking was not necessarily trying to place a competitor at a competitive disadvantage; it was rather acting following a pattern according to which undertakings of the same nationality had to be privileged.

4.99 **The rule.** Pursuant to case law, a dominant undertaking may not favour undertakings or partners on the basis of their nationality. As a corollary, they may not impose on a customer a disadvantage based on nationality. *GVL* is the leading case for this category of discriminatory practice.[82] In this case an undertaking

---

[82] Commission Decision (EEC) 81/1030 relating to a proceeding under Article 86 of the EEC Treaty (IV/29.839—GVL) [1981] OJ L370/49; Case 7/82 *Gesellschaft zur Verwertung von Leistungsschutzrechten mbH (GVL) v Commission* [1983] ECR 483.

dominated the market for services provided to authors in Germany (protection of copyright, etc). The services provided by that undertaking were reserved for artists fulfilling two conditions: they had to have German nationality and, additionally, be resident in Germany. As a result of these conditions, the services in question were not offered to artists of a different nationality and/or artists without a residence in that country. These conditions were found to be discriminatory. For the Commission and the European courts, general competition law must be interpreted consistently with European law in general. As is known, the prohibition on discrimination based on nationality plays an important role in the European legal order.

> *Commission.* 'The prohibition of abuses contained in the first paragraph of Article [82] . . . must . . . be viewed in the light of, and having due regard to, the general principles laid down in the EEC Treaty. One of these principles is embodied in Article [12] . . . of the EEC Treaty,[83] which provides that any discrimination on grounds of nationality shall be prohibited. As a rule, therefore, discriminatory treatment by a dominant undertaking on grounds of nationality must be regarded automatically as an infringement of Article [82] . . .' 'The refusal by GVL as a *de facto* monopoly undertaking to conclude management agreements with foreign artists having no residence in Germany constitutes discrimination on grounds of nationality and hence an abuse within the meaning of Article [82] . . .'[84] *ECJ.* '[A] refusal[85] by an undertaking having a *de facto* monopoly to provide its services for all those who may be in need of them but who do not come within a certain category of persons defined by the undertaking on the basis of nationality or residence must be regarded as an abuse of a dominant position within the meaning of the first paragraph of Article [82] . . . of the Treaty.'[86]

Frequent situations. Practitioners may be tempted to consider that discrimination on the basis of nationality has disappeared with the introduction of competition. In the new, competitive, environment, undertakings have to seek all possible partners. They do not take the risk of rejecting a possible customer for reasons related to nationality or residence. Despite the emergence of this new environment, behaviour of this nature may still be adopted in a context where the former incumbent operators remain, to a large extent, in the hands of public authorities. Situations might thus occur where these undertakings are tempted to deal with specific partners in preference to other undertakings of another nationality. **4.100**

Market partitioning

Geographical partitioning. Another kind of discrimination is where dominant undertakings treat differently customers located in several geographical markets. **4.101**

---

[83] Art 12 EC. 'Within the scope of application of this Treaty, and without prejudice to any special provisions contained therein, any discrimination on grounds of nationality shall be prohibited.'

[84] Decision of the Commission, at [46] and [47] (extracts).

[85] It is interesting to note the use of the term 'refusal' made by the ECJ in the case. The ECJ in substance considers the behaviour adopted by a dominant undertaking as a refusal to deal on a non-discriminatory basis. That formulation indicates how close the concepts, and the categories, of discrimination and refusal to deal are with each other. [86] Judgment of the ECJ, at [56].

In situations of this nature, the Commission and the European courts tend to intervene to the extent that these practices introduce, within the internal market, a division based on geographical criteria. A classic example is *United Brands*.[87] In that case, an undertaking dominated the market for banana imports into the Community. The bananas were imported through two European harbours, where they were sold to distributors. Each distributor was granted a given territory in which the bananas were to be marketed. The products sold in the various countries were identical. Prices diverged to a considerable extent, however (by up to 100 per cent). The reason for that difference was related to the tariff policy practised by the importer. The latter undertaking set for each distributor a tariff which was calculated taking into account the maximum price that could be obtained from the final consumers in the various territories involved.[88]

4.102　**Arguments raised against the undertaking.**　Various arguments were raised against the behaviour adopted by the dominant undertaking. One was that the tariffs charged were too high. That claim is examined in a later section, in connection with excessive prices (see paras 4.185–4.218). Another was the partitioning which was orchestrated by the undertaking on the European territory. Different prices were set for the various countries concerned. Several mechanisms were additionally used by the undertaking in order to prevent distributors and other possible customers from taking advantage of the internal market by buying bananas on one market where prices were low and selling them on another where tariffs were on the high side.[89] The combination of the differences in price, and of the mechanisms making it impossible for undertakings to take advantage of these differences, was found abusive by the Commission. That finding was confirmed

---

[87] Commission Decision (EEC) 76/353 relating to a procedure under Article 86 of the EEC Treaty (IV/26699—Chiquita) [1975] OJ L95/1; Case 27/76 *United Brands Co v Commission* [1978] ECR 207.

[88] In that context, prices were not based, as a result, on costs. As in *Belgacom*, examined earlier, the tariff depended on the revenue that the distributor anticipated he could obtain. That revenue was established on the basis of available information. The wholesale price was set at the level of the final price, *minus* a percentage supposed to represent the profit left to the distributor.

[89] These mechanisms were as follows. The contracts concluded by the dominant undertaking and the distributors did not explicitly mention a prohibition to export bananas to a country where they could be sold against a higher tariff. Neither did they contain a prohibition to import bananas from a country where they would be cheaper. A similar result was however obtained through the use of two mechanisms which were based on the impossibility of transporting bananas when they are mature, given the risk that the cargo may be lost. *(a)* A first mechanism was that distributors were compelled to invest heavily in ripening installations. Having made these installations, these distributors found it more remunerative to use them to the fullest—and thus bring bananas to complete maturation before selling these products. *(b)* A second mechanism was a prohibition included in the contracts with the distributor, to export or import bananas as long as the products were green. That prohibition was justified by the willingness, on the part of the dominant undertaking, to ensure that bananas were brought to maturation by an agreed distributor. The practical result was that bananas had to be kept until ripe—and could not be transported thereafter.

by the ECJ, even though the decision adopted by the Commission was annulled on other accounts.

> *Commission.* '[F]or an undertaking in a dominant position, a policy of systematically setting prices at the highest possible level, resulting in wide price differences, cannot be objectively justified, particularly where that undertaking maintains market segregation.' '[D]ifferences in transport costs, taxes and duties or marketing conditions might justify different levels in price on resale at the retail level. these differences can, however, never justify objectively UBC's [United Brand's] differing prices to its distributor/ripeners for equivalent transactions at Bremerhaven and Rotterdam, and still less so given that the quantities of bananas sold to each such distributor/ripener are approximately the same.'[90]

> *ECJ.* '[T]he mechanisms of the market are adversely affected if the price is calculated by leaving out one stage of the market and taking into account the law of supply and demand as between the vendor and the ultimate consumer and not as between the vendor (UBC) and the purchaser (the ripener/distributors)'; 'thus, by reason of its dominant position UBC, fed with information by its local representatives, was in fact able to impose its selling price on the intermediate purchaser'; 'this price and also the "weekly quota allocated" is only fixed and notified to the customer four days before the vessel carrying the bananas berths'; 'these discriminatory prices, which varied according to the circumstances of the Member States, were just so many obstacles to the free movement of goods and their effect was intensified by the clause forbidding the resale of bananas while still green and by reducing the deliveries of the quantities ordered'; 'a rigid partitioning of national markets was thus created at price levels, which were artificially different, placing certain distributor/ripeners at a competitive disadvantage, since compared with what it should have been competition had thereby been distorted'.[91]

Packaging.   Two further examples are presented briefly in this and the following **4.103** paragraph. The objective is not to analyse the practice in a systematic fashion, but rather to show that it can be designated discriminatory in a variety of situations. In *Tetra Pak II*, the dominant undertaking was found against as a result of the differences that could be observed between the prices charged in respect of different geographical markets. That undertaking was active on several markets for the preparation and packaging of foodstuffs, as well as on adjacent markets such as that for packaging machinery or for the manufacture of the packaging. These various markets, or at least a significant proportion of them, were dominated by the undertaking in question, which was particularly powerful on a worldwide basis.

---

[90] Decision of the Commission, col 15. The Commission states, but does not demonstrate, that 'the marketing conditions in these Member States are in fact broadly comparable'.

[91] Judgment of the ECJ, at [230]–[233]. The partitioning introduced between the national markets seems to constitute the essential argument put forward by the Commission. Partitioning indeed runs counter to an essential objective sought in the EU. The Commission also devotes some attention to the encounter between offer and demand. The remarks which are then made by it appear less important. If the realisation of the internal market is not impaired, there is no reason to impede an undertaking from determining the conditions offered to distributors by taking into account the price that can be charged on the final market.

As a result of the power held by the undertaking, customers had no choice but to accept the conditions imposed on them even if they were unfavourable compared to those offered to customers on other territories. The differences in the tariffs set for the various territories were sometimes substantial,[92] and could not be explained by any objective or acceptable reason.[93]

4.104 **Railways.** Another illustration is *Deutsche Bundesbahn*,[94] concerning the transportation of goods by rail. The Commission found that different prices were charged by the German undertaking as regards containers transported on the German territory, depending on whether the containers transited through a German or a Belgian/Dutch harbour. The difference was based on the length of the journey carried out on German soil. Where the containers transited through a German harbour, the journey on German soil was longer. Given the length of the journey, the total price that should have been charged by the German undertaking would have been relatively high if the normal pricing method had been used. To avoid such a result, and present an acceptable bill, the German undertaking charged a reduced tariff per kilometre. This pricing policy was presented as a sort of rebate for quantity, the longer the journey on German soil the better the price per kilometre. According to the Commission, that tentative justification could not be accepted.[95] Tariffs could not be based on a decision to transit through a given Member State instead of another. The decision taken by the Commission was confirmed by the CFI.

---

[92] For aseptic Tetra Brik boxes, the differences amounted to 40 to 70% of the price. For Tetra Raw boxes, they were often higher than 25% and sometimes reached 50%. As for the non-aseptic Tetra Brik boxes, they were sold in various countries at prices higher than those (20 to 30%) set for the Italian market.

[93] The Commission and the ECJ would have accepted price differences if, as mentioned in their decision and judgment, the differences were due to divergences in the costs incurred by the undertaking on the various markets. However, such cost divergences could not be established in the case at issue. For instance, the undertaking could not demonstrate that the differences could be justified by divergences relating to the size of the boxes concerned, the average quantities purchased by the customers, variations in the transportation costs or variations in the prices applicable on the market for the raw materials necessary to manufacture the products.

[94] *Deutsche Bundesbahn*, Commission Decision (EC) 94/210 relating to a proceeding pursuant to Articles 85 and 86 of the EC Treaty (IV/33.941—HOV SVZ/MCN) [1994] OJ L104/34.

[95] For the Commission, the undertaking was wrong in claiming that the difference could be analysed as a rebate for quantity. In its decision, the Commission submits that the tariff policy set by the dominant undertaking was not based on the distance separating the harbour and the municipality to which the goods had to be transported, or from which they had to be transported to the port. The journey was indeed longer when the transit occurred through a Belgian or Dutch harbour. A rebate, if any, would thus have been relevant for the prices charged for these journeys. The dominant undertaking also sought to justify its pricing policy through a reference to the degree of competition, which was allegedly higher in Germany. According to the presentation given by the German undertaking, that high degree of competition on German soil forced the undertaking to set tariffs at a lower level. Without such a policy, the railway transportation would have been set aside in favour of other forms of transportation (by road, river or air). That argument was not accepted by the Commission, which deemed that the alleged higher degree of competition had not been established by the dominant undertaking.

Conclusion. The case law concerning the prohibition imposed on dominant **4.105**
undertakings to partition the internal market is rather highly developed, due to
the importance afforded by the Commission and the European courts to free
movement within the internal market. Pursuant to the case law, consumers and
businesses must at all times be able to enjoy the advantages they can expect to flow
from a unified market. Any behaviour running counter to that principle is inevitably
condemned where it is adopted by a dominant undertaking. Practitioners representing dominant undertakings should scrutinise carefully any tariff policy practised by a dominant undertaking, to ensure that it does not bring about any
market partitioning, however slight. As a corollary, practitioners representing
competitors should be aware of the potentialities opened up by the case law, and
should examine systematically behaviour adopted by the dominant undertaking to
determine whether its practices can be analysed in terms of market partitioning.

Behaviour directed at competitors' customers

Punitive measures. Dominant undertakings may not impose a disadvantage **4.106**
on competitors' customers. This type of practice is sometimes used by dominant
undertakings to sanction customers which decide to deal, or remain, with a
competitor. The practice may also be used in order to constrain customers to
change suppliers and deal with the dominant undertaking. This practice has been
deemed abusive in several judgments, the clearest of which is probably *Compagnie
maritime belge*.[96] That case concerned a maritime conference, the members of
which sought to monopolise maritime transportation on the route between the
Congo and destinations on the North Sea. In order to achieve their objective, the
members resorted to various practices. One of them was to establish 'blacklists'
of customers dealing with competitors. These customers were then subjected to
unsatisfactory conditions. They could not evade these conditions as the members
of the association held a dominant position jointly. That position afforded those
members the possibility of behaving independently of possible reactions by
dissatisfied customers.[97]

Advantages offered to customers. A symmetrically opposite practice may con- **4.107**
sist of advantages granted to competitors' customers in an attempt to attract them
to the dominant undertaking. These practices are analysed in a later section, in so
far as they concern rebates granted to customers for that purpose. Suffice it to
mention here that specific practices intended to attract competitors' customers are
prohibited where they are adopted by one or several dominant undertakings. This
behaviour can be illustrated with the rulings adopted successively in *Hilti* by the

---

[96] *Cewal*, Commission Decision (EEC) 93/82 relating to a proceeding pursuant to Articles 85
(IV/32.448 and IV/32.450: Cewal, Cowac and Ukwal) and 86 (IV/32.448 and IV/32.450: Cewal)
of the EEC Treaty [1993] OJ L34/20.
[97] See decision of the Commission, at [29] and [86]. See also judgment of the CFI, at [185].

Commission, the CFI and the ECJ.[98] In that case, a dominant undertaking manufactured and sold nails as well as cartridges and nail guns, as mentioned above.[99] As part of the practice was intended to reinforce its position, the undertaking offered exceptional conditions to competitors' customers. The goal was to attract them and make them part of their clientele. The practice was deemed abusive. The reason referred to by the Commission was that ordinary consumers were not treated correctly in that they were granted treatment which was unfavourable compared to the conditions proposed to customers' customers. However, these customers could not shift to another supplier as a result of the absence of an alternative, deriving from the market power held by the undertaking. These customers were thus locked into a situation that could not be accepted, as they were deprived of their economic freedom and the absence of alternatives did not allow competition to flourish and develop.

> *Hilti.* 'On several occasions Hilti singled out some of the main customers of these competitors and offered them especially favourable conditions in order to attract their loyalty, going in certain cases so far as to give away products free of charge. These conditions were selective and discriminatory in that other customers of Hilti buying similar or equivalent quantities did not benefit from these special conditions. The customers of Hilti who did not receive these special offers are discriminated against and effectively bear the cost of the lower prices to other customers. These special offers were not a direct defensive reaction to competitors, but reflected Hilti's pre-established policy of attempting to limit their entry into the market for Hilti-compatible nails. Only a dominant undertaking such as Hilti could carry out such a strategy because it is able, through its market power, to maintain prices to all its other customers unaffected by its selectively discriminatory discounts.'[100]

(6) Situations to compare

4.108 **Relationship between treatment and situation.** As was stated, the case law developed under general competition law imposes on dominant undertakings a prohibition on treating customers placed in identical situations differently. The corollary of that prohibition is that customers placed in different situations should be treated accordingly, that is, differences should thus be established between them as required by the circumstances. In both formulations, it appears that the treatment to be granted by the dominant undertaking depends on an

---

[98] Commission Decision EEC (88/138) relating to a proceeding under Article 86 of the EEC Treaty (IV/30.787 and 31.488—Eurofix-Bauco v Hilti) [1988] OJ L65/19; Case T-30/89 *Hilti AG v Commission* [1991] ECR II-1439; Case C-53/92 P *Hilti AG v Commission* [1994] ECR I-667.

[99] Materials were attached through the use of the nail gun and the cartridges and nails contained therein. The nails were to be introduced in the cartridges, which in turn were introduced in the nail guns. The undertaking held clear dominance on the market for nail guns, where it was protected by intellectual property rights and the level of investment required to start an activity. Its position was less protected on the market for cartridges and even less on the market for nails.

[100] Decision of the Commission, at [80]. The subject matter (offer to clients of competitors) is not addressed by the ECJ or the CFI in their judgments.

assessment of the similarities and differences existing between the situations in which customers are placed. Situations must be compared and conclusions drawn from that comparison as regards the treatment to be granted to each party. The question arises in this context as to what situations can actually be compared. A distinction must be made in this regard between various situations which are analysed in the following paragraphs.

(a) Customers with no link to the undertaking. In the first type of situation, **4.109** the dominant undertaking deals with other undertakings which are not related to it. For instance, an operator grants infrastructure access to service providers. That operator has no specific link with any of these providers. In such a situation, general competition law (case law) implies that the providers must be treated equally. In most circumstances, one can expect this requirement to be complied with because the dominant undertaking has no interest in granting preferential treatment to any of the providers.[101] For that reason, practitioners rarely encounter cases where this kind of situation materialises. It is also for that reason, probably, that no case seems to have been decided by a competition authority or a court regarding this specific situation.

The situation that has just been examined is not addressed only in the case law, **4.110** but is also covered by the NRF. The rules introduced in regulation to counter discriminatory treatment are examined in Chapter 3 dealing with access under sector-specific regulation. These rules address all possible situations, including those where customers have no link with the dominant undertaking.

> *Access Directive.* 'Obligations of non-discrimination shall ensure, in particular, that the operator applies equivalent conditions in equivalent circumstances to other undertakings providing equivalent services.'[102]

(b) Partners. In a second type of situation, dominant undertakings have a rela- **4.111** tionship with several undertakings, some of which are partners. In that sort of context, dominant undertakings may be tempted to grant special treatment to partners.[103] However, the result of special treatment being granted to a partner would be that the other undertakings (the 'non partners') would not have access under identical conditions. Where for example an operator creates a joint venture with an internet provider for the collection and analysis of data concerning possible customers, and that operator offers excellent conditions for access by that internet undertaking to its network, these conditions are part of its willingness to

---

[101] The undertaking has no relation with them—why would it favour one of them?

[102] Access Directive, Art 10(2).

[103] They have specific relations with these undertakings. Economic success depends to a large extent on the alliances that may be entered into. The strength of such alliances in turn depends on the benefits partners can obtain from these links established among them. That context induces partners to favour their allies in all circumstances—particularly when the advantage can be decisive in the struggle carried out by one of these partners with its competitors.

have good relations with its partners. The favourable character of these conditions implies that other internet undertakings seeking access to the network but having no partnership with the operator are disadvantaged.

4.112 **Case law.** According to general competition law (case law), such preferential treatment granted to partners cannot be accepted but should be deemed abusive. Undertakings must treat all other undertakings equally where they are dominant. The existence of a partnership does not provide any objective reason allowing the granting of an advantage. Several cases have been addressed by competition authorities, but most have led to decisions adopted under Article 81 EC. In these cases, the Commission authorises alliances among various telecoms operators, subject to the condition that the facilities or resources created by these undertakings as a result of the joint venture must be made available to third parties under equal conditions.[104]

4.113 **Regulation.** The position adopted by the competition authorities (in particular the Commission) in the context of general competition law fully corresponds to the rules imposed by the European legislator in the NRF. In that framework, the Access Directive specifically provides that operators with significant market power may not discriminate in favour of partners. The consequence of that prohibition is that such operators may not grant any special treatment to undertakings with which they have entered into partnership.

> - *Access Directive.* 'Obligations of non-discrimination shall ensure, in particular, that the operator applies equivalent conditions in equivalent circumstances to other undertakings providing equivalent services, and provides services and information to others under the same conditions and of the same quality as it provides for its . . . partners.'[105]

4.114 **(c) Relations within a single economic group.** In a third category, the chance that better treatment may be granted to certain undertakings becomes even greater as one considers the relations existing among companies belonging to the same economic group. Suppose that a group is made up of several companies carrying out their activities on different electronic communications markets. That group is legally organised in distinct companies each dealing with a specific activity. In this scenario, one company operates a network and another provides internet services. The company entrusted with the provision of internet services asks its sister company for access to the infrastructure. In this type of situation, it can be expected that special prices will be charged by companies belonging to the same group.[106]

---

[104] See for instance *Atlas*, Commission Decision 96/546 relating to a proceeding under Article 85 of the EC Treaty and Article 53 of the EEA Agreement (Case No IV/35.337—Atlas) [1996] OJ L239/23.　　　　　　　　　　　　　　　　　　　[105] Access Directive, Art 10(2).
[106] Undertakings often diversify their activities in order to avoid excessive concentration on one market. (A lack of diversification makes undertakings dependent upon fluctuations in demand). The diversification, however, is generally carried out while maintaining a general orientation. Undertakings in fact develop upstream or downstream—but generally remain in the same industry

Case law.   Pursuant to the case law (general competition law), a dominant under-   **4.115**
taking may not offer special treatment to another company, even if the two entities
belong to the same group. No preferential treatment may thus be granted between
the members of an economic group. This prohibition is formulated clearly in *Stena
Sealink*, which was examined at para 4.34 above. In that case, a company controlling
port facilities had granted access to the company in charge of the relevant maritime
route within its own group, whereas access was refused to a potential competitor.[107]

Regulation.   The approach is identical in the regulation. In the Access   **4.116**
Directive, the provision dealing with discrimination is formulated so as to
address situations where benefits are granted to members of the same economic
group. In that provision, a clear prohibition is established which also covers
intra-group advantages.

> *Access Directive.* 'Obligations of non-discrimination shall ensure, in particular, that
> the operator applies equivalent conditions in equivalent circumstances to other
> undertakings providing equivalent services, and provides services and information
> to others under the same conditions and of the same quality as it provides for . . . its
> subsidiaries.'[108]

(d) Internal transfers.   The last situation is where a single undertaking is   **4.117**
divided into several departments or divisions, each responsible for a given activity.
In that situation, the issue is not really different from that presented above in
connection with intra-group advantages. There is, however, a difference, the degree
of interpenetration among activities is even bigger in the context currently examined, as all divisions and departments are part of the same legal entity.[109] In an
organisation of that kind, there exists a similar incentive for all departments or
divisions to grant each other favours as compared to the treatment provided to
third companies. Additionally, the costs relating to each activity are not always

---

or sector. At the same time, the various activities carried out within the group are generally allocated
to entities which are structured so as to be legally independent. The reason is that groups want each
of these activities to be lucrative. That can only be achieved if the managers of each entity are given
some independence. At the same time, groups want to isolate each activity as regards liability. In
that context, the incorporation of each entity in charge of an activity has an advantage—the other
entities are not in danger if one of them happens to fail.

[107] Another example may be found in *Telemarketing* (n 39 above), where a company responsible
for publicity broadcasting did not agree to renew a contract concluded with a third undertaking.
That company had significant power on the relevant market. The decision taken by that company
was based upon a willingness to reserve that market for a sister company belonging to the same
group. A similar pattern may be observed in *Commercial Solvents* (n 50 above), where the company
producing a substance refused to continue selling it in order to reserve for a sister company the market relating to the end products manufactured with that substance. It should be observed that, in
these two cases, the European institutions place an emphasis on the refusal to deal rather than on the
conditions under which access may be obtained.   [108] Access Directive, Art 10(2).

[109] In the previous situation, there were several entities—all legally independent but participating in a wider economic group. In the situation currently examined, there is only one (legal and
economic) entity.

established with the same rigour where they concern activities carried out within the same entity. There exists a trend to organise internal transfers and be satisfied, for instance, with a smaller return on network operations where activities relating to services are to be launched.[110] The question arises whether that kind of situation—favourable treatment granted to a division or department within a single undertaking—should also be taken into account in order to assess whether conditions proposed to other customers are satisfactory. An answer to that question is provided in the following paragraphs on the basis of various sources—regulation, Article 82 EC, Article 81 EC and the 1998 Competition Guidelines.

4.118 **Regulation.** The first source to examine is the NRF. As observed above, a prohibition on discrimination may be imposed, pursuant to the NRF, by NRAs on undertakings with significant market power. That prohibition entails that conditions offered to customers must be identical in all situations, whatever the relation with the dominant undertaking. Where a prohibition on discrimination is imposed on it, an undertaking with significant market power must offer the same conditions to all customers seeking access. No preferential treatment may be granted to divisions/departments within its own organisation. The prohibition concerns, of course, the tariffs charged for access to facilities or resources necessary for the provision of electronic communications services. It is not limited, however, to these aspects, but covers all other elements of the transactions concluded by the dominant undertakings with other undertakings as regards access.

> *Access Directive.* 'Obligations of non-discrimination shall ensure, in particular, that the operator applies equivalent conditions in equivalent circumstances to other undertakings providing equivalent services, and provides services and information to others under the same conditions and of the same quality as it provides for its own services.'[111]

4.119 **Article 82 EC.** The prohibition is no different in the context of general competition law. A similar prohibition was formulated by the Commission and the European courts in the case law developed on the basis of Article 82 EC. The first occurrence of that obligation seems to have been in the decision adopted by the Commission in *Stena Sealink*.[112] It will be recalled that that case concerned a dominant undertaking refusing to give access to the port facilities necessary to serve a given maritime route. The behaviour adopted by the dominant undertaking was deemed abusive on two counts. On the one hand, the undertaking had to grant access and could not refuse use of the facilities by the undertaking

---

[110] That kind of organisation is frequent. Undertakings often seek vertical integration, in order to develop activities at several stages of the economic chain. When they adopt such an organisation, they hope to enjoy particular benefits. They do not expect, for instance, to be charged a price similar to the one they could obtain with a third undertaking—or where would be the advantage of being integrated?   [111] Access Directive, Art 10(2).

[112] Commission Decision EC (94/19) relating to a proceeding pursuant to Article 86 of the EC Treaty (IV/34.689—Sea Containers v Stena Sealink—Interim measures) [1994] OJ L15/8.

seeking to provide services. On the other hand, access had been refused to that competitor whereas it had been granted to the subsidiary company responsible within the group for the provision of the service. Discrimination had thus been practised to the extent that an advantage had been granted to one undertaking (the subsidiary company) and refused to another (the potential competitor). On that occasion the Commission formulated a principle pursuant to which an undertaking must share access to a facility or resource under its control, subject to conditions equal to those charged to its own divisions or departments responsible for the same activity.

> *Stena Sealink.* 'An undertaking which occupies a dominant position in the provision of an essential facility and itself uses that facility (ie a facility or infrastructure, without access to which competitors cannot provide services to their customers), and which refuses other companies access to that facility without objective justification or grants access to competitors only on terms less favourable than those which it gives its own services, infringes Article [82] . . .'[113]

1998 Competition Guidelines. The same approach was adopted by the Commission in the guidelines concerning the application of general competition law to the telecommunications sector (1998 Competition Guidelines). In that instrument, the Commission analyses Article 82 EC as implying an obligation for dominant operators[114] to share access on a non-discriminatory basis. For the Commission, non-discrimination implies that all undertakings seeking access must be treated equally, as long as they are placed in similar situations. The obligation is not limited to relations with independent parties. Equality must be complied with in the conditions offered to such parties as well as to the divisions or departments which are responsible, within the organisation of the operator, for the task of providing the services concerned. **4.120**

> *1998 Competition Guidelines.* 'In general terms, the dominant company's duty is to provide access in such a way that the goods and services offered to downstream companies are available on terms no less favourable than those given to other parties, including its own corresponding downstream operations.'[115]

Article 81 EC. An obligation to extend to third parties advantages conferred internally on divisions or departments in charge of the activity appears to be in conformity with the case law developed on the basis of Article 81 EC. That provision concerns agreements concluded by undertakings and which may have an **4.121**

---

[113] Decision of the Commission, at [66]. 'The owner of an essential facility which uses its power in one market in order to protect or strengthen its position in another related market, in particular, by refusing to grant access to a competitor, or by granting access on less favourable terms than those of its own services, and thus imposing a competitive disadvantage on its competitor, infringes Article [82] . . .' (ibid).

[114] In general competition law, the obligation is not limited to operators. The situation of operators is emphasised in the 1998 Competition Guidelines to the extent that that instrument specifically deals with access agreements, ie agreements concluded by operators with undertakings seeking access to infrastructure.   [115] 1998 Competition Guidelines, para 86.

effect on the degree of competition existing on the common market. The relevant case law developed in connection with several alliances concluded by major operators seeking to establish global telecoms networks and to provide high-quality services around the world. These agreements were notified to the Commission, in conformity with the rules then in force. After an enquiry, they were authorised by that institution on the basis of Article 81(3) EC. That provision allows for exemptions to be granted where agreements with an effect on competition contribute to economic or technical progress and are compatible with the principle of proportionality. In the various relevant decisions, the Commission introduces an obligation for the parties to share under equal conditions with all interested parties the networks they intend to establish as a result of the alliance.

> *Atlas.* 'DT and FT shall grant any entity created pursuant to the Atlas Agreement and any third party operating a telecommunications facility that apply for the interconnection of such facility with DT or FT's networks such interconnection on non-discriminatory terms that enables such entity or person to provide telecommunications services or provide its telecommunications facilities without limitation in any respect within the reasonable capabilities of the operator concerned.'[116]

4.122 **Towards a general principle.**   As will be clear from the paragraphs above, there is a correlation between regulation and general competition law (Article 81 EC, Article 82 EC and the 1998 Competition Guidelines) regarding the scope and content of the prohibition on discrimination. As a result, a general principle can be considered to exist whereby entities providing a service over a facility or resource must be treated equally where that facility or resource is controlled by a dominant undertaking. The relation that that undertaking may have with one or several of these entities does not provide any justification for granting special treatment.

4.123 **European courts.**   Despite the homogeneity existing between these various parts of the law, a caveat must be expressed. The NRF provisions dealing with discrimination were adopted by the Parliament and Council. The other sources—case law based on Articles 81 and 82 EC, 1998 Competition Guidelines—have been developed by the Commission. On none of these rules has a European court intervened as of now. It must thus be observed that the prohibition to discriminate, and particularly the section implying that an internal benefit has to be extended to other parties, has not yet been tested by the CFI or by the ECJ itself.[117] Does this circumstance affect the validity or force of that prohibition? The absence of a clear position by the European courts does not provide an argument for questioning the legality of the obligation to propose equal conditions whatever the identity of the entity

---

[116] Commission Decision 96/546 relating to a proceeding under Article 85 of the EC Treaty and Article 53 of the EEA Agreement (Case No IV/35.337—Atlas) [1996] OJ L239/23.

[117] No challenge has apparently been launched before the CFI against a decision adopted by the Commission. Similarly, the Access Directive has not been challenged in an application for annulment or a request for a preliminary ruling.

concerned. There is sufficient case law where the courts have expressed the idea that dominance may not be used to acquire an advantage. That case law implies that nothing may justify granting favourable treatment to internal divisions or departments, subsidiaries belonging to the same economic group, partners or simply other undertakings with no special relation to the dominant undertaking.

Practical consequence.   This section cannot be brought to a close without   **4.124** emphasising a practical consequence of the prohibition on discrimination. A remark of the same nature was made regarding the scale of the obligation to grant access. It was emphasised there how important it is for undertakings to develop competitive advantages. Such a strategy must be developed if undertakings want to compete successfully in the market. It should be reckoned that a strategy of that nature loses its importance if, once obtained, the competitive advantage must be shared. The observation is not only valid for the obligation to share—the same may be said of the obligation to set conditions identical for all parties independently of the relationship with the dominant undertaking. As a result of that obligation, not only must competitive advantages be shared, but they must be shared under equal conditions.

Organisation of undertakings.   The conjunction of these rules has a far-reaching   **4.125** consequence for the strategies, and organisation, of undertakings. As a result of the rules imposed in regulation and general competition law, it no longer appears essential for a given undertaking to seek, or keep, vertical integration, where that undertaking dominates a given market. Vertical integration normally has one advantage—undertakings may find within the group the facilities and resources necessary to provide services subject to conditions that are more favourable than those available on the markets. The obligation to share under equal conditions implies that that advantage has disappeared, or at least to a certain extent. A piece of advice to undertakings is not to seek or maintain vertical integration if they reach a stage where they can be found dominant. For business reasons, it is more appropriate for them to develop one or several niches, not necessarily related to one another. Using regulation and competition rules wherever this is needed, they will obtain access under satisfactory conditions to the facilities or resources required. In that context, geographical extension to cover new territories may provide an attractive alternative—more attractive indeed than an extension to other activities downstream or upstream of the main market in the economic chain.

D. Tariff-Related Practices

(1) General presentation

Competitive advantages.   It has been observed in this book that, since the open-   **4.126** ing of telecoms markets, undertakings have striven to develop and/or maintain competitive advantages allowing them to offer goods and services under terms and conditions that other undertakings are not in a position to offer. That attitude is somehow countered by regulation and general competition law pursuant to which facilities and resources are to be shared, to a certain extent at least. The rules involved were developed by public authorities in an attempt to foster the development of communications services.[118] Ideally, obligations would be imposed on all market participants, but such comprehensive intervention would not be accepted, as it would imply significant intervention by public authorities and restrictions imposed on the freedom for businesses and individuals to carry out activities as they wish. Authorities have thus limited the obligation to situations where markets are dominated by one or several undertakings.

4.127 **Public policy *vs* business goals.** It should be realised that the objectives sought by undertakings and the purposes imposed by authorities are not entirely consistent. Undertakings seek exclusivity, as this is an attractive option for surviving competition, whereas authorities want facilities and resources to be made available in an attempt to achieve public policy objectives. The relationship between these attitudes creates a tension—undertakings must, at the same time, comply with the law, and keep on countering rivals. That tension typically conjures up behaviour where rules are not always complied with. A classic situation is that of operators which, as a result of the position they have acquired on the market, must share access to their network, pursuant to the law, but use all possible means to discourage rivals and impede them from competing successfully.

4.128 **Strategic importance of tariffs.** A few examples of this attitude have been examined in previous sections. Some discriminatory practices used by dominant undertakings in that context have also been analysed. Typically, such practices provide an occasion for dominant undertakings to keep or obtain an advantage without going so far as to refuse to deal with a competitor and thus blatantly violate the law. Prices are often determinant in a strategy of this nature. Undertakings are obliged to grant access but they can influence the situation of competitors through the tariffs they apply for access. Looking at tariffs, several patterns can be distinguished. They are presented briefly here and are examined in more detail in the following sections.

4.129 **Low prices.** One pattern is to charge relatively low prices. In certain circumstances, prices set at a low level may bring about difficulties for competitors. This is particularly the case where the latter are not in a position to match the tariffs proposed by the dominant undertaking. The result may be that customers continue to turn to the dominant undertaking, and that competitors are progressively eliminated.

---

[118] We remain focused on that economic sector, although the same remark could be made for other sectors of the economy.

High prices.   At the opposite end of the spectrum, another difficulty is that **4.130** prices are sometimes fixed at a high level. Such prices may also raise concerns, although in a different context. *(a)* In the first option (low prices), one market is concerned. The dominant undertaking may eliminate competition on the market where the prices are set at a low level. *(b)* In the second (high pricing), two markets are concerned. The prices raise difficulties where they are fixed at a high level for the acquisition of goods and services used to carry out an economic activity on a second market. The undertakings present on that second market then face high costs for the access to the facilities and resources to be used on that second market.

Combination of prices.   A third practice is to combine pricing policies on vari- **4.131** ous markets in a context where, again, competitors may be eliminated or discouraged. The practice could be analysed in one of the categories mentioned above, to the extent that it implies prices set at a low or high level. It raises specific difficulties, however, in that a disadvantage is created for competitors as a result of a combination of prices set on different markets. For that reason, this practice is analysed in a specific section.

Rebates.   The last scenario is where advantages are granted to certain undertak- **4.132** ings without being extended to all of them. In this chapter, emphasis is placed on advantages taking the form of price rebates or discounts. Advantages of that nature have been presented, although briefly, in the section dealing with discriminatory practices. They are further analysed below.

(2) Predatory prices

Business strategy

The practice under consideration.   Certain undertakings charge to their cus- **4.133** tomers prices that may be considered low. Such a practice may have a negative effect on competition, where it is adopted by an undertaking holding a dominant position. Various situations may be examined.

Market entry.   One situation is where low prices have an effect on market entry. **4.134** As an example, take the situation of a network operator which, in addition to infrastructure, provides data transmission services. In this scenario, the operator dominates the market for data transmission. Several undertakings are contemplating entering that market, but have refrained from doing so given the low prices charged by the dominant undertaking. They are not in a position to match these prices. The result is that they may sell at a loss, but viability is then at stake. They may also sell at higher prices, but then take the risk of failing to attract customers.

Elimination of competition.   Another situation is where an undertaking dom- **4.135** inates a market where several competitors are present. On that market the dominant undertaking sets prices at a low level that cannot be matched by competitors.

As the prices are low, customers continue to be attracted by the dominant undertaking. The share held by that undertaking on the market keeps growing, and with it that undertaking's ability to behave independently of market players. In view of the dominant undertaking's success, competitors cannot bring in enough revenues to cover their costs. Their financial situation deteriorates, investors lose patience and withdraw their support, and they are as a result eliminated.

> *1998 Competition Guidelines, para 110.* 'Such a problem could, for example, arise in the context of competition between different telecommunications infrastructure networks, where a dominant operator may tend to charge unfairly low prices for access in order to eliminate competition from other (emerging) infrastructure providers.'

4.136 Analysis. The examples examined above provide illustrations without any claim to be exhaustive. What they show is that low prices raise difficulties where they have an effect on existing competition in a context where the degree of competition is already insufficient as a result of dominance. Deterioration occurs where, as a result of low prices, existing competitors are eliminated. It may be less visible, but equally dangerous, where market entry is discouraged.

4.137 1998 Competition Guidelines. The practice whereby prices are set at a predatory level is addressed in the 1998 Competition Guidelines. It will be recalled that that instrument was adopted to announce the position likely to be taken by the Commission in situations where it considered that general competition law was infringed. The attention given by the Commission to that type of behaviour highlights the risks that predatory pricing represents for competition. In the 1998 Competition Guidelines, the Commission stresses the risk that operators may charge predatory prices for access to infrastructure. This may come as a surprise, as it was submitted above that excessive, not predatory, prices are likely to be charged by dominant operators to discourage access. The two practices in fact depend on the strategy carried out by the dominant undertaking, and that strategy varies with the context in which that undertaking is placed.

4.138 Market for services. Where, for example, an operator faces harsh competition on a market for services, it will wish to eliminate some of the competitors present there. This attitude is necessary to improve the position of the operator in question on that market. In order to reach that objective, a strategy might be for the dominant undertaking to set access prices at a high level. These high prices would imply that competitors face high costs to obtain access. This in turn implies that, to cover their expenses, these competitors must charge relatively high prices on the service market. This may facilitate the task of the operator which, on that secondary market, may be able to charge lower tariffs and thereby attract customers.[119]

---

[119] Such a strategy would infringe general competition law on two counts. First, the high prices set for access could be deemed excessive. Second, these prices could also be deemed discriminatory as the operator charges to its own division a lower tariff for access.

Network markets.   Where, by contrast, an operator faces competition on the   **4.139**
network market, charging high prices for access would not be adequate. If high
prices are charged, competitors would believe that they could provide infrastructure at lower prices. A high price policy would thus bring about the emergence of
competition, a result not desired by the operator. The opposite strategy would be
more appropriate, whereby low prices were charged for access to infrastructure.
These prices can hardly be matched by actual or potential competitors. The result
is that these competitors refrain from entering the market (potential competition),
or leave the market if they had already started an activity (actual competition).

Access below cost.   This last strategy is singled out by the Commission in the   **4.140**
1998 Competition Guidelines as a real option for dominant operators. These
operators see infrastructure as their main asset. They want to keep a situation
where they remain the only ones providing networks. One possibility for them to
discourage entry or eliminate existing competition in that context is to charge low
prices on the market for networks. From a regulatory point of view, this sort of
strategy raises concerns because it further complicates the development of alternative infrastructure. Competition will not develop spontaneously and vigor-
ously on the markets for services where service providers are not in a position to
choose the operator they deal with.

> *1998 Competition Guidelines.* 'Predatory pricing occurs, *inter alia*, where a dominant
> undertaking sells a good or service below cost for a sustained period of time, with the
> intention of deterring entry, or putting a rival out of business, enabling the dominant
> undertaking to further increase its market power and later its accumulated profits.
> Such unfairly low prices are in breach of Article [82](a).' 'Such a problem could, for
> example, arise in the context of competition between different telecommunications
> infrastructure networks, where a dominant operator may tend to charge unfairly low
> prices for access in order to eliminate competition from other (emerging) infrastruc-
> ture providers.'[120]

Original stage in the case law

AKZO.   Setting prices below costs is not allowed, under certain circumstances,   **4.141**
pursuant to general competition law principles. This kind of practice was
addressed in *AKZO*.[121] In that case, an undertaking dominated the market for
food additives (flour derivatives). The market covered the Irish and UK territories,
thereby inviting the application of European competition rules. The dominant
undertaking had used various practices to strengthen its position on the relevant
market. One of these was to attract and capture customers from a competitor with
very low tariffs—tariffs that were indeed so low that they were below cost. The

---

[120] 1998 Competition Guidelines, para 110.
[121] Commission Decision (EEC) 85/609 relating to a proceeding under Article 86 of the EEC
Treaty (IV/30.698—ECS/AKZO) [1985] OJ L374/1; Case C-62/86 *AKZO Chemie BV v
Commission* [1991] ECR I-3359.

case was brought to the Commission, which ruled that the practice infringed Article 82 EC. An appeal was lodged before the ECJ, which confirmed the ruling and established a standard for the assessment of predatory prices. Pursuant to that ruling, dominant undertakings may sell, to a certain extent, at a loss. The limit is however infringed where goods or services are sold without recovering fixed costs or, even, a portion of the variable costs.

> *AKZO.* 'Prices below average variable costs (that is to say, those which vary depend-
> ing on the quantities produced) by means of which a dominant undertaking seeks to
> eliminate a competitor must be regarded as abusive. A dominant undertaking has no
> interest in applying such prices except that of eliminating competitors so as to enable
> it subsequently to raise its prices by taking advantage of its monopolistic position,
> since each sale generates a loss, namely the total amount of the fixed costs (that is to
> say, those which remain constant regardless of the quantities produced) and, at least,
> part of the variable costs relating to the unit produced.'[122]

4.142   **Reasoning difficult to understand.**   It is not easy to understand the reasons which led the ECJ to establish this standard, which is peculiar as a result of the technical reference it contains to various categories of costs. For the ECJ, low pricing is allowed up to a certain point, even where it is carried out by a dominant undertaking. Beyond that point, the practice becomes prohibited. That point is reached where, as a result of the price policy it has carried out, the dominant undertaking no longer recovers its fixed costs and a portion of the variable costs. The ECJ deems that, where such a pricing policy is adopted, the dominant undertaking may have only one purpose in mind, the elimination of actual or potential competition.

4.143   **Effect or intention.**   This position makes the ruling somehow fragile. The assessment made by the ECJ ultimately depends on a finding that the dominant undertaking is seeking to eliminate competition. However, there may be a discrepancy between the existence of an eliminatory effect or intention, and the actual cost-related standard which is set in the case law. *(a)* For instance, one may imagine situations where dominant undertakings eliminate competition through low prices but the standard fixed in *AKZO* is not fulfilled.[123] *(b)* One may also imagine situations where prices are set at a level which can be considered as predatory under the *AKZO* standard (below variable costs). Despite that very low level, the undertaking does not have any eliminatory intention.[124]

---

[122] Judgment of the ECJ, at [71].

[123] Where, for instance, a dominant undertaking enjoys significant economies of scale. That situation allows the undertaking to have very low costs. Using that situation, the undertaking sets the prices at the level of its costs. That level may be too low for competitors, which do not enjoy such economies of scale. In such a situation, the practice may be eliminatory. However, the standard fixed in *AKZO* is not fulfilled to the extent that the prices are not set below the variable cost.

[124] The practice may be intended, for instance, to attract customers to a new market. An illustration can be taken from the markets for internet services. For several years, activities were carried out at a loss. This was mainly made possible by buoyant stock markets, as employees and partners were paid with the shares of the undertakings concerned.

Not entirely satisfactory.   From the observations presented above, one can con-   **4.144**
clude that the standard fixed in *AKZO* cannot be found to be totally satisfactory.
Another difficulty with this standard is that it is not totally consistent with the
general developments which have taken place in the interpretation given to the
concept of abuse. In the analysis devoted to those developments it was emphasised
that the case law originally focused on the idea of an infringement. In that phase,
Article 82 EC was used to sanction behaviour adopted by dominant undertakings
and constituting an infringement. One of the infringements sanctioned by the
Commission and the European courts was the adoption of practices intended to
eliminate competitors. Various rulings were adopted in which this kind of behaviour was held to be abusive.[125]

Evolution.   The standard set in *AKZO* does not depart from that interpretation.   **4.145**
There are references in that standard to objective economic criteria. However, these
criteria are chosen for the indications they provide concerning a possible intention
by the dominant undertaking of eliminating one or several competitors.[126] The
ruling adopted by the ECJ in *AKZO* can thus be analysed as being part of the first
phase in the case law developed around the concept of abuse. That ruling gave
forewarning of further developments. It could indeed be expected that the
Commission and the European courts would, sooner or later, develop a standard,
which would be more in line with the new, more pervasive, orientations taken in
the case law.

New standard in the case law

Tetra Pak II.   That evolution took place in *Tetra Pak II*,[127] in which an under-   **4.146**
taking dominated several markets relating to liquid food[128] packaging. From an
enquiry carried out by the Commission, it appeared that the undertaking had
repeatedly sold packaging and machines at a loss. This behaviour was found to be
abusive by the Commission, a position which was successively confirmed, on this

---

[125] Several reasons may be cited as possible explanations for that position. *(a)* A willingness to
eliminate is a manifestation of violence in society. The violence is economic rather than physical—
but the difference of character is not sufficient to allow that kind of violence. *(b)* Competition has
to develop on the merits displayed by undertakings. In a case where an undertaking sells below cost,
the performance is not based on merits but rather on financial power. The undertaking which will
survive is the one which will be able to survive the longest in an environment where revenues are
below costs. However, that undertaking is not necessarily the one which would answer the needs of
customers in the most adequate fashion.
[126] Admittedly, the *AKZO* standard is not exclusively based on an interpretation of the intention
displayed by the dominant undertaking. It is already a compromise to the extent that it provides
objective criteria as a means of interpreting an intention which the undertaking is supposed to have.
In that context, the interpretation cannot be said to be exclusively subjective.
[127] Commission Decision (EEC) 92/163 relating to a proceeding pursuant to Article 86 of the
EEC Treaty (IV/31043—Tetra Pak II) [1991] OJ L72/1. Case T-83/91 *Tetra Pak International SA v
Commission* [1994] ECR II-755. Case C-333/94 P *Tetra Pak International SA v Commission* [1996]
ECR I-5951.   [128] In particular fresh milk and UHT milk.

point, by the CFI and ECJ. In many regards, *Tetra Pak II* appears as a transitional case. It is interesting because it builds on the existing case law, but goes beyond with the establishment of a new, larger standard. In this case the Commission and European courts were confronted with two sorts of predatory pricing-related practices.

4.147 **First category.** The first type of practice could be addressed using the standard established in *AKZO*. In some instances the dominant undertaking had indeed sold machinery and packages at prices which did not allow the recovery of the fixed costs or the whole of the variable costs. These prices could be deemed abusive under the *AKZO* standard.

> *Tetra Pak II.* 'The sale of Tetra Rex cartons constantly below not only their cost price but also their variable direct cost is sufficient evidence that the applicant pursued a policy of eviction.' 'By their scale and their very nature, the purpose of such losses, which cannot reflect any economic rationale other than ousting Elopak, was unquestionably to strengthen Tetra Pak's position on the markets in non-aseptic cartons where it already had a leading position as has already been found . . . , thereby weakening competition on those markets.'[129]

4.148 **Second category.** The situation was more complex for the second category of practice. The Commission and European courts realised that the undertaking had resorted to a variety of techniques intended to discourage and eliminate competitors. Faced with this determination to destroy competition, they felt that the standard established in *AKZO* was not sufficient. From the circumstances of the case it became obvious that low prices can destroy competition in circumstances other than those mentioned in *AKZO*.

4.149 **Non-variable costs.** In a move to extend the prohibition, the ECJ ruled that prices may be deemed abusive not only where prices are below variable costs, but also in other circumstances. The difficulty for the ECJ was to set a criterion, or several criteria, which could be used to establish the abusive character of the price. That criterion could no longer be found in a specific category of costs such as proposed in *AKZO*. In order to replace such an approach, the Commission and the European courts opted for a two-pronged test. *(a)* The first part of the test is that the price must not allow the dominant undertaking to recover the totality of the costs associated with the production and marketing of the good or service concerned. In other words, the transaction(s) must thus be carried out at a loss before one can speak of abusive pricing. *(b)* In a context where losses are incurred, prices can be said to be abusive where, and to the extent that, there exists 'a whole series of important and convergent factors [providing] evidence of the existence of an eliminatory intent'.[130]

---

[129] Judgment of the CFI, at [150].   [130] *Tetra Pak*, Judgment of the CFI, at [151].

AKZO. '[P]rices below average total costs, that is to say, fixed costs plus variable costs, but above average variable costs, must be regarded as abusive if they are determined as part of a plan for eliminating a competitor. Such prices can drive from the market undertakings which are perhaps as efficient as the dominant undertaking but which, because of their smaller financial resources, are incapable of withstanding the competition waged against them.'[131]

Analysis of the new standard

Line to follow.   Low prices can thus be said to be abusive where serious indica-   **4.150**
tors converge to establish the existence of an eliminatory, or predatory, intention. That case law can be analysed along the following lines. *(a)* In an attempt to show that prices are abusive, practitioners should refer to the indicators that are mentioned in the case at issue. *(b)* None of these indicators is sufficient to establish, on its own, the abusive character of a pricing policy. *(c)* Several of these indicators must as a result be used. There is no indication concerning a minimum number of indicators that would have to be used. *(d)* These indicators must converge and show that, in setting its tariffing policy, the undertaking indeed sought to eliminate potential or actual competitors.

A list of indicators.   The indicators mentioned in *Tetra Pak II* provide elements   **4.151**
which, according to the Commission and the European courts, can be used to establish the existence of an eliminatory intention. These indicators are mentioned briefly. They are further analysed in the following paragraphs.

(a) Duration of the practice.

(b) Difference between the price and average cost.

(c) Difference between the price set by the dominant undertaking and those applied by competitors.

(d) Pricing policies carried out by the undertaking in various territories.

(e) Absence of an offer coming from competitors.

(f) Documents establishing the desire by the dominant undertaking to eliminate competitors, or conquer some or all of its customers.

(g) Outcome of the practice—possibly an increase in the market share held by the dominant undertaking to the detriment of competitors.

The extent of the loss.   Among these various indicators, some are not distant   **4.152**
from the standard used in *AKZO*. It will be recalled that *AKZO* provides that prices are predatory where the undertaking cannot recover its fixed or variable

---

[131] *AKZO*, Judgment of the ECJ, at [72].

costs. The requirement seems less demanding in *Tetra Pak II*. In that new approach, the extent of the loss may be used as an indicator, but no minimum loss is required.[132] *Example.* In *Tetra Pak II*, some of the packaging had been sold at a price 11.4 per cent below the average cost. From that illustration, it can probably be concluded that a 10 per cent loss, or difference between the price and costs, provides an indication that the undertaking indeed intended to eliminate, through its pricing policy, one or several competitors.

4.153 **Comparison of pricing patterns (1).** Indications may also be obtained from a comparison between various pricing patterns. A first comparison may be carried out concerning the prices charged by the same dominant undertaking on the various (geographical) markets where it is present.[133] The comparison is then carried out as regards the prices that are charged by the undertaking in various areas for the acquisition of similar items. Pricing discrepancies may show that the undertaking is selling at a loss on some of these markets. The bigger the discrepancy, the greater the probability that a loss is incurred, and that prices are used as an eliminatory mechanism. *Example.* In *Tetra Pak II*, the prices charged in Italy for Tetra Rex boxes were 20 to 50 per cent lower than those applied by the same undertaking for identical products in the other Member States.

4.154 **Comparison of pricing patterns (2).** Another comparison may be made between the prices set by the dominant undertaking and those adopted by other, comparable, undertakings in similar situations.[134] Suppose that the competitors of a dominant undertaking sell goods or services at a price which is higher than the one charged by the latter undertaking. That difference in pricing pattern may indicate that the dominant undertaking is indeed selling at a loss and, hence, that it is using prices as a tool to eliminate competition. According to the case law, a significant discrepancy as compared to the prices charged by competitors indicates that the undertaking is not merely seeking to win an order. Had the order been the target, the practice would have been limited to what was strictly necessary to reach that objective. *Example.* In *Tetra Pak II*, the discrepancy amounted, in some instances, to 30 per cent.[135] In *AKZO*, the dominant undertaking offered prices that were 8.5, 19 and 30 per cent inferior to those charged by the competitor.[136]

4.155 **Documentary evidence.** The predatory character of a price may also be established with the assistance of traditional legal evidence such as documentation.[137] Where, for instance, an undertaking dominates a market and there is a claim that the prices charged by that undertaking are below cost, one possibility for competition

---

[132] That indicator is presented in the list above under *(b)*—difference between the price and the average cost.   [133] That indicator is presented in the list above under *(d)*.
[134] That indicator is presented in the list above under *(c)*.
[135] Judgment of the CFI, at [151].   [136] Judgment of the ECJ, at [108].
[137] That indicator is presented in the list above under *(f)*.

authorities to establish an eliminatory intention is to raid the offices of the under-taking concerned in search of evidence. The case will be deemed to be established if enquirers find e-mails, internal memos or other documents showing that the undertaking engaged in an eliminatory strategy.

Market-related evidence. Finally, some indicators relate to the conditions that 4.156 can be found on the relevant market. One of these indicators is the duration of the practice at stake.[138] In some instances, prices are set at a low level over a very short period. Such a practice may be explained by a willingness, on the part of the dom-inant undertaking, to attract customers, rather than to eliminate competition. If the practice lasts for a longer period, there is a chance that, through low pricing, the undertaking seeks to discourage entry in the long term and/or inflict serious damages on existing competitors. *Example.* In *AKZO*, predatory pricing lasted for three years. In *Tetra Pak II*, Tetra Rex packaging was sold below cost for six years. According to the case law, periods of such duration provide indications of a predatory intent.

Competing offers. Another indicator may be found in the existence, or 4.157 absence, of competing offers. There is no acceptable justification for the dom-inant undertaking to sell at a loss where there is no competitor on the market. If that behaviour is adopted in such a context, there can be only one reason, accord-ing to the Commission and the European courts, and that must be the desire to discourage entry. *Example.* In *AKZO*, the undertaking maintained prices at a very low level over a relatively long period. That behaviour could not be justified by the necessity of responding to a very low offer coming from a rival. There was indeed at that time no competitor on the relevant market. The only reason that could be imagined by the ECJ to explain this behaviour was that the dominant undertak-ing was seeking to discourage entry by showing to potential competitors that they would not make profits on the market.

Degree of success. A final indication is whether or not the practice appears to be 4.158 successful. Suppose that a dominant undertaking sells products at a loss, but com-petitors resist and/or new undertakings even enter the market. There might be no reason, in such a situation, for the authorities to intervene. Imagine on the con-trary that low pricing in effect leads to a situation where competitors are progres-sively eliminated and entry made impossible. The eliminatory effect can be established, and this provides an indicator, pursuant to the case law, concerning the eliminatory intention of the dominant undertaking. *Example.* In *Tetra Pak II*, evidence could be provided that the market for Tetra Rex boxes was expanding. The volume sold by the dominant undertaking increased, in line with that expan-sion. By contrast, the volume sold by the competitor diminished progressively.[139] The discrepancy between these patterns showed that the practice was successful.

---

[138] That indicator is presented in the list above under *(a)*.
[139] See judgment of the CFI, at [151].

Towards a new development of the case law?

4.159   Intention.   The case law examined above concerns prices set at a level which can be considered as predatory. It should be noticed that in the case law the focus is placed on the alleged intention by a dominant undertaking to eliminate competition. In other words, intent remains a central element in the current case law. This observation has already been made with respect to the standard fixed in *AKZO*. It has to be made again as regards *Tetra Pak II*. In that case also, the courts remain attached to the idea that a plan to hinder competition must be established.

4.160   A more objective interpretation.   The analysis is that maintaining such an important role for subjective considerations may not be in line with the trend that appeared, and evolved, in the last phase of the case law.[140] It is stated above that the case law is evolving towards a more objective interpretation of the concept of abuse. The consequence is that subjective considerations will in the future not remain an important factor in the demonstration that predatory pricing has been carried out. The case law can be expected to evolve towards a new stage in which low pricing is deemed abusive where *(a)* tariffs are below costs; *(b)* the practice is adopted by a dominant undertaking; and *(c)* it has, or may have, an effect on the existing degree of competition, which is already insufficient as a result of the dominance held by the undertaking. These criteria are in conformity with recent developments that have occurred in the case law concerning abusive practices. They correspond to a more objective interpretation of the concept, where the effect on competition is the central criterion for assessing a practice.[141] Given this likely evolution, it no longer appears appropriate to refer to the practice using the expression 'predatory pricing'. It seems more adequate to designate the behaviour as 'low pricing'.

---

[140] That idea is clearly expressed in the quotations presented above and which were taken from the two main cases. In *AKZO*, the setting of prices below the level of fixed and variable costs is chosen as a criterion for the establishment of predatory pricing because, as the ECJ says, that sort of practice can only be based on the wish to eliminate competition. A similar remark is made in *Tetra Pak II*, where the Commission and the European courts accept the production of evidence which tends to establish the existence of a plan to eliminate competition.

[141] That new stage would imply that a prohibition is imposed on dominant undertakings. Such a situation would correspond to the *second* pole/step that was identified in the case law (objective interpretation—imposition of prohibitions). It should not be excluded that a further development could occur, which would still bring the case law further away from the standard set in *AKZO* and *Tetra Pak II*. That further development would bring the standard closer to the *third* pole/step that was also examined (objective interpretation—imposition of obligations). In that third pole/step, obligations, rather than prohibitions, are imposed on dominant undertakings. In line with that latest development, it can be predicted that competition authorities, and courts will decide in the future that in some circumstances dominant undertakings must take positive measures to allow, and even foster, the development of competition. In that context, one should not exclude the possibility that obligations will be imposed on such undertakings to set prices at a level higher than costs, where this is necessary to ensure the emergence and/or the development of competition.

What should practitioners do?

What standard?   In the development of the case law, two standards were suc-   **4.161**
cessively established by the Commission and the European courts. The standards
set in *AKZO* and *Tetra Pak II* are not mutually exclusive. By adopting *Tetra Pak II*,
the Commission and the European courts have not repealed *AKZO*. The two
standards remain in existence. How can these standards be assessed as regards
the possibilities opened for practitioners? Their advantages and disadvantages are
examined in the following paragraphs.[142]

Below-variable-cost standard.   As was observed, the first standard, which was   **4.162**
established in *AKZO*, is that prices are abusive (predatory) where they do not
cover the fixed costs or the totality of the variable costs incurred by the dominant
undertaking. *Advantage*. That standard has one advantage—it is decisive. With
this standard, the case is won where challengers can point out the difference
existing between the price and the relevant costs. *Drawbacks*. This advantage is
offset by several difficulties. The first is that the test is economic in nature. This
may create issues for lawyers, who are not always adequately equipped to venture
into this territory. Another difficulty is that costs are not easy to prove. To establish that a dominant undertaking carried out predatory pricing, the demonstration must be made that prices are lower than variable costs. The difficulty is that
the demonstration must be based on accounts held by the dominant undertaking.
There is no guarantee that access can be obtained to these accounts or that they
will identify the costs associated with the relevant activity, etc.

Convergence-of-indicators standard.   The second standard was established in   **4.163**
Tetra Pak II and introduces the possibility of using various criteria as a method to
demonstrate the existence of a predatory activity. *Advantages*. This standard provides an answer to the difficulties mentioned above. The arguments to be presented
under *Tetra Pak II* are not necessarily economic in nature. They may for example be
based on documentary evidence. Practitioners are not restricted to the accounts
held by the opponent. Other forms of evidence, not based on accounts, may be
presented. An additional advantage is that the standard established in *Tetra Pak II*
is not clear-cut. Several criteria may be used. This creates a situation where practitioners may articulate all sorts of arguments, as long as they tend to show that an
eliminatory plan had been drawn up by the dominant undertaking. *Disadvantages*.
Not providing a clear-cut solution is not an advantage in all cases. Under the *Akzo*
standard, challengers could demonstrate in one step the predatory character of the
pricing policy (prices below variable costs). The situation is less certain where
several types of argument may be presented and room for assessment opened.

---

[142] The third standard which, it was announced, is likely to emerge, is not commented on in the
next paragraphs. The intention is to counsel practitioners about the current situation—even if
possible developments are to be taken into account.

4.164 **Strategy.** The strategy to be followed depends on the position to be defended, and on the objectives pursued by the dominant undertaking. *(a)* Where, for instance, a practitioner represents a new competitor excluded from a market as a result of predatory prices, that practitioner can use *Akzo* if the difference between the price and the costs can be established. If the evidence is less certain the practitioner may have to rely on *Tetra Pak II*. *(b)* Imagine that the practitioner is on the contrary defending a dominant undertaking. If *Tetra Pak II* is used, the practitioner will often be able to come forward with arguments in order to defend the behaviour adopted. It will more difficult to articulate a convincing defence on the basis of *Akzo*, but in that context the practitioner has control over the accounting data that may be demanded by the challenger.

4.165 **Relationship with discrimination.** Some difficulties encountered in establishing the existence of predation may be solved by examining the practice from a different angle. Low pricing may be covered, in some circumstances, by the prohibition directed against discriminatory practices. It is often more convenient for challengers to demonstrate that they have not been treated like other undertakings although they were placed in the same situation. The best advice for practitioners is probably to articulate an argument based on two counts (discrimination, predatory practices). As the existence of discrimination is easier to establish, practitioners are more inclined to put that claim to the fore, the other having only a subsidiary or accessory character.

4.166 **Evidence.** In all circumstances, undertakings seeking to demonstrate predation face difficulties regarding evidence. The first issue is who must demonstrate what, that is, how the burden of proof must be allocated. This question has been examined in the context of discriminatory practices, and the issue is no less important in the current context. To determine the allocation of proof, fundamental principles must be taken into account. *(a)* Pursuant to these principles, a claimant has to establish a basis for its claims. In the context of this book, this implies that the challenger[143] must establish the predatory character of the practice. *(b)* Another principle is that, to avoid losing the case, a defendant must demonstrate that the claim is incorrect, or that the behaviour can be justified. In the current context, this implies that, to defend itself, the dominant undertaking has two options: demonstrate that the facts provided by the challenger are incorrect or, where these facts cannot be denied, attempt to justify the behaviour alleged on the basis of reasoning that appears acceptable to competition authorities.

4.167 **Collaboration of the undertaking.** A second evidence-related issue is that evidence mainly depends on data to be provided by the dominant undertaking. In another section, the relationship is examined between general competition law

---

[143] The competition authority of the (actual or potential) competitor seeking to obtain redress against the undertaking.

and the NRF. An idea submitted there is that substantial obligations imposed by general competition law may be enforced with tools established under the NRF. In this context, this idea implies that predatory prices, which are prohibited under general competition law, may be established with tools introduced in the regulation, such as the constraint on undertakings with significant market power to provide explanations for the prices it sets and to publicise accounting information.

Create a serious impression.   An additional idea is that the burden of proof   **4.168** should be interpreted in the light of the context in which the parties are placed. For the reasons indicated above, it is often difficult for (actual or potential) competitors to establish the costs incurred by a dominant undertaking. As a result, it cannot be required from these challengers that they produce a clear analysis of those costs. The maximum which could be required from them is that they create a serious impression that prices are indeed below costs. An accurate relationship between costs and prices would not have to be established formally. It would be sufficient to produce a prima facie case of predatory behaviour. Such evidence may be provided through a comparison between the prices charged by the undertaking on different geographical markets. If the prices differ widely, there is a chance that those fixed at the lowest level may have a predatory character. Other indicators may then be used to reinforce that impression. Once the impression is established, the competition authority may be sufficiently convinced, and will probably start an investigation. At that stage, competitors are discharged from any further duty. The case is taken over by the competition authority, which has various enquiry tools allowing it to gather accounting information rather easily.

Relation with the NRF

Case law more developed.   An analysis is given above of the approach adopted   **4.169** by the Commission and the European courts with respect to predatory pricing in the case law based on general competition law. The case law has evolved in the direction of a prohibition where prices are below costs, provided the undertaking has a dominant position and it appears from circumstances that the intention, or possibly the effect, of the practice is the destruction or weakening of competition. On this point the case law seems more advanced than the NRF. There is in the NRF no provision which would prohibit, clearly and in a general manner, predatory pricing on the part of undertakings with significant market power.

Nuances.   This does not imply that no allusion can be found to predatory pric-   **4.170** ing in the NRF. *(a)* The NRF gives NRAs the power to impose on undertakings with significant market power an obligation to recover costs and base tariffs on costs. That power is generally interpreted in the light of the tendency of several undertakings with significant market power to set prices at a high level. There is no reason, however, to limit the scope of the provision to these situations.

The provision also implies that prohibitions may be imposed in situations where prices are set below costs. *(b)* One allusion is made, in the NRF, to the need for NRAs to monitor the price policies carried of dominant undertakings, in order to see whether excessive prices, or squeeze prices, are imposed.[144] *(c)* A reference is also made in the framework to a method used in the convergence-of-indicators standard (*Tetra Pak II*). Using this method, it is suggested that prices may be compared across undertakings or territories. An idea may be obtained, in this fashion, of the prices that may be considered normal for transactions in Europe.

> *Cost orientation.* 'A national regulatory authority may . . . impose obligations relating to cost recovery and price controls, including obligations for cost orientation of prices.'[145] 'National regulatory authorities shall take into account the investment made by the operator and allow him a reasonable rate of return on adequate capital employed.'[146] *Price squeeze.* 'Such an obligation may be appropriate when the operator concerned might . . . apply a price squeeze, to the detriment of end-users.'[147] *Price comparison.* 'In this regard national regulatory authorities may also take account of prices available in comparable competitive markets.'[148]

4.171 **Combined application of the two bodies of law.** This situation opens interesting perspectives for a combined application of the two bodies of the law. At the end of this chapter, the relationship existing between general competition law and the NRF is examined in a more systematic manner. It can already be stated that, although they are based on a similar approach, the rules contained in the two bodies are not always absolutely identical. This common approach may then serve as an argument to apply them jointly. This joint application could be envisaged as regards substantial provisions, as well as provisions dealing with procedural matters.

4.172 **Example 1.** Suppose that a practitioner wants to use the NRF against an undertaking which resorts to predatory pricing. In the NRF, that practitioner cannot find a clear-cut prohibition of this practice. The elements that are singled out in the paragraph above may be used as indications that the practice raises concerns under the framework. These indications may be interpreted with the assistance of general competition law in order to articulate a clear-cut prohibition.

4.173 **Example 2.** Imagine by contrast that the same practitioner wants to use general competition law against an undertaking using predatory pricing. This body of the law has limitations as regards procedural issues such as proof. There is no provision, in general competition law, stating, for instance, to what extent accounting information must be published by dominant undertaking. These limitations may be addressed with the assistance of the procedural provisions contained in the NRF. On the basis of general competition law, a claim may thus be made that

---

[144] As is examined later, predatory pricing may sometimes be used as part of a larger strategy to squeeze a competitor through low tariffs.   [145] Access Directive, Art 13(1).
[146] ibid, Art 13(1).   [147] ibid, Art 13(1).   [148] ibid, Art 13(2).

a dominant undertaking has unduly resorted to predatory pricing, and be based on evidence obtained through provisions contained in the NRF.

The peculiar situation of emerging markets

Frequent practice.   Low or predatory pricing appears to develop with particular   **4.174** strength on emerging markets. Often, this kind of technique is used by businesses to attract the attention of customers to a new product or service. Through low prices, businesses hope to induce customers to buy the items concerned, if only to try them out. The strategy is followed by all kinds of undertaking, independently of their market share. The practice is generally accepted as it makes possible, and indeed facilitates, the emergence of new activities (new markets are necessary for the economy to grow in general).

Difficulties.   Difficulties arise in various sets of circumstances. One such situation   **4.175** is where an undertaking dominates an emerging market. The authorities are then confronted with a dilemma. They can tolerate the pricing policy carried out by the dominant undertaking. The consequence may be that the market develops, as consumers are attracted by the low tariffs. However, the low prices may have as a consequence that potential competitors are kept out. In this kind of context, a lack of intervention may lead to a situation where competition does not develop.

An already dominant undertaking.   Another situation is where low prices are   **4.176** set on an emerging market by an undertaking which already dominates another market. This kind of behaviour typically takes place where an undertaking uses a dominance held on a given market as a tool to improve its position on the emerging activity. The situation on the two markets involved may be analysed as follows. *(a)* Through low prices, the undertaking attracts customers. *(b)* It is in a position to maintain prices at a low level, despite the losses incurred as a result. This capacity to resist losses is due to the high revenues collected by the undertaking on the market which it dominates.[149]

Regulation.   In the Framework Directive, the Parliament and Council observe   **4.177** that emerging markets may require special treatment. The situation is further analysed in the 2002 Competition Guidelines issued by the Commission. As mentioned in both instruments, an undertaking may acquire in relation to emerging activities a market share which is relatively high. This situation can be due to specific circumstances, such as the rapidity with which the undertaking has developed a presence on this market. Pursuant to the regulation, regulatory obligations

---

[149] On that dominated market, the undertaking can behave independently of possible reactions by other market participants. That position allows the undertaking to set prices at a level higher than what could be expected on a competitive market. These high prices make it possible for the undertaking to obtain substantial profits, which are used to compensate the losses incurred on the emerging market.

should not necessarily be imposed quickly in such a context. The suggestion made by the European legislator to NRAs is to avoid excessive intervention. Intervention would only become necessary, according to these institutions, in situations where the dominance held by the undertaking leads to market foreclosure.

> *Framework Directive.* 'Those guidelines will . . . address the issue of newly emerging markets, where de facto the market leader is likely to have a substantial market share but should not be subjected to inappropriate obligations.'[150]

> *Guidelines.* 'As far as emerging markets are concerned, . . . the Framework Directive notes that emerging markets, where *de facto* the market leader is likely to have a substantial market share, should not be subject to inappropriate *ex-ante* regulation. This is because premature imposition of *ex-ante* regulation may unduly influence the competitive conditions taking shape within a new and emerging market. At the same time, foreclosure of such emerging markets by the leading undertaking should be prevented. Without prejudice to the appropriateness of intervention by the competition authorities in individual cases, NRAs should ensure that they can fully justify any form of early, *ex-ante* intervention in an emerging market, in particular since they retain the ability to intervene at a later stage, in the context of the periodic reassessment of the relevant markets.'[151]

4.178 **General competition law.** The situation is a little different when it comes to the application of competition rules. In normal circumstances, these rules are not applied ex ante. They follow the emergence of a pattern of behaviour adopted by a dominant undertaking and deemed to be unacceptable. In the context of predatory pricing, the rule is, as stated above, that pricing below costs should be considered unacceptable where prices are set by dominant undertakings and form part of a plan carried out by that undertaking to hinder competition. Where it is accused of behaviour of this nature, the dominant undertaking may attempt to justify its attitude. It is, however, difficult to imagine the kind of argument that could be used in order to convince competition authorities that such behaviour should be accepted. In the above analysis concerning the concept of abuse, it was submitted that the main criterion in assessing a given practice is the fear that an already insufficient degree of competition[152] might be further impaired as a result of behaviour adopted by a dominant undertaking. In this context, any behaviour—however appropriate it may be from a business and ethical point of view—is considered as abusive as soon as it is adopted by a dominant undertaking and implies a further restriction of competition.

4.179 **Competition impaired.** Low pricing satisfies these criteria almost by its nature. *(a)* As a result of low pricing, competition is impaired further. The impairment is not necessarily direct or immediate. But it would be doubtful that the practice has no effect whatsoever on the situation of any single actual or potential competitor.

---

[150] Framework Directive, Preamble, recital 27.
[151] 2002 Guidelines on market analysis and significant market power, para 32.
[152] As a result of the existence of a dominant position on the relevant market.

(b) Authorities generally accept that customers make a selection from among businesses as a result of competition. The difficulty with predatory pricing is that this selection does not take place on the merits, but that undertakings may be eliminated, or entry impeded, even though competitors may have been more efficient than the dominant undertaking once the market matured.

Mobile telephony.   An example is the low prices that were charged by mobile   **4.180** operators when mobile telephony started to develop a decade ago. At that time, mobile markets were mainly occupied in each country by a national operator. When the markets were opened to competition, these operators set relatively low tariffs. Their purpose was to capture the market, ie attract a significant proportion of potential customers. As these customers would already have a supplier, it would be more difficult for competitors to attract them, that is, to enter the market and develop, over a reasonable timeframe, a market share sufficient to reimburse entry-related expenses.[153]

Deutsche Telekom.   Another example is the behaviour adopted by the German   **4.181** operator Deutsche Telekom (DT) when competition was introduced on the market for fixed telephony. Just before the market was opened, the undertaking announced a cut in tariffs for business telephony. The purpose was to deter other undertakings from entering the market. The undertaking had realised that business telephony services were essential for its financial stability. That market indeed provided the resources necessary to cover gaps appearing in other segments of activity. To keep these resources, the undertaking was determined to impede, or hinder, entry, even if the strategy implied that losses had to be incurred over a certain period.[154]

Rarely a good business strategy.   In closing this section it is important to   **4.182** emphasise that low pricing, as defined above, is not a good business strategy, and that dominant undertakings should refrain from using it, not only for legal or regulatory reasons, but also because this is rarely in their interest. Low pricing is likely to qualify quickly as an abuse where dominant undertakings are involved and competition is affected. This derives from the current stage of the case law, and it is predicted that the case law will expand in the future. A second reason is that low pricing, even when it is not predatory, is not without cost. It may admittedly imply significant expenses for competitors which the dominant undertaking

---

[153] Being first on a market is often a decisive advantage. Under normal circumstances, it is easier for an undertaking to resist competition when it has acquired a significant position on the market. In such a situation, the undertaking serves as the reference for customers. As a result, customers spontaneously turn to it when they wish to receive the product or service concerned. To that advantage must be added the reluctance of customers to change supplier. Any change in supplier indeed implies transactions costs—such as the time necessary to gather information, etc.

[154] The behaviour was deemed abusive by the Commission. See [1996] Competition Policy Newsletter 26.

seeks to discourage or eliminate. The purpose is clearly to push such competitors into a situation in which they face costs higher than revenues. But low pricing also implies significant losses for the dominant undertaking itself.

4.183 Customers.   It is sometimes submitted that predatory pricing benefits customers. That view must, at least, be qualified. Authorities are aware of the advantages that low pricing has for customers. For that reason, they have decided not to prohibit the practice in all circumstances. The danger only comes where low pricing has an effect on existing or potential competition in a situation where the state of competition is already impaired to an unacceptable degree (existence of a dominant position). Suppose that the authorities decide never to intervene with respect to low pricing (such an attitude could be motivated by populist ideas, that low prices benefit customers and that these benefits should inspire public policy). The result of such an attitude would be that customers would indeed enjoy benefits—they would pay little for what they wanted. That benefit would however be limited in time. In the longer term, low pricing impedes the emergence and development of an environment where competition is durable.[155]

One case concerning electronic communications

4.184 *Wanadoo.*   Before concluding this section, it should be noted that the European Commission recently applied the case law on predatory prices in a case concerning electronic communications—*Wanadoo*.[156] In this case the Commission considered that the relevant market was retail access to the internet through ADSL technology. In its decision the Commission noted that Wanadoo, a subsidiary of France Telecom, was charging low prices contrary to the case law. *(a)* Wanadoo was charging prices below variable costs. This behaviour lasted between 1999 and August 2001. As stated, such behaviour is prohibited *per se*. *(b)* After that period, prices

---

[155] An argument is sometimes presented to criticise the view that low pricing is negative in the long term. That argument is as follows. Suppose that a dominant undertaking sets prices at a low level. As soon as it raises prices, the possibility exists that potential competitors will enter the market. There is thus a pressure on the dominant undertaking to maintain prices at a very low level. Predatory pricing, in that context, would not have negative consequences. That presentation has drawbacks. *(a)* First, it would not be possible for the dominant undertaking to maintain prices below costs over a long period. Should that be the case, the practice would mean that the dominant undertaking is using resources obtained from another market in order to subsidise the relevant activities. However, that cannot be accepted as it would imply that customers of one market are treated less favourably than customers on another. *(b)* In the argument presented at the beginning of this note, the dominant undertaking is described as being under a constraint to maintain prices at a low level to impede entry. However, a situation of that nature implies that the undertaking cannot be considered as dominant. As a reminder, an undertaking is dominant when it is in a position to behave independently of other market participants. In the situation at issue, that undertaking cannot act independently as it remains under a constraint to set prices at a low level.

[156] The decision has not yet been published. Information on the case is currently available only through the press release published by the Commission, and it is accordingly not possible to assess the circumstances of the case with great accuracy. For the text of the press release, see IP/03/1025, accessible on *http://europa.eu.int*.

were set at a level higher than variable costs but lower than average costs. According to the case law on predatory pricing, the latter practice is prohibited where there are signs that, through the application of these prices, the undertaking was attempting to eliminate one or more competitors. In the case at issue, documents were found by the Commission, stating that the undertaking intended to pursue selling at a loss over a significant period. The intention was indeed to pre-empt the emerging market for retail access to the internet in order to make subsequent entry by competitors more difficult. As a result of the practice, Wanadoo's market share rose from 46 per cent to 72 per cent within a few months. Once the practice had ceased as a result of the commencement of the Commission's enquiry, prices increased rapidly by 30 per cent. As competitors were entering the market, the level of activity multiplied by a factor of five and continued to increase thereafter.

(3) Excessive prices

The practice

Relation to costs.   In the previous section, situations were examined where **4.185** dominant undertakings charge prices below costs in an attempt to hinder or eliminate competition. That behaviour normally takes place on an individual market, that is, a market for a given good or product. On that market, the dominant undertakings set prices at a level which, they hope, cannot be matched, in the short term or on a longer period, by actual or potential competitors. Another practice can now be examined, where dominant undertakings set prices at the other end of the spectrum—at a rather high level. As was done for predatory pricing, high prices can be defined as tariffs which cannot be found, in normal circumstances, on markets that are organised on a competitive basis.[157]

Various situations

(a) Business-to-consumer.   Several situations may be examined where high **4.186** prices may be charged by dominant undertakings. A first situation is where high prices are charged to consumers. The issue in this situation is that, as prices are set at a high level, the dominant undertaking is confiscating from consumers a proportion of the resources they would have allocated in another manner had they been allowed to pay a normal price. The underlying argument is that the prices would have been set at a lower level if the relevant market had been organised on

---

[157] In the previous section, it was submitted that predatory prices cannot be found on competitive markets—at least in normal circumstances. That observation is based on the idea that, in principle, undertakings strive to make profits. Losses are somehow prohibited—if they are excessive they imply that the company must be declared bankrupt. (The capitalist system differs in this regard from state-controlled economies, where losses were tolerated.) In that context, predatory pricing appears as a deviation from the commercial standards that may be expected from undertakings competing in the normal way. A similar approach can be used with respect to high tariffs, which would not be encountered on a market organised on a competitive basis.

a competitive basis. The difference between the actual price and that normal competitive price is confiscated by the dominant undertaking.

4.187 **Not in this chapter.** That first situation, and the issue which is associated with it, are not analysed in this chapter but in the chapter dealing with universal service. The NRF indeed contains rules ensuring that the tariffs charged to users by dominant undertakings remain within reasonable limits.

4.188 **(b) Business-to-business.** A second type of situation is where a dominant undertaking charges excessive prices to other businesses. In this business-to-business scenario, two sub-situations may be distinguished. The difference between them is that, in one case, the dominant undertaking is present only on one market, whereas it carries out activities on two markets in the second.

4.189 **Dominant undertaking present on one market.** In some instances, undertakings limit their activities to one market. In the scenario envisaged, the dominant undertaking charges excessive prices on the only market on which it carries out an activity. That practice raises concerns, because the (business) customers which obtain their supply on that market pay a higher tariff than the one they would have presumably had to pay on a competitive market. These concerns (allocation of resources) are identical to those examined in connection with business-to-consumer situations, with the difference that the customers are businesses and not consumers.

4.190 **Dominant undertaking present on two markets.** In other instances, dominant undertakings are present on two—or even more—markets. A practice which is sometimes observed is that they charge excessive prices on one of these markets. In most cases, that practice is intended to support its activities on a second market. For instance, the undertaking seeks high revenues on the market which it dominates with the intention of subsidising, with those revenues, activities which are performed in another market where its position is in danger. Another possibility is that the dominant undertaking may impose excessive tariffs on a first market where the goods or services obtained on that market are necessary for the performance of activities on a second market. The dominance held means that the undertakings present on the second market, on which the dominant undertaking is also present, have to obtain their supplies from the dominant undertaking on the first market. The dominant undertaking may then increase the costs of its competitors on the second market, by raising the prices for access to the necessary resources or facilities on the first market.

4.191 **Analysis.** The behaviour described in the previous paragraphs may be analysed as an abuse of a dominant position under Article 82 EC. From the facts, it indeed appears that behaviour is adopted by a dominant undertaking and that that behaviour has an effect on competition. The conditions are thus fulfilled to consider that an abuse is committed. As stated above, the case law now imposes on dominant undertakings a prohibition on further restraining competition, and even an obligation to co-operate actively in order to support the development of competition.

Variation.   A situation which is close, without being exactly identical, is where   **4.192** the dominant undertaking is present on one market and charges excessive prices on that market in order to support the activities of an allied undertaking on a second market. A difference exists with regard to the situations examined above because the undertaking is only present on one market. The similarity is however that competition is hindered on a second market as a result of behaviour adopted by the dominant undertaking on the first market. The hindrance, in this case, comes from the fact that competition does not develop 'on the merits' on the second market. On that second market, an undertaking receives preferential treatment which has the consequence that a competitor may be eliminated in spite of being organised more efficiently.

Analysis of the case law

Excessive prices.   In this section, the analysis is limited to excessive prices under   **4.193** general competition law. The situation where prices are combined on various markets in order to harm competitors is examined in the next section.

A frequent practice.   Before examining the case law it should be noted that,   **4.194** according to the Commission, excessive prices are likely to be imposed by dominant undertakings on electronic communications markets. This may be expected to be the case, the Commission states, where customers have no alternative. The typical situation is where service providers seek access to a network and have no other option than to negotiate with a former national operator. That operator, which is still dominant in most circumstances, may be tempted to exploit that situation by imposing prices higher than those which could be found in a normal competitive situation.

> *1998 Competition Guidelines, para 105.* 'Pricing problems in connection with access for service providers to a dominant operator's facilities will often revolve around excessively high prices.' 'In the absence of another viable alternative to the facility to which access is being sought by service providers, the dominant or monopolistic operator may be inclined to charge excessive prices.'

A reasonable relation with costs.   Pursuant to general competition law, prices   **4.195** cannot be set at a level which seriously exceeds costs. The rule is formulated in *Ahmed Saaed Flugreisen*.[158] That case, which concerned tariffs charged by airline companies in Germany, was submitted to the ECJ in a preliminary reference. In the ruling, the ECJ provides indications about the criteria to be considered in

---

[158] Case 66/86 *Ahmed Saeed Flugreisen v Zentrale zur Bekämpfung unlauteren Wehbewerbs eV* [1989] ECR 803.

order to conclude that a price is excessive. Two principles may be distinguished. *(a)* According to the ECJ, prices must be set at a level permitting the recovery of the costs incurred in performing the activity. If prices are lower than costs, the undertaking faces bankruptcy. Among the costs, account has to be taken of a satisfactory dividend for shareholders. *(b)* A second principle is that prices should not outweigh costs. This results from the pressure of competition, which forces undertakings to attract customers. One means of attracting customers is to offer prices that are as low as possible, taking into account the costs.[159]

> *Ahmed Saaed Flugreisen.* '[T]ariffs must be reasonably related to the long-term fully allo-
> cated costs of the air carrier, while taking into account the needs of consumers, the need
> for a satisfactory return on capital, the competitive market situation, including the fares
> of the other air carriers operating on the route, and the need to prevent dumping.'[160]

4.196 **Economic value.** In other cases, the European courts have proposed other criteria in order to assess the potentially excessive character of a price. One of these criteria was the relationship with the economic value of the good or service concerned. That criterion was proposed in *United Brands*.[161] In that case, the dominant undertaking imported products (bananas) from third countries. These products were sold to distributors, which had to organise the ripening and subsequent marketing. The focus was placed, in the case, on the price at which the products were sold by the importer to the distributor. These prices were not identical for all transactions, but rather depended upon the Member State for which the cargo was intended.[162] The strategy carried out by the undertaking was to determine, in advance, the revenues that the distributor could be expected to obtain on the specific geographical market where it was to operate. An import price was then established.[163] The practice was adopted as a mechanism to ensure

---

[159] The case under issue arose as a result of the alleged high prices charged by airline companies for flights originating on German territory. As a result of these high tariffs, travel agencies had derived a system where they purchased airline tickets in other Member States. These tickets concerned flights originating from the territory where they were purchased—with a transit stop in Germany where clients could embark. These agencies were sued in Germany. In the national proceeding, a preliminary reference was directed to the ECJ involving Art 82. Tariffs were fixed by a public authority, but a contention was that they had been influenced by a dominant undertaking. The ideas expressed by the ECJ, and in particular the indications provided by the ECJ about criteria to be used, are based on a Council Directive concerning tariffs to be set by national authorities.

[160] At [43].

[161] Commission Decision (EEC) 76/353 relating to a procedure under Art 86 of the EEC Treaty (IV/26699—Chiquita) [1975] OJ L95/1. See also Case 27/76 *United Brands Co v Commission* [1978] ECR 207.

[162] In some instances, the prices varied, according to the Commission, by 30 to 50%, and even 100%. Prices were the only items to vary, because the other elements of the transaction did not change according to the destination (quantity supplied, quality of the products, trade mark under which the products were marketed, etc).

[163] Above the costs some margin was left to the distributors as profit. That margin did not need to be substantial. The undertaking indeed had a dominant position. The distributors could not seek a similar supply from another undertaking. Any attempts to enter discussions with competitors were severely repressed.

that the products would be sold at the highest possible price, given the financial capability of each market for which the products were meant.[164] This behaviour by the dominant undertaking was deemed abusive by the Commission. In the Commission's view the prices were exaggerated compared to the economic value of the products, and the undertaking was sanctioned on the basis of Article 82 EC.

United Brands. 'Prices charged . . . in Germany . . . , Denmark, the Netherlands . . . [,Belgium and Luxembourg] are considerably higher, sometimes by as much as 100%, than the prices charged to customers in Ireland, and accordingly produce a very substantial profit. UBC's [United Brand's] prices are excessive in relation to the economic value of the product supplied.'[165]

Two standards. It is difficult to determine whether there are differences **4.197** between the expressions used by the European courts in their discussion concerning the reasonableness of prices. The reference to costs in order to establish the reasonable character of prices seems rather clear. By contrast, the reference to an economic value appears less certain. That expression could refer to the price which would have been set if the relevant market had been organised on a competitive basis. The reason to choose that interpretation is that the assessment which is made of the value of a good or service is left to markets in normal circumstances, ie where markets function properly. If that interpretation were accepted it would mean that two standards may be used to assess prices: *(a)* the difference as compared to the costs incurred to produce the good/service, and *(b)* the difference as compared to the value that the good/service would have on a competitive market.

Is there a difference? There is no indication in the case law as to which standard **4.198** is preferable. Practitioners are thus invited to refer to the standard which, they consider, would suit their argument better. They should however be aware that the two standards may be rather close to each other. As noted above, prices tend towards costs in a competitive environment. In other words, competition brings prices closer to costs. At some point, undertakings no longer make real profits. The prices at which the good or service is charged, and which represents the value of that good/service on a competitive market, then corresponds to the costs.

General Motors. This case[166] provides an interesting example of the confusion **4.199** that seems to exist between the two expressions in general competition law. It concerned the sale of General Motors vehicles in various Member States of the European Union. In each of these countries, the sale of vehicles was subject to an examination and declaration whereby the producer, or its representative, certified that the vehicle conformed with the model for which an authorisation had been granted by the public authority. In that case, the territory concerned was Belgium and the undertaking authorised to make such an examination and statement was

---

[164] Decision of the Commission, 14, col B and 15, col A.   [165] ibid, 15, col B, in fine.
[166] Case 26/75 *General Motors Continental NV v Commission* [1975] ECR 1367.

the Belgian subsidiary of General Motors. In order to carry out the examination and deliver a certificate, the company charged a price to the individuals or businesses buying the car(s). That price was high. A legal proceeding was started against the company before a national court. A preliminary reference was addressed to the ECJ. In its ruling, the ECJ stated that the price charged to the customer(s) was considerably higher than the cost incurred by the undertaking in examining and certifying the vehicles. It also declared that the difference between the price and the economic value of the service was excessive.[167]

> *General Motors.* 'Such an abuse might lie, *inter alia*, in the imposition of a price which is excessive in relation to the economic value of the service provided, and which has the effect of curbing parallel imports by neutralizing the possibly more favourable level of prices applying in other sales areas in the community, or by leading to unfair trade in the sense of Article [82](2) (a).'[168]

Evidence

4.200 Similar difficulties. Difficulties related to evidence have been mentioned regarding predatory prices. They are similar where a demonstration has to be made that prices are excessively high. *(a)* The first issue is to determine who has to establish the excessive character of the price. As was pointed out in the context of predatory pricing, that element must be established by the party claiming that the price is excessive. The identity of that party depends on the procedure. If the case is being examined by a competition authority, that authority has to establish the excessive character of the price. If the case is brought before a court, the demonstration has to be made by the party initiating the proceedings. *(b)* The second issue is what has to be demonstrated. The two applicable standards—if they can be differentiated—are examined above. Both imply a comparison between the price charged by the undertaking and the costs incurred by the undertaking and/or the price which would have been offered in a competitive environment.

4.201 Comparing prices. Whatever the standard chosen, a question arises as to what elements may be used in a comparison intended to establish the excessive character of a price. The decision adopted by the Commission in *United Brands* contains interesting suggestions on this point. *(a)* A first comparison was made by the Commission between the prices charged by the dominant undertaking in several

---

[167] Ultimately, the ECJ found that Art 82 EC had not been violated. Several reasons were given by the ECJ, to justify and excuse the behaviour of the undertaking. One of them was that the practice had not lasted long.

[168] At [12]. Other cases can be mentioned in connection with the jurisprudence on excessive prices. See, in particular, Case 24/67 *Parke, Davis & Co v Probel* [1968] ECR 81; Case 78-70 *Deutsche Grammophon Gesellschaft Gmbh v Metro SB Grossmarkte Gmbh & Co KG* [1971] ECR 487; Case 30/87 *Bodson v Pompes funèbres des régions libérées* [1988] ECR 2479; Joined Cases 110, 241 & 242/88 *Lucazeau v Société des Auteurs, Compositeurs et Editeurs de Musique (SACEM)* [1989] ECR 2811; Case 395/87 *Ministère Public v Tournier* [1989] ECR 2521.

European countries. In that comparison, the Commission opposed the highest and lowest prices. In the Commission's view, the lowest price provided indications concerning the costs incurred by the undertaking. It could not supposed, indeed, that the undertaking would sell at a loss. The difference with the highest price was striking, and that price was then deemed excessive. *(b)* Another comparison was between the prices charged by the dominant undertaking for the sale of its products under various trademarks (the undertaking had a policy where products were sold under various trademarks[169]). In the course of that comparison, it was again observed that wide differences existed. *(c)* A final comparison was between the prices charged by the dominant undertakings and those charged by competitors. For the competition, the prices charged by competitors provided evidence about the price which could be obtained on a competitive market. As these prices were lower than those charged by the dominant undertaking, one could conclude that these latter prices were, in some instances, excessive.

Commission's reasoning. In all these comparisons, the Commission adopted a similar method. It first sought to establish the difference existing between the prices charged in the contexts mentioned. It then enquired about the possibility for the dominant undertaking of providing a justification explaining the differences that had been observed. In the absence of an acceptable justification, the Commission concluded that the prices were excessive. **4.202**

Justifications put forward by the undertaking. From the decision, it appears that the dominant undertaking had attempted to justify some of the prices which were suspected of being excessive by the Commission. These justifications were however dismissed. The Commission makes clear that only certain justifications may be accepted. For instance, higher prices could be explained by higher costs for the distribution of the products in certain areas.[170] Similarly, differences in prices could have been justified by variations in the quality of the products sold under different trademarks, or in certain geographical areas. None of these justifications was however deemed to be grounded in the case examined, as the products were of a similar quality and no significant differences could be found in the costs incurred in the sale of the products in different areas. **4.203**

Interesting method. The criteria and method proposed by the Commission to establish excessive prices open interesting possibilities for practitioners. They imply the use of data which are not complex and may be found easily (it is on the other hand not easy to compare prices charged by various undertakings, possibly on different territories). No calculation has to be made on the basis of costs. Hence, no sensitive information has to be extracted from the dominant undertaking. **4.204**

---

[169] This is a mechanism which is sometimes used in order to create apparent competition, and choice, on the relevant market, whereas the various brands are in effect managed by the same undertaking. [170] For instance transportation costs.

4.205 **Negative attitude of the ECJ.** In spite of these advantages, the method proposed by the Commission was rejected by the ECJ. The decision taken by the Commission was challenged before the ECJ, which ruled that prices cannot be found excessive on the basis of comparisons such as those made by the Commission. *(a)* The ECJ found that the lowest price charged by a dominant undertaking does not necessarily provide information about the costs incurred by the undertaking. One cannot exclude, in the view of the ECJ, that products may have been sold at a loss. *(b)* A similar conclusion was reached regarding the difference between the prices charged by the dominant undertaking for products sold under different trademarks. That difference was not negligible (30 to 40 per cent), but could be explained by other factors (different images associated with the various trademarks, etc). *(c)* As for the difference between the prices charged by the dominant undertaking and those charged by the competitors (7 per cent), it was not sufficient to establish the existence of an abuse on the part of the dominant undertaking.

4.206 **A more qualified position.** From the judgment issued by the ECJ it can be concluded that no comparison may be made to establish excessive prices. The position defended here is that that conclusion should be nuanced. This opinion is based on several arguments. *(a)* The ruling issued in *United Brands* is rather outdated. Since that time the ECJ has accepted that comparisons can indeed be used as evidence showing that predatory prices have been fixed. There is no reason that the case law could not be extended to excessive prices. *(b)* In other rulings concerning excessive prices, the ECJ has accepted that prices could be compared and that differences could be interpreted as providing an indication that prices may be excessive.

4.207 **Convergence of indicators.** In *Parke*,[171] for instance, a particular medicine was protected by intellectual property rights in the Netherlands. The undertaking enjoying the protection was opposing the importation of the medicine from another European country, where it was sold at a lower price. In that situation, the ECJ observed that there was a significant difference between the price charged on the protected territory and that available in other geographical areas. That difference, the ECJ ruled, provided evidence that the undertaking was abusing its dominant position. The ECJ, however, emphasised that no final conclusion could be drawn as to the existence of an excessive price on the basis of that single element. This appears to indicate that price differences provide an indication that prices may be excessive, but that that indication must be substantiated by other elements. If this interpretation is correct, the position would be similar to that adopted for predatory pricing, where predatory prices must be established using a series of convergent indicators. It however remains to be seen, in this specific context, what other indicators can be used to establish that prices are excessive.

---

[171] Case 24/67 *Parke, Davis & Co v Probel* [1968] ECR 81.

Parke. 'Although the sale price of the protected product may be regarded as a factor to be taken into account in determining the possible existence of an abuse, a higher price for the patented product as compared with the unpatented product does not necessarily constitute an abuse.'[172]

Prima facie case. In other rulings, the ECJ goes further and states that price **4.208** differences provide a prima facie case of abusive conduct. The undertaking charging abusive prices must justify the level at which the tariffs are set. In the absence of a plausible, and acceptable, justification, the conduct is deemed to be in violation of Article 82 EC. That position is illustrated in various cases. The position adopted by the ECJ in that case law is so important that three of the cases are presented here.

Metro. The first case is *Metro,*[173] where an undertaking manufactured sound **4.209** appliances in Germany. The undertaking was also responsible for the distribution of these appliances on German territory. The appliances were marketed by subsidiaries in other European countries. There was a significant difference between the price charged by the undertaking in Germany and the price charged by subsidiaries in the other Member States. Taking advantage of that difference, intermediaries started importing appliances from the Member States where the prices were lower, onto German territory where they were higher. The undertaking attempted to oppose the move and a case arose before a national court. A question was addressed to the ECJ to determine whether or not the imposition of a high price by the manufacturer on German soil could be deemed abusive. The ECJ reiterated the position set out above. *(a)* The existence of a price difference does not establish per se the abusive character of the tariff policy. *(b)* The behaviour may however be deemed abusive if the difference is significant and the undertaking is unable to present an objective justification.

> *Metro.* 'For it to fall within article [82] a dominant position must further be abused. The difference between the controlled price and the price of the product reimported from another member state does not necessarily suffice to disclose such an abuse; it may however, if unjustified by any objective criteria and if it is particularly marked, be a determining factor in such abuse.'[174]

Bodson. *Bodson*[175] provides a second illustration concerning situations where **4.210** price differences can be accepted as evidence of the abusive character of particular conduct. An exclusive right had been granted to an undertaking in various municipalities for the organisation of funerals. There was a contention that the price charged by that undertaking was excessive. A preliminary reference was addressed to the ECJ; in its ruling the Court suggested that a comparison should be made between the prices charged by the dominant undertaking and those applied by other undertakings on other, similar, geographical markets.[176]

---

[172] At [72].   [173] See n 168 above.   [174] At [19].   [175] See n 168 above.

[176] The suggestion was made to the national court which was to carry out the comparison. The ECJ could not make the comparison itself as the preliminary reference contained no relevant

Bodson. '[I]t must be possible to make a comparison between the prices charged by the group of undertakings which hold concessions and prices charged elsewhere. Such a comparison could provide a basis for assessing whether or not the prices charged by the concession holders are fair.'[177]

4.211 *Lucazeau.* The last case, *Lucazeau*,[178] provides interesting indications about price comparisons. According to that ruling, price comparisons may be used to establish excessive prices. They must however be credible, ie they must relate to comparable circumstances. Once the evidence is presented, the burden of proof is reversed. It is then for the dominant undertaking to present acceptable reasons in an attempt to justify the level of prices. The case concerned fees claimed by an undertaking managing copyrights for musical works on French territory. That undertaking held a dominant position on the relevant market. It was alleged by certain discotheques that the fees were excessive. As part of their case, the discotheques presented evidence showing that the fees were significantly higher than those charged for similar usage by similar undertakings in other European countries. In the ruling, the ECJ stated that the difference existing between these various prices could indeed be used as an indication that excessive tariffs were imposed. In such a circumstance, it was for the undertaking in question to justify its behaviour. That behaviour would be deemed abusive in the absence of a convincing objective justification.

> *Lucazeau.* 'When an undertaking holding a dominant position imposes scales of fees for its services which are appreciably higher than those charged in other Member States and where a comparison of the fee levels has been made on a consistent basis, that difference must be regarded as indicative of an abuse of a dominant position. In such a case it is for the undertaking in question to justify the difference by reference to objective dissimilarities between the situation in the Member State concerned and the situation prevailing in all the other Member States.'[179]

What should practitioners do?

4.212 **Summary.** From these cases, it can be concluded that prices can be deemed abusive where there are differences between the prices charged for similar items by various undertakings or, even, by the same undertaking, on different territories. That finding can be questioned by the dominant undertaking, but it is then for that undertaking to establish the reasonable character of the price. That allocation

---

data. The ruling however makes it clear that evidence can be presented about the excessive character of prices through comparisons on prices charged by the dominant undertaking and other companies. The importance of price comparison was thus acknowledged in the judgment, even if the method was not implemented by the ECJ itself.

[177] At [31].   [178] See n 168 above.

[179] At [25]. According to the ECJ, the comparison must be made 'on a consistent basis'. In the case at issue, the parties had not compared identical situations. Thus they had ignored the influence of climatic conditions, social habits and long-term practice as regards entry to discotheques. The ECJ was however satisfied, because the comparison had been made on a systematic basis.

of tasks between the parties has important consequences for practitioners. Practitioners representing challengers must establish a prime facie case of abusive conduct. They can do so using the price comparisons mentioned above. The burden of proof is then placed on the dominant undertaking, which must present objective justifications. Such justifications may be found in a possible difference in the costs incurred by the undertaking(s) concerned in relation to different markets. It can also be related to differences in quality, although these differences are often reflected in costs and the justification thus comes back to a difference in costs.

Justification by the dominant undertaking. An implication of the case law **4.213** is that the justification presented by the dominant undertaking must be based on accounting information. The only possibility for a dominant undertaking to justify its pricing policy is to show that a reasonable relationship exists between prices and costs. To that effect, that undertaking must submit reliable, and convincing, accounting data. In the absence of such a demonstration, the finding will be that excessive prices have indeed been charged.

Allocation of tasks. That allocation of tasks between parties (challengers must **4.214** establish a difference in prices, the defendant must show a reasonable relationship with costs) corresponds to the position adopted by the Commission in the 1991 Competition Guidelines. In these guidelines, the Commission states that prices are abusive where indications are available and a prima facie case can be established to that effect. The burden of proof is then reversed, and the dominant undertaking has to justify its behaviour on the basis of costs.

> *1991 Competition Guidelines.* '[I]f in a specific case there are substantial elements converging in indicating the existence of an abusive . . . pricing, the Commission could establish a presumption of such [abusive] . . . pricing. An appropriate separate accounting system could be important in order to counter this presumption.'[180]

A proper accounting system. This allocation of tasks seems appropriate, as the **4.215** dominant undertaking has access to accounting data. It is logical that, in such a situation, the undertaking which has access to information may be compelled to produce that information to demonstrate whether or not an abuse has been committed. So far the Commission has been reluctant to impose accounting requirements in the case law applying Article 82 EC. Requirements of that nature have been introduced in the liberalisation directives, as well as in some decisions adopted on the basis of Article 81(3) EC (anti-competitive agreements). The Commission has however refrained from imposing general accounting obligations on dominant firms. That situation could change, as the Commission has repeatedly announced that such obligations could be introduced.

---

[180] 1991 Competition Guidelines, para 108. In this extract, the Commission explicitly refers to predatory prices as well as to cross-subsidisation. The statement can also be used, however, for excessive pricing.

1991 Competition Guidelines. 'An appropriate accounting system approach should permit the identification and allocation of all costs between the activities which they support. In this system all products and services should bear proportionally all the relevant costs . . . It should enable the production of recorded figures which can be verified by accountants.'[181] *1998 Competition Guidelines.* 'It is necessary for the Commission to determine what the actual costs for the relevant product are. Appropriate cost allocation is therefore fundamental to determining whether a price is excessive. For example, where a company is engaged in a number of activities, it will be necessary to allocate relevant costs to the various activities, together with an appropriate contribution towards common costs. It may also be appropriate for the Commission to determine the proper cost allocation methodology where this is a subject of dispute.'[182]

4.216 **Link with discrimination.** As was stated in relation to predatory pricing, it may be easier for practitioners to demonstrate the existence of discrimination rather than to establish that a price is excessive. As an illustration, reference may be made to *General Motors*, a case examined above in connection with a claim that the Belgian subsidiary of the producer was charging excessive fees for the service provided. That service can be described as follows: the undertaking examined the conformity of vehicles purchased by buyers with the model agreed by the national authorities and, where appropriate, issued a declaration certifying conformity.

4.217 *General Motors* **revisited.** The case was argued as one where excessive prices were charged. Another basis could however be used. By looking closely at the facts, it will be realised that the case concerns the more important problem of market partitioning. Two kinds of GM cars were sold on the Belgian market: *(a)* cars for which the subsidiary of the producer served as distributor and *(b)* cars coming from distributors located in other European countries and imported onto Belgian territory. The service concerned (examination of the conformity and issuance of a certificate where appropriate) was to be provided for the two sorts of cars. Where it was acting as a distributor (ie selling its own cars), the GM subsidiary performed the service without asking an extra fee from the purchaser. The tariff for the service was included in the price for the car. A different attitude was adopted where the company had to examine and certify GM cars coming from other European countries. As it was not selling these cars, a fee was charged for the service. The difficulty arose because the company was using that occasion as an opportunity to compensate the differences existing between the prices at which cars were sold in Belgium and in other European countries. For the sale of cars, the Belgian subsidiary was in fact charging prices higher than those available in other countries. Intermediaries were using that opportunity to buy abroad and import into Belgium. These cars had to be presented for examination and certification of conformity. The GM subsidiary was using that occasion to compensate the price

---

[181] 1991 Competition Guidelines, para 106, al 3.   [182] Para 107.

differences by imposing a fee which was excessive in view of the service provided and of the fee incorporated for that service in the sale prices for its own cars. In other words, GM was using the fee as a mechanism to hinder parallel import of goods.[183]

Relationship with regulation. From the considerations set out above, it can be **4.218** deduced that the case law on excessive prices does not depart from the position adopted by the Parliament and Council in the NRF. There is in both contexts a strong emphasis on the necessity of ensuring that prices are oriented towards costs.

(4) Combination of prices (price squeeze)

Types of practice. The above sections analyse price-related practices encoun- **4.219** tered on markets dominated by one or several undertakings (predatory and excessive pricing). Some of the cases examined in connection with these practices involve two or more markets rather than a single one. In this section, emphasis is placed on situations where competitors can be squeezed as a result of a strategy implemented by dominant undertakings and implying prices set on various markets. As will be observed, some examples examined in this section are analogous to situations already examined. It is however important to present them in a separate section in order to emphasise the complex pricing strategies applied by dominant undertakings.

Leading case

National Carbonising. The leading case for price combination is *National* **4.220** *Carbonising.*[184] In that case, a company had a quasi-monopoly (97 per cent) on the production of raw coal. After production, the product was transferred to intermediaries for processing and distribution to individual or industrial users. The producer had a subsidiary on that intermediary market. There was vertical integration between the two companies, the producer being present on the primary market, which it dominated, and the intermediary being present on the secondary market. The two companies were part of the same group. Apart from these two companies, there was on the secondary market an independent, and isolated, intermediary. That intermediary depended upon the dominant producer for its supply of raw coal, which it processed and sold on the market for intermediaries.

---

[183] Market partitioning is a form of discrimination. The undertaking in effect charged different fees for the service, whether the car was sold by itself or imported from another Member State.

[184] The decision issued by the Commission in *National Carbonising* is not available in English. Readers may consult the text of the decision in a language that was then officially used within the European Communities. For the French version of the decision, see: décision 76/185/CECA de la Commission, du 29 octobre 1975, adoptant des measures provisoires concernant la National Coal Board, la National Smokeless Fuels Ltd et la National Carbonising Company Ltd [1976] OJ L35/6.

| Primary market—Production of raw coal | Dominant undertaking | |
| Secondary market—Processing and distribution | Subsidiary | Independent intermediary |

4.221 **Price strategy.** At a point in time the dominant producer adopted a strategy whereby prices were increased on the primary market while prices were maintained at a constant level, without change, on the secondary market. The result of the practice was not the same for the parties present.

4.222 **Consequence for the independent intermediary.** The result, for the independent intermediary, was disastrous. It saw an increase in the costs incurred to obtain the product which it processed and distributed. However, that increase could not be carried over to the customers by increasing the price of delivery after processing. An increase in the prices charged to customers would have meant that those customers would have sought their supply from another intermediary. For the independent intermediary, costs thus increased but revenues remained stable. There was no alternative as regards supply, because the dominant producer accounted for 97 per cent of the coal available in the region. Other producers could not increase production to supply the independent intermediary, because there was no excess capacity. No coal could be obtained in another country, given the high transportation costs that importation would have implied.

4.223 **Consequence for the dominant undertaking.** The analysis was different for the group, or undertaking, consisting of the dominant producer and the related intermediary. As stated, these entities were companies integrated in a single group. They thus formed a single undertaking. As a consequence, the situation of that undertaking could not be examined with mere reference to one of the markets involved. The consequence of the strategy had to be examined taking into account the two markets involved. From that perspective, it must be stressed that the revenues obtained by the group depended upon the final price paid by customers on the second market. The level at which the price for the supply of the raw product was set did not really influence the overall economic result obtained by the group. It was merely a transfer price, which could fluctuate without influencing the overall results realised by the undertaking.[185]

---

[185] The increase in transfer price may have corresponded to an increase in the cost incurred by the undertaking to produce raw coal. As will be stated, there is apparently no reason to prevent a dominant undertaking from increasing prices where costs become higher. The difficulty was that the dominant undertaking did not adapt the prices set on the secondary market in order to reflect that cost increase. Normal economic behaviour, when costs increase, is to adapt the final price, particularly where the undertaking is a dominant undertaking and the absence of adaptation in the final price has an effect on competition.

Attitude of the Commission.   The Commission considered that the dominant **4.224**
undertaking had abused its dominant position. In the view of the Commission,
an undertaking dominating a primary market must refrain from adopting behaviour which may hinder competition on a secondary market. In such a context it
must set prices at a level permitting a reasonably efficient competitor to carry out
activities under normal conditions.

> *National Carbonising.*   '[A]n undertaking which occupies a dominant position on
> the market of a raw material . . . , which thereby is in a position to determine freely
> the price at which it supplies goods or services to independent companies manufac-
> turing derived products . . . and which itself manufactures identical derived pro-
> ducts in competition with those supplied by those independent manufacturers,
> could be found to abuse its dominant position where the behaviour adopted by such
> undertaking would have the effect of eliminating the competition coming from
> these independent producers on the market for derived products'; 'an undertaking in
> a situation of dominant position could face an obligation to lower its prices so as to
> leave a reasonably efficient manufacturer of derived products a margin which is
> sufficient to allow it to subsist in the long term'.[186]

1998 Competition Guidelines.   The situation described above regarding **4.225**
National Carbonising is not isolated. According to the 1998 Competition
Guidelines it could occur frequently on electronic communications markets. In
these guidelines the Commission refers to a situation where a dominant operator
could charge high tariffs for access to infrastructure, thereby making it impossible
for independent service providers to carry out activities without losses on downstream markets.

> *1998 Competition Guidelines, para 117.* 'Where the operator is dominant in the
> product or services market, a price squeeze could constitute an abuse. A price
> squeeze could be demonstrated by showing that the dominant company's own
> downstream operations could not trade profitably on the basis of the upstream price
> charged to its competitors by the upstream operating arm of the dominant com-
> pany. A loss-making downstream arm could be hidden if the dominant operator has
> allocated costs to its access operations which should properly be allocated to the
> downstream operations, or has otherwise improperly determined the transfer prices
> within the organisation.'

Further case law

British Sugar.   The second case concerns another product, although the structure **4.226**
of the markets involved remains the same. That case concerns a primary market—
the production of raw sugar—dominated by an undertaking. That product is
processed and distributed by intermediaries on a secondary market. On that
secondary market there are several intermediaries including a subsidiary of the
undertaking dominating the primary market.

---

[186] Decision of the Commission, 7, col b (translation by the authors).

| Primary market—Production of raw sugar | Dominant undertaking | — |
| Secondary market—Processing and distribution | Subsidiary | Independent intermediary |

4.227 **Price strategy.** At some point the dominant undertaking decided to eliminate an independent intermediary.[187] To that effect, prices for the sale of sugar were decreased on the retail market. They were however maintained at a similar level on the market for raw materials. In other words, prices decreased on the secondary market but remained stable on the primary market. Again, the result produced by that strategy varied with the situation of the parties involved.

4.228 **Effect on the independent intermediary.** As prices decreased on the retail market, the independent company had to adapt its behaviour and reduce prices in the same proportion. In the absence of such a measure, customers would have turned to the subsidiary of the dominant undertaking, which offered better conditions. The consequence for the independent intermediary was that revenues decreased. However, costs did not decrease, as prices remained stable on the market on which the raw product was purchased. With diminishing revenues and constant costs, the independent intermediary was squeezed.

4.229 **Consequence for the dominant undertaking.** As was stated in the case above, the situation was different for the dominant undertaking. Admittedly, the final revenues obtained by that undertaking decreased on the secondary market. The prices were however set on that market at a level which allowed the undertaking to remain profitable overall. The difference between the two undertakings was due to what constituted costs for them. For the independent intermediary, the costs were the price charged by the dominant undertaking for the delivery of supplies. For the dominant undertaking, the real cost was not the transfer price, ie the price at which the raw sugar was sold to the subsidiary in charge of distributing the product, but rather the production cost, ie the cost incurred by the undertaking on the primary market for the production of sugar. That cost was lower than that incurred by the independent intermediary. As a result, the price could be set at a lower level on the secondary market without the undertaking undergoing a loss.[188]

---

[187] The move was apparently motivated by the intention, announced by that intermediary, of developing an activity which the undertaking wanted to develop itself.

[188] There is an uncertainty in the case whether the operations of the dominant undertaking remained profitable on the whole. In the extract presented below, the Commission refers to the insufficient level of the prices charged on the secondary market, to cover the 'prices' of industrial sugar. It is not sure whether the Commission thereby means that the prices charged on the secondary market were lower than the prices charged on the primary market, or whether the Commission means that these 'secondary prices' were even lower than the costs of producing industrial sugar. (The price at which industrial sugar was sold on the primary market hopefully reflected the costs incurred to produce sugar, but were normally higher than these costs.) In the case that the 'secondary

Comparison between the cases

Structure of the cases.   Both cases have similar structures. In the two situations, **4.230**
(a) an undertaking dominates a primary market; *(b)* that market involves a
product (it could also be a service) that is necessary for activities on a secondary
market; *(c)* the independent undertaking is present on that secondary market and
depends on supply from the dominant undertaking to carry out activities on that
secondary market; *(d)* the dominant undertaking uses price policies in order to
squeeze the independent intermediary—and reinforce its own position—on the
secondary market; *(e)* the practice would have been successful had no authority
intervened.

Strategies used by the undertakings.   The strategies used by the dominant **4.231**
undertakings are different in the two cases, but they are carried out in order to
produce the same result and were inspired by the same objective. In one case
(*National Carbonising*) the prices are increased on the primary market and are left
constant on the secondary. In the other (*British Sugar*) the prices are decreased on
the secondary market but are left constant on the primary market.

	National Carbonising	British Sugar
Primary market (production)	Price increase	(Prices left constant)
Secondary market (processing, distribution)	(Prices left constant)	Price decrease

Attitude adopted by the competition authority.   The attitude adopted by the **4.232**
competition authority was the same in both instances. In the Commission's view,
a dominant undertaking cannot adopt a price strategy which leads to the elimination of a competitor. It must practise a price policy which allows a reasonably efficient competitor to perform activities in normal circumstances. A dominant
undertaking may increase prices on a primary market, for instance where it faces
increased costs. But it should then increase prices on the secondary market in a
similar proportion (*National Carbonising*). Similarly, dominant undertakings
may decrease prices on the secondary market, but should then decrease prices on
the first market also (*British Sugar*). In the two sets of circumstances the dominant
undertaking must take into account the consequences of its behaviour on competitors. It must adapt its price policy to ensure that the price strategy which is
carried out does not have a negative impact on competition (which is already
insufficient as a result of dominance).

> *1998 Competition Guidelines, para 118.* '[A] price squeeze could . . . be demon-
> strated by showing that the margin between the price charged to competitors on the

---

prices' were lower than costs, the practice could have been challenged on the basis of case law
concerning predatory pricing.

downstream market (including the dominant company's own downstream operations, if any) for access and the price which the network operator charges in the downstream market is insufficient to allow a reasonably efficient service provider in the downstream market to obtain a normal profit (unless the dominant company can show that its downstream operation is exceptionally efficient).'

4.233   **Relationships with other cases.**   *(a) National Carbonising* can be analysed on the basis of the case law prohibiting excessive prices. When that case law was analysed, two sets of circumstances were distinguished—excessive prices charged to final consumers and excessive prices charged to businesses. As concerns the second category,[189] it was submitted that undertakings cannot charge high prices where they undermine the ability of customers to carry out activities on a second market. *(b) British Sugar* can be analysed in connection with the case law on predatory pricing or discrimination. In that case, prices are set on the secondary market at a very low level. Apparently, that level is lower than the prices charged on the primary market for the sale of raw sugar. In a shorter, and more striking sentence, one can say that the 'secondary price' is inferior to the 'primary price'. That 'primary price' corresponds to the cost,[190] as regards the independent intermediary. One can thus say that the price is lower than to the cost, as regards that undertaking. The situation is different, however, for the dominant undertaking. For that undertaking, the 'primary price' is not the cost for the activity developed on the secondary market. That cost is in fact the cost incurred by the undertaking for the production and sale of the raw sugar. There is thus a possibility that the undertaking may not have operated at a loss.

One case concerning electronic communications

4.234   *Deutsche Telekom.*   The European Commission has adopted a decision in a case concerning a price squeeze in electronic communications,[191] in relation to the tariffs set by Deutsche Telekom for access to the local loop. In its decision the Commission distinguishes between access for final users and access for intermediaries. Only the latter is considered in the decision as forming the relevant market. In the Commission's view, Deutsche Telekom has a dominant position on that market. An abuse can be observed to the extent that Deutsche Telekom applies charges for wholesale access which make it impossible for service providers to perform their activities without incurring a loss.

> *Deutsche Telekom.* 'A margin squeeze exists if the charges to be paid to DT for wholesale access, taking monthly charges and one-off charges together, are so expensive that competitors are forced to charge their end-users prices higher than the prices

---

[189] The first category is analysed in Chapter 5 dealing with universal service, as well as in Chapter 7 dealing with specific issues including the protection of users.

[190] In fact, to a part of that cost, because the independent undertaking must face other expenses to process and distribute the product.

[191] Commission Decision (EC) 2003/707 relating to a proceeding under Art 82 of the EC Treaty (Case COMP/C-1/37.451, 37.578, 37.579—Deutsche Telekom AG) [2003] OJ L263/9.

DT charges its own end-users for similar services. If wholesale charges are higher than retail charges, DT's competitors, even if they are at least as efficient as DT, can never make a profit, because on top of the wholesale charges they pay to DT they also have other costs such as marketing, billing, debt collection, etc.'[192] 'In the case of the local network access at issue here, there is an abusive margin squeeze if the difference between the retail prices charged by a dominant undertaking and the wholesale prices it charges its competitors for comparable services is negative, or insufficient to cover the product-specific costs to the dominant operator of providing its own retail services on the downstream market.'[193] 'An insufficient spread between a vertically integrated dominant operator's wholesale and retail charges constitutes anticompetitive conduct especially where other providers are excluded from competition on the downstream market even if they are at least as efficient as the established operator.'[194]

(5) Cross-subsidisation

Description of the mechanism.   Cross-subsidies are operations whereby funds **4.235** obtained on one market are transferred to another one. It appears as a technique where activities are not financed on the basis of revenues acquired on the relevant market, but rather with funds channelled onto that market from another activity. There has been much commotion around cross-subsidies in the electronic communications sector because of the possibility that, through that mechanism, powerful undertakings, and, in particular, former national operators, may hinder the development of competitors by subsidising new activities with funds coming from markets where they still enjoy dominance. In general, the rules concerning cross-subsidisation have the consequence for dominant undertakings and their management of the division into markets of the activities carried out. Activities are divided into markets for the application of competition rules. These markets serve as units within which the degree of competition must be assessed to determine where the environment is conducive to proper market functioning. In that assessment exercise, the position of undertakings is evaluated on each of these markets separately. Undertakings representing a threat to competition because they have acquired, or are bound to acquire, market power, need to take into account that division in their organisation, and in the way they structure activities.

Various situations

The 1991 Competition Guidelines.   In the 1991 Competition Guidelines, the **4.236** Commission takes a clear position against the practice whereby, in the electronic communications sector, dominant undertakings channel funds between markets. Two situations are envisaged. They are analysed below, and the case law developed by the European courts on the subject is also examined.

(a) Undertakings with public prerogatives.   One situation is where the dominant **4.237** undertaking enjoys prerogatives granted by a public authority. These prerogatives

---

[192] Para 102.   [193] Para 107.   [194] Para 108.

may take the form of special and/or exclusive rights.[195] On the market where they enjoy these prerogatives, these undertakings are protected from competition (monopoly) or have advantages which allow them to compete under better conditions than their rivals. As a result of that protection or advantage, these undertakings may obtain substantial revenues. A danger arises where these revenues are used to support the position of the undertakings on other markets, where the undertaking is weaker in the absence of public prerogatives.

4.238 **Attitude of the Commission.**   Cross-subsidisation is generally deemed abusive by the Commission for the reasons set out below. That position is based on various ideas that may be formulated in the following manner. *(a)* In a competitive system, undertakings are to compete 'on the merits', ie on the basis of their capability in providing a satisfactory response to the needs of customers. As a result of cross-subsidisation, the undertakings present on the markets where funds are channelled do not compete on the merits. The dominant undertaking has an advantage which may permit it to maintain and even improve its position despite the presence of—in some cases—more efficient competitors. *(b)* Cross-subsidisation is conduct which, when adopted by a dominant undertaking, may lead to competition being further reduced, in a context where the degree of competition was already insufficient as a result of the existence of dominance. *(c)* The customers on the first market, where the public prerogatives are situated, pay for the goods/services on that first market. As a proportion of the revenues are channelled, they also pay for a proportion of the goods/services sold on the market where the channelled revenues are used. As a result, they are forced to contribute to costs for which they receive no return.

> 1991 *Competition Guidelines*. 'Subsidizing activities under competition, whether concerning services or equipment, by allocating their costs to monopoly activities, however, is likely to distort competition in violation of Article [82] . . . It could amount to an abuse by an undertaking holding a dominant position within the Community. Moreover, users of activities under monopoly have to bear unrelated costs for the provision of these activities. Cross-subsidization can also exist between monopoly provision and equipment manufacturing and sale. Cross-subsidization can be carried out through: (i) funding the operation of the activities in question with capital remunerated substantially below the market rate; (ii) providing for those activities premises, equipment, experts and/or services with a remuneration substantially lower than the market price.'[196]

4.239 **(b) Dominant undertakings.**   A second situation is where undertakings dominate one market and use funds coming from that market to sustain other activities

---

[195] As a result of regulation, special and exclusive rights have been eliminated from electronic communications markets. The only situations where public prerogatives may be encountered is where undertakings enjoy these prerogatives on other, non-electronic communications, markets, which have not been regulated in the same fashion. See the Consolidated Directive, Art 2.

[196] 1991 Competition Guidelines, para 104.

where competition is harsher. The situation is similar, with the difference that the funds are not acquired as a result of a public prerogative but rather through factual dominance. This difference may appear accessory, but has some relevance. *(a)* In one scenario (public prerogatives), funds are acquired through a prerogative granted by public authorities. Principles of administrative law then apply. One principle is that equality must be respected. Equality is however infringed if competition develops on an unequal basis on the market where the funds are channelled. Furthermore, the channelling of funds implies that a public prerogative is being put to a use that was not intended by the grantor.[197] *(b)* In the second scenario, there is no public intervention. An undertaking dominates a market and the issue is whether it can use as it wishes the revenues acquired on the market where that activity is performed.

Attitude of the Commission.   Despite these differences, no distinction is drawn   **4.240** by the Commission between the two scenarios. In both cases, cross-subsidisation is analysed as abusive conduct and prohibited. For the Commission, the main argument against the practice is that cross-subsidisation impedes competition 'on the merits'. With cross-subsidisation, the dominant undertaking uses on a market an advantage which is not related to that market. This creates a risk that competitors may be eliminated, even where they provide a better response to these needs.

> *1991 Competition Guidelines.* 'Cross-subsidization means that an undertaking allocates all or part of the costs of its activity in one product or geographic market to its activity in another product or geographic market. Under certain circumstances, cross-subsidization in telecommunications could distort competition, ie lead to beating other competitors with offers which are made possible not by efficiency and performance but by artificial means such as subsidies. Avoiding cross-subsidization leading to unfair competition is crucial for the development of service provision and equipment supply.'[198]

General case law on abuse

The concept of abuse.   The position described in the paragraphs above seems   **4.241** compatible, and even consistent, with the definition given in the case law to the concept of abuse. Pursuant to that case law, a dominant undertaking must refrain from any behaviour which may reduce further the degree of existing competition. In the most recent cases, that prohibition leads to a positive obligation whereby dominant undertakings must adopt conduct—however irrational that behaviour might seem in the light of traditional business behaviour—which may help competition, and competitors, to develop to a level deemed satisfactory by competition authorities. These principles call for a prohibition on cross-subsidisation. As was observed while analysing the 1991 Competition Guidelines, cross-subsidisation

---

[197] A prerogative is normally granted by a public authority in order to realise a specific end. An exclusive right, for instance, is granted, in most cases, to ensure a concentration of demand on one provider, in a situation where public service obligations make the activity unprofitable should the activity be carried out by several undertakings.   [198] 1991 Competition Guidelines, para 102.

allows dominant undertakings to reduce competition on adjacent markets. Competitors are driven out of business for reasons independent of their ability to service users adequately. Users from the first market are forced to subsidise, against their will, goods/services offered on the second market.

Specific cases on cross-subsidisation

4.242 **Three cases.** One difficulty is that there is little case law dealing specifically with cross-subsidisation; further, these cases do not necessarily correspond altogether to the line set out above in connection with the general case law concerning the concept of abuse. So far the issue has been addressed in three cases, which are examined below. The current state of the case law is then discussed in an attempt to provide some clarity concerning the dangers that dominant undertakings may face if they resort to this practice, together with the possibilities opened to their challengers in case they want to oppose such behaviour.

4.243 **(a) Cross-subsidies involving public funds.** In *Ferring*,[199] the ECJ ruled that an undertaking may not use funds provided by public authorities in relation to activities other than those for which the funds were provided. In other words, cross-subsidies are not allowed where funds have a public origin. The case is analysed thoroughly in Chapter 5 dealing with universal service. At this stage it is sufficient to mention that it concerns the distribution of medicines in France, where that activity is carried out by laboratories and wholesalers. Specific obligations are imposed on wholesalers in the interests of public service.[200] In consideration of these obligations, wholesalers were granted a tax exemption. The issue was whether that exemption was legitimate under general competition law.

4.244 **Correspondence with costs.** In their submissions, laboratories claimed that they suffered discrimination as they had to pay a tax which wholesalers did not. The claim was dismissed by the ECJ. In the Court's view the exemption granted to wholesalers had to be accepted to the extent that it did not exceed the costs represented by the public service obligations imposed on the undertakings concerned. These obligations have a cost and that cost may be compensated by a tax exemption as long as the two amounts (costs—tax exemption) correspond with each other.

> *Ferring.* '[P]rovided that the tax on direct sales imposed on pharmaceutical laboratories corresponds to the additional costs actually incurred by wholesale distributors in discharging their public service obligations, not assessing wholesale distributors to the tax may be regarded as compensation for the services they provide and hence

---

[199] Case C-53/00 *Ferring SA v Agence centrale des organismes de sécurité sociale (ACOSS)* [2001] I-9067.
[200] As part of these obligations, the wholesalers are to make sure that they can deliver in a very short time a list of medicines upon request (security of supply). That obligation, and the others which are attached hereto, imply costs on wholesalers—costs which are additional to those incurred by laboratories.

not State aid within the meaning of Article 92 of the Treaty. Moreover, provided there is the necessary equivalence between the exemption and the additional costs incurred, wholesale distributors will not be enjoying any real advantage for the purposes of Article 92(1) of the Treaty because the only effect of the tax will be to put distributors and laboratories on an equal competitive footing.'[201]

Prohibition of cross-subsidies. A consequence of the ruling is that no excess, **4.245** in terms of tax exemption, is allowed. This aspect of the ruling is important for the treatment of cross-subsidies. Where, for instance, wholesalers receive an exemption exceeding the costs incurred in fulfilling their public service obligations, that excess cannot be used to cover costs other than those associated with the obligations. From the judgment, one can thus consider that, under general competition law, public funds must be used for the purpose for which they were granted. Any use outside of the market concerned—or indeed within that market but not related to the obligations in question—is prohibited.

(b) Funds paid by other undertakings. In another case (*TNT*[202]), the ECJ **4.246** addressed the use of revenues obtained through an obligation imposed on other companies to contribute to given costs. The case concerned the national postal service in Italy. At the time when the ruling was issued, the national postal entity (Poste Italiane) enjoyed an exclusive right for the provision of basic postal services. These services were provided at a loss. To cover that loss, a subsidy was paid by the Italian Government. An obligation was also imposed by the Italian legislation on other undertakings present on more lucrative postal markets to contribute to the costs of the services. A preliminary reference was addressed to the ECJ concerning the legality of the obligation to contribute as imposed by the Italian legislation. In its ruling, the ECJ considered that the mechanism was legal as long as three conditions were satisfied. *(a)* The sums paid to the national entity could not exceed the costs resulting from the public service obligations imposed on that entity.[203] *(b)* The entity receiving these sums (subsidy paid by the Government and contributions paid by the other undertakings) had to be subject to a similar obligation, that is, to pay a contribution on the basis of the revenues obtained on these other, more lucrative, markets.[204] *(c)* The entity could not use these sums in order to subsidise activities other than those which were to be financed through them. The entity could not use on other markets the funds which were granted in order to carry out the tasks associated with the public service. Cross-subsidies were prohibited, in the case of funds coming from the subsidy paid by the Government or from contributions paid by other market participants.

TNT [a] 'Article [86](2) of the Treaty does not allow the total proceeds from postal dues of the kind at issue in the main proceedings, which are paid by economic operators

---

[201] At [27].   [202] Case C-340/99 *TNT Traco SpA v Poste Italiane SpA* [2001] ECR I-4109.
[203] On this point, the case law is similar to the ruling issued in *Ferring* (n 199 above).
[204] The market would have been organised, otherwise, on a discriminatory basis.

supplying an express mail service not forming part of the universal service, to exceed the amount necessary to offset any losses which may be incurred in the operation of the universal postal service by the undertaking responsible therefore.' *[b]* 'In those circumstances, the undertaking responsible for the universal postal service must also be required, when itself supplying an express mail service not forming part of that service, to pay the postal dues.' *[c]* 'It must also ensure that neither all nor part of the costs of its express mail service are subsidised by the universal service, lest charges for the universal service and, consequently, the potential losses of that service be improperly increased.'[205]

4.247 **(c) Funds coming from reserved activities.** The last case concerns the German national postal operator Deutsche Post (DP).[205a] At the time the case was decided, that undertaking still enjoyed prerogatives on reserved markets. On these markets, the undertaking in fact enjoyed a monopoly. It also received from the German Government a subsidy to finance losses incurred in the performance of these public service-related activities. DP was active on other markets and attempted to acquire a company (DHL) on one of those markets. The operation was challenged by a competitor (UPS), which argued that the acquisition was financed with funds coming from reserved markets. These funds had two origins. On the one hand, the undertaking received a subsidy from the Government. That subsidy was supposed to cover costs relating to public service obligation but was used partly, the contention was, to finance the acquisition. On the other hand, as UPS stated, DP enjoyed protection against competition on the market where it had a public monopoly. Given the protection, the undertaking was in a position to acquire substantial revenues which were channelled to another market through the acquisition.

4.248 **Procedure.** The case was examined by the Commission on the first occasion in connection with the authorisation that had to be given for the concentration. A complaint was thereafter addressed by the competitor (UPS) to the Commission, which then had to deal with the matter specifically. In these two procedures the Commission stated that an undertaking must be allowed to use funds coming from reserved markets to finance acquisitions. According to the Commission, the operation could be prohibited only if, and to the extent, that it would create, or reinforce, a dominant position on the market where the acquisition takes place.

4.249 **Confirmation in substance.** The position adopted by the Commission was examined, and confirmed, in substance, by the CFI. According to the CFI, a dominant undertaking may use funds deriving from reserved markets in order to finance acquisitions on other markets which are subject to competition. Cross-subsidies are thus allowed using funds obtained on markets dominated by the undertaking concerned. This general position is however nuanced by the CFI. *(a)* For the CFI, cross-subsidies must be prohibited where the funds channelled have

---

[205] At [57] and [58].   [205a] See footnote 210.

been obtained through anti-competitive behaviour (excessive or discriminatory prices, other abusive practices). *(b)* As a result of the acquisition, the activities carried out by DP had been diversified. The challenger (UPS) feared that diversification would be used by the undertaking to transfer funds in the course of business from the reserved market to the new market.[206] The CFI ruled that cross-subsidisation would be prohibited for future activities carried out by DP, because DP had committed itself, during the procedure leading to the authorisation of the acquisition not to resort to that practice in the future.

> *Cross subsidy allowed to finance acquisitions.* '[T]he mere fact that it [Deutsche Post] used . . . funds to acquire joint control of an undertaking active in a neighbouring market open to competition does not in itself, even if the source of those funds was the reserved market, raise any problem from the standpoint of the competition rules and cannot therefore constitute an infringement of Article 82 EC.'[207] *Prohibition when the funds come from abusive conduct.* '[T]he acquisition of a holding . . . could raise problems in the light of the Community competition rules where the funds used by the undertaking holding the monopoly derived from excessive or discriminatory prices or from other unfair practices in its reserved market.'[208] *Future cross subsidy prohibited as a result of a commitment made by the undertaking.* '[I]t is clear from the undertaking given by Deutsche Post to the Commission . . . that Deutsche Post is prohibited from engaging in any such cross-subsidisation, with the result that, for the purposes of that case, that question is academic. Consequently, if, in the future, the application were able to prove such cross-subsidisation on the part of Deutsche Post, it would be entitled to apply to the Commission or, by virtue of the direct effect of Article 82 EC, to the competent national court for appropriate penalties to be imposed.'

Origin of the funds

(a) Funds or advantages from a public source.   In the three cases examined **4.250** above, two deal with particular situations where an undertaking holds funds coming from a public authority or from other undertakings (and paid, in the latter case, as part of an obligation to finance public service obligations). In that context, the issue raised by cross-subsidisation is specific. That issue is not whether an undertaking may use market power to obtain advantages on other markets. It is rather whether funds granted by a public authority for a particular purpose may be used to another end. The answer given to that question must be negative, as public funds may not be used outside of the use for which they were granted (see above).

Comparison with the guidelines.   That solution is no different from the posi- **4.251** tion adopted by the Commission in the 1991 Competition Guidelines. As stated above, the guidelines prohibit cross-subsidisation where an undertaking has

---

[206] As a result of the acquisition of DHL by DP, UPS had become a challenger of DP on the parcel market. UPS feared that its position would be undermined, if DP was to carry out its parcel activities with resources coming from the reserved market.   [207] At [61].
[208] At [55].

a special or exclusive right on a given market. The idea underlying that prohibition is the same as that examined earlier, ie the necessity of limiting public advantages to markets to which they relate. As the case law and the guidelines converge, it can be concluded that there is, as of now, a prohibition in general competition law on the misappropriation of funds or other advantages from a public source[209] by using them on markets which were not contemplated by the authority when the prerogative or advantage was granted.

4.252 **(b) Funds resulting from dominance.** The second situation does not involve public funds or advantages. It is more common, to the extent that dominant undertakings are often tempted to support their activities on markets where they face competition with revenues obtained on markets where they enjoy relative protection. These practices are prohibited under the 1991 Competition Guidelines. By contrast, it is not certain that the practice has ever been addressed by the Commission, the CFI or the ECJ in a specific case. Several cases are examined above in connection with cross-subsidisation; none of them seems to have given rise to a clear position on the part of these institutions as to the legality of the practice. That observation is clear for *Ferring* and *TNT*, which involve funds from a public source and, as a result, provide information about the first category of situations (see above). *Deutsche Post*[210] is more complex and deserves a more thorough analysis.

4.253 *Deutsche Post re-examined.* The situation addressed in *Deusche Post* is no different from *Ferring* and *TNT*. In all these cases a public prerogative is granted and the issue is whether revenues obtained through that prerogative may be used on other markets. The ruling adopted by the CFI is admittedly more general, as that institution takes an attitude which is not limited to the situation examined. It goes beyond the details and addresses in general terms the issue of cross-subsidisation. The difficulty is, however, that the position adopted by the CFI is not entirely clear.

4.254 **Attitude of the CFI.** In its ruling the CFI does not refer specifically to the 1991 Competition Guidelines. As the case concerns postal services, it refers to a notice concerning the application of competition rules to that sector. The position advocated by the Commission in that notice is no different from that adopted in the guidelines, ie that cross-subsidisation should be deemed abusive when carried out by dominant undertakings. That position is set aside by the CFI. The argument raised by the CFI is that there is an inconsistency in the guidelines on this point. On the one hand, the guidelines would prohibit cross-subsidisation practised by dominant undertakings. On the other hand, it would allow dominant undertakings

---

[209] The funds and advantages are either granted by the public authority or by undertakings acting on the basis of an obligation imposed by a public authority.

[210] *UPS Europe v Commission and Deutsche Post* T-175/99 [2002] ECR II-01915.

to compete on prices. According to the CFI, there is a contradiction and that contradiction could only be solved by adopting a position where cross-subsidisation is prohibited in certain circumstances only, that is, where the funds were obtained through abusive conduct (excessive prices, discrimination, etc).

Commitment made by the undertaking.   In the ruling, the CFI observes that   **4.255** DP committed itself not to transfer funds from the reserved activities (ordinary mail) to the market where the acquisition took place. On the basis of that observation, it states that future cross-subsidisation would be prohibited. DP could not, indeed, use cross-subsidisation as a financing mechanism, in a situation where it had committed itself not to resort to that mechanism. From that commitment, it can be concluded that the Commission, and the CFI, are not indifferent to cross-subsidisation. From the decision and the ruling, one can deduce that, for both institutions,[211] cross-subsidisation indeed raises concerns under general competition law.[212]

Legal basis.   There exists an ambiguity concerning the legal basis that would be   **4.256** used in order to sanction cross-subsidisation, should the undertaking resort to that practice after the acquisition. In its ruling the CFI states that the practice should be prohibited because the authorisation was granted by the Commission on the basis of a commitment, entered into by the undertaking, not to resort to this kind of behaviour. However, the CFI mentions that the practice could be sanctioned by national courts on the basis of Article 82 EC. Two sources of obligation are thus mentioned in the same paragraph—a commitment made by the undertaking and a prohibition deriving directly from Article 82 EC.

Funds obtained through abusive practices.   The CFI submits that cross-   **4.257** subsidisation is abusive where the funds were obtained through abusive practices (excessive pricing, etc). This attitude does not appear to address the specific issues raised by cross-subsidisation. There is no doubt that practices such as excessive pricing or discriminatory behaviour must be deemed abusive. This does not depend, however, on the use which is made by the undertaking of the funds acquired in such an illegal manner. The practices are illegal per se and must be sanctioned as such—they do not become illegal as a result of the transfer. The same observation may be made with respect to the transfer itself. The issue was whether a transfer may be deemed abusive per se where it is made by an undertaking

---

[211] A nuance is that the Commission does not appear certain about the status of cross-subsidisation under general competition law. The Commission seems to have subordinated the operation to a commitment from the undertaking that it would not use cross-subsidisation. However, such an undertaking would not be necessary if the practice were clearly prohibited. In other words, it is not relevant to impose on an undertaking an obligation which is any way applicable as a result of the general law.

[212] Were that not the case, it would not be relevant for these institutions to make the authorisation of the operation dependent upon an undertaking not to resort to cross-subsidisation.

from a market which it dominates. The question is not related to the prohibition possibly breached upstream in collecting the funds. As stated above, dominance is not abusive per se. The question is whether a transfer is abusive where funds are obtained on a dominated market, independently of specific abusive practices.

Relationship with regulation

4.258 **No clear prohibition.**   Cross-subsidies are not clearly prohibited in the regulation. As appears from the extract quoted in the next paragraph, the prohibition is limited to 'abusive' cross-subsidies. That rule appears to imply that cross-subsidies are not per se illegal. They are considered illegal only where they have an 'abusive' character. Regarding that 'abusive' character there is no explanation in the regulation. In other words, the regulation does not contain information concerning criteria allowing the question whether cross-subsidisation is, or is not, legal to be considered.

4.259 **Procedural rules.**   The bulk of the NRF obligations concerning cross-subsidisation have a procedural, or formal, nature. *(a)* The Access Directive provides that an obligation may be imposed on vertically integrated undertakings, where such undertakings are dominant, to ensure transparency in the prices charged internally among divisions responsible for various interrelated activities within the same organisation. That measure must allow authorities, customers and competitors to verify under what conditions goods and services are transferred within the organisation. It is then possible to determine whether subsidies are transferred internally from one division to another.[213] *(b)* The Framework Directive introduces an obligation to keep separate accounts, or to separate activities structurally, where undertakings provide electronic communications networks and/or services, and these undertakings have special or exclusive rights for the performance of their activities in other sectors.

> *Access Directive, Preamble, recital 18.* 'Accounting separation allows internal price transfers to be rendered visible.' *Access Directive, Article 11(1).* '[A] national regulatory authority may require a vertically integrated company to make transparent its wholesale prices and its internal transfer prices . . ., where necessary, to prevent unfair cross-subsidy.' *Framework Directive, Article 13(1).* 'Member States shall require undertakings providing public communications networks or publicly available electronic communications services which have special or exclusive rights for the provision of services in other sectors in the same or another Member State to: *(a)* keep separate accounts for the activities associated with the provision of electronic communications networks or services, . . . so as to identify all elements of cost and revenue, . . ., or *(b)* have structural separation for the activities associated with the provision of electronic communications networks or services.'

---

[213] The obligation also facilitates investigation regarding the possibility that different prices are charged internally and in relations with third parties. If distinctions are drawn between the two kinds of customer, the practice can be deemed discriminatory. See the Access Directive, Art 11.

Complementarities.   Again, there appears to be complementarities between   **4.260**
regulation and general competition law. General competition law introduces
material obligations, the scope and content of which are not always easy to determine. That body of law does not contain, however, procedural, or formal, rules
imposing, for instance, the obligation that certain information must be made
available at all times, or that accounts must be held in a given manner. By contrast,
this aspect may be found in the regulation, which is rather specific on these issues.
On the other hand, the regulation does not contain a *per se* prohibition of the
behaviour. In the regulation, cross-subsidisation is prohibited only where it is
'abusive'. A reference appears to be made to general competition law through this
allusion to abusive conduct.

What should practitioners do?

Case law.   On the basis of the observations made above, the current state of the   **4.261**
case law concerning cross-subsidisation under Article 82 EC may be summarised
as follows. *(a)* The practice is prohibited where the funds transferred have a public source (funds provided by an authority or paid by undertakings on the basis of
an obligation imposed by an authority). *(b)* Cross-subsidisation is also prohibited
where the undertaking committed itself not to use that mechanism. *(c)* Another
circumstance is where the funds were acquired through abusive practices (excessive
prices, discriminatory behaviour, etc). *(d)* Outside of these circumstances, there
is an uncertainty as regards the status of cross-subsidisation. The Commission
prohibits the practice in the electronic communications sector (see the 1991
Competition Guidelines), but the European courts have not adopted a clear position on the subject. The general case law goes in the direction of a general prohibition, as the practice further reduces competition where it is adopted by a dominant
undertaking.

Both areas of the law.   The best solution for practitioners who wish to challenge   **4.262**
such behaviour is to use general competition law and sector-specific regulation
simultaneously, that is, use information available on the basis of regulation and
argue that the practice must be prohibited on the basis of the prohibition which
exists in general competition law. Such a strategy could unfold in various types of
situation.

Past behaviour.   Practitioners could try to establish that past cross-subsidisation   **4.263**
practised by a dominant undertaking must be sanctioned. The sanction would be
imposed on the basis of general competition law, which traditionally operates
ex post. In that context, the procedure for obtaining information would be based
on regulation. The challenge would be greatly helped by the separation of accounts,
and/or structural separation, in situations where these forms of separation are
imposed by regulation.

4.264 **Future behaviour.** Another situation is where practitioners seek to establish that a prohibition should be imposed, as regards future cross-subsidisation, on undertakings with significant market power. Such a prohibition could also be imposed on the basis of general competition law, with the procedural or formal assistance provided by the regulation. General competition law could be used as the material legal basis for the imposition of such an obligation, as that body of law makes it possible to impose interim or provisional measures. That body of law further allows authorities, while they sanction past behaviour, to state that such behaviour may no longer be adopted in the future—a type of intervention which has effects analogous to the regulation of future behaviour.

4.265 **Lack of a general rule.** The difficulty with the above types of intervention, which are both based on general competition law, is that they do not allow the imposition of a general rule which would be valid for several undertakings, active on different markets, or for an entire sector. Intervention of general scope would require NRAs to adopt general rules prohibiting cross-subsidisation in situations where their assessment is that the practice should be deemed abusive. Such intervention would have to be based on regulation. In that case, regulation would provide the material basis, as well as the procedural and formal environment, for action.[214] The regulation would be interpreted in the light of general competition law, as NRAs would base their evaluation of the practice on case law pursuant to which cross-subsidisation is to be considered abusive.

(6) Rebates

4.266 **Description of the mechanism.** Rebates provide dominant undertakings with a subtle mechanism to introduce differences between customers without clearly proposing diverging tariffs. As submitted above, differences in tariffs are abusive where they do not correspond to differences in the situations in which the customers are placed. Dominant undertakings may attempt to circumvent the prohibition by offering rebates to customers in exchange for services, or other advantages. Rebates sometimes have an adverse effect on competition, which explains why they have attracted the attention of competition authorities.

Quantity, fidelity, exclusivity

4.267 **Sizeable orders.** For the Commission, the CFI and the ECJ, rebates are allowed only in circumstances where legitimate consideration is provided by the customer. According to the case law, consideration qualifies as legitimate where it relates to the quantity of orders addressed to the dominant undertaking. In other words, the Commission and the European courts consider that rebates are legitimate where customers purchase a sizeable quantity of goods and/or services from the dominant

---

[214] Provision of information about internal transfer prices, obligation to hold separate accounts.

undertaking. The reasoning underlining this position is as follows. *(a)* The customer has placed significant orders with the undertaking. *(b)* As a result of that situation, the undertaking is able to save on costs (economies of scale). *(c)* Through the rebate, that economy is shared between the undertaking and customers. *(d)* Where it obtains a portion of that economy, the customer receives an amount which is related to its own behaviour. *(e)* The customer remains free to move to another supplier, with which it will probably enjoy the same benefit, as the rebates are linked to its own behaviour. *(f)* For that reason, quantity-related rebates do not raise competition concerns.

Fidelity or exclusivity. A difficulty arises where rebates are granted without a **4.268** connection to a quantity purchased by the customer, but where the dominant undertaking attempts to lock customers in in exchange for certain commitments. In some cases, a rebate is granted if the customer orders goods or services from the undertaking regularly (fidelity). The regularity with which orders have to be addressed to the undertaking is generally set out in writing in the contract. In other instances, the customer must commit itself to addressing its orders to the undertaking without seeking to obtain supplies from any other undertaking (exclusivity). The promise of exclusivity may concern one part,[215] or the totality, of the orders placed by the customer.

Case law. These commitments (fidelity, exclusivity) made by customers in **4.269** exchange for a rebate are unacceptable, since they have an impact on competition on markets which are already affected as a result of dominance. *(a)* Fidelity establishes between the customer and supplier a relationship which somehow prevents, or at least hinders, any move by the customer to another supplier. To that extent the normal rules of competition, whereby customers choose freely with whom they want to deal, are impaired. *(b)* The same remark may be made with respect to exclusivity. Exclusivity implies that customers may deal, for all or one part of their orders, only with one supplier. It excludes the possibility for customers to seek supplies from other undertakings. As a result of this situation, these latter undertakings lose their capacity to attract and win customers, even if they provide better terms and conditions.

Legitimacy of rebates. A debate exists as to the basis on which rebates may be **4.270** accepted. Some commentators state that quantity rebates are acceptable because they provide customers with a chance to recover a proportion of the economies realised by the undertaking. It should however be emphasised that promises of fidelity and exclusivity also provide economies to the undertaking.[216] Where they

---

[215] For instance, a percentage of these orders; the totality of orders concerning a certain material; the orders concerning a given territory; etc.

[216] With fidelity, the undertaking is placed in a situation where it can better organise its production as it knows in advance how much it has to supply. The same goes for exclusivity—with exclusivity suppliers are sure they can supply all needs of certain clients. Suppliers are relieved when they

grant fidelity or exclusivity rebates, the dominant undertakings do nothing other than to pass on a proportion of that economy to the customers concerned. The debate shows that another criterion must be found to explain where rebates may, or may not, be accepted. That criterion lies in the effect of rebates on competition. Rebates granted in exchange for fidelity or exclusivity cannot be accepted because they introduce additional rigidity into a market which was already characterised by an insufficient degree of competition. By contrast, quantity rebates may be accepted, in the current state of the case law, because they do not limit the freedom of customers, which may turn to other suppliers if they wish to do so.[217]

Leading case

4.271 *Hoffman-La Roche.* The leading case for fidelity and exclusivity rebates is *Hoffmann-La Roche*.[218] In that case, the Commission, and subsequently the ECJ, were confronted with rebates granted by a dominant undertaking in exchange for a commitment given by customers that they would purchase their supplies, or at least a substantial part of them, from that undertaking. The behaviour was deemed abusive, for two reasons. *(a)* The rebate could be analysed as a more advantageous treatment compared with the treatment which was granted to other customers. There was thus discrimination, in infringement of competition rules. *(b)* The rebate increased the rigidity which already existed on the market. As a result of these rebates, and more importantly of the commitment in consideration of that advantage, the beneficiaries lost their freedom to act. This was deemed contrary to competition rules, as competition may only function if customers remain free to choose their suppliers.

Effect on consumers

Hoffmann-La Roche. '[T]he effect of fidelity rebates is to apply dissimilar conditions to equivalent transactions with other trading parties in that two purchasers pay a different price for the same quantity of the same product depending on whether they obtain their supplies exclusively from the undertaking in a dominant position or have several sources of supply.'[219]

---

know that can rely on systematic orders and that these orders will not be addressed to competitors. In these situations, a risk inherent to competition is taken away. That represents an economy for the supplier.

[217] This does not exclude that the case law could evolve in the future. As stated, any behaviour—however rational it may be under commercial usages—may be deemed abusive when it has an additional effect on a degree of competition which is already altered as a result of the existence of dominance.

[218] Commission Decision (EEC) 76/642 relating to a proceeding under Article 86 of the Treaty establishing the European Economic Community (IV/29.020—Vitamins) [1976] OJ L223/27. Case 85/76 *Hoffmann-La Roche & Co AG v Commission* [1979] ECR 461.

[219] Judgment of the ECJ, at [90], al 3.

Effect on competitors

Hoffmann - La Roche. '[T]he fact of agreeing with purchasers that they will buy all or a very large proportion of their requirements from only one source by its very nature removes all freedom of choice from purchasers in their selection of sources of supply, and ties them to one supplier. the special price offered by Roche is the consideration for the abandonment by its purchasers of their opportunities to obtain substantial proportions of their requirements from competitors.'[220]

'[S]hould a purchaser not observe his obligation of exclusivity—by purchasing some of his requirements from another vitamin manufacturer—the fidelity rebate is forfeited not only in respect of the amount of such purchase, but in respect of all his purchases from Roche. This restrictive effect is aggravated by the fact that the rebate—and hence the exclusivity—is calculated on the basis of all purchases from Roche so that purchases of vitamins of one group are aggregated with purchases of vitamins of other groups ("across-the-board" rebates).'[221]

'[A]n undertaking which is in a dominant position on a market and ties purchasers—even if it does so at their request—by an obligation or promise on their part to obtain all or most of their requirements exclusively from the said undertaking abuses its dominant position within the meaning of article [82] . . . of the treaty, whether the obligation in question is stipulated without further qualification or whether it is undertaken in consideration of the grant of a rebate.'[222]

'[O]bligations of this kind to obtain supplies exclusively from a particular undertaking, whether or not they are in consideration of rebates or of the granting of fidelity rebates intended to give the purchaser an incentive to obtain his supplies exclusively from the undertaking in a dominant position, are incompatible with the objective of undistorted competition within the common market, because—unless there are exceptional circumstances which may make an agreement between undertakings in the context of article 85 and in particular of paragraph (3) of that article, permissible—they are not based on an economic transaction which justifies this burden or benefit but are designed to deprive the purchaser of or restrict his possible choices of sources of supply and to deny other producers access to the market.'[223]

Other similar cases

Suiker Unie. Fidelity and exclusivity rebates have been examined by the European courts in other cases, some of which are examined briefly below. In *Suiker Unie*,[224] for instance, the producer was seeking to obtain a commitment of exclusivity from most intermediaries located in a particular geographical area in Germany, where it had a quasi monopoly on a given market (production of raw sugar). In order to attain its goal, the producer granted a rebate to all intermediaries

4.272

---

[220] Decision of the Commission, at [24], subpara 2. [221] ibid, at [24], subpara 3.
[222] Judgment of the ECJ, at [89]. [223] ibid, at [90], al 1.
[224] Commission Decision (EEC) 73/109 relating to proceedings under Articles 85 and 86 of the EEC Treaty (IV/26 918—European sugar industry) [1973] OJ L140/17. Joined Cases 40–48, 50, 54–56, 111, 113 & 114/73 *Coöperatieve Vereniging 'Suiker Unie' UA v Commission* [1975] ECR 1663.

who would accept a commitment not to purchase any sugar—whatever the quantity—from another producer.[225] The practice was found abusive.

> *Suiker Unie.* 'The granting of a rebate which does not depend on the amount bought, but only on whether the annual requirements are covered exclusively by the SZV, is an unjustifiable discrimination against buyers who also buy sugar from sources other than SZV. Since the buyers depend for at least part of their supplies on SZV as they have insufficient storage facilities and need regular supplies, the disadvantage of los- ing the rebate is usually greater than the advantage of buying sugar from outsiders even if they offer it at more favourable prices.'[226]

4.273 **Other cases.** The same attitude was adopted in *(a) Hilti,*[227] where rebates were granted to customers who agreed not to buy nails from competitors;[228] *(b) Compagnie maritime belge,*[229] where rebates were limited to customers entrusting members of the maritime conference with all their maritime transports;[230] *British Gypsum,*[231] where subsidies were paid by the dominant undertaking for the pro- motion of its products where they were sold by distributors who would commit themselves to buying exclusively from that undertaking;[232] the same case, where priority was given to orders coming from customers committing themselves to exclusivity for the totality or a substantial part of their supplies; and *ICI*[233] and *Solvay,*[234] where the dominant undertaking sought information about the needs of its customers and provided a rebate for the quantities that would be purchased pursuant to those needs, thereby inducing customers to acquire a supplementary

---

[225] The producer had other arguments to impose its policy. First, the other producers were located farther away. Transportation costs were thus higher for these producers. Second, the other manufactur- ers did not produce much. It was thus impossible for the intermediaries to shift to these manufacturers in case the main producer stopped supplying as a measure of retaliation if they did not accept the con- ditions. Third, the storage capacity of the intermediaries was rather limited. As a result, they could not purchase sugar from other producers and store it. They had to deal, on a frequent basis, with a producer that would not be located far from their premises.

[226] Decision of the Commission, 39 *in fine* and 40.

[227] See *Hilti*, Commission Decision EEC (88/138) relating to a proceeding under Article 86 of the EEC Treaty (IV/30.787 and 31.488—Eurofix-Bauco v Hilti) [1988] OJ L65/19. See also Case T-30/89 *Hilti AG v Commission* [1991] ECR II-1439 and Case C-53/92 P *Hilti AG v Commission* [1994] ECR I-667.   [228] Decision of the Commission, at [82].

[229] *Cewal*, Commission Decision (EEC) 93/82 relating to a proceeding pursuant to Articles 85 (IV/32.448 and IV/32.450: Cewal, Cowac and Ukwal) and 86 (IV/32.448 and IV/32.450: Cewal) of the EEC Treaty [1993] OJ L34/20; Joined Cases T 24-26 & 28/93 *Compagnie Maritime Belge Transports v Commission* [1996] ECR II-1201; Joined Cases C-395 & 396/96 P *Compagnie Maritime Belge v Commission* [2000] ECR I-1365.

[230] See decision of the Commission, at [94]et seq and judgment of the CFI, at [181] et seq.

[231] *British Gypsum*, Commission Decision (EEC) 89/22 relating to a proceeding under Article 86 of the EEC Treaty (IV/31.900, BPB Industries plc) [1989] OJ L010/50. Case T-65/89 *BPB Industries Plc and British Gypsum Ltd v Commission* [1993] ECR II-389. Case C-310/93 P *BPB Industries plc and British Gypsum Ltd v Commission* [1995] I-865.

[232] Judgment of the CFI, at [94].

[233] *ICI*, Commission Decision (EEC) 91/300 relating to a proceeding under Article 86 of the EEC Treaty (IV/33.133-D: Soda-ash—ICI) [1991] OJ L152/40.

[234] *Solvay*, Commission Decision (EEC) 91/299 relating to a proceeding under Article 86 of the EEC Treaty (IV/33.133-C: Soda-ash—Solvay) [1991] OJ L152/21.

proportion of their supply from that undertaking instead of seeking supplies from competitors.

A wide variety of practices

Variety in rebates. Other examples of rebates are provided below. The purpose **4.274** is not to provide an exhaustive analysis, since in this area too, dominant undertakings have displayed considerable ingenuity. It is important, however, to draw practitioners' attention to the variety of practices that can be encountered on electronic communications markets, as well as in other sectors of the economy.

(a) General rebates. It is submitted above that rebates may be granted in **4.275** exchange for sizeable orders. These may not be general and must be limited to a given market. Dominant undertakings may not make the granting of rebates conditional on the purchase of quantities of supplies on several markets. In other words, no link may be established between various markets in calculating a rebate.[235]

Hoffmann-La Roche. An example of this prohibition may be found in **4.276** *Hoffmann-La Roche*, where some rebates granted by the dominant undertaking were calculated on a whole range of products. They were granted only if the customer purchased from the dominant undertaking a given quantity of products on separate markets. The purpose was to induce an overall strategy from the customers. These customers were invited to control centrally the orders placed by the various departments within their organisation. These orders could then be addressed to the dominant undertaking, as clear advantages were offered if this was done.

(b) Progressive rebates. Some undertakings grant progressive rebates, which **4.277** grow in the same proportion as the quantities purchased by the customers. The practice seeks to induce customers into buying ever more from the undertaking concerned. It raises concerns under general competition law because, as a result of this practice, the space left for intervention by competitors—already restricted as a result of the limited degree of competition existing on that market—decreases as customers turn to the dominant undertaking for additional supplies in the hope of obtaining a higher rebate.

Solvay. One example can be found in *Solvay*. According to the Commission, the **4.278** undertaking had established a system where rebates were increased significantly

---

[235] That position can be compared to the prohibition to tie transactions. Dominant undertakings are not allowed to impose a second transaction on customers wishing to obtain a first transaction from them—and to use the domination they hold on that latter market to compel the second transaction. The reason is that customers are then left with a good or a service that they did not really need. Similarly, dominant undertakings cannot establish a link between various markets for the calculation of rebates. Also in such a case, customers are no longer free. They have to remain with the dominant supplier on all the markets concerned—or lose the benefit of the rebate.

on quantities purchased by customers above the level which they would normally order. Pursuant to the analysis provided by the Commission, the practice was particularly dangerous given the characteristics of the relevant market. On that market, competitors were relatively small. The consequence was that their production capacity was limited and they could not serve customers for the totality of the supplies sought by them. In that context, competition was concentrated, to a significant extent, on marginal orders, ie orders placed by customers depending on their turnover during the period in question. As a result of this progressive rebate, the undertaking was in effect impeding competitors from accessing that portion of the orders, while they were already excluded from the bulk of the market as a result of their limited capacity.[236]

4.279 **(c) Cross-rebates.** In some instances, rebates are granted on one market for purchases carried out on another. On the dominated market, the undertaking takes substantial benefits. It may thus grant rebates without jeopardising its position. The rebates are not necessary to support its position on the dominated market, because that position is already strong enough. By contrast, it is necessary to sustain activities on another market where the position occupied by the undertaking is less stable. In order to sustain these activities, advantages are granted to customers on that second market. In return for these rebates, customers rely on the undertaking for supplies on that second market.[237]

4.280 *Michelin.* An example of the practice can be found in *Michelin*,[238] which featured two markets for the distribution of tyres by intermediaries—tyres for touring vehicles and for trucks. The Commission contended that rebates were granted to intermediaries for the purchase of tyres made for the first market (tourism). The issue was that the rebate had been calculated, according to the Commission, on transactions entered into on the second market (trucks). This

---

[236] See decision of the Commission, at [17] and [52]. In order to counterbalance the orders placed by the dominant undertaking, the competitors would have had to offer a rebate which would have been equal to the global rebate granted by that undertaking on all of the purchases made by the customers with that undertaking. That was impossible for them, as they were only selling a small quantity of goods and services compared to that sold by the dominant undertaking.

[237] The practice is close to cross-subsidisation in which revenues are transferred from one division to another within the same undertaking. With cross-rebates, revenues from one division are granted to customers served by another division within the same undertaking. The difference is that, in the second case, the transfer is indirect. The customers are the beneficiaries—but the purpose is to support the activities of the second division, which will receive additional revenues as a result of the orders placed by the customers to that division. In effect, the first division bears a burden which economically belongs to the second. There is cross subsidy in the sense that the rebate may be analysed as a subsidy from the first division to the second, to support sales made by that second division.

[238] *Michelin*, Commission Decision (EEC) 81/969 relating to a proceeding under Article 86 of the EEC Treaty (IV.29.491—Bandengroothandel Frieschebrug BV/NV Nederlandsche Banden-Industrie Michelin) [1981] OJ L353/33. Case 322/81 *Nederlandsche Banden Industrie Michelin v Commission* [1983] ECR 3461.

did not seem acceptable to the Commission, as competition does not unfold, in such a scenario, 'on the merits'.[239] The position adopted by the Commission was confirmed by the ECJ in principle, even if the Court estimated that the Commission had not established the facts correctly.[240]

(d) Collective rebates.   Pursuant to the case law, a dominant undertaking may   **4.281** not calculate rebates collectively on purchases made by various entities even where these entities belong to the same economic undertaking. An example of that prohibition may be found in *British Sugar*,[241] where an undertaking dominated the market for the production and distribution of raw sugar in the United Kingdom. Rebates were granted to intermediaries, where these intermediaries promised to purchase all of their supplies from that undertaking. In order to increase the efficiency of the mechanism, the undertaking imposed the collectivisation of rebates. That collectivisation implied that the rebate was only granted, in the case of several companies belonging to the same economic group, if all of these companies were purchasing their supplies from the dominant undertaking. With that mechanism, a double pressure was exerted—the pressure on each company to place its orders with the dominant undertaking and the pressure on the other members of the group to follow the same policy otherwise the rebate would be lost for the whole group.

(e) Objectives assigned to customers.   In some instances the payment of the   **4.282** rebate is made dependent upon customers reaching one or several objectives assigned by the dominant undertaking in terms of quantity. The practice appears similar to quantity rebates, in that the amount which is paid or discounted to the customer depends on quantities purchased. There is however a difference, in that these quantities are not fixed once and for all for all customers. They are rather established on a customer per customer basis. The idea is to determine the needs of these customers. The objectives are then set taking into account their needs, the purpose being to cover all of the needs of the customers in terms of supply. In *Hoffmann-La Roche*, for instance, a rebate was granted in exchange for a commitment by the customer to seek supplies with the undertaking for a substantial part

---

[239] Competition did not develop on the basis of the activities displayed by tyre producers on each market concerned. It was distorted, according to the Commission, by transfers of revenues, in the form of rebates, from one market to another.

[240] Contrary to what the Commission contended, the rebate was calculated on the basis of the transactions realised on the market where the rebate was granted. As a result, there was no trace of cross-subsidies. '[T]here is no ground for describing the bonus, as the commission has done, as a discount on sales of heavy-vehicle tyres. In granting the bonus Michelin nv did not make a benefit granted on sales on one market dependent upon the attainment of a target for sales on another market. The Commission's argument that the practice in question is akin to a linked obligation within the meaning of article 86 (d) is therefore unfounded' (Judgment of the ECJ, at [98]).

[241] *British Sugar*, Commission Decision (EEC) 88/518 relating to a proceeding under Article 86 of the EEC Treaty (Case No IV/30.178 Napier Brown—British Sugar) [1988] OJ L284/41.

of its needs. The rebate increased with the proportion of the needs satisfied with supplies coming from the dominant undertaking.

4.283 *Michelin.* Similarly, the rebates granted to intermediaries in *Michelin*[242] seemed to be based on quantities. As a result, there was an appearance of legality (case law allowing quantity rebates). The reality was however more complex, as conditions were imposed on intermediaries. These conditions led to a situation where the freedom of the intermediaries, and as a result the degree of existing competition, was limited to an unacceptable degree. According to the Commission, later confirmed by the ECJ, the intermediaries, as a result of these conditions, were no longer in a position to choose freely from among existing suppliers those offering the best terms and conditions. These conditions were as follows. *(a)* The rebate was granted only to intermediaries who purchased a quantity higher than the one they had bought the previous year. It was thus made dependent upon a progression in purchases on an annual basis. *(b)* The rebate was acquired only at the end of the year. Monthly rebate payments were made, but these could be kept only if the objective set for the whole year was reached. As a result of this mechanism, there was a growing pressure on intermediaries to place orders with the undertaking as the year came to an end, otherwise they would have to reimburse the advance payments already made if the final objective was not reached. *(c)* The rebate was calculated on the basis of the total of the purchases made during the entire year. It was thus a significant amount. To combat this strategy, competitors, which were smaller in size, had to offer a higher rebate per unit—something which they could hardly afford to do as they did not enjoy comparable economies of scale. *(d)* There was no transparency. The objectives, for instance, and the final amount paid as a rebate, were not set in writing. The consequence was that, to avoid any risk, intermediaries tended to place all their orders with the dominant undertaking.

> *Michelin.* '[S]uch a situation is calculated to prevent dealers from being able to select freely at any time in the light of the market situation the most favourable of the offers made by the various competitors and to change supplier without suffering any appreciable economic disadvantage. It thus limits the dealers' choice of supplier and makes access to the market more difficult for competitors. Neither the wish to sell more nor the wish to spread production more evenly can justify such a restriction of the customer's freedom of choice and independence. The position of dependence in which dealers find themselves and which is created by the discount system in question, is not therefore based on any countervailing advantage which may be economically justified.'[243]

---

[242] *Michelin*, Commission Decision (EEC) 81/969 relating to a proceeding under Article 86 of the EEC Treaty (IV.29.491—Bandengroothandel Frieschebrug BV/NV Nederlandsche Banden-Industrie Michelin) [1981] OJ L353/33. Case 322/81 *Nederlandsche Banden Industrie Michelin v Commission* [1983] ECR 3461.   [243] Judgment of the ECJ, at [85].

(7) Tying practices

Presentation of the mechanism.   Competition authorities observe that dom-   **4.284**
inant undertakings sometimes establish a link between the goods and services
they provide on different markets. Here, again, the strategy is to use dominance
on one market to obtain an advantage on another. In the context of tying, a link is
established between markets by subjecting transactions on the dominated market
to the conclusion of another transaction on another market.

Underlying reasoning.   The reasoning behind this strategy may be described as   **4.285**
follows. *(a)* The undertaking dominates a market. *(b)* Dominance means that, on
that market, the undertaking may behave independently of the reactions of other
market participants, including customers. *(c)* As a result of dominance, the undertaking is in a position to refuse to sell the good or service concerned if the cus-
tomer(s) do(es) not purchase other goods and services. *(d)* As the first market is
subject to domination, customers find no alternative to the undertaking on the
first market. *(e)* If they want the good or service sold on that first market, they
must accept the second transaction.[244]

1998 Competition Guidelines.   In the 1998 Competition Guidelines, the   **4.286**
Commission emphasises the risk that this practice poses for the development of
communications services. There is a danger, it states, that undertakings dominating network markets will use that dominance to impose on customers services that
could otherwise be provided on a competitive basis. Practitioners representing
dominant undertakings should beware, because the determination of the
Commission to react against these practices is clearly expressed in the guidelines
and that institution can use well-established case law to that effect.

> *1998 Competition Guidelines.* 'This is of particular concern where it involves the
> tying of services for which the TO[245] is dominant with those for which it is not.
> Where the vertically integrated dominant network operator obliges the party
> requesting access to purchase one or more services without adequate justification,
> this may exclude rivals of the dominant access provider from offering those elements
> of the package independently. This requirement could thus constitute an abuse
> under Article [82] . . .'[246]

Following paragraphs.   In the following paragraphs, two typical tie-in cases are   **4.287**
examined. They provide a good illustration of what the practice is and how the
authorities react when confronted with this type of behaviour. Several cases
involving electronic communications are then analysed. Finally, specific issues are

---

[244] It may happen that some customers refuse the second transaction. That is the case where the
said customers do not really need the first good or service. As a result of that renunciation, the dominant undertaking loses part of its turnover. It however calculates that the loss resulting from that
renunciation is inferior to the incremental part due, in its turnover, to customers being obliged to buy
the second good or service.   [245] 'TO' refers to 'Telecommunications Organisation'.
[246] 1998 Competition Guidelines, para 103.

addressed, one of them being how undertakings use dominance to impose a second transaction on customers. Another is whether second transactions may never be imposed, even where they are closely related to the first.

Leading cases

4.288 *Tetra Pak II.* *Tetra Pak II* is examined above in connection with predatory pricing.[247] Another kind of conduct favoured by the undertaking in question was to impose second transactions on customers, using the power it had acquired on a market where a first transaction was to take place. The undertaking dominated the market for the manufacture and sale of machinery to be used for the packaging of liquids. On that market it could behave independently of reactions by customers and/or competitors because there was no real alternative available. The undertaking was also active on the market for the manufacturing and sale of the boxes which were used to package the liquid after processing, as well as on accessory markets such as the hire and repair of the machines. The position of the undertaking was less stable on these various secondary markets, where potential competition was higher.[248]

> *Maintenance, repair and provision of spare parts.* '[T]hose . . . clauses could be considered as abusive in themselves since their object was in particular, depending on the clause, to make the sale of machines and cartons subject to accepting additional services of a different type, such as maintenance and repair and the provision of spare parts.'[249] *Cartons.* '[T]he combined effect of the . . . contractual clauses at issue . . . was an overall strategy aiming to make the customer totally dependant on Tetra Pak for the entire life of the machine once purchased or leased, thereby excluding in particular any possibility of competition at the level both of cartons and of associated products.'[250]

4.289 *British Sugar.* In *British Sugar*,[251] an undertaking dominated the market for the production of raw sugar. It was subordinating the sale of that product to the acceptance of transport services for the delivery of the product to the premises of the intermediary. A link was thus established between the good and the service. The intermediaries could not ensure the transportation themselves and they could not obtain the service from a third undertaking. Forcing customers to accept transport

---

[247] See Commission Decision (EEC) 92/163 relating to a proceeding pursuant to Article 86 of the EEC Treaty (IV/31043—Tetra Pak II) [1991] OJ L72/1. Case T-83/91 *Tetra Pak International SA v Commission* [1994] ECR II-755. Case C-333/94 P *Tetra Pak International SA v Commission* [1996] ECR I-5951.

[248] It is easier for potential competitors to enter the market for boxes than to develop the technology required to carry out an activity in a successful manner in a relatively short term on a market concerning the manufacture of machines. As a result, the undertaking sought to impose, on clients in need of machinery, the boxes it was also making, as well as other services it was providing.

[249] Judgment of the CFI, at [135].   [250] ibid, at [135].

[251] Commission Decision (EEC) 88/518 relating to a proceeding under Article 86 of the EEC Treaty (Case No IV/30.178 Napier Brown—British Sugar) [1988] OJ L284/41.

services had a significant advantage for the undertaking. It had a substantial fleet of trucks which were used for its own purposes. Using them for deliveries to intermediaries made it possible to amortise that fleet under better financial conditions.

> *British Sugar.* 'BS [British Sugar] has accepted that, before the end of 1986, it refused to supply sugar to its customers unless the customer also accepted that BS itself . . . supplied the service of delivery of the sugar. It was thus reserving for itself the separate but ancillary activity of delivering the sugar which could, under normal circumstances be undertaken by an individual contractor acting alone.' 'The Commission is not aware of any objective necessity requiring BS to reserve such an activity to itself, and the fact that following BS's undertaking it has offered a choice to its customers between ex factory or delivered sugar, indicates that no such objective necessity exists.' 'The Commission considers that BS has abused its dominant position on the sugar market by refusing to grant to its customers an option between purchasing sugar on an ex factory or delivered price basis, thereby reserving for itself the ancillary activity of the delivery of that sugar, thus eliminating all competition in relation to the delivery of the products.'[252]

Electronic communications

Cases dealing with electronic communications.   Various cases with special rele- **4.290** vance for this book are examined below, as they concern tying practices adopted in connection with networks. Cases are also analysed in connection with refusal to deal or grant access. This should not come as a surprise, as refusing to deal or grant access is an approach that dominant undertakings sometimes use to impose second transactions on customers.

Services accessory to equipment.   In *Alsatel*,[253] an undertaking imposed various **4.291** accessory services on customers which purchased telephony equipment from it. For instance, customers were obliged to use that undertaking for any subsequent modifications to the equipment. The case was addressed to the ECJ by way of preliminary reference. The ECJ found that the practice could be deemed abusive.[254]

Computer network.   In *Sabena*,[255] the undertaking controlled the computer **4.292** network used by travel agencies established on Belgian territory in order to book

---

[252] Decision of the Commission, at [69] and [71] (extracts).

[253] Case 247/86 *Société alsacienne et lorraine de télécommunications et d'électronique (Alsatel) v SA Novasam* [1988] ECR 5987.

[254] These modifications were to take place under conditions that were not fair for customers. The price of these modifications was unilaterally determined by the undertaking. The contract was automatically renewed if the modification implied an increase of 25% in the price at which the equipment was leased. That latter condition made it possible for the dominant undertaking to determine freely the cases where it thought that a contract renewal was appropriate. These various practices were deemed abusive by the ECJ. The ECJ however formulated doubts about the existence of a dominant position in the case at issue. The elements provided by the national court in the preliminary reference were not insufficient to conclude the existence of dominance.

[255] Commission Decision (EEC) (88/589) relating to a proceeding under Article 86 of the EEC Treaty (IV/32.318, London European—Sabena) [1988] OJ L317/47.

flights originating from the Belgian national airport (Zaventem). That under-taking was the former national airline company, and dominated the market for flight reservations in Belgium, in addition to operating flights itself and providing a series of accessory services (plane maintenance, etc). It was important for com-petitors to be able to access the reservation system, since otherwise they would have no means of ensuring reservations for their flights from Belgium. In this case, Sabena was denying access by a competitor to the reservation system on the ground that that competitor did not entrust to Sabena the maintenance of its planes at the national airport.

> *Sabena.* '[T]he two contracts . . . are not connected: the computer reservation con-tract enables travel agencies to obtain transport services for passengers as quickly and efficiently as possible. The handling contract involves ground assistance for aircraft. One of the reasons for Sabena's refusal is thus clearly the fact that it makes the conclu-sion of a . . . contract subject to the conclusion by London European of a handling contract which is not related to the subject matter of the first contract. This behaviour therefore constitutes an abusive practice expressly covered by Article [82] . . .'[256]

4.293 **Mobile communications network.** In *Racal Decca*, the undertaking controlled a network used for the transmission of signals allowing the geographical position of ships in the North Sea to be plotted. It was also active on the market for the manufacture and sale of the terminals which were placed on the ships to receive the signals.[257] The position acquired by the undertaking was less stable on the sec-ond market, because terminals could be made by other undertakings, whereas the establishment of a network of stations would have required significant invest-ment, as well as cumbersome formalities in order to obtain authorisations from the Member States in which the stations were established. To protect its position on the second market, the undertaking used several practices, including going so far as to change frequencies without warning to ensure that signals could be received only by terminals produced by it. The latter behaviour amounted to tying, as customers (ships) could not access signals (first market) if they used terminals manufactured by another undertaking (second market).

Link with other practices

4.294 **Refusal to deal.** Many tie-in cases are analysed by competition authorities on the basis of the case law concerning refusal to deal. The reason for this is that the practice amounts to a conditional refusal to deal. The undertaking agrees to enter into a transaction only if the customer accepts a second, designated, transaction. It refuses to deal with the customer if that condition is not accepted. In *Sabena*, for

---

[256] Decision of the Commission, para 31.

[257] The geographical position of the ships was obtained through calculation on the basis of the signals received from the different emitting stations—these stations being placed in various countries bordering the North Sea.

instance, the undertaking refused to give access to the reservation system if other transactions were not accepted by the customer. In *Racal Decca*, the undertaking similarly refused to provide the location service to customers which would not use terminals manufactured by it.

Rebates.   Another arrangement used by dominant undertakings to force second   **4.295** transactions is to use rebates. Rebates are granted where customers accept a second transaction. In *AKZO*,[258] for example, the dominant undertaking had concluded contracts concerning the supply of benzoyl peroxide. The undertaking had a dominant position on the market for that product. To customers accepting to purchase that product the undertaking offered to supply other substances with a significant rebate. In such a set of circumstances, use is made of the position of dominance because customers realise that the price offered for the second transaction is limited to those which deal with the undertaking on the first market. They then have the impression that missing the advantage would be a mistake; in other words, they feel obliged, for financial reasons, to enter into the second transaction.

A variety of practices.   A number of other approaches are commonly used to   **4.296** impose second transactions. *Hilti*[259] provides an interesting case in point. As stated above, the undertaking sold nail guns, cartridges and nails for use in the construction sector. Its position was less solid on the latter market, as competitors could manufacture nails more easily for instance than nail guns, for which investment and technology were required. To protect its position on the nail market, the undertaking established a link between nails, cartridges and nail guns. The purpose was to reserve nail guns for customers which would also buy cartridges and nails manufactured by the undertaking. All sorts of practices were used to impose the link between the various markets: the undertaking refused to sell nail guns or cartridges without the accessory products; rebates were refused to customers buying nails without the corresponding number of cartridges; the undertaking refused to provide a guarantee where nail guns were used with nails manufactured by competitors, and so on.

> *Hilti*. 'Making the sale of patented cartridge strips conditional upon taking a corresponding complement of nails constitutes an abuse of a dominant position, as do reduced discounts and other discriminatory policies described above on cartridge-only orders. These policies leave the consumer with no choice over the source of his nails and as such abusively exploit him. In addition, these policies all have the object or effect of excluding independent nail makers who may threaten the dominant position Hilti holds. The tying and reduction of discounts were not isolated incidents but a generally applied policy.'[260]

---

[258] Case C-62/86 *AKZO Chemie BV v Commission* [1991] ECR I-3359.
[259] Commission Decision EEC (88/138) relating to a proceeding under Article 86 of the EEC Treaty (IV/30.787 and 31.488—Eurofix-Bauco v Hilti) [1988] OJ L65/19. Case T-30/89 *Hilti AG v Commission* [1991] ECR II-1439. Case C-53/92 P *Hilti AG v Commission* [1994] ECR I-667.
[260] Decision of the Commission, at [75].

Hilti. 'Hilti's policy of attempting to block the sale of independents' nails took another course in that it was made known that guarantees on nail guns would not be honoured if non-Hilti nails were used. Whilst it may be legitimate not to honour a guarantee if a faulty or sub-standard non-Hilti nail causes malfunctioning, premature wear or breakdown in a particular case, such a general policy in the circumstances of this case amounts to an abuse of a dominant position in that it is yet another indirect means used to hinder customers from having access to different sources of supply. Furthermore, Hilti has not been able to present any data to show that use of any of the non-Hilti nails currently available cause damage, premature wear or malfunctioning of Hilti guns in excess of that expected as a result of using Hilti nails.'[261]

Objective justifications

4.297 **Subject matter.**   On the basis of the case law examined above, it can be considered that tie-in practices are prohibited where they are adopted by dominant undertakings. It is thus not allowed for dominant undertakings to make access to one transaction dependent upon the customer's accepting a second transaction. The question has arisen whether the behaviour adopted by the undertakings in question could be justified objectively. Some indications are provided in this section concerning specific arguments made by dominant undertakings to justify tie-in practices. A further section is devoted to the principles of objective justification in general. Interested readers may consult that general section if they need more analysis on that subject.

4.298 **(a) Natural or commercial links.**   Dominant undertakings have sought to justify tie-in practices on the basis of the link which may exist in some circumstances between the transactions concerned. The argument is that tying in should be permitted where the link existing between the transactions is due to the nature of the transactions concerned or where the link was generally made as part of business practice. In these cases, it is argued, the dominant undertaking does not engage in behaviour which seeks specifically to undermine competition. It merely reflects, in the offers made to customers, links that are made anyway on the markets between the transactions in question.

4.299 **Position adopted by the European courts.**   The argument was addressed in *Tetra Pak II*, where the dominant undertaking produced machines and boxes for packaging liquids. A link was established between the two markets in that customers were compelled to buy boxes when they purchased machines. The undertaking was challenged by the Commission on that count and others. The undertaking contended that a link should be accepted in the circumstances of the case, by virtue of the natural and/or commercial relationship existing between the products concerned. The argument was rejected by the CFI. The position

---

[261] Decision of the Commission, at [79].

adopted by that institution is based on the facts of the case.[262] It also contains a position in principle on the issue. For the CFI, dominant undertakings may not resort to tie-in practices, even if there is a natural or commercial link between the transactions, in situations where these practices may affect competition. The criterion for the practice to be prohibited, or allowed, does not depend, as a result, on the alleged existence of a natural or commercial relationship between the transaction, but rather on the effect which the practice may have on competition.[263]

> *Tetra Pak II.* 'It must . . . be stressed that the list of abusive practices set out in the second paragraph of Article [82] . . . of the Treaty is not exhaustive. Consequently, even where tied sales of two products are in accordance with commercial usage or there is a natural link between the two products in question, such sales may still constitute abuse within the meaning of Article [82] . . . unless they are objectively justified.'[264]

(b) Sales promotions. Another attempt made by dominant undertakings to establish links between transactions without falling under the prohibition is to disguise tie-in practices. In general, such practices must be distinguished from other forms of behaviour where undertakings grant gifts to customers acquiring goods or services. Suppose a mobile equipment manufacturer sells mobile phones and gives buyers free items such as posters. In that transaction, one good is marketed (mobile terminal) and the other is given free. The situation is different where goods or services are tied in. An example could be the decision taken by an operator to reserve fixed telephony for customers purchasing internet services from that same operator. In that kind of transaction, two services are being sold, fixed telephony and internet services. **4.300**

Similarity and differences. In some circumstances, tie-in practices and sales promotions look very similar. The main difference is that two transactions are carried out in one case (tie-in), whereas one only occurs in the second (sales promotion). **4.301**

---

[262] For the CFI, the products could be dissociated. Machines were manufactured by undertakings which did not produce boxes. In addition, boxes could be used with machines manufactured by other producers.

[263] The position adopted by the CFI appears to that extent entirely in line with the trend discovered in the case law on abuse. In the analysis, it was submitted that there now exists a general prohibition to engage in any behaviour, however normal that behaviour may appear on a commercial (and even natural) basis, where competition is likely to be further degraded on the relevant market, or on an adjacent one.

[264] Case C-333/94 P *Tetra Pak International SA v Commission* [1996] ECR I-5951 at [37]. As appears from the extract, the CFI rejects the justification claimed by the dominant undertaking and based on the existence of an alleged link between the two transactions. It however accepts, in the same judgment, more generally, the possibility that the behaviour may be excused in the presence of an objective justification. The question is what justification will be acceptable. There thus does not exist a response to that question, as regards the specific context of tying up practices. A general jurisprudence has been developed around the notion of objective justification in the application of Art 82 EC—that jurisprudence is analysed at paras 4.317–4.324. As a result, the response provided by the CFI to the question of justification should not appear ambiguous. It merely recalls the existence of case law allowing seemingly abusive practices to be excused when an objective justification is available.

Dominant undertakings may attempt to disguise the difference, but this sort of behaviour would not escape the scrutiny of competition authorities. General competition law is concerned with economic realities going beyond legal constructions. It is possible, for competition authorities, to analyse a transaction independently of the description of it given by the parties. Furthermore, competition authorities do not need to designate behaviour as tie-in in order to apply the prohibition. As stated above, what is important is to demonstrate that the undertaking holds dominance and that it is engaged in behaviour which affects competition, in line with the general trend in the case law established around that provision.[265]

4.302 (c) **Limitation of sales to significant quantities.** A question arises in connection with the case law on tie-in concerning the treatment to be granted to certain transactions which appear indivisible because they concern the same good or service. Suppose that dominant operators decide to sell transmission capacity only if a given, substantial, portion of that capacity is purchased. Could such behaviour be analysed according to the tie-in model? A positive answer could be given to that question if the transaction were to be analysed as a series of transactions involving smaller quantities, between which a link would be established by the operator. An analysis along those lines should not be excluded. The practice indeed raises concerns similar to those relating to tie-in. *(a)* Customers are not free in their purchases. They have to buy the designated quantity if they want to acquire access to capacity, and the presence of dominance makes it impossible for them to find an alternative. *(b)* Competition is affected to the extent that demand may be concentrated on the dominant undertaking as a result of that practice, leaving little room for the development of competing offers.

4.303 **No official position.** To date, the issue does not seem to have been addressed by the Commission or a European court. Some elements may be found in *SABAM*.[266] In that case, the undertaking defended the interests of composers of music in Belgium. It was the only undertaking with a similar object on the Belgian territory. The services were accessible only to those who would accept a condition whereby they entrusted the undertaking with the responsibility for the management of all their musical interests. The rights conveyed remained with the undertaking for a period of five years after the composers had severed their agreements with the undertaking. In the view of the ECJ these limitations and requirements were abusive, as they were not essential for the defence of the composers' interests. Furthermore, the composers' freedom was impaired to an excessive degree.

---

[265] The list included in Art 82 EC does not enumerate all possible practices adopted by dominant undertakings and prohibited by the provision it merely provides examples. As a result, there is no obligation, for competition authorities, to establish a link between the practices mentioned in that list and the behaviour they have to address in practice.

[266] Case 127/73 *Belgische Radio & TV v SABAM* [1974] ECR 313.

Sabam. '[I]t must thus be concluded that the fact that an undertaking entrusted with the exploitation of copyrights and occupying a dominant position within the meaning of article [82] . . . imposes on its members obligations which are not absolutely necessary for the attainment of its object and which thus encroach unfairly upon a member's freedom to exercise his copyright can constitute an abuse.'[267]

E. Other Practices

Introduction.   The case law on Article 82 EC addresses other issues which are **4.304** analysed briefly below. Again, the purpose is not to provide an exhaustive account but rather to examine the most frequent practices likely to be adopted by dominant undertakings on markets where electronic communications networks or services are provided.

(a) Exercise of a right.   In some cases the Commission and European courts **4.305** have addressed the situation of dominant undertakings exercising rights allocated to them. The question is to what extent these rights may be used where this implies an effect on competition.

Right created by contract.   In some instances, rights arise out of a contract **4.306** signed by the dominant undertaking with other undertakings. An example may be found in *Compagnie maritime belge,*[268] where a maritime conference[269] concluded a contract with the Zairian entity responsible for the organisation of maritime transportation. That contract provided that maritime transportation of goods was entrusted to the members of the conference. Derogations could be introduced, but had to be authorised by the entity as well as by the conference itself. These clauses—exclusivity for maritime transportation and the possibility of derogations—in effect granted to the conference the right to determine who would be allowed to transport goods on the route concerned. The conference had used this right to prevent goods being transported by a company which was not a member of the association. This behaviour was deemed abusive by the Commission

---

[267] Judgment of the ECJ, at [15]. As can be seen, the prohibition is based on the implications produced in the case at issue by the principle of proportionality. It could have been structured along the lines proposed above in connection with the jurisprudence on tie-in practices. In that context, the ECJ could have said that the undertaking imposed on artists the conclusion of several transactions concerning different interests of theirs—the artists being deprived of the possibility to react, as the undertaking dominated the Belgian market.

[268] *Cewal,* Commission Decision (EEC) 93/82 relating to a proceeding pursuant to Articles 85 (IV/32.448 and IV/32.450: Cewal, Cowac and Ukwal) and 86 (IV/32.448 and IV/32.450: Cewal) of the EEC Treaty [1993] OJ L34/20; Joined Cases T 24-26 & 28/93 *Compagnie Maritime Belge Transports v Commission* [1996] ECR II-1201; Joined Cases C 395 & 396/96 P *Compagnie Maritime Belge v Commission* [2000] ECR I-1365.

[269] A maritime conference is an association of sea transporters which gather in order to regulate matters of common interest. They are generally structured on maritime routes. In this case, the conference was active on maritime links between Africa and North Sea destinations.

and the CFI, in that the use of the right led to a situation where competition was further restricted (presence of a dominant undertaking).

4.307 **Right granted by a public authority.** In other instances, the right is granted by an authority. This situation has already been examined in the context of exclusive rights granted by an authority for the exercise of certain activities—for instance the monopoly which existed previously in most Member States for the provision of telecommunications networks and services. Other forms of right may also be concerned. For instance, the case law contains several cases where dominant undertakings have made abusive use of a right granted by the law to start legal proceedings.

4.308 *Racal Decca.* In *Racal Decca*,[270] the undertaking sued competitors on the basis of a copyright which it claimed to hold over signals emitted by stations under its control. That copyright prohibited competitors, it argued, from manufacturing terminals aimed at receiving those signals without due authorisation. In each of the proceedings initiated, the undertaking posed lengthy legal questions to the opposing parties. In itself the commencement of such proceedings could not be considered abusive, indeed it should rather be conceived as a right for the undertaking to obtain protection from the judicial authorities. It however took place in a context where the undertaking was seeking to avoid the emergence of competition on the market for terminals adapted to the reception of these signals for plotting the position of ships in the North Sea. Through the legal proceedings, and the questions which were raised, the undertaking was seeking to discourage competitors from continuing their activities in view of the legal costs they would face in addition to the damages which would have to be paid if copyright indeed existed and had been violated. The legal proceedings were used as an intimidating mechanism, rather than to obtain due protection.

4.309 **Intellectual property rights.** Dominant undertakings sometimes use intellectual property rights improperly. The issue is whether these rights can be used where they lead to a lessening of competition in a situation where competition is already impaired by the existence of dominance. In *Renault*[271] and *Volvo*,[272] two car manufacturers possessed exclusivity for the manufacture and sale of spare parts for vehicles coming from their factories. For strategic reasons they wished to maintain that exclusivity. As a result, they opposed any attempt by competitive spare parts manufacturers to enter that market. Cases arose before national courts and preliminary references were addressed to the ECJ. In its rulings, the Court did not state that exclusive rights resulting from intellectual property can be

---

[270] Commission Decision (EEC) 89/113 relating to a proceeding under Articles 85 and 86 of the EEC Treaty (IV/30.979 and 31.394, Decca Navigator System) [1988] OJ L43/27.

[271] Case 53/87 *Consorzio italiano della componentistica di ricambio per autoveicoli and Maxicar v Régie nationale des usines Renault* [1988] ECR 6039.

[272] Case 238/87 *AB Volvo v Erik Veng (UK) Ltd* [1988] ECR 6211.

considered abusive per se. It ruled, however, that the use which is made of them may be abusive.

> *Volvo.* '[T]he right of the proprietor of a protected design to prevent third parties from manufacturing and selling or importing, without its consent, products incorporating the design constitutes the very subject-matter of his exclusive right.' 'It follows that an obligation imposed upon the proprietor . . . to grant to third parties, even in return for a reasonable royalty, a licence for the supply of products incorporating the design would lead to the proprietor thereof being deprived of the substance of his exclusive right.' '[A] refusal to grant such a licence cannot in itself constitute an abuse of a dominant position.' '[T]he exercise of an exclusive right . . . may be prohibited by Article 86 if it involves, on the part of an undertaking holding a dominant position, certain abusive conduct such as the arbitrary refusal to supply spare parts to independent repairers, the fixing of prices for spare parts at an unfair level or a decision no longer to produce spare parts for a particular model even though many cars of that model are still in circulation, provided that such conduct is liable to affect trade between Member States.'[273]

Copyright. A similar issue was addressed in three cases concerning broadcasting **4.310** companies which held copyright over the grid presenting the programmes they intended to broadcast during the week.[274] They refused on the basis of that copyright to allow the publication of these programmes in a weekly journal which another, independent, company sought to produce. The practice was deemed abusive, successively, by the Commission, the CFI and the ECJ. The judgment issued by the CFI is particularly interesting in that it analyses the circumstances in which the use of a right may become abusive. In the view of the CFI, rights and, in general, prerogatives, are granted with the attainment of a particular goal in view. The use which is made of them may not lead to the attainment of another purpose. In the cases at issue, the rights were granted to protect information, but were used to avoid the emergence of competition. Furthermore, the use made of rights must be reconciled with other values that are also recognised in the Treaty. Among these values is the importance of the development of markets where relations are based on competition among undertakings. For the CFI, the protection due to a right must in some circumstances be subordinated to the need for competition.[275]

(b) Threats abusive *per se*. It is not necessary in all cases that the dominant **4.311** undertaking actually adopts a practice which may be deemed abusive—in some

---

[273] At [8] and [9]. See also *Renault*, at [15] and [16].

[274] See *Magill*, Commission Decision (EEC) 89/205 relating to a proceeding under Article 86 of the EEC Treaty (IV/31.851—Magill TV Guide/ITP, BBC and RTE) [1989] OJ L078/43. Case T-69/89 *Radio Telefis Eireann v Commission* [1991] ECR II-485. Case T-76/89 *Independent Television Publications Ltd v Commission* [1991] ECR II-100575. Joined Cases C 241 & 241/91 P *Radio Telefis Eireann (RTE) and Independent Television Publications Ltd (ITP) v Commission* [1995] ECR I-743.

[275] Judgment of the CFI, *RTE*, at [65] et seq. Identical paragraphs are included in *BBC*, at [52] et seq and *ITP*, at [50] et seq.

instances the mere threat of resorting to that practice may be deemed contrary to Article 82 EC. In *Suiker Unie*, a dominant producer (of Belgian nationality) was exerting pressure on various intermediaries to induce sales to given customers.[276] A similar practice was carried out by another producer (of German origin) in order to avoid a situation where intermediaries would get some of their supplies from a competitor.[277] Two other producers (of Dutch origin) threatened to hinder the activities of three intermediaries. Under threat, these intermediaries had to sell a given quantity of sugar under conditions decided by the producers, give up another quantity of sugar to these producers and refrain from distributing the product on their own initiative without asking for prior permission from the producers.

4.312 **Further example.** In *AKZO*, the dominant undertaking threatened to lower prices significantly on all markets concerning flour additives if its competitor continued to sell certain substances. As a result of these threats, the competitor was placed in a dilemma. The first possibility was to maintain its behaviour (the sales which were opposed by the dominant undertaking). The result would then be a decision by the dominant undertaking to decrease prices as announced. The competitor would then have to decrease prices to the same extent, for fear of losing market share to the dominant undertaking. It would then suffer a decrease in revenues. The second possibility was to accept the demand made by the dominant undertaking. The competitor would then give up serving certain markets. Total turnover from its activities would then decrease, but probably to a more limited extent than under the first scenario.

4.313 **(c) Contractual rigidities.** Dominant undertakings must avoid including in their contracts clauses which restrict the freedom of customers to an unacceptable degree. Among these clauses, one which is often criticised is the long duration of contracts. The purpose of the dominant undertakings in imposing contracts of long duration is to avoid situations where customers seek other suppliers. These clauses thus, in effect, seek to protect the undertaking, in this case a dominant undertaking, from competition. Such behaviour is not acceptable. This type of clause was deemed abusive, for instance, in *Solvay*,[278] where the dominant undertaking imposed on its customers contracts of indeterminate duration. These contracts could be ended only after a long notice period.[279] Clauses of this type were also condemned in *Alsatel*,[280] where the contract imposed by the dominant

---

[276] See the decision of the Commission, 38, col a and judgment of the ECJ, at [366] et seq.

[277] See the decision of the Commission, 39, col b. The allegation has not been retained by the ECJ. See judgment of the ECJ, at [459] et seq.

[278] *Solvay*, Commission Decision (EEC) 91/299 relating to a proceeding under Article 86 of the EEC Treaty (IV/33.133-C: Soda-ash—Solvay) [1991] OJ L152/21.

[279] See decision of the Commission, at [8].

[280] Case 247/86 *Société alsacienne et lorraine de télécommunications et d'électronique (Alsatel) v SA Novasam* [1988] ECR 5987.

undertaking provided that it would be renewed automatically for a duration of 15 years where modifications were made to the installations placed on customers' premises and these modifications reached a certain value.

(d) Legal proceedings. The question to know whether legal proceedings can amount to an abuse, where these proceedings are initiated by a dominant undertaking, has been examined by the Commission and the CFI in one of the rare cases leading to an official decision in the telecommunications sector. That case, *ITT Promedia*,[281] concerns access to subscriber data for the publication of a directory in Belgium.[282] ITT Promedia sought to obtain from Belgacom data about subscribers to the public electronic communications network in Belgium. The relations between the two parties became intense and several proceedings were initiated. Several complaints were addressed by ITT Promedia to the Commission. In some of them, the complainant argued that Belgacom was abusing its dominant position through the attitude that it was adopting in the course of these legal proceedings.   **4.314**

Attitude of the Commission. In its decision, the Commission considered that legal proceedings qualify as an abuse in exceptional circumstances. Two conditions must be fulfilled. *(a)* First, the only reasonable interpretation of behaviour adopted by the dominant undertaking is to consider that these proceedings are used by that undertaking as a tool to harass its opponent. *(b)* Second, it appears that the legal proceedings do not constitute isolated actions. They are part of a series of actions which, together, indicate the existence of a plan, on the part of that undertaking, to hinder competition.   **4.315**

> *Commission.* '[I]n principle the bringing of an action, which is the expression of the fundamental right of access to a judge, cannot be characterised as an abuse . . . unless . . . an undertaking in a dominant position brings an action (i) which cannot reasonably be considered as an attempt to establish its rights and can therefore only serve to harass the opposite party, and (ii) which is conceived in the framework of a plan whose goal is to eliminate competition.'[283]

Position of the CFI. The position adopted by the Commission was confirmed, in substance, by the CFI. The CFI does not take a stance on the conditions proposed by the Commission to consider whether legal proceedings may be analysed as an abuse. The reason is that these conditions were not challenged by the applicant. It stressed however that the possibility of bringing an action is a fundamental right which can only be limited in exceptional circumstances.   **4.316**

---

[281] Case T-111/96 *ITT Promedia NV v Commission* [1998] ECR II-2937.

[282] The prices charged by Belgacom for the transfer of the relevant data were excessive, and discriminatory, compared to the tariff that Belgacom was charging for an internal transfer of these data to its subsidiary in charge of the same service.

[283] Decision of the Commission, as summarised by the CFI, at [30] of the ruling. The decision taken by the Commission has not been published.

CFI. '[The] ability to assert one's rights through the courts and the judicial control . . . constitute the expression of a general principle of law which underlies the constitutional traditions common to the Member States and which is also laid down in Articles 6 and 13 of the European Convention for the Protection of Human Rights and Fundamental Freedoms of 4 November 1950.' 'As access to the Court is a fundamental right and a general principle ensuring the rule of law, it is only in wholly exceptional circumstances that the fact that legal proceedings are brought is capable of constituting an abuse of an dominant position within the meaning of Article 86 of the Treaty.' '[S]ince the two cumulative criteria constitute an exception to the general principle of access to the courts, which ensures the rule of law, they must be construed and applied strictly, in a manner which does not defeat the application of the general rule.'[284]

F. Objective Justifications

4.317 **An exception to the prohibition.** Various practices qualifying as abusive under Article 82 EC have been examined. In several cases, the institution involved (Commission, CFI or ECJ) has submitted that, although abusive in appearance, the practice could be justified if acceptable reasons were provided. That possibility should be read in connection with the basic regulatory principles examined in the chapter concerning the rules and principles applicable throughout the framework. There it was emphasised that the provisions concerning competition and the internal market are divided into two parts. The first part contains an obligation—or rather, a prohibition, as in most provisions an obligation not to do something is imposed. Into that category falls for instance the prohibition on abuses of a dominant position or the conclusion of anti-competitive agreements. The second part introduces a derogation under which a prohibited practice can be excused if certain conditions are fulfilled. These conditions correspond in substance to requirements analysed in connection with the basic regulatory principles. They are as follows. *(a)* The practice must be adopted in connection with an objective that is acceptable at European level. *(b)* The practice must conform with the various requirements connected to proportionality.[285]

4.318 **Articles 81 and 82 EC.** Authors generally emphasise a difference between the two main provisions dealing with anti-competitive behaviour besides concentrations. Article 81 EC, they say, provides a possibility of granting an exemption, whereas that possibility does not exist for Article 82 EC. The consequence would be that abusive practices may not be excused under the latter provision. A different opinion is defended in this book. Very early in the case law, the Commission

---

[284] At [60] and [61].

[285] These requirements are as follows. There must exist a link between the practice and the purpose. (The practice must make it possible to attain the said goal.) No other measure may be available to ensure the realisation of the same goal while threatening less a European value. European values, competition in particular, may not be affected to an excessive degree.

and European courts introduced the possibility for dominant undertakings to present arguments to justify their behaviour. It is difficult, if not impossible, to provide an exhaustive account of the circumstances which may justify the granting of a derogation. Where they are trying to construe such an excuse, practitioners should not necessarily seek to draw analogies with other cases. The best strategy is to draft arguments on the basis of the principles set out in the paragraphs above. Similarly, practitioners seeking to fend off a tentative justification should rely on these principles and see how the facts may be used to establish that these principles cannot apply in the case at issue.

A typical example.   The possibility of enjoying a justification under Article 82 EC   **4.319** can be analysed using *British Midland*, a case decided on the basis of general competition law.[286] That case concerns the behaviour adopted by Aer Lingus, the then Irish national airline company. In that case, the behaviour at issue was adopted vis-à-vis a potential competitor, British Midland. At the time the case arose, Aer Lingus dominated the market for airline traffic between Ireland and the United Kingdom. That market attracted the attention of British Midland, a newcomer which had developed successfully an activity on internal routes in the United Kingdom after the airline industry had been liberalised in that country. The newcomer sought to expand its activities through the provision of services to other countries. Under normal circumstances, airlines are allowed to issue tickets on flights provided by other companies including competitors (interline). This mechanism is explained by the impossibility for airline companies of organising their own flights to all possible destinations. As a result of such interline agreements, companies may 'interconnect' their routes and offer to the public a network of flights reaching around the world.[287]

The behaviour in question.   In the case at issue, Aer Lingus denied British   **4.320** Midland the right to use this mechanism. The interline mechanism would have been useful for British Midland. That undertaking was not at first in a position to organise frequent flights between London and Dublin. The frequency proposed by that undertaking was then limited to one or two flights per day. That situation

---

[286] *British Midland/Aer Lingus*, Commission Decision 92/213 relating to a procedure pursuant to Articles 85 and 86 of the EEC Treaty (IV/33.544, British Midland v Aer Lingus) [1992] OJ L96/34.

[287] The service is particularly appreciated for unusual, complex, routes. Suppose that a customer wants to fly from London to a city in Brazil. It turns to British Airways. Although that latter undertaking organises a significant number of flights from London, it does not serve all regional airports in Brazil. In order to provide a satisfactory solution to the consumer, the journey is organised in several parts. A first flight is provided by British Airways from London to São Paolo. A connection is then organised to the regional airport by a local company. The journey thus takes place on flights provided by two different companies. It would not be convenient to require the customer to deal with these two separate companies. To avoid that inconvenience, British Airways is allowed to act as an agent for the Brazilian regional company. In that situation, British Airways issues two tickets—one for its own flight and another for the flight ensured by the Brazilian company.

was not considered satisfactory by most customers, who wanted to have a choice between different schedules when they contacted British Midland to organise their journeys. The undertaking thought that using the interline mechanism would allow it to satisfy its customers by combining its own flights with those offered by Aer Lingus. That option was however made impossible as a result of the decision taken by Aer Lingus to refuse the use of the interline agreement by British Midland. The consequence of that decision was that British Midland could only offer its own flights to its customers.

4.321 **Attitude of the Commission.**   The decision taken by Aer Lingus was not deemed compatible with competition rules. In its decision, the Commission points out that that undertaking dominated the market for flights between Ireland and the United Kingdom. It had received a request from another company already active on the same market and seeking to expand its business opportunities. According to the Commission, a dominant undertaking may not refuse business relations with a competitor where that refusal impedes entry into a market or makes it more difficult.

> *British Midland.* 'Whether a duty to interline arises depends on the effects on competition of the refusal to interline; it would exist in particular when the refusal or withdrawal of interline facilities by a dominant airline is objectively likely to have a significant impact on the other airline's ability to start a new service or sustain an existing service on account of its effects on the other airline's costs and revenue in respect of the service in question, and when the dominant airline cannot give any objective commercial reason for its refusal (such as concerns about creditworthiness) other than its wish to avoid helping this particular competitor.'[288]

4.322 **Attempt to justify behaviour.**   In that case, the Commission discussed at length the context in which the behaviour was adopted by the dominant undertaking. Among other important considerations, the Commission noted that the behaviour could not be justified by any acceptable, or objective, reason. The reason invoked by Aer Lingus was that it could not be obliged to help a competitor develop a presence on a market where it was itself carrying out activities.[289] That reason was set aside because, as the Commission states, the purpose of competition is to organise rivalry among undertakings in the hope of constraining market participants to improve their performance for the benefit of consumers.[290]

---

[288] At [26].

[289] In this regard, the Commission underlines the importance of barriers to entry on airline markets. For that authority, a new company seeking to start an airline route will not readily be able to attain profitability. The difficulty is only increased when that undertaking cannot use the interline agreement, as a result of a refusal by the undertakings already present to allow the newcomer to issue tickets on their flights. See [27], para 1.

[290] See [25]. 'Refusing to interline is not normal competition on the merits. Interlining has for many years been accepted industry practice, with widely acknowledged benefits for both airlines and passengers. A refusal to interline for other reasons than problems with currency convertibility or doubts about the creditworthiness of the beneficiary airline is a highly unusual step and has up to now not been considered by the European airline industry as a normal competitive strategy.'

Proportionality.   The Commission further analysed the proportionality of the **4.323** behaviour of the dominant undertaking. In that context it compared the damage that would be suffered by the two undertakings should one or other scenario be adopted (acceptance or refusal of interline). The Commission observed that the refusal to grant the interline service had caused considerable damage to British Midland, which had not been able to provide enough connections to interested customers. By contrast, Aer Lingus would not have suffered great harm if the interline facility had been granted. Admittedly the provision of the interline service would have increased competition between the two undertakings. The consequence would have been, probably, a reduction in the revenues collected by Aer Lingus, as British Midland would have reinforced its presence. But increased competition, and the resulting reallocation of market shares depending on the choices made by customers, are precisely the objectives pursued by general competition law. In that context, the best response for Aer Lingus in the face of a new and threatening presence by British Midland was to improve performance, not hinder competition.[291]

Attention to the context.   Finally, the Commission emphasised the particular cir- **4.324** cumstances in which the behaviour took place. For 35 years Aer Lingus had accepted interline tickets issued by other companies for use on its flights. The refusal to allow the use of this facility by British Midland appeared as an abrupt change in a policy followed for years by the undertaking.[292] The interline agreement was accepted by the vast majority of airline companies worldwide (95 per cent). Not to accept that that agreement could be used on a particular route could be analysed, as a result, as a deviation from the standard usage applicable in the sector.[293] Finally, a third company, British Airways, was present on the air route between London and Dublin. That company had been covering the route for several years already, using the interline agreement with Aer Lingus. The use of that agreement could be interpreted as a sign that the interline mechanism conferred advantages on consumers. As a corollary, it showed that the refusal by Aer Lingus to grant access to British Midland was motivated by a desire to protect its operations against the new competitor. For the Commission, that behaviour could not be accepted under competition rules.[294]

G. The Essential Facilities Doctrine

(1) Principles

Sector-specific regulation.   In the course of this book, it has been made clear **4.325** that several obligations may, pursuant to sector-specific regulation, be imposed on

---

[291] See [25].   [292] See [26] in fine.   [293] See [25](1).
[294] See [29]. It is to be noted that British Airways never seemed to adopt very active commercial policies on that route. It indeed withdrew from the route after British Midland started to operate on it.

undertakings holding significant market power. *(a)* One obligation is to give access to infrastructure or other resources, where access is needed by another undertaking to provide a service. *(b)* Another obligation is to give access under acceptable conditions. To satisfy the latter obligation, access must be granted under satisfactory financial and technical conditions. These conditions may not be discriminatory. This prohibition on the application of discriminatory conditions implies that equivalent conditions must be applied in equivalent circumstances to undertakings providing equivalent services. It also entails an obligation for undertakings holding significant market power to supply other undertakings with services and information under the same conditions as they use for their own services or those of their partners or subsidiaries.[295]

4.326 **The essential facilities doctrine.** These various obligations may be found in the NRF and have been construed as being an application of the 'essential facilities doctrine'. That doctrine was developed in the first instance in the United States, where several authors argued that some cases decided by the American courts supported an obligation for undertakings to share access to essential facilities under their control. Under that doctrine, access would have to be granted under acceptable, and non-discriminatory, conditions.

4.327 **Introduction in the European Union.** This doctrine received a warm echo on the European continent, where the Commission was looking for a sound basis to open existing electronic communications infrastructure to all interested service providers.[296] The European competition rules provided some basis for the development of that doctrine, in the case law relating to the refusal to deal and the prohibition on discrimination. However, there was no explicit reference in the case law to an obligation to share access and avoid discrimination when using scarce infrastructure.

4.328 **Legal basis.** The essential facilities doctrine does not itself provide a legal basis for prohibiting and sanctioning behaviour. In the European Union, rules and sanctions may be imposed in the field of competition only where they are based on a Treaty provision or an instrument adopted in application of such a provision. Most attempts to use the doctrine in the case law have been made in connection with Article 82 EC. Using the doctrine, that provision has been construed, in one part of the case law, as containing an obligation for dominant undertakings to share access where a facility under their control is necessary for the exercise of activities on an adjacent market.[297]

---

[295] See the Access Directive, Art 10(2).

[296] As a reminder, the telecommunications markets had been reserved to national monopolies for decades. The Commission was willing to develop, in the first instance, the markets for telecommunications services. Such a development could only intervene if, and to the extent that, the existing infrastructure could be used by service providers different from the incumbent operators.

[297] The doctrine has also been used in some cases, in connection with Art 81 EC. In that context, the purpose is not to establish an abuse allegedly committed by one or several undertakings.

Following paragraphs. In the following paragraphs the cases that are tradition- **4.329**
ally associated with the essential facilities doctrine are analysed. As will appear,
these cases were decided after a number of authors and, to a certain extent, the
Commission had started to discuss the relevance of the doctrine in the context of
liberalisation. For that reason it is generally assumed that these cases provide a
kind of official position adopted by the European institutions in a binding instrument. There is one leading case per institution with the power to intervene in the
application of general competition law (Commission, CFI, ECJ).

(2) Position of the Commission

Leading case (*Stena Sealink*). The application and development of the essential **4.330**
facilities doctrine is supported by the Commission. Encouraged by various
authors,[298] the Commission undertook to apply the doctrine in the case law. The
first, and clearest, application was made in *Stena Sealink (1994)*. That case is
discussed above in this chapter, in the section dealing with refusal to deal (see
paras 4.49–4.50). In that case, the Commission ruled that an undertaking in a
dominant position has an obligation to share with other undertakings, including
competitors, access to facilities under its control, where that access is necessary to
carry out activities on a derived market. In its ruling, the Commission stated that
that obligation applies where the facility, or resource, concerned, is 'essential'.

> *Decision of the Commission.* 'An undertaking which occupies a dominant position
> in the provision of an *essential facility* and itself uses that facility (ie a facility or
> infrastructure, without access to which competitors cannot provide services to their
> customers), and which refuses other companies access to that facility without objec-
> tive justification or grants access to competitors only on terms less favourable than
> those which it gives its own services, infringes Article [82] . . . if the other conditions
> of that Article are met.' 'The owner of an *essential facility* which uses its power in one
> market in order to protect or strengthen its position in another related market, in
> particular, by refusing to grant access to a competitor, or by granting access on less
> favourable terms than those of its own services, and thus imposing a competitive
> disadvantage on its competitor, infringes Article [82] . . .'[299]

It is rather to demonstrate the scope of the power held by the undertakings concerned. A similar use
could be made of the Merger Regulation, to establish that the merging undertakings are likely to
acquire market power as a result of their operation. This section only refers to cases using the
doctrine in the context of Art 82 EC.

[298] That path has been taken, among others, by a prominent scholar, J Temple Lang, who is also
a former director in DG Competition within the Commission. In his review, J Temple Lang takes
all of Art 82 EC into consideration. He even goes further, by adding some Art 81 EC cases and
other cases examined under the Merger Regulation. See J Temple Lang, 'Defining Legitimate
Competition: Companies' Duties to Supply Competitors and Access to Essential Facilities' [1994]
18 Fordham LJ 437.

[299] *Stena Sealink*, Commission Decision EC (94/19) relating to a proceeding pursuant to
Article 86 of the EC Treaty (IV/34.689—Sea Containers v. Stena Sealink—Interim measures)
[1994] OJ L15/8, at [66] (authors' emphasis).

4.331 **Application to telecommunications.** The decision analysed in the previous paragraph only concerned the adoption of interim measures.[300] These measures are intended to improve the situation of the undertaking requesting access, during the procedure leading to a final decision concerning the behaviour adopted by the dominant undertaking. The transitory character of the decision adopted in *Stena Sealink* has not prevented the Commission from giving prominent status to the case. For the Commission, the case establishes an obligation to share access to essential facilities. Such an obligation may be useful in the telecommunications sector where existing infrastructure must also be shared by service providers.

> *1998 Competition Guidelines.* 'In the transport field . . . , the Commission has ruled that an undertaking controlling an essential facility must give access in certain circumstances.'[301] 'The same principles apply to the telecommunications sector.'[302] 'The principle obliging dominant companies to contract in certain circumstances will often be relevant in the telecommunications sector. Currently, there are monopolies or virtual monopolies in the provision of network infrastructure for most telecom services in the Community. Even where restrictions have already been, or will soon be, lifted, competition in downstream markets will continue to depend upon the pricing and conditions of access to upstream network services that will only gradually reflect competitive market forces. Given the pace of technological change in the telecommunications sector, it is possible to envisage situations where companies would seek to offer new products or services which are not in competition with products or services already offered by the dominant access operator, but for which this operator is reluctant to provide access.'[303]

4.332 **Underlying motives.** Ultimately, the essential facilities doctrine expresses a political desire that the Commission shares with the Council and Parliament to open existing infrastructure to new service providers. The purpose was initially to put an end to the era of telecommunications monopoly. It is now to ensure that existing infrastructures are used efficiently for the benefit of customers.

> *1998 Competition Guidelines.* 'The Commission must ensure that the control over facilities enjoyed by incumbent operators is not used to hamper the development of a competitive telecommunications environment. A company which is dominant on a market for services and which commits an abuse contrary to Article [82] . . . on that market may be required, in order to put an end to the abuse, to supply access to its facility to one or more competitors on that market. In particular, a company may abuse its dominant position if by its actions it prevents the emergence of a new product or service.'[304]

(3) Behaviour concerned

4.333 **Various types of behaviour.** The analysis provided by the Commission in *Stena Sealink* and the 1998 Competition Guidelines provides indications concerning

---

[300] The decision was adopted upon a complaint submitted by Sea Containers and asking for an authorisation to provide the service through the facility owned and operated by Stena Sealink.
[301] At [86].   [302] At [86].   [303] At [88].   [304] At [90].

the types of behaviour falling under the doctrine. Typical behaviour is a refusal to give access to an essential facility under the control of a dominant undertaking. That behaviour tends to be rare, however. It appears in practice that undertakings seldom adopt such a straightforward reaction. They do so, probably, out of a desire to avoid jeopardising relations, undermining their reputation and attracting the attention of the authorities. For these reasons, undertakings generally adopt other attitudes which, even if they appear more courteous, often boil down to a refusal. In *Stena Sealink*, the dominant undertaking used technical arguments constantly to delay giving access. This led the Commission to delineate the sorts of behaviour which it considers may be analysed as a refusal under the doctrine. Three forms of behaviour are envisaged in the 1998 Competition Guidelines: delaying tactics, technical issues and proposing access under unsatisfactory financial conditions.

> *1998 Competition Notice.* 'Three important elements relating to access which could be manipulated by the access provider in order, in effect, to refuse to provide access are timing, technical configuration and price.'

Delays.   In *Stena Sealink*, the dominant undertaking used delaying tactics to **4.334** avoid giving access. In the view of the Commission these tactics may amount to a refusal to deal. They can, as a result, be analysed as an abuse of a dominant position. A similar attitude is adopted in the 1998 Competition Guidelines, where the Commission makes clear that delays are abusive where they are undue, inexplicable or unjustified. Comparisons may be used to establish the abusive character of the delay. *(a)* The Commission may compare the treatment given by the dominant undertaking to applications coming from various entities. Where, for instance, access is granted by the dominant undertakings to one of its departments, to a subsidiary or to a partner, the Commission investigates whether the application from independent undertakings is treated with similar care. *(b)* Independently of the activities carried out by undertakings, the Commission may also investigate the efficiency used in other Member States to answer requests by undertakings seeking access. The purpose in this context is to exert pressure on dominant undertakings to use best-practice standards observed in the European Union.

> *1998 Competition Notice, para 95.* 'Dominant TOs [telecommunications operators] have a duty to deal with requests for access efficiently: undue and inexplicable or unjustified delays in responding to a request for access may constitute an abuse. In particular, however, the Commission will seek to compare the response to a request for access with: *(a)* the usual time frame and conditions applicable when the responding party grants access to its facilities to its own subsidiary or operating branch; *(b)* responses to requests for access to similar facilities in other Member States; *(c)* the explanations given for any delay in dealing with requests for access.'

Technical issues.   Dominant undertakings may also use technical arguments to **4.335** avoid giving access. Again, comparisons may be used to establish a possible abuse.

Raising technical issues to refuse access is abusive if the dominant undertaking has not raised the same difficulty with respect to applications coming from other entities, in particular departments using the facility within its own organisation. Limited capacity may however justify the impossibility for a dominant undertaking of granting access. Moreover, the undertaking may refuse access where the service provider does not comply with technical standards used on the infrastructure. These standards must however be legitimate. This requirement is fulfilled only where the standard is intended to achieve an objective deemed acceptable at European level and where the means used to achieve that end conform with the various tests associated with proportionality.

> *1998 Competition Notice, para 96.* 'Issues of technical configuration will similarly be closely examined in order to determine whether they are genuine. In principle, competition rules require that the party requesting access must be granted access at the most suitable point for the requesting party, provided that this point is technically feasible for the access provider. Questions of technical feasibility may be objective justifications for refusing to supply—for example, the traffic for which access is sought must satisfy the relevant technical standards for the infrastructure—or there may be questions of capacity restraints, where questions of rationing may arise.'

4.336 **Tariffs.** In some cases, access may be granted under conditions which make it financially impossible for the undertaking seeking access to carry out its activities. These excessive tariffs imposed by the dominant undertaking may in themselves be deemed abusive under the classic case law on unfair terms under Article 82 EC. The behaviour may also be analysed as a disguised refusal to deal under the same provision, using the essential facilities doctrine.

> *1998 Competition Notice, para 97.* 'Excessive pricing for access, as well as being abusive in itself, may also amount to an effective refusal to grant access.'

(4) Conditions drawn up by the Commission

4.337 **First indications.** The doctrine signals that dominant undertakings must share access under acceptable and non-discriminatory conditions. In itself, it gives no detail about the circumstances in which that obligation may be imposed. In *Stena Sealink*, two indications are provided on the subject. *(a)* Access can be ordered only where the facilities are essential. That condition is fulfilled where competitors cannot provide services to their customers without access to that facility. *(b)* The development of an ancillary market—that of the services provided through infrastructure—would be jeopardised in the absence of access to the facility.

4.338 **Development of these conditions.** These conditions have been developed in the 1998 Competition Guidelines. In that instrument, the Commission explained which conditions must be fulfilled for the doctrine to apply. *(a)* The facility must be essential for the exercise of activities on an adjacent market. *(b)* Access must be possible to the facility, in terms of capacity (the capacity of the facility must be sufficient to service the interests of the controlling operator and, at the same time, of the undertakings seeking access). *(c)* In the absence of access to the facility, activities on the adjacent market will not develop in a satisfactory manner. *(d)* The undertaking seeking access is ready to pay an acceptable contribution for the use of the facility. *(e)* There is no objective reason to refuse access.

> *1998 Competition Guidelines, para 91.* 'In order to determine whether access should be ordered under the competition rules, account will be taken of . . . the following elements, taken cumulatively: *(a)* access to the facility in question is generally essential in order for companies to compete on that related market'; '*(b)* there is sufficient capacity available to provide access; *(c)* the facility owner fails to satisfy demand on an existing service or product market, blocks the emergence of a potential new service or product, or impedes competition on an existing or potential service or product market; *(d)* the company seeking access is prepared to pay the reasonable and non-discriminatory price and will otherwise in all respects accept non-discriminatory access terms and conditions; *(e)* there is no objective justification for refusing to provide access'.

Comparison of the conditions.   From a comparison, it appears that the positions adopted by the Commission in *Stena Sealink* and the 1998 Competition Guidelines are identical in substance. These positions show that one condition (the essential character of the facility) is central to the application of the doctrine. The other indications, presented as conditions by the Commission, have a less determinant role. **4.339**

Essential character.   The key condition is that the facility must be essential. Under *Stena Sealink*, there must be no alternative to the facility. If an alternative may be found, the facility loses its essential character. That standard was maintained by the Commission in the 1998 Competition Guidelines. Under these guidelines, a facility may be deemed essential where the exercise of the ancillary activity would not be possible in the absence of access. The case can be decided quickly where the facility cannot be duplicated for technical reasons. A further assessment must be made where the impossibility is of an economic nature. In such a context, it is not sufficient to argue that access would help the service provider to exercise its activities at a lower cost. A facility may only be deemed essential for economic reasons where activities would not otherwise be commercially feasible, or would be seriously and unavoidably uneconomic. **4.340**

> *1998 Competition Guidelines.* 'The key issue . . . is . . . what is essential. It will not be sufficient that the position of the company requesting access would be more advantageous if access were granted—but refusal of access must lead to the proposed activities being made either impossible or seriously and unavoidably uneconomic.'[305] 'If there were no commercially feasible alternatives to the access being requested, then unless access is granted, the party requesting access would not be able to operate on the service market.'[306]

---

[305] At [91].   [306] At [89].

4.341 **Absence of objective justification.** Even where the facility is essential, the doctrine does not apply where access may be refused on legitimate grounds. Dominant undertakings are allowed to refuse access where they have an objective reason to do so. This aspect of the case law should come as no surprise. It applies to the more general possibility examined above in connection with Article 82 EC and under which apparently abusive behaviour does not fall under the prohibition where it can be justified on objective grounds.

4.342 **Sufficient capacity.** A concrete difficulty is to determine what reasons can be deemed objective to avoid the application of the doctrine. A typical circumstance is where the capacity available on an infrastructure is not sufficient to serve the needs of all interested undertakings. Various issues may arise in this connection.

4.343 **(a) Allocation among applicants.** A first issue is how capacity may be allocated among undertakings other than the entity controlling the infrastructure. Suppose that an infrastructure is dominated by one entity. Several other undertakings ask for access. There is not enough capacity to satisfy the needs of those applicants. The question is how capacity may be allocated. Under the competition rules there should be no discrimination as between applicants. There will be no discrimination where the allocation is based on objective criteria. One objective criterion could be a percentage of the needs expressed by the undertakings. For instance, each undertaking could be allocated 40 per cent of their needs, if that division ensures that all applicants have access to the facility. Another possible criterion could be the timing of the applications made. Where an undertaking has been using an infrastructure for several years, the proportion allocated to that undertaking should not be reduced abruptly even if the purpose is to provide access to other applicants. Time should be given to that undertaking so that it can adjust to the necessity of sharing capacity with other applicants.[307]

4.344 **(b) Allocation with the dominant undertaking.** In most circumstances, the issue is how to allocate capacity among all interested companies including the dominant undertaking. In these circumstances, it must be decided whether the dominant undertaking should give up part of the available capacity to provide access to other entities. The question is more delicate than the previous situation. The controlling undertaking has contributed time, effort and resources to the establishment and development of an infrastructure. As a result of these investments it may not be considered as a mere applicant. A balance must be struck between the legitimate interests of that undertaking, which must be taken into

---

[307] In the absence of a transitional period, the undertaking would indeed suffer excessive damages. Furthermore, the development of competition may require that one large service provider exists beyond the controlling entity. It is often more difficult for an entity controlling an infrastructure to compete on an adjacent market for services in the presence of a large service provider.

account, and the necessities of competition, which require that other undertakings receive access in order to exercise their activities.

> *1998 Competition Notice, para 91.* 'Relevant justifications . . . could include . . . the need for a facility owner which has undertaken investment aimed at the introduction of a new product or service to have sufficient time and opportunity to use the facility in order to place that new product or service on the market. However, although any justification will have to be examined carefully on a case-by-case basis, it is particularly important in the telecommunications sector that the benefits to end-users which will arise from a competitive environment are not undermined by the actions of the former State monopolists in preventing competition from emerging and developing.'

Assessment. There is no concrete indicator available in the case law to carry out **4.345** that assessment. The assessment depends mainly on circumstances. If the level of competition on the market is low, there is an argument to restrict the capacity allocated to the controlling undertaking and grant it to competitors. If the level of competition is not so low, the interests of the controlling undertaking appear more legitimate. The criterion probably lies in the power held by the controlling undertaking on the market. If, as a result of that power, the controlling undertaking may be said to be dominant, there appears to exist a sufficient reason to order access. That conclusion can be reached on the basis of the general principles underlying the case law on Article 82 EC. According to that case law, dominant undertakings have a special responsibility to avoid actions which may undermine further the already weakened degree of competition. They also have a positive duty to take all action likely to allow the development of competition. That prohibition, and the corresponding obligation, only disappear where dominance ceases to exist, ie where the undertaking controlling the facility loses its dominance.[308]

Proportionality. As was stated during the discussion on objective justifications, **4.346** competition rules may be set aside in the context of Article 82 EC where behaviour adopted by a dominant undertaking may be explained by an objective which can be deemed acceptable at European level. Another requirement is that the means used by the undertaking to reach that end must conform with the principle of proportionality. In order to have an overview of that requirement, developments in relation to proportionality may be referred to in Chapter 2 dealing with the rules and principles applicable throughout the framework.

> *1998 Competition Guidelines, para 93.* 'The question of objective justification will require particularly close analysis in this area. In addition to determining whether difficulties cited in any particular case are serious enough to justify the refusal to

---

[308] In this case, domination is not to be measured on the market where the facility is located. It is rather to be taken into account on the adjacent market for activities carried out with the use of the facility. If the undertaking controlling the facility is one of the players on that adjacent market and competition is developed, there is probably no reason to intervene. By contrast, if the controlling undertaking has used the facility to impose its position on the adjacent market, intervention is mandated.

grant access, the relevant authorities must also decide whether these difficulties are sufficient to outweigh the damage done to competition if access is refused or made more difficult and the downstream service markets are thus limited.'

4.347 **Risk for an adjacent market.**   Under the essential facilities doctrine, access to an infrastructure is granted because that infrastructure is essential for the exercise of activities on an adjacent market. The development of competition on the adjacent market is thus the objective that is sought through the application of the doctrine. The importance of that adjacent market appears in *Stena Sealink*, where the Commission sought to develop the market for maritime services provided through port facilities. It also appears in the 1998 Competition Guidelines, where the Commission endeavoured, as it does still today, to create the best possible regulatory environment for the development of electronic communications services.[309]

(5) Case law of the CFI

4.348 **Leading case (*Tiercé Ladbroke*).**   As stated above, there is one leading case in connection with the essential facility doctrine per institution applying competition rules in the European Union. That case is *Tiercé Ladbroke* as far as the CFI is concerned. It concerned an undertaking organising betting on horse races. The undertaking owned premises where customers could place their bets, and sought permission to show on its Belgian premises television images of races run in France and on which bets were placed. The images belonged to another undertaking, which refused to grant the requested permission. The Commission found the refusal abusive. The decision adopted by that institution was submitted to the CFI, by which it was overruled. For the CFI, horse-race images cannot be deemed a resource essential for the organisation of betting.

> *Judgment of the CFI.* [131] 'The refusal to supply the applicant could not fall within the prohibition laid down by Article [82] . . . unless it concerned a product or service which was either essential for the exercise of the activity in question, in that there was no real or potential substitute, or was a new product whose introduction might be prevented, despite specific, constant and regular potential demand on the part of consumers.' [132] 'In this case, . . . the televised broadcasting of horse races, although constituting an additional, and indeed suitable, service for bettors, it is not in itself indispensable for the exercise of bookmakers' main activity, namely the taking of bets, as is evidenced by the fact that the applicant is present on the Belgian betting market and occupies a significant position as regards bets on French races.

---

[309] The importance of the adjacent market cannot be considered, however, as a separate condition. It is already included in the requirement that the facility must be essential. As stated above, an infrastructure, for instance, satisfies that requirement when it is necessary for the exercise of an activity on an adjacent market. The presence of such an adjacent market may not be considered, as a result, as a separate condition. Nor is the willingness of the authority to encourage the development of competition and economic activities on that market. Pursuant to the EC Treaty, competition must develop on all markets. Exceptions are only accepted when they are provided in the Treaty, or in binding instruments adopted on the basis of the Treaty.

Moreover, transmission is not indispensable, since it takes place after bets are placed, with the result that its absence does not in itself affect the choices made by bettors and, accordingly, cannot prevent bookmakers from pursuing their business.'

Same position as the Commission. In its ruling, the CFI agrees that essential **4.349** resources must be shared. It considers however that the essential facilities doctrine should not apply in the case at issue, as the necessary conditions are not fulfilled. As the Commission had proposed, the CFI rules that the doctrine may apply only where the resource or facility is indispensable for an activity on an adjacent market. In the case at issue, displaying images was not a condition for the organisation of betting. Admittedly, the undertaking seeking access would probably attract more bets if images could be shown. The doctrine is not intended, however, to improve the situation of undertakings on adjacent markets. It only applies where the adjacent activity is not possible in the absence of access to the resource concerned.

Special features. As appears from the extract quoted above, the CFI emphasises **4.350** in the case features that are different from the situations aimed at in the doctrine. As has been stated, the doctrine applies where an undertaking is present on two markets and a resource on the first market is a condition for the activity on an adjacent market. In that situation there is a risk that the undertaking could leverage the power held on the first market (resource or facility) to dominate the second. The context was different in *Tiercé Ladbroke*. In that case, the undertaking controlling access to images was present on the first market (images) but absent from the second (betting), which it (apparently) had no intention of entering. In that situation, there was no risk that the undertaking would leverage the power conferred by the resource at stake in an attempt to develop a presence, and dominance, on the second market (betting).

The essential facilities doctrine and the case law of the CFI **4.351**

Essential facilities doctrine	*Tiercé Ladbroke*
An undertaking controls a facility or resource	→ Idem
That facility or resource is a condition for the exercise of the activity on an adjacent market	→ Idem
The undertaking controlling the facility or resource may use that position to reserve an adjacent market for its own benefit	↔ The undertaking controlling the facility or resource *is not* present on the adjacent market
Access is ordered to allow the presence and development of competitors on the adjacent market	↔ There is *no risk* that the power held as a result of the facility or resource will be leveraged onto the adjacent market

Absence of discrimination. The structure of the cases examined under the **4.352** essential facilities doctrine shows that that doctrine is very close to the prohibition imposed on dominant undertakings from adopting discriminatory behaviour. As stated above, the doctrine implies that access must be granted to ensure the development of activities on a second market which could be monopolised as a result of the undertaking leveraging the power resulting from control over the essential facility. The doctrine thus applies in situations where a dominant undertaking has access to resources or facilities from which other undertakings are barred or which other undertakings may only access under unsatisfactory conditions.

> *Judgment of the CFI.* '[I]n the absence of direct or indirect exploitation by the *sociétés de courses* of their intellectual property rights on the Belgian market, their refusal to supply cannot be regarded as involving any restriction of competition on the Belgian market.'[310] 'It is common ground that the *sociétés de courses* have not granted any licence for the territory of Belgium to date. Accordingly, their refusal to grant a licence to Ladbroke does not constitute discrimination as between operators on the Belgian market.'[311] '[T]he ECJ held that an undertaking abuses a dominant position where, without any objective necessity, it reserves to itself or to an undertaking belonging to the same group an ancillary activity which might be carried out by another undertaking as part of its activities on a neighbouring but separate market. However, in this case the sociétés de courses have not reserved the Belgian market in French sound and pictures to themselves and have not granted access to that market to a third-party undertaking or to an undertaking belonging to them.'[312]

(6) Case law of the ECJ

4.353 **Leading case (*Bronner*).** The leading case adopted by the ECJ is *Bronner*.[313] In that case, the ECJ focuses on the circumstances in which a resource can be deemed necessary for the exercise of an activity. The case concerned the publisher of a newspaper, which sought authorisation to use the distribution system established by another undertaking. The latter undertaking was active on the market for newspaper distribution, and also published newspapers. The case thus presented a structure typical for the application of the doctrine. *(a)* An undertaking was present on two markets (publication of newspapers, distribution of newspapers). *(b)* Another was present on one of these markets (publication). *(c)* That second undertaking sought access to the distribution network established by the first one, by claiming that it would otherwise have to cease its activities.

4.354 **No application of the doctrine.** In the judgment, the ECJ does not apply the essential facilities doctrine. The ECJ merely refers to the Treaty provisions concerned (particularly Article 82 EC) and to its own case law. For the ECJ, an obligation to share access may be imposed only where the resource is indispensable for the exercise of an activity. There must exist no real, or potential, substitute to the resource concerned. That condition did not appear to be fulfilled in the case. The assessment made by the ECJ is based, on this point, on two arguments. *(a)* Other

---

[310] At [130].   [311] At [124].   [312] At [133].
[313] Case C-7/97 *Bronner v Mediaprint* [1998] ECR I-7791.

distribution channels existed. For instance, it was possible for the applicant to deliver newspapers via the postal services. The use of these services would allegedly be more expensive. However, competition rules are not meant to facilitate or render more comfortable the position of some competitors to the detriment of others. *(b)* There was also a possibility of creating a parallel distribution system. It would admittedly be difficult to set up an alternative distribution system. The applicant could however co-operate with other undertakings, thereby sharing costs with other participants.

> *Judgment of the ECJ.* [43] 'In the first place, it is undisputed that other methods of distributing daily newspapers, such as by post and through sale in shops and at kiosks, even though they may be less advantageous for the distribution of certain newspapers, exist and are used by the publishers of those daily newspapers.' [44] 'Moreover, it does not appear that there are any technical, legal or even economic obstacles capable of making it impossible, or even unreasonably difficult, for any other publisher of daily newspapers to establish, alone or in cooperation with other publishers, its own nationwide home-delivery scheme and use it to distribute its own daily newspapers.'

A classic position.   These paragraphs of the judgment do not contain a particu-   **4.355**
larly restrictive position regarding the possibility of imposing obligations regarding access. For such obligations to be imposed, it is required that no real or potential substitute be available. This approach echoes the attitude adopted by the CFI in *Tiercé Ladbroke*, as well as the position advocated by the Commission in *Stena Sealink* or the 1998 Competition Guidelines. There is thus nothing new, at this stage of the analysis, in the position adopted by the ECJ, compared to the case law coming from the other European institutions entitled to apply competition rules.

A criterion for assessment.   Later in the ruling, however, the ECJ sets in *Bronner*   **4.356**
a criterion for the concrete assessment of the circumstances in which resources can be deemed 'indispensable'. In the case in question the undertaking seeking access was arguing that its own situation had to be considered when assessing whether another, competing, distribution channel could be established. The argument was rejected by the ECJ. For the ECJ, access may be ordered only if no alternative distribution channel may be created for a newspaper of a circulation equal to that owned by the controlling undertaking.

> *Judgment of the ECJ.* [45] 'It should be emphasised in that respect that, in order to demonstrate that the creation of such a system is not a realistic potential alternative and that access to the existing system is therefore indispensable, it is not enough to argue that it is not economically viable by reason of the small circulation of the daily newspaper or newspapers to be distributed.' [46] 'For such access to be capable of being regarded as indispensable, it would be necessary at the very least to establish . . . that it is not economically viable to create a second home-delivery scheme for the distribution of daily newspapers with a circulation comparable to that of the daily newspapers distributed by the existing scheme.'

4.357 **Explanation.** The criterion is not entirely clear and deserves some explanation. The undertaking seeking access was publishing a low-circulation newspaper. As the applicant stated, no company would ever be able to establish a distribution channel for the distribution of a low-circulation newspaper. The situation of the controlling undertaking was different, as it was publishing several popular newspapers. In setting aside the argument made by the undertaking seeking access, the ECJ established the situation of the dominant undertaking as the standard for the assessment of the essential character of the resource. Under that interpretation, a resource may be deemed essential if no alternative is possible to provide services, taking into account the financial means available given the turnover of the controlling undertaking on the adjacent markets where the facility is used.

4.358 **An unacceptable criterion.** The criterion proposed by the ECJ does not appear acceptable. As several authors have observed, it restricts unduly the scope of the doctrine. It was stated above that the essential facilities doctrine served as a basis for the liberalisation which has taken place in the electronic communications sector. In the liberalisation process, rules were provided to ensure that existing facilities may be used by service providers other than the undertakings controlling these assets. If the criterion proposed by the ECJ had been used, the reform undertaken in European electronic communications would not have taken place. Using that criterion, the European legislator would have been entitled to order access in the limited circumstances where no alternative was available, taking as a basis for the assessment the turnover of the incumbents.[314]

4.359 **Why has the ECJ chosen this criterion?** The criterion used by the ECJ is inspired by Advocate General (AG) Jacobs, who wrote the opinion in that case. For AG Jacobs, allowing the editor of a small-circulation newspaper to use the network established by a larger competitor would not serve competition in the long term. Access should be ordered only if that publisher is not able to establish a similar distribution network. Losses would be incurred in the short term as the newspaper has only a small circulation and, as a result, the alternative network would not be used fully at the beginning. Access can be made mandatory, however, only if there is no possibility for that publisher of increasing its circulation to a level similar to that reached by the incumbent and to amortise the costs of the distribution network with the profits from that larger circulation.

---

[314] There is little doubt that existing infrastructure is lucrative, if one takes into account the services provided on these infrastructures by the incumbent operators. Under the rules adopted by the European legislator, these infrastructures were to be open to all service providers asking for access. There was no condition in terms of turnover to be realised by the service providers. The critera used by the ECJ in *Bronner* are different. Pursuant to the ruling, access can only be ordered if the service providers cannot *(a)* develop their services to a level identical to the one reached by the incumbent and *(b)* establish a similar infrastructure to provide these services in acceptable financial conditions.

Opinion of the AG, para 68. '[I]t would be necessary to establish that the level of investment required to set up a nation-wide home distribution system would be such as to deter an enterprising publisher who was convinced that there was a market for another large daily newspaper from entering the market. It may well be uneconomic, as Bronner suggests, to establish a nation-wide system for a newspaper with a low circulation. In the short term, therefore, losses might be anticipated, requiring a certain level of investment. But the purpose of establishing a competing nation-wide network would be to allow it to compete on equal terms with Mediaprint's newspapers and substantially to increase geographical coverage and circulation.'

Avoid economic involvement. The reason why that approach was proposed by **4.360** the AG, and then the ECJ, is that ordering access would involve, for a court, the task of determining the conditions under which access should be provided. There is a fear that accepting the existence of the essential facilities doctrine, and using it in the case law, might lead to the involvement of courts in the realm of regulation, which is traditionally reserved for administrative bodies.

Opinion of the AG, para 69. 'To accept Bronner's contention would be to lead the Community and national authorities and courts into detailed regulation of the Community markets, entailing the fixing of prices and conditions for supply in large sectors of the economy. Intervention on that scale would not only be unworkable but would also be anti-competitive in the longer term and indeed would scarcely be compatible with a free market economy.'

The role of courts. Justifying a ruling by a wish to avoid any involvement in **4.361** economic decisions does not appear to provide an adequate basis for the application of competition rules. There is little doubt that an intervention by a public body (court or administrative authority) in a general competition law case implies significant responsibility for that body. The task should not, however, discourage the body concerned from intervening. Competition should be maintained, and consumers should be served. Where intervention is necessary, administrative authorities and courts should not stand to one side on the grounds that they would otherwise face challenges. No decision can be taken in the field of competition law without involvement by the courts and authorities concerned in the details of the businesses in question.[315]

Relationship with dominance. A reason to criticise the approach adopted in **4.362** *Bronner* is the link which exists between the essential facilities doctrine and the concept of dominance. Under the case law based on Article 82 EC, undertakings with a dominant position must refrain from behaviour which would undermine

---

[315] An argument could be that the application of competition rules should be left to administrative bodies, given the involvement that these rules imply in the course of business. Another approach has however been chosen in the European Union. Pursuant to existing legislation, behaviour adopted by economic actors may be examined, under competition rules, at a national level, by administrative bodies as well as by national courts. Guidance is provided by the Commission. But the absence of such guidance does not relieve these bodies and courts of their responsibility.

further the already weakened degree of competition. They must adopt positive action allowing the development of competition. The essential facilities doctrine appears to satisfy the conditions for the application of the case law. The existence of a single infrastructure in a context where duplication is difficult[316] implies that the undertaking dominates the market. The case law on abusive practices should, as a result, apply. A refusal to deal, in these circumstances, has all the characteristics necessary to satisfy the conditions for the application of the case law.

(7) Conclusion

4.363 **Uncertainty.**   The conclusion to the analysis of the case law on the essential facilities doctrine is that some uncertainty exists on the matter. The doctrine is accepted by the Commission. It also seems to have been adopted by the CFI, under conditions which do not appear to differ from those stated by the Commission. The ECJ seems more reserved. The approach adopted by the ECJ in *Bronner* is, however, unclear. In that case, the ruling was adopted by a small chamber (five judges). This shows that the case was not perceived as important by the ECJ (weightier cases are referred to the full court). The judges probably had the impression that they were being asked to handle an ordinary general competition law case.

4.364 **Another criterion.**   Another reason not to consider *Bronner* as a landmark case is that the ECJ merely accepted, in that case, one of the criteria proposed by the AG. The ECJ does not appear to have noticed that, in his opinion, the AG in effect proposed another criterion which, for an unknown reason, he did not advocate at the end of the opinion. As is stated in the opinion, an obligation to grant access may be justified in various circumstances. Clear circumstances are where duplication of the facility is impossible.[317] Another set of circumstances is where duplication is extremely difficult for physical, geographical or legal constraints.[318] The real issue is whether circumstances of an economic nature may be considered. That possibility is not ruled out by the AG. For AG Jacobs, an obligation to grant access may be imposed where duplication would be impossible or extremely difficult for 'any other undertaking', or 'any prudent undertaking'.

> *Opinion of the AG, para 66.* 'I do not rule out the possibility that the cost of duplicating a facility might alone constitute an insuperable barrier to entry . . . However,

---

[316] If duplication is difficult, entry barriers are high and potential competition is, as a result, limited.

[317] See *Bronner*, Opinion of the AG, at [65]. 'It seems to me that intervention of that kind, whether understood as an application of the essential facilities doctrine or, more traditionally, as a response to a refusal to supply goods or services, can be justified in terms of competition policy only in cases in which the dominant undertaking has a genuine stranglehold on the related market. That might be the case for example where duplication of the facility is impossible or extremely difficult owing to physical, geographical or legal constraints or is highly undesirable for reasons of public policy. It is not sufficient that the undertaking's control over a facility should give it a competitive advantage.'   [318] ibid.

the test . . . must be an objective one: . . . in order for refusal of access to amount to an abuse, it must be extremely difficult not merely for the undertaking demanding access but *for any other undertaking* to compete. Thus, if the cost of duplicating the facility alone is the barrier to entry, it must be such as to deter *any prudent undertaking* from entering the market.' (Authors' emphasis.)

Proposal.   The latter criterion proposed by AG Jacobs appears acceptable. As the **4.365** AG states, the application of the doctrine should not result in simply improving the competitive situation of the undertaking seeking access. In that context, it appears legitimate not to take the specific situation of that undertaking into account. The assessment whether or not to grant access should be based on what a normally efficient undertaking can do. There is no reason, however, to state that that assessment must be made taking into account the situation of the controlling undertaking, as the AG proposed at the end of his opinion and as the ECJ submitted in its ruling.

H. The Relationship Between General Competition Law and the NRF

Two legal tools.   As is shown by the analysis set out in the paragraphs above, **4.366** practitioners are presented with two series of tools to argue their cases, where they address a situation where an undertaking has allegedly refused to deal with another or has refused to give access to a facility. The Commission attempts to establish a distinction between these tools based on the circumstances in which the intervention associated with each set of rules takes place. According to that institution, the NRF addresses issues before they arise (ex ante intervention). It also envisages them in a rather general perspective (all undertakings in the same situation). By contrast, general competition law consists of ex post intervention, where an authority reacts against behaviour which has already been adopted and which does not appear to conform to the competition rules. It is also made up of rather individual interventions, where sanctions are applied to one or several of the undertakings concerned without being extended, or extendable, except in particular circumstances, to all undertakings present on a given market.

Ex ante vs ex post.   Nuances should probably be brought to the distinction **4.367** made by the Commission. As regards the timing of intervention, it should be observed that general competition law does not always encompass ex post facto interventions. Competition authorities intervene ex ante in some instances. That is the case, inter alia, where they issue interim measures aimed at organising the relations between the parties during a procedure. Competition authorities also publish instruments (regulations, notices, etc) where they explain how they will apply competition rules in future cases. That technique does not really differ from the tools used in the NRF. On a more fundamental basis, it should not be forgotten that general competition law is based on Treaty provisions as interpreted by the case law. The combination of the provisions and the case law leaves little doubt concerning obligations or prohibitions imposed on dominant undertakings, including those relating to access or refusal to deal. As a result of that combination, the undertakings concerned know in advance whether the behaviour which they envisage is, or is not, lawful.

4.368 **Individual or general interventions.** Similar remarks may be made regarding the individual or general character of the interventions made. General competition law may not be presented as a body of law that is focused on specific or peculiar situations. It is based on Treaty provisions which have general scope. These provisions are determined in instruments which also have general character and cannot be distinguished in this regard from the rules contained in the NRF. The case law also has general character, as it announces the position that all undertakings can expect from the competition authorities should those undertakings be placed in a situation similar to that which forced the public intervention.

4.369 **A type of competition law.** For these various reasons, it appears more appropriate to present the NRF as a part of general competition law—a body of rules which are not different from competition rules as regards the objectives pursued by the two bodies of law as well as the main concepts on which these bodies are based. The difference ultimately has a principally institutional nature. It is related to the institutions or authorities which have the power to adopt, and to implement, the rules (NRAs for the NRF and NCAs for competition). It also relates to the procedures which have to be used in order for the relevant institutions and/or authorities to adopt and apply these rules (the rules for harmonisation in the case of the NRF and the rules relating to general competition law in the other case).

4.370 **Focus on the most convenient body of law.** The consequence is that practitioners should not consider the coexistence of these bodies of law as a cause for legal uncertainty, but rather as an opportunity to be creative. The concepts and rules associated with these bodies of law are in substance identical. It cannot be excluded that discrepancies may appear in specific circumstances. Should that be the case, practitioners should focus on the body of law that is supposed to advance the situation of their clients. In case of conflict, it is for the authorities to decide which must prevail. It cannot be anticipated that a general attitude will necessarily be adopted in response to that issue. The answer may depend on the context in which the issue is raised. In some circumstances, general competition law might prevail, and in others the NRF. Answers may also be different depending on the identity of the authority called to take a position. It should not be excluded that a preference for the regulatory framework will be expressed by NRAs, whereas competition authorities will consider that general competition law should prevail. At some stage the Commission will have to clarify its attitude about possible conflicts between the two bodies of the law. The issue may be brought to the CFI and/or the ECJ in proceedings, and these courts will then have the final say on the matter.

Use one body of law to support the other. Another possibility is to use one **4.371** body of law to support the other. General competition law may be used to support claims based on the NRF. The scenario is that of a practitioner seeking to obtain the application of a provision in the NRF, but for some reason not succeeding. That practitioner has the possibility of using general competition case law to support his claim. *Example.* Suppose that a practitioner claims that a price charged by an undertaking is predatory. That claim is made on the basis of the NRF. It is not accepted by the competent NRA on the ground that sector-specific regulation does not contain an outright prohibition against that kind of practice. The practitioner may submit to that authority that the obligation to base prices on costs does not only imply that prices cannot be excessive, but also entails a prohibition to set prices below costs. In support of that argument, the practitioner should be able to use the case law developed on predatory pricing in general competition law. It could thus be argued that the practice should be prohibited under one of the two standards established for that practice in that area of the law.

Practitioners may also face situations where they are trying to build a case with concepts extracted from general competition law. The question arises whether they should be allowed to use some of the provisions established by regulation to support their attempts. The opinion supported in this book is that practitioners should be allowed to use regulatory provisions in support of their general competition law based claims.

Burden of proof. Using regulatory provisions to support claims based on **4.372** general competition law may be important for reasons relating to the burden of proof. The NRF introduces rules which make it easier for practitioners to establish violations of general competition laws. As an example, the framework provides that undertakings may be compelled to justify prices on markets where they have significant market power.[319] Where that obligation is applied, the contention that abusive prices are charged does not have to be established by the applicant. The burden of proof is reversed and placed on the shoulders of the powerful undertaking. Practitioners arguing that an undertaking abuses its dominant position may use that sector-specific regulatory provision concerning the burden of proof to request from the powerful undertaking a demonstration that its prices are acceptable.

---

[319] See the Access Directive, Art 13(3). 'Where an operator has an obligation regarding the cost orientation of its prices, the burden of proof that charges are derived from costs including a reasonable rate of return on investment shall lie with the operator concerned. For the purpose of calculating the cost of efficient provision of services, NRAs may use cost accounting methods independent of those used by the undertaking. NRAs may require an operator to provide full justification for its prices, and may, where appropriate, require prices to be adjusted.'

4.373 **Accounting obligations.**   Another interesting development is that practitioners may be able to use accounting obligations imposed by the NRF in cases argued on the basis of general competition law. It is stated above that accounting obligations may be imposed on undertakings with significant market power (see Chapter 3 on access under sector-specific regulation). Suppose that a competitor wants to enter a market but its attempts are made difficult, if not impossible, as a result of the very low prices charged by the undertaking in place, which happens to be dominant. On the basis of general competition law, a plea can be formulated to show that the dominant undertaking engages in predatory pricing to avoid the development of competition. The new competitor faces difficulties, however, as a result of the absence of general competition law provisions compelling dominant undertakings to produce accounting evidence or reversing the burden of proof. The opinion defended in this book is that practitioners should be allowed to use the regulatory provisions relating to these procedural aspects.[320]

4.374 **Sector-specific regulation based on competition law.**   The position that the two bodies of law can be used in support of each other ultimately rests on the following contention. There is no clear distinction between the regulation and general competition law. Most of the rules established in the NRF come from general competition law. The links existing between the two areas of the law have become clearer since the acknowledgement, by the Parliament and Council, that the concepts of dominance and relevant markets are to be defined, and established, using the same methodology. The relationship between the two areas of the law is however more deeply rooted than that decision, which has come only recently. It can be submitted confidently that the rules established by regulation find their origin in prior decisions or rules established by the Commission on the basis of general competition law.[321]

I. Compatibility with WTO Provisions

4.375 **Existence of international rules.**   International law contains a few provisions dealing with general competition law. Some of these provisions (those dealing

---

[320] These obligations are: *(a)* the undertakings concerned may be compelled to adopt an accounting system where prices are based on costs; *(b)* they may be obliged to provide for publication of the system which they use—the principles on which that system is based and how the costs and revenues are allocated among the activities; *(c)* as part of the transparency requirements, they may be under a constraint to communicate to the regulatory authorities all accounting documents which are necessary for these authorities to investigate the relations between prices and costs; *(d)* they may be obliged to have their accounts certified by an independent qualified body. For an explanation of these obligations, see Chapter 3 dealing with access to resources and facilities under sector-specific regulation.

[321] Some of these rules were introduced by that institution in the liberalisation directives, which are based on Art 86(3) EC—a general competition law provision. Others were established, even prior to this, in decisions adopted on the basis of Arts 81 or 82 EC, by the same institution, in procedures regarding alliances entered into by telecom operators at the start of the 1990s.

specifically with electronic communications) are worth examining here, although briefly, to show that there is consistency between European and international law as regards the rules applied to electronic communications markets in the name of competition.

Basic telecommunications. Some rules of competition have been inserted at international level in the Reference Paper presented in the introductory chapter (see para 1.176). These rules concern basic telecommunications, ie telecommunications transport networks and services. Pursuant to the Reference Paper, the Members of the Organisation must ensure that major suppliers do not engage in continuing anti-competitive practices. These practices may consist of cross-subsidisation or a failure to give access to relevant commercial or technical information. They may also take the form of a use of sensitive information obtained from competitors. **4.376**

> *Reference Paper, point 1.* 'Appropriate measures shall be maintained for the purpose of preventing suppliers who, alone or together, are a major supplier from engaging in or continuing anti-competitive practices.' 'The anti-competitive practices referred to above shall include in particular: *(a)* engaging in anti-competitive cross-subsidization; *(b)* using information obtained from competitors with anti-competitive results; and *(c)* not making available to other services suppliers on a timely basis technical information about essential facilities and commercially relevant information which are necessary for them to provide services.'

Major supplier. An interesting issue is to determine which undertakings can be considered to be major suppliers on which obligations may be imposed in the name of competition. The concept of 'major supplier' is defined using the essential facilities doctrine. Pursuant to the Reference Paper, a major supplier is an undertaking which may influence the conditions on a market as a result of control over essential facilities. Facilities are considered essential where no alternative facility exists from an economic or technical point of view. **4.377**

> *Reference Paper, point 1.* 'A major supplier is a supplier which has the ability to materially affect the terms of participation (having regard to price and supply) in the relevant market for basic telecommunications services as a result of: *(a)* control over essential facilities; or *(b)* use of its position in the market.' 'Essential facilities mean facilities of a public telecommunications transport network or service that *(a)* are exclusively or predominantly provided by a single or limited number of suppliers; and *(b)* cannot feasibly be economically or technically substituted in order to provide a service.'

Consistency with European law. As appears from the above presentation, competition rules applied in the electronic communications sector are consistent at European and international level. It should not be forgotten that the international rules that have been presented apply to basic telecommunications, whereas the European competition rules examined in this book concern all electronic communications activities. **4.378**

5

UNIVERSAL SERVICE, PUBLIC SERVICE AND SERVICES OF GENERAL INTEREST

A. Introduction

5.01   **An exception to the reform.**   The last major point to analyse before turning to litigation issues is universal service. This would appear in many respects to be an exception under the reform. It is for this reason that it is generally examined in the last instance in the literature. As stated above, the telecommunications sector was formerly organised as a public service in most Member States. Undertakings carried out tasks which, it was expected, would not spontaneously be taken over by market forces in a satisfactory manner. These tasks were not demanded by the markets themselves. They were rather imposed by public authorities, as tools to implement policy objectives. This organisation imposed on markets was justified by a concern that communications services should be made available to the public throughout the national territory on reasonable terms.

This organisation put in place by the Member States has been affected by the introduction of competition as a result of the reform carried out by the European legislator. The change however does not modify the whole construction. Member States and European authorities have not given up public service objectives in the new markets. Where modified, these objectives appear to have been revised only in the light of the changes that have occurred in the economic, social and technological context. In fact, the reform has mainly affected the measures that were used to implement these objectives, not the objectives themselves.

5.02   **Seeking a difficult compromise.**   In the reform, the European legislator has embarked on a difficult enterprise, seeking a compromise between two requirements that are not always easy to reconcile: the fulfilment of public policy objectives in an environment where activities are carried out by players constrained by market forces. The task is set forth with clarity in two Communications adopted by the Commission on services of general interest, as appears from the extracts below. It is still interesting to compare the tone adopted in the two documents, dating respectively from 1996 and 2001. In the first, the Commission states that one issue is to find a compromise between liberalisation and public service. In the second document, it has become more assertive and contends that such a compromise can be reached, and has indeed been implemented in the sectors regulated at European level.

> *First Communication on services of general interest (1996).* 'The real challenge is to ensure a smooth interplay between, on the one hand, the requirements of the single European market and free competition in terms of free movement, economic performance and dynamism and, on the other, the general interest objectives.'[1] *Second Communication on services of general interest (2001).* 'The experience gained so far . . . confirms the full compatibility of the Treaty rules on competition and the internal market with high standards in the provision of services of general interest.'[2]

The conflicting requirements in question. The compromise alluded to above is **5.03** between two requirements. On the one hand are those relating to competition. As was stated above, competition has been introduced because it was believed that efficiency would be enhanced and more wealth created for all. The European economy would be better served and, with it, the European public, in an environment where services which are important for society were performed more efficiently. In addition to this argument, it was emphasised that competition would contribute to internal market objectives, as undertakings from all Member States would be allowed to enter markets throughout Europe. Finally, there was a feeling that competition was of the essence in a society where equality of opportunity is important. This principle of equality was infringed under a system where some undertakings were granted exclusive rights whereas others were excluded from the market.[3]

On the other hand, the European legislator was clearly convinced of the importance of public service in European society. A change admittedly intervened in the terminology, as public services are now termed 'universal service' or 'services of general interest'. This change has, however, not modified fundamentally the goals related to public service. These goals indeed remain fully applicable. Their permanence is explained in the two communications and the report adopted by the Commission. These various documents are analysed later in this chapter. An extract from the most recent of them shows how important services of general interest remain in European society.

---

[1] Commission Communication (EC) 96/C281/03 on services of general interest in Europe [1996] OJ C281/3, para 19.
[2] Commission Communication (EC) 2001/C17/04 on services of general interest in Europe [2001] OJ C17/4, Executive Summary, para 4.
[3] Equality is a fundamental feature in a democracy, from a political but also from an economic point of view. It is understood as implying, for instance, a right of access for all to modern technology. It is also interpreted as implying that all must have access to markets. These two goals appeared better served in a competitive system, where goods are made available in greater quantity and against lower prices and where activities are opened to all interested parties.

Report from the Commission to the Laeken Summit, 2001. '[S]ervices of general interest remain an essential building block of the European model of society. European citizens and businesses have come to expect the availability of a wide spectrum of high-quality services of general interest at affordable prices. These services contribute to the quality of life of citizens and are a prerequisite for fully enjoying many of their fundamental rights. Access to services of general interest by all their members is one of the common values shared by all European societies. Services of general interest contribute to the competitiveness of European industry and strengthen the social and territorial cohesion in the European Union. They are a vital component of the Community's consumer protection policy.'[4]

5.04 **What *did* change?** One may, then, wonder what really changed with the reform. To answer this question, one must realise that, beyond the legal discussion, competition and liberalisation basically operate a specific allocation of resources. The question the European institutions, together with their national counterparts, had to address in the course of the reform was the following. Should incumbents be allowed to continue enjoying the special and/or exclusive rights that were traditionally granted to them? This option would be beneficial to those employed in the undertakings concerned. However, it would be detrimental to consumers whose access is limited as regards output while the prices charged them are excessively high. Nor would the situation be positive for non-privileged undertakings, as they would be barred from entering the market. Should then another option be considered—for instance, opening the market to competition? In such a scenario the situation would be reversed as compared with the first option. Incumbents would lose their protection, whereas newcomers and consumers would probably see their lot improved.

5.05 **Allocation of resources.** The question mentioned above shows what the reform has in essence been doing—changing the allocation of resources as it was organised under the previous system into a new organisation which, it is hoped, will deliver more acceptable results in a modern society. To summarise the analysis in a few words, the public policy objectives do not appear to have been changed by the reform. The position of the various categories of stakeholder represented on the electronic communications markets has, however, been profoundly modified. *(a)* To begin with, consumers have not, one would hope, been affected in a negative fashion. Quite the contrary: as a result of competition, they now seem to have access, under better conditions, to more electronic communications equipment and services. One can also assume that quality has not been lowered, as measures have been adopted to ensure quality improvement.[5] *(b)* Newcomers—ie undertakings starting new activities—should also be better served in the new system. As markets have been opened, the scope for new entry has expanded. The possibilities are real for

---

[4] Commission of the European Communities, Report to the Laeken European Council, services of general interest, COM (2001) 598 final, Brussels, 17 October 2001.

[5] Measures of this type can be found for instance in the provisions concerning universal service. See paras 5.79–5.90 below.

undertakings in other sectors[6] or geographical[7] markets, as well as for undertakings that were previously active in given electronic communications markets and can now broaden their activities. *(c)* Employees have also seen their position affected. Competition has placed them in a more dynamic environment. The consequence is that they are sometimes put under a heavy constraint to perform better. This is not necessarily negative. Previously unemployed people may find a job in undertakings created as a result of competition. More generally, competition gives more opportunities to talented and motivated workers in a system where merits and activity are rewarded. *(d)* The incumbents are clearly the ones that have been the most heavily affected. They had been protected from competition for decades. That protection has now vanished. Furthermore, they are subject to obligations applying as a result of the market power they still hold in some markets or market segments. It is thus the incumbents whose position has changed dramatically in a less favourable direction. It is they that suffer most from the change that has occurred in the means used to ensure the continued pursuit of public objectives.

B. Applicable Instruments

General presentation of the instruments involved.   Several instruments must   **5.06**
be examined when analysing the regime applicable to universal service. Some of them concern universal service as such, particularly the directive on that specific subject adopted by the Parliament and Council and referred to below. Other instruments relate to public service and to services of general interest—two concepts that are often used to describe what is presented as the same or a similar reality. These various instruments are briefly presented in the following paragraphs in an order corresponding with the traditional legislative hierarchy.

Treaty or like provisions.   Under Article 86(2) EC, already referred to above,   **5.07**
a derogation may be obtained to allow a suspension of European law[8] where this is necessary to ensure the performance of services of general economic interest. Another provision, Article 16 EC, introduced by the Amsterdam Treaty, also deals with these services. It mainly emphasises the role played by services of general economic interest in the European model. Finally, Article 36 of the Charter of Fundamental Rights must be mentioned.[9] This provision states that European institutions shall respect and recognise access to services of general economic interest as a fundamental right within the Union.

---

[6] For instance, undertakings active in electricity distribution can now think of using their facilities in order to transmit communications.

[7] American companies, for instance, can now enter European markets.

[8] Including competition rules.

[9] The Charter is deprived of any binding force by itself, but reflects general principles of law, which have a binding character.

5.08 **EC secondary law.** Universal service is also regulated by the European legislator under secondary legislation, in particular European Parliament and Council Directive (EC) 2002/22 on universal service and user's rights relating to electronic communications networks and services, hereinafter the 'Universal Service Directive'.[10] It is analysed extensively in the present chapter. Provisions relating to universal service can also be found in the liberalisation directives adopted by the Commission. As the subject matter has been regulated under two separate legal bases, an issue arising will be the existence of possible divergences between the various provisions.

5.09 **Communications and Report.** Finally, the Commission has issued two non-binding communications on services of general interest in Europe—one in 1996 and a second in 2000.[11] These communications give an interesting insight into the fundamental question posed at the outset of this chapter—how may public policy objectives be carried out in an environment dominated by market forces? In 2001, the Commission made a fresh analysis of the subject matter and proposed its conclusions in a report to the European Summit held in Laeken in December 2001. It contains an inventory of action to be taken by the European institutions in the coming months and/or years to foster the development of universal service.[12]

5.10 **Similarities and differences between the various instruments.** All these instruments have one point in common—they regulate universal service and can be used to that effect in the electronic communications sector. There are, however, differences. The first relates to binding force. As mentioned, three have no binding force in themselves—the two communications and the report drafted by the Commission. Treaty provisions have a higher force but are not as specific as the harmonisation and liberalisation regulation which, for this reason, may ultimately provide the reference for all issues arising in connection with universal service. Another difference is in material scope. The three non-binding documents concern universal service in general and are not limited to the electronic communications sector. The same can be said of the Treaty provisions and those associated with them (Charter). By contrast, the secondary legislation (harmonisation, liberalisation) is limited to the sector analysed in this book. Other rules have been inserted in specific instruments dealing with other sectors of the economy, and are particularly relevant for the implementation of public service objectives.

5.11 **Weight granted to each instrument.** Among the applicable instruments, some are more important than others. The Universal Service Directive adopted by the Parliament and the Council is among them. The relation between these rules and the liberalisation directive, as well as the possibilities opened by Article 86 EC for possible derogations from European rules, are analysed in the following

---

[10] [2002] OJ L108/51.

[11] Commission Communication (EC) 96/C281/03 on services of general interest in Europe [1996] OJ C281/3. Commission Communication (EC) 2001/C17/04 on services of general interest in Europe [2000] OJ C17/4, para 1.   [12] See n 4 above.

paragraphs. The communications and reports drafted by the Commission will serve mainly as explanatory documents concerning the positions adopted by the European institutions. In contrast, less analysis will be provided of the Charter of Fundamental Rights or Article 16 EC, since their scope and force are, as explained in the following paragraphs, uncertain.

Charter of Fundamental Rights.   The first of these instruments is Article 36 of the   **5.12** Charter of Fundamental Rights, which embodies rights that the European institutions have committed themselves to respecting. Member States have not signed this document, and as a result cannot be considered as being bound by it. This result could however be achieved indirectly, via case law. It is indeed expected that the European courts will consider as general principles of law the rights that are embodied in the Charter. As general principles, these rights would then have high binding force that would apply to all—Member States as well as European institutions. Under Article 36 of the Charter, access to services of general economic interest must be recognised and respected by Union institutions. A reference is made to national laws and practices in this area, meaning that national realities must be taken into account in the construction of a European model for these services. The European dimension is present, since emphasis is placed on the continued necessity of complying with Treaty provisions. This means that the recognition given in the Charter to the importance of services of general interest should not be construed in any manner as implying a modification to the interpretation given to Treaty provisions on the subject. Emphasis is also placed on the need to apprehend these services as tools for achieving a certain level of cohesion within European society.

> *Charter of Fundamental Rights, Article 36.* 'The Union recognizes and respects access to services of general economic interest as provided for in national laws and practices, in accordance with the Treaty establishing the European Community, in order to promote the social and territorial cohesion of the Union.'

Article 16 EC.   The second of these instruments is Article 16 EC. Chronologically,   **5.13** this article comes before the Charter of Fundamental Rights, as it was inserted by the Member States in the Amsterdam Treaty, the Charter being adopted subsequently. It is nonetheless analysed in second place because it deserves greater attention.

> *Article 16 EC.* 'Without prejudice to Articles 73, 86 and 87, and given the place occupied by services of general economic interest in the shared values of the Union as well as their role in promoting social and territorial cohesion, the Community and the Member States, each within their respective powers and within the scope of application of this Treaty, shall take care that such services operate on the basis of principles and conditions which enable them to fulfil their missions.'

Provision difficult to interpret.   The content of this new article is difficult to deter-   **5.14** mine. In particular, it is not clear whether it was adopted to support the argument that wider derogations should be accepted when it comes to services of general economic interest, or whether on the contrary it confirms the idea that the existing case law should not be changed. The article itself places emphasis on the role played by services of general economic interest in society. Reference is also made to the importance of these services to enhance cohesion within the Union. Furthermore, allusion is made to 'values' that are presented as being common to the people of Europe, without much precision as to the content of these values. Finally, the necessity is stated of ensuring the fulfilment of their missions by undertakings providing services of this kind. This implies that the principles and conditions relating to the exercise of these services must be chosen and decided on accordingly. As a consequence, it may be assumed that a margin of discretion may be granted in reaching that objective.

On the other hand, the article makes it clear that a status quo must be respected as concerns institutional and material issues. For instance, it is clearly stated that the powers of the States and the European Union are not affected by the provision. This seems to imply that no change is brought to the power of European institutions to intervene with respect to the services in question. If that interpretation were to be chosen, this would mean that the Commission remains competent to intervene as it has done in the past—in electronic communications as well as in other sectors. Similarly, reference is made to three provisions which concern services of general economic interest. This, again, can probably be interpreted as implying that no change should intervene in the interpretation that is given to these provisions in the case law.

5.15 **More flexibility in the application of competition law?** Some authors have argued that the two instruments examined briefly (Charter, Article 16 EC) plead for more flexibility in the application of competition rules as regards services of general economic interest. In the absence of flexibility, it would be impossible to ensure the proper fulfilment of the service. As a result, these authors argue, one should accept that special and exclusive rights, as well as State aids, can be granted to undertakings providing these services, by way of derogation from the normal rules, because the costs associated with these services could otherwise not be covered. In our opinion, the demand made by these authors does not correspond to what is provided in these instruments. In fact, it is not clear how any concrete implication can be deduced from one or the other as regards the legal regime applicable to services of general interest. In our opinion, these texts have a mainly political value. They do not create any right or obligation the application of which individuals or undertakings could enforce before a court or tribunal. The relevance of these texts lies elsewhere, in showing that a considerable debate rages within the Union as to how activities could or should in certain circumstances be carried out outside the conditions imposed by competition.

5.16 **Green Paper.** The Commission has issued a Green Paper on services of general interest.[13] That document adds little to the information contained in the other

---

[13] Commission Green Paper on services of general interest COM(2003)270 final, 21 May 2003.

instruments cited above. It is however important, in that it signals a willingness on the part of that institution to introduce a general framework for all services that can be deemed of general interest in the European Union. The Green Paper asks for comments on a series of questions which indicate the desire of the European Commission to take on a more assertive role in the regulation that is applied to these services.

What should practitioners do?   The first question a practitioner confronted with   **5.17** a universal service-related issue has to solve is to determine what instrument should be consulted first. The answer is relatively simple, despite the impressive number of applicable instruments. In all circumstances, the practitioner should concentrate on the Universal Service Directive (Parliament, Council). This in principle contains all the rules necessary for resolving any universal service issue. If more time is available, a further possibility would be to check within the Consolidated Services Directive whether specific instructions are given by the Commission. Normally, there should not be any substantial difference between the two directives. Lastly, the practitioner may reflect whether arguments may be raised on the basis of general competition law provisions, particularly Article 86(2) EC. All other instruments have a more academic interest. This observation is particularly valid for Article 16 EC and the Charter of Fundamental Rights. There is in principle no specific need to look at the previous versions of the secondary law instruments mentioned above, as the substance has been taken over in the new regulatory framework (NRF).

What should you do when confronted with an issue relating to universal service?

(1) Consult the Universal Service Directive (Parliament, Council).
(2) If you have time, look at the Consolidated Services Directive (Commission).
(3) If no satisfactory answer is found, examine whether an argument may be derived from Article 16(2) EC.
(4) All other texts are of more academic interest.

Method chosen in the following sections.   In this chapter the provisions con-   **5.18** cerning universal service or related concepts (public service, services of general interest) are compared. To be logical, the analysis starts with the rules adopted by the Parliament and Council, since they are the more important as common European provisions. The changes that have taken place with the introduction of the NRF are then examined. Only then are these rules compared with those in the liberalisation directives and the provisions of general competition law. Examining each and every issue, separately, under these three categories would have resulted in sections without a clear thread. The approach chosen has the disadvantage that one cannot define immediately, for each issue, the rules deriving from each category; it does, however, demonstrate the internal coherence of each of these legal bases.

C. Definition and Principles

(1) Definition

5.19 **A package of services.** Universal service is defined as a package of services that are to be made available at a specified quality level to all end users at an affordable price. Various criteria appear in this definition. They provide the basis for the analysis in the next section. The first concerns the items that are included in the universal service. We will have to determine what these services are exactly. A second dimension relates to quality. Clearly, the European institutions have sought to accompany liberalisation so that the introduction of competition does not result in a diminution of the quality available on the markets. A third aspect concerns affordability. The relevant services are to be provided at reasonable prices.

> *Universal Service Directive, Article 3(1).* [The concept of universal service designates] 'services . . . made available at the quality specified to all end-users in their territory, independently of geographical location, and, in the light of specific national conditions, at an affordable price'.

5.20 **Availability for all.** A fourth aspect appears in the definition, as the items included in the universal service are to be made available to all end users throughout the national territories whatever their location. This element refers to difficulties some users may encounter in accessing electronic communications services. These difficulties may be divided into two categories, although they are dealt with by similar mechanisms in the NRF. *(a)* A first difficulty relates to the social conditions in which some users are placed. These users may not have the resources necessary to pay for access to the items included in the universal service. This is not due to the level of the tariffs, which may not be excessive. It is rather related to the low level of the income which is available to them (unemployment allowance, etc). *(b)* A second difficulty has a geographical origin. The costs of providing electronic communications are higher in certain regions.[14] In some instances, the difficulty may also be due to the low density of population in the relevant areas.[15] Whatever the circumstance, people in these regions would not always have enough income to pay for electronic communications if the real costs were charged to them.[16]

---

[14] For instance, installing wires in mountainous terrain implies more investment than in a city.

[15] Suppose wires are established in a city or in the countryside. In our scenario, the cost per kilometre of wire does not vary. There is thus no difference in the nominal costs supported by the operator. (This is not always the case because, as we have seen above, installing a network is more expensive in certain environments than in others.) A difference however appears where one considers the cost per subscriber involved. There are many subscribers in cities and the costs can thus be divided among them. The result is that each urban user can be expected to pay small fees for access to the network. By contrast, there are few inhabitants in the countryside and the costs of the network must thus be divided among a limited number of subscribers. As a result, these costs are higher per subscriber.

[16] In principle, this assessment is not made on an individual basis. Authorities do not try to determine who has enough revenues to pay for higher tariffs due to higher costs in providing electronic communications. The analysis is based on an overall approach where the revenues available in a given region are examined.

Intervention warranted. Intervention is warranted in these two sets of 5.21 circumstances, as the people concerned would otherwise face costs exceeding their resources. In both cases, the intervention will affect tariffs. Prices will be lowered to match the revenues of the people concerned. These prices will in effect be set in both circumstances at a level below costs. The difference between the tariffs and the costs—the loss incurred in the provision of access and services—will be spread over the rest of the population. This shows that the fourth element included in the definition (access for all) cannot be differentiated from another, the affordability of tariffs. Affordability means not only that tariffs should in general be reasonable. It also implies that special efforts must be made where people should be able to afford electronic communications as a result of their social and/or geographic condition.

Availability for all—people facing difficulties in accessing electronic communications 5.22

Origin of the difficulty	Costs incurred in providing access and services	Difficulty	Solution
Social circumstances	Costs can be considered as normal	These costs, however, exceed the income of the people involved	Prices are fixed below cost to ensure access (subsidies to users or special tariffs)
Geographical situation	Costs are high	The costs exceed the income of the people involved, even though they have normal income levels	Prices are fixed below cost to ensure access (geographic averaging)

(2) The relationship with users' rights

Universal service and users' rights. The Universal Service Directive contains 5.23 provisions relating to universal service as well as rules concerning users' rights. The reason for this is apparent from Article 1(1) of the directive. The goal of the directive is to contribute to good electronic communications being made available to end users throughout the Union. This objective is to be reached through a combination of three mechanisms. First, competition is introduced to broaden output and have the effect of decreasing prices. Second, universal service is established through public law measures compelling undertakings to provide goods and services to all in accordance with certain conditions. Third, private law rules are established to ensure the protection of end users in contracts they sign with providers.

Different chapters. These subjects will not be treated as a single topic here. 5.24 Although they are both meant for end users, the two categories of rule have different natures. Public law measures aim at organising markets, whereas private law measures concern the relationship between actors. For these reasons, the different rules are analysed in different chapters.

(3) Division of powers

5.25 **As regards the scope of universal service.** Powers are divided between the Member States and the European institutions within the Universal Service Directive, as regards the determination of the scope to be given to the service. The directive mentions items to be included at European level. These are to be provided in all Member States and are analysed in the following section. Apart from this, the Member States may extend the universal service to other items. The universal service is thus not limited in scope at European level, but can be broadened by the Member States. The harmonisation that has taken place within the Union can be considered as achieving a certain minimum level.[17] It can be supplemented by the Member States, as long as the latter respect the rules established in the NRF or deriving from European law in general.

> *Universal Service Directive, Article 32.* 'Member States may decide to make additional services . . . publicly available in [their] own territory but, in such circumstance, no compensation mechanism involving specific undertaking may be imposed.'[18]

5.26 **Financing methods.** As is apparent from this extract, one limitation is explicitly imposed as regards the mechanism. Member States may use public funds to finance the provision of a national universal service in addition to what is organised at European level. Pursuant to the Universal Service Directive, Member States may not use compensation mechanisms involving specific undertakings. The directive thereby refers to the methods that can be used to finance national obligations going beyond the European universal service. One of these methods is to compel undertakings active in the electronic communications sector to contribute to a fund. The money collected is then used to compensate extra costs incurred in the provision of universal service. This method cannot be used by the Member States in respect of universal service obligations which the latter may decide to introduce and which are additional to those established at European level.

5.27 **Methods to be used to achieve universal service objectives.** Objectives are set at European level, in the Universal Service Directive, as regards the provision of universal service. These objectives are to be attained by the Member States. A choice is left to them as to the means they use to attain these goals. This choice is not unconstrained. Member States have to comply with the basic regulatory principles. Their decisions must thus be objective, transparent and proportionate. Furthermore, Member States must give precedence to market mechanisms. Only

---

[17] Do the Member States have the possibility of introducing obligations other than those described in the directive, as regards the items selected at European or at national level? In other words, may they add rights and obligations over and above those provided for in the directive? Our opinion is that their liberty is limited in this regard. This field of law has been harmonised. As a result, the liberty of Member States is restricted pursuant to case law. States may only intervene with respect to aspects that have not been totally harmonised. In fact, their liberty is restricted to areas where the directive—explicitly or implicitly—confers powers on them.

[18] The title of the provision is: 'Additional mandatory services.'

where the market does not reach goals set in the universal service can Member States resort to public intervention.

> *Universal Service Directive, Article 3(2)*. 'Member States shall determine the most efficient and appropriate approach for ensuring the implementation of universal service, whilst respecting the principles of objectivity, transparency, non-discrimination and proportionality. They shall seek to minimize market distortions, in particular the provision of services at prices or subject to other terms and conditions which depart from normal commercial conditions . . .'[19]

Nature of instrument. This division of powers is in line with the nature of the 5.28 instrument used by the European institutions to regulate universal service. Pursuant to Article 249 EC, directives bind the Member States as to the result to be achieved, whereas national authorities are given a choice as to the forms and methods. Furthermore, the division of powers conforms to Article 86(2) EC. Pursuant to that provision, a derogation may be granted from the application of competition rules to the extent that public policy objectives cannot otherwise be attained. This provision embodies, among others, the principle of proportionality, which states in this context that a given national measure can be accepted only where no other means is available to reach the same objective while hindering competition to a lesser extent.

Market Failure Theory. The conception embodied in the European regulation 5.29 corresponds to the 'Market Failure Theory'. This states that goods and services are normally provided through the interaction of market forces. These forces will unfortunately not be able to produce at all times an outcome that can be deemed satisfactory. Room is then open for authorities to intervene in order to ensure the fulfilment of public policy objectives. This intervention may occur in several circumstances. One of them is where the market does not fully perceive the benefits of a given situation. This is because these benefits do not appear in the short term but only reveal themselves at a later stage. Another situation is where the market does not properly value the benefits society as a whole derives from a given action (for example education). One can also mention the example of museums, which are rarely provided spontaneously by market forces but are organised as a result of public intervention because authorities want to encourage the public good. A final case is the desire on the part of public representatives—and society as whole—that all citizens should have access to certain services, even where this is not possible under normal market conditions.

Reasoning behind universal service. In the light of this theory, the reasoning 5.30 behind universal service may be summarised in the following manner. *(a)* The aim of the reform is to provide services available to the population under reasonable conditions. *(b)* This purpose is normally served by competition, which brings about an increase in output and a diminution of tariffs. *(c)* There are however

---

[19] The provision specifies that the choice as to the methods must be made by Member States 'while safeguarding the public interest'.

situations where the consumer will not be satisfied by the outcome of market interaction. Public intervention will then be necessary. *(d)* Universal service thus appears
as a combination of market mechanisms and public intervention—a combination
that must ensure the availability of fundamental services under set conditions.

> *Universal Service Directive, Article 1(1).* 'Within the framework of Directive
> 2002/21/EC (Framework Directive), this [Universal Service] Directive . . . aim is
> [a] to ensure the availability throughout the Community of good quality publicly
> available services through effective competition and choice and [b] to deal with cir-
> cumstances in which the needs of end-users are not satisfactorily met by the market.'

5.31 **No equivalence between universal service and public intervention.** No trace of
equivalence should thus be assigned to universal service and active public intervention. The relations between market forces and public intervention are rather
complex in the system created by the NRF. Authorities have a wide role, to the
extent that they set the objectives they deem appropriate in modern society. It is
in this context that the European institutions have determined what items are to
be provided in the universal service, and that Member States may establish supplementary goals where they consider this appropriate. At that stage authorities
must however refrain from actively intervening in markets. Their role is limited to
monitoring in order to verify whether objectives are met. Where they are not met,
active intervention may be envisaged. This thus only comes at the end of the scenario, contrary to what happened prior to the reform, where activities were readily
taken over by the authorities and no room was left for market interaction. In the
present system, active intervention by the authorities (themselves providing
some services or compelling certain undertakings to do so) is limited to extreme
circumstances, where competition does not fulfil the goals that have been set.

5.32 **A twofold division of power.** As shown by the discussion above, a twofold division
of power is introduced in the NRF. The first form is classic for constitutional lawyers,
who are accustomed to a division of powers among institutions in complex societies.
In the European Community, the system is that only the European institutions
can act in areas where they have exclusive competence. In other areas, European institutions may act where activities could not be performed adequately by national
bodies.[20] A preference is thus expressed in favour of national action—the European
initiative coming in the second instance where it appears that the first mechanism
will not produce a satisfactory outcome.[21] From the Universal Service Directive it
appears that this condition was satisfied in the case of the rules concerning universal

---

[20] This principle only applies where the Community does not have exclusive competences. In
areas of exclusive competence, Community action is not subject to the principle of subsidiarity.

[21] See Art 5 EC. 'In areas which do not fall within its exclusive competence, the Community shall
take action, in accordance with the principle of subsidiarity, only if and insofar as the objectives of the
proposed action cannot be sufficiently achieved by the Member States and can therefore, by reason of
the scale or effects of the proposed action, be better achieved by the Community. Any action by the
Community shall not go beyond what is necessary to achieve the objectives of this Treaty.'

service.[22] Rules have thus been established at European level. National authorities remain free to introduce additional obligations, but they must then conform to the rules that have been established in the NRF.

Markets or institutions. A second form of power division is introduced in order 5.33 to regulate interventions by public authorities as compared to market forces. The purpose here is no longer to divide powers among institutions, but to express preferences as regards action by institutions or by markets. In the NRF, the system is that authorities may intervene only after markets have been given a chance and where it is observed that policy objectives are not attained in a market-based environment. Public intervention is thus regarded as being subsidiary to the interaction of market forces.

Correct order. In the paragraph above, the two forms of power division are 5.34 presented, starting with the classic form where powers are divided among institutions. This presentation should in fact be reversed, as authorities may intervene only after market forces have been given a chance to operate. The correct presentation should thus be the following. *(a)* Market forces are allowed to interact freely. *(b)* Public intervention comes onto the agenda where the results spontaneously attained are not satisfactory. *(c)* The classic division then comes into play, with a preference for national action where no result can be attained at European level for competences that do not belong exclusively to European institutions.[23]

D. Items Included in Universal Service

Outline. The items included in universal service are examined in the following 5.35 paragraphs. For the sake of clarity, they are divided into categories. In the first the basic right at the core of European universal service is examined—the right for each individual to a private connection at a fixed location. In the second category, the main services that are to be provided through that connection are analysed. The third category comprises other items attached to the connection. In a fourth category, items which may be analysed independently from the private connection (emergency number, public phones) are addressed. Finally, developments that could affect the scope of the universal service in the years ahead are examined.

---

[22] Cf Universal Service Directive, Preamble, recital 51. 'Since the objectives of the proposed action, namely setting a common level of universal service for telecommunications for all European users and of harmonising conditions for access to and use of public telephone networks at a fixed location and related publicly available telephone services and also achieving a harmonised framework for the regulation of electronic communications services, electronic communications networks and associated facilities, cannot be sufficiently achieved by the Member States and can therefore by reason of the scale or effects of the action be better achieved at Community level, the Community may adopt measures in accordance with the principles of subsidiarity as set out in Article 5 of the Treaty.'

[23] The situation is even more complex where authorities decide that priority should be given to market forces. They thus intervene in the first place, be it only to decide that they will refrain from active involvement until it is observed that satisfactory outcomes cannot be attained otherwise.

(1) Private connection at a fixed location

5.36   **Access to a public network.**   End users must be guaranteed access to a public network. As stated above, this is the core item of universal service as defined at European level. As stated above, the purpose of universal service is to provide access for all to basic electronic communications. This can be achieved only where users are given a connection to a network. Connection is thus of the essence where it comes to universal service.

5.37   **Fixed location.**   Pursuant to the Universal Service Directive, the connection must be given at a fixed location. This is because mobile equipment and services are not included in universal service, as of now. The demand for network connection should at all times be met by one undertaking at least. Where several undertakings are present, the connection is provided in competition. If one undertaking only is present, the entity has a de facto monopoly. The behaviour adopted by such undertaking is then monitored under general competition law and sector specific regulation.[24]

> *Universal Service Directive, Article 4(1).* 'Member States shall ensure that all reasonable requests for connection at a fixed location to the public telephone network and for access to publicly available telephone services at a fixed location are met by at least one undertaking.'

5.38   **Reasonable demand.**   As is apparent from the Universal Service Directive, the requirement concerning access is somewhat alleviated by the nuance that requests must be satisfied only where they are 'reasonable'. Member States will not fail to comply with their obligations where they cannot ensure connection for end users making unreasonable demands. This limitation comes as no surprise. One should not expect from undertakings an answer to all requests, whatever the costs or the technical difficulties they may create. If litigation arises, the concept of 'reasonable demand' has to be interpreted by the national regulatory authority (NRA) in the circumstances of the case.[25]

5.39   **One connection per user.**   It should be observed in relation to this issue that Member States may decide to limit universal service to the provision of one connection per user. Some users have several places where they want to

---

[24] These rules are examined in other parts of this book. Specific contexts are provided in the directive, as regards tariffs fixed by undertakings of this kind. They are examined in the section concerning affordability (see paras 5.99–5.137). Mobile technology may be used in order to provide connection at a fixed location, as part of the universal service.

[25] Sometimes, undertakings face technical difficulties that make it impossible to answer a demand for connection. But in most circumstances, the difficulties are of a financial nature. Suppose a citizen decides to build a house on the top of a mountain. On the basis of the universal service provisions, he should be entitled to demand access to a network. Answering this demand positively would, however, imply high costs on the undertaking in charge of the universal service and, indirectly, for society, as the extra costs faced by these undertakings are normally compensated. Member States must have the possibility to decide that, in such circumstances, the demand for access should not be satisfied in the framework of universal service. This does not take away the possibility for the end user involved to finance access with his own revenues outside the universal service framework.

be connected. One connection will have to be given under universal service conditions. The Member States may decide that the other connections will be charged at normal commercial rates.

> *Universal Service Directive, Preamble, recital 8.* 'The requirement is limited to a single . . . network connection, the provision of which may be restricted by Member States to the end-user's primary location/residence.'

'Telephone' network. The connection referred to in the Universal Service **5.40** Directive is to the public 'telephone' network. This may appear surprising, as the NRF builds on the convergence that is taking place among electronic services. These services are progressively converging, in the sense that they are increasingly being provided using different technologies. Given this development, one would expect universal service to imply a connection to a polyvalent facility—a network allowing the transmission of voice and data. This is in fact what the Universal Service Directive provides. Pursuant to Article 4, access must be given to a public 'telephone' network. However, this network is defined in another provision as an installation which must make it possible to transmit voice (voice telephony) as well as other sorts of communications including data and facsimiles.

> *Universal Service Directive, Article 2, subpara 2, letter (b).* ' "[P]ublic telephone network" means an electronic communications network which is used to provide publicly available telephone services; it supports the transfer between network termination points of speech communications, and also other forms of communication, such as facsimile and data.'[26]

Importance of voice telephony. The question remains as to why the European **5.41** authorities have referred to the 'telephone' network despite the ongoing convergence. One reason may be that voice telephony remains the principal service covered by universal service under current usage. Yet the only transmission facility which allows voice telephony across Europe, technically, is the telephone network.[27] Another reason may be that including access to an electronic communications network in the universal service requirement would have compelled undertakings to upgrade their facilities in a very short period—too short a period indeed in view of their financial capabilities.[28]

---

[26] The inclusion of non-voice communications makes sense. The universal service encompasses, as we will see, access to data and facsimile communications. These services are to be provided through the public telephone network, as the connection is to this sort of network. The telephone network thus has to be upgraded, to make the transmission of these services possible.

[27] Progress has been made in adapting public broadcasting networks, to make transmission of voice telephony on these lines possible. However, one is far from the use of this network for public voice telephony in all Member States.

[28] The obligation would have been imposed, probably, on incumbents, which are the sole players in possession of ubiquitous fixed installations. These undertakings would have been compelled to transform their facilities in a relatively short period. This would have raised difficulties, as these incumbents are not necessarily in good financial condition. The extra costs would have had to be paid by the Member States, which cannot afford such expenses at the present time.

(2) Main services to be made available through the private connection

5.42 **Services involved.** The items included in universal service are mentioned in Article 4(2) of the Universal Service Directive. Pursuant to that provision, the connection must be able to perform three kinds of service: voice telephony, data communications and facsimile communications. These services are examined in more detail in the following paragraphs.

> *Universal Service Directive, Article 4(2).* 'The connection . . . shall be capable of allowing end-users to make and receive local, national and international telephone calls, facsimile communications and data communications.'

5.43 **(1) Voice telephony.** The choice of voice telephony as part of the universal service requirement was warranted by the importance of this service for communities and personal relations. Social and territorial cohesion cannot be achieved without good communications. Including voice telephony in universal service also serves the internal market, as people can travel and stay abroad more easily where they can maintain links via voice telephony with family and friends. Pursuant to Article 4(2) of the Universal Service Directive, voice telephony must include local, national and international communications. As part of the universal service requirement, it should thus be possible for end users to access international communications from any private location, once the connection is established.

5.44 **(2) Data communications.** Voice telephony is important not only for personal relations; it is essential for business contacts as well. The importance of business-related criteria is evident from the inclusion of data communications within universal service. By making that choice, the European authorities have manifested their desire to encourage the development of a knowledge- and information-based society. Part of the strategy to reach that goal is to make data transmission facilities widely available to the public. The hope is that consumers, citizens and businesses will turn to these installations in large numbers. Other measures aim at developing the use of these facilities, such as the specific programmes that have been set up by European and national authorities. An example is the 'e-confidence initiative' established by the Commission's Directorate General for Consumer Protection, which seeks to improve the confidence of consumers in internet-based transactions.[29]

5.45 **Criteria.** One difficulty is to determine how fast and powerful data communications ought to be as part of the universal service requirement. Three criteria are mentioned in the Universal Service Directive. First, 'functional' access must be provided to the internet. The requirement is vague, as was access to a private

---

[29] Educational programmes are also directed towards all categories of society with a view to increasing awareness as to the possibilities opened by data communications.

connection at a fixed location. Second, no undertaking can be compelled to provide data communications where this is not technically feasible. Third, requests made by end users must not be unreasonable as regards the technology.

> *Universal Service Directive, Article 4(2).* 'The connection . . . shall be capable of allowing end-users to make and receive . . . data communications, at data rates that are sufficient to permit functional Internet access, taking into account prevailing technologies used by the majority of subscribers and technological feasibility.'

Different purposes.   The criteria mentioned above apparently serve different **5.46** purposes. The first is presented in the Universal Service Directive as an obligation. Pursuant to that criterion, undertakings in charge of the universal service must provide functional access to the internet. The two other criteria impose limitations on this obligation. These limitations are exclusively based on technological considerations.[30] As was the case for connection at a fixed location, one cannot expect data communications to be provided where this is not feasible. Furthermore, several technologies are used to access the internet and exchange data communications. The undertakings involved should not be compelled to adapt to all of them. The offer can be limited to the technology used by a majority of subscribers.

Limited obligations.   In view of these criteria, the obligations imposed by the **5.47** Universal Service Directive appear limited as regards the availability of broadband capacity to all users. We should not forget however that the directive introduces a somewhat minimal harmonisation of what universal service should be in all Member States. National authorities have the possibility of adding further services. They could thus decide that broadband should be included in universal service as an item that has to be made available to all on their national territory. Another possibility for development in this regard is the review that must take place regularly regarding the scope of universal service. On the occasion of such review, the European institutions could decide to include broadband in the universal service requirement.

Flexibility.   A choice is ultimately made in the Universal Service Directive of a **5.48** system where flexibility is of the essence, as regards broadband or narrowband. As noted in the preamble, the data rate ultimately does not depend merely on the connection; it is also related to the equipment used by the consumer. For this reason, it did not appear important to mandate a specific data or bit rate at Community level. At the present time, the average rate is about 56 Kbits/s.[31]

---

[30] The Universal Service Directive does not refer to financial issues in providing data communications. This apparently means that these communications are to be provided, even where this requires heavy investment.

[31] Universal Service Directive, Preamble, recital 8.

5.49   **(3) Facsimile communications.**   Facsimile communications are the third item included in the universal service requirement, alongside voice telephony and data communications. The reason for the inclusion of this service is not clear. Facsimiles ensure the transmission of text. This function is however also available with data communications. In fact, facsimiles can be analysed as a not very advanced data communications technology. It may appear surprising that the European legislator requires the provision of this service where more powerful applications serving the same function must already be provided as part of the universal service requirement. The reason for this may be that facsimile techno-logy is concentrated to a large extent in the terminal equipment. Facsimile com-munications can thus be used as soon as end users have access to adequate equipment. These communications do not require expensive adaptations to be made to the network. From that perspective, the inclusion of facsimile connec-tions may be regarded as an action to encourage data communications while accepting that end users do not have access to the most recent technologies every-where in Europe.

(3) Other services attached to the private connection

5.50   **Accessory services.**   Universal service further includes services that can be analysed as being accessory to the provision of a connection at a fixed location. These services are: the right to be mentioned in the public directory, the right to receive a copy of that directory free of charge, and the right to obtain information about other users through a directory enquiry service. These services are examined below.

5.51   **(1) Being mentioned in the public directory.**   A first item is the right granted to each end user connected to a fixed location to have his details included in a pub-lic directory. This right is open to users that have subscribed to a public telephone service. The purpose is to enhance communications within communities. For rea-sons relating to privacy protection, users may decide not to be mentioned in the directory. This does not take away the right for such users to receive a copy of the public directory, even if their details are not included.[32]

5.52   **Equality.**   End users have a right to equality as regards the references made in the directory. This results from the general prohibition on discrimination, a prohibi-tion imposed on public authorities and on undertakings designated for the provi-sion of the universal service. In the context of the directory, a specific rule provides

---

[32] Universal Service Directive, Art 5(2). Provisions relating to the protection of privacy must be complied with. Persons or entities can thus demand not to be mentioned in the directory. Their request must be respected and no one can provide information on them. See European Parliament and Council Directive (EC) 97/66 concerning the processing of personal data and the protection of privacy in the telecommunications sector [1998] OJ L24/1, Art 11. See also the preamble to Directive (EC) 97/66, recital 11, pursuant to which 'Directive 97/66/EC . . . ensures the subscribers' right to privacy with regard to the inclusion of their personal information in a public directory'.

that the undertaking(s) managing the service may not treat users differently where they are associated with different providers. This rule refers to the following situation. In some instances, the entity in charge of the directory is active on markets where it competes with other providers. A conflict of interest may arise, as the directory manager may be tempted to favour its own clients. The Universal Service Directive makes sure that no such discrimination occurs. The provision was originally meant to protect providers, but also provides a tool for end users to obtain protection against one form of discrimination.

> *Universal Service Directive, Article 5(3).* 'Member States shall ensure that undertaking(s) providing the [directory] services . . . apply the principle of non-discrimination to the treatment of information that has been provided to them by other undertakings.'

(2) Receiving a free copy of the directory.   A second item is the right for each   **5.53** end user to receive a free copy of the public directory. This directory must comply with several requirements. First, it must be comprehensive. It has to contain the details of all persons and entities that have subscribed to a publicly available telephone service and have agreed to be mentioned in the directory. Second, the directory must be updated on a regular basis. It must be reviewed once a year at least. Third, the directory must be made available in a form approved by the NRA in the territory concerned. Several forms may be envisaged. The Universal Service Directive provides that the directory can be distributed in a printed version, electronically or in both forms, as the NRA decides.

> *Universal Service Directive, Article 5(1), letter (a).* 'Member States shall ensure that . . . at least one comprehensive directory is available to end-users in a form approved by the relevant authority, whether printed or electronic, or both, and is updated on a regular basis, and at least once a year.'

(3) Directory enquiry service.   As provided in the Universal Service Directive,   **5.54** Member States must ensure that a directory enquiry service is available to end users. This service is based on the directory, as regards the information provided to end users.[33] In this respect the enquiry service may be regarded as a particular form of communication of the content of the directory. As stated above, information contained in the directory can be communicated in a printed version and/or electronically. A third form of communication is provided through answers given by the enquiry service to end users making use of that facility.

> *Universal Service Directive, Article 5(1), letter (b).* 'Member States shall ensure that . . . at least one comprehensive telephone directory enquiry service is available to all end-users.'

---

[33] As a result, the enquiry service cannot provide information about subscribers that oppose such transmission. This is in application of the privacy protection rules that have been mentioned above, in connection with directory services.

(4) Emergency number and public pay phones

5.55 **(1) Emergency number.** Other services are to be made available to the public in addition to the fixed connection. The first is the availability of an emergency number. A number of this kind has been created at European level ('112'), making it possible for end users to contact emergency services throughout the Union, whatever the country concerned.

5.56 **(2) Public pay telephones.** A second service is access to a public telephone network which is not a private connection. Pursuant to the Universal Service Directive, public pay telephones are to be provided. Access should thus be made possible in public areas in addition to private locations.

> *Universal Service Directive, Article 6(1).* 'Member States shall ensure that national regulatory authorities can impose obligations on undertakings in order to ensure that public pay telephones are provided to meet the reasonable needs of end-users in terms of the geographical coverage, the number of telephones, the accessibility of such telephones to disabled users and the quality of the services.'[34]

5.57 **Means of payment.** No choice is made as regards the means of payment that are to be made possible for the use of public phones. Pursuant to the directive, a selection can be made between coins, debit cards, credit cards or pre-payment cards, at the discretion of the NRAs.

> *Universal Service Directive, Article 2, subpara 2, letter (a).* ' "[P]ublic pay phones" means a telephone available to the general public, for the use of which the means of payment may include coins and/or credit/debit cards and/or pre-payment cards, including cards for use with dialling codes.'

5.58 **Use by non-nationals.** This liberty left to the Member States to choose the means of payment may raise difficulties as regards use of public phones by non-nationals. Where for example a European tourist wants to make a phone call in another Member State, he may have no access to mobile services and want to use a public phone. *(a)* He will normally refrain from using pre-payment cards, since they are generally restricted to the national territory. If he buys one he will not be able to use it in another country. This card is thus not really worth buying, unless the tourist intends to use it up during his stay. *(b)* Debit cards may be used, but possibilities will depend on agreements reached with banks by the operator. As there are many banks, all debit cards are not accepted by all operators. *(c)* Credit cards offer more possibilities. As there are fewer credit cards in circulation, the operator probably has agreements with relevant credit institutions. The use of these cards is not necessarily free, however. Calls may become very expensive if a specific fee is charged to the end-user. *(d)* Ultimately, the easiest means of payment remains coins. This is particularly so since the euro has been introduced in

---

[34] The obligations relating to disabled users and to quality are examined in other sections (see respectively paras 5.62–5.67 and 5.79–5.90).

a significant number of European countries. With the new currency, calls can be made in this way throughout the eurozone via public phones.[35]

Services available through public phones.   We have seen that voice telephony, **5.59** data communications and facsimile connections are to be provided through private connections at a fixed location. The same scope would appear reasonable as regards public pay phones. However, a limitation is introduced in the Universal Service Directive as regards the services to be made available through these phones. Only voice telephony is required in that context. There is thus no obligation to ensure that 'communications centres' are made available where the public could access non-voice telephony communications services.[36]

Number of public phones.   The Universal Service Directive does not specify the **5.60** number of public pay phones that have to be made available, nor the locations that have to be served. The European authorities have opted for a flexible approach, where an obligation regarding 'reasonable' access is formulated. Again, the obligation is vague and has to be construed by the NRAs in the context in which they operate. In this case, the NRAs will have to determine the number of public phones required to comply with an obligation of reasonable access. The directive further provides that NRAs do not need to impose obligations regarding public phones where they consider that the supply is already sufficient. Another reason for them not to impose obligations is where they feel that 'comparable services' are available.[37] The decision must be taken after consultation of all interested parties. The question arises whether NRAs could take into account the mobile phones available, in assessing where public phones should be installed. End users tend to use public phones less intensively where they have access to mobile communications. The difficulty is that mobile phones are, and remain, private connections. They cannot be compared, as a result, with telephones open to the public.[38]

Access to enquiry service and emergency number from a public phone. **5.61** Directory enquiry services must be made available to public pay phone users. The

---

[35] It is not certain that this means of payment is preferred by operators. Pre-payment cards are more advantageous for them. They do not require employees to collect coins in each booth. Selling them is furthermore easy, as agreements can be reached with all sorts of distributors.

[36] This does not mean that 'communications centres' will not exist. Such centres may be created by private initiative. This is indeed what happens in many Member States, where public voice telephony is made available in privately-managed centres which offer a range of communications services. Furthermore, Member States may decide to extend the universal service and include the provision of public communications centres on their national territory.

[37] For instance, public pay phones do not have to be installed in areas where the public has access on a pay basis to private phones (hotels, cafés, restaurants, etc).

[38] Suppose many users have access to mobile communications in an area. It remains true that part of the public is not equipped with mobile access. Public phones should thus be installed. However, the ratio of mobile phones in the area can probably be used as an indicator about the number of people who need access to public phones. This can provide useful information to determine how many public phones should be installed in the relevant area.

same goes for access to the emergency number. The directive goes further on this account, by providing that this number should be made available free of charge and even without having to use means of payment where the call is made from a public pay phone.

> *Universal Service Directive, Article 6(3).* 'Member States shall ensure that it is possible to make emergency calls from public pay telephones using the single European emergency call number "112" and other national emergency numbers, all free of charge and without having to use any means of payment.'[39]

(5) Social needs (mainly disabled users)

5.62 **Social obligations.** Social provisions are included in the universal service requirement.[40] The purpose is to ensure that the items included in that mechanism are made available to all members of society, including those who generally face problems concerning access. These people can generally be divided into two categories, as has been seen earlier. The first category is made up of people with low incomes (social issue). Their incomes are not sufficient to access electronic communications even at standard conditions. Others have standard revenues but cannot afford electronic communications prices if these reflect the costs incurred in providing access and services. This is due to special geographic conditions, which have an effect on the costs of establishing and maintaining the network. In these two situations, the difficulty is solved through mechanisms ensuring the affordability of tariffs. For this reason, it is addressed in this book in the section concerning affordability (see paras 5.91–5.137).

5.63 **Disabled users.** A third category is mentioned in the social provisions, namely disabled users. For these users, tariffs also play a role. Specific measures must be taken to compensate for disability. These measures have a cost, and an issue will arise in determining how this cost has to be financed. Addressing the situation of disabled users in this section however has particular significance because the European approach is not limited to financial measures. Pursuant to the Universal Service Directive, obligations may be imposed by Member States in relation to services meant for disabled users. The purpose is to ensure equivalence with other users. For the European authorities, there is no reason why disabled users should have different access to universal service. Emphasis is placed on the necessity for Member States to improve the ability of these users to take advantage of competition. In recalling this, the European authorities are consistent with their purpose of making market forces responsible in the first instance for the provision of universal service. This does not preclude authorities from intervening in order to ensure

---

[39] In the NRF there is no obligation for Member States to ensure free calls to emergency services from private connections. However, the directive provides that the right to call the emergency number may be maintained in case of disconnection.

[40] Universal Service Directive, chapter II: 'Universal service obligations, including social obligations.'

equivalence. The chances are indeed that equivalence will rarely be reached without intervention, as disabled users do not often attract attention from providers.

> *Universal Service Directive, Article 7(2).* 'Member States may take specific measures . . . to ensure that disabled end-users can also take advantage of the choice of undertakings and service providers available to the majority of end-users.'

Services concerned. The service mentioned in relation to equivalence is in par- **5.64** ticular access to a public voice telephony service. Accessory services are also referred to, in particular access to emergency services, access to directory enquiry services and the possibility of obtaining a directory. The Universal Service Directive further emphasises that measures are to be taken to make public pay phones specifically accessible to disabled users.

> *Universal Service Directive, Article 7(1).* 'Member States shall, where appropriate, take specific measures for disabled end-users in order to ensure access to and afford-ability of publicly available telephone services, including access to emergency ser-vices, directory enquiry services and directories, equivalent to that enjoyed by other end-users.' 'Member States shall ensure that national regulatory authorities can impose obligations on undertakings in order to ensure . . . the accessibility of such [public pay] telephones to disabled users.'[41]

Additional measures. Additional measures may be taken regarding disabled **5.65** users. As an example, Member States may introduce quality requirements in the services intended for these users. In this area the principle is normally that national measures are not allowed where harmonisation has taken place. National measures concerning quality enhancement are, however, allowed as regards dis-abled users. This results from the fact that the possibility of national intervention has been provided for in the Universal Service Directive itself.[42] Suggestions are even made in the preamble regarding specific measures to be taken.

> *Universal Service Directive, Preamble, recital 13.* 'Specific measures for disabled users could include . . . making available accessible public telephones, public text tele-phones or equivalent measures for deaf or speech-impaired people, providing ser-vices such as directory enquiry services or equivalent measures free of charge for blind or partially sighted people.'

Limitations. Despite the scope of the Universal Service Directive, the European **5.66** institutions have clearly been limited in their action concerning disabled users. *(a)* First, the directive states that *equivalence* should be reached, not equality. The precise difference remains to be determined. As of now, the choice of the term 'equivalence' makes it clear that the European institutions were not ready to accept

---

[41] On this specific point, see Universal Service Directive, Art 6(1), end of the sentence.

[42] See paras 5.79–5.90 concerning quality assessment. Other measures concerning quality assessment would be analysed as hindrances to the realisation of the internal market. The measure concerning quality evaluation for disabled users is thus a derogation from the general rule that national initiatives are not allowed where a subject has been (totally) harmonised.

the concrete consequences of a principle that would have required equality. Given the term chosen, disabled users will not be allowed to claim that the directive creates for them a right to equality, a right that Member States would have had to respect by taking all measures necessary to achieve that result. *(b)* Second, not all items included in the universal service requirement are mentioned in the social provisions concerning disabled users. This means that specific measures meant to ensure equivalence are to be taken only with respect to services explicitly designated. Pursuant to the directive, equivalence must be sought as regards public voice telephony. By contrast, data and facsimile communications are not concerned.[43] *(c)* Third, specific measures imply extra costs. An issue arising is how these costs can be financed. No mention is made in the directive of the need for costs to be taken over by Member States or undertakings. The only reference to costs is that affordability must be ensured. This requires Member States to monitor the tariffs charged to disabled users. Where they consider them to be excessive in view of the affordability target, they are required to intervene. The financing schemes introduced with the universal service mechanism can then come into play.

5.67 **Affordability.** It thus has to be concluded from the directive that the specific costs incurred in ensuring equivalence are to be shared by the Member States, the entities designated for that purpose and disabled users themselves. 'Affordability' in effect means that tariffs are to be paid by these users, or partly at least. Only the portion above what is reasonable is taken over through universal service financing schemes. This division would almost appear ironical, if it were not sad. It makes little sense to proclaim equivalence where the means to ensure equivalence are not provided and equivalence is to be financed by the disabled users themselves.

(6) Other obligations

5.68 **Integrity, continuity and quality.** A final obligation is imposed on undertakings designated to provide the universal service. This obligation is not specifically mentioned in the body of the Universal Service Directive, but appears in the preamble, according to which these undertakings have to ensure the integrity of the network. They are also responsible for ensuring the continuity, as well as the quality, of the service. These obligations are intimately related to the concept of universal service. The quality obligation, for example, derives from the desire of the European institutions that liberalisation should not lead to a lower quality of service for end users. Integrity and continuity must also be considered. As stated, universal service implies the provision of fundamental services to all members of the community at reasonable rates. This purpose would not be attained if the network were subject to sudden breakdown.

---

[43] The power of Member States to introduce additional provisions however remains intact, as long as they comply with the basic regulatory principles associated with the provision of the universal service. See Universal Service Directive, Art 8.

Universal Service Directive, Preamble, recital 14. 'It is important that universal service operators maintain the integrity of the network as well as service continuity and quality.'

Link with traditional public service.   These obligations (continuity, integrity, quality) are typical of the requirements that Member States imposed on their national operators before the reform was introduced. In that sense, one can consider that universal service does not altogether terminate the period of public service. The relationship between these two concepts, as well as with services of general interest, is examined in a later section of this book (see paras 5.318–5.334). Some thoughts are also devoted to integrity, continuity and quality in the section concerning the rules adopted by the Commission in the liberalisation framework (see paras 5.237–5.257), which explicitly imposed these requirements on undertakings.

(7) Evolution of the scope of universal service

Concept subject to evolution.   The scope of universal service is the result of a   **5.70** choice regarding objectives considered important as regards access and services. Choices of this nature are made in a given context and bear the mark of this context. Objectives may change as a result of economic, technological or societal evolution. For instance, should third generation mobile technology develop rapidly, the question will arise as to whether access to mobile networks and services should be included in the universal service requirement.

Procedure.   As provided in the Universal Service Directive, the scope of univer-   **5.71** sal service has to be reviewed periodically. An analysis has to be made every three years.[44] It must be performed by the Commission but the final decision is for the Parliament and the Council, as it could imply an amendment of a directive adopted by these authorities.

Universal Service Directive, Article 15(1) and 2. 'The Commission shall periodically review the scope of universal service, in particular with a view to proposing to the European Parliament and the Council that the scope be changed or redefined. A review shall be carried out . . . every three years . . . The Commission shall submit a report to the European Parliament and the Council regarding the outcome of the review.'

Criteria for review.   The Universal Service Directive mentions several criteria to   **5.72** be considered when examining whether the concept should evolve. The question is not left open for discussion, or at least not entirely. This shows that the European authorities have been willing to register their wishes as to what aspects should be considered important in the review. An additional proof, if necessary, is provided in that a serious—and sometimes heated—discussion took place during

---

[44] The first revision process will take place as of July 2005, ie three years after the adoption of the directive and two years after the date set for its implementation in the national legal orders.

the preparation of the directive as to how universal service should be defined and should evolve. The review of universal service is discussed in Article 15 of the directive. This provision is rather sober as concerns the criteria to be used for the review. It provides in particular that social, economic and technological developments should be taken into account.

> *Universal Service Directive, Article 15(2).* 'Th[e] review shall be undertaken in the light of social, economic and technological developments, taking into account, *inter alia*, mobility and data rates in the light of the prevailing technologies used by the majority of subscribers.'

5.73   **Mobile and data technologies.**   Despite this sobriety, emphasis is placed on two areas where developments should occur. The first is mobile technology. The reference made to that technology in Article 15 of the Universal Service Directive shows that mobile networks and services are important in the eyes of the European authorities. They are so important indeed that one might expect them to be included in the next version of the universal service requirement. The second area where developments could take place is data communications. We have seen that functional access to the internet has to be provided as of now. No precision is given, though, as what this implies at the moment. The importance of data communications in the view of the European authorities is likely to grow further in the years ahead, as data rates are mentioned in the directive in connection with changes to be made to universal service. One can thus expect that broadband may be included in future versions of universal service, even if it is difficult to give a target date in this regard.

5.74   **First step.**   More indications can be found in Annex V to the Universal Service Directive as to how the discussion will be structured around possible modifications to universal service. Pursuant to this Annex, the discussion will be divided into two steps. The first is for the Commission to analyse whether a review should be undertaken. The purpose of this analysis is to obtain an overall picture as to what is in demand and what is offered at the time the enquiry is made. In this analysis, the Commission must identify the technology used to provide the services.

> *Universal Service Directive, Annex V, para 1.* 'In considering whether a review of the scope of universal service obligations should be undertaken, the Commission is to take into consideration the following elements: [a] social and market developments in terms of the services used by consumers; [b] social and market developments in terms of the availability and choice of services to consumers; [c] technological developments in terms of the way services are provided to consumers.'

5.75   **Second step.**   The second step can start when the Commission considers that a review should indeed be undertaken. The Commission must identify the changes that should be proposed. To that effect it must answer two questions. One deals with social exclusion. The purpose is to identify services that are not yet included in universal service but are used by a majority of subscribers. Once these services have been identified, the Commission must determine whether the lack of access to these services by a minority of people in society may result in social exclusion for them. The other question relates to economic benefit. Here, the Commission must evaluate the possible consequences of an inclusion of these services in universal service. Suppose that services are included in universal service. Pursuant to the universal service mechanisms, these services will have to be made available to all. Will that provide a benefit to all? What would be the benefit?

> *Universal Service Directive, Annex V, para 2.* 'In considering whether the scope of universal service obligations should be changed or redefined, the Commission is to take into account the following elements: [a] are specific services available to and used by a majority of consumers and does the lack of availability or non-use by a minority of consumers result in social exclusion, and [b] does the availability and use of specific services convey a general net benefit to all consumers such that public intervention is warranted in circumstances where the specific services are not provided to the public under normal market circumstances?'

Social or economic considerations.   As can be seen, the two questions are complementary in their object. The issue is whether both must be satisfied for an extension of universal service to take place. In other words, are the European institutions authorised to broaden the scheme to socially desirable items, even if the extension brings no economic benefit? The answer depends on the status given to the questions mentioned in the Annex. However, as provided there, they are only elements to be considered in deciding whether a change should occur. From this it can be concluded that no decisive weight can be given to either of these questions. If this interpretation is correct, the Commission should be able to propose the inclusion of services that are not used by a majority of subscribers but the general availability of which would create a benefit (such as broadband). A proposal could also be made to extend the universal service to items which do not bring economic benefit but are socially valued (SMS messages, for example). **5.76**

Safeguards.   Safeguards are expressed in the Universal Service Directive concerning criteria that the European institutions should always have in mind when considering whether universal service should be expanded. First, any review should be socially just. Second, any modification should remain technologically neutral. In other words, specific technologies should not be favoured at the expense of others when choices are made as to the inclusion of new items or the broadening of items already included. Finally, reviews should remain modest as to their scope. There is a certain apprehension among the European institutions that the Member States, or at least some of them, may be willing to enlarge the scope significantly. This would imply a substantial additional burden. Member States would probably not be able to finance such a burden from public funds and would thus attempt to apply the contribution mechanism. However, an enlargement of the items to be financed through such a mechanism would imply excessive burdens for undertakings. **5.77**

> *Universal Service Directive, Preamble, recital 25.* 'Care should be taken in any change of the scope of universal service obligations to ensure that certain technological choices are not artificially promoted above others, that a disproportionate financial burden is not imposed on sector undertakings (thereby endangering market developments and innovation) and that any financing burden does not fall unfairly on consumer with lower incomes.'

5.78 **Summary.** By its nature universal service is prone to evolution. Mobile technology and broadband access will probably be included in the years ahead. Change must be agreed by the Parliament and Council, on the basis of a proposal from the Commission. Social considerations will play a role, as well as the economic benefits that would flow from the extension of the service to society as a whole.

E. Quality Requirements

5.79 **European quality standards.** Universal service implies that items included under that concept be made available while complying with certain constraints with respect to quality. This requires oversight; requirements relating to quality cannot be formulated without establishing methods to verify that these requirements are fulfilled. Minimum requirements are established at European level in the form of standards established by a standardisation organisation, ETSI. These standards are referred to in Annex III of the Universal Service Directive, which is in turn referred to in Article 11 of the directive.

> *Universal Service Directive, Article 11(1).* 'National regulatory authorities shall ensure that all designated undertakings with obligations under [the universal service] . . . publish adequate and up-to-date information concerning their performance in the provision of universal service, based on the quality of service parameters, definitions and measurement methods set out in Annex III.'

5.80 **Supplementary requirements at national level.** An additional step can be taken by Member States, in the form of supplementary requirements established at national level. The possibility is however limited to services for disabled end users. In practice, it is for the NRAs to decide whether such additional requirements should be imposed, and which.

> *Universal Service Directive, Article 11(2).* 'National regulatory authorities may specify, *inter alia*, additional quality of service standards, where relevant parameters have been developed, to assess the performance of undertakings in the provision of services to disabled end-users and disabled consumers.'

5.81 **Compatibility with European law.** The reference to national requirements in the Universal Service Directive is useful for the evaluation of the compatibility of these measures with European law. Under the Treaty, Member States are prohibited from enacting rules that may affect the provision of goods or services from other Member States on their national territory. The prohibition is complete where the subject matter has been totally harmonised at European level. In the context of quality assessment within the universal service, this prohibition could not be imposed on Member States deciding to introduce supplementary obligations, since they cannot be considered barriers to the attainment of the internal market.[45]

Limitations. Although it appears ambitious, the measure is limited in practice. **5.82** *(a)* A first limitation is that the standards established by ETSI are not obligatory. Reference is made to them in the Universal Service Directive and the undertakings involved are requested to publish information as to how their performance relates to these standards. However, there is no real obligation for undertakings to comply with them. *(b)* Second, not all items included in universal service must be assessed for quality. As will be seen, standards have been fixed as regards private connection and accessory services. The other aspects have been neglected. As a result, these services will not be assessed as regards their quality, even where universal service is provided not through market forces but by designated undertakings. *(c)* A third limitation is that quality assessment is applicable only to undertakings that have been designated to provide universal service. The European institutions expect market forces to provide the principal mechanism for the fulfilment of universal service objectives. The limitation of quality assessment to designated undertakings means that no quality assessment will have to be made where universal service is ensured in a competitive environment. The reason is probably that the assessment is supposed to be done by market forces themselves in such an environment.[46]

Standards concerning access. Some of the standards to be used for quality **5.83** assessment relate to access. As stated, the provision of an adequate private connection is an important item within universal service. Standards are imposed in order to ensure that the obligation is complied with not merely through the

---

[45] This only applies, as seen above, for requirements concerning disabled persons. In our view, national authorities are not allowed to introduce other technical requirements with respect to product or service quality. The harmonisation that has taken place at European level can indeed be considered as complete. No new measure can thus be introduced by national authorities, without infringing internal market provisions.

[46] Consumers choose the provider that satisfies them. If they are not satisfied, they turn to another provider. In that situation, no assessment needs to be made, pursuant to the philosophy underlying the reform. The situation is different where universal service is provided by one undertaking. Assessment by consumers would have little impact on the behaviour of the undertaking, as consumers could anyway not turn to another provider. An intervention is then necessary, to make sure the performance attains reasonable quality standards. In our view, the publication of information could be an asset for consumers in a competitive environment. The difficulty for consumers is often to compare providers. In the absence of information, the comparison may take place only where the consumer successively 'tests' several providers. This is unfortunately rarely practicable. A solution is for consumer organisations to publish comparative assessments. The fact that such assessment is sometimes carried out does not mean, however, that publication of information would be redundant. It could indeed provide a valuable aid in that exercise.

provision of termination points. Not only must connection be granted; it also has to be of good quality. Quality is to be tested regarding the following aspects: *(a)* supply time for initial connection, *(b)* the fault rate per access line, *(c)* the fault repair time, *(d)* the unsuccessful call ratio, and *(e)* the call set up time.

5.84 **Standards for accessory services.** Other items included in universal service are concerned by the quality assessment exercise. Thus a standard is established for the proportion of public pay phones per region. The purpose is to ensure sufficient access to the public telephone network in addition to private connections. Again, the analysis is not limited to mere provision of public phones; only phones in working order are taken into consideration.[47] A standard is imposed for directory enquiry services. This concerns the time necessary for operators to provide the information requested. This time is generally short if one considers the lapse between the moment the end user speaks to the operator and the moment when the information is provided. An assessment of this aspect will however not be sufficient. One also has to take into account the time between the moment when access to the service is obtained and the moment when the user can speak to the operator.

5.85 **Absence of standards for certain services.** Not all services included in universal service are concerned by the obligation for designated undertakings to perform quality assessment. *(a)* For instance, no such assessment is provided for data communications. Thus no standard is established to help measure the functional internet access to be provided by designated undertakings in the context of universal service. *(b)* Another example concerns directories. No standard is fixed for the provision of information on subscribers. This should not be interpreted as an indication that directory services are perfect within the Union. Standards would have been welcome with respect to, for instance, the type of reference that must be made available. Standards would also be useful to assess the promptness of operators to correct wrong data, as well as the compensation to be paid to end users where false information is provided as a result of a fault within the services of the operator. *(c)* A last instance relates to voice telephony. Quality can diverge significantly in the transmission of speech along telephone lines. However, no standard is fixed in this regard, as those mentioned in Annex III to the Universal Service Directive mainly concern access.

5.86 **Importance of quality assessment.** As can be seen, severe limitations are placed on the assessment which is to be made with respect to quality. The objective of quality assessment is essential in the NRF. As the Commission has repeatedly stated, the liberalisation of electronic communications cannot be equated with the mere introduction of competition. Competition is normally expected to have an influence on prices and output. Prices are supposed to decrease and output to

---

[47] Suppose an undertaking has installed numerous pay phones in a region. These phones will not be counted in the assessment where they are not properly serviced so as to remain in good order.

increase. These advantages, it is sometimes argued, may be outweighed by a decrease in quality. As undertakings have to lower costs, they tend to spare on quality and security. This argument has been taken seriously by the European institutions, and through quality assessment they have sought to prevent a reduction in the level of service from taking place on the European market. This action is worth noting, but further progress could be made: standards could be made obligatory— or some of them at least—and the assessment exercise could be extended.

Technical harmonisation.   The quality assessment system established in the   **5.87** Universal Service Directive is in line with technical harmonisation as it is designed at European level. At the outset, harmonisation was perceived as a technique implying that national rules should be unified by the European Community in all relevant sectors. This objective was, however, impossible to reach. There were not enough civil servants to carry out the work. Furthermore, the available civil servants did not necessarily have the requested technical qualifications. Another reason is that harmonised measures had to be updated regularly in line with technology. Finally, adopting harmonisation measures was a heavy institutional process, as it originally required the consent of all Member States (unanimity). As a result of these difficulties, the European institutions realised that they would not be able to bring about the internal market if they had themselves to adopt all necessary measures. The technique then evolved towards outsourcing, and it was decided to refer to technical standards established by standardisation organisations. The standards were sometimes set by these organisations acting on their own initiative. In other circumstances, the organisations were asked to draft standards by the European institutions.

Legal force.   Generally, the technical standards established by the standardisa-   **5.88** tion bodies are not obligatory per se. Professional associations may decide to give them a compulsory character. The members of these associations will then be compelled to comply with them, to the extent that the standards are compatible with national or European rules. At European level, various mechanisms are used to give standards force. *(a)* A first possibility is for European institutions to impose standards as compulsory. This is done in certain directives. *(b)* Another option is to state that products or services produced in conformity with these standards are to be accepted in all Member States. In such a circumstance, public authorities may thus not oppose the introduction on their territory of a product or service that has been designed or manufactured in conformity with these standards. *(c)* A third possibility can be a reference to standards in a legal instrument, with encouragement of undertakings to comply with them.

Assessment of quality.   This third possibility has been implemented in the   **5.89** Universal Service Directive as regards assessment of quality. The directive refers to standards adopted by a standardisation body. These are not made compulsory.

The obligation is for undertakings to publish information as to how they relate to these standards. In other words, they are to announce publicly whether or not they match, exceed or do not comply with these standards. Pressure is expected from the markets. Should the undertaking be at a lower level than the standard, consumer confidence may be eroded and market share decrease. Investors may also lose confidence in the capacity of the undertaking to provide saleable products or services.

5.90 **Summary.** The Universal Service Directive introduces quality assessment for the provision of universal service. This is important to ensure that quality does not decrease with the introduction of competition. The measure is however limited. No assessment is required where universal service is provided through market forces. The obligation concerns only a few services. Standards are not compulsory; the hope is that undertakings will feel the pressure to improve quality through publication of information.

F. Affordability of Tariffs

(1) Principles

5.91 **The system used in the Universal Service Directive.** The purpose pursued by the European authorities in universal service is to make access possible for all to basic electronic communications services. A consequence of this principle is that access should not be impeded or hindered by tariffs. At the same time, there is no readiness on the part of the European institutions to ensure free access for all. This would contradict another important principle, that market forces must be given precedence and public intervention should be limited. In order to reconcile these sometimes conflicting principles, a compromise has been sought. The result is that, pursuant to the Universal Service Directive, items included in universal service are charged to end users. The latter thus have to support the bulk of the expense as regards their use of electronic communications. The Member States have to ensure, however, that the prices charged by undertakings are not excessive. They must also encourage end users to control their expenditure.

5.92 **In the light of national conditions.** No target is set in the Universal Service Directive at European level as regards affordability. As repeatedly stated, affordability must be assessed by Member States in the light of national conditions.[48] There can thus be considerable differences between tariffs, depending on the European countries where users are located. As a result of the internal market, these differences should probably decrease over time. They will, however, remain, taking into account for instance the accession of new countries.

---

[48] See eg the Universal Service Directive, Art 3(1); Art 9(1), (2) and (4).

Available tools.   Various tools are available for NRAs to ensure affordability.   **5.93**
These are examined below. The system on which they are based can be described
as follows. Normally, NRAs should resort to market mechanisms in order to
ensure affordability. Where this is not possible, controls may be exercised over
tariffs. Special measures may also be taken in order to support certain categories
of consumers. Affordability does not however imply only initiatives from undertakings. Consumers, and users in general, must also play a role. Measures are
included in the NRF to give them the tools necessary to monitor, and limit, their
expenditure.

(2) Market conditions

Market conditions.   A first tool to ensure affordability is to resort to market   **5.94**
forces. These normally exert pressure on prices. As undertakings struggle to gain
market share, they lower their prices to attract consumers. This is in line with the
choice made by the European institutions in favour of a market-oriented strategy.
Member States thus remain under a 'market constraint'. They must resort to market mechanisms for the provision of universal service unless outcomes are unsatisfactory. This constraint has already been analysed above. It appears in several
provisions concerning the organisation of universal service. Among them, Article
3(2) is worth mentioning again.

> *Universal Service Directive, Article 3(2).* 'Member States . . . shall seek to minimize
> market distortions, in particular the provision of services at prices or subject to other
> terms and conditions which depart from normal commercial conditions.'

(3) Controlling tariffs

Excessive prices.   Market forces do not always produce low tariffs. It may hap-   **5.95**
pen that excessive prices are charged. This is the case where undertakings have
market power and abuse it. In these circumstances the objective of affordability
would not be met without public intervention. The Universal Service Directive
provides in this regard that Member States have to verify tariff levels. This is the
second tool that is provided in the directive to attain affordability.

> *Universal Service Directive, Article 9(1).* 'National regulatory authorities shall moni-
> tor the evolution and level of retail tariffs of the services identified . . . as falling
> under the universal service obligations and provided by designated undertakings,
> in particular in relation to national consumer prices and income.'

General competition law.   This oversight can be carried out on the basis of general   **5.96**
competition law. As was stated, Article 82 EC prohibits undertakings in a dominant
position from imposing excessive tariffs. This provision applies as regards relations
between dominant undertakings and other undertakings. A situation of this nature
may be found, for instance, where an operator sells capacity at an excessive price
to a provider with which the operator is in competition on an adjacent market. These

situations will however not be considered, normally, in the context of universal service. This latter context concerns more specifically the tariffs that are set by dominant undertakings in their relations with consumers or, more generally, with end users. These situations can also be analysed under Article 82 EC. That provision can be used in order to prevent dominant undertakings from fixing prices above what could be considered the normal value of the transaction. Such prices will be deemed excessive or, to use the terminology of Article 82 EC, unfair. Further indications as to what this prohibition entails are given in the chapter concerning the application of general competition law to undertakings in the electronic communications sector. At this stage it may however be useful to quote the exact basis for action:

> *Article 82 EC.* 'Any abuse by one or more undertakings of a dominant position with the common market or in a substantial part of it shall be prohibited as incompatible with the common market insofar as it may affect trade between Member States. Such abuse may, in particular, consist in . . . directly or indirectly imposing unfair purchase or selling prices or other unfair trading conditions.'

5.97 **Sector-specific regulation.** In addition to general competition law, certain provisions of the NRF may also be used. The Universal Service Directive, in particular, contains several rules that have been adopted for this purpose. A first rule is that NRAs have to assess the reasonable character of tariffs charged by designated undertakings.[49] This has to be done in the light of available incomes. A comparison has also to be made with the general level of prices charged to consumers in all sectors in the relevant country.[50]

> *Universal Service Directive, Article 9(1).* 'National regulatory authorities shall monitor the evolution and level of retail tariffs of the services identified . . . as falling under the universal service obligations and provided by designated undertakings, in particular in relation to national consumer prices and income.'

5.98 **Tariff unbundling.** More technical rules are also included in the Universal Service Directive. One of them is that designated undertakings should not bundle services and tariffs. Users should at all times have the possibility to choose the specific item they are interested in. They should not be forced to enter into other transactions where they do not have a need for them.

---

[49] Where universal service is provided by market forces, the control is supposed to be made through competition-based mechanisms. A control can take place on the basis of general competition law. The sector-specific regulation does not contain provisions allowing tariff control on non-designated undertakings.

[50] This specific control is limited to undertakings designated to provide universal service. In the absence of designation, no control has to take place under the Universal Service Directive. The idea is that market forces should normally lead to the lowest prices possible. This does not mean that Member States are prevented from carrying out verifications regarding tariffs in normal market conditions. General competition law will be of use in that context, as it prohibits excessive prices charged to consumers by dominant firms. Member States will also have the possibility to use other— national—measures to carry out a control. That control will however have to comply with the traditional basic regulatory principles (transparency, objectivity, non-discrimination, proportionality).

Universal Service Directive, Article 10(1). 'Member States shall ensure that designated undertakings . . . establish terms and conditions in such a way that the subscriber is not obliged to pay for facilities or services which are not necessary or not required for the service requested.'

Significant market power. The unbundling rule is specifically mentioned in the **5.99** Universal Service Directive. Other rules are made applicable through Article 16(1)(a) of the directive, which refers to obligations concerning retail tariffs contained in the ONP Voice Telephony Directive. These apply only where undertakings have significant market power. They apply in the context of the NRF for as long as no decision has been taken to terminate their validity. This decision must be taken by the NRAs, each concerning its territory,[51] after markets have been reviewed in the same manner as required for the review of access-related obligations.

Universal Service Directive, Article 16(1) and (3). 'Member States shall maintain all obligations relating to . . . retail tariffs for the provision of access to and use of the public telephone network, imposed under . . . [the ONP Voice Telephony Directive] until a review has been carried out and a determination made in accordance with . . . this Article.' 'Member States shall ensure that, as soon as possible after the entry into force of this [Universal Service] Directive, and periodically thereafter, national regulatory authorities undertake a market analysis, in accordance with the procedure set out in . . . [the] Framework Directive . . . to determine whether to maintain, amend or withdraw the obligations relating to retail markets.'

Cost orientation. Among these old obligations, the first is that powerful under- **5.100** takings should on each market base their tariffs on the costs incurred in providing the relevant service. This is important, as these undertakings could for instance otherwise include in a tariff for a given service the costs incurred in relation to another service. This obligation of cost orientation was fundamental when the reform was introduced, as former monopolies at that time used to set their tariffs irrespective of the expenses they incurred on a given market. It has now become less essential as competition has forced all undertakings, including powerful ones, to disaggregate their activities and seek profit on each of them separately.

ONP Voice Telephony Directive, Article 17(2). 'Tariffs for use of the . . . public . . . network and . . . public . . . services shall follow the basic principles of cost orientation.'[52]

Independence of application. Another obligation is that tariffs for access to, **5.101** and use of, the public network should be independent of the application that is

---

[51] See Universal Service Directive, Art 18, para 3.

[52] Made applicable through Art 18 of the Universal Service Directive. The original provision refers to the 'fixed' 'telephone' network and services. We have omitted these indications in the quotation because we feel that the provision must be generalised through its application in the NRF. Art 18 of the Universal Service Directive, which makes this provision applicable in the NRF, is not limited, indeed, to 'fixed' 'telephony'.

implemented by the users. As stated above, that obligation comes from the ONP Voice Telephony Directive and is made applicable through the Universal Service Directive until a decision to the contrary after a market review has been carried out. It only concerns undertakings with significant market power. This rule is due to the variety of applications that may be implemented using the network. This variety is even recognised in the context of universal service, since it includes several items which may be considered different applications. Suppose a user decides to use the network in order to send facsimiles or data. No difference should be made between this usage and other possible usages, for instance voice telephony. This of course does not prevent the undertakings involved from charging users where, for the application to work, the latter request items that are additional to those included in universal service.

> *ONP Telephony Directive, Article 17, para 3.* '[T]ariffs for access to and use of the fixed public telephone network shall be independent of the type of application which the users implement, except to the extent that they require different services or facilities.'[53]

5.102 **Notice period.** A third obligation is that tariff changes must be announced in advance. A notice period has to be respected for each change. This period is to be fixed by the NRAs, each for its national territory.

> *ONP Voice Telephony Directive, Article 17(5).* 'Tariff changes shall be implemented only after an appropriate public notice period, set by the national regulatory authority, has been observed.'[54]

5.103 **Other obligations concerning retail services.** Other obligations may be imposed by NRAs on undertakings with significant market power, as regards the conditions, other than those pertaining to tariffs, under which retail service are provided. These obligations do not concern specifically the provision of the universal service. For that reason, they are analysed in the chapter dealing with specific issues (users' rights—see paras 7.02–7.29).[55]

5.104 **The relation between the two bodies of the law.** The obligations examined above are in effect the same, whether they come from general competition law or sector specific regulation. Both bodies of law apply to powerful undertakings.[56]

---

[53] Made applicable through Art 18 of the Universal Service Directive.

[54] A fourth obligation introduced by the ONP Voice Telephony Directive and made applicable through the Universal Service Directive is to avoid any bundling of services. As far as the content is concerned, that obligation adds little to that which is directly imposed, with the same object, by the Universal Service Directive, Art 10. The advantage of taking the obligation over explicitly in the NRF is that this obligation will remain, even where the NRAs decide that former retail tariff obligations no longer have to apply.

[55] These obligations are introduced by the Universal Service Directive, Art 17.

[56] The definition given to this term was different in the old regulatory framework. We do not feel however that this difference matters in the present context. In our view, the obligations contained in the Voice Telephony Directive and made applicable through the Universal Service Directive must be

They are based on similar principles, particularly cost orientation. They can also be used to address the same types of behaviour—bundling, discrimination on the basis of the application, rapid tariff changes, and so on. There is nonetheless a difference between the two bodies of rules in the context of universal service. As regards the NRF, the provisions concerning tariffs apply only to items included in universal service. By contrast, general competition law has wider scope. While there is no obstacle to its application to universal service, it is not limited to these items, and may also apply in respect of any service made available by dominant undertakings to end users. Practitioners are thus advised not to omit referring to the two bodies of law where they argue cases concerning items that are not included in universal service.

(4) Monitoring of expenditure

Monitoring expenditure. A third tool is to induce end users to monitor their **5.105** own expenditure. Bills are sometimes excessive as a result of usage rather than tariffs. Where for example a consumer has access to a variety of electronic communications services he may, as a result of intense usage, receive bills he cannot afford to pay. This may result in service disconnection. The outcome is that access to essential services is lost, even though the disconnection was due to non-payment in respect of applications that are less important in the eyes of the authorities.

> *Universal Service Directive, Article 10(2).* 'Member States shall ensure that designated undertakings . . . provide the specific facilities and services set out in Annex I, Part A, in order that subscribers can monitor and control expenditure and avoid unwarranted disconnection of service.'

Information on expenditure. In order to prevent such an outcome, various **5.106** mechanisms are introduced in the Universal Service Directive. One of them is the provision of information to consumers. Pursuant to Annex I of the directive, designated undertakings must make available information concerning expenditure by consumers. In the market-based philosophy underlying the reform, information is indeed essential, since in its absence rational choices cannot be made.[57] Under the directive, information must be made available free of charge. Standards are to be fixed by NRAs as regards items to be presented in the bill. These standards must make it possible for consumers to carry out a double check: verify

---

adapted to the present situation. One aspect of this is that they have to apply to the undertakings which are now concerned by the obligations imposed in the regulatory framework. For this reason, we consider that the expression 'powerful undertakings' has to be interpreted as it is in the present framework, even if a different meaning was originally given to that expression.

[57] To that extent, the directive does not depart from the market-based mechanisms that are established in the NRF. The hope is that through correct information, consumers will make the best choices and contribute to the production of the most satisfactory outcome. There will thus be no need for public intervention as regards the provision of universal service.

the exact nature of the prices charged; and monitor their expenditure, thereby avoiding excessive bills due to unrestrained usage.[58]

> *Universal Service Directive, Annex I, Part A, letter (a), first sentence.* 'Member States are to ensure that national regulatory authorities . . . may lay down the basic level of itemised bills which are to be provided by designated undertakings . . . to consumers free of charge in order that they can: (i) allow verification and control of the charges incurred in using the public telephone network at a fixed location and/or related publicly available telephone services; (ii) adequately monitor their usage and expenditure and thereby exercise a reasonable degree of control over their bills.'

5.107 **Additional information.** Additional information can be presented, but consumers may be requested to pay for it. Where the undertaking makes use of the possibility of charging clients for extra information, the price must be reasonable.

> *Universal Service Directive, Annex I, Part A, letter (a), second sentence.* 'Where appropriate, additional levels of detail may be offered to subscribers at reasonable tariffs or at no charge.'

5.108 **Technological tool to avoid expenditure.** The Universal Service Directive mentions that technological tools may be used to help users limit their expenditure. A possibility is to prohibit calls to certain numbers.[59] This is particularly useful for parents, who may then limit the calls their children make to premium rate or international numbers. A similar use can be appropriate in communities where telephones are used by several people and it is not always possible to determine who has called where. In such circumstances, anonymity may induce expensive usage, a way to limit this usage being to avoid calls to certain destinations. The technological tools can also be useful for adults who know they have to limit the calls to certain numbers but are not able to resist the temptation. They may then decide to close the line to these numbers.

> *Universal Service Directive, Annex 1, Part A, letter (c).* '[Member States are to ensure that national regulatory authorities may require designated undertakings to provide] the facility whereby the subscriber can, on request to the telephone service provider, bar outgoing calls of defined types or to defined types of numbers free of charge.'

5.109 **Pre-payment cards.** Another tool may be used to ensure that users do not go beyond an acceptable level of expenditure, given their income and spending patterns. Generally, a limitation on expenditure is possible through the provision of information. Users are informed about the state of their account and decide on that basis to limit their usage through self-discipline. The difficulty is that

---

[58] For that reason, calls made free of charge must not be registered on the bill. Such a piece of information is not necessary to control expenditure, as calls are free. Not being under the obligation to register these calls on the bill will allow the undertaking to reduce costs. See Universal Service Directive, Annex I, Part A, letter (a), third sentence.

[59] This can be made through a tuning device placed in the network. All calls from a certain location and directed at specified numbers are then barred.

information is not constantly available in all circumstances. Users have to wait for bills to arrive in order to know where they stand. However, bills only come at the end of determined periods (for example once a month). The ceiling set by the user may already have been reached by then. Another problem is that users may pass their limit even where constant monitoring is possible. They are not always able to respect the limit they have fixed (lack of discipline, unexpected need for extra communications, etc). These various issues may be solved where users resort to pre-payment cards. With cards of this kind, communications stop once the budget is exhausted.[60] There is thus no possibility for users to spend after the limit has been reached and thereafter receive a bill they cannot afford to pay. Furthermore, the card is paid for in advance. With this system, users are not allowed to go beyond what they can afford, unless they have bought the card on credit.

> *Universal Service Directive, Annex 1, Part A, letter (c).* 'Member States are to ensure that national regulatory authorities may require designated undertakings to provide means for consumers to pay for access to the public telephone and use of publicly available telephone services on pre-paid terms.'

Subscriber alert. In the preamble to the Universal Service Directive the **5.110** European institutions allude to another technological tool that could be introduced in the years ahead in connection with expenditure control. This tool implies sending information to consumers as soon as a predetermined level of expenditure is exceeded. Another possibility is to inform consumers electronically that their bill shows an abnormal calling pattern.

> *Universal Service Directive, Preamble, recital 15.* 'Current conditions do not warrant a requirement for operators with universal service obligations to alert subscribers where a predetermined limit of expenditure is exceeded or an abnormal calling pattern occurs. Review of the relevant legislative provisions in future should consider whether there is a possible need to alert subscribers for these reasons.'

(5) Revenue-based measures

All layers of the population. Measures may be taken by Member States to **5.111** ensure that universal service items are actually made available to all layers of the population. Special attention is devoted to two categories of people who sometimes face difficulties in accessing electronic communications. These are subscribers on low incomes and people with special social needs. It is not clear what these categories exactly refer to, nor as a result who could or should be included. Decisions have to be made by Member States in this regard.[61] The first category is

---

[60] In some instances, operators provide consumers/users with electronic access to their own account. Constant monitoring is possible through that technology—at least where the user has constant access to the internet.

[61] No obligation or restriction is imposed on them in this regard in the directive. Other European rules however apply, including those prohibiting national discriminatory measures.

probably not too difficult to determine, as quantitative data can be used. For instance, statistics can be found indicating at what level incomes may be considered low in a given national or regional society. The second category opens more room for interpretation. How can groups with 'special social needs' be defined? Discussions will inevitably emerge on this subject, in the Member States and across the Union.[62]

5.112 **Methods.**   Several methods are mentioned in the Universal Service Directive in connection with the two categories that have been described above. They can be used in order to ensure real access by the people concerned to electronic communications. One implies that support is granted to users. The other consists of special tariffs or packages.

5.113 **(1) Support to end users.**   Pursuant to the Universal Service Directive, support can be granted to the people concerned. A system can be imagined for instance whereby income-based coupons are given by the authorities to people in need. The coupons or more generally the support to these people in need could only be used in order to access items included in the universal service. In this context the directive states that publicly funded advantages can be given to the people concerned.

> *Universal Service Directive, Article 9(3).* 'Member States may . . . ensure that support is provided to consumers identified as having low incomes or social special needs.'

5.114 **State aids.**   This kind of action seems to comply with European law. Compliance derives directly from the fact that the granting of public funds in compensation for the fulfilment of universal service obligations is explicitly accepted in the directive as a method that may contribute to realising the goals that are set in the directive. Granting public funds to that end also conforms to EC provisions on state aids. Pursuant to these rules, aids are financial advantages granted with public money (funds coming from a public authority). The advantage can be direct (subsidy) or indirect (tax deduction, relief, discount). Under European law, aids granted by Member States or through State resources are

---

[62] 'Special social needs' can be interpreted in various fashions. The expression may refer to groups or entities which need help in order to attain a standard social or cultural level in society. Thus one can imagine asylum seekers being granted special treatment for electronic communications as they are temporarily far from home. The expression can also be understood as implying that entities helping these groups should be granted favours. In that hypothesis, one could for example grant assistance to charities helping asylum seekers even where these charities are made up of local people who are remunerated by them. Ultimately, one could also wonder whether another meaning could not be granted to 'special social needs'. Member States have often granted advantages to groups which, although they have few financial difficulties, have indeed a special function in society. Thus, special tariffs have been granted for the use of railways to journalists. The justification is that they make intensive use of railway facilities as a result of their work, and that they should be encouraged to travel to verify information. The same justification was used to explain advantages granted to politicians, who had to travel frequently to their constituencies.

prohibited (Article 87(1) EC). They can, however, be accepted in several circumstances (Article 87(2) EC). One of these circumstances is where the aid has a social character and is granted to individual consumers.[63] That would be the case here, to the extent users are persons (not entities) using telecommunications in a private context (not in the course of a professional activity).

> *Article 87 EC.* [1] 'Save as otherwise provided in this Treaty, any aid granted by a Member State or through State resources in any form whatsoever which distorts or threatens to distort competition by favouring certain undertakings or the production of certain goods shall insofar as it affects trade between Member States, be incompatible with the common market.' [2] 'The following shall be compatible with the common market: (a) aids having a social character, granted to individual consumers, provided that such aid is granted without discrimination related to the origin of the products concerned . . ..'[64]

No discrimination. For the aid to be accepted, one condition must however be **5.115** fulfilled as is apparent from the above. Pursuant to Article 87(2) EC, aids with a social character and attributed to individual consumers must not be discriminatory. No discrimination can be applied relating to the origin or the nationality of the product or service acquired with the aid.[65] This condition is in line with the basic regulatory principles imposed in the NRF. Article 87 EC does not appear to bring any additional condition in this regard. In the context of universal service, the requirement implies that the aid cannot be made conditional upon the beneficiary's choosing a specific operator or provider with the funds granted. The beneficiary must be able to choose the undertaking from which he/she wants to receive the electronic communications services in question.[66]

Compatibility with underlying principle. Support granted to end users is com- **5.116** patible with the philosophy underlying the NRF. In the previous section it was stated that Member States are encouraged to facilitate use by disabled people of competition-based mechanisms. This will tend to assist the social integration of these users, as they would choose their goods and services like any other user in a competitive environment. The same philosophy applies here. Member States are allowed to give support to people with low incomes or special social needs. This support—for example a subsidy—will then be used by the people concerned as a resource allowing them to make a choice among the variety of providers, as other users do.

(2) Special options or packages. Another method of ensuring real access to **5.117** universal service is to offer special tariffs or packages to low income groups or people with special social needs. Reduced rates can for instance be offered for connection and usage.

---

[63] Art 87(2)(a) EC.   [64] Art 87 EC.   [65] ibid.
[66] As we will see, the item for which the aid can be used is limited in this hypothesis to public voice telephony.

Universal Service Directive, Article 9(2). 'Member States may . . . require that designated undertakings provide tariff options or packages to consumers which depart from those provided under normal commercial conditions, in particular to ensure that those on low incomes or with social special needs are not prevented from accessing or using the publicly available telephone service.'

5.118 Exception to market conditions.   This second method introduces mechanisms that are exceptions to normal market conditions. Prices are no longer set by undertakings as a function of market factors, as they were in the first method.[67] The undertakings involved in the provision of universal service are expected to adapt their tariffs and conditions on the basis of social considerations. A certain distortion is thus introduced in the decisions which are to be made by the businesses concerned, as these decisions are further complicated by the integration of non-market conditions. For this reason, the second method does not seem to have the preference of the European authorities. This results from the general principle established in the Universal Service Directive, pursuant to which priority is to be given to market-based mechanisms, with public intervention limited to cases of market failure. The consequence of this is that the second method cannot be used with respect to all items included in universal service. Pursuant to the directive, special tariffs and packages must be limited to public voice telephony.[68]

5.119 Summary.   Member States can facilitate access to universal service as regards people on low incomes or with special social needs. A first possibility is to grant direct support to the people involved (for example a subsidy). A second possibility is to offer special tariffs or packages. In the second case, the measure must be limited to public voice telephony. These are only possibilities. Member States are not obliged to provide access at better conditions for people falling in these categories.

(6) Payment difficulties

5.120 Risk of exclusion.   We have analysed in the previous sections various measures aimed at ensuring real access for people with low incomes and special social needs. There is a possibility that, despite these measures, people may still be incapable of paying their electronic communications bills. The undertakings involved may then be tempted to disconnect the services. This would however lead to a result running counter to the universal service concept—social exclusion. To avoid such an outcome, the Universal Service Directive regulates the reaction undertakings may have where bills remain unpaid. The measures contained in the directive are examined below. They apply only to expenses relating to the items included in

---

[67] Let us recall that in the first method, undertakings would carry out their activities under normal market conditions. They would be approached by people with low incomes or with special social needs. These people would contract with undertakings on normal terms. The difference would be the origin of the funds which are used in order to purchase the connection or the service.

[68] Universal Service Directive, Art 9(2), quoted above.

universal service. No rule is established in the NRF for other services. National laws thus apply in order to determine what is allowed and what is prohibited in these circumstances.

Phased payment. The Universal Service Directive provides that Member States **5.121** may impose phased payment where users cannot pay electronic communications bills outright.[69] The obligation is however limited to the expenses relating to network access. Users thus have a right to phase payments as regards connection fees, but not with respect to other expenses.[70] As stated above, this right can be extended to other items by the Member States for operations concerning their national territory. Most of them in fact have general laws on phased payments. There is no restriction in the directive as to the application of these laws to electronic communications.

> *Universal Service Directive, Annex I, Part A, letter (d).* 'Member States are to ensure that national regulatory authorities may require designated undertakings to allow consumers to pay for connection to the public telephone network on the basis of payments phased over time.'

No payment is made. A second—and more difficult—problem arises where **5.122** the bill is not paid despite the phased payment facility. Guidelines are provided in the Universal Service Directive as to how undertakings may react. One may then expect undertakings[71] to take measures in order to obtain payment.[72] Such measures are to be allowed by Member States. Undertakings must however conform to constraints which correspond to the basic regulatory principles analysed earlier.

> *Universal Service Directive, Annex I, Part A, letter (e).* 'Member States are to authorize specified measures, which are to be proportionate, non-discriminatory and published, to cover non-payment of telephone bills for use of the public telephone network at fixed location.'

Disconnection. Disconnection may finally be carried where no payment is **5.123** made despite these measures. Prior warning must be provided. In the persistent

---

[69] This obligation applies where undertakings are designated for the provision of the universal service. In other cases, undertakings are not bound by the obligation.

[70] The fixed costs faced by end users are thus the only ones with respect to which phased payments are allowed. The reason is that it is essential for the European legislator to ensure access to networks. Once people have access, it is for them to adjust their expenses to their revenues. Expenses made beyond access costs indeed depend on usage. Apparently, there is no desire on the part of the European legislator to encourage usage beyond the financial capabilities of the users.

[71] In practice, most undertakings have within their organisation a department entrusted with the task of recovering unpaid bills. The service may also be provided by a specialised company. After a few attempts, lawyers will be hired to obtain payment. Another possibility is for undertakings to sell unpaid bills for a portion of their nominal value. The buyer will attempt to recover them and will keep the recovered amount.

[72] The reform implies the introduction of market mechanisms. These mechanisms imply that sanctions are attached to non-satisfactory performance. These sanctions apply to undertaking where they do not perform their activities correctly. They then risk being set aside by consumers and partners. A similar mechanism applies with customers or users. The markets cannot accept that bills remain unpaid. A sanction must be applied, which can ultimately take the form of disconnection.

absence of payment, a period of limited disconnection may be decided. During that period, access will be limited to free numbers (such as emergency numbers).[73] Disconnection will then finally be allowed if the debt is not paid. It should be limited to the unpaid services[74] and cannot be extended to all services provided by the undertaking involved. The only exception is where fraud is committed or the issue is recurrent with the same customer (late payment, absence of payment). General disconnection is then allowed. It will affect all services provided by the undertaking, even those for which payments have possibly been made. This will in effect terminate the relation with the end-user concerned.[75]

> *Universal Service Directive, Annex I, Part A, letter (e).* 'Except in case of fraud, persistent late payment or non-payment, these measures are to ensure, as far as is technically feasible, that any service interruption is confined to the service concerned. Disconnection for non-payment of bills should take place only after due warning is given to the subscriber. Member States may allow a period of limited service prior to complete disconnection, during which only calls that do not incur a charge to the subscriber . . . are permitted.'[76]

5.124 **Other national measures.** Other measures may be decided by the Member States in an attempt to ensure access for all to electronic communications. These measures have only to comply with the European rules, in particular those concerning competition. A possibility is directly envisaged in the Universal Service Directive for Member States to provide additional support to certain groups of consumers. One measure could be to allow for debts to be paid off after examination of individual requests.

> *Universal Service Directive.* 'Such measures may also include . . . providing support to identified consumers, for example by means of specific measures, taken after the examination of individual requests, such as the paying off of debts.'[77]

5.125 **Summary.** Measures can be taken by undertakings where bills are not paid by end users. They must conform with the national rules applicable to these situations. These measures are regulated by the Universal Service Directive as concerns items included in the universal service requirement. Phased payments must be granted in relation to connection fees. Subsequently or simultaneously, due warning must be given that disconnection may occur. In the case of persistent default,

---

[73] The only non-free service is then access to the network. Access must normally be paid for. During the period of limited disconnection, it would be provided free of charge.

[74] Suppose a user regularly pays his telephone expenses, but omits to do the same with respect to internet-related expenses. In such a situation, disconnection could only be made with respect to the internet. The measure should not affect the service for which payments have been made.

[75] Where the universal service is provided by several undertakings, the user will have the possibility of turning to another provider. Where one undertaking only is present, he will have no alternative and will thus be deprived of access.

[76] See also the Preamble to the Universal Service Directive, recital 16.

[77] Preamble, recital 7.

full disconnection may then be carried out, but should be limited to the services not paid for.[78]

(7) Other possibilities regarding tariffs

Other techniques. Member States must normally resort to market-based mech- **5.126** anisms in the provision of universal service. Derogations may be introduced, as stated above. They are based on Article 3 of the Universal Service Directive, which allows Member States to determine the most efficient and appropriate approach for ensuring the implementation of universal service. As affordable tariffs must be ensured, they may consider that tariff oversight is not always sufficient. In some instances, they may feel that public intervention should go farther. The path is open in the directive for more intervention as regards tariffs.

Price caps. A first technique is for Member States to impose price caps. This **5.127** technique is explicitly provided for in the Universal Service Directive as a tool that can be used by Member States in order to ensure the attainment of universal service objectives. When they impose price caps Member States in effect fix ceilings. Undertakings may determine their prices as they wish, but cannot exceed the maximum set by the authority. The technique was widely used within the Member States prior to the reform. Telecommunications services were then provided by national administrations or public undertakings. The purpose of these ceilings was to ensure that tariffs would not be in excess of the price authorities found legitimate for such an essential commodity as telecommunications.[79]

> *Universal Service Directive, Article 9(3)*. 'Member States may . . . [introduce] provision for designated undertakings . . . to comply with price caps.'

Geographic averaging. Another technique explicitly envisaged in the Universal **5.128** Service Directive is the use of geographic averaging to ensure affordability of tariffs throughout a given territory. Costs vary across regions. Low-density regions, for instance, are more expensive to supply.[80] Under normal market conditions, these differences are supposed to be reflected in costs. As they are in competition, undertakings fix their prices as close as possible to their costs. In this manner, they hope to recover outgoings but still to attract or retain clients by charging lower tariffs than competitors. Under this hypothesis, electronic communications should thus be more expensive in mountainous regions than in cities. Such an outcome

---

[78] Member States are allowed to impose a period of limited disconnection. A general disconnection (on all services) may take place where fraud has been committed or the issue is recurrent.

[79] Telecommunications were indeed considered an essential commodity in society. Prices were highly sensitive on these markets. Telecommunications were typically an area where promises for lower tariffs were made by politicians.

[80] As these regions have fewer inhabitants, undertakings need to lay down more cables to connect a number of users similar to that which can be found in cities. The cost per user is then higher in low density regions.

is not accepted by all Member States. Some fear that discrepancies may contribute to migration to the cities. The result is that development would not be geographically balanced and a lack of territorial cohesion may be created. These concerns can be addressed through geographic averaging. With this mechanism the same price is fixed across the territory irrespective of the differences in costs. A compensatory mechanism is thus introduced as between regions. Low-cost regions are charged tariffs higher than would have been required under normal market conditions. By contrast, users in high-cost regions receive an advantage and do not have to pay all costs related to the provision of services to them.

> *Universal Service Directive, Article 9(3).* 'Member States may . . . [introduce] provision for designated undertakings . . . to comply with . . . geographic averaging.'

5.129 **Other similar techniques.** The Universal Service Directive provides that other tariff-related mechanisms may be used in addition to those seen above. No detail is however given in this regard. This basically implies that Member States are free to intervene on tariffs wherever they feel this is necessary to ensure the implementation of universal service objectives. They can thus resort to techniques that were used before the reform. They can also bring in new mechanisms without being restricted by the directive.

> *Universal Service Directive, Article 9(3).* 'Member States may . . . [introduce] provision for designated undertakings . . . to comply with . . . other similar schemes [than price caps or geographic averaging].'[81]

5.130 **A setback?** It may come as a surprise to see accepted in the NRF techniques that were in use on national markets prior to the reform. The initiatives taken by the European institutions indeed aimed at setting aside public intervention, which was deemed to have been excessive and to have impeded for decades the development of electronic communications. As has been stated, the goal was not to give up fulfilling policy objectives. Objectives of this kind underlay the reform, as the idea was to open markets to ensure consumers and citizens would have access to the best economic outcome possible. The idea was, however, that such a result could not be attained in an environment where public authorities intervened heavily. A preference was thus expressed in favour of a competitive environment where market forces would interact. The idea apparently suffers a setback to the extent that public intervention seems to be accepted in an area that is very sensitive to market forces, ie tariffs.

5.131 **Do not overestimate intervention.** The possibility for Member States of intervening as regards tariffs should, however, not be overestimated. *(a)* First,

---

[81] A reference to geographic averaging is also made in Annex IV, Part A, of the directive. '[U]niversal service obligations refer to those obligations placed upon an undertaking by a Member State which concern the provision of a network and service throughout a specified geographic area, including, where required, averaged prices in that geographical area.'

intervention may occur only in respect of items included in the universal service requirement. This means that the vast majority of applications already available through electronic communications are provided in a market-based environment where public intervention has no place. *(b)* Second, tariff intervention may come only where market forces have been given a chance to reach the universal service objectives set and have failed to deliver the expected results. Where the markets produce affordable tariffs, there is no need to intervene. *(c)* Third, the NRF does not really change previous policy. The Universal Service Directive merely takes over possibilities that were already provided for at an earlier stage of European regulation.[82]

(8) Observations on powers granted to Member States as regards tariffs

Limitations.   Significant powers are entrusted to the Member States as regards   **5.132** intervention on tariffs. Limitations apply, but they are restricted in scope. Most of them have already been analysed earlier. First, there is the general obligation to respect market mechanisms. This obligation implies that derogations may be introduced only where objectives cannot be attained otherwise (Article 3 of the Universal Service Directive). In order to comply with that principle, Member States have to justify each tariff intervention. As part of this justification, they have to explain why action was necessary and to what extent it could not be replaced by other measures that would have been as effective but would have hindered competition to a lesser extent. Second, Member States are constrained by the basic regulatory principles. As stated, these requirements apply pervasively in the NRF. They express general principles of law which apply to Member States, as well as to dominant or powerful undertakings, across the European legal order.[83]

> *Universal Service Directive, Article 9(5).* 'National regulatory authorities shall ensure that, where a designated undertaking has an obligation to provide special tariff options, common tariffs, including geographical averaging, or to comply with price caps, the conditions are fully transparent and are published and applied in accordance with the principle of non-discrimination. National regulatory authorities may require that specific schemes be modified or withdrawn.'

A possibility, not an obligation.   Social provisions differ on one account from   **5.133** other rules concerning universal service. This difference relates to the character of the task that is entrusted to the Member States. In general, universal service

---

[82] A comparison with the rules formerly in force is carried out later in this chapter (see paras 5.220–5.236). The provisions concerning price caps, price averaging and other tariff-related measures were previously contained in Art 3(1) of the ONP Voice Telephony Directive.

[83] As has been seen, the obligation to resort to market mechanisms is in line with the basic regulatory principles. Among these requirements is the obligation to respect proportionality. However, proportionality requires that preference be given to solutions compatible with competition or the internal market (depending on the context in which the principle is used).

provisions impose obligations. Results are set in the Universal Service Directive and the Member States must ensure that these results are achieved. To that end, they must grant the necessary decision-making powers to the NRAs.[84] The social provisions in the directive are different. They are not phrased in terms of obligations, but rather of possibilities. The concept on which they are based is that Member States *may* provide support[85] or require from undertakings that they offer tariff options or packages.[86]

5.134 **Limited force of social provisions.** The difference has practical consequences. Member States cannot be challenged on the basis of European law where they do not introduce in their national legislation the social provisions that are included in the directive. Consumers or associations will thus not have the possibility of making applications to national courts, claiming that a right has been created for them in the social provisions. This low profile on the social aspects of universal service is probably due to the special status that social provisions generally have in European law. A debate has divided the Member States as to the role the European Union could, or should, play with respect to social policy. This debate has apparently not yet ended, as the Parliament and Council have not been able to agree on further-reaching social measures, although the area provides ample opportunities for action in that regard.[87]

5.135 **Member States and NRAs.** A final observation should be made regarding the division of tasks between the Member States and the NRAs. Most provisions relating to items to be provided as part of the universal service requirement are directed to NRAs.[88] By contrast, the measures concerning tariffs concern Member States. This is probably because national governments and legislators have insisted on retaining the power to make decisions in this area. As far as tariffs are concerned, NRAs are entrusted with limited tasks. One is tariff monitoring.[89] NRAs are better equipped to carry out that task than governments or legislators, as they have the requisite technical expertise.

5.136 **Basic regulatory principles.** A second task is to control the compatibility of national tariff schemes with the basic regulatory principles. An important power

---

[84] For this reason, most provisions are worded in the following manner: 'Member States must ensure that the NRAs have the power to impose on undertakings the following obligations.'

[85] See Universal Service Directive, Art 9(3).   [86] ibid.

[87] Social aspects are however important in the definition of universal service, or services of general interest. See the extracts quoted at the outset of this chapter concerning universal service.

[88] The accurate scheme, in these provisions, is that Member States are to ensure that NRAs have the necessary legal and regulatory powers to take the measures introduced by the directive. The reason for that scheme to appear so frequently in the directive is that the European legislator cannot create rights or obligations for the NRAs directly. The Universal Service Directive provisions have to be addressed to the Member States, which have to take the necessary implementation measures. This is in line with Art 249 EC, pursuant to which directives are binding upon the Member States as to the result to be achieved and leave to national authorities the choice of form and methods.

[89] See Universal Service Directive, Art 9(1).

is granted to the NRAs for this purpose. This power does not encompass a control on what undertakings are doing, but implies that the authorities verify the measures introduced by the Member States as regards tariffs, in order to ensure that they are compatible with the NRF. This goes far, as a power is granted to a national administrative body to oversee measures adopted by the government and/or parliament of the relevant Member State. The Universal Service Directive goes even further and grants NRAs the power to require that specific schemes be modified or withdrawn, where they do not conform to European law.

> *Universal Service Directive, Article 9(5).* 'National regulatory authorities may require that specific schemes be modified or withdrawn.'[90]

Compliance with European law. By granting them these powers, the NRF confers on the NRAs the task of guaranteeing that European rules are complied with. To this extent, NRAs cease to be purely national organs. They acquire a certain European status, as a mission is granted to them which specifically requires them to turn against their national government or legislator where a violation of European law is observed. It is not certain whether the NRAs will be strong enough to resist pressure from the latter authorities, as they are placed in a position of dependency on them in several regards (including financing and appointment of high-ranking personnel). **5.137**

G. Who May Provide Universal Service?

(1) Designation of undertakings

No choice other than to designate in some circumstances. In normal circumstances, universal service must be provided by market forces. The result is that items included in the universal service requirement are provided in some instances under conditions that are not satisfactory, for instance where tariffs are excessive or quality is not sufficient. Measures must then be taken by Member States to ensure that the relevant objectives are fulfilled. As regards tariffs, a typical measure is to impose price caps. Under that system, undertakings may set tariffs as they wish on condition that they do not exceed the ceiling fixed by the authorities. Another situation may be that some services are not provided at all.[91] The Member States must then take the appropriate measures to ensure that the service is indeed made available. The usual scenario is to gather with representatives of the industry and explain **5.138**

---

[90] The other powers granted to the NRAs as regards the control on basic regulatory principles are described in the previous quotation.

[91] This may even be the result of the previous situation examined above. Suppose services are provided but tariffs are deemed excessive by the authority. A ceiling is imposed. In our scenario, the result of that measure is that services would be provided at a loss if the ceiling is respected. The reaction of undertakings may be to stop providing the item.

that additional objectives must be reached. Spontaneous applications should however not be expected. Such applications would emerge if undertakings had a commercial interest in providing the missing item. However, the NRF specifies that all benefits—even the most indirect and immaterial—must be taken into account in calculating the net cost of providing universal service where compensation is requested. The only remaining solution for the Member State is then to organise a procedure at the end of which one or several undertakings will be designated for the provision of the service in question.

> *Universal Service Directive, Preamble, recital 14.* 'In accordance with the principle of subsidiarity, it is for Member States to decide on the basis of objective criteria which undertakings have universal service obligations.'

5.139 **One or several undertakings.** The question arises whether one or several undertakings will be designated. An economic calculation has to be made by the NRA on this point. Where several undertakings are designated, the service will be provided in competition. This will probably result in lower tariffs and costs. Several undertakings may however have to be compensated, as the service is provided on a commercial basis which is outside the norm. It will then be difficult to determine what amount has to be paid to each, as costs probably differ from one undertaking to the other. Another solution would be to designate one undertaking. This undertaking would be in charge of providing a given service in a defined area.

5.140 **Some regions, some items.** The European institutions consider—and hope— that it is possible to fulfil a large proportion of the universal service obligations under normal commercial conditions. These conditions may however not always allow the provision of all items throughout the national territories. For instance, it is relatively easy to ensure access to a public network under reasonable conditions in major cities. The objective will be more difficult to attain in remote areas. Part of the difficulty can probably be resolved through the averaging technique, whereby average tariffs are fixed for access throughout the territory, irrespective of the differences in the costs incurred for connection in cities or in the countryside. The technique will, however, not resolve all difficulties in all Member States. For this reason it may be expected that certain Member States may have to designate undertakings for the provision of part of the universal service in some regions.

> *Universal Service Directive, Article 8(1).* 'Member States may designate one or more undertakings to guarantee the provision of universal service . . . so that the whole of the national territory can be covered.'

5.141 **Division of universal service.** In fact, universal service should not be considered as one monolithic and indivisible bloc. The Member States indeed have the possibility of dividing universal service into items or among regions. For each item or region, different undertakings may be designated. The provision of universal service may thus appear in some Member States as a system implying a variety of actors.

Universal Service Directive, Article 8(1), last sentence. 'Member States may designate different undertakings or sets of undertakings to provide different elements of universal service and/or to cover different parts of the national territory.'

(2) Obligations

Basic regulatory principles. The basic regulatory principles are to be respected **5.142** in the procedure leading to the designation of the undertaking(s) in charge of the universal service. Transparency, objectivity and non-discrimination must thus be complied with. Regarding non-discrimination, the Universal Service Directive specifies that no undertaking can be excluded a priori from designation. The principle of proportionality is not mentioned explicitly in the relevant provision, but applies as a general principle of European law as well as in its capacity as guiding principle for the organisation of universal service.

Universal Service Directive, Article 8(2). 'When Member States designate undertakings in part or all of the national territory as having universal service obligations, they shall do so using an efficient, objective, transparent and non-discriminatory designation mechanism, whereby no undertaking is a priori excluded from being designated.'

Efficiency. Pursuant to the Universal Service Directive, the designation mechan- **5.143** ism must operate in an efficient manner. This is probably to be interpreted as implying that the administrative costs relating to the operation of this mechanism should be as low as possible. One possible consequence is that undertakings applying for the provision of universal service should not be charged any administrative fee or—if at all—the fees should be reduced to a minimum.[92] The requirement also means that the designation must be made so as to ensure that the chosen solution leads to the most efficient provision of the items involved. An appropriate manner of complying with this requirement is to ask candidates to submit bids. These bids should provide financial data, including the costs candidates would wish to be compensated for in the event they are designated. A designation would then be made on the basis of the lowest bid. Such a solution would in fact combine the double requirement related to efficiency. On the one hand, the most efficient solution would be chosen for the implementation of universal service objectives. On the other hand, the designation mechanism would operate in accordance with the efficiency requirement, as it would automatically provide the data necessary for the compensation mechanism to be set in motion.

Universal Service Directive. 'When Member States designate undertakings . . . , they shall do so using an efficient . . . designation mechanism . . . Such designation methods shall ensure that universal service is provided in a cost-effective manner and may be used as a means of determining the net cost of the universal service obligation.'[93]

---

[92] In some instances, undertakings are asked to pay a fee before participating in a contest. It is typical for authorities to charge undertakings for the costs of the procedures in which such undertakings participate.   [93] Universal Service Directive, Art 8(2).

'National regulatory authorities are to consider all means to ensure appropriate incentives for undertakings (designated or not) to provide universal service obligations cost efficiently.'[94] '[U]niversal service obligations could in some cases be allocated to operators demonstrating the most cost-effective means of delivering access and services, including by competitive or comparative selection procedures.'[95]

5.144 **Legislation to expect on this subject.** The ability of Member States to designate undertakings for the provision of services of general interest raises delicate issues. This mechanism makes it possible to reinstate former monopolies in the situation where they were prior to the reform. Suppose a Member State considers that universal service obligations may only be performed if demand is concentrated on one undertaking. It decides that the former national monopoly is in the best position to ensure the fulfilment of these obligations. A procedure is organised which leads to the designation of that undertaking. As a result of the process, the former monopoly may have some of its previous prerogatives restored. It may carry out activities and claim compensation from excluded undertakings wherever abnormal market conditions are encountered.

5.145 **Guidelines to come.** A situation of this nature should be avoided as a result of the obligations that have just been examined. One should, however, not consider that all risks featured in the scenario will never materialise. Being aware of this possibility, the Commission currently envisages the adoption of rules that would draw a clear line between what is allowed and what should be avoided in the designation procedures. Some of the considerations underlying this approach have been made public in the report presented to the European Council for the Laeken Summit (2001).[96] These may be summarised as follows. *(a)* The process whereby the management of a service of general interest is entrusted by a public authority to an undertaking must be analysed as a public contract. The consequence is that the Public Procurement Directives apply. The designation must thus develop in conformity with the conditions set out in these instruments. *(b)* Additionally, the designation mechanism must comply with the rules on competition and those relating to the internal market. Principles of transparency, equal treatment, proportionality and mutual recognition should thus be complied with, together with the rules concerning the free provision of services and the right of establishment.[97]

(3) *Powerful undertakings*

5.146 **Obligations relating to tariffs.** It will be recalled that obligations relating to tariffs may be imposed on undertakings with significant market power under the

---

[94] Universal Service Directive, Annex IV, Part A, para 2.

[95] ibid, Preamble, recital 14.   [96] See n 4 above.

[97] Some of the rules deriving from the internal market and these principles have already been explained in a communication issued by the Commission on the application of Community law to concessions made by Member States. See Commission Interpretative Communication on Concessions in Community law [2000] OJ C121/2.

Universal Service Directive. These obligations were already introduced by the ONP Voice Telephony Directive and are made applicable in the context of the NRF through the Universal Service Directive. They are analysed above in the section dealing with tariff controls (see paras 5.95–5.102).

Retail markets.   Provisions are further set out in the Universal Service Directive   **5.147** to impose obligations on powerful undertakings as regards retail services. The purpose is to ensure that these undertakings do not abuse their dominant position. The obligations can be imposed only where the market is not effectively competitive. These obligations are not examined in this section, because they are not limited to universal service items but apply to all retail markets. They are addressed in the section dealing with users' rights (see paras 7.02–7.29).

H. How Can Universal Service be Financed?

(1) Relevant instruments

Instruments in both frameworks.   Issues relating to financing fall, as do other   **5.148** problems connected with the universal service, under the scope of the provisions of the Universal Service Directive. We will also analyse in a later section (see paras 5.238 and 5.240–5.242) the contribution brought by the Commission in the Consolidated Services Directive. Apart from these, a third instrument should be taken into account, a Communication issued by the Commission on universal service financing.[98] This Communication has no binding force in itself. It may however prove important, because it deals in more detail with issues that are addressed only in general terms within the Universal Service Directive. The communication was adopted in 1996, in the context of the old regulatory framework. However, it has been stated that no substantial differences have been introduced in the NRF as regards universal service, and the communication from the Commission therefore still remains valid.[99] The analysis in the following paragraphs is based on the Universal Service Directive, with the communication being examined whenever it contains a pertinent point.

(2) Methods of financing

Tariff-related issues.   The issue as to how universal service can be financed is to   **5.149** an extent related to the affordability of tariffs, a principle which must be ensured.

---

[98] Commission Communication on Assessment Criteria for National Schemes for the Costing and Financing of Universal Service in Telecommunications and Guidelines for the Member States on Operation of such Schemes, COM(96) 608, Brussels, 27 November 1996.

[99] It is not clear whether this communication has been adopted by the Commission in its capacity as authority with powers to apply competition rules to the sector (Art 86 EC) or as the body entrusted with the task of implementing general rules established in the Universal Service Directive. This debate, however, is not very important, as it appears that, in this communication, the Commission puts forward rules to ensure that the principles are respected in both the harmonisation and the liberalisation frameworks.

As a result of the obligation of affordability, undertakings must provide universal service at tariffs that are sometimes below costs or—at least—below tariffs under normal market conditions. This poses a threat to them. In a competitive environment, undertakings survive only where they recover their costs. Measures are thus to be taken to ensure that they are not disadvantaged compared to other market participants.

> *Universal Service Directive, Preamble, recital 4, first sentence.* 'Ensuring universal service . . . may involve the provision of some services to some end-users at prices that depart from those resulting from normal market conditions.'

5.150 **Losses or abnormal commercial conditions.** The Universal Service Directive appears to allow undertakings to claim compensation as soon as abnormal commercial conditions apply. There would thus be no need for a loss to occur, in order for the possibility of compensation to come into play. This results from the terms used by the European institutions in the Preamble to the directive and in Annex IV of that instrument, where the method is established as to the calculation of costs leading to compensation.

> *Universal Service Directive.* 'Member States should, where necessary, establish mechanisms for financing the net cost of universal service obligations in cases where it is demonstrated that the obligations can only be provided at a loss or at a net cost which falls outside normal commercial standards.'[100] *Annex IV.* 'The calculation is to be based upon the costs attributable to: (i) elements of the identified services which can only be provided at a loss or provided under cost conditions falling outside normal commercial standards . . . ; (ii) . . . end-users who . . . can only be served at a loss or under costs conditions falling outside normal commercial standards.'

5.151 **Criteria.** The difficulty will be to determine criteria to consider that conditions can be deemed abnormal. No indication is given in the directive as to how this expression should be interpreted. This is a significant gap, as it concerns the conditions under which compensation may be claimed. The danger is that the concept of 'abnormal commercial transaction' could be interpreted differently by the NRAs in different Member States. A clue for a European interpretation may perhaps be found in Annex IV of the directive, where the European institutions explain, in connection with items intended for specific end users, that these items may be taken into account only when the said users 'would not be served by a commercial operator which did not have an obligation to provide universal service'.[101] In order to determine where a transaction is abnormal, authorities thus have to engage in economic behaviour where they assess what a normal operator would do in the same context.[102]

---

[100] Universal Service Directive, Preamble, recital 18.

[101] ibid, Annex IV, Part A, para 3, letter (ii).

[102] Some inspiration may be sought in the European case law concerning State aids. Pursuant to that case law, measures taken by national authorities in favour of undertakings can be considered as advantages where a similar move has not been made by a 'Normal Private Investor' in similar circumstances.

An evolution has apparently taken place. There appears to have been some **5.152**
evolution as regards the costs that can ultimately be compensated. In the communication concerning the Costing and Financing of the Universal Service, the
Commission indeed only appears to accept compensation for losses. No similar
possibility seems to have been accepted regarding abnormal costs which would
not lead to a loss.

> *Commission Communication concerning the Costing and Financing of the Universal*
> *Service.* 'The cost of universal service covers the unavoidable net losses incurred by an
> efficient operator in providing universal service to customers or groups of customers.
> These are customers or groups of customers for whom the benefits to the operator of
> providing them with service are outweighed by the costs incurred. Therefore, these
> are customers that an operator, acting solely on commercial principles, would choose
> to disconnect if there was no universal service obligation.'[103]

Reason for the evolution. The reason for the evolution that has taken place **5.153**
between the communication and the NRF is not entirely clear. It may be related
to the possibility that compensation may be lower where intervention is possible
as soon as abnormal conditions are encountered. Suppose an undertaking ceases
to provide a service because it does not realise a sufficient profit, even though no
loss is sustained. Such a possibility should not be excluded, in an era where undertakings generally concentrate on highly profitable markets because this appears to
be the strategy to follow if they want to attract attention from investors. Two scenarios may be distinguished. *(a)* In the first, imagine that the compensation
mechanism may be activated only where losses are suffered. In this case, no compensation may be claimed by the undertaking. The result is that the undertaking
ceases to provide the service. As the service is no longer provided, the national
authorities must designate an undertaking that will be entrusted with the task
of carrying out that activity. In that scenario, the undertaking may demand
compensation for all costs incurred in the provision of the service. *(b)* By contrast,
suppose that compensation may be granted as soon as abnormal costs are
incurred, even where no loss is suffered. The service will not be discontinued by
the undertaking. The latter will be allowed to ask for compensation but it will be
limited: pursuant to the system, the undertaking will be allowed to claim only the
abnormal cost margin, that is, the difference between these abnormal costs and
the costs that the undertaking expects to incur on markets where it continues
activities.

Two mechanisms. Two mechanisms are presented in the Universal Service **5.154**
Directive to find the resources necessary to compensate designated undertakings for the losses or the extra costs they face in fulfilling universal service obligations. The first is to compensate losses with public money. The second is to share

---

[103] Commission Communication concerning the Costing and Financing of the Universal
Service, Guidelines for National Regulatory Authorities, para 1.1.

the costs among the undertakings active on the electronic communications markets.

> *Universal Service Directive, Article 13(1).* 'Where . . . an undertaking is subject to an unfair burden,[104] Member States shall . . . decide: (a) to introduce a mechanism that compensates that undertaking for the determined net costs under transparent conditions from public funds; and/or (b) to share the net cost of universal service obligations between providers of electronic communications networks and services.'

5.155 Combination possible. The Member States do not need to choose between the first and the second mechanisms. They can be combined. For instance, one can imagine a system whereby a Member State resorts to one mechanism for the financing of certain items and to another with respect to other items. The liberty of Member States is thus substantial, to the extent that they respect the requirements examined below.

> *Universal Service Directive, Preamble, recital 21.* 'Member States should be able to finance the net costs of different elements of universal service through different mechanisms, and/or to finance the net costs of some or all elements from either of the mechanisms or a combination of both.'

5.156 Transferring costs. Universal service does not wipe out the losses or extra costs that are incurred where the full costs for providing the service are not paid by the users. These losses or extra costs exist and must be financed. Where they are not covered by the people enjoying the services, the only possibility is to transfer them to others. In this regard universal service may be analysed as a transfer mechanism. Through that mechanism, the costs of providing electronic communications subject to special conditions are transferred to people who are different from those enjoying the services. This is not what is supposed to happen on the markets in a competitive environment, where services are purchased by users.[105]

5.157 Limitations. Transferring costs may have effects on competition on the markets. Suppose one undertaking must face an additional charge which had not been anticipated. This may alter the decision to enter or remain in the market. It may also be that the transfer mechanisms place the burden of universal service on some market participants more than others. In such a situation, competition would be distorted. This is a result the European institutions want by all means to avoid, as the reform is based on the exercise of activity in a healthy competitive environment.

> *Universal Service Directive, Preamble, recital 4.* '[C]ompensating mechanisms designated to provide such services in such circumstances need not result in any distortion of competition, provided that designated undertakings are compensated for the

---

[104] As a result of the provision of universal service.

[105] This supposes that users are able to do so. This is however not always the case. Such a system where people have access to commodities depending on their needs is not accepted by all Member States, where services that are deemed essential in society are concerned.

specific net cost involved and provided that the net cost burden is recovered in a competitively neutral way.'

Not a European preference.   For this reason, the financing mechanisms referred   **5.158** to above are not preferred by the European institutions. As stated repeatedly, the institutions prefer that Member States resort to market-based mechanisms in order to ensure the provision of universal service. The financing should be found only outside of normal market conditions, where no other option is possible. For this reason, limitations are imposed on the introduction of these financing mechanisms.

> *Universal Service Directive, Article 13(1).* 'The mechanisms are set in motion [w]here on the basis of the net cost calculation . . . , national regulatory authorities find that an undertaking is subject to an unfair burden, . . . upon request from a designated undertaking.'

Conditions for the introduction of financing mechanisms.   These limitations   **5.159** can be regarded as conditions that have to be met before financing mechanisms can be established. They appear in the extract quoted in the previous paragraph and are examined below. *(a)* First, these mechanisms may be introduced only where undertakings involved are subject to an unfair burden as a result of the obligation to provide universal service.[106] *(b)* Second, a specific request must be made by the undertaking itself for the introduction of the mechanism. In other words, the mechanisms cannot be set in motion as long as no request is specifically introduced to that effect by the undertaking wishing to receive compensation for the loss or extra costs derived from the performance of universal service. *(c)* Third, the mechanisms can be used only in respect of undertakings that are designated by Member States. This emphasises that the scope of these mechanisms is limited to situations where universal service items are not provided spontaneously by market forces. *(d)* Fourth, the decision to establish the mechanisms cannot be taken by the Member States acting alone. Admittedly, national governments or legislatures are the bodies that have assumed the ultimate political responsibility for this kind of decision. However, the decision must be based on a report drafted by the NRA. Compensation can be introduced only where this report concludes that intervention must take place. *(e)* Fifth, only the net cost of the universal service can be financed via the mechanism. Any expense that is not related to universal service is thus excluded. Similarly, the calculation has to take into account all possible benefits an undertaking may derive from involvement in the provision of universal service.[107]

---

[106]   See also Universal Service Directive, Art 12(1). 'Where national regulatory authorities consider that the provision of universal service . . . may represent an unfair burden on undertakings designated to provide universal service, they shall calculate the net costs of its provision.'

[107]   An additional obligation appeared in the Communication from the Commission concerning the Costing and Financing of the Universal Service. Pursuant to that communication, the financing schemes could only be set in motion where the amount to be paid in compensation exceeded

(3) Use of public funds

Public funds and State aids

5.160 **Public funds.** As stated above, one possible compensation system is that losses or abnormal costs are financed through 'public funds'. This latter expression must probably be understood in broad terms. In the preamble, the Universal Service Directive refers to funds from general government budgets and to other public financing sources such as state lotteries.[108]

5.161 **State aids.** The first mechanism must be assessed in the light of European provisions concerning State aids. First, these provisions may be used to interpret the expression 'public funds'. Pursuant to Article 87 EC, State aids are to be understood as advantages granted with State resources in any form whatsoever. The same criteria must probably be used to determine what the Universal Service Directive means through a financing mechanism implying the payment of 'public funds'. Second, one should be aware of the risk created by the granting of public funds to undertakings. Through these funds, an advantage is conferred on one or several market participants. This implies that competition is—or at least may be—distorted, a situation that is prohibited under Article 87(1) EC.

> *Article 87(1) EC.* '[A]ny aid granted by a Member State or through State resources in any form whatsoever which distorts or threatens to distort competition by favouring certain undertakings or the production of certain goods shall, insofar as it affects trade between Member States, be incompatible with the common market.'[109]

Leading case

5.162 *Ferring.* The position of the ECJ is that funds granted by public authorities to compensate costs derived from public service obligations cannot be considered as State aids under the EC Treaty. That position was established in *Ferring*,[110]

---

the administrative costs relating to the operation of the mechanism. See the communication, para 2.2. This condition seems to have been set aside, although there remains an insistence in the NRF that the mechanisms must be operated as efficiently as possible.

[108] Universal Service Directive, Preamble, recital 22.

[109] Pursuant to Art 87(2) EC, aids having a social character are accepted where they are granted to individual consumers. This possibility has already been examined in connection with the support Member States can give to people with low incomes or special social needs. This support can be accepted on the basis of that provision. The question however remains as regards the other possibilities that are included for universal service. These possibilities do not fall within another exception provided in Art 87(2) EC (these exceptions are limited to natural disasters, exceptional occurrences or the Federal Republic of Germany). Nor do they appear to qualify for a derogation under Art 87(3) EC. Pursuant to that provision, several categories of aids may be deemed compatible with the common market. Among them are projects to develop certain areas, to promote important projects of common interest and to promote culture or heritage conservation. These categories do not encompass the advantages that could be conferred in connection with the provision of universal service.

[110] Case C-53/00 *Ferring SA v Agence centrale des organismes de sécurité sociale (ACOSS)* [2001] ECR I-9067.

where the ECJ was asked its opinion about a tax exemption granted to wholesale distributors of medicinal products in France. Specific obligations were imposed on wholesale distributors as regards products to be held at all times to ensure supply. These obligations did not apply to other sellers. The distribution of medicinal products is taxed in France. The decision was made to exempt wholesale distributors, in order to compensate the extra burden the supply obligations meant for them. In its ruling, the ECJ held that no State aid was in fact granted, since no advantage was conferred on the wholesale distributors. The exemption meant only that a balance was restored with other sellers which did not have to comply with the supply-related obligations.[111]

> *Ferring.* [24] 'It may be recalled that the French regulation requires only wholesale distributors to have at their disposal a permanent range of medicinal products sufficient to meet the requirements of a specific geographic area and to deliver requested supplies within a very short time over the whole of that area, in such a way that the population as a whole can be guaranteed an adequate supply of medicines at all times.' [25] 'Discharging those obligations entails additional costs for wholesale distributors which pharmaceutical laboratories do not have to bear.' [27] '[N]ot assessing . . . [the beneficiaries] to the tax may be regarded as compensation for the [public] services they provide and hence not State aid within the meaning of Article . . . [87] of the Treaty.'

Real costs.   The ruling provides criteria to ensure that the form of financing is   **5.163** appropriate. Pursuant to the ruling, compensation is allowed only where it is limited to the real costs flowing from public service constraints. Any funding granted beyond these costs should be considered an aid falling under the prohibition contained in Article 87(1) EC.[112]

> *Ferring.* '[P]rovided that the tax on direct sales imposed on pharmaceutical laboratories corresponds to the additional costs actually incurred by wholesale distributors in discharging their public service obligations, not assessing wholesale distributors to the tax may be regarded a compensation for the services they provide and hence not

---

[111] The absence of compensation might indeed be considered contrary to the Treaty. Designated undertakings would not be treated equally. This would run counter to the general principle of equality. Furthermore, non-designated undertakings would have a special right, as they would be exempt from certain obligations. Yet we have seen that special rights should be considered as being contrary to the Treaty except where the conditions laid down in Art 86(2) EC are complied with.

[112] Suppose indeed that the public service-related obligations cost less than what is granted as compensation by public authorities. In other words, the compensation exceeds the costs. A net transfer of resources would take place from the authority to the undertaking. This cannot be accepted, as competition would be distorted. The beneficiary indeed receives resources that can be poured into its activities—an opportunity from which competitors are barred. In these circumstances, Art 87(1) EC should apply (prohibition of State aids, obligation to reimburse). What would happen in the other situation? Imagine that the compensation paid by the authority is lower than the obligations imposed in the name of public service. The undertaking would be entitled to challenge the excessive obligations on the basis of the general principle of equality. The challenge could be based on European law where the case had a European dimension. In other circumstances, national laws would apply.

State aid within the meaning of Article [87] . . . of the Treaty. Moreover, provided there is the necessary equivalence between the exemption and the additional costs incurred, whole distributors will not be enjoying any real advantage for the purposes of Article . . . [87](1) of the Treaty because the only effect of the tax will be to put distributors and laboratories on an equal competitive footing.'[113]

5.164 **Legitimate public service obligations.** Another criterion is that the compensation must be connected to obligations that are recognised by the European institutions. It is not certain, therefore, that funds granted by Member States outside the European framework would receive the treatment given by the ECJ to the tax exemption analysed in *Ferring*.[114] In that case, for instance, the obligations imposed on wholesale distributors had been recognised, and accepted, by Community legislation.[115] This appears to have played a significant role in the reasoning developed by the ECJ, in view of the emphasis placed by the ECJ on the existence of EC regulation in the area.

Confirmation of the case law

5.165 *Altmark.* The position adopted by the ECJ in *Ferring* has recently been confirmed in another case, *Altmark*.[116] This new case may be seen as a confirmation, because it has been issued by a full court whereas *Ferring* was decided by only one chamber. The case concerned a German undertaking receiving public funds in connection with the performance of public service obligations. An issue was whether, and to what extent, these funds could be granted to the undertaking under general competition law. In its ruling, the ECJ confirms the general position adopted in *Ferring*, whereby public funds may be granted to compensate the costs created by the obligation imposed on that undertaking to perform a public service.

> *Altmark.* '[W]here a State measure must be regarded as compensation for the services provided by the recipient undertakings in order to discharge public service obligations, so that those undertakings do not enjoy a real financial advantage and the measure thus does not have the effect of putting them in a more favourable competitive position

---

[113] At [27] and [28]. It is for national authorities, in particular national courts, to verify whether the condition is satisfied. See [28]: 'In this case it is for the national court to decide whether that condition is satisfied.' A double control will have to be made. On the one hand, the reality of the costs claimed by the beneficiary will have to be checked. On the other hand, the equivalence between these costs and the compensation will have to be monitored.

[114] This does not mean that the public funds would then be incompatible with EC provisions. An attempt could be made to obtain a derogation through Art 86(2) EC. Pursuant to that provision, derogations may be granted where the application of competition—or other European—rules would obstruct the fulfilment of a mission of general economic interest.

[115] At [3]. Council Directive (EC) 92/25 on the wholesale distribution of medicinal products for human use [1992] OJ L113/1. In this directive, the European legislator accepted that certain Member States could impose on wholesalers public service obligations and asserted that these Member States should be allowed to continue their policy in that regard.

[116] Case C-280/00 *Altmark Trans GmbH v Nahverkehrsgesellschaft Altmark GmbH* [2003] 3 CMLR 12.

than the undertakings competing with them, such a measure is not caught by Article 92(1) of the Treaty.'[117]

List of conditions. *Altmark* is interesting because the ECJ provides a check list **5.166** of conditions under which public funds may be granted in accordance with general competition law. These conditions are as follows. *(a)* First, the funds must be granted in connection with obligations that are actually performed. The undertaking must thus be entrusted with tasks of a general interest, which it actually performs. *(b)* Second, the rules must be established in advance. The public service obligations must be defined at the outset, together with the criteria used to calculate the compensation. *(c)* There must be an equivalence between the costs and the funds granted. To calculate the costs, and the amount due, any receipts obtained by the undertaking must be taken into account.

> *Altmark.* '[T]he recipient undertaking must actually have public service obligations to discharge'; 'the obligations must be clearly defined'; 'the parameters on the basis of which the compensation is calculated must be established in advance in an objective and transparent manner, to avoid it conferring an economic advantage which may favour the recipient undertaking over competing undertakings'; 'the compensation cannot exceed what is necessary to cover all or part of the costs incurred in the discharge of public service obligations'; '[one must take] into account the relevant receipts and a reasonable profit for discharging those obligations'.[118]

Evaluation of case law

Correspondence with criteria set by the Commission. The analysis made by **5.167** the ECJ corresponds to the position that had been adopted by the Commission in the Communication concerning the Costing and Financing of Universal Service (1996).[119] In that Communication, the Commission insisted that compensation mechanisms could cover only the net costs associated with the universal service. Any overcompensation would be considered a State aid subject to the prohibition laid down in the Treaty.

> *Commission Communication.* 'Where Member States decide to fund, directly or indirectly through the State budget, part or all of the net cost of universal service in the telecommunications sector, such interventions must be made in a manner which is

---

[117] At [87].

[118] At [89]–[92]. It is not clear what the ECJ means by the request to take 'a reasonable profit' into account. Does it suggest that the undertaking must be allowed to extract a reasonable benefit from the activity? In other words, should the funds be calculated so as to allow the undertaking to realise such a benefit? A more reasonable interpretation is that the operation should result in no loss, and conversely no benefit, for the undertaking concerned. The public funds must compensate the costs. The possible receipts or benefits realised by the undertaking must be taken into account to calculate these costs. Only the losses should be reimbursed, the receipts and benefits being deducted from the costs incurred by the undertaking.

[119] Commission Communication concerning the Costing and Financing of the Universal Service, para 2.4.3.

consistent with the EC Treaty rules on State aids which are set out in Articles [87 EC] to [88 EC] together with Article [86 EC]. Such funding . . . should not exceed the net costs of the obligations . . . In cases where it will be soundly established that there is no overcompensation (e.g. where there is no compensation of costs which would normally be borne by the relevant activity) . . . , there will normally be no State aid . . . Conversely, when the public intervention will lead to an overcompensation, the Commission will have to determine whether the aid involved can be approved under one of the derogations of Article [87 EC].'[120]

5.168 **Consistency with previous ECJ case law.**   The case is important, as it clarifies the possibility of financing universal service obligations with public funds.[121] The ruling appears to be in accordance with the line already sketched by the ECJ in previous cases. However, the ECJ had never previously been asked a question dealing specifically with compensation for public service obligations. Among previous cases around similar issues, one can mention *ADBHU*, concerning an indemnity granted in the context of environmental protection. In that area of the law the principle is that the polluter pays. In the case in point, the polluter was charged on products transformed into waste oils, or on waste oils. An indemnity could be granted to undertakings collecting and/or disposing of waste oils as compensation for their obligations to collect and/or dispose of the products offered to them by holders. The ECJ ruled that an indemnity of that type did not constitute an aid under Article 87 EC. It was rather to be analysed as a 'consideration' for the services performed by the collection or disposal undertakings.[122]

5.169 **No obligation to notify.**   Beyond more theoretical considerations, the respective positions adopted by the two courts have a practical consequence. Under the EC Treaty, all projects to grant aids must be notified to the Commission by the Member States. The procedure is intended to give the Commission an opportunity to examine whether the aid is compatible with European law before the aid is actually granted. The obligation to notify is, however, dependent on a transfer of funds to be considered aid. This is important in order to determine whether the

---

[120] Commission Communication concerning the Costing and Financing of the Universal Service, para 2.4.3.

[121] In *Ferring* (n 110 above), the funds were provided in the form of a tax exemption. As a result of that exemption, the undertakings involved did not have to make a payment they would otherwise have been constrained to do. This resulted in their having more financial means, as if a subsidy were allocated to them. For this reason, no distinction is drawn in the case law between receiving public funds or being exempted from a payment.

[122] Case 240/83 *Procureur de la République v Association de défense des brûleurs d'huiles usagées (ADBHU)* [1985] ECR 531 at [18]. In this case, the Court thus ruled that special burdens may be compensated by public authorities. These burdens must be in relation to objectives that are deemed acceptable, and even desirable, at European level. They cannot be excessive and will only be accepted where no other means may be used in order to ensure the realisation of the objective while hindering competition to a lesser extent. In the case, a clear reference is made to Community legislation to the extent that the principle that the polluter must pay has been established at European level.

grant of public funds by Member States should be notified where it takes place in connection with the universal service on electronic communications markets. The position adopted by the ECJ implies that no notification needs to take place where the compensation is limited to net costs.[123] This does not mean that the Commission has no chance of verifying the scheme put in place by the Member States. Such schemes must indeed be notified. The notification does not have to be made on the basis of Article 87 EC, for the reason that has been examined. Notification is, however, required under the NRF, given that an obligation has been inserted to that effect in the Commission's Consolidated Services Directive (Article 6(2) EC).

Transferring costs to taxpayers. Beyond strictly legal discussions, a system **5.170** where universal service is financed through public funds implies that the costs of providing the items involved are transferred to tax-payers. Some are likely to be dissatisfied with the mechanism. These are likely to be people paying through taxation an amount equivalent to what they would have paid had the relevant electronic communications services been provided at full tariffs.[124] Corporations are also affected negatively. They pay taxes but do not receive benefits from all provisions included in the universal service requirement.[125] Finally, people who are heavily taxed are concerned; through the money they contribute to the public exchequer, they finance a substantial part of universal service even though they may not necessarily have the highest incomes.[126]

Caveat concerning the consistency of case law

Relative consistency. Practitioners should be aware that, beyond the relative **5.171** consistency of the case law, there are certain difficulties which are not altogether

---

[123] The analysis would have been different if the ECJ had upheld the position adopted by the CFI. In that position, public funds are advantages and qualify thus as State aids under the Treaty. As a result, they must be notified. During the procedure, the Commission will have a chance to consider whether a derogation may be granted on the basis of Art 86(2) EC.

[124] Suppose a user devotes 1,000 euros a year to electronic communications. He receives in fact 1,100 euros-worth of services. This is due to the fact that some services are not charged at full tariffs, as a result of universal service obligations. Each year, this user also pays taxes. In the amount paid to the State, 100 euros are allocated to the financing of the universal service according to the first mechanism (financing through public funds). This taxpayer would probably have preferred paying these 100 euros straight to the undertaking providing the service. This would have avoided administrative costs incurred in collecting taxation and organising the financing mechanism for universal service. (In fact, the user probably has to pay 110 euros in taxation to ensure the payment of the 100 corresponding to the loss incurred by the undertaking on the market.)

[125] They benefit from geographic averaging. By contrast, they normally do not have any specific advantage as a result of the social premiums given to people with low incomes or special social needs. A general advantage should however be considered—living in a society where social cohesion is strong.

[126] People with high revenues are not always taxed at the highest level—or are sometimes not taxed at all. This is due to special categories in the taxation system (diplomats, etc), the difference which may exist among various categories of revenues and the impossibility of ensuring that all frauds are detected.

resolved. Two cases are examined in the following paragraphs to show the extent of these difficulties. They are explained in order to indicate that, in spite of the apparent established case law in the area, practitioners should not refrain from attempting to challenge the current situation in the direction they feel appropriate.

5.172   (a) **Reasoning in two parts.**   A certain duality of approach appears in the ruling adopted by the ECJ in *Ferring*. This ruling is developed in two parts. As a first step, the ECJ considers whether the tax exemption granted by France to wholesale distributors can be considered a State aid, 'leaving aside the public service obligations laid down by French law'. The ECJ thus analyses whether an advantage is conferred on designated undertakings, without considering the obligations that are supposed to be compensated. In that perspective, it comes as no surprise to see the ECJ concluding there is a State aid.[127] A second step is taken where, as stated, the ECJ sets aside the application of that provision on the ground that, taking into account the public service obligations imposed on the undertaking, one has to consider that no advantage was in fact granted, but merely compensation.[128]

5.173   (b) **Which costs?**   Another issue concerns the costs which are to be taken into account in order to establish the level of public funding necessary, and allowed, to compensate public service obligations. Where, for example, an activity is performed by a monopoly, the costs can be higher, or lower, than those which would be found in a competitive environment. Two situations are distinguished by the ECJ in *Altmark*. *(a)* Where the undertaking in charge of public service obligations is chosen in a competitively based selection, the costs incurred by that undertaking can be taken into account. *(b)* Where another procedure has been chosen, the assessment cannot be based on the balance sheet of the undertaking. It must be founded on an analysis of the costs which a typical, well run, undertaking would incur.

> *Altmark*. '[W]here the undertaking which is to discharge public service obligations, in a specific case, is not chosen pursuant to a public procurement procedure which would allow for the selection of the tenderer capable of providing those services at the

---

[127]   N 110 above, at [22]. '[L]eaving aside the public service obligations laid down by French law, the tax on direct sales may in fact constitute State aid within the meaning of Article [87(1) EC] . . . inasmuch as it does not apply to wholesale distributors.'

[128]   Our critique is that it was not necessary to divide the ruling into two steps. Adopting this two-part approach is indeed confusing. You cannot consider that an advantage has been conferred, and then go back on your intermediate conclusion to state that ultimately the advantage was not real, given the extra obligations it was meant to compensate. The reasoning would have been more rigorous had the ECJ successively verified whether each condition was satisfied for the application of the prohibition on State aids. Using that approach, the ECJ would have observed that the condition relating to the presence of an 'advantage' was not fulfilled, as funds merely correspond to the cost of extra obligations. The ECJ could also have ruled that an advantage had been conferred but that competition was not distorted as the exemption only had the effect of putting all market participants on an equal footing.

least cost to the community, the level of compensation needed must be determined on the basis of an analysis of the costs which a typical undertaking, well run and adequately provided with means of transport so as to be able to meet the necessary public service requirements, would have incurred in discharging those obligations, taking into account the relevant receipts and a reasonable profit for discharging the obligations.'[129]

Not always coherent.   The position adopted in *Altmark* seems consistent with the   **5.174** desire, which is apparent in the old and the new regulatory frameworks, that prices should be based on costs and that the costs taken into account should be those which can be found in a competitive environment. From the case law, it appears that circumstances may influence the European institutions (Commission, courts) to adopt decisions or rulings which do not seem to be compatible with the approach delineated in *Altmark*.

SFEI.   An example may be taken from *SFEI*—a case which started a decade ago   **5.175** and is not yet finalised. The case concerns a subsidiary company of La Poste, the national operator entrusted with postal services in France. That subsidiary (SFEI) provided courier services. To carry out these activities, it received logistical and commercial assistance from the parent company. An issue was whether that assistance constituted a State aid. Under Article 87 EC, no advantage whatsoever can be granted to a specific undertaking with funds coming from the State or from entities placed under the control of a public body.

Several procedures.   Several procedures were initiated in relation to that situa-   **5.176** tion. *(a)* First, a complaint was addressed to the Commission by competitors. The purpose of the complaint was to ask the Commission to investigate the possible existence of an aid and to react if that appeared necessary. The complaint was set aside by the Commission. *(b)* A procedure was then initiated before a national court, which addressed preliminary questions to the ECJ. *(c)* On the basis of the judgment issued by the ECJ, the Commission opened a new procedure. A decision was adopted, stating that no aid could be found. *(d)* An application was introduced before the CFI, which annulled the decision adopted by the Commission. *(e)* An appeal was then lodged to the ECJ, which overruled the CFI. *(f)* The case is now pending, again, before the CFI, which must rework its position on the basis of the indications given by the ECJ.

Establishing costs.   In that series of procedures, the issue was not to determine   **5.177** to what extent public service obligations can be funded through public funds granted by authorities. It was rather how costs may, or must, be established. *(a)* As was stated before, the ECJ first ruled that assistance by a public undertaking to a subsidiary company could be regarded as an aid if, and to the extent, the costs

---

[129]   At [93].

relating to that assistance were not entirely reimbursed by the latter company. To evaluate these costs, the authorities must take into account, as the ECJ suggested, 'normal market conditions' ('Normal Market Conditions Test'). *(b)* Using that standard, the CFI considered that one was to take into account the costs incurred by a typical undertaking placed in normal circumstances ('Typical Undertaking Test'). *(c)* In appeal, that position was reversed by the ECJ, which considered that the analysis was to be based on the costs really incurred by the public parent company ('Real Costs Test').

Normal Market Conditions Test (ECJ, first ruling). '[T]he provision of logistical and commercial assistance by a public undertaking to its subsidiaries, which are governed by private law and carry on an activity open to free competition, is capable of constituting State aid . . . if the remuneration received in return is less than that which would have been demanded under normal market conditions.'[130]

Typical Undertaking Test (CFI). 'Given that La Poste might, by virtue of its position as the sole public undertaking in a reserved sector, have been able to provide some of the logistical and commercial assistance at lower cost than a private undertaking not enjoying the same rights, an analysis taking account solely of that public undertaking's costs cannot, in the absence of other evidence, preclude classification of the measures in question as State aid.'[131] 'The Commission should thus have examined whether those full costs took account of the factors which an undertaking acting under normal market conditions should have taken into consideration when fixing the remuneration for the services provided. Hence, the Commission should at least have checked that the payment received in return by La Poste was comparable to that demanded by a private holding company or a private group of undertakings not operating in a reserved sector, pursuing a structural policy—whether general or sectorial—and guided by long-term prospects.'[132]

Real Costs Test (ECJ, second ruling). 'La Poste is entrusted with a service of general economic interest.' 'Such a service essentially consists in the obligation to collect, carry and deliver mail for the benefit of all users throughout the territory of the Member State concerned, at uniform tariffs and on similar conditions as to quality.' 'Because of the characteristics of the service which the La Poste network must be able to ensure, the creation and maintenance of that network are not in line with a purely commercial approach.' '[A] network such as that [one] . . . would never have been created by a private undertaking.' 'Accordingly, in the absence of any possibility of comparing the situation of La Poste with that of a private group of undertakings not operating in a reserved sector, "normal market conditions", which are necessarily hypothetical, must be assessed by reference to the objective and verifiable elements which are available.' 'In the present case, the costs borne by La Poste in respect of the

---

[130] Case C-39/94 *Syndicat Français de l'Express International (SFEI) v La Poste* [1996] ECR I-3547 at [62].

[131] 'On the contrary, it is precisely a relationship in which the parent company operates in a reserved market and its subsidiary carries out its activities in a market open to competition that creates a situation in which State aid is likely to exist' (at [74]).

[132] Case T-613/97 *Ufex v Commission* [2000] ECR II-4055 at [74] and [75].

provision to its subsidiary of logistical and commercial assistance can constitute such objective and verifiable elements.'[133]

Malaise.   The opinions successively adopted by the ECJ and the CFI provide an   **5.178** indication about the malaise which various European institutions still feel when it comes to national public financing. *(a)* The ECJ first ruled that normal market conditions must be taken into account, before suggesting that the situation of La Poste is not normal and that as a result a specific evaluation, based on the costs really incurred by that undertaking, should be used. *(b)* That latter indication that real costs should be used as a basis for an evaluation when the undertaking is a monopoly contradicts the standard established in *Altmark*. In that latter case, the ECJ did not accept that the real costs could be used as a basis for an assessment when the undertaking has not been chosen in a competitive selection procedure. On the contrary, it specifically requested that, in such a situation (absence of a selection based on competition) the analysis should be based on the standard of a typical undertaking.

(4) Sharing mechanism

Sharing mechanism.   Another method of financing the cost of universal service   **5.179** is to share the costs among undertakings active on the electronic communications markets. This mechanism is different from the previous one, to the extent that the burden of universal service is not formally transferred to taxpayers. The difference is however limited, as the sharing mechanism also organises—as does taxation— the transfer of a financial burden. In this case, resources are transferred from the providers paying contributions to the people enjoying the services. As undertakings always have to charge their customers for their costs, these contributions are therefore passed on to users. The sharing mechanism thus operates a transfer between two categories of users. The payers are those who resort to items not included in universal service, or included in that service but provided under normal commercial conditions. These people are in effect asked to contribute indirectly to the cost of universal service. The beneficiaries are the customers who make use of universal service items, where these items are provided under abnormal market conditions. In these situations, these items are subsidised by the sharing mechanism.[134]

A danger to competition.   As is the case with the granting of public funds, shar-   **5.180** ing mechanisms are also a danger to competition. The reason is, however, different. In this case, the danger comes from the fact that an extra burden is imposed

---

[133] Joined Cases C 83, 93 & 94/01 P *Chronopost v Ufex* [2003] 3 CMLR 11 at [34]–[39].

[134] The categories are not closed, as the same users may belong to the first and second depending on the item they resort to. Where he calls locally in a situation where these calls are subsidised, a user is granted an advantage that may be financed by himself in his capacity, for instance, as user resorting to internet communications, where these communications are not subsidised.

on market participants. As a result of this burden, costs are made heavier. However, costs do not have the same effect on all actors. There is clearly a difference in this regard between incumbents and newcomers. First, incumbents have a larger turnover than newcomers because they have been present on the relevant market for a longer period. The consequence is that costs incurred by incumbents may be amortised on a bigger budget. Second, incumbents are already present on the market and they will not leave it, as exit costs would be excessive.[135] By contrast, newcomers have not yet entered the market or have just started an activity. Their situation is thus different with respect to costs. Any additional expenses may be perceived by them as a threat—in fact as an argument not to enter the market or, where the undertaking is already present, to leave it as soon as possible.[136]

5.181 **Current situation in the Member States.** In the Eighth implementation report, the Commission observes that there is an increasing demand on the part of undertakings in charge of universal service to activate sharing mechanisms in order to be compensated for the costs which, they say, they incur in providing universal service. This growing phenomenon is explained by the decreasing market share held by incumbents. As they can progressively be compared to other operators, incumbents do not want to sustain costs which others do not have to bear. The move can probably also be explained by the current difficult financial environment.

> *Eighth implementation report, 43.* 'In the last year, the relevant operators have requested the funding of the net cost of the provision of universal service in Portugal, Belgium, Spain, Ireland and Austria (although in this last case the request was finally withdrawn).' 'A public consultation on this subject has been conducted in Greece and France.' 'However, for the time being only two Member States have required actual payments from other operators to the universal service provider (France and Italy), while two other Member States (Spain and the United Kingdom) have concluded that the provision of the universal service had not implied an unfair burden for the designated operator.'

5.182 **Constraints.** In order to ensure that distortions are minimal, the European institutions have introduced limitations on the use of the sharing mechanism. These limitations are formulated in Article 13 and Annex IV of the Universal Service Directive. Before analysing them it is worth noting that these obligations in fact correspond, for the most part, to constraints that apply to the organisation of universal service in general. They are formulated in the provisions dealing specifically with the sharing mechanism, but would have applied in any case as

---

[135] They have invested so much in the establishment and maintenance of the network over decades.

[136] Exit costs are more limited for newcomers, as they have not invested as heavily as incumbents. The costs to enter a market and to stay there are higher for such an undertaking, in terms of lost opportunities. Any decision to invest in an activity indeed implies a foregone opportunity to engage in another. If additional costs are imposed, the danger is to alter the assessment of opportunities.

a result of the general guidelines governing universal service. This provides a further indication that the sharing mechanism has been a delicate issue to agree. The mechanism has been accepted, but some parties have clearly been anxious to emphasise the limitations that would apply. The practical consequence is that one can expect a tight control on all arrangements established by the various Member States in connection with the compensation to be provided in exchange for the performance of universal service obligations.

(1) The least restrictive measure. A first constraint imposed on the Member **5.183** States is that they have to use the least restrictive measure where they establish the financing mechanism. This is explicitly stated in the context of the sharing mechanism, although a similar obligation could already have been derived from the guiding principle applying to all aspects regarding universal service, that is, Member States must normally resort to market mechanisms. Exceptions may be introduced only where no other option is available. Where such arrangements are set in place, the Member States must minimise market distortions.[137]

> *Universal Service Directive, Annex IV, Part B, para 1.* 'A sharing mechanism shall respect the principle . . . of least market distortion';[138] 'the transfers [must] result in the least distortion to competition and user demand'.

(2) Limitation of net costs. Another limitation is that the scheme must be **5.184** restricted to compensation of the net costs incurred in the performance of universal service obligations.[139] Again, this is by no means a new obligation. A similar constraint applies in respect of financing through public funds (see paras 5.160–5.179 above). The limitation of net costs also derives from the obligation to use the least restrictive measures. If measures are to be limited to what is strictly necessary, they cannot be extended to the financing of items that are not related to universal service. Finally, limitation also appears to be a consequence of the principle of proportionality under which exceptions must be restricted as much as possible.

(3) Basic regulatory principles. Member States further have to comply with the **5.185** basic regulatory principles in organising the sharing mechanism.[140] This hardly

---

[137] Cf Universal Service Directive, Art 3(2). 'Member States shall determine the most efficient and appropriate approach for ensuring the implementation of universal service . . . They shall seek to minimize market distortions.'

[138] See Universal Service Directive, Art 13(3). In fact this obligation is also inherent, as we have seen, in the principle of proportionality. This principle appears in the basic regulatory principles, which apply to all aspects of the universal service and are also taken over, as we will see, in the specific context of universal service.

[139] The obligation appears in several places. See eg Universal Service Directive, Art 13(1)(b). See also Art 13(2), last sentence: 'Only the net cost . . . of the obligations . . . may be financed.'

[140] Universal Service Directive, Art 13(3), first sentence. 'A sharing mechanism shall respect the principles of transparency, least market distortion, non-discrimination and proportionality.'

needs to be repeated, as these requirements appear in almost every provision that concerns the organisation of universal service.[141]

> *Universal Service Directive, Article 13(3).* 'A sharing mechanism shall respect the principles of transparency, . . . non-discrimination and proportionality.' *Universal Service Directive, Annex IV, Part B, para 1.* 'The recovery or financing of any net costs of universal service obligations requires designated undertakings with universal service obligations to be compensated for the services they provide under non-commercial conditions. Because such a compensation involves financial transfers, Member States are to ensure that these are undertaken in an objective, transparent, non-discriminatory and proportionate manner.'

5.186 **(4) Independent administration.** Pursuant to the Universal Service Directive, the mechanism must be administered by a body that is independent from market participants. This can be the NRA, but the European institutions have also accepted that the administration of the mechanism be entrusted to another body. In that case that body must be placed under the supervision of the NRA.[142]

> *Universal Service Directive, Article 13(2).* 'Where the net cost is shared . . . , Member States shall establish a sharing mechanism administered by the national regulatory authority or a body independent from the beneficiaries under the supervision of the national regulatory authority.'

5.187 **Several tasks.** The independent body is to perform several tasks. Pursuant to Annex IV to the directive, this entity is responsible for collecting the dues and transferring them to the undertakings which must be compensated. Other tasks could probably also be entrusted to this entity. Among others, it would be appropriate to designate the independent body to verify the costs claimed by designated undertakings as deserving compensation. This entity could also be responsible for calculating the dues that are to be imposed on each market participant.[143]

> *Universal Service Directive, Annex IV, Part B, para 3.* 'The independent body administering the fund is to be responsible for collecting contributions from undertakings which are assessed as liable to contribute to the net cost of universal service obligations in the Member State and is to oversee the transfer of sums due and/or administrative payments to the undertakings entitled to receive payments from the fund.'

---

[141] Universal Service Directive, Art 3(2).

[142] The European legislator has thereby paved the way for the financing mechanism to be entrusted to private entities, such as consultancy firms. There is no reason, indeed, why this task should be reserved for a public body, as the task of calculating costs and collecting dues could just as well be done by private undertakings.

[143] The two last tasks proposed for the independent body (control on costs, calculation of dues) are not explicitly entrusted to the independent body in the regulation. However, there is in our opinion no argument against this entity performing them. In our view it would be appropriate for all aspects relating to the whole sharing mechanism to be treated by the same body. This suggestion is based on efficiency considerations. It also relates to transparency. It is more difficult to identify the author of a decision and to ensure compliance where responsibilities are divided.

(5) Easily identifiable contributions.   The contributions claimed from market **5.188**
participants must be easily identified. This implies that the amount claimed from
each contributor must be stated clearly. Another aspect is that contributions must
be unbundled. Member States may thus not integrate them with other sums that
would have to be paid by undertakings, for instance fees relating to use of public
resources[144] or rights of entry for access on given markets.[145]

> *Universal Service Directive, Article 13(4).* 'Any charges related to the sharing of the
> cost of the universal service obligations shall be unbundled and identified separately
> for each undertaking.'

Clarity.   In all these aspects, the European legislator has in effect wanted to **5.189**
ensure that clarity is maintained. Clarity is indeed important for newcomers.
Without accurate information, costs may not be calculated and decisions cannot
be taken as regards potential entry or exit. Clarity is also important to mount legal
or political challenges. If undertakings do not know for sure what is claimed from
them for the financing of the universal service, they cannot approach courts or
NRAs and present reasonable arguments. Finally, clarity puts pressure on
Member States to comply with the obligations placed on them, including that of
seeking to distort markets the least. This is perhaps the most important aspect;
without information, it would be impossible for the Commission to verify that
obligations have been fulfilled and the NRF duly implemented.

An obligation to individualise contributions?   The question is whether the **5.190**
European legislator has been willing to go further than transparency and require
that sums claimed from market participants be individualised. Imagine a system
where the costs to be financed were divided into the number of undertakings
active in the relevant markets. Each would then pay an equal share of the burden.
The burden would not be calculated as a function of the characteristics of each
undertaking, for example the profits or turnover realised in electronic communications activities on the national territory.

A system favourable to incumbents.   There is in the Universal Service Directive **5.191**
no provision which prohibits directly or explicitly the installation of such a system.
However, it does not appear that a system of this nature would be compatible with
European law. Such a system would favour incumbents, as they would bear a burden equal to the others in nominal terms, although their operations are more
extensive.[146] This outcome would run counter to the objective of opening markets

---

[144] For instance, the possibility of using rights of way.
[145] For instance, the amount to be paid to be entitled to provide third generation mobile
communications.
[146] In a system of averaged contributions, undertakings would be taxed irrespective of their size.
Two situations might then be distinguished. In the first situation, the tax is small. This would be an
advantage for incumbents as their contribution would be limited to a small amount whereas they

and could be analysed as being contrary to the principle of non-discrimination. This analysis corresponds with the position expressed by the Commission in the Second Communication on Services of General Interest (2001) as well as in the Communication on Costing and Financing of the Universal Service (1996).

> *Second Communication on Services of General Interest.* '[I]t is important that the share borne by any undertaking should be proportionate to its activity in the market and be clearly separated from other charges that it may bear in the normal exercise of its activities.'[147] *Communication on Costing and Financing of Universal Service.* 'National Schemes should apportion contributions amongst eligible market players according to their activity on the relevant market. In order to achieve this, National Schemes must provide procedures for identifying clearly the market upon which such activity is measured and determine in a transparent manner the basis for contribution for each eligible organization to contribute.'[148]

5.192 **(6) Emphasis on transparency.** An emphasis is placed on the transparency that has to be achieved in setting up and administering the sharing mechanism.[149] An entire provision is devoted to that requirement, in addition to references in other paragraphs. This requirement entails public availability of all aspects relating to the mechanism. A report must be published each year by NRAs. This report must contain information about the essential features of the mechanism, ie the net cost to be financed and the contribution paid by each undertaking. Publication is subject to business confidentiality. NRAs must thus refrain from publishing information that would be sensitive under European and national rules.

> *Universal Service Directive, Article 14.* [1] 'Where a mechanism for sharing the cost of the universal service obligations . . . is established, national regulatory authorities shall ensure that the principles for cost sharing, and details of the mechanism used, are publicly available.' [2] 'Subject to Community and national rules on business confidentiality, national regulatory authorities shall ensure that an annual report is published giving the calculated cost of universal service obligations, identifying the contributions made by all undertakings involved, and identifying any market benefits, that may have accrued to the undertaking(s) designed to provide the universal service, where a fund is actually in place and working.'[150]

---

realise a large turnover on the market. The same amount would have to be paid by newcomers, which have a smaller turnover on the relevant markets. In the second situation, the tax to be paid by market participants would be significant. This would again benefit the incumbents. They would incur a heavy burden but this burden could be amortised on a significant turnover. The newcomers would be in a worse position, as they would have to pay the same amount—this amount being amortised on a smaller amount.

[147] Commission Communication (EC) 2001/C17/04 on services of general interest in Europe [2001] OJ C17/4, para 15.

[148] Communication from the Commission concerning the Costing and Financing of the Universal Service, para 3.

[149] For instance, transparency is explicitly mentioned as a requirement in Art 13(3) as well as in Art 14 of the Universal Service Directive. It appears again in Annex IX, Part B, para 2.

[150] ibid, Art 14.

(7) **Avoiding double payment.**   Pursuant to the Universal Service Directive, the   **5.193**
mechanism must avoid hitting the same undertakings twice. This could occur,
depending on the system used in order to calculate the contributions. The difficulty would come from the fact that an obligation to contribute is imposed on both
network operators and service providers. Suppose the contribution is calculated on
the basis of turnover on electronic communications markets. In such a system, it
can be expected that network operators will transfer to their customers the economic weight of the burden they have to bear as part of the contribution to universal service.[151] Some of these customers may however be service providers. In
that capacity these undertakings would then be asked to pay their own contributions on the basis of the services performed. This system would result in providers
having imposed on them the whole weight of universal service financing.[152]

> *Universal Service Directive, Annex IV, Part B, para 2.* '[A] sharing mechanism based
> on a fund should use a transparent and neutral means for collecting contributions
> that avoids the danger of a double imposition of contributions falling on both out-
> puts and inputs of undertakings.'

(8) **No involvement of foreign undertakings.**   Contributions to the cost of   **5.194**
providing the universal service on a national territory may not be imposed on foreign undertakings. For instance, the French NRA could not establish a scheme
where UK undertakings were required to contribute even though they perform no
activity on French electronic communications markets.

> *Universal Service Directive, Article 13(4).* '[C]harges shall not be imposed or collected
> from undertakings that are not providing services in the territory of the Member
> States that has established the sharing mechanism.'[153]

(9) **If possible, avoid imposing obligations on new entrants.**   The Universal   **5.195**
Service Directive mentions the possibility for Member States not to impose an
obligation to contribute on new entrants. This could be regarded as a State aid, as
a financial advantage would be conferred on these undertakings. Suppose that one
Member State makes use of that possibility: this question is how the authorities in
charge of applying competition law—including the Commission—would
react. The probability is that the advantage would be accepted in the name of

---

[151] All costs indeed have to be charged, directly or indirectly, to customers.
[152] The situation of network providers would be different. Two situations should be distinguished in that respect. Part of their activity is devoted to selling capacity to service providers. Their
situation has already been examined, as concerns this activity. They will have to pay a contribution
based on capacity selling and this contribution will be passed on to the purchasers of the capacity—
these purchasers being themselves service providers most of the time. The second part of their activity is providing services. In that capacity, the undertakings have an integrated organisation. They sell
services based on their own transmission capacity. This activity also gives rise to the payment of
a contribution. One contribution only will however be paid as the services appear as one performance.
[153] Pursuant to the Preamble, the financing mechanism should also avoid users being charged
the economic weight of the contribution where they make calls to another Member State. See the
Preamble, recital 21.

competition itself. An argument would probably be made that the aid indeed fosters the possibility for new undertakings to take part in activities and thereby stimulate further competition on the markets.

> *Universal Service Directive.* 'This principle (proportionality) does not prevent Member States from exempting new entrants which have not yet achieved any significant market presence.'[154] 'Member States may choose not to require contributions from undertakings whose national turnover is less than a set limit.'[155]

(5) Compatibility with general competition law

5.196 **Case law examined above.** We have examined above two cases, *Ferring*[156] and *Altmark*,[157] which concern the use of public funds to finance public service obligations. The mechanism was found to be in conformity with general competition law, provided several conditions were satisfied. We will not come back to these cases in the following paragraphs.

5.197 **Sharing mechanism.** The organisation of a sharing mechanism was also found by the ECJ to be compatible with general competition law. An important case in this regard is *TNT*,[158] concerning the organisation of postal services in Italy. The national operator still had at the relevant time[159] a monopoly for the provision of the ordinary postal service. Other services were open to competition as a result of the liberalisation which had already partly taken place in that sector. In order to finance the ordinary service, the national operator was granted a subsidy by the Italian Government. This subsidy was supposed to compensate the losses incurred in the performance of the service.[160] The national operator found that the subsidy was not sufficient. It thus requested, and obtained, the establishment of a sharing mechanism whereby the other undertakings present on non-reserved postal service markets in Italy were compelled to pay a contribution to the national operator.[161]

5.198 **Principle admitted.** In the judgment, the ECJ confirms the possibility for Member States to establish sharing mechanisms whereby undertakings present on some markets may be compelled to contribute financially in order to ensure the financing of universal service obligations performed by one of them, in this case

---

[154] Universal Service Directive, Preamble, recital 21.   [155] ibid, Art 13, para 3.

[156] See n 110 above.   [157] See n 116 above.

[158] Case C-340/99 *TNT Traco SpA v Poste Italiane SpA* [2001] ECR I-4109; Case 395/87 *Ministère Public v Tournier* [1989] ECR 2521.

[159] Again, the issues which were raised date back to 1999. They would not be addressed in the same manner today, as new rules have recently been adopted for the organisation of postal services in Europe.

[160] No issue was raised as to the legality of the subsidy which, we must thus suppose, was compatible with the EC Treaty and in particular with the provisions concerning State aids in the line defined by *Ferring*.

[161] Thus, undertakings delivering express mail on the Italian territory were to pay to the national operator part of the receipts they acquired thereby. In that case, the amount to be paid was equivalent to the normal rate senders would have paid, had they not resorted to the express service.

the incumbent. The scheme established by the Italian Government was thus accepted in principle.

> *TNT.* '[In order to] enable the holder of [universal service obligations] to perform tasks of general economic interest which have been assigned to it under economically acceptable conditions . . . it may prove necessary not only to permit the undertaking entrusted with the task, in the general interest, of operating the universal service to offset profitable sectors against less profitable sectors . . . , but also to require suppliers of postal services not forming part of the universal service to contribute, by paying postal dues of the kind at issue in the main proceedings, to the financing of the universal service and in that way to enable the undertaking entrusted with that task to perform it in conditions of economic stability.'[162]

Conditions. Conditions were however imposed by the ECJ in order to ensure **5.199** compliance with competition rules. These conditions correspond to the analysis which has been made regarding the use of public funds to finance universal service, in the light of general competition law. The first is that contributions must not exceed what is needed to ensure the reimbursement of the net costs of providing universal service. The beneficiary must thus not receive funds in addition to what is needed to cover the expenses actually associated with the provision of universal service.[163]

> *TNT.* '[S]ince Article [86(2) EC] is a provision which permits, in certain circumstances, derogation from the rules of the Treaty, it must be restrictively interpreted.' 'Therefore, Article [86(2) EC] of the Treaty does not allow the total proceeds . . . which are paid by economic operators . . . to exceed the amount necessary to offset any losses which may be incurred in the operation of the universal postal service by the undertaking responsible therefore.'[164]

No discrimination. Another condition is that no discrimination may be prac- **5.200** tised in the operation of the mechanism. This implies that all undertakings must be treated equally. No undertaking could as a result in principle be exempted. The undertaking receiving the funds in particular must also contribute, on the basis of the same criteria as those applied to the other market participants.

---

[162] At [54] and [55].

[163] This condition corresponds to the rule introduced in *Ferring*. The situation was however slightly different. In *Ferring*, the sum paid was a tax exemption. Pursuant to case law, this can be analysed in the same way as a subsidy and be subject to EC provisions concerning State aids. In *TNT*, the payment was not made, however, either directly or indirectly with public funds. Contributions were paid directly by contributors to the beneficiary. (This system was also implemented under the former European telecommunications regulation, where the contributions could be paid directly to the operator with the interconnection charge. This system has however been abandoned, for the reasons we have analysed above.) The issue is, would EC provisions on State aids apply to contributions paid by undertakings directly to an operator? One argument against such application could be that the contributions are not public funds. An argument in favour would be that the sharing mechanism is a public scheme administered by the NRA. On the basis of this last argument, no distinction could be made as regards the treatment under State aid provisions. We concur with this second argument. [164] At [56] and [57].

> *TNT.* 'In those circumstances, the undertaking responsible for the universal postal service must also be required, when itself supplying an express mail service not forming part of that service, to pay the postal dues.'[165]

5.201 **Use made of the proceeds.** A final condition relates to the use that can be made of these proceeds. This, however, cannot be considered as a condition relating to the scheme as such, but rather concerns the behaviour of the designated undertaking. The issue is to determine whether undertakings may use public funds for purposes that were originally not envisaged as the normal destination of these funds. The answer must be in the negative. The argumentation presented in the judgment is that behaviour of this nature would increase universal service costs.

> *TNT.* '[T]he undertaking responsible for the universal postal service . . . must . . . ensure that neither all nor part of the costs of its express mail service are subsidised by the universal service, lest charges for the universal service and, consequently, the potential losses of that service be improperly increased.'[166]

5.202 **No legal basis for action.** This argument does not provide, however, a legal basis for action.[167] A basis of that nature can probably be found in Article 82 EC, which prohibits abuse of a dominant position. It could indeed be considered an abuse to subsidise activities on a competitive market with revenues obtained from public authorities and which were to be used in connection with a protected market. The behaviour would lead to competition being further altered, through unacceptable means. State aid provisions may also provide a basis for a prohibition. The mechanism is meant to ensure proper functioning of markets where services of general interest are imposed. To that extent, it is considered that no advantage is conferred, as the sharing mechanism merely compensates undertakings for the implementation of supplementary obligations. This justification ceases to exist where the subsidy is used for other purposes. The subsidy then becomes an aid which is in principle prohibited.

(6) Calculating the net cost of universal service

5.203 **Limitation to universal service obligations.** Undertakings may be compensated for the costs of providing universal service under arrangements that deviate from normal market conditions. We have examined above the conditions that must be complied with before a decision can be taken to compensate. In substance, the compensation must cover expenses related to the performance of universal service obligations.

---

[165] At [58].   [166] At [58].

[167] One could say that these costs are certainly increased. At that time there was, however, no secondary regulation concerning the calculation of the cost of universal service. Should cross-subsidy occur in electronic communications with proceeds from the sharing mechanism to finance the universal service, one could say that the undertaking had infringed the laws concerning universal service financing. No such regulation however applied in the postal sector, where the case emerged.

Universal Service Directive, Annex IV, Part A, para 1. 'Universal service obligations refer to those obligations placed upon an undertaking by a Member State which concern the provision of a network and service throughout a specified geographic area, including, where required, averaged prices in that geographical area for the provision of that service or provision of specific tariff options for consumers with low incomes or with special social needs.'

Necessity of approval by the Commission. We have seen that, pursuant to the **5.204** subsidiarity principle, the Member States have a certain margin of manoeuvre in order to organise mechanisms whereby they finance universal service obligations. The actions they undertake must, however, conform at all times with European rules. In its general role as guardian of the Treaty, the Commission has the responsibility of ensuring compliance with these rules. In order to perform this task, the Commission must be provided with all necessary information concerning the mechanisms in place. So as to ensure this, the Universal Service Directive places upon the Member States an obligation to communicate to the Commission the mechanisms they have put in place.

Universal Service Directive, Preamble, para 24. 'Member States' schemes for the costing and financing of universal service obligations should be communicated to the Commission for verification of compatibility with the Treaty.'

Burden of proof. We have already seen that no compensation mechanism can **5.205** be established without a specific request presented to that effect by the undertaking(s) asking for compensation. A second obligation applies to these undertakings, that of justifying the funding requested. It is for them to provide information as regards the costs they must incur. These data cannot be general, but must be sufficiently detailed to convince the NRA.

Universal Service Directive, Preamble, recital 24. 'National regulatory authorities should satisfy themselves that those undertakings benefiting from universal service financing provide a sufficient level of detail of the specific elements requiring such funding in order to justify their request.'

Competences. The calculation on which the compensation is based must be **5.206** made by the NRA. In some instances it is based on accounts held by the undertakings involved. These accounts must then be audited. Another possibility is that they are verified by an independent body. If use is made of this second possibility, the accounts must be approved by the NRA. In all cases, the sums claimed by the undertaking for compensation must be published, together with the conclusions reached by the auditors or the independent body.

Main task of the NRAs. '[N]ational regulatory authorities . . . shall calculate the net costs of its provision.'[168] 'The responsibility for verifying the net cost lies with the

---

[168] Universal Service Directive, Art 12(1).

national regulatory authority.'[169] *Accounts.* 'The accounts and/or information serving as the basis for the calculation of the net cost of universal service obligations . . . shall be audited or verified by the national regulatory authority or a body independent of the relevant parties and approved by the national regulatory authority. The results of the cost calculation and the conclusions of the audit shall be publicly available.'[170]

5.207 Link with the designation mechanism. As stated, only the net cost of universal service may be financed. This implies the determination of criteria that will ensure that items are not included unduly in the calculation. This is regulated by Article 12 of the Universal Service Directive. Rules are set out in greater detail in Annex IV, Part A. In substance, the calculation exercise depends on the method that has been chosen to designate the undertakings in charge of universal service provision.

5.208 Competitive selection. In some instances the designation mechanism makes it possible to establish the net cost that will have to be compensated. That is the case, for instance, where the candidates are invited to bid for the provision of universal service by indicating how much would have to be paid out in compensation. In such a situation, the net cost would be available immediately, and NRAs could take the figure as a basis for paying the compensation.

> *Universal Service Directive, Article 12(1), subpara 2, letter (b).* '[N]ational regulatory authorities shall . . . make use of the net costs of providing universal service identified by a designation mechanism.'

5.209 Other forms of designation. Other designation mechanisms may however be used, and not all mechanisms make it possible to determine immediately with accuracy the amount to be paid. In these cases, the net costs have to be calculated. The calculation must then be carried out in conformity with the rules examined in the following paragraphs.[171]

> *Universal Service Directive, Article 12(1), subpara 2, letter (a).* '[N]ational regulatory authorities shall: (a) calculate the net cost of the universal service obligation.'

5.210 (1) Use a general formula. The net costs should be established in the following manner. First, the undertaking should establish the cost of carrying out the activity in accordance with the obligations flowing from the universal service requirements. This will be done on the basis of the accounts which the undertaking must in any case hold. Second, the undertaking should calculate the costs that it would have incurred had it carried out the activities without complying with universal

---

[169] Universal Service Directive, Annex IV, Part A, para 4.   [170] ibid, Art 12, para 2.

[171] From the directive, it thus follows that the calculation exercise must not take place where net costs can be established on the basis of the designation mechanism. This calculation must only be made where the designation mechanism is not such as to allow the determination of the amount to be claimed for the compensation. This constitutes an incentive for NRAs to organise the designation as a procedure where candidates bid for the provision of the universal service obligations, the lowest bid being chosen. For this procedure, see paras 5.138–5.141 above.

service objectives. This step cannot be based on an observation of the accounts, as it is not merely founded on costs actually incurred and reported in the accounts. The third step will consist in calculating the difference between the two amounts previously obtained.

> *Universal Service Directive, Annex IV, Part A, para 2.* 'In undertaking a calculation exercise, the net cost of universal service obligations is to be calculated as the difference between the net cost for a designated undertaking of operating with the universal service obligation and operating without the universal service obligations.'

(2) Divide universal service into items.   The undertakings must present their **5.211** requests for compensation by giving a general amount to be paid. However, this amount must be the sum of the costs that relate to the provision of the various universal service items. In the calculation exercise, the costs—and benefits—relating to each item must be calculated separately.

> *Universal Service Directive, Annex IV, Part A, para 4.* 'The calculation of the net cost of specific aspects of universal service obligations is to be made separately . . . The overall net cost of universal service obligations to any undertaking is to be calculated as the sum of the net costs arising from the specific components of universal service obligations.'

(3) Concentrate on loss-making items.   In the division exercise, attention **5.212** should be limited to items where the undertaking is not able to comply with the universal service obligations in economic equilibrium. Items where profit or economic equilibrium can be obtained should not be counted, as they do not form a basis on which a claim for compensation can be made. As far as loss-making items are concerned, a suggestion is given in the Annex to facilitate identification. In some instances, losses are due to the nature of the service that must be performed, such as the provision of an emergency service. By nature, such an item is bound to give rise to losses, as it must be provided free of charge despite the costs that are attached to it.

> *Universal Service Directive, Annex IV, Part A, para 3.* 'The calculation is to be based upon the costs attributable to: (i) elements of the identified services which can only be provided at a loss or provided under cost conditions falling outside normal commercial standards. This category may include service elements such as access to emergency telephone services, provision of certain public pay telephones, . . . etc.'

Public.   In other circumstances, losses are related to the public concerned, for **5.213** example, end users located in mountainous regions. Providing them with certain universal service items may give rise to a loss,[172] in which case compensation may be claimed.

---

[172] Losses will not be incurred in all circumstances. As we have seen, geographic averaging may ensure that higher costs related to low density regions or regions not easily accessible can be compensated by higher tariffs imposed on other regions.

> *Universal Service Directive, Annex IV, Part A, para 3.* 'The calculation is to be based upon the costs attributable to: (ii) specific end-users or groups of end-users who, taking into account the cost of providing the specified network and service, the revenue generated and any geographical averaging of prices imposed by the Member State, can only be served at a loss or under cost conditions falling outside normal commercial standards. This category includes those end-users or groups of end-users which would not be served by a commercial operator which did not have an obligation to provide universal service.'

5.214 Case law. In *Commission v France*,[173] France was condemned for including profitable accounts in the data concerning non-profitable regions. The ECJ considered that France had not concentrated on loss-making items. To determine whether an intervention was warranted, France should have limited the calculus to non-profitable accounts within these regions.

> *Commission v France.* 'It is common ground that the French Republic included . . . the cost of all residential customers, including, therefore, profitable accounts. On this point the French Government merely makes the general argument that it was impossible for it to distinguish between customers in accordance with the criteria set out.' 'It must be concluded, therefore, that the French Republic included in the cost of universal service provision costs which did not satisfy the criteria.'[174]

5.215 (4) Consider all costs. All costs must be considered in the calculation exercise. This is particularly important for the second step of the calculation exercise, where the undertaking must take into account the costs that would not have been incurred had the activities been performed without complying with the universal service obligations.

> *Universal Service Directive, Annex IV, Part A, para 2.* 'Due attention is to be given to correctly assessing the costs that any designated undertaking would have chosen to avoid had there been no universal service obligation.'

5.216 (5) Take all benefits into account. In the calculation, NRAs must take into account all benefits designated undertakings may obtain with the provision of the services concerned. These benefits must be deducted from the general costs incurred in the provision of universal service.

> *Universal Service Directive, Annex IV, Part A, para 2, last sentence.* 'The net cost calculation should assess the benefits, including intangible benefits, to the universal service operator.'[175]

5.217 What are the benefits concerned? No concrete indication is given in the Universal Service Directive as to what could be considered a benefit flowing from an obligation to provide universal service under conditions other than normal market conditions. Among the benefits concerned are those called 'intangible'. An undertaking providing universal service builds up a certain idea in the public

---

[173] Case 146/00 *Commission v France* [2001] ECR I-9767. [174] At [40].
[175] See also para 4 of the same Annex and Art 12(1)(2)(b) of the directive.

mind of an undertaking close to the people and the community where the services are provided. This can be analysed as image-building investment, from which a certain return might be expected.

Case law.   In *Commission v France*,[176] the ECJ ruled that France had not taken **5.218** into account, to calculate the net cost of providing universal service, a certain number of revenue items. *(a)* Among these items were those derived from ex-directory listing.[177] *(b)* Other omitted items were the revenues obtained by France Telecom on comfort services, which include services such as call diversion, call waiting and caller number display.

> *Commission v France.* The 'French Government ought to have taken into account revenue derived from comfort services and from ex-directory listing in calculating the net cost of universal service provision in order to identify unprofitable areas'.[178]

(6) Avoid double counting.   As each item will be counted separately, there is a **5.219** risk that the same costs, or benefits, will be counted several times, in respect of different items. This aspect is to be verified with particular attention by the NRA. A specific obligation is introduced to that effect in Annex IV of the Universal Service Directive.

> *Universal Service Directive, Annex IV, Part 2, para 2, last sentence.* 'The calculation of the net cost of specific aspects of universal service obligations is to be made . . . so as to avoid the double counting of any direct or indirect benefits and costs.'

I. Comparison with Old Regulation

(1) Introduction

The present section.   This section analyses the major changes that have been **5.220** introduced by the NRF. A table is provided in the Annex, showing the correspondence between the provisions dealing with universal service in the former and the new regulation. The text of the new regulation has also been included. Relevant internet addresses are provided in the Annexes to enable, inter alia, the text of the old regulation to be consulted.

---

[176] See n 173 above. That case concerns the rules established under the old regulatory framework, but the rules have not changed on the point examined.

[177] The operator receives payments from persons or undertakings which do not wish to be included in the directories.

[178] At [69]. Belgium was also condemned by the ECJ for reasons relating, among others, to revenue items not being considered in the calculus concerning the cost of universal service. The ruling is less clear, however, because Belgium adopted new rules during the procedure and concentrated its defence on these rules. The ECJ notes that these rules were introduced after some delay, without really examining the substance of the case. See Case C-384/99 *Commission v Belgium* [2000] ECR I-10633.

5.221 **Old regulation—applicable instruments.** Universal service was formerly organised by two directives from the Parliament and Council: *(a)* European Parliament and Council Directive (EC) 97/33 on interconnection in telecommunications with regard to ensuring universal service and interoperability through application of the principles of Open Network Provision (ONP);[179] *(b)* European Parliament and Council Directive (EC) 98/10 on the application of open network provision (ONP) to voice telephony and on universal service for telecommunications in a competitive environment (ONP Voice Telephony Directive).[180] Among these instruments, the first regulated only the financing of universal service,[181] whereas the content was addressed in the more specific context of the second. The liberalisation directives adopted by the Commission also covered universal service. The main aspects were introduced by Commission Directive (EC) 96/19,[182] which added an Article 4c to Commission Directive (EEC) 90/388 on competition in the markets for telecommunications services (Services Directive).[183] This provision dealt principally with the financing of the universal service obligations, the purpose being to avoid a situation whereby the mechanisms set in place by the Member States would distort competition and thereby undermine the reform.[184]

5.222 **Overall picture of the changes.** The provisions relating to universal service have not undergone any revolutionary change in the preparation and adoption of the NRF. The rules have in substance remained the same as concerns the scope of universal service, the designation of undertakings and the mechanisms that can be used in order to finance the service.

(2) Major changes

5.223 **Emphasis on markets.** Beyond technical issues, an important modification is to be found in the emphasis placed by the European legislator on the requirement for Member States to ensure the performance of universal service obligations to the maximum extent possible through market forces and subject to normal commercial conditions. The old regulation contained a general reference to the proportionality principle. However, no strong statement was made about a possible obligation for Member States always to resort in the first instance to a competitive

---

[179] [1997] OJ L199/32.   [180] [1998] OJ L101/24.

[181] As Art 4c of Services Directive also did in parallel.   [182] [1996] OJ L74/24.

[183] [1990] OJ L192/10.

[184] A communication was adopted in 1996 by the Commission in order to specify the obligations flowing from the former harmonisation and liberalisation directives as regards the financing of universal service. See the Communication on Assessment Criteria for National Schemes for the Costing and Financing of Universal Service in Telecommunications and Guidelines for the Member States on Operation of such Schemes, COM(96) 608, Brussels, 27 November 1996. This communication has been examined together with the Universal Service Directive (see para 5.167). We will not come back to the issues that are dealt with in that document.

environment. Statements to that effect can, however, be found in several places in the NRF. In the Universal Service Directive, for instance, Article 1 introduces the objective of providing a set of services throughout the territory. A reference is made to the use in principle of market forces to attain that result. Other means are admitted, but they must comply with the rules established in the Universal Service Directive. A similar emphasis is placed in Article 3 on the importance of minimising market distortions.

> *Universal Service Directive.* 'The aim is to ensure the availability throughout the Community of good quality publicly available services through effective competition and choice and to deal with circumstances in which the needs of end-users are not satisfactorily met by the market.'[185] 'Member States . . . shall seek to minimize market distortions, in particular the provision of services at prices or subject to other terms and conditions which depart from normal commercial conditions.'[186]

Payment of contributions

Various systems. The two mechanisms described above concerning the financing of universal service obligations (public funds, contributions) already existed in the old regulation. Several differences appear, however, in the NRF as regards the second system, ie the payment of contributions. One of them concerns the arrangements that may be used to secure payment. The Interconnection Directive explicitly provided that these contributions could be paid to a fund administered by an independent body (this system is also provided for in the current regulation). An alternative was to pay the contribution as a supplementary charge added to the interconnection charge. Using that arrangement, service providers paid to the network operator a contribution meant to finance the universal service obligations performed by the latter. The reason for this arrangement was that universal service was then provided essentially by incumbents. As these would anyway receive the money, it was easier—and cheaper—to organise a direct payment rather than establish a complicated mechanism that would only add to the costs claimed from providers. **5.224**

Payment through interconnection charges abandoned. The situation has changed with the development of competition, and some universal service obligations may now be provided by newcomers.[187] A payment via an interconnection **5.225**

---

[185] Universal Service Directive, Art 1(1).

[186] ibid, Art 3(2). A similar idea had already been formulated in the ONP Voice Telephony Directive—albeit not with the same intensity. See Art 4 of that directive. 'Where the services set out in this chapter cannot be commercially provided on the basis of conditions laid down by the Member State, Member States may set up universal service funding schemes for the shared financing of those services.'

[187] Cf Universal Service Directive, Preamble, recital 14. 'The development of greater competition and choice provides more possibilities for all or part of the universal service obligations to be provided by undertakings other than those with significant market power.'

charge thus appears less appropriate. Other reasons made it difficult to maintain the system. In fact, it would not appear surprising that the payment via interconnection charges has not proved appropriate. Providers required to contribute found it difficult to pay a contribution direct to their main competitor.[188] Furthermore, verification was not easy as it depended entirely on the incumbent. These reasons have probably played a role in the decision apparently taken by the European legislator no longer to organise payment though interconnection charges. This method of payment is not specifically prohibited by the NRF. Some could argue that, given the margin for manoeuvre they have for the organisation of the universal service (subsidiarity), Member States may use that silence on the part of the European legislator to continue to organise payments using that arrangement as long as the system is placed under the surveillance of the NRA. The absence of an indication concerning the continued possibility of using this arrangement must probably be interpreted as a desire by the European legislator that payments be made to a fund administered by the NRA or by an independent body placed under the surveillance of that authority.

Identity of contributors

5.226 **Debate between European institutions.** A dispute had emerged under the old regulation between the Commission on the one hand and the Parliament and Council on the other hand, concerning the identity of undertakings which may be required to contribute. For the Commission the obligation had to be limited to undertakings operating public telecommunications networks.[189] For the Parliament and Council the obligation could be extended to undertakings providing public voice telephony services.[190] The dispute was settled through a statement made by the Commission in which it accepted that public voice telephony service providers may be called on to contribute. It made clear, however, that this contribution should be imposed only in proportion to the usage made by such providers of public telecommunications networks.[191]

5.227 **Clarification.** The situation has now been totally clarified with the adoption of the NRF. Pursuant to the Universal Service Directive, an obligation to contribute may be imposed on all undertakings present on electronic communications markets, ie all

---

[188] The argument goes as follows. Not only did the incumbents have the advantage of economic power, of a relation with customers and of a network already installed with the support of public authorities; in addition, they had to receive payments from competitors who were trying to establish themselves, not without difficulty.

[189] Services Directive, Art 4c(1), as introduced by Commission Directive 96/19.

[190] ONP Interconnection Directive, Art 5(1).

[191] Commission Statement to the Minutes of the 1910th Meeting of Council (Telecommunications), on 27 March 1996 on who contributes to universal service, annex C to Communication COM (96)608, al 2.

service providers and network operators. The European institutions—including the Commission—have probably considered that the principle of subsidiarity should apply to the designation of contributors. In application of that principle, it is for the Member States to decide on the actors they want to contribute. The decision made by them has to comply with the basic regulatory principles. Pursuant to these requirements, the principle of objectivity will have to be complied with. Member States will thus have to justify their position. In their justification, they have to explain why they consider that some or all undertakings must be subject to the obligation, and why they consider particular sums are to be claimed from these undertakings.[192]

(3) Other aspects

Scope of universal service.   The scope of universal service has not really evolved **5.228** with the adoption of the NRF, contrary to what might have been expected.[193] Several documents from the European institutions had hinted at developments that would require Member States to ensure the provision of mobile technology to all, together with access to ISDN networks.[194] The decision was however taken not to extend universal service at the present stage. This may be related to the forthcoming accession of new Member States, which for practical reasons cannot be required to comply with far-reaching obligations over too short a time span.

(1) Mobile technology.   The first issue to determine is whether more emphasis **5.229** has been put on mobile technology in the context of the universal service. As stated, access to a mobile network as well as to mobile services is not considered, at this stage of the regulation, as an item to be included in universal service, although indications are provided that developments are likely to occur on this point in the years ahead. In examining the NRF it has been remarked that mobile technology is considered in some circumstances to be a substitute for fixed technology. One may wonder whether an evolution has taken place in that respect. Thus in the old regulation, access had to be provided to a *fixed* public voice telephony network as well as to *fixed* public voice telephony services.[195] By contrast, the only requirement which appears in the NRF is the provision of access to a public voice telephony network and to public voice telephony services. The specific reference to fixed technology has thus been removed.

---

[192] Contributions must normally be individualised.

[193] The only change that has been introduced relates to the inclusion of mobile technology in the obligation to provide connection to a public network as a fixed location as well as access to public voice telephony services. This change is examined below (see para 5.229).

[194] See Universal Service Directive, Preamble, recital 8. 'The requirement is limited to a single narrowband network connection . . . and does not extend to the Integrated Services Digital Network (ISDN) which provides two or more connections capable of being used simultaneously.'

[195] ONP Voice Telephony Directive, Art 5.

5.230 Practical reason.   This development may probably be explained by a practical, rather than a strategic, reason. In some instances, the fixed public network is not yet fully developed. This is particularly so in some accession countries, where the whole territory is not yet covered by a network. In these circumstances, mobile technology can provide a useful alternative. In many instances it will be less expensive to develop a network through mobile technology than requiring the Member States concerned to remain with fixed technology. This is particularly relevant at a time when the European institutions are counting on the rapid development of UMTS.[196]

> *Universal Service Directive, Preamble, recital 8.* 'There should be no constraints on the technical means by which the connection is provided, allowing for wired or wireless technologies.'[197] 'Flexibility . . . is required . . . to allow Member States . . . to exploit the capabilities of wireless technologies (including cellular wireless networks) to deliver universal service to a higher proportion of the population. This may be of particular importance in some accession countries where household penetration of traditional telephone connections remains relatively low.'[198]

5.231 Difference from previous requirements.   Reflecting further, one may wonder whether there is a real difference as compared to the previous requirements, beyond the fact that the explicit reference to fixed technology has been taken away. As submitted above, the old regulation required a connection to a fixed public network to be provided. Access also had to be provided to fixed electronic communications services. These requirements were set out in the ONP Voice Telephony Directive.[199] Indications were already provided, however, in the preamble to that directive concerning the possibility of using wireless technologies in order to fulfil these obligations. Pursuant to that preamble, wireless technologies could be used as tools to provide access to the fixed network as well as to fixed telecommunications services. As the Preamble stated, 'there should be no constraints on the technical means by which the connection is provided, allowing for wire or wireless technologies'.[200]

5.232 Further development expected.   This seems to be exactly what the NRF provides as regards access in the context of universal service. One has thus to conclude that no real progress has been made in the NRF concerning the inclusion of mobile technologies in universal service. This does not imply that nothing is being done, in terms of European policy, as regards these technologies. Substantial measures have been adopted to promote the development of UMTS. There is little doubt that the issue whether or not to include these technologies in the universal service requirement will be raised when they are further developed.

---

[196] UMTS technologies should be able to support the same applications as a fixed broadband network.   [197] Universal Service Directive, Preamble, recital 8.
[198] ibid, Preamble, recital 8.   [199] ibid, Art 5, para 2.
[200] ONP Voice Telephony Directive, Preamble, recital 4.

(2) Internet access.   A second issue to be analysed relates to internet access. We   **5.233**
have seen that no specific requirement is included in the NRF as regards broadband in the universal service. The requirement contained in the Universal Service
Directive is limited to functional internet access. An obligation of this nature
probably remains insufficient in a context where some authorities want to see the
emergence of an information and communications-based society. More could
hardly be done, however, in the light of the expense that would have been added
to the sector had broadband been included within the universal service obligation.
The absence of more specific requirements should also be read in the light of the
future accession of new Member States. Obligations cannot be set at a level that
these countries could take some considerable time to attain.

Little difference.   One should further note that little progress has been made as   **5.234**
compared with the requirements that already appeared in the old regulation.
Pursuant to the ONP Voice Telephony Directive, a connection had to be provided
as part of the universal service requirement, and this connection had to support
data transmission.[201] Pursuant to the Preamble to that directive, data communications were to be made possible 'at rates suitable for access to online information
services'.[202] There is in fact little difference as compared with what is required today.

(3) Quality-oriented measures.   More emphasis also appears to have been placed   **5.235**
on quality in the NRF. Quality was not absent from the old regulation, and indeed
an entire article was included in the Voice Telephony Directive to deal with the
subject. Quality has however become so important in the NRF that it has now been
integrated into the definition of universal service. Universal service is now defined as
a minimum set of services which must comply with specified quality conditions.
Affordability and availability are thus not the only applicable requirements.

> *Universal Service Directive, Article 3(1).* 'Member States shall ensure that the services . . .
> are made available *at the quality specified* to all end-users in their territory . . . and . . . at
> an affordable price.'[203]

(4) More national action regarding disabled users.   One development should   **5.236**
be remarked concerning action Member States are allowed to take in addition to
those already provided for in the NRF, in their support for policies to disabled
users. The Universal Service Directive now makes it clear that action of this nature
is authorised, and in fact even encouraged.[204] This did not appear to be the case in
the old regulation, where obligations were limited at European level in the

---

[201] ibid, Art 5, para 2.

[202] ibid, Preamble, recital 4.

[203] Quality was not included in the definition given to universal service in the ONP Voice
Telephony Directive (Art 3(1)). It already appeared, however, in a definition in the ONP
Interconnection Directive (Art 2(1)(g)).

[204] Universal Service Directive, Art 7(2). In the former regulation, the provisions dealing with
disabled users were contained in the ONP Voice Telephony Directive, Art 8.

absence of authorisation to Member States to go beyond these provisions in the light of national conditions.

J. Universal Service in the Liberalisation Directives

(1) Intervention by the Commission

5.237 **Harmonisation framework.** The rules examined above concerning universal service have been established by the Parliament and Council (harmonisation framework). The Commission has also participated in the process leading to the directives adopted by these institutions,[205] and has clearly had an opportunity to influence the content of the rules adopted by the other institutions. However, the ultimate responsibility for the adoption of these rules (the harmonisation directives) lies with their authors, the Parliament and Council.

5.238 **Consolidated Services Directive.** This is probably the reason why the Commission has sought to establish its own rules in parallel with those adopted by the Parliament and Council. These rules are based on powers concerning the application of European law, in particular European competition rules, to undertakings covered by Article 86 EC. In this capacity the Commission adopted the Terminal Equipment Liberalisation Directives and the Services Directive (services, networks). These directives, which have been described earlier (see paras 1.98–1.107), have been amended several times. Recently, the Services Directive has been replaced by the Consolidated Services Directive. This directive contains provisions dealing with the application of competition rules to electronic communications. Some of these rules relate to universal service. It is important to examine whether they coincide with those adopted by the Parliament and Council.

5.239 **Old liberalisation directives.** Indications will also be given about the rules contained in the old liberalisation directives. These directives remain important in interpreting the rules applicable to the sector. Pursuant to the case law, the liberalisation directives must be seen as determining and specifying obligations which pre-exist and which may be found in the Treaty itself. As a result, the obligations specified in the liberalisation directives in principle remain the same unless the Treaty itself is modified.

(2) The main concern—financing

5.240 **Main concern of the Commission.** The Commission's concern as regards universal service is concentrated on financing issues in the context of the

---

[205] As we have seen, the Commission has a right of initiative to propose draft directives to the European Parliament and the Council in the harmonisation framework. The Commission is also entrusted with the administration of the harmonisation procedure.

Consolidated Services Directive. This is due to the task that is entrusted to the Commission on the basis of Article 86 EC. This is not to regulate an entire economic sector, but rather to ensure the application of European rules, including the competition rules, to the activities mentioned in that provision. Although European law as a whole is referred to in that provision, the Commission focuses on the application of the competition rules. In that context it is not for the Commission to determine a set of fundamental services that should be made available to all at affordable rates. In other words, the task entrusted to the Commission in that framework is not to advance social policy, but rather to ensure that activities are carried out in a competitive environment.

Basic regulatory principles. In the Consolidated Services Directive the **5.241** Commission emphasises three principles. *(a)* First, all actions undertaken by the Member States should conform to the basic regulatory principles which, as has been submitted, are intimately related to competition provisions. *(b)* Second, Member States are required to communicate to the Commission their universal service schemes so that the Commission is in a position to verify the compatibility of such schemes with competition law.

> *Basic regulatory principles.* 'Any national scheme . . . serving to share the net cost of the provision of universal service obligations shall be based on objective, transparent and non-discriminatory criteria and shall be consistent with the principle of proportionality.'[206] *Communication.* 'Member States shall communicate any scheme of the kind referred to in paragraph 1 to the Commission.'[207]

Least market distortion. A third principle is that the distortion imposed on mar- **5.242** kets by the organisation set by the Member States must be minimal. That principle is explicitly stated in the Preamble to the Consolidated Services Directive. One aspect of that is, according to the Commission, the burden imposed on each undertaking participating in the scheme must be as low as possible. This can only be achieved if the burden is allocated on a large number of undertakings.

> *Consolidated Services Directive, Preamble, recital 12.* 'Any national scheme . . . serving to share the net cost of the provision of universal service obligations . . . shall be consistent with the principle . . . of least market distortion.' 'Least market distortion means that contributions should be recovered in a way that as far as possible minimises the impact of the financial burden falling on end-users, for example by spreading contributions as widely as possible.'

(3) Old liberalisation directives

No substantial difference. These principles contained in the Consolidated **5.243** Services Directive coincide with the rules examined in connection with the

---

[206] Consolidated Services Directive, Art 6.
[207] ibid, Art 6. See also the Preamble to that directive, recital 12.

instruments adopted by the Parliament and Council in the harmonisation framework. In these latter instruments, similar insistence is placed on the basic regulatory principles to be respected in the schemes established to finance universal service. No incompatibility thus appears to exist as regards the present state of regulation as between the two sets of regulation. This does not mean that no problem of this kind has ever existed. A few observations need to be made in this regard concerning areas where compatibility was previously not achieved entirely.

5.244 **Identity of contributors.** A first difficulty concerned the determination of undertakings from which a contribution could be required to finance universal service (sharing mechanism). As already mentioned, the Commission originally wished to limit the obligation to undertakings providing public telecommunications networks. This limitation was alleviated when the Commission accepted that the obligation could be extended to undertakings providing public telecommunications services. In the Consolidated Services Directive no indication is provided regarding the identity of contributors. This must probably be understood as implying that the Commission has abandoned any specific requirement on that point. The Commission probably considers that newcomers have now evolved to a degree where they can withstand having to pay their contribution. There is thus no longer any need to limit the obligation to incumbents.

5.245 **Tariff rebalancing.** A second difficulty concerns tariff rebalancing. This concept concerns former national monopolies, and more particularly the situation in which these monopolies were placed after the introduction of the reform. These undertakings had long set their tariffs without taking costs into account, or at least without considering them as the main element in setting their tariffs. This was the result of policy objectives that were imposed on them at that time by national public authorities. As an example one can mention an obligation that was for a long time imposed on former national monopolies, that of giving priority to local communications to the detriment of long-distance communications.[208] This strategy was seen as useful in reinforcing social cohesion and providing cheap communications to residential users. In that system, connection charges and local communications were priced below cost. On the other hand, tariffs for long-distance communications were set at a high level, and the additional profits made on this second market used to compensate the losses incurred on the first.

5.246 **Prices close to costs.** However, competition puts pressure on undertakings to set their tariffs as close as possible to costs. Only if they shadow costs will they recover

---

[208] The system is called *perequation*. The purpose was to have businesses subsidise communications made by individuals. Most local communications were of a private nature whereas long-distance communications were professional. The idea behind the tariff policy was that low prices should be charged to individuals. Local communications should thus be made available for low prices. By contrast, businesses could afford higher tariffs.

their investment, while attracting consumers with low prices. Competition thus made untenable the former system of cross-subsidisation between local and long-distance communications. In this case, the process of adaptation forced former national monopolies to lower their prices on long-distance communications. Had they not done this, they would have lost market share. Since prices on these markets were set at high levels, competitors were entering these markets on a massive scale, as they could set prices lower and still bring in a profit. Conversely, the introduction of competition forced former national monopolies to increase prices for local communications. In the absence of such a rebalancing process they would have incurred losses.

Services Directive.   In the Services Directive, the Commission mandated tariff   **5.247** rebalancing, that is, former national monopolies were required to price their services as a function of their costs. The operation was however not neutral as regards universal service. As tariffs were rebalanced, connection charges increased. Local communications also became more expensive. These are, nonetheless, essential elements in universal service. There was a risk that former monopolists may use rebalancing as a tool to increase the cost of universal service. As they were likely to be designated for the provision of universal service, they would thus receive a bigger subsidy.[209] The Commission accordingly issued a warning. Tariff rebalancing was unavoidable, it admitted. Contributions required of undertakings, however, had to be based on costs actually incurred by former national monopolists.

> *Services Directive, Article (4)c, as amended.* 'Member States shall allow their telecommunications organisations to re-balance tariffs taking account of specific market conditions and of the need to ensure the affordability of a universal service . . . [In particular], Member States shall allow them to adapt current rates which are not in line with costs and which increase the burden of universal service provision, in order to achieve tariffs based on real costs.'

Still an issue.   References to this necessity of rebalancing tariffs have not been   **5.248** taken over in the Consolidated Services Directive. The reason is probably that the operation has been carried out, in some Member States, over the course of the years. It would however be erroneous to consider that the issue no longer needs to be discussed. Tariffs have not been rebalanced in all European countries, as the various Implementation Reports show. Furthermore, tariff rebalancing still has to be implemented in accession countries. For all Member States, the principle remains, that the cost of universal service has to be calculated along strict lines, as was stated above. The absence of a reference to tariff rebalancing in the Consolidated Services

---

[209] In most instances, monopolists were entrusted with the task of providing universal service in the years following the reform. That choice was mandated by necessity, as only those undertakings had a network covering the entire national territory and universal service is often associated with the obligation to provide access to a network across geographic regions.

Directive cannot be interpreted, as a result, as an acceptance on the part of the Commission of any strategy that could be adopted by incumbents or other undertakings to increase artificially the cost of universal service in order to claim higher compensation. Such a claim would have to be set aside, since universal service has to be provided at the lowest possible cost.

(4) Universal service in a liberalised context

5.249 **Tension between the objectives.**   The relations between universal service and liberalisation have long been uncertain. The position set out in the sector-specific regulation has reached maturity. Some time has however been needed before that stage has been attained. The difficulty was that it was not clear how it would be possible to reconcile the necessity of introducing competition with the desire to maintain public policy objectives in a sector long considered fundamental for social cohesion. It should be borne in mind that telecommunications were, prior to the reform, considered as part of the body of 'public services' in all Member States. Telecommunications were thus not left to private undertakings, but taken over by public authorities. As a corollary, activities were subject to specific rules. Entities responsible for telecommunications were granted protection from the forces of competition, and in return were required to fulfil obligations relating to a variety of policy objectives.

5.250 **Two systems possible.**   There was some debate as to how these public policy objectives could be attained in a competitive environment. The provisions adopted in the Terminal Equipment Liberalisation Directive and the Services Directive show that the Commission hesitated long between two systems in order to implement these objectives. In both systems, a key role was played by the Member States within a framework established at European level. *(a)* The first system was to entrust one or several undertakings with the provision of universal service. These undertakings would be designated by the Member States. They would be set objectives and would be required to do whatever was necessary to fulfil these goals. This system is in fact the one that seems to have been chosen in the harmonisation directives adopted by the Parliament and Council. *(b)* The second system was to impose obligations on all undertakings present in a given market where public service objectives were to be attained. These obligations would be imposed by the Member States, using national regulatory tools for the purpose. One possibility for Member States to impose these objectives would have been to insert them in a legislative or regulatory instrument. Another would have been to insert conditions in the authorisations generally required from undertakings before they start their activities on the national territories.

5.251 **Designate undertakings.**   The first possibility entailed the risk that, under cover of the need to provide universal service, exceptions to the reform would be re-introduced by Member States. In that system, some undertakings would be granted exclusive rights to provide certain services. A situation similar to that which the reform sought to eliminate would then be re-created. Admittedly the scope of the services concerned would be more limited.[210] One should however not forget that Member States are granted a significant role in the organisation of universal service. Not only may they choose the methods to achieve the goals set in this context at European level, but in addition to this, they may set supplementary goals on their territory where they consider this is necessary for cohesion in society at national level. The fear was thus that Member States—or at least some of them—would use the concept of universal service as an excuse to revert to the previous system by setting high-level objectives and deciding that substantial derogations were necessary to attain them.

No choice made by the Commission.   No real choice appears to have been made   **5.252** by the Commission between the possibilities opened for the realisation of the policy objectives set out. To a certain extent the two options coexist in the Terminal Equipment Liberalisation Directive and the Services Directive. On the one hand, the Commission accepted in these directives that one or several undertakings—in most cases the incumbent—could be designated to provide universal service. From that perspective, the Commission further acknowledged the possibility of creating a financing mechanism to compensate extra costs allegedly borne by these undertakings. On the other hand, the Commission also envisaged in the Services Directive the possibility for Member States to impose obligations on all undertakings present on markets where universal service items are to be provided. In that scenario, the obligations were not limited to undertakings that would be designated to provide specific items. They were extended to all businesses likely to enter markets where public service objectives could be fulfilled.

Imposition of obligations.   We have examined at length how the first system has   **5.253** been implemented in the NRF and how it is also regulated in the Consolidated Services Directive. No more needs to be said in this regard. On the other hand, it may be useful to provide examples of what the Commission intended with the second system. These may be found in the Services Directive. Article 3 of that Directive,[211] for instance, provided that Member States could impose obligations to be fulfilled by undertakings wishing to obtain a licence to carry out an activity. These obligations could even be imposed on undertakings where no licence was necessary, but where a mere declaration was required to commence activity. They could be introduced in relation to voice telephony and/or the provision of public telecommunications networks. A similar provision was introduced in Article 3a of the same Services Directive. In both instances, the

---

[210] Prior to the reform, all telecommunications markets were organised in the form of a monopoly. By contrast, this monopolistic organisation would have been limited, under this 'new' system, to the items included in the universal service requirement.

[211] As amended by Directive 96/19.

obligations imposed were intended to ensure that essential requirements were complied with.[212] The purpose was also to ensure that the services concerned would be provided while respecting three important principles: quality, permanence and availability.

> *Mobile services.* '[L]icensing conditions must not contain conditions other than those justified on the grounds of the essential requirements and, in the case of systems for use by the general public, *public service requirements* in the form of trade regulation.'[213]

> *Voice telephony and public telecommunications networks.* 'As regards voice telephony and the provision of public telecommunications networks, Member States shall . . . notify to the Commission . . . any licensing or declaration procedure which is aimed at compliance with: essential requirements, or trade regulations relating to conditions of permanence, availability and quality of the service, or financial obligations with regard to universal service . . . The whole of these conditions shall form a set of *public-service specifications.*'[214]

5.254 **Coexistence of both possibilities.** The two systems envisaged by the Commission for the provision of the universal service have been taken over in the harmonisation framework. We have seen that the Universal Service Directive grants Member States a significant margin of manoeuvre in choosing the method they consider best to achieve the universal service objectives on their territory. Among these methods are the possibility of imposing obligations, for instance the obligation to fix prices below a ceiling (price caps). Another is to designate undertakings to provide services that would not otherwise be provided. From this harmonisation framework emerges a certain organisation of the methods likely to be chosen by the Member States. Where a universal service item is not provided, undertakings have to be designated. Where the item is provided but conditions are not satisfactory, obligations may be imposed on providers.

5.255 **Second communication.** This coexistence is acknowledged in the Second Communication on Services of General Interest adopted by the Commission in 2001. Pursuant to that communication, services of general interest may be provided through the imposition of public service obligations on all market participants. Another possibility is to designate undertakings which are subject to special obligations in exchange for which compensation may be granted. In all cases, the European rules must be respected regarding the objectives that are pursued and the means that are used in order to implement them.

> *Commission Communication.* 'Public authorities may decide to apply general interest obligations on all operators in a market or, in some cases, to designate one or a limited number of operators with specific obligations, without granting special or exclusive rights.' 'Where only one or a limited number of all operators competing

---

[212] This concept has been examined in Chapter 2.
[213] Services Directive, Art 3a introduced by Directive 96/2. Authors' emphasis.
[214] ibid, Art 3, as amended by Directive 96/19. Authors' emphasis.

in a certain market are charged with public service obligations while the others are not, it may be appropriate to involve all operators active in that market in the financing of the net extra costs of the service of general interest.'[215]

Market entry. In general terms, the directives adopted by the Parliament and   **5.256**
Council have been rather systematic in organising universal service. By contrast, the liberalisation directives have been more schematic. In these latter directives, the Commission has refrained from intervening in a manner that could have been deemed excessive. Its main focus has been on establishing competition-related constraints to be respected whatever the system chosen. A particular concern was to ensure that universal service could not be used to re-establish a sort of monopolistic system where exclusive rights would be reintroduced. Barriers to entry were to be specifically avoided. The Commission could not accept that undertakings might be deterred from entering electronic communications markets as a result of burdens imposed in the name of universal service.

Communication from the Commission. This concern clearly appears in   **5.257**
the Communication on the Costing and Financing of the Universal Service. In that Communication the Commission lists the policy aims that must be implemented as regards the European universal service. Among these aims, the first is to minimise barriers to entry so as not to impair or undermine the goals pursued in the reform.

> *Commission Communication.* 'National schemes for financing of the universal service should be consistent with certain basic policy aims at a European level. Such schemes must, as far as possible . . . minimise market entry barriers.'[216]

K. The Contribution of General Competition Law

(1) Least disruption and fewest exceptions to competition rules

Until now. Until now, attention has been concentrated on the regime applic-   **5.258**
able to the universal service as part of EC secondary law. We have concentrated on the choices made by the Parliament and Council in establishing common rules as regards access to fundamental electronic communications. These rules are integrated in the harmonisation framework. It was submitted that this framework is based on the principle that Member States should distort markets as little as possible when establishing systems for the provision of universal service. Similar emphasis has been placed on the same principle by the Commission in the

---

[215] Commission Communication (EC) 2001/C17/04 on services of general interest in Europe [2001] OJ C17/4, para 15. See also the Commission Communication (EC) 96/C281/03 on services of general interest in Europe [1996] OJ C281/3, paras 30 and 31.
[216] Communication from the Commission on the Costing and Financing of the Universal Service, para 2.2.

liberalisation directives. These last directives were adopted in order to put an end to an era where telecommunications were distanced from market forces. In adopting the liberalisation directives, the Commission sought to restore these forces as the main actors on the markets. This did not mean that public policy objectives could no longer be defined or implemented. The change was, however, that the tools to be chosen to achieve these objectives were to be found primarily in market forces.

5.259 **Typical process.** Pursuant to the philosophy underlying the reform, market forces are expected to produce the best economic outcome in normal circumstances. Other tools may be used where this outcome does not achieve universal service objectives. The Member States have a certain liberty to choose these tools as they see fit. They must however conform to the rules of the Treaty, including the competition rules. We have seen that several methods could be used to fulfil these goals. These methods were already envisaged in the liberalisation directives and have been taken over in the harmonisation framework. One of these methods is to impose obligations on undertakings active on a market concerned by universal service objectives. For instance, undertakings active on the market for voice telephony may be compelled to respect price caps. A second possibility is to identify services that are not provided subject to satisfactory conditions. One or several undertakings are then designated to provide these services. The losses incurred in the course of these activities may be compensated with public funds or funds transferred through a sharing mechanism.

5.260 **No derogation from the competition rules.** None of the possibilities envisaged in the previous paragraph can be considered as a derogation from the competition rules. We have analysed under general competition law the possibility of granting public funds to compensate universal service obligations. Our observation was that these funds cannot be considered State aids, as no real advantage is conferred upon the undertakings. The funds merely compensate extra obligations and in fact restore competition with other undertakings that are not subject to the same obligation. The same conclusion goes for the second mechanism envisaged to ensure the performance of universal service obligations. This second mechanism—sharing schemes—also does not in itself imply any exception to the competition rules. Imposing on undertakings the payment of contributions may not be analysed as a derogation, any more than the imposition of obligations of any other nature.

5.261 **Least distortion and derogation from the competition rules.** However, one cannot say that no common feature can be found in the principle that distortions to market forces must always be the least possible and that in some instances derogations may be granted from the application of the competition rules. In fact these two ideas have points in common. There is in both cases a certain emphasis on market forces. The principle of least derogation means that public intervention must be reduced to a minimum; market forces must be granted a priority. The idea that derogations to competition rules are necessary in some instances means that competition rules must apply in principle but the application of these rules may be set aside in given circumstances by public authorities. Both ideas refer to the possibility, for Member States, of intervening, and suggest that such intervention must come only in the second instance, where it appears that means more in conformity with the market force priority may not be used with the same efficacy.[217]

Differences between the two ideas.   The features in common between the two   **5.262** ideas do not take away an essential difference that separates them. Take measures which conform to the principle of least distortion. Some of these measures may infringe competition rules. In such a case, legality can be respected only if a derogation is granted as regards the application of these rules.[218] In other instances, the measures adopted to ensure the realisation of universal service objectives conform to the principle of least restriction and do not indeed infringe competition rules. That is in fact the situation for the measures envisaged in the European regulatory framework concerning the implementation of universal service. This framework allows Member States to take measures in order to ensure the realisation of policy objectives. A range of possibilities is opened to them from which they can make a selection—using one or several possibilities in combination. All these possibilities conform to the principle of least distortion. None of them, however, conflicts with competition rules.

Universal service may imply that disruptive measures are adopted in order to ensure the realisation of the public policy objectives that are associated with it. However disruptive they may be, these measures will not necessarily conflict with competition rules so that a derogation should be granted to restore legality.

---

[217] Least distortion of and derogation from competition rules indeed have a second point in common. As we will see, the principle of least distortion intervenes where derogations are decided in regard to competition rules. In our debate, these derogations are based on Art 86 EC. One of the rules to be complied with in that context is proportionality. Pursuant to proportionality, derogations may be introduced only where no other means are available to achieve the result while hindering competition to a lesser extent. This formulation is close, and probably even identical, to the requirement associated with least distortion. In both cases, one may not disrupt markets where another, less disruptive method, may be used.

[218] Suppose a Member State wants to ensure free education for all at all ages and for all degrees within its national society. This Member State considers that the best way to ensure the realisation of this objective is to concentrate demand on a single undertaking, which is as a result entrusted with the task of organising education on the whole national market. This measure may be deemed least restrictive, because we do not see how this result could otherwise be achieved. It conflicts however with competition rules, as these rules are nowadays interpreted as prohibiting exclusive rights. A derogation may however be granted and this derogation will indeed be necessary if legality is to be respected. (In the absence of such derogation, the organisation of education will infringe the prohibition of exclusive rights contained in competition rules.)

5.263 **Universal service, services of general interest.** This idea may appear complex but is important to explain the difference between two concepts that are often erroneously associated in the literature concerning electronic communications— universal service and services of general interest. In our context (electronic communications), the first concept ('universal service') refers to a set of public objectives to be achieved across Europe in connection with the availability of fundamental services for all. The second concept ('services of general interest') has a more technical scope: it refers to a method that can be used in order to make possible the fulfilment of public policy objectives (derogation from competition rules).

5.264 **No synonyms.** The two concepts are often used as synonyms as there is a sort of intuition that a similar reality lies behind them. Again, the intuition cannot simply be set aside, as the two concepts indeed have something in common. This is that universal service and services of general interest refer to situations that, in some respects, appear as exceptions to normal commercial, or competitive, conditions. The two concepts must however be differentiated. As stated above, the universal service regime adopted at European level in electronic communications does not contain, or imply, in itself, any derogation from competition rules. One thus has to conclude that universal service cannot necessarily be considered as a service of general interest in the light of Article 86 EC.

(2) Article 86 EC

5.265 **A principle and a derogation.** We have already encountered Article 86 EC several times in the course of previous sections and chapters. As observed, this provision is made up of three paragraphs. Only the first two have relevance here. In application of the first paragraph, Member States must comply with competition rules[219] as regards public undertakings or undertakings to which they grant special or exclusive rights. A derogation may be granted pursuant to the second paragraph where an undertaking is entrusted with the performance of a service of general economic interest.[220]

> *Article 86 EC.* [1] 'In the case of public undertakings or undertakings to which Member States grant special or exclusive rights, Member States shall neither enact nor maintain in force any measures contrary to the rules contained in this Treaty, in particular to those rules provided for in . . . Articles 81 to 89.' [2] 'Undertakings entrusted with the operation of services of general economic interest or having the character of a revenue-producing monopoly shall be subject to the rules contained in

---

[219] Art 86 EC refers in general to all European rules, 'in particular' those concerning competition. In this section, we concentrate on competition rules.

[220] The third paragraph has an institutional character, as a mission is granted to the Commission to make sure the rules presented above are applied. This paragraph is not relevant here and has already been addressed in previous chapters (see paras 1.101–1.102).

this Treaty, in particular to the rules on competition, insofar as the application of such rules does not obstruct the performance, in law or in fact, of the particular tasks assigned to them. The development of trade must not be affected to such an extent as would be contrary to the interests of the Community.'

A derogation from the competition rules.   We are particularly interested in our   **5.266** current discussion in Article 86(2) EC, and more specifically in the derogation that undertakings may obtain regarding the application of competition law. Pursuant to this provision, several conditions must be fulfilled for the derogation to be granted. These conditions are mentioned in the provision itself and have been further construed in the case law. *(a) Condition 1.* The service must qualify as a service of general economic interest under Article 86 EC. *(b) Condition 2.* A mission regarding a service of that nature must be explicitly granted to the undertaking though an official document coming from a national authority. *(c) Condition 3.* Proportionality must be respected. This entails a test in three parts. First, the derogation must be useful: it must effectively contribute to the realisation of the objective that is sought. Second, it must be necessary: there may not exist any other measure which would be as effective for the realisation of the objective and would hinder competition to a lesser extent. Finally, the derogation cannot be excessive. This means that competition cannot be eliminated. A balance must be struck between the negative effect of the derogation on competition and the value of the objective that is sought through the derogation.

Issues examined in the next paragraphs.   The conditions laid down in   **5.267** Article 86(2) EC have given rise to several issues that have been discussed at length in the case law. These issues mainly concern *condition 3*. The purpose is to determine in what material circumstances a derogation may be granted. We will not spend much time discussing *condition 2*, which does not raise specific difficulties in our context. In a case concerning Article 86 EC, the party concerned has to produce a document stating that a mission has been officially entrusted to the undertaking seeking a derogation. By contrast, *condition 1* will be examined in more depth. This condition is important, as it determines who has the competence to consider that an item qualifies as a service of general interest. Regarding proportionality (*condition 3*), the case law can be divided into two categories depending on the circumstances in which derogations have been upheld. These categories are analysed below. The first concerns scenarios where one market only is involved. The question is to determine whether a derogation from competition may be accepted on that market. The second category concerns scenarios where several markets are involved. One issue is to determine whether a derogation from competition may be accepted on one market in order to finance activities on another.

Exclusive rights.   Most cases concerning Article 86(2) EC in effect concern situ-   **5.268** ations where exclusive rights were granted to undertakings in return for the fulfilment of policy objectives. It is for that reason that Article 86(2) EC has played an important role in the argumentation developed by the Commission to justify the reform. In addition to raising arguments related to the internal market, the Commission in substance asserted that telecommunications monopolies violated competition rules without any reason being present to grant a derogation under Article 86(2) EC. The debate has then evolved in the direction of specific rules to be established at European level in order to administer the markets in the post-monopoly transitional period. The issue of exclusive rights however remained on the agenda as concerns other sectors, where the Commission did not have the resources to introduce a similar movement.

5.269 **The debate.** The fact that Article 86(2) EC cases concern exclusive rights indicates that the debate around services of general interest is not the same as that around universal service. Again, the underlying ideas are similar, as in both cases authorities seek to justify their intervention where market forces are expected to operate. The legal issues are, however, different. Universal service refers to a set of objectives defined at European level that must be implemented without derogation from the competition rules. Services of general interest are items selected by national authorities and the issue is to determine whether they can be implemented through a derogation from rules contained in the EC Treaty.

5.270 **Other situations where the provision applies.** As emphasised below, Article 86(2) EC is not limited to situations where exclusive rights have been granted. This provision has general scope and may apply in all circumstances where a provision under the competition rules, or under any other European rule, would normally lead to a prohibition. As a result of the derogation, the prohibition is then suspended. The mechanism can be illustrated with an example taken from the treatment given to exclusive rights. As stated, these rights are considered under that provision in combination with Article 82 EC, where their compatibility with competition rules is examined. That article prohibits abusive conduct by dominant undertakings. It applies to exclusive rights because the holders of such privileges have a dominant position by definition. It is thought that they will necessarily abuse that position through, for instance, fixing excessive prices, or limiting output. The abuse is, however, excused as a result of the application of Article 86(2) EC, which has the effect of suspending the application of the prohibition contained in Article 82 EC.

5.271 **All EC provisions.** The mechanism may be used with all competition law-based prohibitions, and indeed with all European law provisions, as Article 86(2) EC is not limited to competition rules. Thus, advantages that would be prohibited under Article 87 EC may be authorised as a result of the suspension of the prohibition, where the advantage is considered under Article 86(2) EC and it is demonstrated that the conditions are fulfilled for the derogation to be granted. Similarly, cartels that are normally prohibited may be justified on the basis of Article 86(2) EC even though the conditions for the application of the 'normal' derogations for cartels (Article 81(3) EC) are not fulfilled. A further example is mergers that should normally be prohibited because they create a threat to competition but that may be authorised on the basis of that same provision where the conditions are fulfilled.

(3) One market involved ('concentration-of-demand theory')

One market involved.   Although Article 86(2) EC may be applied in connec-   **5.272** tion with all competition law provisions, the vast majority of cases involving that provision concern exclusive rights. In a first scenario, attention is focused on one market.[221] The leading case concerned here is *Affalds*,[222] where an exclusive right[223] was granted to three undertakings for the treatment of non-dangerous waste in a Danish municipality. This right was challenged by a newcomer willing to enter the market. The issue was whether a derogation could be justified under Article 86(2) EC. If the derogation was justified then these undertakings would be allowed to retain their exclusive right. In the absence of justification they would have to renounce it and possibly repair the consequences that flowed from the existence of an illegal market organisation over several years. The debate before the ECJ focused on whether the exclusive right could be found compatible with the principle of proportionality.

Useful measure test.   This principle, it has been submitted, encompasses three   **5.273** tests that are examined below. First, the ECJ investigated whether the measure can be considered useful to the realisation of the objective sought. The answer was positive on that account. The ECJ noted that the regulation was intended to solve a serious environmental problem. Building-waste had been buried where it could have been recycled. Recycling was however impossible. No undertakings were apparently willing to enter the market, given the size of the investments required and the uncertainty as to the capacity of users to change behaviour (recycle waste and not dump it). Undertakings were nonetheless willing to commit themselves to the extent that they were assured a sufficient flow of waste. This condition was realised by concentrating demand on a few participants. The market was thus reserved for three undertakings, the only ones authorised to treat waste on the territory concerned (concentration of demand).

---

[221] We are thus not concerned with a situation where two or more activities are concerned and with issues related to a transfer of funds between them. In our situation, there is one undertaking with an exclusive right over a given activity and the issue is to determine whether that exclusive right can be authorised on the basis of Art 86(2) EC.

[222] Case C-209/98 *Entreprenørforeningens Affalds/Miljøsektion (FFAD) v Københavns Kommune* [2000] ECR I-3743.

[223] These undertakings were the only ones allowed on the relevant market. Although they were several, the ECJ used the expression 'exclusive rights'.

Affalds. [78] '[W]hen the [waste handling] centre was set up and an exclusive right was granted to a limited number of undertakings, the Municipality . . . was faced with . . . a serious environmental problem, namely the burial of most building waste in the ground when it could have been recycled. Recycling was impossible owing to the lack of undertakings capable of processing the waste. In order to deal with the volumes of waste produced in the municipality and to ensure that it was recycled to a high standard, the municipality considered it necessary to set up a high-capacity centre; and, in order to ensure that this newly-established centre would be profitable, the municipality considered it necessary to ensure that the centre was guaranteed a significant flow of waste by granting it an exclusive processing right.' [79] 'Admittedly, that exclusive right had the effect of excluding even qualified undertakings wishing to enter the market . . . In the absence of undertakings capable of processing the waste at issue in the main proceedings, however, the Municipality . . . considered it necessary to set up a high-capacity centre. Furthermore, in order to ensure that undertakings would be interested in participating in the operation of a high-capacity centre, it was also considered necessary to grant an exclusive right, limited in time to the period over which the investments could foreseeably be written off and in space to the land within the boundaries of the municipality.'

5.274   **Necessary measure test.**   For the ECJ, no other measure could be enacted to ensure the realisation of the goal sought. A challenger had contended that the same result would have been obtained through imposing on users an obligation to recycle. In a system of that kind, undertakings would have remained free to organise their offer as they wished. Thus competition would not have been impaired while the objective of protecting the environment would have been attained. The argument was dismissed by the ECJ. For the ECJ, an obligation to recycle would not have solved the problem. The investments necessary to start the activity were indeed very high. There was no guarantee for investors that demand would be sufficient to amortise their assets, were the market left to competition. It could thus be expected that in a competitive environment, undertakings would not necessarily have put in the required investments.

> *Affalds.* 'A measure having a less restrictive effect on competition, such as rules which merely required undertakings to have their waste recycled, would not necessarily have ensured that most of the waste produced in the municipality would be recycled, precisely because there was not sufficient capacity to process that waste.'[224]

5.275   **Non-excessive effect test.**   The ECJ did not explicitly examine whether the measure adopted by the municipality was excessive or not, as regards effects on competition. Elements can, however, be found in the judgment to attempt our own analysis on this point. An essential element in this regard is that, although competition was admittedly impaired, the distortion seems to have been limited to a minimum. The municipality took three measures to that effect. First, several participants were allowed on the markets. From this it can be concluded that the municipality

---

[224] At [80].

did not unduly limit the number of participants. Second, there was nothing to show that discrimination had been applied at the time the privilege was granted.[225] Third, the exclusion was restricted geographically and in time; it was granted for a limited period and only concerned one municipality (Copenhagen).[226]

Echo in the Communication on services of general interest.   The analysis by **5.276** the ECJ regarding the concentration of demand is similar to that carried out by the Commission in the communications concerning services of general interest. In these communications the Commission stresses that some services of general interest cannot be provided by a plurality of market participants. The solution is, then, to concentrate demand on one provider. In that situation, competition is not totally excluded to the extent that the provider is selected in a procedure where no candidate is excluded and all are given a fair chance.

> *Commission Communication.* '[C]ertain services of general interest do not lend themselves to a plurality of providers, for instance where only one single provider can be economically viable. In these circumstances, public authorities will usually grant exclusive and special rights for providing the service of general interest by awarding concessions for limited periods through tendering procedures. Competition at the moment of the award of the tender is meant to ensure that the missions assigned to a service of general interest are met at low cost to the public.'[227]

(4) Two or more markets involved ('compensation theory')

Several markets involved.   The case law relating to Article 86(2) EC addresses a **5.277** second scenario, where several markets are involved. This scenario is in fact related to the first examined earlier, and can be said to be complementary. In order to understand this relationship, a situation must be imagined where a public authority wants to realise a policy objective, for example, protect the environment or establish a public electronic communications network. Implementing this objective requires funds which, the authority in question argues,[228] cannot be found in a competitive environment. An exclusive right is then granted to one or several

---

[225]   The judgment does not contain any data to examine this aspect. The three undertakings were authorised to handle waste. The operations took place in a high-capacity installation, which was financed by one company ('RGS'). This latter company was founded by several shareholders— themselves waste-handling companies. RGS was one of the undertakings authorised to treat waste. All treatment operations took place in that installation, even where it was performed by companies other than RGS. The capital of RGS was opened to all interested private or public parties when the undertaking was founded to bring about investment for the high-capacity installation.

[226]   Although one municipality only was concerned, European law was affected for several reasons. One was that the quantity of waste produced and treated in that municipality constituted a substantial share of the national market.

[227]   Commission Communication (EC) 2001/C17/04 on services of general interest in Europe [2001] OJ C17/4, para 17.

[228]   And generally also by the undertaking(s) receiving the exclusive right as a result of that situation.

undertakings. As in *Affalds*, the strategy is to concentrate demand on a few undertakings. Costs should then be easier to amortise. In this scenario it however turns out that this measure is not sufficient. Revenues obtained on the relevant market are not high enough to reach economic equilibrium. A second measure must then be taken. Among the available options, the authority decides to extend the exclusive right to another, more lucrative, market. The hope is that, as it is protected from competition, the undertaking will obtain high revenues on this second market, which will be used to compensate losses on the first market.

5.278 **Who is happy with this market organisation?** The first market, it is expected, will not attract many candidates. The activity performed on that market is indeed not deemed to be profitable. The result is that undertakings, which normally seek profits, will not be tempted to enter.[229] By contrast, the second market attracts more attention. As it is said to be lucrative, it appeals to candidates which, as they try to enter the market, find themselves excluded as a result of the exclusive right. Consumers are also frustrated on the second market, as they pay there sums in excess of what is needed to purchase the relevant goods and services. The reason is that part of the price they pay is used to sponsor goods or services on another market, in which they possibly have no interest whatsoever. In fact, the only satisfied party is probably the monopoly which gets higher revenues and more scope for action.[230]

5.279 **Leading case.** *Corbeau* is the leading case as regards derogations for the creation of a monopoly on a second market to finance activities on a first market where a monopoly has already been granted.[231] The case concerns the Belgian legislation regarding postal services, which conferred on the Régie des Postes[232] an exclusive right to collect, carry and distribute throughout the national territory all correspondence of whatever nature. This exclusive right was infringed by Mr Corbeau, who provided, within the city of Liège and the surrounding areas, a service

---

[229] The only possibility of making a profit on that market would be to organise operations better in the hope of lowering costs and attaining economic equilibrium. Another possibility would be to request the authorities to reduce their policy expectations for the market. Public service obligations are then lowered and with them, the costs of exercising the activity. These two options rarely materialise, however. The authority generally hold to their intention of implementing their objectives. Links are in addition very strong with the monopolist, so that the authorities rarely envisage opening the market in the hope that a more efficient undertaking will appear.

[230] Are consumers happy on the first market? On that market, they receive goods and services for a price lower than the real cost. The cost of providing goods and services on the first market is partially covered by revenues from the second market. Consumers on the first market thus pay a price that is lower than the cost incurred to provide the goods or services. However, activities are performed on this first market under conditions which derogate from competition. It is not certain that this system ultimately brings the best products at the lowest price.

[231] Case C-320/91 *Corbeau* [1993] ECR I-2533. We have previously encountered this case with respect to the legality of exclusive rights. As regards this issue, we have stated that *Corbeau* was important because the ECJ confirms in that judgment that exclusive rights are illegal per se.

[232] A legal person under public law.

consisting in collecting mail from the address of the sender and distributing it by noon on the following day, provided that the addressee was located within the district concerned. As regards correspondence to addressees outside that district, Mr Corbeau collected it from the sender's address and sent it by post.

As a general remark, it cannot be denied that public service obligations are imposed in most European countries as regards postal services. These obligations generally imply that market participants must collect, carry and distribute mail on behalf of all users throughout the national territory at uniform tariffs and subject to similar quality conditions, irrespective of the degree of economic profitability of each individual operation. All operations must thus be performed under equal conditions[233] without consideration for the differences in the costs incurred.[234]

The judgment. In its judgment the ECJ addresses the conditions to be fulfilled **5.280** in order for a derogation to be granted under Article 86(2) EC. Our attention will again concentrate on the third condition, which concerns the circumstances in which an exclusive right may be deemed compatible with the principle of proportionality. Three passages are important in the judgment, as regards this aspect.

> *Corbeau.* 'The starting point . . . must be the premise that the obligation on the part of the undertaking entrusted with that task [of general economic interest] to perform its services in conditions of economic equilibrium presupposes that it will be possible to offset less profitable sectors against the profitable sectors and hence justifies a restriction of competition from individual undertakings where the economically profitable sectors are concerned.'[235] 'However, the exclusion of competition is not justified as regards specific services dissociable from the service of general interest which meet special needs of economic operators and which call for certain additional services not offered by the traditional postal service, such as collection from the senders' address, greater speed or reliability of distribution or the possibility of changing the destination in the course of transit.'[236] '[Ultimately] the exclusion of competition is . . . justified . . . in so far as such specific services, by their nature and the conditions in which they are offered, such as the geographical area in which they are provided, do . . . compromise the economic equilibrium of the service of general economic interest performed by the holder of the exclusive right.'[237]

---

[233] The costs are not identical, for instance, where the mail is distributed in a city or in a remote mountainous area. This difference may however not be reflected in the prices charged to users.

[234] The activity falling under this obligation only relates to the basic, traditional and ordinary postal service. The obligation to collect, carry and distribute mail under equal conditions does not apply to all postal activities. The purpose of public service obligations in that sector is to ensure that a minimum service is made available to all citizens whatever their location and status. It is not to transform altogether the conditions for the performance of activities in the whole sector.

[235] At [17].   [236] At [19], first part of the sentence.

[237] At [19], second part of the sentence. The sentence originally read: 'the exclusion of competition is not justified . . . in so far as such specific services . . . do not compromise the economic equilibrium.' The presence of a double negative makes it difficult, however, to understand the position of the ECJ. For that reason, we have opted for a reformulation where the double negative is replaced by an affirmative.

5.281 **Three ideas.** These various passages each contain an idea as to the circumstances in which a derogation might be found to be proportional. *(a)* The first is that a compensation mechanism may be operated in certain circumstances between various markets, whereby a transfer of revenues is organised from a lucrative market to a less profitable activity.[238] For the ECJ, such a transfer may be justified where, in the absence of such a mechanism, economic equilibrium would not be reached on the first market. *(b)* The second is that compensation should not be admitted where 'specific' and 'dissociable' markets are concerned. This apparently means that the second markets are very different from the one where the public service obligation is imposed. The difference, the ECJ suggests, is so important that one could not justify using these markets as compensation tools. *(c)* The final idea is that, all things taken into account, a compensation mechanism involving 'specific' and 'dissociable' markets should ultimately be accepted where economic equilibrium on the first market so requires.

5.282 **Analysis.** These various ideas are set out in the table below in order to analyse their implications. As can be seen, the reasoning developed by the ECJ cannot be deemed entirely consistent. The ECJ starts by allowing compensation. It then imposes a limitation, stating that compensation should not be allowed where it comes to specific and dissociable services. In the last step, it goes back to the initial position and states that a compensation mechanism must finally be accepted in all situations.[239]

Compensation allowed	Compensation *not* allowed
(a) Where required by economic equilibrium	(b) For specific and dissociable services
(c) Even for specific, dissociable services	

5.283 **Evaluation.** The position adopted by the ECJ may be criticised, not least regarding the inconsistency of finally accepting a position earlier rejected in the same judgment. Paragraph 17 starts from the premise that the undertaking entrusted with a service of general economic interest has an obligation to perform this service in conditions of economic equilibrium. It should however be borne in mind that the economic equilibrium obligation is imposed by a national authority. This authority is in fact the body which sets the public service objectives, imposes them, states that economic balance must be reached, does not provide funds to finance them, and establishes a monopoly to reach the balance. The situation in which the undertaking is placed in fact derives from a national public intervention. In accepting that compensation can take place between markets,

---

[238] This implies that the position of the undertaking must be protected on the second market (monopoly). Suppose no protection is granted: the undertaking will not be in a position to charge high tariffs. [239] Even where specific and dissociable services are involved.

and thus granting a derogation as regards competition law, the ECJ in effect acknowledges that the application of competition at European level can be made dependent upon decisions taken by national authorities.[240]

Economic equilibrium. More generally, *Corbeau* states that compensation must be accepted where economic equilibrium so requires. The difficulty is that economic equilibrium is relative, where it comes to one undertaking. In many circumstances monopolies are not profitable because they are not managed adequately. Drawing an argument from the lack of profitability provides an incentive to be as inefficient as possible.[241] The case law ultimately grants to the undertaking itself the tool which can be used to claim the benefit provided by Article 86(2) EC.[242]   **5.284**

(5) Who decides where an item qualifies as a service of general interest?

Back to condition 1. In the cases examined above, the ECJ concentrated on the compatibility of the national legislation with the principle of proportionality (*condition 3* above). As stated, other conditions must be fulfilled for a derogation to be granted. An important one is whether an item falls within the category of service of general interest (*condition 1* above). This condition is a key strategic issue. Suppose the decision is granted to the European institutions—for instance the Commission. The margin left to Member States will be limited. By contrast, any power granted to Member States to decide whether an item qualifies for an Article 86(2) EC derogation implies that they have a substantial margin of manoeuvre in determining how entire sectors of the economy may be organised.   **5.285**

Case law. In application of the principle of subsidiarity, the ECJ has decided that the power to consider that an item qualifies as a service of general interest belongs to the Member States. This was stated in *France v Commission*, where several Member States challenged the validity of the Terminal Equipment Liberalisation Directive and more generally the powers of the Commission to   **5.286**

---

[240] This does not appear to be in line with the principle that European law should never depend on national rules as to its scope of application. Such a principle can be found across the case law. Illustrations may be taken in Art 226 EC actions: Member States are not allowed to invoke internal problems to escape the application of European rules. Other examples can be found in Art 230 EC actions: the ECJ does not accept that the admissibility of actions by individuals be made dependent upon the possibility of obtaining a remedy at national level (Case C-50/00 P *Unión de Pequeños Agricultores v Council of the European Union* [2002] ECR I-6677). The case law on State aids also provides examples: the application of national rules may not be claimed in order to avoid an obligation to reimburse an aid that has not been notified and/or authorised.

[241] Monopolies are only granted to undertakings that claim not to be profitable.

[242] In that respect, the situation created by the European case law appears even worse than appeared from the previous paragraph, where we have seen that national authorities could decide where the derogation would be granted, as it is they who impose the public service obligations. As appeared from the new critique, the case law goes further by making European law provisions dependent upon the goodwill of a national undertaking.

adopt general instruments on the basis of Article 86 EC. The ECJ interpreted that provision as allowing Member States to pursue national policies. These policies could not, however, conflict with European competition policy. The purpose of Article 86(2) EC was to organise a procedure where policies decided by Member States would be checked against constraints derived from competition law. The same position was reasserted in three cases concerning monopolies entrusted with the production and distribution of energy (gas and/or electricity) on national territories. In these judgments, the ECJ stressed that Member States have a right to define services of general interest on the basis of national objectives. It went further in stating that this entailed for the Member States a right to determine in principle what legal regime is appropriate to attain these objectives.

> *France v Commission (Telecommunications).* 'In allowing derogations to be made from the general rules of the Treaty on certain conditions, that provision [Article 86 EC] seeks to reconcile the Member States' interest in using certain undertakings, in particular in the public sector, as an instrument of economic or fiscal policy with the Community's interest in ensuring compliance with the rules on competition and the preservation of the unity of the Common Market.'[243]

> *Commission v Netherlands (Energy).* 'The Member States' interest being so defined, they cannot be precluded, when defining the services of general economic interest which they entrust to certain undertakings, from taking account of objectives pertaining to their national policy or from endeavouring to attain them by means of obligations and constraints which they impose on such undertakings.'[244]

5.287 **Echo in the communications issued by the Commission.** This liberty given to the Member State is also emphasised in the two communications issued by the Commission concerning services of general interest. According to these communications the Member States have the power to make fundamental choices concerning their society. In that context it is up to them to decide whether certain policy objectives are to be pursued. The power of the European institutions is limited to ensuring that European rules are not infringed in the implementation of those objectives.

> *Second Communication on services of general interest (2001).* 'Member States are primarily responsible for defining what they regard as services of general economic interest . . . This definition can only be subject to control for manifest error.'[245]
> *First Communication on services of general interest (1996).* 'The Community's commitment to the European model of society is based on respect for the diversity of the organization of general interest services in Europe.'[246] 'Member States . . . [are free] to define what are general interest services.'[247] 'Respect for national choice over

---

[243] Case C-202/88 *France v Commission* [1991] ECR I-1223 at [12]. The same paragraph appears in Case C-157/94 *Commission v Netherlands* [1997] ECR I-5699 at [39].

[244] Case C-157/94 *Commission v Netherlands* [1997] ECR I-5699 at [40].

[245] Commission Communication (EC) 2001/C17/04 on services of general interest in Europe [2001] OJ C17/4, at para 22.

[246] Commission Communication (EC) 96/C281/03 on services of general interest in Europe [1996] OJ C281/3, para 16.   [247] ibid.

economic and social organization is a clear example of subsidiarity in action. It is for the Member States to make the fundamental choices concerning their society, whereas the job of the Community is merely to ensure that the means they employ are compatible with their European commitments.'[248]

Less power than suggested.   The power granted to the Member States seems **5.288** more limited than suggested in the case law and in the communications. The ECJ admittedly stresses the national responsibility for determining objectives to be attained. However, the ECJ verifies in all Article 86 EC cases whether the objective set by the Member States can be deemed compatible with European law.[249] The power of the Member States is thus asserted in principle but a check is carried out in practice whether national objectives correspond to European priorities.[250]

Pre-emption by European institutions.   A similar trend may be observed in the **5.289** adoption of legislation at European level. As stated, the power of the Member States to define policy objectives has been emphasised in the communications issued by the Commission concerning services of general interest. This power disappears, however, where the European legislator makes use of its prerogative to harmonise national legislation in the interests of the single market. In the harmonisation process the European legislator in effect unifies the policy objectives to be pursued in the areas concerned. The result is that Member States lose their powers

---

[248] ibid, para 17.

[249] A few examples may be given to illustrate the statement. See eg *Affalds*: 'The management of particular waste may properly be considered to be capable of forming the subject of a service of general economic interest, particularly where the service is designed to deal with an environmental problem' (at [75]). See also *Corbeau*: 'As regards the services at issue in the main proceedings, it cannot be disputed that the Régie des Postes is entrusted with a service of general economic interest consisting in the obligation to collect, carry and distribute mail on behalf of all users throughout the territory of the Member State concerned, at uniform tariffs and on similar quality conditions, irrespective of the specific situations or the degree of economic profitability of each individual operation.' See finally *Dusseldorp* (protection of the environment): 'Even if the task conferred on that undertaking could constitute a task of general economic interest, however, it is for the Netherlands Government, as the Advocate General points out at paragraph 108 of his Opinion, to show to the satisfaction of the national court that that objective cannot be achieved equally well by other means. Article . . . [86] (2) of the Treaty can thus apply only if it is shown that, without the contested measure, the undertaking in question would be unable to carry out the task assigned to it.' (Case C-203/96 *Chemische Afvalstoffen Dusseldorp v Minister van Volkshuisvesting, Ruimtelijke Ordening en Milieubeheer* [1998] ECR I-4075.)

[250] In that regard, Art 86 EC is not different from other European provisions concerning derogations Member States may seek. Internal market provisions provide a good example. In these provisions, the issue is whether national measures can be accepted despite the effect they may have on free movement. In cases concerning measures of that nature, a control is carried out by the ECJ. This control bears, in the first instance, on the objective that is sought via the measure. The purpose is then to verify whether this objective can be considered as acceptable under European law. The control also concerns the arrangements that are implemented by the Member States to reach the objective. In that context, the question is whether these arrangements are useful, necessary and proportionate.

to define policy independently. Admittedly they retain in most cases the possibility of adding obligations to those which have been defined at European level. However, their margin of manoeuvre is limited, as these objectives must normally be financed through public funds, which are always lacking. Furthermore, there exists a sort of regulatory competition among the Member States. Pursuant to that process, market participants generally choose the States where regulations are the most favourable. Any State adding obligations thus faces the risk that undertakings may create jobs elsewhere.

5.290 **Objectivity, proportionality.** In the case law as well as in the legislation, the control exercised by the European institution focuses on the objectives that are set by the Member States and the means that are used in order to implement those objectives. The verification of national objectives coincides with the control on objectivity. We have seen that objectivity is a fundamental requirement and that an obligation to respect requirements of this nature is pervasive throughout the NRF. The content of this requirement is no different from what is established in the Article 86 EC case law, where a derogation may be granted only where an objective can be found to be acceptable in European law. We have also examined the links between objectivity and the control carried out on proportionality. Proportionality implies an objective that can be deemed acceptable, as well as arrangements that conform to various tests. Examples of acceptable objectives may be found in the case law. Most of them are also expressed in legislation. This is particularly so for electronic communications, where the European institutions have spelled out in detail what they deem acceptable ('essential requirements').

(6) Burden of proof

5.291 **The principle.** The final issue is to determine who must demonstrate what in an Article 86(2) EC case. The question has been addressed by the ECJ in three judgments concerning energy distribution in France, the Netherlands and Italy.[251] Here again, consistency has unfortunately not always been achieved. In these judgements the ECJ ruled that the obligation to demonstrate that conditions are fulfilled normally rests with the Member States. Among these conditions is the principle of proportionality. In application of that principle, the Member States thus have to demonstrate that the objectives sought could not be reached by measures which are as efficient, but less burdensome.

---

[251] Case C-157/94 *Commission v Netherlands* [1997] ECR I-5699; Case C-158/94 *Commission v Italy* [1997] ECR I-5789; Case C-159/94 *Commission v France* [1997] ECR I-5815. A fourth procedure was directed against Spain, but was rejected because the Commission had not duly demonstrated the existence of the exclusive rights against which the application was directed. See Case C-160/94 *Commission v Spain* [1997] ECR I-5851.

Nuance. In these cases the ECJ however nuances its position. This is due to **5.292** the way the arguments were developed before it in the course of the procedure. Pursuant to the division of proof mentioned above, the Member States had explained why they considered exclusivity was necessary to ensure the fulfilment of the mission of general interest. In reply, the Commission had merely repeated a general, legal argumentation, without going into more detail about the technical justifications put forward by the Member States. For the ECJ, an argument of that nature was not sufficient. The ECJ repeats the principle that it is normally for Member States to establish that the conditions are satisfied under Article 86(2) EC. This does not imply, however, an obligation for them to demonstrate in detail that all other alternatives that can be thought of would not lead to a similar outcome or would result in a lesser burden for competition.

> *Commission v Netherlands.* 'Whilst it is true that it is incumbent upon a Member State which invokes Article [86(2) EC] . . . to demonstrate that the conditions laid down by that provision are met, that burden of proof cannot be so extensive as to require the Member State, when setting out in detail the reasons for which, in the event of elimination of the contested measures, the performance, under economically acceptable conditions, of the tasks of general economic interest which it has entrusted to an undertaking would, in its view, be jeopardized, to go even further and prove, positively, that no other conceivable measure, which by definition would be hypothetical, could enable those tasks to be performed under the same conditions.'[252]

Evaluation. That nuance does not question the general division of proof, as the **5.293** burden is clearly placed on the Member States in the first instance. The ECJ only made it clear that the obligation was not absolute and that the Commission could be forced in some circumstances to bring a more substantial contribution to the discussion. This is particularly so in cases where the Commission has the role of the applicant, and is thus the source of the action. In such a scenario, it may be expected from the Commission that it will contribute substantially to the demonstration. In this regard it must be noted that a position more favourable to the Commission has been developed in preliminary rulings. Thus the ECJ was confronted in *Dusseldorp*[253] with Dutch legislation reserving for one company the treatment of waste in a given geographic area. In its preliminary ruling the ECJ found that it was for the Member States to establish that no other means could be used to attain the objective. Pursuant to that judgment, the obligation for Member States to establish that all conditions are fulfilled to obtain an Article 86(2) EC derogation can thus be confirmed.

---

[252] At [58].
[253] Case C-203/96 *Chemische Afvalstoffen Dusseldorp v Minister van Volkshuisvesting, Ruimtelijke Ordening en Milieubeheer* [1998] ECR I-4075.

Dusseldorp. 'The Netherlands Government submits that the rules in question are intended to reduce the costs of the undertaking responsible for the incineration of dangerous waste and thus to enable it to be economically viable. Even if the task conferred on that undertaking could constitute a task of general economic interest, however, it is for the Netherlands Government . . . to show to the satisfaction of the national court that that objective cannot be achieved equally well by other means. Article [86(2) EC] of the Treaty can thus apply only if it is shown that, without the contested measure, the undertaking in question would be unable to carry out the task assigned to it.'[254]

5.294 **Difficulty for the Member States.** One should emphasise the uncomfortable position of the Member States in view of this burden imposed on them. It could indeed lead to a situation where they are never able to demonstrate that an alternative was possible. The allocation of obligations as regards proof has in fact a significant influence on the outcome of the case. As it is difficult to show that conditions are fulfilled, Member States may be put in a situation where they cannot successfully claim the benefit of a derogation.

5.295 **Substantiation of argument.** Is this a sufficient reason to question the position adopted by the ECJ? On the one hand, the position seems justified for the reason that Article 86(2) EC introduces a derogation and that it is normally for the party seeking the benefit of the derogation to demonstrate that the conditions are fulfilled. On the other hand, the burden imposed on Member States does not seem compatible with the principle that no one can in principle be required to prove a 'negative fact'. This principle implies, for instance, that parties are in normal circumstances not asked to establish that something has *not* happened. The obligation at stake in the energy distribution cases was not different, as the Member States were asked to demonstrate that no alternative existed. An obligation of that nature can hardly be satisfied, as it is easy for the other party to claim that one other measure could at least be envisaged. What the ECJ has done in the energy distribution cases is to impose on the party stating that an alternative exists an obligation to substantiate its argument. In the absence of such an obligation, the Member States would have been placed in a position where they can never obtain an Article 86(2) EC derogation.

(7) Growing complexity

5.296 **Concern for legal certainty.** In closing the subject it should be emphasised how complex the case law has grown as regards exclusive rights and services of general economic interest. This is why the discussion has been limited to clear cases. An illustration of that complexity, which gives rise to some concern regarding legal certainty, is set out below.

---

[254] At [66] and [67].

One illustration.   This case (*Glöckner*[255]) concerns the provision of emergency   **5.297**
transport for patients in a German province (Land). This activity had been
entrusted to four non-profit organisations. The exclusive right[256] was extended to
the adjacent market for non-emergency transport, as the organisations involved
claimed that this second market was more lucrative and would allow them to
bring in profits that could be used to compensate losses incurred on the first,
allegedly non-profitable, market. The case concerns this extension of the exclusive
right to the second market. In the judgment, the ECJ starts with classic reasoning.
The economic character of the activity is established. Then the question is raised
as to the compatibility of exclusive rights with European competition rules. In
conformity with previous case law, the ECJ rules that exclusive rights must normally be considered incompatible, but that a derogation may be sought where the
conditions laid down in Article 86(2) EC are fulfilled.[257]

Following *Corbeau*.   In assessing whether a derogation can be granted, the ECJ   **5.298**
follows the pattern established in *Corbeau*. Pursuant to that judgment, an exclusive right can be accepted on a second market in certain circumstances. The purpose must be to use revenues acquired on the second market in order to finance
losses incurred on the first as a result of special obligations. The second market
cannot concern services that are specific or dissociable from the main service at
issue. Even where this last condition is not fulfilled, an extension may be granted
where economic equilibrium so requires. In the case under consideration, the ECJ
ruled that these conditions were satisfied. The transport in question could not easily be divided depending on whether there was or not an emergency. Furthermore,
economic balance could not be reached on the emergency transport market if no
transfer could be made from the non-emergency market ('Compensation
Theory').

> *Glöckner*. [59] '[In] *Corbeau*, the Court held that the exclusion of competition is not
> justified in certain cases involving specific services, severable from the service of general
> interest in question, if those services do not compromise the economic equilibrium of
> the service of general economic interest performed by the holder of the exclusive rights.'
> [60] 'However, that is not the case with the two services now under consideration, for
> two reasons in particular. First, unlike the situation in *Corbeau*, the two types of service
> in question, traditionally assumed by the medical aid organisations, are so closely
> linked that it is difficult to sever the non-emergency transport services from the task of
> general economic interest constituted by the provision of the public ambulance service,

---

[255] Case 475/99 *Ambulanz Glöckner v Landkreis Sudwestpfalz* [2001] ECR I-8089.

[256] This expression is used in the judgment by the Court, although the right was granted to
several undertakings.

[257] This position is adopted on the basis of the case law analysed in Case C-179/90 *Merci
Convenzionali Porto di Genova SpA v Siderurgica Gabriella SpA* [1991] ECR I-5889 and Case
C-41/90 *Höfner & Else v Mactroton GmbH* [1991] ECR I-1979 (category 2 in the case concerning
exclusive rights).

with which they also have characteristics in common.' [61] 'Second, the extension of the medical aid organisations' exclusive rights to the non-emergency transport sector does indeed enable them to discharge their general-interest task of providing emergency transport in conditions of economic equilibrium. The possibility which would be open to private operators to concentrate, in the non-emergency sector, on more profitable journeys could affect the degree of economic viability of the service provided by the medical aid organisations and, consequently, jeopardise the quality and reliability of that service.'

5.299   **New position.**   Then comes a remark from the ECJ that has led some observers to doubt that it has understood the logic behind the rules on services of general interest. As stated, the ECJ accepts a derogation for the transport in non-emergency situations. This means that an exclusive right is admitted on this market, in addition to the monopoly already granted on the first market. The ECJ however places a limitation. Pursuant to the judgment, the derogation will not be justified should it be demonstrated that the organisations in question are not able to provide a satisfactory service on this second market for transportation outside emergency situations.

> *Glöckner.* '[I]f it were established that the medical aid organisations entrusted with the operation of the public ambulance service were manifestly unable to satisfy demand for emergency ambulance services and for patient transport at all times . . . [,] the justification for extending their exclusive rights, based on the task of general interest, could not be accepted.'[258]

5.300   **Doubts.**   This new orientation taken by the ECJ gives rise to some doubts. Article 86(2) EC consists of a derogation granted where behaviour or a situation arises that normally falls under a prohibition. For instance, a State aid that could not normally be granted under the State aid provisions may be accepted under Article 86(2) EC where it is demonstrated that it is necessary to finance a service of general interest. Article 86(2) EC thus presupposes a 'violation' of competition law and provides an explanation so that this 'violation' is ultimately considered legitimate. After this legitimisation has taken place, the behaviour can no longer be called a 'violation'. Yet this is exactly what the ECJ does in *Glöckner*, where this concept of violation is reintroduced after the derogation has been granted. In the judgment, the reasoning is structured along the following lines. First the ECJ rules that the exclusive right granted to non-profit organisations is incompatible. Second, the conditions for the derogation are considered fulfilled. The situation can thus be deemed admissible, as it conforms to the competition rules. Only then comes the observation about a possible abuse committed by the organisations as a result of the exclusive right conferred on them.

---

[258] At [62].

Normal Article 86 EC case	*Glöckner*
—The entity in question is an undertaking	—Same position
—This undertaking has an exclusive right	—Same position
—This exclusive right can be deemed incompatible with Treaty provisions because it encompasses abusive conduct incompatible with Article 82 EC	—Same position
—A derogation may be granted where conditions are fulfilled under Article 86(2) EC	—Same position
	—*Different position: the derogation will be withdrawn in situations where an abuse is committed*[259]

Inability to serve demand.   The possible abuse is, according to the ECJ, related   **5.302**
to the possible inability of the organisation to serve demand satisfactorily. It will
be remembered that an argument of this nature was made in *Höfner*, which concerned a public placement agency with an exclusive right for the exercise of that
activity. In that case, the exclusive right was found illegal because the agency was
not in a position to serve demand adequately. The question about a derogation
was asked after the ECJ had established the illegal character of the exclusive right.
The ECJ did not raise the issue of abusive conduct, after the derogation had been
granted.

> *Höfner.* '[A] public employment agency engaged in employment procurement activ-
> ities is subject to the prohibition contained in Article 86 of the Treaty, so long as the
> application of that provision does not obstruct the performance of the particular task
> assigned to it. A Member State which has conferred an exclusive right to carry on that
> activity upon the public employment agency is in breach of Article 90(1) of the
> Treaty where it creates a situation in which that agency cannot avoid infringing
> Article 86 of the Treaty.'[260]

(8) Is Article 86(2) EC still relevant for electronic communications cases?

The question of relevance.   After studying the conditions under which   **5.303**
Article 86(2) EC may be used, the question must be raised whether this provision
still has relevance in the electronic communications sector. We have seen that

---

[259] Raising the issue of a possible abuse at this stage is not appropriate, as this issue must be examined *before* a derogation is granted.

[260] At [34]. This justification issue was not explicitly dealt with by the ECJ in *Höfner*. The reason is probably that the question was not asked by the national jurisdiction. However, the justification was examined in *Merci*, which provides a second illustration of the theory according to which
exclusive rights are abusive per se. In *Merci*, the ECJ ruled that the exclusive right granted to several
companies for the organisation of operations in the port of Genoa must be deemed contrary to competition rules (at [8]–[20]). The question then arises as to whether a derogation should be granted.
In casu, the derogation is not granted because it had not been demonstrated that the activities were
different from plain economic tasks (at [25]–[28]).

universal service encompasses the public policy objectives that may be reached in that sector and that the means to be used in order to carry out these policies have been regulated at European level by the Parliament, Council and Commission. In that context one may wonder whether the Member States still have the possibility of seeking the realisation of other policy-oriented goals and of choosing methods that may derogate from the competition rules in order to attain these objectives.

5.304 **Two steps in the discussion.**   As appears from the observation above, Article 86(2) EC gives some leeway to the Member States where the latter can demonstrate that the conditions for the application of that provision are fulfilled. There is however some doubt about whether the Member States can use that provision at all in the context of electronic communications. This issue will be examined in two steps in the following paragraphs. First, we will consider the fulfilment of obligations set at European level concerning universal service. These obligations encompass the policy objectives imposed on the Member States beyond the establishment of a competitive market. The question will be whether these obligations may be fulfilled through a derogation from the competition rules. Second, additional obligations which may be introduced by the Member States will be examined. The same question will be raised regarding the methods that may be used by them in order to ensure the fulfilment of those obligations.

Situations where harmonisation has taken place

5.305 **European obligations exist.**   In the context of obligations that have been established at European level, the possibility of using Article 86(2) EC may be important for the financing of universal service. We have seen that two possible financing mechanisms have been established—payments from public funds and sharing mechanisms. Can a third system be imagined where Member States would be allowed to entrust one undertaking with the provision of the universal service in a monopolistic environment? Going further, could the Member States grant a monopoly on a second, more lucrative, electronic communications market, and use revenues derived from this second market in order to finance extra costs incurred on the first as a result of national additional obligations?

5.306 **(a) Concentration of demand theory.**   The question has not been dealt with explicitly in the NRF, although elements may be found there to address the issue. Under the regulation, Member States can designate undertakings for the provision of universal service where no other option is available. This possibility, which we have examined several times, seems to indicate that a monopoly may indeed be granted for the provision of universal service as provided under the concentration of demand theory. It will be recalled that Member States are allowed, under that (Article 86(2) EC) theory, to reserve an activity for one undertaking where this is necessary to ensure the provision of a service of general interest. This theory is invoked in circumstances where the existence of several undertakings would imply excessive investment, and thus excessive tariffs, thereby creating a situation contrary to the policy objectives at stake. The acceptance of that possibility in the regulation indicates consistency on that point between the various frameworks involved—harmonisation, liberalisation and general competition law.[261] In fact, the regulation seems to have expressed, and further construed, in legislative instruments the conditions that would have applied in the context of Article 86(2) EC.

(b) Compensation theory. A different conclusion must probably be reached **5.307** regarding the second possibility envisaged in the question presented above, ie the possibility of granting a monopoly on the second market to finance costs incurred in the first. The regulation has indeed established two specific mechanisms in order to ensure the financing of activities—public funds and sharing schemes. The issue is whether Member States may claim the application of a general competition law provision, arguing that this provision must continue to apply parallel to, and irrespective of, the rules that have been established in the Community legislation.

General case law. Again, this issue has not been dealt with in the regulation. **5.308** Nor has it been examined in the competition case law. Elements may however be found in cases concerning a similar problem in the context of the internal market. Internal market provisions prohibit national measures from hindering free movement. Derogations may be applied if certain conditions are fulfilled. The question has arisen whether Member States could still claim the benefit of a derogation of that nature in an environment where harmonisation had taken place. The answer has been that the harmonisation process places limits on the liberty of the Member States. The degree to which this liberty is impaired depends on the completeness of the process that has taken place. *(a)* If harmonisation has been complete, then Member States have lost all liberty. They may no longer request an internal market derogation contained in a Treaty provision. The only derogations they may claim are those which have been integrated in the directives in question. *(b)* If harmonisation has not been complete, then the Member States retain a certain degree of liberty. The question will have to be examined on a case-by-case basis. The focus in this context is placed on the rule in question. One generally considers that Member States have lost their liberty where a derogation is requested in connection with a rule that has been construed in the European

---

[261] As we have seen, the regulation imposes requirements to ensure that the designation takes place in the spirit of competition. No undertaking may be excluded a priori, and the basic regulatory principles must be complied with. This is in line with what is also required under the competition rules.

regulation. They may however continue using Treaty derogations for issues that have not been addressed in the regulation.[262]

5.309 **Application to electronic communications.**   There appears to be no reason why this case law should not apply in the electronic communications context. The general idea is indeed that Member States lose their liberty when the European legislator has exercised its competence to regulate. The only possibility for Member States then to react is to challenge the validity of the Community regulation before the ECJ, but this has to be done within strict deadlines. If this case law is applied to our context, it should be considered that the Member States have lost any right to claim the application of Article 86(2) EC regarding the financing of the universal service, as the whole sector has been regulated and— leaving aside the question whether harmonisation has been complete—all aspects relating to this financing issue have been addressed in the European regulation. This implies that no derogation from competition rules may be granted in the form of a monopoly on a second market to finance extra costs related to universal service on a first market.

Additional obligations introduced by Member States

5.310 **No mechanism involving other undertakings.**   We have however seen that Member States are allowed by the European regulation to introduce obligations additional to those established at European level. One constraint applies to them where they decide to resort to this possibility. Under the Universal Service Directive, Member States are then prohibited from resorting to a 'compensation mechanism involving specific undertakings' in order to ensure the financing of these obligations. As the possibilities opened to Member States thus seem more limited, there is a question as to whether Member States can resort to an Article 86(2) EC derogation to ensure financing.[263]

5.311 **Concentration of demand theory.**   In order to address this issue, let us return to the distinction made earlier on the basis of the various theories that may be founded on Article 86(2) EC. There seems no reason why Member States should not be allowed to designate undertakings for the provision of additional national

---

[262] In this debate, the strategic question is to determine whether harmonisation can be deemed to be complete or otherwise. Where harmonisation is not complete, a key issue will also be to determine whether the derogation that the Member State is seeking has indeed been addressed in the European regulation. These findings are normally made by the ECJ in Art 234 EC proceedings (request for a preliminary ruling). More generally, they may be made by national courts acting on request from a legal or natural person with the possibility for these courts of submitting a preliminary question to the ECJ where the answer does not appear obvious.

[263] The question does not vanish as a result of the exclusion of one financing mechanism by the European regulation. Its relevance is in effect increased by that exclusion. As Member States are unlikely to resort to public funds, may they ensure the realisation of their additional policy objectives through derogations from competition rules?

universal service obligations. This mechanism is allowed for European obligations. Why should it not be used for national provisions? If this interpretation is accepted, the Member States could thus grant to one undertaking an exclusive right on given markets to ensure that demand is concentrated on that undertaking. The mechanism would be submitted to the same conditions as seen above. In application of these conditions, the designation could take place only where no other option was available. No candidate should a priori be excluded. And the basic regulatory principles—particularly proportionality—should be respected. The basis for the derogation would not lie in the regulation, as no provision specifically organises that possibility in the harmonisation or the liberalisation directives. It would thus be founded on Article 86(2) EC.

Compensation theory.   Could the Member States grant a monopoly on a sec-   **5.312**
ond market to finance extra costs incurred on the first? This possibility was excluded for obligations relating to universal service. The reason was that the issue had been addressed in European regulation. Member States had thus lost their liberty to introduce new measures in the field. It appears that the same position must be adopted regarding additional national obligations. The matter has indeed also been regulated. Pursuant to the Universal Service Directive, 'no compensation mechanism involving specific undertakings may be imposed' in a context where additional obligations are fixed by the Member States. This sentence means that no sharing mechanism may be used to finance these obligations. The Member States are thus not allowed to impose on market participants an obligation to pay a contribution that would be used to compensate extra costs incurred as a result of additional national obligations. The formulation chosen by the European institutions as regards additional obligations is however wider, and thus refers only to that mechanism. Any scheme implying compensation and involving specific undertakings must be avoided. That is however exactly what a derogation granted on the basis of Article 86(2) EC would imply. Such a derogation would indeed organise *compensation* between markets. It would further involve specific undertakings, as one or several of them would be granted the privilege to carry out their activities while being protected from competition.

Other provisions

Issues other than monopolies.   The discussion above concentrates on a deroga-   **5.313**
tion given in the form of an exclusive right on one or several markets. However, it should be recalled that other possibilities are opened through the application of Article 86(2) EC. From case law it appears that that provision always applies in combination with another rule. Article 86(2) EC introduces the possibility that other EC provisions may be suspended, to the extent that such suspension is necessary to ensure the realisation of policy objectives. This goes for all EC provisions, although a focus has been placed here on general competition law. As a result of

Article 86(2) EC, prohibitions contained in all European competition law provisions may be suspended if the conditions are satisfied.

5.314 **Two provisions combined.** Most cases examined above relate to Article 86 EC in connection with Article 82 EC. The latter provision prohibits abusive conduct adopted by undertakings in a dominant position. It comes into play where exclusive rights are involved. Pursuant to case law, these rights are deemed abusive but they can be redeemed where the conditions under Article 86(2) EC are fulfilled. Other kinds of behaviour that would normally be deemed abusive may be considered under Article 82 EC combined with Article 86(2) EC. Similarly cartels, which are normally prohibited under Article 81 EC, may be allowed where a derogation appears necessary to ensure the fulfilment of a mission of general interest. A similar treatment applies to State aids: advantages normally prohibited can be saved (Article 87 EC). Even mergers follow the same line, with the possibility that an operation may be authorised although it would have been rejected in the absence of the derogation contained in Article 86(2) EC.[264]

The redeeming virtue of Article 86 EC

—Behaviour normally prohibited under competition rules may be exempted where it is necessary to ensure the provision of a service of general interest.
—This process may cover cartels, abuse of dominant position, State aids, mergers.

5.315 **The derogation as applied to these other issues.** The question arises whether the derogation contained in Article 86(2) EC could be used in connection with issues not related to exclusive rights. For instance, could one imagine a possibility for undertakings to abuse a dominant position and ask for a derogation on the ground that it is entrusted with the task of providing a service of general interest? Probably not. Abusive conduct has been regulated in the harmonisation and liberalisation directives. The result is that the rules contained in these regulations must apply. They are considered to have specified and determined the obligations flowing from Treaty provisions. The result is that a separate application of these provisions cannot be demanded any longer. To take another example, could special rights be authorised in derogation from the competition? Again, these privileges have been regulated and the possibility of invoking Treaty provisions directly has, as a result, vanished in connection with these issues.

---

[264] All these rules contain a prohibition but also, within themselves, the possibility of a derogation. For instance, anti-competitive cartels are prohibited under Art 81(1) EC but a derogation may be obtained under Art 81(3) EC where specific conditions, mentioned in that provision, are met. In respect of these provisions, Art 86(2) EC thus opens a second possibility for a derogation to be granted. It should however be noted that this second possibility is more limited in scope, as it applies only to services of general interest.

Articles 86 and 82 EC. From this analysis it appears that no derogation **5.316**
is available on the basis of Article 86(2) EC to excuse behaviour falling under
Article 82 EC. The same conclusion should be reached as regards State aids. The
possibility of conferring advantages financed with public money has been regulated in the harmonisation and liberalisation directives. For instance, it is emphasised in regulation that aids can be given only to cover the net costs relating to
universal service. Public funds are not prohibited for financing additional
national obligations. However, these funds again may not be greater than those
necessary in order to finance the net costs.

Articles 86 and 81 EC. By contrast, a different conclusion may be reached **5.317**
with respect to mergers and cartels prohibited under Article 81 EC. These
operations have not been regulated at all in the harmonisation or liberalisation
framework. The consequence is that Treaty provisions may still be invoked
directly. Undertakings entering cartels or mergers which are normally prohibited could thus claim that a derogation should be granted on the basis
of Article 86(2) EC. For the derogation to be granted, they would have to demonstrate that the conditions are fulfilled. In particular, they would have to show that
no alternative is available to ensure the performance of a service of general
interest.

L. Public Service, Universal Service and Services of General Interest

(1) Introduction

Necessity of a definition. We have examined in the paragraphs above the **5.318**
regime applicable to universal service, as well as that concerning services of general interest. We have also alluded to the concept of public service. It is now time
to define with more rigour the relations between these concepts.[265]

(2) Public service and universal service

Objectives. Public service, and universal service, have features in common. **5.319**
These features mainly concern the objectives to be reached in the two contexts. In
both cases, as regards electronic communications, the purpose is to make available
specified services deemed important for members of society. Public services as
well as universal service must provide a certain level of quality. For instance, quality targets have been fixed in the harmonisation directives, in connection with

---

[265] With regard to public service, we will limit ourselves to the content given to that concept
in the former telecommunications sector. Public service is indeed a wide concept which is used in
several sectors in the Member States and to which several kinds of rules are attached.

standards set by specialised bodies. In both public and universal services, there are also conditions relating to tariffs. Affordability is an objective in the two contexts. Equality is added as a further objective for public services. In that approach, all must have access to the specified services under the same conditions. These services are indeed considered as a corollary to citizenship. All citizens must have access to these services and—as citizens are equal before the law—they should be charged the same tariffs whatever their needs, their social status or the costs incurred to provide the services.[266]

5.320   Objectives in public and universal service

Public service	Universal service
Specific items must be made available for all at affordable and equal conditions	*Idem* *Affordability applies, equality does not appear in the regulation*
Where possible of good quality	*Quality becomes a key objective, with standards established by standardisation bodies*

5.321   **Arrangements—public service.**   Even where objectives can be compared, there are differences between public services and universal service. As stated, telecommunications were considered prior to the reform as part of the 'public service' in many Member States. In those countries they were subject to a 'public service regime'. This regime had two aspects. First, telecommunications activities were not left to private undertakings but were taken over by public authorities. Networks were thus operated, and services provided, by public authorities on the national territories. Second, activities were subject to specific rules. Entities responsible for telecommunications were organised as monopolies. As they were the only entities carrying out activities in that sector, they were protected from competition. In return, obligations were imposed upon them which pursued a variety of objectives. These objectives varied depending on the period involved, the Member States concerned and the political sensibility of the governments in power.[267] Public ownership, specific obligations to comply with and privileges in order to carry these obligations out were thus the main characteristics of the public sector under the former national telecommunications organisation.

5.322   **Arrangements—universal service.**   These arrangements are radically different in the universal service approach. Public ownership is not banned. However, the two other characteristics have been affected. There is no question any longer of protecting

---

[266] Equality does not appear to be emphasised in the universal service requirement. The goal to attain is limited to affordability, with special measures for certain members of society.

[267] Services Directive, Art 3, as amended.

former monopolies against competition—quite the contrary.[268] General obligations have been imposed, with the aim of ensuring the achievement of objectives regarding universal service (provision of specific items, quality, affordability targets). It is expected that these obligations should be met spontaneously by market forces. Where this outcome is not reached, public authorities may intervene. The public intervention should in all cases ensure that no undertaking is discriminated against.

Arrangements in public and universal service   **5.323**

Public service	Universal service
The relevant services are provided by public undertakings	Public ownership is not prohibited—but is not encouraged
These undertakings are protected from competition (special or exclusive rights)	Markets are open to competition and protection from competition is prohibited
Specific obligations are imposed to ensure the performance of the public service	Obligations are imposed on all undertakings

Conclusion.   In the context of telecommunications and/or electronic communications, public service and universal service appear as two approaches, but the latter has replaced the former. Both approaches seek the realisation of similar objectives but cannot be combined because the arrangements put in place are different. Universal service in fact appears to have been set up in order to bring about public service objectives without the arrangements that were attached to these objectives in the era of monopolies. In summary, one can say that universal service is a form of public service in a competitive environment.   **5.324**

(3) Services of general interest

Technical concept.   We have seen above that public service and universal service can somehow be placed on the same level. They designate similar objectives, to be reached by arrangements that are not mutually compatible. The situation is different for services of general interest. This expression designates a technique used in general competition law in order to designate services established by national authorities and functioning under a special regime as regards the application of these rules. Unlike the two other concepts, services of general interest cannot be regarded as a policy-oriented idea. The expression rather designates a technical instrument meant to verify to what extent a national policy may be implemented in derogation of Treaty rules, in particular, competition rules.   **5.325**

---

[268] Not only have their former privileges been abolished, but in addition, special obligations have been imposed on these undertakings as a result of their persistent dominant position on the markets (asymmetric regulation). These obligations do not concern universal service, but the behaviour adopted by these undertakings on the markets. The purpose is to ensure that these undertakings will under no circumstance abuse their dominant position.

5.326 **Application to universal service?** As stated above, this concept cannot be applied in connection with universal service as the latter is defined at European level. This is due to the regulation of the arrangements that may be used by Member States in order to reach the goals fixed by the European legislator as regards universal service. We have seen that Member States may impose tariffs or designate undertakings where the services would not be provided spontaneously. These actions do not however imply any derogation from the competition rules. Financing mechanisms may be set up. However, these mechanisms may not infringe competition rules. Public funds are therefore mere compensation for extra obligations and may not exceed net costs of providing the universal service. There are thus no State aids and competition law is not infringed. The same analysis may be carried out for sharing mechanisms, as all market participants must be treated equally. The conclusion is thus that universal service is not a derogation in application of Article 86(2) EC, and can thus not be analysed as a service of general interest.

5.327 **In the case law.** Admittedly, the concepts are often associated in the case law. We have thus encountered several cases where the ECJ decided that a derogation should be granted for the fulfilment of a service that could be analysed along the lines of universal service. In some instances, the rapprochement between the two concepts has been made by the ECJ itself. This was the case for *TNT*, where the universal postal service was at stake. In other cases, the ECJ has designated as a service of general interest a service that corresponds to what is called a universal service item in the European regulation, even where the expression was not used explicitly. This approach may be found, for instance, in *Corbeau*, as regards the same universal postal service, but is not limited to that judgment.[269]

> *Corbeau—Implicit reference.* '[I]t cannot be disputed that the *Régie des Postes* is entrusted with a service of general economic interest consisting in the obligation to collect, carry and distribute mail on behalf of all users throughout the territory of the Member State concerned, at uniform tariffs and on similar quality conditions, irrespective of the specific situations or the degree of economic profitability of each individual operation.'[270]

> *TNT—Explicit reference.* '[I]n so far as trade between Member States may be affected, Article [82] of the Treaty, read in conjunction with Article [86] thereof, precludes legislation of a Member State which grants a private-law undertaking the exclusive right to operate the universal postal service from making the right of any other economic operator to provide an express mail service not forming part of the universal service subject to payment of postal dues equivalent to the postage charge

---

[269] See for instance as regards the distribution of electricity in the Member States: Case C-157/94 *Commission v Netherlands* [1997] ECR I-5699 at [41] and [42]. Similar paragraphs can be found in the two other 'energy distribution' judgments issued on the same day by the ECJ: Case C-158/94 *Commission v Italy* [1997] ECR I-5789; Case C-159/94 *Commission v France* [1997] ECR I-5815.

[270] *Corbeau*, at [15]. The expression 'universal service' was not used in that judgment, but the description of the service corresponds to the definition generally given to these terms.

normally payable to the undertaking responsible for the universal service, unless it can be shown that the proceeds of such payment are necessary to enable the undertaking to operate the universal postal service in economically acceptable conditions and that the undertaking is required to pay the same dues when itself providing an express mail service not forming part of the universal service.'[271]

The reason for an association in the case law.   The reason why the two concepts **5.328** are sometimes associated in the case law is probably that the cases dealt with by the ECJ have concerned sectors in the course of liberalisation. During these periods there was a transition from public service to universal service. What was traditionally called the public service was progressively transformed into universal service. Where the transformation was complete, there was no longer any need to speak about services of general economic interest because universal service must normally be operated at European level without derogation from competition rules.[272] The situation was different during the transitional periods. Universal service was then not yet organised. Member States still had the power to set policy objectives in the sectors involved and to choose the methods likely to allow the realisation of these results. The question which then arose was whether that power by the Member States went so far as to allow derogations from the European competition rules.

Illustration.   *TNT* provides in this context an excellent example.[273] This case con- **5.329** cerns the performance of postal services in Italy. Pursuant to the Italian legislation, these services were divided into two categories. The first category was made up of value-added services. The market for these services was opened to entry and the activities were carried out in competition on these markets. The second category consisted of the basic postal service, ie collection, carriage and delivery of letter post throughout the territory under equal and reasonable conditions. These latter services were bundled and called explicitly 'universal service' in the Italian legislation. The case emerged after a competitor was fined for carrying out some of the items included in the universal service, even though the task of operating this service was reserved to Poste Italiane. The case dates back to 1997, at which time there was no European legislation organising the conditions under which universal service could be performed in that economic sector.[274] As the subject matter had not been regulated at European level, the question arose whether the organisation given to the postal services in Italy could be found compatible with the Treaty. An essential issue in that regard was to determine whether the monopoly granted to Poste Italiane could be justified as a service of general interest under Article 86(2) EC.

---

[271] *TNT*, at [63].

[272] We have seen that some nuance needs to be brought to that statement, as regards national obligations introduced by Member States in addition to European objectives.

[273] Case C-340/99 *TNT Traco SpA v Poste Italiane SpA* [2001] ECR I-4109.

[274] This legislation was initiated with the adoption of Directive (EC) 97/67 of the European Parliament and of the Council of 15 December 1997 on common rules for the development of the internal market of Community postal services and the improvement of quality of service [1998], OJ L15/14.

5.330 **A largely redundant notion in the electronic communications sector.** Ultimately, the only remaining question regarding universal service and Article 86(2) EC is, as submitted above, whether Member States may introduce derogations from the competition rules in order to ensure the implementation of additional obligations related to universal service. We have seen that the possibilities are rather limited in this regard. A monopoly can indeed be granted on the basis of concentration of demand theory, but not on the basis of compensation theory. The conditions that must be satisfied are far-reaching. It is for the ECJ to give a final answer in that discussion. The position defended in this book is that universal service has made Article 86(2) EC redundant in the sectors where that service has been organised at European level. The organisation of a universal service by the European legislator implies that Member States are to comply with the rules that have been established. Basically, the establishment of a universal service in a given sector means that policy objectives have been harmonised for the activities pertaining to that sector. Admittedly, Member States have not lost all margin of manoeuvre, but this remaining liberty is severely restricted by measures established at European level.

This does not mean that Article 86(2) EC can no longer be used. This provision still has a function in areas where policy objectives remain decided by the Member States, ie where no harmonisation, or at least no substantial harmonisation, has taken place. Take for instance banking services. The idea has been expressed that a sort of universal service could be established in that sector. All consumers would be granted access under reasonable conditions to a minimum set of banking services deemed essential in our society. No regulation has yet been adopted at European level on this subject matter. The Member States thus remain free to organise a universal service—or a public service—of that kind as they see fit. The constraint will be for them to respect the European provisions adopted in the financial sector and not to introduce derogations from the competition rules where the conditions laid down in Article 86(2) EC are not satisfied.

(4) Communications and Report adopted by the Commission

5.331 **Two communications and one report.** As indicated at the outset of this section, the Commission has issued two communications around services of general interest. It has also drafted a report that was submitted to the European Council at the Laeken summit. The purpose of these various documents is to present the analysis made by the Commission of the subject matter and to propose measures that are necessary, according to that institution, in order to regulate the relevant services. These documents are presented briefly below. A more substantial presentation is not needed, as all relevant indications contained in these documents concerning the legal regime applicable to services of general interest have been analysed in other parts of the chapter.

First Communication on services of general interest (1996). The first **5.332**
communication[275] was issued at a time when the Commission was introducing
the idea that full competition should be implemented on the telecommunications
markets within a few years. Progress was also being made in other sectors and
some concern had arisen among Member States and within some sectors of
public opinion that liberalisation would somehow lead to a disappearance of public
service. The communication was drafted as a document to reassure public and
national authorities. An attempt is made in that document to connect what it was
seeking to do in the sectors being liberalised with the public service that was carried out in those sectors beforehand. In the communication, the Commission
asserts the importance of public service within the European Union. It also
stresses that there are divergences in the organisation of the relevant activities
within the Member States. This, according to the Commission, justifies action at
European level. The Commission explains that significant changes are taking
place that make it possible to carry out public service in a competitive environment. Finally, the Commission reviews the various sectors where liberalisation
was then taking place, explaining all actions taken by the European legislator in
order to ensure that objectives relating to the former public service did not disappear but survived, although in a different form, in the new organisation.

Second Communication on services of general interest (2001). In the second **5.333**
communication,[276] the Commission reiterates the analysis provided in the first
document. The purpose is to review developments since 1996 and to convince
that these developments have ensured in a liberalised context the realisation of
objectives underlying the concept of public service. The communication contains
two Annexes, the first of which presents the initiatives adopted by the European
institutions in the various sectors opened to competition.

Report to the Laeken Summit, 2001. A few months after issuing the second **5.334**
Communication, the Commission drafted a new document that contains practical
information about the concrete initiatives planned for the months and/or years
ahead as regards services of general interest.[277]

  (a) A first initiative is to facilitate access to information regarding the treat-
      ment of services of general interest under European law. To that effect, a
      section was created from 2002 on these services in the annual report
      published by the Commission concerning the application of the

---

[275] Commission Communication (EC) 96/C281/03 on services of general interest in Europe
[1996] OJ C281/3.
[276] Commission Communication (EC) 2001/C17/04 on services of general interest in Europe
[2001] OJ C17/4.
[277] Commission Report to the Laeken European Council, on services of general interest COM
(2001) 598 final, Brussels, 17 October 2001.

competition rules. Similarly, cases concerning services of general interest will be identified in the register concerning State aids.

(b) A second initiative planned by the Commission was to increase legal certainty as regards the legal regime applicable to the relevant services. The necessity of adopting additional measures will be considered concerning the rules applicable to the procedure whereby one or several undertakings are selected in order to provide universal service. One may thus not exclude the adoption by the Commission of guidelines on that point. Nothing specific has however been announced regarding electronic communications. Following the same line, the Commission intended to draft and publish a Community framework for State aids granted for services of general interest. The difficulty is that the ECJ has now ruled that public funds granted to compensate costs associated with public service cannot be considered as State aids under the Treaty. It is not sure whether this case law will affect the Commission's plans.

(c) A third initiative will be to carry out effective evaluation of the performance of services of general interest at Community level. To that effect, the Commission will improve the reports concerning the various sectors concerned, including electronic communications. There is also a project to develop a horizontal evaluation aimed at monitoring market structure and performance, assessing public service obligations from an economic and social point of view, and surveying public opinion about the impact of liberalisation on the performance of services of general interest.

(d) Finally, the possibility is considered of adopting a Framework Directive on services of general interest. The purpose would be to concentrate in a binding document all ideas spread across existing legislation regarding these services, together with the ideas explained in the above-mentioned communications. It is not clear whether such a directive would be adopted in the harmonisation framework, in which case the final decision would be for the Parliament and the Council. The probability however appears higher that it would be adopted by the Commission, as services of general interest are articulated in Article 86 EC and the Commission is specifically granted powers to ensure the application of that provision.

M. Services of Non-Economic Interest

(1) The issue

5.335 **The issue.** The situation of services of general interest with an economic character has been examined so far. This is the result of the expression used in Article 86(2) EC, where services are covered only where they have an economic character. The reference to these services however indicates that other services exist which do not have an economic character. The question is what these services are and how they must be treated in the light of the discussions seen above concerning universal service.

Economic character. The determination of the economic character of an activity **5.336** is a classic debate in European law, which has arisen in connection with internal market provisions where an issue was to determine under what circumstances an activity could be considered a service subject to free movement provisions. Article 50 EC provides some indications in this regard. Pursuant to that provision, services are activities of a mainly industrial or commercial character where remuneration is provided.[278] Later on, criteria to determine whether an activity is economic have also been discussed in the competition case law. Pursuant to the Treaty, competition law applies only to undertakings, and the issue was to determine when an entity qualifies under that concept. In the case law, the ECJ considered that an entity could be considered as an undertaking where it carries out an economic activity.

(2) Legal regime applicable to non-economic services

Answer to the question. This already provides an answer to the question raised **5.337** in this section. The economic character of a task—of a service for instance—has the consequence that the entity will be subject to the competition rules. By contrast, entities which do not carry out activities of such a nature cannot be considered undertakings. As a result, they do not fall under the ambit of competition rules. In the light of this interpretation, services of non-economic interest cannot be considered as activities submitted to competition law. There is thus no need to examine whether a derogation should be obtained: these activities in any event fall outside the scope of competition rules.

Whether or not activities fall under competition rules **5.338**

Option 1	Option 2
Activities are economic in nature	Activities are not economic in nature
Example: services of general economic interest	Services of general non-economic interest
This has a consequence on the regime	The undertakings performing these services
applicable to the entity performing them:	are *not* subject to competition rules
this entity is subject to competition rules	
A derogation may be obtained if the conditions	There is thus no need to ask questions about
laid down in Article 86(2) EC are fulfilled	the possibility of a derogation

(3) What are non-economic services?

Criteria. Some content should be given to the concept of 'economic character' **5.339** of an activity. This content is important to determine whether a service falls

---

[278] This in fact leads to a paradox, regarding our question. Activities can be considered as services where they are economic in nature. One can thus hardly speak, in EC terms, about 'non-economic services'.

outside the competition rules (services of non-economic interest) or whether it must be included within them—the possibility then remaining that a derogation could be granted in application of Article 86(2) EC. Pursuant to the case law, a first criterion may be found in the content of the activity performed. In several cases, the ECJ has ruled that activities are economic where they consist in selling goods or services. Another criterion used by the ECJ is whether the activity could be performed by a private entity. According to that criterion, an activity must be deemed economic in situations where a private entity cannot be excluded.

5.340   **Economic tasks vs public authority.**   Through that last criterion, the line for the application of the competition rules has in effect been placed between, on the one hand, activities that can be considered as economic tasks and, on the other hand, missions that are attached to the exercise of a public authority. This case law has been established in *Eurocontrol*, where an organisation[279] was entrusted by several States—not all members of the European Union—with surveillance tasks relating to air navigation. The case law was upheld in *Diego Cali*, where an entity[280] was responsible for anti-pollution surveillance in the oil port of Genoa. In both cases, the ECJ considered that the entities in question had been entrusted with tasks which were intrinsically prerogatives of the State and could not as a result be submitted to the competition rules.

5.341   **Exercise of public authority.**   The result of this case law is that competition law normally applies unless the party concerned specifically demonstrates that the activity is linked intimately to the exercise of public authority and could not, as a result, by any means be carried out by private undertakings. This will be difficult to demonstrate. As tasks covered by this concept, one can think of the provision of national internal and external security, the administration of justice, the conduct of foreign relations and other exercises of official authority. Ultimately, these tasks are connected to the possible use of physical sanctions to ensure that the public authority is respected.[281] All other tasks can in some way be taken over by private entities, and this has, pursuant to the case law, the

---

[279] Eurocontrol.   [280] SEPG : Servizi ecologii porto di Genova.

[281] The case law does not go so far, but we consider that it does not go far enough. Missions relating to surveillance were entrusted to the entity involved in *Eurocontrol* as well as in *Diego Cali*. This sort of mission to our mind corresponds with the idea that only violence-related tasks can be intimately associated with the use of public authority. The State arrogated to itself several centuries ago the exclusive right to resort legitimately to violence. This use of legitimate violence remains a key characteristic of public authority. However, a surveillance mission was entrusted in *Diego Cali* to a private entity. This entity was thus considered to fall outside the scope of competition law. In our view, this solution is not consistent. One cannot consider that an activity relates to public authority and at the same time admit that it can be carried out by private entities. The possibility that an activity may be carried out privately has been consistently used in the case law as an indication that the mission was economic in character.

consequence that they may not be considered as intimately related to public authority.[282]

Non-relevant criteria. Member States sometimes resort to arguments in order   **5.342** to dismiss the application of competition law, but these arguments have so far been resisted. In several judgments, the ECJ has made it clear that it would look only at the character of the activity (economic activity or public authority). Other criteria are not deemed relevant, such as legal status (a public entity can be subject to competition law) or the method used for the financing of activities (for instance tasks where no remuneration is paid by the customer but the entity is compensated for the costs in another fashion).

Public service obligations. An interesting argument raised by some Member   **5.343** States is that some entities are being required to perform tasks of general interest and should as a result escape competition rules. Were they subject to these rules, the activities could not be financed because competition would not allow the undertakings concerned to bring in enough returns to cover their costs. This situation is typical of undertakings designated for the provision of universal service. These undertakings are subject to specific obligations. Some of them would appreciate falling outside competition law in return for implementing these obligations.

Glöckner. The issue was discussed in *Glöckner*, where non-profit organisations   **5.344** were entrusted with an exclusive right to transport patients. A question was whether the activity could be considered as economic in nature. Suppose the answer to this question was negative; the organisations would have escaped the competition rules and the exclusive right granted to them would not have been questioned. The issue of the legitimacy of this right would not even have been raised. Contrary to the expectations of the organisations involved, the ECJ ruled that the activity could indeed be considered as economic. The organisations concerned were thus subject to competition rules. Admittedly, public service obligations were imposed on the relevant organisations. However, these obligations, said the ECJ, did not alter the economic character of the activity, even if they had an impact on the profitability of the operations.

> *General answer.* '[T]he medical aid organisations provide services, for remuneration from users, on the market for emergency transport services and patient transport services. Such activities have not always been, and are not necessarily, carried on by such organisations or by public authorities. . . . The provision of such services therefore constitutes an economic activity for the purposes of the application of the competition

---

[282] The case law concerning the economic character of activities is discussed at length in the Second Communication on Services of general interest in Europe. See paras 28–30. In that Communication, the Commission stresses that compulsory basic social security schemes are excluded from the application of competition. The same analysis should be made, according to the Commission, for activities conducted by organisations performing largely social functions. In both activities, the activities would thus be services of non-economic general interest.

rules laid down by the Treaty.'[283] *Public service obligations.* '[P]ublic service obligations may, of course, render the services provided by a given medical aid organisation less competitive than comparable services rendered by other operators not bound by such obligations, but that fact cannot prevent the activities in question from being regarded as economic activities.'[284]

5.345   **Application of competition rules (in principle).**   Through this ruling, the ECJ indicated that competition rules apply in principle where obligations are imposed on undertakings to ensure the performance of public or universal service. This does not mean that no derogation is possible. However, these derogations will have to be examined under Article 86(2) EC or under the regulation that may have been adopted by the European institutions in the area in question. In its ruling the ECJ emphasised that the questions relating to the application of competition rules were to be asked in relation to these rules, but did not have any influence on the economic, or non-economic, character of the activities.

5.346   **Are there non-economic activities in electronic communications?**   The question remains whether there are tasks which may be considered as non-economic in the electronic communications sector. These tasks would then form a service of general non-economic interest. Entities carrying out these services would not be considered as undertakings and would thus escape the application of all competition rules. To fill this category, it is difficult to think of any other tasks than those that are entrusted to the NRAs. Even within these tasks a selection should probably be made, because all missions entrusted to NRAs do not necessarily imply an exercise of public authority.[285] This shows that only a few activities do not qualify as economic and could be taken out of the hands of entities subject to the competition rules.

5.347   **Essential facilities doctrine.**   One may wonder about the status of activities carried out by dominant undertakings covered by the essential facilities doctrine. Under that doctrine, dominant undertakings must sometimes behave as 'independent authorities'. This expression is used explicitly in decisions adopted by the Commission concerning the doctrine. A good example is *Stena Sealink*,[286]

---

[283] *Glöckner*, at [20].

[284] *Glöckner*, at [21]. The ECJ then went on to analyse whether the exclusive right could be found compatible with competition law and, if not, whether a derogation could be granted. The conclusion was that conditions for a derogation were satisfied but that the derogation could not be maintained if it was demonstrated that the organisations did not serve demand appropriately. This case has been discussed extensively in the previous sections.

[285] For instance, the NRF allows for the intervention of non-public bodies in the performance of given tasks concerning the implementation of the regulation. The control of financial data for the establishment of the net cost of the universal service, for instance, can be entrusted to an independent body, which does not need to be public. Similarly, the sharing mechanism can be operated by an independent body, which does not necessarily have to be a public authority.

[286] Commission Decision EC (94/19) relating to a proceeding pursuant to Article 86 of the EC Treaty (IV/34.689—Sea Containers v Stena Sealink—Interim measures) [1994] OJ L15/8.

where an undertaking owned port facilities giving access to the only practicable maritime route between Ireland and Great Britain. The undertaking was also active on an adjacent market, as it provided a maritime link between the two. On this latter market the undertaking was subject to competition. The litigation arose when a potential competitor asked for authorisation to use the port facilities in order to perform a competing service. The request was not set aside, but was handled in a manner that did not allow the newcomer to perform its activities effectively. The behaviour adopted by the undertaking was analysed by the Commission as an abuse of a dominant position. In its decision the Commission repeatedly points to the existence of an obligation for the undertaking to act as an independent authority as regards access to port facilities placed under its control.

> *Stena Sealink, at [75].* 'It is the Commission's view that in the circumstances of the present case an independent harbour authority, which would of course have had an interest in increasing revenue at the port, would at least have considered whether the interests of existing and proposed users of the port could best be reconciled by a solution involving modest changes in the allocated slot times or in any plans for the development of the harbour. In situations such as the present one, unless a solution is considered fully and discussed with all the interests involved, it is likely that a port authority which is not independent will prefer an arrangement which minimizes inconvenience to itself (especially in relation to its own operations as a user) but which does not necessarily provide non-discriminatory access to the new entrant.'

Competition law not applicable.   One may wonder whether this case—and others relating to the essential facilities doctrine—can be regarded as implying that tasks of a non-economic nature are sometimes imposed on undertakings. As a result of that doctrine, these undertakings would then act in some regards as public authorities and in others as undertakings. However interesting this question may be theoretically, the answer must probably be in the negative. Suppose these tasks were not economic in nature. This would imply that the entities would not be subject to competition rules, and as a result, no special obligations could be imposed on them.[287]   **5.348**

N. Compatibility with WTO Provisions

Freedom, with regulatory constraints.   As stated above, the European Union has committed itself to complying with certain rules in the framework of the WTO, as concerns telecommunications. The instruments containing the content of these commitments are presented above. The difficulty which may derive from the persistent reference in WTO instruments to telecommunications and audiovisual services, rather than to electronic communications, has also been analysed. Among   **5.349**

---

[287] These obligations are imposed on the undertaking in its capacity as holder of a dominant position and accordingly subject to special responsibilities in accordance with the case law.

these instruments, the Reference Paper is important because it contains regulatory options to be respected by Members in their commitments. This paper does not prevent Member States from adopting rules in the area of universal service. The concept is used, but is not defined in the text. It is rather left to the Members to define what universal service entails, each for its own territory. Constraints are however imposed on Members: they correspond in substance to those that have been called 'basic regulatory principles' in the European regulation.

WTO Reference Paper. 'Any Member has the right to define the kind of universal service it wishes to maintain. Such obligations will not be regarded as anti-competitive *per se*, provided they are administered in a transparent, non discriminatory and competitively neutral manner and are not more burdensome than necessary for the kind of universal service defined by the Member.'[288]

Universal Service Directive. 'The Community and its Member States have undertaken commitments on the regulatory framework on telecommunications networks and services in the context of the World Trade Organisation (WTO) agreement on basic telecommunications. Any member of the WTO has the right to define the kind of universal service obligation it wishes to maintain. Such obligations will not be regarded as anti-competitive per se, provided they are administered in a transparent, non-discriminatory and competitively neutral manner and are not more burdensome than necessary for the kind of universal service defined by the member.'[289]

5.350 Correspondence between the old and the new regulatory frameworks as regards universal service

Subject	NRF	Old regulatory framework	
		Voice Telephony Directive	*Interconnection Directive*
Scope and aims	Article 1	Article 1	—
Definitions	Article 2	Article 2	—
Availability of universal service	Article 3	Article 3	—
Provision of access at fixed location	Article 4	Article 5	—
Directory enquiry services and directories	Article 5	Article 6	—
Public pay phones	Article 6	Article 7	—
Special measures for disabled users	Article 7	Article 8	—
Designation of undertakings	Article 8	Article 5, para 1	—
Affordability of tariffs	Article 9	Articles 3 and 17	—
Control of expenditure	Article 10	Article 17[290]	—
Quality of service	Article 11 and Annex III	Article 12 and Annex III	—

(cont.)

---

[288] Reference Paper, para 3.   [289] Universal Service Directive, Preamble, recital 3.
[290] Limited to a prohibition regarding unbundling.

Subject	NRF	Old regulatory framework	
		Voice Telephony Directive	*Interconnection Directive*
Costing of universal service obligations	Article 12 and Annex IV (Part A)	Article 4	Article 5 and Annex III
Financing of universal service obligations	Articles 13 and 14, Annex IV (Part B)	—	Article 5 and Annex III
Review of the scope of universal service	Article 15 and Annex V	Article 31	—
Additional national mandatory services	Article 32	Article 4, in fine	—

6

LITIGATION AND DISPUTE RESOLUTION

A. Introduction

A significant number of conflicts expected. One may expect a significant **6.01** number of conflicts in electronic communications markets in the years ahead, for various reasons. *(a)* New regulation has been established. In such a context, disagreements necessarily emerge regarding the interpretation to be given to the new rules and the differences with the old regulation. *(b)* Electronic communications markets are vibrant. As a result of economic and technological changes, the identity of the actors is constantly, and rapidly, changing. Competition is fierce, forcing undertakings to resort to legal weaponry whereby their position can be improved. *(c)* Undertakings are confronted with a variety of rules to be complied with. These rules are adopted at various levels—national, European and international. They are also divided into sector-specific regulation and general competition law. The relations between these various categories of laws are not always evident—hence litigation in order to clarify them.

6.02 **The approach followed in this book.** The new regulatory framework (NRF) establishes mechanisms to solve conflicts arising between actors intervening on electronic communications markets. These mechanisms are explained in the following paragraphs. The changes that have taken place are then compared with the old framework. Finally, conflicts are divided into categories corresponding to the situations in which undertakings and individuals may be placed, and the procedures available to the parties in these situations examined.

B. Sector-Specific Regulation

(1) Conflicts between undertakings

6.03 **Applicable provisions.** Conflicts between undertakings are addressed under sector-specific regulation in Articles 20 and 21 of the Framework Directive.

6.04 **General competence of national regulatory authorities (NRAs).** The normal procedure for resolving conflicts arising between parties on electronic communications markets is to bring the case to the NRA in the Member State in which the conflict arises. These authorities are specialised in the treatment of difficulties relating to electronic communications. It was logical, and appropriate, for the European institutions to entrust them with the task of resolving conflicts in this sector. The solution applies whatever the identity of the party, undertaking or individual.

> *Framework Directive, Article 20(1).* 'In the event of a dispute arising in connection with obligations arising under this Directive or the Specific Directives between undertakings providing electronic communications networks or services in a Member State, the national regulatory authority concerned shall, at the request of either party . . . , issue a binding decision to resolve the dispute.'

> *Framework Directive, Preamble 32.* 'In the event of a dispute between undertakings in the same Member State in an area covered by this Directive or the Specific Directives, for example relating to obligations for access and interconnection or to the means of transferring subscriber lists, an aggrieved party that has negotiated in good faith but failed to reach agreement should be able to call on the national regulatory authority to resolve the dispute. National regulatory authorities should be able to impose a solution on the parties.'

6.05 **Intervention on the basis of, or without, a complaint.** As appears from the extracts above, NRAs normally intervene at the request of a party. Conflicts are normally brought by one of the parties to the authority entrusted with the power to resolve them. A question however remains—may NRAs intervene in the absence of a complaint or request? An intervention by an NRA on its own initiative would probably be deemed compatible with the provisions contained in the NRF and the inspiration lying behind the framework. NRAs indeed have a general competence to intervene whenever the objectives sought through the NRF are threatened.[1] That general competence would appear to provide a sufficient basis to intervene in the absence of a formal request. The absence of a formal request cannot be used, as a result, in order to challenge a decision taken by an NRA.

Power of the NRAs to adopt binding decisions.   Pursuant to the Framework   **6.06** Directive, cases brought before NRAs must be resolved with the adoption of a binding decision. The failure by parties to respect such a decision constitutes an infringement, to be sanctioned under national administrative (and possibly criminal) laws. In their binding decisions, the NRAs may impose obligations on undertakings where it is necessary to solve the conflict. The NRF does not contain a list laying down all of the obligations NRAs may impose. The absence of such a list may be interpreted as implying that NRAs have the power to impose whatever constraint is deemed necessary. NRAs are limited in their discretion in only two ways. *(a)* The obligations imposed by NRAs must be related to objectives pursued through the NRF. The possibility for NRAs of imposing obligations is thus limited to situations where obligations are necessary to attain these objectives.[2] *(b)* The obligations must conform to the Framework Directive and the other instruments composing the NRF. The latter does not contain a strict limitation on the obligations that may be imposed, and indeed the obligations that NRAs may impose in fulfilment of their regulatory tasks are defined broadly. There is no reason to define more strictly the obligations that may be imposed during a conflict-resolution procedure.

> *Framework Directive, Preamble 32.* 'National regulatory authorities should be able to impose a solution on the parties.' 'The intervention of a national regulatory authority in the resolution of a dispute between undertakings providing electronic communications networks or services in a Member State should seek to ensure compliance with the obligations arising under this Directive or the Specific Directives.'

Non-conventional conflict-resolution mechanisms.   NRAs may attempt to   **6.07** resolve conflicts through non-conventional mechanisms (mediation, etc). The use of these mechanisms is dependent upon the Member States allowing it in the national legislation implementing the NRF. Assuming they are authorised, these mechanisms should not prolong the procedure unduly. They may be tried during a maximum period of four months. If the problem is not then resolved, the NRA must resort to a binding decision. That decision must, again, be taken within four months. This last

---

[1]   See, eg, the Framework Directive, Art 8. 'Member States shall ensure that . . . the NRAs take all reasonable measures which are aimed at achieving the objectives attached to the NRF.'

[2]   This constraint, combined with an obligation to motivate decisions, implies NRAs have to explain how the obligations imposed are likely to solve the conflicts at issue in the way sought in the NRF.

period starts when the NRA has abandoned the use of non-conventional mechanisms. In total, the entire procedure may thus last at most eight months after receipt of the complaint or the own-initiative intervention by the NRA.

> *Framework Directive, Article 20(2).* 'Member States may make provision for national regulatory authorities to decline to resolve a dispute through a binding decision where other mechanisms, including mediation, exist and would better contribute to resolution of the dispute in a timely manner.' 'If after four months the dispute is not resolved, and if the dispute has not been brought before the courts by the party seeking redress, the national regulatory authority shall issue, at the request of either party, a binding decision to resolve the dispute in the shortest possible time frame and in any case within four months.'

6.08 **Constraints to be complied with by the NRAs.** The NRF imposes on NRAs constraints similar to those associated with courts. Thus, pursuant to the Framework Directive, decisions taken by NRAs must be reasoned, that is, the reasons for reaching a particular solution must be explained to the parties. Decisions are to be made public.

> *Framework Directive, Article 20(4).* 'The decision of the national regulatory authority shall be made available to the public, having regard to the requirements of business confidentiality. The parties concerned shall be given a full statement of the reasons on which it is based.'

6.09 **Duration of the procedure.** An important aspect is the timeframe within which solutions are to be found. Rapidity is of the essence, as investments often depend on legal decisions. *(a)* Pursuant to the Framework Directive, cases must be resolved within four months. There is an indication that an even more rapid timeframe is desirable. The four-month period may be extended, but only in exceptional circumstances. *(b)* The procedure may last longer where non-conventional conflict mechanisms are used. As stated above, these mechanisms may be tried for a period up to four months. At the end of that time an assessment must be made. If the conflict has not been solved, the NRA has four additional months to take a binding decision. That second four-month period may not be extended.[3] In this scenario (use of non-conventional means followed by the normal procedure) the procedure cannot last more than eight months in total. *(c)* The eight-month timeframe provides an indication as to the absolute limit for a conflict resolution procedure under the NRF. That time limit is laid down explicitly where a non-conventional followed by a normal procedure is used. There is no explicit limit for situations where NRAs resort solely to normal procedures. In that case the period may last for four months with an extension being possible in exceptional circumstances. There is no reason to accept that these normal procedures may last in total (including extensions) more than the eight months referred to.

---

[3] There is a difference in that regard between the two procedures. The normal procedure usually lasts for four months but may be extended in exceptional circumstances. The procedure leading to a binding decision cannot be prolonged beyond four months when non-conventional mechanisms have been used in the first instance.

Framework Directive, Article 20(1). 'In the event of a dispute arising in connection with obligations arising under this Directive or the Specific Directives between undertakings providing electronic communications networks or services in a Member State, the national regulatory authority . . . issue a binding decision . . . in the shortest possible time frame and in any case within four months except in exceptional circumstances.'

(2) Cross-border conflicts

Co-ordination between NRAs.   Where conflicts arise between parties estab-   **6.10** lished in a single Member State, requests must be addressed to the NRA having authority in the State concerned. Conflicts may also involve parties established in various national territories. The NRAs established in these territories then have the power to intervene. It may in this situation be difficult to avoid conflicting decisions, and the NRF accordingly provides that cross-border conflicts must be resolved through co-ordination among the NRAs concerned.

Framework Directive, Article 21(2). 'Any party may refer the dispute to the national regulatory authorities concerned. The national regulatory authorities shall coordinate their efforts in order to bring about a resolution of the dispute.' *Framework Directive, Preamble, recital 33.* 'In addition to the rights of recourse granted under national or Community law, there is a need for a simple procedure to be initiated at the request of either party in a dispute, to resolve cross-border disputes which lie outside the competence of a single national regulatory authority.'

Which NRAs may intervene?   An issue that arises is the determination of which   **6.11** NRAs are competent to address cross-border conflicts. The criterion provided by the NRF is the place of establishment of the parties involved. Thus an NRA may intervene in a dispute only when that dispute involves a party (undertaking or individual) established on the territory where it has jurisdiction.

Framework Directive, Article 21(1). NRAs must co-ordinate their action '[i]n the event of a cross-border dispute arising under this Directive or the Specific Directives between parties in different Member States, where the dispute lies within the competence of national regulatory authorities from more than one Member State'.

Cross-border dispute-resolution procedure.   The NRF provides little indication   **6.12** concerning the procedures for resolving cross-border disputes. *(a)* The normal procedure will not necessarily lead to the adoption of a binding decision. The purpose is only to come to a 'resolution of the dispute'. *(b)* The timeframe is rather flexible. For instance, the four-month limit applicable to normal procedures concerning national conflicts is not mentioned in connection with cross-border disputes. This appears to imply that NRAs are not bound by the time limit established under the NRF for 'national' conflicts. The reason is probably that time is needed to allow NRAs to co-ordinate their action. *(c)* Under the NRF, NRAs may resort to non-conventional mechanisms (mediation, etc) to resolve cross-border disputes. There is no difference, in this regard, in the treatment of national or cross-border conflicts. A nuance however is that a decision to resort to non-conventional mechanisms has to be taken jointly by all of the NRAs involved. The NRAs thus keep their freedom concerning the mechanisms they want to use. Each of them has the power to block the use of such mechanisms. *(d)* Any attempt to use non-conventional mechanisms must be limited to four months. The time limitation examined for national conflicts thus applies. After the expiry of the four-month period the NRAs may resort to normal procedures. They are not then bound by any time limitation.

> *Framework Directive, Article 21(3)*. 'Member States may make provision for national regulatory authorities jointly to decline to resolve a dispute where other mechanisms, including mediation, exist and would better contribute to resolution of the dispute in a timely manner.' 'If after four months the dispute is not resolved, if the dispute has not been brought before the courts by the party seeking redress, and if either party requests it, the national regulatory authorities shall coordinate their efforts in order to bring about a resolution of the dispute.'

6.13 Duration of the procedures

National conflicts
—Conventional mechanisms (binding decision): four months, if possible less, extension possible in exceptional circumstances.
—Non-conventional means: trial possible for four months; then possibility to turn to the normal procedure; in that case, a binding decision must be taken within four months; total duration: eight months maximum.

Cross-border conflicts
—Normal procedure (not necessarily through binding decision): coordination, no timeframe.
—Non-conventional means: trial possible for four months; possibility to turn to normal procedure; no time frame.

(3) Bringing an action before national courts

6.14 Principle. The NRF further provides that undertakings and individuals may seek redress from national courts. Applicants are not prevented from seeking a remedy in court as a result of a request being addressed to an NRA. The possibility of bringing an action before a national[4] court is not limited to national or to cross-border disputes. In either case, the parties retain the possibility of having their case handled in court.

> *Framework Directive, Article 20(5) and Article 21(4)*. 'The procedure referred to [above] . . . shall not preclude either party from bringing an action before the courts.'

6.15 Rules applicable to the procedure. The rules applicable in procedures before national courts are to be found in national laws. English law, for instance, governs procedures initiated before English courts. English law then determines which court has competence within the English legal system and how the procedure must unfold. The difficulty in cross-border cases is to select a court. As several

---

[4] Under European law, actions may not be brought by undertakings or individuals to the ECJ or the CFI against other undertakings or individuals.

territories are involved, courts from various Member States may claim jurisdiction. There is no indication in the NRF as to how concurrent jurisdiction must be addressed. The matter is thus resolved through a more general instrument, Council Regulation (EC) 44/2001 on jurisdiction and the recognition and enforcement of judgments in civil and commercial matters.[5] Once the jurisdiction is determined, national laws provide the rules applicable to the procedure.[6]

(4) Relations between NRAs and national courts

Concurrent jurisdiction of NRAs and national courts. Concurrence of jurisdiction affects not only courts established in various territories. In some instances, national courts and NRAs are equally competent to handle cases. Suppose a French service provider is denied access to a mobile network belonging to another French operator. Redress may be sought from the French NRA. A case may also be brought before a French court. It cannot be excluded that these instances may reach contradictory conclusions. Similar scenarios may unfold in cross-border disputes. Imagine a German service provider seeking redress from a French network operator charging excessive access fees. A request may be addressed to the French and German NRAs which, as observed earlier, may both be competent to rule, and must co-ordinate their efforts to resolve the conflict. An action could also be brought before a national court, in this case probably a French court, as jurisdiction is based, pursuant to Council Regulation (CE) 44/2001, on the place where the defendant is established.   **6.16**

Little co-ordination in the NRF. Little co-ordination is provided for in the NRF   **6.17**
to resolve concurrent jurisdiction issues between NRAs and national courts in electronic communications matters. *(a)* One principle stated in the framework is that parties are allowed to bring cases to courts in place of, or in addition to, NRAs.[7] This principle indeed causes concurrence in jurisdiction rather than resolving it. *(b)* A second principle is that NRAs must resort to normal procedures only after using non-conventional mechanisms where no action has been brought in the intervening period before a national court. The introduction of an action by a party during the non-conventional phase of the procedure thus implies, pursuant to the NRF, that the NRAs have no power to return to the normal procedure thereafter.[8]

---

[5] [2001] OJ L12/1. Hereinafter 'Council Regulation (EC) 44/2001'.

[6] In the absence of special issues regulated by Council Regulation (EC) 44/2001. Suppose that a dispute arises on interconnection charges due by a British undertaking for access to a network operated by a German undertaking. Pursuant to Council Regulation (EC) 44/2001, the issue is to be heard in the country where the domicile of the defendant is situated. The case should thus be brought before a German court—assuming the British applicant is acting to challenge the access charges. German law applies to the procedure. The case has to be resolved on the merits taking into account the German laws implementing the NRF.

[7] See Framework Directive, Art 20(5) and Art 21(4).

[8] See Framework Directive, Art 20(2). 'If after four months the dispute is not resolved, and if the dispute has not been brought before the courts by the party seeking redress, the national regulatory authority shall issue . . . a binding decision.' A similar provision can be found with respect to transborder disputes in the Framework Directive, Art 21(3).

6.18 **General co-ordination under national laws.** In the absence of a European mechanism, national laws have to be used in order to find ways to solve issues relating to concurrent jurisdiction. In most Member States there are rules for the co-ordination of action by national courts and agencies. These rules generally have wide scope. They apply to all situations where agencies may contradict courts, and vice versa. *(a)* A typical principle, in this regard, is the special powers granted to courts in actions for damages. In most Member States, courts have a specific responsibility in the protection of subjective rights. In that capacity they are entitled to order the reparation of damages caused in violation of rights granted to undertakings or individuals. Such a power is rarely granted to administrative agencies such as NRAs. In the field of reparation, there should thus not exist any cause for concurrent jurisdiction. *(b)* Another technique sometimes used, when a court and an administrative agency are handling a similar case, is to designate which of these two bodies is entitled to proceed. The designation is made in the law, as authorities may act only on the basis of powers allocated to them by the law. *(c)* A third technique is the creation of a superior body which is responsible for consistency in the case law. Through the existence of such a body, Member States attempt to reconcile, at a superior level, the possibly diverging positions adopted by courts and administrative agencies.

6.19 **Necessity of European guidelines.** The absence of European mechanisms to solve concurrent jurisdictional issues between NRAs and national courts is bound to create difficulties. The Parliament and Council have not been willing to interfere in a task which is generally left to the Member States, the organisation of powers within the internal legal orders. However, the absence of European rules does not favour homogeneous solutions across the European Union. Undertakings face different arrangements depending on the territory where the issue is raised. The forging of the internal market is thus affected. Furthermore, satisfactory arrangements do not necessarily exist in all Member States. The observation may be all the more valid with the extension of the Union to new members. In some instances, the absence of satisfactory solutions at national level may impinge on the effectiveness of the law. European institutions would then have power to intervene since, as a result of deadlocks possibly occurring at national level, the effectiveness of the NRF would be affected. It is to be hoped that, to anticipate difficulties of this nature, guidelines will be provided at European level.[9]

---

[9] A similar difficulty emerged in the field of competition law, where agencies and courts have somewhat concurrent jurisdictions to apply competition rules. The relations between these two categories of entities are now organised in a regulation adopted by the Council. Beforehand, guidelines had been issued by the European Commission. See Notice on cooperation between national courts and the Commission in applying Articles 85 and 86 of the EEC Treaty [1993] OJ C39/6 and Commission notice on cooperation between national competition authorities and the Commission in handling cases falling within the scope of Arts 85 or 86 of the EC Treaty [1997] OJ C313/3. These guidelines contain principles that could be used, in our opinion, by national courts and agencies, to organise their relations.

(5) Right of appeal against NRA decisions

Applicable provisions. Decisions adopted by NRAs may be challenged on **6.20** appeal. The NRF goes even further by stating that there must exist a possibility for the parties concerned to challenge NRA decisions. These decisions against which an appeal is available may be those taken by the NRA in fulfilment of its regulatory task. They may also be those adopted by the NRAs in the course of the procedure set up to resolve conflicts. The applicable provisions are Article 4 of the Framework Directive and Article 2 of the Consolidated Services Directive.

Principles. An appeal may be lodged by undertakings or individuals. In either **6.21** case, the applicant needs to demonstrate only that it is 'affected'.[10] The body with which an appeal is lodged must be independent of the parties. It must have the expertise required to fulfil its task. It must be given the resources and personnel necessary to ensure that the appeal process is effective. It must have the power to review all aspects of the case, including the ability to take a decision on the merits of the case and adopt interim measures as necessary.

> *Framework Directive, Article 4(1).* 'Member States shall ensure that effective mechanisms exist at national level under which any user or undertaking providing electronic communications networks and/or services who is affected by a decision of a national regulatory authority has the right of appeal against the decision to an appeal body that is independent of the parties involved. This body, which may be a court, shall have the appropriate expertise available to it to enable it to carry out its functions. Member States shall ensure that the merits of the case are duly taken into account and that there is an effective appeal mechanism. Pending the outcome of any such appeal, the decision of the national regulatory authority shall stand, unless the appeal body decides otherwise.'

The appeal body. In most Member States, the appeal body is a (national) court. **6.22** Other possibilities may be envisaged. One of them is for another administrative body to rule on the case. Several constraints apply where Member States opt for a body which does not have the status of a court. *(a)* That administrative body must be independent of the NRA.[11] *(b)* An additional level must be available for a further review, by a court, of the decision adopted by the administrative appeal body. *(c)* The administrative appeal body is subject to rules generally applicable to courts. A specific reference is made, in this context, to an obligation to provide reasoned decisions.[12]

---

[10] There is no such requirement as those which can be found under normal European rules for access to a European court, where legal or natural persons must demonstrate that they are directly and individually affected by an instrument before being allowed to start an action against such instrument.

[11] A high standard of independence applies. Should that not be the case, the appeal procedure loses credibility and the appeal cannot be said to be effective as required in the NRF.

[12] The parties are told the reasons why decisions were adopted, and are then in a better position to challenge these decisions in court.

Framework Directive, Article 4. 'This [appeal] body . . . may be a court.' 'Where the appeal body . . . is not judicial in character, written reasons for its decision shall always be given. Furthermore, in such a case, its decision shall be subject to review by a court or tribunal within the meaning of Article 234 of the Treaty.'

6.23 **Consolidated Services Directive.**   As stated above, similar rules may be found in the Consolidated Services Directive. The main concern driving the Commission in this regard is to ensure that NRAs do not prevent undertakings from entering markets and performing their activities. To avoid potential difficulties, the Commission has inserted a specific provision ensuring that review must be available against an act taken by an NRA and restricting the right of an undertaking to provide a network and/or a service. The conditions which the review must satisfy are similar to those imposed in the Framework Directive and examined above. *(a)* The review must be carried out by an organ independent of the parties. *(b)* That organ should ideally be a judicial body. *(c)* Should that not be the case, a second level of review must be organised before a judge. *(d)* To make the review possible, and effective, NRAs are obliged to reason their decisions.[13]

Consolidated Services Directive, Article 2(5). 'Reasons shall be given for any decision . . . preventing an undertaking from providing electronic communications services or networks. Any aggrieved party should have the possibility to challenge such a decision before a body that is independent of the parties involved and ultimately before a court or a tribunal.'

6.24 **Current situation in the Member States.**   In the Eighth implementation report, the Commission appears satisfied with the situation as it currently exists in the Member States. In most cases, appeals are lodged with a court. Some countries have organised a first, internal, appeal, where the case is addressed in a first instance within the NRA itself. That system may be in line with the organisation of appeals as it generally exists in the administrative law of these countries. It is not encouraged, however, by the Commission, because time and resources are diverted from the main mission entrusted to NRAs, that is, to regulate markets.[14]

Eighth implementation report, 19. 'In almost all Member States appeals are lodged with a court, normally an administrative tribunal. Denmark is the only country which has established a separate appeals body which is not a court, while in the United Kingdom appeals against decisions by OFTEL using its concurrent competition powers are submitted in the first instance to the Competition Commission. In some further cases appeals are in the first instance dealt with internally in the NRA

---

[13] In their reasoning, NRAs must explain why they have reached a given conclusion. They must also specify the contacts that the undertakings concerned have had with the NRA. In this manner, the appeal body is in position to verify whether the decision has been taken by the NRA in conformity with the obligations introduced by the NRF (in particular the fundamental requirements: objectivity, transparency, non-discrimination, proportionality).

[14] Another reason, not mentioned by the Commission, is that the probability that a decision taken by an organ may be changed by that organ itself is not high. One may wonder why, in these circumstances, the appeal could not be heard directly by another authority.

(Belgium, Spain, Luxembourg, the Netherlands), which may mean time and resources are diverted from pure regulatory oversight.' 'In Germany, the length of the appeals procedure due to confidentiality rules is considered a barrier to competition.'

Procedure and substance.   In many Member States, administrative decisions are   **6.25** reviewed in their formal aspects. The courts determine whether the administrative organ which has taken the decision has respected the formalities prior to adopting a position. That situation, for the Commission, is not satisfactory. For that reason, it has been specified in the NRF that the review should address both the substance and the form where an appeal is lodged against a decision taken by an NRA.

> *Eighth implementation report, 19.* 'The practice under the existing framework has in many cases been for the appeals bodies to examine process rather than substance. This situation must be remedied under the new regime, and is indeed changing: in France for example the Court of Appeal, assisted by an expert, can now examine the substance of an NRA decision in addition to its legality.'

(6) What should undertakings and individuals do?

Procedures before NRAs and national courts in parallel.   Some individuals   **6.26** may be dissatisfied with the services that are provided to them and which they consider to be incompatible with the requirements set forth in the national legislation implementing the NRF. Individuals in this situation should address a request for a decision to the NRA. The procedure is bound to be effective and without cost. Most substantial complaints come, however, from undertakings seeking access or other services from powerful undertakings and finding that these services are not satisfactory. The advice to these undertakings is also to seek redress from the relevant NRA. NRAs have developed a culture where competition is important, since their task is to ensure that competition develops and is maintained. Such undertakings have little to gain from non-conventional mechanisms. In most instances the only effect of these mechanisms is to delay the outcome. A binding decision should be requested and a plea made that the four-month period should not be extended. If the resources are available, the party seeking redress should simultaneously bring an action before a national court and pursue the two procedures in parallel, stopping them or one of them when it is satisfied with the outcome. Showing through the commencement of these procedures that a satisfactory outcome is sought at all costs should exert decisive pressure on the other party.

C. What Has Changed?

Conflicts between parties.   No significant change has been introduced in the   **6.27** NRF regarding conflicts between parties (undertakings, individuals). *(a)* The old framework already provided that conflicts of this nature could be resolved by NRAs. In fulfilling that task, these authorities were to use the regulatory powers conferred on them by the framework. The ONP Interconnection Directive, for instance, gave NRAs the power to intervene on their own initiative or at the request of one party, to specify issues to be covered in an interconnection agreement, or lay down specific conditions to be observed by one or more parties to such an agreement.[15] Pursuant to the same directive, NRAs could, in exceptional cases, require changes to be made to interconnection agreements already concluded, where justified to ensure effective competition and/or interoperability of services for users.[16] Similar possibilities existed under the ONP Voice Telephony Directive and the ONP Leased Lines Directive.[17] *(b)* There is no difference either regarding the requirements imposed on NRAs in the procedures leading to a resolution of conflicts. In the old framework, as in the NRF, conflicts were to be resolved rapidly. The procedures were to be transparent and the rights of the parties were to be respected. Finally, decisions were to be reasoned and were to be notified to the party(ies) before implementation.[18]

6.28 **Appeal against NRA decisions.** The analysis is identical as regards appeals against decisions adopted by NRAs. The possibility of lodging an appeal was introduced in the ONP Framework Directive.[19] In the context of general competition law, the Services Directive adopted by the Commission required Member States to create a channel, where necessary, for undertakings to challenge decisions whereby authorities refused an authorisation to provide a service.[20] Beyond these directives, the possibility for legal or natural persons to bring an application against a decision adopted by a national authority and affecting them may be regarded as a general principle of law. In the electronic communications sector, for instance, the Terminal Equipment Liberalisation Directive stated unequivocally that 'the addressees of any decision taken . . . must be informed of the reasons for such a decision and the means of appeal open to them'.[21]

6.29 **Case law.** In the case law, this principle has been affirmed in *Régie des télégraphes et des téléphones (RTT)*.[22] That case concerned terminal equipment sold in Belgium by a supermarket in violation of national regulations. RTT was a public body entrusted with economic activities, the operation of the national telecommunications network, the provision of telecommunications services and the sale of telecommunications equipment. In addition to these tasks, RTT was also granted

---

[15] See ONP Interconnection Directive, Art 9(4).   [16] ibid.

[17] See ONP Voice Telephony Directive, Art 26 and ONP Leased Lines Directive, Art 12.

[18] For all these requirements, see ONP Leased Lines Directive, Art 8, para 1.

[19] See ONP Framework Directive, Art 5bis(3).   [20] See Services Directive, Art 2(3), al 1.

[21] See Council Directive (EEC) 91/263 on the approximation of the laws of the Member States concerning telecommunications terminal equipment, including the mutual recognition of their conformity [1991] OJ L128/1. That instrument has been abrogated. The instrument currently in force is European Parliament and Council Directive (EC) 1999/5 on radio equipment and telecommunications terminal equipment and the mutual recognition of their conformity [1999] OJ L91/10.

[22] Case C-18/88 *Régie des télégraphes et des téléphones v GB-Inno-BM* [1991] ECR I-5941.

regulatory powers, including the power to specify the technical requirements to be satisfied before connecting terminals to the national network. There was a fear that in using these powers the RTT would adopt rules favouring its own operations. The ECJ ruled that granting regulatory powers to an entity active on the markets was not compatible with the competition rules. Additionally, the ECJ emphasised the obligation for Member States to establish procedures allowing undertakings to seek remedies against decisions adopted by national authorities and affecting the possibility of entering a national market.

> *RTT, Judgment of the ECJ.* '[I]t must be open to traders to challenge before the courts an unjustified failure to grant authorisation for imports. The same possibility must exist with regard to decisions refusing to grant type-approval since they can lead in practice to denial of access to the market of a Member State to telephone equipment imported from another Member State and hence to a barrier to the free movement of goods.'[23]

D. Application of General Competition Law

(1) Introduction and applicable provisions

Proceedings on the basis of general competition law. Parallel to the rules com- **6.30** posing the NRF, undertakings and users alike can act on the basis of the competition rules where these have been infringed. The interaction between these two sets of rules (sector-specific regulation and general competition law) has been examined in earlier sections in connection with particular issues (specifically, access and universal service). The analysis will be continued at the end of this chapter, when an analysis is presented of conflicts that may occur between various bodies or sets of rules. In this section, the purpose is to present the procedures that may be used to exploit the possibilities offered by competition law.

Applicable provisions. The rules concerning proceedings based on general **6.31** competition law that can be used in electronic communications are contained in Regulation 1/2003 on the implementation of the rules on competition laid down in Articles 81 and 82 of the Treaty.[24] This regulation has substantially changed the arrangements that were in force until then. The following presentation is based on these new rules. A short summary is provided at the end of this section to underline the most significant changes that have taken place.

(2) National competition authorities (NCAs)

Recourse to specialised national agencies. Parties contending that the **6.32** European competition rules have been violated can complain to NCAs. These

---

[23] At [34].
[24] [2003] OJ L1/1. Hereinafter 'Regulation 1/2003'. The date for the entry into force of the regulation was 1 May 2004.

authorities are specialised administrative agencies established in the Member States in order to solve competition-related disputes. The purpose is to have a set of agents qualified to deal with the complex issues involved in the application of competition rules. The possibility for parties to complain to a specialised agency in competition matters is not different from the situation examined in connection with sector-specific regulation. In both cases, parties seek redress from an authority specialising in the application of the rules on which the contention is based. A difference should however be noted. In sector-specific regulation applicable on electronic communications markets, national authorities apply national rules. In the area of competition, national authorities apply national *and* European rules alike. In contrast to what was observed for sector-specific regulation, authorities intervening in the context of competition rules act, simultaneously, in their capacity as an entity entrusted with national, and European, powers and obligations.[25]

> *Council Regulation (EC) 1/2003, Article 5.* 'The competition authorities of the Member States shall have the power to apply Articles 81 and 82 of the Treaty in individual cases.' *Regulation 1/2003, Preamble, recital 6.* 'In order to ensure that the Community competition rules are applied effectively, the competition authorities of the Member States should be associated more closely with their application. To this end, they should be empowered to apply Community law.'

	NRAs	NCAs
Do they apply national law?	Yes	Yes
Do they apply European law?	In principle, no[26]	Yes

6.33 **Designation of authorities.** In pursuance of Regulation 1/2003, the Member States must designate the authorities which are responsible for the application of European competition rules on their respective territories. A date was set for the communication of the identity of these authorities to the European Commission (1 May 2004). The list of designated authorities may also be consulted on the website of the European Commission, Directorate General for Competition. The designation must ensure that the authorities in charge of the application of these rules are in a position to function effectively. The Commission is entitled to initiate a procedure against a Member State before the ECJ where that Member State has failed to take the appropriate measures to ensure effective application of European competition rules in its national territory.

---

[25] The difference should not be overestimated. In sector-specific regulation, national authorities admittedly apply national rules. But these rules must conform to European law. In the absent of conformity, NRAs must set aside their national legislation. In that scenario, they can also apply the NRF—at least the provisions of it which have direct effect. On the basis of the latter hypothesis, one can say that, through national rules, NRAs indeed apply European electronic communications laws.

[26] NRAs only have to apply European law directly when the national implementing legislation does not conform with European rules.

Regulation 1/2003, Article 35(1). 'The Member States shall designate the competition authority or authorities responsible for the application of Articles 81 and 82 of the Treaty in such a way that the provisions of this regulation are effectively complied with. The measures necessary to empower those authorities to apply those Articles shall be taken before 1 May 2004.'

The power to apply the competition rules.   Pursuant to Regulation 1/2003,   **6.34**
NCAs are empowered to adopt decisions requiring that an infringement be brought to an end; ordering interim measures; accepting commitments; and imposing fines or penalties.[27] Under the regulation, the Member States may organise these powers as they need. They may, in particular, organise, according to their needs, the institutional structure leading to the application of European competition rules on their national territories. For instance, they may allocate powers and responsibilities between national courts or administrative agencies. In practice, Member States have remained attached to the distinction classically made between the judiciary and the executive branch. For that reason they have entrusted to administrative agencies the tasks attributed to the NCAs in Regulation 1/2003. They have further organised in specific legislation the relations with national courts, which have retained their traditional competences (defence of private interests in civil or commercial litigation).

Regulation 1/2003, Article 5. 'The competition authorities of the Member States shall have the power to apply Articles 81 and 82 of the Treaty in individual cases. For this purpose, acting on their own initiative or on a complaint, they may take the following decisions: requiring that an infringement be brought to an end, ordering interim measures, accepting commitments, imposing fines, periodic penalty payments or any other penalty provided for in their national law.'

Regulation 1/2003, Article 35(2). 'When enforcement of Community competition law is entrusted to national administrative and judicial authorities, the Member States may allocate different powers and functions to those different national authorities, whether administrative or judicial.' *Preamble, recital 35.* 'In order to attain a proper enforcement of Community competition law, Member States should designate and empower authorities to apply Articles 81 and 82 of the Treaty as public enforcers. They should be able to designate administrative as well as judicial authorities to carry out the various functions conferred upon competition authorities in this Regulation. This Regulation recognises the wide variation which exists in the public enforcement systems of Member States.'

Is there an obligation to intervene?   The power for NCAs to apply national and   **6.35**
European competition rules is provided in Regulation 1/2003. An issue arising is whether NCAs are under an obligation to investigate all cases that are brought before them by undertakings and/or individuals. This is, in principle, a matter for the Member States to decide. The Member States retain the power, as has been stated, to organise their institutional structure, as long as the effectiveness of

---

[27] See Regulation 1/2003, Art 5.

European law is not affected. It is generally accepted that, under normal circumstances, administrative authorities are not compelled to pursue all matters. They enjoy a certain margin of action to determine what they want to investigate, and how. This is due to the limited nature of the resources available to these authorities. Their available personnel in particular is limited, and they are accordingly not in a position to investigate all claims in the same manner. Choices have to be made and priorities set. For that reason, NCAs are empowered to select the cases they wish to investigate further.[28]

6.36 **Exception—Obligation to intervene.** An exception is made for the application of European competition law in certain situations. Where national and European competition rules are applicable to a case (ie the conditions for the application of the two sets of laws are fulfilled) and the competent NCA decides to apply national competition rules, the NCA cannot avoid applying European competition rules. European competition law must be applied whenever NCAs decide to apply national competition law and the conditions are fulfilled for the application of the European rules.

> *Council Regulation 1/2003, Article 16(1).* 'Where the competition authorities of the Member States or national courts apply national competition law to agreements, decisions by associations of undertakings or concerted practices within the meaning of Article 81(1) of the Treaty which may affect trade between Member States within the meaning of that provision, they shall also apply Article 81 of the Treaty to such agreements, decisions or concerted practices. Where the competition authorities of the Member States or national courts apply national competition law to any abuse prohibited by Article 82 of the Treaty, they shall also apply Article 82 of the Treaty.'

(3) Relations between NCAs and the European Commission

6.37 **Action by the Commission in the field of competition.** NCAs thus have a substantial role in the application of European competition rules. This does not imply that the Commission is inactive in that field. Its attention focuses on drafting documents of a more general nature to guide national authorities in the fulfilment of their tasks. The Commission also retains the power to apply European rules in specific cases.[29] The power to apply the European competition rules in individual cases was explicitly vested on the Commission by the Treaty itself. It was not in the power of the Council to change that situation in a regulation. Only

---

[28] The only obligation imposed on NCAs is to notify the complainants about the fate of their complaint. Parties that want to have an official decision may bring an action before the national courts, when they cannot obtain a decision from a national agency. Under a general principle of law, courts have to render judgments on cases submitted to them.

[29] That indeed derives from the EC Treaty itself. See Art 85(1) EC. '[T]he Commission shall ensure the application of the principles laid down in Art. 81 and 82.' '[T]he Commission shall investigate cases of suspected infringement of these principles. If it finds that there has been an infringement, it shall propose appropriate measures to bring it to an end.'

through an amendment to the Treaty could the Commission be divested of its power to apply competition laws in concrete cases.

Supervision by the Commission.   Ultimately, the organisational structure estab-   **6.38**
lished in Regulation 1/2003 ensures that the application of European competition rules remains the prime responsibility of the European Commission.
In that organisation, the national authorities act as decentralised organs. They
apply the rules in individual cases under the supervision of the Commission. The
implication is that NCAs are indeed subject to the authority of the Commission
in the fulfilment of their tasks. This is apparent from various mechanisms embodied in Regulation 1/2003. These mechanisms are presented in the following
paragraphs.

Binding individual decisions.   A first mechanism is that the decisions adopted   **6.39**
by the Commission in individual cases are binding on NCAs. The issuance of
a decision by the Commission thus implies that the NCAs may not adopt, in the
same case, a decision running counter to the Commission's prior decision.

> *Regulation 1/2003, Article 16(2).* 'When competition authorities of the Member
> States rule on agreements, decisions or practices under Article 81 or Article 82 of the
> Treaty which are already the subject of a Commission decision, they cannot take
> decisions which would run counter to the decision adopted by the Commission.'

Intervention in concrete cases.   A second mechanism is that the Commission   **6.40**
further has the power to divest NCAs of the competence to handle a given case.
As stated above, the Commission retains the power to intervene in individual
cases. If the Commission decides to make use of that possibility in a particular case,
the initiation of a European procedure automatically suspends the power of the
national authorities to pursue the case. As a consequence of that mechanism, there
cannot, under normal circumstances, be two enquiries pending simultaneously
on the same case, one at European level and the other carried out at national
level.[30]

---

[30] In practice, the Commission is in constant contact with the NCAs. NCAs involved in a case
are thus rapidly informed of the interest of the Commission in a particular case. Regulation 1/2003
signals that, out of courtesy, the Commission must consult national authorities before starting
an investigation when a national procedure is already under way. See Regulation 1/2003, Art 11(6).
'If a competition authority of a Member State is already acting on a case, the Commission shall only
initiate proceedings after consulting with that NCA.' In the same line, the Commission must proceed rapidly if a case is already pending before an NRA. It would not be appropriate to leave the
NRA in uncertainty as to whether the case will be taken over. See Regulation 1/2003, Preamble,
recital 17. 'Where a competition authority of a Member State is already acting on a case and the
Commission intends to initiate proceedings, it [the Commission] should endeavour to do so as soon
as possible.' Cases where the Commission wishes to intervene may also be discussed during a meeting of the Advisory Committee—an organ bringing together representatives of the Commission
and the NCAs. See Regulation 1/2003, Art 14(7). 'A request may in particular be made by a competition authority of a Member State [for a discussion in the Advisory Committee] in respect of a
case where the Commission intends to initiate proceedings.'

> *Regulation 1/2003, Article 11(6).* 'The initiation by the Commission of proceedings for the adoption of a decision . . . shall relieve the competition authorities of the Member States of their competence to apply Articles 81 and 82 of the Treaty.'

6.41 **Obligation to notify.** A third mechanism is that NCAs are under an obligation to notify the Commission concerning their intention to initiate a procedure. This notification gives the Commission a chance to consider whether it is in agreement with the performance of the task by national authorities or whether it considers that the task should be taken over.

> *Regulation 1/2003, Article 11(3).* 'The competition authorities of the Member States shall, when acting under Article 81 or Article 82 of the Treaty, inform the Commission in writing before or without delay after commencing the first formal investigative measure.'

6.42 **Communication of draft decision.** Finally, NCAs must communicate to the Commission, at the end of the procedure, the decision they intend to take in a given case. The Commission then has 30 days to consider whether it wishes to take the case over. If, and when, the Commission takes a case over, the national authorities are relieved of their powers in the case.

> *Regulation 1/2003, Article 11(4).* 'No later than 30 days before the adoption of a decision requiring that an infringement be brought to an end, accepting commitments or withdrawing the benefit of a block exemption Regulation, the competition authorities of the Member States shall inform the Commission. To that effect, they shall provide the Commission with a summary of the case, the envisaged decision or, in the absence thereof, any other document indicating the proposed course of action . . . At the request of the Commission, the acting competition authority shall make available to the Commission other documents it holds which are necessary for the assessment of the case.'

6.43 **Co-operation at the heart of the system.** The mechanisms examined in the previous paragraph are set in place in order to ensure that the Commission prevails where it disagrees with NCAs on the application of European competition rules in a given case. These mechanisms should however be used only in exceptional circumstances. The heart of the system is indeed co-operation, not conflict, between the NCAs and the Commission. *(a)* One way for NCAs to co-operate with the Commission is to consult the latter whenever they consider it appropriate for the resolution of pending cases. Through consultation, authorities maintain contact on pending cases and avoid conflicting interpretations. *(b)* Within Regulation 1/2003, consultation is not considered a unilateral process proceeding from the NCAs to the Commission. Emphasis is placed on obligations imposed on the Commission to provide NCAs with whatever information is necessary. *(c)* Before issuing a decision in an individual case, the Commission must consult the representatives of the NCAs in an Advisory Committee that is convened regularly at the request of the Commission.

> *Regulation 1/2003, Article 11.* [1] 'The Commission and the competition authorities of the Member States shall apply the Community competition rules in close cooperation.'

[5] 'The competition authorities of the Member States may consult the Commission on any case involving the application of Community law.' [2] 'The Commission shall transmit to the competition authorities of the Member States copies of the most important documents it has collected.' 'At the request of the competition authority of a Member State, the Commission shall provide it with a copy of other existing documents necessary for the assessment of the case.'

The Advisory Committee. The Advisory Committee plays an important role **6.44** in applying European competition law. That body was created in order to assist the Commission in its task as agency in charge of implementing the European competition rules. The Committee provides opportunities to bring together specialists to advise the Commission. It also constitutes a forum where NCAs and the Commission can meet and exchange ideas as well as information. One of the main tasks entrusted to the Advisory Committee is to counsel, and place restraints on, the Commission before the adoption, by the latter, of a decision in an individual case.[31] *(a)* When the Committee is examining individual decisions envisaged by the Commission, it is composed of representatives of the NCAs.[32] *(b)* Strict procedural rules must be complied with regarding meetings, which must be convened at least 14 days in advance. Where interim measures are considered, a period of seven days is deemed sufficient. Shorter periods are accepted if no Member State opposes them. The consultation may take place by written procedure, with the rules examined above concerning time-periods then applying. The Committee however has to meet if any Member State so requests. *(c)* Meetings are convened, and chaired, by the Commission. *(d)* Documents must be communicated to participants, including a summary of the case, an indication of the most important documents and a preliminary draft decision. *(e)* The Advisory Committee must deliver a written opinion on the draft decision presented by the Commission. However, the reasons underlying the positions adopted in the opinion must be explained if one or several members so request. *(f)* The Commission is not bound by the opinion delivered. It must however take utmost account of it. The Commission must also inform the Committee as to how the opinion has been taken into account. *(g)* The opinion must be appended to the draft decision, in writing.[33] The written opinion must be published by the Commission, if the Committee so requests. Business secrets must be protected.

---

[31] On the Advisory Committee, see Regulation 1/2003, Art 14.

[32] Art 14(3). When other issues are discussed—where for instance the opinion of the Committee is sought about an important reform envisaged by the Commission—the Committee may also comprise an additional representative per Member State. The purpose is then to gather expertise and ensure that the right specialists are sent by the Member States even if these specialists do not operate within NCAs. See Regulation 1/2003, Art 14(7). 'The Advisory Committee may . . . discuss general issues of Community competition law.'

[33] This precaution ensures that the opinion delivered by the Committee is communicated to all members of the European Commission prior to its taking a decision.

(4) Co-operation between NCAs

6.45 Avoidance of divergent interpretations. As stated, European competition law is applied to a certain extent by NCAs. A risk is thereby created that diverging national case law may develop concerning the interpretation of European competition law. Tools have been established under Regulation 1/2003 to avoid excessive disparities. These tools have been examined in the paragraphs below. Among them are the possibility for the Commission of intervening in cases where NCAs are envisaging adopting decisions which it considers inappropriate.

6.46 Exchange of information. These tools in general concern relations between the NCAs and the Commission. Other devices have been put in place to organise co-operation among NCAs themselves. Classic channels are used for this purpose. One of them is the exchange of information. Regulation 1/2003 stresses the importance for NCAs of exchanging information among themselves. The traditional rules of confidentiality are applicable. For instance, information can be used only for the application of European and national competition laws.

> *Regulation 1/2003, Article 12.* [1] 'For the purpose of applying Articles 81 and 82 of the Treaty . . . the competition authorities of the Member States shall have the power to provide one another with and use in evidence any matter of fact or of law, including confidential information.' [2] 'Information exchanged shall only be used in evidence for the purpose of applying Article 81 or Article 82 of the Treaty and in respect of the subject-matter for which it was collected by the transmitting authority. However, where national competition law is applied in the same case and in parallel to Community competition law and does not lead to a different outcome, information exchanged under this Article may also be used for the application of national competition law.'

6.47 Mutual consultations. Another device provided by Regulation 1/2003 is regular meetings under the auspices of the Advisory Committee.[34] It was observed that the Committee plays an important role in structuring relations between the NCAs and the Commission. The same may be said regarding relations among NCAs. *(a)* Individual cases submitted to NCAs in their respective countries can be discussed during meetings. The Committee thus provides a forum where national cases may be presented spontaneously by NCAs in search of assistance or advice. *(b)* Meetings may also be used to call upon NCAs to justify their attitude in cases pending before them.[35] An invitation to explain a particular attitude may

---

[34] That Committee has been mentioned in connection with decisions envisaged by the Commission on individual competition law cases (obligation for the Commission to consult representatives of all European NCAs).

[35] Suppose that the French NCA is investigating a case involving a British undertaking. It is possible, for the British NCA's representative, to question, through the Advisory Committee, its French counterpart about the treatment given to the case in France and the intentions of the French authority as regards the solution to be given to the case.

be addressed by one NCA to another, or may come from the Commission. Through this rather informal mechanism, NCAs are kept informed as to how European competition rules are applied throughout the European Union. Where they are not satisfied with an explanation given to them, NCAs can ask the Commission to initiate its own proceedings. It will be recalled that the initiation by the Commission of its own proceedings terminates all proceedings started by the national authority(ies) in charge of the case.

> *Regulation 1/2003, Article 14(7)*. 'At the request of a competition authority of a Member State, the Commission shall include on the agenda of the Advisory Committee cases that are being dealt with by a competition authority of a Member State under Article 81 or Article 82 of the Treaty. The Commission may also do so on its own initiative.'[36]

Less pressure on NCAs regarding national cases.   It has been observed that **6.48** considerable pressure can be placed on the Commission by the Advisory Committee in the treatment of individual cases. That pressure results from several mechanisms: the Commission must consult the Advisory Committee before adopting an Article 81 or 82 EC decision; the Committee must adopt a written opinion regarding that draft decision; the opinion must be reasoned, if one or several members of the Committee so request; the opinion must be attached to the draft decision which is circulated within the Commission; the opinion must be published, if the Committee requests it. A legitimate expectation would have been the application of these mechanisms not only to decisions being prepared by the Commission, but also to procedures being handled by NCAs. However, nothing of this kind is provided for in Regulation 1/2003. The only possibility is that of discussing individual national cases or calling upon an NCA to justify its attitude. The regulation stops short of imposing on NCAs a mechanism similar to that applied to the Commission.[37]

Determination of the jurisdiction of the NCAs.   On what basis can it be **6.49** considered that an NCA has jurisdiction to handle a case? No indication can be found on this subject in Regulation 1/2003. In the absence of a European rule, the answer is to be found in national law. It is for the Member States to decide when, and where, their NCAs have the power to intervene. The competence of these national authorities is a matter for the Member States to organise. This does not imply that European law has no influence on these issues. The authority to apply European competition laws is granted to the NCAs by a European regulation.

---

[36] A difference from the procedure concerning the decisions envisaged by the Commission is that, in cases involving national decisions, the Advisory Committee cannot issue opinions on cases treated by competition authorities of the Member States. See Regulation 1/2003, Art 14(7).

[37] The regulation even provides that no opinion can be issued by the Advisory Committee on cases handled by NCAs. See Regulation 1/2003, Art 14(7). 'The Advisory Committee shall not issue opinions on cases dealt with by competition authorities of the Member States.'

Furthermore, that regulation provides that, in some circumstances, NCAs not only have the power to apply these rules, they indeed have an obligation to do so.

6.50 **Concurrent jurisdiction of NCAs from several Member States.**   As the Member States decide when their authorities intervene, the possibility cannot be excluded that national authorities from various States simultaneously declare themselves competent to address the same case. Concurrent jurisdiction inevitably flows from the freedom left to Member States to organise their authorities.[38] The difficulty in such a situation is to avoid conflicting decisions from concurrently competent authorities. Several tools are available in the regulation to address this difficulty; they do not however appear altogether satisfactory. *(a)* Some mechanisms introduced by Regulation 1/2003 to ensure a degree of uniformity in the case law have been examined (exchange of information, possibility for the Commission to initiate its own proceedings). *(b)* These tools are probably sufficient to avoid significant disparities between decisions. As stated, the Commission may take over the responsibility for a case where it feels that an unsatisfactory conclusion would be reached by the competent NCA. *(c)* The regulation however stops short of establishing criteria for the designation, among the various NCAs possibly involved in a case, of the one offering the best forum to decide the case.[39] To this extent, Regulation 1/2003 provides mechanisms to manage some of the consequences brought about by concurrent jurisdiction, but no concrete tools to avoid that concurrence. The only attempt made in that direction is a reference in Regulation 1/2003 to the possibility for NCAs of suspending proceedings, or rejecting a complaint, when the matter is treated concurrently, or has already been treated, by another NCA. Suspension or rejection of a case are authorised, but are not made obligatory.[40]

Regulation 1/2003, Article 13. [2] 'Where a competition authority of a Member State or the Commission has received a complaint against an agreement, decision of an

---

[38] The intervention of several authorities may have drawbacks. Suppose an undertaking obtains a favourable decision from an NCA. That positive outcome may be undone by another NCA taking a stricter attitude vis-à-vis the applicant in the same case. In other situations, the existence of concurrent jurisdiction at least has one advantage: undertakings and individuals can choose the authority likely to produce the most favourable outcome.

[39] Suppose that two NCAs claim jurisdiction in a given case. Imagine that these authorities are envisaging different, if not contradictory, solutions for that case. The dossier is brought by the Commission, or by an NCA, to the Advisory Committee. As a result of the consultation, the Commission takes over responsibility for the case. The initiation of the procedure by the European Commission implies that the NCAs involved are relieved of their tasks and powers in the case at issue. In such a scenario, the conflict between the two NCAs involved is not really solved—it is rather set aside. The mechanism allowing the Commission to intervene is powerful, as it takes the case away from the conflicting authorities. It also has limitations because it does not articulate objective criteria to designate, among the NCAs involved, the one which, it is deemed, would have the greatest merits to decide the case.

[40] The absence of an obligation makes the provision to some extent redundant. As stated, administrative agencies are rarely compelled to pursue a case. As they have limited resources and personnel, they have a margin to determine whether a case is worth pursuing. A decision to suspend proceedings or reject a complaint would be appropriate, in most situations, on that basis, when a case is already handled by another authority.

association or practice which has already been dealt with by another competition authority, it may reject it.' [1] 'Where competition authorities of two or more Member States have received a complaint or are acting on their own initiative under Article 81 or Article 82 of the Treaty against the same agreement, decision of an association or practice, the fact that one authority is dealing with the case shall be sufficient grounds for the others to suspend the proceedings before them or to reject the complaint.' *Regulation 1/2003, Preamble, recital 18.* 'To ensure that cases are dealt with by the most appropriate authorities within the network, a general provision should be laid down allowing a competition authority to suspend or close a case on the ground that another authority is dealing with it or has already dealt with it, the objective being that each case should be handled by a single authority.'

(5) Bringing an action before national courts

Intervention by national courts. Parties may bring an action based on the **6.51** competition rules before national courts to solve issues relating to electronic communications markets. National courts may thus intervene, in addition to NCAs and the Commission, in the application of competition rules. Pursuant to Regulation 1/2003, national courts have the power, and indeed the obligation, to apply European competition rules. In most Member States, national courts have in parallel the power to apply national competition law. The jurisdiction of the courts, and the procedure applicable before them, are matters for the Member States to decide.

> *Regulation 1/2003, Article 6.* 'National courts shall have the power to apply Articles 81 and 82 of the Treaty.'

No hierarchical power of the Commission. The main difference, compared **6.52** to the application of European competition rules by NCAs, is that the Commission lacks any hierarchical power over national courts. This absence of power, or control, is due to the 'division of powers' between the legislature, the executive and the judiciary. In application of that principle, the courts must remain free to apply the law as it stands without interference from the other branches. The principle applies also to the relations between the Commission and the European courts, the ECJ and CFI. It also applies to the relations between, on the one hand, the European legislature or executive and, on the other, the national courts.

Tools for the Commission to influence national courts. This does not mean **6.53** that the Commission has no means of influencing, or attempting to influence, decisions envisaged by national courts. A series of progressive mechanisms are set in place to ensure that the Commission expresses its view.

Avoid conflicting decisions with the Commission. A first tool is a prohibition **6.54** imposed on national courts from issuing judgments conflicting with decisions already taken by the Commission. National courts must also avoid judgments which may contradict possible future decisions in investigations pending before the Commission. In the latter scenario, national courts are invited to stay their proceedings until the end of the procedure before the Commission.

> *Regulation 1/2003, Article16(1).* 'When national courts rule on agreements, decisions or practices under Article 81 or Article 82 of the Treaty which are already the subject of a Commission decision, they cannot take decisions running counter to the decision adopted by the Commission. They must also avoid giving decisions which would conflict with a decision contemplated by the Commission in proceedings it has initiated. To that effect, the national court may assess whether it is necessary to stay its proceedings.'

6.55 **Consultation of the Commission by national courts.** Tools are also given to organise consultations between national courts and the Commission. *(a)* National courts may ask the Commission to supply information in relation to pending cases. If a request of this nature is made, and adequate information provided, national courts can base their assessment on the same documentation as that used by the Commission to examine the case. The existence of an identical background information limits the probability that diverging conclusions will be reached. *(b)* National courts are invited to ask the Commission's opinion on pending cases. The idea is that, competition rules being a technical matter, national courts are satisfied, in most instances, to take over the opinion of the Commission, as that of an expert body specialised in competition issues. *(c)* The Commission may submit observations to national courts whenever necessary for the treatment of pending cases. An interesting element is that the Commission may do so without being invited by the national court. In other words, the Commission has the right to send written observations on its own initiative in national proceedings.[41] National courts have no power to oppose the move. *(d)* A supplementary measure is that the Commission can request national courts to communicate information concerning pending cases. The measure is justified by the need for information in order to enable observations to be prepared. As the Commission has the right to submit observations, it must also be granted the right to request necessary information.

> *Regulation 1/2003, Article 15.* [a and b] 'In proceedings for the application of Article 81 or Article 82 of the Treaty, courts of the Member States may ask the Commission to transmit to them information in its possession or its opinion on questions concerning the application of the Community competition rules.'[42] [c] 'Where the coherent application of Article 81 or Article 82 of the Treaty so requires, the Commission, acting on its own initiative, may submit written observations to courts of the Member States.'[43] [d] 'For the purpose of the preparation of . . . [its] observations only, . . . the Commission may request the relevant court of the Member State to transmit or ensure the transmission to them of any documents necessary for the assessment of the case.'[44]

---

[41] The only limitation is that the observations must be submitted in writing. Oral submissions are allowed, but only if the national court in question so allows. See Regulation 1/2003, Art 15(3). 'With the permission of the court in question, it [the Commission] may . . . make oral observations.'
[42] Para 1.   [43] Para 3.   [44] Para 3.

Supervision by the Commission of the application of competition rules. **6.56** Finally, Member States are required to provide the Commission with a copy of all decisions taken by their national courts concerning the application of European competition rules.[45] This provides the Commission with a mechanism allowing it to supervise the rulings of national courts as regards European competition law. Should it feel that national courts are not issuing the right judgments, the Commission can use various available tools to rectify the situation.[46]

> *Regulation 1/2003, Article 15(2).* 'Member States shall forward to the Commission a copy of any written judgment of national courts deciding on the application of Article 81 or Article 82 of the Treaty.'[47]

Relations between national courts and the Commission 6.57

— National courts must comply with decisions adopted by the Commission in competition law matters.
— To avoid conflicting decisions, they must suspend proceedings when an investigation is pending before the Commission.
— They may ask the Commission for information or for an opinion.
— They must accept observations made by the Commission.
— They must provide the Commission with all information needed to prepare these observations.
— Member States must provide copies of national court decisions applying European competition laws; supervision can then be exercised by the Commission over the rulings of national courts in competition law matters.

Independence of national courts vis-à-vis NCAs. Another complex issue is the **6.58** relations between national courts and NCAs. It is observed above that national courts, and indeed European courts, are independent with respect to the Commission. The observation is based on the principle of 'separation of powers', which requires that judicial entities must be independent vis-à-vis the executive and the legislative branches. That principle also applies to the relations between national courts and national administrative agencies entrusted with the application of (national and European) competition rules (NCAs).

Organisation of relations. Independence does not imply, however, that the **6.59** entities belonging to these groups may carry out their legal activities without co-operation or co-ordination. The risk of conflicting decisions is substantial when various entities have the power to decide in the same cases. Here again, however, Regulation 1/2003 provides few tools for the organisation of these relations.

---

[45] The obligation only concerns the decisions applying European rules, not those applying national competition laws.
[46] One possibility is to adopt notices clarifying the application of competition rules, on points where the Commission considers that national courts may have erred. Another possibility is to seek, from the ECJ, an interpretation, or a clarification, on points of law that are nor entirely clear (Preliminary reference, Art 234 EC).
[47] See Regulation 1/2003, Art 15(2). 'Such copy shall be forwarded without delay after the full written judgment is notified to the parties.'

It is observed above that several devices are introduced by the regulation for the organisation of relations between the Commission and the national courts. Among these devices, two only are applicable regarding relations between the courts and the NCAs. *(a)* Under the regulation, NCAs may submit observations to the national courts about pending cases. *(b)* They may request national courts to transmit documents and provide information in order for them to prepare these observations under adequate conditions.

> *Regulation 1/2003, Article 15(3)*. 'Competition authorities of the Member States, acting on their own initiative, may submit written observations to the national courts of their Member State on issues relating to the application of Article 81 or Article 82 of the Treaty.'[48] 'For the purpose of the preparation of their observations only, the competition authorities of the Member States and the Commission may request the relevant court of the Member State to transmit or ensure the transmission to them of any documents necessary for the assessment of the case.'

6.60 **These relations may be further organised by the Member States.** Beyond the rules provided at European level, Member States can organise further the relations between national courts and NCAs. This task pertains to the sovereignty of the Member States, which can organise their internal institutional structures as they consider appropriate. A constraint is that the organisation chosen by the States must make it possible to implement European law in an adequate fashion. Pursuant to Regulation 1/2003, the Member States may use their freedom to allocate different functions and powers to national courts and NCAs for the application of European competition rules. A traditional division is that courts are competent for actions aimed at obtaining payment of reparation for damages incurred by undertakings or individuals as a result of a violation of competition rules.

> *Regulation 1/2003, Article 35(2)*. 'When enforcement of Community competition law is entrusted to national administrative and judicial authorities, the Member States may allocate different powers and functions to those different national authorities, whether administrative or judicial.' *Regulation 1/2003, Preamble, recital 7*. 'National courts have an essential part to play in applying the Community competition rules. When deciding disputes between private individuals, they protect the subjective rights under Community law, for example by awarding damages to the victims of infringements. The role of the national courts here complements that of the competition authorities of the Member States. They should therefore be allowed to apply Articles 81 and 82 of the Treaty in full. (8) In order to ensure the effective enforcement of the Community.'

(6) Conflicts between national and European competition law

6.61 **Conflicts between national and European competition law.** Conflicts between authorities as a result of concurrent jurisdiction are examined above. Conflicts

---

[48] With the permission of the court in question, they may also submit oral observations. See Regulation 1/2003, Art 15(3).

may also appear between national laws, as well as between national and European competition laws. National competition laws are not necessarily identical one with another. Nor do they coincide in all cases with European laws. Competition laws have not been harmonised; in the absence of harmonisation, the possibility that these laws may be different, and possibly contradictory, cannot be excluded.

(a) Cases where national and European law applies. The first situation to **6.62** consider is that where national and European law are applicable in the same case. Such a situation occurs where the respective conditions for the application of national law, and of European law, are fulfilled.[49] A risk in situations of this nature is that the application of both bodies of law may lead to conflicting outcomes.

Obligation to apply European law. In these situations, NCAs must apply **6.63** European competition law. Under Regulation 1/2003, European competition rules are to be applied whenever NCAs have the intention of applying their national laws.[50] Why has this rule been adopted? *(a)* There was apparently a concern that NCAs may be reluctant to apply European competition laws. The agents working in these authorities have been trained in national law. They may not feel comfortable with European rules, although the latter are not very different in most instances. *(b)* European institutions wanted to avoid a situation where national law would be applied across the European Union in preference to European law. Such a situation would indeed impair the objectives of the internal market. It is preferable, for undertakings and for individuals, to be subject to the same rules throughout the European Union. *(c)* Possible contradictions between national and European rules only come to light, in a clear manner, when both categories of rules apply. Then only is it possible to observe that solutions are different, or even conflicting.

> *Regulation 1/2003, Article 3(1).* 'Where the competition authorities of the Member States or national courts apply national competition law to agreements, decisions by associations of undertakings or concerted practices within the meaning of Article 81(1) of the Treaty which may affect trade between Member States within the meaning of that provision, they shall also apply Article 81 of the Treaty to such agreements, decisions or concerted practices. Where the competition authorities of the Member States or national courts apply national competition law to any abuse prohibited by Article 82 of the Treaty, they shall also apply Article 82 of the Treaty.'

Primacy of European law. Another rule is that European law must prevail where **6.64** there are differences, or contradictions, with national law. Various scenarios may be envisaged in this regard. They are examined in the following paragraphs.

First scenario. In a first scenario, certain behaviour is authorised under national **6.65** competition legislation but prohibited under European competition law. In such

---

[49] Particularly, in that latter case (European law), the condition, which may be found in Arts 81 and 82 EC, that inter-State commerce is affected.

[50] An additional—and evident—requirement is that the conditions for the application of European law are fulfilled.

a situation, precedence must be given to European competition law. In application of that principle, NCAs must prohibit the behaviour.[51]

> *Regulation 1/2003, Article 3.* 'The application of national competition law may not lead to the prohibition of agreements, decisions by associations of undertakings or concerted practices which may affect trade between Member States but which do not restrict competition within the meaning of Article 81(1) of the Treaty, or which fulfil the conditions of Article 81(3) of the Treaty or which are covered by a Regulation for the application of Article 81(3) of the Treaty.'

6.66 **Second scenario.** In a second scenario, certain behaviour is prohibited by national laws but authorised by European law. The same principle prevails. The NCA must authorise the behaviour despite the existence of a more restrictive approach under national law (primacy). An exception is made, however, regarding unilateral behaviour, ie behaviour falling under Article 82 EC. For such behaviour, Regulation 1/2003 accepts that Member States may take a more restrictive approach. In other words, national laws may prohibit unilateral behaviour that is accepted under European law.

> *Regulation 1/2003, Article 3(2).* 'The application of national competition law may not lead to the prohibition of agreements, decisions by associations of undertakings or concerted practices which may affect trade between Member States but which do not restrict competition within the meaning of Article 81(1) of the Treaty, or which fulfil the conditions of Article 81(3) of the Treaty or which are covered by a Regulation for the application of Article 81(3) of the Treaty.' *Exception for unilateral behaviour.* 'Member States shall not under this Regulation be precluded from adopting and applying on their territory stricter national laws which prohibit or sanction unilateral conduct engaged in by undertakings.'

6.67 **Concurrent application of national and European competition laws—Cases dealt with under Articles 81 and 82 EC**

National law	European law	Outcome
Behaviour is authorised under national law	It is prohibited under European law	The behaviour is prohibited (primacy of European law)
Behaviour is prohibited under national law	It is authorised under European law	The behaviour is authorised under Article 81 EC and may be prohibited by the Member States under Article 82 EC

6.68 **(b) Cases where only national laws apply.** In some cases, national competition laws apply exclusively of European competition law. Typically these situations arise where the conditions for the application of European law are not satisfied.[52]

---

[51] The outcome results from the general primacy of European over national law. A European prohibition cannot be set aside as a result of the existence of a national authorisation.

[52] For instance, behaviour is adopted by an undertaking in restriction of competition but that behaviour is limited to a small portion of a national territory and does not affect inter-State commerce.

In situations of this nature, NCAs and/or national courts do not have the power, in principle, to apply European rules. The sole possibility open to them is to apply national competition law. As only one set of rules is applied, there is no risk of an *explicit* contradiction. This does not mean, however, that full consistency exists. In some instances, national laws may lead to conclusions that would have been deemed incompatible had European law applied. A question arises whether one can tolerate a situation where solutions are adopted in conformity with national laws but in *implicit* contradiction with European law. In that interpretation, convergence must exist at all times between national and European laws. As a result, national laws must converge towards European competition law. The effectiveness of European law would otherwise be affected. A doubt would be raised about what is ultimately authorised, or prohibited. Undertakings would adopt behaviour authorised by national laws, believing that it is generally author-ised. However, this behaviour is prohibited under European law and would have to be prosecuted if it is adopted in a setting which allows inter-State commerce to be affected.[53]

(c) Cases where only European law applies. For the sake of completeness, situ-   **6.69**
ations must also be considered where European law only is applicable. These are scenarios where, for instance, behaviour prohibited under European competition law has not been deemed serious enough to warrant a prohibition under national laws. NCAs then only have one set of rules to apply. There is no risk of a possible contradiction in this context.

(d) A special regime for concentrations. In the paragraphs above it is stated   **6.70**
that consistency must exist between national and European competition laws. Special consideration must be given to the rules concerning concentrations. These rules are essential to the economy, as they determine the ability of the authorities to carry out any sort of industrial policy.[54] *(a)* As stated above, the European Merger

---

[53] To illustrate that situation, a scenario examined above may be considered. Suppose national law allows behaviour that is prohibited under European law. Under Regulation 1/2003, the European solution must prevail where both bodies of law apply. The hypothesis, however, in the current case, is that national laws only apply. There is no provision in the NRF dealing with that issue. A solution must thus be found on the basis of general principles of European law. In an interpretation of these principles, the solution examined above should apply and European law should prevail. In the context of a concurrent application of both sets of rules, the prevalence of European law can be justi-fied by the primacy of European law over national law. Primacy implies that European laws must prevail over national laws when the two bodies of law apply concurrently to the same situations. That principle cannot apply, however, in situations where only national laws are applicable. In such a case, there is no concurrent application. In that scenario, the prevalence of European law must be based, arguably, on the effectiveness of European law. One cannot accept that national laws produce con-clusions contradictory to what European laws should entail. Such an outcome would damage the effectiveness of European law.

[54] Such a policy is carried out, mainly, by allowing or encouraging some operations, or on the contrary by prohibiting certain concentrations or submitting them to specific conditions deemed to be in line with public objectives.

Regulation applies to concentrations above certain thresholds. The application of the Merger Regulation is therefore exclusive. This means that national merger control cannot be carried out when the European regulation applies. In that context, there is no risk of concurrent application, and hence of a contradiction, between national and European merger regulations. *(b)* Again, this does not mean, however, that consistency is ensured between the two sets of rules. National laws, if they were applied, could require solutions that would not be compatible with European law. Conversely, European rules require solutions that may be different from, or contradictory with, what national law would impose if the two sets of rules applied concurrently. *(c)* In the previous paragraphs, it is observed that the Council has not accepted such a risk of inconsistency regarding decisions in relation to cartels (Article 81 EC) or, to a lesser extent, unilateral behaviour (Article 82 EC). Under Regulation 1/2003, national solutions must conform to the European solution in cases considered under these provisions. *(d)* Another attitude has been adopted with respect to mergers. The European institutions have accepted in this field that there may be an inconsistency between national and European laws. Under Regulation 1/2003, national merger rules do not need to be identical to European merger regulation.

> *Regulation 1/2003, Article 3(3)*. 'Paragraphs 1 and 2[55] do not apply when the competition authorities and the courts of the Member States apply national merger control laws.'

6.71 Application of national and European merger control

— European and national merger control do not apply concurrently.
— There is no risk of an explicit contradiction.
— Implicit contradiction may occur when, for instance, national rules apply and require treatment different from that which European law would have required had it applied.
— Parliament and Council have accepted the risk of a certain level of inconsistency.
— This is probably due to the desire of Member States to maintain their own industrial policy, possibly independently of that carried out by the Commission.

6.72 **(e) Other competition-related national legislation.** Regulation 1/2003 further states that national courts and NCAs may apply, irrespective of any consideration relating to European competition law, other national rules related to competition, to the extent that these rules pursue predominantly an objective different from that aimed at in Articles 81 and 82 EC. This provision refers to national unfair trading legislation. To a significant extent, that legislation existed prior to the rules prohibiting cartels and abuses of dominant positions which are prohibited in European law as well as in national law (in the latter case under the influence of the European rules). There is no risk of confusion, in the eyes of the European

---

[55] These paragraphs confirm the prevalence of European law in the case of a discrepancy with national laws (with the nuance examined above as regards unilateral behaviour under Art 82 EC).

institutions, between the two categories of legislation. The application of the 'new' competition rules does not impede any application of the old rules. National courts and authorities must however ensure that the national legislation conforms to general European law. It should be recalled in this context that harmonisation directives have been adopted in some areas generally covered by unfair trading legislation (for instance, directives on publicity or on unfair clauses).

> *Regulation 1/2003, Article 3(3).* 'Without prejudice to general principles and other provisions of Community law, paragraphs 1 and 2 do not . . . preclude the application of provisions of national law that predominantly pursue an objective different from that pursued by Articles 81 and 82 of the Treaty.'

> *Regulation 1/2003, Preamble, recital 9.* 'Articles 81 and 82 of the Treaty have as their objective the protection of competition on the market. This Regulation, which is adopted for the implementation of these Treaty provisions, does not preclude Member States from implementing on their territory national legislation, which protects other legitimate interests provided that such legislation is compatible with general principles and other provisions of Community law. In so far as such national legislation pursues predominantly an objective different from that of protecting competition on the market, the competition authorities and courts of the Member States may apply such legislation on their territory. Accordingly, Member States may under this Regulation implement on their territory national legislation that prohibits or imposes sanctions on acts of unfair trading practice, be they unilateral or contractual. Such legislation pursues a specific objective, irrespective of the actual or presumed effects of such acts on competition on the market. This is particularly the case of legislation which prohibits undertakings from imposing on their trading partners, obtaining or attempting to obtain from them terms and conditions that are unjustified, disproportionate or without consideration.'

(7) Final remarks

Horizontal relations yet to be organised. The discussion in the paragraphs **6.73** above shows that the application of European competition law has been organised in a vertical, rather than horizontal, way. *(a)* In that organisation, the horizontal relations remain, to a certain extent, to be organised. It is observed that consultation mechanisms have been established between NCAs. No mechanism is however provided to designate a competent NCA, where several are handling the same case simultaneously. In the same fashion, the adoption of a decision by an NCA in a given case does not prevent another NCA from issuing another, possibly contradictory, decision, in the same case. *(b)* Similar issues may be observed regarding national courts. Under Regulation 1/2003, NCAs can submit observations to national courts. This however seems to be the only co-ordination mechanism established in the European regulation. The organisation of relations between these entities is left, for the rest, to the Member States.

Hierarchical organisation. By contrast, more structure has been introduced **6.74** in the relations between the Commission on the one hand and the NCAs and national courts on the other. These relations are clearly organised on a hierarchical basis as regards the Commission and the NCAs. Thus Regulation 1/2003 establishes the primacy of the Commission, which has the power to overrule NCA decisions. This primacy implies that a transfer of information must be organised from the NCAs to the Commission. Using that information, the Commission may effectively control the work performed at national level. Conversely, the NCAs can carry out surveillance over the actions envisaged by the Commission (Advisory Committee). That surveillance is however designed as an advisory mechanism, rather than a possibility for NCAs collectively to adopt binding decisions.

> *Regulation 1/2003, Preamble, recital 34.* 'The principles laid down in Articles 81 and 82 of the Treaty . . . have given a central role to the Community bodies. This central role should be retained, whilst associating the Member States more closely with the application of the Community competition rules.'

6.75 **Behavioural and structural remedies.** Some observations must be added regarding remedies. Under Regulation 1/2003, a finding that European antitrust laws have been violated gives rise to a decision whereby the Commission orders the undertakings concerned to put an end to the behaviour at stake. Remedies may be ordered. Some of them are behavioural—they concern behaviour that must be halted and refrained from in the future by the undertaking concerned. Other remedies have a more structural nature. Typically, remedies are said to be structural where they imply an obligation for the undertaking in question to divest itself of part of its assets. The structure of the undertaking, and not only its behaviour, is then affected.

6.76 **Proportionality.** Under Regulation 1/2003, structural remedies must conform to the proportionality principle.[56] Under that principle, sanctions may be imposed only if three conditions are fulfilled. *(a)* 'Usefulness': sanctions must be useful to obtain the objective that is sought. *(b)* 'Necessity': they cannot be replaced by another measure which would attain the same result without infringing to the same extent the freedom of undertakings. And *(c)* 'absence of excessive effect': sanctions are admitted only where the consequences for the undertakings concerned are not excessive in the light of the offence leading to the punishment. Regulation 1/2003 specifies how the second test must be interpreted for structural remedies. Under that interpretation, such remedies can be ordered only where there is no equally effective behavioural remedy or where the possible behavioural remedies would be more burdensome for the undertaking concerned.

> *Regulation 1/2003, Article 7(1).* 'Where the Commission . . . finds that there is an infringement of Article 81 or of Article 82 of the Treaty, it may by decision require the undertakings and associations of undertakings concerned to bring such infringement

---

[56] This does not constitute a real difference with respect to other sanctions. All sanctions must indeed conform to that principle. What is interesting regarding structural remedies is the emphasis placed by the European institutions in the regulation on the importance of complying with the tests relating to proportionality.

to an end. For this purpose, it may impose on them any behavioural or structural remedies which are proportionate to the infringement committed and necessary to bring the infringement effectively to an end. Structural remedies can only be imposed either where there is no equally effective behavioural remedy or where any equally effective behavioural remedy would be more burdensome for the undertaking concerned than the structural remedy.'

Main changes introduced by Regulation 1/2003. Regulation 1/2003 has **6.77** changed in a considerable manner the rules for the application of competition law. Two major changes must be singled out. *(a)* General competence for the application of European competition law now rests on NCAs. National courts also have a competence but that competence is limited, in most Member States, in practice, to actions for damages. The European Commission has a more regulatory role, as it is responsible for drafting guidelines to be followed by NCAs. It retains the power to intervene in individual cases, particularly when it considers that NCAs would not handle a case in an appropriate manner. These principles differ from the earlier period. In that earlier period, the competence to apply European competition rules rested mainly on the Commission. The Commission even had an exclusive power to determine whether agreements falling under the prohibition in Article 81(1) EC could be exempted on the basis of Article 81(3) EC. *(b)* A second change concerns formalities to be fulfilled in order to obtain an exemption under Article 81(3) EC. Under the previous regime, an exemption could be obtained only if the agreement was notified to the Commission. Exemptions were thus dependent upon a formality being observed. That system was progressively changed, in the first instance through the adoption of regulations stating under what conditions categories of agreements would be exempted. Agreements conforming to those conditions could be considered exempt.[57] That modification was not deemed sufficient, however, by the Commission. For that reason, Regulation 1/2003 provides that no notification is any longer necessary in order to obtain an exemption. Parties may thus enjoy an exemption without having to notify their agreement to the Commission or any authority.[58]

Other issues regarding the application of European competition law. The **6.78** sections above deal mainly with the issue of determining what action is possible

---

[57] A formal notification would have been necessary, under the previous regulation, to obtain a guarantee that the exemption applies. It was impossible, however, for the Commission to adopt a decision on all agreements being notified. As regulations addressed categories of agreements, it was possible for parties to determine by themselves whether their agreement indeed complied with the due conditions. National courts and NCAs had the power to determine whether the conditions were indeed fulfilled in a particular agreement.

[58] It should be noted that that modification only concerns European law. The procedural aspects concerning the national laws depend, here again, on the national laws themselves. The Member States are free, for instance, to subordinate exemptions to cartel prohibitions (if such prohibitions exist in their national legal orders) to formal conditions such as notification. Regulation 1/2003 only concerns European competition laws. No notification is thus necessary under that body of the law to obtain in the future an exemption to a provision prohibiting cartels.

on the basis of competition rules in order to obtain redress. Many issues relating to judicial or administrative protection have not been covered.[59] They cannot be addressed exhaustively in this book, which focuses on electronic communications rather than some of the wider issues relating to the application of competition rules.

E. Protecting Users and Consumers

6.79 **Consumer-related litigation.** The NRF introduces special procedures for litigation concerning consumers and possibly other categories of final users. These procedures are described in the Universal Service Directive. The reason for specific procedures to be introduced is that, in most cases, it would be too expensive for consumers to litigate against undertakings. To solve that difficulty, the NRF imposes upon the Member States an obligation to create out-of-court dispute resolution mechanisms. These mechanisms must comply with several constraints. First, they must be transparent, simple and inexpensive. Second, they must allow for a rapid, and equitable, solution of the dispute. These mechanisms are normally reserved for consumers, ie users resorting to electronic communications for their private (non-professional) interests. They may however be extended by the Member States to other categories of end user. An effort must be made by the Member States to co-ordinate their efforts when the dispute involves parties established in different Member States.

> *Universal Service Directive, Article 34.* 'Member States shall ensure that transparent, simple and inexpensive out-of-court procedures are available for dealing with unresolved disputes, involving consumers, relating to issues covered by this Directive. Member States shall adopt measures to ensure that such procedures enable disputes to be settled fairly and promptly and may, where warranted, adopt a system of reimbursement and/or compensation. Member States may extend these obligations to cover disputes involving other end-users.'[60] 'Where such disputes involve parties in different Member States, Member States shall coordinate their efforts with a view to bringing about a resolution of the dispute.'[61] 'This Article is without prejudice to national court procedures.'[62]

6.80 **Complaints offices and on-line services.** Another mechanism which is often used for the resolution of disputes involving consumers is the provision of offices where consumers may address their complaints in the hope of a quick resolution. In some instances, these offices may be reached physically. Consumers then have to go to them to present their cases. In other instances, consumers do not need to

---

[59] Including issues relating to the powers of investigation conferred on the NCAs, the national courts and the Commission; the penalties; the hearings and the obligations relating to professional secrecy; review by the ECJ and the CFI, etc.   [60] Para 1.
[61] Para 3.   [62] Para 4.

go to a specific location, but may express their complaint on line to an operator, who records it. These mechanisms are not made obligatory in the NRF for the Member States. There is, as a result, no obligation for the Member States to organise complaints offices or on-line services. There is only a negative obligation on Member States as regards these possibilities. Under the NRF, they may not hamper, through their legislation, the establishment of such offices or services.

> *Universal Service Directive, Article 34(2).* 'Member States shall ensure that their legislation does not hamper the establishment of complaints offices and the provision of on-line services at the appropriate territorial level to facilitate access to dispute resolution by consumers and end-users.'

F. Delineating a Strategy

(1) Choosing an authority and procedure

A variety of procedures and authorities. As appears from the sections above, **6.81** various procedures are open to undertakings and individuals to obtain protection on electronic communications markets from illegal behaviour. This variety finds an echo in the number of entities authorised to intervene in the resolution of these conflicts. In most instances, undertakings and individuals have a choice between several procedures, involving several entities, on the path they want to take to obtain protection. As they are confronted with a number of solutions, parties must make a selection from the various possibilities available to them. In the following paragraphs, advice and suggestions are provided about procedures which offer the best chances for success.

Criteria to be taken into account. Undertakings and individuals should **6.82** determine the criteria on the basis of which they will delineate their legal strategy. *(a)* A first criterion could be the selection of the body of rules likely to provide the best results. In most instances, the NRF provides adequate tools to defend new companies seeking to enter markets. The tools supplied by general competition law are not necessarily different in substance. They do not, however, have a similar degree of specificity.[63] As a result, it is not easy to anticipate solutions provided by competition law. *(b)* A second criterion could be the case law developed by each authority on the territory concerned. Suppose that an undertaking wants to initiate a procedure in a given country. In that country, it has a choice between several authorities (NRA, NCA, national court(s)). Before opting for one among these possibilities, it should examine the case law concerning the precedents set by these authorities in circumstances similar to the conflict in hand.

---

[63] Competition law has been designed as a more general body of rules. The case law developed in that body of the law, on electronic communications, is rather limited.

(2) Major options

6.83 **National regulatory authorities (NRAs).** Taking into account these two criteria, individuals and undertakings are likely to request the application, by NRAs, of the national rules implementing the NRF. NRAs are specialised in the resolution of conflicts related to electronic communications. They have the resources necessary to deal with these conflicts. In most Member States, the NRAs have been created over the past 15 years. They are in most cases not financed by a State budget but through (authorisation) fees paid by undertakings active in the sector. The result is that they have the resources necessary to attract reasonably competent personnel. As to their nature, NRAs are administrative entities. Their task is to apply the national rules implementing the NRF. These rules must be compatible with the European provisions they are intended to implement. Where there is a disparity between national and European rules, the latter must be given precedence (primacy of European law over national law).

6.84 **National competition authorities (NCAs).** A second option would be to address a complaint to an NCA and request the resolution of the conflict through the application of competition law. A disadvantage of this procedure is that competition laws are, by their nature, more general than sector-specific regulation. Outcomes are, as a result, less easy to anticipate. An advantage is that NCAs are not particularly involved in electronic communications markets. As a result, they have few links with operators or other players active on these markets. It may be easier for a new undertaking to obtain redress from that authority in Member States where the links between the former national operator and the NRA remains in place despite the elimination of any structural relation between them.[64]

6.85 **National courts.** Actions may also be brought before national courts. In cases pending before them, these courts may apply three kinds of law: *(a)* national sector-specific legislation; *(b)* the European NRF, in case the NRF is not correctly implemented in the national legislation; *(c)* national competition rules; *(d)* European competition rules. National courts may intervene in cases concerning conflicts between undertakings and/or individuals. Even if they do not intervene in the first instance, national courts are bound to intervene at some stage in the procedure. As stated, the NRF creates a right of appeal against decisions adopted by the NRAs.[65]

---

[64] As was stated, NCAs must apply national and European competition laws. In all cases, they must give precedence to European competition laws. The result of this is that national competition laws are bound to converge towards European rules. In the long run, they are likely to have the same content as European rules. The only remaining difference will be that the European rules apply when inter-State commerce is affected whereas the national roles are limited to purely national cases, ie cases without any European impact whatsoever.

[65] No explicit rule of that nature may be found explicitly in Regulation 1/2003 about decisions adopted by the NCAs. There thus exists no obligation, under European law, for Member States to organise a judicial review mechanism against decisions adopted by NCAs.

Ideally, appeals must be heard and handled by a court. Where that is not the case, a subsequent review must be organised by the Member States before a court.

The European Commission. The European Commission is involved in the draft-   **6.86**
ing of policy guidelines to be complied with by NRAs and NCAs. *(a)* In competition law, the Commission may intervene in individual cases. In that field, it appears
as the superior body charged with ensuring uniformity within the case law.[66] *(b)* The
powers entrusted to the Commission are more limited in the application of sector-
specific regulation. On the basis of the body of European rules, it can use general
European law mechanisms to promote its interpretation of the law (for instance,
initiation of an Article 226 EC procedure against a Member State whose NRA does
not apply correctly, in its view, the NRF as implemented in the national legislation).

Applicable rules and competent authorities   **6.87**

	National sector-specific legislation	European NRF	National competition law	European competition law
NRAs	Yes	Yes[67]	___[68]	___[69]
NCAs	—	—	Yes	Yes
National courts	Yes	Yes	Yes	Yes
European Commission	—	Yes	—	Yes

(3)   The relations between NCAs and NRAs

Cross competences of NCAs and NRAs.   Another issue arising is whether   **6.88**
NRAs and NCAs have 'cross competences', ie the power to apply rules normally
belonging to the jurisdiction of the other national agency. The solution to that
issue is not to be found in European law. European law states only what NCAs and
NRAs must, or may, do. It does not, however, organise the allocation of powers
among the different entities that may serve in these functions. The institutional
organisation has been left to the Member States as regards the application of
sector-specific regulation and general competition law. As a result, the Member
States decide on matters of jurisdiction within their internal administrative
orders. The consequence is that undertakings and individuals cannot expect
a single solution to apply on all national territories across the European Union.

May NCAs apply sector-specific legislation?   Do NCAs have the power to apply   **6.89**
sector-specific regulation, a body of rules the application of which is normally

---

[66] The Commission, of course, carries out its activities under the control of the CFI and the ECJ, which review acts adopted by that authority. See Art 230 EC.

[67] Where national laws do not conform to the NRF and for NRF provisions which have direct effect.

[68] In the absence of special arrangements made in the internal legal order by the Member States.

[69] In the absence of special arrangements made in the internal legal order by the Member States.

managed by NRAs? There are arguments in favour of such an arrangement. Sector-specific regulation is based, indeed, to a large extent, in the current state of the legislation, on concepts that are used in general competition law. This sort of arrangement has not been opted for, however, in the Member States. Sector-specific regulation is now closer to general competition law than it used to be. Before the NRF was adopted, differences, sometimes substantial, existed between the two sets of rules. It did not appear appropriate to Member States to grant to a single authority the power to apply, in the same sector of the economy, rules which, at times, were so different. A situation was thus created where two authorities existed, each responsible for the application of a given set of rules. When the NRF was adopted, it was probably for pragmatic reasons too late to change that institutional organisation altogether.

6.90 May NRAs apply competition laws? The issue is more complex regarding the application of competition laws by NRAs. The first impression is that general competition laws are rather easy to understand and that authorities other than NCAs should as a result be capable of applying them. A survey shows that three types of institutional organisation may be encountered in the Member States. *(a)* In some countries, NRAs have been vested with the power to apply competition rules in addition to sector-specific regulation in parallel with NCAs. In these States, the two authorities thus have concurrent jurisdiction to apply general competition law to electronic communications markets. In such a situation, the risk of conflict between these agencies is real. It is to be hoped that the national legal order of these Member States contains mechanisms allowing, and even compelling, the authorities involved to co-operate. As NCAs and NRAs are administrative bodies, an appeal is normally available, in those countries, to a common superior body, possibly of a judicial nature, which may develop a certain level of convergence between the solutions adopted in the two frameworks. *(b)* In a second category of country, each agency has been left with its core competence[70] but both have reached agreements on how to deal jointly with cases falling under their jurisdiction. This scenario is more satisfactory than the previous situation, as some consistency must in principle flow from the joint intervention of the two authorities. *(c)* In a last category of European country, the power to apply competition rules and sector-specific regulation has been entrusted to one entity. In these countries, a single entity is thus responsible for the application of all rules concerning electronic communications markets (sector-specific regulation and general competition law). Some countries have granted that power to their NRA. In others, the NCA has been preferred. Whatever the choice, the advantage of the solution is that parties—undertakings and users alike—may address themselves to a single entity to obtain a coherent solution.

---

[70] NRAs applying sector-specific regulation and NCAs applying general competition laws.

Clear identification of the responsible authorities. Whatever the division of **6.91** powers decided at national level, there are obligations which the Member States must comply with as regards authorities in charge of the implementation of the various bodies of rules applicable to electronic communications markets. One constraint is that the Member States must identify with clarity who does what. In other words, the Member States are under an obligation, pursuant to the NRF, to designate the entities in charge of the respective regulatory tasks assigned in implementation of the framework. They also have the obligation to make this division of tasks public.

> *Framework Directive, Article 3(4).* 'Where more than one authority has competence to address such matters,[71] Member States shall ensure that the respective tasks of each authority are published in an easily accessible form.'

Co-operation among the various national authorities. Another constraint is **6.92** for the Member States to organise a system of co-operation among the various authorities likely to intervene on electronic communications markets. The authorities in charge of competition, sector-specific regulation and the protection of consumers are specifically concerned by this obligation.

> *Framework Directive, Article 3(4).* 'Member States shall ensure, where appropriate, consultation and cooperation between those authorities, and between those authorities and national authorities entrusted with the implementation of competition law and national authorities entrusted with the implementation of consumer law, on matters of common interest.'

Communication of information. As part of this co-operation, NCAs and **6.93** NRAs must exchange information, where such an exchange is useful or necessary for the implementation of the NRF. *(a)* This implies that NCAs are under an obligation to provide information to NRAs for the application of sector-specific rules such as those concerning the definition of relevant markets or the designation of undertakings with significant market power. Confidentiality must be complied with by all entities concerned. *(b)* Conversely, NCAs may obtain from NRAs information necessary for the resolution of cases pending before them. In these scenarios, the application of competition rules in the electronic communications sector is facilitated as a result of information provided by NRAs pursuant to sector-specific regulation

> *Framework Directive.* [a]'National regulatory authorities and national competition authorities shall provide each other with the information necessary for the application of the provisions of this Directive and the Specific Directives. In respect of the information exchanged, the receiving authority shall ensure the same level of confidentiality as the originating authority.'[72] [b] 'Member States shall ensure that the information submitted to one national regulatory authority can be made available to

---

[71] The regulatory issues relating to competition, sector-specific regulation and the protection of consumers.   [72] Art 3(5).

another such authority in the same or different Member State, after a substantiated request, where necessary to allow either authority to fulfil its responsibilities under Community law.'[73]

6.94 **Current situation in the Member States.** The Commission does not appear frightened by the possibility of conflicting decisions taken by NCAs and NRAs. In the Eighth implementation report it is stated that co-operation works well between the authorities concerned in many of the Member States.

> *Eighth implementation report, 20.* 'Co-operation between the NRA and the national competition authority (NCA) . . . has generally improved since liberalisation and works well in practice in many of the Member States (in particular in Denmark, Greece, France, Ireland, Italy, the Netherlands, Austria, United Kingdom). Two Member States have already introduced formal procedures for such co-operation (Denmark, Ireland), while in two Member States the competition authority provides the NRA with non-binding opinions on matters which affect the competitive conditions of the market (Germany with the exception of SMP designation, where the opinion is binding, and Italy). In others the NCA does not get involved at all in the decision-making process but leaves it to the NRA (Greece, the Netherlands except for market analysis).'

(4) The relations between national and European law

6.95 **National and European law.** National authorities have a general responsibility for the application of national laws. As stated above, these national laws implement, in various circumstances, rules adopted at European level. This is the case for sector-specific regulation. That regulation has been adopted at European level and the European rules have been transposed in the national legal orders through national rules. The situation is more complex for competition law. There has been no harmonisation of competition laws across the European Union. As a result, national authorities have no obligation to implement European competition rules. They must however apply these rules directly, as provided in Regulation 1/2003. Furthermore, there is an obligation for Member States to ensure that their national competition rules do not depart excessively from the rules applicable in that field at European level. Pursuant to Article 10 EC, Member States must take all appropriate measures to ensure the attainment of the goals assigned under the Treaty. These measures include the establishment of authorities capable of applying European rules effectively. The application of European rules by national entities depends on the way in which these rules must be applied. As regards European competition rules, Articles 81 and 82 EC clearly have direct applicability in the national legal orders.

6.96 **Direct effect of sector-specific regulation.** A remaining issue is the potential direct effect of sector-specific regulation. Pursuant to the EC Treaty, the directives

---

[73] Art 5(2), subpara 2.

composing the NRF must be transposed by national instruments in order to produce legal effects in the national orders. However, transposition is not always correct or timely. The question then arises whether these rules may be applied directly, in the absence of transposition. Direct effect is not possible for some rules, which are not clear, precise or unconditional. For others, which have these attributes, direct effect is possible. No general answer can thus be given about the direct effect of the rules contained in the NRF. An assessment has to be made on an ad hoc basis.

(5) Conflicts likely to occur

Categories of situation. This section is devoted to various types of conflicts **6.97** which are bound to occur and is intended to provide advice on the procedure to be followed to obtain redress. In most cases, the attitude to be adopted by the applicant depends on its intentions. *(a)* Does it want a rapid decision to resolve the conflict? The advice would then be to proceed before the competent NRA. *(b)* Does the applicant prefer on the contrary a slow procedure—or does it even wish to drag the procedure out for as long as possible? Use can then be made of the intricacies of the possibilities offered in sector-specific legislation and general competition law. For instance, a procedure can be started as soon as another finishes, especially if the latter procedure has not given a satisfactory result.

New entrants vs powerful undertakings. A significant number of claims come **6.98** from new companies seeking to enter a market and being barred from doing so by a powerful undertaking. These companies normally seek a quick solution. *(a)* The advice in this situation is to use sector-specific regulation. That regulation specific-ally deals with market entry. It was adopted with the aim of facilitating entry and the development of competition. In sector-specific regulation, the challenger will find provisions allowing it to obtain redress. A request for a decision should be addressed to the NRA. *(b)* It cannot be ruled out that the decision adopted by the NRA will not be favourable to the entrant company. Should the decision fail to support the contention of that undertaking, an appeal should be sought to the review body that Member States have to put in place under the NRF. The difficulty, however, is that the appeal procedure is not subject to time limitations. There is thus a risk that the procedure may drag on. *(c)* An alternative would then be to seek intervention from: the European Commission, which remains in close contact with the national authorities; an NRA established in another Member State, the jurisprudence of which seems to be more favourable to the demands made by the applicant;[74] or the NCA of the Member State where the new entrant seeks entry.

---

[74] To have an overview of that jurisprudence, the best advice is to consult the internet site of each NRA potentially involved. These sites contain an explanation of the policy followed on the national territory concerned.

6.99   Dominant undertakings vs NRAs or NCAs.   Applications may also come from powerful undertakings. In most instances, these powerful undertakings submit applications because they are not satisfied with a decision adopted against them by an NRA or NCA. Sector-specific legislation requires Member States to organise an appeal procedure against decisions adopted by NRAs. These procedures must conform to rules generally applicable to judicial review. There is no mention, in Regulation 1/2003, of a similar constraint imposed on Member States for the review of decisions adopted by an NCA. The existence of an appeal depends, in that context, on national law.

6.100   Users vs undertakings.   Users may be dissatisfied with the services provided by undertakings. In most instances, the procedures initiated by that category of applicant concern, under sector-specific regulation, universal service or the provision of the service which is specified in the contract signed with the undertaking. *(a)* For these sorts of conflict, Member States are required to establish out-of-court procedures. The purpose of these procedures is to help consumers. They may however be extended by the Member States to other sorts of users. They are ideal for individuals when it comes to ensuring that a contract(s) signed with the provider(s) is executed correctly. *(b)* In the absence of such arrangements, another possibility is to address a request to the NRA. That procedure should not be used where the purpose of the action is to ensure compliance with contractual obligations. It is more indicated when a user, and particularly a consumer, wants to litigate against an undertaking for reasons relating to the provision of universal service. In that case, addressing a request to the NRA appears an easy, and quick, path to obtain redress. Sector-specific regulation will normally apply, as it is that part of the regulation which provides for universal service. Competition laws would probably be of no use regarding claims concerning universal service, as their core object is to deal with market power. Furthermore, users rarely have the resources needed to address requests to several NRAs and to present their case to these various entities. Addressing a complaint to the Commission is not bound to be successful. As the Commission has limited resources and personnel, it devotes its efforts to cases where markets do not function properly rather than to individual requests. In all cases, the advice would be for users to act in conjunction with a consumer association.

6.101   Users vs NRAs or NCAs.   In some instances, users may not be satisfied with decisions adopted by NRAs or NCAs. As stated, an appeal procedure must be open, in all Member States, against NRA decisions. There is no limitation regarding access to that procedure in the Framework Directive. This must be interpreted as implying that access should be defined broadly. Anyone affected by an NRA decision, including individuals, and thus users, should have the possibility of using the appeal procedure. Nothing is by contrast provided in European law about possible appeals against decisions adopted by NCAs. The national laws have to be consulted in this regard.

G. Other Remedies Based on General European Law

(1) Another source of remedies

Presentation.   In addition to specific remedies created in sector-specific regulation   **6.102**
and competition law, undertakings and users may resort to remedies and procedures
organised in general European law. These possibilities are examined in the following
paragraphs. In each paragraph a general presentation is followed by an attempt to
determine whether they are useful in relation to electronic communications markets.
A table is provided at the end with a summary of all possible procedures available in
general European law. For the application of national rules, readers should refer to the
relevant sections below.

(2) Actions against Member States

Applications by Member States.   Under the EC Treaty, Member States may   **6.103**
take action against other Member States before the ECJ where the latter States have
not complied with obligations they have entered into under European law
(Article 227 EC). That action is useful, for instance, if a Member State fails to
implement the NRF correctly or in a timely manner. Another possible use of that
procedure is if an NCA does not apply the European competition rules correctly.
A similar scenario would be where an NRA does not apply the NRF correctly as
implemented in the national legislation. NCAs and NRAs are organs of the State.
The State can thus be held accountable for the behaviour, or attitude, adopted
by these authorities. In these various cases, an Article 227 EC action could be
launched against the Member State at issue. Before being allowed to bring the case
to the ECJ, the Member State bringing the action must have the case examined by
the Commission. The Commission delivers a reasoned opinion after each of the
States concerned has been given the opportunity to submit its case and observations regarding the other party's case, both orally and in writing. If the Commission
has not delivered an opinion within three months of the date on which the matter
was brought before it, the absence of such an opinion does not prevent the matter
from being brought before the ECJ. If the procedure is successful, the ECJ declares
that the Member State concerned has failed to comply with one or several
European obligations. The State must then take all measures necessary to comply
with the judgment.[75]

Applications by the Commission.   A similar action can be brought to the ECJ   **6.104**
by the European Commission (see Article 226 EC). That action is not available to
other European institutions. The Commission is thus the only European institution
authorised by the EC Treaty to bring a direct action before the ECJ against

---

[75] Art 228(1) EC.

a Member State.[76] Article 226 actions could be used in the scenarios examined above in connection with actions started by Member States. In the context of electronic communications, hypotheses would be where a Member State does not implement the NRF in an appropriate manner; where the NCA does not apply the competition rules correctly;[77] or where the NRA fails to comply with European sector-specific regulation as implemented in the national legislation. The outcome of the procedure is similar to that examined above. If the ECJ finds that the Member State has not complied with European obligations, the State in question is under an obligation to remedy the illegal situation.

6.105 **Second judgment.** Member States do not always comply with an Article 226 or 227 EC judgment issued by the ECJ against them in a procedure started by the Commission or another Member State. In case of non-compliance, the Commission, after giving that State the opportunity to submit its observations, can issue a reasoned opinion specifying the points on which the Member State has not complied with the Court's judgment. The Commission then sets a time limit within which the Member State must take the measures necessary to comply with the judgment. In the absence of compliance, the Commission may take the case to the ECJ. In doing so, it must specify the amount of the lump sum or penalty payment that would have to be paid by the Member State should the ECJ consider that that State has indeed failed to comply with the judgment.[78] The case is then judged by the ECJ, which determines the amount actually to be paid by the State.[79]

6.106 **Applications by undertakings and individuals.** No direct action is available to undertakings or individuals against the Member States before the ECJ. Undertakings and individuals are thus deprived of direct redress against behaviour adopted by a Member State in violation of European law. Various possibilities should however be mentioned. *(a)* Undertakings and individuals may lobby the Commission or a Member State in order to obtain from one of these applicants

---

[76] In practice, the actions directed against Member States are mainly started by the Commission. They rarely come from other Member States. Member States generally prefer solving their disputes through political discussions.

[77] For that hypothesis, the European Commission will probably use the tools made available to it by Regulation 1/2003. Under that regulation, the Commission may initiate its own proceedings when an NCA envisages adopting a decision that does not appear appropriate to the Commission. The initiation by the Commission of its own proceedings automatically relieves the national authority of its power to pursue the case. See Regulation 1/2003, Art 11(6).

[78] The amount is not necessarily that asked by the Commission. There is no indication in the Treaty about criteria to be used in order to fix that amount. The Treaty only mentions that, in the application, the Commission may specify an amount 'which it considers appropriate in the circumstances' (Art 228 EC).

[79] It should be noted that this second procedure (procedure against an absence of compliance with a prior judgment) may only be initiated by the Commission. Member States thus have no *locus standi* to initiate such an action. The second procedure may be started after a first judgment issued by the ECJ in an Art 227 action (by Member States) or Art 228 EC action (by the Commission).

the initiation of an action. There is no obligation, however, for the Commission to start a procedure against a Member State upon request of an undertaking or an individual. Member States may be more prone to accede to demands coming from private individuals or undertakings. They generally prefer solving through negotiation, however, the difficulties they may have with fellow Member States of the Union. *(b)* Another possibility is to use the preliminary procedure to obtain from the ECJ a declaration concerning the behaviour adopted by the national authorities. That procedure supposes that an action is brought before a national court.[80] Where it considers a reference is necessary to obtain an explanation or an interpretation concerning European law, the national court may then stay the proceedings and submit questions to the ECJ. Once a ruling is provided by the ECJ, the national court can continue the procedure. In practice, preliminary references are often made to obtain a declaration from the ECJ that a Member State has not fulfilled its obligations under the Treaty or under instruments adopted on the basis of the Treaty. *(c)* Under European law, it is possible for individuals and undertakings to obtain reparation when they have suffered damage as a result of an intervention by a national authority in violation of European law. That possibility opens an interesting perspective for undertakings which feel they are not being treated correctly by an NRA and/or an NCA as regards the application of European law. These undertakings may seek reparation from the State, arguing that damages have been caused in violation of European rules by an organ under its responsibility.

(3) Actions against European institutions

Applications by Member States.   Member States may challenge the validity   **6.107** of actions adopted by the European institutions (Article 230 EC, action for annulment). They may also bring actions against European institutions when the latter have not adopted an act in a situation where they were under an obligation to do so (Article 232 EC, action for failure to act). Finally, they may seek reparation from European institutions where they have suffered damage as a result of behaviour adopted by the institutions in violation of European law (Articles 235 and 288 EC, action for liability). Despite their availability, these actions are not likely to be used in the electronic communications sector. An action for annulment has to be set in motion within two months of the adoption, notification or publication of the act. That period has now elapsed, making it inadmissible for Member States to challenge the validity of the directives composing the NRF (they were adopted in 2002). The European institutions appear to have adopted all instruments they were required to in the field of competition law and in sector-specific regulation. No claim seems to have been made that damages have been suffered by Member States through the adoption or implementation of the two sets of rules.

---

[80] It was observed that that possibility exists as regards the NRA. Sector-specific regulation requires Member States to make a judicial review available against the decisions adopted by the NRA.

6.108 **Applications by European institutions.** The same actions (annulment, failure to act, liability) are available to the European institutions. They may thus seek the annulment of an act of another institution. They may also seek from the ECJ a declaration that another institution has not acted despite an obligation to do so. They further have *locus standi* to ask for the reparation of damage that may have been inflicted on them by another institution, in violation of European law. The analysis, and reasoning, presented above regarding applications by Member States apply in this context as concerns the probability of seeing such actions being used in the field of competition law and sector-specific regulation. Here again there does not appear to be any concrete reason for European institutions to challenge the NRF or the European rules adopted in implementation of them, even if theoretical considerations may be expressed on the subject. No failure to act seems to have been detected and no damage to have been suffered by a European institution as a result of behaviour adopted by another institution.

6.109 **Applications by undertakings and individuals.** The actions examined above in the context of applications made by Member States and European institutions are available, to a certain extent, for undertakings and individuals. *(a)* Actions for annulment (Article 230 EC) may be brought against European acts. They are only admissible when these acts affect the applicant directly and individually. *(b)* Actions for failure to act (Article 232 EC) are available under corresponding conditions, ie to the extent that the failure concerns acts which would have affected the applicant(s) directly and individually. *(c)* Actions for liability (Articles 235 and 288 EC) are available under the same conditions as those applicable to similar actions brought by Member States or European institutions. These conditions are rather restrictive. Liability of the European institutions is present only where: European law has been violated; the violation is serious; significant damage has been caused; there exists a causal link between the act and the damage. *(d)* A word of caution should be added regarding the court before which the action must be brought. Actions against European institutions must be brought to the ECJ where they come from Member States or other European institutions. By contrast, the CFI is competent for Article 230 or 232 litigation initiated by undertakings and individuals.[81]

6.110 **Competition law.** These actions are useful in fields where the Commission, or other European institutions, adopt decisions affecting directly and individually undertakings or individuals. That is the case in competition law. *(a)* It was stated that the Commission retains the power to adopt decisions in individual cases under the new rules concerning the application of competition law. These decisions may be the subject of judicial review by the CFI. An appeal to the ECJ is open against judgments of the CFI. *(b)* Theoretically, undertakings and/or individuals could attempt to challenge any failure by the Commission to adopt

---

[81] An appeal is available against the judgments of the CFI. It must be brought before the ECJ.

a decision in application of the competition rules. Any such attempt is, however, bound to fail. The reason is that the application of these rules is now the responsibility, primarily, of the NCAs. The European Commission retains the power to intervene in individual cases. But intervention is by no means an obligation. In Regulation 1/2003 there is no provision indicating that the Commission has an obligation to apply European competition rules in a specific case. *(c)* At this stage it does not appear that either European court (ECJ or CFI) has ever held so far that the European Commission, or any other European institution, should be held liable for a violation of European law in the application of the competition rules. Challenging the Commission's liability in this context is theoretically possible. The conditions for damages to be granted are so strict, however, that, in the current state of the case law, no undertaking has ever obtained damages as a result of a wrongful application of European competition law.

Sector-specific regulation. The instruments adopted by the European institutions **6.111** in the NRF are more general in nature than those adopted by the same institutions in the realm of general competition law. This difference has consequences for the procedures that may be initiated in order to challenge action, or inaction, by the European institutions. Applications for annulment (Article 230 EC) may be brought to the CFI by legal and natural persons when the applicants are directly and individually concerned by the acts they claim to challenge. That condition is not fulfilled in the case of the instruments composing the NRF. As stated throughout this book, the NRF consists of directives. However, these instruments have a general character in the context of electronic communications. On the basis of the case law, these instruments may not be considered as having a direct and individual effect on private applicants. They may as a result not be challenged by undertakings and individuals before a European court. This does not mean, however, that undertakings and individuals are deprived of any possibility of challenging the validity of these instruments. European instruments of a general nature may be challenged indirectly by private applicants, in a procedure directed against implementation measures. *(a)* In some instances, implementation is carried out by European institutions. The idea, in that context, is to wait until the moment when implementation reaches the stage where direct and individual measures are adopted and affect undertakings and individuals. Applications may then be introduced by the undertaking(s) and/or the individual(s) against the implementation measure before the CFI. *(b)* In other situations, implementation is carried out by national authorities. A procedure must then be initiated before a national court against the national implementation measure. During the national procedure, a preliminary reference may be addressed by the national court to the ECJ in order to obtain, from the latter institution, an assessment concerning the validity of the European instrument which served as a basis for the adoption of the national measure (Article 234 EC). Through the preliminary reference, a view may be obtained from the ECJ concerning the validity of the European instrument at issue.

6.112 **Applications for failure to act.** As stated above, the situation is rather theoretical for actions for failure to act by European institutions (Article 232 EC). These actions may be initiated, under the EC Treaty, against European institutions which have failed to act, contrary to an obligation imposed on them by European law. In these situations, European institutions are required to take certain action but fail to do so despite the obligation imposed on them. Pursuant to the EC Treaty, such behaviour may be challenged by legal and natural persons if these persons would have been affected directly and individually by the act which should have been adopted had the European institution complied with its obligation. In the context of the NRF, the issue is whether private applicants could challenge a failure by a European institution to adopt an act. It has been observed that acts adopted by the European institutions in this context are of a general nature. It remains unclear how an application, however solid it may be on its merits, could be held admissible. Furthermore, it was observed that no failure to adopt an act seems to have been raised in regard to the European institutions.

6.113 **Applications for liability.** A final word must be devoted to applications for liability. As stated, private applicants may start a procedure before a European court in order to seek damages from a European institution which it is claimed has violated European rules. The conditions for a European institution to be declared liable are rather strict: European law must have been violated; the violation must be serious; there must have been damage; a causal link must exist between the violation and the damage. To these conditions, which are the same as those applicable in similar applications by Member States and European institutions, must be added a specific requirement. Pursuant to the case law, private applicants may obtain damages from European institutions only where the violation involves a superior rule of law which had been introduced in the European legal order in order to protect legal or natural persons. Applications by private persons are thus subject to a stricter standard, which makes their success very rare.

(4) Actions against undertakings and individuals

6.114 **Undertakings and individuals as defendants.** For the sake of being comprehensive, procedures initiated against undertakings and individuals should be examined. *(a)* Procedures started by Member States against such defendants ordinarily have an administrative nature. In the application of European competition law, NCAs may, for instance, issue decisions stating that the law has been infringed, and impose a sanction. This does not take place in the context of a judicial procedure but rather in an administrative setting.[82] *(b)* The same may be said about decisions

---

[82] Administrative procedures are also used by NRAs to apply sector-specific legislation, in some cases, against undertakings and, probably, also, in given contexts, against users. (For instance, a decision that a user or an association of users has no right to claim a given service as part of the universal service.) NRAs then adopt decisions addressed to the undertaking(s) or the user(s)

adopted by the European Commission against undertakings. Such decisions may intervene in the application of competition laws. It was observed that there did not appear to be room for the adoption of decisions addressed to undertakings by the European Commission on the basis of the NRF. Whatever the basis, these decisions are adopted in the context of an administrative procedure. (c) Finally, undertakings and users may be challenged by other private applicants on the basis of European law. The challenge must then take place before an NRA (if the undertaking or user asks for the application of the NRF in the absence of correct or timely implementation in national law); before the NCA (if the application requests the application of European competition law); or before a national court (if the application of European competition law or the NRF[83] is requested).

Remedies available under general European law   6.115

	Defendant Member States	Defendant European Institutions	Defendant Legal and natural persons[84]
Applicant Member States	Article 227 EC action.	Article 230 EC, action for annulment. Article 232 EC, action for failure to act. Articles 235 and 288 EC, action for liability.	Decisions taken by Member States against undertakings adopted by an NRA or NCA in the course of an administrative procedure.
Applicant European Institutions	Article 226 EC action. This action is available only to the European Commission.	Same actions as those available to the Member States (scenarios above).	The European Commission may adopt decisions against undertakings on the basis of European competition law. No decision may be adopted by the European Commission against an undertaking on the basis of sector-specific regulation.
Applicant Legal and natural persons[85]	*(a)* No action available before the ECJ orCFI. *(b)* Legal and natural persons may lobby the Commission or	*(a)* Same actions as those available to the Member States in the event that the legal or natural person is	Conflicts between parties must be brought to the NRA, to the NCA or to a national court.

(cont.)

concerned. In doing so, they normally apply national sector-specific legislation. In the absence of an implementing provision, or if the NRF has not been correctly (or timely) implemented, NRAs may apply European law directly, if the European provisions so permit (direct effect theory).

[83] In the event of an incorrect or later implementation in the national legislation.
[84] Undertakings and individuals.   [85] Undertakings and individuals.

Defendant Member States	Defendant European Institutions	Defendant Legal and natural persons
a Member State for the introduction of an application by them.	directly and individually affected by the act at issue.	
(c) In national proceedings, legal and natural persons may initiate preliminary references.	(b) No direct action against European acts of a general nature. These acts	
(d) In national proceedings, legal and natural persons may ask for the reparation of damages caused by national authorities in violation of European law.	may only be questioned indirectly in a proceeding concerning an implementation measure.[86]	

H. Conflicts Between Various Bodies of Law

(1) Conflicts possible between various sets of rules

6.116 Variety of applicable rules. So far, possible conflicts between authorities as a result of concurrent jurisdiction have been examined. The question must now be asked to what extent bodies of law can conflict. The variety of potentially applicable laws is a characteristic of the situation created by the NRF. Two sets of law, in particular, may claim to be applicable in similar situations: sector-specific regulation and general competition law. That situation is made all the more complex through the coexistence of rules at various levels: laws adopted by the Member States, European law, and international law. Finally, the application of national laws may create difficulties when the laws of several States may be applied.

(2) Sector-specific regulation and general competition law

6.117 Two sets of rules. Electronic communications are subject, in the European Union, to sector-specific legislation and general competition law. These sets of rules may be applied, to a certain extent, in the same situations. Should one fear conflicts between decisions respectively based on the first and the second set? The subject has

---

[86] Two situations may be distinguished. *(a)* If the implementation measure is national, an action must be brought against the national implementing measure before a national court. During that procedure, a preliminary reference is addressed to the ECJ. That reference aims at assessing the validity of the European general act on which the national implementation measure is based (Art 234 EC). *(b)* If the implementation measure is adopted by a European body, that measure must be challenged in a direct action before the CFI. In the course of that procedure, an exception of illegality may be used against the European general act on the basis of which the European implementation measure is adopted (Art 241 EC).

been discussed at length in academic texts. Some authors assert that sector-specific regulation and general competition law are indeed different and that these differences may bring about conflicting decisions.[87] Others claim that sector-specific regulation can be analysed as a special section within the body of rules devoted to competition.[88] Beyond these academic discussions, the concrete issue is whether undertakings and/or individuals may be confronted with discrepancies in decisions, depending on whether these decisions are based on one or the other set of rules.

No major difference between the two sets of rules.   The position adopted in this book is that there is no substantial difference between the two sets of rules. Sector-specific regulation is based, to a significant extent, if not entirely, on general competition law concepts. This statement has gained in relevance since the option taken up, in the NRF, by the European institutions in favour of a definition of sector-specific concepts based on principles and concepts which have existed for decades in European competition law. This is particularly so for the concepts of 'market', and 'powerful undertaking', which are now defined, in substance, as in the law of competition. If discrepancies are observed, they are not due, and will not as a result be due, to the coexistence of two sets of differing rules. The possibility that discrepancies may arise and grow would be due, if such a development occurred, to the plurality of authorities with competence to intervene in similar cases.   **6.118**

Intervention by a myriad of authorities.   A feature of European electronic communications is that they are subject to a myriad of authorities from which one can expect a claim to apply their rules wherever these rules so permit. This has already been stated in the paragraphs above but is worth repeating because of the importance of that situation for the development of consistent case law. The same situation may fall under the jurisdiction of various authorities, pursuant to the rules established in the NRF. *(a)* Under the NRF, NCAs may intervene in many market-oriented difficulties in electronic communications. *(b)* The same may be said of NRAs. *(c)* Interventions by the European Commission cannot be excluded. *(d)* On any occasion that national authorities (NCAs, NRAs) are competent, one has to take into account the possibility that several of them, belonging to various Member States, may seek to intervene in the same case.   **6.119**

Absence of clear co-ordination mechanisms.   The competence of all these authorities does not create an ideal context for the development of a clear, and consistent, body of decisions and case law. The hope in such a situation is that efficient mechanisms are set in place to co-ordinate these interventions. Unfortunately, such mechanisms do not exist at the present time, or barely.   **6.120**

---

[87] Principally P Larouche, *Competition Law and Regulation in European Telecommunications* (2000).

[88] See in particular P Nihoul, *Les télécommunications en Europe: concurrence ou organisation de marché* (2004).

(a) It has already been remarked in the sections above that a decisive mechanism to solve issues deriving from concurrent jurisdiction between NRAs does not appear to exist. Under the Framework Directive, NRAs may intervene when they cover a territory on which one party at least is established. No device has been established at European level to co-ordinate their action.

(b) The institutional structure for the decentralised application of the competition rules has been further construed but is not altogether satisfactory. Regulation 1/2003 has established an Advisory Committee which provides a forum for meetings, discussions and exchanges of ideas and information. The Commission can also take over cases handled by NCAs. Such a decision may be taken, for instance, when handling the case at European level would provide more uniformity and consistency in the decisions taken or rulings adopted. These mechanisms do not take away the risk of inconsistency altogether. Where for example several NCAs are competent, there is no mechanism to designate one NCA from among them to intervene exclusively. Furthermore, NCAs are not only competent to apply European competition rules. They may also apply national rules. One cannot exclude the possibility that decisions based on national rules may be incompatible with European competition law, even though it is stated above that such a contradiction should be regarded as being contrary to the principle of the effectiveness of European law.

(c) The greatest difficulty is that no institutional structure has been established at the European level to articulate relations between NCAs and NRAs. The organisation of the relations between these two kinds of authority has been considered a matter of national sovereignty. Member States have thus retained the entire competence to organise these relations. It has already been observed that the Member States have used that competence in different ways. Some have entrusted the responsibility for the application of the two sets of rules to a single authority. Others have accepted, or encouraged, the development of agreements between authorities, so as to promote an advanced institutional co-operation between them. A third category has been inactive. In that last category, discrepancies can be expected to emerge, and grow, in the decisions taken to apply the two sets of rules.

6.121 Adoption of guidelines desirable. This is a matter serious enough for the European institution to address the issue. The current institutional organisation does not appear to provide a clear framework from which consistency may be expected in the development of the case law. It is difficult to envisage any other possibility for the European institutions than to intervene to provide guidelines as to how the relations between the authorities should be articulated at national level. Some consistency can probably be reached as a result of the presence of the European Commission in the institutional structure in both sets of rules (sector-specific regulation, general competition law). Tools must however be given to the Commission in order to place it in a position to co-ordinate the actions by all relevant authorities effectively.

(3) European and national law

Primacy of European law.   The relations between European and national laws   **6.122**
need not be discussed at length. These relations have been clarified by the case law and academic analysis over previous decades. A clear principle in case law is that European law must prevail on any occasion where there is a conflict between European and national rules (primacy of European law). The consequence is that national laws that are incompatible with European rules must be set aside. The primacy principle is particularly important for advocates and counsellors-at-law. It implies that, whenever national laws do not provide a satisfactory solution to their concerns, they are invited to consult European rules. These rules may well provide a solution. As a result of primacy, the national laws in dispute may be set aside if a contradiction with European law can be demonstrated.

Direct effect.   Pursuant to the case law, European law must be applied directly,   **6.123**
without prior implementation in a national instrument, when national laws are not compatible with the European rules and these rules are clear, precise and unconditional. The doctrine of direct effect applies where European rules in principle require implementation by national instruments in the national legal order. The typical example is provided by directives. These instruments are adopted by European institutions and must be introduced into the national legal orders before they can start producing legal effects for legal and natural persons. In some instances the national authorities do not implement these European rules, in contradiction to European law. The question is then whether legal and natural persons may claim the application of the rights which are granted to them by these European instruments but which have not been introduced in the national legal orders as a result of the (conscious or unconscious) failure to act by the Member State(s) concerned. In these situations the case law provides that the failure to implement European law in national laws should not provide a reason for these legal subjects to lose the rights granted by the European instruments in question. Conditions are however attached for European rules of that nature to produce their effects directly in the national legal orders, without being implemented by national authorities. In substance, the European rules in question must be susceptible of being applied directly. The case law has laid down this general requirement in the form of three conditions. *(a)* The European rule in question must be clear (without ambiguity). *(b)* It must be precise (no choice to be made by the Member State in

the interpretation). *(c)* Finally, it must be unconditional (application not subject to a date still to come or to the occurrence of a forthcoming event).

6.124 **Effectiveness.** Another principle is worth discussing and taking into account in legal strategies: the principle of effectiveness. Under the case law, the effectiveness of European law may not be impaired. On the basis of that principle, the ECJ, for instance, has created new procedures.[89] An implication of that interpretation is that national laws may not create a situation where doubts are raised among undertakings and individuals concerning permissible or, on the contrary, prohibited, behaviour. That principle was used to explain why national competition laws must progressively converge towards the rules that are in force under European competition law. Suppose that discrepancies exist between national and European competition laws. Regulation 1/2003 introduces rules to avoid, to a certain extent, the emergence of discrepancies. These rules are however limited to situations where the national, and European, competition rules are simultaneously applicable to the same situations.[90] No mechanism has been put in place to ensure coherence in situations where national competition laws would apply exclusively. One can thus not exclude the possibility that, in these situations, decisions may be adopted on the basis of national competition laws, in contradiction with the content of European competition rules. The principle of effectiveness appears to require that, in such a situation, the national solutions must be made compatible with European rules. One cannot expect that undertakings and individuals can be subject to various and, in fact, contradictory, prescripts as regards competition, depending on whether national, or European, rules are applied. Legal certainty requires a consistent body of rules and decisions to be developed, so that legal subjects can be asked to adapt their behaviour accordingly. The effectiveness of European law seems to imply that consistency must exist, not only within each legal order (national and European) separately, but also as between these orders.

(4) The relationship with WTO provisions

6.125 **International by nature.** Networks and services provide links, through virtual exchanges, between people located at a distance from one another. These communications imply the mediation of undertakings, which provide the networks and services involved. As exchanges of all kinds grow across borders, arrangements

---

[89] See for instance Case C-221/89 *R v Secretary of State for Transport, ex p Factortame (No 3)* [1991] ECR I-3905. In that judgment, the ECJ ruled that national courts have to suspend national laws when they ask in a preliminary reference whether these laws are compatible with European law and that suspension is necessary to avoid inflicting on the parties irreparable damage.

[90] NCAs are compelled to apply European competition rules whenever they intend to apply the national competition rules and the conditions for these European rules are satisfied. The NCAs thus have no margin for the application of the European competition rules when the latter could be applied and these authorities have decided that they will apply the national rules. See Regulation 1/2003, Art 3(1).

are made at international level between the undertakings concerned, as well as the States and regional organisations where these undertakings are established and carry out their activities.

Conformity of national and European laws. As international rules are adopted, **6.126** the relationship between these rules and European law deserves attention. In addition, as stated above, not all rules concerning electronic communications have been adopted at European level. In the field of spectrum, for instance, powers remain largely in the hands of the Member States. The consequence is that these Member States have concluded international agreements among themselves, as well as with third States. These agreements may be important for practitioners, where national rules are not in conformity with them.

Focus on WTO provisions. Issues relating to compatibility between national, **6.127** European and international rules are numerous. It is not possible, or desirable, to address them all in this book, which focuses on European electronic communications laws. To give a hint of these issues, this section briefly explores the compatibility of European law with WTO provisions. Rather than providing a systematic analysis of the subject, the purpose of this section is to explain to practitioners how important it is to assess rules against other rules coming from a superior legal order. This continuous assessment is a considerable source of argument in legal practice, and this development will continue in the future.

Overall consistency. Rules have been adopted at WTO level which have a sig- **6.128** nificant impact on electronic communications. Among them are those set out in the Reference Paper, which introduces regulatory principles to be complied with by the Members of the Organisation on the markets which they have accepted to liberalise. The rules introduced by the WTO Reference Paper are, in substance, consistent with those which have been adopted at European level. This should not come as a surprise, as the European Union has played a key role in the definition of these international rules. The relevant WTO provisions have been examined in previous chapters, particularly the rules concerning regulators (independence, impartiality), authorisations (basic regulatory principles), interconnection (where no distinction is made from access), competition law (essential facilities doctrine) and universal service (compatibility of national schemes).

Different scope. The main difference remains the scope of the rules. European **6.129** rules apply to all electronic communications networks and services. In the NRF, the European legislator has decided to address regulatory issues arising in the broadcasting and telecommunications sectors, which were formerly subject to differing regimes. In contrast, the Reference Paper covers basic telecommunications, ie core telecommunications services; broadcasting networks and services are not covered.

In case of divergence. Despite overall consistency, divergences may appear **6.130** between WTO and European provisions in the course of specific cases. What should practitioners then do? *(a)* It has been stated that European law prevails in case of incompatibility with national rules. Primacy implies that, in case of incompatibility, contrary national laws may not be applied. It also implies that, where they have direct effect, the relevant European provisions may be applied directly within the national legal orders. *(b)* The possibilities are more limited as regards the relations between European law and WTO provisions. Pursuant to the case law,[91] European institutions are bound by the commitments which they undertake within the WTO. This does not imply, however, that European rules must be set aside where they are incompatible with these provisions.

6.131 **Four principles.** The principles regarding the effect of WTO provisions in the European legal order have been defined in the case law and are as follows. *(a)* Parties to an international agreement can decide that the rules which they adopt must have direct effect on the territories of the signatories. For instance, where it is competent to adopt a provision according to European rules, the European Union may decide, with the other parties, that that provision has direct effect within the European legal order. *(b)* Where such a choice in favour of direct effect has not been made, the ECJ and the CFI have the duty to interpret European law and assess the validity of European provisions by virtue of the powers granted to them by the EC Treaty. *(c)* As regards validity, the European courts accept that WTO provisions are to be taken into account in determining whether European acts are valid. That possibility is however restricted to limited circumstances (see para 6.132 below). *(d)* WTO provisions may not be granted direct effect within the European legal order in the absence of a specific decision to that effect by the European Union and the other parties to the agreement as mentioned in *(a)* above.

> *Portugal v Council.* '[I]n conformity with the principles of public international law Community institutions which have power to negotiate and conclude an agreement with a non-member country are free to agree with that country what effect the provisions of the agreement are to have in the internal legal order of the contracting parties.' 'Only if that question has not been settled by the agreement does it fall to be decided by the courts having jurisdiction in the matter, and in particular by the Court of Justice within the framework of its jurisdiction under the EC Treaty, in the same manner as any question of interpretation relating to the application of the agreement in the Community.'[92]

6.132 **Validity of European acts.** In view of this case law, the possibilities appear limited for practitioners eager to set aside a European rule which does not serve the interests of their clients. The main possibility seems restricted to arguing that the relevant European act is invalid as being contrary to WTO provisions. As

---

[91] In chronological order, see Cases 21–24/72 *International Fruit Company NV v Produktschap voor Groenten en Fruit* [1972] ECR 1226, Case 70/87 *FEDIOL v Commission* [1989] ECR 1781, Case C-69/89 *Nakajima All Precision v Council* [1991] ECR I-2069, Case C-188/88 *NMB Germany v Commission* [1992] ECR I-1689, Case C-280/93 *Germany v Council* [1994] ECR I-4973, Case C-149/96 *Portugal v Council* [1999] ECR I-8395.   [92] At [34].

mentioned in the paragraph above, that possibility is however limited to circumstances where the European legislator intended to implement a particular WTO provision by adopting the relevant European act, or where the European act expressly refers to a WTO provision.

> *Portugal v Council.* '[H]aving regard to their nature and structure, the WTO agreements are not in principle among the rules in the light of which the Court is to review the legality of measures adopted by the Community institutions.' 'It is only where the Community intended to implement a particular obligation assumed in the context of the WTO, or where the Community measure refers expressly to the precise provisions of the WTO agreements, that it is for the Court to review the legality of the Community measure in question in the light of the WTO rules.'[93]

Review possible. These circumstances are present as regards the rules adopted by   **6.133** the European legislator in the electronic communications sector. Most directives composing the NRF refer to international commitments adopted in the WTO framework.[94] This implies that these European rules may be assessed as to their validity against the corresponding WTO provisions. In principle an analysis of compatibility should not lead to a situation where European rules are found incompatible with WTO provisions. As has been seen, European and international rules correspond in substance, although it cannot be excluded that divergences may appear in the course of the application of these European rules in practice.

---

[93] At [47] and [49].
[94] Framework Directive, Preamble, recital 29; Access Directive, Preamble, recital 13; Universal Service Directive, Preamble, recital 3.

7

SPECIFIC ISSUES

A. Introduction

Issues covered. The principal rules composing the NRF have been examined in **7.01**
previous chapters. This chapter analyses specific issues or themes to which special
attention must be devoted by virtue of their special importance in underpinning

687

the principles of the regulatory framework: the protection granted to users in the NRF; the progressive emergence of European policy in the field of radio spectrum; cost accounting obligations; accounting separation and the structural separation that may be imposed on undertakings in particular circumstances; technological neutrality, standardisation and harmonisation; the specific provisions introduced in the NRF regarding public voice telephony; and, finally, provisions regarding (radio and television) broadcasting.

B. Protection of Users

(1) Universal service and the protection of users

7.02 **Link with universal service.**   The services that certain undertakings must provide as part of the universal service requirement have been examined above. Universal service is established in order to ensure that the public receives the services which, it is felt, are necessary in a modern society. Universal service is thus created, and organised, for the benefit of users. In addition to provisions concerning universal service, the Universal Service Directive contains articles devoted to the protection of users.

7.03 **National legislation on contracts.**   The inclusion, in a directive, of provisions concerning the protection of users is worth mentioning. There are not many instances where the European legislator has harmonised national provisions relating to contracts. Some provisions of this nature were adopted at the request of the Commission Directorate General responsible for consumers. Plans are also under discussion concerning the possibility for the European legislator to harmonise the laws of the Member States relating to contracts. Such harmonisation has however not yet taken place on a substantial scale. For this reason the inclusion in the Universal Service Directive of harmonisation provisions concerning electronic communications services contracts for end users has been greeted with enthusiasm, as providing an additional signal that there is room for Community action in this field.

7.04 **A far-reaching transformation.**   Another reason why provisions concerning the protection of users are important is that contracts are not usual in the provision of public services. Before the reform, telecommunications services were provided by administrations. In that context, there was in many cases no provision for the conclusion of a contract. Nor was there any willingness to include provisions to ensure user protection. That context has undergone significant transformation with the advent of competition. With liberalisation, relations between users and providers have changed. They no longer represent a relationship between an administration and members of the public, where administrative law applies with general rules determining the conditions under which public service may be used. These relations have been transformed into a link between an undertaking and customers. To these new relations, civil or commercial law applies. A contract is signed and, as in most cases where a contract creates links between legal or natural persons of different negotiating powers, protective provisions are added in the legislation to ensure consumers are treated according to a proper legal framework.

> *Universal Service Directive, Article 1(2).* 'This [Universal Service] Directive establishes the rights of end-users and the corresponding obligations on undertakings providing publicly available electronic communications networks and services.'

(2) Provision of information

A complement to competition. The course of action decided on by the **7.05** European institutions in relation to user protection is connected with the introduction of competition and efforts to ensure that markets work properly. On a competitive market, consumers and users can choose their service provider. Where a consumer is not satisfied by the service supplied, he can seek better services elsewhere. Information must be provided to ensure adequate choice. It is the responsibility of the Member States, and the national authorities, to ensure transparency on the markets. Transparency in this sense refers to the presence of adequate information on the market so that choices can be made in an appropriate manner.

Same information as in contracts. In substance, information must be provided **7.06** on all important aspects of the contract to be signed with the undertaking providing a service. In that context, it does not come as a surprise that the information to be provided before the conclusion of the contract is approximately the same as that which has to be included in the agreement. A more systematic comparison is carried out in the following paragraphs. The principle that information must be provided is expressed in the body of the Universal Service Directive. That principle is further detailed in Annex II to the directive, where a list of information is provided, together with an explanation as to how the list is to be used.

> *Universal Service Directive, Article 21(1).* 'Member States shall ensure that transparent and up-to-date information on applicable prices and tariffs, and on standard terms and conditions, in respect of access to and use of publicly available telephone services is available to end-users and consumers, in accordance with the provisions of Annex II.'

Three categories. At the present stage it is sufficient to mention that information **7.07** to be provided in principle covers the following three broad categories: tariffs and financial aspects of the transaction; characteristics of the service, including the identity of the provider; and the duration as well as the termination date of the contract.

Tariffs and financial conditions. The main element on which information must **7.08** be provided is prices. These are the main criterion for comparing providers. Customers may sometimes be ready to compromise on quality, but often seem motivated by price or other financial considerations. *(a)* Information must therefore be provided concerning prices and other financial conditions. *(b)* Among the latter are the compensation and refund policies of the undertaking concerned in case of failure to provided the service. *(c)* In many instances consumers select a provider on the basis of their estimate of the cost of the various alternatives open to them.

National regulatory authorities (NRAs) are required to promote systems to help users and consumers to calculate the cost of using one or other supplier (simulation).

> *Universal Service Directive, Annex II.* Information must be provided on (a) 'Standard tariffs covering access, all types of usage charges, maintenance, and including details of standard discounts applied and special and targeted tariff schemes'; and on (b) '[c]ompensation/refund policy, including specific details of any compensation/refund schemes offered'. *Universal Service Directive, Article 21(2).* 'National regulatory authorities shall encourage the provision of information to enable end-users, as far as appropriate, and consumers to make an independent evaluation of the cost of alternative usage patterns, by means of, for instance, interactive guides.'

7.09 **Characteristics of the service.**   Information must also be provided on the service the undertaking is ready to provide. There must be an agreement between the undertaking and the user as to exactly what service will be provided. *(a)* In that context, users must be made aware of the identity of the undertaking providing the service. This may have an impact on the choice by the consumer. Where an undertaking has a bad reputation in terms of reliability as to quality, information of this kind may be decisive for the consumer in making his choice. *(b)* In the Universal Service Directive, emphasis is placed on the relationship between service and price. As a result of the information provided, users must be made aware of what is obtained in exchange for payment. *(c)* Pursuant to the directive, information must also be provided on the type of maintenance offered. In some instances users receive access to a service, but this may be made ineffective where the service needs maintenance to work properly. *(d)* A last item on which information must be provided is the rights granted under universal service. The universal service creates rights for users, who can thus lay claim to the provision of the service. As stated above, this does not mean that the services in question are to be provided free of charge by the undertakings.

> *Universal Service Directive, Annex II.* [a] 'Name(s) and address(es) of undertaking(s), ie names and head office addresses of undertakings providing public telephone networks and/or publicly available telephone services.' [b] 'Description of the publicly available telephone services offered, indicating what is included in the subscription charge and the periodic rental charge (eg operator services, directories, directory enquiry services, selective call barring, itemised billing, maintenance, etc.).' [c] 'Types of maintenance service offered.' [d] 'Information about rights as regards universal service.'

7.10 **Duration and termination of the contract.**   The last category of information concerns the duration of the contract. Information must be provided regarding possible minimum contract periods. Users must also be informed as to how the contract may be terminated in the event that that user wants to deal with another provider. Information about dispute resolution may be relevant in this regard.

> *Universal Service Directive, Annex II.* [a] 'Standard contract conditions, including any minimum contractual period, if relevant.' [b] 'Dispute settlement mechanisms including those developed by the undertaking.'

Quality of service. Information must be provided regarding the quality of the ser- **7.11**
vice provided. One difficulty in this regard is to ensure the comparability of the
information provided by the undertakings concerned. Quality is often assessed sub-
jectively. However, a comparison is necessary to allow a choice by users. *(a)* To solve
this difficulty the Universal Service Directive gives NRAs the power to request from
undertakings the provision of comparable, adequate and up-to-date information on
quality. *(b)* A further step is made by allowing NRAs to provide standards for quality evaluation. Where such standards are provided, the evaluation no longer
depends on the presentation that is made by the undertaking itself, but rather uses
measurements drawn up and made by independent evaluators. *(c)* A suggestion is
set out in the Universal Service Directive that standards applicable for the measurement of universal service quality may be used. There are strong arguments in favour
of using these standards for items other than those covered by universal service. First,
undertakings do not need to adapt to divergent methodologies. They can use the
same standards for all services, independently of whether a service falls under or outside the universal service requirement. Second, the use of the same standards for all
electronic communications services would lead to more coherence in the sector.
Discrepancies in the level of requirements could hardly be avoided if standards from
various organisations were used. A third argument is that the standards proposed by
the European institutions are prepared by ETSI. That organisation specialises in the
production of standards for the electronic communications sector, and no other
organisation appears better equipped for the provision of such evaluation tools.

> *Universal Service Directive, Article 22.* [a] 'Member States shall ensure that national
> regulatory authorities are, after taking account of the views of interested parties, able
> to require undertakings that provide publicly available electronic communications
> services to publish comparable, adequate and up-to-date information for end-users
> on the quality of their services. The information shall, on request, also be supplied to
> the national regulatory authority in advance of its publication.' [b] 'National regula-
> tory authorities may specify, *inter alia*, the quality of service parameters to be meas-
> ured, and the content, form and manner of information to be published, in order to
> ensure that end-users have access to comprehensive, comparable and user-friendly
> information. Where appropriate, the parameters, definitions and measurement
> methods given in Annex III could be used.'[1]

Telephony and services intended for the public. All electronic communica- **7.12**
tions services are not concerned to the same extent by the obligations concerning
the provision of information. *(a)* The obligations examined above apply only for
services which are intended for the public. An inference is that services not meant
for the public do not give rise to the same obligations. Undertakings offering services to private groups are as a result not covered by the provisions examined.
(b) A distinction is drawn in the Universal Service Directive between services on

---

[1] Annex III contains the standards used for the evaluation of quality as regards the universal
service. These standards are drawn up by ETSI. The standard used is ETSI EG 769-1.

the basis of their nature as regards information-related obligations. The measurement of quality applies to all services. There is thus a general position that all electronic communications services should be comparable as regards quality—something that implies that information must be provided on the quality of these services. By contrast, the other obligations appear limited to one category of electronic communications services, that is, voice telephony. The obligations which are introduced in the Universal Service Directive regarding tariffs and other financial conditions, the characteristics of the service and the duration, or termination, of the contract, are limited to that particular service. These obligations as a result do not apply to other activities within the electronic communications sector.

> *Universal Service Directive, Article 21(1).* 'Member States shall ensure that transparent and up-to-date information on applicable prices and tariffs, and on standard terms and conditions, in respect of access to and use of *publicly available telephone services* is available to end-users and consumers.' *Universal Service Directive, Annex II.* 'It is for the national regulatory authority to decide which information is to be published by the undertakings providing *public telephone networks* and/or *publicly available telephone services* and which information is to be published by the national regulatory authority itself.'[2]

7.13 **Why these obligations regarding voice telephony?** It is not clear why the European legislator has imposed specific obligations regarding voice telephony and has not extended them to other services. *(a)* One reason is probably that the European legislator does not want to overburden undertakings on non-traditional electronic communications markets. It takes the view that services should develop to a maximum and that such development will not take place if obligations are imposed on providers. Hence the desire to limit the obligations imposed on the undertakings present on non-voice telephony markets. *(b)* A second reason might be that the provisions examined above, and the obligations they contain, relate to universal service. As stated, universal service at the present stage mainly concerns public voice telephony. That position corresponds with the idea that, in a modern society, access should be obtained to public voice telephony under the best conditions. For that reason, obligations may be imposed regarding these services. A criticism can however be levelled at this position. In a market-driven economy, the authorities have a major role to fulfil, that is, to ensure the correct functioning of the market. However, markets can only perform if adequate information is provided to users. Leaving it up to the markets to produce adequate and comparable information may appear, in this context, naive. Undertakings do not present information—they make marketing presentations.

7.14 **Why distinguish markets?** A similar question might be why information-related obligations are limited to services meant for the public. Markets function properly if, and when, information is provided to users. That principle applies

---

[2] Author's emphasis.

irrespective of the service concerned. There is no reason to ensure, via information-related obligations, that the markets concerning voice telephony work properly, without adopting a similar attitude for markets concerning other services. More generally, one must realise that a distinction is made between markets depending on their public or private character in some instances, or depending on the nature of the service in other circumstances. However, why should a policy be promoted for some markets and not for others? The answer, here again, must be found in the desire, manifested in these provisions, that authorities should refrain as much as possible from intervening. Markets should be left free, unless it appears that a blatant failure would emerge from a lack of intervention. This principle lies at the foundation of the NRF. Some of its manifestations are examined in various chapters above.

Provision by undertakings or by NRAs?   The information referred to above   **7.15** must be provided pursuant to the Universal Service Directive. However, there is no indication as to who has responsibility for providing it. The directive leaves a choice to be made by the Member States on this point. The latter may decide that all information is to be provided by undertakings, or entrust the NRAs with the task of informing the public to a certain extent.

> *Universal Service Directive, Annex II.* 'The national regulatory authority has a respon-sibility to ensure that the information in this Annex is published.' 'It is for the national regulatory authority to decide which information is to be published by the undertakings providing public telephone networks and/or publicly available tele-phone services and which information is to be published by the national regulatory authority itself.'

(3) Contracts with undertakings

Application of general contractual protection.   A key aspect of these provisions   **7.16** is the protection of consumers in the contracts signed by the latter with undertak-ings. The provisions included in the Universal Service Directive are not exclusive of the protection granted in other European instruments. Two directives are men-tioned in the NRF.[3] *(a)* The first is Council Directive (EEC) 93/13 on unfair terms in consumer contracts.[4] That directive concerns the content of the contract which may be signed between a consumer and an undertaking. It contains a list of clauses which may be deemed abusive. The Member States are compelled to intro-duce protection in their internal legal orders against these clauses. *(b)* The second instrument is European Parliament and Council Directive (EC) 97/7 on the pro-tection of consumers in respect of distance contracts.[5] That directive does not concern the content of the contract but rather the circumstances in which the contract has been concluded. Where the seller does not meet the buyer, and the buyer does not see what he is buying, there is a possibility that the buyer may not be satisfied with the object of the transaction when that object is delivered. To

---

[3] See Universal Service Directive, Art 20(1).   [4] [1993] OJ L95/29.
[5] [1997] OJ L144/19.

avoid disappointment, the directive organises the information that must be provided by the seller. It also provides that the buyer has a right to return the goods, where that is possible, without incurring specific cancellation charges.

7.17 Obligation to have a contract. An obligation is imposed on undertakings to sign a contract with consumers when the latter ask for access to a public network. There is thus no possibility for the undertaking to start providing the service without signing an agreement with the consumer. The reasons are as follows. *(a)* First, it ensures consumers know the exact content and scope of their commitments and rights before concluding the agreement. The signing of a contract provides the best instrument to ensure that consumers are made aware of the rights and obligations which they subscribe to in an appropriate way. *(b)* Second, it is not possible for undertakings to modify without notice the conditions of the contract during the provision of the service. In the absence of a contract, changes could be introduced without the consumer being in a position to know that the new provisions indeed introduce a modification in the original arrangement.

> *Universal Service Directive, Article 20(2).* 'Member States shall ensure that, where subscribing to services providing connection and/or access to the public telephone network, consumers have a right to a contract with an undertaking or undertakings providing such services.'

7.18 Information to be provided. Pursuant to the Universal Service Directive, the information to be provided may be divided into two categories. In the first category is information concerning the main elements of the contract: the identity of the parties; the services provided and the tariff to be applied. The second category provides information on how to terminate the contract, obtain possible compensation and start a procedure. That second category is included to provide the consumer with all data necessary in case a dispute arises.

> *Universal Service Directive, Article 20(2).* 'The contract shall specify at least: (a) the identity and address of the supplier; (b) services provided, the service quality levels offered, as well as the time for the initial connection; (c) the types of maintenance service offered; (d) particulars of prices and tariffs and the means by which up-to-date information on all applicable tariffs and maintenance charges may be obtained; (e) the duration of the contract, the conditions for renewal and termination of services and of the contract; (f) any compensation and the refund arrangements which apply if contracted service quality levels are not met; and (g) the method of initiating procedures for settlement of disputes.'

7.19 Changes in contractual conditions. Undertakings must inform consumers when they decide to introduce modifications into the contractual conditions. Information must be provided at least one month before the changes become effective. The consumer accordingly has the right to stop the contract without having to pay an indemnity. The possibility of bringing the contract to an end must be mentioned in the information provided by the undertaking and announcing the changes. There is no indication in the directive about other conditions to be fulfilled for this protective measure to apply. No reference is made, in particular, to any requirement that the modification should be substantial in order to allow for the contract to be terminated. In the absence of a restriction of that nature it seems reasonable to conclude that any change may be sufficient to support a request that the contract be terminated by the consumer. In order to avoid unnecessary harm to the undertaking, a requirement may be laid down that the termination will be possible only where the change affects the position of the consumer and the consumer is in a position to explain why that change in his judgment justifies termination.

> *Universal Service Directive, Article 20(4).* 'Subscribers shall have a right to withdraw from their contracts without penalty upon notice of proposed modifications in the contractual conditions. Subscribers shall be given adequate notice, not shorter than one month, ahead of any such modifications and shall be informed at the same time of their right to withdraw, without penalty, from such contracts, if they do not accept the new conditions.'

Application to all undertakings.   The provision examined above imposes an   **7.20** obligation on undertakings. Thus the absence of a contract with a consumer implies that the undertaking is not in a position to request the payments which it would otherwise have been entitled to request from that consumer. These obligations may be imposed on all undertakings providing services in the electronic communications sectors. The obligations are mentioned explicitly in regard to undertakings providing connection and/or access to the public telephone network. A reference is also made to other undertakings providing electronic communications services.

> *Universal Service Directive, Article 20(3).* 'Where contracts are concluded between consumers and electronic communications services providers other than those providing connection and/or access to the public telephone network, the information . . . shall also be included in such contracts.'

Extension possible to other users.   The protection introduced above applies to   **7.21** consumers. In the NRF, consumers are natural persons using the service for their personal use.[6] Two conditions must thus be fulfilled for a person to obtain the protection granted to consumers. First, the consumer must be a natural person. The protection is not accessible to legal persons. Second, the use must be private. There is no protection possible for professional use. Severe limitations are thus imposed regarding the scope of the protection. These limitations should not be interpreted, however, as implying a prohibition on the Member States to extend the protection to other users. The possibility of an extension is mentioned, in an explicit manner, in the directive.[7] There is thus no opposition on the part of the European legislator to the application of this protection to other persons. Member

---

[6] See Framework Directive, Art 2, letter (i). The expression ' "consumer" means any natural person who uses or requests a publicly available electronic communications service for purposes which are outside his or her trade, business or profession'.

[7] See Universal Service Directive, Art 20(2), al 2. 'Member States may extend these obligations to cover other end-users.'

States may as a result protect legal persons in addition to natural persons. They may also decide that the protection measures apply independently of the private or professional use of the electronic communications services by the legal or natural person.

7.22 Comparison of information to be provided

Information that must be available before the conclusion of the contract[8]	Information that must be included in the contract[9]
Identity and address of the supplier.	Name(s) and address(es) of undertaking(s), ie names and head office addresses of undertakings providing public telephone networks and/or publicly available telephone services.
Services provided, the service quality levels offered and the time taken to provide the initial connection.	Scope of the publicly available telephone service. Description of the publicly available telephone services offered, indicating what is included in the subscription charge and the periodic rental charge (eg operator services, directories, directory enquiry services, selective call barring, itemised billing, maintenance, etc).
Particulars of prices and tariffs and the means by which up-to-date information on all applicable tariffs and maintenance charges may be obtained.	Standard tariffs covering access, all types of usage charges, maintenance, and details of standard discounts applied and special and targeted tariff schemes.
Any compensation and the refund arrangements which apply if contracted service quality levels are not met.	Compensation/refund policy, including specific details of any compensation/refund schemes offered.
Types of maintenance service offered.	Types of maintenance service offered.
Duration of the contract, the conditions for renewal and termination of services and of the contract.	Standard contract conditions, including any minimum contractual period, if relevant.
Method of initiating procedures for settlement of disputes in accordance with Article 34.	Dispute settlement mechanisms including those developed by the undertaking.
	Information about rights as regards universal service.

(4) Regulatory controls on retail services

7.23 Specific obligations. Under the Universal Service Directive, NRAs may impose on undertakings with significant market power specific obligations relating to retail markets. The mechanism which is introduced here is similar to the one that has been examined with respect to access. This mechanism is that an intervention is warranted where market interactions are not likely to produce the best economic results as a result of the absence of a sufficient degree of competition.

---

[8] Universal Service Directive, Art 21 and Annex II.   [9] ibid, Art 20.

Procedure.   The procedure to be followed by NRAs for the imposition of the   **7.24**
obligations is similar to that examined as regards access. Readers may consult the
relevant section in the chapter on access for a complete analysis (see paras
3.213–3.266). It will be recalled that the procedure implies that the degree of
competition existing on the markets must be examined. Where the NRA considers that that degree is not sufficient, and that the issues raised on these markets
could not be solved through the application of general competition law, they may
impose obligations.

Only where competition is not effective.   In the Universal Service Directive,   **7.25**
there is an emphasis on the necessity of limiting obligations to situations where
competition is not effective. A similar emphasis had already been noticed in connection with access-related obligations. The European legislator in this way
ensures that competition remains the main regulatory mechanism to produce
satisfactory outcomes for market participants.

> *Universal Service Directive, Article 17(1).* '[N]ational regulatory authorities shall not
> apply retail control mechanisms . . . to geographical or user markets where they are
> satisfied that there is effective competition.'

Additional conditions.   In the context of retail markets, additional conditions   **7.26**
apply. *(a)* Obligations may be imposed only where the issues observed on the relevant retail market(s) cannot be solved through selection and/or preselection of
the operator. The idea is that where users can change suppliers, the existence of
that choice forces market participants, including undertakings with significant
market power, to adopt a more competitive approach. *(b)* A second condition
is that obligations can be imposed only where the conditions for the provision of
retail services cannot be improved upstream through intervention at the level
of the undertakings. As access conditions improve, new entrants may be tempted
to enter the relevant retail markets, thereby increasing the degree of competition
and producing satisfactory outcomes for consumers.

> *Universal Service Directive, Article 17(1).* 'Member States shall ensure that, where:
> (a) as a result of a market analysis . . . a national regulatory authority determines that a
> given retail market . . . is not effectively competitive, and (b) the national regulatory
> authority concludes that obligations imposed under . . . [the] Access Directive . . .,
> or [the provisions on selection or preselection] of this [Universal Service] Directive
> would not result in the achievement of the objectives . . ., national regulatory
> authorities shall impose appropriate regulatory obligations on undertakings identi-
> fied as having significant market power on a given retail market.'

Tariff-related obligations.   There are few indications about the obligations that   **7.27**
may be introduced at the retail level, where the markets are dominated by undertakings with significant market power. Most illustrations concern tariffs. *(a)* NRAs
may prohibit excessive prices—a prohibition which can also be imposed on
the basis of general competition law. *(b)* Predatory prices may also be prohibited.

The prohibition, in that case, does not aim at protecting end users, at least in the short term. End users would indeed benefit from low prices, even where they were set below cost. It is however important to ensure that competition remains alive. This can be achieved only where enough competitors survive—an outcome which is difficult to maintain where sales at a loss are carried out. *(c)* Depending on the circumstances, maximum prices can be imposed or undertakings may be compelled to set prices above costs.

> *Universal Service Directive, Article 17(2).* 'Obligations . . . shall be based on the nature of the problem identified and be proportionate and justified in the light of the objectives laid down in . . . [the] Framework Directive.' 'The obligations imposed may include requirements that the identified undertakings do not charge excessive prices, inhibit market entry or restrict competition by setting predatory prices.' 'National regulatory authorities may apply to such undertakings appropriate retail price cap measures, measures to control individual tariffs, or measures to orient tariffs towards costs or prices on comparable markets, in order to protect end-user interests whilst promoting effective competition.'

7.28 **Other obligations.**   Other obligations may be imposed, but not many illustrations are given in the Universal Service Directive. These illustrations also concern behaviour which can be prohibited on the basis of general competition law—bundled offers or discrimination.

> *Universal Service Directive, Article 17(2).* 'The obligations imposed may include requirements that the identified undertakings do not . . . show undue preference to specific end-users or unreasonably bundle services.'

7.29 **Accompanying accounting measures.**   Where obligations are imposed on retail markets, accounting measures must also be taken. The purpose is to ensure that costs and tariffs are properly identified. This measure aims, here as well, at establishing the conditions for an efficient exercise of activities, in the hope that activities will later be provided in a competitive environment.

> *Universal Service Directive, Article 17(4).* 'National regulatory authorities shall ensure that, where an undertaking is subject to retail tariff regulation or other relevant retail controls, the necessary and appropriate cost accounting systems are implemented. National regulatory authorities may specify the format and accounting methodology to be used. Compliance with the cost accounting system shall be verified by a qualified independent body. National regulatory authorities shall ensure that a statement concerning compliance is published annually.'

C. Towards a European Spectrum Policy

(1) Spectrum in the NRF

7.30 **Rights of use.**   Radio frequencies are examined above in the discussion concerning authorisation to commence activities. In the course of that discussion it is stated that general authorisation is the rule. The purpose is to avoid formalities and obligations which could discourage undertakings from entering markets or remaining active on them. In some instances, Member States may introduce an obligation for undertakings to obtain rights of use before commencing activity. These rights are different from general authorisation in that they require specific action from undertakings as well as a specific reaction from an authority. That reaction may be an acceptance or refusal to grant the right of use in question.

Limited number of rights.   In exceptional circumstances, Member States may   **7.31** limit the number of rights of use. Such a limitation intervenes as a standard where the rights to be distributed are a scarce resource. The limited number of available resources—for instance frequencies or certain numbers—implies that the candidate undertakings applying for a right do not all receive what they are asking for. Some of them are only designated as beneficiaries. A selection must be made. A scenario of this nature entails risks for the development of competition. It is indeed not guaranteed that the undertakings selected by the Member States will at all times be the best to perform the activities concerned. Furthermore, there is a danger that, as they are limited in number, the selected undertakings will not perform their activities as they would do in a more competitive environment (possibility of cartel or oligopoly).

(2) Legislative history

A European policy.   As stated above, Chapter 2 relating to authorisation covers   **7.32** general authorisation, rights of use and the limitation which Member States may introduce regarding the frequencies allocated to undertakings. In this section, the focus is placed on the progressive development of a European policy for radio frequency.

Disparity among national legislation.   The need for a European policy in the   **7.33** field of radio frequencies appears to have emerged progressively in recent years. An important factor explaining that need has been the process of allocation of frequencies for the development of the third generation of mobile technology across the European continent. The procedures whereby those frequencies were distributed showed that divergences existed between the applicable national legislation. Some Member States emphasised the prices to be paid by the undertakings in order for them to be allowed to perform activities on the markets concerned (auctions). Others considered that attention should be granted to a variety of criteria, the price being only one of them ('beauty contest').

A contested subject.   Before examining the arguments put forward by various   **7.34** authors, it is important to realise that there is some disagreement among observers as to the analysis which can be made of the procedures whereby licences have been distributed for the development of third generation mobile technology. The existence of disagreement is no reason, however, not to explain the arguments, which could be important for the development of spectrum policy in the Member States as well as at European level.

7.35 **Internal market.** To some observers, it appears that this disparity may undermine the attainment of the internal market. How is it possible to speak of an internal market if the rules concerning the development of a major technology are still defined at national level without co-ordination or harmonisation at European level? Third generation mobile technology is expected to evolve as a major communications platform in the years ahead. Can the European Union afford not to develop a common view, if not a common policy, on how that technology could, or should, be developed?

7.36 **Equity among the Member States.** For some, the allocation of frequencies by the Member States has created other difficulties. During the relevant procedures, significant payments were made by operators in some Member States in order to obtain a licence allowing them to provide third generation services. The situation was different in other countries, where payments were not so high.[10] The result was a sense that equity may have been violated between the Member States. *(a)* Some were not able to obtain the sums that their markets would have allowed them to extract, had the procedures developed in a more harmonious manner. *(b)* The reason why these Member States did not obtain the resources which, they believe, they should have been able to obtain, is that other Member States had charged excessive amounts. *(c)* Finally, some Member States simply considered high licence fees as a barrier to entry, and did not wish to charge them. At the same time they deplored the high fees charged in other Member States.

7.37 **Technology and the survival of undertakings.** An additional difficulty, for some observers, is that the discrepancy between national procedures may have contributed to the increase of the perception of the business risks associated with the development of the technology concerned. In some Member States, the candidates chose to pay significant amounts to participate in the development of the markets concerned. *(a)* A consequence may be that these undertakings may no longer have the financial capability to invest the amounts necessary for the development of the technology.[11] *(b)* In some instances, these amounts may have been so large that they may have caused the value of these undertakings to plunge, so

---

[10] The reason for the difference may be related to the identity of the market concerned. Germany being a big market, more operators were interested. They had to pay higher amounts than in, say, Belgium. Another reason was the period during which the procedures unfolded. Some Member States started the procedure when the stock market was already declining and the crisis was looming. In that uncertain context, undertakings have not dared to propose extravagant amounts as they had done in the first instance in Member States which had organised these procedures earlier.

[11] One could thus arrive at a paradoxical situation where the undertakings authorised to develop a technology may not be able to do so, or at least not at the level which they would have reached had they not been forced to hand out large amounts to buy the right to participate in the development of the new markets.

reducing investor value. *(c)* The financial obligations imposed on these undertakings may have been of such a size that their capability to perform standard activities, including universal service related activities, may have been undermined.

Efficient use of scarce resources.   On the other hand, it is observed by the **7.38** Member States that charged high fees through auction procedures that the most efficient way to price a scarce resource is to allow the market to place a value on it. Undertakings that place a high value on spectrum are likely to be those that will strive to make a return on their investment within the shortest possible timescale, ultimately benefiting consumers and society as a whole.

Legislative steps.   These various reasons, or at least some of them, have caused **7.39** European institutions to reflect whether some sort of harmonisation was desirable at European level. Discussions have been carried out with the Member States to assess the necessity of carrying out common action in this field. The European institutions have also attempted to delineate what those common steps could be. *(a)* A first document was drafted by the Commission to ask for opinions from interested parties about the direction European action could take in the field of radio frequencies.[12] *(b)* The Commission then summarised the oral and written observations submitted by the parties.[13] *(c)* A draft decision was later presented to the Parliament and Council. The draft was adopted after several years of discussion. That instrument is European Parliament and Council Decision (EC) 676/2002 on a regulatory framework for radio spectrum policy in the European Community ('Radio Spectrum Decision').[14]

(3) The Radio Spectrum Decision

Frequencies covered.   The rules contained in the Radio Spectrum Decision are **7.40** examined in the following paragraphs. An important aspect is to determine to what frequencies the decision applies. Pursuant to Article 2, frequencies between 9 kHz and 3000 GHz are covered whereas other frequencies are left aside. For these other frequencies there is no specific regulation at European level. The general rules thus apply, ie the rules which have been adopted by the Parliament and Council under the NRF.

---

[12] See the Green Paper on radio spectrum policy in the context of European Community policies such as telecommunications, broadcasting, transport and research and development (R&D) Brussels, 9 December 1998, COM 1998 (596 final).

[13] See the Communication from the Commission to the European Parliament, the Council, the Economic and Social Committee and the Committee of the Regions, 'Next steps in Radio Spectrum Policy—Results of the Public Consultation on the Green Paper', Brussels, 10 November 1999, COM(1999)538.

[14] [2002] OJ L108/1. The European Commission has recently established a Radio Spectrum Policy Group. See Commission Decision (EC) 2002/622 establishing a Radio Spectrum Policy Group [2002] OJ L198/49. The composition and functions of the Group are presented in para 7.80.

Radio Spectrum Decision, Article 2. 'For the purposes of this Decision, "radio spectrum" includes radio waves in frequencies between 9 kHz and 3000 GHz; radio waves are electromagnetic waves propagated in space without artificial guide.'

7.41 **Division of powers.** The Radio Spectrum Decision mirrors the current delicate division of powers between the Member States and the European institutions in the field of radio spectrum. A legal basis for action at European level may be found in Article 95 EC, which provides that harmonisation may be carried out to solve difficulties created by discrepancies among national legislations in areas where this is necessary for the realisation of the internal market. Some Member States have however remained unconvinced, in whole or in part, about the necessity for European institutions to intervene in spectrum. *(a)* Frequencies are important for some Member States for strategic reasons. For instance, some States want to control certain aspects of electronic communications on their territory for defence purposes. *(b)* Policy considerations also come into play. Some Member States want to allocate frequencies as they consider appropriate to ensure the development of certain activities (such as cultural activities). *(c)* Finally, financial reasons also intervene. Some Member States want to be able to charge undertakings for the use of frequencies, in a period where national exchequers are under spending pressure.

7.42 **Scheme.** Under the Radio Spectrum Decision, action must be carried out by the European institutions in order to realise the objectives assigned to them. The institutions must use the legal tools established in the decision. In their actions, the European institutions must also respect certain values which are specifically referred to. These various elements (objectives, values, legal tools, action) are discussed in the following paragraphs.

7.43 **Ambitious objectives.** The result of these hesitant steps is a subtle allocation of power between the Member States and the European institutions. The objectives assigned to the European institutions are ambitious. Pursuant to the Preamble, the decision purports to 'establish a common framework for radio spectrum policy'.[15] That framework is expected to reach specific objectives. *(a)* A first objective is that frequencies must be available, effectively, for the provision of services. *(b)* Another is that, where they are available, frequencies must be used efficiently.

7.44 **Values to respect.** There is also a certain ambition in determining the values which a European policy should respect in the field of spectrum. Pursuant to the Radio Spectrum Decision, such a policy should not focus on technical issues. All sorts of considerations should be taken into account. Among the values to be complied with are freedom of expression and media pluralism. A reference is also made in the decision to the interests of users.

---

[15] See Radio Spectrum Decision, Preamble, recital 22.

Radio Spectrum Decision, Preamble, recital 3. 'Radio spectrum policy in the Community should contribute to freedom of expression, including freedom of opinion and freedom to receive and disseminate information and ideas, irrespective of borders, as well as freedom and plurality of the media.' *Radio Spectrum Decision, Preamble, recital 8.* 'Radio spectrum policy cannot be based only on technical parameters but also needs to take into account economic, political, cultural, health and social considerations. Moreover, the ever increasing demand for the finite supply of available radio spectrum will lead to conflicting pressures to accommodate the various groups of radio spectrum users in sectors such as telecommunications, broadcasting, transport, law enforcement, military and the scientific community. Therefore, radio spectrum policy should take into account all sectors and balance the respective needs.'

Legal tools.   To reach these objectives, legal tools are granted. *(a)* The first, for   **7.45** the European institutions, is the co-ordination of existing national policies. Where that tool is used, national policies remain defined by the Member States. Arrangements are made, however, to ensure that a discussion takes place regarding the policies developed by the Member States. The hope is that, through discussion, Member States will work towards a progressive convergence of their national policies. *(b)* Another tool, going one step further, is harmonisation. The Radio Spectrum Decision introduces the possibility for the European institutions of harmonising elements of national legislation.[16] These institutions may not act in entire liberty. They are bound by limitations, which are mainly of a procedural nature. One of these limitations is that an agreement must be found in the Council, which brings together the representatives of the Member States.[17]

> *Radio Spectrum Decision, Article 1(1).* 'The aim of this [Radio Spectrum] Decision is to establish a policy and legal framework in the Community in order to ensure the coordination of policy approaches and, where appropriate, harmonised conditions with regard to the availability and efficient use of the radio spectrum necessary for the establishment and functioning of the internal market in Community policy areas such as electronic communications, transport and research and development (R & D).'

Action to be undertaken by the European Union.   Pursuant to the Radio   **7.46** Spectrum Decision, action must be taken by the European institutions to bring about the objectives assigned to them. This action is as follows: the provision of adequate information to the undertakings concerned, the harmonisation of technical implementing rules, the co-ordination of the interests of the Member States and the representation of the Community at international level.

---

[16] Harmonisation is different from co-ordination. In the former process, national policies, or legislation, are unified. In the latter, the decisions are no longer taken at national level. The power is instead conferred on the European institutions.

[17] Harmonisation also requires the intervention of the European Parliament. By nature, the European Parliament is however less enthusiastic about leaving national sovereignty on the distribution of frequencies. As a European institution, with no clear link with national entities, it is more concerned with the realisation of the internal market and the necessity to provide satisfactory technology to the European consumer.

(4) Adequate provision of information

7.47 **Availability of information.** A first action is to ensure the availability of information across the European Union concerning frequencies. The availability of information is essential for undertakings to make business decisions. Where business planning is made at European level, it is essential that information concerning frequencies be made available at that level. Information must cover, in that perspective: the availability of frequencies in the various Member States; the way in which the frequencies are allocated in each of these States; the conditions that are attached to the rights of use granted to beneficiaries; and the obligations that are imposed on undertakings authorised to perform services on the frequencies concerned.

7.48 **Tools available for that action.** In the Radio Spectrum Decision, the European institutions are invited to co-ordinate the dissemination of information by the Member States. A specific obligation is imposed on the Member States to publish all relevant information on rights, conditions, procedures, charges and fees. That information must be updated. Databases must be set up to ensure the broad availability of this information. Finally, a procedure is set up for the harmonisation of information to be presented by the Member States.

> *Radio Spectrum Decision, Article 1(2)*. 'In order to meet this aim, this Decision establishes procedures in order to: . . . (c) ensure the coordinated and timely provision of information concerning the allocation, availability and use of radio spectrum in the Community.' *Radio Spectrum Decision, Article 5*. 'Member States shall ensure that their national radio frequency allocation table and information on rights, conditions, procedures, charges and fees concerning the use of radio spectrum, shall be published if relevant.' 'They shall keep this information up to date and shall take measures to develop appropriate databases in order to make such information available to the public, where applicable in accordance with the relevant harmonisation measures.' *Radio Spectrum Decision, Article 4(1)*. The 'Commission shall submit to the Radio Spectrum Committee . . . appropriate technical implementing measures with a view to ensuring harmonised conditions for . . . the availability of information related to the use of radio spectrum'.

7.49 **Co-ordination or harmonisation?** The tools proposed for action in the previous paragraphs are typical of the uncertainty which exists in the decision regarding the powers to be conferred on the European institutions to develop and carry out policy in the field of spectrum across the European Union. Pursuant to the provision cited above, the key mechanism to be used regarding information seems to be co-ordination. The Radio Spectrum Decision indeed emphasises, in the first instance, the need to co-ordinate the provision of information by the Member States. A second tool is however mentioned in connection with that same action—the possibility for the European Commission to use harmonisation procedures to the same effect. A third tool is referred to specifically, as the Radio Spectrum Decision already introduces some sort of harmonisation by compelling the Member States to publish information as detailed in the decision. Co-ordination, harmonisation of technical implementing rules, harmonisation within the decision itself: the reference to three modes of action, in the same instrument, shows that no clear option has been taken as to how the objectives set in the decision should be reached.

(5) Harmonisation of technical implementing measures

Harmonisation of national legislation.   A second action is the harmonisation of   **7.50**
national legislation concerning availability and use of radio frequencies. The Radio Spectrum Decision organises various procedures to be followed in order to harmonise technical implementing measures.

> *Radio Spectrum Decision, Article 4(1)*. '[T]he Commission shall submit to the Radio Spectrum Committee, in accordance with the procedures set out in this Article, appropriate technical implementing measures with a view to ensuring harmonised conditions for the availability and efficient use of radio spectrum, as well as the availability of information related to the use of radio spectrum.'

Two types of standard.   Among these procedures, a distinction is made between   **7.51**
standards drawn up by CEPT and standards prepared by the Commission itself. *(a)* All standards falling under the remit of CEPT are normally prepared by CEPT. This implies that all standards to be prepared in the field of spectrum are normally prepared by CEPT. As will be stated, CEPT indeed works on technical and regulatory matters relating to post and telecommunications. It was granted the competence by its members to intervene in these sectors in order to support the development of regulation at European and international level. *(b)* Non-CEPT standards are prepared by the Commission. The Commission intervenes, in principle, for the preparation of standards in three instances: where the standards do not fall under the remit of CEPT; standards have been prepared by CEPT but are not found satisfactory; or CEPT has been entrusted with a mandate to prepare standards but has not complied with the deadline within which the work was to be terminated, or does not appear to be able to do so.

Two types of standard	7.52

Standards prepared by CEPT	Non-CEPT standards
— Standards falling under the remit of CEPT	— Standards falling outside the remit of CEPT — Standards prepared by CEPT but found unsatisfactory — Standards the drawing up of which was entrusted to CEPT but which were not finished in time by that institution

Procedures for the adoption of decisions.   In the procedures concerning the   **7.53**
adoption of these standards, decisions have to be taken. The procedures for the

adoption of these decisions must conform to another instrument, Council Decision (EC) 1999/468 laying down the procedures for the exercise of implementing powers conferred on the Commission.[18] As will be submitted, different standards are set for the adoption of decisions whether the standards are elaborated, or not, by CEPT. In the following paragraphs, the drawing up of standards by CEPT is described. The drawing up of non-CEPT standards is then examined. The analysis terminates with a comparison between the procedures used in these two situations.

7.54 **Procedures to be used for harmonisation**

(1) The Commission holds general responsibility for the harmonisation of technical implementing measures.

Standards drawn up by CEPT
(2) In most instances, these technical standards are prepared by CEPT upon a mandate issued by the Commission.
(3) Once they have been prepared by CEPT, the standards are examined by the Commission.
(4) If the Commission considers that these standards should be made obligatory, an 'advisory procedure' may be started.
(5) When a standard has been declared obligatory, it must be implemented in all the Member States.

Adoption of non-CEPT standards
(6) Standards may also be adopted in the absence of an intervention by CEPT.
(7) These standards are adopted by the Commission with the Radio Spectrum Committee ('regulatory procedure').
(8) In the absence of agreement, the matter is referred to the Council.

(6) Rules contained in other instruments

7.55 **Authorisations and Framework Directives.** Chronologically, the Radio Spectrum Decision was adopted on the same day as the directives composing the NRF. An interesting development is that, within the NRF, the harmonisation of national legislation concerning spectrum is not envisaged in that decision only. *(a)* In the Framework Directive, the Parliament and Council express the desire that national legislation should be approximated concerning the allocation of frequencies in the European Union. *(b)* In the Authorisations Directive, the same institutions state that Member States must comply with the rules that have been harmonised, once harmonisation has taken place. In case of harmonisation, Member States lose the power to introduce rules that would be additional to those agreed at European level.

Framework Directive, Article 9(2). 'Member States shall promote the harmonisation of use of radio frequencies across the Community, consistent with the need to ensure effective and efficient use thereof and in accordance with the . . . Radio Spectrum Decision.' *Authorisations Directive, Article 8.* 'Where the usage of radio frequencies has been harmonised, access conditions and procedures have been agreed, and

---

[18] [1999] OJ L184/23.

undertakings to which the radio frequencies shall be assigned have been selected in accordance with international agreements and Community rules, Member States shall grant the right of use for such radio frequencies in accordance therewith. Provided that all national conditions attached to the right to use the radio frequencies concerned have been satisfied in the case of a common selection procedure, Member States shall not impose any further conditions, additional criteria or procedures which would restrict, alter or delay the correct implementation of the common assignment of such radio frequencies.'

Ambiguity.   The occurrence of provisions on harmonisation in several instruments **7.56** concerning spectrum shows that the subject matter is on the European agenda. There is a desire to go forward, but the conditions have not yet been satisfied for a further step to be taken. The reasons for that difficulty have already been examined. They are due to the desire on the part of various Member States to maintain control over an area where they have consistently exercised undisputed sovereignty.

(7) Standards drawn up by CEPT

Intervention of CEPT.   Measures to be harmonised may fall under the remit of **7.57** the European Conference of Postal and Telecommunications Administrations (CEPT). That Conference brings together, as the title indicates, the representatives of the national administrations active in the field of communications and postal services. From the Radio Spectrum Decision it appears that that Conference is an official interlocutor of the European institutions regarding the preparation of technical standards for frequencies. Some of the key characteristics of that organisation are examined later (see paras 7.82–7.85). Suffice it to mention at the present stage that issues relating to the availability of information regarding spectrum, or to the procedures for the allocation of frequencies, are addressed by the Conference. CEPT as a result intervenes as the standard-setting institution in procedures for the preparation of standards regarding these issues.

Procedure.   Where standards are prepared by CEPT, the following procedure **7.58** must be complied with. *(a)* The Commission issues a mandate (request that a specific standard be drawn up). That mandate is addressed to CEPT. It must be clear regarding the objectives to be reached. It must also specify the deadline by which the work must be terminated. *(b)* The standard is prepared by CEPT following the procedures and arrangements in force within that organisation. *(c)* When it is finished, the standard is submitted to the Commission. *(d)* A decision then has to be made by that institution. That decision is whether or not the standard can, or should, be made obligatory across the European Union. It is taken by the Commission in a procedure involving the Radio Spectrum Committee.

> *Radio Spectrum Decision, Article 4(2) and (3).* [2] 'For the development of technical implementing measures . . . which fall within the remit of CEPT, such as the harmonisation of radio frequency allocation and of information availability, the Commission shall issue mandates to CEPT, setting out the tasks to be performed and the timetable

therefore.' [3] 'On the basis of the work completed . . . , the Commission shall decide whether the results of the work carried out pursuant to the mandates shall apply in the Community and on the deadline for their implementation by the Member States. These decisions shall be published in the Official Journal of the European Communities.'

7.59 **Decisions to be adopted.**   In these various steps, decisions must be taken by the Commission with regard to CEPT standards in two types of circumstance. First, when a mandate is issued to CEPT asking for specific standards to be drawn up and setting a deadline for the preparation of these technical rules. Second, when the Commission considers that a standard prepared by CEPT should be made obligatory across the European Union.

7.60 **Procedure for the adoption of decisions.**   In these two categories of situation, the 'advisory procedure' is applicable.[19] In that procedure, *(a)* the Commission is assisted by the Radio Spectrum Committee. That Committee is made up of representatives of the Member States. It also includes one representative of the Commission. *(b)* The meetings are chaired by a representative of the Commission. *(c)* A draft decision is proposed by the Commission.[20] *(d)* An opinion is issued on the draft by the Committee. If necessary, a vote is organised to that effect within the Committee. *(e)* On the basis of that opinion, a decision is adopted by the Commission. The link between the decision and the opinion are as follows. The Commission is not bound by the opinion issued by the Committee. It must however take the utmost account of the opinion. It further has the obligation to explain to the Committee why the opinion has not been followed in part or in its entirety. An obligation to provide reasoning is thus imposed on the Commission. The Commission remains free regarding the content of the decision. However, the content must be justified to the Committee, and possibly to the public,[21] when there is a partial, or total, disagreement with the Committee. The reasons why the Commission has departed, partially or totally, from the opinion, must then be explained.

> *Implementing Power Decision, Article 3.* '1. The Commission shall be assisted by an advisory committee composed of the representatives of the Member States and chaired by the representative of the Commission. 2. The representative of the Commission shall submit to the Committee a draft of the measures to be taken. The committee shall deliver its opinion on the draft, within a time-limit which the chairman may lay down according to the urgency of the matter, if necessary by taking a vote. 3. The opinion shall be recorded in the minutes; in addition, each Member State shall have the right to ask to have its position recorded in the minutes. 4. The Commission shall take the utmost account of the opinion delivered by the committee. It shall inform the committee of the manner in which the opinion has been taken into account.'

7.61 **Procedures within CEPT.**   The Radio Spectrum Decision, and the Comitology Decision, organise the procedures whereby the Commission decides, together

---

[19] See Implementing Power Decision, Art 3.
[20] That draft is the instrument whereby the Commission intends to issue a mandate to CEPT or to make CEPT standards compulsory.   [21] In the Preamble to that decision itself.

with the Radio Spectrum Committee, as the case may be, whether technical standards must be prepared and what must be done with these standards. The procedures concerning how CEPT itself works and draws up the standards where a mandate is issued to that effect, are not organised in these Decisions. These latter procedures are organised by CEPT itself. For the sake of completeness, that Conference is further presented in paras 7.82–7.85 below.

(8) Non-CEPT standards

Other standards.   No standards to be prepared for technical implementing meas-   **7.62** ures are entrusted to CEPT. The harmonisation process may concern, in some instances, standards which do not fall under the remit of CEPT. There are also situations where standards are drawn up by CEPT but are not accepted because they do not appear to be satisfactory. Another possible situation is where CEPT has been given a mandate but fails to comply with the deadline set for the preparation of the standard (a variation is where, during the period for the preparation of the standard, indications become available that CEPT will not be able to comply with the deadline).

Another procedure.   In these various cases (non-CEPT standard, unsatisfactory   **7.63** result, non-compliance with the timetable), another procedure has to be used in order to prepare the requested standards. In that procedure the Commission has a greater margin of manoeuvre. In substance, it can itself take the measures that are necessary in order to ensure the preparation of the standards in question. The only obligations which are imposed on that institution are of a procedural nature, that is, the Commission must comply with the steps mentioned in the Radio Spectrum Decision.

> *Radio Spectrum Decision, Preamble, recital 12.* 'Where it is necessary to adopt harmonised measures for the implementation of Community policies which do not fall within the remit of CEPT, the Commission could adopt implementation measures with the assistance of the Radio Spectrum Committee.' *Radio Spectrum Decision, Articles 4(4) and 6.* [4] '[If] the Commission or any Member State considers that the work carried out on the basis of a mandate issued [to CEPT] pursuant to paragraph 2 is not progressing satisfactorily having regard to the set timetable or if the results of the mandate are not acceptable, the Commission may adopt . . . measures to achieve the objectives of the mandate.' [6] 'To achieve the aim set out in [the Radio Spectrum Decision] . . ., the Commission may also adopt technical implementing measures . . . which are not covered by paragraph 2 [CEPT mandates].'

Regulatory procedure.   For these decisions the 'regulatory procedure' is applic-   **7.64** able.[22] As the name indicates, this procedure is more demanding than the 'advisory'. A comparison between the two settings is presented in the table at para 7.69 below. As shown in the table, there is no difference between the two

---

[22] See Implementing Power Decision, Art 5.

procedures in the first aspects examined above. *(a)* In both cases, the Commission is assisted by the Radio Spectrum Committee. The composition of the Committee is identical in the two procedures. In both cases it consists of representatives of the Member States (one per State), to which must be added one representative of the Commission. *(b)* There is also no difference regarding the functioning of the Committee. As in the previous procedure, the meetings are chaired by the representative of the Commission. *(c)* As was stated for the advisory procedure, the draft decision is presented, here also, by the Commission.

7.65 **Force of the opinion submitted by the Committee.** The differences appear in the latter stages, concerning the rules which must be complied with for the adoption of the opinion by the Committee and the force which that opinion must be given in relations with the Commission. *(d)* Pursuant to the Comitology Decision, a vote must be taken for the adoption of the opinion by the Committee. That vote must take place according to the arrangements and procedures relating to qualified majority voting in the EC Treaty. This means that a given weight is attached to the votes expressed by the representatives of the various Member States. The overall number of votes must reach a level specified in the Treaty. *(e)* A difference also appears in the force given to the opinion adopted by the Committee. The agreement of the Committee is necessary in the regulatory procedure. Where the Committee agrees with the draft, the decision proposed by the Commission is adopted. Where the Committee disagrees, the matter must be referred to the Council. The Council must then act. Three possibilities may then be envisaged. The first is that the Council may adopt the draft. In that case, the decision proposed by the Commission is taken as a result of the agreement expressed by the Council. A second possibility is that the Council may reject the draft. The consequence is that the draft is set aside. The Commission may submit a new proposal, although there is no obligation to that effect. A third possibility is that the Council may not react. In that situation, the decision will be considered as having been taken after the expiry of a certain period (three months maximum).

> *Comitology Decision, Article 5.* '1. The Commission shall be assisted by a regulatory committee composed of the representatives of the Member States and chaired by the representative of the Commission. 2. The representative of the Commission shall submit to the committee a draft of the measures to be taken. The committee shall deliver its opinion on the draft within a time-limit which the chairman may lay down according to the urgency of the matter. The opinion shall be delivered by the majority laid down in Article 205(2) of the Treaty in the case of decisions which the Council is required to adopt on a proposal from the Commission. The votes of the representatives of the Member States within the Committee shall be weighted in the manner set out in that Article. The chairman shall not vote. 3. The Commission shall . . . adopt the measures envisaged if they are in accordance with the opinion of the committee. 4. If the measures envisaged are not in accordance with the opinion of the committee, or if no opinion is delivered, the Commission shall, without delay, submit to the Council a proposal relating to the measures to be taken and shall inform the European Parliament. 5. If the European Parliament considers that a proposal submitted by the

Commission pursuant to a basic instrument adopted in accordance with the procedure laid down in Article 251 of the Treaty exceeds the implementing powers provided for in that basic instrument, it shall inform the Council of its position. 6. The Council may, where appropriate in view of any such position, act by qualified majority on the proposal, within a period to be laid down in each basic instrument but which shall in no case exceed three months from the date of referral to the Council. If within that period the Council has indicated by qualified majority that it opposes the proposal, the Commission shall re-examine it. It may submit an amended proposal to the Council, re-submit its proposal or present a legislative proposal on the basis of the Treaty. If on the expiry of that period the Council has neither adopted the proposed implementing act nor indicated its opposition to the proposal for implementing measures, the proposed implementing act shall be adopted by the Commission.'

Qualified majority under the EC Treaty—Article 205 EC **7.66**

Where the Council is required to act by a qualified majority, the votes of its members shall be weighted as follows: Germany 29; United Kingdom 29; France 29; Italy 29; Spain 27; Poland 27; Netherlands 13; Greece 12; Czech Republic 12; Belgium 12; Hungary 12; Portugal 12; Sweden 10; Austria 10; Slovakia 7; Denmark 7; Finland 7; Ireland 7; Lithuania 7; Latvia 4; Slovenia 4; Estonia 4; Cyprus 4; Luxembourg 4; Malta 3.

Acts of the Council shall require for their adoption at least 232 votes in favour, cast by a majority of members, where this Treaty requires them to be adopted on a proposal from the Commission.

In other cases, for their adoption acts of the Council shall require at least 232 votes in favour cast by at least two-thirds of the members.

When a decision is to be adopted by the Council by a qualified majority, a member of the Council may request verification that the Member States constituting the qualified majority represent at least 62% of the total population of the Union. If that condition is shown not to have been met, the decision in question shall not be adopted.

(9) Comparison between the procedures

Opinion submitted by the Committee.   As stated above, the main difference **7.67** between the two procedures concerns the opinion submitted by the Radio Spectrum Committee. *(a)* That opinion must, first, be adopted in the form provided for in the decisions to be taken on a qualified majority pursuant to the Treaty. *(b)* Second, it must be complied with by the Commission. Failure by the Commission to conform to that opinion implies for the Commission that it is impossible to adopt the decision. The matter must then be referred to the Council. Failure by the Council to take a position admittedly creates the possibility that the draft presented by the Commission may be adopted unchanged. Such an outcome would result, however, from a failure of the Council to reach an agreement. In that perspective, the Commission is not deprived of any room for manoeuvre. But the absence of an agreement within the Council remains a matter of circumstance. It is not possible for the Commission to carry out a strategy with the hope that the Council remains undecided.

General provisions concerning all procedures.   Other provisions of a more gen- **7.68** eral character apply to both procedures, independently of the intervention, or not, of CEPT. These general rules, again, are introduced by the Comitology Decision.[23] Pursuant to these rules, *(a)* the Committee adopts its own rules of procedures. These rules must comply, in substance, with a model published in the Official Journal. *(b)* The Committee is assimilated to the Commission regarding the conditions under which access may be sought to its documents. The Committee must thus give access to its documents under the same conditions as the Commission under existing regulation. *(c)* The Parliament must be informed regularly about proceedings involving the Committee.

> *Implementing Power Decision, Article 7.* [1] 'Each committee shall adopt its own rules of procedure on the proposal of its chairman, on the basis of standard rules of procedure which shall be published in the Official Journal of the European Communities.[24] Insofar as necessary existing committees shall adapt their rules of procedure to the standard rules of procedure.' [2] 'The principles and conditions on public access to documents applicable to the Commission shall apply to the committees.' [3] 'The European Parliament shall be informed by the Commission of committee proceedings on a regular basis. To that end, it shall receive agendas for committee meetings, draft measures submitted to the committees for the implementation of instruments adopted by the procedure provided for by Article 251 of the Treaty, and the results of voting and summary records of the meetings and lists of the authorities and organisations to which the persons designated by the Member States to represent them belong. The European Parliament shall also be kept informed whenever the Commission transmits to the Council measures or proposals for measures to be taken.'[25]

7.69 **Transitional periods and special arrangements.** Under the Radio Spectrum Decision, the measures adopted by the Commission regarding technical implementing standards may create transitional regimes and organise special arrangements for certain Member States. A transitional period may be granted to one or several Member States, where these States need some time to adapt to new technical standards imposed by the Commission. Another situation is where radio spectrum sharing is organised between several Member States. In these two situations, measures can be adopted only if certain conditions are fulfilled. *(a)* A request to that effect must be presented by the Member State(s) concerned. *(b)* The request must be reasoned. The justification as to why the Member State(s) is making it must be given with clear and convincing reasons. *(c)* The situation created as a result of the special measures may not delay excessively the implementation of the standards concerned. *(d)* Competition may not be distorted to an extent that would not be deemed acceptable.

> *Radio Spectrum Decision, Article 4(5).* 'The measures [adopted by the Commission] may, where appropriate, provide the possibility for transitional periods and/or radio

---

[23] They are made applicable in the field of electronic communications through a reference made to them in the Radio Spectrum Decision. See Radio Spectrum Decision, Art 3.

[24] See also Radio Spectrum Decision, Art 3(4). 'The Committee shall adopt its rules of procedure.'

[25] These general rules are rendered applicable to advisory and regulatory procedures by the Radio Spectrum Decision, Art 3(2) and (3).

spectrum sharing arrangements in a Member State to be approved by the Commission, where justified, taking into account the specific situation in the Member State, on the basis of a reasoned request by the Member State concerned and provided such exception would not unduly defer implementation or create undue differences in the competitive or regulatory situations between Member States.'

Similarities and differences between the advisory and regulatory procedures   **7.70**

Advisory procedure Comitology Decision, Article 3	Regulatory procedure Comitology Decision, Article 5
SIMILARITIES **Participating organs**. The Commission is assisted by a committee composed of representatives of the Member States and chaired by a representative of the Commission.	→ idem
Right of initiative. The representative of the Commission submits to the committee a draft of the measures to be taken.	→ idem
Role of the Committee. *(a)* The committee delivers an opinion.	→ idem
(b) The opinion must be delivered within a time-limit laid down by the chairman in accordance with the urgency of the matter.	→ idem
(c) The opinion is recorded in the minutes, together with the opinion of the Member States which so request.	→ idem

Advisory procedure Comitology Decision, Article 3	Regulatory procedure Comitology Decision, Article 5
DIFFERENCES **Adoption of the opinion by the Committee**. A vote is organised if necessary.	A vote is organized. The opinion is delivered by the majority laid down in Article 205(2) of the Treaty. The votes of the representatives of the Member States are weighted in the manner set out in that Article. The chairman does not vote.
Force of the opinion issued by the Committee. The Commission is not bound by the opinion. It must take the utmost account of it. The committee is informed concerning the follow up.	*(a)* Where the Committee agrees, the Commission may adopt the decision. *(b)* In the absence of agreement, the draft must be referred to the Council. The Council may vote by a qualified majority. If the draft is adopted, the decision is taken. If the draft is rejected, the Commission may submit another proposal. Where the Council fails to adopt a position, the decision is adopted.

(10) Roll-out of third generation mobile communications

Relax conditions.   As stated above, some electronic communications operators   **7.71**
have suffered significant losses in the negative financial climate of recent years. This

has, it can be argued, endangered the roll-out of third generation mobile communications. To bring a solution to the problem, calls have been made for Member States to relax the obligations that they had attached to the operators obtaining licences.

7.72 **Stable regulatory environment.** The Commission has emphasised in this connection that the regulatory environment must remain stable. Stability does not imply that rules may never change, but changes must unfold in conformity to certain constraints. *(a)* The basic regulatory principles must be respected. For instance, no decision can be taken by Member States to postpone the roll-out of third generation mobile communications without respecting transparency, objectivity and non-discrimination. *(b)* A discussion must also take place at European level, to ensure a co-ordinated approach to roll-out.

> *Eighth implementation report, 38.* '[C]alls have been made for the relaxation of licence conditions and in three Member States (Belgium, Spain and Portugal) there has been a postponement of certain requirements of the original 3G licences relating to roll-out and coverage. In addition, in two Member States (Italy and France) the duration originally provided for the 3G licences has been extended (from 15 to 20 years).' 'In its Communication of June 2002 "Towards the Full Roll-Out of Third Generation Mobile Communications", the Commission stressed the need for stability of the regulatory environment, while acknowledging that adaptation of deployment modalities may become necessary. It stated that such changes need to be undertaken under transparent and objective conditions, which would imply a public consultation on the basis of a reasoned and justified proposal.' 'The Commission also recommended that any changes to licence conditions be discussed with other national administrations in an appropriate forum, in order to facilitate the exchange of information and best practice and to work towards a co-ordinated approach throughout the EU.'

(11) International dimension of spectrum

7.73 **International relevance of spectrum.** Radio spectrum has traditionally attracted much international attention. This is due to the links existing between spectrum and national sovereignty. Providing electronic communications services through frequencies implies that use is made of the national space. Member States have always been keen to preserve their decision-making power in that area. Another reason for spectrum to attract international attention is that fees may be obtained from operators exploiting frequencies. Undertakings accept that payment may be taken in exchange for the right to use public property (air waves) for the exercise of their activities. Finally, radio spectrum requires co-ordination to provide services across borders. Seamless services may not be provided across a continent without the participation of all States concerned. These States must commit themselves to imposing identical technical standards on their territories. In the absence of such a commitment, interoperability between networks and services cannot be ensured.

7.74 **Obligation to comply with international law.** The international relevance of spectrum explains why several provisions are devoted to international issues in the

Radio Spectrum Decision. These provisions organise the relations between European and international obligations, as regards spectrum. A first principle is that the decision does not affect commitments possibly made by the Member States, or the European institutions, in international fora. There is an emphasis in the decision on the fact that the decision does not introduce any right, or obligation, that would contravene these commitments. As a consequence, no provision of the decision may be construed as containing contradictions with commitments of an international nature.

> *Radio Spectrum Decision, Article 1(3).* 'Activities pursued under this Decision shall take due account of the work of international organisations related to radio spectrum management, eg the International Telecommunication Union (ITU) and the European Conference of Postal and Telecommunications Administrations (CEPT).'
> *Radio Spectrum Decision, Article 6(4).* 'Measures . . . shall be without prejudice to the Community's and Member States' rights and obligations under relevant international agreements.'

Obligation to comply with European law. The obligation to comply with **7.75** international law does not mean that the Member States may infringe the commitments that they have undertaken within the European legal order. A reciprocal principle is thus established, wherein it is recalled that Member States are indeed bound by obligations stated in the EC Treaty and in derived instruments. A consequence is that Member States may not enter into international commitments which would not be compatible with European law. The Radio Spectrum Decision confirms in this regard a specific obligation for Member States to indicate, in the international commitments to which they may subscribe, that these commitments may only be taken, and will only be executed, in so far as they comply with European rules.

> *Radio Spectrum Decision, Preamble, recital 19.* 'Member States should accompany any act of acceptance of any agreement or regulation within international *fora* in charge of, or concerned with, radio spectrum management by a joint declaration stating that they will apply such agreement or regulation in accordance with their obligations under the Treaty.'

Mutual information. The Radio Spectrum Decision further entrusts the **7.76** Commission with the task of observing the development of policies regarding spectrum outside the European Union. The information collected by the Commission during the accomplishment of that task is to be shared with the Member States. In return the Member States must inform the Commission whenever they are confronted with attitudes outside the European Union which may have an influence on the policy carried out within the Union as regards spectrum. A specific demand is made that national information must be provided where third countries or international organisations adopt acts or positions which may jeopardise the implementation of the objectives sought through the Radio Spectrum Decision.

Radio Spectrum Decision, Article 1(2). 'The Commission shall monitor developments regarding radio spectrum in third countries and in international organisations, which may have implications for the implementation of this Decision.' *Radio Spectrum Decision, Article 6(2).* 'Member States shall inform the Commission of any difficulties created, *de jure* or *de facto*, by third countries or international organisations for the implementation of this Decision.'

7.77 Co-ordination of interests.   An additional action to be taken by the European institutions is to co-ordinate the interests of the Member States, together, as well as with those of the Union, in international negotiation on spectrum wherever these negotiations may take place. Until the adoption of the decision, co-ordination of that nature had taken place. That co-ordination was however based on the voluntary participation of the Member States. The regime changes with the decision, as co-ordination is made obligatory. As a result of that obligation, Member States are compelled to co-ordinate their positions. They are also forced to take the position of the Union into account. A difficulty is to determine what these obligations may imply in practice. An implication is that Member States must discuss their plans. A mutual exchange of information, as well as discussion, must then take place. Ideally that discussion should take place before the adoption of their positions by the Member States.[26] The discussion may not be a mere juxtaposition of views; the Member States must participate constructively in a dialogue.

Radio Spectrum Decision, Article 6(1). The 'Decision establishes procedures in order to: . . . (d) ensure the effective coordination of Community interests in international negotiations where radio spectrum use affects Community policies.' *Radio Spectrum Decision, Article 6(3).* 'When necessary to meet the aim set out in [the Decision] . . ., common policy objectives shall be agreed to ensure Community coordination among Member States.'

7.78 Representation of the Community.   Beyond co-ordination, the Radio Spectrum Decision requires that the Community must be represented in its own capacity in international negotiations taking place concerning spectrum around the globe. That emphasis on the representation of the Community interest may be explained in several ways. *(a)* It is important, for the Member States and for their undertakings, to obtain satisfactory access to spectrum available in third countries. However, negotiations led by the European Union are more likely to produce satisfactory outcomes than bilateral encounters organised by individual Member States. *(b)* Spectrum raises issues with cross-border services. Co-ordination or, as the case may be, harmonisation, must take place to resolve these issues. The Community seems to provide the best forum where common interests may be defined in a harmonious manner. *(c)* In the field of spectrum, the Community has specific interests that are necessarily identical with those of the Member States.

---

[26] One could not speak, otherwise, of a co-ordination, as unilateral positions would be taken by each Member State, which would only inform their counterparts in the aftermath.

Among these interests are for instance the necessity to have European-wide spectrum in order to carry out projects with a European dimension. Given the existence of these specific interests, it is legitimate for the European Community to seek the organisation of spectrum available across the European Union. The desire to establish such an organisation implies that the Community must be present in international negotiations where spectrum is allocated, and regulated, at an international level, before being further determined at the European and/or national level.

> *Radio Spectrum Decision, Preamble, Recital 18.* 'The Community should therefore be adequately represented in the activities of all relevant international organisations and conferences related to radio spectrum management matters, such as within the International Telecommunication Union (ITU) and its World Radio communications Conferences.' *Reasons for this.* [a] 'Community undertakings should obtain fair and non-discriminatory treatment on access to radio spectrum in third countries.'[27] [b] 'As access to radio spectrum is a key factor for business development and public interest activities, it is also necessary to ensure that Community requirements for radio spectrum are reflected in international planning.'[28] [c] 'Implementation of Community policies may require coordination of radio spectrum use, in particular with regard to the provision of communications services including Community-wide roaming facilities. Moreover, certain types of radio spectrum use entail a geographical coverage which goes beyond the borders of a Member State and allow for trans border services without requiring the movement of persons, such as satellite communications services.'[29]

(12) Organs concerned

Radio Spectrum Committee. The Radio Spectrum Decision sets up the Radio **7.79** Spectrum Committee. The task of that Committee is to assist the Commission in the definition of a Radio Spectrum Policy in the European Community. It is also to assist the Commission in the harmonisation of measures concerning the availability of frequencies as well as the efficiency in the use of available spectrum. The arrangements for the intervention of the Committee in that harmonisation process have been examined above. Suffice it to recall that, in that context, the Committee may intervene in two types of procedure. *(a)* When standards are prepared by CEPT, the Committee intervenes in an advisory procedure. In that procedure, the task entrusted to the Committee is to issue an opinion. That opinion is not binding on the Commission. However, the Commission must explain the reasons when it departs from the opinion, in whole or in part. *(b)* A second possibility is that standards are not drawn up by CEPT. The role devoted to the Committee is then more substantial. The Committee intervenes in a regulatory procedure. Here again, its task is to deliver an opinion. The existence of an agreement between the Commission and the Committee implies that the draft is

---

[27] Recital 17.   [28] Recital 17.   [29] Recital 18.

adopted. In the absence of an agreement, the matter must be referred to the Council.[30]

7.80 **The Radio Spectrum Policy Group.** Parallel to the Radio Spectrum Policy, the Commission has created the Radio Spectrum Policy Group.[31] There are thus two bodies with various responsibilities as regards the development of a spectrum policy in the European Union. These bodies have features in common. *(a)* For instance, they are composed in a similar manner. Both consist of representatives of the Member State (one per State) and one representative for the Commission. *(b)* Another similarity is the functioning of the Group and the Committee. Both bodies adopt opinions on issues raised, or drafts presented, by the Commission.

7.81 **Differences between the two bodies.** There are however significant differences between the two organs. *(a)* The Committee has an official task. The intervention of that Committee is a condition necessary for the adoption of harmonised technical standards. Without an intervention in that procedure, alongside the arrangements examined above, the standards cannot be adopted. *(b)* The role of the Group is, by contrast, more informal. Its purpose is to provide counsel to the Commission. The intervention of the Group is not obligatory by any means for any rule to be adopted or any procedure to be completed. The task is limited to helping the Commission develop its own position. As part of its task, the Group may consult extensively. The consultations may be defined and carried out in a very broad manner. They may compass all kinds of forward-looking enquiries on technological, market and regulatory developments relating to the use of radio spectrum. During these consultations, the Group may consult with all radio spectrum users involved, both commercial and non-commercial, as well as with any other interested parties.

7.82 **CEPT.** CEPT, the European Conference of Postal and Telecommunications Administrations, as its name indicates, brings together representatives of the national administrations dealing with postal and telecommunications matters in European countries. Its main purpose is to provide a forum for discussions on regulatory matters. The conference has 45 members. Its membership thus goes beyond the members of the European Union. As a result of an active membership policy, the Conference covers almost the entire geographical area of Europe. Central and Eastern European Countries are eligible for membership.

> *Members of the Conference.* 'Albania, Andorra, Austria, Azerbaijan, Belgium, Bosnia and Herzegovina, Bulgaria, Croatia, Cyprus, Czech Republic, Denmark, Estonia, Finland, France, Germany, Great Britain, Greece, Hungary, Iceland, Ireland, Italy,

---

[30] See Radio Spectrum Decision, Arts 3 and 4. See also Implementing Power Decision, Arts 3 and 5.
[31] See Commission Decision 2002/622/EC, of 26 July 2002, establishing a Radio Spectrum Policy Group [2002] OJ L198/49.

Latvia, Liechtenstein, Lithuania, Luxembourg, Malta, Moldova, Monaco, Netherlands, Norway, Poland, Portugal, Romania, Russian Federation, San Marino, Slovakia, Slovenia, Spain, Sweden, Switzerland, the former Yugoslav Republic of Macedonia, Turkey, Ukraine, Vatican, Yugoslavia.[32]

History of the organisation. The Conference was established in 1959. The **7.83** original members were the postal and telecommunications administrations. At that stage, however, the members were not limited in their functions to policy or regulatory tasks. They also performed commercial operations. In 1988 CEPT created ETSI—the European Telecommunications Standards Institute. Telecommunications standardisation activities were transferred to that new body. In 1992 it was decided that the Conference would only represent the national administrations in so far as they carry out policy and/or regulatory tasks. The commercial operations were to be represented by two other organisations, which were then created. The first organisation is Post Europe, which gathers the former national operators active in postal services. The second organisation is ETNO— the European Telecommunications Network Operators. That organisation represents the former national telecoms operators. The modifications which intervened in the membership of the Conference coincided with the definition, and the progressive implementation, of the European policy whereby postal and telecommunications operations were separated from policy-making and regulatory functions.

Current function of CEPT. CEPT provides its members with opportunities to: **7.84** *(a)* establish a European forum for discussions on sovereign and regulatory issues in the field of post and telecommunications issues; *(b)* provide mutual assistance among members with regard to the settlement of sovereign/regulatory issues; *(c)* more generally, promote and facilitate relations between European regulators (for example through personal contacts); *(d)* exert an influence on the goals and priorities in the field of European post and telecommunications through common positions addressed to the bodies in charge of defining and implementing policies in those sectors (the European Union but also the EEE and the International Telecommunications Union).

Committees. CEPT has two committees. One concerns the postal industry— **7.85** the CERP (Comité européen des régulateurs postaux). The other relates to electronic communications (Electronic Communications Committee). That latter committee results from the merger between two formerly distinct committees: the European Radio Communications Committee (ERC) and the European Committee for Telecommunications Regulatory Affairs (ECTRA). These two committees conducted research in their respective areas. As a result of convergence, it was decided that the activities should be united. The two remaining committees

---

[32] For a more general presentation of CEPT, see the website http://www.cept.org.

handle harmonisation activities within their respective fields of responsibility. They also adopt recommendations and decisions. These recommendations and decisions are normally prepared by their working groups and project teams.

(13) Is there a common policy?

7.86 **Ambiguity.**   The Radio Spectrum Decision does not take away all ambiguities about the division of powers between the European institutions and the Member States. This ambiguity remains vivid after a careful examination of the provisions contained in the decision. As a result of this ambiguity, one cannot consider that there exists, as of the present time, any real common policy in the field of spectrum.

7.87 **Technical implementation measures.**   This ambiguity appears with some clarity in the provisions concerning the harmonisation of national legislation regarding radio frequencies. Pursuant to the decision, technical implementing measures may be harmonised. It is not sure what these measures are. *(a)* What clearly appears from the denomination chosen in the Radio Spectrum Decision, is that the harmonisation, if any, must be limited to 'technical' matters. *(b)* There is also a reference in the decision to the 'implementing' character of these measures to be harmonised. Again, this reference seems to limit the scope of the harmonisation that is sought. It does not, it is implied, concern policy decisions. *(c)* Finally, it is repeatedly indicated in the decision that these measures can be harmonised only when this is 'appropriate'. This indication implies, once more, that no choice can be made automatically to harmonise some measures. A justification is necessary for each harmonisation step, in order to demonstrate to what extent the harmonisation is indeed legitimate.

7.88 **Preliminary steps.**   All this gives some credit to the opinion on the part of several observers that there is indeed no common policy regarding spectrum in the European Union. One cannot find in the decision, or in any other European instrument, an indication of goals which should be attained by the European institutions, nor a list of adequate instruments that these institutions could use in order to fulfil their mission. The Radio Spectrum Decision establishes only the preliminary steps for European intervention in the field. These steps can indeed be considered as being preliminary to the extent that their main object is to establish procedures for facilitating the common definition of policies, or the establishment of a methodology concerning the use of harmonisation in the field.

> *Radio Spectrum Decision, Article 1(2)*. This 'Decision establishes procedures in order to: (a) facilitate policy making with regard to the strategic planning and harmonisation of the use of radio spectrum in the Community taking into consideration *inter alia* economic, safety, health, public interest, freedom of expression, cultural, scientific, social and technical aspects of Community policies as well as the various interests of radio spectrum user communities with the aim of optimising the use of radio spectrum and of voiding harmful interference; (b) ensure the effective implementation

of radio spectrum policy in the Community, and in particular establish a general methodology to ensure harmonised conditions for the availability and efficient use of radio spectrum'.

Consequences of other policies for spectrum.   The main object of the Radio **7.89** Spectrum Decision is thus to organise procedures leading Member States and the European institutions to discuss the possibility, and need, for further action in common. In the meantime, the concrete actions which can already be taken are restricted to fields where the Parliament and Council act on the basis of their own powers, and which have consequences for the use of spectrum in the European Union. Harmonisation is currently restricted, as regards spectrum, to these scenarios where non-spectrum-related action is taken by a European institution, with a consequence for spectrum, thereby raising the need for a co-ordination of harmonisation of the technical measures which are necessary to ensure the implementation of these choices. These scenarios may be presented in a schematic manner along the following lines. *(a)* The Parliament and/or the Council have the competence to adopt instruments in a given field. *(b)* They decide to make use of that competence. *(c)* The use of that competence has an impact on spectrum. *(d)* That impact is such that European action in the field of spectrum is appropriate. *(e)* Harmonisation may be decided if the discrepancies among the national legislations would jeopardise the implementation of these instruments.

> *Radio Spectrum Decision, Preamble, recital 4.* 'This [Radio Spectrum] Decision is based on the principle that, where the European Parliament and the Council have agreed on a Community policy which depends on radio spectrum, committee procedures should be used for the adoption of accompanying technical implementing measures.' *Radio Spectrum Decision, Preamble, recital 5.* 'Any new Community policy initiative depending on radio spectrum should be agreed by the European Parliament and the Council as appropriate, on the basis of a proposal from the Commission.'

Harmonisation of national legislation regarding spectrum   **7.90**

(1) There is no common policy regarding spectrum.
(2) The Parliament and/or the Council may adopt decisions or instruments in the framework of non-spectrum-related policies.
(3) Some of these decisions or instruments may have implications for the use of spectrum.
(4) Action at European level may then be warranted.
(5) Where appropriate, the Commission may start the process to harmonise the technical measures which are necessary to implement these originally non-spectrum-related choices.

Harmonisation in other situations.   The harmonisation process, which is sup- **7.91** posed to be the core legal tool for the development of a common policy, is thus restricted, as regards spectrum, to very limited circumstances. The limited nature of European intervention is confirmed by the Preamble to the Radio Spectrum Decision, which states simply that harmonisation of non-technical implementing measures may be sought. The Commission, however, is granted no autonomous or independent power to carry out such harmonisation. The only possibility open to it is to present a draft to the Parliament and Council, which will then take a position on the basis of general EC provisions concerning harmonisation.

> *Radio Spectrum Decision, Preamble, recital 7.* 'Where it is necessary to adopt harmonisation measures for the implementation of Community policies which go beyond technical implementing measures, the Commission may submit to the European Parliament and to the Council a proposal on the basis of the Treaty.'

7.92 Powers further limited. A further limitation is imposed on the harmonisation actions which may be decided by the Commission. Pursuant to the Radio Spectrum Decision, the Commission has the power to harmonise, to a certain extent, technical implementing measures. These measures may not concern, however: *(a)* decisions to resort to a competitive procedure for the selection of the undertakings to which frequencies are allocated; *(b)* decisions whereby frequencies are allocated; *(c)* instruments for the organisation of the procedures in the course of which the allocation takes place. These aspects remain within the responsibility of the Member States. In the current state of European legislation, the Member States are, as a result, the only ones holding the power to decide how, and to whom, frequencies are assigned.

> *Radio Spectrum Decision, Preamble, recital 11.* 'Radio spectrum technical management includes the harmonisation and allocation of radio spectrum. Such harmonisation should reflect the requirements of general policy principles identified at Community level. However, radio spectrum technical management does not cover assignment and licensing procedures, nor the decision whether to use competitive selection procedures for the assignment of radio frequencies.'

7.93 Other limitations. Other limitations must be mentioned as regards the possibility for European institutions to intervene. *(a)* Pursuant to the Radio Spectrum Decision, the Member States may reserve competence for all issues relating to spectrum where these issues may have an impact on public order, public security and defence. These limitations do not appear to be exceptional, as it is generally accepted that the Member States may act, by way of derogation from European law, where these interests are affected. *(b)* Another limitation is provided for content regulation and audiovisual policy. One finds, here again, an ambiguity coming from the desire of the European Commission to address all issues relating to electronic communications and, at the same time, leave untouched the possibility for Member States to organise audiovisual services as they wish.

> *Radio Spectrum Decision, Article 1(4).* 'This Decision is without prejudice to measures taken at Community or national level, in compliance with Community law, to pursue general interest objectives, in particular relating to content regulation and audio-visual policy . . . and to the right of Member States to organise and use their radio spectrum for public order and public security purposes and defence.'

Practical consequences. The limitations analysed regarding the existence of **7.94** a common spectrum policy have practical consequences. Not only are they important to determine what the European institutions may, or may not, do. These issues of power and competence also have concrete implications for the validity of measures adopted by these institutions. However, validity-related issues may prove crucial in litigation directed against Community acts. As submitted in the chapter devoted to litigation, undertakings and individuals have the possibility of challenging the validity of acts adopted by the European institutions. Where for example the Commission harmonises national legislation on points going beyond technical implementing measures, the acts whereby the harmonised standard is imposed across the Community could be challenged as to its validity. An argument could be founded on the absence of power of the Commission to use the harmonisation process to approximate the national legislations on the point at issue. The challenge may be brought to the CFI, if the private applicants (undertakings and/or individuals) are directly and individually concerned. In the absence of a direct and individual link with the instrument, an indirect procedure must be used. An action must then be started against an implementing measure. *(a)* If that implementing measure is adopted by a European institution, an application for annulment may be lodged with the CFI against that implementing measure. In the course of the procedure, an exception of illegality may be directed against the basic European instrument (Article 241 EC). *(b)* If the implementing measure is taken by a national authority, the challenge must start before a national court. In the course of the national procedure, a preliminary reference may be addressed to the ECJ, with a request to assess the validity of the basic European instrument (Article 234 EC).

D. Accounting Obligations, Accounting Separation and Structural Separation

(1) Accounting obligations

Cost orientation. One purpose of the NRF is to develop an environment where **7.95** markets function properly. In a correctly functioning market, prices are based on costs.[33] In such a system, having a proper accounting system where costs are clearly identified is essential for undertakings to establish their pricing strategy. The obligation to hold proper accounts is not a part of the NRF. The national measures relating to accounting have been harmonised to some extent at European level. The NRF concerning electronic communications has more specific goals,

---

[33] Prices may not be much higher than costs, because they would be undercut by competitors. They may not be lower than costs, at least for lengthy periods, because the undertakings would then suffer losses, which would undermine their reliability.

limited to the functioning of a given sector of the economy. For that reason, measures have been adopted by the European legislator in connection with accounting only to address specific issues to be dealt with, in that field, to ensure the realisation of the goals pursued by the NRF.

7.96 **Small undertakings.**   An obligation is imposed on undertakings not subject to accounting requirements under the general rules in force in the various Member States. The obligation covers undertakings which are not subject to the requirements of company law. It also covers undertakings which do not satisfy the requirements for the application of the accounting rules as harmonised by the European legislator (small and medium-sized undertakings). A difficulty with these two categories of undertakings is that no correct and independent information may be available about their operations and financial situation. To remedy this, the NRF introduces an obligation for these undertakings to submit financial reports to an independent auditor. These reports have to be published. The auditors must carry out their verification tasks in accordance with the rules applicable to their profession, under national and Community law.

> *Framework Directive, Article 13(2).* 'Where undertakings providing public communications networks or publicly available electronic communications services are not subject to the requirements of company law and do not satisfy the small and medium-sized enterprise criteria of Community law accounting rules, their financial reports shall be drawn up and submitted to independent audit and published. The audit shall be carried out in accordance with the relevant Community and national rules.'

7.97 **Retail market.**   An obligation to hold cost-based accounts is mentioned in the Universal Service Directive. That obligation concerns undertakings with significant market power. It is meant to accompany other obligations imposed on these undertakings, as regards retail tariffs or other conditions at which services are provided to end users.

> *Universal Service Directive, Article 17(4).* 'National regulatory authorities shall ensure that, where an undertaking is subject to retail tariff regulation or other relevant retail controls, the necessary and appropriate cost accounting systems are implemented. National regulatory authorities may specify the format and accounting methodology to be used. Compliance with the cost accounting system shall be verified by a qualified independent body. National regulatory authorities shall ensure that a statement concerning compliance is published annually.'

7.98 **Current situation in the Member States.**   An important aspect is that the accounts of undertakings notified as having significant market power must have their accounts certified. That verification of the accounts is deemed essential by the Commission. The situation that can be observed in the Member States does not appear satisfactory in that regard. Infringement procedures have been initiated against several Member States by the Commission in this regard.

Eighth implementation, report, 37. 'A key element of compliance with the principles contained in EU law regarding costing is the existence of a verification process, including an audit by an independent auditor or the NRA. The Commission has taken action in this regard, opening infringement procedures against several Member States. Currently, audits are generally performed by external independent auditors, although in many cases the NRAs carry out additional verification procedures.'[34]

(2) Accounting separation

Danger of cross-subsidisation.   The proper functioning of electronic commun-   **7.99**
ications markets may require that, in certain circumstances, NRAs impose accounting separation between certain activities. Two situations are envisaged in the NRF. The first situation is where special or exclusive rights have been granted to undertakings performing electronic communications activities. The second situation is where activities are performed by undertakings with significant market power. These two situations are examined in the following paragraphs. In both cases, the danger addressed by the respective provisions is that the undertakings concerned (those which have received special and/or exclusive rights, or those which have significant market power) may be tempted to use cross-subsidisation as a way of financing activities on markets where they are subject to competition. Such a situation would be disastrous for the development of competition, as undertakings would then compete on an unequal basis on the latter markets.

(a) Undertakings with significant market power.   The first situation is where an   **7.100**
undertaking is notified as having significant market power on an electronic communications market. Under the NRF, NRAs may request from such powerful undertakings a communication of accounting information necessary to verify that the obligations of transparency and non-discrimination are complied with. The publication of relevant information may be ordered, subject to the rules of confidentiality in force in the Member States and the European Community.

> *Access Directive, Article 11(2).* '[T]o facilitate the verification of compliance with obligations of transparency and non-discrimination, national regulatory authorities shall have the power to require that accounting records, including data on revenues received from third parties, are provided on request. National regulatory authorities may publish such information as would contribute to an open and competitive market, while respecting national and Community rules on commercial confidentiality.'

Accounting separation.   A further step may be taken, with NRAs ordering such   **7.101**
powerful undertakings to hold separate accounts for some activities. The activities concerned are those relating to access to resources or facilities placed under the control of powerful undertakings. These undertakings may be requested to identify the costs and the revenues relating to these activities, separately from accounting data concerning other activities.

---

[34] Only three NRAs (in Germany, Austria and Finland) verify the accounts themselves. All Member States have verified at least once the accounting systems of the notified operators, except Belgium, Luxembourg and Finland.

Access Directive, Article 11(1). 'A national regulatory authority may . . . impose obligations for accounting separation in relation to specified activities related to interconnection and/or access.'

7.102 **Vertically integrated undertakings.**   A specific provision is devoted, in the NRF, to vertically integrated undertakings holding significant market power. Vertical integration means that the undertaking is present at various stages of the economic chain. As stated above, such an undertaking may be tempted to leverage power held on a market in order to reinforce its position on another, related, activity. One way to leverage that power would be to impose high tariffs for access to essential resources under the control of the undertaking. These tariffs could be higher, for instance, than those charged to partners, subsidiaries or even to its own divisions internally in charge of the activities where the undertaking is in competition with those other companies.

7.103 **Transparency.**   In the context of these vertically integrated undertakings with significant market power, the measure imagined in the NRF to address the risks associated with cross-subsidisation is also to require transparency from the undertakings concerned. Under the rules introduced in the framework, these undertakings may be obliged to make transparent the prices which they charge on the market where they hold significant power. The idea is that, with transparency, it is possible to monitor the tariffs charged by the undertakings and determine, for instance, whether these tariffs are discriminatory or excessive.

Access Directive, Article 11(1). '[A] national regulatory authority may require a vertically integrated company to make transparent its wholesale prices and its internal transfer prices *inter alia* to ensure compliance where there is a requirement for non-discrimination . . . or, where necessary, to prevent unfair cross-subsidy.'

7.104 **A far-reaching measure.**   The accounting obligations which may be imposed on undertakings, in particular the obligation to hold separate accounts for given activities, may appear as a far-reaching measure imposed on economic actors in a context where the priority is left to market forces. These measures indeed imply for the undertakings concerned an administrative burden which may, in some instances, be heavy. To have a clear perception of the burden imposed on the undertakings concerned, it should however be recalled that a more radical idea was submitted by various participants during the negotiation leading to the adoption of the NRF. That idea was that activities relating to networks should be completely severed from service provision. The consequence of that idea was that undertakings would not have been allowed to carry out activities on the two types of markets and divestiture would, as a result, have been imposed on those which are currently present on both of them.[35]

---

[35] As is stated in the following paragraphs, an obligation to separate accounts may be imposed also on undertakings holding special and/or exclusive rights on given markets. Member States may,

(b) Undertakings with special and/or exclusive rights.   An issue similar to that   **7.105**
examined in the paragraphs above is when undertakings have special and/or
exclusive rights on one or several markets while carrying out other activities in
a competitive environment. The danger examined above would also arise in such
a situation, as the undertakings concerned could use funds from the markets
where they hold these privileges to subsidise activities carried out on competitive
markets. The difficulty mentioned above would then arise, with competition being
distorted on the latter markets. A second difficulty would be that the distortion
would come from revenues acquired with the assistance of a public authority—that
which had granted the special and/or exclusive right. Such a situation seems
hardly acceptable in an environment where market participants may not be
discriminated against by public authorities.

Markets concerned.   Under normal circumstances, the scenario should not   **7.106**
occur where special and/or exclusive rights are held on electronic communications markets. As has been made clear, rights of that nature have been eliminated
in the course of the reform. If the European directives are complied with in the
various Member States, no undertaking will enjoy special and/or exclusive rights
on these markets. By contrast, a situation may occur where an undertaking has
special and/or exclusive rights in other sectors of the economy which have not
been similarly regulated.

Accounting separation.   The measure which has been adopted in the NRF to   **7.107**
address that situation is that such an undertaking must hold separate accounts for
electronic communications activities. In other words, the accounts relating to
electronic communications must be held separately from those relating to these
other activities where privileges are held. This accounting separation makes it possible to identify the revenues and costs (including fixed assets and structural costs)
relating to electronic communications. In this fashion, it is possible for NRAs to verify that tariffs charged on electronic communications markets indeed correspond to
the costs which are identified for the activities carried out on these markets.

> *Framework Directive, Article 13(1).* 'Member States shall require undertakings pro-
> viding public communications networks or publicly available electronic communi-
> cations services which have special or exclusive rights for the provision of services in
> other sectors in the same or another Member State to: . . . keep separate accounts for
> the activities associated with the provision of electronic communications networks
> or services, to the extent that would be required if these activities were carried out by
> legally independent companies, so as to identify all elements of cost and revenue,

---

however, decide that accounting separation does not apply to undertakings with a limited turnover.
That possibility to limit the obligation relating to accounting separation is not provided regarding
undertakings with significant market power. As they hold significant market power, the undertakings concerned indeed have, by their nature, turnover higher than that envisaged for the companies
with special or exclusive rights.

with the basis of their calculation and the detailed attribution methods used, related to their activities associated with the provision of electronic communications networks or services including an itemised breakdown of fixed asset and structural costs.'

7.108 **Derogation.** A derogation may be introduced by the Member States to the obligation to hold separate accounts, concerning undertakings with a limited turnover in electronic communications (50 million euros). The purpose of the derogation is to avoid imposing excessive administrative costs on these undertakings. By definition, these undertakings only have a limited presence on electronic communications markets. Their entry on these markets should not be discouraged by excessive burdens. On the contrary, entry should be encouraged on the part of all potentially interested undertakings including those which are currently engaged on other markets where they have public privileges.

> *Framework Directive, Article 13(1), subpara 2.* 'Member States may choose not to apply the requirements referred to in the first subparagraph to undertakings the annual turnover of which in activities associated with electronic communications networks or services in the Member States is less than EUR 50 million.'

7.109 **Trans-boundary activities.** The obligation to hold separate accounts applies whatever the geographic market where the undertakings concerned carry out their activities. Undertakings with activities limited to one national territory are thus subject to the obligation.[36] Another possible situation would be that of an undertaking performing activities under public privileges (special or exclusive rights) in one Member State, and wishing to prolong that activity on electronic communications markets in one or several other Member States. As is apparent from the extract quoted in para 7.107 above, the transboundary character of the activities, and the fact that the public privileges are held in other Member States than those where the electronic communications activities are performed, does not impede the application of the obligation to hold separate accounts.

7.110 **(c) Current situation in the Member States.** In the Eighth implementation report, the Commission states that the obligations concerning accounting separation are not complied with. This is important, as these obligations are considered essential to ensure appropriate access and interconnection.

> *Eighth implementation report, 37.* '[I]t should be pointed out that where separate accounts are prepared in a comprehensive way, these do not seem to include key elements such as transfer charges between business units (Greece, Spain, the Netherlands, Finland), costs or revenues. There are therefore still significant aspects to be improved across the EU before implementation of accounting separation can be regarded as satisfactory.'

---

[36] An example would be an undertaking holding special rights, as is still the case in some Member States, for the exercise of water-related activities in a given territory, and which might decide to use its existing infrastructure to develop an electronic communications network and provide electronic communications services on that territory.

(3) Structural separation

Special and/or exclusive rights on non-electronic communications markets. **7.111**
The NRF provides that structural separation may be imposed where an undertaking active on electronic communications markets also performs activities in
other sectors of the economy where it holds special and/or exclusive rights. The
purpose, again, is to avoid cross-subsidisation with revenues obtained in an environment where competition is not based on the merits, as privileges have
been granted by a public authority.

> *Framework Directive, Article 13(1).* 'Member States shall require undertakings pro-
> viding public communications networks or publicly available electronic communi-
> cations services which have special or exclusive rights for the provision of services in
> other sectors in the same or another Member State to . . . have structural separation
> for the activities associated with the provision of electronic communications
> networks or services.'

Other circumstances where structural separation is required. There are other **7.112**
circumstances in which the NRF provides that structural separation must be
established between activities. These circumstances are analysed in the following
paragraphs. They concern the separation which must be established between
authorities and undertakings, as well as the specific context where rights of way are
granted.

Independence of NRAs. The first circumstance where structural separation is **7.113**
required regards the organisation and status of NRAs. That aspect has been
analysed in detail in Chapter 1 dealing with authorities. It is worth mentioning,
however, in connection with structural obligations imposed on undertakings.
Under the Framework Directive, NRAs must be independent. In the system proposed by the European legislator, independence requires a separation between
authorities and the undertakings which they regulate. As is apparent from the
extract quoted at the end of this paragraph, the separation must be 'legal', 'functional' and 'structural'. The last requirement (structural separation) is associated
with situations where undertakings are owned or controlled by a public authority.
In that context, a feeling of common interest may develop among these public entities. This may endanger the necessity of neutrality on the part of the authority.

> *Framework Directive, Article 3(2).* 'Member States shall guarantee the independence
> of national regulatory authorities by ensuring that they are legally distinct from and
> functionally independent of all organisations providing electronic communications
> networks, equipment or services. Member States that retain ownership or control of
> undertakings providing electronic communications networks and/or services shall
> ensure effective structural separation of the regulatory function from activities asso-
> ciated with ownership or control.'

Rights of way. The same requirements of independence and structural **7.114**
separation appear in connection with rights of way. As was stated, these rights are

authorisations granted by a public authority to establish network equipment or facilities on, above or under private or public property. In some instances, the undertaking applying to receive a right of way may be controlled and/or owned by a public authority. The danger mentioned above (conflict of interest) may then arise, as the authority may be tempted to favour the public undertaking. To avoid that situation, structural separation is required between the entities granting the rights and those applying for them.

> *Framework Directive, Article 11(2).* 'Member States shall ensure that where public or local authorities retain ownership or control of undertakings operating electronic communications networks and/or services, there is effective structural separation of the function responsible for granting the rights [of way] . . . from activities associated with ownership or control.'

7.115 **What does structural separation imply?**   It is difficult to determine the exact implications of the requirement of structural separation or, even, as it is stated in the various relevant provisions, the requirement that structural separation must be 'effective'. There exists on that question a certain ambiguity in the NRF. The reason is probably that the structural separation-related requirement is the result of a compromise. The nature of the compromise appears with clarity for the application of the requirement to the organisation of public authorities (general requirement of a structural separation between authorities and undertakings, as well as specific requirement that authorities granting rights of way must be separate from undertakings applying for these rights). During the negotiations which led to the adoption of the NRF, as well as under the old framework, it had appeared that markets could not be regulated properly if authorities were not independent. There was also an observation that that independence may be undermined, or at least that suspicions of partiality may arise, where governments still control electronic communications operators. A compromise was sought in the form of a requirement where independence would be set as an objective and Member States would remain free to organise their internal powers as they considered appropriate as long as the objective was reached.

7.116 **Undertakings.**   The situation is not different for the application of the requirement to undertakings. In that context, as has been stated, electronic communications activities must be separated structurally from activities carried out on other markets where the undertaking has special and/or exclusive rights. As the risk of cross-subsidisation from these protected markets appeared so important, the ideal solution was probably to prohibit the combination of activities by the undertakings concerned. Such a situation did not appear, however, acceptable. A compromise was found by requiring that the activities should be structurally separated. The hope was that, with that requirement, the activities would be performed as if they were carried out by separate entities even if the Member States maintained some freedom to organise the structural separation as they considered appropriate.

Elements for an interpretation.   As there does not exist a general explanation **7.117**
concerning the exact content of the requirement in sector-specific regulation,
some elements of interpretation may be found in other parts of the law. *(a)* A first
source of inspiration might be the Merger Regulation, in which a concentration is
defined as an operation which modifies the structure of the undertakings
involved. Under that regulation, structural modifications may take the form of
a (real) merger, an acquisition or the creation of an autonomous joint venture
(lasting basis). *(b)* Other elements may be found in the case law,[37] where the ECJ
addressed the issue of electronic communications operators and authorities still
forming part of the same department in a national government (France). Pursuant
to the ruling issued by the ECJ, the presence of an authority and an undertaking
in the same ministerial department could not be considered acceptable in the light
of the requirement of independence. These cases provide useful information, as
they imply that the coexistence of two entities in a single organisational unit cannot be considered as structural separation sufficient to satisfy the requirement of
independence.

> *Merger regulation (1997), Preamble, recital 5.* '[I]t is appropriate to define the concept
> of concentration in such a manner as to cover operations bringing about a lasting
> change in the structure of the undertakings concerned.'[38] *Decoster*[39] *and*
> *Taillandier.*[40] 'So far as concerns the requirement that the body responsible for draw-
> ing up the specifications, monitoring their application and granting type-approval
> must be independent, suffice it to note that the different directorates of a single
> authority cannot be regarded as independent of each other.'

Durable autonomy.   On the basis of these elements, a reasonable interpretation **7.118**
is to define structural separation as a form of separation which must be substantial
and durable. *(a)* The separation must be substantial and may not be merely cos-
metic. It must concern the way the functions are performed by the entities
involved. The exercise of one activity may not have an influence on the performance of the others. The entities involved must be autonomous in their functioning. *(b)* The separation may not be transitory or temporary. If separation is limited
to a short period of time, the risk is that autonomy may only be illusory.

(4) Legal separation

Consolidated Services Directives.   Parallel to the measure adopted by the **7.119**
Parliament and Council, the Commission imposes legal separation in a specific

---

[37] Case C-69/91 *Criminal proceedings against Francine Gillon, née Decoster* [1993] ECR I-5335;
Criminal proceedings against Annick Neny, née Taillandier [1993] ECR I-5383.

[38] See also, on that subject, the Commission notice on the notion of a concentration
under Council Regulation (EEC) 4064/89 of 21 December 1989 on the control of concentrations
between undertakings [1994] OJ C385/5, as well as the Commission Notice on the distinction
between concentrative and co-operative joint ventures under Council Regulation (EEC) 4064/89
of 21 December 1989 on the control of concentrations between undertakings [1994] OJ C385/1.

[39] Para 16.   [40] Para 15.

situation. That situation is where an undertaking operates two, or more, electronic communications networks which, formerly, belonged to the formerly distinguished telecommunications and broadcasting industries.

> *Consolidated Services Directive, Article 8*. 'Each Member State shall ensure that no undertaking providing public electronic communications networks operates its cable television network using the same legal entity as it uses for its other public electronic communications network, when such undertaking: (a) is controlled by that Member State or benefits from special rights; and (b) is dominant in a substantial part of the common market in the provision of public electronic communications networks and publicly available telephone services; and (c) operates a cable television network[41] which has been established under special or exclusive right in the same geographic area.'

7.120 **Cable TV Directives.** That obligation is identical to one earlier introduced by the Commission in Directive (EC) 1999/64 amending Directive 90/388 in order to ensure that telecommunications networks and cable TV networks owned by a single operator are separate legal entities ('Cable TV 2 Directive')[42]. This latter instrument was itself reinforcing a similar obligation introduced by an earlier instrument—Commission Directive (EC) 95/51 amending Directive 90/388 with regard to the abolition of the restrictions on the use of cable television networks for the provision of already liberalised telecommunications services ('Cable TV 1 Directive').[43]

7.121 **Network competition.** The principle underlying, on that point, the Consolidated Services Directive, is that network competition has to be promoted. Services can only develop if, and to the extent that, access can be obtained to networks under satisfactory conditions. Access-related obligations are imposed to that effect. Another strategy is to stimulate competition between networks. Where competition exists between networks, service providers may choose their operators and competition may force the latter to improve the conditions under which access may be obtained.

7.122 **Regulatory intervention.** The difficulty is that establishing complete telecommunications networks requires heavy investment and time. A quicker path to stimulate competition is to ensure convergence among networks. Network convergence means that telecommunications and broadcasting networks, which in the past served different industries, can be used to provide the same services. Convergence requires technical and economic initiatives on the part of market participants. In addition to these initiatives, legal or regulatory measures have to be taken. These measures concern in particular countries where the former

---

[41] Cable television networks are defined in the following manner in the Consolidated Services Directive, Art 1(8): 'any mainly wire-based infrastructure established primarily for the delivery or distribution of radio or television broadcast to the public'. [42] (1999) OJ L1175/39.
[43] (1995) OJ L256/49.

telecommunications and broadcasting networks are controlled by the same undertaking. In most circumstances, that undertaking has no interest in changing the situation. It controls the two networks—and thus dominates two markets where domination allows it to impose conditions to its liking.

Separating the networks. The solution imagined by the Commission is to **7.123** impose legal separation. With that measure, the undertaking(s) concerned have to entrust different companies with the task of managing the different networks. Legal separation is supposed to enhance separate management. Where former broadcasting and telecommunications networks are managed by different teams, it is hoped that these teams will seek to maximise profit for the company (legal entity) they have in charge. It remains that these legal entities may belong to a same economic group and that a feeling of collective interest, justifying a common approach within the group, may still exist and develop. Such an outcome could be examined under Article 82 EC as that provision aims, among others, at behaviour 'limiting production, markets or technical development to the prejudice of consumers' (Article 82, letter c).

Strict conditions. As appears from the extract quoted above, the legal separation **7.124** introduced by the Consolidated Services Directive is subject to stringent conditions. The conditions analysed in this paragraph are mentioned in letters (b) and (c) in the extract quoted above. Pursuant to these conditions, the obligation (legal separation) applies only where *(a)* the undertaking holds a dominant position on one market for electronic communications networks or services; *(b)* that undertaking operates a cable television network in the same geographical market; *(c)* that cable television network has been established with the assistance of special or exclusive rights granted by a public authority.

Special or exclusive rights. That latter condition does not imply that the under- **7.125** taking must still enjoy special or exclusive rights on these cable television networks at the time when legal separation is envisaged. Such prerogatives indeed have to be eliminated as a result of the general prohibition directed against special or exclusive rights for all electronic communications networks and services—a general prohibition which already existed under the old liberalisation directives but has been extended to broadcasting networks and services by the Consolidated Services Directive. The condition means only that legal separation is obligatory where, historically, the cable television network has been built thanks to the assistance of a public authority in the form of a special or an exclusive right.

Supplementary condition. The application of the obligation (legal separation) **7.126** is further subject to one condition, which is mentioned at letter (a) in the extract quoted above. That condition is that the operator to which the obligation applies must be controlled by a public authority or enjoy special rights. That condition is examined separately, because it does not have the same function as those examined in the last paragraph, which aim at ensuring legal separation. By contrast, the condition mentioned at letter (a) relates to the competence for the Commission to intervene. The Consolidated Services Directive has been adopted on the basis of Article 86 EC. That provision concerns special or exclusive rights, as well as public undertakings or undertakings entrusted with a service of general interest. These undertakings are the only ones with respect to which the Commission is entitled to take action on the basis of that provision. A condition thus had to be inserted, in order to limit legal separation to undertakings vis-à-vis which the Commission is entitled to take action on the basis of that provision.[44]

7.127 **Possibility of removing the obligation.** Pursuant to the Consolidated Services Directive, the Commission may decide that, under certain circumstances, the obligation to legally separate the former telecommunications and broadcasting networks may be set aside. One condition has to be fulfilled to that effect—the Commission has to consider, on the basis of information provided by the parties, that competition is effective on the network market.

> *Consolidated Services Directive, Article 8(3) and (4).* 'Member States which consider that there is sufficient competition in the provision of local loop infrastructure and services in their territory shall inform the Commission accordingly.' 'Such information shall include a detailed description of the market structure.' 'The Commission shall decide within a reasonable period, after having heard the comments of these parties, whether the obligation of legal separation may be ended in the Member State concerned.'

E. Technological Neutrality, Standardisation and Harmonisation

(1) Technological neutrality

7.128 **No technological choices by NRAs.** It has been stated that regulatory choices made by NRAs must remain technologically neutral. This requirement implies that these choices may not favour any given technology. Technological neutrality is inspired by several considerations. First, authorities are not always in a position to make the best choices from a technological point of view. Second, markets and

---

[44] Pursuant to the extract presented above, the first possibility is that the undertaking concerned is placed under the control of a public authority. Such a situation still occurs today as all former national incumbents have not been privatised. The Consolidated Services Directive adds another possibility, which is that the undertaking(s) have a special right. On that point, the Commission does not appear entirely consistent. Special rights have been eliminated on all telecommunications markets and the prohibition has been extended, by the Consolidated Services Directive, to broadcasting markets (cable television networks included). If an undertaking still enjoys special rights on one of these markets, the situation should be deemed contrary to the directive. The State concerned should then be found against, instead of an obligation of legal separation being imposed on the undertaking(s).

authorities may not share the same opinion about technology. Assuming that authorities are correctly informed, they may make choices which are subsequently disavowed by markets. Third, technological choices made by authorities may favour certain undertakings—those which have developed the technology concerned or which are ahead in the race in developing that technology. Competition would thereby be distorted.[45]

> *Framework Directive, Article 8(1).* 'Member States shall ensure that in carrying out [their] . . . regulatory tasks . . ., in particular those designed to ensure effective competition, national regulatory authorities take the utmost account of the desirability of making regulations technologically neutral.' *Framework Directive, Preamble, recital 18.* '[N]ational regulatory authorities take the utmost account of the desirability of making regulation technologically neutral, that is to say that it neither imposes nor discriminates in favour of the use of a particular type of technology.'

Difficulty of remaining neutral.   It has not escaped the European legislator that **7.129** remaining entirely neutral from a technological point of view would be difficult, if not impossible. Some, if not all, choices have technological consequences. Promoting a service, for instance, may imply that the technology used to provide that service is indeed promoted. Nuances thus had to be brought to the requirement that regulatory choices should remain neutral. These nuances are expressed in the Preamble to the Framework Directive. Under that preamble, technological neutrality does not preclude NRAs from promoting given services—for instance digital television—even though this might imply the promotion of a given technology. From these statements, it appears that the requirement to maintain neutrality must be understood as a prohibition on adopting stances which, as their main object, imply that a given technology is favoured. A reasonable interpretation is that other choices, with ancillary consequences on technology, could by contrast be accepted.

> *Framework Directive, Preamble, recital 18.* 'The requirement . . . of making regulation technologically neutral . . . does not preclude the taking of proportionate steps to promote certain specific services where this is justified, for example digital television as a means for increasing spectrum efficiency.'

(2) Standardisation

Necessity of common standards.   The development of networks and services in **7.130** the European Union requires the use of technical standards. In the absence of uniformity in the standards used, there is a risk that networks and services may not be

---

[45] To that extent, technological choices made by regulation could be analysed as a special right giving a regulatory advantage to certain undertakings. In Chapter 2 dealing with rules applicable throughout the regulatory framework, it has been stated that special rights are prohibited under the Consolidated Services Directive. Such rights are furthermore prohibited under general competition law, with possible derogation where an acceptable objective can be found and the means to achieve that objective are legitimate.

interoperable. To ensure interoperability, the NRF introduces measures aiming at the determination of common standards.

7.131 **Standards for networks and services.** The provisions examined in the following paragraphs concern standards and specifications regarding networks and services.[46] They do not affect the rules concerning standards relating to electronic communications equipment, since the latter standards are subject to a specific regime which is not examined in this book.[47]

7.132 **(a) Adoption of European standards.** Under the NRF, the European Commission is entrusted with the task of developing standards for electronic communications activities across the European Union. The standards developed by the Commission must be published in the form of a list in the Official Journal of the European Communities. As drawing up standards requires specialised technical expertise, the Commission usually asks standard-setting organisations to prepare the standards in question. In Europe, these organisations are: the European Committee for Standardisation (CEN), the European Committee for Electrotechnical Standardisation (CENELEC), and the European Telecommunications Standards Institute (ETSI).

> *Framework Directive, Article 17(1).* 'The Commission . . . shall draw up and publish in the Official Journal of the European Communities a list of standards and/or specifications to serve as a basis for encouraging the harmonised provision of electronic communications networks, electronic communications services and associated facilities and services. Where necessary, the Commission may . . . request that standards be drawn up by the European standards organisations (European Committee for Standardisation (CEN), European Committee for Electrotechnical Standardisation (CENELEC), and European Telecommunications Standards Institute (ETSI).'

7.133 **Ordinary harmonisation procedure.** A procedure must be followed before the adoption of decisions whereby mandates are given to the organisations to prepare given standards, and of decisions to draw up standards and publish them in the form of a list. This procedure is referred to here as the 'ordinary harmonisation procedure' and unfolds as follows. *(a)* A committee made up of representatives of the Member States and chaired by a representative of the Commission must be consulted. *(b)* The chairman submits to the committee a draft of the measure to

---

[46] The NRF uses these two terms (standards and specifications), without providing a definition of them. These terms are not defined either in the instruments composing the old framework. Specifications appear to be more technical. They are technical rules which must be satisfied in the design and the development of the networks and services concerned. Standards are more general. They refer in a more general manner to any sort of rule adopted by organisations gathering representatives of all stakeholders in the industry concerned. For instance, these standards may establish goals, or objectives, to be reached in given services, in terms or quantity of quality. For examples, see Chapter 5 dealing with universal service.

[47] See Framework Directive, Art 17(7) as well as European Parliament and Council Directive (EC) 1999/5 on radio equipment and telecommunications terminal equipment and the mutual recognition of their conformity [1999] OJ L91/10.

be taken. *(c)* The committee delivers an opinion on the draft, if necessary by taking a vote, within a time limit laid down by the chairman according to the urgency of the matter. *(d)* The opinion is recorded in the minutes, together with the position which the Member States want to be recorded. *(e)* The Commission takes the utmost account of the opinion and informs the committee of the manner in which it has been taken into account.[48]

(b) Application in the Member States. The Member States must encourage the   **7.134**
use of the standards which have been drawn up and published in accordance with the requirements described in the latter paragraph. These measures whereby the use of standards is encouraged may appear to some observers as a limitation imposed on the freedom of economic operators to choose the technology which they see as more appropriate.[49] It should be recalled in this regard that the NRF sees technological neutrality as a requirement to be complied with by NRAs. To alleviate the burden which encouragement measures may represent for economic freedom, the NRF provides that these measures may only be taken if two conditions are fulfilled. *(a)* The standards are necessary to ensure interoperability between the services. *(b)* The use of these standards increases the choice open to users.[50]

> *Framework Directive, Article 17(2).* 'Member States shall encourage the use of the standards and/or specifications [drawn up and published in conformity with the requirements described above] . . . for the provision of services, technical interfaces and/or network functions, to the extent strictly necessary to ensure interoperability of services and to improve freedom of choice for users.'

(c) Imposition of standards. In some circumstances, it may appear that the   **7.135**
standards drawn up and published as described above are not applied by market participants, even though their use has been encouraged by the Member States in conformity with the requirement set forth in the latter paragraph. In that situation, compliance with the standards in question may be made obligatory. As was the case for encouragement measures, the decisions whereby standards are made obligatory may be taken only if the two above-mentioned conditions are satisfied—the measure is strictly necessary to ensure interoperability of the services and improve the choice offered to users.

---

[48] On that procedure, see Framework Directive, Art 17(1) and Art 22(2). See also Council Decision (EC) 1999/468 laying down the procedures for the exercise of implementing powers conferred on the Commission [1999] OJ L184/23, Arts 3 and 7. The committee established under European Parliament and Council Directive (EC) 98/34 laying down a procedure for the provision of information in the field of technical standards and regulations ([1998] OJ L204/37) must also be consulted.

[49] See Framework Directive, Preamble, recital 30. 'Standardisation should remain primarily a market-driven process.'

[50] It might appear that imposing standards restricts the freedom of users. Users are indeed limited by the choices made by the standards organisations. The idea is, however, that standards increase interoperability and efficiency, the mid- and long-term result being an increase in the possibilities opened to users.

Framework Directive, Article 17(3) and (4). 'If the standards and/or specifications . . . have not been adequately implemented so that interoperability of services in one or more Member States cannot be ensured, the implementation of such standards and/or specifications may be made compulsory . . . , to the extent strictly necessary to ensure such interoperability and to improve freedom of choice for users.'

7.136 **Special harmonisation procedure.** An additional procedure has to be followed before standards can be imposed. This procedure is referred to here as the 'procedure to make standards obligatory'. It is rather demanding, in terms of documents and reactions required from intervening institutions. *(a)* A notice must be published in the Official Journal, announcing the intention of the Commission to make compliance with the standards concerned obligatory. *(b)* An opinion must be requested from a regulatory committee composed of representatives of the Member States and chaired by a representative of the Commission. *(c)* The chairman must submit to the committee a draft of the measure to be taken. *(d)* An opinion must be delivered by the committee within the time limit laid down by the chairman according to the urgency of the matter.[51] *(e)* After the opinion has been delivered, various scenarios may unfold. In a first scenario, the measure envisaged by the Commission is in accordance with the opinion of the committee. The measure can then be adopted. The Commission is the author of the measure. In a second scenario, there is no agreement between the Commission and the committee. Another possibility is that the committee has not been in a position to deliver the opinion. In these cases, the Commission must submit without delay to the Council a proposal relating to the measure to be taken. Parallel to that, it must inform the European Parliament. The Council must then act by qualified majority on the proposal. If the Council has indicated by qualified majority that it opposes the proposal, the Commission must re-examine it. It may submit an amended proposal to the Council, re-submit its proposal or present a legislative proposal on the basis of the Treaty. If the Council has neither adopted the proposed implementing act nor indicated its opposition to the proposal for implementing measures, the proposed implementing act is adopted by the Commission.[52]

7.137 **(d) Removal.** After an enquiry, the Commission may consider that one or several standards do not comply with the requirements set forth above (standards to be encouraged in the sole circumstances where they promote interoperability and enlarge the choice of users). If that conclusion is reached, the standard(s) concerned must be removed from the list of those which have been made obligatory

---

[51] The opinion must be delivered by the majority laid down in Art 205(2) EC in the case of decisions which the Council is required to adopt on a proposal from the Commission. The votes of the representatives of the Member States within the Committee are weighted in the manner set out in that article. The chairman does not vote.

[52] For a complete description of the procedure, see the Framework Directive, Art 17(3) and (4). See also Framework Directive, Art 22(3) and Council Decision (EC) 1999/468 laying down the procedures for the exercise of implementing powers conferred on the Commission, Arts 5 and 7.

or which must be encouraged by the Member States. The decision to remove standards may only be taken following a procedure. That procedure is the same as that which has been followed in order to prepare, or make obligatory, the standard concerned. *(a)* Where the standard has not been made obligatory, but was merely encouraged by the Member States, the procedure described for the preparation of standards is applicable (ordinary harmonisation procedure). *(b)* Where the standard(s) have been made obligatory, the more demanding procedure explained in the latter paragraph must be complied with[53] (special harmonisation procedure).

> *Framework Directive, Article 17(5) and (6).* 'Where the Commission considers that standards and/or specifications . . . no longer contribute to the provision of harmonised electronic communications services, or that they no longer meet consumers' needs or are hampering technological development, it shall . . . remove them from the list of standards and/or specifications.'

(e) Absence of European standards. The European standards organisations **7.138** have established, in recent years, a large number of standards based on mandates given by the European Commission. There may however remain areas where mandates have not been given or have not been implemented. An issue then is what standards should be used on the markets. *(a)* To that issue, the NRF brings a solution by stating that, in the absence of standards determined on the basis of mandates given by the European Commission, Member States should encourage the standards established, on their own initiative, by the European standards organisations. *(b)* Where such standards do not exist, those established by the international organisations should be encouraged.[54]

> *Framework Directive, Article 17(2), subpara 2.* 'As long as standards and/or specifications have not been published in accordance with . . . [the formalities examined above], Member States shall encourage the implementation of standards and/or specifications adopted by the European standards organisations.' 'In the absence of such standards and/or specifications, Member States shall encourage the implementation of international standards or recommendations adopted by the International Telecommunication Union (ITU), the International Organisation for Standardisation (ISO) or the International Electrotechnical Commission (IEC).'

European and international standards. A European standardisation policy has **7.139** the advantage of allowing the European institutions to establish standards using technology developed by European undertakings. Using the standardisation process, an industrial policy may be carried out. A difficulty is however that the reasons why interoperability should be promoted are not limited to the European

---

[53] See Framework Directive, Art 17(6) and Art 22(3), as well as Council Decision (EC) 1999/468 laying down the procedures for the exercise of implementing powers conferred on the Commission, Arts 5 and 7.

[54] The NRF does not provide that international standards, or standards established by European standards organisations on their own initiative, can be made obligatory. The possibility to make standards obligatory is thus limited to standards which have been developed by European standards organisations, on the basis of a mandate given by the European Commission.

territory. These reasons indeed extend to the entire world. To take that necessity into account, the NRF urges the European standards organisations to work on the basis of international standards where such standards exist. The only limitation is that international standards must be set aside where they would undermine the goals underlying the standard-related provisions of the NRF, ie if these standards do not improve interoperability and/or broaden the choice of users.

> *Framework Directive, Article 17(2), subpara 3.* 'Where international standards exist, Member States shall encourage the European standards organisations to use them, or the relevant parts of them, as a basis for the standards they develop, except where such international standards or relevant parts would be ineffective.'

(3) Harmonisation

7.140 **Further harmonisation by the Commission.** The NRF establishes common rules for electronic communications markets across the European Union. In the implementation of the framework, a need for additional common rules may appear. It is in that perspective that provisions have been introduced to allow the adoption of common technical standards, as explained in the paragraphs above. Other rules of a common character might be necessary, in less technical areas, to ensure the harmonious development of activities on the European territory in electronic communications markets. To that effect, the European legislator entrusts the Commission with the task of adopting harmonisation measures for the implementation of the directives composing the NRF.

7.141 **(a) Technical implementing measures.** A first possibility is the adoption of technical implementing measures by the Commission. A typical example of a provision allowing the adoption of these measures is Article 10(4) of the Framework Directive. Under that provision, harmonisation measures may be adopted by the Commission in the field of numbering where this is necessary to ensure the development of pan-European services. These measures may be adopted only where the formalities associated with the special harmonisation procedure have been used. That procedure has been described above, in connection with the imposition of an obligation to comply with standards.

> *Framework Directive, Article 10(4).* 'Member States shall support the harmonisation of numbering resources within the Community where that is necessary to support the development of pan European services. The Commission may . . . take the appropriate technical implementing measures on this matter [using the forms associated to the special harmonisation procedure].' *Framework Directive, Article 19(2).* 'Where the Commission finds that divergence at national level in regulations aimed at implementing Article 10(4) creates a barrier to the single market, the Commission may, acting in accordance with the [special harmonisation] procedure, . . . take the appropriate technical implementing measures.'

7.142 **(b) Recommendations.** Another possibility is for the Commission to adopt recommendations for the implementation of the NRF. As is known, recommendations are Community acts having no binding force.[55] As they have no binding force, the Commission may not use recommendations to introduce new obligations. That limitation on the effect which recommendations may produce must be however nuanced. Under the Framework Directive, recommendations adopted by the Commission for the harmonised implementation of the NRF must be taken into account by the Member States. When an NRA decides not to comply with such a recommendation, it must explain the reasons why it has chosen that attitude.

> *Framework Directive, Article 19(1).* '[T]he Commission . . . issues recommendations to Member States on the harmonised application of the provisions in this [Framework] Directive and the Specific Directives in order to further the achievement of the objectives.' 'Member States shall ensure that national regulatory authorities take the utmost account of those recommendations in carrying out their tasks. Where a national regulatory authority chooses not to follow a recommendation, it shall inform the Commission giving the reasoning for its position.'

What measures.   It is uncertain whether the provision examined in the last **7.143** paragraph grants the Commission a general power to issue recommendations for the implementation of the regulatory framework. From a careful analysis of the provisions contained in the framework, it appears that two interpretations are possible. *(a)* A first interpretation would be that the provision examined in the latter paragraphs creates a legal basis for the European Commission, allowing that institution to adopt recommendations wherever it feels that supplementary harmonisation is needed for the implementation of the NRF. *(b)* A second possibility would be that the provision does not create a legal basis but merely regulates how recommendations should be adopted. In that interpretation, a legal basis should be sought by the Commission wherever that institution wishes to adopt a recommendation. That legal basis should be found in other specific provisions granting explicitly to the Commission a power to adopt recommendations for the implementation of the subject matter covered by these specific provisions.

Theoretical discussion.   The discussion between these interpretations does not **7.144** appear to have practical consequences. Under the EC Treaty, the Commission has a general right[56] to issue recommendations on all subjects where it considers that such acts must be adopted.[57] As stated above, the EC Treaty provides that these instruments are deprived of binding force. This does not imply, however, that the

---

[55] See Art 249 EC. 'Recommendations and opinions shall have no binding force.'

[56] There remains a procedural difference between the recommendations adopted on the basis of the EC Treaty and those which are mentioned in connection with harmonisation in the NRF. There is no specific procedure for the adoption of the former recommendations whereas a special, demanding, procedure must be followed for the adoption of the latter recommendations in implementation of the NRF.

[57] Cf Art 211 EC. 'In order to ensure the proper functioning and development of the common market, the Commission shall . . . formulate recommendations or deliver opinions on matters dealt with in this Treaty, if it expressly so provides or if the Commission considers it necessary.'

recommendations adopted by the Commission are deprived of any effect. Pursuant to Article 211 EC, the Commission is the guardian of the Treaty.[58] When that institution adopts a recommendation, it explains to the public concerned its position as to the interpretation which, according to it, should be given to the provisions concerned. Given the status of the institution, it cannot be claimed that such an interpretation is deprived of any effect.[59]

7.145 **Ordinary harmonisation procedure.** Under the NRF, recommendations may be adopted by the Commission in implementation of the NRF only if the forms associated with the ordinary harmonisation procedure have been complied with. That procedure has been described in the paragraphs above, in connection with the definition and publication of standards.[60]

F. Specific Provisions Regarding Public Voice Telephony

7.146 **Specific provisions.** Specific provisions are dedicated to public voice telephony in the NRF. These provisions are discussed in this section. It has been deemed appropriate to gather them and emphasise, in this fashion, their coherence. These provisions concern respectively: number portability, carrier selection and pre-selection, network integrity, operator assistance and enquiry services, directory services in other Member States, non-geographic numbers, the establishment of a single European emergency call number and the use of a common code for international calls.

(1) Number portability

7.147 **Portability.** A first obligation for undertakings providing public voice telephone services is to ensure the portability of the numbers assigned to subscribers. Portability implies that the subscriber may keep the same number when it changes provider. A change of provider thus has no consequence on the number allocated to the user.

---

[58] The 'Commission shall . . . ensure that the provisions of this Treaty and the measures taken by the institutions pursuant thereto are applied.'

[59] That effect must be understood in the light of the right on the part of the Commission, to take decisions and bring actions against those who do not comply with the European provisions as interpreted by it. Pursuant to the EC Treaty, the Commission has the right to start a procedure against Member States or European institutions failing to comply with their obligations. In the application of competition rules, it may take decisions against legal or natural persons infringing European law. Where European law is infringed by such persons in other fields than competition, action must be taken by the competent national authorities. In the absence of due national action, a procedure may be initiated by the Commission against the Member State in question.

[60] On that procedure, see Framework Directive, Art 19(1) and Art 22(2). See also Council Decision (EC) 1999/468 laying down the procedures for the exercise of implementing powers conferred on the Commission [1999] OJ L184/23, Arts 3 and 7.

Universal Service Directive, Article 30(1). 'Member States shall ensure that all sub-scribers of publicly available telephone services, including mobile services, who so request can retain their number(s) independently of the undertaking providing the service: (a) in the case of geographic numbers, at a specific location; and (b) in the case of non-geographic numbers, at any location.'[61]

Fixed and mobile voice telephony.   As appears from the extract above, portability   **7.148** is limited to public voice telephony. No obligation has been introduced for other services in the NRF. One could consider that portability has been designed in a relatively restricted manner. That impression would not be correct, however, in the light of the importance of voice telephony in society. Furthermore, portability has to be ensured, under the NRF, on all telephone services. Fixed services are not the only ones concerned. The obligation also applies on mobile voice telephony services.

Limitations.   The obligation to ensure portability has limitations. (*a*) Portability   **7.149** is not imposed when a user goes from a fixed to a mobile connection.[62] As a result, it cannot be expected that a user may keep for its mobile services the number which had been allocated to it as a subscriber to a fixed voice telephony service. (*b*) A second limitation is that fixed voice telephony-related portability may be limited to the location where the subscriber was established. Under the NRF, there is no obligation to ensure portability across regions—and less even across national boundaries.[63] That limitation affects mobile voice telephony only partially. Pursuant to the framework, portability must be ensured fully for mobile services, regarding a Member State, in all regions of that State, whatever the location of the user within that State.[64]

Tariffs.   Portability is a service. Payment thus has to be made to cover the costs   **7.150** associated with that operation. As is the case for selection and preselection (see next section), portability is financed, in most circumstances, by subscribers. NRAs must ensure that the tariffs charged for that service are not excessive. The tariffs must be cost oriented. They may not be a burden discouraging changes of provider.

Universal Service Directive, Article 30(2) and (3). 'National regulatory authorities shall ensure that pricing for interconnection related to the provision of number

---

[61]   Under the NRF, 'geographic number' means a number from the national numbering plan where part of the digit structure has geographic significance used for routing calls to the physical location of the network termination point. See Universal Service Directive, Art 2(2), letter (d).

[62]   See Universal Service Directive, Art 30(1). 'This paragraph [portability] does not apply to the porting of numbers between networks providing services at a fixed location and mobile networks.'

[63]   As a result of that limitation, a subscriber moving from one region to another, within the same Member State, may not be allowed to keep its number. Numbers contain prefixes which are associated to regions. Changing regions implies that a new prefix must be given to the subscriber.

[64]   A mobile user changing provider may keep its number, wherever that user is located on the national territory. Where it is implemented, that measure implies that it is no longer possible to determine the identity of the operator on the basis of numbers used by the subscribers. This may cause difficulties in Member States where charges depend on whether calls terminate on the same, or another, network than the one from which they originate.

portability is cost oriented and that direct charges to subscribers, if any, do not act as a disincentive for the use of these facilities.' 'National regulatory authorities shall not impose retail tariffs for the porting of numbers in a manner that would distort competition, such as by setting specific or common retail tariffs.'

(2) Carrier selection and carrier preselection

7.151 **Markets for services.** As stated above, the development of the markets for services depends largely, in European electronic communications, on the possibility for service providers of carrying out activities via networks or infrastructure controlled by other undertakings, in most instances incumbent operators. This statement is particularly valid for services requiring access via existing fixed telephony networks. A difficulty already examined in this book is that, often, network operators do not limit their activities to infrastructure markets, but also develop a presence on one or several markets for services. In these situations, the network providers are in competition, on these markets for services, with undertakings which act as their customers on the markets for infrastructure. In most instances, these network operators have significant market power—a circumstance which prompts public intervention to ensure that freedom of choice is maintained.

7.152 **Two mechanisms.** Under the NRF, an obligation must be imposed on undertakings with significant market power to grant final users a choice between providers.[65] *(a)* It must be possible, for users, to select on a call-by-call basis the provider from which they wish to receive a service. That selection must be possible by the mere dialling of a specific code, which must be communicated to the users. *(b)* In addition to that first mechanism, the undertakings concerned must grant users the possibility of preselecting a provider. Preselection means that the user expresses a general choice in favour of a given provider, which then becomes the provider by default.[66]

> *Universal Service Directive, Article 19(1).* 'National regulatory authorities shall require undertakings notified as having significant market power for the provision of connection to and use of the public telephone network at a fixed location . . . to enable their subscribers to access the services of any interconnected provider of publicly available telephone services: (a) on a call-by-call basis by dialling a carrier selection code; and (b) by means of pre-selection, with a facility to override any pre-selected choice on a call-by-call basis by dialling a carrier selection code.'[67]

---

[65] That obligation is imposed directly by the European legislator in the regulatory framework. As a result, there is no possibility for NRAs to determine whether selection and pre-selection should, or should not, be imposed. On that subject, NRAs are deprived of any margin of manoeuvre.

[66] The two mechanisms must be combined. As a result, it must always be possible, for a user, to select a provider, even if it has expressed a given choice for another provider by default.

[67] The obligations relating to selection and pre-selection apply independently of any action taken by an NRA. They were introduced in the ONP Interconnection Directive and are taken over in the context of the NRF by virtue of the Universal Service Directive. A review must take place to determine whether the obligations must be maintained. They have to be suppressed where competition is effective on the market. In case of effective competition, users normally have the possibility to choose their supplier. See Universal Service Directive, Art 16(1), letter a.

Reasonable conditions. Selection and preselection have a cost. An issue already **7.153** addressed in connection with portability is how that cost should be financed. Two principles are introduced on this point in the NRF. These principles correspond to the techniques which may be used by network operators to finance the costs relating to selection and preselection. *(a)* In some instances, network operators may decide that the service must be financed by the user directly. The NRF provides that, in such a situation, the tariff charged to users may not act as a disincentive to use the service. *(b)* In other cases, network operators may decide that providers have to be charged. If that option is chosen, these operators have to use cost-based tariffs.[68] This, again, implies that a proper, cost-based, accounting system must be held.[69]

> *Price charged to subscribers.* 'National regulatory authorities shall ensure that . . . direct charges to subscribers, if any, do not act as a disincentive for the use of these [selection and pre selection] facilities.'[70] *Price charged to service providers.* 'National regulatory authorities shall ensure that pricing for access and interconnection related to the provision of the [selection and preselection] facilities is cost oriented.'[71]

Services concerned. At this stage, selection and preselection mainly concern **7.154** voice telephony services provided through fixed infrastructure. Other services may however be concerned. One can imagine, for instance, the possibility for a user to choose a provider of another service than voice telephony on public fixed infrastructure. Selection and preselection could also be used for voice telephony, or other services, on mobile infrastructure.

Possible extension. The possibility of extending selection and preselection to **7.155** other services is left to the NRAs. Under the NRF, NRAs may impose selection and/or preselection-related obligations on undertakings with significant market power. A decision of that nature may only be taken, pursuant to the general regime introduced by the Access Directive, when the market is found not to be effectively competitive and NRAs consider that imposing these specific obligations is appropriate in the light of market conditions.[72]

> *Universal Service Directive, Article 19(2).* 'User requirements for these facilities to be implemented on other networks or in other ways shall be assessed in accordance with the market analysis procedure laid down in . . . [the] Framework Directive . . . and implemented in accordance with . . . [the] Access Directive.'

---

[68] That obligation is usual for tariffs charged by network operators to service providers. See Chapter 3 on access under sector-specific regulation.

[69] Accounting information may then be used to ascertain that service providers are not charged excessive prices by network providers.   [70] Universal Service Directive, Art 19(3).

[71] ibid, Art 19(3).

[72] The possibility exists, but obligations may only be imposed if it is necessary and if the other conditions for the imposition of obligations are satisfied (in particular, compliance with the basic regulatory principles).

(3) Integrity of the network

7.156 **Continuity of public voice telephony services.** Despite the development of other forms of service, public voice telephony remains essential in the European Union. In many instances, voice telephony remains the main application for connection between individuals across society. Given the importance of that service, a provision has been inserted in the NRF to ensure continuity. Under the Universal Service Directive, public voice telephony must at all times remain possible. Member States must take all measures necessary to ensure continuity as well as, as a result, the integrity of the network.

> *Universal Service Directive, Article 23.* 'Member States shall take all necessary steps to ensure the integrity of the public telephone network at fixed locations and, in the event of catastrophic network breakdown or in cases of *force majeure*, the availability of the public telephone network and publicly available telephone services at fixed locations.'

7.157 **Emergency services.** In a similar manner, access to emergency services must remain available at all times. To ensure permanent availability, obligations may be imposed by the Member States on the undertakings in charge of access to these services.

> *Universal Service Directive, Article 23.* 'Member States shall ensure that undertakings providing publicly available telephone services at fixed locations take all reasonable steps to ensure uninterrupted access to emergency services.'

(4) Operator assistance and enquiry services

7.158 **Operator assistance and enquiry services.** Another set of provisions specifically relating to public voice telephony relates to the universal service. Among these provisions, some deal with the provision of assistance and information to public voice telephony subscribers. Pursuant to these provisions, subscribers have a right to be mentioned in the directory. They also have a right to have access to operator assistance and directory enquiry services. These rights do not differ, in substance, from the general regime examined in connection with the universal service.

> *A mention in the directory.* 'Member States shall ensure that subscribers to publicly available telephone services have the right to have an entry in the publicly available directory referred to above.'[73] *Operator assistance and directory enquiry services.* 'Member States shall ensure that all end-users provided with a connection to the public telephone network can access operator assistance services and directory enquiry services.'[74]

7.159 **Obligations for undertakings.** A corollary of these obligations is that undertakings having information on subscribers must make that information available to companies providing enquiry services. *(a)* The conditions under which information

---

[73] Universal Service Directive, Art 25(1).   [74] ibid, Art 25(3).

must be provided are to be negotiated between the undertakings concerned. *(b)* They must be compatible with the basic regulatory principles. Among these principles, emphasis is placed on objectivity (cost orientation) and the absence of discrimination.[75] *(c)* The European rules concerning privacy must be complied with by all undertakings providing directory enquiry services, as well as by the companies supplying these undertakings with information concerning their subscribers.

> *Make information available.* 'Member States shall ensure that all undertakings which assign telephone numbers to subscribers meet all reasonable requests to make available, for the purposes of the provision of publicly available directory enquiry services and directories, the relevant information.'[76] *Terms and conditions.* The relevant information must be provided 'in an agreed format on terms which are fair, objective, cost oriented and non-discriminatory'.[77] *Protection of privacy.* The provisions 'apply subject to the requirements of Community legislation on the protection of personal data and privacy'.[78]

(5) Directory services in other Member States

Directory services in other Member States. In most Member States, access is **7.160** restricted, as regards directory enquiries, to services provided by national undertakings, even where information is sought about users located in other Member States. A British user, for instance, must consult a British operator to obtain information about users located in other Member States. It is not possible, in general, for users to consult directly by telephone the enquiry services located in the other Member States.

Removal of regulatory restrictions. A first step is made, in the NRF, towards **7.161** making foreign enquiry services available to national users. Under the regulatory framework, regulatory restrictions prohibiting general access to enquiry services throughout the Union, or making that access more difficult, must be set aside. This does not mean that an obligation is imposed on undertakings providing these services to make these services available across the Community. No obligation is imposed in the NRF on undertakings, whatever their power on the market, to provide such access. Nor does it imply that access to enquiry services in other Member States will be made possible, in practice, by the undertakings involved. A decision has to be made by the undertakings themselves, which must consider whether providing such a service is of commercial interest to them.

> *Universal Service Directive, Article 25(4).* 'Member States shall not maintain any regulatory restrictions which prevent end-users in one Member State from accessing directly the directory enquiry service in another Member State.'

---

[75] To these principles, the NRF adds that prices must be reasonable. The purpose is to ensure the development of enquiry services, which are often a condition for an efficient use of the electronic communications applications concerned. [76] See Universal Service Directive, Art 25(2).
[77] See ibid, Art 25(2). [78] ibid, Art 25(5).

(6) *Non-geographic numbers*

7.162 Non-geographic numbers.   Another limitation generally imposed on public voice telephony is that users cannot call non-geographic numbers assigned by operators in other Member States. Non-geographic numbers are numbers which are not preceded by a prefix corresponding to a given region in a Member State. Typical non-geographic numbers are 'freephone' numbers, ie numbers where information can be obtained about a given product or service offered by an under-taking. These numbers may be called free of charge, the costs relating to the calls being borne by the undertaking in question. Other examples are 'premium rate' numbers, where callers not only pay for the calls but also for the provision of a service. These numbers are often used for after sales services, or to obtain infor-mation about bills sent by undertakings.

> *Universal Service Directive, Article 2, subpara 2, letter f.* ' "[N]on-geographic num-bers" means a number from the national numbering plan that is not a geographic number. It includes *inter alia* mobile, freephone and premium rate numbers.'

7.163 Access to foreign numbers.   Under the NRF, the Member States must make it possible for users to access non-geographic numbers in other Member States. As a result of these measures, the Community users must be given access to 'freephone' numbers, as well as 'premium rate' numbers, assigned by operators across the European Union.[79]

> *Universal Service Directive, Article 28.* 'Member States shall ensure that end-users from other Member States are able to access non-geographic numbers within their territory where technically and economically feasible.'[80]

(7) *Single European emergency call number*

7.164 A European number.   The importance of public voice telephony is due, among other reasons, to the role which can be played by that service in contacting emer-gency services. Emphasis is placed in the NRF on the possibility for each user to call the emergency services easily, wherever that user may be located. Under the regulatory framework, a single European emergency call number—112—must be ensured. Access to that number must be free of charge, independent of the ter-minal used (public or private) or the public network involved in the transmission of the call (fixed or mobile infrastructure).

> *Universal Service Directive, Article 26(1).* 'Member States shall ensure that, in addition to any other national emergency call numbers specified by the national regulatory

---

[79] No indication is provided about the charges subject to which access to these numbers must be provided. In conformity with the principles contained in the NRF, the charges are normally fixed by the undertakings providing the service. The rules concerning tariff regulation for these services are not different from the general rules examined in the chapter dealing with universal service.

[80] A subscriber to a non-geographic number may limit access to that number, for users located in designated regions. See Universal Service Directive, Art 28.

authorities, all end-users of publicly available telephone services, including users of public pay telephones, are able to call the emergency services free of charge, by using the single European emergency call number "112".'

Other obligations.   Other obligations are imposed in connection with the   **7.165** single emergency call number. *(a)* Users must be informed about the existence of the European number. In the absence of correct information, it is doubtful that the number will ever be used in a satisfactory manner. *(b)* The Member States must organise their services to ensure that emergency calls are addressed satisfactorily. Creating an emergency number is of no use if emergency calls are not answered appropriately.[81] *(c)* Emergency services must be in a position to identify callers. In some instances, callers are not in a position to give adequate information about their location. In these situations, emergency services cannot be provided if undertakings do not receive adequate caller location information from the operators concerned.

> *Inform users.* 'Member States shall ensure that citizens are adequately informed about the existence and use of the single European emergency call number "112".'[82] *Adequate emergency services.* 'Member States shall ensure that calls to the single European emergency call number "112" are appropriately answered and handled in a manner best suited to the national organisation of emergency systems and within the technological possibilities of the networks.'[83] *Caller location information.* 'Member States shall ensure that undertakings which operate public telephone networks make caller location information available to authorities handling emergencies, to the extent technically feasible, for all calls to the single European emergency call number "112".'[84]

(8) International calls

Access code.   The NRF confirms that telephone calls placed across national   **7.166** borders must be preceded by the prefix '00'. That prefix must be used in all Member States as the standard international access code. The general use of that access code may not impede special arrangements made to facilitate communications between adjacent regions located in different Member States. Such arrangements may be made, or continued. Where such arrangements are made, the users concerned must be informed.

> *Universal Service Directive, Article 27(1).* 'Member States shall ensure that the "00" code is the standard international access code. Special arrangements for making calls between adjacent locations across borders between Member States may be established or continued. The end-users of publicly available telephone services in the locations concerned shall be fully informed of such arrangements.'

---

[81] On that subject, the obligations however remain limited, at European level, for reasons relating to competence. The European legislator has no competence to organise emergency services across the European Union. It remains dependent upon the goodwill of the Member States, regarding the quality of the emergency services which are provided in the national territories.
[82] Universal Service Directive, Art 26(4).   [83] ibid, Art 26(2).   [84] ibid, Art 26(3).

7.167 Call conveyance.   Telephone calls are generally provided by different undertakings in the various Member States. To reach users in other Member States, the calls are conveyed through lines, or networks, operated by different companies. Under the NRF, an obligation is placed on undertakings providing public telephone networks to convey calls in the European numbering space. Conveyance is a service which requires payment. No provision has been inserted in the regulatory framework on that subject, except a general clause specifying that undertakings carrying out conveyance have a right to charge a fee for the performance of the service.[85]

> *Universal Service Directive, Article 27(2).* 'Member States shall ensure that all undertakings that operate public telephone networks handle all calls to the European telephony numbering space, without prejudice to the need for an undertaking that operates a public telephone network to recover the cost of the conveyance of calls on its network.'

G. Specific Provisions Regarding Broadcasting

(1) Broadcasting in a converging environment

7.168 Convergence.   The NRF is based on the idea that telecommunications, broadcasting and information-based services are converging to form a broader sector—the sector of electronic communications. For that reason, it has been decided that, in the absence of exceptional circumstances, all services belonging to these three formerly distinct fields would be subject to the same regime under the NRF. The approach adopted in the framework is that all transmissions are treated alike, irrespective of the regulatory regime to which they were previously subject. By contrast, the content which is provided through electronic transmissions remains outside the scope covered by the NRF.

7.169 Specific provisions.   Convergence does not take away all characteristics of the fields which were formerly separated and are now converging. To address these characteristics, specific provisions have been included in the NRF. For instance, several provisions deal with issues associated with (radio and/or television) broadcasting. Four provisions, or groups of provisions, are concerned. They concern respectively the interoperability of consumer digital television equipment; the interoperability of digital interactive television services; conditional access systems and other facilities involved in broadcasting activities; as well as the possibility for Member States to introduce 'must carry' obligations.

(2) Consumer digital television equipment

7.170 Consumer digital television equipment.   It has been stated that the NRF does not address legal or technical issues relating to equipment. This is so, in general,

---

[85] That fee must be compatible with the general obligations introduced by the NRF. These obligations mainly concern, as regards access to facilities, undertakings with significant market power.

for equipment used in connection with telecommunications or information-based services. There is an exception for digital television equipment meant for consumers. Under the NRF, the Member States must ensure interoperability as regards that type of equipment. Interoperability is an objective, at least, for equipment meant for consumers, ie final subscribers acting in a private capacity.[86] The purpose is to facilitate the use, by consumers, of equipment manufactured by different, and possibly competing, undertakings.

> *Universal Service Directive, Article 24.* 'Member States shall ensure the interoperability of the consumer digital television equipment.'

Unscrambling equipment. One financial technique used for the development **7.171** of digital television is the limitation of TV signals to persons or entities which pay a subscription to that effect. With such a system, the signals are not available to people who do not purchase the programmes concerned. Technically, the system is made feasible by the use of equipment to scramble TV signals. Unscrambling equipment is then sold, or rented, to the subscribers, which have access to programmes via that equipment. An important aspect of European policy is to ensure that common standards are used to manufacture unscrambling equipment. To that effect, the NRF imposes the use of a given, common, algorithm for TV signal unscrambling. Here again, the purpose is to ensure interoperability. Equipment must be polyvalent, so that it can be used to unscramble programmes broadcast by a variety of undertakings.[87]

> *Universal Service Directive, Annex VI, point (1).* 'All consumer equipment intended for the reception of digital television signals, for sale or rent or otherwise made available in the Community, capable of descrambling digital television signals, is to possess the capability to . . . allow the descrambling of such signals according to the common European scrambling algorithm as administered by a recognised European standards organisation, currently ETSI.'

Analogue and digital television sets. The NRF further contains rules aiming at **7.172** ensuring interoperability between television sets. The purpose is to ensure that analogue and digital television sets may be used with a variety of electronic devices already placed on the markets or to be developed in the years ahead. *(a)* Analogue television sets must be designed to allow simple connection of peripherals, especially additional decoders and digital receivers. To that effect, they must be equipped with at least one open interface socket along standards established by European standards organisations. *(b)* Similarly, digital television sets must be equipped with

---

[86] As opposed to intermediaries, or to final users acting in the course of their professional activities.

[87] Another aspect is that the descrambling equipment must make it possible to display messages that have been transmitted in clear. The purpose is to ensure that such equipment is polyvalent and may, as a result, be used for a variety of purposes not limited to descrambling. See Universal Service Directive, Annex VI, point (1). Equipment should 'possess the capability to . . . display signals that have been transmitted in clear provided that, in the event that such equipment is rented, the rentee is in compliance with the relevant rental agreement'.

an open interface socket permitting simple connection of peripherals. The socket must also allow all the elements of a digital television signal, including information relating to interactive and conditionally accessed services, to pass.[88]

(3) Digital interactive television services and equipment

7.173 **Emphasis on interactivity.**   A special emphasis is placed on interoperability, for interactive television services and equipment. Only digital television is concerned at this stage, as the analogue technology does not allow, in principle, in the current stage of research and development, substantial interactivity.

7.174 **Equipment.**   Under the NRF, equipment used for interactive digital television must be open. The idea is that consumers must be able to use that equipment with all forms of tools and devices designed by the undertakings active on the markets concerned. To that effect, the manufacturers of that equipment must use open application programme interfaces (API).

> *Framework Directive, Article 18(1), letter (b).* 'In order to promote the free flow of information, media pluralism and cultural diversity, Member States shall encourage . . . providers of all enhanced digital television equipment deployed for the reception of digital interactive television services on interactive digital television platforms to comply with an open API in accordance with the minimum requirements of the relevant standards or specifications.'

7.175 **Services.**   A similar obligation must be imposed by the Member States on providers of digital interactive television services. These providers are to be obliged, under the NRF, to use open application programme interfaces.

> *Framework Directive, Article 18(1), letter (a).* 'In order to promote the free flow of information, media pluralism and cultural diversity, Member States shall encourage . . . providers of digital interactive television services for distribution to the public in the Community on digital interactive television platforms, regardless of the transmission mode, to use an open API.'

7.176 **Provision of information.**   A supplementary obligation is imposed on undertakings holding intellectual property rights regarding these application programme

---

[88] (a) For analogue television, see Universal Service Directive, Annex VI, point (2), subpara 1. 'Any analogue television set with an integral screen of visible diagonal greater than 42 cm which is put on the market for sale or rent in the Community is to be fitted with at least one open interface socket, as standardised by a recognised European standards organisation, eg as given in the CENELEC EN 50 049–1:1997 standard, permitting simple connection of peripherals, especially additional decoders and digital receivers.' (b) For digital television, see Universal Service Directive, Annex VI, point (2), subpara 2. 'Any digital television set with an integral screen of visible diagonal greater than 30 cm which is put on the market for sale or rent in the Community is to be fitted with at least one open interface socket (either standardised by, or conforming to a standard adopted by, a recognised European standards organisation, or conforming to an industry-wide specification) eg the DVB common interface connector, permitting simple connection of peripherals, and able to pass all the elements of a digital television signal, including information relating to interactive and conditionally accessed services.'

interfaces. These interfaces are considered resources necessary for the provisions of services on the markets concerned (digital interactive television services). Under the NRF, access must be provided to facilities of that nature. Under the Framework Directive, proprietors must make available all API-related information necessary for service providers to use these interfaces in an optimal manner. The conditions for the communication of that information must be fair, reasonable and non-discriminatory.

> *Framework Directive, Article 18(2).* 'Member States shall encourage proprietors of APIs to make available on fair, reasonable and non-discriminatory terms, and against appropriate remuneration, all such information as is necessary to enable providers of digital interactive television services to provide all services supported by the API in a fully functional form.'

Future action.   The way is paved for future action by the Commission if the **7.177** objectives discussed in the above paragraphs are not achieved. Under the NRF, the situation must be reviewed in the course of July 2004. If the objectives have not been reached by then, harmonisation measures may be adopted by the Commission.

> *Framework Directive, Article 18(3).* 'Within one year . . . the Commission shall examine the effects of this Article. If interoperability and freedom of choice for users have not been adequately achieved in one or more Member States, the Commission may take action in accordance with the [special standardisation] procedure.'[89]

(4) Conditional access systems and other facilities

The facilities concerned

Digital services.   This section concerns conditional access systems and like facili-   **7.178** ties. The provisions dealing with these systems and facilities in the NRF concern radio and broadcasting digital services. Unlike in previous paragraphs, the emphasis is thus not placed on equipment. All sorts of services are concerned, as long as they are based on digital technology and imply the transmission of a radio or television programme.

Access to certain resources.   The key principle underlying the Access Directive   **7.179** is that access should be provided to all facilities which are essential for the provision of services. Among these facilities are the conditional access systems. The provisions concerning these systems have already been analysed in Chapter 3 dealing with access under sector-specific regulation. The analysis is not repeated here in full. The presentation is limited, in this section, to some important aspects.

Definition.   Under the NRF, conditional access systems are established on infra-   **7.180** structure to ensure that access to given services (usually radio and/or television programmes) is limited to authorised persons. In that system, people are authorised where they have made a payment (subscription, etc).

---

[89] That procedure is laid down in Art 17(3) and (4) of the Framework Directive.

> *Framework Directive, Article 2, letter (f).* ' "[C]onditional access system" means any technical measure and/or arrangement whereby access to a protected radio or television broadcasting service in intelligible form is made conditional upon subscription or other form of prior individual authorisation.'

7.181 **Content of these systems.** The conditional access is composed of two elements. *(a)* A first element is a hardware box (decoder) serving as an intermediary between a radio or television set, on which the programmes and the network through which the programmes are transmitted are displayed. *(b)* That box itself contains software, which permits the reception of the programmes by organising their translation into signals understood by the radio or television set. In the conditional access systems, the signals must be unscrambled because they have been coded in order to limit transmission to authorised persons.

> *Framework Directive, Article 2, letters (o) and (p).* ' "[E]nhanced digital television equipment" means set-top boxes intended for connection to television sets or integrated digital television sets, able to receive digital interactive television services.' ' "[A]pplication program interface (API)" means the software interfaces between applications, made available by broadcasters or service providers, and the resources in the enhanced digital television equipment for digital television and radio services.'

Obligations to be imposed

7.182 **Open the conditional access systems to all broadcasters.** The first obligation imposed by the NRF is that the conditional access systems must be open to all broadcasters. *(a)* There is no indication that the obligation is limited to undertakings holding significant market power. The consequence is that openness applies to all undertakings providing conditional access services, whatever their position on the market. *(b)* No limitation is imposed either in terms of a minimum number of viewers and/or listeners which should be interested in receiving the broadcasting services concerned. The obligation thus applies whatever the size of the market. *(c)* As regards the conditions, access must be fair, reasonable and non-discriminatory.

> *Access Directive, Article 6 and Annex I, first part.* '[A]ll operators of conditional access services, irrespective of the means of transmission, who provide access services to digital television and radio services and whose access services broadcasters depend on to reach any group of potential viewers or listeners are to . . . offer to all broadcasters, on a fair, reasonable and non-discriminatory basis compatible with Community competition law, technical services enabling the broadcasters' digitally-transmitted services to be received by viewers or listeners authorised by means of decoders administered by the service operators, and comply with Community competition law.'

7.183 **Accounting obligation.** Another obligation is that undertakings providing conditional access services must ensure transparency in their accounts. This is important to monitor the financial transfers which may occur, within these undertakings, from the divisions in charge of these systems to the divisions entrusted with other activities. To avoid transfers, separate accounts are imposed to identify the costs and revenues concerning the conditional access services. The idea is that, as they control a facility which is necessary to organise the reception of radio and/or television programmes, the undertakings providing these conditional access services may charge relatively high tariffs on that market. They may be tempted to channel the revenues from these activities to other markets where their position is less comfortable due to a higher degree of competition. Such a transfer of revenues would distort competition on the latter markets.

> *Access Directive, Annex I, first part.* '[A]ll operators of conditional access services, irrespective of the means of transmission, who provide access services to digital television and radio services and whose access services broadcasters depend on to reach any group of potential viewers or listeners are to: . . . keep separate financial accounts regarding their activity as conditional access providers.'

Open interface.   Under the NRF, the Member States must ensure that the   **7.184** conditional access systems used on their national territory are open. This means that these systems must be equipped with a common interface, allowing a connection with other systems of that nature. The undertakings holding the intellectual property rights on the conditional access systems and leasing these rights through licences may not make the granting of these licences dependant on any condition capable of limiting interconnection between the conditional access systems.

> *Access Directive, Annex I, first part.* 'Taking into account technical and commercial factors, holders of rights are not to subject the granting of licences to conditions prohibiting, deterring or discouraging the inclusion in the same product of: *[a]* a common interface allowing connection with several other access systems, or *[b]* means specific to another access system, provided that the licensee complies with the relevant and reasonable conditions ensuring, as far as he is concerned, the security of transactions of conditional access system operators.'

Limitations.   As appears from the extract presented in the previous paragraph,   **7.185** the obligation to open interfaces must be nuanced. *(a)* A first observation is that undertakings holding intellectual property rights on the systems may find it difficult, or even impossible, for technical or commercial reasons, to satisfy the obligation. These circumstances must be taken into account in order to determine whether the obligation must still be complied with in spite of these difficulties.[90] *(b)* A second, more obvious, observation is that interoperability among conditional access systems may in certain circumstances be undermined by the behaviour adopted by the users themselves. To assess whether interoperability is real, or not, one must refer to the use which would be made by a user complying with

---

[90] There is no detail about the assessment which would have to be made by the authorities in such a situation. A reasonable assumption would be that the assessment should be carried out in the forms required for the evaluation of objective justifications. For an analysis of these forms, see Chapter 4 dealing with access under general competition law.

the instructions provided by the manufacturer, in particular the instructions concerning security.

7.186 **Intellectual property rights.** As was stated above, the European legislator seeks the development of services provided through conditional access systems. A difficulty is that these systems require, for their design, substantial intellectual, and thus financial, investment. In these circumstances, it is important to ensure that the technology used in these systems is used across society in the European Union. A good method to stimulate the availability of that technology is to organise the legal regime so that the conditions under which licences may be acquired are fair, reasonable and non-discriminatory.

> *Access Directive, Annex I, first part.* '[W]hen granting licences to manufacturers of consumer equipment, holders of industrial property rights to conditional access products and systems are to ensure that this is done on fair, reasonable and non-discriminatory terms.'

7.187 **Cost-effective transcontrol.** A final obligation is that conditional access systems must be designed to monitor easily how networks function. That obligation is a technical one. The goal is to ensure that delivery of radio and television signals occurs smoothly and may be promptly repaired in case of difficulty.

> *Access Directive, Annex I, first part.* '[C]onditional access systems operated on the market in the Community are to have the necessary technical capability for cost-effective transcontrol allowing the possibility for full control by network operators at local or regional level of the services using such conditional access systems.'

Removal of obligations

7.188 **Conditions.** If, and where, they consider that markets are effectively competitive, NRAs may remove the obligations analysed in the paragraphs above. The procedure is no different from that which is applicable for the removal of other obligations regarding access to infrastructure. To organise such a removal, a first condition is that the relevant market(s) must be found to be effectively competitive. The degree of existing competition must therefore be analysed. The removal is possible if, and to the extent that, no undertaking holds significant power on the relevant market. Pursuant to the NRF, the analysis must be carried out regularly. It had to be performed, for the first time, shortly after the entry into force of the NRF.

> *Access Directive, Article 6(3), subparas 1 and 2.* 'Member States may permit their national regulatory authority, as soon as possible after the entry into force of this Directive and periodically thereafter, to review the conditions applied in accordance with this Article, by undertaking a market analysis in accordance with the . . . Framework Directive . . . to determine whether to maintain, amend or withdraw the conditions applied.' 'Where, as a result of this market analysis, a national regulatory authority finds that one or more operators do not have significant market power on the relevant market, it may amend or withdraw the conditions with respect to

those operators, in accordance with the procedures referred to in . . . [the] Framework Directive.'

Objectives to be reached.   A second condition is that the removal of obligations   **7.189** may not jeopardise objectives deemed essential for digital activities under the NRF. NRAs are not allowed to remove obligations if, in their absence, there is a possibility that these objectives may no longer be reached. *(a)* Thus, obligations can be removed only where there are prospects for effective competition on the markets concerned: retail radio and television broadcasting services, conditional access systems, associated facilities. *(b)* Furthermore, users must retain access to the programmes which they want to hear or see. The removal of obligations may not endanger or limit that access.

> *Access Directive, Article 6(3), subpara 2.* '[A] national regulatory authority . . . may amend or withdraw the conditions with respect to those operators . . . only to the extent that . . . the prospects for effective competition in the markets for: (i) retail digital television and radio broadcasting services, and (ii) conditional access systems and other associated facilities would not be adversely affected by such amendment or withdrawal.' *Access Directive, Article 6(3), subpara 2.* '[A] national regulatory authority . . . may amend or withdraw the conditions with respect to those operators . . . only to the extent that . . . accessibility for end-users to [specified] radio and television broadcasts and broadcasting channels and services . . . would not be adversely affected by such amendment or withdrawal.'

Differences with access-related obligations

Access.   Obligations concerning conditional access systems (obligations to provide   **7.190** access under fair, reasonable and non-discriminatory conditions) are similar in substance to obligations which may be imposed under the Access Directive for access to resources or facilities deemed essential for the provision of services. Two differences should however be noticed. *(a)* In general, obligations under the Access Directive concern markets which are not effectively competitive. They are imposed on undertakings holding significant market power. In the context of conditional access, obligations must be imposed on all undertakings providing conditional access services irrespective of their position on the market. Obligations thus have a scope of application which is larger than that envisaged under the Access Directive. *(b)* A second difference is that, under the Access Directive, NRAs must remove access-related obligations as soon as it appears that the market concerned may be considered effectively competitive and that no undertaking holds, as a result, significant market power. In contrast, the provisions concerning conditional access provide only that NRAs may remove obligations where these conditions are fulfilled.

Case law

Obligation to register.   The ECJ has issued a ruling concerning national legisla-   **7.191** tion (Spain) compelling conditional-access services to register before they could perform their activities in the country concerned (Spain) (*Canal Satélite Digital*).[91] In that ruling, the ECJ states that such a national provision constitutes a restriction on the free provision of services. Simultaneously, the ECJ considers that the national provision also restricted the free movement of goods as, in addition to registering themselves, the undertaking concerned had to indicate in the register what products it intended to commercialise.

> *Canal Satélite Digital.* 'The requirement imposed on an undertaking wishing to market apparatus, equipment, decoders or digital transmission and reception systems for television signals by satellite to register as an operator of conditional-access services and to state in that register the products which it proposes to market restricts the free movement of goods and the freedom to provide services guaranteed by Articles 30 and 59 of the Treaty respectively.'

7.192 **Justification.** The restriction can however be justified under the relevant EC provisions, if several conditions are fulfilled. *(a)* The regime of prior registration, or a prior authorisation, must be founded on objective and non-discriminatory criteria which are known in advance. *(b)* That regime may not be combined with similar national provisions in existence in the country where the service provider is established. In other words, the Member States may not duplicate a control which already exists in the country of origin. The formalities which have already been accomplished in the country of origin may not be repeated in the State of destination. *(c)* The regime may imply prior authorisation or registration only where it would not be possible to put in place ex post controls. *(d)* The effect on the undertakings concerned may not be excessive. That condition is not fulfilled where the undertakings are discouraged, as a result of the application of the regime, from entering the market concerned.

> *Canal Satélite Digital.*[92] [a] '[A] prior administrative authorisation scheme . . . must be based on objective, non-discriminatory criteria which are known in advance to the undertakings concerned, in such a way as to circumscribe the exercise of the national authorities' discretion, so that it is not used arbitrarily.' [b] '[A] measure introduced by a Member State cannot be regarded as necessary to achieve the aim pursued if it essentially duplicates controls which have already been carried out in the context of other procedures, either in the same State or in another Member State.'[93]

---

[91] Case C-390/99 *Canal Satélite Digital SL v Adminstración General del Estado, and Distribuidora de Televisión Digital SA (DTS)* [2002] ECR I-607.

[92] The extracts are taken from [35]–[42] of the ruling.

[93] Regarding the free movement of products: a product which is lawfully marketed in one Member State must in principle be able to be marketed in any other Member State without being subject to additional controls (see, among others, Case 120/78 *Rewe-Zentral AG v Bundesmonopolverwaltung fur Branntwein* ('Cassis de Dijon') [1979] ECR 649 at [14], and Case C-123/00 *Bellamy and English Shop Wholesale* [2001] ECR I-2795 at [18]. Regarding the free provision of services: it is incompatible in principle with the freedom to provide services to make a provider subject to restrictions for safeguarding the public interest where that interest is already safeguarded by the rules to which the provider is subject in the Member State where he is established (see, in particular, Case 279/80 *Criminal Proceedings Against Webb* [1981] ECR 3305 at [17].

[c] '[A] prior authorisation procedure will be necessary only where a subsequent control is to be regarded as being too late to be genuinely effective and to enable it to achieve the aim pursued.' [d] '[I]t should be noted that, for as long as it lasts, a prior authorisation procedure completely prevents traders from marketing the products and services concerned. It follows that, in order to comply with the fundamental principles of the free movement of goods and the freedom to provide services, such a procedure must not, on account of its duration, the amount of costs to which it gives rise, or any ambiguity as to the conditions to be fulfilled, be such as to deter the operators concerned from pursuing their business plan.'[94]

Products and services.   In the case at issue, the ECJ announced that cases relat-   **7.193**
ing to telecommunications, or electronic communications, will be analysed under EC provisions relating to products as much as EC provisions relating to services. That option is justified by the difficulty, or even the impossibility, for the ECJ to separate, in many instances, the services from the products that are envisaged.

> *Canal Satélite Digital.* 'In the field of telecommunications, . . . it is difficult to determine generally whether it is free movement of goods or freedom to provide services which should take priority.' '[T]he two aspects are often intimately linked.' 'The supply of telecommunication equipment is sometimes more important than the installation or other services connected therewith. In other circumstances, by contrast, it is the economic activities of providing know-how or other services of the operators concerned which are dominant, whilst delivery of the apparatus, equipment or conditional-access telecommunication systems which they supply or market is only accessory.' 'Accordingly, the question . . . must be examined simultaneously in the light of both Article 30 and Article 59 of the Treaty.'[95]

(5) Must carry obligations

Diversity and pluralism.   An objective pursued by the European legislator   **7.194**
regarding broadcasting is that all users, or the great majority of them, should have access to an array of radio and television programmes. This objective relates to media pluralism and cultural diversity, which stand as fundamental values in the Member States across the European Union.

Access-related obligations.   In some instances, this objective may be endan-   **7.195**
gered by the limitations of the infrastructure that may be used to channel radio and television programmes. The Access Directive introduces a series of tools to ensure that users have access to service providers, and services providers to users, when one or several undertakings have significant power on a market for transmission. These tools are provided for all electronic communications services. They thus have a general character and may be used regarding all forms of transmission,

---

[94] The regime must neither delay nor complicate exercise of the right of the undertaking to market products and services. The requirements of entry on a register and the obtaining of certification, assuming they are justified, must not give rise to disproportionate administrative expenses (Case C-58/98 *Corsten Josef* [2000] ECR I-7919 at [47] and [48]).   [95] At [32] and [33].

including those which concern radio or television broadcasting. These obligations are not analysed again here, and readers may consult Chapter 3 on access in order to find more detail.

7.196 **Additional obligation.** To reinforce pluralism and diversity, the NRF introduces an additional tool which is applicable only for the transmission of radio and television programmes. That tool covers situations where a significant number of users resort to a given infrastructure to receive programmes, even if the undertakings controlling that infrastructure do not have significant market power. The directive thus allows the Member States to impose specific obligations in situations where the undertakings concerned do not have market power bringing about the application of the general provisions concerning access.

7.197 **Must carry.** That additional tool is called the 'must carry' obligation. Under the NRF, Member States may impose 'must carry' obligations on undertakings controlling infrastructure used to convey radio and television programmes to a significant number of users. These obligations imply that the undertakings concerned are required to convey these programmes.

> *Universal Service Directive, Article 31(1).* 'Member States may impose reasonable "must carry" obligations, for the transmission of specified radio and television broadcast channels and services, on undertakings under their jurisdiction providing electronic communications networks used for the distribution of radio or television broadcasts to the public where a significant number of end-users of such networks use them as their principal means to receive radio and television broadcasts.'

7.198 **Limitations.** As an obligation with potentially far-reaching consequences is imposed on undertakings, the NRF introduces limitations. These limitations are meant to ensure that the freedom of the undertakings transmitting the programmes is not affected to an excessive extent. *(a)* A first limitation is that 'must carry' obligations may be imposed only in relation to specified services. NRAs may not impose a general obligation to transmit all programmes at the request of all content producers. The specification must be made by the NRA concerned. *(b)* A 'significant' numbers of end users must be concerned. These users must resort to the network concerned as their 'principal' medium to receive the programmes.[96] *(c)* The obligations imposed by the NRAs must conform to the basic regulatory principles. They must, as a result, be objective, proportionate

---

[96] It is unclear how to interpret the requirement that a significant number of users must be concerned. The term used ('significant') is similar to that used in order to designate the undertakings on which obligations may be imposed under the Access Directive ('significant market power'). There is no indication, however, that the term must receive, in both contexts, the same interpretation. It can indeed be argued that they should be interpreted differently. If the interpretation was the same, it would mean that the provisions concerning 'must carry' obligations may only be used in respect of network operators with significant market power, that power being established by taking into account the proportion of users concerned (instead of, for instance, the turnover realised by the undertakings concerned).

and transparent. As for other obligations relating to access, they must be reviewed periodically. *(d)* Access to infrastructure or other facilities generally must be negotiated by the parties concerned. Public intervention is warranted only where these parties cannot agree on conditions. This corresponds to the general scenario which is envisaged under the NRF for all issues regarding access. The basic regulatory principles apply to the conditions established by the NRAs, where the parties cannot agree. For instance, payment has to be made to the operator in consideration of the transmission. That payment must be proportionate, transparent and free of all discrimination.

Universal Service Directive, Article 31(1) and (2). 'Must carry obligations shall only be imposed where they are necessary to meet clearly defined general interest objectives and shall be proportionate and transparent. The obligations shall be subject to periodical review.' The NRF does not 'prejudice the ability of Member States to determine appropriate remuneration, if any, in respect of measures taken in accordance with this Article while ensuring that, in similar circumstances, there is no discrimination in the treatment of undertakings providing electronic communications networks'. 'Where remuneration is provided for, Member States shall ensure that it is applied in a proportionate and transparent manner.'

APPENDIX A

List of Instruments

1. NEW REGULATORY FRAMEWORK—EUROPEAN PARLIAMENT AND COUNCIL DIRECTIVES

European Parliament and Council Directive (EC) 2002/21 on a common regulatory framework for electronic communications networks and services (Framework Directive) [2002] OJ L108/33

European Parliament and Council Directive (EC) 2002/20 on the authorisation of electronic communications networks and services (Authorisations Directive) [2002] OJ L108/21

European Parliament and Council Directive (EC) 2002/19 on access to, and interconnection of, electronic communications networks and associated facilities (Access Directive) [2002] OJ L108/7

European Parliament and Council Directive (EC) 2002/22 on universal service and user's rights relating to electronic communications networks and services (Universal Service Directive) [2002] OJ L108/51

European Parliament and Council Directive (EC) 2002/58 concerning the processing of personal data and the protection of privacy in the electronic communications sector (Directive on privacy and electronic communications) [2002] OJ L201/37

2. SUPPLEMENTARY INSTRUMENTS

Commission Recommendation C(2003)497 on relevant product and service markets within the electronic communications sector susceptible to ex ante regulation in accordance with Directive 2002/21/EC of the European Parliament and of the Council on a common regulatory framework for electronic communication networks and services [2003] OJ L114/45

Commission Guidelines 2002/C165/03 on market analysis and the assessment of significant market power under the Community regulatory framework for electronic communications networks and services [2002] OJ C165/3

Commission Recommendation (EC) 98/195 on interconnection in a liberalised telecommunications market (Part 1—Interconnection pricing) [1998] OJ L73/42[1]

Commission Recommendation (EC) 98/322 on interconnection in a liberalised telecommunications market (Part 2—Accounting separation and cost accounting) [1998] OJ L141/6

Commission Recommendation (EC) C(2002)561 amending Recommendation 98/195/EC, as last amended by Recommendation 2000/263/EC, on Interconnection in a liberalised telecommunications market (Part 1—Interconnection Pricing) [2002] OJ L58/56

Commission Recommendation C(2003)2647 final of 23 July 2003 on notifications, time limits and consultations provided for in Article 7 of Directive 2002/21/EC of the European Parliament and of the Council of 7 March 2002 on a common regulatory framework for electronic communications networks and services

List of standards and/or specifications for electronic communications networks, services and associated facilities and services in accordance with Article 17 of Directive 2002/21/EC of the European Parliament and of the Council on a common regulatory framework for electronic communication networks and services [2003] OJ C331/32

Commission Recommendation (EC) C(2003)2657 on the processing of caller location information in electronic communication networks for the purpose of location-enhanced emergency call services [2003] OJ L189/49

Commission Decision (EC) 2002/62 establishing the European Regulators Group for Electronic Communications Networks and Services [2002] OJ L200/38

3. RADIO SPECTRUM POLICY

European Parliament and Council Decision (EC) 676/2002 on a regulatory framework for radio spectrum policy in the European Community (Radio Spectrum Decision) [2002] OJ L108/1

Commission Decision (EC) 2002/622 establishing a Radio Spectrum Policy Group [2002] OJ L198/49

Commission Recommendation (EC) 2003/203 on the harmonisation of the provision of public R-LAN access to public electronic communications networks and services in the Community [2003] OJ C203/12

Commission Communication, Towards the Full Roll-Out of Third Generation Mobile Communications, June 2002

Green Paper on radio spectrum policy in the context of European Community policies such as telecommunications, broadcasting, transport and research and development (R & D), Brussels, 9 December 1998, COM 1998 (596 final)

'Next steps in Radio Spectrum Policy—Results of the Public Consultation on the Green Paper', Communication from the Commission to the European Parliament, the Council, the Economic and Social Committee and the Committee of the Regions, Brussels 10 November 1999, COM(1999)538

---

[1] This Recommendation has been amended several times—the last time through Commission Recommendation C(2002)561 available on the internet site of the Commission—DG Information Society.

4. INSTRUMENTS ADOPTED BY THE EUROPEAN COMMISSION

Commission Directive 88/301 of 16 May 1988 on competition in the markets in telecommunications terminal equipment [1988] OJ L131/73

Commission Directive (EC) 2002/77 on competition in the markets for electronic communications networks and services [2002] OJ L249/21

Commission Guidelines (EC) 91/C233/02 on the application of EEC competition rules in the telecommunications sector [1991] OJC 233/2

Commission Notice 98/C265/02 on the application of the competition rules to access agreements in the telecommunications sector [1998] OJ C265/2

Commission Communication (EC) 96/C281/03 on services of general interest in Europe [1996] OJ C281/3

Commission Communication (EC) 2001/C17/04 on services of general interest in Europe [2001] OJ C17/4

Commission Communication on Assessment Criteria for National Schemes for the Costing and Financing of Universal Service in Telecommunications and Guidelines for the Member States on Operation of such Schemes COM(96) 608 [1996]

Commission Report to the Laeken European Council, on services of general interest COM (2001) 598 final, Brussels, 17 October 2001

Commission Green paper on services of general interest COM(2003)270 final, 21 May 2003

Commission Notice on the definition of relevant market for the purposes of Community competition law [1997] OJ C372/5

Commission Communication concerning the review under competition rules of the joint provision of telecommunications and cable TV networks by a single operator and the abolition of restrictions on the provision of cable TV capacity over telecommunications networks [1998] OJ C71/4

Commission Recommendation (EC) 2000/417 on unbundled access to the local loop: enabling the competitive provision of a full-range of electronic communications services including broadband multimedia and high-speed Internet [2000] OJ L156/44

5. IMPLEMENTATION REPORTS

Communication from the Commission to the Council, the European Parliament, the Economic and Social Committee and the Committee of the Regions, Fifth Report from the Commission on the Implementation of the Telecommunications Regulatory Package, 11 November 1999, COM(1999)537

Communication from the Commission to the Council, the European Parliament, the Economic and Social Committee and the Committee of the Regions, Sixth Report from the Commission on the Implementation of the Telecommunications Regulatory Package, 7 December 2000, COM(2000)814

Communication from the Commission to the Council, the European Parliament, the Economic and Social Committee and the Committee of the Regions, Seventh Report from the Commission on the Implementation of the Telecommunications Regulatory Package, 26 November 2001, COM(2001)706

Eighth Report from the Commission on the Implementation of the Telecommunications Regulatory Package, 3 December 2002, COM(2002)695 final

European Electronic Communications Regulation and Markets 2003: Report on the Implementation of the EU Electronic Communications Regulatory Package (Ninth Report), 19 November 2003, COM (2003) 715 final

6. BACKGROUND INSTRUMENTS

Council Directive (EEC) 88/361 for the implementation of Article 67 of the Treaty [1988] OJ L178/5[2]

Council Directive (EEC) 89/336 on the approximation of the laws of the Member States relating to electromagnetic compatibility [1989] OJ L139/19

Council Directive (EEC) 89/552 on the coordination of certain provisions laid down by Law, Regulation or Administrative Action in Member States concerning the pursuit of television broadcasting activities [1989] OJ L298/23, amended by European Parliament and Council Directive (EC) 97/36 amending Council Directive 89/552/EEC on the coordination of certain provisions laid down by law, regulation or administrative action in Member States concerning the pursuit of television broadcasting activities [1997] OJ L202/60 ('Directive on Television Broadcasting Activities')

Council Directive (EEC) 93/13 on unfair terms in consumer contracts [1993] OJ L95/29

European Parliament and Council Directive (EC) 95/46 on the protection of individuals with regard to the processing of personal data and on the free movement of such data [1995] OJ L281/31

European Parliament and Council Directive (EC) 97/7 on the protection of consumers in respect of distance contracts [1997] OJ L144/19

European Parliament and Council Directive (EC) 97/66 concerning the processing of personal data and the protection of privacy in the telecommunications sector [1998] OJ L24/1

European Parliament and Council Directive (EC) 98/34 laying down a procedure for the provision of information in the field of technical standards and regulations [1998] OJ L204/37

European Parliament and Council Directive (EC) 2000/31 on certain legal aspects of information society services, in particular electronic commerce, in the internal market [2000] OJ L178/1 ('Directive on electronic commerce')

Council Regulation (EC) 44/2001 on jurisdiction and the recognition and enforcement of judgments in civil and commercial matters [2001] OJ L12/1

Council Regulation (EC) 1/2003 on the implementation of the rules on competition laid down in Articles 81 and 82 of the Treaty [2003] OJ L1/1

Council Decision (EC) 1999/46 laying down the procedures for the exercise of implementing powers conferred on the Commission [1999] OJ L184/23

Council Decision (EC) 1999/468 laying down the procedures for the exercise of implementing powers conferred on the Commission [1999] OJ L184/23

Commission Regulation (EC) No 1400/2002 on the application of Article 81(3) of the Treaty to categories of vertical agreements and concerted practices in the motor vehicle sector [2002] OJ L203/30

Commission Notice on the notion of a concentration under Council Regulation (EEC) No 4064/89 of 21 December 1989 on the control of concentrations between undertakings [1994] OJ C385/5

Commission Notice on the distinction between concentrative and cooperative joint ventures under Council Regulation (EEC) 4064/89 of 21 December 1989 on the control of concentrations between undertakings [1994] OJ C385/1

---

[2] Article 67 EC has been renumbered as Art 56 EC (free movement of capital).

Commission Notice on remedies acceptable under Council Regulation (EEC) No 4064/89 and under Commission Regulation (EC) No 447/98 [2001] OJ C68/3

Communication of the Commission on certain legal aspects concerning intra-EU investment [1997] OJ C220/15

Commission notice on cooperation between national competition authorities and the Commission in handling cases falling within the scope of Articles 85 or 86 of the EC Treaty [1997] OJ C313/3

Commission Interpretative Communication on Concessions in Community law [2000] OJ C121/2

Commission Notice on cooperation between national courts and the Commission in applying Articles 85 and 86 of the EEC Treaty [1993] OJ C39/6

7. Old Regulatory Framework

Council Directive (EEC) 90/387 on the establishment of the internal market for telecommunications services through the implementation of open network provision [1990] OJ L192/1, amended several times

Council Directive (EEC) 92/44 on the application of open network provision to leased lines [1992] OJ L165/27, amended several times

European Parliament and Council Directive (EC) 97/33 on interconnection in telecommunications with regard to ensuring universal service and interoperability through application of the principles of Open Network Provision (ONP) [1997] OJ L199/32[3]

European Parliament and Council Directive (EC) 98/10 on the application of open network provision (ONP) to voice telephony and on universal service for telecommunications in a competitive environment [1998] OJ L101/24

European Parliament and Council Regulation (EC) 2887/2000 on unbundled access to the local loop [2000] OJ L336/4

Commission Communication (EC), Unbundled access to the local loop: enabling the competitive provision of a full range of electronic communication services, including broadband multimedia and high-speed Internet [2000] OJ C272/55

Commission Recommendation (EC) 2000/417 on unbundled access to the local loop: enabling the competitive provision of a full range of electronic communications services including broadband multimedia and high-speed internet [2000] OJ L156/44

European Parliament and Council Decision (EC) 710/97 on a coordinated authorisation approach in the field of satellite personal-communication services in the Community [1997] OJ L105/4

8. Terminal Equipment

Commission Directive 88/301 of 16 May 1988 on competition in the markets in telecommunications terminal equipment [1988] OJ L131/73

European Parliament and Council Directive (EC) 98/13 relating to telecommunications terminal equipment and satellite earth station equipment, including the mutual recognition of their conformity [1998] OJ L74/1

Previous directions

Council Directive (EEC) 86/361 on the initial stage of the mutual recognition of type approval for telecommunications terminal equipment Official Journal [1986] OJ L217/21

---

[3] Amended by European Parliament and Council Directive (EC) 98/61 [1998] OJ L268/37.

Council Directive (EEC) 91/263 on the approximation of the laws of the Member States concerning telecommunications terminal equipment, including the mutual recognition of their conformity [1991] OJ L128/1

Council Directive (EEC) 93/97 supplementing Directive 91/263/EEC in respect of satellite earth station equipment [1993] OJ L290/1

European Parliament and Council Directive (EC) 1999/5 on radio equipment and telecommunications terminal equipment and the mutual recognition of their conformity [1999] OJ L91/10

9. Old Regulatory Framework—Directives Adopted by the Commission

Commission Directive 88/301 of 16 May 1988 on competition in the markets in telecommunications terminal equipment [1988] OJ L131/73

Commission Directive (EEC) 90/388 on competition in the markets for telecommunications services [1990] OJ L192/10[4]

Commission Directive (EEC) 94/46 amending Directive 88/301 and Directive 90/388 in particular with regard to satellite communications [1994] OJ L268/15

Commission Directive (EC) 95/51 amending Directive 90/388 with regard to the abolition of the restrictions on the use of cable television networks for the provision of already liberalised telecommunications services [1995] OJ L256/49

Commission Directive (EC) 96/2 amending Directive 90/388 with regard to personal and mobile communications [1996] OJ L20/59

Commission Directive (EC) 96/19 amending Directive 90/388/EEC with regard to the implementation of full competition in telecommunications markets [1996] OJ L74/24

Commission Directive (EC) 1999/64 amending Directive 90/388 in order to ensure that telecommunications networks and cable TV networks owned by a single operator are separate legal entities [1999] OJ L1175/39

---

[4] Although they have been repealed, this and the following directives contain provisions that are still important for an understanding of the consequences of the liberalisation process for the organisation of markets. This is due to the special status granted by the ECJ to directives adopted by the Commission on the basis of Art 86 EC. Pursuant to case law, these directives do not introduce any new rules but only specify and further determine obligations that existed beforehand in the Treaty.

APPENDIX B

List of Relevant Services in the European Commission

DG Information Society, Directorate B (Electronic communications services policy and regulatory framework)

Unit B1—Policy Development and Regulatory Framework

The unit develops policy for electronic communications services, including telecoms, digital radio and TV and next generation networks.

The main outputs are draft proposals for directives (such as the five European Parliament and Council directives constituting the main pillar of the current EU regulatory framework), recommendations and other regulatory instruments.

Unit mailbox: INFSO-B1@cec.eu.int

Unit B2—Implementation of the regulatory framework (I)

The unit is responsible for the implementation of the EU regulation in:

Austria, Cyprus, Czech Republic, Germany, Hungary, Latvia, Portugal, Slovakia, Spain, United Kingdom

The unit is also responsible for:

Questions of principle relating to the Framework, Access and Interconnection and Universal Service Directives

Coordination of infringement proceedings concerning the five directives

Management of the Communications Committee

Article 7 ('special regulatory procedure') taskforce (DG INFSO)—For all registered notifications, see http://forum.europa.eu.int/Public/irc/infso/ecctf/home

Unit mailbox: INFSO-B2@cec.eu.int

Unit B3—Implementation of the regulatory framework (II)

The unit is responsible for the implementation of the EU regulation in:

Belgium, Denmark, Estonia, Finland, France, Greece, Ireland, Italy, Lithuania, Luxembourg, Malta, Netherlands, Poland, Slovenia, Sweden,

and for questions of principle relating to the Authorisations and e-Privacy Directives.

Unit mailbox: INFSO-B3@cec.eu.int

Unit B4—Radio Spectrum Policy

The unit is responsible for the development of radio spectrum policy pursuant to the Radio Spectrum Decision 676/2002/EC and implementation measures for EU radio spectrum policy; it represents the Commission in international organisations dealing with radio spectrum aspects, notably the CEPT and ITU.

Unit mailbox: INFSO-B4@cec.eu.int

DG COMPETITION, DIRECTORATE C (INFORMATION, COMMUNICATION AND MULTIMEDIA)

Unit C1—Telecommunications and post; Information society coordination

As regards the regulatory framework, the unit oversees the Consolidated Services Directive and is responsible for the Article 7 ('special regulatory procedure') taskforce (DG COMP)

Unit mailbox: COMP-C1@cec.eu.int

APPENDIX C

List of National Competition Authorities

Belgium

Conseil de la Concurrence/Raad voor Mededinging

Square de Méeus, 23—1er étage
B-1000 Bruxelles
Tel. +32-2-5065235
Fax. +32-2-5065791

Denmark

Konkurrencestyrelsen—Danish Competition Authority

Nørregade 49
DK-1165 København-K
Tel. +45-33-177000
Fax. +45-33-326144
E-mail: ks@ks.dk

Germany

Bundeskartellamt

Kaiser-Friedrich-Strasse, 16
D-53113 Bonn
Tel. +49-228-94990
Fax. +49-228-9499400
E-mail: mailbox@bundeskartellamt.bund.de

Greece

Hellenic Competition Commission

Building of Ministry of Commerce (5th floor) 10, Kaningos Square
GR-10181 Athens
Tel. +30-210-3893106
Fax. +30-210-3829654
E-mail: dtzouganatos@epant.gr

Spain

Tribunal de Defensa de la Competencia (España)

Avda. de Pio XII, 17
E-28016 Madrid
Fax. +34-91-3530590
E-mail: secretaria.presidente@tdcompetencia.org

France

Conseil de la Concurrence

11, rue de l'Echelle
F-75001 Paris
Tel. +33-1-55040000

Iceland

Icelandic Competition Authority

Laugavegi 118—Postholf 5120
125 Reykjavik

Ireland

Irish Competition Authority

Parnell House, 14 Parnell Square
IRL Dublin 1
Tel. +353-1-8045400
Fax. +353-1-8045401
E-mail: chair@tca.ie

Italy

Autorità garante della Concorrenza e del Mercato

Piazza Verdi, 6/A
I-00198 Roma
Tel. 39-06-858211
Fax. 39-06-85821256
E-mail: antitrust@agcm.it

Liechtenstein

Office of National Economy (Amt für Volkwirtschaft)
(Liechtenstein)

Kirchstr. 7,
FL-9490 Vaduz
Tel. +4232366881
Fax. 423-2366889
E-mail: Anne-Sophie.Constans@avw.llv.li

Luxembourg

Ministère de l'Economie—Direction de la Concurrence et de Protection des
Consommateurs

Case Postale 97–19–21, Blvd Royal
L-2914 Luxembourg
Tel. +352-4784172
Fax. +352-221607
E-mail: pierre.rauchs@eco.etat.lu

The Netherlands

Nederlandse Mededingingsautoriteit (Nma)

Muzentoren, Wijnhaven, 24—NL-2511 GA Den Haag
Postbus 16326 NL-2500 BH Den Haag
Tel. +31-70-3303330
Fax. +31-70-3303310
E-mail: p.kalbfleisch@nmanet.nl

Norway

Norwegian Competition Authority—Konkurransetilsynet

H. Heyerdahls gate 1—P.O. Box 8132 Dep
0033 Oslo
Tel. +47-22400900
Fax. +47-22400999
E-mail: post@konkurransetilsynet.no

Austria

Bundeswettbewerbsbehörde (Federal Competition Authority)

Praterstrasse, 31
A-1020 WIEN
Tel. +43-1-245080
Fax. +43-1-5874200

Portugal

Autoridade da Concorrência

Rua Laura Alves, nø 4—7ø andar
P-1050-138 LISBOA
Tel. +351-21-7802470
Fax. +351-21-7802471
E-mail: adc@autoridadedaconcorrencia.pt

Finland

Kilpailuvirasto

Pitkänsillanranta 3—P.O. Box 332
FIN-00531 Helsinki
Tel. +358-9-73141
Fax. +358-9-73143328
E-mail: kirjaamo@kilpailuvirasto.fi

Sweden

Konkurrensverket

Sveavägen, 167
S-10385 Stockholm
Tel. +46-8-7001600
Fax. +46-8-245543
E-mail: claes.norgren@kkv.se

United Kingdom

Ofcom—Office of Communications

Riverside House
22 Southwark Bridge Road
London SEI 9HA
United Kingdom
Tel. +44-20-79893000
Fax. +44-20-79893333

The Competition Commission

Victoria House
Southampton Row
London WC1B 4AD
United Kingdom
Tel. +44-20-72710100
Fax. +44-20-72710367

APPENDIX D

List of National Regulatory Authorities

Belgium

IBPT—Institut belge des Services postaux et des Télécommunications

Avenue de l'Astronomie 14—Bte 21
1210 Bruxelles
http://www.ibpt.be
Fax: +32 2 226 88 77

Denmark

IT-& Telestyrelsen

National IT & Telecom Agency
Holsteinsgade 63
DK-2100 København Ø
http://www.itst.dk/
Fax: +45 35 45 00 10

Germany

Reg TP—Regierungsbehörde für Telekommunikation und Post

Tulpenfeld 4
D-53113 Bonn
http://www.regtp.de
Fax: +49 228 14 88 72

Greece

EETT—National Commission for Telecommunications and Post

60 Kifisias Avenue
GR-151 25 Marousi
http://www.eett.gr
Fax: +30 1 615 11 13

Spain

CMT—Comisión del Mercado de las Telecomunicaciones

C/Alcalá n° 37
E-28014 Madrid
http://www.cmt.es
Fax: +34 91 372 42 03

France

ART—Autorité de Régulation des Télécommunications

7, square Max Hymans
F-75730 Paris Cedex 15

http://www.art-telecom.fr
Fax: +33 1 40 47 72 02

Ireland

Commission for Communications Regulation

Block DEF, Abbey Court, Irish Life Centre
Lower Abbey Street
Dublin 1
Ireland
http://www.odtr.ie
Fax: +353 1 804 96 80

Italy

AGC—Autorità per le Garanzie nelle Comunicazioni

Centro Direzionale
Isola B5
Torre Francesco
I-80143 Napoli
http://www.agcom.it
Fax: +39 81 750 71 11

Luxembourg

ILR—Institut Luxembourgeois de Régulation

45a, Avenue Monterey
L-2922 Luxembourg
Fax: +352 45 88 45 88

Netherlands

OPTA—Onafhankelijke Post en Telecommunicatie Autoriteit

Postbus 90420
2509 LK's Gravenhage
Nederland
http://www.opta.nl
Fax: +31 70 315 35 01

Austria

Rundfunk und Telekom Regulierungs-GmbH (RTR-GmbH)

Mariahilfer Strasse 77-79
A-1060 Wien
http://www.rtr.at

Portugal

ANACOM

Avenida José Malhoa, n. 12-21 A
P-1099-017 Lisboa
http://www.icp.pt
Fax: +351 1 721 10 01

Finland

Viestintävirasto

Itämerenkatu 3
FIN-00180 Helsinki
http://www.thk.fi
Fax: +358 9 6966 410

Sweden

PTS—Post-och telestyrelsen

Birger Jarlsgatan 16
SE-102 49 Stockholm
http://www.pts.se
Fax: +46 8 678 55 08

United Kingdom

Ofcom—Office of Communications

Riverside House
2a Southwark Bridge Road
London SE1 9HA
United Kingdom
http://www.ofcom.org.uk
Tel: +44 20 7989 3000
Fax: +44 20 7989 3333

INDEX